DICTIONARY OF LAW

CONTAINING

DEFINITIONS OF THE TERMS AND PHRASES OF AMER- ICAN AND ENGLISH JURISPRUDENCE, ANCIENT AND MODERN

INCLUDING

THE PRINCIPAL TERMS OF INTERNATIONAL, CONSTITUTIONAL, AND COM- MERCIAL LAW; WITH A COLLECTION OF LEGAL MAXIMS AND NUMEROUS SELECT TITLES FROM THE CIVIL LAW AND OTHER FOREIGN SYSTEMS

———————

BY HENRY CAMPBELL BLACK, M. A.

Author of Treatises on "JUDGMENTS," "TAX-TITLES," "CONSTITUTIONAL PROHIBITIONS," etc.

———————

ST. PAUL, MINN.
WEST PUBLISHING CO.
1891

PREFACE.

THE dictionary now offered to the profession is the result of the author's endeavor to prepare a concise and yet comprehensive book of definitions of the terms, phrases, and maxims used in American and English law and necessary to be understood by the working lawyer and judge, as well as those important to the student of legal history or comparative jurisprudence. It does not purport to be an epitome or compilation of the body of the law. It does not invade the province of the text-books, nor attempt to supersede the institutional writings. Nor does it trench upon the field of the English dictionary, although vernacular words and phrases, so far as construed by the courts, are not excluded from its pages. Neither is the book encyclopædic in its character. It is chiefly required in a dictionary that it should be comprehensive. Its value is impaired if any single word that may reasonably be sought between its covers is not found there. But this comprehensiveness is possible (within the compass of a single volume) only on condition that whatever is foreign to the true function of a lexicon be rigidly excluded. The work must therefore contain nothing but the legitimate matter of a dictionary, or else it cannot include all the necessary terms. This purpose has been kept constantly in view in the preparation of the present work. Of the most esteemed law dictionaries now in use, each will be found to contain a very considerable number of words not defined in any other. None is quite comprehensive in itself. The author has made it his aim to include *all* these terms and phrases here, together with some not elsewhere defined.

For the convenience of those who desire to study the law in its historical development, as well as in its relations to political and social philosophy, place has been found for numerous titles of the old English law, and words used in old European and feudal law, and for the principal terminology of the Roman law. And in view of the modern interest in comparative jurisprudence and similar studies, it has seemed necessary to introduce a considerable vocabulary from the civil, canon, French, Spanish, Scotch, and Mexican law and other foreign systems. In order to further adapt the work to the advantage and convenience of all classes of users, many terms of political or public law are here defined, and such as are employed in trade, banking, and commerce, as also the principal phraseology of international and maritime law and forensic medicine. There have also been included numerous words taken from the vernacular, which, in consequence of their interpretation by the courts or in statutes, have acquired a quasi-technical meaning, or which, being frequently used in laws or private documents, have often been referred to the courts for construction. But the main body of the work is given to the definition of the technical terms and phrases used in modern American and English jurisprudence.

In searching for definitions suitable to be incorporated in the work, the author has carefully examined the codes, and the compiled or revised statutes, of the various states, and from these sources much valuable matter has been obtained. The definitions thus enacted by law are for the most part terse, practical, and of course authoritative. Most, if not all, of such statutory interpretations of words and phrases will be found under their appropriate titles. Due prominence has also been given to definitions formulated by the appellate courts and embodied in the reports. Many

(iii)

of these judicial definitions have been literally copied and adopted as the author's definition of the particular term, of course with a proper reference. But as the constant aim has been to present a definition at once concise, comprehensive, accurate, and lucid, he has not felt bound to copy the language of the courts in any instance where, in his judgment, a better definition could be found in treatises of acknowledged authority, or could be framed by adaptation or re-arrangement. But many judicial interpretations have been added in the way of supplementary matter to the various titles.

The more important of the synonyms occurring in legal phraseology have been carefully discriminated. In some cases, it has only been necessary to point out the correct and incorrect uses of these pairs and groups of words. In other cases, the distinctions were found to be delicate or obscure, and a more minute analysis was required.

A complete collection of legal maxims has also been included, comprehending as well those in English and Law French as those expressed in the Latin. These have not been grouped in one body, but distributed in their proper alphabetical order through the book. This is believed to be the more convenient arrangement.

It remains to mention the sources from which the definitions herein contained have been principally derived. For the terms appertaining to old and middle English law and the feudal polity, recourse has been had freely to the older English law dictionaries, (such as those of Cowell, Spelman, Blount, Jacob, Cunningham, Whishaw, Skene, Tomlins, and the "Termes de la Ley,") as also to the writings of Bracton, Littleton, Coke, and the other sages of the early law. The authorities principally relied on for the terms of the Roman and modern civil law are the dictionaries of Calvinus, Scheller, and Vicat, (with many valuable suggestions from Brown and Burrill,) and the works of such authors as Mackeldey, Hunter, Browne, Hallifax, Wolff, and Maine, besides constant reference to Gaius and the *Corpus Juris Civilis*. In preparing the terms and phrases of French, Spanish, and Scotch law, much assistance has been derived from the treatises of Pothier, Merlin, Toullier, Schmidt, Argles, Hall, White, and others, the commentaries of Erskine and Bell, and the dictionaries of Dalloz, Bell, and Escriche. For the great body of terms used in modern English and American law, the author, besides searching the codes and statutes and the reports, as already mentioned, has consulted the institutional writings of Blackstone, Kent, and Bouvier, and a very great number of text-books on special topics of the law. An examination has also been made of the recent English law dictionaries of Wharton, Sweet, Brown, and Mozley & Whitley, and of the American lexicographers, Abbott, Anderson, Bouvier, Burrill, and Rapalje & Lawrence. In each case where aid is directly levied from these sources, a suitable acknowledgment has been made. This list of authorities is by no means exhaustive, nor does it make mention of the many cases in which the definition had to be written entirely *de novo;* but it will suffice to show the general direction and scope of the author's researches.

H. C. B.

Washington, D. C., August 1, 1891.

A TABLE

OF

BRITISH REGNAL YEARS.

Sovereign.	Accession.	Length of reign.	Sovereign.	Accession.	Length of reign.
William I	Oct. 14, 1066	21	Henry VII	Aug. 22, 1485	24
William II	Sept. 26, 1087	13	Henry VIII	April 22, 1509	38
Henry I	Aug. 5, 1100	36	Edward VI	Jan. 28, 1547	7
Stephen	Dec. 26, 1135	19	Mary	July 6, 1553	6
Henry II	Dec. 19, 1154	35	Elizabeth	Nov. 17, 1558	45
Richard I	Sept. 23, 1189	10	James I	March 24, 1603	23
John	May 27, 1199	18	Charles I.	March 27, 1625	24
Henry III	Oct. 28, 1216	57	The Commonwealth	Jan. 30, 1649	11
Edward I	Nov. 20, 1272	35	Charles II	May 29, 1660	37
Edward II	July 8, 1307	20	James II	Feb. 6, 1685	4
Edward III	Jan. 25, 1326	51	William and Mary	Feb. 13, 1689	14
Richard II	June 22, 1377	23	Anne	March 8, 1702	13
Henry IV	Sept. 30, 1399	14	George I	Aug. 1, 1714	13
Henry V	March 21, 1413	10	George II	June 11, 1727	34
Henry VI	Sept. 1, 1422	39	George III	Oct. 25, 1760	60
Edward IV	March 4, 1461	23	George IV	Jan. 29, 1820	11
Edward V	April 9, 1483		William IV	June 26, 1830	7
Richard III	June 26, 1483	3	Victoria	June 20, 1837	

(v)*

BIBLIOGRAPHICAL LIST

OF THE

PRINCIPAL LAW DICTIONARIES

IN

ENGLISH AND FOREIGN LANGUAGES.

ABBOTT, Benj. Vaughan. Dictionary of terms and phrases used in American or English Jurisprudence. 2 vols. 8vo. Boston, 1879.

ADAMS, Henry C. A juridical glossary; being an exhaustive compilation of the most celebrated maxims, aphorisms, doctrines, precepts, technical phrases and terms employed in the Roman, Civil, Feudal, Canon, and Common Law, and quoted in the standard elementary works and reports of the British and American courts. Vol. 1, A to E. 8vo. Albany, 1886.

ANDERSON, William C. A dictionary of law, consisting of judicial definitions and explanations of words, phrases, and maxims, and an exposition of the principles of law; comprising a dictionary and compendium of American and English jurisprudence. 1 vol. 8vo. Chicago, 1889.

BACON, Francis, Lord. The maxims of the law. [Printed in Bacon's Law Tracts, 1 vol. 12mo. London, 1737.]

BADEN, Gustav Ludvig. Forsög til et dansk-norsk juridisk ord- og sag-leksikon. 1 vol. 16mo. Odense, 1814.

BELL, William. A dictionary and digest of the law of Scotland, with short explanations of the most ordinary English law terms. 1 vol. 8vo. Edinburgh, 1861.

BIRET, Aimé Charles Louis Modeste. Vocabulaire des Cinq Codes, ou définitions simplifiées des termes de droit et de jurisprudence exprimés dans ces codes. 1 vol. 8vo. Paris, 1826.

BLOUNT, Thomas. A law dictionary and glossary, interpreting such difficult and obscure words and terms as are found either in our common or statute, ancient or modern, laws. 3d Edn. 1 vol. folio. London, 1717.

BOUSQUET, J. Nouveau dictionaire de droit. 2d Edn. 1 vol. 4to. Paris, 1847.

BOUVIER, John. A law dictionary adapted to the constitution and laws of the United States of America and of the several states of the American Union, with references to the civil and other systems of foreign law. 1st Edn. 2 vols. 8vo. Philadelphia, 1839.

——, Same. 14th Edn. 2 vols. 8vo. Philadelphia, 1882.

BRILLON, Pierre Jacques. Nouveau dictionaire civil et canonique de droit et de pratique. 1 vol. 4to. Paris, 1707.

BRISSONIUS, Barnabas. De verborum quæ ad jus civile pertinent significatione. 1st Edn. 1 vol. folio. Leyden, 1559. [Other editions, 1578, 1683, 1697, 1721.]

——, Same. 6th Edn. By J. G. Heineccius. 1 vol. folio. Halae Magdeburgicae, 1743.

BROOM, Herbert. A selection of legal maxims, classified and illustrated. 2d Edn. 1 vol. 8vo. London, 1848.

——, Same. 8th Edn.

BROWN, Archibald. A new law dictionary and institute of the whole law, for the use of students, the legal profession, and the public. 1 vol. 8vo. London, 1874.

——, Same. American edition, by A. P. Sprague. 1 vol. 8vo. Albany, 1875.

BURN, Richard and John. A new law dictionary, intended for general use as well as for gentlemen of the profession. 2 vols. 8vo. London, 1792.

BURRILL, Alexander M. A new law dictionary and glossary, containing full definitions of the principal terms of the common and civil law, together with translations and explanations of the various technical phrases in different languages occurring in the ancient and modern reports and standard treatises; embracing also all the principal common and civil law maxims. 1st Edn. 2 vols. 8vo. New York, 1850.

——, Same. 2d Edn. 2 vols. 8vo. New York, 1867.

CALVINUS, (or Kahl,) John. Lexicon juridicum juris Cæsarei, simul et canonici, feudalis, item, civilis, criminalis, theoretici ac practici, et in schola et in foro usitatarum. 1 vol. folio. ——, 1669.

COWELL, John. Nomothetes: The Interpreter, containing the genuine signification of such obscure words and terms used either in the common or statute laws of this realm. 1st Edn. 1 vol. folio. Cambridge, 1607.

——, Same. 2d Edn. London, 1672. 3d Edn. London, 1708.

CRAMER, Andreas Wilhelm. Supplementi ad Barnabæ Brissonii opus, De verborum quæ ad jus civile pertinent significatione, specimen. 1 vol. 4to. Kiliae, 1813.

CUNNINGHAM, T. A new and complete law dictionary or general abridgment of the law. 3d Edn. 2 vols. 4to. London, 1783.

DALLOZ, Armand. Dictionnaire general et raisonné de legislation, de doctrine, et de jurisprudence, en matière civile, commerciale, criminelle, administrative, et de droit public. 4 vols. 4to. Paris, 1835.

ESCRICHE, Joaquin. Diccionario razonado de legislacion y jurisprudencia. 3d Edn. 2 vols. 4to. Madrid, 1847.

FERRIÈRE, Claude Joseph. Dictionnaire de droit et de pratique. 1st Edn. 1734. 2d Edn. 1740. 3d Edn. 2 vols. 4to. Paris, 1762.

GOIRAND, Leopold. Glossary of French judicial terms. [In his work on the French Code of Commerce. 1 vol. 8vo. London, 1880.]

HALKERSTON, Peter. A collection of Latin maxims and rules in law and equity, selected from the most eminent authors on the civil, canon, feudal, English, and Scots law, with an English translation. 1 vol. 8vo. Edinburgh, 1823.

HOLTHOUSE, Henry James. A new law dictionary, containing explanations of such technical terms and phrases as occur in the works of legal authors, in the practice of the courts, and in the parliamentary proceedings of the houses of Lords and Commons. 1st Edn. London, 1839.

——, Same. American edn. from 2d English edn. 1 vol. 12mo. Philadelphia, 1847.

HOLTZENDORFF, Franz von. Rechts-Lexicon. [Part second of his Encyclopædie der Rechts-wissenschaft.] 2 vols. 8vo. Leipsic, 1875.

JACOB, Giles. A new law dictionary, containing the interpretation and definition of words and terms used in the law, as also the law and practice under the proper heads and titles; together with such learning as explains the history and antiquity of the law, our manners, customs, and original government. 10th Edn. By J. Morgan. 1 vol. folio. London, 1782.

——, Same. 1st American edn. from [Tomlin's] 2d English edn. 6 vols. 8vo. Philadelphia, 1811.

KELHAM, Robert. A dictionary of the Norman or old French language. 1 vol. 8vo. London, 1779.

LAWSON, John D. A concordance of words and phrases construed in the judicial reports, and of legal definitions contained therein. 1 vol. 8vo. St. Louis, 1883.

LEE, Thomas. A dictionary of the practice in civil actions in the courts of King's Bench and Common Pleas, with practical directions and forms, arranged under each title. 2d Edn. 2 vols. 8vo. London, 1825.

LLOYD, A. Parlett. Glossary of words and terms frequently used by builders, architects, etc. [Printed in his Treatise on the Law of Building. 1 vol. 8vo. Boston, 1888.]

LOFFT, Capel. Maxims and rules of the law of England and principles of equity. [In his reports of cases adjudged in the court of King's Bench. 1 vol. folio. London, 1776. Same, 1 vol. 8vo. Dublin, 1790.]

MAXWELL, John Irwing. A pocket dictionary of the law of bills of exchange, promissory notes, bank notes, checks, etc. 1 vol. 12mo. Philadelphia, 1808.

MONTEFIORE, Joshua. A commercial dictionary, containing the present state of mercantile law, practice, and custom. 1st Amer. Edn. 3 vols. 8vo. Philadelphia, 1804.

MOZLEY (Herbert Newman) and WHITLEY, (George Crispe.) A concise law dictionary. 1 vol. 8vo. London, 1876.

OSTERSEN, Christian. Glossarium juridico-Danicum. 1 vol. 4to. Kjöbeniavn, 1641. *Note.* A second, revised edition was printed in 1652, and this was reprinted in 1665 and subsequently.

POTTS, Thomas. A compendious law dictionary, containing both an explanation of the terms and the law itself. Intended for the use of the country gentleman, the merchant, and the professional man. 1 vol. 16mo. London, 1803.

RAPALJE (Stewart) and LAWRENCE, (Robert L.) A dictionary of American and English law. 2 vols. 8vo. Jersey City, 1883.

RASTELL, John. Terms of the law; or certain difficult and obscure words and terms of the common and statute laws expounded and explained in French and English. 1 vol. 16mo. London,

1721. *Note.* This work is also known as "Termes de la Ley."

RAWSON, Henry Gilbert. The pocket law lexicon, explaining technical words, phrases, and maxims of the English, Scotch, and Roman law. 2d Edn. 1 vol. 16mo. London, 1884.

SCHLYTER, Carl Johan. Glossarium ad corpus juris Sueo-Gotorum antiqui. Ordbok till Samlingen of Sweriges Gamla Lagar. 1 vol. 4to. Lund, 1877.

SKENE, John. De verborum significatione; the exposition of the termes and difficill wordes conteined in the foure buiks of "Regiam Majestatem" and uthers, in the acts of parliament, etc. 1 vol. 4to. London, 1641.

——, Same. Printed at the end of the collection of the laws of James I. Folio. Edinburgh, 1597.

SPELMAN, Sir Henry. Glossarium archaiologicum; continens Latino-Barbara, peregrina, obsoleta, et novatæ significationis vocabula. 1st Edn. 1 vol. 4to. London, 1626.

——, Same. 3d Edn. 1 vol. folio. London, 1687.

STIMSON, F. J. Glossary of technical terms, phrases, and maxims of the common law. 1 vol. 12mo. Boston, 1881.

SWEET, Charles. A dictionary of English law, containing definitions of the technical terms in modern use and a concise statement of the rules of law affecting the principal subjects, with historical and etymological notes. 1 vol. 8vo. London, 1882.

TAYLER, Thomas. A law-glossary of the Latin, Greek, Norman, French, and other languages, interspersed in the commentaries by Sir W. Blackstone, Knt., and various law treatises upon each branch of the profession, translated into English and alphabetically arranged. 1 vol. 8vo. London, 1819.

——, Same. American edition. Albany, 1833.

TERMES DE LA LEY. See RASTELL.

TOLLUIRE (R. S.) and BOULET (J. B. E.) Nouveau dictionnaire des termes de droit et de pratique: ou *Ferrière* moderne. 1 vol. 8vo. Paris, 1841.

TOMLINS, Sir Thomas E. The law dictionary, explaining the rise, progress, and present state of the British law, defining and interpreting the terms or words of art. 4th Edn. 2 vols. 4to. London, 1835.

——, **Same.** 1st American from 4th English Edn. 3 vols. 8vo. Philadelphia, 1836.

TRAYNER, John. Latin phrases and maxims, collected from the institutional and other writers on Scotch law, with translations and illustrations. 2d Edn. 1 vol. 12mo. Edinburgh, 1876.

VICAT, Philip. Vocabularium juris utriusque, ex variis ante editis. 2d Edn. 4 vols. 8vo. Naples, 1760.

WHARTON, J. J. S. The law lexicon, forming an epitome of the law of England, and containing full explanations of the technical terms and phrases thereof, both ancient and modern. 1st Edn. 1 vol. 8vo. London, 1848.

WHARTON, J. J. S. Same. 7th Edn. by J. M. Lely. 1 vol. 8vo. London, 1883.

——, **Same.** 1st American from 1st English Edn. 1 vol. 8vo. Philadelphia, 1854.

WHISHAW, James. A new law dictionary, containing a concise exposition of the mere terms of art and such obsolete words as occur in old legal, historical, and antiquarian writers. 1 vol. 8vo. London, 1829.

WILLIAMS, Thomas Walter. A compendious and comprehensive law dictionary, elucidating the terms and general principles of law and equity. 1 vol. 8vo. London, 1816.

WINFIELD, Charles H. Adjudged words and phrases, being a collection of adjudicated definitions of terms used in the law, with references to authorities. 1 vol. 8vo. Jersey City, 1882.

WINGATE, Edmond. Maxims of reason, or the reason of the common law of England. 1 vol. 4to. London, 1658.

†

BLACK'S DICTIONARY OF LAW.

A.

A. The first letter of the English alphabet; used to distinguish the first page of a folio from the second, marked b, or the first page of a book, the first foot-note on a printed page, the first of a series of subdivisions, etc., from the following ones, which are marked b, c, d, e, etc.

A. Lat. The letter marked on the ballots by which, among the Romans, the people voted against a proposed law. It was the initial letter of the word "*antiquo*," I am for the old law. Tayl. Civil Law, 191.

A. Lat. The letter inscribed on the ballots by which, among the Romans, jurors voted to acquit an accused party. It was the initial letter of "*absolvo*," I acquit. Tayl. Civil Law, 192.

"A." The English indefinite article. This particle is not necessarily a singular term; it is often used in the sense of "any," and is then applied to more than one individual object. 141 Mass. 266, 4 N. E. Rep. 794; 101 N. Y. 458, 5 N. E. Rep. 322; 60 Iowa, 223, 14 N. W. Rep. 247.

A. D. Lat. Contraction for *Anno Domini*, (in the year of our Lord.)

A. R. *Anno regni*, the year of the reign; as, A. R. V. R. 22, (*Anno Regni Victoriæ Reginæ vicesimo secundo*,) in the twenty-second year of the reign of Queen Victoria.

A 1. Of the highest qualities. An expression which originated in a practice of underwriters of rating vessels in three classes,—A, B, and C; and these again in ranks numbered. Abbott.

A AVER ET TENER. L. Fr. (L. Lat. *habendum et tenendum.*) To have and to hold. Co. Litt. §§ 523, 524. *A aver et tener a luy et a ses heires, a touts jours*,—to have and to hold to him and his heirs forever. Id. § 625. See AVER ET TENER.

AM. DICT. LAW—1

A CŒLO USQUE AD CENTRUM. From the heavens to the center of the earth.

A communi observantia non est recedendum. From common observance there should be no departure; there must be no departure from common usage. 2 Coke, 74; Co. Litt. 186a, 229b, 365a; Wing. Max. 752, max. 203. A maxim applied to the practice of the courts, to the ancient and established forms of pleading and conveyancing, and to professional usage generally. Id. 752-755. Lord Coke applies it to common professional opinion. Co. Litt. 186a, 364b.

A CONSILIIS. (Lat. *consilium*, advice.) Of counsel; a counsellor. The term is used in the civil law by some writers instead of *a responsis*. Spelman, "*Apocrisarius.*"

A CUEILLETTE. In French law. In relation to the contract of affreightment, signifies when the cargo is taken on condition that the master succeeds in completing his cargo from other sources. Arg. Fr. Merc. Law, 543.

A DATU. L. Lat. From the date. 2 Salk. 413. *A die datûs*, from the day of the date. Id.; 2 Crabb, Real Prop. p. 248, § 1301; 1 Ld. Raym. 84, 480; 2 Ld. Raym. 1242. *A dato*, from the date. Cro. Jac. 135.

A digniori fieri debet denominatio. Denomination ought to be from the more worthy. The description (of a place) should be taken from the more worthy subject, (as from a will.) Fleta, lib. 4, c. 10, § 12.

A digniori fieri debet denominatio et resolutio. The title and exposition of a thing ought to be derived from, or given, or made with reference to, the more worthy degree, quality, or species of it. Wing. Max. 265, max. 75.

A FORFAIT ET SANS GARANTIE. In French law. A formula used in indorsing commercial paper, and equivalent to "without recourse."

A FORTIORI. By a stronger reason. A term used in logic to denote an argument to the effect that because one ascertained fact exists, therefore another, which is included in it, or analogous to it, and which is less improbable, unusual, or surprising, must also exist.

A GRATIA. From grace or favor; as a matter of indulgence, not of right.

A LATERE. Lat. From the side. In connection with the succession to property, the term means "collateral." Bract. fol. 20b. Also, sometimes, "without right." Id. fol. 42b. In ecclesiastical law, a legate *a latere* is one invested with full apostolic powers; one authorized to represent the pope as if the latter were present. Du Cange.

A LIBELLIS. L. Lat. An officer who had charge of the *libelli* or petitions addressed to the sovereign. Calvin. A name sometimes given to a chancellor, (*cancellarius*,) in the early history of that office. Spelman, "*Cancellarius.*"

A l'impossible nul n'est tenu. No one is bound to do what is impossible.

A ME. (Lat. *ego*, I.) A term denoting direct tenure of the superior lord. 2 Bell, H. L. Sc. 133. Unjustly detaining from me. He is said to withhold *a me* (from me) who has obtained possession of my property unjustly. Calvin.

A MENSA ET THORO. From bed and board. Descriptive of a limited divorce or separation by judicial sentence.

A NATIVITATE. From birth, or from infancy. Denotes that a disability, status, etc., is congenital.

A non posse ad non esse sequitur argumentum necessarie negative. From the impossibility of a thing to its non-existence, the inference follows necessarily in the negative. That which cannot be done is not done. Hob. 336b. Otherwise, in the affirmative. Id.

A PALATIO. L. Lat. From *palatium*, (a palace.) Counties palatine are hence so called. 1 Bl. Comm. 117. See PALATIUM.

A piratis aut latronibus capti liberi permanent. Persons taken by pirates or robbers remain free. Dig. 49, 15, 19, 2; Gro. de J. B. lib. 3, c. 3, § 1.

A piratis et latronibus capta dominium non mutant. Things taken or captured by pirates and robbers do not change their ownership. Bynk. bk. 1, c. 17; 1 Kent, Comm. 108, 184. No right to the spoil vests in the piratical captors; no right is derivable from them to any recaptors in prejudice o. the original owners. 2 Wood. Lect. 428.

A POSTERIORI. A term used in logic to denote an argument founded on experiment or observation, or one which, taking ascertained facts as an effect, proceeds by synthesis and induction to demonstrate their cause.

A PRENDRE. L. Fr. To take. *Bref à prendre la terre*, a writ to take the land. Fet Ass. § 51. A right to take something out of the soil of another is a profit *à prendre*, or a right coupled with a profit. 1 Crabb, Real Prop. p. 125, § 115. Distinguished from an easement. 5 Adol. & E. 758. Sometimes written as one word, *apprendre*, *apprender*.

A PRIORI. A term used in logic to denote an argument founded on analogy, or abstract considerations, or one which, positing a general principle or admitted truth as a cause, proceeds to deduce from it the effects which must necessarily follow.

A QUO. A term used, with the correlative *ad quem*, (to which,) in expressing the computation of time, and also of distance in space. Thus, *dies à quo*, the day from which, and *dies ad quem*, the day to which, a period of time is computed. So, *terminus à quo*, the point or limit from which, and *terminus ad quem*, the point or limit to which, a distance or passage in space is reckoned.

A QUO; A QUA. From which. The judge or court from which a cause has been brought by error or appeal, or has otherwise been removed, is termed the judge or court *a quo; a qua.* Abbott.

A RENDRE. (Fr. to render, to yield.) That which is to be rendered, yielded, or paid. *Profits à rendre* comprehend rents and services. Ham. N. P. 192.

A rescriptis valet argumentum. An argument drawn from original writs in the register is good. Co. Litt. 11a.

A RESPONSIS. L. Lat. In ecclesiastical law. One whose office it was to give or convey answers; otherwise termed *responsalis*, and *apocrisiarius*. One who, being consulted on ecclesiastical matters, gave answers, counsel, or advice; otherwise termed *a consiliis.* Spelman, "*Apocrisiarius.*"

A RETRO. L. Lat. Behind; in arrear. *Et reditus proveniens inde à retro fuerit,* and the rent issuing therefrom be in arrear. Fleta, lib. 2, c. 55, § 2.

A RUBRO AD NIGRUM. Lat. From the red to the black; from the rubric or title of a statute, (which, anciently, was in *red* letters,) to its body, which was in the ordinary *black.* Tray. Lat. Max.; Bell, "*Rubric.*"

A summo remedio ad inferiorem actionem non habetur regressus, neque auxilium. From (after using) the highest remedy, there can be no recourse (going back) to an inferior action, nor assistance, (derived from it.) Fleta, lib. 6, c. 1, § 2. A maxim in the old law of real actions, when there were grades in the remedies given; the rule being that a party who brought a writ of right, which was the highest writ in the law, could not afterwards resort or descend to an inferior remedy. Bract. 112*b;* 3 Bl. Comm. 193, 194.

A TEMPORE CUJUS CONTRARII MEMORIA NON EXISTET. From time of which memory to the contrary does not exist.

A verbis legis non est recedendum. From the words of the law there must be no departure. 5 Coke, 119; Wing. Max. 25. A court is not at liberty to disregard the express letter of a statute, in favor of a supposed intention. 1 Steph. Comm. 71; Broom, Max. 268.

A VINCULO MATRIMONII. (Lat. from the bond of matrimony.) A term descriptive of a kind of divorce, which effects a complete dissolution of the marriage contract. See DIVORCE.

Ab abusu ad usum non valet consequentia. A conclusion as to the use of a thing from its abuse is invalid. Broom, Max. 17.

AB ACTIS. Lat. An officer having charge of *acta,* public records, registers, journals, or minutes; an officer who entered on record the *acta* or proceedings of a court; a clerk of court; a notary or actuary. Calvin. Lex. Jurid. See "*Acta.*" This, and the similarly formed epithets *à cancellis, à secretis, à libellis,* were also anciently the titles of a chancellor, (*cancellarius,*) in the early

history of that office. Spelman, "*Cancellarius.*"

AB AGENDO. Disabled from acting; unable to act; incapacitated for business or transactions of any kind.

AB ANTE. In advance. Thus, a legislature cannot agree *ab ante* to any modification or amendment to a law which a third person may make. 1 Sum. 308.

AB ANTECEDENTE. Beforehand; in advance.

AB ANTIQUO. Of old; of an ancient date.

Ab assuetis non fit injuria. From things to which one is accustomed (or in which there has been long acquiescence) no legal injury or wrong arises. If a person neglect to insist on his right, he is deemed to have abandoned it. Amb. 645; 3 Brown, Ch. 639.

AB EPISTOLIS. Lat. An officer having charge of the correspondence (*epistolæ*) of his superior or sovereign; a secretary. Calvin.; Spiegelius.

AB EXTRA. (Lat. *extra,* beyond, without.) From without. 14 Mass. 151.

AB INCONVENIENTI. From hardship, or inconvenience. An argument founded upon the hardship of the case, and the inconvenience or disastrous consequences to which a different course of reasoning would lead.

AB INITIO. L. Lat. From the beginning; from the first act. A party is said to be a trespasser *ab initio,* an estate to be good *ab initio,* an agreement or deed to be void *ab initio,* a marriage to be unlawful *ab initio,* and the like. Plow. 6*a,* 16*a;* 1 Bl. Comm. 440.

AB INITIO MUNDI. Lat. From the beginning of the world. *Ab initio mundi usque ad hodiernum diem,* from the beginning of the world to this day. Y. B. M. 1 Edw. III. 24.

AB INTESTATO. Lat. In the civil law. From an intestate; from the intestate; in case of intestacy. *Hæreditas ab intestato,* an inheritance derived from an intestate. Inst. 2, 9, 6. *Successio ab intestato,* succession to an intestate, or in case of intestacy. Id. 3, 2, 3; Dig. 38, 6, 1. This answers to the descent or inheritance of real estate at common law. 2 Bl. Comm. 490, 516; Story, Confl. Laws, § 480. "Heir *ab intestato.*"

1 Burr. 420. The phrase *"ab intestato"* is generally used as the opposite or alternative of *ex testamento,* (from, by, or under a will.) *Vel ex testamento, vel ab intestato [hæreditates]* *pertinent,*—inheritances are derived either from a will or from an intestate, (one who dies without a will.) Inst. 2, 9, 6; Dig. 29, 4; Cod. 6, 14, 2.

AB INVITO. Lat. By or from an unwilling party. A transfer *ab invito* is a compulsory transfer.

AB IRATO. By one who is angry. A devise or gift made by a man adversely to the interest of his heirs, on account of anger or hatred against them, is said to be made *ab irato.* A suit to set aside such a will is called an action *ab irato.* Merl. Repert. *"Ab irato."*

ABACTOR. In Roman law. A cattle thief; a driver away of cattle and other animals; one who stole cattle in numbers; one who abstracted cattle from the herd, intending to steal them. Also called *ubigeus.* Blount; Cowell.

ABADENGO. In Spanish law. Land owned by an ecclesiastical corporation, and therefore exempt from taxation. In particular, lands or towns under the dominion and jurisdiction of an abbot.

ABALIENATIO. In Roman law. The perfect conveyance or transfer of property from one Roman citizen to another. This term gave place to the simple *alienatio,* which is used in the Digest and Institutes, as well as in the feudal law, and from which the English "alienation" has been formed. Inst. 2, 8, pr.; Id. 2, 1, 40; Dig. 50, 16, 28.

ABAMITA. Lat. In the civil law. A great-great-grandfather's sister, (*abavi soror.*) Inst. 3, 6, 6; Dig. 38, 10, 3. Called *amita maxima.* Id. 38, 10, 10, 17. Called, in Bracton, *abamita magna.* Bract. fol. 68*b.*

ABANDON. To desert, surrender, relinquish, give up, or cede. See ABANDONMENT.

ABANDONEE. A party to whom a right or property is abandoned or relinquished by another. Applied to the insurers of vessels and cargoes. Lord Ellenborough, C. J., 5 Maule & S. 82; Abbott, J., Id. 87; Holroyd, J., Id. 89.

ABANDONMENT. The surrender, relinquishment, disclaimer, or cession of property or of rights.

The giving up a thing absolutely, without reference to any particular person or purpose; as throwing a jewel into the highway; leaving a thing to itself, as a vessel at sea; desertion, or dereliction. (2 Bl. Comm. 9, 10.) Burrill.

In marine insurance. A relinquishment or cession of property by the owner to the insurer of it, in order to claim as for a total loss, when in fact it is so by construction only. 2 Steph. Comm. 178. The exercise of a right which a party having insured goods or vessels has to call upon the insurers, in cases where the property insured has, by perils of the sea, become so much damaged as to be of little value, to accept of what is or may be saved, and to pay the full amount of the insurance, as if a total loss had actually happened. Park, Ins. 143; 2 Marsh. Ins. 559; 3 Kent, Comm. 318–335, and notes.

Abandonment is the act by which, after a constructive total loss, a person insured by contract of marine insurance declares to the insurer that he relinquishes to him his interest in the thing insured. Civil Code Cal. § 2716.

The term is used only in reference to risks in navigation; but the principle is applicable in fire insurance, where there are remnants, and sometimes, also, under stipulations in life policies in favor of creditors.

In maritime law. The surrender of a vessel and freight by the owner of the same to a person having a claim thereon arising out of a contract made with the master. See Poth. Chart. § 2, art. 3, § 51.

By husband or wife. The act of a husband or wife who leaves his or her consort willfully, and with an intention of causing perpetual separation.

"Abandonment, in the sense in which it is used in the statute under which this proceeding was commenced, may be defined to be the act of willfully leaving the wife, with the intention of causing a palpable separation between the parties, and implies an actual desertion of the wife by the husband." 60 Ind. 279.

In French law. The act by which a debtor surrenders his property for the benefit of his creditors. Merl. Repert. "Abandonment."

ABANDONMENT FOR TORTS. In the civil law. The act of a person who was sued in a noxal action, *i. e.,* for a tort or trespass committed by his slave or his animal, in relinquishing and abandoning the slave or animal to the person injured, whereby he saved himself from any further responsibility. See Inst. 4, 8, 9; 11 La. Ann. 396.

ABANDUN, or ABANDUM. Anything sequestered, proscribed, or abandoned. *Abandon, i. e., in bannum res missa*, a thing banned or denounced as forfeited or lost, whence to *abandon, desert*, or *forsake*, as lost and gone. Cowell.

ABARNARE. Lat. To detect or discover, and disclose to a magistrate, any secret crime. Leges Canuti, cap. 10.

ABATAMENTUM. L. Lat. In old English law. An abatement of freehold; an entry upon lands by way of interposition between the death of the ancestor and the entry of the heir. Co. Litt. 277a; Yel. 151.

ABATEMENT. In pleading. The effect produced upon an action at law, when the defendant pleads matter of fact showing the writ or declaration to be defective and incorrect. This defeats the action for the time being, but the plaintiff may proceed with it after the defect is removed, or may recommence it in a better way. In England, in equity pleading, declinatory pleas to the jurisdiction and dilatory to the persons were (prior to the judicature act) sometimes, by analogy to common law, termed "pleas in abatement."

In chancery practice. The determination, cessation, or suspension of all proceedings in a suit, from the want of proper parties capable of proceeding therein, as upon the death of one of the parties pending the suit. See 2 Tidd, Pr. 932; Story, Eq. Pl. § 354.

In mercantile law. A drawback or rebate allowed in certain cases on the duties due on imported goods, in consideration of their deterioration or damage suffered during importation, or while in store. A diminution or decrease in the amount of tax imposed upon any person.

In contracts. A reduction made by the creditor for the prompt payment of a debt due by the payor or debtor. Wesk. Ins. 7.

Of legacies and debts. A proportional diminution or reduction of the pecuniary legacies, when the funds or assets out of which such legacies are payable are not sufficient to pay them in full. Ward, Leg. p. 369, c. 6, § 7; 1 Story, Eq. Jur. § 555; 2 Bl. Comm. 512, 513. In equity, when equitable assets are insufficient to satisfy fully all the creditors, their debts must abate in proportion, and

they must be content with a dividend; for *æquitas est quasi æqualitas*.

ABATEMENT OF A NUISANCE. The removal, prostration, or destruction of that which causes a nuisance, whether by breaking or pulling it down, or otherwise removing, disintegrating, or effacing it.

The remedy which the law allows a party injured by a nuisance of destroying or removing it by his own act, so as he commits no riot in doing it, nor occasions (in the case of a private nuisance) any damage beyond what the removal of the inconvenience necessarily requires. 3 Bl. Comm. 5, 168; 3 Steph. Comm. 361; 2 Salk. 458.

ABATEMENT OF FREEHOLD. This takes place where a person dies seised of an inheritance, and, before the heir or devisee enters, a stranger, having no right, makes a wrongful entry, and gets possession of it. Such an entry is technically called an "abatement," and the stranger an "abator." It is, in fact, a figurative expression, denoting that the rightful possession or freehold of the heir or devisee is overthrown by the unlawful intervention of a stranger. *Abatement* differs from *intrusion*, in that it is always to the prejudice of the *heir* or immediate *devisee*, whereas the latter is to the prejudice of the *reversioner* or *remainder-man;* and *disseisin* differs from them both, for to *disseise* is to put forcibly or fraudulently a person seised of the freehold out of possession. 1 Co. Inst. 277a; 3 Bl. Comm. 166. By the ancient laws of Normandy, this term was used to signify the act of one who, having an apparent right of possession to an estate, took possession of it immediately after the death of the actual possessor, before the heir entered. (Howard, Anciennes Lois des Français, tome 1, p. 539.) Bouvier.

ABATOR. In real property law, a stranger who, having no right of entry, contrives to get possession of an estate of freehold, to the prejudice of the heir or devisee, before the latter can enter, after the ancestor's death. Litt. § 397. In the law of torts, one who abates, prostrates, or destroys a nuisance.

ABATUDA. Anything diminished. *Moneta abatuda* is money clipped or diminished in value. Cowell; Dufresne.

ABAVIA. Lat. In the civil law. A great-great-grandmother. Inst. 3, 6, 4; Dig. 38, 10, 1, 6, Bract. fol. 68b.

ABAVITA. A great-great-grandfather's sister. Bract. fol. 68b. This is a misprint for *abamita*, (q. v.) Burrill.

ABAVUNCULUS. Lat. In the civil law A great-great-grandmother's brother, (*abaviæ frater.*) Inst. 3, 6, 6; Dig. 38, 10, 3. Called *avunculus maximus*. Id. 38, 10, 10, 17. Called by Bracton and Fleta *abavunculus magnus*. Bract. fol. 68b; Fleta, lib. 6, c. 2, § 19.

ABAVUS. Lat. In the civil law. A great-great-grandfather. Inst. 3, 6, 4; Dig. 38, 10, 1, 6; Bract. fol. 67a.

ABBACY. The government of a religious house, and the revenues thereof, subject to an abbot, as a bishopric is to a bishop. Cowell. The rights and privileges of an abbot.

ABBEY. A society of religious persons, having an abbot or abbess to preside over them.

ABBOT. The spiritual superior or governor of an abbey or monastery. Feminine, *Abbess*.

ABBREVIATE OF ADJUDICATION. In Scotch law. An abstract of the decree of adjudication, and of the lands adjudged, with the amount of the debt. Adjudication is that diligence (execution) of the law by which the real estate of a debtor is adjudged to belong to his creditor in payment of a debt; and the abbreviate must be recorded in the register of adjudications.

ABBREVIATIO PLACITORUM. An abstract of ancient judicial records, prior to the Year Books. See Steph. Pl. Append. xvi.

ABBREVIATIONS. Shortened conventional expressions, employed as substitutes for names, phrases, dates, and the like, for the saving of space, of time in transcribing, etc. Abbott.

Abbreviationum, ille numerus et sensus accipiendus est, ut concessio non sit inanis. In abbreviations, such number and sense is to be taken that the grant be not made void. 9 Coke, 48.

ABBREVIATORS. In ecclesiastical law. Officers whose duty it is to assist in drawing up the pope's briefs, and reducing petitions into proper form to be converted into papal bulls. Bouvier.

ABBROCHMENT, or ABBROACHMENT. The act of forestalling a market, by buying up at wholesale the merchandise intended to be sold there, for the purpose of selling it at retail. See FORESTALLING.

ABDICATION. The act of a sovereign in renouncing and relinquishing his government or throne, so that either the throne is left entirely vacant, or is filled by a successor appointed or elected beforehand.

Also, where a magistrate or person in office voluntarily renounces or gives it up before the time of service has expired. It differs from resignation, in that resignation is made by one who has received his office from another and restores it into his hands, as an inferior into the hands of a superior; abdication is the relinquishment of an office which has devolved by act of law. It is said to be a renunciation, quitting, and relinquishing, so as to have nothing further to do with a thing, or the doing of such actions as are inconsistent with the holding of it. Chambers.

ABDUCTION. In criminal law. The offense of taking away a man's wife, child, or ward, by fraud and persuasion, or open violence. 3 Bl. Comm. 139–141.

The unlawful taking or detention of any female for the purpose of marriage, concubinage, or prostitution.

ABEARANCE. Behavior; as a recognizance to be of good abearance signifies to be of good behavior. 4 Bl. Comm. 251, 256

ABEREMURDER. (From Sax. *abere*, apparent, notorious; and *mord*, murder.) Plain or downright murder, as distinguished from the less heinous crime of manslaughter, or chance medley. It was declared a capital offense, without fine or commutation, by the laws of Canute, c. 93, and of Hen. I. c. 13. Spelman.

ABESSE. Lat. In the civil law. To be absent; to be away from a place. Said of a person who was *extra continentia urbis*, (beyond the suburbs of the city.)

ABET. In criminal law. To encourage, incite, or set another on to commit a crime. To abet another to commit a murder is to command, procure, or counsel him to commit it. Old Nat. Brev. 21; Co. Litt. 475.

ABETTATOR. L. Lat. In old English law. An abettor. Fleta, lib. 2, c. 65, § 7. See ABETTOR.

ABETTOR. In criminal law. An instigator, or setter on; one who promotes or procures a crime to be committed; one who commands, advises, instigates, or encourages another to commit a crime; a person who, being present or in the neighborhood, incites another to commit a crime, and thus becomes a principal.

The distinction between abettors and accessaries is the presence or absence at the commission of the crime. Cowell; Fleta, lib. 1, c. 34. Presence and participation are necessary to constitute a person an abettor. 4 Shars. Bl. Comm. 33; Russ. & R. 99; 9 Bing. N. C. 440; 13 Mo. 382; 1 Wis. 159; 10 Pick. 477.

ABEYANCE. In the law of estates. Expectation; waiting; suspense; remembrance and contemplation in law. Where there is no person in existence in whom an inheritance can vest, it is said to be in *abeyance*, that is, in expectation; the law considering it as always potentially existing, and ready to vest whenever a proper owner appears. 2 Bl. Comm. 107. Or, in other words, it is said to be in the remembrance, consideration, and intendment of the law. Co. Litt. §§ 646, 650. The term "abeyance" is also sometimes applied to personal property. Thus, in the case of maritime captures during war, it is said that, until the capture becomes invested with the character of prize by a sentence of condemnation, the right of property is in *abeyance*, or in a state of legal sequestration. 1 Kent, Comm. 102. It has also been applied to the franchises of a corporation. "When a corporation is to be brought into existence by some future acts of the corporators, the franchises remain in *abeyance*, until such acts are done; and, when the corporation is brought into life, the franchises instantaneously attach to it." Story, J., 4 Wheat. 691.

ABIATICUS, or Aviaticus. L. Lat. In feudal law. A grandson; the son of a son. Spelman; Lib. Feud., Baraterii, tit. 8, cited Id.

ABIDE. To "abide the order of the court" means to perform, execute, or conform to such order. 8 Cush. 297; 7 Tex. App. 38; 108 Mass. 585.

A stipulation in an arbitration bond that the parties shall "abide by" the award of the arbitrators means only that they shall await the award of the arbitrators, without revoking the submission, and not that they shall acquiesce in the award when made. 6 N. H. 162; 48 N. H. 40.

ABIDING BY. In Scotch law. A judicial declaration that the party abides by the deed on which he founds, in an action where the deed or writing is attacked as forged.

Unless this be done, a decree that the deed is false will be pronounced. Pat. Comp. It has the effect of pledging the party to stand the consequences of founding on a forged deed. Bell.

ABIGEATORES. In the civil law. Cattle stealers; those who drove away cattle or other animals, with the intention of stealing them. A rarer form of *abigei*, (q. v.) Calvin.

ABIGEATUS. Lat. (From *abigere*, to drive away.) In the civil law. The offense of stealing or driving away cattle. Dig. 47, 14, 2.

ABIGEI. Lat. In the civil law. Cattle stealers. Dig. 47, 14, 1, 1. Calvin.; Brissonius; 4 Bl. Comm. 239. See ABIGEUS.

ABIGERE. Lat. (From *ab*, from; and *agere*, to drive.) In the civil law. To drive away. Applied to those who drove away animals with the intention of stealing them. Dig. 47, 14, "*De abigeis.*" Applied, also, to the similar offense of cattle stealing on the borders between England and Scotland. Scott's Minstrelsy of the Scottish Border, Introd. Append. No. vii.

ABIGERE. To drive out; to expel by force; to produce abortion. Dig. 47, 11, 4.

ABIGEUS. Lat. (From *abigere*, to drive away.) In the civil law. A stealer of cattle; one who drove or drew away (*subtraxit*) cattle from their pastures, as horses or oxen from the herds, and made booty of them, and who followed this as a business or trade. Dig. 47, 14, 1, 1. The term was applied also to those who drove away the smaller animals, as swine, sheep, and goats. Id. 47, 14, 1, 2. In the latter case, it depended on the *number* taken, whether the offender was *fur* (a common thief) or *abigeus.* Id. 47, 14, 3. But the taking of a single horse or ox seems to have constituted the crime of *abigeatus.* Dig. 47, 14, 3. And those who *frequently* did this were clearly *abigei*, though they took but an animal or two at a time. Id. 47, 14, 3, 2. See Cod. 9, 37; Nov. 22, c. 15, § 1.

ABILITY. When a statute makes it a ground of divorce that the husband has neglected to provide for his wife the common necessaries of life, having the ability to provide the same, the word "ability" has reference to the possession by the husband of the means in property to provide such necessaries, not to his capacity of acquiring such means by labor. 9 Cal. 476.

ABISHERING, or ABISHERSING. Quit of amercements. It originally signified a forfeiture or amercement, and is more properly *mishering, mishersing,* or *miskering,* according to Spelman. It has since been termed a liberty of freedom, because, wherever this word is used in a grant, the persons to whom the grant is made have the forfeitures and amercements of all others, and are themselves free from the control of any within their fee. Termes de la Ley, 7.

ABJUDICATIO. In old English law. The depriving of a thing by the judgment of a court; a putting out of court; the same as *forisjudicatio,* forjudgment, forjudger. Co. Litt. 100a, b; Townsh. Pl. 49.

ABJURATION OF ALLEGIANCE. One of the steps in the process of naturalizing an alien. It consists in a formal declaration, made by the party under oath before a competent authority, that he renounces and abjures all the allegiance and fidelity which he owes to the sovereign whose subject he has theretofore been.

ABJURATION OF THE REALM. In ancient English law. A renunciation of one's country, a species of self-imposed banishment, under an oath never to return to the kingdom unless by permission. This was formerly allowed to criminals, as a means of saving their lives, when they had confessed their crimes, and fled to sanctuary. See 4 Bl. Comm. 332.

ABJURE. To renounce, or abandon, by or upon oath. See ABJURATION.

"The decision of this court in Arthur v. Broadnax, 3 Ala. 557, affirms that if the husband has *abjured* the state, and remains abroad, the wife, meanwhile trading as a *feme sole,* could recover on a note which was given to her as such. We must consider the term 'abjure,' as there used, as implying a total abandonment of the state; a departure from the state without the intention of returning, and not a renunciation of one's country, upon an oath of perpetual banishment, as the term originally implied." 15 Ala. 148.

ABLE-BODIED. As used in a statute relating to service in the militia, this term does not imply an absolute freedom from all physical ailment. It imports an absence of those palpable and visible defects which evidently incapacitate the person from performing the ordinary duties of a soldier. 10 Vt. 152.

ABLEGATI. Papal ambassadors of the second rank, who are sent to a country where there is not a nuncio, with a less extensive commission than that of a nuncio.

ABLOCATIO. A letting out to hire, or leasing for money. Calvin. Sometimes used in the English form "ablocation."

ABMATERTERA. Lat. In the civil law. A great-great-grandmother's sister, (*abaviæ soror.*) Inst. 3, 6, 6; Dig. 38, 10, 3. Called *matertera maxima.* Id. 38, 10, 10, 17. Called, by Bracton, *abmatertera magna.* Bract. fol. 68b.

ABNEPOS. Lat. A great-great-grandson. The grandson of a grandson or granddaughter. Calvin.

ABNEPTIS. Lat. A great-great-granddaughter. The granddaughter of a grandson or granddaughter. Calvin.

ABODE. The place where a person dwells.

ABOLITION. The destruction, abrogation, or extinguishment of anything; also the leave given by the sovereign or judges to a criminal accuser to desist from further prosecution. 25 Hen. VIII. c. 21.

ABORDAGE. Fr. In French commercial law. Collision of vessels.

ABORTION. In criminal law. The miscarriage or premature delivery of a woman who is quick with child. When this is brought about with a malicious design, or for an unlawful purpose, it is a crime in law.

The act of bringing forth what is yet imperfect; and particularly the delivery or expulsion of the human *fœtus* prematurely, or before it is yet capable of sustaining life. Also the thing prematurely brought forth, or product of an untimely process. Sometimes loosely used for the offense of procuring a premature delivery; but, strictly, the early delivering is the abortion; causing or procuring abortion is the full name of the offense. Abbott.

ABORTIVE TRIAL. A term descriptive of the result when a case has gone off, and no verdict has been pronounced, without the fault, contrivance, or management of the parties. Jebb & B. 51.

ABORTUS. Lat. The fruit of an abortion; the child born before its time, incapable of life.

ABOUT. Nearly; approximating to; in the neighborhood of; not much more or less than. An expression constantly used where a time or sum cannot be precisely stated, importing the possibility of a small variation from it.

ABOUTISSEMENT. Fr. An abuttal or abutment. See Guyot, Répert. Univ. "*Aboutissans.*"

ABOVE. (Lat. *super, supra.*) In practice. Higher; superior. The court to which a cause is removed by appeal or writ of error is called the court *above.* Principal; as distinguished from what is auxiliary or instrumental. Bail to the action, or special bail, is otherwise termed bail *above.* 3 Bl. Comm. 291. See BELOW.

ABOVE CITED or MENTIONED. Quoted before. A figurative expression taken from the ancient manner of writing books on scrolls, where whatever is mentioned or cited before in the same roll must be *above.* Encyc. Lond.

ABPATRUUS. Lat. In the civil law. A great-great-grandfather's brother, (*abavi frater.*) Inst. 3, 6, 6; Dig. 38, 10, 3. Called *patruus maximus.* Id. 38, 10, 10, 17. Called, by Bracton and Fleta, *abpatruus magnus.* Bract. fol. 68b; Fleta, lib. 6, c. 2, § 17.

ABRIDGE. To reduce or contract; usually spoken of written language.

In copyright law, to abridge means to epitomize; to reduce; to contract. It implies preserving the substance, the essence, of a work, in language suited to such a purpose. In making *extracts* there is no condensation of the author's language, and hence no abridgment. To abridge requires the exercise of the mind; it is not *copying.* Between a compilation and an abridgment there is a clear distinction. A compilation consists of selected extracts from different authors; an abridgment is a condensation of the views of one author. 4 McLean, 306, 310.

In practice. To shorten a declaration or count by taking away or severing some of the substance of it. Brooke, Abr. "Abridgment."

ABRIDGMENT. An epitome or compendium of another and larger work, wherein the principal ideas of the larger work are summarily contained.

Abridgments of the law are brief digests of the law, arranged alphabetically. The oldest are those of Fitzherbert, Brooke, and Rolle; the more modern those of Viner, Comyns, and Bacon. (1 Steph. Comm. 51.) The term "digest" has now supplanted that of "abridgment." Sweet.

ABRIDGMENT OF DAMAGES. The right of the court to reduce the damages in certain cases. *Vide* Brooke, tit. "Abridgment."

ABROGATE. To annul, repeal, or destroy; to annul or repeal an order or rule issued by a subordinate authority; to repeal a former law by legislative act, or by usage.

ABROGATION. The annulment of a law by constitutional authority. It stands opposed to *rogation;* and is distinguished from *derogation,* which implies the taking away only some part of a law; from *subrogation,* which denotes the adding a clause to it; from *dispensation,* which only sets it aside in a particular instance; and from *antiquation,* which is the refusing to pass a law. Encyc. Lond.

ABSCOND. To go in a clandestine manner out of the jurisdiction of the courts, or to lie concealed, in order to avoid their process.

To hide, conceal, or absent oneself clandestinely, with the intent to avoid legal process. 2 Sneed, 153. See, also, 8 Kan. 262; 1 Ala. 200.

ABSCONDING DEBTOR. One who absconds from his creditors.

An absconding debtor is one who lives without the state, or who has intentionally concealed himself from his creditors, or withdrawn himself from the reach of their suits, with intent to frustrate their just demands. Thus, if a person departs from his usual residence, or remains absent therefrom, or conceals himself in his house, so that he cannot be served with process, with intent unlawfully to delay or defraud his creditors, he is an absconding debtor; but if he departs from the state or from his usual abode, with the intention of again returning, and without any fraudulent design, he has not absconded, nor absented himself, within the intendment of the law. 5 Conn. 121.

A party may abscond, and subject himself to the operation of the attachment law against absconding debtors, without leaving the limits of the state. 7 Md. 209.

A debtor who is shut up from his creditors in his own house is an absconding debtor. 2 Root, 133.

ABSENCE. The state of being absent, removed, or away from one's domicile, or usual place of residence.

Absence is of a fivefold kind: (1) A *necessary absence,* as in banished or transported persons; this is entirely necessary. (2) *Necessary and voluntary,* as upon the account of the commonwealth, or in the service of the church. (3) A *probable absence,* according to the civilians, as that of students on the score of study. (4) *Entirely voluntary,* on account of trade, merchandise, and the like. (5) *Absence cum dolo et culpâ*, as not appearing to a writ, *subpœna*, citation, etc., or to delay or defeat creditors, or avoiding arrest, either on civil or criminal process. Ayliffe.

Where the statute allows the vacation of a judgment rendered against a defendant "in his absence," the term "absence" means non-appearance to the action, and not merely that the party was not present in court. 12 Neb. 423, 11 N. W. Rep. 867.

ABSENCE. In Scotch law. Want or default of appearance. A decree is said to be *in absence* where the defender (defendant) does not appear. Ersk. Inst. bk. 4, tit. 3, § 6. See DECREET.

ABSENTE. Lat. (Abl. of *absens*.) Being absent. A common term in the old reports. "The three justices, *absente* North, C. J., were clear of opinion." 2 Mod. 14.

ABSENTEE. One who dwells abroad; a landlord who resides in a country other than that from which he draws his rents. The discussions on the subject have generally had reference to Ireland. McCul. Pol. Econ.; 33 Brit. Quar. Rev. 455.

One who is absent from his usual place of residence or domicile.

In Louisiana law and practice. A person who has resided in the state, and has departed without leaving any one to represent him. Also, a person who never was domiciliated in the state and resides abroad. Civil Code La. art. 3556; 18 La. Ann. 696; 30 La. Ann. 880.

ABSENTEES, or DES ABSENTEES. A parliament so called was held at Dublin, 10th May, 8 Hen. VIII. It is mentioned in letters patent 29 Hen. VIII.

Absentem accipere debemus eum qui non est eo loci in quo petitur. We ought to consider him absent who is not in the place where he is demanded. Dig. 50, 16, 199.

Absentia ejus qui reipublicæ causâ abest, neque ei neque alii damnosa esse debet. The absence of him who is away in behalf of the republic (on business of the state) ought neither to be prejudicial to him nor to another. Dig. 50, 17, 140.

ABSOILE—ASSOILE. To pardon or set free; used with respect to deliverance from excommunication. Cowell; Kelham.

Absoluta sententia expositore non indiget. An absolute sentence or proposition (one that is plain without any scruple, or absolute without any saving) needs not an expositor. 2 Inst. 533.

ABSOLUTE. Unconditional; complete and perfect in itself, without relation to, or dependence on, other things or persons,—as an *absolute* right; without condition, exception, restriction, qualification, or limitation, —as an *absolute* conveyance, an *absolute* estate; final, peremptory,—as an *absolute* rule

ABSOLUTE CONVEYANCE. A conveyance by which the right or property in a thing is transferred, free of any condition or qualification, by which it might be defeated or changed; as an ordinary deed of lands, in contradistinction to a mortgage, which is a conditional conveyance. Burrill.

ABSOLUTE COVENANT. A covenant which is unconditional or unqualified.

ABSOLUTE ESTATE. An estate in lands not subject to be defeated upon any condition.

In this phrase the word "absolute" is not used legally to distinguish a fee from a life-estate, but a qualified or conditional fee from a fee-simple. 71 Pa. St. 483.

ABSOLUTE INTEREST. That is an absolute interest in property which is so completely vested in the individual that he can by no contingency be deprived of it without his own consent. So, too, he is the owner of such absolute interest who must necessarily sustain the loss if the property is destroyed. The terms "interest" and "title" are not synonymous. A mortgagor in possession, and a purchaser holding under a deed defectively executed, have, both of them, absolute, as well as insurable, interests in the property, though neither of them has the legal title. "Absolute" is here synonymous with "vested," and is used in contradistinction to contingent or conditional. 29 Conn. 20.

ABSOLUTE LAW. The true and proper law of nature, immutable in the abstract or in principle, in theory, but not in application; for very often the object, the reason, situation, and other circumstances, may vary its exercise and obligation. 1 Steph. Comm. 21 et seq.

ABSOLUTE PROPERTY. Absolute property is where a man hath solely and exclusively the right, and also the occupation, of movable chattels; distinguished from a qualified property, as that of a bailee. 2 Bl. Comm. 388; 2 Kent, Comm. 347.

ABSOLUTE RIGHTS. Absolute rights are such as appertain and belong to particular persons merely as individuals or single persons, as distinguished from relative rights, which are incident to them as members of society. 1 Bl. Comm. 123; 1 Chit. Pl. 364; 1 Chit. Pr. 32.

ABSOLUTE RULE. In practice. A rule of court commanding something to be done *absolutely*, and at all events, as distinguished from a rule *nisi*, which commands something to be done, *unless* cause be shown against it; or, as the latter is more commonly called, a rule to *show cause* why a thing should not be done. 3 Steph. Comm. 680.

ABSOLUTE WARRANDICE. In Scotch law. A warranting or assuring of property against all mankind. It is, in effect, a covenant of title.

ABSOLUTELY. Completely; wholly; without qualification; without reference or relation to, or dependence upon, any other person, thing, or event.

ABSOLUTION. In the civil law. A sentence whereby a party accused is declared innocent of the crime laid to his charge.

In canon law. A juridical act whereby the clergy declare that the sins of such as are penitent are remitted.

In French law. The dismissal of an accusation. The term "acquitment" is employed when the accused is declared not guilty and "absolution" when he is recognized as guilty but the act is not punishable by law, or he is exonerated by some defect of intention or will. Merl. Repert.; Bouvier.

ABSOLUTISM. Any system of government, be it a monarchy or democracy, in which one or more persons, or a class, govern absolutely, and at pleasure, without check or restraint from any law, constitutional device, or co-ordinate body.

ABSOLVITOR. In Scotch law. An acquittal; a decree in favor of the defender in any action.

ABSQUE. Without. Occurs in phrases taken from the Latin; such as the following:

ABSQUE ALIQUO INDE REDENDO. (Without rendering anything therefrom.) A grant from the crown reserving no rent. 2 Rolle, Abr. 502.

ABSQUE CONSIDERATIONE CURIÆ. In old practice. Without the con-

sideration of the court; without judgment. Fleta, lib. 2, c. 47, § 13.

ABSQUE HOC. Without this. These are technical words of denial, used in pleading at common law by way of special traverse, to introduce the negative part of the plea, following the affirmative part or inducement.

ABSQUE IMPETITIONE VASTI. Without impeachment of waste; without accountability for waste; without liability to suit for waste. A clause anciently often inserted in leases, (as the equivalent English phrase sometimes is,) signifying that the tenant or lessee shall not be liable to suit, (*impetitio*,) or challenged, or called to account, for committing waste. 2 Bl. Comm. 283; 4 Kent, Comm. 78; Co. Litt. 220a; Litt. § 352.

ABSQUE TALI CAUSA. (Lat. without such cause.) Formal words in the now obsolete replication *de injuria*. Steph. Pl. 191.

ABSTENTION. In French law. Keeping an heir from possession; also tacit renunciation of a succession by an heir. Merl. Repert.

ABSTRACT. An abstract is a less quantity containing the virtue and force of a greater quantity. A transcript is generally defined a copy, and is more comprehensive than an abstract. 10 S. C. 283.

ABSTRACT OF A FINE. In old conveyancing. One of the parts of a fine, being an abstract of the writ of covenant, and the concord, naming the parties, the parcels of land, and the agreement. 2 Bl. Comm. 351; Shep. Touch. 3. More commonly called the "note" of the fine. See FINE; CONCORD.

ABSTRACT OF TITLE. A condensed history of the title to land, consisting of a synopsis or summary of the material or operative portion of all the conveyances, of whatever kind or nature, which in any manner affect said land, or any estate or interest therein, together with a statement of all liens, charges, or liabilities to which the same may be subject, and of which it is in any way material for purchasers to be apprised. Warv. Abst. § 2.

An abstract of a judgment or title is not the same as a copy of a judgment or title. An "abstract of a title" is a brief account of all the deeds upon which the title rests; a synopsis of the distinctive portions of the various instruments which constitute the muniments of title. See Prest. Abst.; Whart. Law Dict. (2d Lond. Ed.;) Bouv.

Law Dict. 47. An abstract, ordinarily, means a mere brief, and not a copy of that from which it is taken. 7 W. Va. 413.

Abundans cautela non nocet. Extreme caution does no harm. 11 Coke, 6*b.* This principle is generally applied to the construction of instruments in which superfluous words have been inserted more clearly to express the intention.

ABUSE, *v.* To make excessive or improper use of a thing, or to employ it in a manner contrary to the natural or legal rules for its use; to make an extravagant or excessive use, as to abuse one's authority.

In the civil law, the borrower of a chattel which, in its nature, cannot be used without consuming it, such as wine or grain, is said to abuse the thing borrowed if he uses it.

ABUSE, *n.* Everything which is contrary to good order established by usage. Merl. Repert. Departure from use; immoderate or improper use.

The "abuse or misuse" of its franchises by a corporation signifies any positive act in violation of the charter and in derogation of public right, willfully done, or caused to be done, by those appointed to manage the general concerns of the corporation. 3 Pittsb. R. 20; 26 Pa. St. 318.

Abuse of judicial discretion, and especially gross and palpable abuse of discretion, which are the terms ordinarily employed to justify an interference with the exercise of discretionary power, implies not merely error of judgment, but perversity of will, passion, prejudice, partiality, or moral delinquency. The exercise of an honest judgment, however erroneous it may appear to be, is not an abuse of discretion. 29 N. Y. 431.

ABUSE OF A FEMALE CHILD. An injury to the genital organs in an attempt at carnal knowledge, falling short of actual penetration. 58 Ala. 376.

ABUSE OF DISTRESS. The using an animal or chattel distrained, which makes the distrainer liable as for a conversion.

ABUSE OF PROCESS. There is said to be an abuse of process when an adversary, through the malicious and unfounded use of some regular legal proceeding, obtains some advantage over his opponent. Wharton.

A malicious abuse of legal process is where the party employs it for some unlawful object, not the purpose which it is intended by the law to effect; in other words, a perversion of it. 64 Pa. St. 285.

ABUT. To reach, to touch. In old law, the ends were said to abut, the sides to adjoin. Cro. Jac. 184.

ABUTMENTS. The ends of a bridge, or those parts of it which touch the land.

ABUTTALS. (From *abut,* q. v.) Commonly defined "the buttings and boundings of lands, east, west, north, and south, showing on what other lands, highways, or places they *abut,* or are limited and bounded." Cowell; Toml.

AC ETIAM. (Lat. And also.) Words used to introduce the statement of the real cause of action, in those cases where it was necessary to allege a fictitious cause of action to give the court jurisdiction, and also the real cause, in compliance with the statutes.

AC SI. (Lat. As if.) Townsh. Pl. 23, 27. These words frequently occur in old English statutes. Lord Bacon expounds their meaning in the statute of uses: "The statute gives entry, not *simpliciter,* but with an *ac si.*" Bac. Read. Uses, Works, iv. 195.

ACADEMY. In its original meaning, an association formed for mutual improvement, or for the advancement of science or art; in later use, a species of educational institution, of a grade between the common school and the college.

ACAPTE. In French feudal law. A species of relief; a seignorial right due on every change of a tenant. A feudal right which formerly prevailed in Languedoc and Guyenne, being attached to that species of heritable estates which were granted on the contract of *emphyteusis.* Guyot, Inst. Feod. c. 5, § 12.

ACCEDAS AD CURIAM. An original writ out of chancery, directed to the sheriff, for the removal of a replevin suit from a hundred court or court baron to one of the superior courts. See Fitzh. Nat. Brev. 18; 3 Bl. Comm. 34; 1 Tidd, Pr. 38.

ACCEDAS AD VICE COMITEM. L. Lat. (You go to the sheriff.) A writ formerly directed to the coroners of a county in England, commanding them to go to the sheriff, where the latter had suppressed and neglected to return a writ of *pone,* and to deliver a writ to him requiring him to return it. Reg. Orig. 83. See PONE.

ACCELERATION. The shortening of the time for the vesting in possession of an expectant interest.

ACCEPT. To receive with approval or satisfaction; to receive with intent to retain. Also, in the capacity of drawee of a bill, to recognize the draft, and engage to pay it when due.

ACCEPTANCE. The taking and receiving of anything in good part, and as it were a tacit agreement to a preceding act, which might have been defeated or avoided if such acceptance had not been made. Brooke, Abr.

The act of a person to whom a thing is offered or tendered by another, whereby he receives the thing with the intention of retaining it, such intention being evidenced by a sufficient act.

The acceptance of goods sold under a contract which would be void by the statute of frauds without delivery and acceptance involves something more than the act of the vendor in the delivery. It requires that the vendee should also act, and that his act should be of such a nature as to indicate that he receives and accepts the goods delivered as his property. He must receive and retain the articles delivered, intending thereby to assume the title to them, to constitute the acceptance mentioned in the statute. 40 N. Y. 524. See, also, 10 Metc. 132.

In marine insurance, the acceptance of an abandonment by the underwriter is his assent, either express or to be implied from the surrounding circumstances, to the sufficiency and regularity of the abandonment. Its effect is to perfect the insured's right of action as for a total loss, if the cause of loss and circumstances have been truly disclosed. Rap. & Law.

Acceptance of a bill of exchange. In mercantile law. The act by which the person on whom a bill of exchange is drawn (called the "drawee") assents to the request of the drawer to pay it, or, in other words, engages, or makes himself liable, to pay it when due. 4 East, 57, 72; 2 Bl. Comm. 469. It may be by parol or in writing, and either general or special, absolute or conditional; and it may be impliedly, as well as expressly, given. 3 Kent, Comm. 83, 85; Story, Bills, §§ 238, 251. But the usual and regular mode of acceptance is by the drawee's writing across the face of the bill the word "acceptance," and subscribing his name; after which he is termed the *acceptor.* Id. § 243.

The following are the principal varieties of acceptances:

Absolute. An express and positive agreement to pay the bill according to its tenor.

Conditional. An engagement to pay the bill on the happening of a condition.

Express. An absolute acceptance.

Implied. An acceptance inferred by law from the acts or conduct of the drawee.

Partial. An acceptance varying from the tenor of the bill.

Qualified. One either conditional or partial, and which introduces a variation in the sum, time, mode, or place of payment.

Special. One which specifies a particular place for payment.

Supra protest. An acceptance by a third person, after protest of the bill for non-acceptance by the drawee, to save the honor of the drawer or some particular indorser.

ACCEPTANCE AU BESOIN. Fr. In French law. Acceptance in case of need; an acceptance by one on whom a bill is drawn *au besoin,* that is, in case of refusal or failure of the drawee to accept. Story, Bills, §§ 65, 254, 255.

ACCEPTARE. Lat. In old pleading. To accept. *Acceptavit,* he accepted. 2 Strange, 817. *Non acceptavit,* he did not accept. 4 Man. & G. 7.

In the civil law. To accept; to assent; to assent to a promise made by another. Gro. de J. B. lib. 2, c. 11, § 14.

ACCEPTEUR PAR INTERVENTION. In French law. Acceptor of a bill for honor.

ACCEPTILATION. In the civil and Scotch law. A release made by a creditor to his debtor of his debt, without receiving any consideration. Ayl. Pand. tit. 26, p. 570. It is a species of donation, but not subject to the forms of the latter, and is valid unless in fraud of creditors. Merl. Repert.

The verbal extinction of a verbal contract, with a declaration that the debt has been paid when it has not; or the acceptance of something merely imaginary in satisfaction of a verbal contract. Sanders' Just. Inst. (5th Ed.) 386.

ACCEPTOR. The person who accepts a bill of exchange, (generally the drawee,) or who engages to be primarily responsible for its payment.

ACCEPTOR SUPRA PROTEST. One who accepts a bill which has been protested, for the honor of the drawer or any one of the indorsers.

ACCESS. Approach; or the means, power, or opportunity of approaching. Sometimes importing the occurrence of sexual intercourse; otherwise as importing opportunity of communication for that purpose as between husband and wife.

In real property law, the term "access" denotes the right vested in the owner of land which adjoins a road or other highway to go and return from his own land to the highway without obstruction.

ACCESSARY. In criminal law. Contributing to or aiding in the commission of a crime. One who, without being present at the commission of a felonious offense, becomes guilty of such offense, not as a chief actor, but as a participator, as by command, advice, instigation, or concealment; either before or after the fact or commission; a *particeps criminis.* 4 Bl. Comm. 35; Cowell.

An accessary is one who is not the chief actor in the offense, nor present at its performance, but in some way concerned therein, either *before* or *after* the act committed. Code Ga. 1882, § 4306.

ACCESSARY AFTER THE FACT. An accessary after the fact is a person who, having full knowledge that a crime has been committed, conceals it from the magistrate, and harbors, assists, or protects the person charged with, or convicted of, the crime. Code Ga. 1882, § 4308.

All persons who, after the commission of any felony, conceal or aid the offender, with knowledge that he has committed a felony, and with intent that he may avoid or escape from arrest, trial, conviction, or punishment, are accessaries. Pen. Code Dak. § 28.

All persons who, after full knowledge that a felony has been committed, conceal it from the magistrate, or harbor and protect the person charged with or convicted thereof, are accessaries. Pen. Code Cal. § 32.

An accessary *after the fact* is a person who, knowing a felony to have been committed by another, receives, relieves, comforts or assists the felon, in order to enable him to escape from punishment, or the like. 1 Russ. Crimes, 171; Steph. 27; 39 Miss. 702.

ACCESSARY BEFORE THE FACT. In criminal law. One who, being absent at the time a crime is committed, yet procures, counsels, or commands another to commit it; and, in this case, absence is necessary to constitute him an accessary, for, if he be present at any time during the transaction, he is guilty of the crime as principal. Plow. 97. 1 Hale, P. C. 615, 616; 4 Steph. Comm. 90, note *n.*

An accessary before the fact is one who, being absent at the time of the crime committed, doth yet procure, counsel, or command another to commit a crime. Code Ga. 1882, § 4307.

ACCESSARY TO ADULTERY. A phrase used in the law of divorce, and derived from the criminal law. It implies more than connivance, which is merely knowledge with consent. A conniver abstains from interference; an accessary directly commands, advises, or procures the adultery. A husband or wife who has been accessary to the adultery of the other party to the marriage cannot obtain a divorce on the ground of such adultery. 20 & 21 Vict. c. 85, §§ 29, 31. See Browne, Div.

ACCESSIO. In Roman law. An increase or addition; that which lies next to a thing, and is supplementary and necessary to the principal thing; that which arises or is produced from the principal thing. Calvin. Lex. Jurid.

One of the modes of acquiring property, being the extension of ownership over that which grows from, or is united to, an article which one already possesses.

ACCESSION. The right to all which one's own property produces, whether that property be movable or immovable; and the right to that which is united to it by accession, either naturally or artificially. 2 Kent, 360; 2 Bl. Comm. 404.

A principle derived from the civil law, by which the owner of property becomes entitled to all which it produces, and to all that is added or united to it, either naturally or artificially, (that is, by the labor or skill of another,) even where such addition extends to a change of form or materials; and by which, on the other hand, the possessor of property becomes entitled to it, as against the original owner, where the addition made to it by his skill and labor is of greater value than the property itself, or where the change effected in its form is so great as to render it impossible to restore it to its original shape. Burrill.

In international law. The absolute or conditional acceptance by one or several states of a treaty already concluded between other sovereignties. Merl. Repert. Also the commencement or inauguration of a sovereign's reign.

ACCESSION, DEED OF. In Scotch law. A deed executed by the creditors of a bankrupt or insolvent debtor, by which they approve of a trust given by their debtor for the general behoof, and bind themselves to concur in the plans proposed for extricating his affairs. Bell, Dict.

Accessorium non ducit, sed sequitur suum principale. Co. Litt. 152. That which is the accessory or incident does not lead, but follows, its principal.

Accessorius sequitur naturam sui principalis. An accessary follows the nature of his principal. 3 Inst. 139. One who is accessary to a crime cannot be guilty of a higher degree of crime than his principal.

ACCESSORY. Anything which is joined to another thing as an ornament, or to render it more perfect, or which accompanies it, or is connected with it as an incident, or as subordinate to it, or which belongs to or with it.

In criminal law. An accessary. The latter spelling is preferred. See that title.

ACCESSORY ACTION. In Scotch practice. An action which is subservient or auxiliary to another. Of this kind are actions of "proving the tenor," by which lost deeds are restored; and actions of "transumpts," by which copies of principal deeds are certified. Bell, Dict.

ACCESSORY CONTRACT. In the civil law. A contract which is incident or auxiliary to another or principal contract; such as the engagement of a surety. Poth. Obl. pt. 1, c. 1, § 1, art. 2.

A principal contract is one entered into by both parties on their own accounts, or in the several qualities they assume. An accessory contract is made for assuring the performance of a prior contract, either by the same parties or by others; such as suretyship, mortgage, and pledge. Civil Code La. art. 1771.

ACCESSORY OBLIGATION. In the civil law. An obligation which is incident to another or principal obligation; the obligation of a surety. Poth. Obl. pt. 2, c. 1, § 6.

In Scotch law. Obligations to antecedent or primary obligations, such as obligations to pay interest, etc. Ersk. Inst. lib. 3, tt. 3, § 60.

ACCIDENT. An unforeseen event, occurring without the will or design of the person whose mere act causes it; an unexpected, unusual, or undesigned occurrence; the effect of an unknown cause, or, the cause being known, an unprecedented consequence of it; a casualty.

There is nothing in the definition of the word "accident" that excludes the negligence of the injured party as one of the elements contributing to produce the result. A very large proportion of those events which are universally called "accidents" happen through some carelessness of the party injured, which contributes to produce them. Thus, men are injured by the careless use of fire-arms, of explosive substances, of machinery, the careless management of horses, and in a thousand ways, where it can readily be seen afterwards that a little greater care on their part would have prevented it. Yet such injuries, having been unexpected, and not caused intentionally or by design, are always called "accidents," and properly so. 24 Wis. 28.

In equity practice. Such an unforeseen event, misfortune, loss, act, or omission as is not the result of any negligence or misconduct in the party. Fran. Max. 87; Story, Eq. Jur. § 78.

The meaning to be attached to the word "accident," in relation to equitable relief, is any unforeseen and undesigned event, productive of disadvantage. Wharton.

An accident relievable in equity is such an occurrence, not the result of negligence or misconduct of the party seeking relief in relation to a contract, as was not anticipated by the parties when the same was entered into, and which gives an undue advantage to one of them over another in a court of law. Code Ga. 1882, § 3112.

Accipere quid ut justitiam facias, non est tam accipere quam extorquere. To accept anything as a reward for doing justice is rather extorting than accepting. Lofft, 72.

ACCIPITARE. To pay relief to lords of manors. *Capitali domino accipitare, i. e.,* to pay a relief, homage, or obedience to the chief lord on becoming his vassal. Fleta, lib. 2, c. 50.

ACCOLA. In the civil law. One who inhabits or occupies land near a place, as one who dwells by a river, or on the bank of a river. Dig. 43, 13, 3, 6.

In feudal law. A husbandman; an agricultural tenant; a tenant of a manor. Spelman. A name given to a class of villeins in Italy. Barr. St. 302.

ACCOMENDA. In maritime law. A contract between the owner of goods and the master of a ship, by which the former intrusts the property to the latter to be sold by him on their joint account.

In such case, two contracts take place: First, the contract called *mandatum,* by which the owner of the property gives the master power to dispose of it; and the contract of partnership, in virtue of which the profits are to be divided between them. One party runs the risk of losing his capital; the other, his labor. If the sale produces no more than first cost, the owner takes all the proceeds. It is only the profits which are to be divided. Emerig. Mar. Loans, § 5.

ACCOMMODATION. An arrangement or engagement made as a favor to another, not upon a consideration received; something done to oblige, usually spoken of a loan of money or commercial paper; also a friendly agreement or composition of differences. Abbott.

ACCOMMODATION LANDS. Land bought by a builder or speculator, who erects houses thereon, and then leases portions thereof upon an improved ground-rent.

ACCOMMODATION PAPER. An accommodation bill or note is one to which the accommodating party, be he acceptor, drawer, or indorser, has put his name, without consideration, for the purpose of benefiting or accommodating some other party who desires to raise money on it, and is to provide for the bill when due.

ACCOMMODATION WORKS. Works which a railway company is required to make and maintain for the accommodation of the owners or occupiers of land adjoining the railway, e. g., gates, bridges, culverts, fences, etc. 8 Vict. c. 20, § 68.

ACCOMPLICE. (From *ad*, to, and *complicare*, to fold up, or wrap together.) In criminal law. One who is joined or united with another; one of several concerned in a felony; an associate in a crime; one who co-operates, aids, or assists in committing it. Tomlins; Jacob. This term includes all the *participes criminis*, whether considered in strict legal propriety as principals or as accessaries. 1 Russ. Crimes, 26. It is generally applied to those who are admitted to give evidence against their fellow criminals. 4 Bl. Comm. 331; Hawk. P. C. bk. 2, c. 37, § 7.

One who is in some way concerned in the commission of a crime, though not as a principal; and this includes all persons who have been concerned in its commission, whether they are considered, in strict legal propriety, as principals in the first or second degree, or merely as accessaries before or after the fact. 47 Ill. 152; 71 Cal. 20, 11 Pac. Rep. 799.

ACCORD, v. In practice. To agree or concur, as one judge with another. "I accord." Eyre, C. J., 12 Mod. 7. "The rest accorded." 7 Mod. 361.

ACCORD, n. A satisfaction agreed upon between the party injuring and the party injured which, when performed, is a bar to all actions upon this account. 75 N. Y. 576.

ACCORD AND SATISFACTION. An agreement between two persons, one of whom has a right of action against the other, that the latter should do or give, and the former accept, something in satisfaction of the right of action different from, and usually less than, what might be legally enforced. When the agreement is executed, and satisfaction has been made, it is called "accord and satisfaction."

An accord and satisfaction may be briefly defined as "the settlement of a dispute or the satisfaction of a claim, by an executed agreement between the party injuring and the party injured;" or, to give a definition indicating more definitely its peculiar nature, it is "something of legal value to which the creditor before had no right, received in full satisfaction of the debt, without regard to the magnitude of the satisfaction." 1 Smith, Lead. Cas. (10th Amer. Ed.,) 558; 43 Conn. 462.

Accord and satisfaction is the substitution of another agreement between the parties in satisfaction of the former one, and an execution of the latter agreement. Such is the definition of this sort of defense, usually given. But a broader application of the doctrine has been made in later times, where one promise or agreement is set up in satisfaction of another. The rule is that an agreement or promise of the same grade will not be held to be in satisfaction of a prior one, unless it has been expressly accepted as such; as, where a new promissory note has been given in lieu of a former one, to have the effect of a satisfaction of the former, it must have been accepted on an express agreement to that effect. 50 Miss. 257.

An accord is an agreement to accept, in extinction of an obligation, something different from or less than that to which the person agreeing to accept is entitled. Civil Code Cal. § 1521; Civil Code Dak. § 859.

ACCORDANT. Fr. and Eng. Agreeing; concurring. "Baron Parker, *accordant*," Hardr. 93; "Holt, C. J., *accordant*," 6 Mod. 299; "Powys, J., *accord*," "Powell, J., *accord*," Id. 298.

ACCOUCHEMENT. The act of a woman in giving birth to a child. The fact of the accouchement, proved by a person who was present, is often important evidence in proving the parentage of a person.

ACCOUNT. A detailed statement of the mutual demands in the nature of debt and credit between parties, arising out of contracts or some fiduciary relation. 1 Metc. (Mass.) 216; 1 Hemp. 114; 32 Pa. St. 202.

A statement in writing, of debts and credits, or of receipts and payments; a list of items of debts and credits, with their respective dates. 5 Cow. 593.

The word is sometimes used to denote the balance, or the right of action for the balance, appearing due upon a statement of dealings; as where one speaks of an assignment of accounts; but there is a broad distinction between an account and the mere balance of an account, resembling the distinction in logic between the premises of an argument and the conclusions drawn therefrom. A balance is but the conclusion or result of the debit and credit sides of an account. It implies mutual dealings, and the existence of debt and credit, without which there could be no balance. 45 Mo. 574.

The word is often used in the sense of "behalf," or "charge;" as in saying that an agent acts upon account of his principal; that a policy is issued on account of whom it may concern. Abbott.

ACCOUNT. In practice. A writ or action at common law, (sometimes called "account render,") which lies against a person who, by reason of his office or business as bailiff, receiver, or guardian, ought to render an account to another, but refuses to do so. Fitzh. Nat. Brev. 116; Co. Litt. 172.

Account is a writ or action brought against a person who, by means of his office as a guardian, or for some business he has undertaken as an agent, or some money he has received for another, ought to render an account to him, and refuses to do it; and he that calls him to an account shall recover of him not only what shall be found due, but also damages for the wrong done him. 1 Amer. & Eng. Enc. Law, 128.

ACCOUNT-BOOK. A book kept by a merchant, trader, mechanic, or other person, in which are entered from time to time the transactions of his trade or business. Such books, when regularly kept, may be admitted in evidence. Greenl. Ev. §§ 115–118.

ACCOUNT CURRENT. An open or running or unsettled account between two parties.

ACCOUNT DUTIES. Duties payable by the English customs and inland revenue act, 1881, (44 Vict. c. 12, § 38,) on a *donatio mortis causa*, or on any gift, the donor of which dies within three months after making it, or on joint property voluntarily so created, and taken by survivorship, or on property taken under a voluntary settlement in which the settlor had a life-interest.

ACCOUNT RENDERED. An account made out by the creditor, and presented to the debtor for his examination and acceptance. When accepted, it becomes an account stated.

ACCOUNT STATED. The settlement of an account between the parties, with a balance struck in favor of one of them; an account rendered by the creditor, and by the debtor assented to as correct, either expressly, or by implication of law from the failure to object.

This was also a common count in a declaration upon a contract under which the plaintiff might prove an absolute acknowledgment by the defendant of a liquidated demand of a fixed amount, which implies a promise to pay on request. It might be joined with any other count for a money demand. The acknowledgment or admission must have been made to the plaintiff or his agent. Wharton.

ACCOUNTABLE. Subject to pay; responsible; liable. Where one indorsed a note "A. C. accountable," it was held that, under this form of indorsement, he had waived demand and notice. 42 N. H. 74.

ACCOUNTABLE RECEIPT. An instrument acknowledging the receipt of money or personal property, coupled with an obligation to account for or pay or deliver the whole or some part of it to some person. 27 Minn. 315, 7 N. W. Rep. 262.

ACCOUNTANT. One who keeps accounts; a person skilled in keeping books or accounts; an expert in accounts or bookkeeping.

A person who renders an account. When an executor, guardian, etc., renders an account of the property in his hands and his administration of the trust, either to the beneficiary or to a court, he is styled, for the purpose of that proceeding, the "accountant."

ACCOUNTANT GENERAL, or ACCOMPTANT GENERAL. An officer of the court of chancery, appointed by act of parliament to receive all money lodged in court, and to place the same in the Bank of England for security. 12 Geo. I. c. 32; 1 Geo. IV. c. 35; 15 & 16 Vict. c. 87, §§ 18–22, 39. See Daniell, Ch. Pr. (4th Ed.) 1607 et seq. The office, however, has been abolished by 35 & 36 Vict. c. 44, and the duties transferred to her majesty's paymaster general.

ACCOUNTING. The making up and rendition of an account, either voluntarily or by order of a court.

ACCOUPLE. To unite; to marry. *Ne unques accouple*, never married.

ACCREDIT. In international law. (1) To receive as an envoy in his public character, and give him credit and rank accordingly. Burke. (2) To send with credentials as an envoy. Webst. Dict.

ACCREDULITARE. L. · Lat. In old records. To purge an offense by oath. Blount; Whishaw.

ACCRESCERE. In the civil and old English law. To grow to; to pass to, and become united with, as soil to land *per alluvionem*. Dig. 41, 1, 30, pr.

ACCRETION. The act of growing to a thing; usually applied to the gradual and imperceptible accumulation of land by natural causes, as out of the sea or a river. Accretion of land is of two kinds: By *alluvion*, *i. e.*, by the washing up of sand or soil, so as to form firm ground; or by *dereliction*, as when the sea shrinks below the usual watermark.

The increase of real estate by the addition of portions of soil, by gradual deposition through the operation of natural causes, to that already in possession of the owner. 2 Washb. Real Prop. 451.

ACCROACH. To encroach; to exercise power without due authority.

To attempt to exercise royal power. 4 Bl. Comm. 76. A knight who forcibly assaulted and detained one of the king's subjects till he paid him a sum of money was held to have committed treason, on the ground of accroachment. 1 Hale, P. C. 80.

ACCROCHER. Fr. In French law. To delay; retard; put off. *Accrocher un procès*, to stay the proceedings in a suit.

ACCRUE. To grow to; to be added to; to attach itself to; as a subordinate or accessory claim or demand arises out of, and is joined to, its principal; thus, costs accrue to a judgment, and interest to the principal debt.

The term is also used of independent or original demands, and then means to arise, to happen, to come into force or existence; as in the phrase, "The right of action did not *accrue* within six years."

ACCRUER, CLAUSE OF. An express clause, frequently occurring in the case of gifts by deed or will to persons as tenants in common, providing that upon the death of one or more of the beneficiaries his or their shares shall go to the survivor or survivors. Brown. The share of the decedent is then said to *accrue* to the others.

ACCRUING. Inchoate; in process of maturing. That which will or may, at a future time, ripen into a vested right, an available demand, or an existing cause of action. 13 Ohio St. 382.

ACCRUING COSTS. Costs and expenses incurred after judgment.

ACCUMULATED SURPLUS. In statutes relative to the taxation of corporations, this term refers to the fund which the company has in excess of its capital and liabilities. 34 N. J. Law, 493; 35 N. J. Law, 577.

ACCUMULATIONS. When an executor or other trustee masses the rents, dividends, and other income which he receives, treats it as a capital, invests it, makes a new capital of the income derived therefrom, invests that, and so on, he is said to accumulate the fund, and the capital and accrued income thus procured constitute *accumulations*.

ACCUMULATIVE. That which accumulates, or is heaped up; additional. Said of several things heaped together, or of one thing added to another.

ACCUMULATIVE JUDGMENT. Where a person has already been convicted and sentenced, and a second or additional judgment is passed against him, the execution of which is postponed until the completion of the first sentence, such second judgment is said to be *accumulative*.

ACCUMULATIVE LEGACY. A second, double, or additional legacy; a legacy given in addition to another given by the same instrument, or by another instrument.

Accusare nemo se debet, nisi coram Deo. No one is bound to accuse himself, except before God. See Hardres, 139.

ACCUSATION. A formal charge against a person, to the effect that he is guilty of a punishable offense, laid before a court or magistrate having jurisdiction to inquire into the alleged crime.

Accusator post rationabile tempus non est audiendus, nisi se bene de omissione excusaverit. Moore, 817. An accuser ought not to be heard after the expiration of a reasonable time, unless he can account satisfactorily for the delay.

ACCUSE. To bring a formal charge of crime against a person, before a competent court or officer. 30 Mich. 468. See 5 Rich. 492.

ACCUSED. The person against whom an accusation is made.
"Accused" is the generic name for the defendant in a criminal case, and is more appropriate than either "prisoner" or "defendant." 1 Car. & K. 131.

ACCUSER. The person by whom an accusation is made.

ACEPHALI. The levelers in the reign of Hen. I., who acknowledged no head or superior. Leges H. 1; Cowell. Also certain ancient heretics, who appeared about the beginning of the sixth century, and asserted that there was but one substance in Christ, and one nature. Wharton.

ACEQUIA. In Mexican law. A ditch, channel, or canal, through which water, diverted from its natural course, is conducted, for use in irrigation or other purposes.

ACHAT. Fr. A purchase or bargain. Cowell.

ACHERSET. In old English law. A measure of corn, conjectured to have been the same with our quarter, or eight bushels. Cowell.

ACKNOWLEDGE. To own, avow, or admit; to confess; to recognize one's acts, and assume the responsibility therefor.

ACKNOWLEDGMENT. In conveyancing. The act by which a party who has executed an instrument of conveyance as grantor goes before a competent officer or court, and declares or acknowledges the same as his genuine and voluntary act and deed. The certificate of the officer on such instrument that it has been so acknowledged.
The term is also used of the act of a person who avows or admits the truth of certain facts which, if established, will entail a civil liability upon him. Thus, the debtor's *acknowledgment* of the creditor's demand or right of action will toll the statute of limitations. *Admission* is also used in this sense. To denote an avowal of criminal acts, or the concession of the truth of a criminal charge, the word "confession" seems more appropriate.

ACKNOWLEDGMENT MONEY. A sum paid in some parts of England by copyhold tenants on the death of their lords, as a recognition of their new lords, in like manner as money is usually paid on the attornment of tenants. Cowell.

ACOLYTE. An inferior ministrant or servant in the ceremonies of the church, whose duties are to follow and wait upon the priests and deacons, etc.

ACQUEST. An estate acquired newly, or by purchase. 1 Reeve, Eng. Law, 56.

ACQUETS. In the civil law. Property which has been acquired by purchase, gift, or otherwise than by succession. Immovable property which has been acquired otherwise than by succession. Merl. Repert.
Profits or gains of property, as between husband and wife. Civil Code La. § 2369.

ACQUIESCE. To give an implied consent to a transaction, to the accrual of a right, or to any act, by one's mere silence, or without express assent or acknowledgment.

ACQUIESCENCE. Acquiescence is where a person who knows that he is entitled to impeach a transaction or enforce a right neglects to do so for such a length of time that, under the circumstances of the case, the other party may fairly infer that he has waived or abandoned his right. Sweet.

ACQUIETANDIS PLEGIIS. A writ of justices, formerly lying for the surety against a creditor who refuses to acquit him after the debt has been satisfied. Reg. Writs, 158; Cowell; Blount.

ACQUIRE. In the law of contracts and of descents; to become the owner of property; to make property one's own.

ACQUIRED. Coming to an intestate in any other way than by gift, devise, or descent from a parent or the ancestor of a parent. 2 Lea, 54.

ACQUISITION. The act of becoming the owner of certain property; the act by which one acquires or procures the property in anything. Used also of the thing acquired.

Original acquisition is where the title to the thing accrues through occupancy or accession, (*q. v.*,) or by the creative labor of the individual, as in the case of patents and copyrights.

Derivative acquisition is where property in a thing passes from one person to another. It may transpire by the act of the law, as in cases of forfeiture, insolvency, intestacy, judgment, marriage, or succession, or by the act of the parties, as in cases of gift, sale, or exchange.

ACQUIT. To release, absolve, or discharge one from an obligation or a liability; or to legally certify the innocence of one charged with crime.

ACQUIT À CAUTION. In French law. Certain goods pay higher export duties when exported to a foreign country than when they are destined for another French port. In order to prevent fraud, the administration compels the shipper of goods sent from one French port to another to give security that such goods shall not be sent to a foreign country. The certificate which proves the receipt of the security is called "*acquit à caution.*" Argles, Fr. Merc. Law, 543.

ACQUITTAL. In contracts. A release, absolution, or discharge from an obligation, liability, or engagement.

In criminal practice. The legal and formal certification of the innocence of a person who has been charged with crime; a deliverance or setting free a person from a charge of guilt.

The absolution of a party accused on a trial before a traverse jury. 1 Nott & McC. 36; 3 McCord, 461.

Acquittals in fact are those which take place when the jury, upon trial, finds a verdict of not guilty.

Acquittals in law are those which take place by mere operation of law; as where a man has been charged merely as an accessary, and the principal has been acquitted. 2 Co. Inst. 364.

In feudal law. The obligation on the part of a mesne lord to protect his tenant from any claims, entries, or molestations by lords paramount arising out of the services due to them by the mesne lord. See Co. Litt. 100*a*.

ACQUITTANCE. In contracts. A written discharge, whereby one is freed from an obligation to pay money or perform a duty. It differs from a *release* in not requiring to be under seal.

This word, though perhaps not strictly speaking synonymous with "receipt," includes it. A receipt is one form of an acquittance; a discharge is another. A receipt in full is an acquittance, and a receipt for a part of a demand or obligation is an acquittance *pro tanto.* 51 Vt. 104.

ACQUITTED. Released; absolved; purged of an accusation; judicially discharged from accusation; released from debt, etc. Includes both civil and criminal prosecutions. 26 Wend. 383, 399.

ACRE. A quantity of land containing 160 square rods of land, in whatever shape. Serg. Land Laws Pa. 185; Cro. Eliz. 476, 665; 6 Coke, 67; Poph. 55; Co. Litt. 5*b*.

Originally the word "acre" (*acer, aker,* or Sax. *æcer*) was not used as a measure of land, or to signify any determinate quantity of land, but to denote any open ground, (*latum quantumvis agrum,*) wide champaign, or field; which is still the meaning of the German *acker,* derived probably from the same source, and is preserved in the names of some places in England, as Castle Acre, South Acre, etc. Burrill.

ACREFIGHT, or ACRE. A camp or field fight; a sort of duel, or judicial combat, anciently fought by single combatants, English and Scotch, between the frontiers of the two kingdoms with sword and lance. Called "campfight," and the combatants "champions," from the open *field* that was the stage of trial. Cowell.

ACROSS. Under a grant of a right of way *across* the plaintiff's lot of land, the grantee has not a right to enter at one place, go partly across, and then come out at another place on the same side of the lot. 5 Pick. 163. See 10 Me. 391.

ACT, n. In its most general sense, this noun signifies something done voluntarily by a person: the exercise of an individual's power; an effect produced in the external world by an exercise of the power of a person objectively, prompted by intention, and proximately caused by a motion of the will. In a more technical sense, it means something done voluntarily by a person, and of such a nature that certain legal consequences attach to it. Thus a grantor acknowledges the conveyance to be his "*act* and deed," the terms being synonymous.

In the civil law. An *act* is a writing which states in a legal form that a thing has been said, done, or agreed. Merl. Repert.

In practice. Anything done by a court and reduced to writing; a decree, judgment, resolve, rule, order, or other judicial proceeding. In Scotch law, the orders and decrees of a court, and in French and German law, all the records and documents in an action, are called "acts."

In legislation. A written law, formally ordained or passed by the legislative power of a state, called in England an "act of parliament," and in the United States an "act of congress," or of the "legislature;" a statute.

Acts are either public or private. Public acts (also called general acts, or general statutes, or statutes at large) are those which relate to the community generally, or establish a universal rule for the governance of the whole body politic.

Private acts (formerly called special, Co. Litt. 126a) are those which relate either to particular persons (personal acts) or to particular places, (local acts,) or which operate only upon specified individuals or their private concerns.

In Scotch practice. An abbreviation of *actor*, (proctor or advocate, especially for a plaintiff or pursuer,) used in records. "*Act.* A. *Alt.* B." an abbreviation of *Actor*, A. *Alter*, B.; that is, for the pursuer or plaintiff, A., for the defender, B. 1 Broun, 336, note.

ACT, *v.* In Scotch practice. To do or perform judicially; to enter of record. Surety "acted in the Books of Adjournal." 1 Broun, 4.

ACT BOOK. In Scotch practice. The minute book of a court. 1 Swin. 81.

ACT IN PAIS. An act done or performed out of court, and not a matter of record.

A deed or an assurance transacted between two or more private persons in the country, that is, according to the old common law, upon the very spot to be transferred, is matter *in pais.* 2 Bl. Comm. 294.

ACT OF ATTAINDER. A legislative act, attainting a person. See ATTAINDER.

ACT OF BANKRUPTCY. Any act which renders a person liable to be proceeded against as a bankrupt, or for which he may be adjudged bankrupt. These acts are usual-

ly defined and classified in statutes on the subject.

ACT OF CURATORY. In Scotch law. The act extracted by the clerk, upon any one's acceptance of being curator. Forb. Inst. pt. 1, b. 1, c. 2, tit. 2. 2 Kames, Eq. 291. Corresponding with the order for the appointment of a guardian, in English and American practice.

ACT OF GOD. Inevitable accident; *vis major.* Any misadventure or casualty is said to be caused by the "act of God" when it happens by the direct, immediate, and exclusive operation of the forces of nature, uncontrolled or uninfluenced by the power of man and without human intervention, and is of such a character that it could not have been prevented or escaped from by any amount of foresight or prudence, or by any reasonable degree of care or diligence, or by the aid of any appliances which the situation of the party might reasonably require him to use.

Inevitable accident, or casualty; any accident produced by any physical cause which is irresistible, such as lightning, tempests, perils of the seas, an inundation, or earthquake; and also the sudden illness or death of persons. Story, Bailm. § 25; 2 Bl. Comm. 122; Broom, Max. 108.

Under the term "act of God" are comprehended all misfortunes and accidents arising from inevitable necessity, which human prudence could not foresee or prevent. 1 Conn. 491.

ACT OF GRACE. In Scotch law. A term applied to the act of 1696, c. 32, by which it was provided that where a person imprisoned for a civil debt is so poor that he cannot aliment [maintain] himself, and will make oath to that effect, it shall be in the power of the magistrates to cause the creditor by whom he is incarcerated to provide an aliment for him, or consent to his liberation; which, if the creditor delay to do for 10 days, the magistrate is authorized to set the debtor at liberty. Bell.

The term is often used to designate a general act of parliament, originating with the crown, such as has often been passed at the commencement of a new reign, or at the close of a period of civil troubles, declaring pardon or amnesty to numerous offenders. Abbott.

ACT OF HONOR. When a bill has been protested, and a third person wishes to take it up, or accept it, for honor of one or more of the parties, the notary draws up an instrument, evidencing the transaction, called by this name.

ACT OF INDEMNITY. A statute by which those who have committed illegal acts which subject them to penalties are protected from the consequences of such acts.

ACT OF INSOLVENCY. Within the meaning of the national currency act, an act of insolvency is an act which shows the bank to be insolvent; such as non-payment of its circulating notes, bills of exchange, or certificates of deposit; failure to make good the impairment of capital, or to keep good its surplus or reserve; in fact, any act which shows that the bank is unable to meet its liabilities as they mature, or to perform those duties which the law imposes for the purpose of sustaining its credit. 5 Biss. 504.

ACT OF LAW. The operation of fixed legal rules upon given facts or occurrences, producing consequences independent of the design or will of the parties concerned; as distinguished from "act of parties."

ACT OF PARLIAMENT. A statute, law, or edict, made by the British sovereign, with the advice and consent of the lords spiritual and temporal, and the commons, in parliament assembled. Acts of parliament form the *leges scriptæ, i. e.,* the written laws of the kingdom.

ACT OF SETTLEMENT. The statute (12 & 13 Wm. III. c. 2) limiting the crown to the Princess Sophia of Hanover, and to the heirs of her body being Protestants.

ACT OF STATE. An act done by the sovereign power of a country, or by its delegate, within the limits of the power vested in him. An act of state cannot be questioned or made the subject of legal proceedings in a court of law.

ACT OF SUPREMACY. The statute (1 Eliz. c. 1) by which the supremacy of the British crown in ecclesiastical matters within the realm was declared and established.

ACT OF UNIFORMITY. In English law. The statute of 13 & 14 Car. II. c. 4, enacting that the book of common prayer, as then recently revised, should be used in every parish church and other place of public worship, and otherwise ordaining a uniformity in religious services, etc. 3 Steph. Comm. 104.

ACT OF UNION. In English law. The statute of 5 Anne, c. 8, by which the articles of union between the two kingdoms of England and Scotland were ratified and confirmed. 1 Bl. Comm. 97.

ACT ON PETITION. A form of summary proceeding formerly in use in the high court of admiralty, in England, in which the parties stated their respective cases briefly, and supported their statements by affidavit. 2 Dod. Adm. 174, 184; 1 Hagg. Adm. 1, note.

ACTA DIURNA. Lat. In the Roman law. Daily acts; the public registers or journals of the daily proceedings of the senate, assemblies of the people, courts of justice, etc. Supposed to have resembled a modern newspaper. Brande.

Acta exteriora indicant interiora secreta. 8 Coke, 146*b*. External acts indicate undisclosed thoughts.

Acta in uno judicio non probant in alio nisi inter easdem personas. Things done in one action cannot be taken as evidence in another, unless it be between the same parties. Tray. Lat. Max. 11.

ACTA PUBLICA. Lat. Things of general knowledge and concern; matters transacted before certain public officers. Calvin.

ACTE. In French law, denotes a document, or formal, solemn writing, embodying a legal attestation that something has been done, corresponding to one sense or use of the English word "act." Thus, *actes de naissance* are the certificates of birth, and must contain the day, hour, and place of birth, together with the sex and intended christian name of the child, and the names of the parents and of the witnesses. *Actes de mariage* are the marriage certificates, and contain names, professions, ages, and places of birth and domicile of the two persons marrying, and of their parents; also the consent of these latter, and the mutual agreements of the intended husband and wife to take each other for better and worse, together with the usual attestations. *Actes de décès* are the certificates of death, which are required to be drawn up before any one may be buried. *Les actes de l' état civil* are public documents. Brown.

ACTE AUTHENTIQUE. In French law. A deed, executed with certain prescribed formalities, in the presence of a notary, mayor, *greffier, huissier,* or other functionary qualified to act in the place in which it is drawn up. Argles, Fr. Merc. Law, 50.

ACTE DE FRANCISATION. In French law. The certificate of registration of a ship, by virtue of which its French nationality is established.

ACTE D' HÉRITIER. In French law. Act of inheritance. Any action or fact on the part of an heir which manifests his intention to accept the succession; the acceptance may be express or tacit. Duverger.

ACTE EXTRAJUDICIAIRE. In French law. A document served by a *huissier*, at the demand of one party upon another party, without legal proceedings.

ACTING. A term employed to designate a *locum tenens* who is performing the duties of an office to which he does not himself claim title; *e. g.*, "*Acting* Supervising Architect." 16 Ct. of Cl. 514.

ACTIO. Lat. In the civil law. An action or suit; a right or cause of action. It should be noted that this term means both the proceeding to enforce a right in a court and the right itself which is sought to be enforced.

ACTIO AD EXHIBENDUM. In the civil law. An action for the purpose of compelling a defendant to exhibit a thing or title in his power. It was preparatory to another action, which was always a real action in the sense of the Roman law; that is, for the recovery of a thing, whether it was movable or immovable. Merl. Quest. tome i. 84.

ACTIO ÆSTIMATORIA. ACTIO QUANTI MINORIS. In the civil law. Two names of an action which lay in behalf of a buyer to reduce the contract price, not to cancel the sale; the *judex* had power, however, to cancel the sale. Hunter, Rom. Law, 332.

ACTIO ARBITRARIA. In the civil law. Action depending on the discretion of the judge. In this, unless the defendant would make amends to the plaintiff as dictated by the judge in his discretion, he was liable to be condemned. Hunter, Rom. Law, 825.

ACTIO BONÆ FIDEI. (Lat. An action of good faith.) In the civil law. A class of actions in which the judge might at the trial, *ex officio*, take into account any equitable circumstances that were presented to him affecting either of the parties to the action. 1 Spence, Eq. Jur. 218.

ACTIO CALUMNIÆ. In the civil law. An action to restrain the defendant from prosecuting a groundless proceeding or trumped-up charge against the plaintiff. Hunter, Rom. Law, 859.

ACTIO CIVILIS. In the common law. A civil action, as distinguished from a criminal action. Bracton divides personal actions into *criminalia et civilia*, according as they grow out of crimes or contracts, (*secundum quod descendunt ex maleficiis vel contractibus*.) Bract. fol. 101*b*.

ACTIO COMMODATI. In the civil law. Included several actions appropriate to enforce the obligations of a borrower or a lender. Hunter, Rom. Law, 305.

ACTIO COMMODATI CONTRARIA. In the civil law. An action by the borrower against the lender, to compel the execution of the contract. Poth. *Prêt à Usage*, n. 75.

ACTIO COMMODATI DIRECTA. In the civil law. An action by a lender against a borrower, the principal object of which is to obtain a restitution of the thing lent. Poth. *Prêt à Usage*, nn. 65, 68.

ACTIO COMMUNI DIVIDUNDO. In the civil law. An action to procure a judicial division of joint property. Hunter, Rom. Law, 194. It was analogous in its object to proceedings for partition in modern law.

ACTIO CONDICTIO INDEBITATI. In the civil law. An action by which the plaintiff recovers the amount of a sum of money or other thing he paid by mistake. Poth. Promutuum, n. 140; Merl. Repert.

ACTIO CONFESSORIA. In the civil law. An affirmative petitory action for the recognition and enforcement of a servitude. So called because based on the plaintiff's affirmative allegation of a right in defendant's land. Distinguished from an *actio negatoria*, which was brought to repel a claim of the defendant to a servitude in the plaintiff's land. Mackeld. Rom. Law, § 324.

ACTIO DAMNI INJURIA. In the civil law. The name of a general class of actions for damages, including many species of suits for losses caused by wrongful or negligent acts. The term is about equivalent to our "action for damages."

ACTIO DE DOLO MALO. In the civil law. An action of fraud; an action which lay for a defrauded person against the defrauder and his heirs, who had been enriched by the fraud, to obtain the restitution of the thing of which he had been fraudulently deprived, with all its accessions (*cum omni causa;*) or, where this was not practicable, for compensation in damages. Mackeld. Rom. Law, § 227.

ACTIO DE PECULIO. In the civil law. An action concerning or against the *peculium,* or separate property of a party.

ACTIO DE PECUNIA CONSTITU-TA. In the civil law. An action for money engaged to be paid; an action which lay against any person who had engaged to pay money for himself, or for another, without any formal stipulation, (*nulla stipulatione interposita.*) Inst. 4, 6, 9; Dig. 13, 5; Cod. 4, 18.

ACTIO DEPOSITI CONTRARIA. In the civil law. An action which the depositary has against the depositor, to compel him to fulfil his engagement towards him. Poth. *Du Dépôt,* n. 69.

ACTIO DEPOSITI DIRECTA. In the civil law. An action which is brought by the depositor against the depositary, in order to get back the thing deposited. Poth. *Du Dépôt,* n. 60.

ACTIO DIRECTA. In the civil law. A direct action; an action founded on strict law, and conducted according to fixed forms; an action founded on certain legal obligations which from their origin were accurately defined and recognized as actionable.

ACTIO EMPTI. In the civil law. An action employed in behalf of a buyer to compel a seller to perform his obligations or pay compensation; also to enforce any special agreements by him, embodied in a contract of sale. Hunter, Rom. Law, 332.

ACTIO EX CONDUCTO. In the civil law. An action which the bailor of a thing for hire may bring against the bailee, in order to compel him to redeliver the thing hired.

ACTIO EX CONTRACTU. In the civil and common law. An action of contract; an action arising out of, or founded on, contract. Inst. 4, 6, 1; Bract. fol. 102; 3 Bl. Comm. 117.

ACTIO EX DELICTO. In the civil and common law. An action of tort; an action arising out of fault, misconduct, or malfeasance. Inst. 4, 6, 15; 3 Bl. Comm. 117. *Ex maleficio* is the more common expression

of the civil law; which is adopted by Bracton. Inst. 4, 6, 1; Bract. fols. 102, 103.

ACTIO EX LOCATO. In the civil law. An action upon letting; an action which the person who let a thing for hire to another might have against the hirer. Dig. 19, 2; Cod. 4, 65.

ACTIO EX STIPULATU. In the civil law. An action brought to enforce a stipulation.

ACTIO EXERCITORIA. In the civil law. An action against the *exercitor* or employer of a vessel.

ACTIO FAMILIÆ ERCISCUNDÆ. In the civil law. An action for the partition of an inheritance. Inst. 4, 6, 20; Id. 4, 17, 4. Called, by Bracton and Fleta, a mixed action, and classed among actions arising *ex quasi contractu.* Bract. fol. 100b; Id. fols. 443b, 444; Fleta, lib. 2, c. 60, § 1.

ACTIO FURTI. In the civil law. An action of theft; an action founded upon theft. Inst. 4, 1, 13–17; Bract. fol. 444. This could only be brought for the penalty attached to the offense, (*tantum ad poenæ persecutionem pertinet,*) and not to recover the thing stolen itself, for which other actions were provided. Inst. 4, 1, 19.

ACTIO HONORARIA. In the civil law. An honorary, or prætorian action. Dig. 44, 7, 25, 35.

ACTIO IN FACTUM. In the civil law. An action adapted to the particular case, having an analogy to some *actio in jus,* the latter being founded on some subsisting acknowledged law. Spence, Eq. Jur. 212. The origin of these actions is similar to that of actions on the case at common law.

ACTIO IN PERSONAM. In the civil law. An action against the person, founded on a personal liability; an action seeking redress for the violation of a *jus in personam* or right available against a particular individual.

In admiralty law. An action directed against the particular person who is to be charged with the liability. It is distinguished from an *actio in rem,* which is a suit directed against a specific *thing* (as a vessel) irrespective of the ownership of it, to enforce a claim or lien upon it, or to obtain, out of the thing or out of the proceeds of its sale, satisfaction for an injury alleged by the claimant.

ACTIO IN REM. In the civil and common law. An action *for a thing;* an action for the recovery of a thing possessed by another. Inst. 4, 6, 1. An action for the enforcement of a right (or for redress for its invasion) which was originally available against all the world, and not in any special sense against the individual sued, until he violated it. See IN REM.

ACTIO JUDICATI. In the civil law. An action instituted, after four months had elapsed after the rendition of judgment, in which the judge issued his warrant to seize, first, the movables, which were sold within eight days afterwards; and then the immovables, which were delivered in pledge to the creditors, or put under the care of a curator, and if, at the end of two months, the debt was not paid, the land was sold. Dig. 42, 1; Code, 8, 34.

ACTIO LEGIS AQUILIÆ. In the civil law. An action under the Aquilian law; an action to recover damages for maliciously or injuriously killing or wounding the slave or beast of another, or injuring in any way a thing belonging to another. Otherwise called *damni injuriæ actio.*

ACTIO MANDATI. In the civil law. Included actions to enforce contracts of mandate, or obligations arising out of them. Hunter, Rom. Law, 316.

ACTIO MIXTA. In the civil law. A mixed action; an action brought for the recovery of a thing, or compensation for damages, and also for the payment of a penalty; partaking of the nature both of an *actio in rem* and *in personam.* Inst. 4, 6, 16, 18, 19, 20; Mackeld. Rom. Law, § 209.

ACTIO NEGATORIA. In the civil law. An action brought to repel a claim of the defendant to a servitude in the plaintiff's land. Mackeld. Rom. Law, § 324.

ACTIO NEGOTIORUM GESTORUM. In the civil law. Included actions between principal and agent and other parties to an engagement, whereby one person undertook the transaction of business for another.

ACTIO NON. In pleading. The Latin name of that part of a special plea which follows next after the statement of appearance and defense, and declares that the plaintiff "ought not to have or maintain his aforesaid action," etc.

ACTIO NON ACCREVIT INFRA SEX ANNOS. The name of the plea of the statute of limitations, when the defendant alleges that the plaintiff's action has not accrued within six years.

Actio non datur non damnificato. An action is not given to one who is not injured. Jenk. Cent. 69.

Actio non facit reum, nisi mens sit rea. An action does not make one guilty, unless the intention be bad. Lofft. 37.

ACTIO NON ULTERIUS. In English pleading. A name given to the distinctive clause in the plea to the *further maintenance* of the action, introduced in place of the plea *puis darrein continuance;* the averment being that the plaintiff ought not *further* (*ulterius*) to have or maintain his action. Steph. Pl. 64, 65, 401.

ACTIO NOXALIS. In the civil law. A noxal action; an action which lay against a master for a crime committed or injury done by his slave; and in which the master had the alternative either to pay for the damage done or to deliver up the slave to the complaining party. Inst. 4, 8, pr.; Heinecc. Elem. lib. 4, tit. 8. So called from *noxa,* the offense or injury committed. Inst. 4, 8, 1.

ACTIO PERSONALIS. In the civil and common law. A personal action. The ordinary term for this kind of action in the civil law is *actio in personam,* (*q. v.*,) the word *personalis* being of only occasional occurrence. Inst. 4, 6, 8, *in tit.;* Id. 4, 11, pr. 1. Bracton, however, uses it freely, and hence the *personal action* of the common law. Bract. fols. 102a, 159b. See PERSONAL ACTION.

Actio personalis moritur cum persona. A personal right of action dies with the person. Noy, Max. 14.

ACTIO PIGNORATITIA. In the civil law. An action of pledge; an action founded on the contract of pledge, (*pignus.*) Dig. 13, 7; Cod. 4, 24.

Actio pœnalis in hæredem non datur, nisi forte ex damno locupletior hæres factus sit. A penal action is not given against an heir, unless, indeed, such heir is benefited by the wrong.

ACTIO PRÆJUDICIALIS. In the civil law. A preliminary or preparatory action. An action instituted for the determination of some preliminary matter on which other litigated matters depend, or for the determination of some point or question arising in another or principal action; and so called from its being *determined before*, (*prius*, or *præ judicari*.)

ACTIO PRÆSCRIPTIS VERBIS. In the civil law. A form of action which derived its force from continued usage or the *responsa prudentium*, and was founded on the unwritten law. 1 Spence, Eq. Jur. 212.

ACTIO PRÆTORIA. In the civil law. A prætorian action; one introduced by the prætor, as distinguished from the more ancient *actio civilis*, (*q. v.*) Inst. 4, 6, 3; Mackeld. Rom. Law, § 207.

ACTIO PRO SOCIO. In the civil law. An action of partnership. An action brought by one partner against his associates to compel them to carry out the terms of the partnership agreement.

ACTIO PUBLICIANA. In the civil law. An action which lay for one who had lost a thing of which he had *bona fide* obtained possession, before he had gained a property in it, in order to have it restored, under color that he had obtained a property in it by prescription. Inst. 4, 6, 4; Heinecc. Elem. lib. 4, tit. 6, § 1131; Halifax, Anal. b. 3, c. 1, n. 9. It was an honorary action, and derived its name from the prætor Publicius, by whose edict it was first given. Inst. 4, 6, 4.

Actio quælibet it sua via. Every action proceeds in its own way. Jenk. Cent. 77.

ACTIO QUOD JUSSU. In the civil law. An action given against a master, founded on some business done by his slave, acting under his *order*, (*jussu*.) Inst. 4, 7, 1; Dig. 15, 4; Cod. 4, 26.

ACTIO QUOD METUS CAUSA. In the civil law. An action granted to one who had been compelled by unlawful force, or fear (*metûs causa*) that was not groundless, (*metus probabilis* or *justus*,) to deliver, sell, or promise a thing to another. Bract. fol. 103*b*; Mackeld. Rom. Law, § 226.

ACTIO REALIS. A real action. The proper term in the civil law was *Rei Vindicatio*. Inst. 4, 6, 3.

ACTIO REDHIBITORIA. In the civil law. An action to cancel a sale in consequence of defects in the thing sold. It was prosecuted to compel complete restitution to the seller of the thing sold, with its produce and accessories, and to give the buyer back the price, with interest, as an equivalent for the restitution of the produce. Hunter, Rom. Law, 332.

ACTIO RERUM AMOTARUM. In the civil law. An action for things removed; an action which, in cases of divorce, lay for a husband against a wife, to recover things carried away by the latter, in contemplation of such divorce, (*divortii consilio*.) Dig. 25, 2; Id. 25, 2, 25, 30. It also lay for the wife against the husband in such cases. Id. 25, 2, 7, 11; Cod. 5, 21.

ACTIO RESCISSORIA. In the civil law. An action for restoring the plaintiff to a right or title which he has lost by prescription, in a case where the equities are such that he should be relieved from the operation of the prescription. Mackeld. Rom. Law, § 226.

ACTIO SERVIANA. In the civil law. An action which lay for the lessor of a farm, or rural estate, to recover the goods of the lessee or farmer, which were pledged or bound for the rent. Inst. 4, 6, 7.

ACTIO STRICTI JURIS. In the civil law. An action of strict right. The class of civil law personal actions, which were adjudged only by the strict law, and in which the judge was limited to the precise language of the formula, and had no discretionary power to regard the *bona fides* of the transaction. See Inst. 4, 6, 28; Gaius, iii. 137; Mackeld. Rom. Law, § 210.

ACTIO TUTELÆ. In the civil law. Action founded on the duties or obligations arising on the relation analogous to that of guardian and ward.

ACTIO UTILIS. In the civil law. A beneficial action or equitable action. An action founded on equity instead of strict law, and available for those who had equitable rights or the beneficial ownership of property.

Actions are divided into *directæ* or *utiles* actions. The former are founded on certain legal obligations which from their origin were accurately defined and recognized as actionable. The latter were formed analogically in imitation of the former. They were permitted in legal obligations for which the *actiones directæ* were not originally intended, but which resembled the legal obligations which formed the basis of the direct action. Mackeld. Rom. Law, § 207.

ACTIO VENDITI. In the civil law. An action employed in behalf of a seller, to compel a buyer to pay the price, or perform any special obligations embodied in a contract of sale. Hunter, Rom. Law, 332.

ACTIO VI BONORUM RAPTORUM. In the civil law. An action for goods taken by force; a species of mixed action, which lay for a party whose goods or movables (*bona*) had been taken from him by force, (*vi*) to recover the things so taken, together with a penalty of triple the value. Inst. 4, 2; Id. 4, 6, 19. Bracton describes it as lying *de rebus mobilibus vi ablatis sive robbatis.* (for movable things taken away by force, or robbed.) Bract. fol. 103b.

ACTIO VULGARIS. In the civil law. A legal action; a common action. Sometimes used for *actio directa.* Mackeld. Rom. Law, § 207.

ACTION. Conduct; behavior; something done; the condition of acting; an act or series of acts.

In practice. The legal and formal demand of one's right from another person or party made and insisted on in a court of justice.

An action is an ordinary proceeding in a court of justice by which one party prosecutes another for the enforcement or protection of a right, the redress or prevention of a wrong, or the punishment of a public offense. Code Civil Proc. Cal. § 22; Code N. Y. § 2; Code N. C. 1883, § 126.

An action is merely the judicial means of enforcing a right. Code Ga. 1882, § 3151.

Action is the form of a suit given by law for the recovery of that which is one's due; the lawful demand of one's right. Co. Litt. 284b, 285a.

Classification of actions. Civil actions are such as lie in behalf of persons to enforce their rights or obtain redress of wrongs in their relation to individuals.

Criminal actions are such as are instituted by the sovereign power, for the purpose of punishing or preventing offenses against the public.

Penal actions are such as are brought, either by the state or by an individual under permission of a statute, to enforce a penalty imposed by law for the commission of a prohibited act.

Common law actions are such as will lie, on the particular facts, at common law, without the aid of a statute.

Statutory actions are such as can only be based upon the particular statutes creating them.

Popular actions, in English usage, are those actions which are given upon the breach of a penal statute, and which any man that will may sue on account of the king and himself, as the statute allows and the case requires. Because the action is not given to one especially, but generally to any that will prosecute, it is called "action popular;" and, from the words used in the process, (*qui tam pro domino rege sequitur quam pro se ipso,* who sues as well for the king as for himself,) it is called a *qui tam* action. Tomlins.

Real, personal, mixed. Actions are divided into real, personal, and mixed; real actions being those brought for the specific recovery of lands or other realty; personal actions, those for the recovery of a debt, personal chattel, or damages; and mixed actions, those for the recovery of real property, together with damages for a wrong connected with it. Litt. § 494; 3 Bl. Comm. 117.

Local actions are those founded upon a cause of action which necessarily refers to, and could only arise in, some particular place, *e. g.*, trespass to land.

Transitory actions are those founded upon a cause of action not necessarily referring to or arising in any particular locality.

Actions are called, in common-law practice, *ex contractu,* when they are founded on a contract; *ex delicto,* when they arise out of a wrong.

"Action" and "Suit." The terms "action" and "suit" are now nearly, if not entirely synonymous. (3 Bl. Comm. 3, 116, et passim.) Or, if there be a distinction, it is that the term "action" is generally confined to proceedings in a court of law, while "suit" is equally applied to prosecutions at law or in equity. Formerly, however, there was a more substantial distinction between them. An *action* was considered as terminating with the giving of judgment, and the execution formed no part of it. (Litt. § 504; Co. Litt. 289a.) A *suit,* on the other hand, included the execution. (Id. 291a.) So, an action is termed by Lord Coke, "the *right* of a *suit.*" (2 Inst. 40.) Burrill.

In French commercial law. Stock in a company, or shares in a corporation.

ACTION FOR POINDING OF THE GROUND. A term of the Scotch law. See POINDING.

ACTION OF A WRIT. A phrase used when a defendant pleads some matter by which he shows that the plaintiff had no cause to have the writ sued upon, although it may be that he is entitled to another writ or action for the same matter. Cowell.

ACTION OF ABSTRACTED MULT-URES. In Scotch law. An action for multures or tolls against those who are thirled to a mill, *i. e.*, bound to grind their corn at a certain mill, and fail to do so. Bell.

ACTION OF ADHERENCE. In Scotch law. An action competent to a husband or wife, to compel either party to adhere in case of desertion. It is analogous to the English suit for restitution of conjugal rights. Wharton.

ACTION OF BOOK DEBT. A form of action for the recovery of claims, such as are usually evidenced by a book-account; this action is principally used in Vermont and Connecticut.

ACTION ON THE CASE. A species of personal action of very extensive application, otherwise called "trespass on the case," or simply "case," from the circumstance of the plaintiff's whole *case* or cause of complaint being set forth at length in the original writ by which formerly it was always commenced. 3 Bl. Comm. 122.

ACTION REDHIBITORY. In the civil law. An action instituted to avoid a sale on account of some vice or defect in the thing sold, which renders it either absolutely useless or its use so inconvenient and imperfect that it must be supposed the buyer would not have purchased it had he known of the vice. Civil Code La. art. 2496.

ACTIONABLE. That for which an action will lie; furnishing legal ground for an action; *e. g.*, words are *actionable per se*, in slander, when an action may be brought upon them without alleging special damage.

ACTIONARE. L. Lat. (From *actio*, an action.) In old records. To bring an action; to prosecute, or sue. Thorn's Chron.; Whishaw.

ACTIONARY. A foreign commercial term for the proprietor of an *action* or share of a public company's stock; a stockholder.

ACTIONES LEGIS. In the Roman law. Legal or lawful actions; actions of or at law, (*legitimæ actiones*.) Dig. 1, 2, 2, 6.

ACTIONES NOMINATÆ. In the English chancery. Writs for which there were precedents. The statute of Westminster, 2, c. 24, gave chancery authority to form new writs *in consimili casu;* hence the action on the case.

ACTIONS ORDINARY. In Scotch law. All actions which are not rescissory. Ersk. Inst. 4, 1, 18.

ACTIONS RESCISSORY. In Scotch law. These are either (1) actions of proper improbation for declaring a writing false or forged; (2) actions of reduction-improbation for the production of a writing in order to have it set aside or its effect ascertained under the certification that the writing if not produced shall be declared false or forged; and (3) actions of simple reduction, for declaring a writing called for null until produced. Ersk. Prin. 4, 1, 5.

ACTIVE. That is in action; that demands action; actually subsisting; the opposite of passive. An active debt is one which draws interest. An active trust is a confidence connected with a duty. An active use is a present legal estate.

ACTON BURNEL, Statute of. In English law. A statute, otherwise called "*Statutum de Mercatoribus*," made at a parliament held at the castle of Acton Burnel in Shropshire, in the 11th year of the reign of Edward I. 2 Reeves, Eng. Law, 158–162.

ACTOR. In Roman law. One who acted for another; one who attended to another's business; a manager or agent. A slave who attended to, transacted, or superintended his master's business or affairs, received and paid out moneys, and kept accounts. Burrill.

A plaintiff or complainant. In a civil or private action the plaintiff was often called by the Romans "*petitor;*" in a public action (*causa publica*) he was called "*accusator.*" The defendant was called "*reus,*" both in private and public causes; this term, however, according to Cicero, (*De Orat.* ii. 43,) might signify either party, as indeed we might conclude from the word itself. In a private action, the defendant was often called "*adversarius,*" but either party might be called so.

Also, the term is used of a party who, for the time being, sustains the burden of proof, or has the initiative in the suit.

In old European law. A proctor, advocate, or pleader; one who acted for another in legal matters; one who represented a party and managed his cause. An attorney, bailiff, or steward; one who managed or acted for another. The Scotch "doer" is the literal translation.

Actor qui contra regulam quid adduxit, non est audiendus. A plaintiff is not to be heard who has advanced anything against authority, (or against the rule.)

Actor sequitur forum rei. According as *rei* is intended as the genitive of *res*, a thing, or *reus*, a defendant, this phrase means: The plaintiff follows the forum of the property in suit, or the forum of the defendant's residence. Branch, Max. 4.

Actore non probante reus absolvitur. When the plaintiff does not prove his case the defendant is acquitted. Hob. 103.

Actori incumbit onus probandi. The burden of proof rests on the plaintiff, (or on the party who advances a proposition affirmatively.) Hob. 103.

ACTORNAY. In old Scotch law. An attorney. Skene.

ACTRIX. Lat. A female actor; a female plaintiff. Calvin.

Acts indicate the intention. 8 Co. 146*b*; Broom, Max. 301.

ACTS OF COURT. Legal memoranda made in the admiralty courts in England, in the nature of pleas.

ACTS OF SEDERUNT. In Scotch law. Ordinances for regulating the forms of proceeding, before the court of session, in the administration of justice, made by the judges, who have the power by virtue of a Scotch act of parliament passed in 1540. Ersk. Prin § 14

ACTUAL. Real; substantial; existing presently in act; having a valid objective existence; as opposed to that which is merely theoretical or possible.

Something real, in opposition to constructive or speculative; something existing in act. 31 Conn. 213.

ACTUAL CASH VALUE. In insurance. The sum of money the insured goods would have brought for cash, at the market price, at the time when and place where they were destroyed by fire. 4 Fed. Rep. 59.

ACTUAL COST. The actual price paid for goods by a party, in the case of a real *bona fide* purchase, and not the market value of the goods. 2 Story, 422, 429; 2 Mas. 48; 9 Gray, 226.

ACTUAL DAMAGES. Real, substantial, and just damages. The amount adjudged to a complainant in compensation for his actual and real loss or damage; opposed to "nominal damages," which is a trifling sum awarded as a matter of course, and not in compensation, but merely in recognition of the fact that his right has been technically violated; and opposed also to "exemplary" or "punitive" damages, the latter being in excess of the real loss, and intended as a punishment to the wrong-doer, or (from motives of public policy) to discourage a repetition of such acts.

ACTUAL DELIVERY. In the law of sales, actual delivery consists in the giving real possession of the thing sold to the vendee or his servants or special agents who are identified with him in law and represent him. Constructive delivery is a general term, comprehending all those acts which, although not truly conferring a real possession of the thing sold on the vendee, have been held, by construction of law, equivalent to acts of real delivery. In this sense constructive delivery includes symbolical delivery and all those *traditiones fictæ* which have been admitted into the law as sufficient to vest the absolute property in the vendee and bar the rights of lien and stoppage *in transitu*, such as marking and setting apart the goods as belonging to the vendee, charging him with warehouse rent, etc. 1 Rawle, 19.

ACTUAL FRAUD. Actual fraud implies deceit, artifice, trick, design, some direct and active operation of the mind. Constructive fraud is indirect, and may be implied from some other act or omission to act, which may be, in moral contemplation, entirely innocent, but which, without the explanation or actual proof of its innocence, is evidence of fraud. 35 Barb. 457.

ACTUAL NOTICE. A notice expressly and actually given, and brought home to the party directly, in distinction from one inferred or imputed by the law on account of the existence of means of knowledge.

ACTUAL OCCUPATION. An open, visible occupancy as distinguished from the constructive one which follows the legal title.

ACTUAL OUSTER. By "actual ouster" is not meant a physical eviction, but a possession attended with such circumstances as to evince a claim of exclusive right and title, and a denial of the right of the other tenants to participate in the profits. 45 Iowa, 287.

ACTUAL POSSESSION. This term, as used in the provisions of Rev. St. N. Y.

p. 312, § 1, authorizing proceedings to compel the determination of claims to real property, means a possession in fact effected by actual entry upon the premises; an actual occupation. 59 N. Y. 134.

It means an actual occupation or possession in fact, as contradistinguished from that constructive one which the legal title draws after it. The word "actual" is used in the statute in opposition to virtual or constructive, and calls for an open, visible occupancy. 7 Hun, 616.

ACTUAL SALE. Lands are "actually sold" at a tax sale, so as to entitle the treasurer to the statutory fees, when the sale is completed; when he has collected from the purchaser the amount of the bid. 5 Neb. 272.

ACTUAL TOTAL LOSS. In marine insurance. The total loss of the vessel covered by a policy of insurance, by its real and substantive destruction, by injuries which leave it no longer existing *in specie*, by its being reduced to a wreck irretrievably beyond repair, or by its being placed beyond the control of the insured and beyond his power of recovery. Distinguished from a *constructive* total loss, which occurs where the vessel, though injured by the perils insured against, remains *in specie* and capable of repair or recovery, but at such an expense, or under such other conditions, that the insured may claim the whole amount of the policy upon abandoning the vessel to the underwriters.

"An *actual* total loss is where the vessel ceases to exist *in specie*,—becomes a ' mere congeries of planks,' incapable of being repaired; or where, by the peril insured against, it is placed beyond the control of the insured and beyond his power of recovery. A *constructive* total loss is where the vessel remains *in specie*, and is susceptible of repairs or recovery, but at an expense, according to the rule of the English common law, exceeding its value when restored, or, according to the terms of this policy, where ' the injury is equivalent to fifty per cent. of the agreed value in the policy,' and where the insured abandons the vessel to the underwriter. In such cases the insured is entitled to indemnity as for a total loss. An exception to the rule requiring abandonment is found in cases where the loss occurs in foreign ports or seas, where it is impracticable to repair. In such cases the master may sell the vessel for the benefit of all concerned, and the insured may claim as for a total loss by accounting to the insurer for the amount realized on the sale. There are other exceptions to the rule, but it is sufficient now to say that we have found no case in which the doctrine of constructive total loss without abandonment has been admitted, where the injured vessel remained *in specie* and was brought to its home port by the insured. A well marked distinction between an actual and a constructive total loss is therefore found in this: that in the former no abandonment is necessary, while in the latter it is essential, unless the case be brought within some exception to the rule requiring it. A *partial* loss is where an injury results to the vessel from a peril insured against, but where the loss is neither actually nor constructively total." 25 Ohio St. 64. See, also, 96 U. S. 645; 9 Hun, 383.

ACTUARIUS. In Roman law. A notary or clerk. One who drew the acts or statutes, or who wrote in brief the public acts.

ACTUARY. In English ecclesiastical law. A clerk that registers the acts and constitutions of the lower house of convocation; or a registrar in a court christian.

Also an officer appointed to keep savings banks accounts; the computing officer of an insurance company; a person skilled in calculating the value of life interests, annuities, and insurances.

ACTUM. A deed; something done.

ACTUS. In the civil law. A species of right of way, consisting in the right of driving cattle, or a carriage, over the land subject to the servitude. Inst. 2, 3, pr. It is sometimes translated a "road," and included the kind of way termed "*iter*," or path. Lord Coke, who adopts the term "*actus*" from Bracton, defines it a foot and horse way, vulgarly called "pack and prime way;" but distinguishes it from a cart-way. Co. Litt. 56a.

In old English law. An act of parliament; a statute. A distinction, however, was sometimes made between *actus* and *statutum*. *Actus parliamenti* was an act made by the lords and commons; and it became *statutum*, when it received the king's consent. Barring. Obs. St. 46, note *b*.

ACTUS. In the civil law. An act or action. *Non tantum verbis, sed etiam actu;* not only by words, but also by act. Dig. 46, 8, 5.

Actus curiæ neminem gravabit. An act of the court shall prejudice no man. Jenk. Cent. 118. Where a delay in an action is the act of the court, neither party shall suffer for it.

Actus Dei nemini est damnosus. The act of God is hurtful to no one. 2 Inst. 287.

Actus Dei nemini facit injuriam. The act of God does injury to no one. 2 Bl. Comm. 122. A thing which is inevitable by the act of God, which no industry can avoid, nor policy prevent, will not be construed to the prejudice of any person in whom there was no laches. Broom, Max. 230.

Actus inceptus, cujus perfectio pendet ex voluntate partium, revocari potest; si autem pendet ex voluntate tertiæ personæ, vel ex contingenti, revocari non potest. An act already begun, the completion of which depends on the will of the parties, may be revoked; but if it depend on the will of a third person, or on a contingency, it cannot be revoked. Bac. Max. reg. 20.

Actus judiciarius coram non judice irritus habetur, de ministeriali autem a quocunque provenit ratum esto. A judicial act by a judge without jurisdiction is void; but a ministerial act, from whomsoever proceeding, may be ratified. Lofft, 458.

Actus legis nemini est damnosus. The act of the law is hurtful to no one. An act in law shall prejudice no man. 2 Inst. 287.

Actus legis nemini facit injuriam. The act of the law does injury to no one. 5 Coke, 116.

Actus legitimi non recipiunt modum. Acts required to be done by law do not admit of qualification. Hob. 153; Branch, Princ.

Actus me invito factus non est meus actus. An act done by me, against my will, is not my act. Branch, Princ.

Actus non facit reum, nisi mens sit rea. An act does not make [the doer of it] guilty, unless the mind be guilty; that is, unless the intention be criminal. 3 Inst. 107. The intent and the act must both concur to constitute the crime. Lord Kenyon, C. J., 7 Term 514; Broom, Max. 306.

Actus repugnus non potest in esse produci. A repugnant act cannot be brought into being, *i. e.*, cannot be made effectual. Plowd. 355.

Actus servi in iis quibus opera ejus communiter adhibita est, actus domini habetur. The act of a servant in those things in which he is usually employed, is considered the act of his master. Lofft, 227.

AD. Lat. At; by; for; near; on account of; to; until; upon.

AD ABUNDANTIOREM CAUTELAM. L. Lat. For more abundant caution. 2 How. State Tr. 1182. Otherwise expressed, *ad cautelam ex superabundanti.* Id. 1163.

AD ADMITTENDUM CLERICUM. For the admitting of the clerk. A writ in the nature of an execution, commanding the bishop to admit his clerk, upon the success of the latter in a *quare impedit.*

AD ALIUD EXAMEN. To another tribunal; belonging to another court, cognizance, or jurisdiction.

AD ALIUM DIEM. At another day. A common phrase in the old reports. Yearb. P. 7 Hen. VI. 13.

AD ASSISAS CAPIENDAS. To take assises; to take or hold the assises. Bract. fol. 110a; 3 Bl. Comm. 185. *Ad assisam capiendam;* to take an assise. Bract. fol. 110b.

AD AUDIENDUM ET TERMINANDUM. To hear and determine. St. Westm. 2, cc. 29, 30.

AD BARRAM. To the bar; at the bar. 3 How. State Tr. 112.

AD CAMPI PARTEM. For a share of the field or land, for champert. Fleta, lib. 2, c. 36, § 4.

AD CAPTUM VULGI. Adapted to the common understanding.

AD COLLIGENDUM BONA DEFUNCTI. To collect the goods of the deceased. Special letters of administration granted to one or more persons, authorizing them to *collect* and preserve the goods of the deceased, are so called. 2 Bl. Comm. 505; 2 Steph. Comm. 241. These are otherwise termed "letters *ad colligendum*," and the party to whom they are granted, a "collector."

AD COMMUNEM LEGEM. At common law. The name of a writ of entry (now obsolete) brought by the reversioners after the death of the life tenant, for the recovery of lands wrongfully alienated by him.

AD COMPARENDUM. To appear. *Ad comparendum, et ad standum juri*, to appear and to stand to the law, or abide the judgment of the court. Cro. Jac. 67.

AD COMPOTUM REDDENDUM. To render an account. St. Westm. 2, c. 11.

AD CURIAM. At a court. 1 Salk. 195. To court. *Ad curiam vocare*, to summon to court.

AD CUSTAGIA. At the costs. Toullier; Cowell; Whishaw.

AD CUSTUM. At the cost. 1 Bl. Comm. 314.

AD DAMNUM. In pleading. "To the damage." The technical name of that clause of the writ or declaration which contains a statement of the plaintiff's money loss, or the damages which he claims.

AD DEFENDENDUM. To defend. 1 Bl. Comm. 227.

AD DIEM. At a day; at the day. Townsh. Pl. 23. *Ad certum diem*, at a certain day. 2 Strange, 747. *Solvit ad diem;* he paid at or on the day. 1 Chit. Pl. 485.

Ad ea quæ frequentius accidunt jura adaptantur. Laws are adapted to those cases which most frequently occur. 2 Inst. 137; Broom, Max. 43.

Laws are adapted to cases which frequently occur. A statute, which, construed according to its plain words, is, in all cases of ordinary occurrence, in no degree inconsistent or unreasonable, should not be varied by construction in every case, merely because there is one possible but highly improbable case in which the law would operate with great severity and against our notions of justice. The utmost that can be contended is that the construction of the statute should be varied in that particular case, so as to obviate the injustice. 7 Exch. 549; 8 Exch. 778.

AD EFFECTUM. To the effect, or end. Co. Litt. 204a; 2 Crabb, Real Prop. p. 802, § 2143. *Ad effectum sequentem*, to the effect following. 2 Salk. 417.

AD EXCAMBIUM. For exchange; for compensation. Bract. fol. 12b, 37b.

AD EXHÆREDATIONEM. To the disherison, or disinheriting; to the injury of the inheritance. Bract. fol. 15a; 3 Bl. Comm. 288. Formal words in the old writs of waste.

AD EXITUM. At issue; at the end (of the pleadings.) Steph. Pl. 24.

AD FACIENDUM. To do. Co. Litt. 204a. *Ad faciendum, subjiciendum et recipiendum;* to do, submit to, and receive. *Ad faciendam juratam illam;* to make up that jury. Fleta, lib. 2, c. 65, § 12.

AD FACTUM PRÆSTANDUM. In Scotch law. A name descriptive of a class of obligations marked by unusual severity. A debtor who is under an obligation of this kind cannot claim the benefit of the act of grace, the privilege of sanctuary, or the *cessio bonorum.* Ersk. Inst. lib. 3, tit. 3, § 62.

AD FEODI FIRMAM. To fee farm. Fleta, lib. 2, c. 50, § 30.

AD FIDEM. In allegiance. 2 Kent, Comm. 56. Subjects born *ad fidem* are those born in allegiance.

AD FILUM AQUÆ. To the thread of the water; to the central line, or middle of the stream. *Usque ad filum aquæ*, as far as the thread of the stream. Bract. fol. 208b; 235a. A phrase of frequent occurrence in modern law; of which *ad medium filum aquæ* (q. v.) is another form.

AD FILUM VIÆ. To the middle of the way; to the central line of the road. 8 Metc. (Mass.) 260.

AD FINEM. Abbreviated *ad fin.* To the end. It is used in citations to books, as a direction to read from the place designated to the end of the chapter, section, etc. *Ad finem litis*, at the end of the suit.

AD FIRMAM. To farm. Derived from an old Saxon word denoting rent. *Ad firmam noctis* was a fine or penalty equal in amount to the estimated cost of entertaining the king for one night. Cowell. *Ad feodi firmam*, to fee farm. Spelman.

AD GAOLAS DELIBERANDAS. To deliver the gaols; to empty the gaols. Bract. fol. 109b. *Ad gaolam deliberandam;* to deliver the gaol; to make gaol delivery. Bract. fol. 110b.

AD GRAVAMEN. To the grievance, injury, or oppression. Fleta, lib. 2, c. 47, § 10.

AD HOMINEM. To the person. A term used in logic with reference to a personal argument.

AD HUNC DIEM. At this day. 1 Leon. 90.

AD IDEM. To the same point, or effect. *Ad idem facit*, it makes to or goes to establish the same point. Bract. fol. 27b.

AD INDE. Thereunto. *Ad inde requisitus*, thereunto required. Townsh. Pl. 22.

AD INFINITUM. Without limit; to an infinite extent; indefinitely.

AD INQUIRENDUM. To inquire; a writ of inquiry; a judicial writ, commanding inquiry to be made of any thing relating to a cause pending in court. Cowell.

AD INSTANTIAM. At the instance. 2 Mod. 44. *Ad instantiam partis*, at the instance of a party. Hale, Com. Law, 28.

AD INTERIM. In the mean time. An officer *ad interim* is one appointed to fill a temporary vacancy, or to discharge the duties of the office during the absence or temporary incapacity of its regular incumbent.

AD JUDICIUM. To judgment; to court. *Ad judicium provocare;* to summon to court; to commence an action; a term of the Roman law. Dig. 5, 1, 13, 14.

AD JUNGENDUM AUXILIUM. To joining in aid; to join in aid. See AID PRAYER.

AD JURA REGIS. To the rights of the king; a writ which was brought by the king's clerk, presented to a living, against those who endeavored to eject him, to the prejudice of the king's title. Reg. Writs, 61.

AD LARGUM. At large; at liberty; free, or unconfined. *Ire ad largum*, to go at large. Plowd. 37.

At large; giving details, or particulars; *in extenso*. A special verdict was formerly called a verdict at large. Plowd. 92.

AD LITEM. For the suit; for the purposes of the suit; pending the suit. A guardian *ad litem* is a guardian appointed to prosecute or defend a suit on behalf of a party incapacitated by infancy or otherwise.

AD LUCRANDUM VEL PERDENDUM. For gain or loss. Emphatic words in the old warrants of attorney. Reg. Orig. 21, et seq. Sometimes expressed in English, "to lose and gain." Plowd. 201.

AD MAJOREM CAUTELAM. For greater security. 2 How. State Tr. 1182.

AD MANUM. At hand; ready for use. *Et querens sectam habeat ad manum;* and the plaintiff immediately have his suit ready. Fleta, lib. 2, c. 44, § 2.

AD MEDIUM FILUM AQUÆ. To the middle thread of the stream.

AD MEDIUM FILUM VIÆ. To the middle thread of the way.

AD MELIUS INQUIRENDUM. A writ directed to a coroner commanding him to hold a second inquest. See 45 Law J. Q. B. 711.

AD MORDENDUM ASSUETUS. Accustomed to bite. Cro. Car. 254. A material averment in declarations for damage done by a dog to persons or animals. 1 Chit. Pl. 388; 2 Chit. Pl. 597.

AD NOCUMENTUM. To the nuisance, or annoyance. Fleta, lib. 2, c. 52, § 19. *Ad nocumentum liberi tenementi sui*, to the nuisance of his freehold. Formal words in the old assise of nuisance. 3 Bl. Comm. 221.

Ad officium justiciariorum spectat, unicuique coram eis placitanti justitiam exhibere. It is the duty of justices to administer justice to every one pleading before them. 2 Inst. 451.

AD OSTENDENDUM. To show. Formal words in old writs. Fleta, lib. 4, c. 65, § 12.

AD OSTIUM ECCLESIÆ. At the door of the church. One of the five species of dower formerly recognized by the English law. 1 Washb. Real Prop. 149; 2 Bl. Comm. 132.

Ad proximum antecedens fiat relatio nisi impediatur sententiâ. Relative words refer to the nearest antecedent, unless it be prevented by the context. Jenk. Cent. 180.

AD QUÆRIMONIAM. On complaint of.

AD QUEM. To which. A term used in the computation of time or distance, as correlative to *a quo;* denotes the end or terminal point. See A QUO.

Ad questiones facti non respondent judices; ad questiones legis non respondent juratores. Judges do not answer questions of fact; juries do not answer questions of law. 8 Coke, 308; Co. Litt. 295.

AD QUOD CURIA CONCORDAVIT. To which the court agreed. Yearb. P. 20 Hen. VI. 27.

AD QUOD DAMNUM. The name of a writ formerly issuing from the English chancery, commanding the sheriff to make inquiry "to what damage" a specified act, if done, will tend. *Ad quod damnum* is a writ which ought to be sued before the king grants certain liberties, as a fair, market, or such like, which may be prejudicial to others, and thereby it should be inquired whether it will be a prejudice to grant them, and to whom it will be prejudicial, and what prejudice will come thereby. There is also another writ of *ad quod damnum*, if any one will turn a common highway and lay out another way as beneficial. Termes de la Ley.

AD QUOD NON FUIT RESPONSUM. To which there was no answer. A phrase used in the reports, where a point advanced in argument by one party was not denied by the other; or where a point or argument of counsel was not met or noticed by the court; or where an objection was met by the court, and not replied to by the counsel who raised it. 3 Coke, 9; 4 Coke, 40.

AD RATIONEM PONERE. A technical expression in the old records of the Exchequer, signifying, to put to the bar and interrogate as to a charge made; to arraign on a trial.

AD RECOGNOSCENDUM. To recognize. Fleta, lib. 2, c. 65, § 12. Formal words in old writs.

Ad recte docendum oportet, primum inquirere nomina, quia rerum cognitio a nominibus rerum dependet. In order rightly to comprehend a thing, inquire first into the names, for a right knowledge of things depends upon their names. Co. Litt. 68.

AD REPARATIONEM ET SUSTENTATIONEM. For repairing and keeping in suitable condition.

AD RESPONDENDUM. For answering; to make answer; words used in certain writs employed for bringing a person before the court to make answer in defense in a proceeding. Thus there is a *capias ad respondendum, q. v.;* also a *habeas corpus ad respondendum.*

AD SATISFACIENDUM. To satisfy. The emphatic words of the writ of *capias ad satisfaciendum,* which requires the sheriff to *take* the person of the defendant *to satisfy* the plaintiff's claim.

AD SECTAM. At the suit of. Commonly abbreviated to *ads.* Used in entering and indexing the names of cases, where it is desired that the name of the defendant should come first. Thus, "B. *ads.* A." indicates that B. is defendant in an action brought by A., and the title so written would be an inversion of the more usual form "A. *v.* B."

An affidavit of merits, on the same paper with the pleas, by a defendant, entitled "C. D. *ads.* A. B.," is the same in law as if entitled "A. B. *v.* C. D.," and is properly entitled, and it is error to strike the pleas from the files as for want of a sufficient affidavit. 86 Ill. 11.

AD STUDENDUM ET ORANDUM. For studying and praying; for the promotion of learning and religion. A phrase applied to colleges and universities. 1 Bl. Comm. 467; T. Raym. 101.

AD TERMINUM ANNORUM. For a term of years.

AD TERMINUM QUI PRETERIT. For a term which has passed. Words in the Latin form of the writ of entry employed at common law to recover, on behalf of a landlord, possession of premises, from a tenant holding over after the expiration of the term for which they were demised. See Fitzh. Nat. Brev. 201.

Ad tristem partem strenua est suspicio. Suspicion lies heavy on the unfortunate side.

AD TUNC ET IBIDEM. In pleading. The Latin name of that clause of an indictment containing the statement of the subject-matter "then and there being found."

AD ULTIMAM VIM TERMINORUM. To the most extended import of the terms; in a sense as universal as the terms will reach. 2 Eden, 54.

AD USUM ET COMMODUM. To the use and benefit.

AD VALENTIAM. To the value. See AD VALOREM.

AD VALOREM. According to value. Duties are either *ad valorem* or *specific;* the former when the duty is laid in the form of a percentage on the value of the property; the latter where it is imposed as a fixed sum on each article of a class without regard to its value.

The term *ad valorem* tax is as well defined and fixed as any other used in political economy or legislation, and simply means a tax or duty upon the value of the article or thing subject to taxation. 24 Miss. 501.

AD VENTREM INSPICIENDUM. To inspect the womb. A writ for the summoning of a jury of matrons to determine the question of pregnancy.

Ad vim majorem vel ad casus fortuitus non tenetur quis, nisi sua culpa intervenerit. No one is held to answer for the effects of a superior force, or of accidents, unless his own fault has contributed. Fleta, lib. 2, c. 72, § 16.

AD VITAM. For life. Bract. fol. 13*b*. *In feodo, vel ad vitam;* in fee, or for life. Id.

AD VITAM AUT CULPAM. For life or until fault. This phrase describes the tenure of an office which is otherwise said to be held "for life or during good behavior." It is equivalent to *quamdiu bene se gesserit.*

AD VOLUNTATEM. At will. Bract. fol. 27*a.* *Ad voluntatem domini,* at the will of the lord.

AD WARACTUM. To fallow. Bract. fol. 228*b.* See WARACTUM.

ADAWLUT. Corrupted from *Adalat,* justice, equity; a court of justice. The terms "Dewanny Adawlut" and "Foujdarry Adawlut" denote the civil and criminal courts of justice in India. Wharton.

ADCORDABILIS DENARII. Money paid by a vassal to his lord upon the selling or exchanging of a feud. Enc. Lond.

ADDICERE. Lat. In the civil law. To adjudge or condemn; to assign, allot, or deliver; to sell. In the Roman law, *addico* was one of the three words used to express the extent of the civil jurisdiction of the prætors.

ADDICTIO. In the Roman law. The giving up to a creditor of his debtor's person by a magistrate; also the transfer of the debtor's goods to one who assumes his liabilities.

Additio probat minoritatem. An addition [to a name] proves or shows minority or inferiority. 4 Inst. 80; Wing. Max. 211, max. 60. This maxim is applied by Lord Coke to courts, and terms of law; *minoritas* being understood in the sense of difference, inferiority, or qualification. Thus, the style of the king's bench is *coram rege,* and the style of the court of chancery is *coram domino rege in cancellaria;* the addition showing the difference. 4 Inst. 80. By the word "fee" is intended *fee-simple,* fee-tail not being intended by it, unless there be added to it the *addition* of the word "tail." 2 Bl. Comm. 106; Litt. § 1.

ADDITION. Whatever is added to a man's name by way of title or description, as additions of mystery, place, or degree. Cowell.

In English law, there are four kinds of *additions,*—additions of *estate,* such as yeoman, gentleman, esquire; additions of *degree,* or names of dignity, as knight, earl, marquis, duke; additions of *trade,* mystery, or occupation, as scrivener, painter, mason, carpenter; and additions of *place* of residence, as London, Chester, etc. The only additions recognized in American law are those of mystery and residence.

In the law of liens. Within the meaning of the mechanic's lien law, an "addition" to a building must be a lateral addition. It must occupy ground without the limits of the building to which it constitutes an addition, so that the lien shall be upon the building formed by the addition and the land upon which it stands. An alteration in a former building, by adding to its height, or to its depth, or to the extent of its interior accommodations, is merely an "alteration," and not an "addition." Putting a new story on an old building is not an addition. 27 N. J. Law, 132.

In French law. A supplementary process to obtain additional information. Guyot, Repert.

ADDITIONAL., This term embraces the idea of joining or uniting one thing to another, so as thereby to form one aggregate. Thus, "additional security" imports a security, which, united with or joined to the former one, is deemed to make it, as an aggregate, sufficient as a security from the beginning. 53 Miss. 626.

ADDITIONALES. In the law of contracts. Additional terms or propositions to be added to a former agreement.

ADDONE, Addonne. L. Fr. Given to. Kelham.

ADDRESS. That part of a bill in equity wherein is given the appropriate and technical description of the court in which the bill is filed.

The word is sometimes used as descriptive of a formal document, embodying a request, presented to the governor of a state by one or both branches of the legislative body, desiring him to perform some executive act.

A place of business or residence.

ADDUCED. "The word 'adduced' is broader in its signification than the word 'offered,' and, looking to the whole statement in relation to the evidence below, we think it sufficiently appears that all of the evidence is in the record." 106 Ind. 84, 5 N. E. Rep. 882.

ADEEM. To take away, recall, or revoke. To satisfy a legacy by some gift or substituted disposition, made by the testator, in advance. See ADEMPTION.

ADELANTADO. In Spanish law. A governor of a province; a president or president judge; a judge having jurisdiction over a kingdom, or over certain provinces only. So called from having authority over the judges of those places. Las Partidas, pt. 3, tit. 4, l. 1.

ADELING or **ATHELING.** Noble; excellent. A title of honor among the Anglo-Saxons, properly belonging to the king's children. Spelman.

ADEMPTIO. Lat. In the civil law. A revocation of a legacy; an ademption. Inst. 2, 21, pr. Where it was expressly transferred from one person to another, it was called *translatio.* Id. 2, 21, 1; Dig. 34, 4.

ADEMPTION. The revocation, recalling, or cancellation of a legacy, according to the apparent intention of the testator, implied by the law from acts done by him in his life, though such acts do not amount to an express revocation of it.

"The word 'ademption' is the most significant, because, being a term of art, and never used for any other purpose, it does not suggest any idea foreign to that intended to be conveyed. It is used to describe the act by which the testator pays to his legatee, in his life-time, a general legacy which by his will he had proposed to give him at his death. (1 Rop. Leg. p. 365.) It is also used to denote the act by which a specific legacy has become inoperative on account of the testator having parted with the subject." 16 N. Y. 40.

Ademption, in strictness, is predicable only of specific, and satisfaction of general legacies. 9 Barb. 35, 56; 3 Duer, 477, 541.

ADEO. Lat. So, as. *Adeo plene et integre,* as fully and entirely. 10 Coke, 65.

"ADEQUATE CAUSE." In criminal law. Adequate cause for the passion which reduces a homicide committed under its influence from the grade of murder to manslaughter, means such cause as would commonly produce a degree of anger, rage, resentment, or terror, in a person of ordinary temper, sufficient to render the mind incapable of cool reflection. Insulting words or gestures, or an assault and battery so slight as to show no intention to inflict pain or injury, or an injury to property unaccompanied by violence are not adequate causes. 2 Tex. App. 100; 7 Tex. App. 396; 10 Tex. App. 421.

ADEQUATE CONSIDERATION. One which is equal, or reasonably proportioned, to the value of that for which it is given. 1 Story, Eq. Jur. §§ 244–247.

ADEQUATE REMEDY. One vested in the complainant, to which he may at all times resort at his own option, fully and freely, without let or hindrance. 54 Conn. 249.

ADESSE. In the civil law. To be present; the opposite of *abesse.* Calvin.

ADFERRUMINATIO. In the civil law. The welding together of iron; a species of *adjunctio,* (*q. v.*) Called also *ferruminatio.* Mackeld. Rom. Law. § 276; Dig. 6, 1, 23, 5.

ADHERENCE. In Scotch law. The name of a form of action by which the mutual obligation of marriage may be enforced by either party. Bell. It corresponds to the English action for the restitution of conjugal rights.

ADHERING. Joining, leagued with, cleaving to; as, "adhering to the enemies of the United States."

Rebels, being citizens, are not "enemies," within the meaning of the constitution; hence a conviction for treason, in promoting a rebellion, cannot be sustained under that branch of the constitutional definition which speaks of "adhering to their enemies, giving them aid and comfort." 2 Abb. (U. S.) 364.

ADHIBERE. In the civil law. To apply; to employ; to exercise; to use. *Adhibere diligentiam,* to use care. *Adhibere vim,* to employ force.

ADIATION. A term used in the laws of Holland for the application of property by an executor. Wharton.

ADIEU. L. Fr. Without day. A common term in the Year Books, implying final dismissal from court.

ADIRATUS. Lost; strayed; a price or value set upon things stolen or lost, as a recompense to the owner. Cowell.

ADIT. In mining law. A lateral entrance or passage into a mine; the opening by which a mine is entered, or by which water and ores are carried away; a horizontal excavation in and along a lode. 9 Colo. 207, 11 Pac. Rep. 80; 6 Colo. 278.

ADITUS. An approach; a way; a public way. Co. Litt. 56a.

ADJACENT. Lying near or close to; contiguous. The difference between *adjacent* and *adjoining* seems to be that the former implies that the two objects are not widely separated, though they may not actually touch, while *adjoining* imports that they are so joined or united to each other that no third object intervenes.

ADJECTIVE LAW. The aggregate of rules of procedure or practice. As opposed to that body of law which the courts are established to administer, (called "substantive law,") it means the rules according to which the substantive law is administered. That part of the law which provides a method for enforcing or maintaining rights, or obtaining redress for their invasion.

ADJOINING. The word "adjoining," in its etymological sense, means touching or contiguous, as distinguished from lying near to or adjacent. And the same meaning has been given to it when used in statutes. 52 N. Y. 397. See ADJACENT.

ADJOURN. To put off; defer; postpone. To postpone action of a convened court or body until another time specified, or indefinitely, the latter being usually called to adjourn *sine die*.

The primary signification of the term "adjourn" is to put off or defer to another day specified. But it has acquired also the meaning of suspending business for a time,—deferring, delaying. Probably, without some limitation, it would, when used with reference to a sale on foreclosure, or any judicial proceeding, properly include the fixing of the time to which the postponement was made. 14 How. Pr. 58. See, also, 5 N. Y. 22.

ADJOURNAL. A term applied in Scotch law and practice to the records of the criminal courts. The original records of criminal trials were called "bukis of adiornale," or "books of adjournal," few of which are now extant. An "act of adjournal" is an order of the court of justiciary entered on its minutes.

Adjournamentum est ad diem dicere seu diem dare. An adjournment is to appoint a day or give a day. 4 Inst. 27. Hence the formula *"eat sine die."*

ADJOURNATUR. L. Lat. It is adjourned. A word with which the old reports very frequently conclude a case. 1 Ld. Raym. 602; 1 Show. 7; 1 Leon. 88.

ADJOURNED SUMMONS. A summons taken out in the chambers of a judge, and afterwards taken into court to be argued by counsel.

ADJOURNED TERM. In practice. A continuance, by adjournment, of a regular term. 4 Ohio St. 473. Distinguished from an "additional term," which is a distinct term. Id. An *adjourned term* is a continuation of a previous or regular term; it is the same term prolonged, and the power of the court over the business which has been done, and the entries made at the regular term, continues. 22 Ala. 57.

ADJOURNMENT. A putting off or postponing of business or of a session until another time or place; the act of a court, legislative body, public meeting, or officer, by which the session or assembly is dissolved, either temporarily or finally, and the business in hand dismissed from consideration, either definitively or for an interval. If the adjournment is final, it is said to be *sine die*.

In the civil law. A calling into court; a summoning at an appointed time. Du Cange.

ADJOURNMENT DAY. A further day appointed by the judges at the regular sittings at *nisi prius* to try issues of fact not then ready for trial.

ADJOURNMENT DAY IN ERROR. In English practice. A day appointed some days before the end of the term at which matters left undone on the affirmance day are finished. 2 Tidd, Pr. 1176.

ADJOURNMENT IN EYRE. The appointment of a day when the justices in eyre mean to sit again. Cowell; Spelman.

ADJUDGE. To pass upon judicially; to decide, settle, or decree; to sentence or condemn.

ADJUDICATAIRE. In Canadian law. A purchaser at a sheriff's sale. See 1 Low. Can. 241; 10 Low. Can. 325.

ADJUDICATE. To settle in the exercise of judicial authority. To determine finally. Synonymous with *adjudge* in its strictest sense.

ADJUDICATIO. In the civil law. An adjudication. The judgment of the court that the subject-matter is the property of one of the litigants; confirmation of title by judgment. Mackeld. Rom. Law, § 204.

ADJUDICATION. The giving or pronouncing a judgment or decree in a cause; also the judgment given. The term is principally used in bankruptcy proceedings, the adjudication being the order which declares the debtor to be a bankrupt.

In French law. A sale made at public auction and upon competition. Adjudications are voluntary, judicial, or administrative. Duverger.

In Scotch law. A species of diligence, or process for transferring the estate of a debtor to a creditor, carried on as an ordinary action before the court of session. A species of judicial sale, redeemable by the debtor. A decreet of the lords of session, adjudging and appropriating a person's lands, hereditaments, or any heritable right to belong to his creditor, who is called the "adjudger," for payment or performance. Bell; Ersk. Inst. c. 2, tit. 12, §§ 39–55; Forb. Inst. pt. 3, b. 1, c. 2, tit. 6.

ADJUDICATION CONTRA HÆREDITATEM JACENTEM. In Scotch law. When a debtor's heir apparent renounces the succession, any creditor may obtain a decree *cognitionis causâ*, the purpose of which is that the amount of the debt may be ascertained so that the real estate may be adjudged.

ADJUDICATION IN IMPLEMENT. In Scotch law. An action by a grantee against his grantor to compel him to complete the title.

ADJUNCTIO. In the civil law. Adjunction; a species of *accessio*, whereby two things belonging to different proprietors are brought into firm connection with each other; such as interweaving, (*intertextura;*) welding together, (*adferruminatio;*) soldering together, (*applumbatura;*) painting, (*pictura;*) writing, (*scriptura;*) building, (*inædificatio;*) sowing, (*satio;*) and planting, (*plantatio.*) Inst. 2, 1, 26–34; Dig. 6, 1, 23; Mackeld. Rom. Law, § 276. See ACCESSIO.

ADJUNCTS. Additional judges sometimes appointed in the English high court of delegates. See Shelf. Lun. 310.

ADJUNCTUM ACCESSORIUM. An accessory or appurtenance.

ADJURATION. A swearing or binding upon oath.

ADJUST. To bring to proper relations; to settle; to determine and apportion an amount due.

ADJUSTMENT. In the law of insurance, the adjustment of a loss is the ascertainment of its amount and the ratable distribution of it among those liable to pay it; the settling and ascertaining the amount of the indemnity which the assured, after all allowances and deductions made, is entitled to receive under the policy, and fixing the proportion which each underwriter is liable to pay. Marsh. Ins. (4th Ed.) 499; 2 Phil. Ins. §§ 1814, 1815.

Adjuvari quippe nos, non decipi, beneficio oportet. We ought to be favored, not injured, by that which is intended for our benefit. (The species of bailment called "loan" must be to the advantage of the borrower, not to his detriment.) Story, Bailm. § 275. See 8 El. & Bl. 1051.

ADLAMWR. In Welsh law. A proprietor who, for some cause, entered the service of another proprietor, and left him after the expiration of a year and a day. He was liable to the payment of 30 pence to his patron. Wharton.

ADLEGIARE. To purge one's self of a crime by oath.

ADMANUENSIS. A person who swore by laying his hands on the book.

ADMEASUREMENT. Ascertainment by measure; measuring out; assignment or apportionment by measure, that is, by fixed quantity or value, by certain limits, or in definite and fixed proportions.

ADMEASUREMENT, WRIT OF. It lay against persons who usurped more than their share, in the two following cases: Admeasurement of dower, where the widow held from the heir more land, etc., as dower, than rightly belonged to her; and admeasurement of pasture, which lay where any one having common of pasture surcharged the common. Termes de la Ley.

ADMEASUREMENT OF DOWER. In practice. A remedy which lay for the heir on reaching his majority to rectify an assignment of dower made during his minority, by which the doweress had received more than she was legally entitled to. 2 Bl. Comm. 136; Gilb. Uses, 379.

In some of the states the statutory proceeding enabling a widow to compel the assignment of dower is called "admeasurement of dower."

ADMEASUREMENT OF PASTURE. In English law. A writ which lies between those that have common of pasture appendant, or by vicinage, in cases where any one or more of them surcharges the common with more cattle than they ought. Bract. fol. 229a; 1 Crabb, Real Prop. p. 318, § 358.

ADMENSURATIO. In old English law. Admeasurement. Reg. Orig. 156, 157.

ADMEZATORES. In old Italian law. Persons chosen by the consent of contending parties, to decide questions between them. Literally, mediators. Spelman.

ADMINICLE. In Scotch law. An aid or support to something else. A collateral deed or writing, referring to another which has been lost, and which it is in general necessary to produce before the tenor of the lost deed can be proved by parol evidence. Ersk. Inst. b. 4, tit. 1, § 55.

Used as an English word in the statute of 1 Edw. IV. c. 1, in the sense of aid, or support.

In the civil law. Imperfect proof. Merl. Repert.

ADMINICULAR. (From *adminiculum, q. v.*) Auxiliary to. "The murder would be *adminicular* to the robbery," (*i. e.,* committed to accomplish it.) 3 Mason, 121.

ADMINICULAR EVIDENCE. In ecclesiastical law. Auxiliary or supplementary evidence; such as is presented for the purpose of explaining and completing other evidence.

ADMINICULATE. To give adminicular evidence.

ADMINICULATOR. An officer in the Romish church, who administered to the wants of widows, orphans, and afflicted persons. Spelman.

ADMINICULUM. An adminicle; a prop or support; an accessory thing. An aid or support to something else, whether a right or the evidence of one. It is principally used to designate evidence adduced in aid or support of other evidence, which without it is imperfect. Brown.

ADMINISTER. To discharge the duties of an office; to take charge of business; to manage affairs; to serve in the conduct of affairs, in the application of things to their uses; to settle and distribute the estate of a decedent.

In physiology, and in criminal law, to administer means to cause or procure a person to take some drug or other substance into his or her system; to direct and cause a medicine, poison, or drug to be taken into the system. 8 Ohio St. 131; 34 N. Y. 223; 11 Fla. 247; 1 Moody, 114.

Neither fraud nor deception is a necessary ingredient in the act of administering poison. To force poison into the stomach of another; to compel another by threats of violence to swallow poison; to furnish poison to another for the purpose and with

the intention that the person to whom it is delivered shall commit suicide therewith, and which poison is accordingly taken by the suicide for that purpose; or to be present at the taking of poison by a suicide, participating in the taking thereof, by assistance, persuasion, or otherwise,—each and all of these are forms and modes of "administering" poison. 23 Ohio St. 146.

ADMINISTRATION. In public law. The administration of government means the practical management and direction of the executive department, or of the public machinery or functions, or of the operations of the various organs of the sovereign. The term "administration" is also conventionally applied to the whole class of public functionaries, or those in charge of the management of the executive department.

ADMINISTRATION OF ESTATES. The management and settlement of the estate of an intestate, or of a testator who has no executor, performed under the supervision of a court, by a person duly qualified and legally appointed, and usually involving (1) the collection of the decedent's assets; (2) payment of debts and claims against him and expenses; (3) distributing the remainder of the estate among those entitled thereto.

The term is applied broadly to denote the management of an estate by an executor, and also the management of estates of minors, lunatics, etc., in those cases where trustees have been appointed by authority of law to take charge of such estates in place of the legal owners. Bouvier.

Administration is principally of the following kinds, viz.:

Ad colligendum. That which is granted temporarily, for the purpose of collecting and preserving property of a perishable nature.

Ancillary administration is auxiliary and subordinate to the administration at the place of the decedent's domicile; it may be taken out in any foreign state or country where assets are locally situated, and is merely for the purpose of collecting such assets and paying debts there.

Cum testamento annexo. Administration with the will annexed. Administration granted in cases where a testator makes a will, without naming any executors; or where the executors who are named in the will are incompetent to act, or refuse to act; or in case of the death of the executors, or the survivor of them. 2 Bl. Comm. 503, 504.

De bonis non. Administration of the goods not administered. Administration granted for the purpose of administering such *of the goods* of a deceased person as were *not administered* by the former executor or administrator. 2 Bl. Comm. 506.

De bonis non cum testamento annexo. That which is granted when an executor dies leaving a part of the estate unadministered. 3 Cush. 28; 4 Watts, 34, 38, 39.

Durante absentia. That which is granted during the absence of the executor and until he has proved the will.

Durante minori œtate. Where an infant is made executor; in which case administration with will annexed is granted to another, during the minority of such executor, and until he shall attain his lawful age to act. See Godo. 102.

Foreign administration. That which is exercised by virtue of authority properly conferred by a foreign power.

Pendente lite. Administration during the suit. Administration granted during the pendency of a suit touching the validity of a will. 2 Bl. Comm. 503.

Public administration is such as is conducted (in some jurisdictions) by an officer called the public administrator, who is appointed to administer in cases where the intestate has left no person entitled to apply for letters.

ADMINISTRATION SUIT. In English practice. A suit brought in chancery, by any one interested, for administration of a decedent's estate, when there is doubt as to its solvency. Stimson.

ADMINISTRATIVE LAW. That branch of public law which deals with the various organs of the sovereign power considered as in motion, and prescribes in detail the manner of their activity, being concerned with such topics as the collection of the revenue, the regulation of the military and naval forces, citizenship and naturalization, sanitary measures, poor laws, coinage, police, the public safety and morals, etc. See Holl. Jur. 305–307.

ADMINISTRATOR, in the most usual sense of the word, is a person to whom letters of administration, that is, an authority to administer the estate of a deceased person, have been granted by the proper court. He resembles an executor, but, being appointed by the court, and not by the deceased, he has to give security for the due administration of the estate, by entering into a bond with sureties, called the administration bond. (Browne, Prob. Pr. 150.) Sweet.

By the law of Scotland the father is what is called the "administrator-in-law" for his children. As such, he is *ipso jure* their tutor while they are pupils, and their curator during their minority. The father's power extends over whatever estate may descend to his children, unless where that estate has been placed by the donor or grantor under the charge of special trustees or managers. This power in the father ceases by the child's discontinuing to reside with him, unless he continues to live at the father's expense; and with regard to daughters, it ceases on their marriage, the husband being the legal curator of his wife. Bell.

A public administrator is an officer authorized by the statute law of several of the states to superintend the settlement of estates of persons dying without relatives entitled to administer.

ADMINISTRATOR. In the civil law. A manager or conductor of affairs, especially the affairs of another, in his name or behalf. A manager of public affairs in behalf of others. Calvin. A public officer, ruler, or governor. Nov. 95, gl.; Cod. 12, 8.

ADMINISTRATRIX. A female who administers, or to whom letters of administration have been granted.

ADMIRAL. In European law. An officer who presided over the *admiralitas,* or *collegium ammiralitatis.* Locc. de Jur. Mar. lib. 2, c. 2, § 1.

In English law. A high officer or magistrate that hath the government of the king's navy, and the hearing of all causes belonging to the sea. Cowell.

In the navy. Admiral is also the title of high naval officers; they are of various grades, —rear admiral, vice-admiral, admiral, admiral of the fleet, the latter being the highest.

ADMIRALITAS. L. Lat. Admiralty; the admiralty, or court of admiralty.

In European law. An association of private armed vessels for mutual protection and defense against pirates and enemies.

ADMIRALTY. A court exercising jurisdiction over maritime causes, both civil and criminal, and marine affairs, commerce and navigation, controversies arising out of acts done upon or relating to the sea, and over questions of prize.

Also, the system of jurisprudence relating to and growing out of the jurisdiction and practice of the admiralty courts.

In English law. The executive department of state which presides over the naval forces of the kingdom. The normal head is the lord high admiral, but in practice the functions of the great office are discharged by several commissioners, of whom one is the chief, and is called the "First Lord." He is assisted by other lords and by various secretaries. Also, the court of the admiral.

The building where the lords of the admiralty transact business.

In American law. A tribunal exercising jurisdiction over all maritime contracts, torts, injuries, or offenses. 2 Pars. Mar. Law, 508.

ADMISSIBLE. Proper to be received. As applied to evidence, the term means that it is of such a character that the court or judge is bound to receive it; that is, allow it to be introduced.

ADMISSIBILITY. An objection to the *admissibility* of evidence in any cause can only be properly founded on the hypothesis that such testimony violates the law of evidence in this: that the law prohibits the proof of the particular fact in the manner proposed, or because of its irrelevancy to the subject-matter of the inquiry. 7 Md. 87.

ADMISSION. In evidence. A voluntary acknowledgment, confession, or concession of the existence of a fact or the truth of an allegation made by a party to the suit.

In pleading. The concession or acknowledgment by one party of the truth of some matter alleged by the opposite party, made in a pleading, the effect of which is to narrow the area of facts or allegations requiring to be proved by evidence.

In practice. The formal act of a court, by which attorneys or counsellors are recognized as officers of the court and are licensed to practice before it.

In corporations. The act of a corporation or company by which an individual acquires the rights of a member of such corporation or company.

In English ecclesiastical law. The act of the bishop, who, on approval of the clerk presented by the patron, after examination, declares him fit to serve the cure of the church to which he is presented, by the words "*admitto te habilem,*" I admit thee able. Co. Litt. 344a; 4 Coke, 79; 1 Crabb, Real Prop. p. 138, § 123.

ADMISSIONALIS. In European law. An usher. Spelman.

ADMIT. To allow, receive, or take; to suffer one to enter; to give possession; to license. See ADMISSION.

ADMITTANCE. In English law. The act of giving possession of a copyhold estate. It is of three kinds: (1) Upon a *voluntary grant by the lord,* where the land has escheated or reverted to him. (2) Upon *surrender* by the former tenant. (3) Upon *descent,* where the heir is tenant on his ancestor's death.

ADMITTENDO CLERICO. A writ of execution upon a right of presentation to a benefice being recovered in *quare impedit,* addressed to the bishop or his metropolitan, requiring him to *admit* and institute the clerk or presentee of the plaintiff. Reg. Orig. 33a.

ADMITTENDO IN SOCIUM. A writ for associating certain persons, as knights and other gentlemen of the county, to justices of assize on the circuit. Reg. Orig. 206.

ADMONITIO TRINA. A triple or threefold warning, given, in old times, to a prisoner standing mute, before he was subjected to the *peine forte et dure.* 4 Bl. Comm. 325; 4 Steph. Comm. 391.

ADMONITION. In ecclesiastical law, this is the lightest form of punishment, consisting in a reprimand and warning administered by the judge to the defendant. If the latter does not obey the admonition, he may be more severely punished, as by suspension, etc.

ADMORTIZATION. The reduction of property of lands or tenements to mortmain, in the feudal customs.

ADNEPOS. The son of a great-great-grandson. Calvin.

ADNEPTIS. The daughter of a great-great-granddaughter. Calvin.

ADNICHILED. Annulled, cancelled, made void. 28 Hen. VIII.

ADNIHILARE. In old English law. To annul; to make void; to reduce to nothing; to treat as nothing; to hold as or for nought.

ADNOTATIO. In the civil law. The subscription of a name or signature to an instrument. Cod. 4, 19, 5, 7.

A rescript of the prince or emperor, signed with his own hand, or sign-manual. Cod. 1, 19, 1. "In the imperial law, casual homicide was excused by the indulgence of the emperor, signed with his own sign-manual, *annotatione principis.*" 4 Bl. Comm. 187.

ADOLESCENCE. That age which follows puberty and precedes the age of majority. It commences for males at 14, and for females at 12 years completed, and continues till 21 years complete.

ADOPT. To accept, appropriate, choose, or select; to make that one's own (property or act) which was not so originally; to take another's child and give him the rights and duties of one's own.

To adopt a route for the transportation of the mail means to take the steps necessary to cause the mail to be transported over that route. Dev. Ct. Cl. 47.

To adopt a contract is to accept it as binding, notwithstanding some defect which entitles the party to repudiate it. Thus, when a person affirms a voidable contract, or ratifies a contract made by his agent beyond his authority, he is said to adopt it. Sweet.

ADOPTION. The act of one who takes another's child into his own family, treating him as his own, and giving him all the rights and duties of his own child.

A juridical act creating between two persons certain relations, purely civil, of paternity and filiation. 6 Demol. § 1.

ADOPTIVE ACT. An act of parliament which comes into operation within a limited area upon being adopted, in manner prescribed therein, by the inhabitants of that area.

ADOPTIVUS. Lat. Adoptive. Applied both to the parent adopting, and the child adopted. Inst. 2, 13, 4; Id. 3, 1, 10–14.

ADPROMISSOR. In the civil and Scotch law. A guarantor, surety, or cautioner; a peculiar species of *fidejussor;* one who adds his own promise to the promise given by the principal debtor, whence the name.

ADQUIETO. Payment. Blount.

ADRECTARE. To do right, satisfy, or make amends.

ADRHAMIRE. In old European law. To undertake, declare, or promise solemnly; to pledge; to pledge one's self to make oath. Spelman.

ADRIFT. Sea-weed, between high and low water-mark, which has not been deposited on the shore, and which during flood-tide is moved by each rising and receding wave, is *adrift,* although the bottom of the mass may touch the beach. 2 Allen, 549.

ADROGATION. In the civil law. The adoption of one who was *impubes;* that is,

if a male, under fourteen years of age; if a female, under twelve. Dig. 1, 7, 17, 1.

ADSCENDENTES. Lat. In the civil law. Ascendants. Dig. 23, 2, 68; Cod. 5, 5, 6.

ADSCRIPTI GLEBÆ. Slaves who served the master of the soil, who were annexed to the land, and passed with it when it was conveyed. Calvin.

In Scotland, as late as the reign of George III., laborers in collieries and salt works were bound to the coal-pit or salt work in which they were engaged, in a manner similar to that of the *adscripti* of the Romans. Bell.

ADSCRIPTUS. In the civil law. Added, annexed, or bound by or in writing; enrolled, registered; united, joined, annexed, bound to, generally. *Servus colonæ adscriptus,* a slave annexed to an estate as a cultivator. Dig. 19, 2, 54, 2. *Fundus adscriptus,* an estate bound to, or burdened with a duty. Cod. 11, 2, 3.

ADSESSORES. Side judges. Assistants or advisers of the regular magistrates, or appointed as their substitutes in certain cases. Calvin.

ADSTIPULATOR. In Roman law. An accessory party to a promise, who received the same promise as his principal did, and could equally receive and exact payment; or he only stipulated for a part of that for which the principal stipulated, and then his rights were co-extensive with the amount of his own stipulation. Sandars, Just. Inst. (5th Ed.) 348.

ADULT. In the civil law. A male infant who has attained the age of fourteen; a female infant who has attained the age of twelve. Dom. Liv. Prel. tit. 2, § 2, n. 8.

In the common law. One of the full age of twenty-one. Swanst. Ch. 533.

"The authorities all agree, so far as we are advised, that at common law the word 'adult' signifies a person who has attained the full age of 21 years. The word 'adult' seems to have a well-defined meaning, both in law and in common acceptation. Mr. Bouvier defines the meaning of the word in the civil law, with which we have no present concern, and says: 'In the common law an adult is considered one of full age.' Mr. Wharton defines the word as signifying 'a person of full age.' Mr. Webster gives as one of the meanings 'one who has reached the years of manhood.' " 10 Tex. App. 411; 11 Tex. App. 95.

ADULTER. Lat. One who corrupts; one who seduces another man's wife. *Adulter solidorum.* A corruptor of metals; a counterfeiter. Calvin.

ADULTERA. In the civil law. An adulteress; a woman guilty of adultery. Dig. 48, 5, 4, pr.; Id. 48, 5, 15, 8.

ADULTERATION. The act of corrupting or debasing. The term is generally applied to the act of mixing up with food or drink intended to be sold other matters of an inferior quality, and usually of a more or less deleterious quality.

It is not clear that the addition of a wholesome article, as of pure water to milk, is adulterating. 5 Park. Crim. R. 311.

ADULTERATOR. Lat. In the civil law. A forger; a counterfeiter. *Adulteratores monetæ,* counterfeiters of money. Dig. 48, 19, 16, 9.

ADULTERINE. Begotten in an adulterous intercourse. In the Roman and canon law, adulterine bastards were distinguished from such as were the issue of two unmarried persons, and the former were treated with more severity, not being allowed the *status* of natural children, and being ineligible to holy orders.

ADULTERINE GUILDS. Traders acting as a corporation without a charter, and paying a fine annually for permission to exercise their usurped privileges. Smith, Wealth Nat. b. 1, c. 10.

ADULTERIUM. A fine anciently imposed as a punishment for the commission of adultery.

ADULTEROUS BASTARDY. Adulterous bastards are those produced by an unlawful connection between two persons, who, at the time when the child was conceived, were, either of them or both, connected by marriage with some other person. Civil Code La. art. 182.

ADULTERY. Adultery is the voluntary sexual intercourse of a married person with a person other than the offender's husband or wife. Civil Code Cal. § 93; 1 Bish. Mar. & Div. § 703; 6 Metc. 243; 36 Me. 261; 11 Ga. 56.

Adultery is the unlawful voluntary sexual intercourse of a married person with one of the opposite sex, and when the crime is committed between parties, only one of whom is married, both are guilty of adultery. Pen. Code Dak. § 333.

It is to be observed, however, that in some of the states it is held that this crime is committed only when the *woman* is married to a third person, and the unlawful commerce of a married man with an unmarried woman is not of the grade of adultery. In some jurisdictions, also, a distinction is made between double and single adultery, the former being committed where both parties are married to other persons, the latter where one only is so married.

ADVANCE, v. To pay money or render other value before it is due; or to furnish capital in aid of a projected enterprise, in expectation of return from it.

ADVANCEMENT. Money or property given by a father to his child or presumptive heir, or expended by the former for the latter's benefit, by way of anticipation of the share which the child will inherit in the father's estate and intended to be deducted therefrom. It is the latter circumstance which differentiates an advancement from a gift or a loan.

Advancement, in its legal acceptation, does not involve the idea of obligation or future liability to answer. It is a pure and irrevocable gift made by a parent to a child in anticipation of such child's future share of the parent's estate. 13 Pa. St. 580.

An advancement is any provision by a parent made to and accepted by a child out of his estate, either in money or property, during his life-time, over and above the obligation of the parent for maintenance and education. Code Ga. 1882, § 2579.

An "advancement by portion," within the meaning of the statute, is a sum given by a parent to establish a child in life, (as by starting him in business,) or to make a provision for the child, (as on the marriage of a daughter.) L. R. 20 Eq. 155.

ADVANCES. Moneys paid before or in advance of the proper time of payment; money or commodities furnished on credit; a loan or gift, or money advanced to be repaid conditionally. See 51 Barb. 597, 612; 10 Barb. 73.

This word, when taken in its strict legal sense, does not mean gifts, (advancements,) and does mean a sort of loan; and, when taken in its ordinary and usual sense, it includes both loans and gifts, — loans more readily, perhaps, than gifts. 25 Ga. 355.

Payments advanced to the owner of property by a factor or broker on the price of goods which the latter has in his hands, or is to receive, for sale.

ADVANTAGIUM. In old pleading. An advantage. Co. Ent. 484; Townsh. Pl. 50.

ADVENA. In Roman law. One of foreign birth, who has left his own country and settled elsewhere, and who has not acquired citizenship in his new locality; often called *albanus.* Du Cange.

ADVENT. A period of time recognized by the English common and ecclesiastical law, beginning on the Sunday that falls either upon St. Andrew's day, being the 30th of November, or the next to it, and continuing to Christmas day. Wharton.

ADVENTITIOUS. That which comes incidentally, fortuitously, or out of the regular course.

ADVENTITIUS. Lat. Fortuitous; incidental; that which comes from an unusual source. *Adventitia bona* are goods which fall to a man otherwise than by inheritance. *Adventitia dos* is a dowry or portion given by some friend other than the parent.

ADVENTURA. An adventure. 2 Mon. Angl. 615; Townsh. Pl. 50. Flotson, jetson, and lagon are styled *adventuræ maris,* (adventures of the sea.) Hale, De Jure Mar. pt. 1, c. 7.

ADVENTURE. In mercantile law. Sending goods abroad under charge of a supercargo or other agent, at the risk of the sender, to be disposed of to the best advantage for the benefit of the owners.

The goods themselves so sent.

In marine insurance. A very usual word in policies of marine insurance, and everywhere used as synonymous, or nearly so, with "perils." It is often used by the writers to describe the enterprise or voyage as a "marine adventure" insured against. 14 Fed. Rep. 233.

ADVENTURE, BILL OF. In mercantile law. A writing signed by a merchant, stating that the property in goods shipped in his name belongs to another, to the adventure or chance of which the person so named is to stand, with a covenant from the merchant to account to him for the produce.

ADVERSARIA. (From Lat. *adversa,* things remarked or ready at hand.) Rough memoranda, common-place books.

ADVERSARY. A litigant-opponent, the opposite party in a writ or action.

ADVERSARY PROCEEDING. One having opposing parties; contested, as distinguished from an *ex parte* application; one of which the party seeking relief has given legal warning to the other party, and afforded the latter an opportunity to contest it.

ADVERSE. Opposed; contrary; in resistance or opposition to a claim, application, or proceeding.

ADVERSE CLAIM. A claim set up by a stranger to goods upon which the sheriff has levied an execution or attachment.

ADVERSE ENJOYMENT. The possession or exercise of an easement, under a claim of right against the owner of the land out of which such easement is derived. 2 Washb. Real Prop. 42.

ADVERSE POSSESSION. The possession and enjoyment of real property, or of any estate lying in grant, continued for a certain length of time, held adversely and in denial and opposition to the title of another claimant, or under circumstances which indicate an assertion or color of right or title on the part of the person maintaining it, as against another person who is out of possession.

ADVERSE USER. An adverse user is such a use of the property as the owner himself would make, asking no permission, and disregarding all other claims to it, so far as they conflict with this use. 63 Me. 434.

ADVERSE VERDICT. Where a party, appealing from an allowance of damages by commissioners, recovers a verdict in his favor, but for a less amount of damages than had been originally allowed, such verdict is *adverse* to him, within the meaning of his undertaking to pay costs if the verdict should be adverse to him. 16 Gray, 256.

ADVERSE WITNESS. A witness whose mind discloses a bias hostile to the party examining him; not a witness whose evidence, being honestly given, is adverse to the case of the examinant. Brown.

ADVERSUS. In the civil law. Against, (*contra.*) *Adversus bonos mores,* against good morals. Dig. 47, 10, 15.

ADVERTISEMENT. Notice given in a manner designed to attract public attention; information communicated to the public, or to an individual concerned, by means of handbills or the newspaper.

A sign-board, erected at a person's place of business, giving notice that lottery tickets are for sale there, is an "advertisement," within the meaning of a statute prohibiting the advertising of lotteries. In such connection the meaning of the word is not confined to notices printed in newspapers. 5 Pick. 42.

ADVERTISEMENTS OF QUEEN ELIZABETH. Certain articles or ordinances drawn up by Archbishop Parker and some of the bishops in 1564, at the request of Queen Elizabeth, the object of which was to enforce decency and uniformity in the ritual of the church. The queen subsequently refused to give her official sanction to these advertisements, and left them to be enforced by the bishops under their general powers. Phillim. Ecc. Law, 910; 2 Prob. Div. 276; Id. 354.

ADVICE. View; opinion; the counsel given by lawyers to their clients; an opinion expressed as to wisdom of future conduct.

The instruction usually given by one merchant or banker to another by letter, informing him of shipments made to him, or of bills or drafts drawn on him, with particulars of date, or sight, the sum, and the payee. Bills presented for acceptance or payment are frequently dishonored for *want of advice*.

ADVISARE, ADVISARI. To consult, deliberate, consider, advise; to be advised. Occurring in the phrase *curia advisari vult,* (usually abbreviated *cur. adv. vult,* or *C. A. V.,*) the court wishes to be advised, or to consider of the matter.

ADVISE. To give an opinion or counsel, or recommend a plan or course of action; also to give notice.

This term is not synonymous with "direct" or "instruct." Where a statute authorizes the trial court to *advise* the jury to acquit, the court has no power to *instruct* the jury to acquit. The court can only counsel, and the jury are not bound by the advice. 70 Cal. 17, 11 Pac. Rep. 470.

ADVISED. Prepared to give judgment, after examination and deliberation. "The court took time to be advised." 1 Leon. 187.

ADVISEMENT. Deliberation, consideration, consultation; the consultation of a court, after the argument of a cause by counsel, and before delivering their opinion.

ADVISORY. Counselling, suggesting, or advising, but not imperative. A verdict on an issue out of chancery is advisory. 101 U. S. 252.

ADVOCARE. Lat. To defend; to call to one's aid; to vouch; to warrant.

ADVOCASSIE. L. Fr. The office of an advocate; advocacy. Kelham.

ADVOCATA. In old English law. A patroness; a woman who had the right of presenting to a church. Spelman.

ADVOCATE. One who assists, defends, or pleads for another; one who renders legal advice and aid and pleads the cause of another before a court.

A person learned in the law, and duly admitted to practice, who assists his client with advice, and pleads for him in open court. Holthouse.

The *College or Faculty of Advocates* is a corporate body in Scotland, consisting of the members of the bar in Edinburgh. A large portion of its members are not active practitioners, however. 2 Bankt. Inst. 486.

In the civil and ecclesiastical law. An officer of the court, learned in the law, who is engaged by a suitor to maintain or defend his cause.

ADVOCATE GENERAL. The adviser of the crown in England on questions of naval and military law.

ADVOCATE, LORD. The principal crown lawyer in Scotland, and one of the great officers of state of Scotland. It is his duty to act as public prosecutor; but private individuals injured may prosecute upon obtaining his concurrence. He is assisted by a solicitor general and four junior counsel, termed "advocates-depute." He has the power of appearing as public prosecutor in any court in Scotland, where any person can be tried for an offense, or in any action where the crown is interested. Wharton.

ADVOCATE, QUEEN'S. A member of the College of Advocates, appointed by letters patent, whose office is to advise and act as counsel for the crown in questions of civil, canon, and international law. His rank is next after the solicitor general.

ADVOCATI. In Roman law. Patrons; pleaders; speakers. Anciently, any one who lent his aid to a friend, and who was supposed to be able in any way to influence a judge, was called *advocatus.*

ADVOCATI ECCLESIÆ. A term used in the ecclesiastical law to denote the patrons of churches who presented to the living on an avoidance. This term was also applied to those who were retained to argue the cases of the church.

ADVOCATI FISCI. In the civil law. Advocates of the fisc, or revenue; fiscal advocates, (*qui causam fisci egissent.*) Cod. 2,

9, 1; Id. 2, 7, 13. Answering, in some measure, to the king's counsel in English law. 3 Bl. Comm. 27.

ADVOCATIA. In the civil law. The quality, function, privilege, or territorial jurisdiction of an advocate.

ADVOCATION. In Scotch law. A process by which an action may be carried from an inferior to a superior court before final judgment in the former.

ADVOCATIONE DECIMARUM. A writ which lay for tithes, demanding the fourth part or upwards, that belonged to any church.

ADVOCATOR. In old practice. One who called on or vouched another to warrant a title; a voucher. *Advocatus;* the person called on, or vouched; a vouchee. Spelman; Townsh. Pl. 45.

In Scotch practice. An appellant. 1 Broun, R. 67.

ADVOCATUS. In the civil law. An advocate; one who managed or assisted in managing another's cause before a judicial tribunal. Called also *"patronus."* Cod. 2, 7, 14. But distinguished from *causidicus.* Id. 2, 6, 6.

ADVOCATUS DIABOLI. The devil's advocate; the advocate who argues against the canonization of a saint.

Advocatus est, ad quem pertinet jus advocationis alicujus ecclesiæ, ut ad ecclesiam, nomine proprio, non alieno, possit præsentare. A patron is he to whom appertains the right of presentation to a church, in such a manner that he may present to such a church in his own name, and not in the name of another. Co. Litt. 119.

ADVOWEE, or AVOWEE. The person or patron who has a right to present to a benefice. Fleta, lib. 5, c. 14.

ADVOWEE PARAMOUNT. The sovereign, or highest patron.

ADVOWSON. In English ecclesiastical law. The right of presentation to a church or ecclesiastical benefice; the right of presenting a fit person to the bishop, to be by him admitted and instituted to a certain benefice within the diocese, which has become vacant. 2 Bl. Comm. 21; Co. Litt. 119b, 120a. The person enjoying this right is called the "patron" (*patronus*) of the church, and was formerly termed *"advocatus,"* the advocate or defender, or in English, *"advowee."* Id.; 1 Crabb, Real Prop. p. 129, § 117.

Advowsons are of the following several kinds, viz.:

Advowson appendant. An advowson annexed to a manor, and passing with it, as incident or appendant to it, by a grant of the manor only, without adding any other words. 2 Bl. Comm. 22; Co. Litt. 120, 121; 1 Crabb, Real Prop. p. 130, § 118.

Advowson collative. Where the bishop happens himself to be the patron, in which case (presentation being impossible, or unnecessary) he does by one act, which is termed *"collation,"* or conferring the benefice, all that is usually done by the separate acts of presentation and institution. 2 Bl. Comm. 22, 23; 1 Crabb, Real Prop. p. 131, § 119.

Advowson donative. Where the patron has the right to put his clerk in possession by his mere gift, or deed of donation, without any presentation to the bishop, or institution by him. 2 Bl. Comm. 23; 1 Crabb, Real Prop. p. 131, § 119.

Advowson in gross. An advowson separated from the manor, and annexed to the person. 2 Bl. Comm. 22; Co. Litt. 120; 1 Crabb, Real Prop. p. 130, § 118; 3 Steph. Comm. 116.

Advowson presentative. The usual kind of advowson, where the patron has the right of *presentation* to the bishop, or ordinary, and moreover to demand of him to institute his clerk, if he finds him canonically qualified. 2 Bl. Comm. 22; 1 Crabb, Real Prop. p. 131, § 119.

ADVOWTRY, or ADVOUTRY. The offense, by an adulteress, of continuing to live with the man with whom she committed the adultery. Cowell; Termes de la Ley.

ÆDES. Lat. In the civil law. A house, dwelling, place of habitation, whether in the city or country. Dig. 30, 41, 5. In the country everything upon the surface of the soil passed under the term *"ædes."* Du Cange; Calvin.

ÆDIFICARE. Lat. In civil and old English law. To make or build a house; to erect a building. Dig. 45, 1, 75, 7.

Ædificare in tuo proprio solo non licet quod alteri noceat. 3 Inst. 201. To build upon your own land what may injure another is not lawful. A proprietor of land has no right to erect an edifice on his own ground, interfering with the due enjoyment of adjoining premises, as by overhanging them, or by throwing water from the roof and eaves upon them, or by obstructing ancient lights and windows. Broom, Max. 369.

ÆdIficatum solo solo cedit. What is built upon land belongs to or goes with land. Broom, Max. 172; Co. Litt. 4*a*.

ÆdIficia solo cedunt. Buildings belong to [go with] the soil. Fleta, lib. 3, c. 2, § 12.

ÆDILE. In Roman law. An officer who attended to the repairs of the temples and other public buildings; the repairs and cleanliness of the streets; the care of the weights and measures; the providing for funerals and games; and regulating the prices of provisions. Ainsw. Lex.; Smith, Lex.; Du Cange.

ÆDILITUM EDICTUM. In the Roman law. The Ædilitian Edict; an edict providing remedies for frauds in sales, the execution of which belonged to the curule ædiles. Dig. 21, 1. See Cod. 4, 58.

ÆFESN. In old English law. The remuneration to the proprietor of a domain for the privilege of feeding swine under the oaks and beeches of his woods.

ÆGROTO. Lat. Being sick or indisposed. A term used in some of the older reports. "Holt *ægroto*." 11 Mod. 179.

ÆGYLDE. Uncompensated, unpaid for, unavenged. From the participle of exclusion, *a*, *æ*, or *ex*, (Goth.,) and *gild*, payment, requital. Anc. Inst. Eng.

ÆL. A Norman French term signifying "grandfather." It is also spelled "*aieul*" and "*ayle.*" Kelham.

Æquior est dispositio legis quam hominis. The disposition of the law is more equitable than that of man. 8 Coke, 152.

ÆQUITAS. In the civil law. Equity, as opposed to *strictum* or *summum jus*, (*q. v.*) Otherwise called *æquum*, *æquum bonum*, *æquum et bonum*, *æquum et justum*. Calvin.

Æquitas agit in personam. Equity acts upon the person. 4 Bouv. Inst. n. 3733.

Æquitas est correctio legis generaliter latæ, qua parte deficit. Equity is the correction of that wherein the law, by reason of its generality, is deficient. Plowd. 375.

Æquitas est correctio quædam legi adhibita, quia ab eâ abest aliquid propter generalem sine exceptione comprehen- sionem. Equity is a certain correction applied to law, because on account of its general comprehensiveness, without an exception, something is absent from it. Plowd. 467.

Æquitas est perfecta quædam ratio quæ jus scriptum interpretatur et emendat; nulla scriptura comprehensa, sed solum in verâ ratione consistens. Equity is a certain perfect reason, which interprets and amends the written law, comprehended in no writing, but consisting in right reason alone. Co. Litt. 24*b*.

Æquitas est quasi æqualitas. Equity is as it were equality; equity is a species of equality or equalization. Co. Litt. 24.

Æquitas ignorantiæ opitulatur, oscitantiæ non item. Equity assists ignorance, but not carelessness.

Æquitas non facit jus, sed juri auxiliatur. Equity does not make law, but assists law. Lofft, 379.

Æquitas nunquam contravenit leges. Equity never counteracts the laws.

Æquitas sequitur legem. Equity follows the law. Gilb. 186.

Æquitas supervacua odit. Equity abhors superfluous things. Lofft, 282.

Æquitas uxoribus, liberis, creditoribus maxime favet. Equity favors wives and children, creditors most of all.

Æquum et bonum est lex legum. What is equitable and good is the law of laws. Hob. 224.

ÆRA, or ERA. A fixed point of chronological time, whence any number of years is counted; thus, the Christian era began at the birth of Christ, and the Mohammedan era at the flight of Mohammed from Mecca to Medina. The derivation of the word has been much contested. Wharton.

ÆRARIUM. Lat. In the Roman law. The treasury, (*fiscus.*) Calvin.

ÆS. Lat. In the Roman law. Money, (literally, brass;) metallic money in general, including gold. Dig. 9, 2, 2, pr.; Id. 9, 2, 27, 5; Id. 50, 16, 159.

ÆS ALIENUM. A civil law term signifying a debt; the property of another; borrowed money, as distinguished from *æs suum*, one's own money.

ÆS SUUM. One's own money. In the Roman law. Debt; a debt; that which others owe to us, (*quod alii nobis debent.*) Dig. 50, 16, 213.

ÆSNECIA. In old English law. Esnecy; the right or privilege of the eldest born. Spelman; Glanv. lib. 7, c. 3; Fleta, lib. 2, c. 66, §§ 5, 6.

ÆSTIMATIO CAPITIS. In Saxon law. The estimation or valuation of the head; the price or value of a man. By the laws of Athelstan, the life of every man, not excepting that of the king himself, was estimated at a certain price, which was called the *were,* or *œstimatio capitis.* Crabb, Eng. Law, c. 4.

Æstimatio præteriti delicti ex postremo facto nunquam crescit. The weight of a past offense is never increased by a subsequent fact. Bacon.

ÆTAS INFANTIÆ PROXIMA. In the civil law. The age next to infancy; the first half of the period of childhood, (*pueritia,*) extending from seven years to ten and a half. Inst. 3, 20, 9; 4 Bl. Comm. 22.

ÆTAS LEGITIMA. In the civil law. Lawful age; the age of twenty-five. Dig. 3, 5, 27, pr.; Id. 26, 2, 32, 2; Id. 27, 7, 1, pr.

ÆTAS PERFECTA. In the civil law, Complete age; full age; the age of twenty-five. Dig. 4, 4, 32; Id. 22, 3, 25, 1.

ÆTAS PRIMA. In the civil law. The first age; infancy, (*infantia.*) Cod. 6, 61, 8, 3.

ÆTAS PUBERTATI PROXIMA. In the civil law. The age next to puberty; the last half of the period of childhood, (*pueritia,*) extending from ten years and a half to fourteen. Inst. 3, 20, 9; 4 Bl. Comm. 22.

ÆTATE PROBANDA. A writ which inquired whether the king's tenant holding in chief by chivalry was of full age to receive his lands. It was directed to the escheater of the county. Now disused.

ÆTHELING. In Saxon law. A noble; generally a prince of the blood.

AFFAIRS. A person's concerns in trade or property; business.

AFFECT. This word is often used in the sense of acting injuriously upon persons and things. 93 U. S. 84.

Affectio tua nomen imponit operi tuo. Your disposition (or intention) gives name (or character) to your work or act. Bract. fol. 2*b*, 101*b*.

AFFECTION. The making over, pawning, or mortgaging a thing to assure the payment of a sum of money, or the discharge of some other duty or service. Crabb, Technol. Dict.

AFFECTUS. Disposition; intention, impulse or affection of the mind. One of the causes for a challenge of a juror is *propter affectum,* on account of a suspicion of *bias* or favor. 3 Bl. Comm. 363; Co. Litt. 156.

Affectus punitur licet non sequatur effectus. The intention is punished although the intended result does not follow. 9 Coke, 55.

AFFEER. To assess, liquidate, appraise, fix in amount.

To affeer an amercement. To establish the amount which one amerced in a court-leet should pay.

To affeer an account. To confirm it on oath in the exchequer. Cowell; Blount; Spelman.

AFFEERORS. Persons who, in courtleets, upon oath, settle and moderate the fines and amercements imposed on those who have committed offenses arbitrarily punishable, or that have no express penalty appointed by statute. They are also appointed to moderate fines, etc., in courts-baron. Cowell.

AFFERMER. L. Fr. To let to farm. Also to make sure, to establish or confirm. Kelham.

AFFIANCE. A plighting of troth between man and woman. Litt. § 39. An agreement by which a man and woman promise each other that they will marry together. Poth. Traité du Mar. n. 24.

AFFIANT. The person who makes and subscribes an affidavit. The word is used, in this sense, interchangeably with "deponent." But the latter term should be reserved as the designation of one who makes a deposition.

AFFIDARE. To swear faith to; to pledge one's faith or do fealty by making oath. Cowell.

AFFIDARI. To be mustered and enrolled for soldiers upon an oath of fidelity.

AFFIDATIO. A swearing of the oath of fidelity or of fealty to one's lord, under whose protection the quasi-vassal has voluntarily come. Brown.

AFFIDATIO DOMINORUM. An oath taken by the lords in parliament.

AFFIDATUS. One who is not a vassal, but who for the sake of protection has connected himself with one more powerful. Spelman; 2 Bl. Comm. 46.

AFFIDAVIT. A written or printed declaration or statement of facts, made voluntarily, and confirmed by the oath or affirmation of the party making it, taken before an officer having authority to administer such oath.

An affidavit is a written declaration under oath, made without notice to the adverse party. Code Civil Proc. Cal. § 2003; Code Civil Proc. Dak. § 464.

An affidavit is an oath in writing, sworn before and attested by him who hath authority to administer the same. 1 Mich. N. P. 189.

An affidavit is always taken *ex parte*, and in this respect it is distinguished from a deposition, the matter of which is elicited by questions, and which affords an opportunity for cross-examination.

AFFIDAVIT OF DEFENSE. An affidavit stating that the defendant has a good defense to the plaintiff's action on the merits of the case. Also called an affidavit of merits.

AFFIDAVIT OF SERVICE. An affidavit intended to certify the service of a writ, notice, or other document.

AFFIDAVIT TO HOLD TO BAIL. An affidavit made to procure the arrest of the defendant in a civil action.

AFFILARE. L. Lat. To file or affile. *Affiletur*, let it be filed. 8 Coke, 160. *De recordo affilatum*, affiled of record. 2 Ld. Raym. 1476.

AFFILE. A term employed in old practice, signifying to put on file. 2 Maule & S. 202. In modern usage it is contracted to *file*.

AFFILIATION. The fixing any one with the paternity of a bastard child, and the obligation to maintain it.

In French law. A species of adoption which exists by custom in some parts of France. The person affiliated succeeded equally with other heirs to the property acquired by the deceased to whom he had been affiliated, but not to that which he inherited. Bouvier.

In ecclesiastical law. A condition which prevented the superior from removing the person affiliated to another convent. Guyot, Repert.

AFFINAGE. A refining of metals. Blount.

AFFINES. In the civil law. Connections by marriage, whether of the persons or their relatives. Calvin.

Neighbors, who own or occupy adjoining lands. Dig. 10, 1, 12.

Affinis mei affinis non est mihi affinis. One who is related by marriage to a person related to me by marriage, has no affinity to me. Shelf. Mar. & Div. 174.

AFFINITAS. In the civil law. Affinity; relationship by marriage. Inst. 1, 10, 6.

AFFINITAS AFFINITATIS. Remote relationship by marriage. That connection between parties arising from marriage which is neither consanguinity nor affinity.

AFFINITY. Relationship by marriage between the husband and the blood relations of the wife, and between the wife and the blood relations of the husband. 1 Bl. Comm. 434. Affinity is distinguished into three kinds: (1) *Direct*, or that subsisting between the husband and his wife's relations by blood, or between the wife and the husband's relations by blood; (2) *secondary*, or that which subsists between the husband and his wife's relations by marriage; (3) *collateral*, or that which subsists between the husband and the relations of his wife's relations. Wharton.

The connection which arises by marriage between each person of the married pair and the kindred of the other. Mackeld. Rom. Law, § 147. A husband is related by affinity to all the *consanguinei* of his wife, and *vice versa*, the wife to the husband's *consanguinei*; for the husband and wife being considered one flesh, those who are related to the one by blood are related to the other by affinity. Gib. Cod. 412; 1 Bl. Comm. 435.

In a larger sense, consanguinity or kindred. Co. Litt. 157a.

Affinity means the tie which arises from the marriage between the husband and the blood relations of the wife, and between wife and the blood relations of the husband. 45 N. Y. Super. Ct. 84.

AFFIRM. To ratify, make firm, confirm, establish, reassert.

To ratify or confirm a former law or judgment. Cowell.

In the practice of appellate courts, to *affirm* a judgment, decree, or order, is to declare that it is valid and right, and must stand as rendered below; to ratify and reassert it; to concur in its correctness and confirm its efficacy.

In pleading. To allege or aver a matter of fact; to state it affirmatively; the opposite of *deny* or *traverse*.

In practice. To make affirmation; to make a solemn and formal declaration or asseveration that an affidavit is true, that the witness will tell the truth, etc., this being substituted for an oath in certain cases. Also, to give testimony on affirmation.

In the law of contracts. A party is said to affirm a contract, the same being voidable at his election, when he ratifies and accepts it, waives his right to annul it, and proceeds under it as if it had been valid originally.

AFFIRMANCE. In practice. The confirming, or ratifying a former law, or judgment. Cowell; Blount.

The confirmation and ratification by an appellate court of a judgment, order, or decree of a lower court brought before it for review. See AFFIRM.

A dismissal of an appeal for want of prosecution is not an "affirmance" of the judgment. 14 N. Y. 60.

The ratification or confirmation of a voidable contract or act by the party who is to be bound thereby.

The term is in accuracy to be distinguished from *ratification*, which is a recognition of the validity or binding force as against the party ratifying, of some act performed by another person; and from *confirmation*, which would seem to apply more properly to cases where a doubtful authority has been exercised by another in behalf of the person ratifying; but these distinctions are not generally observed with much care. Bouvier.

AFFIRMANCE DAY GENERAL. In the English court of exchequer, is a day appointed by the judges of the common pleas, and barons of the exchequer, to be held a few days after the beginning of every term for the general affirmance or reversal of judgments. 2 Tidd, Pr. 1091.

AFFIRMANT. A person who testifies on affirmation, or who affirms instead of taking an oath. See AFFIRMATION. Used in affidavits and depositions which are *affirmed*, instead of sworn to in place of the word "deponent."

Affirmanti, non neganti incumbit probatio. The [burden of] proof lies upon him who affirms, not upon one who denies. Steph. Pl. 84.

Affirmantis est probare. He who affirms must prove. 9 Cush. 535.

AFFIRMATION. In practice. A solemn and formal declaration or asseveration that an affidavit is true, that the witness will tell the truth, etc., this being substituted for an oath in certain cases.

A solemn religious asseveration in the nature of an oath. 1 Greenl. Ev. § 371.

AFFIRMATIVE. That which declares positively; that which avers a fact to be true; that which establishes; the opposite of negative.

The party who, upon the allegations of pleadings joining issue, is under the obligation of making proof, in the first instance, of matters alleged, is said to hold the affirmative, or, in other words, to sustain the burden of proof. Abbott.

AFFIRMATIVE PREGNANT. In pleading. An affirmative allegation implying some negative in favor of the adverse party.

AFFIRMATIVE STATUTE. In legislation. A statute couched in affirmative or mandatory terms; one which directs the doing of an act, or declares what shall be done; as a *negative* statute is one which prohibits a thing from being done, or declares what shall not be done. Blackstone describes affirmative acts of parliament as those "wherein justice is directed to be done according to the law of the land." 1 Bl. Comm. 142.

AFFIRMATIVE WARRANTY. In the law of insurance, warranties may be either affirmative or promissory. Affirmative warranties may be either express or implied, but they usually consist of positive representations in the policy of the existence of some fact or state of things at the time, or previous to the time, of the making of the policy; and they are, in general, conditions precedent, which, if untrue, whether material to the risk or not, the policy does not attach, as it is not the contract of the insurer. 4 Cliff. 281.

AFFIXUS. In the civil law. Affixed, fixed, or fastened to.

AFFORARE. To set a price or value on a thing. Blount.

AFFORATUS. Appraised or valued, as things vendible in a market. Blount.

AFFORCE. To add to; to increase; to strengthen; to add force to.

AFFORCE THE ASSISE. In old English practice. A method of securing a verdict, where the jury disagreed, by adding other jurors to the panel until twelve could be found who were unanimous in their opinion. Bract. fol. 185*b*, 292*a;* Fleta, lib. 4, c. 9, § 2; 2 Reeve, Hist. Eng. Law, 267.

AFFORCIAMENTUM. In old English law. A fortress or stronghold, or other fortification. Cowell.

The calling of a court upon a solemn or extraordinary occasion. Id.

AFFOREST. To convert land into a forest in the legal sense of the word.

AFFOUAGE. In French law. The right of the inhabitants of a commune or section of a commune to take from the forest the fire-wood which is necessary for their use. Duverger.

AFFRANCHIR. L. Fr. To set free. Kelham.

AFFRANCHISE. To liberate; to make free.

AFFRAY. In criminal law. The fighting of two or more persons in some public place to the terror of the people.

It differs from a riot in not being premeditated; for if any persons meet together upon any lawful or innocent occasion, and happen on a sudden to engage in fighting, they are not guilty of a riot, but an affray only; and in that case none are guilty except those actually engaged in it. Hawk. P. C. bk. 1, c. 65, § 3; 4 Bl. Comm. 146; 1 Russ. Crimes, 271.

If two or more persons voluntarily or by agreement engage in any fight, or use any blows or violence towards each other in an angry or quarrelsome manner, in any public place to the disturbance of others, they are guilty of an affray, and shall be punished by imprisonment in the county jail not exceeding thirty days, or by fine not exceeding one hundred dollars. Rev. Code Iowa 1880, § 4065.

AFFRECTAMENTUM. Affreightment; a contract for the hire of a vessel. From the Fr. *fret*, which, according to Cowell, meant tons or tonnage.

AFFREIGHTMENT. A contract of affreightment is a contract with a ship-owner to hire his ship, or part of it, for the carriage of goods. Such a contract generally takes the form either of a charter-party or of a bill of lading. Maude & P. Mer. Shipp. 227; Smith, Merc. Law. 295.

In French law, freighting and affreighting are distinguished. The owner of a ship freights it, (*le frete;*) he is called the freighter, (*freteur;*) he is the letter or lessor, (*locateur, locator.*) The merchant affreights (*af frete*) the ship, and is called the affreighter, (*affreteur;*) he is the hirer, (*locataire, conductor.*) Emerig. Tr. des Ass. c. 11, § 3.

AFFRETEMENT. Fr. In French law. The hiring of a vessel; affreightment. Called also *nolissement.* Ord. Mar. liv. 1, tit. 2, art. 2; Id. liv. 3, tit. 1, art. 1.

AFFRI. In old English law. Plow cattle, bullocks or plow horses. *Affri*, ot *afri carucæ;* beasts of the plow. Spelman.

AFORESAID. Before, or already said, mentioned, or recited; premised. Plowd. 67. *Foresaid* is used in Scotch law.

Although the words "preceding" and "aforesaid" generally mean next before, and "following" means next after, yet a different signification will be given to them if required by the context and the facts of the case. 35 Ga. 180.

AFORETHOUGHT. In criminal law. Deliberate; planned; premeditated; prepense.

AFTER-ACQUIRED. Acquired after a particular date or event. Thus, a judgment is a lien on after-acquired realty, *i. e.,* land acquired by the debtor after entry of the judgment.

AFTER-DISCOVERED. Discovered or made known after a particular date or event.

AFTERMATH. A second crop of grass mown in the same season; also the right to take such second crop. See 1 Chit. Gen. Pr. 181.

AFTERNOON. This word has two senses. It may mean the whole time from noon to midnight; or it may mean the earlier part of that time, as distinguished from the evening. When used in a statute, its meaning must be determined by the context and the circumstances of the subject-matter. 2 El. & Bl. 451.

AGAINST THE FORM OF THE STATUTE. When the act complained of is prohibited by a statute, these technical words must be used in an indictment under it. The Latin phrase is *contra formam statuti.*

AGAINST THE PEACE. A technical phrase used in alleging a breach of the peace. See CONTRA PACEM.

AGAINST THE WILL. Technical words which must be used in framing an indictment for robbery from the person. 1 Chit. Crim. Law, 244.

AGALMA. An impression or image of anything on a seal. Cowell.

AGARD. L. Fr. An award. *Nul fait agard;* no award made.

AGARDER. L. Fr. To award, adjudge, or determine; to sentence, or condemn.

AGE. Signifies those periods in the lives of persons of both sexes which enable them to do certain acts which, before they had arrived at those periods, they were prohibited from doing.

The length of time during which a person has lived or a thing has existed.

In the old books, "age" is commonly used to signify "full age;" that is, the age of twenty-one years. Litt. § 259.

AGE, Awe, Aive. L. Fr. Water. Kelham.

AGE PRAYER. A suggestion of non-age, made by an infant party to a real action, with a prayer that the proceedings may be deferred until his full age. It is now abolished. St. 11 Geo. IV.; 1 Wm. IV. c. 37, § 10; 1 Lil. Reg. 54; 3 Bl. Comm. 300.

AGENCY. The contract of agency may be defined to be a contract by which one of the contracting parties confides the management of some affair, to be transacted on his account, to the other party, who undertakes to do the business and render an account of it. 1 Liverm. Prin. & Ag. 2.

A contract by which one person, with greater or less discretionary power, undertakes to represent another in certain business relations. Whart. Ag. 1.

A relation between two or more persons, by which one party, usually called the agent or attorney, is authorized to do certain acts for, or in relation to the rights or property of the other, who is denominated the principal, constituent, or employer. Bouvier, quoting Prof. Joel Parker, MS. Lect. 1851.

AGENCY, DEED OF. A revocable and voluntary trust for payment of debts. Wharton.

AGENFRIDA. Sax. The true master or owner of a thing. Spelman.

AGENHINA. In Saxon law. A guest at an inn, who, having stayed there for three nights, was then accounted one of the family. Cowell.

AGENS. Lat. An agent, a conductor, or manager of affairs. Distinguished from *factor,* a workman. A plaintiff. Fleta, lib. 4, c. 15, § 8.

AGENT. One who undertakes to transact some business, or to manage some affair, for another, by the authority and on account of the latter, and to render an account of it. 1 Liverm. Prin. & Ag. 67; 2 Bouv. Inst. 3.

An agent is one who represents another called the "principal," in dealings with third persons. Such representation is called agency. Civil Code Dak. § 1337.

The terms "agent" and "attorney" are often used synonymously. Thus, a letter c power of attorney is constantly spoken of a. the formal instrument by which an agency is created. Paley, Ag. (Dunl. Ed.) 1, n.

Classification. Agents are either general or special. A general agent is one employed in his capacity as a professional man or master of an art or trade, or one to whom the principal confides his whole business or all transactions or functions of a designated class. A special agent is one employed to conduct a particular transaction or authorized to perform a specified act.

Agents employed for the sale of goods or merchandise are called "mercantile agents," and are of two principal classes,—brokers and factors, (*q. v.;*) a factor is sometimes called a "commission agent," or "commission merchant." Russ. Merc. Ag. 1.

Synonyms. The term "agent" is to be distinguished from its synonyms "servant," "representative," and "trustee." A servant acts in behalf of his master and under the latter's direction and authority, but is regarded as a mere instrument, and not as the substitute or proxy of the master. A representative (such as an executor or an assignee in bankruptcy) owes his power and authority to the law, which puts him in the place of the person represented, although the latter may have designated or chosen the representative. A trustee acts in the interest and for the benefit of one person, but by an authority derived from another person.

In international law. A diplomatic *agent* is a person employed by a sovereign to manage his private affairs, or those of his subjects in his name, at the court of a foreign government. Wolff, Inst. Nat. § 1237.

In the practice of the house of lords and privy council. In appeals, solicitors and other persons admitted to practise in those courts in a similar capacity to that of solicitors in ordinary courts, are technically called "agents." Macph. Priv. Coun. 65.

AGENT AND PATIENT. A phrase indicating the state of a person who is required to do a thing, and is at the same time the person to whom it is done.

Agentes et consentientes pari pœna plectentur. Acting and consenting parties are liable to the same punishment. 5 Coke, 80.

AGER. Lat. In the civil law. A field; land generally. A portion of land inclosed by definite boundaries.

In old English law. An acre. Spelman.

AGGER. Lat. In the civil law. A dam, bank or mound. Cod. 9, 38; Townsh. Pl. 48.

AGGRAVATED ASSAULT. An assault with circumstances of aggravation, or of a heinous character, or with intent to commit another crime. See ASSAULT.

Defined in Pennsylvania as follows: "If any person shall unlawfully and maliciously inflict upon another person, either with or without any weapon or instrument, any grievous bodily harm, or unlawfully cut, stab, or wound any other person, he shall be guilty of a misdemeanor," etc. Brightly, Purd. Dig. p. 434, § 167.

AGGRAVATION. Any circumstance attending the commission of a crime or tort which increases its guilt or enormity or adds to its injurious consequences, but which is above and beyond the essential constituents of the crime or tort itself.

Matter of aggravation, correctly understood, does not consist in acts of the same kind and description as those constituting the gist of the action, but in something done by the defendant, on the occasion of committing the trespass, which is, to some extent, of a different legal character from the principal act complained of. 19 Vt. 107.

In pleading. The introduction of matter into the declaration which tends to increase the amount of damages, but does not affect the right of action itself. Steph. Pl. 257; 12 Mod. 597.

AGGREGATE. Composed of several; consisting of many persons united together. 1 Bl. Comm. 469.

AGGREGATIO MENTIUM. The meeting of minds. The moment when a contract is complete. A supposed derivation of the word "agreement."

AGGRESSOR. The party who first offers violence or offense. He who begins a quarrel or dispute, either by threatening or striking another.

AGGRIEVED. Having suffered loss or injury; damnified; injured.

AGGRIEVED PARTY. Under statutes granting the right of appeal to the party aggrieved by an order or judgment, the party aggrieved is one whose pecuniary interest is directly affected by the adjudication; one whose right of property may be established or divested thereby. 6 Metc. (Mass.) 197; 16 Pick. 264; 6 N. H. 116; 25 N. J. Eq. 505; 64 N. C. 110. Or one against whom error has been committed. 67 Mo. 99. See, also, 27 Wis. 670; 2 Paine, 315; 17 Cal. 250; 3 Allen, 556.

AGILD. In Saxon law. Free from penalty, not subject to the payment of *gild*, or *weregild;* that is, the customary fine or pecuniary compensation for an offense. Spelman; Cowell.

AGILER. In Saxon law. An observer or informer.

AGILLARIUS. L. Lat. In old English law. A hayward, herdward, or keeper of the herd of cattle in a common field. Cowell.

AGIO. In commercial law. A term used to express the difference in point of value between metallic and paper money, or between one sort of metallic money and another. McCul. Dict.

AGIOTAGE. A speculation on the rise and fall of the public debt of states, or the public funds. The speculator is called "*agioteur.*"

AGIST. In ancient law. To take in and feed the cattle of strangers in the king's forest, and to collect the money due for the same to the king's use. Spelman; Cowell.

In modern law. To take in cattle to feed, or pasture, at a certain rate of compensation. Jacob; 13 East, 159.

AGISTATIO ANIMALIUM IN FORESTA. The drift or numbering of cattle in the forest.

AGISTERS or GIST TAKERS. Officers appointed to look after cattle, etc. See Williams, Common, 232.

AGISTMENT. The taking in of another person's cattle to be fed, or to pasture, upon one's own land, in consideration of an agreed price to be paid by the owner. Also the profit or recompense for such pasturing of cattle.

There is also agistment of sea-banks, where lands are charged with a tribute to keep out the sea; and *terræ agistatæ* are lands whose owners must keep up the sea-banks. Holthouse.

AGISTOR. One who takes in horses or other animals to pasture at certain rates. Story, Bailm. § 443.

AGNATES. In the law of descents. Relations by the father. This word is used in the Scotch law, and by some writers as an English word, corresponding with the Latin *agnati*, (*q. v.*) Ersk. Inst. b. 1, tit. 7, § 4.

AGNATI. In Roman law. The term included "all the cognates who trace their connection exclusively through males. A table of *cognates* is formed by taking each lineal ancestor in turn and including all his descendants of both sexes in the tabular view. If, then, in tracing the various branches of such a genealogical table or tree, we stop whenever we come to the name of a female, and pursue that particular branch or ramification no further, all who remain after the descendants of women have been excluded are *agnates*, and their connection together is agnatic relationship." Maine, Anc. Law, 142.

All persons are agnatically connected together who are under the same *patria potestas*, or who have been under it, or who might have been under it if their lineal ancestor had lived long enough to exercise his empire. Maine, Anc. Law, 144.

The agnate family consisted of all persons, living at the same time, who would have been subject to the *patria potestas* of a common ancestor, if his life had been continued to their time. Hadl. Rom. Law, 131.

Between *agnati* and *cognati* there is this difference: that, under the name of agnati, *cognati* are included, but not *è converso;* for instance, a father's brother, that is, a paternal uncle, is both *agnatus* and *cognatus*, but a mother's brother, that is, a maternal uncle, is a *cognatus* but not *agnatus.* (Dig. 38, 7, 5, pr.) Burrill.

AGNATIC. [From *agnati*, *q. v.*] Derived from or through males. 2 Bl. Comm. 236.

AGNATIO. In the civil law. Relationship on the father's side; agnation. *Agnatio a patre est.* Inst. 3, 5, 4; Id. 3, 6, 6.

AGNATION. Kinship by the father's side. See AGNATES; AGNATI.

AGNOMEN. Lat. An additional name or title; a nickname. A name or title which a man gets by some action or peculiarity; the last of the four names sometimes given a Roman. Thus, Scipio *Africanus*, (the African,) from his African victories. Ainsworth; Calvin.

AGNOMINATION. A surname; an additional name or title; agnomen.

AGNUS DEI. Lat. Lamb of God. A piece of white wax, in a flat, oval form, like a small cake, stamped with the figure of a lamb, and consecrated by the pope. Cowell.

AGRARIAN. Relating to land, or to a division or distribution of land; as an agrarian law.

AGRARIAN LAWS. In Roman law. Laws for the distribution among the people, by public authority, of the lands constituting the public domain, usually territory conquered from an enemy.

In common parlance the term is frequently applied to laws which have for their object the more equal division or distribution of landed property; laws for subdividing large properties and increasing the number of landholders.

AGRARIUM. A tax upon or tribute payable out of land.

AGREAMENTUM. In old English law. Agreement; an agreement. Spelman.

AGREE. To concur; to come into harmony; to give mutual assent; to unite in mental action; to exchange promises; to make an agreement.

To assent to a thing, or undertake to do it; to promise. 1 Denio, 226, 228, 229. This is a loose and incorrect sense of the term. 5 East, 11.

To concur or acquiesce in; to approve or adopt. *Agreed, agreed to,* are frequently used in the books, (like *accord,*) to show the concurrence or harmony of cases. *Agreed per curiam* is a common expression.

To harmonize or reconcile. "You will *agree* your books." 8 Coke, 67.

AGRÉÉ. In French law. A solicitor practising solely in the tribunals of commerce.

AGREEANCE. In Scotch law. Agreement; an agreement or contract.

AGREED. Settled or established by agreement. This word in a deed creates a covenant.

This word is a technical term, and it is synonymous with "contracted." Meigs, 433. It means, *ex vi termini*, that it is the agreement of both parties, whether both sign it or not, each and both consenting to it. 26 Barb. 298.

AGREED STATEMENT OF FACTS. A statement of facts, agreed on by the parties as true and correct, to be submitted to a court for a ruling on the law of the case.

AGREEMENT. A concord of understanding and intention, between two or more parties, with respect to the effect upon their relative rights and duties, of certain past or future facts or performances. The act of two or more persons, who unite in expressing a mutual and common purpose, with the view of altering their rights and obligations.

A coming together of parties in opinion or determination; the union of two or more minds in a thing done or to be done; a mutual assent to do a thing. Com. Dig. "Agreement," A 1.

The consent of two or more persons concurring, the one in parting with, the other in receiving, some property, right, or benefit. Bac. Abr.

A promise, or undertaking. This is a loose and incorrect sense of the word. 5 East, 11. See 3 Brod. & B. 14; 3 N. Y. 335.

The writing or instrument which is evidence of an agreement.

Agreements are of the following several descriptions, viz.:

Conditional agreements, the operation and effect of which depend upon the existence of a supposed state of facts, or the performance of a condition, or the happening of a contingency.

Executed agreements, which have reference to past events, or which are at once closed and where nothing further remains to be done by the parties.

Executory agreements are such as are to be performed in the future. They are commonly preliminary to other more formal or important contracts or deeds, and are usually evidenced by memoranda, parol promises, etc.

Express agreements are those in which the terms and stipulations are specifically declared and avowed by the parties at the time of making the agreement.

Implied agreements are those which the law infers the parties to have made, although the terms were not openly expressed.

Synonyms distinguished. The term "agreement" is often used as synonymous with "contract." Properly speaking, however, it is a wider term than "contract" (Anson, Cont. 4.) An agreement might not be a contract, because not fulfilling some requirement of the law of the place in which it is made. So, where a contract embodies a series of mutual stipulations or constituent clauses, each of these clauses might be denominated an "agreement."

"*Agreement*" is seldom applied to specialties; "*contract*" is generally confined to simple contracts; and "*promise*" refers to the engagement of a party without reference to the reasons or considerations for it, or the duties of other parties. Pars. Cont. 6.

"Agreement" is more comprehensive than "promise;" signifies a mutual contract, on consideration, between two or more parties. A statute (of frauds) which requires the agreement to be in writing includes the consideration. 5 East, 10.

"Agreement" is not synonymous with "promise" or "undertaking," but, in its more proper and correct sense, signifies a mutual contract, on consideration, between two or more parties, and implies a consideration. 24 Wend. 285.

AGREEMENT FOR INSURANCE. A brief agreement entered into between the insurer and insured, preliminary to the filling up and delivery of a policy.

AGREER. Fr. In French marine law. To rig or equip a vessel. Ord. Mar. liv. 1, tit. 2, art. 1.

AGREZ. Fr. In French marine law. The rigging or tackle of a vessel. Ord. Mar. liv. 1, tit. 2, art. 1; Id. tit. 11, art. 2; Id. liv. 3, tit. 1, art. 11.

AGRI. Arable lands in common fields.

AGRI LIMITATI. In Roman law. Lands belonging to the state by right of conquest, and granted or sold in plots. Sandars, Just. Inst. (5th Ed.) 98.

AGRICULTURE. A person actually engaged in the "science of agriculture" (within the meaning of a statute giving him special exemptions) is one who derives the support of himself and his family, in whole or in part, from the tillage and cultivation of fields. He must cultivate something more than a garden, although it may be much less than a farm. If the area cultivated can be called a field, it is agriculture, as well in contemplation of law as in the etymology of the word. And if this condition be fulfilled, the uniting of any other business, not inconsistent with the pursuit of agriculture, does not take away the protection of the statute. 22 Pa. St. 193. See, also, 7 Heisk. 515; 62 Me. 526; 64 Ga. 128.

AGUSADURA. In ancient customs, a fee, due from the vassals to their lord for sharpening their plowing tackle.

AHTEID. In old European law. A kind of oath among the Bavarians. Spelman. In Saxon law. One bound by oath, *q. d.* "oath-tied." From *ath*, oath, and *tied*. Id.

AID, *v.* To support, help, or assist. This word must be distinguished from its synonym "encourage," the difference being that the former connotes active support and assistance, while the latter does not; and also from "abet," which last word imports necessary criminality in the act furthered, while "aid," standing alone, does not.

AID AND COMFORT. Help; support; assistance; counsel; encouragement.

As an element in the crime of treason, the giving of "aid and comfort" to the enemy may consist in a mere attempt. It is not essential to constitute the giving of aid and comfort that the enterprise commenced should be successful and actually render assistance. 4 Sawy. 472; 97 U. S. 62.

AID OF THE KING. The king's tenant prays this, when rent is demanded of him by others.

AID PRAYER. In English practice. A proceeding formerly made use of, by way of petition in court, praying in aid of the tenant for life, etc., from the reversioner or remainder-man, when the title to the inheritance was in question. It was a plea in suspension of the action. 3 Bl. Comm. 300.

AIDER BY VERDICT. The healing or remission, by a verdict rendered, of a defect or error in pleading which might have been objected to before verdict.

The presumption of the proof of all facts necessary to the verdict as it stands, coming to the aid of a record in which such facts are not distinctly alleged.

AIDING AND ABETTING. In criminal law. That kind of connection with the commission of a crime which, at common

law, rendered the person guilty as a principal in the second degree. It consisted in being present at the time and place, and doing some act to render aid to the actual perpetrator of the crime, though without taking a direct share in its commission. See 4 Bl. Comm. 34.

AIDS. In feudal law, originally mere benevolences granted by a tenant to his lord, in times of distress; but at length the lords claimed them as of right. They were principally three: (1) To ransom the lord's person, if taken prisoner; (2) to make the lord's eldest son and heir apparent a knight; (3) to give a suitable portion to the lord's eldest daughter on her marriage. Abolished by 12 Car. II. c. 24.

Also, extraordinary grants to the crown by the house of commons, and which were the origin of the modern system of taxation. 2 Bl. Comm. 63, 64.

AIEL, Aieul, Aile, Ayle. L. Fr. A grandfather.

A writ which lieth where the grandfather was seised in his demesne as of fee of any lands or tenements in fee-simple the day that he died, and a stranger abateth or entereth the same day and dispossesseth the heir. Fitzh. Nat. Brev. 222; Spelman; Termes de la Ley; 3 Bl. Comm. 186.

AIELESSE. A Norman French term signifying "grandmother." Kelham.

AINESSE. In French feudal law. The right or privilege of the eldest born; primogeniture; esnecy. Guyot, Inst. Feud. c. 17.

AIR. That fluid transparent substance which surrounds our globe.

AIRE. In old Scotch law. The court of the justices itinerant, corresponding with the English *eyre*, (*q. v.*) Skene de Verb. Sign. voc. *Iter.*

AIRT AND PAIRT. In old Scotch criminal law. Accessary; contriver and partner. 1 Pitc. Crim. Tr. pt. 1, p. 133; 3 How. State Tr. 601. Now written *art and part*, (*q. v.*)

AIR-WAY. In English law. A passage for the admission of air into a mine. To maliciously fill up, obstruct, or damage, with intent to destroy, obstruct, or render useless the air-way to any mine, is a felony punishable by penal servitude or imprisonment at the discretion of the court. 24 & 25 Vict. c. 97, § 28.

AISIAMENTUM. In old English law. An easement. Spelman.

AISNE or EIGNE. In old English law, the eldest or first born.

AJOURNEMENT. In French law. The document pursuant to which an action or suit is commenced, equivalent to the writ of summons in England. Actions, however, are in some cases commenced by *requête* or petition. Arg. Fr. Merc. Law, 545.

AJUAR. In Spanish law. Paraphernalia. The jewels and furniture which a wife brings in marriage.

AJUTAGE. A tube, conical in form, intended to be applied to an aperture through which water passes, whereby the flow of the water is greatly increased. See 2 Whart. 477.

AKIN. In old English law. Of kin. "Next-a-kin." 7 Mod. 140.

AL. L. Fr. At the; to the. *Al barre;* at the bar. *Al huis d'esglise;* at the church-door.

ALÆ ECCLESIÆ. The wings or side aisles of a church. Blount.

ALANERARIUS. A manager and keeper of dogs for the sport of hawking; from *alanus,* a dog known to the ancients. A falconer. Blount.

ALARM LIST. The list of persons liable to military watches, who were at the same time exempt from trainings and musters. See Prov. Laws 1775-76, c. 10, § 18; Const. Mass. c. 11, § 1, art. 10; Pub. St. Mass. 1882, p. 1287.

ALBA FIRMA. In old English law. White rent; rent payable in silver or white money, as distinguished from that which was anciently paid in corn or provisions, called black mail, or black rent. Spelman; Reg. Orig. 319*b*.

ALBANAGIUM. In old French law. The state of alienage; of being a foreigner or alien.

ALBANUS. In old French law. A stranger, alien, or foreigner.

ALBINATUS. In old French law. The state or condition of an alien or foreigner.

ALBINATUS JUS. In old French law. The *droit d'aubaine* in France, whereby the king, at an alien's death, was entitled to all his property, unless he had peculiar exemption. Repealed by the French laws in June, 1791.

ALBUM BREVE. A blank writ; a writ with a blank or omission in it.

ALBUS LIBER. The white book; an ancient book containing a compilation of the law and customs of the city of London. It has lately been reprinted by order of the master of the rolls.

ALCABALA. In Spanish law. A duty of a certain per cent. paid to the treasury on the sale or exchange of property.

ALCALDE. The name of a judicial officer in Spain, and in those countries which have received their laws and institutions from Spain. His functions somewhat resembled those of mayor in small municipalities on the continent, or justice of the peace in England and most of the United States.

ALDERMAN. A judicial or administrative magistrate. Originally the word was synonymous with "elder," but was also used to designate an earl, and even a king.

In English law. An associate to the chief civil magistrate of a corporate town or city.

In American cities. The aldermen are generally a legislative body, having limited judicial powers as a body, as in matters of internal police regulation, laying out and repairing streets, constructing sewers, and the like; though in many cities they hold separate courts, and have magisterial powers to a considerable extent. Bouvier.

ALDERMANNUS CIVITATIS VEL BURGI. L. Lat. Alderman of a city or borough, from which the modern office of alderman has been derived. T. Raym. 435, 437.

ALDERMANNUS COMITATUS. The alderman of the county. According to Spelman, he held an office intermediate between that of an earl and a sheriff. According to other authorities, he was the same as the earl. 1 Bl. Comm. 116.

ALDERMANNUS HUNDREDI SEU WAPENTACHII. Alderman of a hundred or wapentake. Spelman.

ALDERMANNUS REGIS. Alderman of the king. So called, either because he received his appointment from the king or because he gave the judgment of the king in the premises allotted to him.

ALDERMANNUS TOTIUS ANGLIÆ. Alderman of all England. An officer among the Anglo-Saxons, supposed by Spelman to be the same with the chief justiciary of England in later times. Spelman.

ALE-CONNER. An officer appointed by the court-leet, sworn to look to the assise and goodness of ale and beer within the precincts of the leet. Kitch. Courts, 46; Whishaw.

An officer appointed in every court-leet, and sworn to look to the assise of bread, ale, or beer within the precincts of that lordship. Cowell.

ALE-HOUSE. A place where ale is sold to be drunk on the premises where sold.

ALE SILVER. A rent or tribute paid annually to the lord mayor of London, by those who sell ale within the liberty of the city.

ALE-STAKE. A maypole or long stake driven into the ground, with a sign on it for the sale of ale. Cowell.

ALEA. Lat. In the civil law. A game of chance or hazard. Dig. 11, 5, 1. See Cod. 3, 43. The chance of gain or loss in a contract.

ALEATOR. Lat. (From *alea, q. v.*) In the civil law. A gamester; one who plays at games of hazard. Dig. 11, 5; Cod. 3, 43.

ALEATORY CONTRACT. A mutual agreement, of which the effects, with respect both to the advantages and losses, whether to all the parties or to some of them, depend on an uncertain event. Civil Code La. art. 2982.

A contract, the obligation and performance of which depend upon an uncertain event, such as insurance, engagements to pay annuities, and the like.

A contract is aleatory or hazardous when the performance of that which is one of its objects depends on an uncertain event. It is certain when the thing to be done is supposed to depend on the will of the party, or when in the usual course of events it must happen in the manner stipulated. Civil Code La. art. 1776.

ALER A DIEU. L. Fr. In old practice. To be dismissed from court; to go quit. Literally, "to go to God."

ALER SANS JOUR. In old practice, a phrase used to indicate the final dismissal of a case from court without continuance. "To go without day."

ALEU. Fr. In French feudal law. An allodial estate, as distinguished from a feudal estate or benefice.

ALFET. A cauldron into which boiling water was poured, in which a criminal plunged his arm up to the elbow, and there held it for some time, as an ordeal. Du Cange.

ALGARUM MARIS. Probably a corruption of *Laganum maris, lagan* being a right, in the middle ages, like *jetsam* and *flotsam,* by which goods thrown from a vessel in distress became the property of the king, or the lord on whose shores they were stranded. Spelman; Jacob; Du Cange.

ALGO. Span. In Spanish law. Property. White, Nov. Recop. b. 1, tit. 5, c. 3, § 4.

ALIA ENORMIA. Other wrongs. The name given to a general allegation of injuries caused by the defendant with which the plaintiff in an action of trespass under the common law practice concluded his declaration. Archb. Crim. Pl. 694.

ALIAMENTA. A liberty of passage, open way, water-course, etc., for the tenant's accommodation. Kitchen.

ALIAS. In practice. Formerly; hitherto; at another time. An *alias* writ is a second writ issued in the same cause, where a former writ of the same kind had been issued without effect. In such case, the language of the second writ is, "We command you, as we have *before* [*sicut alias*] commanded you," etc.

ALIAS DICTUS. "Otherwise called." This phrase (or its shorter and more usual form, *alias,*) when placed between two names in a pleading or other paper, indicates that the same person is known by both those names. A fictitious name assumed by a person is colloquially termed an "*alias.*"

ALIBI. Lat. In criminal law. Elsewhere; in another place. A term used to express that mode of defense to a criminal prosecution, where the party accused, in order to prove that he could not have committed the crime with which he is charged, offers evidence to show that he was *in another place* at the time; which is termed setting up an *alibi.* Tomlins.

ALIEN, *n.* A foreigner; one born abroad; a person resident in one country, but owing allegiance to another. In England, one born out of the allegiance of the king. In the United States, one born out of the jurisdiction of the United States, and who has not been naturalized under their constitution and laws. 2 Kent, Comm. 50.

ALIEN AMY. In international law. Alien friend. An alien who is the subject or citizen of a foreign government at peace with our own.

ALIEN AND SEDITION LAWS. Acts of congress of July 6 and July 14, 1798. See Whart. State Tr. 22.

ALIEN ENEMY. In international law. An alien who is the subject or citizen of some hostile state or power. See Dyer, 2b; Co. Litt. 129b. A person who, by reason of owing a permanent or temporary allegiance to a hostile power, becomes, in time of war, impressed with the character of an enemy, and, as such, is disabled from suing in the courts of the adverse belligerent. See 1 Kent, Comm. 74; 2 Id. 63; 10 Johns. 183.

ALIEN FRIEND. The subject of a nation with which we are at peace; an *alien amy.*

ALIEN NEE. A man born an alien.

ALIEN or ALIENE. *v.* To transfer or make over to another; to convey or transfer the property of a thing from one person to another; to alienate. Usually applied to the transfer of lands and tenements. Co. Litt. 118; Cowell.

Aliena negotia exacto officio geruntur. The business of another is to be conducted with particular attention. Jones, Bailm. 83; 79 Pa. St. 118.

ALIENABLE. Proper to be the subject of alienation or transfer.

ALIENAGE. The condition or state of an alien.

ALIENATE. To convey; to transfer the title to property. Co. Litt. 118b. *Alien* is very commonly used in the same sense. 1 Washb. Real Prop. 53.

"Sell, *alienate*, and dispone" are the formal words of transfer in Scotch conveyances of heritable property. Bell.

"The term *alienate* has a technical legal meaning, and any transfer of real estate, short of a conveyance of the title, is not an alienation of the estate. No matter in what form the sale may be made, unless the title is conveyed to the purchaser, the estate is not alienated." 11 Barb. 630.

Alienatio licet prohibeatur, consensu tamen omnium, in quorum favorem prohibita est, potest fieri, et quilibet potest renunciare juri pro se introducto. Although alienation be prohibited, yet, by the consent of all in whose favor it is prohibited, it may take place; for it is in the power of any man to renounce a law made in his own favor. Co. Litt. 98.

Alienatio rei præfertur juri accrescendi. Alienation is favored by the law rather than accumulation. Co. Litt. 185.

ALIENATION. In real property law. The transfer of the property and possession of lands, tenements, or other things, from one person to another. Termes de la Ley. It is particularly applied to absolute conveyances of real property. 1 N. Y. 290, 294.

The act by which the title to real estate is voluntarily resigned by one person to another and accepted by the latter, in the forms prescribed by law. See 24 N. H. 558; 11 Barb. 629; 31 Ill. 119.

In medical jurisprudence. A generic term denoting the different kinds of aberration of the human understanding. 1 Beck, Med. Jur. 535.

ALIENATION OFFICE. In English practice. An office for the recovery of fines levied upon writs of covenant and entries.

Alienation pending a suit is void. 2 P. Wms. 482; 2 Atk. 174; 3 Atk. 392; 11 Ves. 194; 1 Johns. Ch. 566, 580.

ALIENEE. One to whom an alienation, conveyance, or transfer of property is made.

ALIENI GENERIS. Lat. Of another kind. 3 P. Wms. 247.

ALIENI JURIS. Under the control, or subject to the authority, of another person; *e. g.*, an infant who is under the authority of his father or guardian; a wife under the power of her husband. The term is contrasted with SUI JURIS, (*q. v.*)

ALIENIGENA. One of foreign birth; an alien. 7 Coke, 31.

ALIENISM. The state, condition, or character of an alien. 2 Kent, Comm. 56, 64, 69.

ALIENOR. He who makes a grant, transfer of title, conveyance, or alienation.

ALIENUS. Lat. Another's; belonging to another; the property of another. *Alienus homo*, another's man, or slave. Inst. 4, 3, pr. *Aliena res*, another's property. Bract. fol. 13b.

ALIMENT. In Scotch law. To maintain, support, provide for; to provide with necessaries. As a noun, maintenance, support; an allowance from the husband's estate for the support of the wife. Paters. Comp. §§ 845, 850, 893.

ALIMENTA. Lat. In the civil law. Aliments; means of support, including food, (*cibaria*,) clothing, (*vestitus*,) and habitation, (*habitatio*.) Dig. 34, 1, 6.

ALIMONY. The allowance made to a wife out of her husband's estate for her support, either during a matrimonial suit, or at its termination, when she proves herself entitled to a separate maintenance, and the fact of a marriage is established.

Alimony is an allowance out of the husband's estate, made for the support of the wife when living separate from him. It is either temporary or permanent. Code Ga. 1882, § 1736.

The allowance which is made by order of court to a woman for her support out of her husband's estate, upon being separated from him by divorce, or pending a suit for divorce. Pub. St. Mass. 1882, p. 1287.

By *alimony* we understand what is necessary for the nourishment, lodging, and support of the person who claims it. It includes education, when the person to whom the alimony is due is a minor. Civil Code La. art. 230.

The term is commonly used as equally applicable to all allowances, whether annual or in gross, made to a wife upon a decree in divorce. 107 Mass. 432.

Alimony pendente lite is that ordered during the pendency of a suit.

Permanent alimony is that ordered for the use of the wife after the termination of the suit during their joint lives.

ALIO INTUITU. Lat. In a different view; under a different aspect. 4 Rob. Adm. & Pr. 151.

With another view or object. 7 East, 558; 6 Maule & S. 234.

Aliquid conceditur ne injuria remaneat impunita, quod alias non concederetur. Something is (will be) conceded, to prevent a wrong remaining unredressed, which otherwise would not be conceded. Co. Litt. 197*b*.

ALIQUID POSSESSIONIS ET NIHIL JURIS. Somewhat of possession, and nothing of right, (but no right.) A phrase used by Bracton to describe that kind of possession which a person might have of a thing as a guardian, creditor, or the like; and also that kind of possession which was granted for a term of years, where nothing could be demanded but the usufruct. Bract. fols. 39*a*, 160*a*.

Aliquis non debet esse judex in propriâ causâ, quia non potest esse judex et pars. A person ought not to be judge in his own cause, because he cannot act as judge and party. Co. Litt. 141; 3 Bl. Comm. 59.

ALITER. Lat. Otherwise. A term often used in the reports.

Aliud est celare, aliud tacere. To conceal is one thing; to be silent is another thing. Lord Mansfield, 3 Burr. 1910.

Aliud est distinctio, aliud separatio. Distinction is one thing; separation is another. It is one thing to make things distinct, another thing to make them separable.

Aliud est possidere, aliud esse in possessione. It is one thing to possess; it is another to be in possession. Hob. 163.

Aliud est vendere, aliud vendenti consentire. To sell is one thing; to consent to a sale (seller) is another thing. Dig. 50, 17, 160.

ALIUD EXAMEN. A different or foreign mode of trial. 1 Hale, Com. Law, 38.

ALIUNDE. Lat. From another source; from elsewhere; from outside. Evidence *aliunde* (*i. e.,* from without the will) may be received to explain an ambiguity in a will. 1 Greenl. Ev. § 291.

"ALL FAULTS." A sale of goods with "all faults" covers, in the absence of fraud on the part of the vendor, all such faults and defects as are not inconsistent with the identity of the goods as the goods described. 118 Mass. 242.

ALL FOURS. Two cases or decisions which are alike in all material respects, and precisely similar in all the circumstances affecting their determination, are said to be or to run on "all fours."

ALL THE ESTATE. The name given in England to the short clause in a conveyance or other assurance which purports to convey "all the estate, right, title, interest, claim, and demand" of the grantor, lessor, etc., in the property dealt with. Dav. Conv. 93.

Allegans contraria non est audiendus. One alleging contrary or contradictory things (whose statements contradict each other) is not to be heard. 4 Inst. 279. Applied to the statements of a witness.

Allegans suam turpitudinem non est audiendus. One who alleges his own infamy is not to be heard. 4 Inst. 279.

Allegari non debuit quod probatum non relevat. That ought not to be alleged which, if proved, is not relevant. 1 Ch. Cas. 45.

ALLEGATA. In Roman law. A word which the emperors formerly signed at the bottom of their rescripts and constitutions; under other instruments they usually wrote *signata* or *testata*. Enc. Lond.

ALLEGATA ET PROBATA. Lat. Things alleged and proved. The allegations made by a party to a suit, and the proof adduced in their support.

Allegatio contra factum non est admittenda. An allegation contrary to the deed (or fact) is not admissible.

ALLEGATION. The assertion, declaration, or statement of a party to an action, made in a pleading, setting out what he expects to prove.

A material allegation in a pleading is one essential to the claim or defense, and which could not be stricken from the pleading without leaving it insufficient. Code Civil Proc. Cal. § 463.

In ecclesiastical law. The statement of the facts intended to be relied on in support of the contested suit.

In English ecclesiastical practice the word seems to designate the pleading as a whole; the three pleadings are known as the allegations; and the defendant's plea is distinguished as the defensive, or sometimes the responsive, allegation, and the complainant's reply as the rejoining allegation.

ALLEGATION OF FACULTIES. A statement made by the wife of the property of her husband, in order to her obtaining alimony. 11 Ala. 763; 3 Tex. 168.

ALLEGE. To state, recite, assert, or charge; to make an allegation.

ALLEGED. Stated; recited; claimed; asserted; charged.

ALLEGIANCE. By allegiance is meant the obligation of fidelity and obedience which the individual owes to the government under which he lives, or to his sovereign in return for the protection he receives. It may be an absolute and permanent obligation, or it may be a qualified and temporary one. The citizen or subject owes an absolute and permanent allegiance to his government or sovereign, or at least until, by some open and distinct act, he renounces it and becomes a citizen or subject of another government or another sovereign. The alien, while domiciled in the country, owes a local and temporary allegiance, which continues during the period of his residence. 16 Wall. 154.

"The tie or *ligamen* which binds the subject [or citizen] to the king [or government] in return for that protection which the king [or government] affords the subject, [or citizen."] 1 Bl. Comm. 366. It consists in "a true and faithful obedience of the subject due to his sovereign." 7 Coke, 4*b*.

Allegiance is the obligation of fidelity and obedience which every citizen owes to the state. Pol. Code Cal. § 55.

In Norman French. Alleviation; relief; redress. Kelham.

ALLEGIARE. To defend and clear one's self; to wage one's own law.

ALLEGING DIMINUTION. The allegation in an appellate court, of some error in a subordinate part of the *nisi prius* record.

ALLEVIARE. L. Lat. In old records. To levy or pay an accustomed fine or composition; to redeem by such payment. Cowell.

ALLIANCE. The relation or union between persons or families contracted by intermarriage.

In international law. A union or association of two or more states or nations, formed by league or treaty, for the joint prosecution of a war, or for their mutual assistance and protection in repelling hostile attacks. The league or treaty by which the association is formed. The act of confederating, by league or treaty, for the purposes mentioned.

If the alliance is formed for the purpose of mutual aid in the prosecution of a war against a common enemy, it is called an "offensive" alliance. If it contemplates only the rendition of aid and protection in resisting the assault of a hostile power, it is called a "defensive" alliance. If it combines both these features, it is denominated an alliance "offensive and defensive."

ALLISION. The running of one vessel into or against another, as distinguished from a collision, *i. e.*, the running of two vessels against each other.

ALLOCATION. An allowance made upon an account in the English exchequer. Cowell.

ALLOCATIONE FACIENDA. In old English practice. A writ for allowing to an accountant such sums of money as he hath lawfully expended in his office; directed to the lord treasurer and barons of the exchequer upon application made. Jacob.

ALLOCATO COMITATU. In old English practice. In proceedings in outlawry, when there were but two county courts holden between the delivery of the writ of *exigi facias* to the sheriff and its return, a special *exigi facias*, with an *allocato comitatu* issued to the sheriff in order to complete the proceedings. See EXIGENT.

ALLOCATUR. Lat. It is allowed. A word formerly used to denote that a writ or order was allowed.

A word denoting the allowance by a master or prothonotary of a bill referred for his consideration, whether touching costs, damages, or matter of account. Lee.

ALLOCATUR EXIGENT. A species of writ anciently issued in outlawry proceedings, on the return of the original writ of exigent. 1 Tidd, Pr. 128.

ALLOCUTUS. In criminal procedure, when a prisoner is convicted on a trial for treason or felony, the court is bound to demand of him what he has to say as to why the court should not proceed to judgment against him; this demand is called the "*allocutus*," and is entered on the record. Archb. Crim. Pl. 173.

ALLODARII. Owners of allodial lands. Owners of estates as large as a subject may have. Co. Litt. 1; Bac. Abr. "*Tenure,*" A.

ALLODIAL. Free; not holden of any lord or superior; owned without obligation of vassalage or fealty; the opposite of feudal.

ALLODIUM. Land held absolutely in one's own right, and not of any lord or superior; land not subject to feudal duties or burdens.

An estate held by absolute ownership, without recognizing any superior to whom any duty is due on account thereof. 1 Washb. Real Prop. 16.

ALLOGRAPH. A document not written by any of the parties thereto; opposed to autograph.

ALLONGE. When the indorsements on a bill or note have filled all the blank space, it is customary to annex a strip of paper, called an "*allonge,*" to receive the further indorsements.

ALLOT. To apportion, distribute; to divide property previously held in common among those entitled, assigning to each his ratable portion, to be held in severalty; to set apart specific property, a share of a fund, etc., to a distinct party.

In the law of corporations, to allot shares, debentures, etc., is to appropriate them to the applicants or persons who have applied for them; this is generally done by sending to each applicant a letter of allotment, informing him that a certain number of shares have been allotted to him. Sweet.

ALLOTMENT. Partition, apportionment, division; the distribution of land under an inclosure act, or shares in a public undertaking or corporation.

ALLOTMENT NOTE. A writing by a seaman, whereby he makes an assignment of part of his wages in favor of his wife, father or mother, grandfather or grandmother, brother or sister. Every allotment note must be in a form sanctioned by the board of trade. The allottee, that is, the person in whose favor it is made, may recover the amount in the county court. Mozley & Whitley.

ALLOTMENT SYSTEM. Designates the practice of dividing land in small portions for cultivation by agricultural laborers and other cottagers at their leisure, and after they have performed their ordinary day's work. Wharton.

ALLOTMENT WARDEN. By the English general inclosure act, 1845, § 108, when an allotment for the laboring poor of a district has been made on an inclosure under the act, the land so allotted is to be under the management of the incumbent and church warden of the parish, and two other persons elected by the parish, and they are to be styled "the allotment wardens" of the parish. Sweet.

ALLOTTEE. One to whom an allotment is made, who receives a ratable share under an allotment; a person to whom land under an inclosure act or shares in a public undertaking are allotted.

ALLOW. To grant, approve, or permit; as to allow an appeal or a marriage; to allow an account. Also to give a fit portion out of a larger property or fund.

ALLOWANCE. A deduction, an average payment, a portion assigned or allowed; the act of allowing.

ALLOWANCE PENDENTE LITE. In the English chancery division, where property which forms the subject of proceedings is more than sufficient to answer all claims in the proceedings, the court may allow to the parties interested the whole or part of the income, or (in the case of personalty) part of the property itself. St. 15 & 16 Vict. c. 86, § 57; Daniell, Ch. Pr. 1070.

ALLOY. An inferior or cheaper metal mixed with gold or silver in manufacturing or coining. As respects coining, the amount of alloy is fixed by law, and is used to increase the hardness and durability of the coin.

ALLOYNOUR. L. Fr. One who conceals, steals, or carries off a thing privately. Britt. c. 17.

ALLUVIO MARIS. Lat. In the civil and old English law. The washing up of the sea; formation of soil or land from the sea; maritime increase. Hale, Anal. § 8. "*Alluvio maris* is an increase of the land adjoining, by the projection of the sea, casting up and adding sand and slubb to the adjoining land, whereby it is increased, and for the most part by insensible degrees." Hale, de Jure Mar. pt. 1, c. 6.

ALLUVION. That increase of the earth on a shore or bank of a river, or to the shore of the sea, by the force of the water, as by a current or by waves, which is so gradual that no one can judge how much is added at each moment of time. Inst. l. 2, t. 1, § 20. Ang. Watercourses, 53.

The term is chiefly used to signify a gradual increase of the shore of a running stream, produced by deposits from the waters.

By the common law, alluvion is the addition made to land by the washing of the sea, or a navigable river or other stream, whenever the increase is so gradual that it cannot be perceived in any one moment of time. 64 Ill. 58.

Alluvion differs from avulsion in this: that the latter is sudden and perceptible. 23 Wall. 46. See AVULSION.

ALLY. A nation which has entered into an alliance with another nation. 1 Kent, Comm. 69.

A citizen or subject of one of two or more allied nations.

ALMANAC. A publication, in which is recounted the days of the week, month, and year, both common and particular, distinguishing the fasts, feasts, terms, etc., from the common days by proper marks, pointing out also the several changes of the moon, tides, eclipses, etc.

ALMESFEOH. In Saxon law. Almsfee; alms-money. Otherwise called "Peter-pence." Cowell.

ALMOIN. Alms; a tenure of lands by divine service. See FRANKALMOIGNE.

ALMOXARIFAZGO. In Spanish law. A general term, signifying both export and import duties, as well as excise.

ALMS. Charitable donations. Any species of relief bestowed upon the poor. That which is given by public authority for the relief of the poor.

ALNAGER or ULNAGER. A sworn officer of the king whose duty it was to look to the assise of woolen cloth made throughout the land, and to the putting on the seals for that purpose ordained, for which he collected a duty called "alnage." Cowell; Termes de la Ley.

ALNETUM. In old records, a place where alders grow, or a grove of alder trees. Doomsday Book; Co. Litt. 4b.

ALODE, Alodes, Alodis. L. Lat. In feudal law. Old forms of *alodium*, or *allodium*, (*q. v.*)

ALONG. This term means "by," "on," or "over," according to the subject-matter and the context. 34 Conn. 425; 1 Barn. & Adol. 448; 67 Mo. 58.

ALT. In Scotch practice. An abbreviation of *Alter*, the other: the opposite party; the defender. 1 Broun, 336, note.

ALTA PRODITIO. L. Lat. In old English law. High treason. 4 Bl. Comm. 75. See HIGH TREASON.

ALTA VIA. L. Lat. In old English law. A highway; the highway. 1 Salk. 222. *Alta via regia;* the king's highway; "the king's high street." Finch, Law, b. 2. c. 9.

ALTARAGE. In ecclesiastical law. Offerings made on the altar; all profits which accrue to the priest by means of the altar. Ayliffe, Parerg. 61.

ALTER. To make a change in; to modify; to vary in some degree; to change some of the elements or ingredients or details, without substituting an entirely new thing or destroying the identity of the thing affected.

This term is to be distinguished from its synonyms "change" and "amend." To change may import the substitution of an entirely different thing, while to alter is to operate upon a subject-matter which continues objectively the same while modified in some particular. If a check is raised, in respect to its amount, it is altered; if a new check is put in its place, it is changed. To "amend" implies that the modification made in the subject improves it, which is not necessarily the case with an alteration. An amendment always involves an alteration, but an alteration does not always amend.

ALTERATION. Variation; changing; making different.

An act done upon a written instrument, which, without destroying the identity of the document, introduces some change into its terms, meaning, language, or details. This may be done either by the mutual agreement of the parties concerned, or by a person interested under the writing without the consent, or without the knowledge, of the others. In either case it is properly denominated an alteration; but if performed by a mere stranger, it is more technically described as a spoliation or mutilation. The term is not properly applied to any change which involves the substitution of a practically new document. And it should in strictness be reserved for the designation of changes in form or language, and not used with reference to modifications in matters of substance.

An alteration is an act done upon the instrument by which its meaning or language is changed. If what is written upon or erased from the instrument has no tendency to produce this result, or to mislead any person, it is not an alteration. 5 Neb. 444.

An alteration is said to be *material* when it affects, or may possibly affect, the rights of the persons interested in the document.

Alterius circumventio alii non præbet actionem. The deceiving of one person does not afford an action to another. Dig. 50, 17, 49.

ALTERNAT. A usage among diplomatists by which the rank and places of different powers, who have the same right and pretensions to precedence, are changed from time to time, either in a certain regular order or one determined by lot. In drawing up treaties and conventions, for example, it is the usage of certain powers to alternate, both in the preamble and the signatures, so that each power occupies, in the copy intended to be delivered to it, the first place. Wheat. Int. Law, § 157.

ALTERNATIM. L. Lat. Interchangeably. Litt. § 371; Townsh. Pl. 37.

Alternativa petitio non est audienda. An alternative petition or demand is not to be heard. 5 Coke, 40.

ALTERNATIVE. One or the other of two things; giving an option or choice; allowing a choice between two or more things or acts to be done.

ALTERNATIVE OBLIGATION. An obligation allowing the obligor to choose which of two things he will do, the performance of either of which will satisfy the instrument.

Where the things which form the object of the contract are separated by a disjunctive, then the obligation is *alternative*. A promise to deliver a certain thing or to pay a specified sum of money, is an example of this kind of obligation. Civil Code La. art. 2066.

ALTERNATIVE REMEDY. Where a new remedy is created in addition to an existing one, they are called "alternative" if only one can be enforced; but if both, "cumulative."

ALTERNATIVE WRIT. A writ commanding the person against whom it is issued to do a specified thing, or show cause to the court why he should not be compelled to do it.

ALTERNIS VICIBUS. L. Lat. By alternate turns; at alternate times; alternately. Co. Litt. 4a; Shep. Touch. 206.

ALTERUM NON LÆDERE. Not to injure another. This maxim, and two others, *honeste vivere*, and *suum cuique tribuere*, (*q. v.*,) are considered by Justinian as fundamental principles upon which all the rules of law are based. Inst. 1, 1, 3.

ALTIUS NON TOLLENDI. In the civil law. A servitude due by the owner of a house, by which he is restrained from building beyond a certain height. Dig. 8, 2, 4; Sandars, Just. Inst. 119.

ALTIUS TOLLENDI. In the civil law. A servitude which consists in the right, to him who is entitled to it, to build his house as high as he may think proper. In general, however, every one enjoys this privilege, unless he is restrained by some contrary title. Sandars, Just. Inst. 119.

ALTO ET BASSO. High and low. This phrase is applied to an agreement made between two contending parties to submit all matters in dispute, *alto et basso*, to arbitration. Cowell.

ALTUM MARE. L. Lat. In old English law. The high sea, or seas. Co. Litt. 260b. The deep sea. *Super altum mare*, on the high seas. Hob. 212b.

ALUMNUS. A child which one has nursed; a foster-child. Dig. 40, 2, 14. One educated at a college or seminary is called an "*alumnus*" thereof.

ALVEUS. The bed or channel through which the stream flows when it runs within its ordinary channel. Calvin.

Alveus derelictus, a deserted channel. Mackeld. Rom. Law, § 274.

AMALGAMATION. A term applied in England to the merger or consolidation of two incorporated companies or societies.

In the case of the Empire Assurance Corporation, (1867,) L. R. 4 Eq. 347, the vice-chancellor said: "It is difficult to say what the word 'amalgamate' means. I confess at this moment I have not the least conception of what the full legal effect of the word is. We do not find it in any law dictionary, or expounded by any competent authority. But I am quite sure of this: that the word 'amalgamate' cannot mean that the execution of a deed shall make a man a partner in a firm in which he was not a partner before, under conditions of which he is in no way cognizant, and which are not the same as those contained in the former deed."

AMALPHITAN CODE. A collection of sea-laws, compiled about the end of the eleventh century, by the people of Amalphi. It consists of the laws on maritime subjects, which were or had been in force in countries bordering on the Mediterranean; and was for a long time received as authority in those countries. Azuni; Wharton.

AMANUENSIS. One who writes on behalf of another that which he dictates.

AM. DICT. LAW—5

AMBACTUS. A messenger; a servant sent about; one whose services his master hired out. Spelman.

AMBASCIATOR. A person sent about in the service of another; a person sent on a service. A word of frequent occurrence in the writers of the middle ages. Spelman.

AMBASSADOR. In international law. A public officer, clothed with high diplomatic powers, commissioned by a sovereign prince or state to transact the international business of his government at the court of the country to which he is sent.

Ambassador is the commissioner who represents one country in the seat of government of another. He is a public minister, which, usually, a consul is not. Brown.

Ambassador is a person sent by one sovereign to another, with authority, by letters of credence, to treat on affairs of state. Jacob.

The United States have always been represented by ministers plenipotentiary, never having sent a person of the rank of an ambassador, in the diplomatic sense. 1 Kent, Comm. 39, note.

AMBER, or AMBRA. In old English law. A measure of four bushels.

AMBIDEXTER. Skillful with both hands; one who plays on both sides. Applied anciently to an attorney who took pay from both sides, and subsequently to a juror guilty of the same offense. Cowell.

Ambigua responsio contra proferentem est accipie da. An ambiguous answer is to be taken against (is not to be construed in favor of) him who offers it. 10 Coke, 59.

Ambiguis casibus semper præsumitur pro rege. In doubtful cases, the presumption always is in behalf of the crown. Lofft, Append. 248.

AMBIGUITAS. Lat. From *ambiguus*, doubtful, uncertain, obscure. Ambiguity; uncertainty of meaning.

Ambiguitas verborum latens verificatione suppletur; nam quod ex facto oritur ambiguum verificatione facti tollitur. A latent ambiguity in the language may be removed by evidence; for whatever ambiguity arises from an extrinsic fact may be explained by extrinsic evidence. Bac. Max. reg. 23.

Ambiguitas verborum patens nullâ verificatione excluditur. A patent ambiguity cannot be cleared up by extrinsic evidence. Lofft, 249.

AMBIGUITY. Doubtfulness; doubleness of meaning; indistinctness or uncertainty of meaning of an expression used in a written instrument.

Latent ambiguity is where the language employed is clear and intelligible and suggests but a single meaning, but some extrinsic fact or evidence *aliunde*, creates a necessity for interpretation or a choice among two or more possible meanings.

Patent ambiguity is that which appears on the face of the instrument, and arises from the defective, obscure, or insensible language used.

Ambiguity of language is to be distinguished from unintelligibility and inaccuracy, for words cannot be said to be ambiguous unless their signification seems doubtful and uncertain to persons of competent skill and knowledge to understand them. Story, Contr. 272.

The term "ambiguity" does not include mere *inaccuracy*, or such uncertainty as arises from the use of peculiar words, or of common words in a peculiar sense. Wig. Wills, 174.

Ambiguum pactum contra venditorem interpretandum est. An ambiguous contract is to be interpreted against the seller.

Ambiguum placitum interpretari debet contra proferentem. An ambiguous plea ought to be interpreted against the party pleading it. Co. Litt. 303b.

AMBIT. A boundary line, as going around a place; an exterior or inclosing line or limit.

The limits or circumference of a power or jurisdiction; the line circumscribing any subject-matter.

AMBITUS. In the Roman law. A going around; a path worn by going around. A space of at least two and a half feet in width, between neighboring houses, left for the convenience of going around them. Calvin.

The procuring of a public office by money or gifts; the unlawful buying and selling of a public office. Inst. 4, 18, 11; Dig. 48, 14.

Ambulatoria est voluntas defuncti usque ad vitæ supremum exitum. The will of a deceased person is ambulatory until the latest moment of life. Dig. 34, 4, 4.

AMBULATORY. Movable; revocable; subject to change.

Ambulatoria voluntas (a changeable will) denotes the power which a testator possesses of altering his will during his life-time.

The court of king's bench in England was formerly called an "ambulatory court," because it followed the king's person, and was held sometimes in one place and sometimes in another. So, in France, the supreme court or parliament was originally *ambulatory*. 3 Bl. Comm. 38, 39, 41.

The return of a sheriff has been said to be *ambulatory* until it is filed. Wilmot, J., 3 Burr. 1644.

AMBUSH. The noun "ambush" means (1) the act of attacking an enemy unexpectedly from a concealed station; (2) a concealed station, where troops or enemies lie in wait to attack by surprise, an ambuscade; (3) troops posted in a concealed place for attacking by surprise. The verb "ambush" means to lie in wait, to surprise, to place in ambush. 46 Ala. 142.

AMELIORATIONS. Betterments; improvements. 6 Low. Can. 294; 9 Id. 503.

AMENABLE. Subject to answer to the law; accountable; responsible; liable to punishment.

Also means tractable, that may be easily led or governed; formerly applied to a wife who is governable by her husband. Cowell.

AMEND. To improve; to make better by change or modification. See ALTER.

AMENDE HONORABLE. In old English law. A penalty imposed upon a person by way of disgrace or infamy, as a punishment for any offense, or for the purpose of making reparation for any injury done to another, as the walking into church in a white sheet, with a rope about the neck and a torch in the hand, and begging the pardon of God, or the king, or any private individual, for some delinquency. Bouvier.

In French law. A species of punishment to which offenders against public decency or morality were anciently condemned.

AMENDMENT. In practice. The correction of an error committed in any process, pleading, or proceeding at law, or in equity, and which is done either of course, or by the consent of parties, or upon motion to the court in which the proceeding is pending. 3 Bl. Comm. 407, 448; 1 Tidd, Pr. 696.

Any writing made or proposed as an improvement of some principal writing.

In legislation. A modification or alteration proposed to be made in a bill on its passage, or an enacted law; also such modification or change when made.

AMENDS. A satisfaction given by a wrong-doer to the party injured, for a wrong committed. 1 Lil. Reg. 81.

AMENTIA. In medical jurisprudence. Insanity; idiocy.

AMERALIUS. L. Lat. A naval commander, under the eastern Roman empire, but not of the highest rank; the origin, according to Spelman, of the modern title and office of admiral. Spelman.

AMERCE. To impose an amercement or fine; to punish by a fine or penalty.

AMERCEMENT. A pecuniary penalty, in the nature of a fine, imposed upon a person for some fault or misconduct, he being "in mercy" for his offense. It was assessed by the peers of the delinquent, or the affeerors, or imposed arbitrarily at the discretion of the court or the lord.

The difference between *amercements* and *fines* is as follows: The latter are certain, and are created by some statute; they can only be imposed and assessed by courts of record; the former are arbitrarily imposed by courts not of record, as courts-leet. Termes de la Ley, 40.

The word "amercement" has long been especially used of a mulct or penalty, imposed by a court upon its own officers for neglect of duty, or failure to pay over moneys collected. In particular, the remedy against a sheriff for failing to levy an execution or make return of proceeds of sale is, in several of the states, known as "amercement." In others, the same result is reached by process of attachment. Abbott.

AMERICAN CLAUSE. In marine insurance. A proviso in a policy to the effect that, in case of any subsequent insurance, the insurer shall nevertheless be answerable for the full extent of the sum subscribed by him, without right to claim contribution from subsequent underwriters. 14 Wend. 399.

AMEUBLISSEMENT. In French law. A species of agreement which by a fiction gives to immovable goods the quality of movable. Merl. Repert.; 1 Low. Can. 25, 58.

AMI; AMY. A friend; as *alien ami*, an alien belonging to a nation at peace with us;

prochein ami, a next friend suing or defending for an infant, married woman, etc.

AMICABLE ACTION. In practice. An action between friendly parties. An action brought and carried on by the mutual consent and arrangement of the parties, in order to obtain the judgment of the court on a doubtful question of law, the facts being usually settled by agreement.

AMICABLE COMPOUNDERS. In Louisiana law and practice. "There are two sorts of arbitrators,—the arbitrators properly so called, and the amicable compounders. The arbitrators ought to determine as judges, agreeably to the strictness of law. Amicable compounders are authorized to abate something of the strictness of the law in favor of natural equity. Amicable compounders are in other respects subject to the same rules which are provided for the arbitrators by the present title." Civil Code La. arts. 3109, 3110.

AMICABLE SUIT. The words "arbitration" and "amicable lawsuit," used in an obligation or agreement between parties, are not convertible terms. The former carries with it the idea of settlement by disinterested third parties, and the latter by a friendly submission of the points in dispute to a judicial tribunal to be determined in accordance with the forms of law. 20 La. Ann. 535.

AMICUS CURIÆ. Lat. A friend of the court. A by-stander (usually a counsellor) who interposes and volunteers information upon some matter of law in regard to which the judge is doubtful or mistaken, or upon a matter of which the court may take judicial cognizance.

When a judge is doubtful or mistaken in matter of law, a by-stander may inform the court thereof as *amicus curiæ*. Counsel in court frequently act in this capacity when they happen to be in possession of a case which the judge has not seen, or does not at the moment remember. Holthouse.

It is also applied to persons who have no right to appear in a suit, but are allowed to introduce evidence to protect their own interests. 11 Tex. 699, 701, 702.

AMIRAL. Fr. In French maritime law. Admiral. Ord. de la Mar. liv. 1, tit. 1, § 1.

AMITA. Lat. A paternal aunt. An aunt on the father's side. *Amita magna.* A great-aunt on the father's side. *Amita* *major.* A great-great aunt on the father's side. *Amita maxima.* A great-great-great aunt, or a great-great-grandfather's sister. Calvin.

AMITINUS. The child of a brother or sister; a cousin; one who has the same grandfather, but different father and mother. Calvin.

AMITTERE. Lat. In the civil law. To lose. Hence the old Scotch "amitt."

AMITTERE CURIAM. To lose the court; to be deprived of the privilege of attending the court.

AMITTERE LEGEM TERRÆ. To lose the protection afforded by the law of the land.

AMITTERE LIBERAM LEGEM. To lose one's frank-law. A term having the same meaning as *amittere legem terræ,* (*q. v.*) He who lost his law lost the protection extended by the law to a freeman, and became subject to the same law as thralls or serfs attached to the land.

AMNESTY. A sovereign act of pardon and oblivion for past acts, granted by a government to all persons (or to certain persons) who have been guilty of crime or delict, generally political offenses,—treason, sedition, rebellion,—and often conditioned upon their return to obedience and duty within a prescribed time.

A declaration of the person or persons who have newly acquired or recovered the sovereign power in a state, by which they pardon all persons who composed, supported, or obeyed the government which has been overthrown.

The word "amnesty" properly belongs to international law, and is applied to treaties of peace following a state of war, and signifies there the burial in oblivion of the particular cause of strife, so that that shall not be again a cause for war between the parties; and this signification of "amnesty" is fully and poetically expressed in the Indian custom of burying the hatchet. And so amnesty is applied to rebellions which by their magnitude are brought within the rules of international law, and in which multitudes of men are the subjects of the clemency of the government. But in these cases, and in all cases, it means only "oblivion," and never expresses or implies a grant. 10 Ct. of Cl. 407.

"Amnesty" and "pardon" are very different. The former is an act of the sovereign power, the object of which is to efface and to cause to be for-

gotten a crime or misdemeanor; the latter is an act of the same authority, which exempts the individual on whom it is bestowed from the punishment the law inflicts for the crime he has committed. Bouvier.

AMONG. Intermingled with. "A thing which is *among* others is intermingled with them. Commerce *among* the states cannot stop at the external boundary line of each state, but may be introduced into the interior." 9 Wheat. 194.

Where property is directed by will to be distributed *among* several persons, it cannot be all given to one, nor can any of the persons be wholly excluded from the distribution. 6 Munf. 352.

AMORTIZATION. An alienation of lands or tenements in mortmain. The reduction of the property of lands or tenements to mortmain.

In its modern sense, amortization is the operation of paying off bonds, stock, or other indebtedness of a state or corporation. Sweet.

AMORTIZE. To alien lands in mortmain.

AMOTIO. In the civil law. A moving or taking away. "The slightest *amotio* is sufficient to constitute theft, if the *animus furandi* be clearly established." 1 Swint. 205.

AMOTION. A putting or turning out; dispossession of lands. Ouster is an *amotion* of possession. 3 Bl. Comm. 199, 208.

A moving or carrying away; the wrongful taking of personal chattels. Archb. Civil Pl. Introd. c. 2, § 3.

In corporation law. The act of removing an officer, or official representative, of a corporation from his office or official station, before the end of the term for which he was elected or appointed, but without depriving him of membership in the body corporate. In this last respect the term differs from "disfranchisement," (or expulsion,) which imports the removal of the party from the corporation itself, and his deprivation of all rights of membership.

AMOUNT COVERED. In insurance. The amount that is insured, and for which underwriters are liable for loss under a policy of insurance.

AMOUNT OF LOSS. In insurance. The diminution, destruction, or defeat of the value of, or of the charge upon, the insured subject to the assured, by the direct consequence of the operation of the risk insured against, according to its value in the policy, or in contribution for loss, so far as its value is covered by the insurance.

AMOVEAS MANUS. Lat. That you remove your hands. After office found, the king was entitled to the things forfeited, either lands or personal property; the remedy for a person aggrieved was by "petition," or "*monstrans de droit*," or "*traverses*," to establish his superior right. Thereupon a writ issued, *quod manus domini regis amoveantur*. 3 Bl. Comm. 260.

AMPARO. In Spanish-American law. A document issued to a claimant of land as a protection to him, until a survey can be ordered, and the title of possession issued by an authorized commissioner. 1 Tex. 790.

AMPLIATION. In the civil law. A deferring of judgment until a cause be further examined. Calvin.; Cowell. An order for the rehearing of a cause on a day appointed, for the sake of more ample information. Halifax, Anal. b. 3, c. 13, n. 32.

In French law. A duplicate of an acquittance or other instrument. A notary's copy of acts passed before him, delivered to the parties.

AMPLIUS. In the Roman law. More; further; more time. A word which the prætor pronounced in cases where there was any obscurity in a cause, and the *judices* were uncertain whether to condemn or acquit: by which the case was deferred to a day named. Adam, Rom. Ant. 287.

AMPUTATION OF RIGHT HAND. An ancient punishment for a blow given in a superior court; or for assaulting a judge sitting in the court.

AMY. See AMI; PROCHEIN AMY.

AN ET JOUR. Fr. Year and day; a year and a day.

AN, JOUR, ET WASTE. In feudal law. Year, day, and waste. A forfeiture of the lands to the crown incurred by the felony of the tenant, after which time the land escheats to the lord. Termes de la Ley, 40.

ANACRISIS. In the civil law. An investigation of truth, interrogation of witnesses, and inquiry made into any fact, especially by torture.

ANAGRAPH. A register, inventory, or commentary.

ANALOGY. In logic. Identity or similarity of proportion. Where there is no precedent in point, in cases on the same subject, lawyers have recourse to cases on a different subject-matter, but governed by the same general principle. This is reasoning by analogy. Wharton.

ANARCHY. The destruction of government; lawlessness; the absence of all political government; by extension, confusion in government. See 122 Ill. 253.

ANATHEMA. An ecclesiastical punishment by which a person is separated from the body of the church, and forbidden all intercourse with the members of the same.

ANATHEMATIZE. To pronounce anathema upon; to pronounce accursed by ecclesiastical authority; to excommunicate.

ANATOCISM. In the civil law. Repeated or doubled interest; compound interest; usury. Cod. 4, 32, 1, 30.

ANCESTOR. One who has preceded another in a direct line of descent; a lineal ascendant.

A former possessor; the person last seised. Termes de la Ley; 2 Bl. Comm. 201.

A deceased person from whom another has inherited land. A former possessor.

The term differs from "predecessor," in that it is applied to a natural person and his progenitors, while the latter is applied also to a corporation and those who have held *offices* before those who now fill them. Co. Litt. 78*b*.

ANCESTRAL. Relating to ancestors, or to what has been done by them; as *homage ancestrel*.

Derived from ancestors. Ancestral estates are such as are transmitted by descent, and not by purchase. 4 Kent, Comm. 404.

ANCHOR. A measure containing ten gallons.

ANCHOR WATCH. A watch, consisting of a small number of men, (from one to four,) kept constantly on deck while the vessel is riding at single anchor, to see that the stoppers, painters, cables, and buoy-ropes are ready for immediate use. 2 Low. 220.

ANCHORAGE. In English law. A prestation or toll for every anchor cast from a ship in a port; and sometimes, though there be no anchor. Hale, de Jure Mar. pt. 2, c. 6. See 1 W. Bl. 413 et seq.; 4 Term, 262.

ANCIENT. Old; that which has existed from an indefinitely early period, or which by age alone has acquired certain rights or privileges accorded in view of long continuance.

ANCIENT DEMESNE. Manors which in the time of William the Conqueror were in the hands of the crown, and are so recorded in the Domesday Book. Fitzh. Nat. Brev. 14, 56.

Tenure in *ancient demesne* may be pleaded in abatement to an action of ejectment. 2 Burr. 1046.

Also a species of copyhold, which differs, however, from common copyholds in certain privileges, but yet must be conveyed by surrender, according to the custom of the manor. There are three sorts: (1) Where the lands are held freely by the king's grant; (2) customary freeholds, which are held of a manor in ancient demesne, but not at the lord's will, although they are conveyed by surrender, or deed and admittance; (3) lands held by copy of court-roll at the lord's will, denominated copyholds of base tenure.

ANCIENT HOUSE. One which has stood long enough to acquire an easement of support against the adjoining land or building. 3 Kent, Comm. 437; 2 Washb. Real Prop. 74, 76.

In England this term is applied to houses or buildings erected before the time of legal memory, (Cooke, Incl. Acts, 35, 109,) that is, before the reign of Richard I., although practically any house is an ancient messuage if it was erected before the time of living memory, and its origin cannot be proved to be modern.

ANCIENT LIGHTS. Lights or windows in a house, which have been used in their present state, without molestation or interruption, for twenty years, and upwards. To these the owner of the house has a right by prescription or occupancy, so that they cannot be obstructed or closed by the owner of the adjoining land which they may overlook.

ANCIENT READINGS. Readings or lectures upon the ancient English statutes, formerly regarded as of great authority in law. Litt. § 481; Co. Litt. 280.

ANCIENT RENT. The rent reserved at the time the lease was made, if the building was not then under lease. 2 Vern. 542.

ANCIENT SERJEANT. In English law. The eldest of the queen's serjeants.

ANCIENT WALL. A wall built to be used, and in fact used, as a party-wall, for more than twenty years, by the express permission and continuous acquiescence of the owners of the land on which it stands. 4 Duer, 53, 63.

ANCIENT WRITINGS. Wills, deeds, or other documents upwards of thirty years old. These are presumed to be genuine without express proof, when coming from the proper custody.

ANCIENTS. In English law. Gentlemen of the inns of court and chancery. In Gray's Inn the society consists of benchers, ancients, barristers, and students under the bar; and here the ancients are of the oldest barristers. In the Middle Temple, those who had passed their readings used to be termed "ancients." The Inns of Chancery consist of ancients and students or clerks; from the ancients a principal or treasurer is chosen yearly. Wharton.

ANCIENTY. Eldership; seniority. Used in the statute of Ireland, 14 Hen. VIII. Cowell.

ANCILLARY. Aiding; auxiliary; attendant upon; subordinate; a proceeding attendant upon or which aids another proceeding considered as principal.

ANCILLARY ADMINISTRATION. When a decedent leaves property in a foreign state, (a state other than that of his domicile,) administration may be granted in such foreign state for the purpose of collecting the assets and paying the debts there, and bringing the residue into the general administration. This is called "ancillary" (auxiliary, subordinate) administration.

ANCIPITIS USUS. Lat. In international law. Of doubtful use; the use of which is doubtful; that may be used for a civil or peaceful, as well as military or warlike, purpose. Gro. de Jure B. lib. 3, c. 1, § 5, subd. 3; 1 Kent, Comm. 140.

ANDROCHIA. In old English law. A dairy-woman. Fleta, lib. 2, c. 87.

ANDROGYNUS. An hermaphrodite.

ANDROLEPSY. The taking by one nation of the citizens or subjects of another, in order to compel the latter to do justice to the former. Wolffius, § 1164; Moll. de Jure Mar. 26.

ANECIUS. L. Lat. Spelled also *æsnecius, enitius, æneas, eneyus.* The eldest-born; the first-born; senior, as contrasted with the *puis-ne,* (younger.) Spelman.

ANGARIA. A term used in the Roman law to denote a forced or compulsory service exacted by the government for public purposes; as a forced rendition of labor or goods for the public service. See Dig. 50, 4, 18, 4.

In maritime law. A forced service, (*onus,*) imposed on a vessel for public purposes; an impressment of a vessel. Locc. de Jure Mar. lib. 1, c. 5, §§ 1–6.

In feudal law. Any troublesome or vexatious personal service paid by the tenant to his lord. Spelman.

ANGEL. An ancient English coin, of the value of ten shillings sterling. Jacob.

ANGILD. In Saxon law. The single value of a man or other thing; a single were-gild; the compensation of a thing according to its single value or estimation. Spelman. The double gild or compensation was called "*twigild,*" the triple, "*trigild,*" etc. Id.

ANGLESCHERIA. In old English law. Englishery; the fact of being an Englishman.

Angliæ jura in omni casu libertatis dant favorem. The laws of England in every case of liberty are favorable, (favor liberty in all cases.) Fortes. c. 42.

ANGLICE. In English. A term formerly used in pleading when a thing is described both in Latin and English, inserted immediately after the Latin and as an introduction of the English translation.

ANGLO - INDIAN. An Englishman domiciled in the Indian territory of the British crown.

ANGYLDE. In Saxon law. The rate fixed by law at which certain injuries to person or property were to be paid for; in injuries to the person, it seems to be equivalent to the "were," *i. e.,* the price at which every man was valued. It seems also to have been the fixed price at which cattle and other goods were received as currency, and to have been much higher than the market price, or *ceap-gild.* Wharton.

ANHLOTE. In old English law. A single tribute or tax, paid according to the custom of the country as scot and lot.

ANIENS, or ANIENT. Null, void, of no force or effect. Fitzh. Nat. Brev. 214.

ANIMAL. Any animate being which is endowed with the power of voluntary motion. In the language of the law the term includes all living creatures not human.

Domitæ are those which have been tamed by man; domestic.

Feræ naturæ are those which still retain their wild nature.

Mansuetæ naturæ are those gentle or tame by nature, such as sheep and cows.

Animalia fera, si facta sint mansueta et ex consuetudine eunt et redeunt, volant et revolant, ut cervi, cygni, etc., eo usque nostra sunt, et ita intelliguntur quamdiu habuerunt animum revertendi. Wild animals, if they be made tame, and are accustomed to go out and return, fly away and fly back, as stags, swans, etc., are considered to belong to us so long as they have the intention of returning to us. 7 Coke, 16.

ANIMALS OF A BASE NATURE. Animals in which a right of property may be acquired by reclaiming them from wildness, but which, at common law, by reason of their base nature, are not regarded as possible subjects of a larceny. 3 Inst. 109; 1 Hale, P. C. 511, 512.

ANIMO. Lat. With intention, disposition, design, will. *Quo animo,* with what intention. *Animo cancellandi,* with intention to cancel. 1 Pow. Dev. 603. *Furandi,* with intention to steal. 4 Bl. Comm. 230; 1 Kent, Comm. 183. *Lucrandi,* with intention to gain or profit. 3 Kent, Comm. 357. *Manendi,* with intention to remain. 1 Kent, Comm. 76. *Morandi,* with intention to stay, or delay. *Republicandi,* with intention to republish. 1 Pow. Dev. 609. *Revertendi,* with intention to return. 2 Bl. Comm. 392. *Revocandi,* with intention to revoke. 1 Pow Dev. 595. *Testandi,* with intention to make a will. See ANIMUS and the titles which follow it.

ANIMO ET CORPORE. By the mind, and by the body; by the intention and by the physical act. Dig. 50, 17, 153; Id. 41, 2, 3, 1; Fleta, lib. 5, c. 5, §§ 9, 10.

ANIMO FELONICO. With felonious intent. Hob. 134.

ANIMUS. Lat. Mind; intention; disposition; design; will. *Animo,* (q. v.;) with the intention or design. These terms are derived from the civil law.

Animus ad se omne jus ducit. It is to the intention that all law applies. Law always regards the intention.

ANIMUS CANCELLANDI. The intention of destroying or canceling, (applied to wills.)

ANIMUS CAPIENDI. The intention to take or capture. 4 C. Rob. Adm. 126, 155.

ANIMUS DEDICANDI. The intention of donating or dedicating.

ANIMUS DEFAMANDI. The intention of defaming. The phrase expresses the malicious intent which is essential in every case of verbal injury to render it the subject of an action for libel or slander.

ANIMUS DERELINQUENDI. The intention of abandoning. 4 C. Rob. Adm. 216.

ANIMUS DIFFERENDI. The intention of obtaining delay.

ANIMUS DONANDI. The intention of giving. Expressive of the intent to give which is necessary to constitute a gift.

ANIMUS ET FACTUS. Intention and act; will and deed. Used to denote those acts which become effective only when accompanied by a particular intention.

ANIMUS FURANDI. The intention to steal.

Animus hominis est anima scripti. The intention of the party is the soul of the instrument. 3 Bulst. 67; Pitm. Prin. & Sur. 26. In order to give life or effect to an instrument, it is essential to look to the intention of the individual who executed it.

ANIMUS LUCRANDI. The intention to make a gain or profit.

ANIMUS MANENDI. The intention of remaining; intention to establish a permanent residence. 1 Kent, Comm. 76. This is the point to be settled in determining the domicile or residence of a party. Id. 77.

ANIMUS MORANDI. The intention to remain, or to delay.

ANIMUS POSSIDENDI. The intention of possessing.

ANIMUS QUO. The intent with which.

ANIMUS RECIPIENDI. The intention of receiving.

ANIMUS RECUPERANDI. The intention of recovering. Locc. de Jure Mar. lib. 2, c. 4, § 10.

ANIMUS REPUBLICANDI. The intention to republish.

ANIMUS RESTITUENDI. The intention of restoring. Fleta, lib. 3, c. 2, § 3.

ANIMUS REVERTENDI. The intention of returning. A man retains his domicile if he leaves it *animo revertendi*. 3 Rawle, 312; 4 Bl. Comm. 225; 2 Russ. Crimes, 18; Poph. 42, 52; 4 Coke, 40.

Also, a term employed in the civil law, in expressing the rule of ownership in tamed animals.

ANIMUS REVOCANDI. The intention to revoke.

ANIMUS TESTANDI. An intention to make a testament or will.

ANKER. A measure containing ten gallons.

ANN. In Scotch law. Half a year's stipend, over and above what is owing for the incumbency, due to a minister's relict, or child, or next of kin, after his decease. Whishaw.

ANNA. In East Indian coinage, a piece of money, the sixteenth part of a rupee.

ANNALES. Lat. Annuals; a title formerly given to the Year Books.

In old records. Yearlings; cattle of the first year. Cowell.

ANNALY. In Scotch law. To alienate; to convey.

ANNATES. In ecclesiastical law. First-fruits paid out of spiritual benefices to the pope, so called because the value of one year's profit was taken as their rate.

ANNEX. To add to; to unite; to attach one thing permanently to another. The word expresses the idea of joining a smaller or subordinate thing with another, larger, or of higher importance.

In the law relating to fixtures, the expression "annexed to the freehold" means fastened to or connected with it; mere juxtaposition, or the laying of an object, however heavy, on the freehold, does not amount to annexation. 14 Cal. 64.

ANNEXATION. The act of attaching, adding, joining, or uniting one thing to another; generally spoken of the connection of a smaller or subordinate thing with a larger or principal thing. The attaching an illustrative or auxiliary document to a deposition, pleading, deed, etc., is called "annexing" it. So the incorporation of newly-acquired territory into the national domain, as an integral part thereof, is called "annexation," as in the case of the addition of Texas to the United States.

In the law relating to fixtures: *Actual annexation* includes every movement by which a chattel can be joined or united to the freehold. *Constructive annexation* is the union of such things as have been holden parcel of the realty, but which are not actually annexed, fixed, or fastened to the freehold. Shep. Touch. 469; Amos & F. Fixt. 2.

In Scotch law. The union of lands to the crown, and declaring them inalienable. Also the appropriation of the church-lands by the crown, and the union of lands lying at a distance from the parish church to which they belong, to the church of another parish to which they are contiguous.

ANNI ET TEMPORA. Lat. Years and terms. An old title of the Year Books.

ANNI NUBILES. A woman's marriageable years. The age at which a girl becomes by law fit for marriage; the age of twelve.

ANNICULUS. A child a year old. Calvin.

Anniculus trecentesimo sexagesimoquinto die dicitur, incipiente plane non exacto die, quia annum civiliter non ad momenta temporum sed ad dies numeramur. We call a child a year old on the three hundred and sixty-fifth day, when the day is fairly begun but not ended, because we calculate the civil year not by moments, but by days. Dig. 50, 16, 134; Id. 132; Calvin.

ANNIENTED. Made null, abrogated, frustrated, or brought to nothing. Litt. c. 3, § 741.

ANNIVERSARY. An annual day, in old ecclesiastical law, set apart in memory of a deceased person. Also called "year day" or "mind day." Spelman.

ANNO DOMINI. In the year of the Lord. Commonly abbreviated A. D. The computation of time, according to the Christian era, dates from the birth of Christ.

ANNONA. Grain; food. An old English and civil law term to denote a yearly contribution by one person to the support of another.

ANNONÆ CIVILES. A species of yearly rents issuing out of certain lands, and payable to certain monasteries.

ANNOTATIO. In the civil law. The sign-manual of the emperor; a rescript of the emperor, signed with his own hand. It is distinguished both from a rescript and pragmatic sanction, in Cod. 4, 59, 1.

ANNOTATION. A remark, note, or commentary on some passage of a book, intended to illustrate its meaning. Webster.

In the civil law. An imperial rescript signed by the emperor. The answers of the prince to questions put to him by private persons respecting some doubtful point of law.

Summoning an absentee. Dig. 1, 5.

The designation of a place of deportation. Dig. 32, 1, 3.

Annua nec debitum judex non separat ipsum. A judge (or court) does not divide annuities nor debt. 8 Coke, 52; 1 Salk. 36, 65. Debt and annuity cannot be divided or apportioned by a court.

ANNUA PENSIONE. An ancient writ to provide the king's chaplain, if he had no preferment, with a pension. Reg. Orig. 165, 307.

ANNUAL ASSAY. An annual trial of the gold and silver coins of the United States, to ascertain whether the standard fineness and weight of the coinage is maintained. See Rev. St. U. S. § 3547.

ANNUAL INCOME. Annual income is annual receipts from property. Income means that which comes in or is received from any business, or investment of capital, without reference to the outgoing expenditures. 4 Abb. N. C. 400.

ANNUAL PENSION. In Scotch law. A yearly profit or rent.

ANNUALLY. The meaning of this term, as applied to interest, is not an undertaking to pay interest at the end of one year only, but to pay interest at the end of each and every year during a period of time, either fixed or contingent. 6 Gray, 164. See, also, 19 S. C. 89; 16 Ohio St. 348.

ANNUITANT. The recipient of an annuity; one who is entitled to an annuity.

ANNUITIES OF TIENDS. In Scotch law; annuities of tithes; 10s. out of the boll of tiend wheat, 8s. out of the boll of beer, less out of the boll of rye, oats, and peas, allowed to the crown yearly of the tiends not paid to the bishops, or set apart for other pious uses.

ANNUITY. A yearly sum stipulated to be paid to another in fee, or for life, or years, and chargeable only on the person of the grantor. Co. Litt. 144*b*.

An annuity is different from a rent-charge, with which it is sometimes confounded, the annuity being chargeable on the person merely, and so far personalty; while a rent-charge is something reserved out of realty, or fixed as a burden upon an estate in land. 2 Bl. Comm. 40; Rolle, Abr. 226; 10 Watts, 127.

The contract of *annuity* is that by which one party delivers to another a sum of money, and agrees not to reclaim it so long as the receiver pays the rent agreed upon. This annuity may be either perpetual or for life. Civil Code La. arts. 2793, 2794.

The name of an action, now disused, (L. Lat. *breve de annuo redditu*,) which lay for the recovery of an annuity. Reg. Orig. 158*b*; Bract. fol. 203*b*; 1 Tidd, Pr. 3.

ANNUITY-TAX. An impost levied annually in Scotland for the maintenance of the ministers of religion.

ANNUL. To cancel; make void; destroy. To annul a judgment or judicial proceeding is to deprive it of all force and operation, either *ab initio* or prospectively as to future transactions.

ANNULUS. Lat. In old English law. A ring; the ring of a door. *Per haspam vel annulum hostii exterioris;* by the hasp or ring of the outer door. Fleta, lib. 3, c. 15, § 5.

ANNULUS ET BACULUS. (Lat. ring and staff.) The investiture of a bishop was *per annulum et baculum*, by the prince's delivering to the prelate a ring and pastoral staff, or crozier. 1 Bl. Comm. 378; Spelman.

ANNUS. Lat. In civil and old English law. A year; the period of three hundred and sixty-five days. Dig. 40, 7, 4, 5; Calvin.; Bract. fol. 359*b*.

ANNUS DELIBERANDI. In Scotch law. A year of deliberating; a year to deliberate. The year allowed by law to the heir to deliberate whether he will enter and represent his ancestor. It commences on the death of the ancestor, unless in the case of a posthumous heir, when the year runs from his birth. Bell.

ANNUS, DIES, ET VASTUM. In old English law. Year, day, and waste. See YEAR, DAY, AND WASTE.

Annus est mora motus quo suum planeta pervolvat circulum. A year is the duration of the motion by which a planet revolves through its orbit. Dig. 40, 7, 4, 5; Calvin.; Bract. 359*b*.

ANNUS ET DIES. A year and a day.

Annus inceptus pro completo habetur. A year begun is held as completed. Tray. Lat. Max. 45.

ANNUS LUCTUS. The year of mourning. It was a rule among the Romans, and also the Danes and Saxons, that widows should not marry *infra annum luctûs*, (within the year of mourning.) Code 5, 9, 2; 1 Bl. Comm. 457.

ANNUS UTILIS. A year made up of available or serviceable days. Brissonius; Calvin. In the plural, *anni utiles* signifies the years during which a right can be exercised or a prescription grow.

ANNUUS REDITUS. A yearly rent; annuity. 2 Bl. Comm. 41; Reg. Orig. 158*b*.

ANON., AN., A. Abbreviation for anonymous.

ANONYMOUS. Nameless; wanting a name or names. A publication, withholding the name of the author, is said to be anonymous. Cases are sometimes reported anonymously, *i. e.*, without giving the names of the parties. Abbreviated to "*Anon.*"

ANOYSANCE. Annoyance; nuisance. Cowell; Kelham.

ANSEL, ANSUL, or AUNCEL. In old English law. An ancient mode of weighing by hanging scales or hooks at either end of a beam or staff, which, being lifted with one's finger or hand by the middle, showed the equality or difference between the weight at one end and the thing weighed at the other. Termes de la Ley, 66.

ANSWER. In pleading. Any pleading setting up matters of fact by way of defense. In chancery pleading, the term denotes a defense in writing, made by a defendant to the allegations contained in a bill or information filed by the plaintiff against him.

In pleading, under the Codes of Civil Procedure, the answer is the formal written statement made by a defendant setting forth the grounds of his defense; corresponding to what, in actions under the common-law practice, is called the "plea."

In Massachusetts, the term denotes the statement of the matter intended to be relied upon by the defendant in avoidance of the plaintiff's action, taking the place of special pleas in bar, and the general issue, except in real and mixed actions. Pub. St. Mass. 1882, p. 1287.

In matrimonial suits in the (English) probate, divorce, and admiralty division, an answer is the pleading by which the respondent puts forward his defense to the petition. Browne. Div. 223.

Under the old admiralty practice in England, the defendant's first pleading was called his "answer." Williams & B. Adm. Jur. 246.

In practice. A reply to interrogatories; an affidavit in answer to interrogatories. The declaration of a fact by a witness after a question has been put, asking for it.

As a verb, the word denotes an assumption of liability, as to "answer" for the debt or default of another.

ANTAPOCHA. In the Roman law. A transcript or counterpart of the instrument called "*apocha*," signed by the debtor and delivered to the creditor. Calvin.

ANTE. Lat. Before. Usually employed in old pleadings as expressive of time, as *præ* (before) was of place, and *coram* (before) of person. Townsh. Pl. 22.

Occurring in a report or a text-book, it is used to refer the reader to a previous part of the book.

ANTE EXHIBITIONEM BILLÆ. Before the exhibition of the bill. Before suit begun.

ANTE-FACTUM or ANTE-GESTUM. Done before. A Roman law term for a previous act, or thing done before.

ANTE LITEM MOTAM. Before suit brought; before controversy instituted.

ANTECESSOR. An ancestor, (*q. v.*)

ANTEDATE. To date an instrument as of a time before the time it was written.

ANTEJURAMENTUM. In Saxon law. A preliminary or preparatory oath, (called also "*præjuramentum*," and "*juramentum calumniæ*,") which both the accuser and accused were required to make before any trial or purgation; the accuser swearing that he would prosecute the criminal, and the accused making oath on the very day that he was to undergo the ordeal that he was innocent of the crime with which he was charged. Whishaw.

ANTENATUS. Lat. From *ante* and *natus*. Born before. A person born before another person or before a particular event. The term is particularly applied to one born in a country before a revolution, change of government or dynasty, or other political event, such that the question of his rights, *status*, or allegiance will depend upon the date of his birth with reference to such event. In England, the term commonly denotes one born before the act of union with Scotland; in America, one born before the declaration of independence. Its opposite is *postnatus*, one born after the event.

ANTENUPTIAL. Made or done before a marriage. *Antenuptial settlements* are settlements of property upon the wife, or upon her and her children, made before and in contemplation of the marriage.

ANTI MANIFESTO. A term used in international law to denote a proclamation or manifesto published by one of two belligerent powers, alleging reasons why the war is defensive on its part.

ANTICHRESIS. In the civil law. A species of mortgage, or pledge of immovables. An agreement by which the debtor gives to the creditor the income from the property which he has pledged, in lieu of the interest on his debt. Guyot, Repert.

A debtor may give as security for his debt any immovable which belongs to him, the creditor having the right to enjoy the use of it on account of the interest due, or of the capital if there is no interest due; this is called "anticresis." Civil Code Mex. art. 1927.

By the law of Louisiana, there are two kinds of pledges,—the pawn and the antichresis. A pawn relates to movables, and the antichresis to immovables. The antichresis must be reduced to writing; and the creditor thereby acquires the right to the fruits, etc., of the immovables, deducting yearly their proceeds from the interest, in the first place, and afterwards from the principal of his debt. He is bound to pay taxes on the property, and keep it in repair, unless the contrary is agreed. The creditor does not become the proprietor of the property by failure to pay at the agreed time, and any clause to that effect is void. He can only sue the debtor, and obtain sentence for sale of the property. The possession of the property is, however, by the contract, transferred to the creditor. 11 Pet. 351.

ANTICIPATION. The act of doing or taking a thing before its proper time.

In conveyancing, anticipation is the act of assigning, charging, or otherwise dealing with income before it becomes due.

In patent law, a person is said to have been anticipated when he patents a contrivance already known within the limits of the country granting the patent.

ANTIGRAPHUS. In Roman law. An officer whose duty it was to take care of tax money. A comptroller.

ANTIGRAPHY. A copy or counterpart of a deed.

ANTINOMIA. In Roman law. A real or apparent contradiction or inconsistency in the laws. Merl. Repert. Conflicting laws or provisions of law; inconsistent or conflicting decisions or cases.

ANTINOMY. A term used in logic and law to denote a real or apparent inconsistency or conflict between two authorities or propositions; same as *antinomia*, (*q. v.*)

ANTIQUA CUSTUMA. In English law. Ancient custom. An export duty on wool, wool-felts, and leather, imposed during the reign of Edw. I. It was so called by way of distinction from an increased duty on the same articles, payable by foreign merchants, which was imposed at a later period of the same reign and was called "*custuma nova.*" 1 Bl. Comm. 314.

ANTIQUA STATUTA. Also called "*Vetera Statuta.*" English statutes from the time of Richard I. to Edward III. 1 Reeve, Eng. Law, 227.

ANTIQUARE. In Roman law. To restore a former law or practice; to reject or vote against a new law; to prefer the old law. Those who voted against a proposed law wrote on their ballots the letter "A," the initial of *antiquo*, I am for the old law. Calvin.

ANTIQUUM DOMINICUM. In old English law. Ancient demesne.

ANTITHETARIUS. In old English law. A man who endeavors to discharge himself of the crime of which he is accused, by retorting the charge on the accuser. He differs from an approver in this: that the latter does not charge the accuser, but others. Jacob.

ANTRUSTIO. In early feudal law. A confidential vassal. A term applied to the followers or dependents of the ancient German chiefs, and of the kings and counts of the Franks. Burrill.

ANUELS LIVRES. L. Fr. The Year Books. Kelham.

APANAGE. In old French law. A provision of lands or feudal superiorities assigned by the kings of France for the maintenance of their younger sons. An allowance assigned to a prince of the reigning house for his proper maintenance out of the public treasury. 1 Hallam, Mid. Ages, pp. ii, 88; Wharton.

APARTMENT. A part of a house occupied by a person, while the rest is occupied by another, or others. As to the meaning of this term, see 7 Man. & G. 95; 6 Mod. 214; 42 Ala. 356; 10 Pick. 293; 10 Mass. 190; 38 Cal. 137.

APATISATIO. An agreement or compact. Du Cange.

APERTA BREVIA. Open, unsealed writs.

APERTUM FACTUM. An overt act.

APERTURA TESTAMENTI. In the civil law. A form of proving a will, by the witnesses acknowledging before a magistrate their having sealed it.

APEX. The summit or highest point of anything; the top; *e. g.*, in mining law, "apex of a vein." See 26 N. W. Rep. 887.

APEX JURIS. The summit of the law; a legal subtlety; a nice or cunning point of law; close technicality; a rule of law carried to an extreme point, either of severity or refinement.

Apices juris non sunt jura, [jus.] Extremities, or mere subtleties of law, are not rules of law, [are not law.] Co. Litt. 304*b*; 10 Coke, 126; Wing. Max. 19, max. 14; Broom, Max. 188.

APICES LITIGANDI. Extremely fine points, or subtleties of litigation. Nearly equivalent to the modern phrase "sharp practice." "It is unconscionable in a defendant to take advantage of the *apices litigandi*, to turn a plaintiff around and make him pay costs when his demand is just." Per Lord Mansfield, in 3 Burr. 1243.

APOCHA. Lat. In the civil law. A writing acknowledging payments; acquittance. It differs from acceptilation in this: that acceptilation imports a complete discharge of the former obligation whether payment be made or not; *apocha*, discharge only upon payment being made. Calvin.

APOCHÆ ONERATORIÆ. In old commercial law. Bills of lading.

APOCRISARIUS. In ecclesiastical law. One who answers for another. An officer whose duty was to carry to the emperor messages relating to ecclesiastical matters, and to take back his answer to the petitioners. An officer who gave advice on questions of ecclesiastical law. An ambassador or legate of a pope or bishop. Spelman.

APOCRISARIUS CANCELLARIUS. In the civil law. An officer who took charge of the royal seal and signed royal dispatches.

APOGRAPHIA. A civil law term signifying an inventory or enumeration of things in one's possession. Calvin.

APOPLEXY. In medical jurisprudence. The failure of consciousness and suspension of voluntary motion from suspension of the functions of the cerebrum.

APOSTACY. In English law. The total renunciation of Christianity, by embracing either a false religion or no religion at all. This offense can only take place in such as have once professed the Christian religion. 4 Bl. Comm. 43; 4 Steph. Comm. 231.

APOSTATA. In civil and old English law. An apostate; a deserter from the faith; one who has renounced the Christian faith. Cod. 1, 7; Reg. Orig. 71b.

APOSTATA CAPIENDO. An obsolete English writ which issued against an apostate, or one who had violated the rules of his religious order. It was addressed to the sheriff, and commanded him to deliver the defendant into the custody of the abbot or prior. Reg. Orig. 71, 267; Jacob; Wharton.

APOSTILLE, Appostille. L. Fr. An addition; a marginal note or observation. Kelham.

APOSTLES. In English admiralty practice. A term borrowed from the civil law, denoting brief dismissory letters granted to a party who appeals from an inferior to a superior court, embodying a statement of the case and a declaration that the record will be transmitted.

This term is still sometimes applied in the admiralty courts of the United States to the papers sent up or transmitted on appeals.

APOSTOLI. In the civil law. Certificates of the inferior judge from whom a cause is removed, directed to the superior. Dig. 49, 6. See APOSTLES.

APOSTOLUS. A messenger; an ambassador, legate, or nuncio. Spelman.

APOTHECA. In the civil law. A repository; a place of deposit, as of wine, oil, books, etc. Calvin.

APOTHECARY. Any person who keeps a shop or building where medicines are compounded or prepared according to prescriptions of physicians, or where medicines are sold. Act Cong. July 13, 1866, § 9; 14 St. at Large, 119.

The term "druggist" properly means one whose occupation is to buy and sell drugs without compounding or preparing them. The term therefore has a much more limited and restricted meaning than the word "apothecary," and there is little difficulty in concluding that the term "druggist" may be applied in a technical sense to persons who buy and sell drugs. 28 La. Ann. 767.

APPARATOR. A furnisher or provider. Formerly the sheriff, in England, had charge of certain county affairs and disbursements, in which capacity he was called "*apparator comitatus*," and received therefor a considerable emolument. Cowell.

APPARENT. That which is obvious, evident, or manifest; what appears, or has been made manifest. In respect to facts involved in an appeal or writ of error, that which is stated in the record.

APPARENT DANGER, as used with reference to the doctrine of self-defense in homicide, means such overt actual demonstration, by conduct and acts, of a design to take life or do some great personal injury, as would make the killing apparently necessary to self-preservation. 44 Miss. 762.

APPARENT DEFECTS, in a thing sold, are those which can be discovered by simple inspection. Code La. art. 2497.

APPARENT EASEMENT. Apparent or continuous easements are those depending upon some artificial structure upon, or natural formation of, the servient tenement, obvious and permanent, which constitutes the easement or is the means of enjoying it; as the bed of a running stream, an overhanging roof, a pipe for conveying water, a drain, or a sewer. Non-apparent or non-continuous easements are such that have no means specially constructed or appropriated to their enjoyment, and that are enjoyed at intervals, leaving between these intervals no visible sign of their existence, such as a right of way, or right of drawing a seine upon the shore. 18 N. J. Eq. 262.

APPARENT HEIR. In English law. One whose right of inheritance is indefeasible, provided he outlive the ancestor. 2 Bl. Comm. 208.

In Scotch law. He is the person to whom the succession has actually opened. He is so called until his regular entry on the lands by service or infeftment on a precept of *clare constat.*

APPARENT MATURITY. The apparent maturity of a negotiable instrument payable at a particular time is the day on which, by its terms, it becomes due, or, when that is a holiday, the next business day. Civil Code Cal. § 3132.

APPARITIO. In old practice. Appearance; an appearance. *Apparitio in judicio,* an appearance in court. Bract. fol. 344. *Post apparitionem,* after appearance. Fleta, lib. 6, c. 10, § 25.

APPARITOR. An officer or messenger employed to serve the process of the spiritual courts in England and summon offenders. Cowell.

In the civil law. An officer who waited upon a magistrate or superior officer, and executed his commands. Calvin.; Cod. 12, 53–57.

APPARLEMENT. In old English law. Resemblance; likelihood; as apparlement of war. St. 2 Rich. II. st. 1, c. 6; Cowell.

APPARURA. In old English law the apparura were furniture, implements, tackle, or apparel. *Carucarum apparura,* plow-tackle. Cowell.

APPEAL. In civil practice. The complaint to a superior court of an injustice done or error committed by an inferior one, whose judgment or decision the court above is called upon to correct or reverse.

The removal of a cause from a court of inferior to one of superior jurisdiction, for the purpose of obtaining a review and retrial. 3 Dall. 321; 7 Cranch, 110; 10 Pet. 205; 14 Mass. 414; 1 Serg. & R. 78; 1 Bin. 219; 3 Bin. 48.

The distinction between an appeal and a writ of error is that an appeal is a process of civil law origin, and removes a cause entirely, subjecting the facts, as well as the law, to a review and revisal; but a writ of error is of common law origin, and it removes nothing for re-examination but the law. 3 Dall. 321; 7 Cranch, 108.

But appeal is sometimes used to denote the nature of appellate jurisdiction, as distinguished from original jurisdiction, without any particular regard to the mode by which a cause is transmitted to a superior jurisdiction. 1 Gall. 5, 12.

In criminal practice. A formal accusation made by one private person against another of having committed some heinous crime. 4 Bl. Comm. 312.

Appeal was also the name given to the proceeding in English law where a person, indicted of treason or felony, and arraigned for the same, confessed the fact before plea pleaded, and *appealed,* or accused others, his accomplices in the same crime, in order to obtain his pardon. In this case he was called an "approver" or "prover," and the party appealed or accused, the "*appellee.*" 4 Bl. Comm. 330.

In legislation. The act by which a member of a legislative body who questions the correctness of a decision of the presiding officer, or "chair," procures a vote of the body upon the decision.

In old French law. A mode of proceeding in the lords' courts, where a party was dissatisfied with the judgment of the peers, which was by accusing them of having given a false or malicious judgment, and offering to make good the charge by the duel or combat. This was called the "appeal of false judgment." Montesq. Esprit des Lois, liv. 28, c. 27.

APPEAL BOND. The bond given on taking an appeal, by which the appellant binds himself to pay damages and costs if he fails to prosecute the appeal with effect.

APPEALED. In a sense not strictly technical, this word may be used to signify the exercise by a party of the right to remove a litigation from one forum to another; as where he removes a suit involving the title to real estate from a justice's court to the common pleas. 8 Metc. (Mass.) 166.

APPEAR. In practice. To be properly before a court; as a fact or matter of which it can take notice. To be in evidence; to be proved. "Making it *appear* and proving are the same thing." Freem. 53.

To be regularly in court; as a defendant in an action. See APPEARANCE.

APPEARANCE. In practice. A coming into court as party to a suit, whether as plaintiff or defendant.

The formal proceeding by which a defendant submits himself to the jurisdiction of the court.

According to Bouvier, appearance may be of the following kinds:

Compulsory. That which takes place in consequence of the service of process.

Conditional. One which is coupled with conditions as to its becoming general.

De bene esse. One which is to remain an appearance, except in a certain event. See DE BENE ESSE.

General. A simple and absolute submission to the jurisdiction of the court.

Gratis. One made before the party has been legally notified to appear.

Optional. One made where the party is not under any obligation to appear, but does so to save his rights. It occurs in chancery practice, especially in England.

Special. That which is made for certain purposes only, and does not extend to all the purposes of the suit.

Subsequent. An appearance by the defendant after one has already been entered for him by the plaintiff. See Daniell, Ch. Pr.

Voluntary. That which is made in answer to a *subpœna* or summons without process. 1 Barb. Ch. Pr. 77.

APPEARANCE DAY. The day for appearing; that on which the parties are bound to come into court.

APPEARAND HEIR. In Scotch law. An apparent heir. See APPARENT HEIR.

APPELLANT. The party who takes an appeal from one court or jurisdiction to another.

APPELLATE. Pertaining to or having cognizance of appeals and other proceedings for the judicial review of adjudications.

APPELLATE COURT. A court having jurisdiction of appeal and review; a court to which causes are removable by appeal, *certiorari*, or error.

APPELLATE JURISDICTION. Jurisdiction on appeal; jurisdiction to revise or correct the proceedings in a cause already instituted and acted upon by an inferior court, or by a tribunal having the attributes of a court. 6 Kan. 505.

APPELLATIO. Lat. An appeal.

APPELLATOR. An old law term having the same meaning as "appellant." (*q. v.*)

In the civil law, the term was applied to the judge *ad quem*, or to whom an appeal was taken. Calvin.

APPELLEE. The party in a cause against whom an appeal is taken; also called the "respondent."

APPELLO. Lat. In the civil law. I appeal. The form of making an appeal *apud acta*. Dig. 49, 1, 2.

APPELLOR. In old English law. A criminal who accuses his accomplices, or who challenges a jury.

APPENDAGE. Something added as an accessory to or the subordinate part of another thing. 28 N. J. Law, 26; 30 N. W. Rep. (Iowa,) 633.

APPENDANT. A thing annexed to or belonging to another thing and passing with it; a thing of inheritance belonging to another inheritance which is more worthy; as an advowson, common, etc., which may be appendant to a manor, common of fishing to a freehold, a seat in a church to a house, etc. It differs from appurtenance, in that appendant must ever be by prescription, *i. e.*, a personal usage for a considerable time, while an appurtenance may be created at this day; for if a grant be made to a man and his heirs, of common in such a moor for his beasts levant or couchant upon his manor, the commons are appurtenant to the manor, and the grant will pass them. Co. Litt. 121*b*. See APPURTENANCE.

APPENDITIA. The appendages or appurtenances of an estate or house. Cowell.

APPENDIX. A printed volume, used on an appeal to the English house of lords or privy council, containing the documents and other evidence presented in the inferior court and referred to in the cases made by the parties for the appeal. Answering in some respects to the "paper-book" or "case" in American practice.

APPENSURA. Payment of money by weight instead of by count. Cowell.

APPERTAINING. Belonging to; appurtenant. See APPURTENANT.

APPLICABLE. When a constitution or court declares that the common law is in force in a particular state so far as it is *applicable*, it is meant that it must be applicable to the habits and conditions of the community, as well as in harmony with the genius, the spirit, and the objects of their institutions. 3 Iowa, 402; 3 Scam. 121; 5 Gilman, 130.

When a constitution prohibits the enactment of local or special laws in all cases where a general law would be *applicable*, a general law should always be construed to be applicable, in this sense, where the entire people of the state have an interest in the subject, such as regulating interest, statutes of frauds or limitations, etc. But where only a portion of the people are affected, as in locating a county-seat, it will depend upon the facts and circumstances of each particular case whether such a law would be applicable. 8 Nev. 322.

APPLICARE. Lat. In old English law. To fasten to; to moor (a vessel.) Anciently rendered, "to apply." Hale, de Jure Mar.

Applicatio est vita regulæ. Application is the life of a rule. 2 Bulst. 79.

APPLICATION. A putting to, placing before, preferring a request or petition to or before a person. The act of making a request for something.

A written request to have a certain quantity of land at or near a certain specified place. 3 Bin. 21; 5 Id. 151.

The use or disposition made of a thing.

A bringing together, in order to ascertain some relation or establish some connection; as the *application* of a rule or principle to a case or fact.

In insurance. The preliminary request, declaration, or statement made by a party applying for an insurance on life, or against fire.

Of purchase money. The disposition made of the funds received by a trustee on a sale of real estate held under the trust.

APPLICATION OF PAYMENTS. Appropriation of a payment to some particular debt; or the determination to which of several demands a general payment made by a debtor to his creditor shall be applied.

APPLY. 1. To make a formal request or petition, usually in writing, to a court, officer, board, or company, for the granting of some favor, or of some rule or order, which is within his or their power or discretion. For example, to apply for an injunction, for a pardon, for a policy of insurance.

2. To use or employ for a particular purpose; to appropriate and devote to a particular use, object, demand, or subject-matter. Thus, to apply payments to the reduction of interest.

3. To put, use, or refer, as suitable or relative; to co-ordinate language with a particular subject-matter; as to apply the words of a statute to a particular state of facts.

APPOINTEE. A person who is appointed or selected for a particular purpose; as the appointee under a power is the person who is to receive the benefit of the power.

APPOINTMENT. In chancery practice. The exercise of a right to designate the person or persons who are to take the use of real estate. 2 Washb. Real Prop. 302.

The act of a person in directing the disposition of property, by limiting a use, or by substituting a new use for a former one, in pursuance of a power granted to him for that purpose by a preceding deed, called a "power of appointment;" also the deed or other instrument by which he so conveys.

Where the power embraces several permitted objects, and the appointment is made to one or more of them, excluding others, it is called "exclusive."

Appointment may signify an appropriation of money to a specific purpose. 3 N. Y. 93, 119.

In public law. The selection or designation of a person, by the person or persons having authority therefor, to fill an office or public function and discharge the duties of the same.

The term "appointment" is to be distinguished from "election." The former is an executive act, whereby a person is named as the incumbent of an office and invested therewith, by one or more individuals who have the sole power and right to select and constitute the officer. Election means that the person is chosen by a principle of selection in the nature of a vote, participated in by the public generally or by the entire class of persons qualified to express their choice in this manner.

APPOINTOR. The person who appoints, or executes a power of appointment; as *appointee* is the person to whom or in whose favor an appointment is made. 1 Steph. Comm. 506, 507; 4 Kent. Comm. 316.

One authorized by the donor, under the statute of uses, to execute a power. 2 Bouv. Inst. n. 1923.

APPORT. L. Fr. In old English law. Tax; tallage; tribute; imposition; payment; charge; expenses. Kelham.

APPORTIONMENT. The division, partition, or distribution of a subject-matter in proportionate parts. Co. Litt. 147; 1 Swanst. 37, n.; 1 Story, Eq. Jur. 475a.

Of contracts. The allowance, in case of a severable contract, partially performed, of a part of the entire consideration proportioned to the degree in which the contract was carried out.

Of rent. The allotment of their shares in a rent to each of several parties owning it. The determination of the amount of rent to be paid when the tenancy is terminated at some period other than one of the regular intervals for the payment of rent.

Of incumbrances. Where several persons are interested in an estate, apportionment, as between them, is the determination of the respective amounts which they shall contribute towards the removal of the incumbrance.

Of corporate shares. The *pro tanto* division among the subscribers of the shares allowed to be issued by the charter, where more than the limited number have been subscribed for.

Of common. A division of the right of common between several persons, among whom the land to which, as an entirety, it first belonged has been divided.

Of representatives. The determination upon each decennial census of the number of representatives in congress which each state shall elect, the calculation being based upon the population. See Const. U. S. art. 1, § 2.

APPORTS EN NATURE. In French law. That which a partner brings into the partnership other than cash; for instance, securities, realty or personalty, cattle, stock, or even his personal ability and knowledge. Argl. Fr. Merc. Law, 545.

APPORTUM. In old English law. The revenue, profit, or emolument which a thing brings to the owner. Commonly applied to a corody or pension. Blount.

APPOSAL OF SHERIFFS. The charging them with money received upon their account in the exchequer. St. 22 & 23 Car. II.; Cowell.

APPOSER. An officer in the exchequer, clothed with the duty of examining the sheriffs in respect of their accounts. Usually called the "foreign apposer." Termes de la Ley.

APPOSTILLE, or APOSTILLE. In French law, an addition or annotation made in the margin of a writing. Merl. Repert.

AM. DICT. LAW—6

APPRAISE. In practice. To fix or set a price or value upon; to fix and state the true value of a thing, and, usually, in writing.

APPRAISEMENT. A just and true valuation of property. A valuation set upon property under judicial or legislative authority.

APPRAISER. A person appointed by competent authority to make an appraisement, to ascertain and state the true value of goods or real estate.

APPREHEND. To take hold of, whether with the mind, and so to conceive, believe, fear, dread; or actually and bodily, and so to take a person on a criminal process; to seize; to arrest. 1 Amer. & Eng. Enc. Law, 636.

APPREHENSIO. Lat. In the civil and old English law. A taking hold of a person or thing; apprehension; the seizure or capture of a person. Calvin.

One of the varieties or subordinate forms of *occupatio*, or the mode of acquiring title to things not belonging to any one.

APPREHENSION. In practice. The seizure, taking, or arrest of a person on a criminal charge. The term "apprehension" is applied exclusively to criminal cases, and "arrest" to both criminal and civil cases.

In the civil law. A physical or corporal act, (*corpus*,) on the part of one who intends to acquire possession of a thing, by which he brings himself into such a relation to the thing that he may subject it to his exclusive control; or by which he obtains the physical ability to exercise his power over the thing whenever he pleases. One of the requisites to the acquisition of judicial possession, and by which, when accompanied by intention, (*animus*,) possession is acquired. Mackeld. Rom. Law, §§ 248, 249, 250.

APPRENDRE. A fee or profit taken or received. Cowell.

APPRENTICE. A person, usually a minor, bound in due form of law to a master, to learn from him his art, trade, or business, and to serve him during the time of his apprenticeship. 1 Bl. Comm. 426; 2 Kent, Comm. 211; 3 Rawle, 307; 4 Term. 735.

APPRENTICE EN LA LEY. An ancient name for students at law, and afterwards applied to counselors, *apprentici ad barras,* from which comes the more modern word "barrister."

APPRENTICESHIP. A contract by which one person, usually a minor, called the "apprentice," is bound to another person, called the "master," to serve him during a prescribed term of years in his art, trade, or business, in consideration of being instructed by the master in such art or trade, and (commonly) of receiving his support and maintenance from the master during such term.

The term during which an apprentice is to serve.

The *status* of an apprentice; the relation subsisting between an apprentice and his master.

APPRENTICIUS AD LEGEM. An apprentice to the law; a law student; a counselor below the degree of serjeant; a barrister. See APPRENTICE EN LA LEY.

APPRIZING. In Scotch law. A form of process by which a creditor formerly took possession of the estates of the debtor in payment of the debt due. It is now superseded by adjudications.

APPROACH. In international law. The right of a ship of war, upon the high sea, to visit another vessel for the purpose of ascertaining the nationality of the latter. 1 Kent, Comm. 153, note.

APPROBATE AND REPROBATE. In Scotch law. To approve and reject; to take advantage of one part, and reject the rest. Bell. Equity suffers no person to *approbate and reprobate* the same deed. 1 Kames, Eq. 317; 1 Bell, Comm. 146.

APPROPRIATE. 1. To make a thing one's own; to make a thing the subject of property; to exercise dominion over an object to the extent, and for the purpose, of making it subserve one's own proper use or pleasure. The term is properly used in this sense to denote the acquisition of property and a right of exclusive enjoyment in those things which before were without an owner or were *publici juris*.

2. To prescribe a particular use for particular moneys; to designate or destine a fund or property for a distinct use, or for the payment of a particular demand.

In its use with reference to payments or moneys, there is room for a distinction between this term and "apply." The former properly denotes the setting apart of a fund or payment for a particular use or purpose, or the mental act of resolving that it shall be so employed, while "apply" signifies the actual expenditure of the fund, or using the payment, for the purpose to which it has been appropriated. **Practically, however, the words are used interchangeably.**

3. To *appropriate* is also used in the sense of to distribute; in this sense it may denote the act of an executor or administrator who distributes the estate of his decedent among the legatees, heirs, or others entitled, in pursuance of his duties and according to their respective rights.

APPROPRIATION. The act of appropriating or setting apart; prescribing the destination of a thing; designating the use or application of a fund.

In public law. The act by which the legislative department of government designates a particular fund, or sets apart a specified portion of the public revenue or of the money in the public treasury, to be applied to some general object of governmental expenditure, (as the civil service list, etc.,) or to some individual purchase or expense.

When money is appropriated (*i. e.*, set apart) for the purpose of securing the payment of a specific debt or class of debts, or for an individual purchase or object of expense, it is said to be specifically appropriated for that purpose.

A specific appropriation is an act of the legislature by which a named sum of money has been set apart in the treasury, and devoted to the payment of a particular demand. 45 Cal. 149.

Appropriation of payments. This means the application of a payment to the discharge of a particular debt. Thus, if a creditor has two distinct debts due to him from his debtor, and the latter makes a general payment on account, without specifying at the time to which debt he intends the payment to apply, it is optional for the creditor to *appropriate* (apply) the payment to either of the two debts he pleases. (1 Mer. 585.) Brown.

In English ecclesiastical law. The perpetual annexing of a benefice to some spiritual corporation either sole or aggregate, being the patron of the living. 1 Bl. Comm. 384; 3 Steph. Comm. 70–75; 1 Crabb, Real Prop. p. 144, § 129. Where the annexation is to the use of a lay person, it is usually called an "impropriation." 1 Crabb, Real Prop. p. 145, § 130.

APPROPRIATOR. In English ecclesiastical law. A spiritual corporation entitled to the profits of a benefice.

APPROVAL. The act of a judge or magistrate in sanctioning and accepting as satisfactory a bond, security, or other instrument which is required by law to pass his inspection and receive his approbation before it becomes operative.

APPROVE. To take to one's proper and separate use. To improve; to enhance the value or profits of anything. To inclose and cultivate common or waste land.

To *approve common* or waste land is to inclose and convert it to the purposes of husbandry, which the owner might always do, provided he left common sufficient for such as were entitled to it. St. Mert. c. 4; St. Westm. 2, c. 46; 2 Bl. Comm. 34; 3 Bl. Comm. 240; 2 Steph. Comm. 7; 3 Kent, Comm. 406.

In old criminal law. To accuse or prove; to accuse an accomplice by giving evidence against him.

APPROVED INDORSED NOTES. Notes indorsed by another person than the maker, for additional security.

APPROVEMENT. By the common law, approvement is said to be a species of confession, and incident to the arraignment of a prisoner indicted for treason or felony, who confesses the fact before plea pleaded, and appeals or accuses others, his accomplices in the same crime, in order to obtain his own pardon. In this case he is called an "approver," or "prover," "probator," and the party appealed or accused is called the "appellee." Such approvement can only be in capital offenses, and it is, as it were, equivalent to an indictment, since the appellee is equally called upon to answer it. 26 Ill. 347.

APPROVER. Approvement; improvement. "There can be no *approver* in derogation of a right of common of turbary." 1 Taunt. 435.

APPROVER. L. Fr. To approve or prove; to vouch. Kelham.

APPROVER. In criminal law. An accomplice in crime who accuses others of the same offense, and is admitted as a witness at the discretion of the court to give evidence against his companions in guilt. He is vulgarly called "Queen's Evidence."

He is one who confesses himself guilty of felony and accuses others of the same crime to save himself from punishment. 26 Ill. 175.

In old English law. Certain men sent into the several counties to increase the farms (rents) of hundreds and wapentakes, which formerly were let at a certain value to the sheriff. Cowell.

APPROVERS. In old English law. Bailiffs of lords in their franchises. Sheriffs were called the king's "approvers" in 1 Edw. III. st. 1, c. 1. Termes de la Ley, 49.

Approvers in the Marches were those who had license to sell and purchase beasts there.

APPRUARE. To take to one's use or profit. Cowell.

APPULSUS. In the civil law. A driving to, as of cattle to water. Dig. 8, 3, 1, 1.

APPURTENANCE. That which belongs to something else; an adjunct; an appendage; something annexed to another thing more worthy as principal, and which passes as incident to it, as a right of way or other easement to land; an out-house, barn, garden, or orchard, to a house or messuage. Webster.

Appurtenances of a ship include whatever is on board a ship for the objects of the voyage and adventure in which she is engaged, belonging to her owner.

Appurtenant is substantially the same in meaning as *accessory*, but it is more technically used in relation to property, and is the more appropriate word for a conveyance.

APPURTENANT. Belonging to; accessory or incident to; adjunct, appended, or annexed to; answering to *accessorium* in the civil law. 2 Steph. Comm. 30 note.

A thing is deemed to be incidental or *appurtenant* to land when it is by right used with the land for its benefit, as in the case of a way, or water-course, or of a passage for light, air, or heat from or across the land of another. Civil Code Cal. § 662.

In common speech, appurtenant denotes annexed or belonging to; but in law it denotes an annexation which is of convenience merely and not of necessity, and which may have had its origin at any time, in both which respects it is distinguished from appendant, (*q. v.*)

APT TIME. Apt time sometimes depends upon *lapse* of time; as, where a thing is required to be done at the first term, or within a given time, it cannot be done afterwards. But the phrase more usually refers to the *order* of proceedings, as fit or suitable. 74 N. C. 383.

APT WORDS. Words proper to produce the legal effect for which they are intended; sound technical phrases.

APTA VIRO. Fit for a husband; marriageable; a woman who has reached marriageable years.

APUD ACTA. Among the acts; among the recorded proceedings. In the civil law, this phrase is applied to appeals taken orally, in the presence of the judge, at the time of judgment or sentence.

AQUA. In the civil and old English law. Water; sometimes a stream or water-course.

AQUA ÆSTIVA. In Roman law. Summer water; water that was used in summer only. Dig. 43, 20, 1, 3, 4.

Aqua cedit solo. Water follows the land. A sale of land will pass the water which covers it. 2 Bl. Comm. 18; Co. Litt. 4.

AQUA CURRENS. Running water.

Aqua currit et debet currere, ut currere solebat. Water runs, and ought to run, as it has used to run. 3 Bulst. 339; 3 Kent, Comm. 439. A running stream should be left to flow in its natural channel, without alteration or diversion. A fundamental maxim in the law of water-courses.

AQUÆ DUCTUS. In the civil law. A servitude which consists in the right to carry water by means of pipes or conduits over or through the estate of another. Dig. 8, 3, 1; Inst. 2, 3.

AQUA DULCIS or FRISCA. Fresh water. Reg. Orig. 97; Bract. fols. 117, 135.

AQUA FONTANEA. Spring water. Fleta, lib. 4, c. 27, § 8.

AQUÆ HAUSTUS. In the civil law. A servitude which consists in the right to draw water from the fountain, pool, or spring of another. Inst. 2, 3, 2; Dig. 8, 3, 1, 1.

AQUÆ IMMITTENDÆ. A civil law easement or servitude, consisting in the right of one whose house is surrounded with other buildings to cast waste water upon the adjacent roofs or yards. Similar to the common law easement of drip. 15 Barb. 96.

AQUA PROFLUENS. Flowing or running water. Dig. 1, 8, 2.

AQUA QUOTIDIANA. In Roman law. Daily water; water that might be drawn at all times of the year, (*qua quis quotidie possit uti, si vellet.*) Dig. 43, 20, 1–4.

AQUA SALSA. Salt water.

AQUAGIUM. A canal, ditch, or water-course running through marshy grounds. A mark or gauge placed in or on the banks of a running stream, to indicate the height of the water, was called "*aquagaugium.*" Spelman.

AQUATIC RIGHTS. Rights which individuals have to the use of the sea and rivers, for the purpose of fishing and navigation, and also to the soil in the sea and rivers.

ARABANT. They plowed. A term of feudal law, applied to those who held by the tenure of plowing and tilling the lord's lands within the manor. Cowell.

ARAHO. In feudal law. To make oath in the church or some other holy place. All oaths were made in the church upon the relics of saints, according to the Ripuarian laws. Cowell; Spelman.

ARALIA. Plow-lands. Land fit for the plow. Denoting the character of land, rather than its condition. Spelman.

ARATOR. A plow-man; a farmer of arable land.

ARATRUM TERRÆ. In old English law. A plow of land; a plow land; as much land as could be tilled with one plow. Whishaw.

ARATURA TERRÆ. The plowing of land by the tenant, or vassal, in the service of his lord. Whishaw.

ARATURIA. Land suitable for the plow; arable land. Spelman.

ARBITER. A person chosen to decide a controversy; an arbitrator, referee.

A person bound to decide according to the rules of law and equity, as distinguished from an arbitrator, who may proceed wholly at his own discretion, so that it be according to the judgment of a sound man. Cowell.

According to Mr. Abbott, the distinction is as follows: "Arbitrator" is a technical name of a person selected with reference to an established system for friendly determination of controversies, which, though not judicial, is yet regulated by law; so that the powers and duties of the arbitrator, when once he is chosen, are prescribed by law, and his doings may be judicially revised if he has exceeded his authority. "Arbiter" is an untechnical designation of a person to whom a controversy is referred, irrespective of any law to govern the decision; and is the proper word to signify a referee of a question outside of or above municipal law.

But it is elsewhere said that the distinction between arbiters and arbitrators is not observed in modern law. Russ. Arb. 112.

In the Roman law. A judge invested with a discretionary power. A person appointed by the prætor to examine and decide that class of causes or actions termed "*bonæ fidei*," and who had the power of judging according to the principles of equity, (*ex æquo et bono;*) distinguished from the *judex*, (*q. v.,*) who was bound to decide according to strict law. Inst. 4, 6, 30, 31.

ARBITRAMENT. The award or decision of arbitrators upon a matter of dispute, which has been submitted to them. Termes de la Ley.

ARBITRAMENT AND AWARD. A plea to an action brought for the same cause which had been submitted to arbitration and on which an award had been made. Wats. Arb. 256.

Arbitramentum æquum tribuit cuique suum. A just arbitration renders to every one his own. Noy, Max. 248.

ARBITRARY. Not supported by fair, solid, and substantial cause, and without reason given. L. R. 9 Exch. 155.

ARBITRARY PUNISHMENT. That punishment which is left to the decision of the judge, in distinction from those defined by statute.

ARBITRATION. In practice. The investigation and determination of a matter or matters of difference between contending parties, by one or more unofficial persons, chosen by the parties, and called "arbitrators," or "referees." Worcester; 3 Bl. Comm. 16.

Compulsory arbitration is that which takes place when the consent of one of the parties is enforced by statutory provisions.

Voluntary arbitration is that which takes place by mutual and free consent of the parties.

In a wide sense, this term may embrace the whole method of thus settling controversies, and thus include all the various steps. But in more strict use, the decision is separately spoken of, and called an "award," and the "arbitration" denotes only the submission and hearing.

ARBITRATION OF EXCHANGE. This takes place where a merchant pays his debts in one country by a bill of exchange upon another.

ARBITRATOR. A private, disinterested person, chosen by the parties to a disputed question, for the purpose of hearing their contention, and giving judgment between them; to whose decision (award) the litigants submit themselves either voluntarily, or, in some cases, compulsorily, by order of a court.

"Referee" is of frequent modern use as a synonym of arbitrator, but is in its origin of broader signification and less accurate than arbitrator.

ARBITRIUM. The decision of an arbiter, or arbitrator; an award; a judgment.

Arbitrium est judicium. An award is a judgment. Jenk. Cent. 137.

Arbitrium est judicium boni viri, secundum æquum et bonum. An award is the judgment of a good man, according to justice. 3 Bulst. 64.

ARBOR. Lat. A tree; a plant; something larger than an herb; a general term including vines, osiers, and even reeds. The mast of a ship. Brissonius. Timber. Ainsworth; Calvin.

ARBOR CONSANGUINITATIS. A table, formed in the shape of a tree, showing the genealogy of a family. See the *arbor civilis* of the civilians and canonists. Hale, Com. Law, 335.

Arbor dum crescit, lignum cum crescere nescit. [That which is] a tree while it grows, [is] wood when it ceases to grow. Cro. Jac. 166; Hob. 77*b*, in marg.

ARBOR FINALIS. In old English law. A boundary tree; a tree used for making a boundary line. Bract. fols. 167, 207*b*.

ARCA. Lat. In the civil law. A chest or coffer; a place for keeping money. Dig. 30, 30, 6; Id. 32, 64. Brissonius.

ARCANA IMPERII. State secrets. 1 Bl. Comm. 337.

ARCARIUS. In civil and old English law. A treasurer; a keeper of public money. Cod. 10, 70, 15; Spelman.

ARCHAIONOMIA. A collection of Saxon laws, published during the reign of Queen Elizabeth, in the Saxon language, with a Latin version by Lambard.

ARCHBISHOP. In English ecclesiastical law. The chief of the clergy in his province, having supreme power under the king or queen in all ecclesiastical causes.

ARCHDEACON. A dignitary of the church who has ecclesiastical jurisdiction immediately subordinate to that of the bishop, either throughout the whole of his diocese or in some particular part of it.

ARCHDEACON'S COURT. In English ecclesiastical law. A court held before a judge appointed by the archdeacon, and called his official. Its jurisdiction comprises the granting of probates and administrations, and ecclesiastical causes in general, arising within the archdeaconry. It is the most inferior court in the whole ecclesiastical polity of England. 3 Bl. Comm. 64; 3 Steph. Comm. 430.

ARCHDEACONRY. A division of a diocese, and the circuit of an archdeacon's jurisdiction.

ARCHERY. In feudal law. A service of keeping a bow for the lord's use in the defense of his castle. Co. Litt. 157.

ARCHES COURT. In English ecclesiastical law. A court of appeal belonging to the Archbishop of Canterbury, the judge of which is called the "Dean of the Arches," because his court was anciently held in the church of Saint Mary-le-Bow, (*Sancta Maria de Arcubus*,) so named from the steeple, which is raised upon pillars built archwise. The court was until recently held in the hall belonging to the College of Civilians, commonly called "Doctors' Commons." It is now held in Westminster Hall. Its proper jurisdiction is only over the thirteen peculiar parishes belonging to the archbishop in London, but, the office of Dean of the Arches having been for a long time united with that of the archbishop's principal official, the Judge of the Arches, in right of such added office, it receives and determines appeals from the sentences of all inferior ecclesiastical courts within the province. 3 Bl. Comm. 64.

ARCHETYPE. The original copy.

ARCHICAPELLANUS. L. Lat. In old European law. A chief or high chancellor, (*summus cancellarius*.) Spelman.

ARCHIVES. The Rolls; any place where ancient records, charters, and evidences are kept. In libraries, the private depository. Cowell; Spelman.

The derivative meaning of the word (now the more common) denotes the writings themselves thus preserved; thus we say the archives of a college, of a monastery, etc.

ARCHIVIST. The custodian of archives.

ARCTA ET SALVA CUSTODIA. Lat. In strict and safe custody or keeping.

When a defendant is arrested on a *capias ad satisfaciendum*, (*ca. sa.*,) he is to be kept *arcta et salva custodia*. 3 Bl. Comm. 415.

ARDENT SPIRITS. This phrase, in a statute, does not include alcohol, which is not a liquor of any kind. 34 Ark. 340.

ARDOUR. In old English law. An incendiary; a house burner.

ARE. A surface measure in the French law, in the form of a square, equal to 1076.441 square feet.

AREA. An inclosed yard or opening in a house; an open place adjoining a house. 1 Chit. Pr. 176.

In the civil law. A vacant space in a city; a place not built upon. Dig. 50, 16, 211.

The site of a house; a site for building; the space where a house has stood. The ground on which a house is built, and which remains after the house is removed. Brissonius; Calvin.

ARENALES. In Spanish law. Sandy beaches; or grounds on the banks of rivers. White, Recop. b. 2, tit. 1, c. 6.

ARENIFODINA. In the civil law. A sand-pit. Dig. 7, 1, 13, 5.

ARENTARE. Lat. To rent; to let out at a certain rent. Cowell. *Arentatio.* A renting.

AREOPAGITE. In ancient Greek law. A lawyer or chief judge of the Areopagus in capital matters in Athens; a tribunal so called after a hill or slight eminence, in a street of that city dedicated to Mars, where the court was held in which those judges were wont to sit. Wharton.

ARETRO. In arrear; behind. Also written *a retro*.

ARG. An abbreviation of *arguendo*.

ARGENT. In heraldry. Silver.

ARGENTARIUS. In the Roman law, a money lender or broker; a dealer in money; a banker. *Argentarium*, the instrument of the loan, similar to the modern word "bond" or "note."

ARGENTARIUS MILES. A money porter in the English exchequer, who carries the money from the lower to the upper exchequer to be examined and tested. Spelman.

ARGENTEUS. An old French coin, answering nearly to the English shilling. Spelman.

ARGENTUM. Silver; money.

ARGENTUM ALBUM. Bullion; uncoined silver; common silver coin; silver coin worn smooth. Cowell; Spelman.

ARGENTUM DEI. Lat. God's money; God's penny; money given as earnest in making a bargain. Cowell.

ARGUENDO. In arguing; in the course of the argument. A statement or observation made by a judge as a matter of argument or illustration, but not directly bearing upon the case at bar, or only incidentally involved in it, is said (in the reports) to be made *arguendo*, or, in the abbreviated form, *arg*.

ARGUMENT. In rhetoric and logic, an inference drawn from premises, the truth of which is indisputable, or at least highly probable.

The argument of a demurrer, special case, appeal, or other proceeding involving a question of law, consists of the speeches of the opposed counsel; namely, the "opening" of the counsel having the right to begin, (*q. v.*,) the speech of his opponent, and the "reply" of the first counsel. It answers to the trial of a question of fact. Sweet.

ARGUMENT AB INCONVENIENTI. An argument arising from the inconvenience which the proposed construction of the law would create.

ARGUMENTATIVE. In pleading. Indirect; inferential. Steph. Pl. 179.

A pleading is so called in which the statement on which the pleader relies is implied instead of being expressed, or where it contains, in addition to proper statements of facts, reasoning or arguments upon those facts and their relation to the matter in dispute, such as should be reserved for presentation at the trial.

Argumentum a communiter accidentibus in jure frequens est. An argument drawn from things commonly happening is frequent in law. Broom, Max. 44.

Argumentum a divisione est fortissimum in jure. An argument from division [of the subject] is of the greatest force in law. Co. Litt. 213*b*; 6 Coke, 60.

Argumentum a majori ad minus negative non valet; valet e converso. An argument from the greater to the less is of no force negatively; affirmatively it is. Jenk. Cent. 281.

Argumentum a simili valet in lege. An argument from a like case (from analogy) is good in law. Co. Litt. 191.

Argumentum ab auctoritate est fortissimum in lege. An argument from authority is the strongest in the law. "The book cases are the best proof of what the law is." Co. Litt. 254*a*.

Argumentum ab impossibili valet in lege. An argument drawn from an impossibility is forcible in law. Co. Litt. 92*a*.

Argumentum ab inconvenienti est validum in lege; quia lex non permittit aliquod inconveniens. An argument drawn from what is inconvenient is good in law, because the law will not permit any inconvenience. Co. Litt. 66*a*, 258.

Argumentum ab inconvenienti plurimum valet [est validum] in lege. An argument drawn from inconvenience is of the greatest weight [is forcible] in law. Co. Litt. 66*a*, 97*a*, 152*b*, 258*b*; Broom, Max. 184. If there be in any deed or instrument equivocal expressions, and great inconvenience must necessarily follow from one construction, it is strong to show that such construction is not according to the true intention of the grantor; but where there is no equivocal expression in the instrument, and the words used admit only of one meaning, arguments of inconvenience prove only want of foresight in the grantor. 3 Madd. 540; 7 Taunt. 496.

ARIBANNUM. In feudal law. A fine for not setting out to join the army in obedience to the summons of the king.

ARIERBAN, or ARRIERE-BAN. An edict of the ancient kings of France and Germany, commanding all their vassals, the noblesse, and the vassals' vassals, to enter the army, or forfeit their estates on refusal. Spelman.

ARIMANNI. A mediæval term for a class of agricultural owners of small allodial farms, which they cultivated in connection with larger farms belonging to their lords, paying rent and service for the latter, and being under the protection of their superiors. Military tenants holding lands from the emperor. Spelman.

ARISTOCRACY. A government in which a class of men rules supreme.

A form of government which is lodged in a council composed of select members or nobles, without a monarch, and exclusive of the people.

A privileged class of the people; nobles and dignitaries; people of wealth and station.

ARISTO-DEMOCRACY. A form of government where the power is divided between the nobles and the people.

ARLES. Earnest. Used in Yorkshire in the phrase "Arles-penny." Cowell. In Scotland it has the same signification. Bell.

ARM OF THE SEA. A portion of the sea projecting inland, in which the tide ebbs and flows. 5 Coke, 107.

An arm of the sea is considered as extending as far into the interior of a country as the water of fresh rivers is propelled backwards by the ingress of the tide. Ang. Tide-waters, 73.

ARMA. Lat. Arms; weapons, offensive and defensive; armor; arms or cognizances of families.

ARMA DARE. To dub or make a knight.

Arma in armatos sumere jura sinunt. The laws permit the taking up of arms against armed persons. 2 Inst. 574.

ARMA MOLUTA. Sharp weapons that cut, in contradistinction to such as are blunt, which only break or bruise. Fleta, lib. 1, c. 33, par. 6.

ARMA REVERSATA. Reversed arms, a punishment for a traitor or felon. Cowell.

ARMATA VIS. In the civil law. Armed force. Dig. 43, 16, 3; Fleta, lib. 4, c. 4.

ARMED. A vessel is "armed" when she is fitted with a full armament for fighting purposes. She may be equipped for warlike purposes, without being "armed." By "armed" it is ordinarily meant that she has cannon, but if she had a fighting crew, muskets, pistols, powder, shot, cutlasses, and boarding appliances, she might well be said to be equipped for warlike purposes, though not armed. 2 Hurl. & C. 537; 2 Cranch, 121.

ARMIGER. An armor-bearer; an esquire. A title of dignity belonging to gentlemen authorized to bear arms. Cowell.

In its earlier meaning, a servant who carried the arms of a knight. Spelman.

A tenant by scutage; a servant or valet; applied, also, to the higher servants in convents. Spelman.

ARMISCARA. An ancient mode of punishment, which was to carry a saddle at the back as a token of subjection. Spelman.

ARMISTICE. A suspending or cessation of hostilities between belligerent nations or forces for a considerable time.

ARMORIAL BEARINGS. In English law. A device depicted on the (now imaginary) shield of one of the nobility, of which gentry is the lowest degree. The criterion of nobility is the bearing of arms, or armorial bearings, received from ancestry.

Armorum appellatione, non solum scuta et gladii et galeæ, sed et fustes et lapides continentur. Under the name of arms are included, not only shields and swords and helmets, but also clubs and stones. Co. Litt. 162.

ARMS. Anything that a man wears for his defense, or takes in his hands, or uses in his anger, to cast at or strike at another. Co. Litt. 161b, 162a; Cromp. Just. Peace, 65.

This term, as it is used in the constitution, relative to the right of citizens to bear arms, refers to the arms of a militiaman or soldier, and the word is used in its military sense. The arms of the infantry soldier are the musket and bayonet; of cavalry and dragoons, the sabre, holster pistols, and carbine; of the artillery, the field-piece, siege-gun, and mortar, with side arms. The term, in this connection, cannot be made to cover such weapons as dirks, daggers, slung-shots, sword-canes, brass knuckles, and bowie-knives. These are not military arms. 37 Tex. 476; 3 Heisk. 179.

Arms, or coat of arms, signifies *insignia, i. e.*, ensigns of honor, such as were formerly assumed by soldiers of fortune, and painted on their shields to distinguish them; or nearly the same as armorial bearings, (*q. v.*)

ARMY. The armed forces of a nation intended for military service on land.

"The term 'army' or 'armies' has never been used by congress, so far as I am advised, so as to include the navy or marines, and there is nothing in the act of 1862, or the circumstances which led to its passage, to warrant the conclusion that it was used therein in any other than its long established and ordinary sense,—the land force, as distinguished from the navy and marines." 2 Sawy. 205.

AROMATARIUS. A word formerly used for a grocer. 1 Vent. 142.

AROMATIC. This word, when employed to express one of the qualities of a liquor, cannot be protected as a trade-mark. 45 Cal. 467.

ARPEN, Arpent. A measure of land of uncertain quantity, mentioned in Domesday and other old books; by some called an "acre," by others "half an acre," and by others a "furlong." Spelman; Cowell; Blount.

A measure of land in Louisiana. 6 Pet. 763.

A French measure of land, containing one hundred square perches, of eighteen feet each, or about an acre. But the quantity varied in different provinces. Spelman.

ARPENTATOR. A measurer or surveyor of land. Cowell; Spelman.

ARRA. In the civil law. Earnest; earnest-money; evidence of a completed bargain. Used of a contract of marriage, as well as any other. Spelled, also, *Arrha, Arræ.* Calvin.

ARRACK. A spirit procured from distillation of the cocoa-nut tree, rice, or sugarcane, and imported from India.

ARRAIGN. In criminal practice. To bring a prisoner to the bar of the court to answer the matter charged upon him in the indictment. The arraignment of a prisoner consists of calling upon him by name, and reading to him the indictment, (in the English tongue,) and demanding of him whether he be guilty or not guilty, and entering his plea.

In old English law. To order, or set in order; to conduct in an orderly manner; to prepare for trial. *To arraign an assise* was to cause the tenant to be called to make the plaint, and to set the cause in such order as the tenant might be enforced to answer thereunto. Litt. § 442; Co. Litt. 262*b*.

ARRAIGNMENT. In criminal practice. Calling the defendant to the bar of the court, to answer the accusation contained in the indictment.

ARRAIGNS, CLERK OF. In English law. An assistant to the clerk of assise.

ARRAMEUR. In old French law. An officer employed to superintend the loading of vessels, and the safe stowage of the cargo. 1 Pet. Adm. Append. XXV.

ARRAS. In Spanish law. The donation which the husband makes to his wife, by reason or on account of marriage, and in consideration of the *dote*, or portion, which he receives from her. Aso & M. Inst. b. 1, t. 7, c. 3.

ARRAY. The whole body of jurors summoned to attend a court, as they are *arrayed* or arranged on the panel. Dane, Abr. Index; 1 Chit. Crim. Law, 536; Com. Dig. "Challenge," B.

A ranking, or setting forth in order; the order in which jurors' names are ranked in the panel containing them. Co. Litt. 156*a;* 3 Bl. Comm. 359.

ARREARS, or **ARREARAGES.** Money unpaid at the due time, as rent behind; the remainder due after payment of a part of an account; money in the hands of an accounting party. Cowell.

ARRECT. To accuse or charge with an offense. *Arrectati,* accused or suspected persons.

ARRENDAMIENTO. In Spanish law. The contract of letting and hiring an estate or land, (*heredad.*) White, Recop. b. 2, tit. 14, c. 1.

ARREST. In criminal practice. The stopping, seizing, or apprehending a person by lawful authority; the act of laying hands upon a person for the purpose of taking his body into custody of the law; the restraining of the liberty of a man's person in order to compel obedience to the order of a court of justice, or to prevent the commission of a crime, or to insure that a person charged or suspected of a crime may be forthcoming to answer it.

Arrest is well described in the old books as "the beginning of imprisonment, when a man is first taken and restrained of his liberty, by power of a lawful warrant." 2 Shep. Abr. 299; Wood, Inst. Com. Law, 575.

In civil practice. The apprehension of a person by virtue of a lawful authority to answer the demand against him in a civil action.

In admiralty practice. In admiralty actions a ship or cargo is *arrested* when the marshal has served the writ in an action *in rem.* Williams & B. Adm. Jur. 193.

Synonyms distinguished. The term "apprehension" seems to be more peculiarly appropriate to seizure on criminal process; while "arrest" may apply to either a civil or criminal action, but is perhaps better confined to the former.

As ordinarily used, the terms "arrest" and "attachment" coincide in meaning to some extent, though in strictness, as a distinction, an arrest may be said to be the act resulting from the service of an attachment; and, in the more extended sense which is sometimes given to attachment, including the act of taking, it would seem to differ from arrest, in that it is more peculiarly applicable to a taking of property, while *arrest* is more commonly used in speaking of persons. Bouvier.

By *arrest* is to be understood to take the party into custody. To *commit* is the separate and distinct act of carrying the party to prison, after having taken him into custody by force of the execution. 1 Metc. (Mass.) 502.

ARREST OF INQUEST. Pleading in arrest of taking the inquest upon a former issue, and showing cause why an inquest should not be taken.

ARREST OF JUDGMENT. In practice. The act of staying a judgment, or refusing to render judgment in an action at law, after verdict, for some matter intrinsic appearing on the face of the record, which would render the judgment, if given, erroneous or reversible. 3 Bl. Comm. 393; 3 Steph. Comm. 628; 2 Tidd, Pr. 918.

ARRESTANDIS BONIS NE DISSIPENTUR. In old English law. A writ which lay for a person whose cattle or goods were taken by another, who during a contest was likely to make away with them, and who had not the ability to render satisfaction. Reg. Orig. 126.

ARRESTANDO IPSUM QUI PECUNIAM RECEPIT. In old English law. A writ which issued for apprehending a person who had taken the king's prest money to serve in the wars, and then hid himself in order to avoid going.

ARRESTATIO. In old English law. An arrest, (*q. v.*)

ARRESTEE. In Scotch law. The person in whose hands the movables of another, or a debt due to another, are arrested by the creditor of the latter by the process of *arrestment.* 2 Kames, Eq. 173, 175.

ARRESTER. In Scotch law. One who sues out and obtains an arrestment of his debtor's goods or movable obligations. Ersk. Inst. 3, 6, 1.

ARRESTMENT. In Scotch law. Securing a criminal's person till trial, or that of a debtor till he give security *judicio sisti.* The order of a judge, by which he who is debtor in a movable obligation to the arrester's debtor is prohibited to make payment or delivery till the debt due to the arrester be paid or secured. Ersk. Inst. 3, 6, 2.

ARRESTMENT JURISDICTIONIS FUNDANDÆ CAUSÂ. In Scotch law. A process to bring a foreigner within the jurisdiction of the courts of Scotland. The warrant attaches a foreigner's goods within the jurisdiction, and these will not be released unless caution or security be given.

ARRESTO FACTO SUPER BONIS MERCATORUM ALIENIGENORUM. In old English law. A writ against the goods of aliens found within this kingdom, in recompense of goods taken from a denizen in a foreign country, after denial of restitution. Reg. Orig. 129. The ancient civilians called it "*clarigatio,*" but by the moderns it is termed "*reprisalia.*"

ARRÊT. Fr. A judgment, sentence, or decree of a court of competent jurisdiction. The term is derived from the French law, and is used in Canada and Louisiana. *Saisie arrêt* is an attachment of property in the hands of a third person. Code Prac. La. art. 209; 2 Low. Can. 77; 5 Low. Can. 198, 218.

ARRETTED. Charged; charging. The convening a person charged with a crime before a judge. Staundef. P. C. 45. It is used sometimes for *imputed* or *laid unto;* as no folly may be *arretted* to one under age. Cowell.

ARRHABO. In the civil law. Earnest; money given to bind a bargain. Calvin.

ARRHÆ. In the civil law. Money or other valuable things given by the buyer to the seller, for the purpose of evidencing the contract; earnest.

ARRIAGE AND CARRIAGE. In English and Scotch law. Indefinite services formerly demandable from tenants, but prohibited by statute, (20 Geo. II. c. 50, §§ 21, 22.) Holthouse; Ersk. Inst. 2, 6, 42.

ARRIER BAN. A second summons to join the lord, addressed to those who had neglected the first. A summons of the inferiors or vassals of the lord. Spelman.

ARRIERE FIEF, or FEE. In feudal law. A fief or fee dependent on a superior one; an inferior fief granted by a vassal of the king, out of the fief held by him. Montesq. Esprit des Lois, liv. 31, cc. 26, 32.

ARRIERE VASSAL. In feudal law. The vassal of a vassal.

ARRIVAL. In marine insurance. The arrival of a vessel means an arrival for purposes of business, requiring an entry and clearance and stay at the port so long as to require some of the acts connected with business, and not merely touching at a port for advices, or to ascertain the state of the market, or being driven in by an adverse wind and sailing again as soon as it changes. 9 How. 372. See, also, 1 Ware, 281; 1 Mason, 482; 2 Sum. 422; 2 Cush. 453; 15 Fed. Rep. 265.

"A vessel arrives at a port of discharge when she comes, or is brought, to a place where it is intended to discharge her, and where is the usual and customary place of discharge. When a vessel is insured to one or two ports, and sails for one, the risk terminates on her arrival there. If a vessel is insured to a particular port of discharge, and is destined to discharge cargo successively at two different wharves, docks, or places, within that port, each being a distinct place for the delivery of cargo, the risk ends when she has been moored twenty-four hours in safety at the first place. But if she is destined to one or more places for the delivery of cargo, and delivery or discharge of a portion of her cargo is necessary, not by reason of her having reached any destined place of delivery, but as a necessary and usual nautical measure, to enable her to reach such usual and destined place of delivery, she cannot properly be considered as having arrived at the usual and customary place of discharge, when she is at anchor for the purpose only of using such means as will better enable her to reach it. If she cannot get to the destined and usual place of discharge in the port because she is too deep, and must be lightered to get there, and, to aid in prosecuting the voyage, cargo is thrown overboard or put into lighters, such discharge does not make that the place of arrival; it is only a stopping-place in the voyage. When the vessel is insured to a particular port of discharge, arrival within the limits of the harbor does not terminate the risk, if the place is not one where vessels are discharged and voyages completed. The policy covers the vessel through the port navigation, as well as on the open sea, until she reaches the destined place." 1 Holmes, 137.

ARRIVE. To reach or come to a particular place of destination by traveling towards it. 1 Brock. 411.

In insurance law. To reach that particular place or point in a harbor which is the ultimate destination of a vessel. 2 Cush. 439, 453.

The words "arrive" and "enter" are not always synonymous; there certainly may be an arrival without an actual entry or attempt to enter. 5 Mason, 120, 132. See, also, 1 Brock. 407, 411.

ARROGATION. In the civil law. The adoption of a person who was of full age or *sui juris.* 1 Browne, Civil & Adm. Law, 119; Dig. 1, 7, 5; Inst. 1, 11, 3.

ARRONDISSEMENT. In France, one of the subdivisions of a department.

ARSÆ ET PENSATÆ. Burnt and weighed. A term formerly applied to money tested or assayed by fire and by weighing.

ARSENALS. Store-houses for arms; dock-yards, magazines, and other military stores.

ARSER IN LE MAIN. Burning in the hand. The punishment by burning or branding the left thumb of lay offenders who claimed and were allowed the benefit of clergy, so as to distinguish them in case they made a second claim of clergy. 5 Coke, 51; 4 Bl. Comm. 367.

ARSON. Arson, at common law, is the act of unlawfully and maliciously burning the *house* of another man. 4 Steph. Comm. 99; 2 Russ. Crimes, 896; Steph. Crim. Dig. 298.

Arson, by the common law, is the willful and malicious burning of the house of another. The word "house," as here understood, includes not merely the dwelling-house, but all outhouses which are parcel thereof. 20 Conn. 246.

Arson is the malicious and willful burning of the house or outhouse of another. Code Ga. 1882, § 4375.

Arson is the willful and malicious burning of a building with intent to destroy it. Pen. Code Cal. § 447.

ARSURA. The trial of money by heating it after it was coined.

The loss of weight occasioned by this process. A pound was said to *burn* so many pence (*tot ardere denarios*) as it lost by the fire. Spelman. The term is now obsolete.

ART. A principle put in practice and applied to some art, machine, manufacture, or composition of matter. 4 Mason, 1. See Act Cong. July 8, 1870.

In the law of patents, this term means a useful art or manufacture which is beneficial, and which is described with exactness in its mode of operation. Such an art can be protected only in the mode and to the extent thus described. 1 Fish. Pat. Cas. 64. See, also, 15 How. 267; 7 Wall. 295.

ART, WORDS OF. Words used in a technical sense; words scientifically fit to carry the sense assigned them.

ART AND PART. In Scotch law. The offense committed by one who aids and assists the commission of a crime, but who is not the principal or chief actor in its actual commission. An accessary. A principal in the second degree. Paters. Comp.

ARTHEL, ARDHEL, or ARDDELIO. To avouch; as if a man were taken with stolen goods in his possession he was allowed a lawful *arthel, i. e.,* vouchee, to clear him of the felony; but provision was made against it by 28 Hen. VIII. c. 6. Blount.

ARTICLE. A separate and distinct part of an instrument or writing comprising two or more particulars; one of several things presented as connected or forming a whole.

In English ecclesiastical law. A complaint exhibited in the ecclesiastical court by way of libel. The different parts of a libel, responsive allegation, or counter allegation in the ecclesiastical courts. 3 Bl. Comm. 109.

In Scotch practice. A subject or matter; competent matter. "Article of dittay." 1 Broun, 62. A "point of dittay." 1 Swint. 128, 129.

ARTICLED CLERK. In English law. A clerk bound to serve in the office of a solicitor in consideration of being instructed in the profession.

ARTICLES. 1. A connected series of propositions; a system of rules. The subdivisions of a document, code, book, etc. A specification of distinct matters agreed upon or established by authority or requiring judicial action.

2. A statute; as having its provisions articulately expressed under distinct heads. Several of the ancient English statutes were called "articles," (*articuli*.)

3. A system of rules established by legal authority; as *articles* of war, *articles* of the navy, *articles* of faith, (*q. v.*)

4. A contractual document executed between parties, containing stipulations or terms of agreement; as *articles* of agreement, *articles* of partnership.

It is a common practice for persons to enter into articles of agreement, preparatory to the execution of a formal deed, whereby it is stipulated that one of the parties shall convey to the other certain lands, or release his right to them, or execute some other disposition of them.

5. In chancery practice. A formal written statement of objections filed by a party, after depositions have been taken, showing ground for discrediting the witnesses.

ARTICLES APPROBATORY. In Scotch law. That part of the proceedings which corresponds to the answer to the charge in an English bill in chancery. Paters. Comp.

ARTICLES IMPROBATORY. In Scotch law. Articulate averments setting forth the facts relied upon. Bell. That part of the proceedings which corresponds to the charge in an English bill in chancery to set aside a deed. Paters. Comp. The answer is called "articles approbatory."

ARTICLES, LORDS OF. A committee of the Scottish parliament, which, in the mode of its election, and by the nature of its powers, was calculated to increase the influence of the crown, and to confer upon it a power equivalent to that of a negative before debate. This system appeared inconsistent with the freedom of parliament, and at the revolution the convention of estates declared it a grievance, and accordingly it was suppressed by Act 1690, c. 3. Wharton.

ARTICLES OF AGREEMENT. A written memorandum of the terms of an agreement. See ARTICLES, 4.

ARTICLES OF ASSOCIATION. Articles subscribed by the members of a joint-stock company or corporation organized under a general law, and which create the corporate union between them. Such articles are in the nature of a partnership agreement, and commonly specify the form of organization, amount of capital, kind of business to be pursued, location of the company, etc. Articles of association are to be distinguished from a charter, in that the latter is a grant of power from the sovereign or the legislature.

ARTICLES OF CONFEDERATION. The name of the instrument embodying the compact made between the thirteen original states of the Union, before the adoption of the present constitution.

ARTICLES OF FAITH. In English law. The system of faith of the Church of England, more commonly known as the "Thirty-Nine Articles."

ARTICLES OF IMPEACHMENT. A formal written allegation of the causes for impeachment; answering the same office as an indictment in an ordinary criminal proceeding.

ARTICLES OF PARTNERSHIP. A written agreement by which the parties enter into a copartnership upon the terms and conditions therein stipulated.

ARTICLES OF RELIGION. In English ecclesiastical law. Commonly called the "Thirty-Nine Articles;" a body of divinity drawn up by the convocation in 1562, and confirmed by James I.

ARTICLES OF ROUP. In Scotch law. The terms and conditions under which property is sold at auction.

ARTICLES OF SET. In Scotch law. An agreement for a lease. Paters. Comp.

ARTICLES OF THE CLERGY. The title of a statute passed in the ninth year of Edward II. for the purpose of adjusting and settling the great questions of cognizance then existing between the ecclesiastical and temporal courts. 2 Reeve, Hist. Eng. Law, 291–296.

ARTICLES OF THE NAVY. A system of rules prescribed by act of parliament for the government of the English navy; also, in the United States, there are articles for the government of the navy.

ARTICLES OF THE PEACE. A complaint made or exhibited to a court by a person who makes oath that he is in fear of death or bodily harm from some one who has threatened or attempted to do him injury. The court may thereupon order the person complained of to find sureties for the peace, and, in default, may commit him to prison. 4 Bl. Comm. 255.

ARTICLES OF UNION. In English law. Articles agreed to, A. D. 1707, by the parliaments of England and Scotland, for the union of the two kingdoms. They were twenty-five in number. 1 Bl. Comm. 96.

ARTICLES OF WAR. Codes framed for the government of a nation's army are commonly thus called.

ARTICULATE ADJUDICATION. In Scotch law. Where the creditor holds several distinct debts, a separate adjudication for each claim is thus called.

ARTICULATELY. Article by article; by distinct clauses or articles; by separate propositions.

ARTICULI. Lat. Articles; items or heads. A term applied to some old English statutes, and occasionally to treatises.

ARTICULI CLERI. Articles of the clergy, (*q. v.*)

ARTICULI DE MONETA. Articles concerning money, or the currency. The title of a statute passed in the twentieth year of Edward I. 2 Reeve, Hist. Eng. Law, 228; Crabb, Eng. Law, (Amer. Ed.) 167.

ARTICULI MAGNÆ CHARTÆ. The preliminary articles, forty-nine in number, upon which the *Magna Charta* was founded.

ARTICULI SUPER CHARTAS. Articles upon the charters. The title of a statute passed in the twenty-eighth year of Edward I. st. 3, confirming or enlarging many particulars in *Magna Charta*, and the *Charta de Foresta*, and appointing a method for enforcing the observance of them, and for the punishment of offenders. 2 Reeve, Hist. Eng. Law, 103, 233.

ARTICULO MORTIS. (Or more commonly *in articulo mortis.*) In the article of death; at the point of death.

ARTIFICER. One who buys goods in order to reduce them, by his own art or industry, into other forms, and then to sell them. 3 T. B. Mon. 335.

One who is actually and personally engaged or employed to do work of a mechanical or physical character, not including one who takes contracts for labor to be performed by others. 7 El. & Bl. 135.

One who is master of his art, and whose employment consists chiefly in manual labor. Wharton; Cunningham.

ARTIFICIAL. Created by art, or by law; existing only by force of or in contemplation of law.

ARTIFICIAL PERSONS. Persons created and devised by human laws for the purposes of society and government, as distinguished from natural persons. Corporations are examples of artificial persons. 1 Bl. Comm. 123.

ARTIFICIAL PRESUMPTIONS. Also called "legal presumptions;" those which derive their force and effect from the law, rather than their natural tendency to produce belief. 3 Starkie, Ev. 1235.

ARTIFICIALLY. Technically; scientifically; using terms of art. A will or contract is described as "artificially" drawn if it is couched in apt and technical phrases and exhibits a scientific arrangement.

ARURA. An old English law term, signifying a day's work in plowing.

ARVIL-SUPPER. A feast or entertainment made at a funeral in the north of England; *arvil bread* is bread delivered to the poor at funeral solemnities, and *arvil, arval,* or *arfal,* the burial or funeral rites. Cowell.

AS. Lat. In the Roman and civil law. A pound weight; and a coin originally weighing a pound, (called also "*libra;*") divided into twelve parts, called "*unciæ.*"

Any integral sum, subject to division in certain proportions. Frequently applied in the civil law to inheritances; the whole inheritance being termed "as," and its several proportionate parts "*sextans,*" "*quadrans,*" etc. Burrill.

The term "as," and the multiples of its *unciæ,* were also used to denote the rates of interest. 2 Bl. Comm. 462, note *m.*

AS AGAINST; AS BETWEEN. These words contrast the relative position of two persons, with a tacit reference to a different relationship between one of them and a third person. For instance, the temporary bailee of a chattel is entitled to it *as between* himself and a stranger, or *as against* a stranger; reference being made by this form of words to the rights of the bailor. Wharton.

ASCEND. To go up; to pass up or upwards; to go or pass in the ascending line. 4 Kent, Comm. 393, 397.

ASCENDANTS. Persons with whom one is related in the ascending line; one's parents, grandparents, great-grandparents, etc.

ASCENDIENTES. In Spanish law. Ascendants; ascending heirs; heirs in the ascending line. Schm. Civil Law, 259.

ASCENT. Passage upwards; the transmission of an estate from the ancestor to the heir in the ascending line. See 4 Kent, Comm. 393, 397.

ASCERTAIN. To fix; to render certain or definite; to estimate and determine; to clear of doubt or obscurity.

ASCRIPTITIUS. In Roman law. A foreigner who had been registered and naturalized in the colony in which he resided. Cod. 11, 47.

ASPECT. View; object; possibility. Implies the existence of alternatives. Used in the phrases "bill with a double aspect" and "contingency with a double aspect."

ASPHYXIA. In medical jurisprudence. Swooning, suspended animation, produced by the non-conversion of the venous blood of the lungs into arterial.

ASPORTATION. The removal of things from one place to another. The carrying away of goods; one of the circumstances requisite to constitute the offense of larceny. 4 Bl. Comm. 231.

ASPORTAVIT. He carried away. Sometimes uses as a noun to denote a carrying away. An "*asportavit* of personal chattels." 2 H. Bl. 4.

ASSACH. In old Welsh law. An oath made by compurgators. Brown.

ASSART. In English law. The offense committed in the forest, by pulling up the trees by the roots that are thickets and coverts for deer, and making the ground plain as arable land. It differs from waste, in that waste is the cutting down of coverts which may grow again, whereas assart is the plucking them up by the roots and utterly destroying them, so that they can never afterward grow. This is not an offense if done with license to convert forest into tillage ground. Consult *Manwood's Forest Laws,* pt. I. p. 171. Wharton.

ASSASSINATION. Murder committed for hire, without provocation or cause of resentment given to the murderer by the person upon whom the crime is committed. Ersk. Inst. 4, 4, 45.

A murder committed treacherously, or by stealth or surprise, or by lying in wait.

ASSATH. An ancient custom in Wales, by which a person accused of crime could clear himself by the oaths of three hundred men. It was abolished by St. 1 Hen. V. c. 6. Cowell; Spelman.

ASSAULT. An unlawful attempt or offer, on the part of one man, with force or violence, to inflict a bodily hurt upon another.

An attempt or offer to beat another, without touching him; as if one lifts up his cane or his fist in a threatening manner at another; or strikes at him, but misses him. 3 Bl. Comm. 120; 3 Steph. Comm. 469.

Aggravated assault is one committed with the intention of committing some additional crime; or one attended with circumstances of peculiar outrage or atrocity. *Simple assault* is one committed with no intention to do any other injury.

An assault is an unlawful attempt, coupled with a present ability, to commit a violent injury on the person of another. Pen. Code Cal. § 240.

An assault is an attempt to commit a violent injury on the person of another. Code Ga. 1882, § 4357.

An assault is any willful and unlawful attempt or offer, with force or violence, to do a corporal hurt to another. Pen. Code Dak. § 305.

An assault is an offer or an attempt to do a corporal injury to another; as by striking at him with the hand , or with a stick, or by shaking the fist at him , or presenting a gun or other weapon within such distance as that a hurt might be given, or drawing a sword and brandishing it in a menacing manner; provided the act is done with intent to do some corporal hurt. 2 Wash. C. C. 435.

An assault is an attempt, with force or violence, to do a corporal injury to another, and may consist of any act tending to such corporal injury, accompanied with such circumstances as denote at the time an intention, coupled with the present ability, of using actual violence against the person. 1 Hill, 351.

An assault is an attempt or offer, with force or violence, to do a corporal hurt to another, whether from malice or wantonness, with such circumstances as denote, at the time, an intention to do it, coupled with a present ability to carry such intention into effect. 43 Ala. 354.

An assault is an intentional attempt, by violence, to do an injury to the person of another. It must be *intentional;* for, if it can be collected, notwithstanding appearances to the contrary, that there is not a *present* purpose to do an injury, there is no assault. 1 Ired. 127.

In order to constitute an assault there must be something more than a mere menace. There must be violence begun to be executed. But, where there is a clear intent to commit violence, accompanied by acts which if not interrupted will be followed by personal injury, the violence is commenced and the assault is complete. 27 Cal. 633.

ASSAY. The proof or trial, by chemical experiments, of the purity or fineness of metals,—particularly of the precious metals, gold and silver.

A trial of weights and measures by a standard; as by the constituted authorities, clerks of markets, etc. Reg. Orig. 280.

A trial or examination of certain commodities, as bread, cloths, etc. Cowell; Blount.

ASSAY OFFICE. The staff of persons by whom (or the building in which) the process of assaying gold and silver, required by government, incidental to maintaining the coinage, is conducted.

ASSAYER. One whose business it is to make assays of the precious metals.

ASSAYER OF THE KING. An officer of the royal mint, appointed by St. 2 Hen. VI. c. 12; who received and tested the bullion taken in for coining; also called "*assayator regis.*" Cowell; Termes de la Ley.

ASSECURARE. To assure, or make secure by pledges, or any solemn interposition of faith. Cowell; Spelman.

ASSECURATION. In European law. Assurance; insurance of a vessel, freight, or cargo. Ferriere.

ASSECURATOR. In maritime law. An insurer, (*aversor periculi.*) Locc. de Jure Mar. lib. 2, c. 5, § 10.

ASSEDATION. In Scotch law. An old term, used indiscriminately to signify a lease or feu-right. Bell; Ersk. Inst. 2, 6, 20.

ASSEMBLY. The concourse or meeting together of a considerable number of persons at the same place. Also the persons so gathered.

Popular assemblies are those where the people meet to deliberate upon their rights; these are guaranteed by the constitution. Const. U. S. Amend. art. 1.

The lower or more numerous branch of the legislature in many of the states is also called the "Assembly" or "House of Assembly," but the term seems to be an appropriate one to designate any political meeting required to be held by law.

ASSEMBLY GENERAL. The highest ecclesiastical court in Scotland, composed of a representation of the ministers and elders of the church, regulated by Act 5th Assem. 1694.

ASSEMBLY, UNLAWFUL. In criminal law. The assembling of three or more persons together to do an unlawful act, who separate without actually doing it, or making any motion towards it. 3 Inst. 176; 4 Bl. Comm. 146.

It differs from a riot or rout, because in each of the latter cases there is some act done besides the simple meeting. See 1 Ired. 30; 9 Car. & P. 91, 431; 5 Car. & P. 154; 1 Bish. Crim. Law, § 535; 2 Bish. Crim. Law, §§ 1256, 1259.

ASSENT. Compliance; approval of something done; a declaration of willingness to do something in compliance with a request.

ASSERTORY COVENANT. One which affirms that a particular state of facts exists; an affirming promise under seal.

ASSESS. 1. To ascertain, adjust, and settle the respective shares to be contributed by several persons toward an object beneficial to them all, in proportion to the benefit received.

2. To adjust or fix the proportion of a tax which each person, of several liable to it, has to pay; to apportion a tax among several; to distribute taxation in a proportion founded on the proportion of burden and benefit.

3. To place a valuation upon property for the purpose of apportioning a tax.

4. To impose a pecuniary payment upon persons or property; to tax.

ASSESSED. Where the charter of a corporation provides for the payment by it of a state tax, and contains a proviso that "no other tax or impost shall be levied or assessed upon the said company," the word "assessed" in the proviso cannot have the force and meaning of describing special levies for public improvements, but is used merely to describe the act of levying the tax or impost. 42 N. J. Law, 97.

ASSESSMENT. In a general sense, denotes the process of ascertaining and adjusting the shares respectively to be contributed by several persons towards a common beneficial object according to the benefit received.

In taxation. The listing and valuation of property for the purpose of apportioning a tax upon it, either according to value alone or in proportion to benefit received. Also determining the share of a tax to be paid by each of many persons; or apportioning the entire tax to be levied among the different taxable persons, establishing the proportion due from each.

Assessment, as used in juxtaposition with taxation in a state constitution, includes all the steps necessary to be taken in the legitimate exercise of the power to tax. 4 Neb. 386.

Assessment is also popularly used as a synonym for taxation in general,—the authoritative imposition of a rate or duty to be paid. But in its technical signification it denotes only taxation for a special purpose or local improvement; local taxation, as distinguished from general taxation; taxation on the principle of apportionment according to the relation between burden and benefit.

As distinguished from other kinds of taxation, assessments are those special and local impositions upon property in the immediate vicinity of municipal improvements which are necessary to pay for the improvement, and are laid with reference to the special benefit which the property is supposed to have derived therefrom. 29 Wis. 599.

Assessment and tax are not synonymous. An assessment is doubtless a tax, but the term implies something more; it implies a tax of a particular kind, predicated upon the principle of equivalents, or benefits, which are peculiar to the persons or property charged therewith, and which are said to be assessed or appraised, according to the measure or proportion of such equivalents; whereas a simple tax is imposed for the purpose of supporting the government generally, without reference to any special advantage which may be supposed to accrue to the persons taxed. Taxes must be levied, without discrimination, equally upon all the subjects of property; whilst assessments are only levied upon lands, or some other specific property, the subjects of the supposed benefits; to repay which the assessment is levied. 1 Handy, 464.

In corporations. Instalments of the money subscribed for shares of stock, called for from the subscribers by the directors, from time to time as the company requires money,

are called "assessments," or, in England, "calls."

The periodical demands made by a mutual insurance company, under its charter and by-laws, upon the makers of premium notes, are also denominated "assessments."

Of damages. Fixing the amount of damages to which the successful party in a suit is entitled after an interlocutory judgment has been taken.

Assessment of damages is also the name given to the determination of the sum which a corporation proposing to take lands for a public use must pay in satisfaction of the demand proved or the value taken.

In insurance. An apportionment made in general average upon the various articles and interests at risk, according to their value at the time and place of being in safety, for contribution for damage and sacrifices purposely made, and expenses incurred for escape from impending common peril. 2 Phil. Ins. c. xv.

ASSESSOR. An officer chosen or appointed to appraise, value, or assess property.

In civil and Scotch law. Persons skilled in law, selected to advise the judges of the inferior courts. Bell; Dig. 1, 22; Cod. 1, 51.

A person learned in some particular science or industry, who sits with the judge on the trial of a cause requiring such special knowledge and gives his advice.

In England it is the practice in admiralty business to call in assessors, in cases involving questions of navigation or seamanship. They are called "nautical assessors," and are always Brethren of the Trinity House.

ASSETS. In probate law. Property of a decedent available for the payment of debts and legacies; the estate coming to the heir or personal representative which is chargeable, in law or equity, with the obligations which such heir or representative is required, in his representative capacity, to discharge.

In an accurate and legal sense, all the personal property of the deceased which is of a salable nature, and may be converted into ready money, is deemed assets. But the word is not confined to such property; for all other property of the deceased which is chargeable with his debts or legacies, and is applicable to that purpose, is, in a large sense, assets. 1 Story, Eq. Jur. § 531.

Assets per descent. That portion of the ancestor's estate which descends to the heir, and which is sufficient to charge him, as far as it goes, with the specialty debts of his ancestors. 2 Williams, Ex'rs, 1011.

Equitable assets. The term includes equities of any sort and rights and claims which are available only by the aid of a court of equity, and which are to be divided, *pari passu,* among all the creditors.

Legal assets. Such as constitute the fund, for the payment of debts, that can be reached in an action at law.

Personal assets. Goods and personal chattels to which the executor or administrator is entitled.

Real assets. Such as descend to the heir, as an estate in fee-simple.

In commercial law. The aggregate of available property, stock in trade, cash, etc., belonging to a merchant or mercantile company.

The word "assets," though more generally used to denote everything which comes to the representatives of a deceased person, yet is by no means confined to that use, but has come to signify everything which can be made available for the payment of debts, whether belonging to the estate of a deceased person or not. Hence we speak of the assets of a bank or other monied corporation, the assets of an insolvent debtor, and the assets of an individual or private copartnership; and we always use this word when we speak of the means which a party has, as compared with his liabilities or debts. 26 Conn. 449.

The property or effects of a bankrupt or insolvent, applicable to the payment of his debts.

The term "assets" includes all property of every kind and nature, chargeable with the debts of the bankrupt, that comes into the hands of and under the control of the assignee; and the value thereof is not to be considered a less sum than that actually realized out of said property, and received by the assignee for it. 16 N. B. R. 351.

ASSETS ENTRE MAINS. L. Fr. Assets in hand; assets in the hands of executors or administrators, applicable for the payment of debts. Termes de la Ley; 2 Bl. Comm. 510; 1 Crabb, Real Prop. 23.

ASSEVERATION. An affirmation; a positive assertion; a solemn declaration. This word is seldom, if ever, used for a declaration made under oath, but denotes a declaration accompanied with solemnity or an appeal to conscience.

ASSEWIARE. To draw or drain water from marsh grounds. Cowell.

ASSIGN, v. In conveyancing. To make or set over to another; to transfer; as to assign property, or some interest therein. Cowell; 2 Bl. Comm. 326.

In practice. To appoint, allot, select, or designate for a particular purpose, or duty.

AM. DICT. LAW—7

Thus, in England, justices are said to be "*assigned* to take the assises," "*assigned* to hold pleas," "*assigned* to make gaol delivery," "*assigned* to keep the peace," etc. St. Westm. 2, c. 30; Reg. Orig. 68, 69; 3 Bl. Comm. 58, 59, 353; 1 Bl. Comm. 351.

To transfer persons, as a sheriff is said to assign prisoners in his custody.

To point at, or point out; to set forth, or specify; to mark out or designate; as to *assign errors* on a writ of error; to *assign breaches* of a covenant. 2 Tidd, Pr. 1168; 1 Tidd, 686.

ASSIGNABLE. That may be assigned or transferred; transferable; negotiable, as a bill of exchange. Comb. 176; Story, Bills, § 17.

ASSIGNATION. A Scotch law term equivalent to assignment, (*q. v.*)

Assignatus utitur jure auctoris. An assignee uses the right of his principal; an assignee is clothed with the rights of his principal. Halk. Max. p. 14; Broom, Max. 465.

ASSIGNAY. In Scotch law. An assignee.

ASSIGNEE. A person to whom an assignment is made. The term is commonly used in reference to personal property; but it is not incorrect, in some cases, to apply it to realty, *e. g.,* "assignee of the reversion."

Assignee in fact is one to whom an assignment has been made in fact by the party having the right.

Assignee in law is one in whom the law vests the right; as an executor or administrator.

The word has a special and distinctive use as employed to designate one to whom, under an insolvent or bankrupt law, the whole estate of a debtor is transferred to be administered for the benefit of creditors.

In old law. A person deputed or appointed by another to do any act, or perform any business. Blount. An *assignee,* however, was distinguished from a *deputy,* being said to occupy a thing in his own right, while a deputy acted in right of another. Cowell.

ASSIGNMENT. In contracts. 1. The act by which one person transfers to another, or causes to vest in that other, the whole of the right, interest, or property which he has in any realty or personality, in possession or in action, or any share, interest, or subsidiary estate therein. More particularly, a *written* transfer of property, as distinguished from a transfer by mere delivery.

2. In a narrower sense, the transfer or making over of the estate, right, or title which one has in lands and tenements; and, in an especially technical sense, the transfer of the unexpired residue of a term or estate for life or years.

Assignment does not include testamentary transfers. The idea of an assignment is essentially that of a transfer by one existing party to another existing party of some species of property or valuable interest, except in the case of an executor. 34 N. Y. 447.

3. A transfer or making over by a debtor of all his property and effects to one or more *assignees* in trust for the benefit of his creditors. 2 Story, Eq. Jur. § 1036.

4. The instrument or writing by which such a transfer of property is made.

5. A transfer of a bill, note, or check, not negotiable.

6. In bankruptcy proceedings, the word designates the setting over or transfer of the bankrupt's estate to the assignee.

ASSIGNMENT FOR BENEFIT OF CREDITORS. An assignment whereby a debtor, generally an insolvent, transfers to another his property, in trust to pay his debts or apply the property upon their payment.

ASSIGNMENT OF DOWER. Ascertaining a widow's right of dower by laying out or marking off one-third of her deceased husband's lands, and setting off the same for her use during life.

ASSIGNMENT OF ERRORS. In practice. The statement of the plaintiff's case on a writ of error, setting forth the errors complained of; corresponding with the declaration in an ordinary action. 2 Tidd, Pr. 1168; 3 Steph. Comm. 644.

There is not, in the strict common-law sense of the term, any assignment of errors required to be filed by the appellant. What is meant by the term, as heretofore used by this court, is that a specification must be filed of the errors upon which the appellant will rely, with such fullness as to give aid to the court in the examination of the transcript. 10 Cal. 298.

ASSIGNMENT WITH PREFERENCES. An assignment for the benefit of creditors, with directions to the assignee to prefer a specified creditor or class of creditors, by paying their claims in full before the others receive any dividend, or in some other manner. More usually termed a "preferential assignment."

ASSIGNOR. One who makes an assignment of any kind; one who assigns or transfers property.

ASSIGNS. Assignees; those to whom property shall have been transferred. Now seldom used except in the phrase, in deeds, "heirs, administrators, and assigns." 8 R. I. 36.

ASSISA. In old English and Scotch law. An assise; a kind of jury or inquest; a writ; a sitting of a court; an ordinance or statute; a fixed or specific time, number, quantity, quality, price, or weight; a tribute, fine, or tax; a real action; the name of a writ. See ASSISE.

ASSISA ARMORUM. Assise of arms. A statute or ordinance requiring the keeping of arms for the common defense. Hale, Com. Law, c. 11.

ASSISA CADERE. To fail in the assise; *i. e.*, to be nonsuited. Cowell; 3 Bl. Comm. 402.

ASSISA CADIT IN JURATUM. The assise falls (turns) into a jury; hence to submit a controversy to trial by jury.

ASSISA CONTINUANDA. An ancient writ addressed to the justices of assise for the continuation of a cause, when certain facts put in issue could not have been proved in time by the party alleging them. Reg. Orig. 217.

ASSISA DE CLARENDON. The assise of Clarendon. A statute or ordinance passed in the tenth year of Henry II., by which those that were accused of any heinous crime, and not able to purge themselves, but must abjure the realm, had liberty of forty days to stay and try what succor they could get of their friends towards their sustenance in exile. Bract. fol. 136; Co. Litt. 159*a*; Cowell.

ASSISA DE FORESTA. Assise of the forest; a statute concerning orders to be observed in the royal forests.

ASSISA DE MENSURIS. Assise of measures. A common rule for weights and measures, established throughout England by Richard I., in the eighth year of his reign. Hale, Com. Law, c. 7.

ASSISA DE NOCUMENTO. An assise of nuisance; a writ to abate or redress a nuisance.

ASSISA DE UTRUM. An obsolete writ, which lay for the parson of a church whose predecessor had alienated the land and rents of it.

ASSISA FRISCÆ FORTIÆ. Assise of fresh force, which see.

ASSISA MORTIS D'ANCESTORIS. Assise of *mort d'ancestor*, which see.

ASSISA NOVÆ DISSEYSINÆ. Assise of novel disseisin, which see.

ASSISA PANIS ET CEREVISIÆ. Assise of bread and ale, or beer. The name of a statute passed in the fifty-first year of Henry III., containing regulations for the sale of bread and ale; sometimes called the "statute of bread and ale." Co. Litt. 159b; 2 Reeve, Hist. Eng. Law, 56; Cowell; Bract. fol. 155.

ASSISA PROROGANDA. An obsolete writ, which was directed to the judges assigned to take assises, to stay proceedings, by reason of a party to them being employed in the king's business. Reg. Orig. 208.

ASSISA ULTIMÆ PRÆSENTATIONIS. Assise of darrein presentment, (*q. v.*)

ASSISA VENALIUM. The assise of salable commodities, or of things exposed for sale.

ASSISE, or ASSIZE. 1. An ancient species of court, consisting of a certain number of men, usually twelve, who were summoned together to try a disputed cause, performing the functions of a jury, except that they gave a verdict from their own investigation and knowledge and not upon evidence adduced. From the fact that they sat together, (*assideo*,) they were called the "assise." See Bract. 4, 1, 6; Co. Litt. 153b, 159b.

A court composed of an assembly of knights and other substantial men, with the baron or justice, in a certain place, at an appointed time. Grand Cou. cc. 24, 25.

2. The verdict or judgment of the jurors or recognitors of assise. 3 Bl. Comm. 57, 59.

3. In modern English law, the name "assises" or "assizes" is given to the court, time, or place where the judges of assise and *nisi prius*, who are sent by special commission from the crown on circuits through the kingdom, proceed to take indictments, and to try such disputed causes issuing out of the courts at Westminster as are then ready for trial, with the assistance of a jury from the particular county; the regular sessions of the judges at *nisi prius*.

4. Anything reduced to a certainty in respect to time, number, quantity, quality, weight, measure, etc. Spelman.

5. An ordinance, statute, or regulation. Spelman gives this meaning of the word the first place among his definitions, observing that *statutes* were in England called "assises" down to the reign of Henry III.

6. A species of writ, or real action, said to have been invented by Glanville, chief justice to Henry II., and having for its object to determine the right of possession of lands, and to recover the possession. 3 Bl. Comm. 184, 185.

7. The whole proceedings in court upon a writ of assise. Co. Litt. 159b. The verdict or finding of the jury upon such a writ. 3 Bl. Comm. 57.

ASSISE OF CLARENDON. See Assisa de Clarendon.

ASSISE OF DARREIN PRESENTMENT. A writ of assise which formerly lay when a man or his ancestors under whom he claimed presented a clerk to a benefice, who was instituted, and afterwards, upon the next avoidance, a stranger presented a clerk and thereby disturbed the real patron. 3 Bl. Comm. 245; St. 13 Edw. I. (Westm. 2) c. 5. It has given way to the remedy by *quare impedit*.

ASSISE OF FRESH FORCE. In old English practice. A writ which lay by the usage and custom of a city or borough, where a man was disseised of his lands and tenements in such city or borough. It was called "fresh force," because it was to be sued within forty days after the party's title accrued to him. Fitzh. Nat. Brev. 7 C.

ASSISE OF MORT D'ANCESTOR. A real action which lay to recover land of which a person had been deprived on the death of his ancestor by the abatement or intrusion of a stranger. 3 Bl. Comm. 185; Co. Litt. 159a. It was abolished by St. 3 & 4 Wm. IV. c. 27.

ASSISE OF NOVEL DISSEISIN. A writ of assise which lay for the recovery of lands or tenements, where the claimant had been lately disseised.

ASSISE OF NUISANCE. A writ of assise which lay where a nuisance had been committed to the complainant's freehold; either for abatement of the nuisance or for damages.

ASSISE OF THE FOREST. A statute touching orders to be observed in the king's forests. Manwood, 35.

ASSISE RENTS. The certain established rents of the freeholders and ancient copyholders of a manor; so called because they are *assised*, or made precise and certain.

ASSISER. An assessor; juror; an officer who has the care and oversight of weights and measures.

ASSISORS. In Scotch law. Jurors; the persons who formed that kind of court which in Scotland was called an "assise," for the purpose of inquiring into and judging divers civil causes, such as perambulations, cognitions, molestations, purprestures, and other matters; like jurors in England. Holthouse.

ASSISTANCE. The name of a writ which issues from the court of chancery, in aid of the execution of a judgment at law, to put the complainant into possession of lands adjudged to him, when the sheriff cannot execute the judgment.

ASSISTANT JUDGE. A judge of the English court of general or quarter sessions in Middlesex. He differs from the other justices in being a barrister of ten years' standing, and in being salaried. St. 7 & 8 Vict. c. 71; 22 & 23 Vict. c. 4; Pritch. Quar. Sess. 31.

ASSISUS. Rented or farmed out for a specified assise; that is, a payment of a certain assessed rent in money or provisions.

ASSITHMENT. Weregeld or compensation by a pecuniary mulct. Cowell.

ASSIZE. In the practice of the criminal courts of Scotland, the fifteen men who decide on the conviction or acquittal of an accused person are called the "assize," though in popular language, and even in statutes, they are called the "jury." Wharton. See ASSISE.

ASSIZES. Sessions of the justices or commissioners of assize. See ASSISE.

ASSIZES DE JERUSALEM. A code of feudal jurisprudence prepared by an assembly of barons and lords A. D. 1099, after the conquest of Jerusalem.

ASSOCIATE. An officer in each of the English courts of common law, appointed by the chief judge of the court, and holding his office during good behavior, whose duties were to superintend the entry of causes, to attend the sittings of *nisi prius*, and there receive and enter verdicts, and to draw up the posteas and any orders of *nisi prius*. The associates are now officers of the Supreme Court of Judicature, and are styled "Masters of the Supreme Court." Wharton.

A person associated with the judges and clerk of assise in the commission of general jail delivery. Mozley & Whitley.

The term is frequently used of the judges of appellate courts, other than the presiding judge or chief justice.

ASSOCIATION. The act of a number of persons who unite or join together for some special purpose or business. The union of a company of persons for the transaction of designated affairs, or the attainment of some common object.

An unincorporated society; a body of persons united and acting together without a charter, but upon the methods and forms used by incorporated bodies for the prosecution of some common enterprise.

In English law. A writ directing certain persons (usually the clerk and his subordinate officers) to associate themselves with the justices and sergeants for the purposes of taking the assises. 3 Bl. Comm. 59, 60.

ASSOCIÉ EN NOM. In French law. In a *société en commandité* an *associé en nom* is one who is liable for the engagements of the undertaking to the whole extent of his property. This expression arises from the fact that the names of the *associés* so liable figure in the firm-name or form part of the *société en nom collectif*. Arg. Fr. Merc. Law, 546.

ASSOIL. To absolve; acquit; to set free; to deliver from excommunication. St. 1 Hen. IV. c. 7; Cowell.

ASSOILZIE. In Scotch law. To acquit the defendant in an action; to find a criminal not guilty.

ASSUME. To undertake; engage; promise. 1 Ld. Raym. 122; 4 Coke, 92.

A stipulation in a deed, accepted by the grantee, that he shall "assume" an outstanding mortgage on the premises conveyed, is broken by a failure to pay the mortgage debt within a reasonable time after its maturity. 12 Cush. 227.

ASSUMPSIT. Lat. He undertook; he promised. A promise or engagement by which one person assumes or undertakes to do some act or pay something to another. It may be either oral or in writing, but is not under seal. It is *express* if the promisor puts his engagement in distinct and definite language; it is *implied* where the law infers a promise (though no formal one has passed) from the conduct of the party or the circumstances of the case.

In practice. A form of action which lies for the recovery of damages for the non-performance of a parol or simple contract; or a contract that is neither of record nor under seal. 7 Term, 351; 3 Johns. Cas. 60.

The ordinary division of this action is into (1) common or *indebitatus assumpsit*, brought for the most part on an implied promise; and (2) special *assumpsit*, founded on an express promise. Steph. Pl. 11, 13.

The action of *assumpsit* differs from *trespass* and *trover*, which are founded on a tort, not upon a contract; from *covenant* and *debt*, which are appropriate where the ground of recovery is a sealed instrument, or special obligation to pay a fixed sum; and from *replevin*, which seeks the recovery of specific property, if attainable, rather than of damages.

ASSURANCE. In conveyancing. A deed or instrument of conveyance. The legal evidences of the transfer of property are in England called the "common assurances" of the kingdom, whereby every man's estate is *assured* to him, and all controversies, doubts, and difficulties are either prevented or removed. 2 Bl. Comm. 294.

In contracts. A making secure; insurance. The term was formerly of very frequent use in the modern sense of insurance, particularly in English maritime law, and still appears in the policies of some companies, but is otherwise seldom seen of late years. There seems to be a tendency, however, to use *assurance* for the contracts of life insurance companies, and *insurance* for risks upon property.

ASSURED. A person who has been insured by some insurance company, or underwriter, against losses or perils mentioned in the policy of insurance.

ASSURER. An insurer against certain perils and dangers; an underwriter; an indemnifier.

ASSYTHEMENT. In Scotch law. Damages awarded to the relative of a murdered person from the guilty party, who has not been convicted and punished. Paters. Comp.

ASTIPULATION. A mutual agreement, assent, and consent between parties; also a witness or record.

ASTITRARIUS HÆRES. An heir apparent who has been placed, by conveyance, in possession of his ancestor's estate during such ancestor's life-time. Co. Litt. 8.

ASTITUTION. An arraignment, (*q. v.*)

ASTRARIUS. In old English law. A householder; belonging to the house; a person in actual possession of a house.

ASTRER. In old English law. A householder, or occupant of a house or hearth.

ASTRICT. In Scotch law. To assign to a particular mill.

ASTRICTION TO A MILL. A servitude by which grain growing on certain lands or brought within them must be carried to a certain mill to be ground, a certain multure or price being paid for the same. Jacob.

ASTRIHILTET. In Saxon law. A penalty for a wrong done by one in the king's peace. The offender was to replace the damage twofold. Spelman.

ASTRUM. A house, or place of habitation. Bract. fol. 267*b*; Cowell.

ASYLUM. 1. A sanctuary, or place of refuge and protection, where criminals and debtors found shelter, and from which they could not be taken without sacrilege. 6 Neb. 291.

2. Shelter; refuge; protection from the hand of justice. The word includes not only place, but also shelter, security, protection; and a fugitive from justice, who has committed a crime in a foreign country, "seeks an asylum" at all times when he claims the use of the territories of the United States. 12 Blatchf. 395.

3. An institution for the protection and relief of unfortunates, as asylums for the poor, for the deaf and dumb, or for the insane.

AT ARM'S LENGTH. Beyond the reach of personal influence or control. Parties are said to deal "at arm's length" when each stands upon the strict letter of his rights, and conducts the business in a formal manner, without trusting to the other's fairness or integrity, and without being subject to the other's control or overmastering influence.

AT BAR. Before the court. "The case at bar," etc. Dyer, 31.

AT LARGE. (1) Not limited to any particular place, district, person, matter, or question. (2) Free; unrestrained; not under corporal control; as a ferocious animal so free from restraint as to be liable to do mischief. (3) Fully; in detail; in an extended form.

AT LAW. According to law; by, for, or in law; particularly in distinction from that which is done in or according to equity; or in titles such as sergeant at law, barrister at law, attorney or counsellor at law.

AT SEA. Out of the limits of any port or harbor on the sea-coast. 1 Story, 251.

ATAMITA. In the civil law. A great-great-great-grandfather's sister.

ATAVIA. In the civil law. A great-grandmother's grandmother.

ATAVUNCULUS. The brother of a great-grandfather's grandmother.

ATAVUS. The great-grandfather's or great-grandmother's grandfather; a fourth grandfather. The ascending line of lineal ancestry runs thus: *Pater, Avus, Proavus, Abavus, Atavus, Tritavus.* The seventh generation in the ascending scale will be *Tritavi-pater,* and the next above it *Proavi-atavus.*

ATHA. In Saxon law. An oath; the power or privilege of exacting and administering an oath. Spelman.

ATHEIST. One who does not believe in the existence of a God.

ATIA. Hatred or ill-will. See DE ODIO ET ATIA.

ATILIUM. The tackle or rigging of a ship; the harness or tackle of a plow. Spelman.

ATMATERTERA. A great-grandfather's grandmother's sister, (*ataviæ soror;*) called by Bracton "*atmatertera magna.*" Bract. fol. 68b.

ATPATRUUS. The brother of a great-grandfather's grandfather.

ATTACH. To take or apprehend by commandment of a writ or precept.

It differs from *arrest,* because it takes not only the body, but sometimes the goods, whereas an arrest is only against the person; besides, he who attaches keeps the party attached in order to produce him in court on the day named, but he who arrests lodges the person arrested in the custody of a higher power, to be forthwith disposed of. Fleta, lib. 5, c. 24. See ATTACHMENT.

ATTACHÉ. A person attached to the suite of an ambassador or to a foreign legation.

ATTACHIAMENTA BONORUM. A distress formerly taken upon goods and chattels, by the legal *attachiators* or bailiffs, as security to answer an action for personal estate or debt.

ATTACHIAMENTA DE SPINIS ET BOSCIS. A privilege granted to the officers of a forest to take to their own use thorns, brush, and windfalls, within their precincts. Kenn. Par. Antiq. 209.

ATTACHMENT. The act or process of taking, apprehending, or seizing persons or property, by virtue of a writ, summons, or other judicial order, and bringing the same into the custody of the law; used either for the purpose of bringing a person before the court, of acquiring jurisdiction over the property seized, to compel an appearance, to furnish security for debt or costs, or to arrest a fund in the hands of a third person who may become liable to pay it over.

Also the writ or other process for the accomplishment of the purposes above enumerated, this being the more common use of the word.

Of persons. A writ issued by a court of record, commanding the sheriff to bring before it a person who has been guilty of contempt of court, either in neglect or abuse of its process or of subordinate powers. 3 Bl. Comm. 280; 4 Bl. Comm, 283.

Of property. A species of mesne process, by which a writ is issued at the institution or during the progress of an action, commanding the sheriff to seize the property, rights, credits, or effects of the defendant to be held as security for the satisfaction of such judgment as the plaintiff may recover. It is principally used against absconding, concealed, or fraudulent debtors.

To give jurisdiction. Where the defendant is a non-resident, or beyond the territorial jurisdiction of the court, his goods or land within the territory may be seized upon process of attachment; whereby he will be compelled to enter an appearance, or the court acquires jurisdiction so far as to dispose of the property attached. This is sometimes called "foreign attachment."

Domestic and foreign. In some jurisdictions it is common to give the name "domestic attachment" to one issuing against a resident debtor, (upon the special ground of fraud, intention to abscond, etc.,) and to designate an attachment against a non-resident, or his property, as "foreign." But the term "foreign attachment" more properly belongs to the process otherwise familiarly known as "garnishment." It was a peculiar and ancient remedy open to creditors within the jurisdiction of the city of London, by which they were enabled to satisfy their own debts by attaching or seizing the money or goods of the debtor in the hands of a third person within the jurisdiction of the city. This power and process survive in modern law, in all common-law jurisdictions, and are variously denominated "garnishment," "trustee process," or "factorizing."

ATTACHMENT OF PRIVILEGE. In English law. A process by which a man, by virtue of his privilege, calls another to litigate in that court to which he himself belongs, and who has the privilege to answer there.

A writ issued to apprehend a person in a privileged place. Termes de la Ley.

ATTACHMENT OF THE FOREST. One of the three courts formerly held in forests. The highest court was called "justice in eyre's seat;" the middle, the "swainmote;" and the lowest, the "attachment." Manwood, 90, 99.

ATTAINDER. That extinction of civil rights and capacities which takes place whenever a person who has committed treason or felony receives sentence of death for his crime. 1 Steph. Comm. 408; 1 Bish. Crim. Law, § 641.

It differs from conviction, in that it is *after* judgment, whereas conviction is upon the verdict of guilty, but *before* judgment pronounced, and may be quashed upon some point of law reserved, or judgment may be arrested. The consequences of attainder are forfeiture of property and corruption of blood. 4 Bl. Comm. 380.

At the common law, attainder resulted in three ways, viz.: *by confession, by verdict,* and *by process* or *outlawry.* The first case was where the prisoner pleaded guilty at the bar, or having fled to sanctuary, confessed his guilt and abjured the realm to save his life. The second was where the prisoner pleaded not guilty at the bar, and the jury brought in a verdict against him. The third, when the person accused made his escape and was outlawed.

ATTAINDER, BILL OF. See BILL OF ATTAINDER.

ATTAINT. In old English practice. A writ which lay to inquire whether a jury of twelve men had given a false verdict, in order that the judgment might be reversed. 3 Bl. Comm. 402; Bract. fol. 288b–292. This inquiry was made by a grand assise or jury of twenty-four persons, and, if they found the verdict a false one, the judgment was that the jurors should become infamous, should forfeit their goods and the profits of their lands, should themselves be imprisoned, and their wives and children thrust out of doors, should have their houses razed, their trees extirpated, and their meadows plowed up, and that the plaintiff should be restored to all that he lost by reason of the unjust verdict. 3 Bl. Comm. 404; Co. Litt. 294b.

A person was said to be attaint when he was under attainder, (*q. v.*) Co. Litt. 390b.

ATTAINT D'UNE CAUSE. In French law. The gain of a suit.

ATTEMPT. In criminal law. An effort or endeavor to accomplish a crime, amounting to more than mere preparation or planning for it, and which, if not prevented, would have resulted in the full consummation of the act attempted, but which, in fact, does not bring to pass the party's ultimate design.

An intent to do a particular criminal thing combined with an act which falls short of the thing intended. 1 Bish. Crim. Law, § 728.

There is a marked distinction between "attempt" and "intent." The former conveys the idea of physical effort to accomplish an act; the latter, the quality of mind with which an act was done. To charge, in an indictment, an assault with an attempt to murder, is not equivalent to charging an assault with intent to murder. 14 Ala. 411.

ATTENDANT. One who owes a duty or service to another, or in some sort depends upon him. Termes de la Ley. One who follows and waits upon another.

ATTENDANT TERMS. In English law. Terms, (usually mortgages,) for a long period of years, which are created or kept outstanding for the purpose of *attending* or waiting upon and protecting the inheritance. 1 Steph. Comm. 351.

A phrase used in conveyancing to denote estates which are kept alive, after the objects for which they were originally created have ceased, so that they might be deemed merged or satisfied, for the purpose of protecting or strengthening the title of the owner. Abbott.

ATTENTAT. Lat. He attempts. In the civil and canon law. Anything wrongfully innovated or *attempted* in a suit by an inferior judge, (or judge *a quo,*) pending an appeal. 1 Addams, 22, note; Shelf. Mar. & Div. 562.

ATTERMINARE. In old English law. To put off to a succeeding term; to prolong the time of payment of a debt. St. Westm. 2, c. 4; Cowell; Blount.

ATTERMINING. In old English law. A putting off; the granting of a time or term, as for the payment of a debt. Cowell.

ATTERMOIEMENT. In canon law. A making terms; a composition, as with creditors. 7 Low. Can. 272, 306.

ATTEST. To witness the execution of a written instrument, at the request of him who makes it, and subscribe the same as a witness. This is also the technical word by which, in the practice in many of the states, a certifying officer gives assurance of the genuineness and correctness of a copy.

An "attested" copy of a document is one which has been examined and compared with the original, with a certificate or memorandum of its correctness, signed by the persons who have examined it.

ATTESTATION. The act of witnessing an instrument in writing, at the request of the party making the same, and subscribing it as a witness. 3 P. Wms. 254; 2 Ves. Sr. 454; 17 Pick. 373.

Execution and *attestation* are clearly distinct formalities; the former being the act of the *party*, the latter of the *witnesses* only.

ATTESTATION CLAUSE. That clause wherein the witnesses certify that the instrument has been executed before them, and the manner of the execution of the same.

ATTESTING WITNESS. One who signs his name to an instrument, at the request of the party or parties, for the purpose of proving and identifying it.

ATTESTOR OF A CAUTIONER. In Scotch practice. A person who attests the sufficiency of a cautioner, and agrees to become *subsidiarie* liable for the debt. Bell.

ATTILE. In old English law. Rigging; tackle. Cowell.

ATTORN. In feudal law. To transfer or turn over to another. Where a lord aliened his seigniory, he might, with the consent of the tenant, and in some cases without, *attorn* or transfer the homage and service of the latter to the alienee or new lord. Bract. fols. 81b, 82.

In modern law. To consent to the transfer of a rent or reversion. A tenant is said to *attorn* when he agrees to become the tenant of the person to whom the reversion has been granted. See ATTORNMENT.

ATTORNARE. In feudal law. To attorn; to transfer or turn over; to appoint an attorney or substitute.

ATTORNARE REM. To turn over money or goods, *i. e.*, to assign or appropriate them to some particular use or service.

ATTORNATO FACIENDO VEL RECIPIENDO. In old English law. An obsolete writ, which commanded a sheriff or steward of a county court or hundred court to receive and admit an attorney to appear for the person who owed suit of court. Fitzh. Nat. Brev. 156.

ATTORNE. L. Fr. In old English law. An attorney. Britt. c. 126.

ATTORNEY. In the most general sense this term denotes an agent or substitute, or one who is appointed and authorized to act in the place or stead of another.

It is "an ancient English word, and signifieth one that is set in the turne, stead, or place of another; and of these some be private * * * and some be publike, as attorneys at law." Co. Litt. 51b, 128a; Britt. 285b.

One who is appointed by another to do something in his absence, and who has authority to act in the place and turn of him by whom he is delegated.

Attorneys, in the modern use, are of two sorts, attorneys at law and attorneys in fact, as to which see those titles.

ATTORNEY AT LARGE. In old practice. An attorney who practised in all the courts. Cowell.

ATTORNEY AT LAW. An advocate, counsel, official agent employed in preparing, managing, and trying cases in the courts. An officer in a court of justice, who is employed by a party in a cause to manage the same for him.

In English law. An attorney at law was a public officer belonging to the superior courts of common law at Westminster, who conducted legal proceedings on behalf of others, called his clients, by whom he was retained; he answered to the solicitor in the courts of chancery, and the proctor of the admiralty, ecclesiastical, probate, and divorce courts. An attorney was almost invariably also a solicitor. It is now provided by the judicature act, 1873, § 87, that solicitors, attorneys, or proctors of, or by law empowered to practise in, any court the jurisdiction of which is by that act transferred to the high court of justice or the court of appeal, shall be called "solicitors of the supreme court." Wharton.

The term is in use in America, and in most of the states includes "barrister," "counsellor," and "solicitor," in the sense in which those terms are used in England. In some states, as well as in the United States supreme court, "attorney" and "counsellor" are distinguishable, the former term being applied to the younger members of the bar, and to those who carry on the practice and formal parts of the suit, while "counsellor" is the adviser, or special counsel retained to try the cause. In some jurisdictions one must have been an attorney for a given time before he can be admitted to practise as a counsellor. Rap. & L.

ATTORNEY GENERAL. In English law. The chief law officer of the realm, being created by letters patent, whose office is to exhibit informations and prosecute for the crown in matters criminal, and to file bills in the exchequer in any matter concerning the king's revenue.

In American law. The attorney general of the United States is the head of the department of justice, appointed by the president, and a member of the cabinet. He appears in behalf of the government in all cases in the supreme court in which it is interested, and gives his legal advice to the president and heads of departments upon questions submitted to him.

In each state also there is an attorney general, or similar officer, who appears for the people, as in England the attorney general appears for the crown.

ATTORNEY IN FACT. A private attorney authorized by another to act in his place and stead, either for some particular purpose, as to do a particular act, or for the transaction of business in general, not of a legal character. This authority is conferred by an instrument in writing, called a "letter of attorney," or more commonly a "power of attorney." Bac. Abr. "Attorney;" Story, Ag. § 25.

ATTORNEY OF THE WARDS AND LIVERIES. In English law. This was the third officer of the Duchy court. Bac. Abr. "Attorney."

ATTORNEY'S CERTIFICATE. In English law. A certificate that the attorney named has paid the annual tax or duty. This is required to be taken out every year by all practising attorneys under a penalty of fifty pounds.

ATTORNEYSHIP. The office of an agent or attorney.

ATTORNMENT. In feudal and old English law. A turning over or transfer by a lord of the services of his tenant to the grantee of his seigniory.

Attornment is the act of a person who holds a leasehold interest in land, or estate for life or years, by which he agrees to become the tenant of a stranger who has acquired the fee in the land, or the remainder or reversion, or the right to the rent or services by which the tenant holds.

AU BESOIN. In case of need. A French phrase sometimes incorporated in a bill of exchange, pointing out some person from whom payment may be sought in case the drawee fails or refuses to pay the bill. Story, Bills, § 65.

AUBAINE. See DROIT D'AUBAINE.

AUCTION. A public sale of land or goods, at public outcry, to the highest bidder.

A sale by auction is a sale by public outcry to the highest bidder on the spot. Civil Code Cal. § 1792; Civil Code Dak. § 1022.

The sale by auction is that which takes place when the thing is offered publicly to be sold to whoever will give the highest price. Civil Code La. art. 2601.

Auction is very generally defined as a sale to the *highest* bidder, and this is the usual meaning. There may, however, be a sale to the *lowest* bidder, as where land is sold for non-payment of taxes to whomsoever will take it for the shortest term; or where a contract is offered to the one who will perform it at the lowest price. And these appear fairly included in the term "auction." Abbott.

AUCTIONARIÆ. Catalogues of goods for public sale or auction.

AUCTIONARIUS. One who bought and sold again at an increased price; an auctioneer. Spelman.

AUCTIONEER. A person authorized or licensed by law to sell lands or goods of other persons at public auction; one who sells at auction.

Auctioneers differ from *brokers*, in that the latter may both buy and sell, whereas auctioneers can only sell; also brokers may sell by private contract only, and auctioneers by public auction only. Auctioneers can only sell goods for ready money, but factors may sell upon credit.

AUCTOR. In the Roman law. An auctioneer.

In the civil law. A grantor or vendor of any kind.

In old French law. A plaintiff. Kelham.

AUCTORITAS. In the civil law. Authority.

In old European law. A diploma, or royal charter. A word frequently used by Gregory of Tours and later writers. Spelman.

Auctoritates philosophorum, medicorum, et poetarum, sunt in causis allegandæ et tenendæ. The opinions of philosophers, physicians, and poets are to be alleged and received in causes. Co. Litt. 264.

Aucupia verborum sunt judice indigna. Catching at words is unworthy of a judge. Hob. 343.

Audi alteram partem. Hear the other side; hear both sides. No man should be condemned unheard. Broom, Max. 113. See L. R. 2 P. C. 106.

AUDIENCE. In international law. A hearing; interview with the sovereign. The king or other chief executive of a country grants an audience to a foreign minister who comes to him duly accredited; and, after the recall of a minister, an "audience of leave" ordinarily is accorded to him.

AUDIENCE COURT. In English law. A court belonging to the Archbishop of Canterbury, having jurisdiction of matters of form only, as the confirmation of bishops, and the like. This court has the same authority with the Court of Arches, but is of inferior dignity and antiquity. The Dean of the Arches is the official auditor of the Audience court. The Archbishop of York has also his Audience court.

AUDIENDO ET TERMINANDO. A writ or commission to certain persons to appease and punish any insurrection or great riot. Fitzh. Nat. Brev. 110.

AUDIT. As a verb; to make an official investigation and examination of accounts and vouchers.

As a noun; the process of auditing accounts; the hearing and investigation had before an auditor.

AUDITA QUERELA. The name of a writ constituting the initial process in an action brought by a judgment defendant to obtain relief against the consequences of the judgment, on account of some matter of defense or discharge, arising since its rendition, and which could not be taken advantage of otherwise. See 1 Amer. & Eng. Enc. Law, 1003; Bac. Abr. *sub voce;* 3 Bl. Comm. 405.

AUDITOR. A public officer whose function is to examine and pass upon the accounts and vouchers of officers who have received and expended public money by lawful authority.

In practice. An officer (or officers) of the court, assigned to state the items of debit and credit between the parties in a suit where accounts are in question, and exhibit the balance. 1 Metc. (Mass.) 218.

In English law. An officer or agent of the crown, or of a private individual, or corporation, who examines periodically the accounts of under officers, tenants, stewards, or bailiffs, and reports the state of their accounts to his principal.

AUDITOR OF THE RECEIPTS. An officer of the English exchequer. 4 Inst. 107.

AUDITORS OF THE IMPREST. Officers in the English exchequer, who formerly had the charge of auditing the accounts of the customs, naval and military expenses, etc., now performed by the commissioners for auditing public accounts.

AUGMENTATION. The increase of the crown's revenues from the suppression of religious houses and the appropriation of their lands and revenues.

Also the name of a court (now abolished) erected 27 Hen. VIII., to determine suits and controversies relating to monasteries and abbey-lands.

Augusta legibus soluta non est. The empress or queen is not privileged or exempted from subjection to the laws. 1 Bl. Comm. 219; Dig. 1, 3, 31.

AULA. In old English law. A hall, or court; the court of a baron, or manor; a court baron. Spelman.

AULA ECCLESIÆ. A nave or body of a church where temporal courts were anciently held.

AULA REGIS. The chief court of England in early Norman times. It was established by William the Conqueror in his own hall. It was composed of the great officers of state, resident in the palace, and followed the king's household in all his expeditions.

AULNAGE. See ALNAGE.

AULNAGER. See ALNAGER.

AUMEEN. In Indian law. Trustee; commissioner; a temporary collector or supervisor, appointed to the charge of a country on the removal of a zemindar, or for any other particular purpose of local investigation or arrangement.

AUMIL. In Indian law. Agent; officer; native collector of revenue; superintendent of a district or division of a country, either on the part of the government zemindar or renter.

AUMILDAR. In Indian law. Agent; the holder of an office; an intendant and collector of the revenue, uniting civil, military, and financial powers under the Mohammedan government.

AUMONE, SERVICE IN. Where lands are given in alms to some church or religious house, upon condition that a service or prayers shall be offered at certain times for the repose of the donor's soul. Britt. 164.

AUNCEL WEIGHT. In English law. An ancient mode of weighing, described by Cowell as "a kind of weight with scales hanging, or hooks fastened to each end of a staff, which a man, lifting up upon his forefinger or hand, discerneth the quality or difference between the weight and the thing weighed."

AUNT. The sister of one's father or mother, and a relation in the third degree, correlative to niece or nephew.

AURES. A Saxon punishment by cutting off the ears, inflicted on those who robbed churches, or were guilty of any other theft.

AURUM REGINÆ. Queen's gold. A royal revenue belonging to every queen consort during her marriage with the king.

AUTER, Autre. L. Fr. Another; other.

AUTER ACTION PENDANT. L. Fr. In pleading. Another action pending. A species of plea in abatement. 1 Chit. Pl. 454.

AUTER DROIT. In right of another, *e. g.*, a trustee holds trust property in right of his *cestui que trust.* A *prochein amy* sues in right of an infant. 2 Bl. Comm. 176.

AUTHENTIC. Genuine; true; having the character and authority of an original; duly vested with all necessary formalities and legally attested; competent, credible, and reliable as evidence.

AUTHENTIC ACT. In the civil law. An act which has been executed before a notary or other public officer authorized to execute such functions, or which is testified by a public seal, or has been rendered public by the authority of a competent magistrate, or which is certified as being a copy of a public register. Nov. 73, c. 2; Cod. 7, 52, 6, 4, 21; Dig. 22, 4.

The *authentic act*, as relates to contracts, is that which has been executed before a notary public or other officer authorized to execute such functions, in presence of two witnesses, free, male, and aged at least fourteen years, or of three witnesses, if the party be blind. If the party does not know how to sign, the notary must cause him to affix his mark to the instrument. All *procès verbals* of sales of succession property, signed by the sheriff or other person making the same, by the purchaser and two witnesses, are authentic acts. Civil Code La. art. 2234.

AUTHENTICATION. In the law of evidence. The act or mode of giving authority or legal authenticity to a statute, record, or other written instrument, or a certified copy thereof, so as to render it legally admissible in evidence.

An attestation made by a proper officer by which he certifies that a record is in due form of law, and that the person who certifies it is the officer appointed so to do.

AUTHENTICS. In the civil law. A Latin translation of the Novels of Justinian by an anonymous author; so called because the Novels were translated *entire*, in order to distinguish it from the epitome made by Julian.

There is another collection so called, compiled by Irnier, of incorrect extracts from the Novels and inserted by him in the Code, in the places to which they refer.

AUTHENTICUM. In the civil law. An original instrument or writing; the original of a will or other instrument, as distinguished from a copy. Dig. 22, 4, 2; Id. 29, 3, 12.

AUTHOR. One who produces, by his own intellectual labor applied to the materials of his composition, an arrangement or compilation new in itself. 2 Blatchf. 39.

AUTHORITIES. Citations to statutes, precedents, judicial decisions, and text-books of the law, made on the argument of questions of law or the trial of causes before a court, in support of the legal positions contended for.

B

C

D

E

F

G

H

I

J

K

L

M

AUTHORITY. In contracts. The lawful delegation of power by one person to another.

In the English law relating to public administration, an authority is a body having jurisdiction in certain matters of a public nature.

In governmental law. Legal power; a right to command or to act; the right and power of public officers to require obedience to their orders lawfully issued in the scope of their public duties.

Authority to execute a deed must be given by deed. Com. Dig. "Attorney," C, 5; 4 Term, 313; 7 Term, 207; 1 Holt, 141; 9 Wend. 68, 75; 5 Mass. 11; 5 Bin. 613.

AUTO ACORDADO. In Spanish colonial law. An order emanating from some superior tribunal, promulgated in the name and by the authority of the sovereign. Schm. Civil Law, 93.

AUTOCRACY. The name of an unlimited monarchical government. A government at the will of one man, (called an "autocrat,") unchecked by constitutional restrictions or limitations.

AUTOGRAPH. The handwriting of any one.

AUTONOMY. The political independence of a nation; the right (and condition) of self-government.

AUTOPSY. The dissection of a dead body for the purpose of inquiring into the cause of death. Pub. St. Mass. 1882, p. 1288.

AUTRE. L. Fr. Another.

AUTRE VIE. L. Fr. Another's life. A person holding an estate for or during the life of another is called a tenant "*pur autre vie*," or "*pur terme d'autre vie*." Litt. § 56; 2 Bl. Comm. 120.

AUTREFOIS. At another time; formerly; before; heretofore.

AUTREFOIS ACQUIT. In criminal law. Formerly acquitted. The name of a plea in bar to a criminal action, stating that the defendant has been once already indicted and tried for the same alleged offense and has been acquitted.

AUTREFOIS ATTAINT. In criminal law. Formerly attainted. A plea that the defendant has already been attainted for one felony, and therefore cannot be criminally prosecuted for another. 4 Bl. Comm. 336.

AUTREFOIS CONVICT. Formerly convicted. In criminal law. A plea by a criminal in bar to an indictment that he has been formerly convicted of the same identical crime. 4 Bl. Comm. 336; 4 Steph. Comm. 404.

AUXILIUM. In feudal and old English law. Aid; a kind of tribute paid by the vassal to his lord, being one of the incidents of the tenure by knight's service. Spelman.

AUXILIUM AD FILIUM MILITEM FACIENDUM ET FILIAM MARITANDAM. An ancient writ which was addressed to the sheriff to levy compulsorily an aid towards the knighting of a son and the marrying of a daughter of the tenants *in capite* of the crown.

AUXILIUM CURIÆ. In old English law. A precept or order of court citing and convening a party, at the suit and request of another, to warrant something.

AUXILIUM REGIS. In English law. The king's aid or money levied for the royal use and the public service, as taxes granted by parliament.

AUXILIUM VICE COMITI. An ancient duty paid to sheriffs. Cowell.

AVAIL OF MARRIAGE. In feudal law. The right of marriage, which the lord or guardian in chivalry had of disposing of his infant ward in matrimony. A guardian in socage had also the same right, but not attended with the same advantage. 2 Bl. Comm. 88.

In Scotch law. A certain sum due by the heir of a deceased ward vassal, when the heir became of marriageable age. Ersk. Inst. 2, 5, 18.

AVAILABLE MEANS. This phrase, among mercantile men, is a term well understood to be anything which can readily be converted into money; but it is not necessarily or primarily money itself. 13 N. Y. 219; 32 N. Y. 224.

AVAILS. Profits, or proceeds. This word seems to have been construed only in reference to wills, and in them it means the *corpus* or proceeds of the estate after the payment of the debts. 1 Amer. & Eng. Enc. Law, 1039. See 3 N. Y. 276; 34 N. Y. 201.

AVAL. In French law. The guaranty of a bill of exchange; so called because usually placed at the foot or bottom (*aval*) of the bill. Story, Bills, § 394, 454.

The act of subscribing one's signature at

the bottom of a promissory note or of a bill of exchange; properly an act of suretyship, by the party signing, in favor of the party to whom the note or bill is given. 1 Low. Can. 221.

AVANTURE. Chance; hazard; mischance.

AVARIA, AVARIE. Average; the loss and damage suffered in the course of a navigation. Poth. Mar. Louage, 105.

AVENAGE. A certain quantity of oats paid by a tenant to his landlord as rent, or in lieu of some other duties.

AVENTURE, or ADVENTURE. A mischance causing the death of a man, as where a person is suddenly drowned or killed by any accident, without felony. Co. Litt. 391.

AVER. In pleading. To declare or assert; to set out distinctly and formally; to allege.

In old pleading. To avouch or verify. Litt. § 691; Co. Litt. 362b. To make or prove true; to make good or justify a plea.

AVER. In old English and French. A working beast; a horse or bullock.

AVER CORN. A rent reserved to religious houses, to be paid by their tenants in corn.

AVER ET TENER. In old conveyancing. To have and to hold.

AVER LAND. In feudal law. Land plowed by the tenant for the proper use of the lord of the soil.

AVER PENNY. Money paid towards the king's averages or carriages, and so to be freed thereof.

AVER SILVER. A custom or rent formerly so called.

AVERAGE. A medium, a mean proportion.

In old English law. A service by horse or carriage, anciently due by a tenant to his lord. Cowell. A labor or service performed with working cattle, horses, or oxen, or with wagons and carriages. Spelman.

Stubble, or remainder of straw and grass left in corn-fields after harvest. In Kent it is called "*gratten,*" and in other parts "*roughings.*"

In maritime law. Loss or damage accidentally happening to a vessel or to its cargo during a voyage.

Also a small duty paid to masters of ships, when goods are sent in another man's ship, for their care of the goods, over and above the freight.

In marine insurance. Where loss or damage occurs to a vessel or its cargo at sea, *average* is the adjustment and apportionment of such loss between the owner, the freight, and the cargo, in proportion to their respective interests and losses, in order that one may not suffer the whole loss, but each contribute ratably. It is of the following kinds:

General average (also called "gross") consists of expense purposely incurred, sacrifice made, or damage sustained for the common safety of the vessel, freight, and cargo, or the two of them, at risk, and is to be contributed for by the several interests in the proportion of their respective values exposed to the common danger, and ultimately surviving, including the amount of expense, sacrifice, or damage so incurred in the contributory value. 2 Phil. Ins. § 1269 et seq.

Particular average is a loss happening to the ship, freight, or cargo which is not to be shared by contribution among all those interested, but must be borne by the owner of the subject to which it occurs. It is thus called in contradistinction to *general* average.

Petty average is a term sometimes applied to small charges which were formerly assessed upon the cargo, viz., pilotage, towage, light-money, beaconage, anchorage, bridge-toll, quarantine, pier-money.

AVERAGE CHARGES. "Average charges for toll and transportation" are understood to mean, and do mean, charges made at a mean rate, obtained by dividing the entire receipts for toll and transportation by the whole quantity of tonnage carried, reduced to a common standard of tons moved one mile. 74 Pa. St. 190.

AVERAGE LOSS. In maritime law. A partial loss of goods or vessels insured, for which the insurers are bound to compensate the insured in the proportion which the loss bears to the whole insurance. 2 Steph. Comm. 178.

AVERAGE PRICES. Such as are computed on all the prices of any articles sold within a certain period or district.

AVERIA. In old English law. This term was applied to working cattle, such as horses, oxen, etc.

AVERIA CARRUCÆ. Beasts of the plow.

AVERIIS CAPTIS IN WITHERNAM. A writ granted to one whose cattle were unlawfully distrained by another and driven out of the county in which they were taken, so that they could not be replevied by the sheriff. Reg. Orig. 82.

AVERMENT. In pleading. A positive statement of facts, in opposition to argument or inference. 1 Chit. Pl. 320.

In old pleading. An offer to prove a plea, or pleading. The concluding part of a plea, replication, or other pleading, containing new affirmative matter, by which the party offers or declares himself "ready to *verify.*"

AVERRARE. In feudal law. A duty required from some customary tenants, to carry goods in a wagon or upon loaded horses.

AVERSIO. In the civil law. An averting or turning away. A term applied to a species of sale in gross or bulk. Letting a house altogether, instead of in chambers. 4 Kent, Comm. 517.

AVERSIO PERICULI. A turning away of peril. Used of a contract of insurance. 3 Kent, Comm. 263.

AVERUM. Goods, property, substance; a beast of burden. Spelman.

AVET. A term used in the Scotch law, signifying to abet or assist.

AVIA. In the civil law. A grandmother. Inst. 3, 6, 3.

AVIATICUS. In the civil law. A grandson.

AVIZANDUM. In Scotch law. To make *avizandum* with a process is to take it from the public court to the private consideration of the judge. Bell.

AVOCAT. Fr. Advocate; an advocate.

AVOID. To annul; cancel; make void; to destroy the efficacy of anything.

AVOIDANCE. A making void, or of no effect; annulling, cancelling; escaping or evading.

In English ecclesiastical law. The term describes the condition of a benefice when it has no incumbent.

In parliamentary language, avoidance of a decision signifies evading or superseding a question, or escaping the coming to a decision upon a pending question. Holthouse.

In pleading. The allegation or statement of new matter, in opposition to a former pleading, which, admitting the facts alleged in such former pleading, shows cause why they should not have their ordinary legal effect.

AVOIRDUPOIS. The name of a system of weights (sixteen ounces to the pound) used in weighing articles other than medicines, metals, and precious stones.

AVOUCHER. The calling upon a warrantor of lands to fulfil his undertaking.

AVOUÉ. In French law. A barrister, advocate, attorney. An officer charged with representing and defending parties before the tribunal to which he is attached. Duverger.

AVOW. In pleading. To acknowledge and justify an act done.

To make an avowry. For example, when replevin is brought for a thing distrained, and the party taking claims that he had a right to make the distress, he is said to avow.

AVOWANT. One who makes an avowry.

AVOWEE. In ecclesiastical law. An advocate of a church benefice.

AVOWRY. A pleading in the action of replevin, by which the defendant *avows*, that is, acknowledges, the taking of the distress or property complained of, where he took it in his own right, and sets forth the reason of it; as for rent in arrear, damage done, etc. 3 Bl. Comm. 149; 1 Tidd, Pr. 645.

Avowry is the setting forth, as in a declaration, the nature and merits of the defendant's case, showing that the distress taken by him was lawful, which must be done with such sufficient authority as will entitle him to a *retorno habendo.* 6 Hill, 284.

An avowry must be distinguished from a *justification.* The former species of plea admits the plaintiff's ownership of the property, but alleges a right in the defendant sufficient to warrant him in taking the property and which still subsists. A justification, on the other hand, denies that the plaintiff had the right of property or possession in the subject-matter, alleging it to have been in the defendant or a third person, or avers a right sufficient to warrant the defendant in taking it, although such right has not continued in force to the time of making answer.

AVOWTERER. In English law. An adulterer with whom a married woman continues in adultery. Termes de la Ley.

AVOWTRY. In old English law. Adultery. Termes de la Ley.

AVULSION. The removal of a considerable quantity of soil from the land of one man, and its deposit upon or annexation to the land of another, suddenly and by the perceptible action of water. 2 Washb. Real Prop. 452.

The property of the part thus separated continues in the original proprietor, in which respect avulsion differs from alluvion, by which an addition is insensibly made to a property by the gradual washing down of the river, and which addition becomes the property of the owner of the lands to which the addition is made. Wharton.

AVUNCULUS. In the civil law. A mother's brother. 2 Bl. Comm. 230. *Avunculus magnus,* a great-uncle. *Avunculus major,* a great-grandmother's brother. *Avunculus maximus,* a great-great-grandmother's brother. See Dig. 38, 10, 10; Inst. 3, 6, 2.

AVUS. In the civil law. A grandfather. Inst. 3, 6, 1.

AWAIT. A term used in old statutes, signifying a lying in wait, or waylaying.

AWARD, *v.* To grant, concede, adjudge to. Thus, a jury *awards* damages; the court *awards* an injunction.

AWARD, *n.* The decision or determination rendered by arbitrators or commissioners, or other private or extrajudicial deciders, upon a controversy submitted to them; also the writing or document embodying such decision.

AWAY-GOING CROP. A crop sown before the expiration of a tenancy, which cannot ripen until after its expiration, to which, however, the tenant is entitled. Broom, Max. 412.

AWM. In old English statutes. A measure of wine, or vessel containing forty gallons.

AXIOM. In logic. A self-evident truth; an indisputable truth.

AYANT CAUSE. In French law. This term signifies one to whom a right has been assigned, either by will, gift, sale, exchange, or the like; an assignee. An *ayant cause* differs from an heir who acquires the right by inheritance. 8 Toullier, n. 245. The term is used in Louisiana.

AYLE. See AIEL.

AYRE. In old Scotch law. Eyre; a circuit, eyre, or iter.

AYUNTAMIENTO. In Spanish law. A congress of persons; the municipal council of a city or town. 1 White, Coll. 416; 12 Pet. 442, notes.

AZURE. A term used in heraldry, signifying blue.

B

C

D

E

F

G

H

I

J

K

L

M

B.

B. The second letter of the English alphabet: is used to denote the second of a series of pages, notes, etc.; the subsequent letters, the third and following numbers.

B. C. An abbreviation for "before Christ," "bail court," and "bankruptcy cases."

B. E. An abbreviation for "Baron of the Court of Exchequer."

B. F. An abbreviation for *bonum factum,* a good or proper act, deed, or decree; signifies "approved."

B. R. An abbreviation for *Bancus Regis,* (King's Bench,) or *Bancus Reginæ,* (Queen's Bench.) It is frequently found in the old books as a designation of that court. In more recent usage, the initial letters of the English names are ordinarily employed, *i. e.,* K. B. or Q. B.

B. S. *Bancus Superior,* that is, upper bench.

" BABY ACT." A plea of infancy, interposed for the purpose of defeating an action upon a contract made while the person was a minor, is vulgarly called "pleading the baby act." By extension, the term is applied to a plea of the statute of limitations.

BACHELERIA. In old records. Commonalty or yeomanry, in contradistinction to baronage.

BACHELOR. The holder of the first or lowest degree conferred by a college or university, *e. g.,* a bachelor of arts, bachelor of law, etc.
A kind of inferior knight; an esquire.
A man who has never been married.

BACKWATER. Water in a stream which, in consequence of some dam or obstruction below, is detained or checked in its course, or flows back.
Water caused to flow backward from a steam-vessel by reason of the action of its wheels or screw.

BACKBEAR. In forest law. Carrying on the back. One of the cases in which an offender against vert and venison might be arrested, as being taken with the mainour, or manner, or found carrying a deer off on his *back.* Manwood; Cowell.

BACKBEREND. Sax. Bearing upon the back or about the person. Applied to a thief taken with the stolen property in his immediate possession. Bract. 1, 3, tr. 2, c. 32. Used with *handhabend,* having in the hand.

BACKBOND. In Scotch law. A deed attaching a qualification or condition to the terms of a conveyance or other instrument. This deed is used when particular circumstances render it necessary to express in a separate form the limitations or qualifications of a right. Bell. The instrument is equivalent to a declaration of trust in English conveyancing.

BACKING. Indorsement; indorsement by a magistrate.

BACKING A WARRANT. The warrant of a justice of the peace cannot be enforced or executed outside of his territorial jurisdiction unless a magistrate of the jurisdiction where it is to be executed indorses or writes on the back of such warrant an authority for that purpose, which is thence termed "backing the warrant."

BACKSIDE. In English law. A term formerly used in conveyances and also in pleading; it imports a yard at the back part of or behind a house, and belonging thereto.

BACKWARDATION. In the language of the stock exchange, this term signifies a consideration paid for delay in the delivery of stock contracted for, when the price is lower for time than for cash. Dos Passos, Stock-Brok. 270.

BACKWARDS. In a policy of marine insurance, the phrase "forwards and backwards at sea" means from port to port in the course of the voyage, and not merely from one terminus to the other and back. 1 Taunt. 475.

BACULUS. A rod, staff, or wand, used in old English practice in making livery of seisin where no building stood on the land, (Bract. 40;) a stick or wand, by the erection of which on the land involved in a real action the defendant was summoned to put in his appearance; this was called *"baculus nuntiatorius."* 3 Bl. Comm. 279.

BAD, (in substance.) The technical word for unsoundness in pleading.

BADGE. A mark or cognizance worn to show the relation of the wearer to any person or thing; the token of anything; a distinctive mark of office or service.

BADGE OF FRAUD. A term used relatively to the law of fraudulent conveyances made to hinder and defraud creditors. It is defined as a fact tending to throw suspicion upon a transaction, and calling for an explanation. Bump, Fraud. Conv. 31.

BADGER. In old English law. One who made a practice of buying corn or victuals in one place, and carrying them to another to sell and make profit by them.

BAG. A certain and customary quantity of goods and merchandise in a sack. Wharton.

BAGA. In English law. A bag or purse. Thus there is the petty-bag-office in the common-law jurisdiction of the court of chancery, because all original writs relating to the business of the crown were formerly kept in a little sack or bag, *in parvâ bagâ.* 1 Madd. Ch. 4.

BAGGAGE. In the law of carriers. This term comprises such articles of personal convenience or necessity as are usually carried by passengers for their personal use, and not merchandise or other valuables, although carried in the trunks of passengers, which are not designed for any such use, but for other purposes, such as a sale and the like. Story, Bailm. § 499. See, also, Hutch. Carr. § 679; L. R. 6 Q. B. 612; 6 Hill, 586; 9 Humph. 621; 23 Fed. Rep. 765. See cases collected in 1 Amer. & Eng. Enc. Law, 1042.

The term includes whatever the passenger takes with him for his personal use or convenience according to the habits or wants of the particular class to which he belongs, either with reference to the immediate necessities or ultimate purpose of the journey. L. R. 6 Q. B. 612.

BAHADUM. A chest or coffer. Fleta.

BAIL, *v.* To procure the release of a person from legal custody, by undertaking that he shall appear at the time and place designated and submit himself to the jurisdiction and judgment of the court.

To set at liberty a person arrested or imprisoned, on security being taken for his appearance on a day and a place certain, which security is called "bail," because the party arrested or imprisoned is delivered into the hands of those who bind themselves for his forthcoming, (that is, become bail for his due

appearance when required,) in order that he may be safely protected from prison. Wharton.

BAIL, *n.* In practice. The sureties who procure the release of a person under arrest, by becoming responsible for his appearance at the time and place designated. Those persons who become sureties for the appearance of the defendant in court.

Upon those contracts of indemnity which are taken in legal proceedings as security for the performance of an obligation imposed or declared by the tribunals, and known as undertakings or recognizances, the sureties are called "bail." Civil Code Cal. § 2780.

The taking of bail consists in the acceptance by a competent court, magistrate, or officer, of sufficient bail for the appearance of the defendant according to the legal effect of his undertaking, or for the payment to the state of a certain specified sum if he does not appear. Code Ala. 1886, § 4407.

Bail is of various kinds, such as:

Civil bail. That taken in civil actions.

Special bail, being persons who undertake that if the defendant is condemned in the action he shall pay the debt or surrender himself for imprisonment.

Bail in error. That given by a defendant who intends to bring error on the judgment and desires a stay of execution in the mean time.

See, further, the following titles.

In Canadian law. A lease. *Bail emphyt'otique.* A lease for years, with a right to prolong indefinitely. 5 Low. Can. 381. It is equivalent to an alienation. 6 Low. Can. 58.

BAIL À CHEPTEL. In French law. A contract by which one of the parties gives to the other cattle to keep, feed, and care for, the borrower receiving half the profit of increase, and bearing half the loss. Duverger.

BAIL A FERME. In French law. A contract of letting lands.

BAIL À LOYER. In French law. A contract of letting houses.

BAIL À RENTE. In French law. A contract partaking of the nature of the contract of sale, and that of the contract of lease; it is translative of property, and the rent is essentially redeemable. 4 La. 286; Poth. Bail à Rente, 1, 3.

BAIL ABSOLUTE. Sureties whose liability is conditioned upon the failure of the principal to duly account for money coming to his hands as administrator, guardian, etc.

BAIL-BOND. In practice. A bond executed by a defendant who has been arrested, together with other persons as sureties, naming the sheriff, constable, or marshal as obligee, in a penal sum proportioned to the damages claimed or penalty denounced, conditioned that the defendant shall duly appear to answer to the legal process in the officer's hands, or shall cause special bail to be put in, as the case may be.

BAIL, COMMON. In practice. A fictitious proceeding, intended only to express the appearance of a defendant, in cases where special bail is not required. It is put in in the same form as special bail, but the sureties are merely nominal or imaginary persons, as John Doe and Richard Roe. 3 Bl. Comm. 287.

BAIL COURT. In English law and practice. An auxiliary court of the court of queen's bench at Westminster, wherein points connected more particularly with pleading and practice are argued and determined. Holthouse.

BAIL PIECE. In practice. A formal entry or memorandum of the recognizance or undertaking of special bail in civil actions, which, after being signed and acknowledged by the bail before the proper officer, is filed in the court in which the action is pending. 3 Bl. Comm. 291; 1 Tidd, Pr. 250.

BAIL TO THE ACTION, BAIL ABOVE, OR SPECIAL BAIL. In practice. Persons who undertake jointly and severally in behalf of a defendant arrested on mesne process in a civil action that, if he be condemned in the action, he shall pay the costs and condemnation, (that is, the amount which may be recovered against him,) or render himself a prisoner, or that they will pay it for him. 3 Bl. Comm. 291; 1 Tidd, Pr. 245.

BAIL TO THE SHERIFF, OR BAIL BELOW. In practice. Persons who undertake that a defendant arrested upon mesne process in a civil action shall duly appear to answer the plaintiff; such undertaking being in the form of a bond given to the sheriff, termed a "bail-bond," (q. v.) 3 Bl. Comm. 290; 1 Tidd, Pr. 221.

BAILABLE. Capable of being bailed; admitting of bail; authorizing or requiring bail. A bailable *action* is one in which the defendant cannot be released from arrest except on furnishing bail. Bailable *process* is such as requires the officer to take bail, after arresting the defendant. A bailable *offense*

is one for which the prisoner may be admitted to bail.

BAILEE. In the law of contracts. One to whom goods are bailed; the party to whom personal property is delivered under a contract of bailment.

BAILIE. In the Scotch law. A bailie is (1) a magistrate having inferior criminal jurisdiction, similar to that of an alderman, (q. v.;) (2) an officer appointed to confer infeoffment, (q. v.;) a bailiff, (q. v.;) a server of writs. Bell.

BAILIFF. In a general sense, a person to whom some authority, care, guardianship, or jurisdiction is delivered, committed, or intrusted; one who is deputed or appointed to take charge of another's affairs; an overseer or superintendent; a keeper, protector, or guardian; a steward. Spelman.

A sheriff's officer or deputy. 1 Bl. Comm. 344.

A magistrate, who formerly administered justice in the parliaments or courts of France, answering to the English sheriffs as mentioned by Bracton.

In the action of account render. A person who has by delivery the custody and administration of lands or goods for the benefit of the owner or bailor, and is liable to render an account thereof. Co. Litt. 271; Story, Eq. Jur. § 446.

A bailiff is defined to be "a servant that has the administration and charge of lands, goods, and chattels, to make the best benefit for the owner, against whom an action of account lies, for the profits which he has raised or made, or might by his industry or care have raised or made." 25 Conn. 149.

BAILIFF-ERRANT. A bailiff's deputy.

BAILIFFS OF FRANCHISES. In English law. Officers who perform the duties of sheriffs within liberties or privileged jurisdictions, in which formerly the king's writ could not be executed by the sheriff. Spelman.

BAILIFFS OF HUNDREDS. In English law. Officers appointed over hundreds, by the sheriffs, to collect fines therein, and summon juries; to attend the judges and justices at the assises and quarter sessions; and also to execute writs and process in the several hundreds. 1 Bl. Comm. 345; 3 Steph. Comm. 29; Bract. fol. 116.

BAILIFFS OF MANORS. In English law. Stewards or agents appointed by the lord (generally by an authority under seal) to superintend the manor, collect fines, and quit rents, inspect the buildings, order repairs, cut down trees, impound cattle trespassing, take an account of wastes, spoils, and misdemeanors in the woods and demesne lands, and do other acts for the lord's interest. Cowell.

BAILIVIA. In old law. A bailiff's jurisdiction, a bailiwick; the same as *bailium.* Spelman. See BAILIWICK.

In old English law. A liberty, or exclusive jurisdiction, which was exempted from the sheriff of the county, and over which the lord of the liberty appointed a bailiff with such powers within his precinct as an under-sheriff exercised under the sheriff of the county. Whishaw.

BAILIWICK. The territorial jurisdiction of a sheriff or bailiff. 1 Bl. Comm. 344.

BAILLEUR DE FONDS. In Canadian law. The unpaid vendor of real estate.

BAILLI. In old French law. One to whom judicial authority was assigned or delivered by a superior.

BAILMENT. A delivery of goods or personal property, by one person to another, in trust for the execution of a special object upon or in relation to such goods, beneficial either to the bailor or bailee or both, and upon a contract, express or implied, to perform the trust and carry out such object, and thereupon either to redeliver the goods to the bailor or otherwise dispose of the same in conformity with the purpose of the trust. See Code Ga. 1882, § 2058.

A delivery of goods in trust upon a contract, expressed or implied, that the trust shall be faithfully executed on the part of the bailee. 2 Bl. Comm. 455.

Bailment, from the French *bailler*, to deliver, is a delivery of goods for some purpose, upon a contract, express or implied, that, after the purpose has been fulfilled, they shall be redelivered to the bailor, or otherwise dealt with, according to his directions, or (as the case may be) kept till he reclaims them. 2 Steph. Comm. 80.

A delivery of goods in trust upon a contract, expressed or implied, that the trust shall be duly executed, and the goods restored by the bailee as soon as the purposes of the bailment shall be answered. 2 Kent, Comm. 559.

Bailment is a delivery of a thing in trust for some special object or purpose, and upon a contract, express or implied, to conform to the object or purpose of the trust. Story, Bailm. 3.

A delivery of goods in trust on a contract, either expressed or implied, that the trust shall be duly executed, and the goods redelivered as soon as the time or use for which they were bailed shall have elapsed or be performed. Jones, Bailm. 117.

Bailment is a word of French origin, significant of the curtailed transfer, the delivery or mere handing over, which is appropriate to the transaction. Schouler, Pers. Prop. 695.

The test of a bailment is that the identical thing is to be returned; if another thing of equal value is to be returned, the transaction is a sale. 6 Thomp. & C. 29; 3 Hun, 550.

Sir William Jones has divided bailments into five sorts, namely: *Depositum,* or deposit; *mandatum,* or commission without recompense; *commodatum,* or loan for use without pay; *pignori acceptum,* or pawn; *locatum,* or hiring, which is always with reward. This last is subdivided into *locatio rei,* or hiring, by which the hirer gains a temporary use of the thing; *locatio operis faciendi,* when something is to be done to the thing delivered; *locatio operis mercium vehendarum,* when the thing is merely to be carried from one place to another. Jones, Bailm. 36.

Lord Holt divided bailments thus:

(1) *Depositum,* or a naked bailment of goods, to be kept for the use of the bailor.

(2) *Commodatum.* Where goods or chattels that are useful are lent to the bailee *gratis,* to be used by him.

(3) *Locatio rei.* Where goods are lent to the bailee to be used by him for hire.

(4) *Vadium.* Pawn or pledge.

(5) *Locatio operis faciendi.* Where goods are delivered to be carried, or something is to be done about them, for a reward to be paid to the bailee.

(6) *Mandatum.* A delivery of goods to somebody who is to carry them, or do something about them, *gratis.* 2 Ld. Raym. 909.

Another division, suggested by Bouvier, is as follows: *First,* those bailments which are for the benefit of the bailor, or of some person whom he represents; *second,* those for the benefit of the bailee, or some person represented by him; *third,* those which are for the benefit of both parties.

BAILOR. The party who *bails* or delivers goods to another, in the contract of bailment.

BAIR-MAN. In old Scotch law. A poor insolvent debtor, left bare and naked, who was obliged to swear in court that he was not worth more than five shillings and fivepence.

BAIRNS. In Scotch law. A known term, used to denote one's whole issue. Ersk. Inst. 3, 8, 48. But it is sometimes used in a more limited sense. Bell.

BAIRN'S PART. In Scotch law. Children's part; a third part of the defunct's free movables, debts deducted, if the wife survive, and a half if there be no relict.

BAITING ANIMALS. In English law. Procuring them to be worried by dogs. Punishable on summary conviction, under 12 & 13 Vict. c. 92, § 3.

BALÆNA. A large fish, called by Blackstone a "whale." Of this the king had the head and the queen the tail as a perquisite whenever one was taken on the coast of England. 1 Bl. Comm. 222.

BALANCE. The amount remaining due from one person to another on a settlement of the accounts involving their mutual dealings; the difference between the two sides (debit and credit) of an account.

A balance is the conclusion or result of the debit and credit sides of an account. It implies mutual dealings, and the existence of debt and credit, without which there could be no balance. 45 Mo. 574. See, also, 71 Pa. St. 69.

The term is also frequently used in the sense of residue or remainder; as when a will speaks of "the balance of my estate." 3 Ired. 155; 23 S. C. 269.

BALANCE OF TRADE. The difference between the value of the exports from and imports into a country.

BALANCE-SHEET. When it is desired to ascertain the exact state of a merchant's business, or other commercial enterprise, at a given time, all the ledger accounts are closed up to date and balances struck; and these balances, when exhibited together on a single page, and so grouped and arranged as to close into each other and be summed up in one general result, constitute the "balance-sheet."

BALCANIFER, or BALDAKINIFER. The standard-bearer of the Knights Templar.

BALCONIES. Small galleries of wood or stone on the outside of houses. The erection of them is regulated in London by the building acts.

BALDIO. In Spanish law. Waste land; land that is neither arable nor pasture. White, New Recop. b. 2, tit. 1, c. 6, § 4, and note.

BALE. A pack or certain quantity of goods or merchandise, wrapped or packed up in cloth and corded round very tightly, marked and numbered with figures corresponding to those in the bills of lading for the purpose of identification. Wharton.

A bale of cotton is a certain quantity of that commodity compressed into a cubical form, so as to occupy less room than when in bags. 2 Car. & P. 525.

BALISE. Fr. In French marine law. A buoy.

BALIUS. In the civil law. A teacher; one who has the care of youth; a tutor; a guardian. Du Cange; Spelman.

BALIVA. L. Lat. In old English law. A bailiwick, or jurisdiction.

BALLAST. In marine insurance. There is considerable analogy between *ballast* and *dunnage.* The former is used for trimming the ship, and bringing it down to a draft of water proper and safe for sailing. Dunnage is placed under the cargo to keep it from being wetted by water getting into the hold, or between the different parcels to keep them from bruising and injuring each other. 13 Wall. 674.

BALLASTAGE. A toll paid for the privilege of taking up ballast from the bottom of a port or harbor.

BALLIVO AMOVENDO. An ancient writ to remove a bailiff from his office for want of sufficient land in the bailiwick. Reg. Orig. 78.

BALLOT. In the law of elections. A slip of paper bearing the names of the offices to be filled at the particular election and the names of the candidates for whom the elector desires to vote; it may be printed, or written, or partly printed and partly written, and is deposited by the voter in a "ballot-box" which is in the custody of the officers holding the election.

Also the act of voting by balls or tickets.

A ballot is a ticket folded in such a manner that nothing written or printed thereon can be seen. Pol. Code Cal. § 1186.

A ballot is defined to be "a paper ticket containing the names of the persons for whom the elector intends to vote, and designating the office to which each person so named is intended by him to be chosen." Thus a ballot, or a ticket, is a single piece of paper containing the names of the candidates and the offices for which they are running. If the elector were to write the names of the candidates upon his ticket twice or three or more times, he does not thereby make it more than one ticket. 28 Cal. 136.

BALLOT-BOX. A case made of wood for receiving ballots.

BALNEARII. In the Roman law. Those who stole the clothes of bathers in the public baths. 4 Bl. Comm. 239.

BAN. 1. In old English and civil law. A proclamation; a public notice; the announcement of an intended marriage. Cowell. An excommunication; a curse, publicly pronounced. A proclamation of silence made by a crier in court before the meeting of champions in combat. Id. A statute, edict, or command; a fine, or penalty.

2. In French law. The right of announcing the time of mowing, reaping, and gathering the vintage, exercised by certain seignorial lords. Guyot, Repert. Univ.

3. An expanse; an extent of space or territory; a space inclosed within certain limits; the limits or bounds themselves. Spelman.

4. A privileged space or territory around a town, monastery, or other place.

5. In old European law. A military standard; a thing unfurled, a banner. Spelman. A summoning to a standard; a calling out of a military force; the force itself so summoned; a national army levied by proclamation.

BANAL. In Canadian and old French law. Pertaining to a *ban* or privileged place; having qualities or privileges derived from a *ban*. Thus, a banal mill is one to which the lord may require his tenant to carry his grain to be ground.

BANALITY. In Canadian law. The right by virtue of which a lord subjects his vassals to grind at his mill, bake at his oven, etc. Used also of the region within which this right applied. Guyot, Repert. Univ.

BANC. Bench; the seat of judgment; the place where a court permanently or regularly sits.

The full bench, full court. A "sitting *in banc*" is a meeting of all the judges of a court, usually for the purpose of hearing arguments on demurrers, points reserved, motions for new trial, etc., as distinguished from the sitting of a single judge at the assises or at *nisi prius* and from trials at bar.

BANCI NARRATORES. In old English law. Advocates; countors; serjeants. Applied to advocates in the common pleas courts. 1 Bl. Comm. 24; Cowell.

BANCO. Ital. See Banc. A seat or bench of justice; also, in commerce, a word of Italian origin signifying a bank.

BANCUS. In old English law and practice. A bench or seat in the king's hall or palace. Fleta, lib. 2, c. 16, § 1.

A high seat, or seat of distinction; a seat of judgment, or tribunal for the administration of justice.

The English court of common pleas was formerly called "*Bancus.*"

A sitting *in banc;* the sittings of a court with its full judicial authority, or in full form, as distinguished from sittings at *nisi prius.*

A stall, bench, table, or counter, on which goods were exposed for sale. Cowell.

BANCUS REGINÆ. L. Lat. The queen's bench. See Queen's Bench.

BANCUS REGIS. Lat. The king's bench; the supreme tribunal of the king after parliament. 3 Bl. Comm. 41.

BANCUS SUPERIOR. The upper bench. The king's bench was so called during the Protectorate.

BAND. In old Scotch law. A proclamation calling out a military force.

BANDIT. An outlaw; a man *banned*, or put under a ban; a brigand or robber. *Banditti*, a band of robbers.

BANE. A malefactor. Bract. l. 1, t. 8, c. 1.

Also a public denunciation of a malefactor; the same with what was called "*hutesium*," hue and cry. Spelman.

BANERET, or BANNERET. In English law. A knight made in the field, by the ceremony of cutting off the point of his standard, and making it, as it were, a banner. Knights so made are accounted so honorable that they are allowed to display their arms in the royal army, as barons do, and may bear arms with supporters. They rank next to barons; and were sometimes called "*vexillarii.*" Wharton.

BANI. Deodands, (*q. v.*)

BANISHMENT. In criminal law. A punishment inflicted upon criminals, by compelling them to quit a city, place, or country for a specified period of time, or for life. See 4 Dall. 14.

It is inflicted principally upon political offenders, "transportation" being the word used to express a similar punishment of ordinary criminals. Banishment, however, merely forbids the return of the person banished before the expiration of the sentence, while transportation involves the idea of deprivation of liberty after the convict arrives at the place to which he has been carried. Rap. & L.

BANK. 1. A bench or seat; the bench or tribunal occupied by the judges; the seat of judgment; a court. The full bench, or full court; the assembly of all the judges of a court. A "sitting *in bank*" is a meeting of all the judges of a court, usually for the purpose of hearing arguments on demurrers, points reserved, motions for new trial, etc., as distinguished from the sitting of a single judge at the assises or at *nisi prius* and from trials at bar. But, in this sense, *banc* is the more usual form of the word.

2. An institution, of great value in the commercial world, empowered to receive deposits of money, to make loans, and to issue its promissory notes, (designed to circulate as money, and commonly called "bank-notes" or "bank-bills,") or to perform any one or more of these functions.

The term "bank" is usually restricted in its application to an incorporated body; while a private individual making it his business to conduct banking operations is denominated a "banker."

Also the house or place where such business is carried on.

Banks in the commercial sense are of three kinds, to-wit: (1) Of deposit; (2) of discount; (3) of circulation. Strictly speaking, the term "bank" implies a place for the deposit of money, as that is the most obvious purpose of such an institution. Originally the business of banking consisted only in receiving deposits, such as bullion, plate, and the like, for safe-keeping until the depositor should see fit to draw it out for use, but the business, in the progress of events, was extended, and bankers assumed to discount bills and notes, and to loan money upon mortgage, pawn, or other security, and, at a still later period, to issue notes of their own, intended as a circulating currency and a medium of exchange, instead of gold and silver. Modern bankers frequently exercise any two or even all three of those functions, but it is still true that an institution prohibited from exercising any more than one of those functions is a bank, in the strictest commercial sense. 17 Wall. 118; Rev. St. U. S. § 3407.

3. An acclivity; an elevation or mound of earth; usually applied in this sense to the raised earth bordering the sides of a watercourse.

BANK-ACCOUNT. A sum of money placed with a bank or banker, on deposit, by a customer, and subject to be drawn out on the latter's check. The statement or computation of the several sums deposited and those drawn out by the customer on checks, entered on the books of the bank and the depositor's pass-book.

BANK-BILLS. Promissory notes issued by a bank designed to circulate as money, and payable to the bearer on demand.

The term "bank-bills" is familiar to every man in this country, and conveys a definite and certain meaning. It is a written promise on the part of the bank to pay to the bearer a certain sum of money, on demand. This term is understood by the community generally to mean a written promise for the payment of money. So universal is this understanding that the term "bank-bills" would be rendered no more certain by adding the words "for the payment of money." 3 Scam. 328.

The words "bank-bill" and "bank-note," in their popular sense, are used synonymously. 21 Ind. 176; 2 Park. Crim. R. 37.

Bank-notes, bank-bills, and promissory notes, such as are issued by the directors of a bank incorporated by the legislature of Vermont, mean the same thing; so that the expression in a statute "bank-bill or promissory note" is an evident tautology. 17 Vt. 151.

BANK-BOOK. A book kept by a customer of a bank, showing the state of his account with it.

BANK-CREDITS. Accommodations allowed to a person on security given to a bank, to draw money on it to a certain extent agreed upon.

BANK-NOTE. A promissory note issued by a bank or authorized banker, payable to bearer on demand, and intended to circulate as money.

BANK-STOCK. Shares in the capital of a bank; shares in the property of a bank.

BANKABLE. In mercantile law Notes, checks, bank-bills, drafts, and other securities for money, received as cash by the banks. Such commercial paper as is considered worthy of discount by the bank to which it is offered is termed "bankable."

BANKER. A private person who keeps a bank; one who is engaged in the business of banking.

BANKER'S NOTE. A commercial instrument resembling a bank-note in every particular except that it is given by a private banker or unincorporated banking institution.

BANKEROUT. O. Eng. Bankrupt; insolvent; indebted beyond the means of payment.

BANKING. The business of receiving money on deposit, loaning money, discounting notes, issuing notes for circulation, collecting money on notes deposited, negotiating bills, etc.

BANKRUPT. A person who has committed an act of bankruptcy; one who has done some act or suffered some act to be done in consequence of which, under the laws of his country, he is liable to be proceeded against by his creditors for the seizure and distribution among them of his entire property.

A trader who secretes himself or does certain other acts tending to defraud his creditors. 2 Bl. Comm. 471.

In a looser sense, an insolvent person; a broken-up or ruined trader. 3 Story, 453.

A person who, by the formal decree of a court, has been declared subject to be proceeded against under the bankruptcy laws, or entitled, on his voluntary application, to take the benefit of such laws.

BANKRUPT LAW. A law relating to bankrupts and the procedure against them in the courts. A law providing a remedy for the creditors of a bankrupt, and for the relief and restitution of the bankrupt himself.

A law which, upon a bankrupt's surrendering all his property to commissioners for the benefit of his creditors, discharges him from the payment of his debts, and all liability to arrest or suit for the same, and secures his future acquired property from a liability to the payment of his past debts. Webster.

A bankrupt law is distinguished from the ordinary law between debtor and creditor, as involving these three general principles: (1) A summary and immediate seizure of all the debtor's property; (2) a distribution of it among the creditors in general, instead of merely applying a portion of it to the payment of the individual complainant; and (3) the discharge of the debtor from future liability for the debts then existing.

The leading distinction between a bankrupt law and an insolvent law, in the proper technical sense of the words, consists in the character of the persons upon whom it is designed to operate,—the former contemplating as its objects bankrupts only, that is, traders of a certain description; the latter, insolvents in general, or persons unable to pay their debts. This has led to a marked separation between the two systems, in principle and in practice, which in England has always been carefully maintained, although in the United States it has of late been effectually disregarded. In further illustration of this distinction, it may be observed that a bankrupt law, in its proper sense, is a remedy intended primarily for the benefit of creditors; it is set in motion at their instance, and operates upon the debtor against his will, (*in invitum,*) although in its result it effectually discharges him from his debts. An insolvent law, on the other hand, is chiefly intended for the benefit of the debtor, and is set in motion at his instance, though less effective as a discharge in its final result. 5 Hill, 327.

The only substantial difference between a strictly bankrupt law and an insolvent law lies in the circumstance that the former affords relief upon the application of the creditor, and the latter upon the application of the debtor. In the general character of the remedy, there is no difference, however-

er much the modes by which the remedy may be administered may vary. 37 Cal. 222.

BANKRUPTCY. 1. The state or condition of one who is a bankrupt; amenability to the bankrupt laws; the condition of one who has committed an act of bankruptcy, and is liable to be proceeded against by his creditors therefor, or of one whose circumstances are such that he is entitled, on his voluntary application, to take the benefit of the bankrupt laws. The term is used in a looser sense as synonymous with "insolvency,"—inability to pay one's debts; the stopping and breaking up of business because the trader is broken down, insolvent, ruined. See 2 Story, 354, 359.

2. The term denotes the proceedings taken, under the bankrupt law, against a person (or firm or company) to have him adjudged a bankrupt, and to have his estate administered for the benefit of the creditors, and divided among them.

3. That branch of jurisprudence, or system of law and practice, which is concerned with the definition and ascertainment of acts of bankruptcy and the administration of bankrupts' estates for the benefit of their creditors and the absolution and restitution of bankrupts.

As to the distinction between bankruptcy and insolvency, it may be said that insolvent laws operate at the instance of an imprisoned debtor; bankrupt laws, at the instance of a creditor. But the line of partition between bankrupt and insolvent laws is not so distinctly marked as to define what belongs exclusively to the one and not to the other class of laws. 4 Wheat. 122.

Insolvency means a simple inability to pay, as debts should become payable, whereby the debtor's business would be broken up; bankruptcy means the particular legal *status,* to be ascertained and declared by a judicial decree. 2 Ben. 196.

BANKRUPTCY COURTS. Courts for the administration of the bankrupt laws. The present English bankruptcy courts are the London bankruptcy court, the court of appeal, and the local bankruptcy courts created by the bankruptcy act, 1869.

BANLEUCA. An old law term, signifying a space or tract of country around a city, town, or monastery, distinguished and protected by peculiar privileges. Spelman.

BANLIEU, or BANLIEUE. A French and Canadian law term, having the same meaning as *banleuca,* (*q. v.*)

BANNERET. See BANERET.

BANNI OR BANNITUS. In old law, one under a ban, (*q. v.*;) an outlaw or banished man. Britt. cc. 12, 13; Calvin.

BANNI NUPTIARUM. L. Lat. In old English law. The bans of matrimony.

BANNIMUS. We ban or expel. The form of expulsion of a member from the University of Oxford, by affixing the sentence in some public places, as a promulgation of it. Cowell.

BANNIRE AD PLACITA, AD MOLENDINUM. To summon tenants to serve at the lord's courts, to bring corn to be ground at his mill.

BANNUM. A ban, (q. v.)

BANNUS. In old English law. A proclamation. *Bannus regis;* the king's proclamation, made by the voice of a herald, forbidding all present at the trial by combat to interfere either by motion or word, whatever they might see or hear. Bract. fol. 142.

BANQUE. A bench; the table or counter of a trader, merchant, or banker. *Banque route;* a broken bench or counter; bankrupt.

BANS OF MATRIMONY. A public announcement of an intended marriage, required by the English law to be made in a church or chapel, during service, on three consecutive Sundays before the marriage is celebrated. The object is to afford an opportunity for any person to interpose an objection if he knows of any impediment or other just cause why the marriage should not take place. The publication of the bans may be dispensed with by procuring a special license to marry.

BANYAN. In East Indian law. A Hindoo merchant or shop-keeper. The word is used in Bengal to denote the native who manages the money concerns of a European, and sometimes serves him as an interpreter.

BAR. 1. A partition or railing running across a court-room, intended to separate the general public from the space occupied by the judges, counsel, jury, and others concerned in the trial of a cause. In the English courts it is the partition behind which all outer-barristers and every member of the public must stand. Solicitors, being officers of the court, are admitted within it; as are also queen's counsel, barristers with patents of precedence, and serjeants, in virtue of their ranks. Parties who appear in person also are placed within the bar on the floor of the court.

2. The term also designates a particular part of the court-room; for example, the place where prisoners stand at their trial, whence the expression "prisoner at the bar."

3. It further denotes the presence, actual or constructive, of the court. Thus, a trial *at bar* is one had before the full court, distinguished from a trial had before a single judge at *nisi prius.* So the "case at bar" is the case now before the court and under its consideration; the case being tried or argued.

4. In the practice of legislative bodies, the *bar* is the outer boundary of the house, and therefore all persons, not being members, who wish to address the house, or are summoned to it, appear *at the bar* for that purpose.

5. In another sense, the whole body of attorneys and counsellors, or the members of the legal profession, collectively, are figuratively called the "bar," from the place which they usually occupy in court. They are thus distinguished from the "bench," which term denotes the whole body of judges.

6. In the law of contracts, "bar" means an impediment, an obstacle, or preventive barrier. Thus, relationship within the prohibited degrees is a *bar* to marriage.

7. It further means that which defeats, annuls, cuts off, or puts an end to. Thus, a provision "in bar of dower" is one which has the effect of defeating or cutting off the dower-rights which the wife would otherwise become entitled to in the particular land.

8. In pleading, it denoted a special plea, constituting a sufficient answer to an action at law; and so called because it *barred, i. e.,* prevented, the plaintiff from further prosecuting it with effect, and, if established by proof, defeated and destroyed the action altogether. Now called a special "plea in bar." See PLEA IN BAR.

BAR FEE. In English law. A fee taken by the sheriff, time out of mind, for every prisoner who is acquitted. Bac. Abr. "Extortion." Abolished by St. 14 Geo. III. c. 26; 55 Geo. III. c. 50; 8 & 9 Vict. c. 114.

BARAGARIA. Span. A concubine, whom a man keeps alone in his house, unconnected with any other woman. Las Partidas, pt. 4, tit. 14.

Baratriam committit qui propter pecuniam justitiam baractat. He is guilty of barratry who for money sells justice. Bell.

BARBANUS. In old Lombardic law. An uncle, (*patruus.*)

BARBICANAGE. In old European law. Money paid to support a barbican or watch-tower.

BARE TRUSTEE. A person to whose fiduciary office no duties were originally attached, or who, although such duties were originally attached to his office, would, on the requisition of his *cestuis qui trust*, be compellable in equity to convey the estate to them or by their direction. 1 Ch. Div. 279.

BARET. L. Fr. A wrangling suit. Britt. c. 92; Co. Litt. 368b.

BARGAIN. A mutual undertaking, contract, or agreement.

A contract or agreement between two parties, the one to sell goods or lands, and the other to buy them. 5 Mass. 360. See, also, 6 Conn. 91; 5 East, 10; 6 East, 307.

"If the word ' agreement ' imports a mutual act of two parties, surely the word ' bargain ' is not less significative of the consent of two. In a popular sense, the former word is frequently used as declaring the engagement of one only. A man may agree to pay money or to perform some other act, and the word is then used synonymously with ' promise ' or ' engage.' But the word ' bargain ' is seldom used, unless to express a mutual contract or undertaking." 17 Mass. 131.

BARGAIN AND SALE. In conveyancing. The transferring of the property of a thing from one to another, upon valuable consideration, by way of sale. Shep. Touch. (by Preston,) 221. ·

A contract or bargain by the owner of land, in consideration of money or its equivalent paid, to sell land to another person, called the "bargainee," whereupon a use arises in favor of the latter, to whom the seisin is transferred by force of the statute of uses. 2 Washb. Real Prop. 128.

The expression "bargain and sale" is also applied to transfers of personalty, in cases where there is first an executory agreement for the sale, (the bargain,) and then an actual and completed sale.

The proper and technical words to denote a bargain and sale are "bargain and sell;" but any other words that are sufficient to raise a use upon a valuable consideration are sufficient. 2 Wood. Conv. 15; 3 Johns. 484.

BARGAINEE. The party to a bargain to whom the subject-matter of the bargain or thing bargained for is to go; the grantee in a deed of bargain and sale.

BARGAINOR. The party to a bargain who is to perform the contract by delivery of the subject-matter.

BARK. Is sometimes figuratively used to denote the mere words or letter of an instrument, or outer covering of the ideas sought to be expressed, as distinguished from its inner substance or essential meaning. "If the *bark* makes for them, the pith makes for us." Bacon.

BARLEYCORN. In linear measure. The third of an inch.

BARMOTE COURTS. Courts held in certain mining districts belonging to the Duchy of Lancaster, for regulation of the mines, and for deciding questions of title and other matters relating thereto. 3 Steph. Comm. 347, note b.

BARNARD'S INN. An inn of chancery. See INNS OF CHANCERY.

BARO. An old law term signifying, originally, a "man," whether slave or free. In later usage, a "freeman," a "strong man," a "good soldier," a "baron;" also a "vassal," or "feudal tenant or client," and "husband," the last being the most common meaning of the word.

BARON. A lord or nobleman; the most general title of nobility in England. 1 Bl. Comm. 398, 399.

A particular degree or title of nobility, next to a viscount.

A judge of the court of exchequer. 3 Bl. Comm. 44; Cowell.

A freeman. Co. Litt. 58a. Also a vassal holding directly from the king.

A husband; occurring in this sense in the phrase "*baron et feme*," husband and wife.

BARON AND FEME. Husband and wife. A wife being under the protection and influence of her *baron*, lord, or husband, is styled a "*feme-covert*," (*fœmina viro cooperta*,) and her state of marriage is called her "coverture."

BARONAGE. In English law. The collective body of the barons, or of the nobility at large. Spelman.

BARONET. An English name or title of dignity, (but not a title of nobility,) established A. D. 1611 by James I. It is created by letters patent, and descends to the male heir. Spelman.

BARONS OF THE CINQUE PORTS. Members of parliament from these ports, viz.: Sandwich, Romney, Hastings, Hythe, and Dover. Winchelsea and Rye have been added.

BARONS OF THE EXCHEQUER. The six judges of the court of exchequer in England, of whom one is styled the "chief baron;" answering to the justices and chief justice of other courts.

BARONY. The dignity of a baron; a species of tenure; the territory or lands held by a baron. Spelman.

BARONY OF LAND. In England, a quantity of land amounting to 15 acres. In Ireland, a subdivision of a county.

BARRA, or BARRE. In old practice. A plea in bar. The bar of the court. A barrister.

BARRATOR. One who is guilty of the crime of barratry.

BARRATROUS. Fraudulent; having the character of barratry.

BARRATRY. In maritime law. An act committed by the master or mariners of a vessel, for some unlawful or fraudulent purpose, contrary to their duty to the owners, whereby the latter sustain injury. It may include negligence, if so gross as to evidence fraud. 8 Cranch, 49; 2 Cush. 511; 3 Pet. 230.

Barratry is some fraudulent act of the master or mariners, tending to their own benefit, to the prejudice of the owner of the vessel, without his privity or consent. 2 Caines, 67.

Barratry is a generic term, which includes many acts of various kinds and degrees. It comprehends any unlawful, fraudulent, or dishonest act of the master or mariners, and every violation of duty by them arising from gross and culpable negligence contrary to their duty to the owner of the vessel, and which might work loss or injury to him in the course of the voyage insured. A mutiny of the crew, and forcible dispossession by them of the master and other officers from the ship, is a form of barratry. 9 Allen, 217.

In criminal law. Common barratry is the practice of exciting groundless judicial proceedings. Pen. Code Cal. § 158; Pen. Code Dak. § 191.

Also spelled "Barretry," which see.

In Scotch law. The crime committed by a judge who receives a bribe for his judgment. Skene; Brande.

BARREL. A measure of capacity, equal to thirty-six gallons.

In agricultural and mercantile parlance, as also in the inspection laws, the term "barrel" means, *prima facie*, not merely a certain quantity, but, further, a certain state of the article; namely, that it is in a cask. 11 Ired. 72.

BARREN MONEY. In the civil law. A debt which bears no interest.

BARRENNESS. Sterility; the incapacity to bear children.

BARRETOR. In criminal law. A common mover, exciter, or maintainer of suits and quarrels either in courts or elsewhere in the country; a disturber of the peace who spreads false rumors and calumnies, whereby discord and disquiet may grow among neighbors. Co. Litt. 368.

BARRETRY. In criminal law. The act or offense of a barretor, (*q. v.*;) usually called "common barretry." The offense of frequently exciting and stirring up suits and quarrels, either at law or otherwise. 4 Bl. Comm. 134; 4 Steph. Comm. 262.

BARRIER. In mining law and the usage of miners, is a wall of coal left between two mines.

BARRISTER. In English law. An advocate; one who has been called to the bar. A counsellor learned in the law who pleads at the bar of the courts, and who is engaged in conducting the trial or argument of causes. To be distinguished from the *attorney*, who draws the pleadings, prepares the testimony, and conducts matters out of court.

Inner barrister. A serjeant or king's counsel who pleads within the bar.

Ouster barrister. One who pleads "ouster" or without the bar.

Vacation barrister. A counsellor newly called to the bar, who is to attend for several long vacations the exercise of the house.

BARTER. A contract by which parties exchange goods or commodities for other goods. It differs from *sale*, in this: that in the latter transaction goods or property are always exchanged for money.

This term is not applied to contracts concerning land, but to such only as relate to goods and chattels. Barter is a contract by which the parties exchange goods. 4 Biss. 123.

BARTON. In old English law. The demesne land of a manor; a farm distinct from the mansion.

BAS CHEVALIERS. In old English law. Low, or inferior knights, by tenure of a base military fee, as distinguished from *barons* and *bannerets*, who were the chief or superior knights. Cowell.

BAS VILLE. In French law. The suburbs of a town.

BASE COURT. In English law. Any inferior court that is not of record, as a court baron, etc. Kitch. 95, 96; Cowell.

BASE ESTATE. The estate which "base tenants" (*q. v.*) have in their land. Cowell.

BASE FEE. In English law. An estate or fee which has a qualification subjoined thereto, and which must be determined whenever the qualification annexed to it is at an end. 2 Bl. Comm. 109.

BASE-INFEFTMENT. In Scotch law. A disposition of lands by a vassal, to be held of himself.

BASE RIGHT. In Scotch law. A subordinate right; the right of a subvassal in the lands held by him. Bell.

BASE SERVICES. In feudal law. Such services as were unworthy to be performed by the nobler men, and were performed by the peasants and those of servile rank. 2 Bl. Comm. 61.

BASE TENANTS. Tenants who performed to their lords services in villenage; tenants who held at the will of the lord, as distinguished from *frank* tenants, or freeholders. Cowell.

BASE TENURE. A tenure by villenage, or other customary service, as distinguished from tenure by military service; or from tenure by free service. Cowell.

BASILEUS. A Greek word, meaning "king." A title assumed by the emperors of the Eastern Roman Empire. It is used by Justinian in some of the Novels; and is said to have been applied to the English kings before the Conquest. See 1 Bl. Comm. 242.

BASILICA. The name given to a compilation of Roman and Greek law, prepared about A. D. 880 by the Emperor Basilius, and published by his successor, Leo the Philosopher. It was written in Greek, was mainly an abridgment of Justinian's *Corpus Juris*, and comprised sixty books, only a portion of which are extant. It remained the law of the Eastern Empire until the fall of Constantinople, in 1453.

BASILS. In old English law. A kind of money or coin abolished by Henry II.

BASIN. In admiralty law and marine insurance. A part of the sea inclosed in rocks. 13 Amer. Jur. 286.

BASKET TENURE. In feudal law. Lands held by the service of making the king's baskets.

BASSE JUSTICE. In feudal law. Low justice; the right exercised by feudal lords of personally trying persons charged with trespasses or minor offenses.

BASTARD. An illegitimate child; a child born of an unlawful intercourse, and while its parents are not united in marriage.

A child born after marriage, but under circumstances which render it impossible that the husband of his mother can be his father. 6 Bin. 283.

One begotten and born out of lawful wedlock. 2 Kent, Comm. 208.

One born of an illicit union. Civil Code La. arts. 29, 199.

A bastard is a child born out of wedlock, and whose parents do not subsequently intermarry, or a child the issue of adulterous intercourse of the wife during wedlock. Code Ga. 1882, § 1797.

BASTARD EIGNE. In old English law. Bastard elder. If a child was born of an illicit connection, and afterwards the parents intermarried and had another son, the elder was called "*bastard eigne*," and the younger "*mulier puisne*," *i. e.*, afterwards born of the wife. See 2 Bl. Comm. 248.

BASTARDA. In old English law. A female bastard. Fleta, lib. 5, c. 5, § 40.

BASTARDIZE. To declare one a bastard, as a court does. To give evidence to prove one a bastard. A mother (married) cannot bastardize her child.

Bastardus nullius est filius, aut filius populi. A bastard is nobody's son, or the son of the people.

Bastardus non potest habere hæredem nisi de corpore suo legitime procreatum. A bastard can have no heir unless it be one lawfully begotten of his own body. Tray. Lat. Max. 51.

BASTARDY. The offense of begetting a bastard child. The condition of a bastard.

BASTARDY PROCESS. The method provided by statute of proceeding against the putative father to secure a proper maintenance for the bastard.

BASTON. In old English law, a baton, club, or staff. A term applied to officers of the wardens of the prison called the "Fleet," because of the staff carried by them. Cowell; Spelman; Termes de la Ley.

BATABLE-GROUND. Land that is in controversy, or about the possession of which there is a dispute, as the lands which were situated between England and Scotland before the Union. Skene.

BATAILLE. In old English law. Battel; the trial by combat or *duellum*.

BATH, KNIGHTS OF THE. In English law. A military order of knighthood, instituted by Richard II. The order was newly regulated by notifications in the London Gazette of 25th May, 1847, and 16th August, 1850. Wharton.

BATIMENT. In French marine law. A vessel or ship.

BATONNIER. The chief of the French bar in its various centres, who presides in the council of discipline. Arg. Fr. Merc. Law, 546.

BATTEL. Trial by combat; wager of battel.

BATTEL, WAGER OF. In old English law. A form of trial anciently used in military cases, arising in the court of chivalry and honor, in appeals of felony, in criminal cases, and in the obsolete real action called a "writ of action." The question at issue was decided by the result of a personal combat between the parties, or, in the case of a writ of right, between their champions.

BATTERY. Any unlawful beating, or other wrongful physical violence or constraint, inflicted on a human being without his consent. 2 Bish. Crim. Law, § 71.

A battery is a willful and unlawful use of force or violence upon the person of another. Pen. Code Cal. § 242; Pen. Code Dak. § 306.

The actual offer to use force to the injury of another person is *assault;* the use of it is *battery;* hence the two terms are commonly combined in the term "assault and battery."

BATTURE. In Louisiana. A marine term used to denote a bottom of sand, stone, or rock mixed together and rising towards the surface of the water; an elevation of the bed of a river under the surface of the water, since it is rising towards it; sometimes, however, used to denote the same elevation of the bank when it has risen above the surface of the water, or is as high as the land on the outside of the bank. In this latter sense it is synonymous with "alluvion." It means, in common-law language, land formed by accretion. 2 Amer. & Eng. Enc. Law, 157. See 6 Mart. (La.) 216; 3 Woods, 117.

BAWD. One who procures opportunities for persons of opposite sexes to cohabit in an illicit manner; who may be, while exercising the trade of a bawd, perfectly innocent of committing in his or her own proper person

the crime either of adultery or of fornication. See 4 Mo. 216.

BAWDY-HOUSE. A house of prostitution; a brothel. A house or dwelling maintained for the convenience and resort of persons desiring unlawful sexual connection.

BAY. A pond-head made of a great height to keep in water for the supply of a mill, etc., so that the wheel of the mill may be turned by the water rushing thence, through a passage or flood-gate. St. 27 Eliz. c. 19. Also an arm of the sea surrounded by land except at the entrance.

In admiralty law and marine insurance. A bending or curving of the shore of the sea or of a lake. 14 N. H. 477. An opening into the land, where the water is shut in on all sides except at the entrance. 13 Amer. Jur. 286.

BAYLEY. In old English law. Bailiff. This term is used in the laws of the colony of New Plymouth, Mass., A. D. 1670, 1671. Burrill.

BAYOU. A species of creek or stream common in Louisiana and Texas. An outlet from a swamp, pond, or lagoon, to a river, or the sea. See 8 How. 48, 70.

BEACH. This term, in its ordinary signification, when applied to a place on tide-waters, means the space between ordinary high and low water mark, or the space over which the tide usually ebbs and flows. It is a term not more significant of a sea margin than "shore." 13 Gray, 257.

The term designates land washed by the sea and its waves; is synonymous with "shore." 28 Me. 180.

When used in reference to places near the sea, beach means the land between the lines of high water and low water, over which the tide ebbs and flows. 48 Me. 68.

Beach means the shore or strand. 15 Me. 237.

Beach, when used in reference to places anywhere in the vicinity of the sea, means the territory lying between the lines of high water and low water, over which the tide ebbs and flows. It is in this respect synonymous with "shore," "strand," or "flats." 5 Gray, 328, 335.

Beach generally denotes land between high and low water mark. 6 Hun, 257.

To "beach" a ship is to run it upon the beach or shore; this is frequently found necessary in case of fire, a leak, etc.

BEACON. A light-house, or sea-mark, formerly used to alarm the country, in case of the approach of an enemy, but now used for the guidance of ships at sea, by night, as well as by day.

BEACONAGE. Money paid for the maintenance of a beacon or signal-light.

BEADLE. In English ecclesiastical law. An inferior parish officer, who is chosen by the vestry, and whose business is to attend the vestry, to give notice of its meetings, to execute its orders, to attend upon inquests, and to assist the constables. Wharton.

BEAMS AND BALANCE. Instruments for weighing goods and merchandise.

BEAR. In the language of the stock exchange, this term denotes one who speculates for a fall in the market.

BEARER. One who carries or holds a thing. When a check, note, draft, etc., is payable to "bearer," it imports that the contents thereof shall be payable to any person who may present the instrument for payment.

BEARERS. In old English law. Those who bore down upon or oppressed others; maintainers. Cowell.

BEARING DATE. Disclosing a date on its face; having a certain date. These words are often used in conveyancing, and in pleading, to introduce the date which has been put upon an instrument.

BEAST. An animal; a domestic animal; a quadruped, such as may be used for food or in labor or for sport.

BEASTGATE. In Suffolk, England, imports land and common for one beast. 2 Strange, 1084; Rosc. Real Act. 485.

BEASTS OF THE CHASE. In English law. The buck, doe, fox, martin, and roe. Co. Litt. 233a.

BEASTS OF THE FOREST. In English law. The hart, hind, hare, boar, and wolf. Co. Litt. 233a.

BEASTS OF THE PLOW. An old term for animals employed in the operations of husbandry.

BEASTS OF THE WARREN. In English law. Hares, coneys, and roes. Co. Litt. 233; 2 Bl. Comm. 39.

BEAT. To beat, in a legal sense, is not merely to whip, wound, or hurt, but includes any unlawful imposition of the hand or arm. The slightest touching of another in anger is a battery. 60 Ga. 511.

BEAU-PLEADER, (to plead fairly.) In English law. An obsolete writ upon the statute of Marlbridge, (52 Hen. III. c. 11,) which enacts that neither in the circuits of the justices, nor in counties, hundreds, or courts-baron, any fines shall be taken for fair-pleading, i. e., for not pleading fairly or aptly to the purpose; upon this statute, then, this writ was ordained, addressed to the sheriff, bailiff, or him who shall demand such fine, prohibiting him to demand it; an *alias*, *pluries*, and attachment followed. Fitzh. Nat. Brev. 596.

BED. The hollow or channel of a watercourse; the depression between the banks worn by the regular and usual flow of the water.

"The *bed* is that soil so usually covered by water as to be distinguishable from the banks by the character of the soil, or vegetation, or both, produced by the common presence and action of flowing water." Curtis, J., 13 How. 426.

The term also occurs in the phrase "divorce from bed and board," *a mensa et thoro;* where it seems to indicate the right of cohabitation or marital intercourse.

BED OF JUSTICE. In old French law. The seat or throne upon which the king sat when personally present in parliament; hence it signified the parliament itself.

BEDEL. In English law. A crier or messenger of court, who summons men to appear and answer therein. Cowell.

An officer of the forest, similar to a sheriff's special bailiff. Cowell.

A collector of rents for the king. Plowd. 199, 200.

A well-known parish officer. See BEADLE.

BEDELARY. The jurisdiction of a bedel, as a bailiwick is the jurisdiction of a bailiff. Co. Litt. 234b; Cowell.

BEDEREPE. A service which certain tenants were anciently bound to perform, as to reap their landlord's corn at harvest. Said by Whishaw to be still in existence in some parts of England. Blount; Cowell; Whishaw.

BEER. A liquor compounded of malt and hops.

In its ordinary sense, denotes a beverage which is intoxicating, and is within the fair meaning of the words "strong or spirituous liquors," used in the statutes on this subject. 3 Park. Crim. R. 9; 3 Denio, 437; 21 N. Y. 173. To the contrary, 20 Barb. 246.

BEER-HOUSE. In English law. A place where beer is sold to be consumed on the premises; as distinguished from a "beer-shop," which is a place where beer is sold to be consumed off the premises. 16 Ch. Div. 721.

BEFORE. Prior to; preceding. In the presence of; under the official purview of; as in a magistrate's jurat, "*before* me personally appeared,*" etc.

In the absence of any statutory provision governing the computation of time, the authorities are uniform that, where an act is required to be done a certain number of days or weeks *before* a certain other day upon which another act is to be done, the day upon which the first act is done is to be excluded from the computation, and the whole number of the days or weeks must intervene before the day fixed for doing the second act. 63 Wis. 44, 22 N. W. Rep. 844, and cases cited.

BEG. To solicit alms or charitable aid. The act of a cripple in passing along the sidewalk and silently holding out his hand and receiving money from passers-by is "begging for alms," within the meaning of a statute which uses that phrase. 3 Abb. N. C. 65.

BEGA. A land measure used in the East Indies. In Bengal it is equal to about a third part of an acre.

BEGGAR. One who lives by begging charity, or who has no other means of support than solicited alms.

BEGUM. In India. A lady, princess, woman of high rank.

BEHALF. A witness testifies on "behalf" of the party who calls him, notwithstanding his evidence proves to be adverse to that party's case. 65 Ill. 274. See, further, 12 Q. B. 693; 18 Q. B. 512.

BEHAVIOR. Manner of behaving, whether good or bad; conduct; manners; carriage of one's self, with respect to propriety and morals; deportment. Webster.

Surety to be of good *behavior* is said to be a larger requirement than surety to keep the peace.

BEHETRIA. In Spanish law. Lands situated in places where the inhabitants had the right to select their own lords.

BEHOOF. Use; benefit; profit; service; advantage. It occurs in conveyances, *e. g.*, "to his and their use and behoof."

BELIEF. A conviction of the truth of a proposition, existing subjectively in the mind, and induced by argument, persuasion,

or proof addressed to the judgment. Belief is to be distinguished from "proof," "evidence," and "testimony." See EVIDENCE.

With regard to things which make not a very deep impression on the memory, it may be called "belief." "Knowledge" is nothing more than a man's firm belief. The difference is ordinarily merely in the degree; to be judged of by the court, when addressed to the court; by the jury, when addressed to the jury. 9 Gray, 274.

The distinction between the two mental conditions seems to be that knowledge is an assurance of a fact or proposition founded on perception by the senses, or intuition; while belief is an assurance gained by evidence, and from other persons. Abbott.

BELLIGERENT. In international law. A term used to designate either of two nations which are actually in a state of war with each other, as well as their allies actively co-operating; as distinguished from a nation which takes no part in the war and maintains a strict indifference as between the contending parties, called a "neutral."

Bello parta cedunt reipublicæ. Things acquired in war belong or go to the state. 1 Kent, Comm. 101; 5 C. Rob. Adm. 173, 181; 1 Gall. 558. The right to all captures vests primarily in the sovereign. A fundamental maxim of public law.

BELLUM. In public law. War. An armed contest between nations; the state of those who forcibly contend with each other. *Jus belli,* the law of war.

BELOW. In practice. Inferior; of inferior jurisdiction, or jurisdiction in the first instance. The court from which a cause is removed for review is called the "court *below.*"

Preliminary; auxiliary or instrumental. Bail to the sheriff is called "bail *below,*" as being preliminary to and intended to secure the putting in of bail above, or special bail.

BENCH. A seat of judgment or tribunal for the administration of justice; the seat occupied by judges in courts; also the court itself, as the "King's Bench," or the aggregate of the judges composing a court, as in the phrase "before the full bench."

The collective body of the judges in a state or nation, as distinguished from the body of attorneys and advocates, who are called the "bar."

In English ecclesiastical law. The aggregate body of bishops.

BENCH WARRANT. Process issued by the court itself, or "from the bench," for the attachment or arrest of a person; either in case of contempt, or where an indictment has been found, or to bring in a witness who does not obey the *subpœna*. So called to distinguish it from a warrant issued by a justice of the peace, alderman, or commissioner.

BENCHERS. In English law. Seniors in the inns of court, usually, but not necessarily, queen's counsel, elected by co-optation, and having the entire management of the property of their respective inns.

BENE. Lat. Well; in proper form; legally; sufficiently.

Benedicta est expositio quando res redimitur à destructione. 4 Coke, 26. Blessed is the exposition when anything is saved from destruction. It is a laudable interpretation which gives effect to the instrument, and does not allow its purpose to be frustrated.

BENEFICE. In ecclesiastical law. In its technical sense, this term includes ecclesiastical preferments to which rank or public office is attached, otherwise described as ecclesiastical dignities or offices, such as bishoprics, deaneries, and the like; but in popular acceptation, it is almost invariably appropriated to rectories, vicarages, perpetual curacies, district churches, and endowed chapelries. 3 Steph. Comm. 77.

"Benefice" is a term derived from the feudal law, in which it signified a permanent stipendiary estate, or an estate held by feudal tenure. 3 Steph. Comm. 77, note *i;* 4 Bl. Comm. 107.

BÉNÉFICE DE DISCUSSION. In French law. Benefit of discussion. The right of a guarantor to require that the creditor should exhaust his recourse against the principal debtor before having recourse to the guarantor himself.

BÉNÉFICE DE DIVISION. In French law. Benefit of division; right of contribution as between co-sureties.

BÉNÉFICE D'INVENTAIRE. In French law. A term which corresponds to the *beneficium inventarii* of Roman law, and substantially to the English law doctrine that the executor properly accounting is only liable to the extent of the assets received by him.

BÉNÉFICIAIRE. In French law. The person in whose favor a promissory note or bill of exchange is payable; or any person in whose favor a contract of any description is executed. Arg. Fr. Merc. Law, 547.

BENEFICIAL. Tending to the benefit of a person; yielding a profit, advantage, or benefit; enjoying or entitled to a benefit or profit. This term is applied both to estates (as a "beneficial interest") and to persons, (as "the beneficial owner.")

BENEFICIAL ENJOYMENT. The enjoyment which a man has of an estate in his own right and for his own benefit, and not as trustee for another. 11 H. L. Cas. 271.

BENEFICIAL INTEREST. Profit, benefit, or advantage resulting from a contract, or the ownership of an estate as distinct from the legal ownership or control.

BENEFICIAL POWER. In New York law and practice. A power which has for its object the donee of the power, and which is to be executed solely for his benefit; as distinguished from a trust power, which has for its object a person other than the donee, and is to be executed solely for the benefit of such person. 73 N. Y. 234; Rev. St. N. Y. § 79.

BENEFICIARY. A term suggested by Judge Story as a substitute for *cestui que trust,* and adopted to some extent. 1 Story, Eq. Jur. § 321.

He that is in possession of a benefice; also a *cestui que trust,* or person having the enjoyment of property, of which a trustee, executor, etc., has the legal possession.

BENEFICIO PRIMO [ECCLESIASTICO HABENDO.] In English law. An ancient writ, which was addressed by the king to the lord chancellor, to bestow the benefice that should *first* fall in the royal gift, above or under a specified value, upon a person named therein. Reg. Orig. 307.

BENEFICIUM. In early feudal law. A benefice; a permanent stipendiary estate; the same with what was afterwards called a "fief," "feud," or "fee." 3 Steph. Comm. 77, note *i;* Spelman.

In the civil law. A benefit or favor; any particular privilege. Dig. 1, 4, 3; Cod. 7, 71; Mackeld. Rom. Law, § 196.

A general term applied to ecclesiastical livings. 4 Bl. Comm. 107; Cowell.

BENEFICIUM ABSTINENDI. In Roman law. The power of an heir to abstain from accepting the inheritance. Sandars, Just. Inst. (5th Ed.) 214.

BENEFICIUM CEDENDARUM ACTIONUM. In Roman law. The privilege by which a surety could, before paying the creditor, compel him to make over to him the actions which belonged to the stipulator, so as to avail himself of them. Sandars, Just. Inst. (5th Ed.) 332, 351.

BENEFICIUM CLERICALE. Benefit of clergy, which see.

BENEFICIUM COMPETENTIÆ. In Scotch law. The privilege of competency. A privilege which the grantor of a gratuitous obligation was entitled to, by which he might retain sufficient for his subsistence, if, before fulfilling the obligation, he was reduced to indigence. Bell.

In the civil law. The right which an insolvent debtor had, among the Romans, on making cession of his property for the benefit of his creditors, to retain what was required for him to live honestly according to his condition. 7 Toullier, n. 258.

BENEFICIUM DIVISIONIS. In civil and Scotch law. The privilege of one of several co-sureties (cautioners) to insist upon paying only his *pro rata* share of the debt. Bell.

BENEFICIUM INVENTARII. See BENEFIT OF INVENTORY.

Beneficium non datum nisi propter officium. Hob. 148. A remuneration not given, unless on account of a duty performed.

BENEFICIUM ORDINIS. In civil and Scotch law. The privilege of order. The privilege of a surety to require that the creditor should first proceed against the principal and exhaust his remedy against him, before resorting to the surety. Bell.

BENEFICIUM SEPARATIONIS. In the civil law. The right to have the goods of an heir separated from those of the testator in favor of creditors.

BENEFIT BUILDING SOCIETY. The original name for what is now more commonly called a "building society," (*q. v.*)

BENEFIT OF CESSION. In the civil law. The release of a debtor from future imprisonment for his debts, which the law operates in his favor upon the surrender of his property for the benefit of his creditors. Poth. Proc. Civil, pt. 5, c. 2, § 1.

BENEFIT OF CLERGY. In its original sense, the phrase denoted the exemption which was accorded to clergymen from the jurisdiction of the secular courts, or from arrest or attachment on criminal process issu-

ing from those courts in certain particular cases. Afterwards, it meant a privilege of exemption from the punishment of death accorded to such persons as were *clerks*, or who could read.

This privilege of exemption from capital punishment was anciently allowed to clergymen only, but afterwards to all who were connected with the church, even to its most subordinate officers, and at a still later time to all persons who could read, (then called "clerks,") whether ecclesiastics or laymen. It does not appear to have been extended to cases of high treason, nor did it apply to mere misdemeanors. The privilege was claimed after the person's conviction, by a species of motion in arrest of judgment, technically called "praying his clergy." As a means of testing his clerical character, he was given a psalm to read, (usually, or always, the fifty-first,) and, upon his reading it correctly, he was turned over to the ecclesiastical courts, to be tried by the bishop or a jury of twelve clerks. These heard him on oath, with his witnesses and compurgators, who attested their belief in his innocence. This privilege operated greatly to mitigate the extreme rigor of the criminal laws, but was found to involve such gross abuses that parliament began to enact that certain crimes should be felonies "without benefit of clergy," and finally, by St. 7 Geo. IV. c. 28, § 6, it was altogether abolished. The act of congress of April 30, 1790, § 30, provided that there should be no benefit of clergy for any capital crime against the United States, and, if this privilege formed a part of the common law of the several states before the Revolution, it no longer exists.

BENEFIT OF DISCUSSION. In the civil law. The right which a surety has to cause the property of the principal debtor to be applied in satisfaction of the obligation in the first instance. Civil Code La. arts. 3014–3020.

In Scotch law. That whereby the antecedent heir, such as the heir of line in a pursuit against the heir of tailzie, etc., must be first pursued to fulfill the defunct's deeds and pay his debts. This benefit is likewise competent in many cases to cautioners.

BENEFIT OF DIVISION. Same as *beneficium divisionis*, (*q. v.*)

BENEFIT OF INVENTORY. In the civil law. The privilege which the heir obtains of being liable for the charges and debts of the succession, only to the value of the effects of the succession, by causing an inventory of these effects within the time and manner prescribed by law. Civil Code La. art. 1032.

BENEFIT SOCIETIES. Under this and several similar names, in various states, corporations exist to receive periodical payments from members, and hold them as a fund to be loaned or given to members needing pecuniary relief. Such are beneficial societies of Maryland, fund associations of Missouri, loan and fund associations of Massachusetts, mechanics' associations of Michigan, protection societies of New Jersey. Friendly societies in Great Britain are a still more extensive and important species belonging to this class. Abbott.

BENERTH. A feudal service rendered by the tenant to his lord with plow and cart. Cowell.

BENEVOLENCE. The doing a kind or helpful action towards another, under no obligation except an ethical one.

Is no doubt distinguishable from the words "liberality" and "charity;" for, although many charitable institutions are very properly called "benevolent," it is impossible to say that every object of a man's benevolence is also an object of his charity. 3 Mer. 17.

In public law. Nominally a voluntary gratuity given by subjects to their king, but in reality a tax or forced loan.

BENEVOLENT. This word is certainly more indefinite, and of far wider range, than "charitable" or "religious;" it would include all gifts prompted by good-will or kind feeling towards the recipient, whether an object of charity or not. The natural and usual meaning of the word would so extend it. It has no legal meaning separate from its usual meaning. "Charitable" has acquired a settled limited meaning in law, which confines it within known limits. But in all the decisions in England on the subject it has been held that a devise or bequest for benevolent objects, or in trust to give to such objects, is too indefinite, and therefore void. 19 N. J. Eq. 307, 313; 20 N. J. Eq. 489.

This word, as applied to objects or purposes, may refer to those which are in their nature charitable, and may also have a broader meaning and include objects and purposes not charitable in the legal sense of that word. Acts of kindness, friendship, forethought, or good-will might properly be described as benevolent. It has therefore been held that gifts to trustees to be applied for "benevolent purposes" at their discretion, or to such "benevolent purposes" as they could agree upon, do not create a public charity. But where the word is used in connection with other words explanatory of its meaning, and indicating the intent of the donor to limit it to purposes strictly charitable, it has been held to be synonymous with, or equivalent to, "charitable." 132 Mass. 413. See, also,

111 Mass. 268; 31 N. J. Eq. 695; 23 Minn. 92.

BENEVOLENT SOCIETIES. In English law. Societies established and registered under the friendly societies act, 1875, for any charitable or benevolent purposes.

Benigne faciendæ sunt interpretationes chartarum, ut res magis valeat quam pereat; et quælibet concessio fortissime contra donatorem interpretanda est. Liberal interpretations are to be made of deeds, so that the purpose may rather stand than fall; and every grant is to be taken most strongly against the grantor. 4 Mass. 134; 1 Sandf. Ch. 258, 268.

Benigne faciendæ sunt interpretationes, propter simplicitatem laicorum, ut res magis valeat quam pereat. Constructions [of written instruments] are to be made liberally, on account of the simplicity of the laity, [or common people,] in order that the thing [or subject-matter] may rather have effect than perish, [or become void.] Co. Litt. 36a; Broom, Max. 540.

Benignior sententia in verbis generalibus seu dubiis, est præferenda. 4 Coke, 15. The more favorable construction is to be placed on general or doubtful expressions.

Benignius leges interpretandæ sunt quo voluntas earum conservetur. Laws are to be more liberally interpreted, in order that their intent may be preserved. Dig. 1, 3, 18.

BEQUEATH. To give personal property by will to another. 13 Barb. 106. The word may be construed *devise*, so as to pass real estate. Wig. Wills, 11.

BEQUEST. A gift by will of personal property; a legacy.

A *specific* bequest is one whereby the testator gives to the legatee all his property of a certain class or kind; as all his pure personalty.

A *residuary* bequest is a gift of all the remainder of the testator's personal estate, after payment of debts and legacies, etc.

An *executory* bequest is the bequest of a future, deferred, or contingent interest in personalty.

BERCARIA. In old English law, a sheepfold; also a place where the bark of trees was laid to tan.

BERCARIUS, OR BERCATOR. A shepherd.

BEREWICHA, or BEREWICA. In old English law. A term used in Domesday for a village or hamlet belonging to some town or manor.

BERGHMAYSTER. An officer having charge of a mine. A bailiff or chief officer among the Derbyshire miners, who, in addition to his other duties, executes the office of coroner among them. Blount; Cowell.

BERGHMOTH, or BERGHMOTE. The ancient name of the court now called "barmote," (*q. v.*)

BERNET. In Saxon law. Burning; the crime of house burning, now called "arson." Cowell; Blount.

BERRA. In old law. A plain; open heath. Cowell.

BERRY, or BURY. A villa or seat of habitation of a nobleman; a dwelling or mansion house; a sanctuary.

BERTON. A large farm; the barn-yard of a large farm.

BES. Lat. In the Roman law. A division of the *as*, or pound, consisting of eight *unciæ*. or duodecimal parts, and amounting to two-thirds of the *as*. 2 Bl. Comm. 462, note *m*.

Two-thirds of an inheritance. Inst. 2, 14, 5.

Eight per cent. interest. 2 Bl. Comm. ubi supra.

BESAILE, BESAYLE. The great-grandfather, *proavus*. 1 Bl. Comm. 186.

BESAYEL, Besaiel, Besayle. In old English law. A writ which lay where a great-grandfather died seised of lands and tenements in fee-simple, and on the day of his death a stranger abated, or entered and kept out the heir. Reg. Orig. 226; Fitzh. Nat. Brev. 221 D; 3 Bl. Comm. 186.

BEST EVIDENCE. Primary evidence, as distinguished from secondary; original, as distinguished from substitutionary; the best and highest evidence of which the nature of the case is susceptible. A written instrument is itself always regarded as the primary or best possible evidence of its existence and contents; a copy, or the recollection of a witness, would be secondary evidence.

BESTIALITY. Bestiality is the carnal knowledge and connection against the order of nature by man or woman in any manner with a beast. Code Ga. 1882, § 4354.

We take it that there is a difference in signification between the terms "bestiality," and the "crime against nature." *Bestiality* is a connection between a human being and a brute of the opposite sex. *Sodomy* is a connection between two human beings of the same sex,—the male,—named from the prevalence of the sin in *Sodom*. Both may be embraced by the term "crime against nature," as felony embraces murder, larceny, etc., though we think that term is more generally used in reference to sodomy. *Buggery* seems to include both sodomy and bestiality. 10 Ind. 356.

BET. Bet and wager are synonymous terms, and are applied both to the contract of betting or wagering and to the thing or sum bet or wagered. For example, one bets or wagers, or lays a bet or wager of so much, upon a certain result. But these terms cannot properly be applied to the act to be done, or event to happen, upon which the bet or wager is laid. Bets or wagers may be laid upon acts to be done, events to happen, or facts existing or to exist. The bets or wagers may be illegal, and the acts, events, or facts upon which they are laid may not be. Bets or wagers may be laid upon games, and things that are not games. Everything upon which a bet or wager may be laid is not a game. 11 Ind. 16. See, also, 81 N. Y. 539.

BETROTHMENT. Mutual promise of marriage; the plighting of troth; a mutual promise or contract between a man and woman competent to make it, to marry at a future time.

BETTER EQUITY. The right which, in a court of equity, a second incumbrancer has who has taken securities against subsequent dealings to his prejudice, which a prior incumbrancer neglected to take although he had an opportunity. 1 Ch. Prec. 470, n.; 4 Rawle, 144. See 3 Bouv. Inst. n. 2462.

BETTERMENTS. Improvements put upon an estate which enhance its value more than mere repairs. The term is also applied to denote the additional value which an estate acquires in consequence of some public improvement, as laying out or widening a street, etc.

BETWEEN. As a measure or indication of distance, this word has the effect of excluding the two termini. 1 Mass. 93; 12 Me. 366. Compare 31 N. J. Law, 212.

If an act is to be done "between" two certain days, it must be performed before the commencement of the latter day. In computing the time in such a case, both the days named are to be excluded. 14 Ill. 332; 16 Barb. 352.

In case of a devise to A. and B. "between them," these words create a tenancy in common. 2 Mer. 70.

BEVERAGE. This term is properly used to distinguish a sale of liquors to be drunk for the pleasure of drinking, from liquors to be drunk in obedience to a physician's advice. 142 Mass. 469, 8 N. E. Rep. 327.

BEWARED. O. Eng. Expended. Before the Britons and Saxons had introduced the general use of money, they traded chiefly by exchange of wares. Wharton.

BEYOND SEA. Beyond the limits of the kingdom of Great Britain and Ireland; outside the United States; out of the state.

Beyond sea, beyond the four seas, beyond the seas, and out of the realm, are synonymous. Prior to the union of the two crowns of England and Scotland, on the accession of James I., the phrases "beyond the four seas," "beyond the seas," and "out of the realm," signified out of the limits of the realm of England. 1 Har. & J. 350.

In Pennsylvania, it has been construed to mean "without the limits of the United States," which approaches the literal signification. 2 Dall. 217; 1 Yeates, 329; 6 Pet. 291, 300. The same construction has been given to it in Missouri. 20 Mo. 530. See Ang. Lim. §§ 200, 201.

The term "beyond seas," in the proviso or saving clause of a statute of limitations, is equivalent to without the limits of the state where the statute is enacted; and the party who is without those limits is entitled to the benefit of the exception. 3 Cranch, 174; 3 Wheat. 541; 11 Wheat. 361; 1 McLean, 146; 2 McCord, 331; 8 Ark. 488; 26 Ga. 182; 13 N. H. 79.

BIAS. This term is not synonymous with "prejudice." By the use of this word in a statute declaring disqualification of jurors, the legislature intended to describe another and somewhat different ground of disqualification. A man cannot be prejudiced against another without being biased against him; but he may be biased without being prejudiced. Bias is "a particular influential power, which sways the judgment; the inclination of the mind towards a particular object." It is not to be supposed that the legislature expected to secure in the juror a state of mind absolutely free from all inclination to one side or the other. The statute means that, although a juror has not formed a judgment for or against the prisoner, before the evidence is heard on the trial, yet, if he is under such an influence as so sways his mind to the one side or the other as to prevent his deciding the cause according to the evidence, he is incompetent. 12 Ga. 444.

BID. An offer by an intending purchaser to pay a designated price for property which is about to be sold at auction.

BIDAL, or BIDALL. An invitation of friends to drink ale at the house of some poor man, who hopes thereby to be relieved by charitable contribution. It is something like "house-warming," i. e., a visit of friends to a person beginning to set up house-keeping. Wharton.

BIDDER. One who offers to pay a specified price for an article offered for sale at a public auction. 11 Ill. 254.

BIDDINGS. Offers of a designated price for goods or other property put up for sale at auction.

BIELBRIEF. Germ. In European maritime law. A document furnished by the builder of a vessel, containing a register of her admeasurement, particularizing the length, breadth, and dimensions of every part of the ship. It sometimes also contains the terms of agreement between the party for whose account the ship is built, and the ship-builder. It has been termed in English the "grand bill of sale;" in French, "*contrat de construction ou de la vente d'un vaisseau*," and corresponds in a great degree with the English, French, and American "register," (*q. v.*,) being an equally essential document to the lawful ownership of vessels. Jac. Sea Laws, 12, 13, and note. In the Danish law, it is used to denote the contract of bottomry.

BIENNIALLY. This term, in a statute, signifies, not duration of time, but a period for the happening of an event; once in every two years. 9 Hun, 573; 68 N. Y. 479.

BIENS. In English law. Property of every description, except estates of freehold and inheritance. Sugd. Vend. 495; Co. Litt. 119b.

In French law. This term includes all kinds of property, real and personal. *Biens* are divided into *biens meubles*, movable property; and *biens immeubles*, immovable property. The distinction between movable and immovable property is recognized by the continental jurists, and gives rise, in the civil as well as in the common law, to many important distinctions as to rights and remedies. Story, Confl. Laws, § 13, note 1.

BIGA, or BIGATA. A cart or chariot drawn with two horses, coupled side to side; but it is said to be properly a cart with two wheels, sometimes drawn by one horse; and in the ancient records it is used for any cart, wain, or wagon. Jacob.

BIGAMUS. In the civil law. A man who was twice married; one who at different times and successively has married two wives. 4 Inst. 88. One who has two wives living. One who marries a widow.

Bigamus seu trigamus, etc., est qui diversis temporibus et successivè duas seu tres uxores habuit. 4 Inst. 88. A bigamus or trigamus, etc., is one who at different times and successively has married two or three wives.

BIGAMY. The criminal offense of willfully and knowingly contracting a second marriage (or going through the form of a second marriage) while the first marriage, to the knowledge of the offender, is still subsisting and undissolved.

The state of a man who has two wives, or of a woman who has two husbands, living at the same time.

The offense of having a plurality of wives at the same time is commonly denominated "polygamy;" but the name "bigamy" has been more frequently given to it in legal proceedings. 1 Russ. Crimes, 185.

The use of the word "bigamy" to describe this offense is well established by long usage, although often criticised as a corruption of the true meaning of the word. Polygamy is suggested as the correct term, instead of bigamy, to designate the offense of having a plurality of wives or husbands at the same time, and has been adopted for that purpose in the Massachusetts statutes. But as the substance of the offense is marrying a second time, while having a lawful husband or wife living, without regard to the number of marriages that may have taken place, bigamy seems not an inappropriate term. The objection to its use urged by Blackstone (4 Bl. Comm. 163) seems to be founded not so much upon considerations of the etymology of the word as upon the propriety of distinguishing the ecclesiastical offense termed "bigamy" in the canon law, and which is defined below, from the offense known as "bigamy" in the modern criminal law. The same distinction is carefully made by Lord Coke, (4 Inst. 88.) But, the ecclesiastical offense being now obsolete, this reason for substituting polygamy to denote the crime here defined ceases to have weight. Abbott.

In the canon law, the term denoted the offense committed by an ecclesiastic who married two wives successively. It might be committed either by marrying a second wife after the death of a first or by marrying a widow.

BIGOT. An obstinate person, or one that is wedded to an opinion, in matters of religion, etc.

BILAGINES. By-laws of towns; municipal laws.

BILAN. A term used in Louisiana, derived from the French. A book in which bankers, merchants, and traders write a statement of all they owe and all that is due them; a balance-sheet. See 3 Mart. (N. S.) 446.

BILANCIIS DEFERENDIS. In English law. An obsolete writ addressed to a corporation for the carrying of weights to such a haven, there to weigh the wool anciently licensed for transportation. Reg. Orig. 270.

BILATERAL CONTRACT. A term, used originally in the civil law, but now generally adopted, denoting a contract in which both the contracting parties are bound to fulfill obligations reciprocally towards each other; as a contract of sale, where one becomes bound to deliver the thing sold, and the other to pay the price of it.

"Every convention properly so called consists of a promise or mutual promises proffered and accepted. Where one only of the agreeing parties gives a promise, the convention is said to be 'unilateral.' Wherever mutual promises are proffered and accepted, there are, in strictness, two or more conventions. But where the performance of either of the promises is made to depend on the performance of the other, the several conventions are commonly deemed one convention, and the convention is then said to be 'bilateral.'" Aust. Jur. § 308.

BILGED. In admiralty law and marine insurance. That state or condition of a vessel in which water is freely admitted through holes and breaches made in the planks of the bottom, occasioned by injuries, whether the ship's timbers are broken or not. 3 Mass. 39.

BILINE. A word used by Britton in the sense of "collateral." *En line biline*, in the collateral line. Britt. c. 119.

BILINGUIS. Of a double language or tongue; that can speak two languages. A term applied in the old books to a jury composed partly of Englishmen and partly of foreigners, which, by the English law, an alien party to a suit is, in certain cases, entitled to; more commonly called a "jury *de medietate linguæ*." 3 Bl. Comm. 360; 4 Steph. Comm. 422.

BILL. A formal declaration, complaint, or statement of particular things in writing. As a legal term, this word has many meanings and applications, the more important of which are enumerated below.

1. A formal written statement of complaint to a court of justice.

In the ancient practice of the court of king's bench, the usual and orderly method of beginning an action was by a *bill*, or original bill, or plaint. This was a written statement of the plaintiff's cause of action, like a declaration or complaint, and always alleged a trespass as the ground of it, in order to give the court jurisdiction. 3 Bl. Comm. 43.

2. A formal written declaration by a court to its officers, in the nature of process; as the old *bill of Middlesex.*

3. A record or certified written account of the proceedings in an action, or a portion of the same; as *a bill of exceptions.*

4. In equity practice. A formal written complaint, in the nature of a petition, addressed by a suitor in chancery to the chancellor or to a court of equity or a court having equitable jurisdiction, showing the names of the parties, stating the facts which make up the case and the complainant's allegations, averring that the acts disclosed are contrary to equity, and praying for process and for specific relief, or for such relief as the circumstances demand.

Bills are said to be original, not original, or in the nature of original bills. They are original when the circumstances constituting the case are not already before the court, and relief is demanded, or the bill is filed for a subsidiary purpose.

5. In legislation and constitutional law, the word means a draft of an act of the legislature before it becomes a law; a proposed or projected law. A draft of an act presented to the legislature, but not enacted. An *act* is the appropriate term for it, after it has been acted on by, and passed by, the legislature. 26 Pa. St. 450.

Also a special act passed by a legislative body in the exercise of a *quasi* judicial power. Thus, bills of attainder, bills of pains and penalties, are spoken of.

In England, "bill" also signifies the draft of a patent for a charter, commission, dignity, office, or appointment; such a bill is drawn up in the attorney general's patent bill office, is submitted by a secretary of state for her majesty's signature, when it is called the "queen's bill;" it is countersigned by the secretary of state, and sealed by the privy seal, and then the patent is prepared and sealed. Sweet.

6. A solemn and formal legislative declaration of popular rights and liberties, promulgated on certain extraordinary occasions; as the famous *Bill of Rights* in English history.

7. As a contract. An obligation; a deed, whereby the obligor acknowledges himself to owe unto the obligee a certain sum of money or some other thing, in which, besides the names of the parties, are to be considered the sum or thing due, the time, place, and manner of payment or delivery thereof. It may be indented or poll, and with or without a penalty. West, Symb. §§ 100, 101.

8. A written statement of the terms of a contract, or specification of the items of a demand, or counter-demand.

Also the creditor's written statement of his claim, specifying the items.

9. By the English usage, it is applied to the statement of the charges and disbursements of an attorney or solicitor incurred in the conduct of his client's business, and which might be taxed upon application, even though not incurred in any suit. Thus, conveyancing costs might be taxed. Wharton.

BILL-BOOK. In mercantile law. A book in which an account of bills of exchange and promissory notes, whether payable or receivable, is stated.

BILL CHAMBER. In Scotch law. A department of the court of session in which petitions for suspension, interdict, etc., are entertained. It is equivalent to sittings in chambers in the English and American practice. Paters. Comp.

BILL FOR A NEW TRIAL. In equity practice. A bill in equity in which the specific relief asked is an injunction against the execution of a judgment rendered at law and a new trial in the action, on account of some fact which would render it inequitable to enforce the judgment, but which was not available to the party on the trial at law, or which he was prevented from presenting by fraud or accident, without concurrent fraud or negligence on his own part.

BILL FOR FORECLOSURE. In equity practice. One which is filed by a mortgagee against the mortgagor, for the purpose of having the estate sold, thereby to obtain the sum mortgaged on the premises, with interest and costs. 1 Madd. Ch. Pr. 528.

BILL-HEAD. A printed form on which merchants and traders make out their bills and render accounts to their customers.

BILL IN CHANCERY. See BILL, 4.

BILL IN EQUITY. See BILL, 4.

BILL IN NATURE OF A BILL OF REVIEW. A bill in equity, to obtain a re-examination and reversal of a decree, filed by one who was not a party to the original suit, nor bound by the decree.

C

D

E

F

G

H

I

J

K

L

M

BILL IN NATURE OF A BILL OF REVIVOR. Where, on the abatement of a suit, there is such a transmission of the interest of the incapacitated party that the title to it, as well as the person entitled, may be the subject of litigation in a court of chancery, the suit cannot be continued by a mere bill of revivor, but an original bill upon which the title may be litigated must be filed. This is called a "bill in the nature of a bill of revivor." It is founded on privity of estate or title by the act of the party. And the nature and operation of the whole act by which the privity is created is open to controversy. Story, Eq. Pl. §§ 378-380; 2 Amer. & Eng. Enc. Law, 271.

BILL IN NATURE OF A SUPPLEMENTAL BILL. A bill filed when new parties, with new interests, arising from events happening since the suit was commenced, are brought before the court; wherein it differs from a supplemental bill, which is properly applicable to those cases only where the same parties or the same interests remain before the court. Story, Eq. Pl. (5th Ed.) § 345 *et seq*.

BILL OBLIGATORY. A bond absolute for the payment of money. It is called also a "single bill," and differs from a promissory note only in having a seal. 2 Serg. & R. 115.

BILL OF ADVENTURE. A written certificate by a merchant or the master or owner of a ship, to the effect that the property and risk in goods shipped on the vessel in his own name belong to another person, to whom he is accountable for the proceeds alone.

BILL OF ADVOCATION. In Scotch practice. A bill by which the judgment of an inferior court is appealed from, or brought under review of a superior. Bell.

BILL OF APPEAL. An ancient, but now abolished, method of criminal prosecution. See BATTEL.

BILL OF ATTAINDER. A legislative act, directed against a designated person, pronouncing him guilty of an alleged crime, (usually treason,) without trial or conviction according to the recognized rules of procedure, and passing sentence of death and attainder upon him.

"Bills of attainder," as they are technically called, are such special acts of the legislature as inflict capital punishments upon persons supposed to be guilty of high offenses, such as treason and felony, without any conviction in the ordinary course of judicial proceedings. If an act inflicts a milder degree of punishment than death, it is called a "bill of pains and penalties," but both are included in the prohibition in the Federal constitution. Story, Const. § 1344.

BILL OF CERTIORARI. A bill, the object of which is to remove a suit in equity from some inferior court to the court of chancery, or some other superior court of equity, on account of some alleged incompetency of the inferior court, or some injustice in its proceedings. Story, Eq. Pl. (5th Ed.) § 298.

BILL OF CONFORMITY. In equity practice. One filed by an executor or administrator, who finds the affairs of the deceased so much involved that he cannot safely administer the estate except under the direction of a court of chancery. This bill is filed against the creditors, generally, for the purpose of having all their claims adjusted, and procuring a final decree settling the order of payment of the assets. 1 Story, Eq. Jur. § 440.

BILL OF COSTS. A certified, itemized statement of the amount of costs in an action or suit.

BILL OF CREDIT. In constitutional law. A bill or promissory note issued by the government of a state or nation, upon its faith and credit, designed to circulate in the community as money, and redeemable at a future day.

In mercantile law. A license or authority given in writing from one person to another, very common among merchants, bankers, and those who travel, empowering a person to receive or take up money of their correspondents abroad.

BILL OF DEBT. An ancient term including promissory notes and bonds for the payment of money. Com. Dig. "Merchant," F. 2.

BILL OF DISCOVERY. A bill in equity filed to obtain a discovery of facts resting in the knowledge of the defendant, or of deeds or writings, or other things in his custody or power. Story, Eq. Pl. (5th Ed.) § 311.

BILL OF ENTRY. An account of the goods entered at the custom house, both incoming and outgoing. It must state the name of the merchant exporting or importing, the quantity and species of merchandise, and whither transported, and whence.

BILL OF EXCEPTIONS. A formal statement in writing of the objections or exceptions taken by a party during the trial of a cause to the decisions, rulings, or instructions of the trial judge, stating the objection, with the facts and circumstances on which it is founded, and, in order to attest its accuracy, signed and sealed by the judge; the object being to put the controverted rulings or decisions upon the record for the information of the appellate court. 2 Dak. 470, 11 N. W. Rep. 497; Pow. App. Proc. 211.

BILL OF EXCHANGE. A written order from A. to B., directing B. to pay to C. a certain sum of money therein named. Byles, Bills, 1.

An open (that is, unsealed) letter addressed by one person to another directing him, in effect, to pay, absolutely and at all events, a certain sum of money therein named, to a third person, or to any other to whom that third person may order it to be paid, or it may be payable to bearer or to the drawer himself. 1 Daniel, Neg. Inst. 27.

A bill of exchange is an instrument, negotiable in form, by which one, who is called the "drawer," requests another, called the "drawee," to pay a specified sum of money. Civil Code Cal. § 3171.

A bill of exchange is an order by one person, called the "drawer" or "maker," to another, called the "drawee" or "acceptor," to pay money to another, (who may be the drawer himself,) called the "payee," or his order, or to the bearer. If the payee, or a bearer, transfers the bill by indorsement, he then becomes the "indorser." If the drawer or drawee resides out of this state, it is then called a "foreign bill of exchange." Code Ga. 1882, § 2773.

BILL OF GROSS ADVENTURE. In French maritime law. Any written instrument which contains a contract of bottomry, *respondentia*, or any other kind of maritime loan. There is no corresponding English term. Hall, Marit. Loans, 182, n.

BILL OF HEALTH. An official certificate, given by the authorities of a port from which a vessel clears, to the master of the ship, showing the state of the port, as respects the public health, at the time of sailing, and exhibited to the authorities of the port which the vessel next makes, in token that she does not bring disease. If the bill alleges that no contagious or infectious disease existed, it is called a "clean" bill; if it admits that one was suspected or anticipated,

or that one actually prevailed, it is called a "touched" or a "foul" bill.

In Scotch law. An application of a person in custody to be discharged on account of ill health. Where the health of a prisoner requires it, he may be indulged, under proper regulations, with such a degree of liberty as may be necessary to restore him. 2 Bell, Comm. (5th Ed.) 549; Paters. Comp. § 1129.

BILL OF INDEMNITY. In English law. An act of parliament, passed every session until 1869, but discontinued in and after that year, as having been rendered unnecessary by the passing of the promissory oaths act, 1868, for the relief of those who have unwittingly or unavoidably neglected to take the necessary oaths, etc., required for the purpose of qualifying them to hold their respective offices. Wharton.

BILL OF INDICTMENT. A formal written document accusing a person or persons named of having committed a felony or misdemeanor, lawfully laid before a grand jury for their action upon it. If the grand jury decide that a trial ought to be had, they indorse on it "a true bill;" if otherwise, "not a true bill" or "not found."

BILL OF INFORMATION. In chancery practice. Where a suit is instituted on behalf of the crown or government, or of those of whom it has the custody by virtue of its prerogative, or whose rights are under its particular protection, the matter of complaint is offered to the court by way of information by the attorney or solicitor general, instead of by petition. Where a suit immediately concerns the crown or government alone, the proceeding is purely by way of information, but, where it does not do so immediately, a relator is appointed, who is answerable for costs, etc., and, if he is interested in the matter in connection with the crown or government, the proceeding is by information and bill. Informations differ from bills in little more than name and form, and the same rules are substantially applicable to both. See Story, Eq. Pl. 5; 1 Daniell, Ch. Pr. 2, 8, 288; 3 Bl. Comm. 261.

BILL OF INTERPLEADER. The name of a bill in equity to obtain a settlement of a question of right to money or other property adversely claimed, in which the party filing the bill has no interest, although it may be in his hands, by compelling such adverse claimants to litigate the right or title between themselves, and relieve him from liability or litigation.

BILL OF LADING. In common law. The written evidence of a contract for the carriage and delivery of goods sent by sea for a certain freight. 1 H. Bl. 359.

A written memorandum, given by the person in command of a merchant vessel, acknowledging the receipt on board the ship of certain specified goods, in good order or "apparent good order," which he undertakes, in consideration of the payment of freight, to deliver in like good order (dangers of the sea excepted) at a designated place to the consignee therein named or to his assigns.

The term is often applied to a similar receipt and undertaking given by a carrier of goods by land.

A bill of lading is an instrument in writing, signed by a carrier or his agent, describing the freight so as to indentify it, stating the name of the consignor, the terms of the contract for carriage, and agreeing or directing that the freight be delivered to the order or assigns of a specified person at a specified place. Civil Code Cal. § 2126; Civil Code Dak. § 1229.

BILL OF MIDDLESEX. An old form of process similar to a *capias*, issued out of the court of king's bench in personal actions, directed to the sheriff of the county of Middlesex, (hence the name,) and commanding him to take the defendant and have him before the king at Westminster on a day named, to answer the plaintiff's complaint.

BILL OF MORTALITY. A written statement or account of the number of deaths which have occurred in a certain district during a given time. In some places, births as well as deaths are included.

BILL OF PAINS AND PENALTIES. A special act of the legislature which inflicts a punishment, less than death, upon persons supposed to be guilty of treason or felony, without any conviction in the ordinary course of judicial proceedings. It differs from a bill of attainder in this: that the punishment inflicted by the latter is death.

BILL OF PARCELS. A statement sent to the buyer of goods, along with the goods, exhibiting in detail the items composing the parcel and their several prices, to enable him to detect any mistake or omission; an invoice.

BILL OF PARTICULARS. In practice. A written statement or specification of the particulars of the demand for which an action at law is brought, or of a defendant's set-off against such demand, (including dates, sums, and items in detail,) furnished by one of the parties to the other, either voluntarily or in compliance with a judge's order for that purpose. 1 Tidd. Pr. 596-600; 2 Archb. Pr. 221.

BILL OF PEACE. In equity practice. One which is filed when a person has a right which may be controverted by various persons, at different times, and by different actions.

BILL OF PRIVILEGE. In old English law. A method of proceeding against attorneys and officers of the court not liable to arrest. 3 Bl. Comm. 289.

BILL OF PROOF. In English practice. The name given, in the mayor's court of London, to a species of intervention by a third person laying claim to the subject-matter in dispute between the parties to a suit.

BILL OF REVIVOR. In equity practice. One which is brought to continue a suit which has abated before its final consummation, as, for example, by death, or marriage of a female plaintiff.

BILL OF REVIVOR AND SUPPLEMENT. In equity practice. One which is a compound of a supplemental bill and bill of revivor, and not only continues the suit, which has abated by the death of the plaintiff, or the like, but supplies any defects in the original bill arising from subsequent events, so as to entitle the party to relief on the whole merits of his case. 5 Johns. Ch. 334; Mitf. Eq. Pl. 32, 74.

BILL OF REVIEW. In equity practice. One which is brought to have a decree of the court reviewed, corrected, or reversed.

BILL OF RIGHTS. A formal and emphatic legislative assertion and declaration of popular rights and liberties usually promulgated upon a change of government; particularly the statute 1 W. & M. St. 2, c. 2. Also the summary of the rights and liberties of the people, or of the principles of constitutional law deemed essential and fundamental, contained in many of the American state constitutions.

BILL OF SALE. In contracts. A written agreement under seal, by which one person assigns or transfers his right to or interest in goods and personal chattels to another.

An instrument by which, in particular, the property in ships and vessels is conveyed.

BILL OF SIGHT. When an importer of goods is ignorant of their exact quantity or quality, so that he cannot make a perfect entry of them, he may give to the customs officer a written description of them, according to the best of his information and belief. This is called a "bill of sight."

BILL OF STORE. In English law. A kind of license granted at the custom-house to merchants, to carry such stores and provisions as are necessary for their voyage, custom free. Jacob.

BILL OF SUFFERANCE. In English law. A license granted at the custom-house to a merchant, to suffer him to trade from one English port to another, without paying custom. Cowell.

BILL PAYABLE. In a merchant's accounts, all bills which he has accepted, and promissory notes which he has made, are called "bills payable," and are entered in a ledger account under that name, and recorded in a book bearing the same title.

BILL PENAL. In contracts. A written obligation by which a debtor acknowledges himself indebted in a certain sum, and binds himself for the payment thereof, in a larger sum, called a "penalty."

BILL QUIA TIMET. A bill invoking the aid of equity "because he fears," that is, because the complainant apprehends an injury to his property rights or interests, from the fault or neglect of another. Such bills are entertained to guard against possible or prospective injuries, and to preserve the means by which existing rights may be protected from future or contingent violations; differing from injunctions, in that the latter correct past and present or imminent and certain injuries. Bisp. Eq. § 568; 2 Story, Eq. Jur. § 826.

BILL RECEIVABLE. In a merchant's accounts, all notes, drafts, checks, etc., payable to him, or of which he is to receive the proceeds at a future date, are called "bills receivable," and are entered in a ledger-account under that name, and also noted in a book bearing the same title.

BILL RENDERED. A bill of items rendered by a creditor to his debtor; an "account rendered," as distinguished from "an account stated."

BILL SINGLE. A written promise to pay to a person or persons named a stated sum at a stated time, without any condition. When under seal, as is usually the case, it is sometimes called a "bill obligatory," (*q. v.*) It differs from a "bill penal," (*q. v.*,) in that it expresses no penalty.

BILL TO CARRY A DECREE INTO EXECUTION. In equity practice. One which is filed when, from the neglect of parties or some other cause, it may become impossible to carry a decree into execution without the further decree of the court. Hind, Ch. Pr. 68; Story, Eq. Pl. § 42.

BILL TO PERPETUATE TESTIMONY. A bill in equity filed in order to procure the testimony of witnesses to be taken as to some matter not at the time before the courts, but which is likely at some future time to be in litigation. Story, Eq. Pl. (5th Ed.) § 300 et seq.

BILL TO SUSPEND A DECREE. In equity practice. One brought to avoid or suspend a decree under special circumstances.

BILL TO TAKE TESTIMONY DE BENE ESSE. In equity practice. One which is brought to take the testimony of witnesses to a fact material to the prosecution of a suit at law which is actually commenced, where there is good cause to fear that the testimony may otherwise be lost before the time of trial. 2 Story, Eq. Jur. § 1813, n.

BILLA. L. Lat. A bill; an original bill.

BILLA CASSETUR, or QUOD BILLA CASSETUR. (That the bill be quashed.) In practice. The form of the judgment rendered for a defendant on a plea in abatement, where the proceeding is *by bill;* that is, where the suit is commenced by *capias*, and not by original writ. 2 Archb. Pr. K. B. 4.

BILLA EXCAMBII. A bill of exchange.

BILLA EXONERATIONIS. A bill of lading.

BILLA VERA. (A true bill.) In old practice. The indorsement anciently made on a bill of indictment by a grand jury, when they found it sufficiently sustained by evidence. 4 Bl. Comm. 306.

BILLET. A soldier's quarters in a civilian's house; or the ticket which authorizes him to occupy them.

In French law. A bill or promissory note. *Billet à ordre,* a bill payable to order. *Billet à vue,* a bill payable at sight. *Billet de complaisance,* an accommodation bill.

BILLET DE CHANGE. In French law. An engagement to give, at a future time, a bill of exchange, which the party is not at the time prepared to give. Story, Bills, § 2, n.

BILLETA. In old English law. A bill or petition exhibited in parliament. Cowell.

BILLETING SOLDIERS. Quartering them in the houses of private citizens; finding quarters for them.

BI-METALLIC. Pertaining to, or consisting of, two metals used as money at a fixed relative value.

BI-METALLISM. The legalized use of two metals in the currency of a country at a fixed relative value.

BIND. To obligate; to bring or place under definite duties or legal obligations, particularly by a bond or covenant; to affect one in a constraining or compulsory manner with a contract or a judgment. So long as a contract, an adjudication, or a legal relation remains in force and virtue, and continues to impose duties or obligations, it is said to be "*binding*." A man is *bound* by his contract or promise, by a judgment or decree against him, by his bond or covenant, by an estoppel, etc.

BIND OUT. To place one under a legal obligation to serve another; as to *bind out* an apprentice.

BINDING OVER. The act by which a court or magistrate requires a person to enter into a recognizance or furnish bail to appear for trial, to keep the peace, to attend as a witness, etc.

BIPARTITE. Consisting of, or divisible into, two parts. A term in conveyancing descriptive of an instrument in two parts, and executed by both parties.

BIRRETUM, BIRRETUS. A cap or coif used formerly in England by judges and serjeants at law. Spelman.

BIRTH. The act of being born or wholly brought into separate existence.

BIS. Lat. Twice.

Bis idem exigi bona fides non patitur; et in satisfactionibus non permittitur amplius fieri quam semel factum est. Good faith does not suffer the same thing to be demanded twice; and in making satisfaction [for a debt or demand] it is not allowed to be done more than once. 9 Coke, 53.

BISAILE. The father of one's grandfather or grandmother.

BISANTIUM, BESANTINE, BEZANT. An ancient coin, first issued at Constantinople; it was of two sorts,—gold, equivalent to a ducat, valued at 9s. 6d.; and silver, computed at 2s. They were both current in England. Wharton.

BI-SCOT. In old English law. A fine imposed for not repairing banks, ditches, and causeways.

BISHOP. An English ecclesiastical dignitary, being the chief of the clergy within his diocese, subject to the archbishop of the province in which his diocese is situated. Most of the bishops are also members of the house of lords.

A bishop has three powers: (1) A power of ordination, gained on his consecration, by which he confers orders, etc., in any place throughout the world; (2) a power of jurisdiction throughout his see or his bishopric; (3) a power of administration and government of the revenues thereof, gained on confirmation. He has, also, a consistory court, to hear ecclesiastical causes, and visits and superintends the clergy of his diocese. He consecrates churches and institutes priests, confirms, suspends, excommunicates, and grants licenses for marriages. He has his archdeacon, dean, and chapter, chancellor, who holds his courts and assists him in matters of ecclesiastical law, and vicar-general. He grants leases for three lives, or twenty-one years, reserving the accustomed yearly rent. Wharton.

BISHOPRIC. In ecclesiastical law. The diocese of a bishop, or the circuit in which he has jurisdiction; the office of a bishop. 1 Bl. Comm. 377–382.

BISHOP'S COURT. In English law. An ecclesiastical court, held in the cathedral of each diocese, the judge whereof is the bishop's chancellor, who judges by the civil canon law; and, if the diocese be large, he has his commissaries in remote parts, who hold *consistory courts*, for matters limited to them by their commission.

BISSEXTILE. The day which is added every fourth year to the month of February, in order to make the year agree with the course of the sun.

Leap year, consisting of 366 days, and happening every fourth year, by the addition of a day in the month of February, which in that year consists of twenty-nine days.

BLACK ACRE and WHITE ACRE. Fictitious names applied to pieces of land, and used as examples in the old books.

BLACK ACT. The statute 9 Geo. I. c. 22, so called because it was occasioned by the outrages committed by persons with their faces blacked or otherwise disguised, who appeared in Epping Forest, near Waltham, in Essex, and destroyed the deer there, and committed other offenses. Repealed by 7 & 8 Geo. IV. c. 27.

BLACK ACTS. Old Scotch statutes passed in the reigns of the Stuarts and down to the year 1586 or 1587, so called because printed in black letter. Bell.

BLACK BOOK OF HEREFORD. In English law. An old record frequently referred to by Cowell and other early writers.

BLACK BOOK OF THE ADMIRALTY. A book of the highest authority in admiralty matters, generally supposed to have been compiled during the reign of Edward III. with additions of a later date. It contains the laws of Oleron, a view of crimes and offenses cognizable in the admiralty, and many other matters. See 2 Gall. 404.

BLACK BOOK OF THE EXCHEQUER. The name of an ancient book kept in the English exchequer, containing a collection of treaties, conventions, charters, etc.

BLACK CAP. It is a vulgar error that the head-dress worn by the judge in pronouncing the sentence of death is assumed as an emblem of the sentence. It is part of the judicial full dress, and is worn by the judges on occasions of especial state. Wharton.

BLACK GAME. In English law. Heath fowl, in contradistinction to red game, as grouse.

BLACK-LIST. A list of persons marked out for special avoidance, antagonism, or enmity on the part of those who prepare the list or those among whom it is intended to circulate; as where a trades-union "black-lists" workmen who refuse to conform to its rules, or where a list of insolvent or untrustworthy persons is published by a commercial agency or mercantile association.

BLACK-MAIL. 1. In one of its original meanings, this term denoted a tribute paid by English dwellers along the Scottish border to influential chieftains of Scotland, as a condition of securing immunity from raids of marauders and border thieves.

2. It also designated rents payable in cattle, grain, work, and the like. Such rents were called "black-mail," (*reditus nigri*,) in distinction from white rents, (*blanche firmes*,) which were rents paid in silver.

3. The extortion of money by threats or overtures towards criminal prosecution or the destruction of a man's reputation or social standing.

In common parlance, the term is equivalent to, and synonymous with, "extortion,"—the exaction of money, either for the performance of a duty, the prevention of an injury, or the exercise of an influence. It supposes the service to be unlawful, and the payment involuntary. Not infrequently it is extorted by threats, or by operating upon the fears or the credulity, or by promises to conceal, or offers to expose, the weaknesses, the follies, or the crimes of the victim. 26 How. Pr. 431; 17 Abb. Pr. 226.

BLACK MARIA. A closed wagon or van in which prisoners are carried to and from the jail, or between the court and the jail.

BLACK RENTS. In old English law. Rents reserved in work, grain, provisions, or baser money, in contradistinction to those which were reserved in *white* money or silver, which were termed "white rents," (*reditus albi*,) or blanch farms. Tomlins; Whishaw.

BLACK-ROD, GENTLEMAN USHER OF. In England, the title of a chief officer of the queen, deriving his name from the *Black Rod* of office, on the top of which reposes a golden lion, which he carries.

BLACK WARD. A subvassal, who held ward of the king's vassal.

"BLACKLEG." "The word 'blackleg' has been used long enough to be understood, not only by experts in slang, but by the public at large, and therefore it was for the judge to expound its meaning. I have always understood the word 'blackleg' to mean a person who gets his living by frequenting race-courses and places where games of chance are played, getting the best odds, and giving the least he can, but not necessarily cheating. That is not indictable either by statute or at common law." Pollock, C. B., 3 Hurl. & N. 379.

BLADA. In old English law. Growing crops of grain of any kind. Spelman. All manner of annual grain. Cowell. Harvested grain. Bract. 217*b*; Reg. Orig. 94*b*, 95.

BLADARIUS. In old English law. A corn-monger; meal-man or corn-chandler; a bladier, or engrosser of corn or grain. Blount.

BLANC SEIGN. In Louisiana, a paper signed at the bottom by him who intends to bind himself, give acquittance, or compromise, at the discretion of the person whom he intrusts with such *blanc seign*, giving him power to fill it with what he may think proper, according to agreement. 6 Mart. (La.) 718.

BLANCH HOLDING. An ancient tenure of the law of Scotland, the duty payable being trifling, as a penny or a pepper-corn, etc., if required; similar to free and common socage.

BLANCHE FIRME. White rent; a rent reserved, payable in silver.

BLANCUS. In old law and practice. White; plain; smooth; blank.

BLANK. A space left unfilled in a written document, in which one or more words or marks are to be inserted to complete the sense.

Also a skeleton or printed form for any legal document, in which the necessary and invariable words are printed in their proper order, with blank spaces left for the insertion of such names, dates, figures, additional clauses, etc., as may be necessary to adapt the instrument to the particular case and to the design of the party using it.

BLANK ACCEPTANCE. An acceptance of a bill of exchange written on the paper before the bill is made, and delivered by the acceptor.

BLANK BAR. Also called the "common bar." The name of a plea in bar which in an action of trespass is put in to oblige the plaintiff to assign the certain place where the trespass was committed. It was most in practice in the common bench. See Cro. Jac. 594.

BLANK BONDS. Scotch securities, in which the creditor's name was left blank, and which passed by mere delivery, the bearer being at liberty to put in his name and sue for payment. Declared void by Act 1696, c. 25.

BLANK INDORSEMENT. The indorsement of a bill of exchange or promissory note, by merely writing the name of the indorser, without mentioning any person to whom the bill or note is to be paid; called "blank," because a blank or space is left *over* it for the insertion of the name of the indorsee, or of any subsequent holder. Otherwise called an indorsement "in blank." 3 Kent, Comm. 89; Story, Prom. Notes, § 138.

BLANKET POLICY. In the law of fire insurance. A policy which contemplates that the risk is shifting, fluctuating, or varying, and is applied to a class of property, rather than to any particular article or thing. 1 Wood, Ins. § 40. See 93 U. S. 541.

BLANKS. A kind of white money, (value 8d.,) coined by Henry V. in those parts of France which were then subject to England; forbidden to be current in that realm by 2 Hen. VI. c. 9. Wharton.

BLASARIUS. An incendiary.

BLASPHEMY. In English law. Blasphemy is the offense of speaking matter relating to God, Jesus Christ, the Bible, or the Book of Common Prayer, intended to wound the feelings of mankind or to excite contempt and hatred against the church by law established, or to promote immorality. Sweet.

In American law. Any oral or written reproach maliciously cast upon God, his name, attributes, or religion. 2 Bish. Crim. Law, § 76; 2 Har. (Del.) 553; 20 Pick. 206; 11 Serg. & R. 394; 8 Johns. 290.

Blasphemy consists in wantonly uttering or publishing words casting contumelious reproach or profane ridicule upon God, Jesus Christ, the Holy Ghost, the Holy Scriptures, or the Christian religion. Pen. Code Dak., § 31.

In general, blasphemy may be described as consisting in speaking evil of the Deity with an impious purpose to derogate from the divine majesty, and to alienate the minds of others from the love and reverence of God. It is purposely using words concerning God calculated and designed to impair and destroy the reverence, respect, and confidence due to him as the intelligent creator, governor, and judge of the world. It embraces the idea of detraction, when used towards the Supreme Being, as "calumny" usually carries the same idea when applied to an individual. It is a willful and malicious attempt to lessen men's reverence of God by denying his existence, or his attributes as an intelligent creator, governor, and judge of men, and to prevent their having confidence in him as such. 20 Pick. 211, 212.

The use of this word is, in modern law exclusively confined to sacred subjects; but *blasphemia* and *blasphemare* were anciently used to signify the reviling by one person of another. Nov. 77, c. 1, § 1; Spelman.

BLEES. Grain; particularly corn.

BLENCH, BLENCH HOLDING. See BLANCH HOLDING.

BLENDED FUND. In England, where a testator directs his real and personal estate to be sold, and disposes of the proceeds as forming one aggregate, this is called a "blended fund."

BLIND. One who is deprived of the sense or faculty of sight.

BLINKS. In old English law. Boughs broken down from trees and thrown in a way where deer are likely to pass. Jacob.

BLOCKADE. In international law. A marine investment or beleaguering of a town or harbor. A sort of circumvallation round a place by which all foreign connection and correspondence is, as far as human power can effect it, to be cut off. 1 C. Rob. Adm. 151. It is not necessary, however, that the place should be invested by land, as well as by sea, in order to constitute a legal blockade; and, if a place be blockaded by sea only, it is no violation of belligerent rights for the neutral to carry on commerce with it by inland communications. 1 Kent, Comm. 147.

The actual investment of a port or place by a hostile force fully competent, under ordinary circumstances, to cut off all communication therewith, so arranged or disposed as to be able to apply its force to every point of practicable access or approach to the port or place so invested. Bouvier.

It is called a "blockade *de facto*" when the usual notice of the blockade has not been given to the neutral powers by the government causing the investment, in consequence of which the blockading squadron has to warn off all approaching vessels.

BLOOD. Kindred; consanguinity; family relationship; relation by descent from a common ancestor. One person is "of the blood" of another when they are related by lineal descent or collateral kinship.

Brothers and sisters are said to be of the whole blood if they have the same father and mother, and of the half blood if they have only one parent in common. 5 Whart. 477.

BLOOD MONEY. A weregild, or pecuniary mulct paid by a slayer to the relatives of his victim.

Also used, in a popular sense, as descriptive of money paid by way of reward for the apprehension and conviction of a person charged with a capital crime.

BLOODWIT. An amercement for bloodshed. Cowell.

The privilege of taking such amercements. Skene.

A privilege or exemption from paying a fine or amercement assessed for bloodshed. Cowell.

BLOODY HAND. In forest law. The having the hands or other parts bloody, which, in a person caught trespassing in the forest against venison, was one of the four kinds of circumstantial evidence of his having killed deer, although he was not found in the act of chasing or hunting. Manwood.

BLUE LAWS. A supposititious code of severe laws for the regulation of religious and personal conduct in the colonies of Connecticut and New Haven; hence any rigid Sunday laws or religious regulations. The assertion by some writers of the existence of the blue laws has no other basis than the adoption, by the first authorities of the New Haven colony, of the Scriptures as their code of law and government, and their strict application of Mosaic principles. Century Dict.

BOARD. A committee of persons organized under authority of law in order to exercise certain authorities, have oversight or control of certain matters, or discharge certain functions of a magisterial, representative, or fiduciary character. Thus, "board of aldermen," "board of health," "board of directors," "board of works."

Also lodging, food, entertainment, furnished to a guest at an inn or boardinghouse.

BOARD OF HEALTH. A board or commission created by the sovereign authority or by municipalities, invested with certain powers and charged with certain duties in relation to the preservation and improvement of the public health.

General boards of health are usually charged with general and advisory duties, with the collection of vital statistics, the investigation of sanitary conditions, and the methods of dealing with epidemic and other diseases, the quarantine laws, etc. Such are the national board of health, created by act of congress of March 3, 1879, (20 St. at Large, 484,) and the state boards of health created by the legislatures of most of the states.

Local boards of health are charged with more direct and immediate means of securing the public health, and exercise inquisitorial and executive powers in relation to sanitary regulations, offensive nuisances, markets, adulteration of food, slaughterhouses, drains and sewers, and similar subjects. Such boards are constituted in most American cities either by general law, by their charters, or by municipal ordinance, and in England by the statutes, 11 & 12 Vict.

c. 63, and 21 & 22 Vict. c. 98, and other acts amending the same.

BOARD OF SUPERVISORS. Under the system obtaining in some of the northern states, this name is given to an organized committee, or body of officials, composed of delegates from the several townships in a county, constituting part of the county government, and having special charge of the revenues of the county.

BOARD OF TRADE. An organization of the principal merchants, manufacturers, tradesmen, etc., of a city, for the purpose of furthering its commercial interests, encouraging the establishment of manufactures, promoting trade, securing or improving shipping facilities, and generally advancing the prosperity of the place as an industrial and commercial community.

In England, one of the administrative departments of government, being a committee of the privy council which is appointed for the consideration of matters relating to trade and foreign plantations.

BOARD OF WORKS. The name of a board of officers appointed for the better local management of the English metropolis. They have the care and management of all grounds and gardens dedicated to the use of the inhabitants in the metropolis; also the superintendence of the drainage; also the regulation of the street traffic, and, generally, of the buildings of the metropolis. Brown.

BOARDER. One who, being the inhabitant of a place, makes a special contract with another person for food with or without lodging. 7 Cush. 424; 36 Iowa, 651.

One who has food and lodging in the house or with the family of another for an agreed price, and usually under a contract intended to continue for a considerable period of time. 1 Tex. App. 220; 7 Rob. (N. Y.) 561.

The distinction between a guest and a boarder is this: The guest comes and remains without any bargain *for time*, and may go away when he pleases, paying only for the actual entertainment he receives; and the fact that he may have remained a long time in the inn, in this way, does not make him a boarder, instead of a guest. 25 Iowa, 553.

BOARDING-HOUSE. A boarding-house is not in common parlance, or in legal meaning, every private house where one or more boarders are kept occasionally only and upon special considerations. But it is a *quasi* public house, where boarders are generally and habitually kept, and which is held out and known as a place of entertainment of that kind. 1 Lans. 486.

A boarding-house is not an inn, the distinction being that a boarder is received into a house by a voluntary contract, whereas an innkeeper, in the absence of any reasonable or lawful excuse, is bound to receive a guest when he presents himself. 2 El. & Bl. 144.

The distinction between a boarding-house and an inn is that in a boarding-house the guest is under an express contract, at a certain rate for a certain period of time, while in an inn there is no express agreement; the guest, being on his way, is entertained from day to day, according to his business, upon an implied contract. 2 E. D. Smith, 148.

BOAT. A small open vessel, or watercraft, usually moved by oars or rowing. It is commonly distinguished in law from a ship or vessel, by being of smaller size and without a deck. 5 Mason, 120, 137.

BOC. In Saxon law. A book or writing; a deed or charter. *Boc land*, deed or charter land. *Land boc*, a writing for conveying land; a deed or charter: a land-book.

BOC HORDE. A place where books, writings, or evidences were kept. Cowell.

BOC LAND. In Saxon law. Allodial lands held by deed or other written evidence of title.

BOCERAS. Sax. A scribe, notary, or chancellor among the Saxons.

BODMERIE, BODEMERIE, BODDE-MEREY. Belg. and Germ. Bottomry, (*q. v.*)

BODY. A person. Used of a natural body, or of an artificial one created by law, as a corporation.

Also the main part of any instrument; in deeds it is spoken of as distinguished from the recitals and other introductory parts and signatures; in *affidavits*, from the title and jurat.

The main part of the human body; the trunk. 22 N. Y. 149.

BODY CORPORATE. A corporation.

BODY OF A COUNTY. A county at large, as distinguished from any particular place within it. A county considered as a territorial whole.

BODY OF AN INSTRUMENT. The main and operative part; the substantive provisions, as distinguished from the recitals, title, jurat, etc.

BODY OF LAWS. An organized and systematic collection of rules of jurisprudence; as, particularly, the body of the civil law, or *corpus juris civilis.*

BODY POLITIC. A term applied to a corporation, which is usually designated as a "body corporate and politic."

The term is particularly appropriate to a *public* corporation invested with powers and duties of government. It is often used, in a rather loose way, to designate the state or nation or sovereign power, or the government of a county or municipality, without distinctly connoting any express and individual corporate character.

BOILARY. Water arising from a salt well belonging to a person who is not the owner of the soil.

BOIS, or BOYS. Wood; timber; brush.

BOLHAGIUM, or BOLDAGIUM. A little house or cottage. Blount.

BOLT. The desertion by one or more persons from the political party to which he or they belong; the permanent withdrawal before adjournment of a portion of the delegates to a political convention. Rap. & L.

BOLTING. In English practice. A term formerly used in the English inns of court, but more particularly at Gray's Inn, signifying the private arguing of cases, as distinguished from *mooting*, which was a more formal and public mode of argument. Cowell; Tomlins; Holthouse.

BOMBAY REGULATIONS. Regulations passed for the presidency of Bombay, and the territories subordinate thereto. They were passed by the governors in council of Bombay until the year 1834, when the power of local legislation ceased, and the acts relating thereto were thenceforth passed by the governor general of India in council. Mozley & Whitley.

BON. Fr. In old French law. A royal order or check on the treasury, invented by Francis I. *Bon pour mille livres,* good for a thousand livres. Step. Lect. 387.

In modern law. The name of a clause (*bon pour ——,* good for so much) added to a cedule or promise, where it is not in the handwriting of the signer, containing the amount of the sum which he obliges himself to pay. Poth. Obl. part 4, ch. 1, art. 2, § 1.

BONA. Goods; property; possessions. In the Roman law, this term was used to designate all species of property, real, personal, and mixed, but was more strictly applied to real estate. In modern civil law, it includes both personal property (technically so called) and chattels real, thus corresponding to the French *biens.* In the common law, its use was confined to the description of movable goods.

BONA CONFISCATA. Goods confiscated or forfeited to the imperial *fisc* or treasury. 1 Bl. Comm. 299.

BONA ET CATALLA. Goods and chattels. Movable property.

This expression includes all personal things that belong to a man. 16 Mees. & W. 68.

BONA FELONUM. In English law. Goods of felons; the goods of one convicted of felony. 5 Coke, 110.

BONA FIDE. In or with good faith; honestly, openly, and sincerely; without deceit or fraud.

Truly; actually; without simulation or pretense.

Innocently; in the attitude of trust and confidence; without notice of fraud, etc.

The phrase "*bona fide*" is often used ambiguously; thus, the expression "a *bona fide* holder for value" may either mean a holder for real value, as opposed to a holder for pretended value, or it may mean a holder for real value without notice of any fraud, etc. Byles, Bills, 121.

Bona fide possessor facit fructus consumptos suos. By good faith a possessor makes the fruits consumed his own. Tray. Lat. Max. 57.

BONA FIDE PURCHASER. A purchaser for a valuable consideration paid or parted with in the belief that the vendor had a right to sell, and without any suspicious circumstances to put him on inquiry. 12 Barb. 605.

One who acts without covin, fraud, or collusion; one who, in the commission of or connivance at no fraud, pays full price for the property, and in good faith, honestly, and in fair dealing buys and goes into possession. 42 Ga. 250.

A *bona fide* purchaser is one who buys property of another without notice that some third person has a right to, or interest in, such property, and pays a full and fair price for the same, at the time of such purchase, or before he has notice of the claim or interest of such other in the property. 65 Barb. 231.

BONA FIDES. Good faith; integrity of dealing; honesty; sincerity; the opposite of *mala fides* and of *dolus malus.*

Eona fides exigit ut quod convenit fiat. Good faith demands that what is agreed upon shall be done. Dig. 19, 20, 21; Id. 19, 1, 50; Id. 50, 8, 2, 13.

Bona fides non patitur ut bis idem exigatur. Good faith does not allow us to demand twice the payment of the same thing. Dig. 50, 17, 57; Broom, Max. 338, note; 4 Johns. Ch. 143.

BONA FORISFACTA. Goods forfeited.

BONA FUGITIVORUM. In English law. Goods of fugitives; the proper goods of him who flies for felony. 5 Coke, 109b.

BONA GESTURA. Good abearance or behavior.

BONA GRATIA. In the Roman law. By mutual consent; voluntarily. A term applied to a species of divorce where the parties separated by mutual consent; or where the parties renounced their marital engagements without assigning any cause, or upon mere pretexts. Tayl. Civil Law, 361, 362; Calvin.

BONA MEMORIA. Good memory. Generally used in the phrase *sanæ mentis et bonæ memoriæ,* of sound mind and good memory, as descriptive of the mental capacity of a testator.

BONA MOBILIA. In the civil law. Movables. Those things which move themselves or can be transported from one place to another, and not permanently attached to a farm, heritage, or building.

BONA NOTABILIA. In English probate law. Notable goods; property worthy of notice, or of sufficient value to be accounted for, that is, amounting to £5.

Where a decedent leaves goods of sufficient amount (*bona notabilia*) in different dioceses, administration is granted by the metropolitan, to prevent the confusion arising from the appointment of many different administrators. 2 Bl. Comm. 509; Rolle, Abr. 908.

BONA PATRIA. In the Scotch law. An assize or jury of good neighbors. Bell.

BONA PERITURA. Goods of a perishable nature; such goods as an executor or trustee must use diligence in disposing of and converting them into money.

BONA UTLAGATORUM. Goods of outlaws; goods belonging to persons outlawed.

BONA VACANTIA. Vacant, unclaimed, or stray goods. Those things in which nobody claims a property, and which belong to the crown, by virtue of its prerogative. 1 Bl. Comm. 298.

BONA WAVIATA. In English law. Waived goods; goods stolen and *waived,* that is, thrown away by the thief in his flight, for fear of being apprehended, or to facilitate his escape; and which go to the sovereign. 5 Coke, 109b; 1 Bl. Comm. 296.

BONÆ FIDEI. In the civil law. Of good faith; in good faith. This is a more frequent form than *bona fide.*

BONÆ FIDEI CONTRACTS. In civil and Scotch law. Those contracts in which equity may interpose to correct inequalities, and to adjust all matters according to the plain intention of the parties. 1 Kames, Eq. 200.

BONÆ FIDEI EMPTOR. A purchaser in good faith. One who either was ignorant that the thing he bought belonged to another or supposed that the seller had a right to sell it. Dig. 50, 16, 109. See Id. 6, 2, 7, 11.

BONÆ FIDEI POSSESSOR. A possessor in good faith. One who believes that no other person has a better right to the possession than himself. Mackeld. Rom. Law, § 243.

Bonæ fidei possessor in id tantum quod sese pervenerit tenetur. A possessor in good faith is only liable for that which he himself has obtained. 2 Inst. 285.

BONANZA. In mining parlance, the widening out of a vein of silver, suddenly, and extraordinarily; hence any sudden, unexpected prosperity in mining. Webster.

BOND. A contract by specialty to pay a certain sum of money; being a deed or instrument under seal, by which the maker or obligor promises, and thereto *binds* himself, his heirs, executors, and administrators, to pay a designated sum of money to another; usually with a clause to the effect that upon performance of a certain condition (as to pay another and smaller sum) the obligation shall be void.

The word "bond" shall embrace every written undertaking for the payment of money or acknowledgment of being bound for money, conditioned to be void on the performance of any duty, or the occurrence of anything therein expressed, and subscribed and delivered by the party making it, to take effect as his obligation, whether it be sealed or unsealed; and, when a bond is required by law, an undertaking in writing without seal shall be sufficient. Rev. Code Miss. 1880, § 19.

The word "bond" has with us a definite legal signification. It has a clause, with a sum fixed as a penalty, binding the parties to pay the same, conditioned, however, that the payment of the penalty may be avoided by the performance by some one or more of the parties of certain acts. 3 Redf. Sur. 459.

Bonds are either single (simple) or double, (conditional.)

A *single* bond is one in which the obligor binds himself, his heirs, etc., to pay a certain sum of money to another person at a specified day.

A *double* (or conditional) bond is one to which a condition is added that if the obligor does or forbears from doing some act the obligation shall be void. Formerly such a condition was sometimes contained in a separate instrument, and was then called a "defeasance."

The term is also used to denote debentures or certificates of indebtedness issued by public and private corporations, governments, and municipalities, as security for the repayment of money loaned to them. Thus, "railway aid bonds" are bonds issued by municipal corporations to aid in the construction of railroads likely to benefit them, and exchanged for the company's stock.

BOND. In old Scotch law. A bond-man; a slave. Skene.

BOND, v. To give bond for, as for duties on goods; to secure payment of duties, by giving bond. *Bonded*, secured by bond. Bonded goods are those for the duties on which bonds are given.

BOND AND DISPOSITION IN SECURITY. In Scotch law. A bond and mortgage on land.

BOND AND MORTGAGE. A species of security, consisting of a bond conditioned for the repayment of a loan of money, and a mortgage of realty to secure the performance of the stipulations of the bond.

BOND CREDITOR. A creditor whose debt is secured by a bond.

BOND TENANTS. In English law. Copyholders and customary tenants are sometimes so called. 2 Bl. Comm. 148.

AM.DICT.LAW—10

BONDAGE. Slavery; involuntary personal servitude; captivity. In old English law, villenage, villein tenure. 2 Bl. Comm. 92.

BONDED WAREHOUSE. See WAREHOUSE SYSTEM.

BONDSMAN. A surety; one who has entered into a bond as surety. The word seems to apply especially to the sureties upon the bonds of officers, trustees, etc., while *bail* should be reserved for the sureties on recognizances and bail-bonds.

BONES GENTS. L. Fr. In old English law. Good men, (of the jury.)

BONI HOMINES. In old European law. Good men; a name given in early European jurisprudence to the tenants of the lord, who judged each other in the lord's courts. 3 Bl. Comm. 349.

Boni judicis est ampliare jurisdictionem. It is the part of a good judge to enlarge (or use liberally) his remedial authority or jurisdiction. Ch. Prec. 329; 1 Wils. 284.

Boni judicis est ampliare justitiam. It is the duty of a good judge to enlarge or extend justice. 1 Burr. 304.

Boni judicis est judicium sine dilatione mandare executioni. It is the duty of a good judge to cause judgment to be executed without delay. Co. Litt. 289.

Boni judicis est lites dirimere, ne lis ex lite oritur, et interest reipublicæ ut sint fines litium. It is the duty of a good judge to prevent litigations, that suit may not grow out of suit, and it concerns the welfare of a state that an end be put to litigation. 4 Coke, 15b; 5 Coke, 31a.

BONIS CEDERE. In the civil law. To make a transfer or surrender of property, as a debtor did to his creditors. Cod. 7, 71.

BONIS NON AMOVENDIS. A writ addressed to the sheriff, when a writ of error has been brought, commanding that the person against whom judgment has been obtained be not suffered to remove his goods till the error be tried and determined. Reg. Orig. 131.

BONITARIAN OWNERSHIP. In Roman law. A species of equitable title to things, as distinguished from a title acquired according to the strict forms of the municipal law; the property of a Roman citizen in a subject capable of quiritary property, acquired by a title not known to the civil law, but introduced by the prætor, and protected by his *imperium* or supreme executive power, *e. g.*, where *res mancipi* had been transferred by mere tradition. Poste's Gaius Inst. 187. See QUIRITARIAN OWNERSHIP.

BONO ET MALO. A special writ of jail delivery, which formerly issued of course for each particular prisoner. 4 Bl. Comm. 270.

Bonum defendentis ex integra causa; malum ex quolibet defectu. The success of a defendant depends on a perfect case; his loss arises from some defect. 11 Coke, 68a.

Bonum necessarium extra terminos necessitatis non est bonum. A good thing required by necessity is not good beyond the limits of such necessity. Hob. 144.

BONUS. A gratuity. A premium paid to a grantor or vendor.

An extra consideration given for what is received.

Any premium or advantage; an occasional extra dividend.

A premium paid by a company for a charter or other franchises.

"A definite sum to be paid at one time, for a loan of money for a specified period, distinct from and independently of the interest." 24 Conn. 147.

A bonus is not a gift or gratuity, but a sum paid for services, or upon some other consideration, but in addition to or in excess of that which would ordinarily be given. 16 Wall. 452.

Bonus judex secundum æquum et bonum judicat, et æquitatem stricto juri præfert. A good judge decides according to what is just and good, and prefers equity to strict law. Co. Litt. 34.

BOOK. 1. A general designation applied to any literary composition which is printed, but appropriately 'to a printed composition bound in a volume.

2. A bound volume consisting of sheets of paper, not printed, but containing manuscript entries; such as a merchant's account-books, dockets of courts, etc.

3. A name often given to the largest subdivisions of a treatise or other literary composition.

4. In practice, the name of "book" is given to several of the more important papers prepared in the progress of a cause, though entirely written, and not at all in the book form;

such as demurrer-books, error-books, paper-books, etc.

BOOK DEBT. In Pennsylvania practice. The act of 28th March, 1835, § 2, in using the words, "book debt" and "book entries," refers to their usual signification, which includes goods sold and delivered, and work, labor, and services performed, the evidence of which, on the part of the plaintiff, consists of entries in an original book, such as is competent to go to a jury, were the issue trying before them. 2 Miles, 102.

BOOK OF ACTS. A term applied to the records of a surrogate's court. 8 East, 187.

BOOK OF ADJOURNAL. In Scotch law. The original records of criminal trials in the court of justiciary.

BOOK OF RATES. An account or enumeration of the duties or tariffs authorized by parliament. 1 Bl. Comm. 316.

BOOK OF RESPONSES. In Scotch law. An account which the directors of the chancery kept to enter all non-entry and relief duties payable by heirs who take precepts from chancery.

BOOKLAND. In English law. Land, also called "charter-land," which was held by deed under certain rents and free services, and differed in nothing from free socage land. 2 Bl. Comm. 90.

BOOKS. All the volumes which contain authentic reports of decisions in English courts, from the earliest times to the present, are called, *par excellence*, "The Books." Wharton.

BOOKS OF ACCOUNT. The books in which merchants, traders, and business men generally keep their accounts.

BOOM. An inclosure formed upon the surface of a stream or other body of water, by means of piers and a chain of spars, for the purpose of collecting or storing logs or timber.

BOOM COMPANY. A company formed for the purpose of improving streams for the floating of logs, by means of booms and other contrivances, and for the purpose of running, driving, booming, and rafting logs.

BOON DAYS. In English law. Certain days in the year (sometimes called "due days") on which tenants in copyhold were obliged to perform corporal services for the lord. Whishaw.

BOOT, or BOTE. An old Saxon word, equivalent to "estovers."

BOOTING, or BOTING, CORN. Certain rent corn, anciently so called. Cowell.

BOOTY. Property captured from the enemy in war, on land, as distinguished from "prize," which is a capture of such property on the sea.

BORD. An old Saxon word, signifying a cottage; a house; a table.

BORDAGE. In old English law. A species of base tenure, by which certain lands (termed "bord lands,") were anciently held in England, the tenants being termed "*bordarii;*" the service was that of keeping the lord in small provisions.

BORDARIA. A cottage.

BORDARII, or BORDIMANNI. In old English law. Tenants of a less servile condition than the *villani*, who had a bord or cottage, with a small parcel of land, allowed to them, on condition they should supply the lord with poultry and eggs, and other small provisions for his board or entertainment. Spelman.

BORD-BRIGCH. In Saxon law. A breach or violation of suretyship; pledgebreach, or breach of mutual fidelity.

BORDER WARRANT. A process granted by a judge ordinary, on either side of the border between England and Scotland, for arresting the person or effects of a person living on the opposite side, until he find security, *judicio sisti.* Bell.

BORDEREAU. In French law. A note enumerating the purchases and sales which may have been made by a broker or stockbroker. This name is also given to the statement given to a banker with bills for discount or coupons to receive. Arg. Fr. Merc. Law, 547.

BORD-HALFPENNY. A customary small toll paid to the lord of a town for setting up boards, tables, booths, etc., in fairs or markets.

BORDLANDS. The demesnes which the lords keep in their hands for the maintenance of their board or table. Cowell.

Also lands held in bordage. Lands which the lord gave to tenants on condition of their supplying his table with small provisions, poultry, eggs, etc.

BORDLODE. A service anciently required of tenants to carry timber out of the woods of the lord to his house; or it is said to be the quantity of food or provision which the *bordarii* or bordmen paid for their bordlands. Jacob.

BORDSERVICE. A tenure of bordlands.

BOREL-FOLK. Country people; derived from the French *bourre,* (Lat. *floccus,*) a lock of wool, because they covered their heads with such stuff. Blount.

BORG. In Saxon law. A pledge, pledge giver, or surety. The name given among the Saxons to the head of each family composing a tithing or decennary, each being the pledge for the good conduct of the others. Also the contract or engagement of suretyship; and the pledge given.

BORGBRICHE. A breach or violation of suretyship, or of mutual fidelity. Jacob.

BORGESMON. In Saxon law. The name given to the head of each family composing a tithing.

BORGH OF HAMHALD. In old Scotch law. A pledge or surety given by the seller of goods to the buyer, to make the goods forthcoming as his own proper goods, and to warrant the same to him. Skene.

BOROUGH. In English law. A town, a walled town. Co. Litt. 108*b.* A town of note or importance; a fortified town. Cowell. An ancient town. Litt. 164. A corporate town that is not a city. Cowell. An ancient town, corporate or not, that sends burgesses to parliament. Co. Litt. 109*a;* 1 Bl. Comm. 114, 115. A city or other town sending burgesses to parliament. 1 Steph. Comm. 116. A town or place organized for local government.

A parliamentary borough is a town which returns one or more members to parliament.

In Scotch law. A corporate body erected by the charter of the sovereign, consisting of the inhabitants of the territory erected into the borough. Bell.

In American law. In Pennsylvania, the term denotes a part of a township having a charter for municipal purposes; and the same is true of Connecticut. 23 Conn. 128. See, also, 1 Dill. Mun. Corp. § 41, n.

"Borough" and "village" are duplicate or cumulative names of the same thing; proof of either will sustain a charge in an indictment employing the other term. 18 Ohio St. 496.

BOROUGH COURTS. In English law. Private and limited tribunals, held by prescription, charter, or act of parliament, in particular districts for the convenience of the inhabitants, that they may prosecute small suits and receive justice at home.

BOROUGH ENGLISH. A custom prevalent in some parts of England, by which the youngest son inherits the estate in preference to his older brothers. 1 Bl. Comm. 75.

BOROUGH FUND. In English law. The revenues of a municipal borough derived from the rents and produce of the land, houses, and stocks belonging to the borough in its corporate capacity, and supplemented where necessary by a borough rate.

BOROUGH-HEADS. Borough-holders, bors-holders, or burs-holders.

BOROUGH-REEVE. The chief muncipal officer in towns unincorporated before the municipal corporations act, (5 & 6 Wm. IV. c. 76.)

BOROUGH SESSIONS. Courts of limited criminal jurisdiction, established in English boroughs under the municipal corporations act.

BORROW. This word is often used in the sense of returning the thing borrowed *in specie,* as to borrow a book or any other thing to be returned again. But it is evident that where money is borrowed, the identical money loaned is not to be returned, because, if this were so, the borrower would derive no benefit from the loan. In the broad sense of the term, it means a contract for the use of money. 13 Neb. 88, 12 N. W. Rep. 812; 39 Leg. Int. 98; 78 N. Y. 177.

BORROWE. In old Scotch law. A pledge.

BORROWER. One to whom money or other property is loaned at his request.

BORSHOLDER. In Saxon law. The borough's ealder, or headborough, supposed to be the discreetest man in the borough, town, or tithing.

BOSCAGE. In English law. The food which wood and trees yield to cattle; browse-wood, mast, etc. Spelman.

An ancient duty of wind-fallen wood in the forest. Manwood.

BOSCARIA. Wood-houses, or ox-houses.

BOSCUS. Wood; growing wood of any kind, large or small, timber or coppice. Cowell; Jacob.

BOTE. In old English law. A recompense or compensation, or profit or advantage. Also reparation or amends for any damage done. Necessaries for the maintenance and carrying on of husbandry. An allowance; the ancient name for estovers.

House-bote is a sufficient allowance of wood from off the estate to repair or burn in the house, and sometimes termed "fire-bote;" *plow-bote* and *cart-bote* are wood to be employed in making and repairing all instruments of husbandry; and *hay-bote* or *hedge-bote* is wood for repairing of hays, hedges, or fences. The word also signifies reparation for any damage or injury done, as *man-bote,* which was a compensation or amends for a man slain, etc.

BOTELESS. In old English law. Without amends; without the privilege of making satisfaction for a crime by a pecuniary payment; without relief or remedy. Cowell.

BOTHA. In old English law. A booth, stall, or tent to stand in, in fairs or markets. Cowell.

BOTHAGIUM, or BOOTHAGE. Customary dues paid to the lord of a manor or soil, for the pitching or standing of booths in fairs or markets.

BOTHNA, or BUTHNA. In old Scotch law. A park where cattle are inclosed and fed. Bothna also signifies a barony, lordship, etc. Skene.

BOTTOMAGE. L. Fr. Bottomry.

BOTTOMRY. In maritime law. A contract in the nature of a mortgage, by which the owner of a ship borrows money for the use, equipment, or repair of the vessel, and for a definite term, and pledges the ship (or the keel or *bottom* of the ship, *pars pro toto*) as a security for its repayment, with maritime or extraordinary interest on account of the marine risks to be borne by the lender; it being stipulated that if the ship be lost in the course of the specified voyage, or during the limited time, by any of the perils enumerated in the contract, the lender shall also lose his money. 2 Hagg. Adm. 48, 53; 2 Sum. 157.

Bottomry is a contract by which a ship or its freightage is hypothecated as security for a loan, which is to be repaid only in case the ship survives a particular risk, voyage, or period. Civil Code Cal. § 3017; Civil Code Dak. § 1783.

When the loan is not made upon the ship, but on the goods laden on board, and which are to be sold or exchanged in the course of the voyage, the borrower's personal *responsibility* is deemed the principal security for the performance of the contract, which is therefore called "*respondentia*," which see. And in a loan upon *respondentia* the lender must be paid his principal and interest though the ship perish, provided the goods are saved. In most other respects the contracts of *bottomry* and of *respondentia* stand substantially upon the same footing. Bouvier.

BOTTOMRY BOND. The instrument embodying the contract or agreement of bottomry.

The true definition of a bottomry bond, in the sense of the general maritime law, and independent of the peculiar regulations of the positive codes of different commercial nations, is that it is a contract for a loan of money on the bottom of the ship, at an extraordinary interest, upon maritime risks, to be borne by the lender for a voyage, or for a definite period. 2 Sum. 157.

BOUCHE. Fr. The mouth. An allowance of provision. *Avoir bouche à court;* to have an allowance at court; to be in ordinary at court; to have meat and drink scot-free there. Blount; Cowell.

BOUCHE OF COURT, or BUDGE OF COURT. A certain allowance of provision from the king to his knights and servants, who attended him on any military expedition.

BOUGH OF A TREE. In feudal law. A symbol which gave seisin of land, to hold of the donor *in capite*.

BOUGHT AND SOLD NOTES. When a broker is employed to buy and sell goods, he is accustomed to give to the buyer a note of the sale, commonly called a "sold note," and to the seller a like note, commonly called a "bought note," in his own name, as agent of each, and thereby they are respectively bound, if he has not exceeded his authority. Story, Ag. § 28.

BOULEVARD. The word "boulevard," which originally indicated a bulwark or rampart, and was afterwards applied to a public walk or road on the site of a demolished fortification, is now employed in the same sense as public drive. A park is a piece of ground adapted and set apart for purposes of ornament, exercise, and amusement. It is not a street or road, though carriages may pass through it.

So a boulevard or public drive is adapted and set apart for purposes of ornament, exercise, and amusement. It is not technically a street, avenue, or highway, though a carriage-way over it is a chief feature. 52 How. Pr. 445.

BOUND. As an *adjective*, denotes the condition of being constrained by the obligations of a bond or a covenant. In the law of shipping, "bound to" or "bound for" denotes that the vessel spoken of is intended or designed to make the voyage to the place named.

As a *noun*, the term denotes a limit or boundary, or a line inclosing or marking off a tract of land. In the familiar phrase "metes and bounds," the former term properly denotes the measured distances, and the latter the natural or artificial marks which indicate their beginning and ending. A distinction is sometimes taken between "bound" and "boundary," to the effect that, while the former signifies the limit itself, (and may be an imaginary line,) the latter designates a visible mark which indicates the limit. But no such distinction is commonly observed.

BOUND BAILIFFS. In English law. Sheriffs' officers are so called, from their being usually *bound* to the sheriff in an obligation with sureties, for the due execution of their office. 1 Bl. Comm. 345, 346.

BOUNDARY. By boundary is understood, in general, every separation, natural or artificial, which marks the confines or line of division of two contiguous estates. Trees or hedges may be planted, ditches may be dug, walls or inclosures may be erected, to serve as boundaries. But we most usually understand by boundaries stones or pieces of wood inserted in the earth on the confines of the two estates. Civil Code La. art. 826.

Boundaries are either natural or artificial. Of the former kind are water-courses, growing trees, beds of rock, and the like. Artificial boundaries are landmarks or signs erected by the hand of man, as a pole, stake, pile of stones, etc.

BOUNDED TREE. A tree marking or standing at the corner of a field or estate.

BOUNDERS. In American law. Visible marks or objects at the ends of the lines drawn in surveys of land, showing the courses and distances. Burrill.

BOUNDS. In the English law of mines, the trespass committed by a person who excavates minerals under-ground beyond the boundary of his land is called "working out of bounds."

BOUNTY. A gratuity, or an unusual or additional benefit conferred upon, or compensation paid to, a class of persons.

A premium given or offered to induce men

to enlist into the public service. The term is applicable only to the payment made to the enlisted man, as the inducement for his service, and not to a premium paid to the man through whose intervention, and by whose procurement, the recruit is obtained and mustered. 39 How. Pr. 488.

It is not easy to discriminate between bounty, reward, and bonus. The former is the appropriate term, however, where the services or action of many persons are desired, and each who acts upon the offer may entitle himself to the promised gratuity, without prejudice from or to the claims of others; while reward is more proper in the case of a single service, which can be only once performed, and therefore will be earned only by the person or co-operating persons who succeed while others fail. Thus, bounties are offered to all who will enlist in the army or navy; to all who will engage in certain fisheries which government desire to encourage; to all who kill dangerous beasts or noxious creatures. A reward is offered for rescuing a person from a wreck or fire; for detecting and arresting an offender; for finding a lost chattel.

Bonus, as compared with bounty, suggests the idea of a gratuity to induce a money transaction between individuals; a percentage or gift, upon a loan or transfer of property, or a surrender of a right. Abbott.

BOUNTY LANDS. Portions of the public domain given to soldiers for military services, by way of bounty.

BOUNTY OF QUEEN ANNE. A name given to a royal charter, which was confirmed by 2 Anne, c. 11, whereby all the revenue of first-fruits and tenths was vested in trustees, to form a perpetual fund for the augmentation of poor ecclesiastical livings. Wharton.

BOURG. In old French law. An assemblage of houses surrounded with walls; a fortified town or village.

In old English law. A borough, a village.

BOURGEOIS. In old French law. The inhabitant of a *bourg*, (*q. v.*)

A person entitled to the privileges of a municipal corporation; a burgess.

BOURSE. Fr. An exchange; a stock-exchange.

BOURSE DE COMMERCE. In the French law. An aggregation, sanctioned by government, of merchants, captains of vessels, exchange agents, and courtiers, the two latter being nominated by the government, in each city which has a *bourse*. Brown.

BOUSSOLE. In French marine law. A compass; the mariner's compass.

BOUWERYE. Dutch. In old New York law. A farm; a farm on which the farmer's family resided.

BOUWMEESTER. Dutch. In old New York law. A farmer.

BOVATA TERRÆ. As much land as one ox can cultivate. Said by some to be thirteen, by others eighteen, acres in extent. Skene; Spelman; Co. Litt. 5a.

BOW-BEARER. An under-officer of the forest, whose duty it is to oversee and true inquisition make, as well of sworn men as unsworn, in every bailiwick of the forest; and of all manner of trespasses done, either to vert or venison, and cause them to be presented, without any concealment, in the next court of attachment, etc. Cromp. Jur. 201.

BOWYERS. Manufacturers of bows and shafts. An ancient company of the city of London.

BOYCOTT. In criminal law. A conspiracy formed and intended directly or indirectly to prevent the carrying on of any lawful business, or to injure the business of any one by wrongfully preventing those who would be customers from buying anything from or employing the representatives of said business, by threats, intimidation, or other forcible means. 11 Va. Law J. 329.

BOZERO. In Spanish law. An advocate; one who pleads the causes of others, or his own, before courts of justice, either as plaintiff or defendant.

BRACHIUM MARIS. An arm of the sea.

BRACINUM. A brewing; the whole quantity of ale brewed at one time, for which *tolsestor* was paid in some manors. *Brecina,* a brew-house.

BRAHMIN, BRAHMAN, or BRAMIN. In Hindu law. A divine; a priest; the first Hindu caste.

BRANCH. A branch of a family stock is a group of persons, related among themselves by descent from a common ancestor, and related to the main stock by the fact that that common ancestor descends from the original founder or progenitor.

BRAND. To stamp; to mark, either with a hot iron or with a stencil plate. 11 Hun, 575.

BRANDING. An ancient mode of punishment by inflicting a mark on an offender with a hot iron. It is generally disused in civil law, but is a recognized punishment for some military offenses.

BRANKS. An instrument formerly used in some parts of England for the correction of scolds; a scolding bridle. It inclosed the head and a sharp piece of iron entered the mouth and restrained the tongue.

BRASIATOR. A maltster, a brewer.

BRASIUM. Malt.

BRAWL. The popular meanings of the words "brawls" and "tumults" are substantially the same and identical. They are correlative terms, the one employed to express the meaning of the other, and are so defined by approved lexicographers. Legally, they mean the same kind of disturbance to the public peace, produced by the same class of agents, and can be well comprehended to define one and the same offense. 42 N. H. 464.

Brawling is quarrelling or chiding, or creating a disturbance, in a church, or churchyard, (4 Bl. Comm. 146; 4 Steph. Comm. 253.) Mozley & Whitley.

BREACH. The breaking or violating of a law, right, or duty, either by commission or omission.

In contracts. The violation or non-fulfilment of an obligation, contract, or duty.

A *continuing* breach occurs where the state of affairs, or the specific act, constituting the breach, endures for a considerable period of time, or is repeated at short intervals.

A *constructive* breach of contract takes place when the party bound to perform disables himself from performance by some act, or declares, before the time comes, that he will not perform.

In pleading. This name is sometimes given to that part of the declaration which alleges the violation of the defendant's promise or duty, immediately preceding the *ad damnum* clause.

BREACH OF CLOSE. The unlawful or unwarrantable entry on another person's soil, land, or close. 3 Bl. Comm. 209.

BREACH OF COVENANT. The non-performance of any covenant agreed to be performed, or the doing of any act covenanted not to be done. Holthouse.

BREACH OF DUTY. In a general sense, any violation or omission of a legal or moral duty. More particularly, the neglect or failure to fulfill in a just and proper manner the duties of an office or fiduciary employment.

BREACH OF POUND. The breaking any pound or place where cattle or goods distrained are deposited, in order to take them back. 3 Bl. Comm. 146.

BREACH OF PRISON. The offense of actually and forcibly breaking a prison or gaol, with intent to escape. 4 Chit. Bl. 130, notes; 4 Steph. Comm. 255. The escape from custody of a person lawfully arrested on criminal process.

BREACH OF PRIVILEGE. An act or default in violation of the privilege of either house of parliament, of congress, or of a state legislature.

BREACH OF PROMISE. Violation of a promise; chiefly used as an elliptical expression for "breach of promise of marriage."

BREACH OF THE PEACE. A violation of the public tranquillity and order. The offense of breaking or disturbing the public peace by any riotous, forcible, or unlawful proceeding. 4 Bl. Comm. 142, et seq.; 4 Steph. Comm. 273, et seq.

A *constructive* breach of the peace is an unlawful act which, though wanting the elements of actual violence or injury to any person, is yet inconsistent with the peaceable and orderly conduct of society. Various kinds of misdemeanors are included in this general designation, such as sending challenges to fight, going armed in public without lawful reason and in a threatening manner, etc.

An *apprehended* breach of the peace is caused by the conduct of a man who threatens another with violence or physical injury, or who goes about in public with dangerous and unusual weapons in a threatening or alarming manner, or who publishes an aggravated libel upon another, etc.

BREACH OF TRUST. Any act done by a trustee contrary to the terms of his trust, or in excess of his authority and to the detriment of the trust; or the wrongful omission by a trustee of any act required of him by the terms of the trust.

Also the wrongful misappropriation by a trustee of any fund or property which had been lawfully committed to him in a fiduciary character.

BREAD ACTS. Laws providing for the sustenance of persons kept in prison for debt.

BREAKING. Forcibly separating, parting, disintegrating, or piercing any solid substance. In the law as to housebreaking and burglary, it means the tearing away or removal of any part of a house or of the locks, latches, or other fastenings intended to secure it, or otherwise exerting force to gain an entrance, with the intent to commit a felony; or violently or forcibly breaking out of a house, after having unlawfully entered it, in the attempt to escape.

BREAKING A CASE. The expression by the judges of a court, to one another, of their views of a case, in order to ascertain how far they are agreed, and as preliminary to the formal delivery of their opinions. "We are breaking the case, that we may show what is in doubt with any of us." Holt, C. J., addressing Dolbin, J., 1 Show. 423.

BREAKING BULK. The offense committed by a bailee (particularly a carrier) in opening or unpacking the chest, parcel, or case containing goods intrusted to his care, and removing the goods and converting them to his own use.

BREAKING DOORS. Forcibly removing the fastenings of a house, so that a person may enter.

BREAKING JAIL. The act of a prisoner in effecting his escape from a place of lawful confinement. *Escape*, while denoting the offense of the prisoner in unlawfully leaving the jail, may also connote the fault or negligence of the sheriff or keeper, and hence is of wider significance than "breaking jail" or "prison-breach."

BREAKING OF ARRESTMENT. In Scotch law. The contempt of the law committed by an arrestee who disregards the arrestment used in his hands, and pays the sum or delivers the goods arrested to the debtor. The breaker is liable to the arrester in damages. See ARRESTMENT.

BREAST OF THE COURT. A metaphorical expression, signifying the conscience, discretion, or recollection of the judge. During the term of a court, the record is said to remain "in the breast of the judges of the court and in their remembrance." Co. Litt. 260a; 3 Bl. Comm. 407.

BREATH. In medical jurisprudence. The air expelled from the lungs at each expiration.

BREDWITE. In Saxon and old English law. A fine, penalty, or amercement imposed for defaults in the assise of bread. Cowell.

BREHON. In old Irish law. A judge. 1 Bl. Comm. 100. Brehons, (*breitheamhuin*,) judges.

BREHON LAW. The name given to the ancient system of law of Ireland as it existed at the time of its conquest by Henry II.; and derived from the title of the judges, who were denominated "Brehons."

BRENAGIUM. A payment in bran, which tenants anciently made to feed their lords' hounds.

BREPHOTROPHI. In the civil law. Persons appointed to take care of houses destined to receive foundlings.

BRETHREN. This word, in a will, may include sisters, as well as brothers, of the person indicated; it is not necessarily limited to the masculine gender. 1 Rich. Eq. 78.

BRETTS AND SCOTTS, LAWS OF THE. A code or system of laws in use among the Celtic tribes of Scotland down to the beginning of the fourteenth century, and then abolished by Edward I. of England.

BRETTWALDA. In Saxon law. The ruler of the Saxon heptarchy.

BREVE. L. Lat. A writ. An original writ. A writ or precept of the king issuing out of his courts.

A writ by which a person is summoned or attached to answer an action, complaint, etc., or whereby anything is commanded to be done in the courts, in order to justice, etc. It is called "*breve*," from the brevity of it, and is addressed either to the defendant himself, or to the chancellors, judges, sheriffs, or other officers. Skene.

BREVE DE RECTO. A writ of right, or license for a person ejected out of an estate, to sue for the possession of it.

BREVE INNOMINATUM. A writ making only a general complaint, without the details or particulars of the cause of action.

Breve ita dicitur, quia rem de qua agitur, et intentionem petentis, paucis verbis breviter enarrat. A writ is so called because it briefly states, in few words, the matter in dispute, and the object of the party seeking relief. 2 Inst. 39.

Breve judiciale debet sequi suum originale, et accessorium suum principale. Jenk. Cent. 292. A judicial writ ought to follow its original, and an accessory its principal.

Breve judiciale non cadit pro defectu formæ. Jenk. Cent. 43. A judicial writ fails not through defect of form.

BREVE NOMINATUM. A named writ. A writ stating the circumstances or details of the cause of action, with the time, place, and demand, very particularly.

BREVE ORIGINALE. An original writ; a writ which gave *origin* and commencement to a suit.

BREVE PERQUIRERE. To purchase a writ or license of trial, in the king's courts, by the plaintiff, *qui breve perquisivit.*

BREVE TESTATUM. A written memorandum introduced to perpetuate the tenor of the conveyance and investiture of lands. 2 Bl. Comm. 307.

In Scotch law. A similar memorandum made out at the time of the transfer, attested by the *pares curiæ* and by the seal of the superior. Bell.

BREVET. In military law. A commission by which an officer is promoted to the next higher rank, but without conferring a right to a corresponding increase of pay.

In French law. A privilege or warrant granted by the government to a private person, authorizing him to take a special benefit or exercise an exclusive privilege. Thus a *brevet d'invention* is a patent for an invention.

BREVIA. Lat. Writs. The plural of *breve*, which see.

BREVIA ADVERSARIA. Adversary writs; writs brought by an adversary to recover land. 6 Coke, 67.

BREVIA AMICABILIA. Amicable or friendly writs; writs brought by agreement or consent of the parties.

BREVIA ANTICIPANTIA. At common law. Anticipating or preventive writs. Six were included in this category, viz.: Writ of *mesne; warrantia chartæ; monstraverunt; audita querela; curia claudenda;* and *ne injuste vexes.*

BREVIA DE CURSU. Writs of course. Formal writs issuing as of course.

BREVIA FORMATA. Certain writs of approved and established form which were granted of course in actions to which they were applicable, and which could not be changed but by consent of the great council of the realm. Bract. fol. 413b.

BREVIA JUDICIALIA. Judicial writs. Auxiliary writs issued from the court during the progress of an action, or in aid of the judgment.

BREVIA MAGISTRALIA. Writs occasionally issued by the *masters* or clerks of chancery, the form of which was varied to suit the circumstances of each case. Bract. fol. 413b.

BREVIA SELECTA. Choice or selected writs or processes. Often abbreviated to Brev. Sel.

Brevia, tam originalia quam judicialia, patiuntur Anglica nomina. 10 Coke, 132. Writs, as well original as judicial, bear English names.

BREVIA TESTATA. The name of the short memoranda early used to show grants of lands, out of which the deeds now in use have grown. Jacob.

BREVIARIUM ALARICIANUM. A compilation of Roman law made by order of Alaric II., king of the Visigoths, in Spain, and published for the use of his Roman subjects in the year 506.

BREVIARIUM ANIANI. Another name for the Brevarium Alaricianum, (*q. v.*) Anian was the referendery or chancellor of Alaric, and was commanded by the latter to authenticate, by his signature, the copies of the breviary sent to the *comites.* Mackeld. Rom. Law, § 68.

BREVIATE. A brief; brief statement, epitome, or abstract. A short statement of contents, accompanying a bill in parliament. Holthouse.

BREVIBUS ET ROTULIS LIBERANDIS. A writ or mandate to a sheriff to deliver to his successor the county, and appurtenances, with the rolls, briefs, remembrance, and all other things belonging to his office. Reg. Orig. 295.

BREWER. One who manufactures fermented liquors of any name or description, for sale, from malt, wholly or in part, or from any substitute therefor. Act July 13, 1866, § 9, (14 St. at Large, 117.)

BRIBE. Any valuable thing given or promised, or any preferment, advantage, privilege, or emolument, given or promised corruptly and against the law, as an inducement to any person acting in an official or public capacity to violate or forbear from his duty, or to improperly influence his behavior in the performance of such duty.

The term "bribe" signifies any money, goods, right in action, property, thing of value, or advantage, present or prospective, or any promise or undertaking to give any, asked, given, or accepted, with a corrupt intent to influence unlawfully the person to whom it is given, in his action, vote, or opinion, in any public or official capacity. Pen. Code Dak. § 774.

BRIBERY. In criminal law. The receiving or offering any undue reward by or to any person whomsoever, whose ordinary profession or business relates to the administration of public justice, in order to influence his behavior in office, and to incline him to act contrary to his duty and the known rules of honesty and integrity. 1 Russ. Crimes, 154; 1 Hawk. P. C. 414; 3 Co. Inst. 149; 29 Ark. 302.

The term "bribery" now extends further, and includes the offense of giving a bribe to many other classes of officers; it applies both to the actor and receiver, and extends to voters, cabinet ministers, legislators, sheriffs, and other classes. 2 Whart. Crim. Law, § 1858.

The offense of taking any undue reward by a judge, juror, or other person concerned in the administration of justice, or by a public officer, to influence his behavior in his office. 4 Bl. Comm. 139, and note.

Bribery is the giving or receiving any undue reward to influence the behavior of the person receiving such reward in the discharge of his duty, in any office of government or of justice. Code Ga. 1882, § 4469.

The crime of offering any undue reward or remuneration to any public officer of the crown, or other person intrusted with a public duty, with a view to influence his behavior in the discharge of his duty. The taking such reward is as much bribery as the offering it. It also sometimes signifies the taking or giving a reward for public office. The offense is not confined, as some have supposed, to judicial officers. Brown.

BRIBERY AT ELECTIONS. The offense committed by one who gives or promises or offers money or any valuable inducement to an elector, in order to corruptly induce the latter to vote in a particular way or to abstain from voting, or as a reward to the voter for having voted in a particular way or abstained from voting.

BRIBOUR. One that pilfers other men's goods; a thief.

BRICOLIS. An engine by which walls were beaten down. Blount.

BRIDEWELL. In England. A house of correction.

BRIDGE. A structure erected over a river, creek, stream, ditch, ravine, or other place, to facilitate the passage thereof; including by the term both arches and abutments. 40 N. J. Law, 305.

A building of stone or wood erected across a river, for the common ease and benefit of travelers. Jacob.

Bridges are either public or private. Public bridges are such as form a part of the highway, common, according to their character as foot, horse, or carriage bridges, to the public generally, with or without toll. 2 East, 342.

A private bridge is one erected by one or more private persons for their own use and convenience.

BRIDGE-MASTERS. Persons chosen by the citizens, to have the care and supervision of bridges, and having certain fees and profits belonging to their office, as in the case of London Bridge.

BRIDLE ROAD. In the location of a private way laid out by the selectmen, and accepted by the town, a description of it as a "bridle road" does not confine the right of way to a particular class of animals or special mode of use. 16 Gray, 175.

BRIEF. In general. A written document; a letter; a writing in the form of a letter. A summary, abstract, or epitome. A condensed statement of some larger document, or of a series of papers, facts, or propositions.

An epitome or condensed summary of the facts and circumstances, or propositions of law, constituting the case proposed to be set up by either party to an action about to be tried or argued.

In English practice. A document prepared by the attorney, and given to the barrister, before the trial of a cause, for the instruction and guidance of the latter. It contains, in general, all the information necessary to enable the barrister to successfully conduct their client's case in court, such as a statement of the facts, a summary of the pleadings, the names of the witnesses, and an outline of the evidence expected from them, and any suggestions arising out of the peculiarities of the case.

In American practice. A written or printed document, prepared by counsel to serve as the basis for an argument upon a cause in an appellate court, and usually filed for the information of the court. It embodies the points of law which the counsel desires to establish, together with the arguments and authorities upon which he rests his contention.

A brief, within a rule of court requiring counsel to furnish briefs, before argument, implies some kind of statement of the case for the information of the court. 43 Ind. 356.

In Scotch law. Brief is used in the sense of "writ," and this seems to be the sense in which the word is used in very many of the ancient writers.

In ecclesiastical law. A papal rescript sealed with wax. See Bull.

BRIEF A L'EVESQUE. A writ to the bishop which, in *quare impedit,* shall go to remove an incumbent, unless he recover or be presented *pendente lite.* 1 Keb. 386.

BRIEF OF TITLE. In practice. A methodical epitome of all the patents, conveyances, incumbrances, liens, court proceedings, and other matters affecting the title to a certain portion of real estate.

BRIEF OUT OF THE CHANCERY. In Scotch law. A writ issued in the name of the sovereign in the election of tutors to minors, the cognoscing of lunatics or of idiots, and the ascertaining the widow's terce; and sometimes in dividing the property belonging to heirs-portioners. In these cases only brieves are now in use. Bell.

BRIEF, PAPAL. In ecclesiastical law. The pope's letter upon matters of discipline.

BRIEVE. In Scotch law. A writ. 1 Kames, Eq. 146.

BRIGA. In old European law. Strife, contention, litigation, controversy.

BRIGANDINE. A coat of mail or ancient armour, consisting of numerous jointed scale-like plates, very pliant and easy for the body, mentioned in 4 & 5 P. & M. c. 2.

BRIGBOTE. In Saxon and old English law. A tribute or contribution towards the repairing of bridges.

BRINGING MONEY INTO COURT. The act of depositing money in the custody of a court or of its clerk or marshal, for the purpose of satisfying a debt or duty, or to await the result of an interpleader.

BRIS. In French maritime law. Literally, breaking; wreck. Distinguished from *naufrage,* (*q. v.*)

BRISTOL BARGAIN. In English law. A contract by which A. lends B. £1,000 on good security, and it is agreed that £500, together with interest, shall be paid at a time stated; and, as to the other £500, that B., in consideration thereof, shall pay to A. £100 *per annum* for seven years. Wharton.

BRITISH COLUMBIA. The territory on the north-west coast of North America, once known by the designation of "New Caledonia." Its government is provided for by 21 & 22 Vict. c. 99. Vancouver Island is united to it by the 29 & 30 Vict. c. 67. See 33 & 34 Vict. c. 66.

BROCAGE. The wages, commission, or pay of a broker, (also called "brokerage.") Also the avocation or business of a broker.

BROCARIUS, BROCATOR. In old English and Scotch law. A broker; a middleman between buyer and seller; the agent of both transacting parties. Bell; Cowell.

BROCELLA. In old English law. A wood, a thicket or covert of bushes and brushwood. Cowell; Blount.

BROKEN STOWAGE. In maritime law. That space in a ship which is not filled by her cargo.

BROKER. An agent employed to make bargains and contracts between other persons, in matters of trade, commerce, or navigation, for a compensation commonly called "brokerage." Story, Ag. § 28.

Those who are engaged for others in the negotiation of contracts relative to property, with the custody of which they have no concern. Paley, Prin. & Ag. 13.

The *broker* or *intermediary* is he who is employed to negotiate a matter between two parties, and who, for that reason, is considered as the mandatary of both. Civil Code La. art. 3016.

One whose business is to negotiate purchases or sales of stocks, exchange, bullion, coined money, bank-notes, promissory notes, or other securities, for himself or for others. Ordinarily, the term "broker" is applied to one acting for others; but the part of the definition which speaks of purchases and sales for himself is equally important as that which speaks of sales and purchases for others. 91 U. S. 710.

A broker is a mere negotiator between

other parties, and does not act in his own name, but in the name of those who employ him. 50 Ind. 234.

Brokers are persons whose business it is to bring buyer and seller together; they need have nothing to do with negotiating the bargain. 68 Pa. St. 42.

The difference between a *factor* or commission merchant and a *broker* is this: A factor may buy and sell in his own name, and he has the goods in his possession; while a broker, as such, cannot ordinarily buy or sell in his own name, and has no possession of the goods sold. 23 Wall. 321, 330.

The legal distinction between a broker and a factor is that the factor is intrusted with the property the subject of the agency; the broker is only employed to make a bargain in relation to it. 50 Ala. 154, 156.

Brokers are of many kinds, the most important being enumerated and defined as follows:

Exchange brokers, who negotiate foreign bills of exchange.

Insurance brokers, who procure insurances for those who employ them and negotiate between the party seeking insurance and the companies or their agents.

Merchandise brokers, who buy and sell goods and negotiate between buyer and seller, but without having the custody of the property.

Note brokers, who negotiate the discount or sale of commercial paper.

Pawnbrokers, who lend money on goods deposited with them in pledge, taking high rates of interest.

Real-estate brokers, who procure the purchase or sale of land, acting as intermediary between vendor and purchaser to bring them together and arrange terms; and who negotiate loans on real-estate security, manage and lease estates, etc.

Ship-brokers, who transact business between the owners of ships and freighters or charterers, and negotiate the sale of vessels.

Stock-brokers, who are employed to buy and sell for their principals all kinds of stocks, corporation bonds, debentures, shares in companies, government securities, municipal bonds, etc.

BROKERAGE. The wages or commissions of a broker; also, his business or occupation.

BROSSUS. Bruised, or injured with blows, wounds, or other casualty. Cowell.

BROTHEL. A bawdy-house; a house of ill fame; a common habitation of prostitutes.

BROTHER. One person is a brother "of the whole blood" to another, the former being a male, when both are born from the same father and mother. He is a brother "of the half blood" to that other (or half-brother) when the two are born to the same father by different mothers or by the same mother to different fathers.

In the civil law, the following distinctions are observed: Two brothers who descend from the same father, but by different mothers, are called "consanguine" brothers. If they have the same mother, but are begotten by different fathers, they are called "uterine" brothers. If they have both the same father and mother, they are denominated brothers "germane."

BROTHER-IN-LAW. A wife's brother or a sister's husband. There is not any relationship, but only affinity, between brothers-in-law.

BRUARIUM. In old English law. A heath ground; ground where heath grows. Spelman.

BRUGBOTE. See BRIGBOTE.

BRUILLUS. In old English law. A wood or grove; a thicket or clump of trees in a park or forest. Cowell.

BRUISE. In medical jurisprudence. A contusion; an injury upon the flesh of a person with a blunt or heavy instrument, without solution of continuity, or without breaking the skin.

BRUKBARN. In old Swedish law. The child of a woman conceiving after a rape, which was made legitimate. Literally, the child of a struggle. Burrill.

BRUTUM FULMEN. An empty noise; an empty threat.

BUBBLE. An extravagant or unsubstantial project for extensive operations in business or commerce, generally founded on a fictitious or exaggerated prospectus, to ensnare unwary investors. Companies formed on such a basis or for such purposes are called "bubble companies." The term is chiefly used in England.

BUBBLE ACT. The statute 6 Geo. I. c. 18, "for restraining several extravagant and unwarrantable practices herein mentioned," was so called. It prescribed penalties for the formation of companies with little or no capital, with the intention, by means of alluring advertisements, of obtaining money from the public by the sale of shares. Such undertakings were then commonly called "bubbles." This legislation was prompted by the collapse of the "South Sea Project," which, as Blackstone says, "had beggared half the nation." It was mostly repealed by the statute 6 Geo. IV. c. 91.

BUCKSTALL. A toil to take deer. 4 Inst. 306.

BUDGET. A name given in England to the statement annually presented to parliament by the chancellor of the exchequer, containing the estimates of the national revenue and expenditure.

BUGGERY. A carnal copulation against nature; and this is either by the confusion of species,—that is to say, a man or a woman with a brute beast,—or of sexes, as a man with a man, or man unnaturally with a woman. 3 Inst. 58; 12 Coke, 36.

BUILDING. A structure or edifice erected by the hand of man, composed of natural materials, as stone or wood, and intended for use or convenience.

BUILDING LEASE. A lease of land for a long term of years, usually 99, at a rent called a "ground rent," the lessee covenanting to erect certain edifices thereon according to specification, and to maintain the same, etc., during the term.

BUILDING SOCIETY. An association in which the subscriptions of the members form a capital stock or fund out of which advances may be made to members desiring them, on mortgage security.

BUL. In the ancient Hebrew chronology, the eighth month of the ecclesiastical, and the second of the civil, year. It has since been called "*Marshevan,*" and answers to our October.

BULK. Unbroken packages. Merchandise which is neither counted, weighed, nor measured.

Bulk is said of that which is neither counted, weighed, nor measured. A sale by the bulk is the sale of a quantity such as it is, without measuring, counting, or weighing. Civil Code La. art. 3556, par. 6.

BULL. In ecclesiastical law. An instrument granted by the pope of Rome, and sealed with a seal of lead, containing some decree, commandment, or other public act, emanating from the pontiff. Bull, in this sense, corresponds with edict or letters patent from other governments. Cowell; 4 Bl. Comm. 110; 4 Steph. Comm. 177, 179.

This is also a cant term of the Stock Exchange, meaning one who speculates for a rise in the market.

BULLA. A seal used by the Roman emperors, during the lower empire; and which was of four kinds,—gold, silver, wax, and lead.

BULLETIN. An officially published notice or announcement concerning the progress of matters of public importance. In France, the registry of the laws.

BULLETIN DES LOIS. In France, the official sheet which publishes the laws and decrees; this publication constitutes the promulgation of the law or decree.

BULLION. Gold and silver intended to be coined. The term is usually applied to a quantity of these metals ready for the mint, but as yet lying in bars, plates, lumps, or other masses; but it may also include ornaments or dishes of gold and silver, or foreign coins not current as money, when intended to be descriptive of its adaptability to be coined, and not of other purposes to which it may be put.

BULLION FUND. A fund of public money maintained in connection with the mints, for the purpose of purchasing precious metals for coinage.

BUM-BAILIFF. A person employed to dun one for a debt; a bailiff employed to arrest a debtor. Probably a vulgar corruption of "bound-bailiff," (*q. v.*)

BUNDA. In old English law. A bound, boundary, border, or limit, (*terminus, limes.*)

BUNGALOW. A country-house in the East Indies.

BUOY. In maritime law. A piece of wood or cork, or a barrel, raft, or other thing, made secure and floating upon a stream or bay, intended as a guide and warning to mariners, by marking a spot where the water is shallow, or where there is a reef or other danger to navigation, or to mark the course of a devious channel.

BURDEN OF PROOF. (Lat. *onus probandi.*) In the law of evidence. The necessity or duty of affirmatively proving a fact or facts in dispute on an issue raised between the parties in a cause.

The term "burden of proof" is not to be confused with "*prima facie* case." When the party upon whom the burden of proof rests has made out a *prima facie* case, this will, in general, suffice to shift the burden.

In other words, the former expression denotes the necessity of establishing the latter.

BUREAU. An office for the transaction of business. A name given to the several departments of the executive or administrative branch of government, or to their larger subdivisions.

BUREAUCRACY. A system in which the business of government is carried on in departments, each under the control of a chief, in contradistinction from a system in which the officers of government have a coordinate authority.

BURG, BURGH. A term anciently applied to a castle or fortified place; a borough, (*q. v.*) Spelman.

BURGAGE. A name anciently given to a dwelling-house in a borough town. Blount.

BURGAGE-HOLDING. A tenure by which lands in royal boroughs in Scotland were held of the sovereign. The service was watching and warding, and was done by the burgesses within the territory of the borough, whether expressed in the charter or not.

BURGAGE-TENURE. In English law. One of the three species of free socage holdings; a tenure whereby houses and lands which were formerly the site of houses, in an ancient borough, are held of some lord by a certain rent. There are a great many customs affecting these tenures, the most remarkable of which is the custom of Borough English. See Litt. § 162; 2 Bl. Comm. 82.

BURGATOR. One who breaks into houses or inclosed places, as distinguished from one who committed robbery in the open country. Spelman.

BURGBOTE. In old English law. A term applied to a contribution towards the repair of castles or walls of defense, or of a borough.

BURGENSES. In old English law. Inhabitants of a *burgus* or borough; burgesses. Fleta, lib. 5, c. 6, § 10.

BURGERISTH. A word used in Domesday, signifying a breach of the peace in a town. Jacob.

BURGESS. In English law. An inhabitant or freeman of a borough or town; a person duly and legally admitted a member of a municipal corporation. Spelman; 3 Steph. Comm. 188, 189.

A magistrate of a borough. Blount.

An elector or voter; a person legally qualified to vote at elections. The word in this sense is particularly defined by the statute 5 & 6 Wm. IV. c. 76, §§ 9, 13. 3 Steph. Comm. 192.

A representative of a borough or town, in parliament. Co. Litt. 109*a;* 1 Bl. Comm. 174.

In American law. The chief executive officer of a borough, bearing the same relation to its government and affairs that the *mayor* does to those of a city. So used in Pennsylvania.

BURGESS ROLL. A roll, required by the St. 5 & 6 Wm. IV. c. 76, to be kept in corporate towns or boroughs, of the names of burgesses entitled to certain new rights conferred by that act.

BURGH-BRECHE. A fine imposed on the community of a town, for a breach of the peace, etc.

BURGH ENGLISH. See BOROUGH ENGLISH.

BURGH ENGLOYS. Borough English, (*q. v.*)

BURGHMAILS. Yearly payments to the crown of Scotland, introduced by Malcolm III., and resembling the English fee-farm rents.

BURGHMOTE. In Saxon law. A court of justice held semi-annually by the bishop or lord in a *burg*, which the thanes were bound to attend without summons.

BURGLAR. One who commits burglary. One who breaks into a dwelling-house in the night-time with intent to commit a felony.

BURGLARIOUSLY. In pleading. A technical word which must be introduced into an indictment for burglary at common law.

BURGLARITER. L. Lat. (Burglariously.) In old criminal pleading. A necessary word in indictments for burglary.

BURGLARY. In criminal law. The breaking and entering the house of another in the night-time, with intent to commit a felony therein, whether the felony be actually committed or not. 3 Inst. 63; 1 Hale, P. C. 549; 1 Hawk. P. C. c. 38, § 1.

Burglary is the breaking and entering the dwelling-house of another, in the night-time, with intent to commit a felony. 29 Ind. 80; 1 N. J. Law, 441; 9 Ired. 463; 1 Dev. 253; 7 Mass. 247.

The common-law definition has been much modified by statute in several of the states.

For example: "Every person who enters any house, room, apartment, tenement, shop, warehouse, store, mill, barn, stable, outhouse, or other building, tent, vessel, or railroad car, with intent to commit grand or petit larceny, or any felony, is guilty of burglary." Pen. Code Cal. § 459.

BURGOMASTER. The title given in Germany to the chief executive officer of a borough, town, or city; corresponding to our "mayor."

BURGUNDIAN LAW. See LEX BURGUNDIONUM.

BURGWHAR. A burgess, (*q. v.*)

BURIAL. Sepulture; the act of interring dead human bodies.

BURKISM, (from the name of its first perpetrator.) The practice of killing persons for the purpose of selling their bodies for dissection.

BURLAW COURTS. In Scotch law. Courts consisting of neighbors selected by common consent to act as judges in determining disputes between neighbor and neighbor.

BURLAWS. In Scotch law. Laws made by neighbors elected by common consent in the burlaw courts. Skene.

BURN. To consume with fire. The verb "to burn," in an indictment for arson, is to be taken in its common meaning of "to consume with fire." 17 Ga. 130.

Burning and *setting fire to* are not legal synonyms. 5 Grat. 664.

BURNING FLUID. As used in policies of insurance, this term does not mean any fluid which will burn, but it means a recognized article of commerce, called by that name, and which is a different article from naphtha or kerosene. 4 Fed. Rep. 766; 24 Hun. 569.

BURNING IN THE HAND. In old English criminal law, laymen, upon being accorded the benefit of clergy, were burned with a hot iron in the brawn of the left thumb, in order that, being thus marked, they could not again claim their clergy. 4 Bl. Comm. 367.

BURROCHIUM. A burroch, dam, or small wear over a river, where traps are laid for the taking of fish. Cowell.

BURROWMEALIS. In Scotch law. A term used to designate the rents paid into the king's private treasury by the burgesses or inhabitants of a borough.

BURSA. A purse.

BURSAR. A treasurer of a college.

BURSARIA. The exchequer of collegiate or conventual bodies; or the place of receiving, paying, and accounting by the bursars. Also stipendiary scholars, who live upon the burse, fund, or joint-stock of the college.

BURYING ALIVE. In English law. The ancient punishment of sodomites, and those who contracted with Jews. Fleta, lib. 1, c. 27, § 3.

BURYING-GROUND. A place set apart for the interment of the dead; a cemetery.

BUSCARL. In Saxon and old English law. Seamen or marines. Spelman.

BUSHEL. A dry measure, containing four pecks, eight gallons, or thirty-two quarts. But the dimensions of a bushel, and the weight of a bushel of grain, etc., vary in the different states in consequence of statutory enactments.

BUSINESS. This word embraces everything about which a person can be employed. 23 N. Y. 242, 244.

That which occupies the time, attention, and labor of men for the purpose of a livelihood or profit. The doing of a single act pertaining to a particular business will not be considered engaging in or carrying on the business; yet a series of such acts would be so considered. 50 Ala. 130. See, also, 2 Allen, 395; 38 N. J. Law, 237.

Labor, business, and work are not synonyms. Labor may be business, but it is not necessarily so; and business is not always labor. Making an agreement for the sale of a chattel is not within a prohibition of labor upon Sunday, though it is (if by a merchant in his calling) within a prohibition upon business. 2 Ohio St. 387.

BUSINESS HOURS. Those hours of the day during which, in a given community, commercial, banking, professional, public, or other kinds of business are ordinarily carried on.

This phrase is declared to mean not the time during which a principal requires an employee's services, but the business hours of the community generally. 18 Minn. 133, (Gil. 119.)

BUSONES COMITATUS. In old English law. The barons of a county.

BUSSA. A term used in the old English law, to designate a large and clumsily constructed ship.

BUTLERAGE. A privilege formerly allowed to the king's butler, to take a certain part of every cask of wine imported by an alien.

BUTLER'S ORDINANCE. In English law. A law for the heir to punish waste in the life of the ancestor. "Though it be on record in the parliament book of Edward I., yet it never was a statute, nor ever so received; but only some constitution of the king's council, or lords in parliament, which never obtained the strength or force of an act of parliament." Hale, Hist. Eng. Law, p. 18.

BUTT. A measure of liquid capacity, equal to one hundred and eight gallons; also a measure of land.

BUTTALS. The bounding lines of land at the end; abuttals, which see.

BUTTED AND BOUNDED. A phrase sometimes used in conveyancing, to introduce the boundaries of lands. See BUTTS AND BOUNDS.

BUTTS. In old English law. Short pieces of land left unplowed at the *ends* of fields, where the plow was turned about, (otherwise called "headlands,") as sidelings were similar unplowed pieces on the sides. Burrill.

Also a place where bowmen meet to shoot at a mark.

BUTTS AND BOUNDS. A phrase used in conveyancing, to describe the end lines or circumscribing lines of a certain piece of land. The phrase "metes and bounds" has the same meaning.

BUTTY. A local term in the north of England, for the associate or deputy of another; also of things used in common.

BUY. To acquire the ownership of property by giving an accepted price or consideration therefor; or by agreeing to do so; to acquire by the payment of a price or value; to purchase. Webster.

BUY IN. To purchase, at public sale, property which is one's own or which one has caused or procured to be sold.

BUYER. One who buys; a purchaser, particularly of chattels.

BUYING TITLES. The purchase of the rights or claims to real estate of a person who is not in possession of the land or is disseised. Void, and an offense, at common law.

BY. This word, when descriptively used in a grant, does not mean "in immediate contact with," but "near" to, the object to which it relates; and "near" is a relative term, meaning, when used in land patents, very unequal and different distances. 6 Gill, 121; 48 N. H. 491.

A contract to complete work *by* a certain time, means that it shall be done before that time. 3 Pen. & W. 48.

By an acquittance for the last payment all other arrearages are discharged. Noy, 40.

BY-BIDDING. In the law relating to sales by auction, this term is equivalent to "puffing." The practice consists in making fictitious bids for the property, under a secret arrangement with the owner or auctioneer, for the purpose of misleading and stimulating other persons who are bidding in good faith.

BY BILL, BY BILL WITHOUT WRIT. In practice. Terms anciently used to designate actions commenced by original *bill*, as distinguished from those commenced by original *writ*, and applied in modern practice to suits commenced by *capias ad respondendum.* 1 Arch. Pr. pp. 2, 337; 5 Hill, 213.

BY ESTIMATION. In conveyancing. A term used to indicate that the quantity of land as stated is estimated only, not exactly measured; has the same meaning and effect as the phrase "more or less."

BY GOD AND MY COUNTRY. In old English criminal practice. The established formula of reply by a prisoner, when arraigned at the bar, to the question, "Culprit, how wilt thou be tried?"

BY-LAWS. Regulations, ordinances, or rules enacted by a private corporation for its own government.

A by-law is a rule or law of a corporation, for its government, and is a legislative act, and the solemnities and sanction required by the charter must be observed. A resolution is not necessarily a by-law, though a by-law may be in the form of a resolution. 7 Barb. 508.

"That the reasonableness of a by-law of a corporation is a question of law, and not of fact, has always been the established rule; but in the case of State v. Overton, 24 N. J. Law, 435, a distinction was taken in this respect between a by-law and a regulation, the validity of the former being a judicial question, while the latter was regarded as a matter *in pais.* But although, in one of the opinions read in the case referred to, the view was clearly expressed that the reasonableness of a corporate regulation was properly for the consideration of the jury, and not of the court, yet it was nevertheless stated that the point was not involved in the controversy then to be decided. There is no doubt that the rule thus intimated is in opposition to recent American authorities. Nor have I been able to find in the English books any such distinction as that above stated between a by-law and a regulation of a corporation." 34 N. J. Law, 135.

The word has also been used to designate the local laws or municipal statutes of a city or town. But of late the tendency is to employ the word "ordinance" exclusively for this class of enactments, reserving "by-law" for the rules adopted by private corporations.

BY LAW MEN. In English law. The chief men of a town, representing the inhabitants.

BY-ROAD. The statute law of New Jersey recognizes three different kinds of roads:

AM.DICT.LAW—11

A public road, a private road, and a by-road. A by-road is a road used by the inhabitants, and recognized by statute, but not laid out. Such roads are often called "driftways." They are roads of necessity in newly-settled countries. 29 N. J. Law, 516. See, also, Id. 68.

An obscure or neighborhood road in its earlier existence, not used to any great extent by the public, yet so far a public road that the public have of right free access to it at all times. 34 N. J. Law, 89.

BY THE BY. Incidentally; without new process. A term used in former English practice to denote the method of filing a declaration against a defendant who was already in the custody of the court at the suit of a different plaintiff or of the same plaintiff in another cause.

BYE-BIL-WUFFA. In Hindu law. A deed of mortgage or conditional sale.

C.

C. The initial letter of the word "*Codex*," used by some writers in citing the Code of Justinian. Tayl. Civil Law, 24.

It was also the letter inscribed on the ballots by which, among the Romans, jurors voted to condemn an accused party. It was the initial letter of *condemno,* I condemn. Tayl. Civil Law, 192.

C, as the third letter of the alphabet, is used as a numeral, in like manner with that use of A and B, (*q. v.*)

The letter is also used to designate the *third* of a series of propositions, sections, etc., as A, B, and the others are used as numerals.

It is used as an abbreviation of many words of which it is the initial letter; such as cases, civil, circuit, code, common, court, criminal, chancellor, crown.

C. A. V. An abbreviation for *curia advisari vult,* the court will be advised, will consider, will deliberate.

C. B. In reports and legal documents, an abbreviation for common bench. Also an abbreviation for chief baron.

C. C. Various terms or phrases may be denoted by this abbreviation; such as circuit court, (or city or county court;) criminal cases, (or crown or civil or chancery cases;) civil code; chief commissioner; and the return of *cepi corpus.*

C. C. P. An abbreviation for Code of Civil Procedure; also for court of common pleas.

C. J. An abbreviation for chief justice; also for circuit judge.

C. L. An abbreviation for civil law.

C. L. P. Common law procedure, in reference to the English acts so entitled.

C. O. D. "Collect on delivery." These letters are not cabalistic, but have a determinate meaning. They import the carrier's liability to return to the consignor either the goods or the charges. 59 Ind. 263.

C. P. An abbreviation for common pleas.

C. R. An abbreviation for *curia regis;* also for chancery reports.

C. T. A. An abbreviation for *cum testamento annexo,* in describing a species of administration.

CABAL. A small association for the purpose of intrigue; an intrigue. This name was given to that ministry in the reign of Charles II. formed by Clifford, Ashley, Buckingham, Arlington, and Lauderdale, who concerted a scheme for the restoration of popery. The initials of these five names form the word "cabal;" hence the appellation. Hume, Hist. Eng. ix. 69.

CABALIST. In French commercial law. A factor or broker.

CABALLARIA. Pertaining to a horse. It was a feudal tenure of lands, the tenant furnishing a horseman suitably equipped in time of war, or when the lord had occasion for his service.

CABALLERIA. In Spanish law. An allotment of land acquired by conquest, to a horse soldier. It was a strip one hundred feet wide by two hundred feet deep. The term has been sometimes used in those parts of the United States which were derived from Spain. See 12 Pet. 444, note.

CABALLERO. In Spanish law. A knight. So called on account of its being more honorable to go on horseback (*à caballo*) than on any other beast.

CABINET. The advisory board or council of a king or other chief executive. In the government of the United States the cabinet is composed of the secretary of state, the secretary of the treasury, the secretary of the interior, the secretary of war, the secretary of the navy, the secretary of agriculture, the attorney general, and the postmaster general.

The select or secret council of a prince or executive government; so called from the apartment in which it was originally held. Webster.

CABINET COUNCIL. In English law. A private and confidential assembly of the most considerable ministers of state, to concert measures for the administration of public affairs; first established by Charles I. Wharton.

CABLE. The great rope of a ship, to which the anchor is fastened.

CABLISH. Brush-wood, or more properly windfall-wood.

CACHEPOLUS, or CACHERELLAS. An inferior bailiff, or catchpoll. Jacob.

CACHET, LETTRES DE. Letters issued and signed by the kings of France, and countersigned by a secretary of state, authorizing the imprisonment of a person. Abolished during the revolution of 1789.

CACICAZGOS. In Spanish-American law. Property entailed on the *caciques*, or heads of Indian villages, and their descendants. Schm. Civil Law, 309.

CADASTRE. In Spanish law. An official statement of the quantity and value of real property in any district, made for the purpose of justly apportioning the taxes payable on such property. 12 Pet. 428, note.

CADASTU. In French law. An official statement of the quantity and value of realty made for purposes of taxation; same as *cadastre*, (*q. v.*)

CADERE. Lat. To end; cease; fail. As in the phrases *cadit actio*, (or *breve*,) the action (or writ) fails; *cadit assisa*, the assise abates; *cadit quæstio*, the discussion ends, there is no room for further argument.

To be changed; to be turned into. *Cadit assisa in juratum*, the assise is changed into a jury.

CADET. In the United States laws, students in the military academy at West Point are styled "cadets;" students in the naval academy at Annapolis, "cadet midshipmen." Rev. St. §§ 1309, 1512.

In England. The younger son of a gentleman; particularly applied to a volunteer in the army, waiting for some post. Jacob.

CADI. The name of a Turkish civil magistrate.

CADIT. It falls, abates, fails, ends, ceases. See CADERE.

CADUCA. In the civil law. Property of an inheritable quality; property such as descends to an heir. Also the lapse of a testamentary disposition or legacy. Also an escheat; escheated property.

CADUCARY. Relating to or of the nature of escheat, forfeiture, or confiscation. 2 Bl. Comm. 245.

CÆDUA. In the civil and old common law. Kept for cutting; intended or used to be cut. A term applied to wood.

CÆSAR. In the Roman law. A cognomen in the Gens Julia, which was assumed by the successors of Julius. Tayl. Civil Law, 31.

CÆSAREAN OPERATION. A surgical operation whereby the fœtus, which can neither make its way into the world by the ordinary and natural passage, nor be extracted by the attempts of art, whether the mother and fœtus be yet alive, or whether either of them be dead, is, by a cautious and well-timed operation, taken from the mother, with a view to save the lives of both, or either of them. If this operation be performed after the mother's death, the husband cannot be tenant by the curtesy; since his right begins from the birth of the issue, and is consummated by the death of the wife; but, if mother and child are saved, then the husband would be entitled after her death. Wharton.

CÆTERIS PARIBUS. Other things being equal.

CÆTERIS TACENTIBUS. Lat. The others being silent; the other judges expressing no opinion. Comb. 186.

CÆTERORUM. When a limited administration has been granted, and all the property cannot be administered under it, administration *cæterorum* (as to the residue) may be granted.

CAHIER. In old French law. A list of grievances prepared for deputies in the states-general. A petition for the redress of grievances enumerated.

CAIRNS' ACT. An English statute for enabling the court of chancery to award damages. 21 & 22 Vict. c. 27.

CALCETUM, CALCEA. A causeway, or common hard-way, maintained and repaired with stones and rubbish.

CALE. In old French law. A punishment of sailors, resembling the modern "keel-hauling."

CALEFAGIUM. In old law. A right to take fuel yearly. Cowell.

CALENDAR. The established order of the division of time into years, months, weeks, and days; or a systematized enumeration of such arrangement; an almanac.

D

E

F

G

H

I

J

K

L

M

CALENDAR MONTH. One of the months of the year as enumerated in the calendar, — January, February, March, etc., — without reference to the number of days it may contain; as distinguished from a lunar month, of twenty-eight days, or a month for business purposes, which may contain thirty, at whatever part of the year it occurs.

CALENDAR OF CAUSES. In practice. A list of the causes instituted in the particular court, and now ready for trial, drawn up by the clerk shortly before the beginning of the term, exhibiting the titles of the suits, arranged in their order for trial, with the nature of each action, the date of issue, and the names of the counsel engaged; designed for the information and convenience of the court and bar. It is sometimes called the "trial-list," or "docket."

CALENDAR OF PRISONERS. In English practice. A list kept by the sheriffs containing the names of all the prisoners in their custody, with the several judgments against each in the margin. Staundef. P. C. 182; 4 Bl. Comm. 403.

CALENDS. Among the Romans the first day of every month, being spoken of by itself, or the very day of the new moon, which usually happen together. And if *pridie*, the day before, be added to it, then it is the last day of the foregoing month, as *pridie calend. Septemb.* is the last day of August. If any number be placed with it, it signifies that day in the former month which comes so much before the month named, as the tenth calends of October is the 20th day of September; for if one reckons backwards, beginning at October, that 20th day of September makes the 10th day before October. In March, May, July, and October, the calends begin at the sixteenth day, but in other months at the fourteenth; which calends must ever bear the name of the month following, and be numbered backwards from the first day of the said following months. Jacob.

CALENDS, GREEK. A metaphorical expression for a time never likely to arrive.

CALL. 1. In English law. The election of students to the degree of barrister at law, hence the ceremony or epoch of election, and the number of persons elected.

2. In conveyancing. A visible natural object or landmark designated in a patent, entry, grant, or other conveyance of lands, as a limit or boundary to the land described, with which the points of surveying must correspond. Also the courses and distances designated.

3. In corporation law. A demand made by the directors of a stock company upon the persons who have subscribed for shares, requiring a certain portion or installment of the amount subscribed to be paid in. The word, in this sense, is synonymous with "assessment," (*q. v.*)

A call is an assessment on shares of stock, usually for unpaid installments of the subscription thereto. The word is said to be capable of three meanings: (1) The resolution of the directors to levy the assessment; (2) its notification to the persons liable to pay; (3) the time when it becomes payable. 4 Exch. 543.

4. In the language of the stock exchange, a "call" is an option to claim stock at a fixed price on a certain day. Bid. Stock-Brok. 70.

CALL OF THE HOUSE. A call of the names of all the members of a legislative body, made by the clerk in pursuance of a resolution requiring the attendance of members. The names of absentees being thus ascertained, they are imperatively summoned (and, if necessary, compelled) to attend the session.

CALLING A SUMMONS. In Scotch practice. See this described in Bell, Dict.

CALLING THE JURY. Successively drawing out of a box into which they have been previously put the names of the jurors on the panels annexed to the *nisi prius* record, and calling them over in the order in which they are so drawn. The twelve persons whose names are first called, and who appear, are sworn as the jury, unless some just cause of challenge or excuse, with respect to any of them, shall be brought forward.

CALLING THE PLAINTIFF. In practice. A formal method of causing a nonsuit to be entered.

When a plaintiff or his counsel, seeing that sufficient evidence has not been given to maintain the issue, withdraws, the crier is ordered to call or demand the plaintiff, and if neither he, nor any person for him, appear, he is nonsuited, the jurors are discharged without giving a verdict, the action is at an end, and the defendant recovers his costs.

CALLING TO THE BAR. In English practice. Conferring the dignity or degree of barrister at law upon a member of one of the inns of court. Holthouse.

CALLING UPON A PRISONER. When a prisoner has been found guilty on an indictment, the clerk of the court addresses him and calls upon him to say why judgment should not be passed upon him.

CALPES. In Scotch law. A gift to the head of a clan, as an acknowledgment for protection and maintenance.

CALUMNIA. In the civil law. Calumny, malice, or ill design; a false accusation; a malicious prosecution.

In the old common law. A claim, demand, challenge to jurors.

CALUMNIÆ JURAMENTUM. In the old canon law. An oath similar to the *calumniæ jusjurandum*, (*q. v.*)

CALUMNIÆ JUSJURANDUM. The oath of calumny. An oath imposed upon the parties to a suit that they did not sue or defend with the intention of calumniating, (*calumniandi animo*,) i. e., with a malicious design, but from a firm belief that they had a good cause. Inst. 4, 16.

CALUMNIATOR. In the civil law. One who accused another of a crime without cause; one who brought a false accusation. Cod. 9, 46.

CALUMNY. Defamation; slander; false accusation of a crime or offense. "There was a word called 'calumny' in the civil law, which signified an unjust prosecution or defense of a suit, and the phrase is said to be still used in the courts of Scotland and the ecclesiastical and admiralty courts of England, though we do not find cases of the kind in the reports." 30 Ohio St. 117.

CAMARA. In Spanish law. A treasury. Las Partidas, pt. 6, tit. 3, l. 2.

The exchequer. White, New Recop. b. 3, tit. 8, c. 1.

CAMBELLANUS, or CAMBELLARIUS. A chamberlain. Spelman.

CAMBIATOR. In old English law. An exchanger. *Cambiatores monetæ*, exchangers of money; money-changers.

CAMBIO. In Spanish law. Exchange. Schm. Civil Law, 148.

CAMBIPARTIA. Champerty; from *campus*, a field, and *partus*, divided. Spelman.

CAMBIPARTICEPS. A champertor.

CAMBIST. In mercantile law. A person skilled in exchanges; one who trades in promissory notes and bills of exchange.

CAMBIUM. In the civil law. Change or exchange. A term applied indifferently to the exchange of land, money, or debts.

Cambium reale or *manuale* was the term generally used to denote the technical common-law exchange of lands; *cambium locale, mercantile,* or *trajectitium,* was used to designate the modern mercantile contract of exchange, whereby a man agrees, in consideration of a sum of money paid him in one place, to pay a like sum in another place. Poth. *de Change,* n. 12; Story, Bills, § 2, et seq.

CAMERA. In old English law. A chamber, room, or apartment; a judge's chamber; a treasury; a chest or coffer. Also, a stipend payable from vassal to lord; an annuity.

CAMERA REGIS. In old English law. A chamber of the king; a place of peculiar privileges especially in a commercial point of view.

CAMERA SCACCARII. The old name of the exchequer chamber, (*q. v.*)

CAMERA STELLATA. The star chamber, (*q. v.*)

CAMERALISTICS. The science of finance or public revenue, comprehending the means of raising and disposing of it.

CAMERARIUS. A chamberlain; a keeper of the public money; a treasurer.

Also a bailiff or receiver.

CAMINO. In Spanish law. A road or highway. Las Partidas, pt. 3, tit. 2, l. 6.

CAMPANA. In old European law. A bell. Spelman.

CAMPANA BAJULA. A small hand-bell used in the ceremonies of the Romish church; and, among Protestants, by sextons, parish clerks, and criers. Cowell.

CAMPANARIUM, CAMPANILE. A belfry, bell tower, or steeple; a place where bells are hung. Spelman; Townsh. Pl. 191, 213.

CAMPARTUM. A part of a larger field or ground, which would otherwise be in gross or in common.

CAMPBELL'S (LORD) ACTS. English statutes, for amending the practice in prosecutions for libel, 9 & 10 Vict. c. 93; also 6 & 7 Vict. c. 96, providing for compensation to relatives in the case of a person having been killed through negligence; also 20 & 21 Vict. c. 83, in regard to the sale of obscene books, etc.

CAMPERS. A share; a champertor's share; a champertous division or sharing of land.

CAMPERTUM. A corn-field; a field of grain. Blount; Cowell; Jacob.

CAMPFIGHT. In old English law. The fighting of two champions or combatants in the field; the judicial combat, or *duellum*. 3 Inst. 221.

CAMPUS. In old European law. An assembly of the people; so called from being anciently held in the open air, in some *plain* capable of containing a large number of persons.

In feudal and old English law. A field, or plain. The field, ground, or lists marked out for the combatants in the *duellum*, or trial by battle.

CAMPUS MAII. L. Lat. The field of May. An anniversary assembly of the Saxons, held on May-day, when they confederated for the defense of the kingdom against all its enemies.

CAMPUS MARTII. The field of March. See CHAMP DE MARS.

CAN. A promise to pay as soon as the debtor possibly *can* is in contemplation of law a promise to pay presently; the law supposes every man able to pay his debts. 1 Bibb, 396.

CANA. A distance in the measure of ground.

CANAL. An artificial ditch or trench in the earth, for confining water to a defined channel, to be used for purposes of transportation.

The meaning of this word, when applied to artificial passages for water, is a trench or excavation in the earth, for conducting water and confining it to narrow limits. It is unlike the words "river," "pond," "lake," and other words used to designate natural bodies of water, the ordinary meaning of which is confined to the water itself; but it includes also the banks, and has reference rather to the excavation or channel as a receptacle for the water; it is an artificial thing. 18 Conn. 394. See, also, 103 U. S. 604.

CANCEL. To obliterate, strike, or cross out; to destroy the effect of an instrument

by defacing, obliterating, expunging, or erasing it. See 18 Cal. 451.

In equity. Courts of equity frequently cancel instruments which have answered the end for which they were created, or instruments which are void or voidable, in order to prevent them from being vexatiously used against the person apparently bound by them. Snell, Eq. 498.

CANCELLARIA. Chancery; the court of chancery. *Curia cancellaria* is also used in the same sense. See 4 Bl. Comm. 46; Cowell.

Cancellarii Angliæ dignitas est, ut secundus a rege in regno habetur. The dignity of the chancellor of England is that he is deemed the second from the sovereign in the kingdom. 4 Inst. 78.

CANCELLARIUS. A chancellor; a scrivener, or notary. A janitor, or one who stood at the door of the court and was accustomed to carry out the commands of the judges.

CANCELLATION. The act of crossing out a writing. The manual operation of tearing or destroying a written instrument. 1 Eq. Cas. Abr. 409; Rob. Wills, 367, n.

According to Bartolus, an expunging or wiping out of the contents of an instrument by two lines drawn in the manner of a cross; also used to signify any manner of obliteration and defacement.

CANCELLATURA. In old English law. A cancelling. Bract. 398b.

CANCELLI. The rails or lattice work or balusters inclosing the bar of a court of justice or the communion table. Also the lines drawn on the face of a will or other writing, with the intention of revoking or annulling it.

CANDIDATE. A person who offers himself, or is presented by others, to be elected to an office. Derived from the Latin *candidus*, (white,) because in Rome it was the custom for those who sought office to clothe themselves in white garments.

One who seeks or aspires to some office or privilege, or who offers himself for the same. A man is a candidate for an office when he is seeking such office. It is not necessary that he should have been *nominated* for the office. 112 Pa. St. 624, 4 Atl. Rep. 607.

CANDLEMAS-DAY. A festival appointed by the church to be observed on the second day of February in every year, in honor of the purification of the Virgin Mary, being forty days after her miraculous delivery. At this festival, formerly, the Protestants went, and the Papists now go, in procession with lighted candles; they also consecrate candles on this day for the service of the ensuing year. It is the fourth of the four cross quarter-days of the year. Wharton.

CANFARA. In old records. A trial by hot iron, formerly used in England. Whishaw.

CANON. A law, rule, or ordinance in general, and of the church in particular. An ecclesiastical law or statute.

One of the dignitaries of the English church; being a prebendary or member of a chapter.

In the civil, Spanish, and Mexican law. An annual charge or rent; an emphyteutic rent. See 15 Cal. 556.

In old English records. A prestation, pension, or customary payment. Cowell.

CANON LAW. A body of ecclesiastical jurisprudence which, in countries where the Roman Catholic church is established, is composed of maxims and rules drawn from patristic sources, ordinances and decrees of general councils, and the decretals and bulls of the popes. In England, according to Blackstone, there is a kind of national canon law, composed of legatine and provincial constitutions enacted in England prior to the reformation, and adapted to the exigencies of the English church and kingdom. 1 Bl. Comm. 82.

The canon law consists partly of certain rules taken out of the Scripture, partly of the writings of the ancient fathers of the church, partly of the ordinances of general and provincial councils, and partly of the decrees of the popes in former ages; and it is contained in two principal parts,—the decrees and the decretals. The decrees are ecclesiastical constitutions made by the popes and cardinals. The decretals are canonical epistles written by the pope, or by the pope and cardinals, at the suit of one or more persons, for the ordering and determining of some matter of controversy, and have the authority of a law. As the decrees set out the origin of the canon law, and the rights, dignities, and decrees of ecclesiastical persons, with their manner of election, ordination, etc., so the decretals contain the law to be used in the ecclesiastical courts. Jacob.

CANON RELIGIOSORUM. Lat. In ecclesiastical records. A book wherein the religious of every greater convent had a fair transcript of the rules of their order, frequently read among them as their local statutes. Kennett, Gloss.; Cowell.

CANONICAL. Pertaining to, or in conformity to, the canons of the church.

CANONICAL OBEDIENCE. That duty which a clergyman owes to the bishop who ordained him, to the bishop in whose diocese he is beneficed, and also to the metropolitan of such bishop. Wharton.

CANONICUS. In old English law. A canon. Fleta, lib. 2, c. 69, § 2.

CANONIST. One versed and skilled in the canon law; a professor of ecclesiastical law.

CANONRY. In English ecclesiastical law. An ecclesiastical benefice, attaching to the office of canon. Holthouse.

CANONS OF DESCENT. The legal rules by which inheritances are regulated, and according to which estates are transmitted by descent from the ancestor to the heir.

CANONS OF INHERITANCE. The legal rules by which inheritances are regulated, and according to which estates are transmitted by descent from the ancestor to the heir. 2 Bl. Comm. 208.

CANT. In the civil law. A method of dividing property held in common by two or more joint owners. See 9 Mart. (La.) 87.

CANTEL, or CANTLE. A lump, or that which is added above measure; also a piece of anything, as "cantel of bread," or the like. Blount.

CANTERBURY, ARCHBISHOP OF. In English ecclesiastical law. The primate of all England; the chief ecclesiastical dignitary in the church. His customary privilege is to crown the kings and queens of England; while the Archbishop of York has the privilege to crown the queen consort, and be her perpetual chaplain. The Archbishop of Canterbury has also, by 25 Hen. VIII. c. 21, the power of granting dispensations in any case not contrary to the holy scriptures and the law of God, where the pope used formerly to grant them, which is the foundation of his granting special licenses to marry at any place or time; to hold two livings, (which must be confirmed under the great seal,) and the like; and on this also is founded the right he exercises of conferring degrees in prejudice of the two universities. Wharton.

CANTRED. A district comprising a hundred villages; a hundred. A term used in Wales in the same sense as "hundred" is in England. Cowell; Termes de la Ley.

CANUM. In feudal law. A species of duty or tribute payable from tenant to lord, usually consisting of produce of the land.

CANVASS. The act of examining and counting the returns of votes cast at a public election.

CAP OF MAINTENANCE. One of the regalia or ornaments of state belonging to the sovereigns of England, before whom it is carried at the coronation and other great solemnities. Caps of maintenance are also carried before the mayors of several cities in England. Enc. Lond.

CAPACITY. Legal capacity is the attribute of a person who can acquire new rights, or transfer rights, or assume duties, according to the mere dictates of his own will, as manifested in juristic acts, without any restraint or hindrance arising from his *status* or legal condition.

Ability; qualification; legal power or right. Applied in this sense to the attribute of persons (natural or artificial) growing out of their *status* or juristic condition, which enables them to perform civil acts; as capacity to hold lands, capacity to devise, etc.

CAPAX DOLI. Lat. Capable of committing crime, or capable of criminal intent. The phrase describes the condition of one who has sufficient intelligence and comprehension to be held criminally responsible for his deeds.

CAPAX NEGOTII. Competent to transact affairs; having business capacity.

CAPE. In English practice. A judicial writ touching a plea of lands or tenements, divided into *cape magnum*, or the *grand cape*, which lay before appearance to summon the tenant to answer the default, and also over to the demandant; the *cape ad valentiam* was a species of grand cape; and *cape parvum*, or *petit cape*, after appearance or view granted, summoning the tenant to answer the default only. Termes de la Ley; 3 Steph. Comm. 606, note.

CAPE AD VALENTIAM. A species of *cape magnum*. See CAPE.

CAPELLA. In old records. A box, cabinet, or repository in which were preserved the relics of martyrs. Spelman. A small building in which relics were preserved; an oratory or chapel. Id.

In old English law. A chapel. Fleta, lib. 5, c. 12, § 1; Spelman; Cowell.

CAPERS. Vessels of war owned by private persons, and different from ordinary privateers only in size, being smaller. Beawes, Lex Merc. 230.

CAPIAS. Lat. "That you take." The general name for several species of writs, the common characteristic of which is that they require the officer to take the body of the defendant into custody; they are writs of attachment or arrest.

In English practice. A *capias* is the process on an indictment when the person charged is not in custody, and in cases not otherwise provided for by statute. 4 Steph. Comm. 383.

CAPIAS AD AUDIENDUM JUDICIUM. In practice. A writ issued, in a case of misdemeanor, after the defendant has appeared and is found guilty, to bring him to hear judgment if he is not present when called. 4 Bl. Comm. 368.

CAPIAS AD COMPUTANDUM. In the action of account render, after judgment of *quod computet*, if the defendant refuses to appear personally before the auditors and make his account, a writ by this name may issue to compel him.

CAPIAS AD RESPONDENDUM. In practice. A judicial writ, (usually simply termed a "*capias*,") by which actions at law were frequently commenced; and which commands the sheriff to *take* the defendant, and him safely keep, so that he may have his body before the court on a certain day, to *answer* the plaintiff in the action. 3 Bl. Comm. 282; 1 Tidd, Pr. 128. The name of this writ is commonly abbreviated to *ca. resp.*

CAPIAS AD SATISFACIENDUM. In practice. A writ of execution, (usually termed, for brevity, a "*ca. sa.*,") which a party may issue after having recovered judgment against another in certain actions at law. It commands the sheriff to *take* the party named, and keep him safely, so that he may have his body before the court on a certain day, to *satisfy* the party by whom it is issued, the damages or debt and damages recovered by the judgment. Its effect is to deprive the party taken of his liberty until he makes the satisfaction awarded. 3 Bl. Comm. 414, 415; 2 Tidd, Pr. 993, 1025; Litt. § 504; Co. Litt. 289a.

CAPIAS EXTENDI FACIAS. A writ of execution issuable in England against a debtor to the crown, which commands the sheriff to "take" or arrest the body, and "cause to be extended" the lands and goods of the debtor. Man. Exch. Pr. 5.

CAPIAS IN WITHERNAM. A writ, in the nature of a reprisal, which lies for one whose goods or cattle, taken under a distress, are removed from the county, so that they cannot be replevied, commanding the sheriff to seize other goods or cattle of the distrainor of equal value.

CAPIAS PRO FINE. (That you take for the fine or in mercy.) Formerly, if the verdict was for the defendant, the plaintiff was adjudged to be amerced for his false claim; but, if the verdict was for the plaintiff, then in all actions *vi et armis*, or where the defendant, in his pleading, had falsely denied his own deed, the judgment contained an award of a *capiatur pro fine;* and in all other cases the defendant was adjudged to be amerced. The insertion of the *misericordia* or of the *capiatur* in the judgment is now unnecessary. Wharton.

CAPIAS UTLAGATUM. (You take the outlaw.) In English practice. A writ which lies against a person who has been *outlawed* in an action, by which the sheriff is commanded to *take* him, and keep him in custody until the day of the return, and then present him to the court, there to be dealt with for his contempt. Reg. Orig. 138*b;* 3 Bl. Comm. 284.

CAPIATUR PRO FINE. (Let him be taken for the fine.) In English practice. A clause inserted at the end of old judgment records in actions of debt, where the defendant denied his deed, and it was found against him upon his false plea, and the jury were troubled with the trial of it. Cro. Jac. 64.

CAPITA. Heads, and, figuratively, entire bodies, whether of persons or animals. Spelman.

Persons individually considered, without relation to others, (polls;) as distinguished from *stirpes* or stocks of descent. The term in this sense, making part of the common phrases, *in capita, per capita,* is derived from the civil law. Inst. 3, 1, 6.

CAPITA, PER. By heads; by the poll; as individuals. In the distribution of an intestate's personalty, the persons legally entitled to take are said to take *per capita* when they claim, each in his own right, as in equal degree of kindred; in contradistinction to claiming by right of representation, or *per stirpes.*

CAPITAL, n. In political economy, that portion of the produce of industry existing in a country, which may be made directly available, either for the support of human existence, or the facilitating of production: but, in commerce, and as applied to individuals, it is understood to mean the sum of money which a merchant, banker, or trader adventures in any undertaking, or which he contributes to the common stock of a partnership. Also the fund of a trading company or corporation, in which sense the word "stock" is generally added to it. McCul. Dict.; 2 Bouv. Inst. 1458.

The actual estate, whether in money or property, which is owned by an individual or a corporation. In reference to a corporation, it is the aggregate of the sum subscribed and paid in, or secured to be paid in, by the shareholders, with the addition of all gains or profits realized in the use and investment of those sums, or, if losses have been incurred, then it is the residue after deducting such losses. 23 N. Y. 219.

When used with respect to the property of a corporation or association, the term has a settled meaning. It applies only to the property or means contributed by the stockholders as the fund or basis for the business or enterprise for which the corporation or association was formed. As to them the term does not embrace temporary loans, though the moneys borrowed be directly appropriated in their business or undertakings. And, when used with respect to the property of individuals in any particular business, the term has substantially the same import; it then means the property taken from other investments or uses and set apart for and invested in the special business, and in the increase, proceeds, or earnings of which property beyond expenditures incurred in its use consist the profits made in the business. It does not, any more than when used with respect to corporations, embrace temporary loans made in the regular course of business. 21 Wall. 286.

The principal sum of a fund of money; money invested at interest.

Also the political and governmental metropolis of a state or country; the seat of government; the place where the legislative department holds its sessions, and where the chief offices of the executive are located.

CAPITAL, adj. Affecting or relating to the head or life of a person; entailing the ultimate penalty. Thus, a capital crime is one punishable with death. See Bract. fol. 101*b.*

Also principal; leading; chief; as "capital burgess." 10 Mod. 100.

CAPITAL CRIME. A crime for which the punishment of death is provided by law.

CAPITAL PUNISHMENT. The punishment of death.

CAPITAL STOCK. The common stock or fund of a corporation. The sum of money raised by the subscriptions of the stockholders, and divided into shares. It is said to be the sum upon which calls may be made upon the stockholders, and dividends are to be paid. 1 Sandf. Ch. 280; Ang. & A. Corp. §§ 151, 556.

Originally "the capital stock of the bank" was all the property of every kind, everything, which the bank possessed. And this "capital stock," all of it, in reality belonged to the contributors, it being intrusted to the bank to be used and traded with for their exclusive benefit; and thus the bank became the agent of the contributors, so that the transmutation of the money originally advanced by the subscribers into property of other kinds, though it altered the form of the investment, left its beneficial ownership unaffected; and every new acquisition of property, by exchange or otherwise, was an acquisition for the original subscribers or their representatives, their respective interests in it all always continuing in the same proportion as in the aggregate capital originally advanced. So that, whether in the form of money, bills of exchange, or any other property in possession or in action into which the money originally contributed has been changed, or which it has produced, all is, as the original contribution was, the capital stock of the bank, held, as the original contribution was, for the exclusive benefit of the original contributors and those who represent them. The original contributors and those who represent them are the stockholders. 31 Conn. 109.

Capital stock, as employed in acts of incorporation, is never used to indicate the value of the property of the company. It is very generally, if not universally, used to designate the amount of capital prescribed to be contributed at the outset by the stockholders, for the purposes of the corporation. The value of the corporate assets may be greatly increased by surplus profits, or be diminished by losses, but the amount of the capital stock remains the same. The funds of the company may fluctuate; its capital stock remains invariable, unless changed by legislative authority. 23 N. J. Law, 195.

CAPITALE. A thing which is stolen, or the value of it. Blount.

CAPITALE VIVENS. Live cattle. Blount.

CAPITALIS. In old English law. Chief, principal; at the *head.* A term applied to persons, places, judicial proceedings, and some kinds of property.

CAPITALIS BARO. In old English law. Chief baron. *Capitalis baro scaccarii domini regis,* chief baron of the exchequer. Townsh. Pl. 211.

CAPITALIS CUSTOS. Chief warden or magistrate; mayor. Fleta, lib. 2, c. 64, § 2.

CAPITALIS DEBITOR. The chief or principal debtor, as distinguished from a surety, (*plegius.*)

CAPITALIS DOMINUS. Chief lord. Fleta, lib. 1, c. 12, § 4; Id. c. 28, § 5.

CAPITALIS JUSTICIARIUS. The chief justiciary; the principal minister of state, and guardian of the realm in the king's absence.

This office originated under William the Conqueror; but its power was greatly diminished by *Magna Charta,* and finally distributed among several courts by Edward I. Spelman; 3 Bl. Comm. 38.

CAPITALIS JUSTICIARIUS AD PLACITA CORAM REGE TENENDA. Chief justice for holding pleas before the king. The title of the chief justice of the king's bench, first assumed in the latter part of the reign of Henry III. 2 Reeve, Eng. Law, 91, 285.

CAPITALIS JUSTICIARIUS BANCI. Chief justice of the bench. The title of the chief justice of the (now) court of common pleas, first mentioned in the first year of Edward I. 2 Reeve, Eng. Law, 48.

CAPITALIS JUSTICIARIUS TOTIUS ANGLIÆ. Chief justice of all England. The title of the presiding justice in the court of *aula regis.* 3 Bl. Comm. 38; 1 Reeve, Eng. Law, 48.

CAPITALIS PLEGIUS. A chief pledge; a head borough. Townsh. Pl. 35.

CAPITALIS REDITUS. A chief rent.

CAPITALIS TERRA. A head-land. A piece of land lying at the head of other land.

CAPITANEUS. A tenant *in capite.* He who held his land or title directly from the king himself. A captain; a naval commander.

CAPITARE. In old law and surveys. To head, front, or abut; to touch at the head, or end.

CAPITATIM. Lat. By the head; by the poll; severally to each individual.

CAPITATION. (Lat. *caput,* head.) A poll-tax. An imposition periodically laid upon each person.

A tax or imposition raised on each person in consideration of his labor, industry, office, rank, etc. It is a very ancient kind of tribute, and answers to what the Latins called "*tributum*," by which taxes on persons are distinguished from taxes on merchandise, called "*vectigalia.*" Wharton.

CAPITATION TAX. One which is levied upon the person simply, without any reference to his property, real or personal, or to any business in which he may be engaged, or to any employment which he may follow. Phillips, 22.

CAPITE. By the head. Tenure *in capite* was an ancient feudal tenure, whereby a man held lands of the king immediately. It was of two sorts,—the one, principal and general, or of the king as the source of all tenure; the other, special and subaltern, or of a particular subject. It is now abolished. Jacob. As to distribution *per capita*, see CAPITA.

CAPITE MINUTUS. In the civil law. One who had suffered *capitis diminutio*, one who lost *status* or legal attributes. See Dig. 4, 5.

CAPITIS DIMINUTIO. In Roman law. A diminishing or abridgment of personality. This was a loss or curtailment of a man's *status* or aggregate of legal attributes and qualifications, following upon certain changes in his civil condition. It was of three kinds, enumerated as follows:

Capitis diminutio maxima. The highest or most comprehensive loss of *status*. This occurred when a man's condition was changed from one of freedom to one of bondage, when he became a slave. It swept away with it all rights of citizenship and all family rights.

Capitis diminutio media. A lesser or medium loss of *status*. This occurred where a man lost his rights of citizenship, but without losing his liberty. It carried away also the family rights.

Capitis diminutio minima. The lowest or least comprehensive degree of loss of *status*. This occurred where a man's family relations alone were changed. It happened upon the arrogation of a person who had been his own master, (*sui juris*,) or upon the emancipation of one who had been under the *patria potestas*. It left the rights of liberty and citizenship unaltered. See Inst. 1, 16, pr.; 1, 2, 3; Dig. 4, 5, 11; Mackeld. Rom Law, § 144.

CAPITITIUM. A covering for the head, mentioned in St. 1 Hen. IV. and other old statutes, which prescribe what dresses shall be worn by all degrees of persons. Jacob.

CAPITULA. Collections of laws and ordinances drawn up under heads of divisions. Spelman.

The term is used in the civil and old English law, and applies to the ecclesiastical law also, meaning chapters or assemblies of ecclesiastical persons. Du Cange.

CAPITULA CORONÆ. Chapters of the crown. Chapters or heads of inquiry, resembling the *capitula itineris*, (*q.v.*,) but of a more minute character.

CAPITULA DE JUDÆIS. A register of mortgages made to the Jews. 2 Bl. Comm. 343; Crabb, Eng. Law, 130, et seq.

CAPITULA ITINERIS. Articles of inquiry which were anciently delivered to the justices in eyre when they set out on their circuits. These schedules were designed to include all possible varieties of crime. 2 Reeve, Eng. Law, p. 4, c. 8.

CAPITULA RURALIA. Assemblies or chapters, held by rural deans and parochial clergy, within the precinct of every deanery; which at first were every three weeks, afterwards once a month, and subsequently once a quarter. Cowell.

CAPITULARY. In French law. A collection and code of the laws and ordinances promulgated by the kings of the Merovingian and Carlovingian dynasties.

Any orderly and systematic collection or code of laws.

In ecclesiastical law. A collection of laws and ordinances orderly arranged by divisions. A book containing the beginning and end of each Gospel which is to be read every day in the ceremony of saying mass. Du Cange.

CAPITULATION. In military law. The surrender of a fort or fortified town to a besieging army; the treaty or agreement between the commanding officers which embodies the terms and conditions on which the surrender is made.

In the civil law. An agreement by which the prince and the people, or those who have the right of the people, regulate the manner in which the government is to be administered. Wolffius, § 989.

CAPITULI AGRI. Head-fields; lands lying at the head or upper end of furrows, etc.

Capitulum est clericorum congregatio sub uno decano in ecclesia cathedrali. A chapter is a congregation of clergy under one dean in a cathedral church. Co. Litt. 98.

CAPPA. In old records. A cap. *Cappa honoris*, the cap of honor. One of the solemnities or ceremonies of creating an earl or marquis.

CAPTAIN. A head-man; commander; commanding officer. The captain of a war-vessel is the officer first in command. In the United States navy, the rank of "captain" is intermediate between that of "commander" and "commodore." The governor or controlling officer of a vessel in the merchant service is usually styled "captain" by the inferior officers and seamen, but in maritime business and admiralty law is more commonly designated as "master." In foreign jurisprudence his title is often that of "patron." In the United States army (and the militia) the captain is the commander of a company of soldiers, one of the divisions of a regiment. The term is also used to designate the commander of a squad of municipal police.

CAPTATION. In French law. The act of one who succeeds in controlling the will of another, so as to become master of it; used in an invidious sense.

CAPTATOR. A person who obtains a gift or legacy through artifice.

CAPTIO. In old English law and practice. A taking or seizure; arrest; receiving; holding of court.

CAPTION. In practice. That part of a legal instrument, as a commission, indictment, etc., which shows where, when, and by what authority it is taken, found, or executed.

When used with reference to an indictment, caption signifies the style or preamble or commencement of the indictment; when used with reference to a commission, it signifies the certificate to which the commissioners' names are subscribed, declaring when and where it was executed. Brown.

The caption of a pleading, deposition, or other paper connected with a case in court, is the heading or introductory clause which shows the names of the parties, name of the court, number of the case on the docket or calendar, etc.

Also signifies a taking, seizure, or arrest of a person. 2 Salk. 498. The word in this sense is now obsolete in English law.

In Scotch law. Caption is an order to incarcerate a debtor who has disobeyed an order, given to him by what are called "letters of horning," to pay a debt or to perform some act enjoined thereby. Bell.

CAPTIVES. Prisoners of war. As in the goods of an enemy, so also in his person, a sort of qualified property may be acquired, by taking him a prisoner of war, at least till his ransom be paid. 2 Bl. Comm. 402.

CAPTOR. In international law. One who takes or seizes property in time of war; one who takes the property of an enemy. In a stricter sense, one who takes a prize at sea. 2 Bl. Comm. 401; 1 Kent, Comm. 86, 96, 103.

CAPTURE. In international law. The taking or wresting of property from one of two belligerents by the other. It occurs either on land or at sea. In the former case, the property captured is called "booty;" in the latter case, "prize."

Capture, in technical language, is a taking by military power; a seizure is a taking by civil authority. 35 Ga. 844.

In some cases, this is a mode of acquiring property. Thus, every one may, as a general rule, on his own land, or on the sea, capture any wild animal, and acquire a qualified ownership in it by confining it, or absolute ownership by killing it. 2 Steph. Comm. 79.

CAPUT. A head; the head of a person; the whole person; the life of a person; one's personality; *status;* civil condition.

At common law. A head.
Caput comitatis, the head of the county; the sheriff; the king. Spelman.
A person; a life. The upper part of a town. Cowell. A castle. Spelman.

In the civil law. It signified a person's civil condition or *status*, and among the Romans consisted of three component parts or elements,—*libertas*, liberty; *civitas*, citizenship; and *familia*, family.

CAPUT ANNI. The first day of the year.

CAPUT BARONIÆ. The castle or chief seat of a baron.

CAPUT JEJUNII. The beginning of the Lent fast, *i. e.*, Ash Wednesday.

CAPUT LOCI. The head or upper part of a place.

CAPUT LUPINUM. In old English law. A wolf's head. An outlawed felon was said to be *caput lupinum*, and might be knocked on the head, like a wolf.

CAPUT MORTUUM. A dead head; dead; obsolete.

CAPUT PORTUS. In old English law. The head of a port. The town to which a port belongs, and which gives the denomination to the port, and is the head of it. Hale de Jure Mar. pt. 2, (*de portubus maris*,) c. 2.

CAPUT, PRINCIPIUM, ET FINIS. The head, beginning, and end. A term applied in English law to the king, as head of parliament. 4 Inst. 3; 1 Bl. Comm. 188.

CAPUTAGIUM. In old English law. Head or poll money, or the payment of it. Cowell; Blount.

CAPUTIUM. In old English law. A head of land; a headland. Cowell.

CARABUS. In old English law. A kind of raft or boat. Spelman.

CARAT. A weight of four grains, used in weighing diamonds. Webster. A weight equal to three and one-sixth grains. Wharton.

CARCAN. In French law. An instrument of punishment, somewhat resembling a pillory. It sometimes signifies the punishment itself. Biret, Vocab

CARCANUM. A gaol; a prison.

CARCARE. In old English law. To load; to load a vessel; to freight.

CARCATUS. Loaded; freighted, as a ship.

CARCEL-AGE. Gaol-dues; prison-fees.

CARCER. A prison or gaol. Strictly, a place of detention and safe-keeping, and not of punishment. Co. Litt. 620.

Carcer ad homines custodiendos, non ad puniendos, dari debet. A prison should be used for keeping persons, not for punishing them. Co. Litt. 260a.

Carcer non supplicii causâ sed custodiæ constitutus. A prison is ordained not for the sake of punishment, but of detention and guarding. Lofft, 119.

CARDINAL. In ecclesiastical law. A dignitary of the court of Rome, next in rank to the pope.

CARDS. In criminal law. Small papers or pasteboards of an oblong or rectangular shape, on which are printed figures or points, used in playing certain games. See 2 Humph. 496; 4 Pick. 251; 19 Mo. 377; 12 Wis. 434.

CARE. As a legal term, this word means diligence, prudence, discretion, attentiveness, watchfulness, vigilance. It is the opposite of negligence or carelessness.

There are three degrees of care in the law, corresponding (inversely) to the three degrees of negligence, viz.: slight care, ordinary care, and great care.

Slight care or diligence is such as persons of ordinary prudence usually exercise about their own affairs of slight importance; ordinary care or diligence is such as they usually exercise about their own affairs of ordinary importance; and great care or diligence is such as they usually exercise about their own affairs of great importance. Civil Code Dak. § 2100.

The exact boundaries between the several degrees of care, and their correlative degrees of carelessness, or negligence, are not always clearly defined or easily pointed out. We think, however, that by "ordinary care" is meant that degree of care which may reasonably be expected from a person in the party's situation,—that is, "reasonable care;" and that "gross negligence" imports not a malicious intention or design to produce a particular injury, but a thoughtless disregard of consequences, the absence, rather than the actual exercise, of volition with reference to results. 23 Conn. 443.

Slight care is such as is usually exercised by persons of common sense, but careless habits, under circumstances similar to those of the particular case in which the question arises, and where their own interests are to be protected from a similar injury.

Ordinary care is such as is usually exercised in the like circumstances by the majority of the community, or by persons of careful and prudent habits.

Great care is such as is exercised under such circumstances by persons of unusually careful and prudent habits. Abbott.

CARENA. A term used in the old ecclesiastical law to denote a period of forty days.

CARENCE. In French law. A *procès-verbal de carence* is a document setting out that the *huissier* attended to issue execution upon a judgment, but found nothing upon which to levy. Arg. Fr. Merc. Law, 547.

CARETA, (spelled, also, *Carreta* and *Carecta*.) A cart; a cart-load.

CARETORIUS, or CARECTARIUS. A carter. Blount.

CARGA. In Spanish law. An incumbrance; a charge. White, New Recop. b. 2, tit. 13, c. 2, § 2.

CARGAISON. In French commercial law. Cargo; lading.

CARGARE. In old English law. To charge. Spelman.

CARGO. In mercantile law. The load or lading of a vessel; goods and merchandise put on board a ship to be carried to a certain port.

The lading or freight of a ship; the goods, merchandise, or whatever is conveyed in a ship or other merchant vessel. See 1 Mason, 142; 4 Pick. 429; 9 Metc. (Mass.) 366; 103 Mass. 406.

A cargo is the loading of a ship or other vessel, the bulk of which is to be ascertained from the capacity of the ship or vessel. The word embraces all that the vessel is capable of carrying. 3 Rob. (N. Y.) 173.

The term may be applied in such a sense as to include passengers, as well as freight, but in a technical sense it designates goods only.

CARIAGIUM. In old English law. Carriage; the carrying of goods or other things for the king.

CARISTIA. Dearth, scarcity, dearness. Cowell.

CARK. In old English law. A quantity of wool, whereof thirty make a sarplar. (The latter is equal to 2,240 pounds in weight.) St. 27 Hen. VI. c. 2. Jacob.

CARLISLE TABLES. Life and annuity tables, compiled at Carlisle, England, about 1780. Used by actuaries, etc.

CARMEN. In the Roman law. Literally, a verse or song. A formula or form of words used on various occasions, as of divorce. Tayl. Civil Law, 349.

CARNAL. Of the body; relating to the body; fleshly; sexual.

CARNAL KNOWLEDGE. The act of a man in having sexual bodily connection with a woman.

Carnal knowledge and sexual intercourse held equivalent expressions. 22 Ohio St. 541.

From very early times, in the law, as in common speech, the meaning of the words "carnal knowledge" of a woman by a man has been sexual bodily connection; and these words, without more, have been used in that sense by writers of the highest authority on criminal law, when undertaking to give a full and precise definition of the crime of rape, the highest crime of this character. 97 Mass. 61.

CARNALITER. In old criminal law. Carnally. *Carnaliter cognovit,* carnally knew. Technical words in indictments for rape, and held essential. 1 Hale, P. C. 637–639.

CARNALLY KNEW. In pleading. A technical phrase essential in an indictment to charge the defendant with the crime of rape.

CARNO. In old English law. An immunity or privilege. Cowell.

CAROOME. In English law. A license by the lord mayor of London to keep a cart.

CARPEMEALS. Cloth made in the northern parts of England, of a coarse kind, mentioned in 7 Jac. I. c. 16. Jacob.

CARRERA. In Spanish law. A carriage-way; the right of a carriage-way. Las Partidas, pt. 3, tit. 31, 1. 3.

CARRIAGE. A vehicle used for the transportation of persons either for pleasure or business, and drawn by horses or other draught animals over the ordinary streets and highways of the country; not including cars used exclusively upon railroads or street railroads expressly constructed for the use of such cars. 63 Wis. 97, 23 N. W. Rep. 425; 8 Kan. 84; 47 N. Y. 122; 46 N. H. 523; 5 Q. B. Div. 176.

The act of carrying, or a contract for transportation of persons or goods.

The contract of carriage is a contract for the conveyance of property, persons, or messages from one place to another. Civil Code Cal. § 2085; Civil Code Dak. § 1208.

CARRICLE, or CARRACLE. A ship of great burden.

CARRIER. One who undertakes to transport goods from one place to another. 1 Pars. Cont. 632.

One who carries or agrees to carry the goods of another, from one place to another, for hire, or without hire.

Carriers are either common or private. Private carriers are persons who undertake for the transportation in a particular instance only, not making it their vocation, nor holding themselves out to the public as ready to act for all who desire their services.

To bring a person within the description of a common carrier, he must exercise it as a public employment; he must undertake to carry goods for persons generally; and he must hold himself out as ready to transport goods for hire, as a business, not as a casual occupation, *pro hac vice.*

"CARRY AWAY." A technical phrase in an indictment for larceny, translating the Lat. *asportavit.* 7 Gray, 45.

CARRYING AWAY. In criminal law. The act of removal or asportation, by which the crime of larceny is completed, and which is essential to constitute it.

CARRYING AWAY INFANT FE-MALES. See ABDUCTION.

CARRYING COSTS. A verdict is said to carry costs when the party for whom the verdict is given becomes entitled to the payment of his costs as incident to such verdict.

CART. A carriage for luggage or burden, with two wheels, as distinguished from a wagon, which has four wheels. The vehicle in which criminals are taken to execution.

This word, in its ordinary and primary acceptation, signifies a carriage with two wheels; yet it has also a more extended signification, and may mean a carriage in general. 22 Ala. 624.

CART BOTE. Wood or timber which a tenant is allowed by law to take from an estate, for the purpose of repairing instruments, (including necessary vehicles,) of husbandry. 2 Bl. Comm. 35.

CARTA. In old English law. A charter, or deed. Any written instrument.

In Spanish law. A letter; a deed; a power of attorney. Las Partidas, pt. 3, tit. 18, l. 30.

CARTA DE FORESTA. In old English law. The charter of the forest. More commonly called "*Charta de Foresta,*" (*q. v.*)

CARTE. In French marine law. A chart.

CARTE BLANCHE. A white sheet of paper; an instrument signed, but otherwise left blank. A sheet given to an agent, with the principal's signature appended, to be filled up with any contract or engagement as the agent may see fit. Hence, metaphorically, unlimited authority.

CARTEL. An agreement between two hostile powers for the delivery of prisoners or deserters. Also a written challenge to fight a duel.

CARTEL-SHIP. A vessel commissioned in time of war to exchange the prisoners of any two hostile powers; also to carry any particular proposal from one to another. For this reason, the officer who commands her is particularly ordered to carry no cargo, ammunition, or implements of war, except a single gun for the purpose of signals. Enc. Lond.

CARTMEN. Carriers who transport goods and merchandise in carts, usually for short distances, for hire.

CARTULARY. A place where papers or records are kept.

CARUCA, or CARUA. A plow.

CARUCAGE. In old English law. A kind of tax or tribute anciently imposed upon every plow, (*carue* or plow-land,) for the public service. Spelman.

CARUCATA. A certain quantity of land used as the basis for taxation. As much land as may be tilled by a single plow in a year and a day. Also, a team of cattle, or a cart-load.

CARUCATARIUS. One who held lands in *carvage,* or plow-tenure. Cowell.

CARUE. A carve of land; plow-land. Britt. c. 84.

CARVAGE. The same as carucage, (*q. v.*) Cowell.

CARVE. In old English law. A carucate or plow-land.

CAS FORTUIT. Fr. In the law of insurance. A fortuitous event; an inevitable accident.

CASATA. In old English law. A house with land sufficient for the support of one family. Otherwise called "*hida,*" a hide of land, and by Bede, "*familia.*" Spelman.

CASATUS. A vassal or feudal tenant possessing a *casata;* that is, having a house, household, and property of his own.

CASE. 1. A general term for an action, cause, suit, or controversy, at law or in equity. A question contested before a court of justice.

The primary meaning of "case" is "cause." When applied to legal proceedings, it imports a state of facts which furnishes occasion for the exercise of the jurisdiction of a court of justice. In its generic sense, the word includes all cases, special or otherwise. 12 N. Y. 592, 596.

2. A statement of the facts involved in a transaction or series of transactions, drawn up in writing in a technical form, for submission to a court or judge for decision or opinion. Under this meaning of the term are included a "case made" for a motion for new trial, a "case reserved" on the trial of

a cause, an "agreed case" for decision without trial, etc.

3. A form of action which lies to recover damages for injuries for which the more ancient forms of action will not lie. Steph. Pl. 15. See TRESPASS ON THE CASE.

CASE AGREED ON. A formal written enumeration of the facts in a case, assented to by both parties as correct and complete, and submitted to the court by their agreement, in order that a decision may be rendered, without a trial, upon the court's conclusions of law upon the facts as stated.

CASE FOR MOTION. In English divorce and probate practice, when a party desires to make a motion, he must file, among other papers, a case for motion, containing an abstract of the proceedings in the suit or action, a statement of the circumstances on which the motion is founded, and the prayer, or nature of the decree or order desired. Browne, Div. 251; Browne, Prob. Pr. 295.

CASE LAW. A professional name for the aggregate of reported cases as forming a body of jurisprudence; or for the law of a particular subject as evidenced or formed by the adjudged cases; in distinction to statutes and other sources of law.

CASE ON APPEAL. In American practice. Before the argument in the appellate court of a case brought there for review, the appellant's counsel prepares a document or brief, bearing this name, for the information of the court, detailing the testimony and the proceedings below.

In English practice. The "case on appeal" is a printed statement prepared by each of the parties to an appeal to the house of lords or the privy council, setting out methodically the facts which make up his case, with appropriate references to the evidence printed in the "appendix." The term also denotes a written statement, prepared and transmitted by an inferior court or judge, raising a question of law for the opinion of a superior court.

CASE RESERVED. A statement in writing of the facts proved on the trial of a cause, drawn up and settled by the attorneys and counsel for the respective parties under the supervision of the judge, for the purpose of having certain points of law, which arose at the trial, and could not then be satisfactorily decided, determined upon full argument before the court in *banc*. This is otherwise called a "special case;" and it is usual for the parties, where the law of the case is doubtful, to agree that the jury shall find a general verdict for the plaintiff, subject to the opinion of the court upon such a case to be made, instead of obtaining from the jury a special verdict. 3 Bl. Comm. 378; 3 Steph. Comm. 621; Steph. Pl. 92, 93; 1 Burrill, Pr. 242, 463.

CASE STATED. In practice. An agreement in writing, between a plaintiff and defendant, that the facts in dispute between them are as therein agreed upon and set forth. 3 Whart. 143. A case agreed upon. See CASE AGREED ON.

CASE TO MOVE FOR NEW TRIAL. In practice. A case prepared by the party against whom a verdict has been given, upon which to move the court to set aside the verdict and grant a new trial.

CASH. Ready money; whatever can be used as money without being converted into another form; that which circulates as money, including bank-bills.

Cash payment means the opposite of credit. 6 Md. 37; 24 N. J. Law, 96.

CASH-ACCOUNT. A record, in book-keeping, of all cash transactions; an account of moneys received and expended.

CASH-BOOK. In book-keeping, an account-book in which is kept a record of all cash transactions, or all cash received and expended. The object of the cash-book is to afford a constant facility to ascertain the true state of a man's cash. Pardessus, n. 87.

CASH-NOTE. In England. A bank-note of a provincial bank or of the Bank of England.

CASH-PRICE. A price payable in cash at the time of sale of property, in opposition to a barter or a sale on credit.

CASHIER, *n.* An officer of a moneyed institution, or commercial house, or bank, who is intrusted with, and whose duty it is to take care of, the cash or money of such institution or bank.

The cashier of a bank is the executive officer, through whom the whole financial operations of the bank are conducted. He receives and pays out its moneys, collects and pays its debts, and receives and transfers its commercial securities. Tellers and other subordinate officers may be appointed, but they are under his direction, and are, as it were, the arms by which designated portions of his various functions are discharged. The directors may limit his authority as they deem proper, but this would not affect those to whom the limitation was unknown. 10 Wall. 650.

CASHIER, *v.* In military law. To deprive a military officer of his rank and office.

CASHLITE. An amercement or fine; a mulct.

CASSARE. To quash; to render void; to break.

CASSATION. In French law. Annulling; reversal; breaking the force and validity of a judgment. A decision emanating from the sovereign authority, by which a decree or judgment in the court of last resort is broken or annulled. Merl. Repert.

CASSATION, COURT OF. (Fr. *cour de cassation.*) The highest court in France; so termed from possessing the power to quash (*casser*) the decrees of inferior courts. It is a court of appeal in criminal as well as civil cases.

CASSETUR BILLA. (Lat. That the bill be quashed.) In practice. The form of the judgment for the defendant on a plea in abatement, where the action was commenced by bill, (*billa.*) 3 Bl. Comm. 303; Steph. Pl. 128, 131. The form of an entry made by a plaintiff on the record, after a plea in abatement, where he found that the plea could not be confessed and avoided, nor traversed, nor demurred to; amounting in fact to a discontinuance of the action. 2 Archb. Pr. K. B. 3, 236; 1 Tidd, Pr. 683.

CASSETUR BREVE. (Lat. That the writ be quashed.) In practice. The form of the judgment for the defendant on a plea in abatement, where the action was commenced by original writ, (*breve.*) 3 Bl. Comm. 303; Steph. Pl. 107, 109.

CASSOCK, or CASSULA. A garment worn by a priest.

CAST, *v.* In old English practice. To allege, offer, or present; to proffer by way of excuse, (as to "cast an essoin.")

This word is now used as a popular, rather than a technical, term, in the sense of to overcome, overthrow, or defeat in a civil action at law.

CAST, *p. p.* Overthrown, worsted, or defeated in an action.

CASTEL, or CASTLE. A fortress in a town; the principal mansion of a nobleman. 3 Inst. 31.

CASTELLAIN. In old English law. The lord, owner, or captain of a castle; the constable of a fortified house; a person having the custody of one of the crown mansions; an officer of the forest.

CASTELLANUS. A castellain; the keeper or constable of a castle. Spelman.

CASTELLARIUM, CASTELLATUS. In old English law. The precinct or jurisdiction of a castle. Blount.

CASTELLORUM OPERATIO. In Saxon and old English law. Castle work. Service and labor done by inferior tenants for the building and upholding castles and public places of defense. One of the three necessary charges, (*trinoda necessitas,*) to which all lands among the Saxons were expressly subject. Cowell.

CASTIGATORY. An engine used to punish women who have been convicted of being common scolds. It is sometimes called the "trebucket," "tumbrel," "ducking-stool," or "cucking-stool."

CASTING. Offering; alleging by way of excuse. Casting an essoin was alleging an excuse for not appearing in court to answer an action. Holthouse.

CASTING VOTE. Where the votes of a deliberative assembly or legislative body are equally divided on any question or motion, it is the privilege of the presiding officer to cast one vote (if otherwise he would not be entitled to any vote) on either side, or to cast one additional vote, if he has already voted as a member of the body. This is called the "casting vote."

By the common law, a casting vote sometimes signifies the single vote of a person who never votes; but, in the case of an equality, sometimes the double vote of a person who first votes with the rest, and then, upon an equality, creates a majority by giving a second vote. 48 Barb. 606.

CASTLEGUARD. In feudal law. An imposition anciently laid upon such persons as lived within a certain distance of any castle, towards the maintenance of such as watched and warded the castle.

CASTLEGUARD RENTS. In old English law. Rents paid by those that dwelt within the precincts of a castle, towards the maintenance of such as watched and warded it.

CASTRATION. The act of depriving a man of the testicles.

CASTRENSIS. In the Roman law. Relating to the camp or military service.

Castrense peculium, a portion of property which a son acquired in war, or from his connection with the camp. Dig. 49, 17.

CASTRUM. Lat. In Roman law. A camp.

In old English law. A castle. Bract. fol. 69*b*. A castle, including a manor. 4 Coke, 88.

CASU CONSIMILI. In old English law. A writ of entry, granted where tenant by the curtesy, or tenant for life, alienated in fee, or in tail, or for another's life, which was brought by him in reversion against the party to whom such tenant so alienated to his prejudice, and in the tenant's life-time. Termes de la Ley.

CASU PROVISO. A writ of entry framed under the provisions of the statute of Gloucester, (6 Edw. I.,) c. 7, which lay for the benefit of the reversioner when a tenant in dower aliened in fee or for life.

CASUAL. That which happens accidentally, or is brought about by causes unknown; fortuitous; the result of chance.

CASUAL EJECTOR. In practice. The nominal defendant in an action of ejectment; so called because, by a fiction of law peculiar to that action, he is supposed to come *casually* or by accident upon the premises, and to turn out or eject the lawful possessor. 3 Bl. Comm. 203; 3 Steph. Comm. 670.

CASUAL EVIDENCE. A phrase used to denote (in contradistinction to "preappointed evidence") all such evidence as happens to be adducible of a fact or event, but which was not prescribed by statute or otherwise arranged beforehand to be the evidence of the fact or event. Brown.

CASUAL PAUPER. A poor person who, in England, applies for relief in a parish other than that of his settlement. The ward in the work-house to which they are admitted is called the "casual ward."

CASUAL POOR. In English law. Those who are not settled in a parish.

Such poor persons as are suddenly taken sick, or meet with some accident, when away from home, and who are thus providentially thrown upon the charities of those among whom they happen to be. 17 N. J. Law, 405.

CASUALTIES OF SUPERIORITY. In Scotch law. Payments from an inferior to a superior, that is, from a tenant to his lord, which arise upon uncertain events, as opposed to the payment of rent at fixed and stated times. Bell.

CASUALTIES OF WARDS. In Scotch law. The mails and duties due to the superior in ward-holdings.

CASUALTY. Inevitable accident; an event not to be foreseen or guarded against. A loss from such an event or cause; as by fire, shipwreck, lightning, etc. Story, Bailm. § 240.

CASUS. Lat. Chance; accident; an event; a case; a case contemplated.

CASUS BELLI. An occurrence giving rise to or justifying war.

CASUS FŒDERIS. In international law. The case of the treaty. The particular event or situation contemplated by the treaty, or stipulated for, or which comes within its terms.

In commercial law. The case or event contemplated by the parties to an individual contract, or stipulated for by it, or coming within its terms.

CASUS FORTUITUS. Lat. An inevitable accident, a chance occurrence, or fortuitous event. A loss happening in spite of all human effort and sagacity. 3 Kent, Comm. 217, 300; Whart. Neg. §§ 113, 553.

Casus fortuitus non est sperandus, et nemo tenetur devinare. A fortuitous event is not to be expected, and no one is bound to foresee it. 4 Coke, 66.

Casus fortuitus non est supponendus. A fortuitous event is not to be presumed. Hardr. 82, arg.

CASUS MAJOR. In the civil law. A casualty; an extraordinary casualty, as fire, shipwreck, etc. Dig. 44, 7, 1, 4.

CASUS OMISSUS. A case omitted; an event or contingency for which no provision is made; particularly a case not provided for by the statute on the general subject, and which is therefore left to be governed by the common law.

Casus omissus et oblivioni datus dispositioni juris communis relinquitur. A case omitted and given to oblivion (forgotten) is left to the disposal of the common law. 5 Coke, 38. A particular case, left unprovided for by statute, must be disposed of according to the law as it existed prior to such statute. Broom, Max. 46.

Casus omissus pro omisso habendus est. A case omitted is to be held as (intentionally) omitted. Tray. Lat. Max. 67.

CAT. An instrument with which criminals are flogged. It consists of nine lashes of whip-cord, tied on to a wooden handle.

CATALLA. In old English law. Chattels. The word among the Normans primarily signified only beasts of husbandry, or, as they are still called, "cattle," but, in a secondary sense, the term was applied to all movables in general, and not only to these, but to whatever was not a fief or feud. Wharton.

Catalla juste possessa amitti non possunt. Chattels justly possessed cannot be lost. Jenk. Cent. 28.

CATALLA OTIOSA. Dead goods or chattels, as distinguished from animals. Idle cattle, that is, such as were not used for working, as distinguished from beasts of the plow; called also *animalia otiosa*. Bract. fols. 217, 217*b;* 3 Bl. Comm. 9.

Catalla reputantur inter minima in lege. Chattels are considered in law among the least things. Jenk. Cent. 52.

CATALLACTICS. The science of political economy.

CATALLIS CAPTIS NOMINE DISTRICTIONIS. An obsolete writ that lay where a house was within a borough, for rent issuing out of the same, and which warranted the taking of doors, windows, etc., by way of distress.

CATALLIS REDDENDIS. For the return of the chattels; an obsolete writ that lay where goods delivered to a man to keep till a certain day were not upon demand redelivered at the day. Reg. Orig. 39.

CATALLUM. A chattel. Most frequently used in the plural form, *catalla*, (*q. v.*)

CATALS. Goods and chattels. See CATALLA.

CATANEUS. A tenant *in capite.* A tenant holding immediately of the crown. Spelman.

CATAPULTA. A catapult. A warlike engine to shoot darts; a cross-bow.

CATASCOPUS. An old name for an archdeacon.

CATCHING BARGAIN. A bargain by which money is loaned, at an extortionate or extravagant rate, to an heir or any one who has an estate in reversion or expectancy, to be repaid on the vesting of his interest; or a similar unconscionable bargain with such person for the purchase outright of his expectancy.

CATCHINGS. Things caught, and in the possession, custody, power, and dominion of the party, with a present capacity to use them for his own purposes. The term includes blubber, or pieces of whale flesh cut from the whale, and stowed on or under the deck of a ship. A policy of insurance upon outfits, and catchings substituted for the outfits, in a whaling voyage, protects the blubber. 1 Story, 603; 4 Law Rep. 297.

CATCHLAND. Land in Norfolk, so called because it is not known to what parish it belongs, and the minister who first seizes the tithes of it, by right of preoccupation, enjoys them for that year. Cowell.

CATCHPOLL. A name formerly given to a sheriff's deputy, or to a constable, or other officer whose duty it is to arrest persons. He was a sort of serjeant. The word is not now in use as an official designation. Minshew.

CATEGORICAL. A term of logic, meaning direct; unqualified; unconditional.

CATEGORY. In logic. A series or order of all the predicates or attributes contained under a genus.

CATER COUSIN. A expression used to designate a very distant relation.

CATHEDRAL. In English ecclesiastical law. The church of the bishop of the diocese, in which is his *cathedra*, or throne, and his special jurisdiction; in that respect the principal church of the diocese.

CATHEDRAL PREFERMENTS. In English ecclesiastical law. All deaneries, archdeaconries, and canonries, and generally all dignities and offices in any cathedral or collegiate church, below the rank of a bishop.

CATHEDRATIC. In English ecclesiastical law. A sum of 2s. paid to the bishop by the inferior clergy; but from its being usually paid at the bishop's *synod*, or visitation, it is commonly named *synodals*. Wharton.

CATHOLIC CREDITOR. In Scotch law. A creditor whose debt is secured on all or several distinct parts of the debtor's property. Bell.

CATHOLIC EMANCIPATION ACT. The statute of 10 Geo. IV. c. 7, by which Roman Catholics were restored, in general, to the full enjoyment of all civil rights, except that of holding ecclesiastical offices, and certain high appointments in the state. 3 Steph. Comm. 109.

CATONIANA REGULA. In Roman law. The rule which is commonly expressed in the maxim, *Quod ab initio non valet tractu temporis non convalebit*, meaning that what is at the beginning void by reason of some technical (or other) legal defect will not become valid merely by length of time. The rule applied to the institution of *hæredes*, the bequest of legacies, and such like. The rule is not without its application also in English law; *e. g.*, a married woman's will (being void when made) is not made valid merely because she lives to become a widow. Brown.

CATTLE. A term which includes the domestic animals generally; all the animals used by man for labor or food.

Animals of the bovine genus. In a wider sense, all domestic animals used by man for labor or food, including sheep, (2 Sawy. 148,) and hogs, (21 Wall. 294.)

CATTLE-GATE. In English law. A right to pasture cattle in the land of another. It is a distinct and several interest in the land, passing by lease and release. 13 East, 159; 5 Taunt. 811.

CATTLE-GUARD. A device to prevent cattle from straying along a railroad-track at a highway-crossing. Century Dict. See 31 Kan. 337, 2 Pac. Rep. 800.

CAUDA TERRÆ. A land's end, or the bottom of a ridge in arable land. Cowell.

CAULCEIS. Highroads or ways pitched with flint or other stones.

CAUPO. In the civil law. An innkeeper. Dig. 4, 9, 4, 5.

CAUPONA. In the civil law. An inn or tavern. Inst. 4, 5, 3.

CAUPONES. In the civil law. Innkeepers. Dig. 4, 9; Id. 47, 5; Story, Ag. § 458.

CAURSINES. Italian merchants who came into England in the reign of Henry III., where they established themselves as money lenders, but were soon expelled for their usury and extortion. Cowell; Blount.

CAUSA. 1. A cause, reason, occasion, motive, or inducement.

2. In the civil law and in old English law. The word signified a source, ground, or mode of acquiring property; hence a title; one's title to property. Thus, "*Titulus est justa causa possidendi id quod nostrum est;*" title is the lawful ground of possessing that which is ours. 8 Coke, 153. See Mackeld. Rom. Law, §§ 242, 283.

3. A condition; a consideration; motive for performing a juristic act. Used of contracts, and found in this sense in the Scotch law also. Bell.

4. In old English law. A cause; a suit or action pending. *Causa testamentaria*, a testamentary cause. *Causa matrimonialis*, a matrimonial cause. Bract. fol. 61.

5. In old European law. Any movable thing or article of property.

6. Used with the force of a preposition, it means by virtue of, on account of. Also with reference to, in contemplation of. *Causa mortis*, in anticipation of death.

Causa causæ est causa causati. The cause of a cause is the cause of the thing caused. 12 Mod. 639. The cause of the cause is to be considered as the cause of the effect also.

CAUSA CAUSANS. The immediate cause; the last link in the chain of causation.

Causa causantis, causa est causati. The cause of the thing causing is the cause of the effect. 4 Camp. 284; 4 Gray, 398.

CAUSA DATA ET NON SECUTA. In the civil law. Consideration given and not followed, that is, by the event upon which it was given. The name of an action by which a thing given in the view of a certain event was reclaimed if that event did not take place. Dig. 12, 4; Cod. 4, 6.

Causa ecclesiæ publicis æquiparatur; et summa est ratio quæ pro religione facit. The cause of the church is equal to public cause; and paramount is the reason which makes for religion. Co. Litt. 341.

Causa et origo est materia negotii. The cause and origin is the substance of the thing; the cause and origin of a thing are a material part of it. The law regards the original act. 1 Coke, 99.

CAUSA HOSPITANDI. For the purpose of being entertained as a guest. 4 Maule & S. 310.

CAUSA JACTITATIONIS MARITA-GII. A form of action which anciently lay against a party who boasted or gave out that he or she was married to the plaintiff, whereby a common reputation of their marriage might ensue. 3 Bl. Comm. 93.

CAUSA MATRIMONII PRÆLO-CUTI. A writ lying where a woman has given lands to a man in fee-simple with the intention that he shall marry her, and he refuses so to do within a reasonable time, upon suitable request. Cowell. Now obsolete. 3 Bl. Comm. 183, note.

CAUSA MORTIS. In contemplation of approaching death. In view of death. Commonly occurring in the phrase *donatio causa mortis*, (q. v.)

CAUSA PATET. The reason is open, obvious, plain, clear, or manifest. A common expression in old writers. Perk. c. 1, §§ 11, 14, 97.

CAUSA PROXIMA. The immediate, nearest, or latest cause.

Causa proxima, non remota, spectatur. The immediate, not the remote, cause, is looked at, or considered. 12 East, 648; 3 Kent, Comm. 302; Story, Bailm. § 515; Bac. Max. reg. 1.

CAUSA REI. In the civil law. The accessions, appurtenances, or fruits of a thing; comprehending all that the claimant of a principal thing can demand from a defendant in addition thereto, and especially what he would have had, if the thing had not been withheld from him. Inst. 4, 17, 3; Mackeld. Rom. Law, § 166.

CAUSA REMOTA. A remote or mediate cause; a cause operating indirectly by the intervention of other causes.

CAUSA SCIENTIÆ PATET. The reason of the knowledge is evident. A technical phrase in Scotch practice, used in depositions of witnesses.

CAUSA SINE QUA NON. A necessary or inevitable cause; a cause without which the effect in question could not have happened.

CAUSA TURPIS. A base (immoral or illegal) cause or consideration.

Causa vaga et incerta non est causa rationabilis. 5 Coke, 57. A vague and uncertain cause is not a reasonable cause.

Causæ dotis, vitæ, libertatis, fisci sunt inter favorabilia in lege. Causes of dower, life, liberty, revenue, are among the things favored in law. Co. Litt. 341.

CAUSAM NOBIS SIGNIFICES QUARE. A writ addressed to a mayor of a town, etc., who was by the king's writ commanded to give seisin of lands to the king's grantee, on his delaying to do it, requiring him to show cause why he so delayed the performance of his duty. Blount; Cowell.

CAUSARE. In the civil and old English law. To be engaged in a suit; to litigate; to conduct a cause.

CAUSATOR. In old European law. One who manages or litigates another's cause. Spelman.

CAUSE. That which produces an effect; whatever moves, impels, or leads. The origin or foundation of a thing, as of a suit or action; a ground of action. 1 N. Y. 47.

The consideration of a contract, that is, the inducement to it, or motive of the contracting party for entering into it, is, in the civil and Scotch law, called the "cause."

The civilians use the term "cause," in relation to obligations, in the same sense as the word "consideration" is used in the jurisprudence of England and the United States. It means the motive, the inducement to the agreement,—*id quod inducet ad contrahendum*. In contracts of mutual interest, the cause of the engagement is the thing given or done, or engaged to be given or done, or the risk incurred by one of the parties. 1 La. Ann. 192.

In pleading. Reason; motive; matter of excuse or justification.

In practice. A suit, litigation, or action. Any question, civil or criminal, contested before a court of justice.

Cause imports a judicial proceeding entire, and is nearly synonymous with *lis* in Latin, or suit in English. Although allied to the word "case," it differs from it in the application of its meaning. A cause is pending, postponed, appealed, gained, lost, etc.; whereas a case is made, rested, argued, decided, etc. Case is of a more limited signification, importing a collection of facts, with the conclusion of law thereon. Both terms may be used with propriety in the same sentence; e. g., on the trial of the *cause*, the plaintiff introduced certain evidence, and there rested his *case*. 18 Conn. 10.

A distinction is sometimes taken between "cause" and "action." Burrill observes that a cause is not, like an action or suit, said to be commenced, nor is an action, like a cause, said to be tried. But, if there is any substantial difference between these terms, it must lie in the fact that "action" refers more peculiarly to the *legal procedure* of a controversy; "cause" to its *merits* or the state of facts involved. Thus, we cannot say "the *cause* should have been replevin." Nor would it be correct to say "the plaintiff pleaded his own *action.*"

CAUSE-BOOKS. Books kept in the central office of the English supreme court, in which are entered all writs of summons issued in the office. Rules of Court, v 8.

CAUSE LIST. In English practice. A printed roll of actions, to be tried in the order of their entry, with the names of the solicitors for each litigant. Similar to the calendar of causes, or docket, used in American courts.

CAUSE OF ACTION. Matter for which an action may be brought. The ground on which an action may be sustained. The right to bring a suit.

Cause of action is properly the ground on which an action can be maintained; as when we say that such a person has no cause of action. But the phrase is often used to signify the matter of the complaint or claim on which a given action is in fact grounded, whether or not legally maintainable. Mozley & Whitley.

It sometimes means a person having a right of action. Thus, where a legacy is left to a married woman, and she and her husband bring an action to recover it, she is called in the old books the "meritorious cause of action." 1 H. Bl. 108.

The term is synonymous with right of action, right of recovery. 26 How. Pr. 501.

Cause of action is not synonymous with chose in action; the latter includes debts, etc., not due, and even stocks. 10 How. Pr. 1.

CAUSES CÉLÈBRES. Celebrated cases. A work containing reports of the decisions of interest and importance in French courts in the seventeenth and eighteenth centuries.

Secondarily a single trial or decision is often called a "*cause célèbre,*" when it is remarkable on account of the parties involved, or the unusual, interesting, or sensational character of the facts.

CAUSIDICUS. In the civil law. A pleader; one who argued a cause *ore tenus.*

CAUTELA. Lat. Care; caution; vigilance; prevision.

CAUTIO. In the civil and French law. Security given for the performance of any thing; bail; a bond or undertaking by way of surety. Also the person who becomes a surety.

In Scotch law. A pledge, bond, or other security for the performance of an obligation, or completion of the satisfaction to be obtained by a judicial process. Bell.

CAUTIO FIDEJUSSORIA. Security by means of bonds or pledges entered into by third parties. Du Cange.

CAUTIO PIGNORATITIA. Security given by pledge, or deposit, as plate, money, or other goods.

CAUTIO PRO EXPENSIS. Security for costs, charges, or expenses.

CAUTIO USUFRUCTUARIA. Security, which tenants for life give, to preserve the property rented free from waste and injury. Ersk. Inst. 2, 9, 59.

CAUTION. In Scotch law, and in admiralty law. Surety; security; bail; an undertaking by way of surety. 6 Mod. 162. See Cautio.

CAUTION JURATORY. In Scotch law. Security given by oath. That which a suspender swears is the best he can afford in order to obtain a suspension. Ersk. Pract. 4, 3, 6.

CAUTIONARY. In Scotch law. An instrument in which a person binds himself as surety for another.

CAUTIONE ADMITTENDA. In English ecclesiastical law. A writ that lies against a bishop who holds an excommunicated person in prison for contempt, notwithstanding he offers sufficient caution or security to obey the orders and commandment of the church for the future. Reg. Orig. 66; Cowell.

CAUTIONER. In Scotch law. A surety; a bondsman. One who binds himself in a bond with the principal for greater security. He is still a cautioner whether the bond be to pay a debt, or whether he undertake to produce the person of the party for whom he is bound. Bell.

CAUTIONNEMENT. In French law. The same as becoming surety in English law.

CAUTIONRY. In Scotch law. Suretyship.

CAVEAT. Lat. Let him beware. A formal notice or warning given by a party interested to a court, judge, or ministerial officer against the performance of certain acts within his power and jurisdiction. This process may be used in the proper courts to prevent (temporarily or provisionally) the proving of a will or the grant of administration, or to arrest the enrollment of a decree in chancery when the party intends to take an appeal, to prevent the grant of letters patent, etc. It is also used, in the American practice, as a kind of equitable process, to stay the granting of a patent for lands.

In patent law. A caveat is a formal written notice given to the officers of the patent-office, requiring them to refuse letters patent on a particular invention or device to to any other person, until the party filing the caveat (called the "caveator") shall have an opportunity to establish his claim to priority of invention.

CAVEAT ACTOR. Let the doer, or actor, beware.

CAVEAT EMPTOR. Let the buyer take care. This maxim summarizes the rule that the purchaser of an article must examine, judge, and test it for himself, being bound to discover any obvious defects or imperfections. Hob. 99; Co. Litt. 102a.

Caveat emptor, qui ignorare non debuit quod jus alienum emit. Hob. 99. Let a purchaser beware, who ought not to be ignorant that he is purchasing the rights of another.

CAVEAT VENDITOR. In Roman law. A maxim, or rule, casting the responsibility for defects or deficiencies upon the *seller* of goods, and expressing the exact opposite of the common law rule of *caveat emptor.* See 18 Wend. 449.

In English and American jurisprudence. *Caveat venditor* is sometimes used as expressing, in a rough way, the rule which governs all those cases of sales to which *caveat emptor* does not apply.

CAVEAT VIATOR. Let the traveler beware. This phrase has been used as a concise expression of the duty of a traveler on the highway to use due care to detect and avoid defects in the way. 10 Exch. 771, 774.

CAVEATOR. One who files a caveat.

Cavendum est a fragmentis. Beware of fragments. Bac. Aph. 26.

CAVERE. In the civil and common law. To take care; to exercise caution; to take care or provide for; to provide by law; to provide against; to forbid by law; to give security; to give caution or security on arrest.

CAVERS. Persons stealing ore from mines in Derbyshire, punishable in the bergh-mote or miners' court; also officers belonging to the same mines. Wharton.

CAYA. In old English **law.** A quay, kay, key, or wharf. Cowell.

CAYAGIUM. In old English law. Cayage or kayage; a toll or duty anciently paid for landing goods at a quay or wharf. Cowell.

CEAP. A bargain; anything for sale; a chattel; also cattle, as being the usual medium of barter. Sometimes used instead of ceapgild, (*q. v.*)

CEAPGILD. Payment or forfeiture of an animal. An ancient species of forfeiture.

CEDE. To yield up; to assign; to grant. Generally used to designate the transfer of territory from one government to another.

CEDENT. In Scotch law. An assignor. One who transfers a chose in action.

CEDO. I grant. The word ordinarily used in Mexican conveyances to pass title to lands. 26 Cal. 88, 108.

CEDULA. In old English law. A schedule.

In Spanish law. An act under private signature, by which a debtor admits the amount of the debt, and binds himself to discharge the same on a specified day or on demand.

Also the notice or citation affixed to the door of a fugitive criminal requiring him to appear before the court where the accusation is pending.

CEDULE. In French law. The technical name of an act under private signature. 3 La. Ann. 458.

CELATION. In medical jurisprudence. Concealment of pregnancy or delivery.

CELDRA. In old English law, a chaldron. In old Scotch law, a measure of grain, otherwise called a "chalder." See 1 Kames, Eq. 215.

CELEBRATION OF MARRIAGE. The formal act by which a man and woman take each other for husband and wife, according to law; the solemnization of a marriage. The term is usually applied to a marriage ceremony attended with ecclesiastical functions.

CELIBACY. The condition or state of life of an unmarried person.

CELLERARIUS. A butler in a monastery; sometimes in universities called "manciple" or "caterer."

CEMETERY. A place of burial, differing from a churchyard by its locality and incidents,—by its locality, as it is separate and apart from any sacred building used for the performance of divine service; by its incidents that, inasmuch as no vault or burying-place in an ordinary churchyard can be purchased for a perpetuity, in a cemetery a permanent burial place can be obtained. Wharton.

Six or more human bodies being buried at one place constitutes the place a cemetery. Pol. Code Cal. § 3106.

CENDULÆ. Small pieces of wood laid in the form of tiles to cover the roof of a house; shingles. Cowell.

CENEGILD. In Saxon law. An expiatory mulct or fine paid to the relations of a murdered person by the murderer or his relations. Spelman.

CENELLÆ. In old records. Acorns.

CENNINGA. A notice given by a buyer to a seller that the things which had been sold were claimed by another, in order that he might appear and justify the sale. Blount; Whishaw.

CENS. In French Canadian law. An annual tribute or due reserved to a seignior or lord, and imposed merely in recognition of his superiority. Guyot, Inst. c. 9.

CENSARIA. In old English law. A farm, or house and land let at a standing rent. Cowell.

CENSARII. In old English law. Farmers, or such persons as were liable to pay a census, (tax.) Blount; Cowell.

CENSERE. In the Roman law. To ordain; to decree. Dig. 50, 16, 111.

CENSITAIRE. In Canadian law. A tenant by *cens,* (*q. v.*)

CENSIVE. In Canadian law. Tenure by *cens,* (*q. v.*)

CENSO. In Spanish and Mexican law. An annuity. A ground rent. The right which a person acquires to receive a certain annual pension, for the delivery which he makes to another of a determined sum of money or of an immovable thing. Civil Code Mex. art. 3206. See Schm. Civil Law,

149, 309; White, New Recop. bk. 2, c. 7, § 4; 13 Tex. 655.

CENSO CONSIGNATIVO. In Spanish and Mexican law. A *censo* (*q. v.*) is called "*consignativo*" when he who receives the money assigns for the payment of the pension (annuity) the estate the fee in which he reserves. Civil Code Mex. art. 3207.

CENSO ENFITEUTICO. In Spanish and Mexican law. An emphyteutic annuity. That species of *censo* (annuity) which exists where there is a right to require of another a certain canon or pension annually, on account of having transferred to that person forever certain real estate, but reserving the fee in the land. The owner who thus transfers the land is called the "*censualisto,*" and the person who pays the annuity is called the "*censatario.*" Hall, Mex. Law, § 756.

CENSUALES. In old European law. A species of *oblati* or voluntary slaves of churches or monasteries; those who, to procure the protection of the church, bound themselves to pay an annual tax or quit-rent only of their estates to a church or monastery.

CENSUERE. In Roman law. They have decreed. The term of art, or technical term for the judgment, resolution, or decree of the senate. Tayl. Civil Law, 566.

CENSUMETHIDUS, or **CENSUMORTHIDUS.** A dead rent, like that which is called "mortmain." Blount; Cowell.

CENSURE. In ecclesiastical law. A spiritual punishment, consisting in withdrawing from a baptized person (whether belonging to the clergy or the laity) a privilege which the church gives him, or in wholly expelling him from the Christian communion. The principal varieties of censures are admonition, degradation, deprivation, excommunication, penance, sequestration, suspension. Phillim. Ecc. Law, 1367.

A custom observed in certain manors in Devon and Cornwall, where all persons above the age of sixteen years are cited to swear fealty to the lord, and to pay 11d. per poll, and 1d. per annum.

CENSUS. The official counting or enumeration of the people of a state or nation, with statistics of wealth, commerce, education, etc.

In Roman law. A numbering or enrollment of the people, with a valuation of their fortunes.

In old European law. A tax, or tribute; a toll. Montesq. Esprit des Lois, liv. 30, c. 14.

CENSUS REGALIS. In English law. The annual revenue or income of the crown.

CENT. A coin of the United States, the least in value of those now minted. It is the one-hundredth part of a dollar. Its weight is 72 gr., and it is composed of copper and nickel in the ratio of 88 to 12.

CENTENA. A hundred. A district or division containing originally a hundred freemen, established among the Goths, Germans, Franks, and Lombards, for military and civil purposes, and answering to the Saxon "hundred." Spelman; 1 Bl. Comm. 115.

Also, in old records and pleadings, a hundred weight.

CENTENARII. Petty judges, undersheriffs of counties, that had rule of a hundred, (*centena*,) and judged smaller matters among them. 1 Vent. 211.

CENTENI. The principal inhabitants of a *centena*, or district composed of different villages, originally in number a hundred, but afterwards only called by that name.

CENTESIMA. In Roman law. The hundredth part.

Usuriæ centesimæ. Twelve per cent. per annum; that is, a hundredth part of the principal was due each month,—the month being the unit of time from which the Romans reckoned interest. 2 Bl. Comm. 462, note.

CENTIME. The name of a denomination of French money, being the one-hundredth part of a franc.

CENTRAL CRIMINAL COURT. An English court, having jurisdiction for the trial of crimes and misdemeanors committed in London and certain adjoining parts of Kent, Essex, and Sussex, and of such other criminal cases as may be sent to it out of the queen's bench, though arising beyond its proper jurisdiction. It was constituted by the acts 4 & 5 Wm. IV. c. 36, and 19 & 20 Vict. c. 16, and superseded the "Old Bailey."

CENTRAL OFFICE. The central office of the supreme court of judicature in England is the office established in pursuance of the recommendation of the legal departments commission in order to consolidate the offices of the masters and associates of the common-law divisions, the crown office of the queen's bench division, the record and writ clerk's report, and enrollment offices of the chancery division, and a few others. The central office is divided into the following departments, and the business and staff of the office are distributed accordingly: (1) Writ, appearance, and judgment; (2) summons and order, for the common-law divisions only; (3) filing and record, including the old chancery report office; (4) taxing, for the common-law divisions only; (5) enrollment; (6) judgments, for the registry of judgments, executions, etc.; (7) bills of sale; (8) married women's acknowledgments; (9) queen's remembrancer; (10) crown office; and (11) associates. Sweet.

CENTRALIZATION. This word is used to express the system of government prevailing in a country where the management of local matters is in the hands of functionaries appointed by the ministers of state, paid by the state, and in constant communication and under the constant control and inspiration of the ministers of state, and where the funds of the state are largely applied to local purposes. Wharton.

CENTUMVIRI. In Roman law. The name of an important court consisting of a body of one hundred and five judges. It was made up by choosing three representatives from each of the thirty-five Roman tribes. The judges sat as one body for the trial of certain important or difficult questions, (called, *"causæ centumvirales,"*) but ordinarily they were separated into four distinct tribunals.

CENTURY. One hundred. A body of one hundred men. The Romans were divided into *centuries*, as the English were divided into hundreds.

Also a cycle of one hundred years.

CEORL. In Anglo Saxon law. The freemen were divided into two classes,—thanes and ceorls. The thanes were the proprietors of the soil, which was entirely at their disposal. The ceorls were men personally free, but possessing no landed property. Guizot, Rep. Govt.

A tenant at will of free condition, who held land of the thane on condition of paying rent or services. Cowell.

A freeman of inferior rank occupied in husbandry. Spelman.

CEPI. Lat. I have taken. This word was of frequent use in the returns of sheriffs when they were made in Latin.

CEPI CORPUS. I have taken the body. The return of a sheriff who has arrested a person upon a *capias.*

CEPI CORPUS ET PARATUM HABEO. I have taken the body and have it ready. A return made by the sheriff upon an attachment, *capias,* etc., when he has the person against whom the process was issued in custody.

CEPIT. In civil practice. He took. This was the characteristic word employed in (Latin) writs of trespass for goods taken, and in declarations in trespass and replevin.

Replevin *in the cepit* is a form of replevin which is brought for carrying away goods merely. Wells, Repl. § 53.

In criminal practice. This was a technical word necessary in an indictment for larceny. The charge must be that the defendant took the thing stolen with a felonious design. Bac. Abr. "Indictment," G, 1.

CEPIT ET ABDUXIT. He took and led away. The emphatic words in writs in trespass or indictments for larceny, where the thing taken was a living chattel, *i. e.,* an animal.

CEPIT ET ASPORTAVIT. He took and carried away. Applicable in a declaration in trespass or an indictment for larceny where the defendant has carried away goods without right. 4 Bl. Comm. 231.

CEPIT IN ALIO LOCO. In pleading. A plea in replevin, by which the defendant alleges that he took the thing replevied in another place than that mentioned in the declaration. 1 Chit. Pl. 490.

CEPPAGIUM. In old English law. The stumps or roots of trees which remain in the ground after the trees are felled. Fleta, lib. 2, c. 41, § 24.

CERA, or **CERE.** In old English law. Wax; a seal.

CERAGRUM. In old English law. A payment to provide candles in the church. Blount.

CEREVISIA. In old English law. Ale or beer.

CERT MONEY. In old English law. Head money or common fine. Money paid yearly by the residents of several manors to the lords thereof, for the certain keeping of the leet, (*pro certo letæ;*) and sometimes to the hundred. Blount; 6 Coke, 78.

Certa debet esse intentio, et narratio, et certum fundamentum, et certa res quæ deducitur in judicium. The design and narration ought to be certain, and the foundation certain, and the matter certain, which is brought into court to be tried. Co. Litt. 303*a.*

CERTA RES. In old English law. A certain thing. Fleta, lib. 2, c. 60, §§ 24, 25.

CERTAIN SERVICES. In feudal and old English law. Such services as were stinted (limited or defined) in quantity, and could not be exceeded on any pretense; as to pay a stated annual rent, or to plow such a field for three days. 2 Bl. Comm. 61.

CERTAINTY. In pleading. Distinctness; clearness of statement; particularity. Such precision and explicitness in the statement of alleged facts that the pleader's averments and contention may be readily understood by the pleader on the other side, as well as by the court and jury.

This word is technically used in pleading in two different senses, signifying either distinctness, or particularity, as opposed to undue generality.

Certainty is said to be of three sorts: (1) *Certainty to a common intent* is such as is attained by using words in their ordinary meaning, but is not exclusive of another meaning which might be made out by argument or inference. (2) *Certainty to a certain intent in general* is that which allows of no misunderstanding if a fair and reasonable construction is put upon the language employed without bringing in facts which are possible, but not apparent. (3) *Certainty to a certain intent in particular* is the highest degree of technical accuracy and precision. Co. Litt. 303; 2 H. Bl. 530; 9 Johns. 317.

In contracts. The quality of being specific, accurate, and distinct.

A thing is certain when its essence, quality, and quantity are described, distinctly set forth, etc. Dig. 12, 1, 6. It is uncertain when the description is not that of an individual object, but designates only the kind. Civil Code La. art. 3522, no. 8; 5 Coke, 121.

CERTIFICANDO DE RECOGNITIONE STAPULÆ. In English law. A writ commanding the mayor of the staple to certify to the lord chancellor a statute-staple taken before him where the party himself detains it, and refuses to bring in the same. There is a like writ to certify a statute-merchant, and in divers other cases. Reg. Orig. 148, 151, 152.

CERTIFICATE. A written assurance, or official representation, that some act has or has not been done, or some event occurred, or some legal formality been complied with. Particularly, such written assurance made or issuing from some court, and designed as a notice of things done therein, or as a warrant or authority, to some other court, judge, or officer.

A document in use in the English custom-house. No goods can be exported *by certifi- cate*, except foreign goods formerly imported, on which the whole or a part of the customs paid on importation is to be drawn back. Wharton.

CERTIFICATE FOR COSTS. In English practice. A certificate or memorandum drawn up and signed by the judge before whom a case was tried, setting out certain facts the existence of which must be thus proved before the party is entitled, under the statutes, to recover costs.

CERTIFICATE INTO CHANCERY. In English practice. This is a document containing the opinion of the common-law judges on a question of law submitted to them for their decision by the chancery court.

CERTIFICATE OF DEPOSIT. In the practice of bankers. This is a writing acknowledging that the person named has deposited in the bank a specified sum of money, and that the same is held subject to be drawn out on his own check or order, or that of some other person named in the instrument as payee.

CERTIFICATE OF HOLDER OF ATTACHED PROPERTY. A certificate required by statute, in some states, to be given by a third person who is found in possession of property subject to an attachment in the sheriff's hands, setting forth the amount and character of such property and the nature of the defendant's interest in it. Code Civil Proc. N. Y. § 650.

CERTIFICATE OF REGISTRY. In maritime law. A certificate of the registration of a vessel according to the registry acts, for the purpose of giving her a national character. 3 Steph. Comm. 274; 3 Kent, Comm. 139–150.

CERTIFICATE OF STOCK. A certificate of a corporation or joint-stock company that the person named is the owner of a designated number of shares of its stock; given when the subscription is fully paid and the "scrip-certificate" taken up.

CERTIFICATE, TRIAL BY. This is a mode of trial now little in use; it is resorted to in cases where the fact in issue lies out of the cognizance of the court, and the judges, in order to determine the question, are obliged to rely upon the solemn averment or information of persons in such a station as affords them the clearest and most competent knowledge of the truth. Brown.

CERTIFICATION. In Scotch practice. This is the assurance given to a party of the course to be followed in case he does not appear or obey the order of the court.

CERTIFICATION OF ASSISE. In English practice. A writ anciently granted for the re-examining or retrial of a matter passed by assise before justices, now entirely superseded by the remedy afforded by means of a new trial.

CERTIFICATS DE COÛTUME. In French law. Certificates given by a foreign lawyer, establishing the law of the country to which he belongs upon one or more fixed points. These certificates can be produced before the French courts, and are received as evidence in suits upon questions of foreign law. Arg. Fr. Merc. Law, 548.

CERTIFIED CHECK. In the practice of bankers. This is a depositor's check recognized and accepted by the proper officer of the bank as a valid appropriation of the amount specified to the payee named, and as drawn against funds of such depositor held by the bank. The usual method of certification is for the cashier or teller to write his name across the face of the check.

CERTIFIED COPY. A copy of a document, signed and certified as a true copy by the officer to whose custody the original is intrusted.

CERTIORARI. Lat. (To be informed of, to be made certain in regard to.) The name of a writ issued by a superior court directing an inferior court to send up to the former some pending proceeding, or all the record and proceedings in a cause before verdict, with its certificate to the correctness and completeness of the record, for review or trial; or it may serve to bring up the record of a case already terminated below, if the inferior court is one not of record, or in cases where the procedure is not according to the course of the common law.

Originally, and in English practice, a *certiorari* is an original writ, issuing out of the court of chancery or the king's bench, and directed in the king's name to the judges or officers of inferior courts, commanding them to certify or to return the records or proceedings in a cause depending before them, for the purpose of a judicial review of their action. Jacob.

In Massachusetts it is defined by statute as a writ issued by the supreme judicial court to any inferior tribunal, commanding it to certify and return to the supreme judicial court its records in a particular case, in order that any errors or irregularities which appear in the proceedings may be corrected. Pub. St. Mass. 1882, p. 1288.

CERTIORARI, BILL OF. In English chancery practice. An original bill praying relief. It was filed for the purpose of removing a suit pending in some inferior court of equity into the court of chancery, on account of some alleged incompetency or inconvenience.

Certum est quod certo reddi potest. That is certain which can be reduced to a certainty. 3 Rep. Ch. 142.

Certum est quod certum reddi potest. That is certain which can be rendered certain. 9 Coke, 47; Broom, Max. 623.

CERURA. A mound, fence, or inclosure.

CERVISARII. In Saxon law. Tenants who were bound to supply drink for their lord's table. Cowell.

CERVISIA. Ale, or beer. Sometimes spelled "*cerevisia.*"

CERVISIARIUS. In old records. An ale-house keeper. A beer or ale brewer. Blount.

CERVUS. Lat. A stag or deer.

CESIONARIO. In Spanish law. An assignee. White, New Recop. b. 3, tit. 10, c. 1, § 3.

CESS, *v.* In old English law. To cease, stop, determine, fail.

CESS, *n.* An assessment or tax. In Ireland, it was anciently applied to an exaction of victuals, at a certain rate, for soldiers in garrison.

Cessa regnare, si non vis judicare. Cease to reign, if you wish not to adjudicate. Hob. 155.

Cessante causa, cessat effectus. The cause ceasing, the effect ceases. Broom, Max. 160.

Cessante ratione legis, cessat et ipsa lex. The reason of the law ceasing, the law itself ceases also. Co. Litt. 70*b*; 2 Bl. Comm. 390, 391; Broom, Max. 159.

Cessante statu primitivo, cessat derivativus. When the primitive or original estate determines, the derivative estate determines also. 8 Coke, 34; Broom, Max. 495.

CESSARE. L. Lat. To cease, stop, or stay.

CESSAVIT PER BIENNIUM. In practice. An obsolete writ, which could formerly have been sued out when the defendant had for two years *ceased* or neglected to perform such service or to pay such rent as he was bound to do by his tenure, and had not upon his lands sufficient goods or chattels to be distrained. Fitzh. Nat. Brev. 208. It also lay where a religious house held lands on condition of performing certain spiritual services which it failed to do. 3 Bl. Comm. 232.

CESSE. (1) An assessment or tax; (2) a tenant of land was said to *cesse* when he neglected or *ceased* to perform the services due to the lord. Co. Litt. 373*a*, 380*b*.

CESSER. Neglect; a ceasing from, or omission to do, a thing. 3 Bl. Comm. 232.

The determination of an estate. 1 Coke, 84; 4 Kent, Comm. 33, 90, 105, 295.

The "cesser" of a term, annuity, or the like, takes place when it determines or comes to an end. The expression is chiefly used (in England) with reference to long terms of a thousand years or some similar period, created by a settlement for the purpose of securing the income, portions, etc., given to the objects of the settlement. When the trusts of a term of this kind are satisfied, it is desirable that the term should be put an end to, and with this object it was formerly usual to provide in the settlement itself that, as soon as the trusts of the term had been satisfied, it should cease and determine. This was called a "proviso for cesser." Sweet.

CESSER, PROVISO FOR. Where terms for years are raised by settlement, it is usual to introduce a proviso that they shall *cease* when the trusts end. This proviso generally expresses three events: (1) The trusts never arising; (2) their becoming unnecessary or incapable of taking effect; (3) the performance of them. Sugd. Vend. (14th Ed.) 621–623.

CESSET EXECUTIO. (Let execution stay.) In practice. A stay of execution; or an order for such stay; the entry of such stay on record. 2 Tidd, Pr. 1104.

CESSET PROCESSUS. (Let process stay.) A stay of proceedings entered on the record.

CESSIO. Lat. A cession; a giving up, or relinquishment; a surrender; an assignment.

CESSIO BONORUM. In Roman law. Cession of goods. A surrender, relinquishment, or assignment of all his property and effects made by an insolvent debtor for the benefit of his creditors. The effect of this voluntary action on the debtor's part was to secure him against imprisonment or any bodily punishment, and from infamy, and to cancel his debts to the extent of the property ceded. It much resembled our voluntary bankruptcy or assignment for creditors. The term is commonly employed in modern continental jurisprudence to designate a bankrupt's assignment of property to be distributed among his creditors, and is used in the same sense by some English and American writers, but here rather as a convenient than as a strictly technical term. See 2 Bl. Comm. 473; 1 Kent, Comm. 247, 422; Ersk. Inst. 4, 3, 26.

CESSIO IN JURE. In Roman law. A fictitious suit, in which the person who was to acquire the thing claimed (*vindicabat*) the thing as his own, the person who was to transfer it acknowledged the justice of the claim, and the magistrate pronounced it to be the property (*addicebat*) of the claimant. Sandars' Just. Inst. (5th Ed.) 89, 122.

CESSION. The act of ceding; a yielding or giving up; surrender; relinquishment of property or rights.

In the civil law. An assignment. The act by which a party transfers property to another. The surrender or assignment of property for the benefit of one's creditors.

In ecclesiastical law. A giving up or vacating a benefice, by accepting another without a proper dispensation. 1 Bl. Comm. 392; Latch, 234.

In public law. The assignment, transfer, or yielding up of territory by one state or government to another.

CESSION DES BIENS. In French law. The surrender which a debtor makes of all his goods to his creditors, when he finds himself in insolvent circumstances. It

is of two kinds, either voluntary or compulsory, (*judiciaire,*) corresponding very nearly to liquidation by arrangement and bankruptcy in English and American law.

CESSION OF GOODS. The surrender of property; the relinquishment that a debtor makes of all his property to his creditors, when he finds himself unable to pay his debts. Civil Code La. art. 2170.

CESSIONARY. In Scotch law. An assignee. Bell.

CESSIONARY BANKRUPT. One who gives up his estate to be divided among his creditors.

CESSMENT. An assessment, or tax.

CESSOR. One who ceases or neglects so long to perform a duty that he thereby incurs the danger of the law. O. N. B. 136.

CESSURE. L. Fr. A receiver; a bailiff. Kelham.

C'EST ASCAVOIR. L. Fr. That is to say, or to-wit. Generally written as one word, *cestascavoir, cestascavoire.*

C'est le crime qui fait la honte, et non pas l'echafaud. It is the offense which causes the shame, and not the scaffold.

CESTUI, CESTUY. He. Used frequently in composition in law French phrases.

CESTUI QUE TRUST. He who has a right to a beneficial interest in and out of an estate the legal title to which is vested in another. 2 Washb. Real Prop. 163.

The person who possesses the equitable right to property and receives the rents, issues, and profits thereof, the legal estate of which is vested in a trustee.

It has been proposed to substitute for this uncouth term the English word "beneficiary," and the latter, though still far from universally adopted, has come to be quite frequently used. It is equal in precision to the antiquated and unwieldy Norman phrase, and far better adapted to the genius of our language.

CESTUI QUE USE. He for whose use and benefit lands or tenements are held by another. The *cestui que use* has the right to receive the profits and benefits of the estate, but the legal title and possession (as well as the duty of defending the same) reside in the other.

CESTUI QUE VIE. He whose life is the measure of the duration of an estate. 1 Washb. Real Prop. 88.

The person for whose life any lands, tenements, or hereditaments are held.

Cestuy que doit inheriter al père doit inheriter al fils. He who would have been heir to the father of the deceased shall also be heir of the son. Fitzh. **Abr.** "Descent," **2**; 2 Bl. Comm. 239, 250.

CF. An abbreviated form of the Latin word *conferre*, meaning "compare." Directs the reader's attention to another part of the work, to another volume, case, etc., where contrasted, analogous, or explanatory views or statements may be found.

CH. This abbreviation most commonly stands for "chapter," or "chancellor," but it may also mean "chancery," or "chief."

CHACE. L. Fr. A chase or hunting ground.

CHACEA. In old English law. A station of game, more extended than a park, and less than a forest; also the liberty of chasing or hunting within a certain district; also the way through which cattle are driven to pasture, otherwise called a "drove-way." Blount.

Chacea est ad communem legem. A chase is by common law. Reg. Brev. 806.

CHACEABLE. L. Fr. That may be chased or hunted.

CHACER. To drive, compel, or oblige; also to chase or hunt.

CHACURUS. A horse for the chase, or a hound, dog, or courser.

CHAFEWAX. An officer in the English chancery whose duty was to fit the wax to seal the writs, commissions, and other instruments thence issuing. The office was abolished by St. 15 & 16 Vict. c. 87, § 23.

CHAFFERS. An ancient term for goods, wares, and merchandise.

CHAFFERY. Traffic; the practice of buying and selling.

CHAIN. A measure used by engineers and surveyors, being twenty-two yards in length.

CHAIRMAN. A name given to the presiding officer of an assembly, public meeting, convention, deliberative or legislative body, board of directors, committee, etc.

CHAIRMAN OF COMMITTEES OF THE WHOLE HOUSE. In English parliamentary practice. In the commons, this officer, always a member, is elected by the house on the assembling of every new parliament. When the house is in committee on bills introduced by the government, or in committee of ways and means, or supply, or in committee to consider preliminary resolutions, it is his duty to preside.

CHALDRON, CHALDERN, or CHALDER. Twelve sacks of coals, each holding three bushels, weighing about a ton and a half. In Wales they reckon 12 barrels or pitchers a ton or chaldron, and 29 cwt. of 120 lbs. to the ton. Wharton.

CHALKING, or CAULKING. The process or method of stopping the seams in a ship or a vessel.

CHALLENGE. 1. To object or except to; to prefer objections to a person, right, or instrument; to formally call into question the capability of a person for a particular function, or the existence of a right claimed, or the sufficiency or validity of an instrument.

2. As a noun, the word signifies the objection or exception so advanced.

3. An exception taken against legal documents, as a declaration, count, or writ. But this use of the word is now obsolescent.

4. An exception or objection preferred against a person who presents himself at the polls as a voter, in order that his right to cast a ballot may be inquired into.

5. An objection or exception to the personal qualification of a judge or magistrate about to preside at the trial of a cause; as on account of personal interest, his having been of counsel, bias, etc.

6. An exception or objection taken to the jurors summoned and returned for the trial of a cause, either individually, (to the polls,) or collectively, (to the array.)

AT COMMON LAW. The causes for principal challenges fall under four heads: (1) *Propter honoris respectum.* On account of respect for the party's social rank. (2) *Propter defectum.* On account of some legal disqualification, such as infancy or alienage. (3) *Propter affectum.* On account of partiality; that is, either expressed or implied bias or prejudice. (4) *Propter delictum.* On account of crime; that is, disqualification arising from the conviction of an infamous crime.

CHALLENGE FOR CAUSE. A challenge to a juror for which some cause or reason is alleged. Termes de la Ley; 4 Bl. Comm. 353. Thus distinguished from a peremptory challenge.

CHALLENGE PEREMPTORY. A privilege allowed to a prisoner in criminal cases, of challenging peremptorily a certain number of jurors, without assigning any cause. Termes de la Ley; 4 Bl. Comm. 353; Co. Litt. 156b.

CHALLENGE, PRINCIPAL. Such as is made for a cause which when substantiated is of itself sufficient evidence of bias in favor of or against the party challenging. Co. Litt. 156b. See 3 Bl. Comm. 363; 4 Bl. Comm. 353.

CHALLENGE TO FIGHT. A summons or invitation, given by one person to another, to engage in a personal combat; a request to fight a duel. A criminal offense. See Steph. Crim. Dig. 40; 3 East, 581; 6 Blackf. 20.

CHALLENGE TO THE ARRAY. An exception to the whole panel in which the jury are *arrayed*, or set in order by the sheriff in his return, upon account of partiality, or some default in the sheriff, coroner, or other officer who arrayed the panel or made the return. 3 Bl. Comm. 359; Co. Litt. 155b.

CHALLENGE TO THE FAVOR. Is where the party has no principal challenge, but objects only some probable circumstances of suspicion, as acquaintance, and the like, the validity of which must be left to the determination of triors, whose office it is to decide whether the juror be favorable or unfavorable. 3 Bl. Comm. 363; 4 Bl. Comm. 353.

CHALLENGE TO THE POLL. A challenge made separately to an individual juror; as distinguished from a challenge to the array.

CHAMBER. A room or apartment in a house. A private repository of money; a treasury. Sometimes used to designate a court, a commission, or an association of persons habitually meeting together in an apartment, *e. g.*, the "star chamber," "chamber of deputies," "chamber of commerce."

CHAMBER OF ACCOUNTS. In French law. A sovereign court, of great antiquity, in France, which took cognizance of and registered the accounts of the king's revenue; nearly the same as the English court of exchequer. Enc. Brit.

CHAMBER OF COMMERCE. An association (which may or may not be incorporated) comprising the principal merchants, manufacturers, and traders of a city, designed for convenience in buying, selling, and exchanging goods, and to foster the commercial and industrial interests of the place.

CHAMBER, WIDOW'S. A portion of the effects of a deceased person, reserved for the use of his widow, and consisting of her apparel, and the furniture of her bed-chamber, is called in London the "widow's chamber." 2 Bl. Comm. 518.

CHAMBERDEKINS, or CHAMBER DEACONS. In old English law. Certain poor Irish scholars, clothed in mean habit, and living under no rule; also beggars banished from England. (1 Hen. V. cc. 7, 8.) Wharton.

CHAMBERLAIN. Keeper of the chamber. Originally the chamberlain was the keeper of the treasure chamber (*camera*) of the prince or state; otherwise called "treasurer." Cowell.

The name of several high officers of state in England, as the lord great chamberlain of England, lord chamberlain of the household, chamberlain of the exchequer. Cowell; Blount.

The word is also used in some American cities as the title of an officer corresponding to "treasurer."

CHAMBERLARIA. Chamberlainship; the office of a chamberlain. Cowell.

CHAMBERS. In practice. The private room or office of a judge; any place in which a judge hears motions, signs papers, or does other business pertaining to his office, when he is not holding a session of court. Business so transacted is said to be done "in chambers." The term is also applied, in England, to the private office of a barrister.

In international law. Portions of the sea cut off by lines drawn from one promontory to another, or included within lines extending from the point of one cape to the next, situate on the sea-coast of the same nation, and which are claimed by that nation as asylums for merchant vessels, and exempt from the operations of belligerents.

CHAMBIUM. In old English law. Change, or exchange. Bract. fols. 117, 118.

CHAMBRE DEPEINTE. A name anciently given to St. Edward's chamber, called the "Painted Chamber," destroyed by fire with the houses of parliament.

CHAMP DE MAI. (Lat. *Campus Maii*.) The field or assembly of May. The national assembly of the Franks, held in the month of May.

CHAMP DE MARS. (Lat. *Campus Martii*.) The field or assembly of March.

D

E

F

G

H

I

J

K

L

M

The national assembly of the Franks, held in the month of March, in the open air.

CHAMPART. In French law. The grant of a piece of land by the owner to another, on condition that the latter would deliver to him a portion of the crops. 18 Toullier, n. 182.

CHAMPERT. In old English law. A share or division of land; champerty.

In old Scotch law. A gift or bribe, taken by any great man or judge from any person, for delay of just actions, or furthering of wrongous actions, whether it be lands or any goods movable. Skene.

CHAMPERTOR. In criminal law. One who makes pleas or suits, or causes them to be moved, either directly or indirectly, and sues them at his proper costs, upon condition of having a part of the gain. One guilty of champerty. St. 33 Edw. I. c. 2.

CHAMPERTOUS. Of the nature of champerty; affected with champerty.

CHAMPERTY. A bargain made by a stranger with one of the parties to a suit, by which such third person undertakes to carry on the litigation at his own cost and risk, in consideration of receiving, if he wins the suit, a part of the land or other subject sought to be recovered by the action.

The purchase of an interest in a thing in dispute, with the object of maintaining and taking part in the litigation. 7 Bing. 378.

The act of assisting the plaintiff or defendant in a legal proceeding in which the person giving the assistance has no valuable interest, on an agreement that, if the proceeding is successful, the proceeds shall be divided between the plaintiff or defendant, as the case may be, and the assisting person. Sweet.

Champerty is the carrying on a suit in the name of another, but at one's own expense, with the view of receiving as compensation a certain share of the avails of the suit. 4 Duer, 275.

The distinction between *champerty* and *maintenance* lies in the interest which the interfering party is to have in the issue of the suit. In the former case, he is to receive a share or portion of what may be recovered; in the latter case, he is in no way benefited by the success of the party aided, but simply intermeddles officiously. Thus every champerty includes maintenance, but not every maintenance is champerty. See 2 Inst. 208.

CHAMPION. A person who fights a combat in his own cause, or in place of another. The person who, in the trial by bat-

tel, fought either for the tenant or demandant. 3 Bl. Comm. 339.

CHAMPION OF THE KING OR QUEEN. An ancient officer, whose duty it was to ride armed *cap-à-piè*, into Westminster Hall at the coronation, while the king was at dinner, and, by the proclamation of a herald, make a challenge "that, if any man shall deny the king's title to the crown, he is there ready to defend it in single combat." The king drank to him, and sent him a gilt cup covered, full of wine, which the champion drank, retaining the cup for his fee. This ceremony, long discontinued, was revived at the coronation of George IV., but not afterwards. Wharton.

CHANCE. In criminal law. An accident; an unexpected, unforeseen, or unintended consequence of an act; a fortuitous event. The opposite of intention, design, or contrivance.

There is a wide difference between *chance* and *accident.* The one is the intervention of some unlooked-for circumstance to prevent an expected result; the other is the uncalculated effect of mere luck. The shot discharged at random strikes its object by chance; that which is turned aside from its well-directed aim by some unforeseen circumstance misses its mark by accident. Pure chance consists in the entire absence of all the means of calculating results; accident, in the unusual prevention of an effect naturally resulting from the means employed. Morris, (Iowa,) 173.

CHANCE-MEDLEY. In criminal law. A sudden affray. This word is sometimes applied to any kind of homicide by misadventure, but in strictness it is applicable to such killing only as happens in defending one's self. 4 Bl. Comm. 184.

CHANCEL. In ecclesiastical law. The part of a church in which the communion table stands; it belongs to the rector or the impropriator. 2 Broom & H. Comm. 420.

CHANCELLOR. In American law, this is the name given in some states to the judge (or the presiding judge) of a court of chancery. In England, besides being the designation of the chief judge of the court of chancery, the term is used as the title of several judicial officers attached to bishops or other high dignitaries and to the universities. (See the following titles.) In Scotch practice, it denotes the foreman of an assise or jury.

CHANCELLOR OF A CATHEDRAL. In English ecclesiastical law. One of the *quatuor personæ*, or four chief dignitaries of the cathedrals of the old foundation. The duties assigned to the office by the statutes of the different chapters vary, but they are chiefly of an educational character, with a special reference to the cultivation of theology.

CHANCELLOR OF A DIOCESE. In ecclesiastical law. Is the officer appointed to assist a bishop in matters of law, and to hold his consistory courts for him. 1 Bl. Comm. 382; 2 Steph. Comm. 672.

CHANCELLOR OF A UNIVERSITY. In English law. The official head of a university. His principal prerogative is to hold a court with jurisdiction over the members of the university, in which court the vice-chancellor presides. The office is for the most part honorary.

CHANCELLOR OF THE DUCHY OF LANCASTER. In English law. An officer before whom, or his deputy, the court of the duchy chamber of Lancaster is held. This is a special jurisdiction concerning all manner of equity relating to lands holden of the king in right of the duchy of Lancaster. Hob. 77; 3 Bl. Comm. 78.

CHANCELLOR OF THE EXCHEQUER. In English law. A high officer of the crown, who formerly sat in the exchequer court, and, together with the regular judges of the court, saw that things were conducted to the king's benefit. In modern times, however, his duties are not of a judicial character, but such as pertain to a minister of state charged with the management of the national revenue and expenditure.

CHANCELLOR OF THE ORDER OF THE GARTER, and other military orders, in England, is an officer who seals the commissions and the mandates of the chapter and assembly of the knights, keeps the register of their proceedings, and delivers their acts under the seal of their order.

CHANCELLOR, THE LORD HIGH. In England, this is the highest judicial functionary in the kingdom, and superior, in point of precedency, to every temporal lord. He is appointed by the delivery of the queen's great seal into his custody. He may not be a Roman Catholic. He is a cabinet minister, a privy counsellor, and prolocutor of the house of lords by prescription, (but not necessarily, though usually, a peer of the realm,)

and vacates his office with the ministry by which he was appointed. To him belongs the appointment of all justices of the peace throughout the kingdom. Being, in the earlier periods of English history, usually an ecclesiastic, (for none else were then capable of an office so conversant in writings,) and presiding over the royal chapel, he became keeper of the sovereign's conscience, visitor, in right of the crown, of the hospitals and colleges of royal foundation, and patron of all the crown livings under the value of twenty marks *per annum* in the king's books. He is the general guardian of all infants, idiots, and lunatics, and has the general superintendence of all charitable uses, and all this, over and above the vast and extensive jurisdiction which he exercises in his judicial capacity in the supreme court of judicature, of which he is the head. Wharton.

CHANCELLOR'S COURTS IN THE TWO UNIVERSITIES. In English law. Courts of local jurisdiction in and for the two universities of Oxford and Cambridge in England.

CHANCERY. Equity; equitable jurisdiction; a court of equity; the system of jurisprudence administered in courts of equity. See COURT OF CHANCERY.

CHANGE. 1. An alteration; substitution of one thing for another. This word does not connote either improvement or deterioration as a result. In this respect it differs from *amendment*, which, in law, always imports a change for the better.

2. Exchange of money against money of a different denomination. Also small coin. Also an abbreviation of *exchange*.

CHANGER. An officer formerly belonging to the king's mint, in England, whose business was chiefly to *exchange* coin for bullion brought in by merchants and others.

CHANNEL. This term refers rather to the bed in which the main stream of a river flows than to the deep water of the stream as followed in navigation. 55 Iowa, 558, 8 N. W. Rep. 443.

The "main channel" of a river is that bed of the river over which the principal volume of water flows. Many great rivers discharge themselves into the sea through more than one channel. They all, however, have a main channel, through which the principal volume of water passes. 31 Fed. Rep. 757.

CHANTER. The chief singer in the choir of a cathedral. Mentioned in 13 Eliz. c. 10.

CHANTRY. A church or chapel endowed with lands for the maintenance of priests to say mass daily for the souls of the donors. Termes de la Ley; Cowell.

CHAPEL. A place of worship; a lesser or inferior church, sometimes a part of or subordinate to another church. Webster.

CHAPEL OF EASE. In English ecclesiastical law. A chapel founded in general at some period later than the parochial church itself, and designed for the accommodation of such of the parishioners as, in course of time, had begun to fix their residence at some distance from its site; and so termed because built *in aid* of the original church. 3 Steph. Comm. 151.

CHAPELRY. The precinct and limits of a chapel. The same thing to a chapel as a parish is to a church. Cowell; Blount.

CHAPERON. A hood or bonnet anciently worn by the Knights of the Garter, as part of the habit of that order; also a little escutcheon fixed in the forehead of horses drawing a hearse at a funeral. Wharton.

CHAPITRE. A summary of matters to be inquired of or presented before justices in eyre, justices of assise, or of the peace, in their sessions. Also articles delivered by the justice in his charge to the inquest. Brit. c. iii.

CHAPLAIN. An ecclesiastic who performs divine service in a chapel; but it more commonly means one who attends upon a king, prince, or other person of quality, for the performance of clerical duties in a private chapel. 4 Coke, 90.

A clergyman officially attached to a ship of war, to an army, (or regiment,) or to some public institution, for the purpose of performing divine service. Webster.

CHAPMAN. An itinerant vendor of small wares. A trader who trades from place to place. Say. 191, 192.

CHAPTER. In ecclesiastical law. A congregation of ecclesiastical persons in a cathedral church, consisting of canons, or prebendaries, whereof the dean is the head, all subordinate to the bishop, to whom they act as assistants in matters relating to the church, for the better ordering and disposing the things thereof, and the confirmation of such leases of the temporalty and offices relating to the bishopric, as the bishop shall make from time to time. And they are termed "*capitulum*," as a kind of head, instituted not only to assist the bishop in manner aforesaid, but also anciently to rule and govern the diocese in the time of vacation. Burn, Dict.

CHARACTER. The aggregate of the moral qualities which belong to and distinguish an individual person; the general result of the one's distinguishing attributes.

That moral predisposition or habit, or aggregate of ethical qualities, which is believed to attach to a person, on the strength of the common opinion and report concerning him.

The opinion generally entertained of a person derived from the common report of the people who are acquainted with him. 3 Serg. & R. 336; 3 Mass. 192.

Character and *reputation* are not synonymous terms. Character is what a man or woman is morally, while reputation is what he or she is reputed to be. Yet reputation is the estimate which the community has of a person's character; and it is the belief that moral character is wanting in an individual that renders him unworthy of belief; that is to say, that reputation is evidence of character, and if the reputation is bad for truth, or reputation is bad in other respects affecting the moral character, then the jury may infer that the character is bad and the witness not reliable. General character has always been proved by proving general reputation. 6 Or. 213.

The word "character" no doubt has an objective and subjective import, which are quite distinct. As to the object, character is its quality. As to man, it is the quality of his mind, and his affections, his capacity and temperament. But as a subjective term, certainly in the minds of others, one's character is the aggregate, or the abstract, of other men's opinions of one. And in this sense, when a witness speaks of the character of another witness for truth, he draws not upon his memory alone, but his judgment also. It is the conclusion of the mind of the witness, in summing up the amount of all the reports he has heard of the man, and declaring his character for truth, as held in the minds of his neighbors and acquaintances, and in this sense character, general character, and general report or reputation are the same, as held in the books. 26 Vt. 278.

CHARGE. *v.* To impose a burden, obligation, or lien; to create a claim against property; to claim, to demand; to accuse; to instruct a jury on matters of law.

CHARGE, *n.* In general. An incumbrance, lien, or burden; an obligation or duty; a liability; an accusation.

In contracts. An obligation, binding upon him who enters into it, which may be removed or taken away by a discharge. Termes de la Ley.

An undertaking to keep the custody of another person's goods.

An obligation entered into by the owner of an estate, which binds the estate for its performance. Com. Dig. "Rent," c. 6; 2 Ball & B. 223.

In the law of wills. A responsibility or liability imposed by the testator upon a devisee personally, or upon the land devised.

In equity pleading. An allegation in the bill of matters which disprove or avoid a defense which it is alleged the defendant is supposed to pretend or intend to set up. Story, Eq. Pl. § 31.

In equity practice. A paper presented to a master in chancery by a party to a cause, being a written statement of the items with which the opposite party should be debited or should account for, or of the claim of the party making it. It is more comprehensive than a *claim*, which implies only the amount due to the person producing it, while a charge may embrace the whole liabilities of the accounting party. Hoff. Mast. 36.

In common-law practice. The final address made by a judge to the jury trying a case, before they make up their verdict, in which he sums up the case, and instructs the jury as to the rules of law which apply to its various issues, and which they must observe, in deciding upon their verdict, when they shall have determined the controverted matters of fact. The term also applies to the address of the court to a grand jury, in which the latter are instructed as to their duties.

In Scotch law. The command of the king's letters to perform some act; as a *charge* to enter heir. Also a messenger's execution, requiring a person to obey the order of the king's letters; as a *charge* on letters of horning, or a *charge* against a superior. Bell.

CHARGE AND DISCHARGE. Under the former system of equity practice, this phrase was used to characterize the usual method of taking an account before a master. After the plaintiff had presented his "charge," a written statement of the items of account for which he asked credit, the defendant filed a counter-statement, called a "discharge," exhibiting any claims or demands he held against the plaintiff. These served to define the field of investigation, and constituted the basis of the report.

CHARGÉ DES AFFAIRES, or CHARGÉ D'AFFAIRES. The title of a diplomatic representative of inferior rank. He has not the title or dignity of a minister, though he may be charged with the functions and offices of the latter, either as a temporary substitute for a minister or at a court to

which his **government** does not **accredit** a minister.

CHARGE-SHEET. A paper kept at a police-station to receive each night the names of the persons brought and given into custody, the nature of the accusation, and the name of the accuser in each case. It is under the care of the inspector on duty. Wharton.

CHARGE TO ENTER HEIR. In Scotch law. A writ commanding a person to enter heir to his predecessor within forty days, otherwise an action to be raised against him as if he had entered.

CHARGEABLE. This word, in its ordinary acceptation, as applicable to the imposition of a duty or burden, signifies capable of being charged, subject to be charged, liable to be charged, or proper to be charged. 46 Vt. 625; 107 Mass. 419.

CHARGEANT. Weighty; heavy; penal; expensive. Kelham.

CHARGES. The expenses which have been incurred, or disbursements made, in connection with a contract, suit, or business transaction. Spoken of an action, it is said that the term includes more than what falls under the technical description of "costs."

CHARGING ORDER. The name bestowed, in English practice, upon an order allowed by St. 1 & 2 Vict. c. 110, § 14, and 3 & 4 Vict. c. 82, to be granted to a judgment creditor, that the property of a judgment debtor in government stock, or in the stock of any public company in England, corporate or otherwise, shall (whether standing in his own name or in the name of any person in trust for him) stand charged with the payment of the amount for which judgment shall have been recovered, with interest. 3 Steph. Comm. 587, 588.

CHARITABLE USES, CHARITIES. Gifts to general public uses, which may extend to the rich, as well as the poor. Amb. 651; 2 Sneed, 305.

Gifts to such purposes as are enumerated in the act 43 Eliz. c. 4, or which, by analogy, are deemed within its spirit or intendment. Boyle, Char. 17.

CHARITY. Subjectively, the sentiment or motive of benevolence and philanthropy; the disposition to relieve the distressed. Objectively, alms-giving; acts of benevolence; relief, assistance, or services accorded to the needy without return. Also gifts for the promotion of philanthropic and humanitarian purposes.

The meaning of the word "charity," in its legal sense, is different from the signification which it ordinarily bears. In its legal sense, it includes not only gifts for the benefit of the poor, but endowments for the advancement of learning, or institutions for the encouragement of science and art, and, it is said, for any other useful and public purpose. 25 Ohio St. 243.

Charity, in its widest sense, denotes all the good affections men ought to bear towards each other; in a restricted and common sense, relief of the poor. 9 Ves. 399.

Charity, as used in the Massachusetts Sunday law, includes whatever proceeds from a sense of moral duty or a feeling of kindness and humanity, and is intended wholly for the purpose of the relief or comfort of another, and not for one's own benefit or pleasure. 118 Mass. 195, 197.

CHARRE OF LEAD. A quantity consisting of 36 pigs of lead, each pig weighing about 70 pounds.

CHART. The word "chart," as used in the copyright law, does not include sheets of paper exhibiting tabulated or methodically arranged information. 24 Fed. Rep. 632.

CHARTA. In old English law. A charter or deed; an instrument written and sealed; the formal evidence of conveyances and contracts. Also any signal or token by which an estate was held. The term came to be applied, by way of eminence, to such documents as proceeded from the sovereign, granting liberties or privileges, and either where the recipient of the grant was the whole nation, as in the case of *Magna Charta,* or a public body, or private individual, in which case it corresponded to the modern word "charter."

In the civil law. Paper, suitable for the inscription of documents or books; hence, any instrument or writing. See Dig. 32, 52, 6; Nov. 44, 2.

CHARTA COMMUNIS. In old English law. A common or mutual charter or deed; one containing mutual covenants, or involving mutuality of obligation; one to which both parties might have occasion to refer, to establish their respective rights. Bract. fols. 33b, 34.

CHARTA CYROGRAPHATA. In old English law. A chirographed charter; a charter executed in two parts, and cut through the middle, (*scinditur per medium,*) where the word "*cyrographum,*" or "*chirographum,*" was written in large letters. Bract. fol. 34; Fleta, lib. 3, c. 14, § 3.

CHARTA DE FORESTA. A collection of the laws of the forest, made in the 9th Hen. III., and said to have been originally a part of *Magna Charta.*

Charta de non ente non valet. Co. Litt. 36. A charter concerning a thing not in existence avails not.

CHARTA DE UNA PARTE. A deed-poll.

Charta non est nisi vestimentum donationis. A deed is nothing else than the vestment of a gift. Co. Litt. 36.

CHARTA PARTITA. (Literally, a deed divided.) A charter-party. 3 Kent, Comm. 201.

CHARTÆ LIBERTATUM. These are *Magna Charta* and *Charta de Foresta.*

Chartarum super fidem, mortuis testibus, ad patriam de necessitudine recurrendum est. Co. Litt. 36. The witnesses being dead, the truth of charters must of necessity be referred to the country, *i. e.,* a jury.

CHARTE. A chart, or plan, which mariners use at sea.

CHARTE-PARTIE. Fr. In French marine law. A charter-party.

CHARTEL. A challenge to a single combat; also an instrument or writing between two states for settling the exchange of prisoners of war.

CHARTER, v. In mercantile law. To hire or lease a vessel for a voyage. A "chartered" is distinguished from a "seeking" ship. 7 East, 24.

CHARTER, n. An instrument emanating from the sovereign power, in the nature of a grant, either to the whole nation, or to a class or portion of the people, or to a colony or dependency, and assuring to them certain rights, liberties, or powers. Such was the "Great Charter" or "*Magna Charta,*" and such also were the charters granted to certain of the English colonies in America. See Story, Const. § 161.

An act of the legislative department of government, creating a corporation, is called the "charter" of the corporation.

In old English law. The term denoted a deed or other written instrument under seal; a conveyance, covenant, or contract.

In old Scotch law. A disposition made by a superior to his vassal, for something to be performed or paid by him. 1 Forb. Inst. pt. 2, b. 2, c. 1, tit. 1. A writing which contains the grant or transmission of the feudal right to the vassal. Ersk. Inst. 2, 3, 19.

CHARTER-HOUSE. Formerly a convent of Carthusian monks in London; now a college founded and endowed by Thomas Sutton. The governors of the charter-house are a corporation aggregate without a head, president, or superior, all the members being of equal authority. 3 Steph. Comm. (7th Ed.) 14, 97.

CHARTER-LAND. Otherwise called "book-land," is property held by deed under certain rents and free services. It, in effect, differs nothing from the free socage lands, and hence have arisen most of the freehold tenants, who hold of particular manors, and owe suit and service to the same. 2 Bl. Comm. 90.

CHARTER OF PARDON. In English law. An instrument under the great seal, by which a pardon is granted to a man for a felony or other offense.

CHARTER OF THE FOREST. See Charta de Foresta.

CHARTER-PARTY. A contract by which an entire ship, or some principal part thereof, is let to a merchant for the conveyance of goods on a determined voyage to one or more places. Abb. Shipp. (241,) 315. A contract of affreightment in writing, by which the owner of a ship lets the whole or a part of her to a merchant, for the conveyance of goods on a particular voyage, in consideration of the payment of freight. 3 Kent, Comm. 201.

A written agreement, not usually under seal, by which a ship-owner lets an entire ship, or a part of it, to a merchant for the conveyance of goods, binding himself to transport them to a particular place for a sum of money which the merchant undertakes to pay as freight for their carriage. Maude & P. Mer. Shipp. 227.

The contract by which a ship is let is termed a "charter-party." By it the owner may either let the capacity or burden of the ship, continuing the employment of the owner's master, crew, and equipments, or may surrender the entire ship to the charterer, who then provides them himself. The master or part owner may be a charterer. Civil Code Cal. § 1959; Civil Code Dak. § 1127.

CHARTER ROLLS. Ancient English records of royal charters, granted between the years 1199 and 1516.

CHARTERED SHIP. A ship hired or freighted; a ship which is the subject-matter of a charter-party.

CHARTERER. In mercantile law. One who charters (i. e., hires or engages) a vessel for a voyage; a freighter. 2 Steph. Comm. 184; 3 Kent, Comm. 137.

CHARTIS REDDENDIS. (For returning the charters.) An ancient writ which lay against one who had charters of feoffment intrusted to his keeping and refused to deliver them. Reg. Orig. 159.

CHARTOPHYLAX. In old European law. A keeper of records or public instruments; a chartulary; a registrar. Spelman.

CHARUE. In old English law. A plow. *Bestes des charues;* beasts of the plow.

CHASE. The liberty or franchise of hunting, one's self, and keeping protected against all other persons, beasts of the chase within a specified district, without regard to the ownership of the land. 2 Bl. Comm. 414-416.

A privileged place for the preservation of deer and beasts of the forest, of a middle nature between a forest and a park. It is commonly less than a forest, and not endowed with so many liberties, as officers, laws, courts; and yet it is of larger compass than a park, having more officers and game than a park. Every forest is a chase, but every chase is not a forest. It differs from a park in that it is not inclosed, yet it must have certain metes and bounds, but it may be in other men's grounds, as well as in one's own. Manwood, 49.

CHASTITY. Purity; continence. That virtue which prevents the unlawful intercourse of the sexes. Also the state of purity or abstinence from unlawful sexual connection.

CHATTEL. An article of personal property; any species of property not amounting to a freehold or fee in land.

The name given to things which in law are deemed personal property. Chattels are divided into chattels real and chattels personal; chattels real being interests in land which devolve after the manner of personal estate, as leaseholds. As opposed to freeholds, they are regarded as personal estate. But, as being interests in real estate, they are called "chattels real," to distinguish them from movables, which are called "chattels personal." Mozley & Whitley.

Chattels personal are movables only; chattels real are such as savor only of the realty. 19 Johns. 73.

The term "chattels" is a more comprehensive one than "goods," as it includes animate as well as inanimate property. 2 Chit. Bl. Comm. 383, note. In a devise, however, they seem to be of the same import. Shep. Touch. 447; 2 Fonbl. Eq. 835.

CHATTEL INTEREST.
An interest in corporeal hereditaments less than a freehold. 2 Kent, Comm. 342.

CHATTEL MORTGAGE.
An instrument of sale of personalty conveying the title of the property to the mortgagee with terms of defeasance; and, if the terms of redemption are not complied with, then, at common law, the title becomes absolute in the mortgagee.

A transfer of personal property as security for a debt or obligation in such form that, upon failure of the mortgagor to comply with the terms of the contract, the title to the property will be in the mortgagee. Thomas, Mortg. 427.

An absolute pledge, to become an absolute interest if not redeemed at a fixed time. 2 Caines Cas. 200, per Kent, Ch.

A conditional sale of a chattel as security for the payment of a debt or the performance of some other obligation. Jones, Chat. Mortg. § 1.

A chattel mortgage is a conditional transfer or conveyance of the property itself. The chief distinctions between it and a pledge are that in the latter the title, even after condition broken, does not pass to the pledgee, who has only a lien on the property, but remains in the pledgeor, who has the right to redeem the property at any time before its sale. Besides, the possession of the property must, in all cases, accompany the pledge, and, at a sale thereof by the pledgee to satisfy his demand, he cannot become the purchaser; while by a chattel mortgage the title of the mortgagee becomes absolute at law, on the default of the mortgagor, and it is not essential to the validity of the instrument that possession of the property should be delivered, and, on the foreclosure of the mortgage, the mortgagee is at liberty to become the purchaser. 36 Cal. 414, 428, 441.

The material distinction between a pledge and a mortgage of chattels is that a mortgage is a conveyance of the legal title upon condition, and it becomes absolute in law if not redeemed by a given time; a pledge is a deposit of goods, redeemable on certain terms, either with or without a fixed period for redemption. In pledge, the general property does not pass, as in the case of mortgage, and the pawnee has only a special property in the thing deposited. The pawnee must choose between two remedies,—a bill in chancery for a judicial sale under a decree of foreclosure, or a sale without judicial process, on the refusal of the debtor to redeem, after reasonable notice to do so. 5 Blackf. 320. See, also, 3 Blackf. 309.

In a *conditional sale* the purchaser has merely a right to repurchase, and no debt or obligation exists on the part of the vendor; this distinguishes such a sale from a mortgage. 40 Miss. 462; 4 Daly, 77.

CHAUD-MEDLEY.
A homicide committed in the heat of an affray and while under the influence of passion; it is thus distinguished from *chance-medley*, which is the killing of a man in a casual affray in self-defense. 4 Bl. Comm. 184. See 1 Russ. Crimes, 660.

CHAUMPERT.
A kind of tenure mentioned in a patent of 35 Edw. III. Cowell; Blount.

CHAUNTRY RENTS.
Money paid to the crown by the servants or purchasers of chauntry-lands. See CHANTRY.

CHEAT.
Swindling; defrauding. "Deceitful practices in defrauding or *endeavoring* to defraud another of his known right, by some *willful device*, contrary to the plain rules of common honesty." Hawk. P. C. b. 2, c. 23, § 1. "The fraudulent obtaining the property of another by any deceitful and illegal practice or token (short of felony) which affects or may affect the public." Steph. Crim. Law, 93.

Cheats, punishable at common law, are such cheats (not amounting to felony) as are effected by deceitful or illegal symbols or tokens which may affect the public at large, and against which common prudence could not have guarded. 2 Whart. Crim. Law, § 1116; 2 East, P. C. 818.

CHEATERS, or ESCHEATORS,
were officers appointed to look after the king's escheats, a duty which gave them great opportunities of fraud and oppression, and in consequence many complaints were made of their misconduct. Hence it seems that a *cheater* came to signify a fraudulent person, and thence the verb to *cheat* was derived. Wharton.

CHECK, v.
To control or restrain; to hold within bounds. To verify or audit. Particularly used with reference to the control or supervision of one department, bureau, or office over another.

CHECK, n.
A draft or order upon a bank or banking-house, purporting to be drawn upon a deposit of funds, for the payment at all events of a certain sum of money to a certain person therein named, or to him or his order, or to bearer, and payable in-

stantly 'on demand.   2 Daniel, Neg. Inst. § 1566.

A check is a bill of exchange drawn upon a bank or banker, or a person described as such upon the face thereof, and payable on demand, without interest.   Civil Code Cal. § 3254; Civil Code Dak. § 1933.

A check differs from an ordinary bill of exchange in the following particulars: (1) It is drawn on a bank or bankers, and is payable immediately on presentment, without any days of grace. (2) It is payable immediately on presentment, and no acceptance as distinct from payment is required. (3) By its terms it is supposed to be drawn upon a previous deposit of funds, and is an absolute appropriation of so much money in the hands of the bankers to the holder of the check, to remain there until called for, and cannot after notice be withdrawn by the drawer. 2 Story, 502; 8 Bush, 357.

CHECK-BOOK. A book containing blank checks on a particular bank or banker, with an inner margin, called a "stub," on which to note the number of each check, its amount and date, and the payee's name, and a memorandum of the balance in bank.

CHECK-ROLL. In English law. A list or book, containing the names of such as are attendants on, or in the pay of, the queen or other great personages, as their household servants.

CHECKER. The old Scotch form of exchequer.

CHEFE. In Anglo-Norman law. Were or weregild; the price of the head or person, (*capitis pretium.*)

CHEMERAGE. In old French law. The privilege or perogative of the eldest. A provincial term derived from *chemier*, (*q. v.*) Guyot, Inst.

CHEMIER. In old French law. The eldest born. A term used in Poitou and other places. Guyot, Inst.

CHEMIN. The road wherein every man goes; the king's highway.

CHEMIS. In old Scotch law. A chief dwelling or mansion house.

CHEVAGE. A sum of money paid by villeins to their lords in acknowledgment of their bondage.

Chevage seems also to have been used for a sum of money yearly given to a man of power for his countenance and protection as a chief or leader. Termes de la Ley; Cowell.

CHEVANTIA. In old records. A loan or advance of money upon credit. Cowell.

CHEVISANCE. An agreement or composition; an end or order set down between a creditor or debtor; an indirect gain in point of usury, etc.; also an unlawful bargain or contract. Wharton.

CHEVITIÆ. In old records. Pieces of ground, or *heads* at the end of plowed lands. Cowell.

CHEZÉ. A homestead or homesfall which is accessory to a house.

CHICANE. Swindling; shrewd cunning. The use of tricks and artifice.

CHIEF. Principal; leading; head; eminent in power or importance; the most important or valuable of several.

Declaration in chief is a declaration for the principal cause of action. 1 Tidd, Pr. 419.

Examination in chief is the first examination of a witness by the party who produces him. 1 Greenl. Ev. § 445.

CHIEF BARON. The presiding judge of the English court of exchequer; answering to the chief justice of other courts. 3 Bl. Comm. 44; 3 Steph. Comm. 401.

CHIEF CLERK. The principal clerical officer of a bureau or department, who is generally charged, subject to the direction of his superior officer, with the superintendence of the administration of the business of the office.

CHIEF JUDGE. The judge of the London bankruptcy court is so called.

CHIEF JUSTICE. The presiding, eldest, or principal judge of a court of justice.

CHIEF JUSTICE OF ENGLAND. The presiding judge in the queen's bench division of the high court of justice, and, in the absence of the lord chancellor, president of the high court, and also an *ex officio* judge of the court of appeals. The full title is "Lord Chief Justice of England."

CHIEF JUSTICE OF THE COMMON PLEAS. In England. The presiding judge in the court of common pleas, and afterwards in the common pleas division of the high court of justice, and one of the *ex officio* judges of the high court of appeal.

CHIEF JUSTICIAR. In old English law. A high judicial officer and special magistrate, who presided over the *aula regis* of the Norman kings, and who was also the principal minister of state, the second man in the kingdom, and, by virtue of his office, guardian of the realm in the king's absence. 3 Bl. Comm. 38.

CHIEF LORD. The immediate lord of the fee, to whom the tenants were directly and personally responsible.

CHIEF PLEDGE. The borsholder, or chief of the borough. Spelman.

CHIEF RENTS. In English law. Were the annual payments of freeholders of manors; and were also called "quit-rents," because by paying them the tenant was freed from all other rents or services. 2 Bl. Comm. 42.

CHIEF, TENANT IN. In English feudal law. All the land in the kingdom was supposed to be holden mediately or immediately of the king, who was styled the "Lord Paramount," or "Lord Above All;" and those that held immediately under him, in right of his crown and dignity, were called his tenants "*in capite*" or "in chief," which was the most honorable species of tenure, but at the same time subjected the tenant to greater and more burdensome services than inferior tenures did. Brown.

CHIEFRIE. In feudal law. A small rent paid to the lord paramount.

CHILD. This word has two meanings in law: (1) In the law of the domestic relations, and as to descent and distribution, it is used strictly as the correlative of "parent," and means a son or daughter considered as in relation with the father or mother. (2) In the law of negligence, and in laws for the protection of children, etc., it is used as the opposite of "adult," and means the young of the human species, (generally under the age of puberty,) without any reference to parentage and without distinction of sex.

CHILDREN. Offspring; progeny. Legitimate offspring; children born in wedlock. 7 Ves. 458; 5 Scott, N. R. 990.

The general rule is that "children," in a bequest or devise, means legitimate children. Under a devise or bequest to children, as a class, natural children are not included, unless the testator's intention to include them is manifest, either by express designation or necessary implication. 14 N. J. Eq. 159; 2 Paige, 11.

In deeds, the word "children" signifies the immediate descendants of a person, in the ordinary sense of the word, as contradistinguished from *issue;* unless there be some accompanying expressions, evidencing that the word is used in an enlarged sense. Lewis, Perp. 196.

In wills, where greater latitude of construction is allowed, in order to effect the obvious intention of the testator, the meaning of the word has sometimes been extended, so as to include *grandchildren,* and it has been held to be synonymous with *issue.* Lewis, Perp. 195, 196; 2 Crabb, Real Prop. pp. 38, 39, §§ 988, 989; 4 Kent, Comm. 345, 346, note.

The word "heirs," in its natural signification, is a word of limitation; and it is presumed to be used in that sense, unless a contrary intention appears. But the term "children," in its natural sense, is a word of purchase, and is to be taken to have been used as such, unless there are other expressions in the will showing that the testator intended to use it as a word of limitation only. 4 Paige, 293; 3 Wend. 503.

In the natural and primary sense of the word "children," it implies immediate offspring, and, in its legal acceptation, is not a word of limitation, unless it is absolutely necessary so to construe it in order to give effect to the testator's intention. 39 Ala. 24.

"Children" is ordinarily a word of description, limited to persons standing in the same relation, and has the same effect as if all the names were given; but heirs, in the absence of controlling or explanatory words, includes more remote descendants, and is to be applied *per stirpes.* 14 Allen, 204.

CHILDWIT. In Saxon law. The right which a lord had of taking a fine of his bondwoman gotten with child without his license. Termes de la Ley; Cowell.

CHILTERN HUNDREDS. In English law. The stewardship of the Chiltern Hundreds is a nominal office in the gift of the crown, usually accepted by members of the house of commons desirous of vacating their seats. By law a member once duly elected to parliament is compelled to discharge the duties of the trust conferred upon him, and is not enabled at will to resign it. But by statute, if any member accepts any office of profit from the crown, (except officers in the army or navy accepting a new commission,) his seat is vacated. If, therefore, any member wishes to retire from the representation of the county or borough by which he was sent to parliament, he applies to the lords of the treasury for the stewardship of one of the Chiltern Hundreds, which having received, and thereby accomplished his purpose, he again resigns the office. Brown.

CHIMIN. In old English law. A road, way, highway. It is either the queen's highway (*chiminus reginæ*) or a private way. The first is that over which the subjects of the realm, and all others under the protection of the crown, have free liberty to pass, though the property in the soil itself belong to some private individual; the last is that in which one person or more have liberty to pass over the land of another, by prescription or charter. Wharton.

CHIMINAGE. A toll for passing on a way through a forest; called in the civil law *"pedagium."* Cowell.

CHIMINUS. The way by which the king and all his subjects and all under his protection have a right to pass, though the property of the soil of each side where the way lieth may belong to a private man. Cowell.

CHIMNEY MONEY, or HEARTH MONEY. A tax upon chimneys or hearths; an ancient tax or duty upon houses in England, now repealed.

CHIPPINGAVEL. In old English law. A tax upon trade; a toll imposed upon traffic, or upon goods brought to a place to be sold.

CHIRGEMOT, CHIRCHGEMOT. In Saxon law. An ecclesiastical assembly or court. Spelman. A synod or meeting in a church or vestry. 4 Inst. 321.

CHIROGRAPH. In old English law. A deed or indenture; also the last part of a fine of land.

An instrument of gift or conveyance attested by the subscription and crosses of the witnesses, which was in Saxon times called *"chirographum,"* and which, being somewhat changed in form and manner by the Normans, was by them styled *"charta."* Anciently when they made a chirograph or deed which required a counterpart, as we call it, they engrossed it twice upon one piece of parchment contrariwise, leaving a space between, in which they wrote in capital letters the word "chirograph," and then cut the parchment in two through the middle of the word, giving a part to each party. Cowell.

In Scotch law. A written voucher for a debt. Bell.

In civil and canon law. An instrument written out and subscribed by the hand of the party who made it, whether the king or a private person. Cowell.

CHIROGRAPHA. In Roman law. Writings emanating from a single party, the debtor.

CHIROGRAPHER OF FINES. In English law. The title of the officer of the common pleas who engrossed fines in that court so as to be acknowledged into a perpetual record. Cowell.

CHIROGRAPHUM. In Roman law. A handwriting; that which was written with

a person's own hand. An obligation which a person wrote or subscribed with his own hand; an acknowledgment of debt, as of money received, with a promise to repay.

An evidence or voucher of debt; a security for debt. Dig. 26, 7, 57, pr.

A right of action for debt.

Chirographum apud debitorem repertum præsumitur solutum. An evidence of debt found in the debtor's possession is presumed to be paid. Halk. Max. 20; Bell, Dict.

Chirographum non extans presumitur solutum. An evidence of debt not existing is presumed to have been discharged. Tray. Lat. Max. 73.

CHIRURGEON. The ancient denomination of a surgeon.

CHIVALRY. In feudal law. Knight-service. Tenure in chivalry was the same as tenure by knight-service. 2 Bl. Comm. 61, 62.

CHIVALRY, COURT OF. In English law. The name of a court anciently held as a court of honor merely, before the earl-marshal, and as a criminal court before the lord high constable, jointly with the earl-marshal. It had jurisdiction as to contracts and other matters touching deeds of arms or war, as well as pleas of life or member. It also corrected encroachments in matters of coat-armor, precedency, and other distinctions of families. It is now grown entirely out of use, on account of the feebleness of its jurisdiction and want of power to enforce its judgments, as it could neither fine nor imprison, not being a court of record. 3 Bl. Comm. 68; 4 Broom. & H. Comm. 360, note.

CHOP-CHURCH. A word mentioned in 9 Hen. VI. c. 65, by the sense of which it was in those days a kind of trade, and by the judges declared to be lawful. But Brooke, in his abridgment, says it was only permissible by law. It was, without doubt, a nickname given to those who used to change benefices, as to "chop and change" is a common expression. Jacob.

CHOPS. The mouth of a harbor. Pub. St. Mass. 1882, p. 1288.

CHORAL. In ancient times a person admitted to sit and worship in the choir; a chorister.

CHOREPISCOPUS. In old European law. A rural bishop, or bishop's vicar. Spelman; Cowell.

CHOSE. A thing; an article of property. A chose is a chattel personal, (Williams, Pers. Prop. 4,) and is either in possession or in action.

CHOSE IN ACTION. A right to personal things of which the owner has not the possession, but merely a right of action for their possession. 2 Bl. Comm. 389, 397; 1 Chit. Pr. 99.

A right to receive or recover a debt, demand, or damages on a cause of action *ex contractu*, or for a tort connected with contract, but which cannot be made available without recourse to an action.

Personalty to which the owner has a right of possession in future, or a right of immediate possession, wrongfully withheld, is termed by the law a "chose in action." Code Ga. 1882, § 2239.

Chose in action is a phrase which is sometimes used to signify a right of bringing an action, and, at others, the thing itself which forms the subject-matter of that right, or with regard to which that right is exercised; but it more properly includes the idea both of the thing itself and of the right of action as annexed to it. Thus, when it is said that a debt is a chose in action, the phrase conveys the idea, not only of the thing itself, *i. e.*, the debt, but also of the right of action or of recovery possessed by the person to whom the debt is due. When it is said that a chose in action cannot be assigned, it means that a thing to which a right of action is annexed cannot be transferred to another, together with such right. Brown.

A chose in action is any right to damages, whether arising from the commission of a tort, the omission of a duty, or the breach of a contract. 4 Ala. 350; 8 Port. 36.

CHOSE IN POSSESSION. A thing in possession, as distinguished from a thing in action. See CHOSE IN ACTION. Taxes and customs, if paid, are a chose in possession; if unpaid, a chose in action. 2 Bl. Comm. 408.

CHOSE LOCAL. A local thing; a thing annexed to a place, as a mill. Kitchin, fol. 18; Cowell; Blount.

CHOSE TRANSITORY. A thing which is movable, and may be taken away or carried from place to place. Cowell; Blount.

CHOSEN FREEHOLDERS. Under the municipal organization of the state of New Jersey, each county has a board of officers, called by this name, composed of representatives from the cities and townships within its limits, and charged with administering the revenues of the county. They correspond to the "county commissioners" or "supervisors" in other states.

CHOUT. In Hindu law. A fourth, a fourth part of the sum in litigation. The "Mahratta chout" is a fourth of the revenues exacted as tribute by the Mahrattas.

CHREMATISTICS. The science of wealth.

CHRENECRUDA. Under the Salic law. This was a ceremony performed by a person who was too poor to pay his debt or fine, whereby he applied to a rich relative to pay it for him. It consisted (after certain preliminaries) in throwing green herbs upon the party, the effect of which was to bind him to pay the whole demand.

CHRISTIAN. Pertaining to Jesus Christ or the religion founded by him; professing Christianity. The adjective is also used in senses more remote from its original meaning. Thus a "court Christian" is an ecclesiastical court; a "Christian name" is that conferred upon a person at baptism into the Christian church. As a noun, it signifies one who accepts and professes to live by the doctrines and principles of the Christian religion.

CHRISTIAN NAME. The baptismal name distinct from the surname. It has been said from the bench that a Christian name may consist of a single letter. Wharton.

CHRISTIANITATIS CURIA. The court Christian. An ecclesiastical court, as opposed to a civil or lay tribunal. Cowell.

CHRISTIANITY. The religion founded and established by Jesus Christ.

Christianity has been judicially declared to be a part of the common law.

CHRISTMAS-DAY. A festival of the Christian church, observed on the 25th of December, in memory of the birth of Jesus Christ.

CHRYSOLOGY. That branch of the science of political economy which relates to the production of wealth.

CHURCH. In its most general sense, the religious society founded and established by Jesus Christ, to receive, preserve, and propagate his doctrines and ordinances.

A body or community of Christians, united under one form of government by the profession of the same faith, and the observance of the same ritual and ceremonies.

The term may denote either a society of persons who, professing Christianity, hold certain doctrines or observances which differentiate them from other like groups, and who use a common discipline, or the building in which such persons habitually assemble for public worship.

The body of communicants gathered into church order, according to established usage in any town, parish, precinct, or religious society, established according to law, and actually connected and associated therewith for religious purposes, for the time being, is to be regarded as the church of such society, as to all questions of property depending upon that relation. 10 Pick. 193. See, also, 3 Me. 247.

A congregational church is a voluntary association of Christians united for discipline and worship, connected with, and forming a part of, some religious society, having a legal existence. 3 Me. 248.

In English ecclesiastical law. An institution established by the law of the land in reference to religion. 3 Steph. Comm. 54. The word "church" is said to mean, in strictness, not the material fabric, but the cure of souls and the right of tithes. 1 Mod. 201.

CHURCH BUILDING ACTS. Statutes passed in England in and since the year 1818, with the object of extending the accommodation afforded by the national church, so as to make it more commensurate with the wants of the people. 3 Steph. Comm. 152–164.

CHURCH DISCIPLINE ACT. The statute 3 & 4 Vict. c. 86, containing regulations for trying clerks in holy orders charged with offenses against ecclesiastical law, and for enforcing sentences pronounced in such cases. Phillim. Ecc. Law, 1314.

CHURCH OF ENGLAND. The Church of England is a distinct branch of Christ's church, and is also an institution of the state, (see the first clause of *Magna Charta*,) of which the sovereign is the supreme head by act of parliament, (26 Hen. VIII. c. 1,) but in what sense is not agreed. The sovereign must be a member of the church, and every subject is in theory a member. Wharton.

CHURCH RATE. In English law. A sum assessed for the repair of parochial churches by the representatives of the parishioners in vestry assembled.

CHURCH REEVE. A church warden; an overseer of a church. Now obsolete. Cowell.

CHURCH-SCOT. In old English law. Customary obligations paid to the parish priest; from which duties the religious some-

times purchased an exemption for themselves and their tenants.

CHURCH WARDENS. A species of ecclesiastical officers who are intrusted with the care and guardianship of the church building and property. These, with the rector and vestry, represent the parish in its corporate capacity.

CHURCHESSET. In old English law. A certain portion or measure of wheat, anciently paid to the church on St. Martin's day; and which, according to Fleta, was paid as well in the time of the Britons as of the English. Fleta, lib. 1, c. 47, § 28.

CHURCHYARD. See CEMETERY.

CHURL. In Saxon law. A freeman of inferior rank, chiefly employed in husbandry. 1 Reeve, Eng. Law, 5. A tenant at will of free condition, who held land from a thane, on condition of rents and services. Cowell. See CEORL.

CI. Fr. So; here. *Ci Dieu vous eyde*, so help you God. *Ci devant*, heretofore. *Ci bien*, as well.

CIBARIA. Lat. In the civil law. Food; victuals. Dig. 34, 1.

CINQUE PORTS. Five (now seven) ports or havens on the south-east coast of England, towards France, formerly esteemed the most important in the kingdom. They are Dover, Sandwich, Romney, Hastings, and Hythe, to which Winchelsea and Rye have been since added. They had similar franchises, in some respects, with the counties palatine, and particularly an exclusive jurisdiction, (before the mayor and jurats, corresponding to aldermen, of the ports,) in which the king's ordinary writ did not run. 3 Bl. Comm. 79.

The 18 & 19 Vict. c. 48, (amended by 20 & 21 Vict. c. 1,) abolishes all jurisdiction and authority of the lord warden of the Cinque Ports and constable of Dover Castle, in or in relation to the administration of justice in actions, suits, or other civil proceedings at law or in equity.

CIPPI. An old English law term for the stocks, an instrument in which the wrists or ankles of petty offenders were confined.

CIRCADA. A tribute anciently paid to the bishop or archbishop for visiting churches. Du Fresne.

CIRCAR. In Hindu law. Head of affairs; the state or government; a grand division of a province; a headman. A name

D

E

F

G

H

I

J

K

L

M

used by Europeans in Bengal to denote the Hindu writer and accountant employed by themselves, or in the public offices. Wharton.

CIRCUIT. A division of the country, appointed for a particular judge to visit for the trial of causes or for the administration of justice. Bouvier.

Circuits, as the term is used in England, may be otherwise defined to be *the periodical progresses of the judges* of the superior courts of common law, through the several counties of England and Wales, for the purpose of administering civil and criminal justice.

CIRCUIT COURTS. The name of a system of courts of the United States, invested with general original jurisdiction of such matters and causes as are of Federal cognizance, except the matters specially delegated to the district courts.

The United States circuit courts are held by one of the justices of the supreme court appointed for the circuit, (and bearing the name, in that capacity, of *circuit justice,*) together with the circuit judge and the district judge of the district in which they are held. Their business is not only the supervision of trials of issues in fact, but the hearing of causes as a court in *banc;* and they have equity as well as common-law jurisdiction, together with appellate jurisdiction from the decrees and judgments of the district courts. 1 Kent, Comm. 301–303.

In several of the states, *circuit court* is the name given to a tribunal, the territorial jurisdiction of which comprises several counties or districts, and whose sessions are held in such counties or districts alternately. These courts usually have general original jurisdiction.

CIRCUIT COURTS OF APPEALS. A system of courts of the United States (one in each circuit) created by act of congress of March 3, 1891, composed of the circuit justice, the circuit judge, and an additional circuit judge appointed for each such court, and having appellate jurisdiction from the circuit and district courts except in certain specified classes of cases.

CIRCUIT PAPER. In English practice. A paper containing a statement of the time and place at which the several assises will be held, and other statistical information connected with the assises. Holthouse.

Circuitus est evitandus; et boni judicis est lites dirimere, ne lis ex lite oriatur. 5 Coke, 31. Circuity is to be avoided; and it is the duty of a good judge to deter-

mine litigations, lest one lawsuit arise out of another.

CIRCUITY OF ACTION. This occurs where a litigant, by a complex, indirect, or roundabout course of legal proceeding, makes two or more actions necessary, in order to effect that adjustment of rights between all the parties concerned in the transaction which, by a more direct course, might have been accomplished in a single suit.

CIRCULAR NOTES. Similar instruments to "letters of credit." They are drawn by resident bankers upon their foreign correspondents, in favor of persons traveling abroad. The correspondents must be satisfied of the identity of the applicant, before payment; and the requisite proof of such identity is usually furnished, upon the applicant's producing a letter with his signature, by a comparison of the signatures. Brown.

CIRCULATING MEDIUM. This term is more comprehensive than the term "money," as it is the medium of exchanges, or purchases and sales, whether it be gold or silver coin or any other article.

CIRCUMDUCTION. In Scotch law. A closing of the period for lodging papers, or doing any other act required in a cause. Paters. Comp.

CIRCUMDUCTION OF THE TERM. In Scotch practice. The sentence of a judge, declaring the time elapsed within which a proof ought to have been led, and precluding the party from bringing forward any further evidence. Bell.

CIRCUMSPECTE AGATIS. The title of a statute passed 13 Edw. I., A. D. 1285, and so called from the initial words of it, the object of which was to ascertain the boundaries of ecclesiastical jurisdiction in some particulars, or, in other words, to regulate the jurisdiction of the ecclesiastical and temporal courts. 2 Reeve, Eng. Law, 215, 216.

CIRCUMSTANCES. A principal fact or event being the object of investigation, the *circumstances* are the related or accessory facts or occurrences which attend upon it, which closely precede or follow it, which surround and accompany it, which depend upon it, or which support or qualify it.

The terms "circumstance" and "fact" are, in many applications, synonymous; but the true distinction of a circumstance is its *relative* character. "Any fact may be a circumstance with reference to any other fact." 1 Benth. Jud. Evid. 42, note; Id. 142.

Thrift, integrity, good repute, business capacity, and stability of character, for example, are "circumstances" which may be very properly considered in determining the question of "adequate security." 5 Redf. Sur. 600.

CIRCUMSTANTIAL EVIDENCE.

Evidence directed to the attending circumstances; evidence which inferentially proves the principal fact by establishing a condition of surrounding and limiting circumstances, whose existence is a premise from which the existence of the principal fact may be concluded by necessary laws of reasoning.

When the existence of any fact is attested by witnesses, as having come under the cognizance of their senses, or is stated in documents, the genuineness and veracity of which there seems no reason to question, the evidence of that fact is said to be direct or positive. When, on the contrary, the existence of the principal fact is only inferred from one or more circumstances which have been established directly, the evidence is said to be circumstantial. And when the existence of the principal fact does not follow from the evidentiary facts as a necessary consequence of the law of nature, but is deduced from them by a process of probable reasoning, the evidence and proof are said to be presumptive. Best, Pres. 246; Id. 12.

All presumptive evidence is circumstantial, because necessarily derived from or made up of *circumstances*, but all circumstantial evidence is not presumptive, that is, it does not operate in the way of *presumption*, being sometimes of a higher grade, and leading to necessary conclusions, instead of probable ones. Burrill.

CIRCUMSTANTIBUS, TALES DE.
See TALES.

CIRCUMVENTION.
In Scotch law. Any act of fraud whereby a person is reduced to a deed by decreet. It has the same sense in the civil law. Dig. 50, 17, 49, 155.

CIRIC-BRYCE.
In old English law. Any violation of the privileges of a church.

CIRIC SCEAT.
In old English law. Church-scot, or shot; an ecclesiastical due, payable on the day of St. Martin, consisting chiefly of corn.

CIRLISCUS.
A ceorl, (*q. v.*)

CISTA.
A box or chest for the deposit of charters, deeds, and things of value.

CITACION.
In Spanish law. Citation; summons; an order of a court requiring a person against whom a suit has been brought to appear and defend within a given time.

CITATIO.
A citation or summons to court.

CITATIO AD REASSUMENDAM CAUSAM.
A summons to take up the cause. A process, in the civil law, which issued when one of the parties to a suit died before its determination, for the plaintiff against the defendant's heir, or for the plaintiff's heir against the defendant, as the case might be; analogous to a modern bill of revivor.

Citatio est de juri naturali. A summons is by natural right. Cases in Banco Regis Wm. III. 453.

CITATION.
In practice. A writ issued out of a court of competent jurisdiction, commanding a person therein named to appear on a day named and do something therein mentioned, or show cause why he should not. Proc. Prac.

The act by which a person is so summoned or cited.

It is used in this sense, in American law, in the practice upon writs of error from the United States supreme court, and in the proceedings of courts of probate in many of the states.

This is also the name of the process used in the English ecclesiastical, probate, and divorce courts to call the defendant or respondent before them. 3 Bl. Comm. 100; 3 Steph. Comm. 720.

In Scotch practice. The calling of a party to an action done by an officer of the court under a proper warrant.

The service of a writ or bill of summons. Paters. Comp.

CITATION OF AUTHORITIES.
The reading of, or reference to, legal authorities and precedents, (such as constitutions, statutes, reported cases, and elementary treatises,) in arguments to courts, or in legal text-books, to establish or fortify the propositions advanced.

Citationes non concedantur priusquam exprimatur super qua re fieri debet citatio. Citations should not be granted before it is stated about what matter the citation is to be made. A maxim of ecclesiastical law. 12 Coke, 44.

CITE.
L. Fr. City; a city. *Cite de Loundr'*, city of London.

CITE.
To summon; to command the presence of a person; to notify a person of legal proceedings against him and require his appearance thereto.

To read or refer to legal authorities, in an argument to a court or elsewhere, in support of propositions of law sought to be established.

CITIZEN. In general. A member of a free city or jural society, (*civitas*,) possessing all the rights and privileges which can be enjoyed by any person under its constitution and government, and subject to the corresponding duties.

In American law. One who, under the constitution and laws of the United States, has a right to vote for civil officers, and himself is qualified to fill elective offices.

One of the sovereign people. A constituent member of the sovereignty, synonymous with the people. 19 How. 404.

A member of the civil state entitled to all its privileges. Cooley, Const. Law, 77.

The term "citizen" has come to us derived from antiquity. It appears to have been used in the Roman government to designate a person who had the freedom of the city, and the right to exercise all political and civil privileges of the government. There was also, at Rome, a partial citizenship, including civil, but not political, rights. Complete citizenship embraced both. 15 Ind. 451.

All persons born or naturalized in the United States, and subject to the jurisdiction thereof, are citizens of the United States and of the state wherein they reside. Amend. XIV. Const. U. S.

There is in our political system a government of each of the several states, and a government of the United States. Each is distinct from the others, and has citizens of its own, who owe it allegiance, and whose rights, within its jurisdiction, it must protect. The same person may be at the same time a citizen of the United States and a citizen of a state; but his rights of citizenship under one of these governments will be different from those he has under the other. The government of the United States, although it is, within the scope of its powers, supreme and beyond the states, can neither grant nor secure to its citizens rights or privileges which are not expressly or by implication placed under its jurisdiction. All that cannot be so granted or secured are left to the exclusive protection of the states. 92 U. S. 542.

"Citizen" and "inhabitant" are not synonymous. One may be a citizen of a state without being an inhabitant, or an inhabitant without being a citizen. 4 Har. (Del.) 383.

"Citizen" is sometimes used as synonymous with "resident;" as in a statute authorizing funds to be distributed among the religious societies of a township, proportionally to the number of their members who are citizens of the township. 11 Ohio, 24.

In English law. An inhabitant of a city. 1 Rolle, 138. The representative of a city, in parliament. 1 Bl. Comm. 174. It will be perceived that, in the English usage, the word adheres closely to its original meaning, as shown by its derivation, (*civis*, a free inhabitant of a city.) When it is designed to designate an inhabitant of the *country*, or one amenable to the laws of the nation, "subject" is the word there employed.

CITIZENSHIP. The *status* of being a citizen, (*q. v.*)

CITY. In England. An incorporated town or borough which is or has been the see of a bishop. Co. Litt. 108; 1 Bl. Comm. 114; Cowell.

A large town incorporated with certain privileges. The inhabitants of a city. The citizens. Worcester.

In America. A city is a municipal corporation of a larger class, the distinctive feature of whose organization is its government by a chief executive (usually called "mayor") and a legislative body, composed of representatives of the citizens, (usually called a "council" or "board of aldermen,") and other officers having special functions.

CITY OF LONDON COURT. A court having a local jurisdiction within the city of London. It is to all intents and purposes a county court, having the same jurisdiction and procedure.

CIVIL. In its original sense, this word means pertaining or appropriate to a member of a *civitas* or free political community; natural or proper to a *citizen*. Also, relating to the community, or to the policy and government of the citizens and subjects of a state.

In the language of the law, it has various significations. In contradistinction to *barbarous* or *savage*, it indicates a state of society reduced to order and regular government; thus, we speak of civil life, civil society, civil government, and civil liberty. In contradistinction to *criminal*, it indicates the private rights and remedies of men, as members of the community, in contrast to those which are public and relate to the government; thus, we speak of civil process and criminal process, civil jurisdiction and criminal jurisdiction.

It is also used in contradistinction to *military* or *ecclesiastical*, to *natural* or *foreign*; thus, we speak of a civil station, as opposed to a military or an ecclesiastical station; a civil death, as opposed to a natural death; a civil war, as opposed to a foreign war. Story, Const. § 791.

CIVIL ACTION. In the civil law. A personal action which is instituted to compel payment, or the doing some other thing which is purely civil.

At common law. As distinguished from a *criminal* action, it is one which seeks the establishment, recovery, or redress of private and civil rights.

Civil suits relate to and affect, as to the parties against whom they are brought, only individual rights which are within their individual control, and which they may part with at their pleasure. The design of such suits is the enforcement of merely private obligations and duties. Criminal prosecutions, on the other hand, involve public wrongs, or a breach and violation of public rights and duties, which affect the whole community, considered as such in its social and aggregate capacity. The end they have in view is the prevention of similar offenses, not atonement or expiation for crime committed. 18 N. Y. 128.

Civil cases are those which involve disputes or contests between man and man, and which only terminate in the adjustment of the rights of plaintiffs and defendants. They include all cases which cannot legally be denominated "criminal cases." T. U. P. Charlt. 175.

In code practice. A civil action is a proceeding in a court of justice in which one party, known as the "plaintiff," demands against another party, known as the "defendant," the enforcement or protection of a private right, or the prevention or redress of a private wrong. It may also be brought for the recovery of a penalty or forfeiture. Rev. Code Iowa 1880, § 2505.

The distinction between actions at law and suits in equity, and the forms of all such actions and suits, heretofore existing, is abolished; and there shall be in this state, hereafter, but one form of action for the enforcement or protection of private rights and the redress of private wrongs, which shall be denominated a "civil action." Code N.Y. § 69.

CIVIL BILL COURT. A tribunal in Ireland with a jurisdiction analogous to that of the county courts in England. The judge of it is also chairman of quarter sessions, (where the jurisdiction is more extensive than in England,) and performs the duty of revising barrister. Wharton.

CIVIL COMMOTION. An insurrection of the people for general purposes, though it may not amount to rebellion where there is a usurped power. 2 Marsh. Ins. 793.

CIVIL CORPORATIONS. An old English term for all lay corporations which are not eleemosynary or charitable.

Civil corporations are those which relate to temporal police; such are the corporations of the cities, the companies for the advancement of commerce and agriculture, literary societies, colleges or universities founded for the instruction of youth, and the like. Re-

ligious corporations are those whose establishment relates only to religion; such are the congregations of the different religious persuasions. Civil Code La. art. 431.

CIVIL DAMAGE ACTS. Acts passed in many of the United States which provide an action for damages against a vendor of intoxicating liquors, (and, in some cases, against his lessor,) on behalf of the wife or family of a person who has sustained injuries by reason of his intoxication.

CIVIL DEATH. That change in a person's legal and civil condition which deprives him of civic rights and juridical capacities and qualifications, as natural death extinguishes his natural condition. It follows as a consequence of being attainted of treason or felony, in English law, and anciently of entering a monastery or abjuring the realm. The person in this condition is said to be *civiliter mortuus*, civilly dead, or dead in law.

CIVIL INJURY. Injuries to person or property, resulting from a breach of contract, delict, or criminal offense, which may be redressed by means of a civil action.

CIVIL LAW. The "Roman Law" and the "Civil Law" are convertible phrases, meaning the same system of jurisprudence; it is now frequently denominated the "Roman Civil Law."

The word "civil," as applied to the laws in force in Louisiana, before the adoption of the Civil Code, is not used in contradistinction to the word "criminal," but must be restricted to the Roman law. It is used in contradistinction to the laws of England and those of the respective states. 5 La. 493.

1. The system of jurisprudence held and administered in the Roman empire, particularly as set forth in the compilation of Justinian and his successors,—comprising the Institutes, Code, Digest, and Novels, and collectively denominated the "*Corpus Juris Civilis*,"—as distinguished from the common law of England and the canon law.

2. That rule of action which every particular nation, commonwealth, or city has established peculiarly for itself; more properly called "municipal" law, to distinguish it from the "law of nature," and from international law.

The law which a people enacts is called the "civil law" of that people, but that law which natural reason appoints for all mankind is called the "law of nations," because all nations use it. Bowyer, Mod. Civil Law, 19.

3. That division of municipal law which is occupied with the exposition and enforce-

ment of *civil rights*, as distinguished from *criminal law*.

CIVIL LIBERTY. The liberty of a member of society, being a man's natural liberty, so far restrained by human laws (and no further) as is necessary and expedient for the general advantage of the public. 1 Bl. Comm. 125; 2 Steph. Comm. 487. The power of doing whatever the laws permit. 1 Bl. Comm. 6; Inst. 1, 3, 1. See LIBERTY.

CIVIL LIST. In English public law. An annual sum granted by parliament, at the commencement of each reign, for the expense of the royal household and establishment, as distinguished from the general exigencies of the state, being a provision made for the crown out of the taxes in lieu of its proper patrimony, and in consideration of the assignment of that patrimony to the public use. 2 Steph. Comm. 591; 1 Bl. Comm. 332.

CIVIL OBLIGATION. An obligation binding in law, and enforceable in a court of justice. Poth. Obl. 173, 191.

CIVIL OFFICER. Any officer of the United States who holds his appointment under the national government, whether his duties are executive or judicial, in the highest or the lowest departments of the government, with the exception of officers of the army and navy. 1 Story, Const. § 792.

CIVIL REMEDY. The remedy afforded by law to a private person in the civil courts, in so far as his private and individual rights have been injured by a delict or crime; as distinguished from the remedy by criminal prosecution for the injury to the rights of the public.

CIVIL RESPONSIBILITY. The liability to be called upon to respond to an action at law for an injury caused by a delict or crime, as opposed to criminal responsibility, or liability to be proceeded against in a criminal tribunal.

CIVIL RIGHTS. Rights appertaining to a person in virtue of his citizenship in a state or community. Rights capable of being enforced or redressed in a civil action. Also a term applied to certain rights secured to citizens of the United States by the thirteenth and fourteenth amendments to the constitution, and by various acts of congress made in pursuance thereof.

CIVIL SERVICE. This term properly includes all functions under the government, except military functions. In general it is confined to functions in the great administrative departments of state. Wharton.

CIVIL SIDE. When the same court has jurisdiction of both civil and criminal matters, proceedings of the first class are often said to be on the civil side; those of the second, on the criminal side.

CIVIL WAR. An internecine war. A war carried on between opposing masses of citizens of the same country or nation.

Before the declaration of independence, the war between Great Britain and the United Colonies was a civil war; but instantly on that event the war changed its nature, and became a public war between independent governments. 3 Dall. 199, 224.

CIVILIAN. One who is skilled or versed in the civil law. A doctor, professor, or student of the civil law. Also a private citizen, as distinguished from such as belong to the army and navy or (in England) the church.

CIVILIS. Civil, as distinguished from criminal. *Civilis actio,* a civil action. Bract. fol. 101b.

CIVILISTA. In old English law. A civil lawyer, or civilian. Dyer, 267.

CIVILITER. Civilly. In a person's civil character or position, or by civil (not criminal) process or procedure. This term is used in distinction or opposition to the word *"criminaliter,"*—criminally,—to distinguish civil actions from criminal prosecutions.

CIVILITER MORTUUS. Civilly dead; dead in the view of the law. The condition of one who has lost his civil rights and capacities, and is accounted dead in law.

CIVILIZATION. In practice. A law; an act of justice, or judgment which renders a criminal process civil; performed by turning an information into an inquest, or the contrary. Wharton.

In public law. This is a term which covers several states of society; it is relative, and has not a fixed sense, but it implies an improved and progressive condition of the people, living under an organized government, with systematized labor, individual ownership of the soil, individual accumulations of property, humane and somewhat cultivated manners and customs, the institution of the family, with well-defined and respected domestic and social relations, institutions of learning, intellectual activity, etc. 19 Ind. 56.

CIVIS. Lat. In the Roman law. A citizen; as distinguished from *incola*, (an inhabitant;) origin or birth constituting the former, domicile the latter. Code, 10, 40, 7.

CIVITAS. Lat. In the Roman law. Any body of people living under the same laws; a state. *Jus civitatis*, the law of a state; civil law. Inst. 1, 2, 1, 2. *Civitates fœderatæ*, towns in alliance with Rome, and considered to be free. Butl. Hor. Jur. 29.

Citizenship; one of the three *status*, conditions, or qualifications of persons. Mackeld. Rom. Law, § 131.

Civitas et urbs in hoc differunt, quod incolæ dicuntur civitas, urbs vero complectitur ædificia. Co. Litt. 409. A city and a town differ, in this: that the inhabitants are called the "city," but town includes the buildings.

CLAIM, *v*. To demand as one's own; to assert a personal right to any property or any right; to demand the possession or enjoyment of something rightfully one's own, and wrongfully withheld.

CLAIM, *n*. 1. A challenge of the property or ownership of a thing which is wrongfully withheld from the possession of the claimant. Plowd. 359.

A claim is a right or title, actual or supposed, to a debt, privilege, or other thing in the possession of another; not the possession, but the means by or through which the claimant obtains the possession or enjoyment. 2 N. Y. 245, 254.

A claim is, in a just, juridical sense, a demand of some matter as of right made by one person upon another, to do or to forbear to do some act or thing as a matter of duty. A more limited, but at the same time an equally expressive, definition was given by Lord Dyer, that "a claim is a challenge by a man of the propriety or ownership of a thing, which he has not in possession, but which is wrongfully detained from him." 16 Pet. 615.

"Claim" has generally been defined as a demand for a thing, the ownership of which, or an interest in which, is in the claimant, but the possession of which is wrongfully withheld by another. But a broader meaning must be accorded to it. A demand for damages for criminal conversation with plaintiff's wife is a claim; but it would be doing violence to language to say that such damages are property of plaintiff which defendant withholds. In common parlance the noun "claim" means an assertion, a pretension; and the verb is often used (not quite correctly) as a synonym for "state," "urge," "insist," or "assert." In a statute authorizing the courts to order a bill of particulars of the "claim" of either party, "claim" is co-extensive with "case," and embraces all causes of action and all grounds of defense, the pleas of both parties, and pleas in confession and avoidance, no less than complaints and counter-claims. It warrants the court in requiring a defendant who justifies

in a libel suit to furnish particulars of the facts relied upon in justification. 6 Daly, 446.

2. Under the mechanic's lien law of Pennsylvania, a demand put on record by a mechanic or material-man against a building for work or material contributed to its erection is called a "claim."

3. Under the land laws of the United States, the tract of land taken up by a preemptioner or other settler (and also his possession of the same) is called a "claim."

CLAIM IN EQUITY. In English practice. In simple cases, where there was not any great conflict as to facts, and a discovery from a defendant was not sought, but a reference to chambers was nevertheless necessary before final decree, which would be as of course, all parties being before the court, the summary proceeding by claim was sometimes adopted, thus obviating the recourse to plenary and protracted pleadings. This summary practice was created by orders 22d April, 1850, which came into operation on the 22d May following. See Smith, Ch. Pr. 664. By Consolid. Ord. 1860, viii. r. 4, claims were abolished. Wharton.

CLAIM OF CONUSANCE. In practice. An intervention by a third person in a suit, claiming that he has rightful jurisdiction of the cause which the plaintiff has commenced out of the claimant's court. Now obsolete. 2 Wils. 409; 3 Bl. Comm. 298.

CLAIM OF LIBERTY. In English practice. A suit or petition to the queen, in the court of exchequer, to have liberties and franchises confirmed there by the attorney general.

CLAIMANT. In admiralty practice. The name given to a person who lays claim to property seized on a libel *in rem*, and who is authorized and admitted to defend the action.

CLAM. In the civil law. Covertly; secretly.

Clam delinquentes magis puniuntur quam palam. 8 Coke, 127. Those sinning secretly are punished more severely than those sinning openly.

CLAM, VI, AUT PRECARIO. A technical phrase of the Roman law, meaning by force, stealth, or importunity.

CLAMEA ADMITTENDA IN ITINERE PER ATTORNATUM. An ancient writ by which the king commanded the justices in eyre to admit the claim by attorney of a person who was in the royal service, and could not appear in person. Reg. Orig. 19.

CLAMOR. In old English law. A claim or complaint; an outcry; clamor.

In the civil law. A claimant. A debt; anything claimed from another. A proclamation; an accusation. Du Cange.

CLARE CONSTAT. (It clearly appears.) In Scotch law. The name of a precept for giving seisin of lands to an heir; so called from its initial words. Ersk. Inst. 3, 8, 71.

CLAREMETHEN. In old Scotch law. The warranty of stolen cattle or goods; the law regulating such warranty. Skene.

CLARENDON, CONSTITUTIONS OF. The constitutions of Clarendon were certain statutes made in the reign of Henry II. of England, at a parliament held at Clarendon, (A. D. 1164,) by which the king checked the power of the pope and his clergy, and greatly narrowed the exemption they claimed from secular jurisdiction. 4 Bl. Comm. 422.

CLARIFICATIO. Lat. In old Scotch law. A making clear; the purging or clearing (clenging) of an assise. Skene.

CLASS. The order or rank according to which persons or things are arranged or assorted. Also a group of persons or things, taken collectively, having certain qualities in common, and constituting a unit for certain purposes; e. g., a class of legatees.

CLASSIARIUS. A seaman or soldier serving at sea.

CLASSICI. In the Roman law. Persons employed in servile duties on board of vessels. Cod. 11, 12.

CLASSIFICATION. In the practice of the English chancery division, where there are several parties to an administration action, including those who have been served with notice of the decree or judgment, and it appears to the judge (or chief clerk) that any of them form a class having the same interest, (e. g., residuary legatees,) he may require them to be represented by one solicitor, in order to prevent the expense of each of them attending by separate solicitors. This is termed "classifying the interests of the parties attending," or, shortly, "classifying," or "classification." In practice the term is also applied to the directions given by the chief clerk as to which of the parties are

to attend on each of the accounts and inquiries directed by the judgment. Sweet.

CLAUSE. A single paragraph or subdivision of a legal document, such as a contract, deed, will, constitution, or statute. Sometimes a sentence or part of a sentence.

CLAUSE IRRITANT. In Scotch law. By this clause, in a deed or settlement, the acts or deeds of a tenant for life or other proprietor, contrary to the conditions of his right, become null and void; and by the "resolutive" clause such right becomes resolved and extinguished. Bell.

CLAUSE POTESTATIVE. In French law. The name given to the clause whereby one party to a contract reserves to himself the right to annul it.

CLAUSE ROLLS. In English Law. Rolls which contain all such matters of record as were committed to close writs; these rolls are preserved in the Tower.

CLAUSULA. A clause; a sentence or part of a sentence in a written instrument or law.

Clausula generalis de residuo non ea complectitur quæ non ejusdem sint generis cum iis quæ speciatim dicta fuerant. A general clause of remainder does not embrace those things which are not of the same kind with those which had been specially mentioned. Lofft, Appendix, 419.

Clausula generalis non refertur ad expressa. 8 Coke, 154. A general clause does not refer to things expressed.

Clausula quæ abrogationem excludit ab initio non valet. A clause [in a law] which precludes its abrogation is void from the beginning. Bac. Max. 77.

Clausula vel dispositio inutilis per presumptionem remotam, vel causam ex post facto non fulcitur. A useless clause or disposition [one which expresses no more than the law by intendment would have supplied] is not supported by a remote presumption, [or foreign intendment of some purpose, in regard whereof it might be material,] or by a cause arising afterwards, [which may induce an operation of those idle words.] Bac. Max. 82, regula 21.

Clausulæ inconsuetæ semper inducunt suspicionem. Unusual clauses [in an instrument] always induce suspicion. 3 Coke, 81.

CLAUSUM. Close, closed up, sealed. Inclosed, as a parcel of land.

CLAUSUM FREGIT. L. Lat. (He broke the close.) In pleading and practice. Technical words formerly used in certain actions of trespass, and still retained in the phrase *quare clausum fregit.* (*q. v.*)

CLAUSUM PASCHIÆ. In English law. The morrow of the *utas*, or eight days of Easter; the end of Easter; the Sunday after Easter-day. 2 Inst. 157.

CLAUSURA. In old English law. An inclosure. *Clausura heyæ*, the inclosure of a hedge. Cowell.

CLAVES CURIÆ. The keys of the court. They were the officers of the Scotch courts, such as clerk, doomster, and serjeant. Burrill.

CLAVES INSULÆ. In Manx law. The keys of the Island of Man, or twelve persons to whom all ambiguous and weighty causes are referred.

CLAVIA. In old English law. A club or mace; tenure *per serjeantiam claviæ*, by the serjeanty of the club or mace. Cowell.

CLAVIGERATUS. A treasurer of a church.

CLAWA. A close, or small inclosure. Cowell.

CLEAN HANDS. It is a rule of equity that a plaintiff must come with "clean hands," *i. e.*, he must be free from reproach in his conduct. But there is this limitation to the rule: that his conduct can only be excepted to in respect to the subject-matter of his claim; everything else is immaterial.

CLEAR. In a devise of money for the purchase of an annuity, this term means free from taxes. 2 Atk. 376.

In the phrase "clear yearly value," clear means free from all outgoings like a rent-charge, as losses by tenants and management, to which a rent charge is not liable. 2 Ves. 499.

CLEAR DAYS. If a certain number of clear days be given for the doing of any act, the time is to be reckoned exclusively, as well of the first day as the last.

CLEARANCE. In maritime law. A document in the nature of a certificate given by the collector of customs to an outward-bound vessel, to the effect that she has com-plied with the law, and is duly authorized to depart.

CLEARING. The departure of a vessel from port, after complying with the customs and health laws and like local regulations.

In mercantile law. A method of making exchanges and settling balances, adopted among banks and bankers.

CLEARING-HOUSE. An institution organized by the banks of a city, where their messengers may meet daily, adjust balances of accounts, and receive and pay differences.

CLEMENTINES. In canon law. The collection of decretals or constitutions of Pope Clement V., made by order of John XXII., his successor, who published it in 1317.

CLEMENT'S INN. An inn of chancery. See INNS OF CHANCERY.

CLENGE. In old Scotch law. To clear or acquit of a criminal charge. Literally, to cleanse or clean.

CLEP AND CALL. In old Scotch practice. A solemn form of words prescribed by law, and used in criminal cases, as in pleas of wrong and unlaw.

CLERGY. The whole body of clergymen or ministers of religion. Also an abbreviation for "benefit of clergy."

CLERGYABLE. In old English law. Admitting of clergy, or benefit of clergy. A clergyable felony was one of that class in which clergy was allowable. 4 Bl. Comm. 371–373.

CLERICAL. Pertaining to clergymen; or pertaining to the office or labor of a clerk.

CLERICAL ERROR. A mistake in writing or copying; the mistake of a clerk or writer. 1 Ld. Raym. 183.

CLERICAL TONSURE. The having the head shaven, which was formerly peculiar to clerks, or persons in orders, and which the coifs worn by serjeants at law are supposed to have been introduced to conceal. 1 Bl. Comm. 24, note *t;* 4 Bl. Comm. 367.

CLERICALE PRIVILEGIUM. In old English law. The clerical privilege; the privilege or benefit of clergy.

CLERICI DE CANCELLARIA. Clerks of the chancery.

Clerici non ponantur in officiis. Co. Litt. 96. Clergymen should not be placed in offices; *i. e.*, in secular offices. See Lofft, 508.

D

E

F

G

H

I

J

K

L

M

CLERICI PRÆNOTARII. The six clerks in chancery. 2 Reeve, Eng. Law, 251.

CLERICO ADMITTENDO. See AD-MITTENDO CLERICO.

CLERICO CAPTO PER STATUTUM MERCATORUM. A writ for the delivery of a clerk out of prison, who was taken and incarcerated upon the breach of a statute merchant. Reg. Orig. 147.

CLERICO CONVICTO COMMISSO GAOLÆ IN DEFECTU ORDINARII DELIBERANDO. An ancient writ, that lay for the delivery to his ordinary of a clerk convicted of felony, where the ordinary did not challenge him according to the privilege of clerks. Reg. Orig. 69.

CLERICO INFRA SACROS ORDINES CONSTITUTO, NON ELIGENDO IN OFFICIUM. A writ directed to those who had thrust a bailiwick or other office upon one in holy orders, charging them to release him. Reg. Orig. 143.

CLERICUS. In Roman law. A minister of religion in the Christian church; an ecclesiastic or priest. Cod. 1, 3; Nov. 3, 123, 137. A general term, including bishops, priests, deacons, and others of inferior order. Brissonius.

In old English law. A clerk or priest; a person in holy orders; a secular priest; a clerk of a court.

An officer of the royal household, having charge of the receipt and payment of moneys, etc. Fleta enumerates several of them, with their appropriate duties; as *clericus coquinæ*, clerk of the kitchen; *clericus panetr' et butelr'*, clerk of the pantry and buttery. Lib. 2, cc. 18, 19.

Clericus et agricola et mercator, tempore belli, ut oret, colat, et commutet, pace fruuntur. 2 Inst. 58. Clergymen, husbandmen, and merchants, in order that they may preach, cultivate, and trade, enjoy peace in time of war.

CLERICUS MERCATI. In old English law. Clerk of the market. 2 Inst. 543.

Clericus non connumeretur in duabus ecclesiis. 1 Rolle. A clergyman should not be appointed to two churches.

CLERICUS PAROCHIALIS. In old English law. A parish clerk.

CLERIGOS. In Spanish law. Clergy; men chosen for the service of God. White, New Recop. b. 1, tit. 5, ch. 4.

CLERK. In ecclesiastical law. A person in holy orders; a clergyman; an individual attached to the ecclesiastical state, and who has the clerical tonsure. See 4 Bl. Comm. 366, 367.

In practice. A person employed in a public office, or as an officer of a court, whose duty is to keep records or accounts.

In commercial law. A person employed by a merchant, or in a mercantile establishment, as a salesman, book-keeper, accountant, amanuensis, etc., invested with more or less authority in the administration of some branch or department of the business, while the principal himself superintends the whole.

CLERK OF ARRAIGNS. In English law. An assistant to the clerk of assise. His duties are in the crown court on circuit.

CLERK OF ASSISE. In English law. Officers who officiate as associates on the circuits. They record all judicial proceedings done by the judges on the circuit.

CLERK OF COURT. An officer of a court of justice who has charge of the clerical part of its business, who keeps its records and seal, issues process, enters judgments and orders, gives certified copies from the records, etc.

CLERK OF ENROLLMENTS. In English law. The former chief officer of the English enrollment office, (*q. v.*) He now forms part of the staff of the central office.

CLERK OF THE CROWN IN CHANCERY. See CROWN OFFICE IN CHANCERY.

CLERK OF THE HOUSE OF COMMONS. An important officer of the English house of commons. He is appointed by the crown as under-clerk of the parliaments to attend upon the commons. He makes a declaration, on entering upon his office, to make true entries, remembrances, and journals of the things done and passed in the house. He signs all orders of the house, indorses the bills sent or returned to the lords, and reads whatever is required to be read in the house. He has the custody of all records and other documents. May, Parl. Pr. 236.

CLERK OF THE MARKET. The overseer or superintendent of a public market. In old English law, he was a *quasi* judicial officer, having power to settle controversies arising in the market between persons dealing there. Called "*clericus mercati.*" 4 Bl. Comm. 275.

CLERK OF THE PARLIAMENTS. One of the chief officers of the house of lords. He is appointed by the crown, by letters patent. On entering office he makes a declaration to make true entries and records of the things done and passed in the parliaments, and to keep secret all such matters as shall be treated therein. May, Parl. Pr. 238.

CLERK OF THE PEACE. In English law. An officer whose duties are to officiate at sessions of the peace, to prepare indictments, and to record the proceedings of the justices, and to perform a number of special duties in connection with the affairs of the county.

CLERK OF THE PETTY BAG. See PETTY BAG.

CLERK OF THE PRIVY SEAL. There are four of these officers, who attend the lord privy seal, or, in the absence of the lord privy seal, the principal secretary of state. Their duty is to write and make out all things that are sent by warrant from the signet to the privy seal, and which are to be passed to the great seal; and also to make out privy seals (as they are termed) upon any special occasion of his majesty's affairs, as for the loan of money and such like purposes. Cowell.

CLERK OF THE SIGNET. An officer, in England, whose duty it is to attend on the king's principal secretary, who always has the custody of the privy signet, as well for the purpose of sealing his majesty's private letters, as also grants which pass his majesty's hand by bill signed; there are four of these officers. Cowell.

CLERKS OF INDICTMENTS. Officers attached to the central criminal court in England, and to each circuit. They prepare and settle indictments against offenders, and assist the clerk of arraigns.

CLERKS OF RECORDS AND WRITS. Officers formerly attached to the English court of chancery, whose duties consisted principally in sealing bills of complaint and writs of execution, filing affidavits, keeping a record of suits, and certifying office copies of pleadings and affidavits. They were three in number, and the business was distributed among them according to the letters of the alphabet. By the judicature acts, 1873, 1875, they were transferred to the chancery division of the high court. Now, by the judicature (officers') act, 1879, they have been transferred to the central office of the supreme court, under the title of "Masters of the Supreme Court," and the office of clerk of records and writs has been abolished. Sweet.

CLERKS OF SEATS, in the principal registry of the probate division of the English high court, discharge the duty of preparing and passing the grants of probate and letters of administration, under the supervision of the registrars. There are six seats, the business of which is regulated by an alphabetical arrangement, and each seat has four clerks. They have to take bonds from administrators, and to receive *caveats* against a grant being made in a case where a will is contested. They also draw the "acts," *i. e.*, a short summary of each grant made, containing the name of the deceased, amount of assets, and other particulars. Sweet.

CLERKSHIP. The period which must be spent by a law-student in the office of a practising attorney before admission to the bar. 1 Tidd, Pr. 61, et seq.

In old English practice. The art of drawing pleadings and entering them on record in Latin, in the ancient court hand; otherwise called "skill of pleading in actions at the common law."

CLIENS. Lat. In the Roman law. A client or dependent. One who depended upon another as his patron or protector, adviser or defender, in suits at law and other difficulties; and was bound, in return, to pay him all respect and honor, and to serve him with his life and fortune in any extremity. Dionys. ii. 10; Adams, Rom. Ant. 33.

CLIENT. A person who employs or retains an attorney, or counsellor, to appear for him in courts, advise, assist, and defend him in legal proceedings, and to act for him in any legal business.

CLIENTELA. In old English law. Clientship, the state of a client; and, correlatively, protection, patronage, guardianship.

CLIFFORD'S INN. An inn of chancery. See INNS OF CHANCERY.

CLITO. In Saxon law. The son of a king or emperor. The next heir to the throne; the Saxon adeling. Spelman.

CLOERE. A gaol; a prison or dungeon.

CLOSE, *adj.* In practice. Close or sealed up. A term applied to writs and letters, as distinguished from those that are open or patent.

CLOSE, *n.* A portion of land, as a field, inclosed, as by a hedge, fence, or other visible inclosure. 3 Bl. Comm. 209. The interest of a person in any particular piece of ground, whether actually inclosed or not. 7 East, 207.

The noun "close," in its legal sense, imports a portion of land inclosed, but not necessarily inclosed by actual or visible barriers. The invisible, ideal boundary, founded on limit of title, which surrounds every man's land, constitutes it his close, irrespective of walls, fences, ditches, or the like.

In practice. The word means termination; winding up. Thus the close of the pleadings is where the pleadings are finished, *i. e.,* when issue has been joined.

CLOSE COPIES. Copies of legal documents which might be written closely or loosely at pleasure; as distinguished from *office* copies, which were to contain only a prescribed number of words on each sheet.

CLOSE-HAULED. In admiralty law, this nautical term means the arrangement or trim of a vessel's sails when she endeavors to make a progress in the nearest direction possible towards that point of the compass from which the wind blows. But a vessel may be considered as close-hauled, although she is not quite so near to the wind as she could possibly lie. 6 El. & Bl. 771.

CLOSE ROLLS. Rolls containing the record of the close writs (*literæ clausæ*) and grants of the king, kept with the public records. 2 Bl. Comm. 346.

CLOSE WRITS. In English law. Certain letters of the king, sealed with his great seal, and directed to particular persons and for particular purposes, which, not being proper for public inspection, are closed up and sealed on the outside, and are thence called "writs close." 2 Bl. Comm. 346; Sewell, Sheriffs, 372.

Writs directed to the sheriff, instead of to the lord. 3 Reeve, Eng. Law, 45.

CLOTURE. The procedure in deliberative assemblies whereby debate is closed. Introduced in the English parliament in the session of 1882.

CLOUD ON TITLE. An outstanding claim or incumbrance which, if valid, would affect or impair the title of the owner of a particular estate, and which apparently and on its face has that effect, but which can be shown by extrinsic proof to be invalid or inapplicable to the estate in question. A conveyance, mortgage, judgment, tax-levy, etc., may all, in proper cases, constitute a cloud on title.

CLOUGH. A valley. Also an allowance for the turn of the scale, on buying goods wholesale by weight.

CLUB. A voluntary, unincorporated association of persons for purposes of a social, literary, or political nature, or the like. A club is not a partnership. 2 Mees. & W. 172.

The word "club" has no very definite meaning. Clubs are formed for all sorts of purposes, and there is no uniformity in their constitutions and rules. It is well known that clubs exist which limit the number of the members and select them with great care, which own considerable property in common, and in which the furnishing of food and drink to the members for money is but one of many conveniences which the members enjoy. 137 Mass. 567.

CLUB-LAW. Rule of violence; regulation by force; the law of arms.

CLYPEUS, or CLIPEUS. In old English law. A shield; metaphorically one of a noble family. *Clypei prostrati,* noble families extinct. Mat. Paris, 463.

CO. A prefix to words, meaning "with" or "in conjunction" or "joint;" *e. g.,* co-trustees, co-executors.

COACH. Coach is a generic term. It is a kind of carriage, and is distinguished from other vehicles, chiefly, as being a covered box, hung on leathers, with four wheels. 9 Ohio, 12.

COADJUTOR. An assistant, helper, or ally; particularly a person appointed to assist a bishop who from age or infirmity is unable to perform his duty. Also an overseer, (coadjutor of an executor,) and one who disseises a person of land not to his own use, but to that of another.

CO-ADMINISTRATOR. One who is a joint administrator with one or more others.

COADUNATIO. A uniting or combining together of persons; a conspiracy. 9 Coke, 56.

COAL NOTE. A species of promissory note, formerly in use in the port of London, containing the phrase "value received in coals." By the statute 3 Geo. II. c. 26, §§ 7, 8, these were to be protected and noted as inland bills of exchange. But this was repealed by the statute 47 Geo. III. sess. 2, c. 68, § 28.

COALITION. In French law. An unlawful agreement among several persons not to do a thing except on some conditions agreed upon; particularly, industrial combinations, strikes, etc.; a conspiracy.

CO-ASSIGNEE. One of two or more assignees of the same subject-matter.

COAST. The edge or margin of a country bounding on the sea. It is held that the term includes small islands and reefs naturally connected with the adjacent land, and rising above the surface of the water, although their composition may not be sufficiently firm and stable to admit of their being inhabited or fortified; but not shoals which are perpetually covered by the water. 5 C. Rob. Adm. 385c.

This word is particularly appropriate to the edge of the sea, while "shore" may be used of the margins of inland waters.

COAST-GUARD. In English law. A body of officers and men raised and equipped by the commissioners of the admiralty for the defense of the coasts of the realm, and for the more ready manning of the navy in case of war or sudden emergency, as well as for the protection of the revenue against smugglers. Mozley & Whitley.

COASTING TRADE. In maritime law. Commerce and navigation between different places along the coast of the United States, as distinguished from commerce with ports in foreign countries.

Commercial intercourse carried on between different districts in different states, different districts in the same state, or different places in the same district, on the sea-coast or on a navigable river. 3 Cow. 713; 1 Newb. Adm. 241.

COASTWISE. Vessels "plying coastwise" are those which are engaged in the domestic trade, or plying between port and port in the United States, as contradistinguished from those engaged in the foreign trade, or plying between a port of the United States and a port of a foreign country. 10 Cal. 504.

COAT ARMOR. Heraldic ensigns, introduced by Richard I. from the Holy Land, where they were first invented. Originally they were painted on the shields of the Christian knights who went to the Holy Land during the crusades, for the purpose of identifying them, some such contrivance being necessary in order to distinguish knights when clad in armor from one another. Wharton.

COCKBILL. To place the yards of a ship at an angle with the deck. Pub. St. Mass. 1882, p. 1288.

COCKET. In English law. A seal belonging to the custom-house, or rather a scroll of parchment, sealed and delivered by the officers of the custom-house to merchants, as a warrant that their merchandises are entered; likewise a sort of measure. Fleta, lib. 2, c. ix.

COCKPIT. A name which used to be given to the judicial committee of the privy council, the council-room being built on the old cockpit of Whitehall Place.

COCKSETUS. A boatman; a cockswain. Cowell.

CODE. A collection or compendium of laws. A complete system of positive law, scientifically arranged, and promulgated by legislative authority.

The collection of laws and constitutions made by order of the Emperor Justinian is distinguished by the appellation of "The Code," by way of eminence. See CODE OF JUSTINIAN.

A body of law established by the legislative authority, and intended to set forth, in generalized and systematic form, the principles of the entire law, whether written or unwritten, positive or customary, derived from enactment or from precedent. Abbott.

A *code* is to be distinguished from a *digest*. The subject-matter of the latter is usually reported decisions of the courts. But there are also digests of statutes. These consist of an orderly collection and classification of the existing statutes of a state or nation, while a code is promulgated as one new law covering the whole field of jurisprudence.

CODE CIVIL. The code which embodies the civil law of France. Framed in the first instance by a commission of jurists appointed in 1800. This code, after having passed both the tribunate and the legislative body, was promulgated in 1804 as the "Code Civil des Français." When Napoleon became emperor, the name was changed to that of "Code Napoleon," by which it is still often designated, though it is now officially styled by its original name of "Code Civil."

CODE DE COMMERCE. A French code, enacted in 1807, as a supplement to the Code Napoleon, regulating commercial transactions, the laws of business, bankruptcies, and the jurisdiction and procedure of the courts dealing with these subjects.

CODE DE PROCÉDURE CIVIL. That part of the Code Napoleon which regulates the system of courts, their organization, civil procedure, special and extraordinary remedies, and the execution of judgments.

CODE D'INSTRUCTION CRIMINELLE. A French code, enacted in 1808, regulating criminal procedure.

CODE NAPOLEON. See CODE CIVIL.

CODE OF JUSTINIAN. The Code of Justinian (*Codex Justinianeus*) was a collection of imperial constitutions, compiled, by order of that emperor, by a commission of ten jurists, including Tribonian, and promulgated A. D. 529. It comprised twelve books, and was the first of the four compilations of law which make up the *Corpus Juris Civilis.*

This name is often met in a connection indicating that the entire *Corpus Juris Civilis* is intended, or, sometimes, the *Digest;* but its use should be confined to the *Codex.*

CODE PÉNAL. The penal or criminal code of France, enacted in 1810.

CODEX. Lat. A code or collection of laws; particularly the Code of Justinian. Also a roll or volume, and a book written on paper or parchment.

CODEX GREGORIANUS. A collection of imperial constitutions made by Gregorius, a Roman jurist of the fifth century, about the middle of the century. It contained the constitutions from Hadrian down to Constantine. Mackeld. Rom. Law, § 63.

CODEX HERMOGENIANUS. A collection of imperial constitutions made by Hermogenes, a jurist of the fifth century. It was nothing more than a supplement to the Codex Gregorianus, (supra,) containing the constitutions of Diocletian and Maximilian. Mackeld. Rom. Law, § 63.

CODEX JUSTINIANEUS. A collection of imperial constitutions, made by a commission of ten persons appointed by Justinian, A. D. 528.

CODEX REPETITÆ PRÆLECTIONIS. The new code of Justinian; or the new edition of the first or old code, promulgated A. D. 534, being the one now extant. Mackeld. Rom. Law, § 78. Tayl. Civil Law, 22.

CODEX THEODOSIANUS. A code compiled by the emperor Theodosius the younger, A. D. 438, being a methodical collection, in sixteen books, of all the imperial constitutions then in force. It was the only body of civil law publicly received as authentic in the western part of Europe till the twelfth century, the use and authority of the Code of Justinian being during that interval confined to the East. 1 Bl. Comm. 81.

CODEX VETUS. The old code. The first edition of the Code of Justinian; now lost. Mackeld. Rom. Law, § 70.

CODICIL. A testamentary disposition subsequent to a will, and by which the will is altered, explained, added to, subtracted from, or confirmed by way of republication, but in no case totally revoked. 2 Woodd. Lect. 284.

A codicil is an addition or supplement to a will, either to add to, take from, or alter the provisions of the will. It must be executed with the same formality as a will, and, when admitted to probate, forms a part of the will. Code Ga. 1882, § 2404.

CODICILLUS. In the Roman law. A codicil; an informal and inferior kind of will, in use among the Romans.

CODIFICATION. The process of collecting and arranging the laws of a country or state into a code, *i. e.,* into a complete system of positive law, scientifically ordered, and promulgated by legislative authority.

COEMPTIO. Mutual purchase. One of the modes in which marriage was contracted among the Romans. The man and the woman delivered to each other a small piece of money. The man asked the woman whether she would become to him a *materfamilias,* (mistress of his family,) to which she replied that she would. In her turn she asked the man whether he would become to her a *paterfamilias,* (master of a family.) On his replying in the affirmative, she delivered her piece of money and herself into his hands, and so became his wife. Adams, Rom. Ant. 501.

CO-EMPTION. The act of purchasing the whole quantity of any commodity. Wharton.

COERCION. Compulsion; force; duress. It may be either *actual,* (direct or positive,) where physical force is put upon a man to compel him to do an act against his will, or *implied,* (legal or constructive,) where the relation of the parties is such that one is under subjection to the other, and is thereby constrained to do what his free will would refuse.

CO-EXECUTOR. One who is a joint executor with one or more others.

COFFEE-HOUSE. A house of entertainment where guests are supplied with coffee and other refreshments, and sometimes with lodging. Century Dict. A coffee-house is not an inn. 4 Camp. 76.

COFFERER OF THE QUEEN'S HOUSEHOLD. In English law. A principal officer of the royal establishment, next under the controller, who, in the counting-house and elsewhere, had a special charge and oversight of the other officers, whose wages he paid.

Cogitationis pœnam nemo patitur. No one is punished for his thoughts. Dig. 48, 19, 18.

COGNATES. (Lat. *cognati.*) Relations by the mother's side, or by females. Mackeld. Rom. Law, § 144. A common term in Scotch law. Ersk. Inst. 1, 7, 4.

COGNATI. Lat. In the civil law. Cognates relations by the mother's side. 2 Bl. Comm. 235. Relations in the line of the mother. Hale, Com. Law, c. xi. Relations by or through females.

COGNATIO. Lat. In the civil law. Cognation. Relationship, or kindred generally. Dig. 38, 10, 4, 2; Inst. 3, 6, pr. Relationship through females, as distinguished from *agnatio*, or relationship through males. *Agnatio a patre sit, cognatio a matre.* Inst. 3, 5, 4. See AGNATIO.

In canon law. Consanguinity, as distinguished from affinity. 4 Reeve, Eng. Law, 56–58.

Consanguinity, as including affinity. Id.

COGNATION. In the civil law. Signifies generally the kindred which exists between two persons who are united by ties of blood or family, or both.

COGNATUS. Lat. In the civil law. A relation by the mother's side; a cognate. A relation, or kinsman, generally.

COGNITIO. In old English law. The acknowledgment of a fine; the certificate of such acknowledgment.

In the Roman law. The judicial examination or hearing of a cause.

COGNITIONES. Ensigns and arms, or a military coat painted with arms. Mat. Par. 1250.

COGNITIONIBUS MITTENDIS. In English law. A writ to a justice of the common pleas, or other, who has power to take a fine, who, having taken the fine, defers to certify it, commanding him to certify it. Now abolished. Reg. Orig. 68.

COGNITIONIS CAUSÆ. In Scotch practice. A name given to a judgment or decree pronounced by a court, ascertaining the amount of a debt against the estate of a deceased landed proprietor, on cause shown, or after a due investigation. Bell.

COGNITOR. In the Roman law. An advocate or defender in a private cause; one who defended the cause of a person who was present. Calvin. Lex. Jurid.

COGNIZANCE. In old practice. That part of a fine in which the defendant *acknowledged* that the land in question was the right of the complainant. From this the fine itself derived its name, as being *sur* cognizance *de droit*, etc., and the parties their titles of *cognizor* and *cognizee.*

In modern practice. Judicial notice or knowledge; the judicial hearing of a cause; jurisdiction, or right to try and determine causes; acknowledgment; confession; recognition.

Of pleas. Jurisdiction of causes. A privilege granted by the king to a city or town to hold pleas within the same.

Claim of cognizance (or of conusance) is an intervention by a third person, demanding judicature in the cause against the plaintiff, who has chosen to commence his action out of claimant's court. 2 Wils. 409; 2 Bl. Comm. 350, note.

In pleading. A species of answer in the action of replevin, by which the defendant acknowledges the taking of the goods which are the subject-matter of the action, and also that he has no title to them, but justifies the taking on the ground that it was done by the command of one who was entitled to the property.

In the process of levying a fine, it is an acknowledgment by the deforciant that the lands in question belong to the complainant.

In the language of American jurisprudence, this word is used chiefly in the sense of jurisdiction, or the exercise of jurisdiction; the judicial examination of a matter, or power and authority to make it.

Judicial cognizance is judicial notice, or knowledge upon which a judge is bound to act without having it proved in evidence.

COGNIZEE. The party to whom a fine was levied. 2 Bl. Comm. 351.

COGNIZOR. In old conveyancing. The party levying a fine. 2 Bl. Comm. 350, 351.

COGNOMEN. In Roman law. A man's family name. The first name (*prænomen*) was the proper name of the individual; the second (*nomen*) indicated the *gens* or tribe to which he belonged; while the third (*cognomen*) denoted his family or house.

In English law. A surname. A name added to the *nomen* proper, or name of the individual; a name descriptive of the family.

Cognomen majorum est ex sanguine tractum, hoc intrinsecum est; agnomen extrinsecum ab eventu. 6 Coke, 65. The cognomen is derived from the blood of ancestors, and is intrinsic; an agnomen arises from an event, and is extrinsic.

COGNOVIT ACTIONEM. (He has confessed the action.) A defendant's written confession of an action brought against him, to which he has no available defense. It is usually upon condition that he shall be allowed a certain time for the payment of the debt or damages, and costs. It is supposed to be given in court, and it impliedly authorizes the plaintiff's attorney to sign judgment and issue execution.

COHABIT. To live together as husband and wife; to live together at bed and board. Burrows, Sett. Cas. 26.

To live together, as in the same house. "That his sisters, the Lady Turner and Arabella Clerk, might *cohabit* in the capital house." 2 Vern. 323.

COHABITATION. Living together; living together as husband and wife.

Cohabitation means having the same habitation, not a sojourn, a habit of visiting or remaining for a time; there must be something more than mere meretricious intercourse. 75 Pa. St. 207.

Cohæredes una persona censentur, propter unitatem juris quod habent. Co. Litt. 163. Co-heirs are deemed as one person, on account of the unity of right which they possess.

COHÆRES. In old English law. A co-heir, or joint heir.

CO-HEIR. One of several to whom an inheritance descends.

CO-HEIRESS. A joint heiress. A woman who has an equal share of an inheritance with another woman.

COHUAGIUM. A tribute made by those who meet promiscuously in a market or fair. Du Cange.

COIF. A title given to serjeants at law, who are called "serjeants of the coif," from the coif they wear on their heads. The use of this coif at first was to cover the clerical tonsure, many of the practising serjeants being clergymen who had abandoned their profession. It was a thin linen cover, gathered together in the form of a skull or helmet; the material being afterwards changed into white silk, and the form eventually into the black patch at the top of the forensic wig, which is now the distinguishing mark of the degree of serjeant at law. (Cowell; Foss, Judg.; 3 Steph. Comm. 272, note.) Brown.

COIN, *v.* To fashion pieces of metal into a prescribed shape, weight, and degree of fineness, and stamp them with prescribed devices, by authority of government, in order that they may circulate as money. See 2 Duv. 29; 22 Ind. 306; 25 How. Pr. 105.

COIN, *n.* Pieces of gold, silver, or other metal, fashioned into a prescribed shape, weight, and degree of fineness, and stamped, by authority of government, with certain marks and devices, and put into circulation as money at a fixed value.

Strictly speaking, coin differs from money, as the species differs from the genus. Money is any matter, whether metal, paper, beads, shells, etc., which has currency as a medium in commerce. Coin is a particular species, always made of metal, and struck according to a certain process called "coinage." Wharton.

COINAGE. The process or the function of coining metallic money; also the great mass of metallic money in circulation.

COJUDICES. Lat. In old English law. Associate judges having equality of power with others.

COLD WATER ORDEAL. The trial which was anciently used for the common sort of people, who, having a cord tied about them under their arms, were cast into a river; if they sank to the bottom until they were drawn up, which was in a very short time, then were they held guiltless; but such as did remain upon the water were held culpable, being, as they said, of the water rejected and kept up. Wharton.

COLIBERTUS. In feudal law. One who, holding in free socage, was obliged to do certain services for the lord. A middle class of tenants between servile and free, who held their freedom of tenure on condition of performing certain services. Said to be the same as the *conditionales.* Cowell.

COLLATERAL. By the side; at the side; attached upon the side. Not lineal, but upon a parallel or diverging line. Additional or auxiliary; supplementary; co-operating.

COLLATERAL ACT. In old practice. The name "collateral act" was given to any act (except the payment of money) for the performance of which a bond, recognizance, etc., was given as security.

COLLATERAL ANCESTORS A phrase sometimes used to designate uncles and aunts, and other collateral antecessors, who are not strictly ancestors. 3 Barb. Ch. 438, 446.

COLLATERAL ASSURANCE. That which is made over and above the principal assurance or deed itself.

COLLATERAL CONSANGUINITY. That relationship which subsists between persons who have the same ancestors but not the same descendants, who do not descend one from the other. 2 Bl. Comm. 203.

Lineal consanguinity being usually represented by a perpendicular or *right line,* (*linea recta,*) in which the kindred are ranked relatively, one above or below the other, as father, son, grandson, *collateral* consanguinity is properly denoted by one or more *transverse* lines, crossing this, or proceeding *obliquely* from it *on the side* (*a latere*) upon which the kindred are ranked in their order. Burrill.

COLLATERAL DESCENT. Descent in a collateral or oblique line, *i. e.,* up through the common ancestor and then down from him; descent to collaterals.

COLLATERAL ESTOPPEL. The collateral determination of a question by a court having general jurisdiction of the subject. See 26 Vt. 209.

COLLATERAL FACTS. Such as are outside the controversy, or are not directly connected with the principal matter or issue in dispute.

COLLATERAL IMPEACHMENT. A collateral impeachment of a judgment or de-

cree is an attempt made to destroy or evade its effect as an estoppel, by reopening the merits of the cause or by showing reasons why the judgment should not have been rendered or should not have a conclusive effect, in a *collateral* proceeding, *i. e.,* in any action other than that in which the judgment was rendered; for, if this be done upon appeal, error, or *certiorari,* the impeachment is *direct.*

COLLATERAL INHERITANCE TAX. A tax levied upon the collateral devolution of property by will or under the intestate law.

COLLATERAL ISSUE. In practice. An issue taken upon matter *aside* from the intrinsic merits of the action, as upon a plea in abatement; or *aside* from the direct and regular order of the pleadings, as on a demurrer. 2 Archb. Pr. K. B. 1, 6, bk. 2, pts. 1, 2.

The term "collateral" is also applied in England to an issue raised upon a plea of diversity of person, pleaded by a criminal who has been tried and convicted, in bar of execution, viz., that he is not the same person who was attainted, and the like. 4 Bl. Comm. 396.

COLLATERAL KINSMEN. Those who descend from one and the same common ancestor, but not from one another.

COLLATERAL LIMITATION. One which gives an interest in an estate for a specified period, but makes the right of enjoyment to depend on some collateral event, as an estate to A. till B. shall go to Rome. Park, Dower, 163; 4 Kent, Comm. 128.

COLLATERAL SECURITY. A security given in addition to the direct security, and subordinate to it, intended to guaranty its validity or convertibility or insure its performance; so that, if the direct security fails, the creditor may fall back upon the collateral security.

Collateral security, in bank phraseology, means some security additional to the personal obligation of the borrower. 2 Abb. (U. S.) 423.

COLLATERAL UNDERTAKING. "Collateral" and "original" have become the technical terms whereby to distinguish promises that are within, and such as are not within, the statute of frauds. 7 Har. & J. 391.

COLLATERAL WARRANTY, in old conveyancing, was where the heir's title to the land neither was nor could have been derived from the warranting ancestor. Thus where a younger brother released to his father's disseisor, with warranty, this was collateral to the elder brother. The whole doctrine of collateral warranty seems repugnant to plain and unsophisticated reason and justice; and even its technical grounds are so obscure that the ablest legal writers are not agreed upon the subject. Wharton.

COLLATERALIS ET SOCII. The ancient title of masters in chancery.

COLLATIO BONORUM. A joining together or contribution of goods into a common fund. This occurs where a portion of money, advanced by the father to a son or daughter, is brought into *hotchpot*, in order to have an equal distributory share of his personal estate at his death. See COLLATION.

COLLATIO SIGNORUM. In old English law. A comparison of marks or seals. A mode of testing the genuineness of a seal, by comparing it with another known to be genuine. Adams. See Bract. fol. 389*b*.

COLLATION. In the civil law. The collation of goods is the supposed or real return to the mass of the succession which an heir makes of property which he received in advance of his share or otherwise, in order that such property may be divided together with the other effects of the succession. Civil Code La. art. 1227.

The term is sometimes used also in common-law jurisdictions in the sense given above. It is synonymous with "hotchpot."

In practice. The comparison of a copy with its original to ascertain its correctness; or the report of the officer who made the comparison.

COLLATION OF SEALS. When upon the same label one seal was set on the back or reverse of the other. Wharton.

COLLATION TO A BENEFICE. In ecclesiastical law. This occurs where the bishop and patron are one and the same person, in which case the bishop cannot present the clergyman to himself, but does, by the one act of collation or conferring the benefice, the whole that is done in common cases both by presentation and institution. 2 Bl. Comm. 22.

COLLATIONE FACTÂ UNI POST MORTEM ALTERIUS. A writ directed to justices of the common pleas, commanding them to issue their writ to the bishop, for the admission of a clerk in the place of another presented by the crown, where there had been a demise of the crown during a suit; for judgment once passed for the king's clerk, and he dying before admittance, the king may bestow his presentation on another. Reg. Orig. 31.

COLLATIONE HEREMITAGII. In old English law. A writ whereby the king conferred the keeping of an hermitage upon a clerk. Reg. Orig. 303, 308.

COLLECT. To gather together; to bring scattered things (assets, accounts, articles of property) into one mass or fund.

To collect a debt or claim is to obtain payment or liquidation of it, either by personal solicitation or legal proceedings.

COLLECTOR. One authorized to receive taxes or other impositions; as "collector of taxes." A person appointed by a private person to collect the credits due him.

COLLECTOR OF DECEDENT'S ESTATE. A person temporarily appointed by the probate court to collect rents, assets, interest, bills receivable, etc., of a decedent's estate, and act for the estate in all financial matters requiring immediate settlement. Such collector is usually appointed when there is protracted litigation as to the probate of the will, or as to the person to take out administration, and his duties cease as soon as an executor or administrator is qualified.

COLLECTOR OF THE CUSTOMS. An officer of the United States, appointed for the term of four years. Act May 15, 1820, § 1; 3 Story, U. S. Laws, 1790.

COLLEGA. In the civil law. One invested with joint authority. A colleague; an associate.

COLLEGATARIUS. Lat. In the civil law. A co-legatee. Inst. 2, 20, 8.

COLLEGATORY. A co-legatee; a person who has a legacy left to him in common with other persons.

COLLEGE. An organized assembly or collection of persons, established by law, and empowered to co-operate for the performance of some special function or for the promotion of some common object, which may be educational, political, ecclesiastical, or scientific in its character.

The assemblage of the cardinals at Rome is called a "college." So, in the United States, the body of presidential electors is called the "electoral college."

In the most common use of the word, it designates an institution of learning (usually incorporated) which offers instruction in the liberal arts and humanities and in scientific branches, but not in the technical arts or those studies preparatory to admission to the professions.

In England, it is a civil corporation, company, or society of men, having certain privileges, and endowed with certain revenues, founded by royal license. An assemblage of several of these colleges is called a "university." Wharton.

COLLEGIA. In the civil law. The guild of a trade.

COLLEGIALITER. In a corporate capacity. 2 Kent, Comm. 296.

COLLEGIATE CHURCH. In English ecclesiastical law. A church built and endowed for a society or body corporate of a dean or other president, and secular priests, as canons or prebendaries in the said church; such as the churches of Westminster, Windsor, and others. Cowell.

COLLEGIUM. In the civil law. A word having various meanings; e. g., an assembly, society, or company; a body of bishops; an army; a class of men. But the principal idea of the word was that of an association of individuals of the same rank and station, or united for the pursuit of some business or enterprise.

COLLEGIUM AMMIRALITATIS. The college or society of the admiralty.

Collegium est societas plurium corporum simul habitantium. Jenk. Cent. 229. A college is a society of several persons dwelling together.

COLLEGIUM ILLICITUM. One which abused its right, or assembled for any other purpose than that expressed in its charter.

COLLEGIUM LICITUM. An assemblage or society of men united for some useful purpose or business, with power to act like a single individual. 2 Kent, Comm. 269.

COLLIERY. This term is sufficiently wide to include all contiguous and connected veins and seams of coal which are worked as one concern, without regard to the closes or pieces of ground under which they are carried, and apparently also the engines and machinery in such contiguous and connected veins. MacSwin. Mines, 25. See 58 Pa. St. 85.

COLLIGENDUM BONA DEFUNCTI. See AD COLLIGENDUM, etc.

COLLISION. In maritime law. The act of ships or vessels striking together.

In its strict sense, collision means the impact of two vessels both moving, and is distinguished from *allision*, which designates the striking of a moving vessel against one that is stationary. But collision is used in a broad sense, to include allision, and perhaps other species of encounters between vessels.

The term is not inapplicable to cases where a stationary vessel is struck by one under way, strictly termed "allision;" or where one vessel is brought into contact with another by swinging at anchor. And even an injury received by a vessel at her moorings, in consequence of being violently rubbed or pressed against by a second vessel lying along-side of her, in consequence of a collision against such second vessel by a third one under way, may be compensated for, under the general head of "collision," as well as an injury which is the direct result of a "blow," properly so called. Abb. Adm. 73.

COLLISTRIGIUM. The pillory.

COLLITIGANT. One who litigates with another.

COLLOBIUM. A hood or covering for the shoulders, formerly worn by serjeants at law.

COLLOCATION. In French law. The arrangement or marshaling of the creditors of an estate in the order in which they are to be paid according to law. Merl. Repert.

COLLOQUIUM. One of the usual parts of the declaration in an action for slander. It is a general averment that the words complained of were spoken "of and concerning the plaintiff," or concerning the extrinsic matters alleged in the inducement, and its office is to connect the whole publication with the previous statement.

An averment that the words in question are spoken of or concerning some usage, report, or fact which gives to words otherwise indifferent the peculiar defamatory meaning assigned to them. 16 Pick. 6.

COLLUSION. A deceitful agreement or compact between two or more persons, for the one party to bring an action against the other for some evil purpose, as to defraud a third party of his right. Cowell.

A secret arrangement between two or more persons, whose interests are apparently conflicting, to make use of the forms and proceedings of law in order to defraud a third person, or to obtain that which justice would not give them, by deceiving a court or its officers.

In divorce proceedings, collusion is an agreement between husband and wife that one of them shall commit, or appear to have committed, or be represented in court as having committed, acts constituting a cause of divorce, for the purpose of enabling the other to obtain a divorce. Civil Code Cal. § 114. But it also means connivance or conspiracy in initiating or prosecuting the suit, as where there is a compact for mutual aid in carrying it through to a decree.

COLLYBISTA. In the civil law. A money-changer; a dealer in money.

COLLYBUM. In the civil law. Exchange.

COLNE. In Saxon and old English law. An account or calculation.

COLONIAL LAWS. In America, this term designates the body of law in force in the thirteen original colonies before the Declaration of Independence. In England, the term signifies the laws enacted by Canada and the other present British colonies.

COLONIAL OFFICE. In the English government, this is the department of state through which the sovereign appoints colonial governors, etc., and communicates with them. Until the year 1854, the secretary for the colonies was also secretary for war.

COLONUS. In old European law. A husbandman; an inferior tenant employed in cultivating the lord's land. A term of Roman origin, corresponding with the Saxon ceorl. 1 Spence, Ch. 51.

COLONY. A dependent political community, consisting of a number of citizens of the same country who have emigrated therefrom to people another, and remain subject to the mother-country. 3 Wash. C. C. 287.

A settlement in a foreign country possessed and cultivated, either wholly or partially, by immigrants and their descendants, who have a political connection with and subordination to the mother-country, whence they emigrated. In other words, it is a place peopled from some more ancient city or country. Wharton.

COLOR. An appearance, semblance, or *simulacrum*, as distinguished from that which is real. A *prima facie* or apparent right. Hence, a deceptive appearance; a plausible,

assumed exterior, concealing a lack of reality; a disguise or pretext.

In pleading. Ground of action admitted to subsist in the opposite party by the pleading of one of the parties to an action, which is so set out as to be apparently valid, but which is in reality legally insufficient.

This was a term of the ancient rhetoricians, and early adopted into the language of pleading. It was an apparent or *prima facie* right; and the meaning of the rule that pleadings in confession and avoidance should give color was that they should confess the matter adversely alleged, to such an extent, at least, as to admit some apparent right in the opposite party, which required to be encountered and avoided by the allegation of new matter. Color was either express, *i. e.*, inserted in the pleading, or implied, which was naturally inherent in the structure of the pleading. Steph. Pl. 233.

The word also means the dark color of the skin showing the presence of negro blood; and hence it is equivalent to African descent or parentage.

COLOR OF OFFICE. An act unjustly done by the countenance of an office, being grounded upon corruption, to which the office is as a shadow and color. Plow. 64.

A claim or assumption of right to do an act by virtue of an office, made by a person who is legally destitute of any such right.

The phrase implies, we think, some official power vested in the actor,—he must be at least officer *de facto*. We do not understand that an act of a mere pretender to an office, or false personator of an officer, is said to be done by color of office. And it implies an illegal claim of authority, by virtue of the office, to do the act or thing in question. 23 Wend. 606.

COLOR OF TITLE. The appearance, semblance, or *simulacrum* of title. Any fact, extraneous to the act or mere will of the claimant, which has the appearance, on its face, of supporting his claim of a present title to land, but which, for some defect, in reality falls short of establishing it.

"Color of title is anything in writing purporting to convey title to the land, which defines the extent of the claim, it being immaterial how defective or imperfect the writing may be, so that it is a sign, semblance, or color of title." 70 Ga. 809.

Color of title is that which the law considers *prima facie* a good title, but which, by reason of some defect, not appearing on its face, does not in fact amount to title. An absolute nullity, as a void deed, judgment, etc., will not constitute color of title. 33 Cal. 668.

"Any instrument having a grantor and grantee, and containing a description of the lands intended to be conveyed, and apt words for their conveyance, gives color of title to the lands described. Such an instrument purports to be a conveyance of the title, and because it does not, for some reason, have that effect, it passes only color or the semblance of a title." 35 Ill. 392.

It is not synonymous with "claim of title." To the former, a paper title is requisite; but the latter may exist wholly in parol. 80 Iowa, 480.

COLORABLE. That which has or gives color. That which is in appearance only, and not in reality, what it purports to be.

COLORABLE ALTERATION. One which makes no real or substantial change, but is introduced only as a subterfuge or means of evading the patent or copyright law.

COLORABLE IMITATION. In the law of trade-marks, this phrase denotes such a close or ingenious imitation as to be calculated to deceive ordinary persons.

COLORABLE PLEADING. The practice of giving *color* in pleading.

COLORE OFFICII. By color of office.

"COLORED MAN." There is no legal, technical signification in this phrase which the courts are bound judicially to know. 31 Tex. 74.

COLORED PERSON. A person of African descent or negro blood.

COLPICES. Young poles, which, being cut down, are made levers or lifters. Blount.

COLPINDACH. In old Scotch law. A young beast or cow, of the age of one or two years; in later times called a "cowdash."

COLT. An animal of the horse species, whether male or female, not more than four years old. Russ. & R. 416.

COMBARONES. In old English law. Fellow-barons; fellow-citizens. The citizens or freemen of the Cinque Ports being anciently called "barons;" the term "*combarones*" is used in this sense in a grant of Henry III. to the barons of the port of Fevresham. Cowell.

COMBAT. A forcible encounter between two or more persons; a battle; a duel. Trial by battel.

COMBATERRÆ. A valley or piece of low ground between two hills. Kennett, Gloss.

COMBE. A small or narrow valley.

COMBINATION. A conspiracy, or confederation of men for unlawful or violent deeds.

A union of different elements. A patent may be taken out for a new combination of existing machines. 2 Mason, 112.

COMBUSTIO. Burning.
In old English law. The punishment inflicted upon apostates.

COMBUSTIO DOMORUM. House-burning; arson. 4 Bl. Comm. 272.

COMBUSTIO PECUNIÆ. Burning of money; the ancient method of testing mixed and corrupt money, paid into the exchequer, by melting it down.

COME. To present oneself; to appear in court. In modern practice, though such presence may be constructive only, the word is still used to indicate participation in the proceedings. Thus, a pleading may begin, "Now *comes* the defendant," etc. In case of a default, the technical language of the record is that the party "*comes* not, but makes default."

COMES, v. A word used in a pleading to indicate the defendant's presence in court. See COME.

COMES, n. Lat. A follower or attendant; a count or earl.

COMES AND DEFENDS. This phrase, anciently used in the language of pleading, and still surviving in some jurisdictions, occurs at the commencement of a defendant's plea or demurrer; and of its two verbs the former signifies that he appears in court, the latter that he defends the action.

COMINUS. Lat. Immediately; hand-to-hand; in personal contact.

COMITAS. Lat. Comity, courtesy, civility. *Comitas inter communitates;* or *comitas inter gentes;* comity between communities or nations; comity of nations. 2 Kent, Comm. 457.

COMITATU COMMISSO. A writ or commission, whereby a sheriff is authorized to enter upon the charges of a county. Reg. Orig. 295.

COMITATU ET CASTRO COMMISSO. A writ by which the charge of a county, together with the keeping of a castle, is committed to the sheriff.

COMITATUS. In old English law. A county or shire; the body of a county. The territorial jurisdiction of a *comes, i. e.,* count or earl. The county court, a court of great antiquity and of great dignity in early times.

Also, the retinue or train of a prince or high governmental official.

COMITES. Counts or earls. Attendants or followers. Persons composing the retinue of a high functionary. Persons who are attached to the suite of a public minister.

COMITES PALEYS. Counts or earls palatine; those who had the government of a county palatine.

COMITIA. In Roman law. An assembly, either (1) of the Roman curiæ, in which case it was called the "*comitia curiata vel calata;*" or (2) of the Roman centuries, in which case it was called the "*comitia centuriata;*" or (3) of the Roman tribes, in which case it was called the "*comitia tributa.*" Only patricians were members of the first *comitia*, and only plebians of the last; but the *comitia centuriata* comprised the entire populace, patricians and plebians both, and was the great legislative assembly passing the *leges*, properly so called, as the senate passed the *senatus consulta*, and the *comitia tributa* passed the *plebiscita.* Under the *Lex Hortensia*, 287 B. C., the *plebiscitum* acquired the force of a *lex.* Brown.

COMITISSA. In old English law. A countess; an earl's wife.

COMITIVA. In old English law. The dignity and office of a *comes*, (count or earl;) the same with what was afterwards called "*comitatus.*"

Also a companion or fellow-traveler; a troop or company of robbers. Jacob.

COMITY. Courtesy; complaisance; respect; a willingness to grant a privilege, not as a matter of right, but out of deference and good will. See next title.

COMITY OF NATIONS. The most appropriate phrase to express the true foundation and extent of the obligation of the laws of one nation within the territories of another. It is derived altogether from the voluntary consent of the latter; and it is inadmissible when it is contrary to its known policy, or prejudicial to its interests. In the silence of any positive rule affirming or denying or restraining the operation of foreign laws, courts of justice presume the tacit adoption of them by their own government, unless repugnant to its policy, or prejudicial to its interests. It is not the comity of the courts, but the comity of the nation, which is administered and ascertained in the same

way, and guided by the same reasoning, by which all other principles of the municipal law are ascertained and guided. Story, Confl. Laws, § 38.

The comity of nations (*comitas gentium*) is that body of rules which states observe towards one another from courtesy or mutual convenience, although they do not form part of international law. Holtz. Enc. *s. v.*

COMMAND. An order, imperative direction, or behest.

COMMANDEMENT. In French law. A writ served by the *huissier* pursuant to a judgment or to an executory notarial deed. Its object is to give notice to the debtor that if he does not pay the sum to which he has been condemned by the judgment, or which he engaged to pay by the notarial deed, his property will be seized and sold. Arg. Fr. Merc. Law, 550.

COMMANDER IN CHIEF. By article 2, § 2, of the constitution it is declared that the president shall be commander in chief of the army and navy of the United States. The term implies supreme control of military operations during the progress of a war, not only on the side of strategy and tactics, but also in reference to the political and international aspects of the war.

COMMANDERY. In old English law. A manor or chief messuage with lands and tenements thereto appertaining, which belonged to the priory of St. John of Jerusalem, in England; he who had the government of such a manor or house was styled the "commander," who could not dispose of it, but to the use of the priory, only taking thence his own sustenance, according to his degree. The manors and lands belonging to the priory of St. John of Jerusalem were given to Henry the Eighth by 32 Hen. VIII. c. 20, about the time of the dissolution of abbeys and monasteries; so that the name only of commanderies remains, the power being long since extinct. Wharton.

COMMANDITAIRES. Special partners; partners *en commandité.* See COMMANDITÉ.

COMMANDITÉ. In French law. A special or limited partnership, where the contract is between one or more persons who are general partners, and jointly and severally responsible, and one or more other persons who merely furnish a particular fund or capital stock, and thence are called "*commandataires*," or "*commendataires*," or "partners *en commandité;*" the business being carried on under the social name or firm of the general partners only, composed of the names of the general or complementary partners, the partners in *commandit:* being liable to losses only to the extent of the funds or capital furnished by them. Story, Partn. § 78; 3 Kent, Comm. 34.

COMMANDMENT. In practice. An authoritative order of a judge or magisterial officer.

In criminal law. The act or offense of one who commands another to transgress the law, or do anything contrary to law, as theft, murder, or the like. Particularly applied to the act of an accessary before the fact, in inciting, procuring, setting on, or stirring up another to do the fact or act. 2 Inst. 182.

COMMARCHIO. A boundary; the confines of land.

COMMENDA. In French law. The delivery of a benefice to one who cannot hold the legal title, to keep and manage it for a time limited and render an account of the proceeds. Guyot, Rép. Univ.

In mercantile law. An association in which the management of the property was intrusted to individuals. Troub. Lim. Partn. c. 3, § 27.

Commenda est facultas recipiendi et retinendi beneficium contra jus positivum à supremâ potestate. Moore, 905. A commendam is the power of receiving and retaining a benefice contrary to positive law, by supreme authority.

COMMENDAM. In ecclesiastical law. The appointment of a suitable clerk to hold a void or vacant benefice or church living until a regular pastor, be appointed. Hob. 144; Latch, 236.

In commercial law. The limited partnership (or *Société en commandité*) of the French law has been introduced into the Code of Louisiana under the title of "Partnership *in Commendam.*" Civil Code La. art. 2810.

COMMENDATIO. In the civil law. Commendation, praise, or recommendation.

COMMENDATION. In feudal law. This was the act by which an owner of allodial land placed himself and his land under the protection of a lord, so as to constitute himself his vassal or feudal tenant.

COMMENDATORS. Secular persons upon whom ecclesiastical benefices were bestowed in Scotland; called so because the benefices were commended and intrusted to their supervision.

COMMENDATORY. He who holds a church living or preferment *in commendam.*

COMMENDATORY LETTERS. In ecclesiastical law. Such as are written by one bishop to another on behalf of any of the clergy, or others of his diocese traveling thither, that they may be received among the faithful, or that the clerk may be promoted, or necessaries administered to others, etc. Wharton.

COMMENDATUS. In feudal law. One who intrusts himself to the protection of another. Spelman. A person who, by voluntary homage, put himself under the protection of a superior lord. Cowell.

COMMERCE. The various agreements which have for their object facilitating the exchange of the products of the earth or the industry of man, with an intent to realize a profit. Pard. Droit Com. n. 1. A general term including the specific contracts of sale and exchange.

The intercourse of nations in each other's produce and manufactures, in which the superfluities of one are given for those of another, and then re-exchanged with other nations for mutual wants. Wharton.

Commerce is the interchange or mutual change of goods, productions, or property of any kind between nations or individuals. Transportation is the means by which commerce is carried on. 45 Iowa, 338.

Commerce is a term of the largest import. It comprehends intercourse for the purposes of trade in any and all its forms, including the transportation, purchase, sale, and exchange of commodities between the citizens of our country and the citizens or subjects of other countries, and between the citizens of different states. The power to regulate it embraces all the instruments by which such commerce may be conducted. 91 U. S. 275.

Commerce is not limited to an exchange of commodities only, but includes, as well, intercourse with foreign nations and between the states; and includes the transportation of passengers. 3 Cow. 713; 34 Cal. 492.

The words "commerce" and "trade" are synonymous, but not identical. They are often used interchangeably; but, strictly speaking, commerce relates to intercourse or dealings with foreign nations, states, or political communities, while trade denotes business intercourse or mutual traffic within the limits of a state or nation, or the buying, selling, and exchanging of articles between members of the same community. See 4 Denio, 353; Jacob; Wharton.

COMMERCIA BELLI. War contracts. Compacts entered into by belligerent nations to secure a temporary and limited peace. 1 Kent, Comm. 159. Contracts between nations at war, or their subjects.

COMMERCIAL LAW. A phrase used to designate the whole body of substantive jurisprudence applicable to the rights, intercourse, and relations of persons engaged in commerce, trade, or mercantile pursuits. It is not a very scientific or accurate term. As foreign commerce is carried on by means of shipping, the term has come to be used occasionally as synonymous with "maritime law;" but, in strictness, the phrase "commercial law" is wider, and includes many transactions or legal questions which have nothing to do with shipping or its incidents.

COMMERCIAL PAPER. The term "commercial paper" means bills of exchange, promissory notes, bank-checks, and other negotiable instruments for the payment of money, which, by their form and on their face, purport to be such instruments as are, by the law-merchant, recognized as falling under the designation of "commercial paper." 6 N. B. R. 338.

Commercial paper means negotiable paper given in due course of business, whether the element of negotiability be given it by the law-merchant or by statute. A note given by a merchant for money loaned is within the meaning. 5 Biss. 113.

COMMERCIAL TRAVELER. Where an agent simply exhibits samples of goods kept for sale by his principal, and takes orders from purchasers for such goods, which goods are afterwards to be delivered by the principal to the purchasers, and payment for the goods is to be made by the purchasers to the principal on such delivery, such agent is generally called a "drummer" or "commercial traveler." 34 Kan. 434, 8 Pac. Rep. 865; 93 N. C. 511.

COMMERCIUM. Lat. In the civil law. Commerce; business; trade; dealings in the nature of purchase and sale; a contract.

Commercium jure gentium commune esse debet, et non in monopolium et privatum paucorum quæstum convertendum. 3 Inst. 181. Commerce, by the law of nations, ought to be common, and not converted to monopoly and the private gain of a few.

COMMINALTY. The commonalty or the people.

COMMINATORIUM. In old practice. A clause sometimes added at the end of writs, admonishing the sheriff to be faithful in executing them. Bract. fol. 398.

COMMISE. In old French law. Forfeiture; the forfeiture of a fief; the penalty attached to the ingratitude of a vassal. Guyot, Inst. Feod. c. 12.

COMMISSAIRE. In French law. A person who receives from a meeting of shareholders a special authority, viz., that of checking and examining the accounts of a manager or of valuing the *apports en nature*, (q. v.) The name is also applied to a judge who receives from a court a special mission, e. g., to institute an inquiry, or to examine certain books, or to supervise the operations of a bankruptcy. Arg. Fr. Merc. Law, 551.

COMMISSAIRES-PRISEURS. In French law. Auctioneers, who possess the exclusive right of selling personal property at public sale in the towns in which they are established; and they possess the same right concurrently with notaries, *greffiers*, and *huissiers*, in the rest of the arrondissement. Arg. Fr. Merc. Law, 551.

COMMISSARIAT. The whole body of officers who make up the commissaries' department of an army.

COMMISSARY. In ecclesiastical law. One who is sent or delegated to execute some office or duty as the representative of his superior; an officer of the bishop, who exercises spiritual jurisdiction in distant parts of the diocese.

In military law. An officer whose principal duties are to supply an army with provisions and stores.

COMMISSARY COURT. A Scotch ecclesiastical court of general jurisdiction, held before four commissioners, members of the Faculty of Advocates, appointed by the crown.

COMMISSION. A warrant or authority or letters patent, issuing from the government, or one of its departments, or a court, empowering a person or persons named to do certain acts, or to exercise jurisdiction, or to perform the duties and exercise the authority of an office, (as in the case of an officer in the army or navy.)

Also, in private affairs, it signifies the authority or instructions under which one person transacts business or negotiates for another.

In a derivative sense, a body of persons to whom a commission is directed. A board or committee officially appointed and empowered to perform certain acts or exercise certain jurisdiction of a public nature or relation; as a "commission of assise."

In the civil law. A species of bailment, being an undertaking, without reward, to do something in respect to an article bailed; equivalent to "mandate."

In commercial law. The recompense or reward of an agent, factor, broker, or bailee, when the same is calculated as a percentage on the amount of his transactions or on the profit to the principal. But in this sense the word occurs more frequently in the plural.

In criminal law. Doing or perpetration; the performance of an act.

In practice. An authority or writ issuing from a court, in relation to a cause before it, directing and authorizing a person or persons named to do some act or exercise some special function; usually to take the depositions of witnesses.

A commission is a process issued under the seal of the court and the signature of the clerk, directed to some person designated as commissioner, authorizing him to examine the witness upon oath on interrogatories annexed thereto, to take and certify the deposition of the witness, and to return it according to the directions given with the commission. Pen. Code Cal. § 1351.

COMMISSION DAY. In English practice. The opening day of the assises.

COMMISSION DEL CREDERE, in commercial law, is where an agent of a seller undertakes to guaranty to his principal the payment of the debt due by the buyer. The phrase "*del credere*" is borrowed from the Italian language, in which its signification is equivalent to our word "guaranty" or "warranty." Story, Ag. 28.

COMMISSION MERCHANT. A term which is synonymous with "factor." It means one who receives goods, chattels, or merchandise for sale, exchange, or other disposition, and who is to receive a compensation for his services, to be paid by the owner, or derived from the sale, etc., of the goods. 50 Ala. 154.

COMMISSION OF ANTICIPATION. In English law. An authority under the great seal to collect a tax or subsidy before the day.

COMMISSION OF APPRAISEMENT AND SALE. Where property has been arrested in an admiralty action *in rem* and ordered by the court to be sold, the order is carried out by a commission of appraisement and sale; in some cases (as where the property is to be released on bail and the value is disputed) a commission of appraisement only is required. Sweet.

COMMISSION OF ARRAY. In English law. A commission issued to send into every county officers to muster or set in military order the inhabitants. The introduction of commissions of lieutenancy, which contained, in substance, the same powers as these commissions, superseded them. 2 Steph. Comm. (7th Ed.) 582.

COMMISSION OF ASSISE. Those issued to judges of the high court or court of appeal, authorizing them to sit at the assises for the trial of civil actions.

COMMISSION OF BANKRUPT. A commission or authority formerly granted by the lord chancellor to such persons as he should think proper, to examine the bankrupt in all matters relating to his trade and effects, and to perform various other important duties connected with bankruptcy matters. But now, under St. 1 & 2 Wm. IV. c. 56, § 12, a fiat issues instead of such commission.

COMMISSION OF CHARITABLE USES. This commission issues out of chancery to the bishop and others, where lands given to charitable uses are misemployed, or there is any fraud or dispute concerning them, to inquire of and redress the same, etc.

COMMISSION OF DELEGATES. When any sentence was given in any ecclesiastical cause by the archbishop, this commission, under the great seal, was directed to certain persons, usually lords, bishops, and judges of the law, to sit and hear an appeal of the same to the king, in the court of chancery. But latterly the judicial committee of the privy council has supplied the place of this commission. Brown.

COMMISSION OF LUNACY. A writ issued out of chancery, or such court as may have jurisdiction of the case, directed to a proper officer, to inquire whether a person named therein is a lunatic or not. 1 Bouv. Inst. n. 382, et seq.

COMMISSION OF PARTITION. In the former English equity practice, this was a commission or authority issued to certain persons, to effect a division of lands held by tenants in common desiring a partition; when the commissioners reported, the parties were ordered to execute mutual conveyances to confirm the division.

COMMISSION OF REBELLION. In English law. An attaching process, formerly issuable out of chancery, to enforce obedience to a process or decree; abolished by order of 26th August, 1841.

COMMISSION OF REVIEW. In English ecclesiastical law. A commission formerly sometimes granted in extraordinary cases, to revise the sentence of the court of delegates. 3 Bl. Comm. 67. Now out of use, the privy council being substituted for the court of delegates, as the great court of appeal in all ecclesiastical causes. 3 Steph. Comm. 432.

COMMISSION OF THE PEACE. In English law. A commission from the crown, appointing certain persons therein named, jointly and severally, to keep the *peace*, etc. Justices of the peace are always appointed by special commission under the great seal, the form of which was settled by all the judges, A. D. 1590, and continues with little alteration to this day. 1 Bl. Comm. 351; 3 Steph. Comm. 39, 40.

COMMISSION OF TREATY WITH FOREIGN PRINCES. Leagues and arrangements made between states and kingdoms, by their ambassadors and ministers, for the mutual advantage of the kingdoms in alliance. Wharton.

COMMISSION OF UNLIVERY. In an action in the English admiralty division, where it is necessary to have the cargo in a ship unladen in order to have it appraised, a commission of unlivery is issued and executed by the marshal. Williams & B. Adm. Jur. 233.

COMMISSION TO EXAMINE WITNESSES. In practice. A commission issued out of the court in which an action is pending, to direct the taking of the depositions of witnesses who are beyond the territorial jurisdiction of the court.

COMMISSION TO TAKE ANSWER IN CHANCERY. In English law. A commission issued when defendant lives abroad to swear him to such answer. 15 & 16 Vict. c. 86, § 21. Obsolete. See Jud. Acts, 1873, 1875.

COMMISSION TO TAKE DEPOSITIONS. A written authority issued by a court of justice, giving power to take the testimony of witnesses who cannot be personally produced in court.

COMMISSIONER. A person to whom a commission is directed by the government or a court.

In the governmental system of the United States, this term denotes an officer who is charged with the administration of the laws relating to some particular subject-matter, or the management of some bureau or agency of the government. Such are the commissioners of education, of patents, of pensions, of fisheries, of the general land-office, of Indian affairs, etc.

In the state governmental systems, also, and in England, the term is quite extensively used as a designation of various officers having a similar authority and similar duties.

COMMISSIONER OF PATENTS. An officer of the United States government, being at the head of the bureau of the patent-office.

COMMISSIONERS OF BAIL. Officers appointed to take recognizances of bail in civil cases.

COMMISSIONERS OF BANKRUPTS. The name given, under the former English practice in bankruptcy, to the persons appointed under the great seal to execute a commission of bankruptcy, (*q. v.*)

COMMISSIONERS OF CIRCUIT COURTS. Officers appointed by and attached to the circuit courts of the United States, performing functions partly ministerial and partly judicial. To a certain extent they represent the judge in his absence. In the examination of persons arrested for violations of the laws of the United States they have the powers of committing magistrates. They also take bail, recognizances, affidavits, etc., and hear preliminary proceedings for foreign extradition.

COMMISSIONERS OF DEEDS. Officers empowered by the government of one state to reside in another state, and there take acknowledgments of deeds and other papers which are to be used as evidence or put on record in the former state.

COMMISSIONERS OF HIGHWAYS. Officers appointed in each county or township, in many of the states, with power to take charge of the altering, opening, repair, and vacating of highways within such county or township.

COMMISSIONERS OF SEWERS. In English law. Commissioners appointed under the great seal, and constituting a court of special jurisdiction; which is to overlook the repairs of the banks and walls of the seacoast and navigable rivers, or, with consent of a certain proportion of the owners and occupiers, to make new ones, and to cleanse such rivers, and the streams communicating therewith. St. 3 & 4 Wm. IV. c. 22, § 10; 3 Steph. Comm. 442.

COMMISSIONS. The compensation or reward paid to a factor, broker, agent, bailee, executor, trustee, receiver, etc., when the same is calculated as a percentage on the amount of his transactions or the amount received or expended.

COMMISSORIA LEX. In Roman law. A clause which might be inserted in an agreement for a sale upon credit, to the effect that the vendor should be freed from his obligation, and might rescind the sale, if the vendee did not pay the purchase price at the appointed time. Also a similar agreement between a debtor and his pledgee that, if the debtor did not pay at the day appointed, the pledge should become the absolute property of the creditor. This, however, was abolished by a law of Constantine. Cod. 8, 35, 3. See Dig. 18, 3; Mackeld. Rom. Law, §§ 447, 461; 2 Kent, Comm. 583.

COMMIT. In practice. To send a person to prison by virtue of a lawful authority, for any crime or contempt. 4 Bl. Comm. 295, 300; 1 Tidd, Pr. 479, 481.

To deliver a defendant to the custody of the sheriff or marshal, on his surrender by his bail. 1 Tidd, Pr. 285, 287.

COMMITMENT. In practice. The warrant or *mittimus* by which a court or magistrate directs an officer to take a person to prison.

The act of sending a person to prison by means of such a warrant or order. 9 N. H. 204.

COMMITTEE. In practice. An assembly or board of persons to whom the consideration or management of any matter is committed or referred by some court.

An individual or body to whom others have delegated or committed a particular duty, or who have taken on themselves to perform it

in the expectation of their act being confirmed by the body they profess to represent or act for. 15 Mees. & W. 529.

The term is especially applied to the person or persons who are invested, by order of the proper court, with the guardianship of the person and estate of one who has been adjudged a lunatic.

In parliamentary law. A portion of a legislative body, comprising one or more members, who are charged with the duty of examining some matter specially referred to them by the house, or of deliberating upon it, and reporting to the house the result of their investigations or recommending a course of action. A committee may be appointed for one special occasion, or it may be appointed to deal with all matters which may be referred to it during a whole session or during the life of the body. In the latter case, it is called a "standing committee." It is usually composed of a comparatively small number of members, but may include the whole house.

COMMITTITUR. In practice. An order or minute, setting forth that the person named in it *is committed* to the custody of the sheriff.

COMMITTITUR PIECE. An instrument in writing on paper or parchment, which charges a person, already in prison, in execution at the suit of the person who arrested him. 2 Chit. Archb. Pr. (12th Ed.) 1208.

COMMIXTIO. In the civil law. The mixing together or confusion of things, dry or solid, belonging to different owners, as distinguished from *confusio*, which has relation to liquids.

COMMODATE. In Scotch law. A gratuitous loan for use. Ersk. Inst. 3, 1, 20. Closely formed from the Lat. *commodatum*, (q. v.)

COMMODATI ACTIO. Lat. In the civil law. An action of loan; an action for a thing lent. An action given for the recovery of a thing loaned, (*commodatum*,) and not returned to the lender. Inst. 3, 15, 2; Id. 4, 1, 16.

COMMODATO. In Spanish law. A contract by which one person lends gratuitously to another some object not consumable, to be restored to him in kind at a given period; the same contract as *commodatum*, (q. v.)

COMMODATUM. In the civil law. He who lends to another a thing for a definite time, to be enjoyed and used under certain conditions, without any pay or reward, is called "*commodans;*" the person who receives the thing is called "*commodatarius,*" and the contract is called "*commodatum.*" It differs from *locatio* and *conductio,* in this: that the use of the thing is gratuitous. Dig. 13, 6; Inst. 3, 2, 14; Story, Bailm. § 221.

COMMODITIES. Goods, wares, and merchandise of any kind; movables; articles of trade or commerce.

Commodum ex injuriâ suâ nemo habere debet. Jenk. Cent. 161. No person ought to have advantage from his own wrong.

COMMON. As an *adjective,* this word denotes usual, ordinary, accustomed; shared among several; owned by several jointly.

COMMON, *n.* An incorporeal hereditament which consists in a profit which one man has in connection with one or more others in the land of another. 12 Serg. & R. 32; 10 Wend. 647; 11 Johns. 498.

Common, in English law, is an incorporeal right which lies in grant, originally commencing on some agreement between lords and tenants, which by time has been formed into prescription, and continues good, although there be no deed or instrument to prove the original contract. 4 Coke, 37; 1 Crabb, Real Prop. p. 258, § 268.

Common, or a right of common, is a right or privilege which several persons have to the produce of the lands or waters of another. Thus, common of pasture is a right of feeding the beasts of one person on the lands of another; common of estovers is the right a tenant has of taking necessary wood and timber from the woods of the lord for fuel, fencing, etc. 10 Wend. 647.

The word "common" also denotes an uninclosed piece of land set apart for public or municipal purposes, in many cities and villages of the United States.

COMMON APPENDANT. A right annexed to the possession of arable land, by which the owner is entitled to feed his beasts on the lands of another, usually of the owner of the manor of which the lands entitled to common are a part. 10 Wend. 648; 2 Bl. Comm. 33.

COMMON APPURTENANT. A right of feeding one's beasts on the land of another, (in common with the owner or with others,) which is founded on a grant, or a prescription which supposes a grant. 1 Crabb, Real Prop. p. 264, § 277. This kind of common arises from no connection of

tenure, and is against common right; it may commence by grant within time of memory, or, in other words, may be created at the present day; it may be claimed as annexed to any kind of land, and may be claimed for beasts not commonable, as well as those that are. 2 Bl. Comm. 33.

COMMON ASSURANCES. The several modes or instruments of conveyance established or authorized by the law of England. Called "common" because thereby *every man's* estate is assured to him. 2 Bl. Comm. 294.

The legal evidences of the translation of property, whereby every person's estate is assured to him, and all controversies, doubts, and difficulties are either prevented or removed. Wharton.

COMMON BAIL. In practice. The form of entering merely fictitious bail, in cases where special bail is not required. A species of bail intended only to express the appearance of a defendant.

COMMON BAR. In pleading. (Otherwise called "blank bar.") A plea to compel the plaintiff to assign the particular place where the trespass has been committed. Steph. Pl. 256.

COMMON BARRETOR. In criminal law. One who frequently excites and stirs up groundless suits and quarrels, either at law or otherwise.

COMMON BECAUSE OF VICINAGE is where the inhabitants of two townships which lie contiguous to each other have usually intercommoned with one another, the beasts of the one straying mutually into the other's fields, without any molestation from either. This is, indeed, only a permissive right, intended to excuse what, in strictness, is a trespass in both, and to prevent a multiplicity of suits, and therefore either township may inclose and bar out the other, though they have intercommoned time out of mind. 2 Bl. Comm. 33; Co. Litt. 122a.

COMMON BENCH. The English court of common pleas was formerly so called. Its original title appears to have been simply "The Bench," but it was designated "Common Bench" to distinguish it from the "King's Bench," and because in it were tried and determined the causes of *common* persons, *i. e.,* causes between subject and subject, in which the crown had no interest.

COMMON CARRIERS. A common carrier is one whose regular business or calling it is to carry chattels for all persons who may choose to employ and remunerate him. Schouler, Bailm. 297.

Every one who offers to the public to carry persons, property, or messages, excepting only telegraphic messages, is a common carrier of whatever he thus offers to carry. Civil Code Cal. § 2168.

A common carrier is one who holds himself out to the public to carry persons or freight for hire. 24 Conn. 479.

At common law, a common carrier is an insurer of the goods intrusted to him, and he is responsible for all losses of the same, save such as are occasioned by the act of God or the public enemy. 15 Minn. 279, (Gil. 208.)

Common carriers are of two kinds,—by *land*, as owners of stages, stage-wagons, railroad cars, teamsters, cartmen, draymen, and porters; and by *water*, as owners of ships, steam-boats, barges, ferrymen, lightermen, and canal boatmen. 2 Kent, Comm. 597.

COMMON CARRIERS OF PASSENGERS. Common carriers of passengers are such as undertake for hire to carry all persons indifferently who may apply for passage. Thomp. Carr. p. 26, n. § 1.

COMMON CHASE. In old English law. A place where all alike were entitled to hunt wild animals.

COMMON COUNCIL. In American law. The lower or more numerous branch of the legislative assembly of a city.

In English law. The councillors of the city of London. The parliament, also, was anciently called the "common council of the realm." Fleta, 2, 13.

COMMON COUNTS. Certain general counts or forms inserted in a declaration in an action to recover a money debt, not founded on the circumstances of the individual case, but intended to guard against a possible variance, and to enable the plaintiff to take advantage of any ground of liability which the proof may disclose, within the general scope of the action. In the action of *assumpsit*, these counts are as follows: For goods sold and delivered, or bargained and sold; for work done; for money lent; for money paid; for money received to the use of the plaintiff; for interest; or for money due on an account stated.

COMMON DAY. In old English practice. An ordinary day in court. Cowell; Termes de la Ley.

COMMON DEBTOR. In Scotch law. A debtor whose effects have been arrested by

several creditors. In regard to these creditors, he is their common debtor, and by this term is distinguished in the proceedings that take place in the competition. Bell.

COMMON ERROR. (Lat. *communis error, q. v.*) An error for which there are many precedents. "Common error goeth for a law." Finch, Law, b. 1, c. 3, no. 54.

COMMON FINE. In old English law. A certain sum of money which the residents in a leet paid to the lord of the leet, otherwise called "head silver," "cert money," (*q. v.*,) or "*certum letæ*." Termes de la Ley; Cowell. A sum of money paid by the inhabitants of a manor to their lord, towards the charge of holding a court leet. Bailey, Dict.

COMMON FISHERY. A fishing ground where all persons have a right to take fish. Not to be confounded with "common of fishery," as to which see COMMON OF PISCARY.

COMMON FORM. A will is said to be proved in common form when the executor proves it on his own oath; as distinguished from "proof by witnesses," which is necessary when the paper propounded as a will is disputed.

COMMON HALL. A court in the city of London, at which all the citizens, or such as are free of the city, have a right to attend.

COMMON HIGHWAY. By this term is meant a road to be used by the community at large for any purpose of transit or traffic. Ham. N. P. 239.

COMMON IN GROSS, OR AT LARGE. A species of common which is neither appendant nor appurtenant to *land*, but is annexed to a man's *person*, being granted to him and his heirs by deed; or it may be claimed by prescriptive right, as by a parson of a church or the like corporation sole. 2 Bl. Comm. 34. It is a separate inheritance, entirely distinct from any other landed property, vested in the person to whom the common right belongs. 2 Steph. Comm. 6.

COMMON INFORMER. A common prosecutor. A person who habitually ferrets out crimes and offenses and lays information thereof before the ministers of justice, in order to set a prosecution on foot, not because of his office or any special duty in the matter, but for the sake of the share of the fine or penalty which the law allots to the informer in certain cases.

COMMON INTENDMENT. The natural and usual sense; the common meaning or understanding; the plain meaning of any writing as apparent on its face without straining or distorting the construction.

COMMON INTENT. The natural sense given to words.

COMMON JURY. In practice. The ordinary kind of jury by which issues of fact are generally tried, as distinguished from a *special jury.* (*q. v.*)

COMMON LAW 1. As distinguished from the Roman law, the modern civil law, the canon law, and other systems, the common law is that body of law and juristic theory which was originated, developed, and formulated and is administered in England, and has obtained among most of the states and peoples of Anglo-Saxon stock.

2. As distinguished from law created by the enactment of legislatures, the common law comprises the body of those principles and rules of action, relating to the government and security of persons and property, which derive their authority solely from usages and customs of immemorial antiquity, or from the judgments and decrees of the courts recognizing, affirming, and enforcing such usages and customs; and, in this sense, particularly the ancient unwritten law of England.

3. As distinguished from equity law, it is a body of rules and principles, written or unwritten, which are of fixed and immutable authority, and which must be applied to controversies rigorously and in their entirety, and cannot be modified to suit the peculiarities of a specific case, or colored by any judicial discretion, and which rests confessedly upon custom or statute, as distinguished from any claim to ethical superiority.

4. As distinguished from ecclesiastical law, it is the system of jurisprudence administered by the purely secular tribunals.

5. As concerns its force and authority in the United States, the phrase designates that portion of the common law of England (including such acts of parliament as were applicable) which had been adopted and was in force here at the time of the Revolution. This, so far as it has not since been expressly abrogated, is recognized as an organic part of the jurisprudence of most of the United States.

6. In a wider sense than any of the foregoing, the "common law" may designate all that part of the positive law, juristic theory, and ancient custom of any state or nation which is of general and universal application, thus marking off special or local rules or customs.

COMMON-LAW PROCEDURE ACTS. Three acts of parliament, passed in the years 1852, 1854, and 1860, respectively, for the amendment of the procedure in the common-law courts. The common-law procedure act of 1852 is St. 15 & 16 Vict. c. 76; that of 1854, St. 17 & 18 Vict. c. 125, and that of 1860, St. 23 & 24 Vict. c. 126. Mozley & Whitley.

COMMON LAWYER. A lawyer learned in the common law.

COMMON LEARNING. Familiar law or doctrine. Dyer, 27b, 33.

COMMON NUISANCE. One which affects the public in general, and not merely some particular person. 1 Hawk. P. C. 197. See NUISANCE.

COMMON OF DIGGING. Common of digging, or common in the soil, is the right to take for one's own use part of the soil or minerals in another's land; the most usual subjects of the right are sand, gravel, stones, and clay. It is of a very similar nature to common of estovers and of turbary. Elton, Com. 109.

COMMON OF ESTOVERS. A liberty of taking necessary wood for the use or furniture of a house or farm from off another's estate, in common with the owner or with others. 2 Bl. Comm. 35. It may be claimed, like common of pasture, either by grant or prescription. 2 Steph. Comm. 10.

COMMON OF FOWLING. In some parts of the country a right of taking wild animals (such as conies or wildfowl) from the land of another has been found to exist; in the case of wildfowl, it is called a "common of fowling." Elton, Com, 118.

COMMON OF PASTURE. The right or liberty of pasturing one's cattle upon another man's land. It may be either appendant, appurtenant, in gross, or because of vicinage.

COMMON OF PISCARY, or FISHERY. The right or liberty of fishing in another man's water, in common with the owner or with other persons. 2 Bl. Comm. 34. A liberty or right of fishing in the water covering the soil of another person, or in a river running through another's land. 3 Kent, Comm. 409. It is quite different from a common fishery, with which, however, it is frequently confounded.

COMMON OF SHACK. A species of common by vicinage prevailing in the counties of Norfolk, Lincoln, and Yorkshire, in England; b ing the right of persons occupying lands lying together in the same common field to turn out their cattle after harvest to feed promiscuously in that field. 2 Steph. Comm. 6, 7; 5 Coke, 65.

COMMON OF TURBARY. Common of turbary, in its modern sense, is the right of taking peat or turf from the waste land of another, for fuel in the commoner's house. Williams, Common, 187.

Common opinion is good authority in law. Co. Litt. 186a; 3 Barb. Ch. 528, 577.

COMMON PLACE. Common pleas. The English court of common pleas is sometimes so called in the old books.

COMMON PLEAS. The name of a court of record having general original jurisdiction in civil suits.

Common causes or suits. A term anciently used to denote civil actions, or those depending between subject and subject, as distinguished from *pleas of the crown.*

COMMON PLEAS, THE COURT OF. In English law. (So called because its original jurisdiction was to determine controversies between subject and subject.) One of the three superior courts of common law at Westminster, presided over by a lord chief justice and five (formerly four, until 31 & 32 Vict. c. 125, § 11, subsec. 8) *puisné* judges. It was detached from the king's court (*aula regis*) as early as the reign of Richard I., and the fourteenth clause of *Magna Charta* enacted that it should not follow the king's court, but be held in some certain place. Its jurisdiction was altogether confined to civil matters, having no cognizance in criminal cases, and was concurrent with that of the queen's bench and exchequer in personal actions and ejectment. Wharton.

COMMON PRAYER. The liturgy, or public form of prayer prescribed by the Church of England to be used in all churches and chapels, and which the clergy are enjoined to use under a certain penalty.

COMMON RECOVERY. In conveyancing. A species of common assurance, or mode of conveying lands by matter of rec-

ord, formerly in frequent use in England. It was in the nature and form of an action at law, carried regularly through, and ending in a *recovery* of the lands against the tenant of the freehold; which recovery, being a supposed adjudication of the right, bound all persons, and vested a free and absolute fee-simple in the recoverer. 2 Bl. Comm. 357. Common recoveries were abolished by the statute 3 & 4 Wm. IV. c. 74.

COMMON SANS NOMBRE. Common without number, that is, without *limit* as to the *number* of cattle which may be turned on; otherwise called "common without stint." Bract. fols. 53b, 222b; 2 Steph. Comm. 6, 7; 2 Bl. Comm. 34.

COMMON SCHOOLS. Schools maintained at the public expense and administered by a bureau of the state, district, or municipal government, for the gratuitous education of the children of all citizens without distinction.

COMMON SCOLD. One who, by the practice of frequent scolding, disturbs the neighborhood. Bish. Crim. Law, § 147. A quarrelsome, brawling, vituperative person.

COMMON SEAL. A seal adopted and used by a corporation for authenticating its corporate acts and executing legal instruments.

COMMON SENSE. Sound practical judgment; that degree of intelligence and reason, as exercised upon the relations of persons and things and the ordinary affairs of life, which is possessed by the generality of mankind, and which would suffice to direct the conduct and actions of the individual in a manner to agree with the behavior of ordinary persons.

COMMON SERJEANT. A judicial officer attached to the corporation of the city of London, who assists the recorder in disposing of the criminal business at the Old Bailey sessions, or central criminal court. Brown.

COMMON, TENANTS IN. See TENANTS IN COMMON.

COMMON TRAVERSE. See TRAVERSE.

COMMON VOUCHEE. In common recoveries, the person who is vouched to warranty. In this fictitious proceeding the crier of the court usually performs the office of a common vouchee. 2 Bl. Comm. 358; 2 Bouv. Inst. n. 2093.

COMMON WEAL. The public or common good or welfare.

COMMONABLE. Entitled to common. Commonable beasts are either beasts of the plow, as horses and oxen, or such as manure the land, as kine and sheep. Beasts not commonable are swine, goats, and the like. Co. Litt. 122*a*; 2 Bl. Comm. 33.

COMMONAGE. In old deeds. The right of common. See COMMON.

COMMONALTY. In English law. The great body of citizens; the mass of the people, excluding the nobility.

In American law. The body of people composing a municipal corporation, excluding the corporate officers.

COMMONANCE. The commoners, or tenants and inhabitants, who have the right of common or commoning in open field. Cowell.

COMMONERS. In English law. Persons having a right of *common*. So called because they have a right to pasture on the waste, in common with the lord. 2 H. Bl. 389.

COMMONS. 1. The class of subjects in Great Britain exclusive of the royal family and the nobility. They are represented in parliament by the house of commons.

2. Part of the demesne land of a manor, (or land the property of which was in the lord,) which, being uncultivated, was termed the "lord's waste," and served for public roads and for common of pasture to the lord and his tenants. 2 Bl. Comm. 90.

COMMONS HOUSE OF PARLIAMENT. In the English parliament. The lower house, so called because the commons of the realm, that is, the knights, citizens, and burgesses returned to parliament, representing the whole body of the commons, sit there.

COMMONTY. In Scotch law. Land possessed in common by different proprietors, or by those having acquired rights of servitude. Bell.

COMMONWEALTH. The public or common weal or welfare. This cannot be regarded as a technical term of public law, though often used in political science. It generally designates, when so employed, a republican frame of government,—one in which the welfare and rights of the entire mass of people are the main consideration, rather than the privileges of a class or the will of a monarch; or it may designate the body of citizens living under such a government. Sometimes it may denote the corporate entity, or the government, of a jural society (or state) possessing powers of self-government in respect of its immediate concerns, but forming an integral part of a larger government, (or nation.) In this latter sense, it is the official title of several of the United States, (as Pennsylvania and Massachusetts,) and would be appropriate to them all. In the former sense, the word was used to designate the English government during the protectorate of Cromwell. See GOVERNMENT; NATION; STATE.

COMMORANCY. The dwelling in any place as an inhabitant; which consists in usually lying there. 4 Bl. Comm. 273. In American law it is used to denote a mere temporary residence. 19 Pick. 247, 248.

COMMORANT. Staying or abiding; dwelling temporarily in a place.

COMMORIENTES. Several persons who perish at the same time in consequence of the same calamity.

COMMORTH, or COMORTH. A contribution which was gathered at marriages, and when young priests said or sung the first masses. Prohibited by 26 Hen. VIII. c. 6. Cowell.

COMMOTE. Half a cantred or hundred in Wales, containing fifty villages. Also a great seignory or lordship, and may include one or divers manors. Co. Litt. 5.

COMMUNE. A self-governing town or village. The name given to the committee of the people in the French revolution of 1793; and again, in the revolutionary uprising of 1871, it signified the attempt to establish absolute self-government in Paris, or the mass of those concerned in the attempt. In old French law, it signified any municipal corporation. And in old English law, the commonalty or common people.

COMMUNE CONCILIUM REGNI. The common council of the realm. One of the names of the English parliament.

COMMUNE FORUM. The common place of justice. The seat of the principal courts, especially those that are fixed.

COMMUNE PLACITUM. In old English law. A common plea or civil action, such as an action of debt.

COMMUNE VINCULUM. A common or mutual bond. Applied to the common stock of consanguinity, and to the feudal bond of fealty, as the common bond of union between lord and tenant. 2 Bl. Comm. 250; 3 Bl. Comm. 230.

COMMUNI CUSTODIA. In English law. An obsolete writ which anciently lay for the lord, whose tenant, holding by knight's service, died, and left his eldest son under age, against a stranger that entered the land, and obtained the ward of the body. Reg. Orig. 161.

COMMUNI DIVIDUNDO. In the civil law. An action which lies for those who have property in common, to procure a division. It lies where parties hold land in common but not in partnership. Calvin.

COMMUNIA. In old English law. Common things, *res communes.* Such as running water, the air, the sea, and sea shores. Bract. fol. 7*b.*

COMMUNIA PLACITA. In old English law. Common pleas or actions; those between one subject and another, as distinguished from pleas of the crown.

COMMUNIA PLACITA NON TENENDA IN SCACCARIO. An ancient writ directed to the treasurer and barons of the exchequer, forbidding them to hold pleas between common persons (*i. e.,* not debtors to the king, who alone originally sued and were sued there) in that court, where neither of the parties belonged to the same. Reg. Orig. 187.

COMMUNIÆ. In feudal law on the continent of Europe, this name was given to towns enfranchised by the crown, about the twelfth century, and formed into free corporations by grants called "charters of community."

COMMUNIBUS ANNIS. In ordinary years; on the annual average.

COMMUNICATION. Information given; the sharing of knowledge by one with another; conference; consultation or bargaining preparatory to making a contract. Also intercourse; connection.

In French law. The production of a merchant's books, by delivering them either to a person designated by the court, or to his adversary, to be examined in all their parts, and as shall be deemed necessary to the suit. Arg. Fr. Merc. Law, 552.

COMMUNINGS. In Scotch law. The negotiations preliminary to the entering into a contract.

COMMUNIO BONORUM. In the civil law. A term signifying a community (*q. v.*) of goods.

COMMUNION OF GOODS. In Scotch law. The right enjoyed by married persons in the movable goods belonging to them. Bell.

Communis error facit jus. Common error makes law. 4 Inst. 240; Noy, Max. p. 37, max. 27. Common error goeth for a law. Finch, Law, b. 1, c. 3, no. 54. Common error sometimes passes current as law. Broom, Max. 139, 140.

COMMUNIS OPINIO. Common opinion; general professional opinion. According to Lord Coke, (who places it on the footing of observance or usage,) common opinion is good authority in law. Co. Litt. 186*a.*

COMMUNIS PARIES. In the civil law. A common or party wall. Dig. 8, 2, 8, 13.

COMMUNIS RIXATRIX. In old English law. A common scold, (*q. v.*) 4 Bl. Comm. 168.

COMMUNIS SCRIPTURA. In old English law. A common writing; a writing common to both parties; a chirograph. Glan. lib. 8, c. 1.

COMMUNIS STIPES. A common stock of descent; a common ancestor.

COMMUNISM. A name given to proposed systems of life or social organization based upon the fundamental principle of the non-existence of private property and of a community of goods in a society.

An equality of distribution of the physical means of life and enjoyment as a transition to a still higher standard of justice that all should work according to their capacity and receive according to their wants. 1 Mill, Pol. Ec. 248.

COMMUNITAS REGNI ANGLIÆ. The general assembly of the kingdom of England. One of the ancient names of the English parliament. 1 Bl. Comm. 148.

COMMUNITY. A society of people living in the same place, under the same laws and regulations, and who have common rights and privileges.

In the civil law. A corporation or body politic. Dig. 3, 4.

In French law. A species of partnership which a man and a woman contract when they are lawfully married to each other.

COMMUNITY PROPERTY. Community property is property acquired by husband and wife, or either, during marriage, when not acquired as the separate property of either. Civil Code Cal. § 687.

This partnership or community consists of the profits of all the effects of which the husband has the administration and enjoyment, either of right or in fact, of the produce of the reciprocal industry and labor of both husband and wife, and of the estates which they may acquire during the marriage, either by donations made jointly to them both, or by purchase, or in any other similar way, even although the purchase be only in the name of one of the two, and not of both, because in that case the period of time when the purchase is made is alone attended to, and not the person who made the purchase. Civil Code La. art. 2402.

COMMUTATION. In criminal law. Change; substitution. The substitution of one punishment for another, after conviction of the party subject to it. The change of a punishment from a greater to a less; as from hanging to imprisonment.

Commutation of a punishment is not a conditional pardon, but the substitution of a lower for a higher grade of punishment, and is presumed to be for the culprit's benefit. 31 Ohio St. 206; 1 Nev. 321.

In civil matters. The conversion of the right to receive a variable or periodical payment into the right to receive a fixed or gross payment. Commutation may be effected by private agreement, but it is usually done under a statute.

COMMUTATION OF TITHES. Signifies the conversion of tithes into a fixed payment in money.

COMMUTATIVE CONTRACT. In the civil law. One in which each of the contracting parties gives and receives an equivalent.

Commutative contracts are those in which what is done, given, or promised by one party is considered as equivalent to, or a consideration for, what is done, given, or promised by the other. Civil Code La. art. 1768.

COMMUTATIVE JUSTICE. See JUSTICE.

COMPACT. An agreement or contract. Usually applied to conventions between nations or sovereign states.

A compact is a mutual consent of parties concerned respecting some property or right that is the object of the stipulation, or something that is to be done or forborne. 4 Gill & J. 1.

The terms "compact" and "contract" are synonymous. 8 Wheat. 1, 92.

COMPANAGE. All kinds of food, except bread and drink. Spelman.

COMPANIES CLAUSES CONSOLIDATION ACT. An English statute, (8 Vict. c. 16,) passed in 1845, which consolidated the clauses of previous laws still remaining in force on the subject of public companies. It is considered as incorporated into all subsequent acts authorizing the execution of undertakings of a public nature by companies, unless expressly excepted by such later acts. Its purpose is declared by the preamble to be to avoid repeating provisions as to the constitution and management of the companies, and to secure greater uniformity in such provisions. Wharton.

COMPANION OF THE GARTER. One of the knights of the Order of the Garter.

COMPANIONS. In French law. A general term, comprehending all persons who compose the crew of a ship or vessel. Poth. Mar. Cont. no. 163.

COMPANY. A society or association of persons, in considerable number, interested in a common object, and uniting themselves for the prosecution of some commercial or industrial undertaking, or other legitimate business.

The proper signification of the word "company," when applied to persons engaged in trade, denotes those united for the same purpose or in a joint concern. It is so commonly used in this sense, or as indicating a partnership, that few persons accustomed to purchase goods at shops, where they are sold by retail, would misapprehend that such was its meaning. 33 Me. 32.

Joint stock companies. Joint stock companies are those having a joint stock or capital, which is divided into numerous transferable shares, or consists of transferable stock. Lindl. Partn. 6.

The term is not identical with "partnership," although every unincorporated society is, in its legal relations, a partnership. In common use a distinction is made, the name "partnership" being reserved for business associations of a limited number of persons (usually not more than four or five) trading under a name composed of their individual names set out in succession; while "company" is appropriated as the designation of a society comprising a larger number of persons, with greater capital, and engaged in more extensive enterprises, and trading under a title not disclosing the names of the individuals.

Sometimes the word is used to represent those members of a partnership whose names do not appear in the name of the firm. See 12 Toullier, 97.

COMPARATIO LITERARUM. In the civil law. Compar'son of writings, or handwritings. A mode of proof allowed in certain cases.

COMPARATIVE JURISPRUDENCE. The study of the principles of legal science by the comparison of various systems of law.

COMPARATIVE NEGLIGENCE. That doctrine in the law of negligence by which the negligence of the parties is compared, in the degrees of "slight," "ordinary," and "gross" negligence, and a recovery permitted, notwithstanding the contributory negligence of the plaintiff, when the negligence of the plaintiff is slight and the negligence of the defendant gross, but refused when the plaintiff has been guilty of a want of ordinary care, thereby contributing to his injury, or when the negligence of the defendant is not gross, but only ordinary or slight, when compared, under the circumstances of the case, with the contributory negligence of the plaintiff. 3 Amer. & Eng. Enc. Law, 367. See 103 Ill. 512; 115 Ill. 358, 3 N. E. Rep. 456; 82 Ill. 198; 1 Shear. & R. Neg. §§ 102, 103; Whart. Neg. § 334.

COMPARISON OF HANDWRITING. A comparison by the juxtaposition of two writings, in order, by such comparison, to ascertain whether both were written by the same person.

A method of proof resorted to where the genuineness of a written document is disputed; it consists in comparing the handwriting of the disputed paper with that of another instrument which is proved or admitted to be in the writing of the party sought to be charged, in order to infer, from their identity or similarity in this respect, that they are the work of the same hand.

COMPASCUUM. Belonging to commonage. *Jus compascuum,* the right of common of pasture.

COMPASS, THE MARINER'S. An instrument used by mariners to point out the course of a ship at sea. It consists of a magnetized steel bar called the "needle," attached to the under side of a card, upon which are drawn the points of the compass, and supported by a fine pin, upon which it turns freely in a horizontal plane.

COMPASSING. Imagining or contriving, or plotting.

COMPATERNITAS. In the canon law. A kind of spiritual relationship contracted by baptism.

COMPATERNITY. Spiritual affinity, contracted by sponsorship in baptism.

COMPATIBILITY. Such relation and consistency between the duties of two offices that they may be held and filled by one person.

COMPEAR. In Scotch law. To appear.

COMPEARANCE. In Scotch practice. Appearance; an appearance made for a defendant; an appearance by counsel. Bell.

COMPELLATIVUS. An adversary or accuser.

Compendia sunt dispendia. Co. Litt. 305. Abbreviations are detriments.

COMPENDIUM. An abridgment, synopsis, or digest.

COMPENSACION. In Spanish law. Compensation; set-off. The extinction of a debt by another debt of equal dignity.

COMPENSATIO. In the civil law. Compensation, or set-off. A proceeding resembling a set-off in the common law, being a claim on the part of the defendant to have an amount due to him from the plaintiff deducted from his demand. Dig. 16, 2; Inst. 4, 6, 30, 39; 3 Bl. Comm. 305.

COMPENSATIO CRIMINIS. (Set-off of crime or guilt.) In practice. The plea of recrimination in a suit for a divorce; that is, that the complainant is guilty of the same kind of offense with which the respondent is charged.

COMPENSATION. Indemnification; payment of damages; making amends; that which is necessary to restore an injured party to his former position. An act which a court orders to be done, or money which a court orders to be paid, by a person whose acts or omissions have caused loss or injury to another, in order that thereby the person damnified may receive equal value for his loss, or be made whole in respect of his injury.

Also that equivalent in money which is paid to the owners and occupiers of lands taken or injuriously affected by the operations of companies exercising the power of eminent domain.

In the constitutional provision for "just compensation" for property taken under the power of eminent domain, this term means a payment in money. Any benefit to the remaining property of the owner, arising from public works for which a part has been taken, cannot be considered as compensation. 42 Ala. 83.

As compared with consideration and damages, compensation, in its most careful use, seems to be between them. Consideration is amends for something given by consent, or by the owner's choice. Damages is amends exacted from a wrong-doer for a tort. Compensation is amends for something which was taken without the owner's choice, yet without commission of a tort. Thus, one should say, consideration for land sold; compensation for land taken for a railway; damages for a trespass. But such distinctions are not uniform. Land damages is a common expression for compensation for lands taken for public use. Abbott.

The word also signifies the remuneration or wages given to an employe or officer. But it is not exactly synonymous with "salary." See 76 Ill. 548.

In the civil, Scotch, and French law. Recoupment; set-off. The meeting of two debts due by two parties, where the debtor in the one debt is the creditor in the other; that is to say, where one person is both debtor and creditor to another, and therefore, to the extent of what is due to him, claims allowance out of the sum that he is due. Bell; 1 Kames, Eq. 395, 396.

Compensation is of three kinds,—legal, or by operation of law; compensation by way of exception; and by reconvention. 16 La. Ann. 181.

COMPERENDINATIO. In the Roman law. The adjournment of a cause, in order to hear the parties or their advocates a second time; a second hearing of the parties to a cause. Calvin.

COMPERTORIUM. In the civil law. A judicial inquest made by delegates or commissioners to find out and relate the truth of a cause.

COMPERUIT AD DIEM. In practice. A plea in an action of debt on a bail bond that the defendant appeared at the day required.

COMPETENCY. In the law of evidence. The presence of those characteris-

tics, or the absence of those disabilities, which render a witness legally fit and qualified to give testimony in a court of justice. The term is also applied, in the same sense, to documents or other written evidence.

Competency differs from credibility. The former is a question which arises before considering the evidence given by the witness; the latter concerns the degree of credit to be given to his story. The former denotes the personal qualification of the witness; the latter his veracity. A witness may be competent, and yet give incredible testimony; he may be incompetent, and yet his evidence, if received, be perfectly credible. Competency is for the court; credibility for the jury. Yet in some cases the term "credible" is used as an equivalent for "competent." Thus, in a statute relating to the execution of wills, the term "credible witness" is held to mean one who is entitled to be examined and to give evidence in a court of justice; not necessarily one who is personally worthy of belief, but one who is not disqualified by imbecility, interest, crime, or other cause. 1 Jarm. Wills, 124; 23 Pick. 18.

In French law. Competency, as applied to a court, means its right to exercise jurisdiction in a particular case.

COMPETENT AND OMITTED. In Scotch practice. A term applied to a plea which might have been urged by a party during the dependence of a cause, but which had been omitted. Bell.

COMPETENT EVIDENCE. That which the very nature of the thing to be proven requires, as the production of a writing where its contents are the subject of inquiry. 1 Greenl. Ev. § 2; 1 Lea, 504.

COMPETENT WITNESS. One who is legally qualified to be heard to testify in a cause. See COMPETENCY.

COMPETITION. In Scotch practice. The contest among creditors claiming on their respective diligences, or creditors claiming on their securities. Bell.

COMPILE. To compile is to copy from various authors into one work. Between a compilation and an abridgment there is a clear distinction. A compilation consists of selected extracts from different authors; an abridgment is a condensation of the views of one author. 4 McLean, 306, 314.

COMPILATION. A literary production, composed of the works of others and arranged in a methodical manner.

COMPLAINANT. In practice. One who applies to the courts for legal redress; one who exhibits a bill of complaint. This is the proper designation of one suing in equity, though "plaintiff" is often used in equity proceedings as well as at law.

COMPLAINT. In civil practice. In those states having a Code of Civil Procedure, the complaint is the first or initiatory pleading on the part of the plaintiff in a civil action. It corresponds to the declaration in the common-law practice. Code N. Y. § 141.

The complaint shall contain: (1) The title of the cause, specifying the name of the court in which the action is brought, the name of the county in which the trial is required to be had, and the names of the parties to the action, plaintiff and defendant. (2) A plain and concise statement of the facts constituting a cause of action, without unnecessary repetition; and each material allegation shall be distinctly numbered. (3) A demand of the relief to which the plaintiff supposes himself entitled. If the recovery of money be demanded, the amount thereof must be stated. Code N. C. 1883, § 233.

In criminal law. A charge, preferred before a magistrate having jurisdiction, that a person named (or an unknown person) has committed a specified offense, with an offer to prove the fact, to the end that a prosecution may be instituted. It is a technical term, descriptive of proceedings before a magistrate. 11 Pick. 436.

The complaint is an allegation, made before a proper magistrate, that a person has been guilty of a designated public offense. Code Ala. 1886, § 4255.

COMPLICE. One who is united with others in an ill design; an associate; a confederate; an accomplice.

COMPOS MENTIS. Sound of mind. Having use and control of one's mental faculties.

COMPOS SUI. Having the use of one's limbs, or the power of bodily motion. *Si fuit ita compos sui quod itinerare potuit de loco in locum.* if he had so far the use of his limbs as to be able to travel from place to place. Bract. fol. 14*b*.

COMPOSITIO MENSURARUM. The ordinance of measures. The title of an ancient ordinance, not printed, mentioned in the statute 23 Hen. VIII. c. 4; establishing a standard of measures. 1 Bl. Comm. 275.

COMPOSITIO ULNARUM ET PERTICARUM. The statute of ells and perches. The title of an English statute establishing a standard of measures. 1 Bl. Comm. 275.

COMPOSITION. An agreement, made upon a sufficient consideration, between an insolvent or embarrassed debtor and his creditors, whereby the latter, for the sake of immediate payment, agree to accept a dividend less than the whole amount of their claims, to be distributed *pro rata*, in discharge and satisfaction of the whole.

"Composition" should be distinguished from "accord." The latter properly denotes an arrangement between a debtor and a single creditor for a discharge of the obligation by a part payment or on different terms. The former designates an arrangement between a debtor and the whole body of his creditors (or at least a considerable proportion of them) for the liquidation of their claims by the dividend offered.

In ancient law. Among the Franks, Goths, Burgundians, and other barbarous peoples, this was the name given to a sum of money paid, as satisfaction for a wrong or personal injury, to the person harmed, or to his family if he died, by the aggressor. It was originally made by mutual agreement of the parties, but afterwards established by law, and took the place of private physical vengeance.

COMPOSITION DEED. An agreement embodying the terms of a composition between a debtor and his creditors.

COMPOSITION IN BANKRUPTCY. An arrangement between a bankrupt and his creditors, whereby the amount he can be expected to pay is liquidated, and he is allowed to retain his assets, upon condition of his making the payments agreed upon.

COMPOSITION OF MATTER. A mixture or chemical combination of materials.

COMPOSITION OF TITHES, or **REAL COMPOSITION.** This arises in English ecclesiastical law, when an agreement is made between the owner of lands and the incumbent of a benefice, with the consent of the ordinary and the patron, that the lands shall, for the future, be discharged from payment of tithes, by reason of some land or other real recompense given in lieu and satisfaction thereof. 2 Bl. Comm. 28; 3 Steph. Comm. 129.

COMPOST. Several sorts of soil or earth and other matters mixed, in order to make a fine kind of mould for fertilizing lands.

COMPOTARIUS. In old English law. A party accounting. Fleta, lib. 2, c. 71, § 17.

COMPOUND. To compromise; to effect a composition with a creditor; to obtain discharge from a debt by the payment of a smaller sum.

COMPOUND INTEREST. Interest upon interest, *i. e.*, when the interest of a sum of money is added to the principal, and then bears interest, which thus becomes a sort of secondary principal.

COMPOUNDER. In Louisiana. The maker of a composition, generally called the "amicable compounder."

COMPOUNDING A FELONY. The offense committed by a person who, having been directly injured by a felony, agrees with the criminal that he will not prosecute him, on condition of the latter's making reparation, or on receipt of a reward or bribe not to prosecute.

The offense of taking a reward for forbearing to prosecute a felony; as where a party robbed takes his goods again, or other amends, upon an agreement not to prosecute. 29 Ark. 301; 4 Steph. Comm. 259.

COMPRA Y VENTA. In Spanish law. Purchase and sale.

COMPRINT. A surreptitious printing of another book-seller's copy of a work, to make gain thereby, which was contrary to common law, and is illegal. Wharton.

COMPRIVIGNI. In the civil law. Children by a former marriage, (individually called "*privigni*," or "*privignæ*,") considered relatively to each other. Thus, the son of a husband by a former wife, and the daughter of a wife by a former husband, are the *comprivigni* of each other. Inst. 1, 10, 8.

COMPROMISE. An arrangement arrived at, either in court or out of court, for settling a dispute upon what appears to the parties to be equitable terms, having regard to the uncertainty they are in regarding the facts, or the law and the facts together. Brown.

An agreement between two or more persons, who, for preventing or putting an end to a lawsuit, adjust their difficulties by mutual consent in the manner which they agree on, and which every one of them prefers to the hope of gaining, balanced by the danger of losing. 4 La. 456.

In the civil law. An agreement whereby two or more persons mutually bind themselves to refer their legal dispute to the decision of a designated third person, who is termed "umpire" or "arbitrator." Dig. 4, 8; Mackeld. Rom. Law, § 471.

Compromissarii sunt judices. Jenk. Cent. 128. Arbitrators are judges.

COMPROMISSARIUS. In the civil law. An arbitrator.

COMPROMISSUM. A submission to arbitration.

Compromissum ad similitudinem judiciorum redigitur. A compromise is brought into affinity with judgments. 9 Cush. 571.

COMPTE ARRÊTÉ. Fr. A *compte arrêté* is an account stated in writing, and acknowledged to be correct on its face by the party against whom it is stated. 9 La. Ann. 484.

COMPTER. In Scotch law. An accounting party.

COMPTROLLER. A public officer of a state or municipal corporation, charged with certain duties in relation to the fiscal affairs of the same, principally to examine and audit the accounts of collectors of the public money, to keep records, and report the financial situation from time to time. There are also officers bearing this name in the treasury department of the United States.

COMPTROLLER IN BANKRUPTCY. An officer in England, whose duty it is to receive from the trustee in each bankruptcy his accounts and periodical statements showing the proceedings in the bankruptcy, and also to call the trustee to account for any misfeasance, neglect, or omission in the discharge of his duties. Robs. Bankr. 13; Bankr. Act 1869, § 55.

COMPTROLLERS OF THE HANAPER. In English law. Officers of the court of chancery; their offices were abolished by 5 & 6 Vict. c. 103.

COMPULSION. Constraint; objective necessity. Forcible inducement to the commission of an act.

COMPULSORY. In ecclesiastical procedure, a compulsory is a kind of writ to compel the attendance of a witness, to undergo examination. Phillim. Ecc. Law, 1258.

COMPURGATOR. One of several neighbors of a person accused of a crime, or charged as a defendant in a civil action, who appeared and swore that they believed him on his oath. 3 Bl. Comm. 341.

COMPUTATION. The act of computing, numbering, reckoning, or estimating.

The account or estimation of time by rule of law, as distinguished from any arbitrary construction of the parties. Cowell.

COMPUTUS. A writ to compel a guardian, bailiff, receiver, or accountant to yield up his accounts. It is founded on the statute Westm. 2, c. 12; Reg. Orig. 135.

COMTE. Fr. A count or earl. In the ancient French law, the *comte* was an officer having jurisdiction over a particular district or territory, with functions partly military and partly judicial.

CON BUENA FE. In Spanish law. With (or in) good faith.

CONACRE. In Irish practice. The payment of wages in land, the rent being worked out in labor at a money valuation. Wharton.

Conatus quid sit, non definitur in jure. 2 Bulst. 277. What an attempt is, is not defined in law.

CONCEAL. To hide; secrete; withhold from the knowledge of others.

The word "conceal," according to the best lexicographers, signifies to withhold or keep secret mental facts from another's knowledge, as well as to hide or secrete physical objects from sight or observation. 57 Me. 339.

CONCEALED. The term "concealed" is not synonymous with "lying in wait." If a person conceals himself for the purpose of shooting another unawares, he is lying in wait; but a person may, while concealed, shoot another without committing the crime of murder. 55 Cal. 207.

The term "concealed weapons" means weapons willfully or knowingly covered or kept from sight. 31 Ala. 387.

CONCEALERS. In old English law. Such as find out concealed lands; that is, lands privily kept from the king by common persons having nothing to show for them. They are called "a troublesome, disturbant sort of men; turbulent persons." Cowell.

CONCEALMENT. The improper suppression or disguising of a fact, circumstance, or qualification which rests within the knowledge of one only of the parties to a contract, but which ought in fairness and good faith to be communicated to the other, whereby the party so concealing draws the other into an engagement which he would not make but for his ignorance of the fact concealed.

A neglect to communicate that which a

AM.DICT.LAW—16

party knows, and ought to communicate, is called a "concealment." Civil Code Cal. § 2561.

The terms "misrepresentation" and "concealment" have a known and definite meaning in the law of insurance. Misrepresentation is the statement of something as fact which is untrue in fact, and which the assured states, knowing it to be not true, with an intent to deceive the underwriter, or which he states positively as true, without knowing it to be true, and which has a tendency to mislead, such fact in either case being material to the risk. Concealment is the designed and intentional withholding of any fact material to the risk, which the assured, in honesty and good faith, ought to communicate to the underwriter; mere silence on the part of the assured, especially as to some matter of fact which he does not consider it important for the underwriter to know, is not to be considered as such concealment. If the fact so untruly stated or purposely suppressed is not material, that is, if the knowledge or ignorance of it would not naturally influence the judgment of the underwriter in making the contract, or in estimating the degree and character of the risk, or in fixing the rate of the premium, it is not a "misrepresentation" or "concealment," within the clause of the conditions annexed to policies. 12 Cush. 416.

CONCEDO. I grant. A word used in old Anglo-Saxon grants, and in statutes merchant.

CONCEPTUM. In the civil law. A theft (*furtum*) was called "*conceptum*," when the thing stolen was searched for, and found upon some person in the presence of witnesses. Inst. 4, 1, 4.

CONCESSI. Lat. I have granted. At common law, in a feoffment or estate of inheritance, this word does not imply a warranty; it only creates a covenant in a lease for years. Co. Litt. 384a; 2 Caines, 194.

CONCESSIMUS. Lat. We have granted. A term used in conveyances, the effect of which was to create a joint covenant on the part of the grantors.

CONCESSIO. In old English law. A grant. One of the old common assurances, or forms of conveyance.

Concessio per regem fieri debet de certitudine. 9 Coke, 46. A grant by the king ought to be made from certainty.

Concessio versus concedentem latam interpretationem habere debet. A grant ought to have a broad interpretation (to be liberally interpreted) against the grantor. Jenk. Cent. 279.

CONCESSION. A grant; ordinarily applied to the grant of specific privileges by a government; French and Spanish grants in Louisiana.

CONCESSIT SOLVERE. (He granted and agreed to pay.) In English law. An action of debt upon a simple contract. It lies by custom in the mayor's court, London, and Bristol city court.

CONCESSOR. In old English law. A grantor.

CONCESSUM. Accorded: conceded. This term, frequently used in the old reports, signifies that the court admitted or assented to a point or proposition made on the argument.

CONCESSUS. A grantee.

CONCILIABULUM. A council house.

CONCILIATION. In French law. The formality to which intending litigants are subjected in cases brought before the *juge de paix.* The judge convenes the parties and endeavors to reconcile them. Should he not succeed, the case proceeds. In criminal and commercial cases, the preliminary of conciliation does not take place. Arg. Fr. Merc. Law, 552.

CONCILIUM. A council. Also argument in a cause, or the sitting of the court to hear argument; a day allowed to a defendant to present his argument; an imparlance.

CONCILIUM ORDINARIUM. In Anglo-Norman times. An executive and residuary judicial committee of the *Aula Regis,* (*q. v.*)

CONCILIUM REGIS. An ancient English tribunal, existing during the reigns of Edward I. and Edward II., to which was referred cases of extraordinary difficulty. Co. Litt. 304.

CONCIONATOR. In old records. A common council man; a freeman called to a legislative hall or assembly. Cowell.

CONCLUDE. To finish; determine; to estop; to prevent.

CONCLUDED. Ended; determined; estopped; prevented from.

CONCLUSION. The end; the termination; the act of finishing or bringing to a close. The conclusion of a declaration or complaint is all that part which follows the statement of the plaintiff's cause of action. The conclusion of a plea is its final clause, in which the defendant either "puts himself upon the country" (where a material aver-

ment of the declaration is traversed and issue tendered) or offers a verification, which is proper where new matter is introduced.

In trial practice. It signifies making the final or concluding address to the jury or the court. This is, in general, the privilege of the party who has to sustain the burden of proof.

Conclusion also denotes a bar or estoppel; the consequence, as respects the individual, of a judgment upon the subject-matter, or of his confession of a matter or thing which the law thenceforth forbids him to deny.

CONCLUSION AGAINST THE FORM OF THE STATUTE. The proper form for the conclusion of an indictment for an offense created by statute is the technical phrase "against the form of the statute in such case made and provided;" or, in Latin, *contra formam statuti.*

CONCLUSION TO THE COUNTRY. In pleading. The tender of an issue to be tried by jury. Steph. Pl. 230.

CONCLUSIVE. Shutting up a matter; shutting out all further evidence; not admitting of explanation or contradiction; putting an end to inquiry; final; decisive.

CONCLUSIVE EVIDENCE. Evidence which, in its nature, does not admit of explanation or contradiction; such as what is called "certain circumstantial" evidence. Burrill, Circ. Ev. 89.

Evidence which, of itself, whether contradicted or uncontradicted, explained or unexplained, is sufficient to determine the matter at issue. 6 Lond. Law Mag. 373.

CONCLUSIVE PRESUMPTION. A rule of law determining the quantity of evidence requisite for the support of a particular averment which is not permitted to be overcome by any proof that the fact is otherwise. 1 Greenl. Ev. § 15.

CONCORD. In the old process of levying a fine of lands, the concord was an agreement between the parties (real or feigned) in which the deforciant (or he who keeps the other out of possession) acknowledges that the lands in question are the right of complainant; and, from the acknowledgment or admission of right thus made, the party who levies the fine is called the "cognizor," and the person to whom it is levied the "cognizee." 2 Bl. Comm. 350.

The term also denotes an agreement between two persons, one of whom has a right of action against the other, settling what amends shall be made for the breach or wrong; a compromise or an accord.

In old practice. An agreement between two or more, upon a trespass committed, by way of amends or satisfaction for it. Plowd. 5, 6, 8.

Concordare leges legibus est optimus interpretandi modus. To make laws agree with laws is the best mode of interpreting them. Halk. Max. 70.

CONCORDAT. In public law. A compact or convention between two or more independent governments.

An agreement made by a temporal sovereign with the pope, relative to ecclesiastical matters.

In French law. A compromise effected by a bankrupt with his creditors, by virtue of which he engages to pay within a certain time a certain proportion of his debts, and by which the creditors agree to discharge the whole of their claims in consideration of the same. Arg. Fr. Merc. Law, 553.

CONCORDIA. Lat. In old English law. An agreement, or concord. Fleta, lib. 5, c. 3, § 5. The agreement or unanimity of a jury. *Compellere ad concordiam.* Fleta, lib. 4, c. 9, § 2.

CONCORDIA DISCORDANTIUM CANONUM. The harmony of the discordant canons. A collection of ecclesiastical constitutions made by Gratian, an Italian monk, A. D. 1151; more commonly known by the name of "*Decretum Gratiani.*"

Concordia parvæ res crescunt et opulentia lites. 4 Inst. 74. Small means increase by concord and litigations by opulence.

CONCUBARIA. A fold, pen, or place where cattle lie. Cowell.

CONCUBEANT. Lying together, as cattle.

CONCUBINAGE. A species of loose or informal marriage which took place among the ancients, and which is yet in use in some countries. See CONCUBINATUS.

The act or practice of cohabiting, in sexual commerce, without the authority of law or a legal marriage.

An exception against a woman suing for dower, on the ground that she was the concubine, and not the wife, of the man of whose land she seeks to be endowed. Britt. c. 107.

CONCUBINATUS. In Roman law. An informal, unsanctioned, or "natural" marriage, as contradistinguished from the *justæ nuptiæ,* or *justum matrimonium,* the civil marriage.

CONCUBINE. (1) A woman who cohabits with a man to whom she is not married. (2) A sort of inferior wife, among the Romans, upon whom the husband did not confer his rank or quality.

CONCUR. In Louisiana. To join with other claimants in presenting a demand against an insolvent estate.

CONCURATOR. In the civil law. A joint or co-curator, or guardian.

CONCURRENCE. In French law. The possession, by two or more persons, of equal rights or privileges over the same subject-matter.

CONCURRENT. Having the same authority; acting in conjunction; agreeing in the same act; contributing to the same event; contemporaneous.

CONCURRENT JURISDICTION. The jurisdiction of several different tribunals, both authorized to deal with the same subject-matter at the choice of the suitor.

CONCURRENT WRITS. Duplicate originals, or several writs running at the same time for the same purpose, for service on or arrest of a person, when it is not known where he is to be found; or for service on several persons, as when there are several defendants to an action. Mozley & Whitley.

CONCURSUS. In the civil law. (1) A running together; a collision, as *concursus creditorum,* a conflict among creditors. (2) A concurrence, or meeting, as *concursus actionum,* concurrence of actions.

CONCUSS. In Scotch law. To coerce.

CONCUSSIO. In the civil law. The offense of extortion by threats of violence. Dig. 47, 13.

CONCUSSION. In the civil law. The unlawful forcing of another by threats of violence to give something of value. It differs from robbery, in this: that in robbery the thing is taken by force, while in concussion it is obtained by threatened violence. Heinec. Elem. § 1071.

CONDEDIT. In ecclesiastical law. The name of a plea entered by a party to a libel filed in the ecclesiastical court, in which it is pleaded that the deceased made the will which is the subject of the suit, and that he was of sound mind. 2 Eng. Ecc. R. 438; 6 Eng. Ecc. R. 431.

CONDEMN. To find or adjudge guilty. 3 Leon. 68. To adjudge or sentence. 3 Bl. Comm. 291. To adjudge (as an admiralty court) that a vessel is a prize, or that she is unfit for service. 1 Kent, Comm. 102; 5 Esp. 65. To set apart or expropriate property for public use, in the exercise of the power of eminent domain.

CONDEMNATION. In admiralty law. The judgment or sentence of a court having jurisdiction and acting *in rem*, by which (1) it is declared that a vessel which has been captured at sea as a prize was lawfully so seized and is liable to be treated as prize; or (2) that property which has been seized for an alleged violation of the revenue laws, neutrality laws, navigation laws, etc., was lawfully so seized, and is, for such cause, forfeited to the government; or (3) that the vessel which is the subject of inquiry is unfit and unsafe for navigation.

In the civil law. A sentence or judgment which condemns some one to do, to give, or to pay something, or which declares that his claim or pretensions are unfounded.

CONDEMNATION MONEY. In practice. The damages which the party failing in an action is adjudged or *condemned* to pay; sometimes simply called the "condemnation."

As used in an appeal-bond, this phrase means the damages which should be awarded against the appellant by the judgment of the court. It does not embrace damages not included in the judgment. 6 Blackf. 8.

CONDESCENDENCE. In the Scotch law. A part of the proceedings in a cause, setting forth the facts of the case on the part of the pursuer or plaintiff.

CONDICTIO. In Roman law. A general term for actions of a personal nature, founded upon an obligation to give or do a certain and defined thing or service. It is distinguished from *vindicatio rei*, which is an action to vindicate one's right of property in a thing by regaining (or retaining) possession of it against the adverse claim of the other party.

CONDICTIO CERTI. In the civil law. An action which lies upon a promise to do a thing, where such promise or stipulation is

certain, (*si certa sit stipulatio*.) Inst. 3, 16, pr.; Id. 3, 15, pr.; Dig. 12, 1; Bract. fol. 103b.

CONDICTIO EX LEGE. In the civil law. An action arising where the law gave a remedy, but provided no appropriate form of action. Calvin.

CONDICTIO INDEBITATI. In the civil law. An action which lay to recover anything which the plaintiff had given or paid to the defendant, by mistake, and which he was not bound to give or pay, either in fact or in law.

CONDICTIO REI FURTIVÆ. In the civil law. An action which lay to recover a thing stolen, against the thief himself, or his heir. Inst. 4, 1, 19.

CONDICTIO SINE CAUSA. In the civil law. An action which lay in favor of a person who had given or promised a thing without consideration, (*causa*.) Dig. 12, 7; Cod. 4, 9.

CONDITIO. Lat. A condition.

Conditio beneficialis, quæ statum construit, benignè secundum verborum intentionem est interpretanda; odiosa autem, quæ statum destruit, stricte secundum verborum proprietatem accipienda. 8 Coke, 90. A beneficial condition, which creates an estate, ought to be construed favorably, according to the intention of the words; but a condition which destroys an estate is odious, and ought to be construed strictly according to the letter of the words.

Conditio dicitur, cum quid in casum incertum qui potest tendere ad esse aut non esse, confertur. Co. Litt. 201. It is called a "condition," when something is given on an uncertain event, which may or may not come into existence.

Conditio illicita habetur pro non adjectâ. An unlawful condition is deemed as not annexed.

Conditio præcedens adimpleri debet prius quam sequatur effectus. Co. Litt. 201. A condition precedent must be fulfilled before the effect can follow.

CONDITION. In the civil law. The rank, situation, or degree of a particular person in some one of the different orders of society.

An agreement or stipulation in regard to some uncertain future event, not of the essential nature of the transaction, but annexed to it by the parties, providing for a change or modification of their legal relations upon its occurrence. Mackeld. Rom. Law, § 184.

In the civil law, conditions are of the following several kinds:

The *casual* condition is that which depends on chance, and is in no way in the power either of the creditor or of the debtor. Civil Code La. art. 2023.

A *mixed* condition is one that depends at the same time on the will of one of the parties and on the will of a third person, or on the will of one of the parties and also on a casual event. Civil Code La. art. 2025.

The *potestative* condition is that which makes the execution of the agreement depend on an event which it is in the power of the one or the other of the contracting parties to bring about or to hinder. Civil Code La. art. 2024.

A *resolutory* condition is one which destroys or releases an obligation already vested, as soon as the condition is fulfilled.

A *suspensive* condition is one which postpones the obligation until the happening of a future and uncertain event, or a present but unknown event.

In French law. In French law, the following peculiar distinctions are made: (1) A condition is *casuelle* when it depends on a chance or hazard; (2) a condition is *potestative* when it depends on the accomplishment of something which is in the power of the party to accomplish; (3) a condition is *mixte* when it depends partly on the will of the party and partly on the will of others; (4) a condition is *suspensive* when it is a future and uncertain event, or present but unknown event, upon which an obligation takes or fails to take effect; (5) a condition is *resolutoire* when it is the event which undoes an obligation which has already had effect as such. Brown.

In common law. The rank, situation, or degree of a particular person in some one of the different orders of society; or his *status* or situation, considered as a juridicial person, arising from positive law or the institutions of society.

A clause in a contract or agreement which has for its object to suspend, rescind, or modify the principal obligation, or, in case of a will, to suspend, revoke, or modify the devise or bequest. 1 Bouv. Inst. no. 730.

A *modus* or quality annexed by him that hath an estate, or interest or right to the same, whereby an estate, etc., may either be defeated, enlarged, or created upon an uncertain event. Co. Litt. 201a.

A qualification or restriction annexed to a conveyance of lands, whereby it is provided that in case a particular event does or does not happen, or in case the grantor or grantee does or omits to do a particular act, an estate shall commence, be enlarged, or be defeated. Greenl. Cruise, Dig. tit. xiii. c. i. § 1.

The different kinds of conditions known to the common law are defined under their appropriate names in the following titles. A further classification is, however, here subjoined:

Conditions are either *express* or *implied.* They are express when they appear in the contract; they are implied whenever they result from the operation of law, from the nature of the contract, or from the presumed intent of the parties. Civil Code La. art. 2026.

They are *possible* or *impossible;* the former when they admit of performance in the ordinary course of events; the latter when it is contrary to the course of nature or human limitations that they should ever be performed.

They are *lawful* or *unlawful;* the former when their character is not in violation of any rule, principle, or policy of law; the latter when they are such as the law will not allow to be made.

They are *consistent* or *repugnant;* the former when they are in harmony and concord with the other parts of the transaction; the latter when they contradict, annul, or neutralize the main purpose of the contract. Repugnant conditions are also called "insensible."

They are *independent, dependent,* or *mutual;* the first when each of the two conditions must be performed without any reference to the other; the second when the performance of one is not obligatory until the actual performance of the other; the third when neither party need perform his condition unless the other is ready and willing to perform his.

Synonyms distinguished. A "condition" is to be distinguished from a *limitation,* in that the latter may be to or for the benefit of a stranger, who may then take advantage of its determination, while only the grantor, or those who stand in his place, can take advantage of a condition, (16 Me. 158;) and in that a limitation ends the estate without entry or claim, which is not true of a condition. It also differs from a *conditional limitation:*

for in the latter the estate is limited over to a third person, while in case of a simple condition it reverts to the grantor, or his heirs or devisees. It differs also from a *covenant*, which can be made by either grantor or grantee, while only the grantor can make a condition, (Co. Litt. 70.) A *charge* is a devise of land with a bequest out of the subject-matter, and a charge upon the devisee personally, in respect of the estate devised, gives him an estate on condition. A condition also differs from a *remainder;* for, while the former may operate to defeat the estate before its natural termination, the latter cannot take effect until the completion of the preceding estate.

CONDITION AFFIRMATIVE. A condition which consists in doing a thing; as provided that the lessee shall pay rent, etc. Shep. Touch. 118.

CONDITION COLLATERAL. A condition where the act to be done is a collateral act. Shep. Touch. 118.

CONDITION COMPULSORY. A condition expressly requiring a thing to be done; as that a lessee shall pay £10 such a day, or his lease shall be void. Shep. Touch. 118.

CONDITION COPULATIVE. A condition to do divers things. Shep. Touch. 118.

CONDITION DISJUNCTIVE. A condition requiring one of several things to be done. Shep. Touch. 118.

CONDITION EXPRESSED. A condition expressed in the deed by which it is created, (*conditio expressa.*) 2 Crabb, Real Prop. p. 792, § 2127; Bract. fol. 47. A condition annexed, by express words, to any feoffment, lease, or grant. Termes de la Ley.

CONDITION IMPLIED. One which the law infers or presumes, from the nature of the transaction or the conduct of the parties, to have been tacitly understood between them as a part of the agreement, although not expressly mentioned.

CONDITION IN DEED. Fr. *condition en fait.* A condition expressed in a deed, (as a feoffment, lease, or grant,) in plain words, or legal terms of law. Cowell; Co. Litt. 201a. See CONDITION EXPRESSED.

CONDITION IN LAW. A condition tacitly created or annexed to a grant, by law, without any words used by the party. Co. Litt. 201a. See CONDITION IMPLIED.

CONDITION INHERENT. A condition annexed to the rent reserved out of the land whereof the estate is made; or rather to the estate in the land, in respect of rent, etc. Shep. Touch. 118.

CONDITION NEGATIVE. A condition which consists in not doing a thing; as provided that the lessee shall not alien, etc. Shep. Touch. 118.

CONDITION POSITIVE. One which requires that an event shall happen or an act be done.

CONDITION PRECEDENT. A condition precedent is one which is to be performed before some right dependent thereon accrues, or some act dependent thereon is performed. Civil Code Cal. § 1436.

A condition which must happen or be performed *before* the estate to which it is annexed can vest or be enlarged.

Conditions may be precedent or subsequent. In the former, the condition must be performed before the contract becomes absolute and obligatory upon the other party. In the latter, the breach of the condition may destroy the party's rights under the contract, or may give a right to damages to the other party, according to a true construction of the intention of the parties. Code Ga. 1882, § 2722.

CONDITION RESTRICTIVE. A condition for not doing a thing; as that the lessee shall not alien or do waste, or the like. Shep. Touch. 118.

CONDITION SINGLE. A condition to do one thing only. Shep. Touch. 118.

CONDITION SUBSEQUENT. A condition subsequent is one referring to a future event, upon the happening of which the obligation becomes no longer binding upon the other party, if he chooses to avail himself of the condition. Civil Code Cal. § 1438.

A condition annexed to an estate already vested, by the performance of which such estate is kept and continued, and by the failure or non-performance of which it is defeated. Co. Litt. 201; 2 Bl. Comm. 154.

CONDITIONAL. That which is dependent upon or granted subject to a condition.

CONDITIONAL CREDITOR. In the civil law. A creditor having a future right of action, or having a right of action in expectancy. Dig. 50, 16, 54.

CONDITIONAL DEVISE. A conditional disposition is one which depends upon the occurrence of some uncertain event, by which it is either to take effect or be defeated. Civil Code Cal. § 1345.

CONDITIONAL FEE. An estate restrained to some particular heirs, exclusive of others, as to the heirs of a man's body, by which only his lineal descendants were admitted, in exclusion of collateral; or to the heirs male of his body, in exclusion of heirs female, whether lineal or collateral. It was called a "conditional fee," by reason of the condition expressed or implied in the donation of it that, if the donee died without such particular heirs, the land should revert to the donor. 2 Bl. Comm. 110.

CONDITIONAL LEGACY. One which is liable to take effect or to be defeated according to the occurrence or non-occurrence of some uncertain event.

CONDITIONAL LIMITATION. A condition followed by a limitation over to a third person in case the condition be not fulfilled or there be a breach of it.

A conditional limitation is where an estate is so expressly defined and limited by the words of its creation that it cannot endure for any longer time than till the contingency happens upon which the estate is to fail. 1 Steph. Comm. 309. Between conditional limitations and estates depending on conditions subsequent there is this difference: that in the former the estate determines as soon as the contingency happens; but in the latter it endures until the grantor or his heirs take advantage of the breach. Id. 310.

CONDITIONAL OBLIGATION. An obligation is conditional when the rights or duties of any party thereto depend upon the occurrence of an uncertain event. Civil Code Cal. § 1434.

The Louisiana Code defines conditional obligations as those which result from the operation of law, from the nature of the contract, or from the presumed intent of the parties. 2 La. Ann. 989.

CONDITIONAL SALE. A sale in which the transfer of title is made to depend upon the performance of a condition.

Conditional sales are distinguishable from mortgages. They are to be taken strictly as independent dealings between strangers. A mortgage is a security for a debt, while a conditional sale is a purchase for a price paid, or to be paid, to become absolute on a particular event; or a purchase accompanied by an agreement to resell upon particular terms. 9 Ala. 24.

CONDITIONAL STIPULATION. In the civil law. A stipulation to do a thing upon condition, as the happening of any event.

Conditiones quælibet odiosæ; maxime autem contra matrimonium et commercium. Any conditions are odious, but especially those which are against [in restraint of] marriage and commerce. Lofft, Appendix, 644.

CONDITIONS CONCURRENT. Conditions concurrent are those which are mutually dependent, and are to be performed at the same time. Civil Code Cal. § 1437.

CONDITIONS OF SALE. The terms upon which sales are made at auction; usually written or printed and exposed in the auction room at the time of sale.

CONDOMINIA. In the civil law. Co-ownerships or limited ownerships, such as *emphyteusis, superficies, pignus, hypotheca, ususfructus, usus,* and *habitatio.* These were more than mere *jura in re alienâ,* being portion of the *dominium* itself, although they are commonly distinguished from the *dominium* strictly so called. Brown.

CONDONACION. In Spanish law. The remission of a debt, either expressly or tacitly.

CONDONATION. The conditional remission or forgiveness, by one of the married parties, of a matrimonial offense committed by the other, and which would constitute a cause of divorce; the condition being that the offense shall not be repeated. See Civil Code Cal. § 115; 3 Hagg. Ecc. 351, 629.

"A blotting out of an offense [against the marital relation] imputed so as to restore the offending party to the same position he or she occupied before the offense was committed." 1 Swab. & T. 334.

Condonation is a conditional forgiveness founded on a full knowledge of all antecedent guilt. 36 Ga. 286.

CONDONE. To make condonation of.

CONDUCT MONEY. In English practice. Money paid to a witness who has been subpœnaed on a trial, sufficient to defray the reasonable expenses of going to, staying at, and returning from the place of trial. Lush, Pr. 460; Archb. New Pr. 639.

CONDUCTI ACTIO. In the civil law. An action which the hirer (*conductor*) of a thing might have against the letter, (*locator.*) Inst. 3, 25, pr. 2.

CONDUCTIO. In the civil law. A hiring. Used generally in connection with the term *locatio,* a letting. *Locatio et conductio,* (sometimes united as a compound word, "*locatio-conductio,*") a letting and hiring.

D

E

F

G

H

I

J

K

L

M

Inst. 3, 25; Bract. fol. 62, c. 28; Story, Bailm. §§ 8, 368.

CONDUCTOR. In the civil law. A hirer.

CONDUCTOR OPERARUM. In the civil law. A person who engages to perform a piece of work for another, at a stated price.

CONDUCTUS. A thing hired.

CONE AND KEY. In old English law. A woman at fourteen or fifteen years of age may take charge of her house and receive *cone* and *key;* that is, keep the accounts and keys. Cowell. Said by Lord Coke to be *cover* and *keye*, meaning that at that age a woman knew what in her house should be kept under lock and key. 2 Inst. 203.

CONFARREATIO. In Roman law. A sacrificial rite resorted to by marrying persons of high patrician or priestly degree, for the purpose of clothing the husband with the *manus* over his wife; the civil modes of effecting the same thing being *coemptio,* (formal,) and *usus mulieris,* (informal.) Brown.

CONFECTIO. The making and completion of a written instrument. 5 Coke, 1.

CONFEDERACY. In criminal law. The association or banding together of two or more persons for the purpose of committing an act or furthering an enterprise which is forbidden by law, or which, though lawful in itself, becomes unlawful when made the object of the confederacy. *Conspiracy* is a more technical term for this offense.

The act of two or more who combine together to do any damage or injury to another, or to do any unlawful act. Jacob. See 52 How. Pr. 353; 41 Wis. 284.

In equity pleading. An improper combination alleged to have been entered into between the defendants to a bill in equity.

In international law. A league or agreement between two or more independent states whereby they unite for their mutual welfare and the furtherance of their common aims. The term may apply to a union so formed for a temporary or limited purpose, as in the case of an offensive and defensive alliance; but it is more commonly used to denote that species of political connection between two or more independent states by which a central government is created, invested with certain powers of sovereignty, (mostly external,) and acting upon the several component states as its units, which,

however, retain their sovereign powers for domestic purposes and some others. See FEDERAL GOVERNMENT.

CONFEDERATION. A league or compact for mutual support, particularly of princes, nations, or states. Such was the colonial government during the Revolution.

CONFERENCE. A meeting of several persons for deliberation, for the interchange of opinion, or for the removal of differences or disputes. Thus, a meeting between a counsel and solicitor to advise on the cause of their client.

In the practice of legislative bodies, when the two houses cannot agree upon a pending measure, each appoints a committee of "conference," and the committees meet and consult together for the purpose of removing differences, harmonizing conflicting views, and arranging a compromise which will be accepted by both houses.

In international law. A personal meeting between the diplomatic agents of two or more powers, for the purpose of making statements and explanations that will obviate the delay and difficulty attending the more formal conduct of negotiations.

In French law. A concordance or identity between two laws or two systems of laws.

CONFESS. To admit the truth of a charge or accusation. Usually spoken of charges of tortious or criminal conduct.

CONFESSING ERROR. A plea to an assignment of error, admitting the same.

CONFESSIO. Lat. A confession. *Confessio in judicio,* a confession made in or before a court.

Confessio facta in judicio omni probatione major est. A confession made in court is of greater effect than any proof. Jenk. Cent. 102.

CONFESSION. In criminal law. A voluntary statement made by a person charged with the commission of a crime or misdemeanor, communicated to another person, wherein he acknowledges himself to be guilty of the offense charged, and discloses the circumstances of the act or the share and participation which he had in it.

Also the act of a prisoner, when arraigned for a crime or misdemeanor, in acknowledging and avowing that he is guilty of the offense charged.

Judicial confessions are those made before

a magistrate or in court in the due course of legal proceedings.

Extra-judicial confessions are those made by the party elsewhere than before a magistrate or in open court. 1 Greenl. Ev. § 216.

CONFESSION AND AVOIDANCE. A plea in confession and avoidance is one which avows and confesses the truth of the averments of fact in the declaration, either expressly or by implication, but then proceeds to allege new matter which tends to deprive the facts admitted of their ordinary legal effect, or to obviate, neutralize, or *avoid* them.

CONFESSION OF DEFENSE. In English practice. Where defendant alleges a ground of defense arising since the commencement of the action, the plaintiff may deliver confession of such defense and sign judgment for his costs up to the time of such pleading, unless it be otherwise ordered. Jud. Act 1875, Ord. XX. r. 3.

CONFESSION OF JUDGMENT. The act of a debtor in permitting judgment to be entered against him by his creditor, for a stipulated sum, by a written statement to that effect or by warrant of attorney, without the institution of legal proceedings of any kind.

CONFESSO, BILL TAKEN PRO. In equity practice. An order which the court of chancery makes when the defendant does not file an answer, that the plaintiff may take such a decree as the case made by his bill warrants.

CONFESSOR An ecclesiastic who receives auricular confessions of sins from persons under his spiritual charge, and pronounces absolution upon them. The secrets of the confessional are not privileged communications at common law, but this has been changed by statute in some states. See 1 Greenl. Ev. §§ 247, 248.

CONFESSORIA ACTIO. Lat. In the civil law. An action for enforcing a servitude. Mackeld. Rom. Law, § 324.

Confessus in judicio pro judicato habetur, et quodammodo sua sententiâ damnatur. 11 Coke, 30. A person confessing his guilt when arraigned is deemed to have been found guilty, and is, as it were, condemned by his own sentence.

CONFIDENCE. Trust; reliance; ground of trust. In the construction of wills, this word is considered peculiarly appropriate to create a trust. "It is as applicable to the subject of a trust, as nearly a synonym, as the English language is capable of. Trust is a confidence which one man reposes in another, and confidence is a trust." 2 Pa. St. 133.

CONFIDENTIAL COMMUNICATIONS. These are certain classes of communications, passing between persons who stand in a confidential or fiduciary relation to each other, (or who, on account of their relative situation, are under a special duty of secrecy and fidelity,) which the law will not permit to be divulged, or allow them to be inquired into in a court of justice, for the sake of public policy and the good order of society. Examples of such privileged relations are those of husband and wife and attorney and client.

CONFIDENTIAL RELATION. A fiduciary relation. These phrases are used as convertible terms. It is a peculiar relation which exists between client and attorney, principal and agent, principal and surety, landlord and tenant, parent and child, guardian and ward, ancestor and heir, husband and wife, trustee and *cestui que trust*, executors or administrators and creditors, legatees, or distributees, appointer and appointee under powers, and partners and part owners. In these and like cases, the law, in order to prevent undue advantage from the unlimited confidence or sense of duty which the relation naturally creates, requires the utmost degree of good faith in all transactions between the parties. 57 Cal. 497; 1 Story, Eq. Jur. 218.

CONFINEMENT. Confinement may be by either a moral or a physical restraint, by threats of violence with a present force, or by physical restraint of the person. 1 Sum. 171.

CONFIRM. To complete or establish that which was imperfect or uncertain; to ratify what has been done without authority or insufficiently.

Confirmare est id firmum facere quod prius infirmum fuit. Co. Litt. 295. To confirm is to make firm that which was before infirm.

Confirmare nemo potest prius quam jus ei acciderit. No one can confirm before the right accrues to him. 10 Coke, 48.

Confirmat usum qui tollit abusum. He confirms the use [of a thing] who removes the abuse, [of it.] Moore, 764.

CONFIRMATIO. The conveyance of an estate, or the communication of a right that one hath in or unto lands or tenements, to another that hath the possession thereof, or some other estate therein, whereby a voidable estate is made sure and unavoidable, or whereby a particular estate is increased or enlarged. Shep. Touch. 311; 2 Bl. Comm. 325.

CONFIRMATIO CHARTARUM. Lat. Confirmation of the charters. A statute passed in the 25 Edw. 1., whereby the Great Charter is declared to be allowed as the common law; all judgments contrary to it are declared void; copies of it are ordered to be sent to all cathedral churches and read twice a year to the people; and sentence of excommunication is directed to be as constantly denounced against all those that, by word or deed or counsel, act contrary thereto or in any degree infringe it. 1 Bl. Comm. 128.

CONFIRMATIO CRESCENS. An enlarging confirmation; one which enlarges a rightful estate. Shep. Touch. 311.

CONFIRMATIO DIMINUENS. A diminishing confirmation. A confirmation which tends and serves to diminish and abridge the services whereby a tenant doth hold, operating as a release of part of the services. Shep. Touch. 311.

Confirmatio est nulla ubi donum præcedens est invalidum. Moore, 764; Co. Litt. 295. Confirmation is void where the preceding gift is invalid.

Confirmatio omnes supplet defectus, licet id quod actum est ab initio non valuit. Co. Litt. 295b. Confirmation supplies all defects, though that which had been done was not valid at the beginning.

CONFIRMATIO PERFICIENS. A confirmation which makes valid a wrongful and defeasible title, or makes a conditional estate absolute. Shep. Touch. 311.

CONFIRMATION. A contract by which that which was infirm, imperfect, or subject to be avoided is made firm and unavoidable.

A conveyance of an estate or right *in esse*, whereby a voidable estate is made sure and unavoidable, or whereby a particular estate is increased. Co. Litt. 295b.

In English ecclesiastical law. The ratification by the archbishop of the election of a bishop by dean and chapter under the king's letter missive prior to the investment and consecration of the bishop by the archbishop. 25 Hen. VIII. c. 20.

CONFIRMAVI. Lat. I have confirmed. The emphatic word in the ancient deeds of confirmation. Fleta, lib. 3, c. 14, § 5.

CONFIRMEE. The grantee in a deed of confirmation.

CONFIRMOR. The grantor in a deed of confirmation.

CONFISCARE. In civil and old English law. To confiscate; to claim for or bring into the fisc, or treasury. Bract. fol. 150.

CONFISCATE. To appropriate property to the use of the state. To adjudge property to be forfeited to the public treasury; to seize and condemn private forfeited property to public use.

Formerly, it appears, this term was used as synonymous with "forfeit," but at present the distinction between the two terms is well marked. Confiscation supervenes upon forfeiture. The person, by his act, forfeits his property; the state thereupon appropriates it, that is, confiscates it. Hence, to confiscate property implies that it has first been forfeited; but to forfeit property does not necessarily imply that it will be confiscated.

"Confiscation" is also to be distinguished from "condemnation" as prize. The former is the act of the sovereign against a rebellious subject; the latter is the act of a belligerent against another belligerent. Confiscation may be effected by such means, summary or arbitrary, as the sovereign, expressing its will through lawful channels, may please to adopt. Condemnation as prize can only be made in accordance with principles of law recognized in the common jurisprudence of the world. Both are proceedings *in rem*, but confiscation recognizes the title of the original owner to the property, while in prize the tenure of the property is qualified, provisional, and destitute of absolute ownership. 14 Ct. Cl. 48.

CONFISCATION. The act of confiscating; or of condemning and adjudging to the public treasury.

CONFISK. An old form of *confiscate*.

CONFITENS REUS. An accused person who admits his guilt.

CONFLICT OF LAWS. 1. An opposition, conflict, or antagonism between different laws of the same state or sovereignty upon the same subject-matter.

2. A similar inconsistency between the municipal laws of different states or countries, arising in the case of persons who have acquired rights or a *status*, or made contracts, or incurred obligations, within the territory of two or more states.

3. That branch of jurisprudence, arising from the diversity of the laws of different na-

tions in their application to rights and remedies, which reconciles the inconsistency, or decides which law or system is to govern in the particular case, or settles the degree of force to be accorded to the law of a foreign country, (the acts or rights in question having arisen under it,) either where it varies from the domestic law, or where the domestic law is silent or not exclusively applicable to the case in point. In this sense, it is more properly called "private international law."

CONFLICT OF PRESUMPTIONS. In this conflict certain rules are applicable, viz.: (1) Special take precedence of general presumptions; (2) constant of casual ones; (3) presume in favor of innocence; (4) of legality; (5) of validity; and, when these rules fail, the matter is said to be at large. Brown.

CONFORMITY. In English ecclesiastical law. Adherence to the doctrines and usages of the Church of England.

CONFORMITY, BILL OF. See BILL OF CONFORMITY.

CONFRAIRIE. Fr. In old English law. A fraternity, brotherhood, or society. Cowell.

CONFRERES. Brethren in a religious house; fellows of one and the same society. Cowell.

CONFRONTATION. In criminal law. The act of setting a witness face to face with the prisoner, in order that the latter may make any objection he has to the witness, or that the witness may identify the accused.

CONFUSIO. In the civil law. The inseparable intermixture of property belonging to different owners; it is properly confined to the pouring together of fluids, but is sometimes also used of a melting together of metals or any compound formed by the irrecoverable commixture of different substances.

It is distinguished from *commixtion* by the fact that in the latter case a separation may be made, while in a case of *confusio* there cannot be. 2 Bl. Comm. 405.

CONFUSION. In Roman and French law. A mode of extinguishing a debt, by the concurrence in the same person of two qualities which mutually destroy one another. This may occur in several ways, as where the creditor becomes the heir of the debtor, or the debtor the heir of the creditor, or either accedes to the title of the other by any other mode of transfer.

This term, as used in the civil law, is syn-

onymous with "merger," as used in the common law. It arises where two titles to the same property unite in the same person. 1 Woods, 182.

CONFUSION OF BOUNDARIES. The title of that branch of equity jurisdiction which relates to the discovery and settlement of conflicting, disputed, or uncertain boundaries.

CONFUSION OF GOODS. The inseparable intermixture of property belonging to different owners; properly confined to the pouring together of fluids, but used in a wider sense to designate any indistinguishable compound of elements belonging to different owners.

The term "confusion" is applicable to a mixing of chattels of one and the same general description, differing thus from "accession," which is where various materials are united in one product. Confusion of goods arises wherever the goods of two or more persons are so blended as to have become undistinguishable. 1 Schouler, Pers. Prop. 41.

CONFUSION OF RIGHTS. A union of the qualities of debtor and creditor in the same person. The effect of such a union is, generally, to extinguish the debt. 1 Salk. 306; Cro. Car. 551.

CONFUSION OF TITLES. A civil-law expression, synonymous with "merger," as used in the common law, applying where two titles to the same property unite in the same person. 1 Woods, 179.

CONGÉ. In the French law. Permission, leave, license; a passport or clearance to a vessel; a permission to arm, equip, or navigate a vessel.

CONGÉ D'ACCORDER. Leave to accord. A permission granted by the court, in the old process of levying a fine, to the defendant to agree with the plaintiff.

CONGÉ D'EMPARLER. Fr. Leave to imparl. The privilege of an imparlance, (*licentia loquendi.*) 3 Bl. Comm. 299.

CONGÉ D'ESLIRE. A permission or license from the British sovereign to a dean and chapter to elect a bishop, in time of vacation; or to an abbey or priory which is of royal foundation, to elect an abbot or prior.

CONGEABLE. L. Fr. Lawful; permissible; allowable. "Disseisin is properly where a man entereth into any lands or tenements where his entry is not *congeable*, and putteth out him that hath the freehold." Litt. § 279. See 7 Wheat. 107.

CONGILDONES. In Saxon law. Fellow-members of a guild.

CONGIUS. An ancient measure containing about a gallon and a pint. Cowell.

CONGREGATION. An assembly or society of persons who together constitute the principal supporters of a particular parish, or habitually meet at the same church for religious exercises.

In the ecclesiastical law, this term is used to designate certain bureaus at Rome, where ecclesiastical matters are attended to.

CONGRESS. In international law. An assembly of envoys, commissioners, deputies, etc., from different sovereignties who meet to concert measures for their common good, or to adjust their mutual concerns.

In American law. The name of the legislative assembly of the United States, composed of the senate and house of representatives, (*q. v.*)

CONGRESSUS. The extreme practical test of the truth of a charge of impotence brought against a husband by a wife. It is now disused. Causes Célèbres, 6, 183.

CONJECTIO. In the civil law of evidence. A throwing together. Presumption; the putting of things together, with the inference drawn therefrom.

CONJECTIO CAUSÆ. In the civil law. A statement of the case. A brief synopsis of the case given by the advocate to the judge in opening the trial. Calvin.

CONJECTURE. A slight degree of credence, arising from evidence too weak or too remote to cause belief.

Supposition or surmise. The idea of a fact, suggested by another fact; as a possible cause, concomitant, or result. Burrill, Circ. Ev. 27.

CONJOINTS. Persons married to each other. Story, Confl. Laws, § 71.

CONJUDEX. In old English law. An associate judge. Bract. 403.

CONJUGAL RIGHTS. Matrimonial rights; the right which husband and wife have to each other's society, comfort, and affection.

CONJUGIUM. One of the names of marriage, among the Romans. Tayl. Civil Law, 284.

CONJUNCT. In Scotch law. Joint.

CONJUNCTA. In the civil law. Things joined together or united; as distinguished from *disjuncta*, things disjoined or separated. Dig. 50, 16, 53.

CONJUNCTIM. Lat. In old English law. Jointly. Inst. 2, 20, 8.

CONJUNCTIM ET DIVISIM. L. Lat. In old English law. Jointly and severally.

CONJUNCTIO. In the civil law. Conjunction; connection of words in a sentence. See Dig. 50, 16, 29, 142.

Conjunctio mariti et feminæ est de jure naturæ. The union of husband and wife is of the law of nature.

CONJUNCTIVE. A grammatical term for particles which serve for joining or connecting together. Thus, the conjunction "and" is called a "conjunctive," and "or" a "disjunctive," conjunction.

CONJUNCTIVE OBLIGATION. A conjunctive obligation is one in which the several objects in it are connected by a copulative, or in any other manner which shows that all of them are severally comprised in the contract. This contract creates as many different obligations as there are different objects; and the debtor, when he wishes to discharge himself, may force the creditor to receive them separately. Civil Code La. art. 2063.

CONJURATIO. In old English law. A swearing together; an oath administered to several together; a combination or confederacy under oath. Cowell.

In old European law. A compact of the inhabitants of a commune, or municipality, confirmed by their oaths to each other, and which was the basis of the commune. Steph. Lect. 119.

CONJURATION. In old English law. A plot or compact made by persons combining by oath to do any public harm. Cowell.

The offense of having conference or commerce with evil spirits, in order to discover some secret, or effect some purpose. Id. Classed by Blackstone with witchcraft, enchantment, and sorcery, but distinguished from each of these by other writers. 4 Bl. Comm. 60; Cowell.

CONJURATOR. In old English law. One who swears or is sworn with others; one bound by oath with others; a compurgator; a conspirator.

CONNECTIONS. Relations by blood or marriage, but more commonly the relations of a person with whom one is connected by marriage. In this sense, the relations of a wife are "connections" of her husband. The term is vague and indefinite. See 1 Pa. St. 507.

CONNEXITÉ. In French law. This exists when two actions are pending which, although not identical as in *lis pendens*, are so nearly similar in object that it is expedient to have them both adjudicated upon by the same judges. Arg. Fr. Merc. Law, 553.

CONNIVANCE. The secret or indirect consent or permission of one person to the commission of an unlawful or criminal act by another.

Literally, a winking at; intentional forbearance to see a fault or other act; generally implying consent to it. Webster.

Connivance is the corrupt consent of one party to the commission of the acts of the other, constituting the cause of divorce. Civil Code Cal. § 112.

Connivance differs from condonation, though the same legal consequences may attend it. Connivance necessarily involves criminality on the part of the individual who connives; condonation may take place without imputing the slightest blame to the party who forgives the injury. Connivance must be the act of the mind before the offense has been committed; condonation is the result of a determination to forgive an injury which was not known until after it was inflicted. 3 Hagg. Ecc. 350.

CONNOISSEMENT. In French law. An instrument similar to our bill of lading.

CONNUBIUM. In the civil law. Marriage. Among the Romans, a lawful marriage as distinguished from "concubinage," (*q. v.*,) which was an inferior marriage.

CONOCIAMENTO. In Spanish law. A recognizance. White, New Recop. b. 3, tit. 7, c. 5, § 3.

CONOCIMIENTO. In Spanish law. A bill of lading. In the Mediterranean ports it is called "*poliza de cargamiento.*"

CONPOSSESSIO. In modern civil law. A joint possession. Mackeld. Rom. Law, § 245.

CONQUEREUR. In Norman and old English law. The first purchaser of an estate; he who first brought an estate into his family.

CONQUEROR. In old English and Scotch law. The first purchaser of an estate; he who brought it into the family owning it. 2 Bl. Comm. 242, 243.

CONQUEST. In feudal law. Conquest; acquisition by purchase; any method of acquiring the ownership of an estate other than by descent. Also an estate acquired otherwise than by inheritance.

In international law. The acquisition of the sovereignty of a country by force of arms, exercised by an independent power which reduces the vanquished to the submission of its empire.

In Scotch law. Purchase. Bell.

CONQUESTOR. Conqueror. The title given to William of Normandy.

CONQUÊTS. In French law. The name given to every acquisition which the husband and wife, jointly or severally, make during the conjugal community. Thus, whatever is acquired by the husband and wife, either by his or her industry or good fortune, inures to the extent of one-half for the benefit of the other. Merl. Repert. "*Conquêt.*"

CONQUISITIO. In feudal and old English law. Acquisition. 2 Bl. Comm. 242.

CONQUISITOR. In feudal law. A purchaser, acquirer, or conqueror. 2 Bl. Comm. 242, 243.

CONSANGUINEUS. A person related by blood; a person descended from the same common stock.

Consanguineus est quasi eodem sanguine natus. Co. Litt. 157. A person related by consanguinity is, as it were, sprung from the same blood.

CONSANGUINEUS FRATER. In civil and feudal law. A half-brother by the father's side, as distinguished from *frater uterinus*, a brother by the mother's side.

CONSANGUINITY. The connection or relation of persons descended from the same stock or common ancestor. It is either lineal or collateral. Lineal is that which subsists between persons of whom one is descended in a direct line from the other, as between son, father, grandfather, great-grandfather, and so upwards in the direct ascending line; or between son, grandson, great-grandson, and so downwards in the direct descending line. Collateral agree with the lineal in this, that they descend from the same stock or ancestor; but differ in this, that they do not descend one from the other. 2 Bl. Comm. 202.

CONSCIENCE. This term is not synonymous with "principle." An "objection on principle" is not the same thing as a "conscientious scruple" or opinion. 7 Cal. 140.

CONSCIENCE, COURTS OF. Courts, not of record, constituted by act of parliament in the city of London, and other towns, for the recovery of small debts; otherwise and more commonly called "Courts of Requests." 3 Steph. Comm. 451.

Conscientia dicitur a con et scio, quasi scire cum Deo. 1 Coke, 100. Conscience is called from *con* and *scio*, to know, as it were, with God.

CONSCIENTIA REI ALIENI. In Scotch law. Knowledge of another's property; knowledge that a thing is not one's own, but belongs to another. He who has this knowledge, and retains possession, is chargeable with "violent profits."

CONSCRIPTION. Drafting into the military service of the state; compulsory service falling upon all male subjects evenly, within or under certain specified ages.

CONSECRATE. In ecclesiastical law. To dedicate to sacred purposes, as a bishop by imposition of hands, or a church or churchyard by prayers, etc. Consecration is performed by a bishop or archbishop.

Consecratio est periodus electionis; electio est præambula consecrationis. 2 Rolle, 102. Consecration is the termination of election; election is the preamble of consecration.

CONSEIL DE FAMILLE. In French law. A family council. Certain acts require the sanction of this body. For example, a guardian can neither accept nor reject an inheritance to which the minor has succeeded without its authority, (Code Nap. 461;) nor can he accept for the child a gift *inter vivos* without the like authority, (Id. 463.)

CONSEIL JUDICIAIRE. In French law. When a person has been subjected to an interdiction on the ground of his insane extravagance, but the interdiction is not absolute, but limited only, the court of first instance, which grants the interdiction, appoints a council, called by this name, with whose assistance the party may bring or defend actions, or compromise the same, alienate his estate, make or incur loans, and the like. Brown.

CONSEILS DE PRUDHOMMES. In French law. A species of trade tribunals, charged with settling differences between masters and workmen. They endeavor, in the first instance, to conciliate the parties. In default, they adjudicate upon the questions in dispute. Their decisions are final up to 200*f.* Beyond that amount, appeals lie to the tribunals of commerce. Arg. Fr. Merc. Law, 553.

CONSENSUAL CONTRACT. A term derived from the civil law; denoting a contract founded upon and completed by the mere consent of the contracting parties, without any external formality or symbolic act to fix the obligation.

Consensus est voluntas plurium ad quos res pertinet, simul juncta. Lofft, 514. Consent is the conjoint will of several persons to whom the thing belongs.

Consensus facit legem. Consent makes the law. (A contract is law between the parties agreeing to be bound by it.) Branch. Princ.

Consensus, non concubitus, facit nuptias vel matrimonium, et consentire non possunt ante annos nubiles. 6 Coke, 22. Consent, and not cohabitation, constitutes nuptials or marriage, and persons cannot consent before marriageable years. 1 Bl. Comm. 434.

Consensus tollit errorem. Co. Litt. 126. Consent (acquiescence) removes mistake.

Consensus voluntas multorum ad quos res pertinet, simul juncta. Consent is the united will of several interested in one subject-matter. Davis, 48; Branch, Princ.

CONSENT. A concurrence of wills.
Express consent is that directly given, either *viva voce* or in writing.
Implied consent is that manifested by signs, actions, or facts, or by inaction or silence, which raise a presumption that the consent has been given.
Consent is an act of reason, accompanied with deliberation, the mind weighing as in a balance the good or evil on each side. 1 Story, Eq. Jur. § 222.

There is a difference between consenting and submitting. Every consent involves a submission; but a mere submission does not necessarily involve consent. 9 Car. & P. 722.

CONSENT-RULE. In English practice. A superseded instrument, in which a defendant in an action of ejectment specified for what purpose he intended to defend, and undertook to confess not only the fictitious lease, entry, and ouster, but that he was in possession.

Consentientes et agentes pari pœna plectentur. They who consent to an act, and they who do it, shall be visited with equal punishment. 5 Coke, 80.

Consentire matrimonio non possunt infra [ante] annos nubiles. Parties cannot consent to marriage within the years of marriage, [before the age of consent.] 6 Coke, 22.

Consequentiæ non est consequentia. Bac. Max. The consequence of a consequence exists not.

CONSEQUENTIAL DAMAGE. Such damage, loss, or injury as does not flow directly and immediately from the act of the party, but only from some of the consequences or results of such act.

The term "consequential damage" means sometimes damage which is so remote as not to be actionable; sometimes damage which, though somewhat remote, is actionable; or damage which, though actionable, does not follow immediately, in point of time, upon the doing of the act complained of. 51 N. H. 504.

CONSEQUENTS. In Scotch law. Implied powers or authorities. Things which follow, usually by implication of law. A commission being given to execute any work, every power necessary to carry it on is implied. 1 Kames, Eq. 242.

CONSERVATOR. A guardian; protector; preserver.

"When any person having property shall be found to be incapable of managing his affairs, by the court of probate in the district in which he resides, * * * it shall appoint some person to be his *conservator*, who, upon giving a probate bond, shall have the charge of the person and estate of such incapable person." Gen. St. Conn. 1875, p. 346, § 1.

CONSERVATORS OF RIVERS. Commissioners or trustees in whom the control of a certain river is vested, in England, by act of parliament.

CONSIDERATIO CURIÆ. The judgment of the court.

CONSIDERATION. The inducement to a contract. The cause, motive, price, or impelling influence which induces a contracting party to enter into a contract. The reason or material cause of a contract.

Any benefit conferred, or agreed to be con- ferred, upon the promisor, by any other person, to which the promisor is not lawfully entitled, or any prejudice suffered, or agreed to be suffered, by such person, other than such as he is at the time of consent lawfully bound to suffer, as an inducement to the promisor, is a good consideration for a promise. Civil Code Cal. § 1605.

Any act of the plaintiff from which the defendant or a stranger derives a benefit or advantage, or any labor, detriment, or inconvenience sustained by the plaintiff, however small, if such act is performed or inconvenience suffered by the plaintiff by the consent, express or implied, of the defendant. 3 Scott, 250.

Considerations are classified and defined as follows:

They are either *express* or *implied;* the former when they are specifically stated in a deed, contract, or other instrument; the latter when inferred or supposed by the law from the acts or situation of the parties.

They are either *executed* or *executory;* the former being acts done or values given before or at the time of making the contract; the latter being promises to give or do something in future.

They are either *good* or *valuable.* A good consideration is such as is founded on natural duty and affection, or on a strong moral obligation. A valuable consideration is founded on money, or something convertible into money, or having a value in money, except marriage, which is a valuable consideration. Code Ga. 1882, § 2741. See Chit. Cont. 7.

A *continuing* consideration is one consisting in acts or performances which must necessarily extend over a considerable period of time.

Concurrent considerations are those which arise at the same time or where the promises are simultaneous.

Equitable or *moral* considerations are devoid of efficacy in point of strict law, but are founded upon a moral duty, and may be made the basis of an express promise.

A *gratuitous* consideration is one which is not founded upon any such loss, injury, or inconvenience to the party to whom it moves as to make it valid in law.

Past consideration is an act done before the contract is made, and is really by itself no consideration for a promise. Anson, Cont. 82.

CONSIDERATUM EST PER CURIAM. (It is considered by the court.) The formal and ordinary commencement of a judgment.

CONSIDERATUR. L. Lat. It is considered. Held to mean the same with *consideratum est.* 2 Strange, 874.

CONSIGN. In the civil law. To deposit in the custody of a third person a thing belonging to the debtor, for the benefit of the creditor, under the authority of a court of justice. Poth. Obl. pt. 3, c. 1, art. 8.

In commercial law. To deliver goods to a carrier to be transmitted to a designated factor or agent.

To deliver or transfer as a charge or trust; to commit, intrust, give in trust; to transfer from oneself to the care of another; to send or transmit goods to a merchant or factor for sale. 4 Daly, 320.

CONSIGNATION. In Scotch law. The payment of money into the hands of a third party, when the creditor refuses to accept of it. The person to whom the money is given is termed the "consignatory." Bell.

In French law. A deposit which a debtor makes of the thing that he owes into the hands of a third person, and under the authority of a court of justice. 1 Poth. Obl. 536; 1 N. H. 304.

CONSIGNEE. In mercantile law. One to whom a consignment is made. The person to whom goods are shipped for sale.

CONSIGNMENT. The act or process of consigning goods; the transportation of goods consigned; an article or collection of goods sent to a factor to be sold; goods or property sent, by the aid of a common carrier, from one person in one place to another person in another place. See CONSIGN.

CONSIGNOR. One who sends or makes a consignment. A shipper of goods.

Consilia multorum quæruntur in magnis. 4 Inst. 1. The counsels of many are required in great things.

CONSILIARIUS. In the civil law. A counsellor, as distinguished from a pleader or advocate. An assistant judge. One who participates in the decisions. Du Cange.

CONSILIUM. A day appointed to hear the counsel of both parties. A case set down for argument.

It is commonly used for the day appointed for the argument of a demurrer, or errors assigned. 1 Tidd, Pr. 438.

CONSIMILI CASU. In practice. A writ of entry, framed under the provisions of the statute Westminster 2, (13 Edw. I.,)

c. 24, which lay for the benefit of the reversioner, where a tenant by the curtesy aliened in fee or for life.

CONSISTING. Being composed or made up of. This word is not synonymous with "including;" for the latter, when used in connection with a number of specified objects, always implies that there may be others which are not mentioned. 6 Mo. App. 331.

CONSISTORIUM. The state council of the Roman emperors. Mackeld. Rom. Law, § 58.

CONSISTORY. In ecclesiastical law. An assembly of cardinals convoked by the pope.

CONSISTORY COURTS. Courts held by diocesan bishops within their several cathedrals, for the trial of ecclesiastical causes arising within their respective dioceses. The bishop's chancellor, or his commissary, is the judge; and from his sentence an appeal lies to the archbishop. Mozley & Whitley.

CONSOBRINI. In the civil law. Cousins-german, in general; brothers' and sisters' children, considered in their relation to each other.

CONSOLATO DEL MARE. The name of a code of sea-laws, said to have been compiled by order of the kings of Arragon (or, according to other authorities, at Pisa or Barcelona) in the fourteenth century, which comprised the maritime ordinances of the Roman emperors, of France and Spain, and of the Italian commercial powers. This compilation exercised a considerable influence in the formation of European maritime law.

CONSOLIDATE. To consolidate means something more than rearrange or redivide. In a general sense, it means to unite into one mass or body, as to consolidate the forces of an army, or various funds. In parliamentary usage, to consolidate two bills is to unite them into one. In law, to consolidate benefices is to combine them into one. 45 Iowa, 56.

CONSOLIDATED FUND. In England. A fund for the payment of the public debt.

CONSOLIDATED ORDERS. The orders regulating the practice of the English court of chancery, which were issued, in 1860, in substitution for the various orders which had previously been promulgated from time to time.

CONSOLIDATION. In the civil law. The union of the usufruct with the estate out of which it issues, in the same person; which happens when the usufructuary acquires the estate, or *vice versa*. In either case the usufruct is extinct. Lec. El. Dr. Rom. 424.

In Scotch law. The junction of the property and superiority of an estate, where they have been disjoined. Bell.

CONSOLIDATION OF ACTIONS. The act or process of uniting several actions into one trial and judgment, by order of a court, where all the actions are between the same parties, pending in the same court, and turning upon the same or similar issues; or the court may order that one of the actions be tried, and the others decided without trial according to the judgment in the one selected.

CONSOLIDATION OF BENEFICES. The act or process of uniting two or more of them into one.

CONSOLIDATION OF CORPORATIONS. The union or merger into one corporate body of two or more corporations which had been separately created for similar or connected purposes. In England this is termed "amalgamation."

When the rights, franchises, and effects of two or more corporations are, by legal authority and agreement of the parties, combined and united into one whole, and committed to a single corporation, the stockholders of which are composed of those (so far as they choose to become such) of the companies thus agreeing, this is in law, and according to common understanding, a consolidation of such companies, whether such single corporation, called the consolidated company, be a new one then created, or one of the original companies, continuing in existence with only larger rights, capacity, and property. 64 Ala. 656.

CONSOLIDATION RULE. In practice. A rule or order of court requiring a plaintiff who has instituted separate suits upon several claims against the same defendant, to consolidate them in one action, where that can be done consistently with the rules of pleading.

CONSOLS. An abbreviation of the expression "consolidated annuities," and used in modern times as a name of various funds united in one for the payment of the British national debt.

Consortio malorum me quoque malum facit. Moore, 817. The company of wicked men makes me also wicked.

CONSORTIUM. In the civil law. A union of fortunes; a lawful Roman marriage. Also, the joining of several persons as parties to one action. In old English law, the term signified company or society. In the language of pleading, (as in the phrase *per quod consortium amisit*) it means the companionship or society of a wife.

CONSPIRACY. In criminal law. A combination or confederacy between two or more persons formed for the purpose of committing, by their joint efforts, some unlawful or criminal act, or some act which is innocent in itself, but becomes unlawful when done by the concerted action of the conspirators, or for the purpose of using criminal or unlawful means to the commission of an act not in itself unlawful.

The agreement or engagement of persons to co-operate in accomplishing some unlawful purpose, or some purpose which may not be unlawful, by unlawful means. 48 Me. 218.

Conspiracy is a consultation or agreement between two or more persons, either falsely to accuse another of a crime punishable by law; or wrongfully to injure or prejudice a third person, or any body of men, in any manner; or to commit any offense punishable by law; or to do any act with intent to prevent the course of justice; or to effect a legal purpose with a corrupt intent, or by improper means. Hawk. P. C. c. 72, § 2; Archb. Crim. Pl. 390, adding also combinations by journeymen to raise wages. 6 Ala. 765.

CONSPIRATIONE. An ancient writ that lay against conspirators. Reg. Orig. 134; Fitzh. Nat. Brev. 114.

CONSPIRATORS. Persons guilty of a conspiracy.

Those who bind themselves by oath, covenant, or other alliance that each of them shall aid the other falsely and maliciously to indict persons; or falsely to move and maintain pleas, etc. 33 Edw. I. St. 2. Besides these, there are conspirators in treasonable purposes; as for plotting against the government. Wharton.

CONSTABLE. In medieval law. The name given to a very high functionary under the French and English kings, the dignity and importance of whose office was only second to that of the monarch. He was in general the leader of the royal armies, and had cognizance of all matters pertaining to war and arms, exercising both civil and military jurisdiction. He was also charged with the conservation of the peace of the nation. Thus there was a "Constable of France" and a "Lord High Constable of England."

In English law. A public civil officer, whose proper and general duty is to keep the peace within his district, though he is frequently charged with additional duties. 1 Bl. Comm. 356.

High constables, in England, are officers appointed in every hundred or franchise, whose proper duty seems to be to keep the king's peace within their respective hundreds. 1 Bl. Comm. 356, 3 Steph. Comm. 47.

Petty constables are inferior officers in every town and parish, subordinate to the high constable of the hundred, whose principal duty is the preservation of the peace, though they also have other particular duties assigned to them by act of parliament, particularly the service of the summonses and the execution of the warrants of justices of the peace. 1 Bl. Comm. 356; 3 Steph. Comm. 47, 48.

Special constables are persons appointed (with or without their consent) by the magistrates to execute warrants on particular occasions, as in the case of riots, etc.

In American law. An officer of a municipal corporation (usually elected) whose duties are similar to those of the sheriff, though his powers are less and his jurisdiction smaller. He is to preserve the public peace, execute the process of magistrates' courts, and of some other tribunals, serve writs, attend the sessions of the criminal courts, have the custody of juries, and discharge other functions sometimes assigned to him by the local law or by statute.

CONSTABLE OF A CASTLE. In English law. An officer having charge of a castle; a warden, or keeper; otherwise called a "castellain."

CONSTABLE OF ENGLAND. (Called, also, "Marshal.") His office consisted in the care of the common peace of the realm in deeds of arms and matters of war. Lamb. Const. 4.

CONSTABLE OF SCOTLAND. An officer who was formerly entitled to command all the king's armies in the absence of the king, and to take cognizance of all crimes committed within four miles of the king's person or of parliament, the privy council, or any general convention of the states of the kingdom. The office was hereditary in the family of Errol, and was abolished by the 20 Geo. III. c. 43. Bell.; Ersk. Inst. 1, 3, 37.

CONSTABLE OF THE EXCHEQUER. An officer mentioned in Fleta, lib. 2, c. 31.

CONSTABLEWICK. In English law. The territorial jurisdiction of a constable; as bailiwick is of a bailiff or sheriff. 5 Nev. & M. 261.

CONSTABULARIUS. An officer of horse; an officer having charge of foot or horse; a naval commander; an officer having charge of military affairs generally. Spelman.

CONSTAT. It is clear or evident; it appears; it is certain; there is no doubt. *Non constat*, it does not appear.

A certificate which the clerk of the pipe and auditors of the exchequer made, at the request of any person who intended to plead or move in that court, for the discharge of anything. The effect of it was the certifying what appears (*constat*) upon record, touching the matter in question. Wharton.

CONSTAT D'HUISSIER. In French law. An affidavit made by a *huissier*, setting forth the appearance, form, quality, color, etc., of any article upon which a suit depends. Arg. Fr. Merc. Law, 554.

CONSTATE. To establish, constitute, or ordain. "Constating instruments" of a corporation are its charter, organic law, or the grant of powers to it. See examples of the use of the term, Green's Brice, Ultra Vires, p. 39; 37 N. J. Eq. 363.

CONSTITUENT. A word used as a correlative to "attorney," to denote one who constitutes another his agent or invests the other with authority to act for him.

It is also used in the language of politics, as a correlative to "representative," the constituents of a legislator being those whom he represents and whose interests he is to care for in public affairs; usually the electors of his district.

CONSTITUERE. To appoint, constitute, establish, ordain, or undertake. Used principally in ancient powers of attorney, and now supplanted by the English word "constitute."

CONSTITUIMUS. A Latin term, signifying *we constitute* or *appoint*.

CONSTITUTED AUTHORITIES. Officers properly appointed under the constitution for the government of the people.

CONSTITUTIO. In the civil law. An imperial ordinance or constitution, distinguished from *Lex, Senatus-Consultum*, and other kinds of law, and having its effect from the sole will of the emperor.

An establishment or settlement. Used of controversies settled by the parties without a trial. Calvin.

A sum paid according to agreement. Du Cange.

In old English law. An ordinance or statute. A provision of a statute.

CONSTITUTIO DOTIS. Establishment of dower.

CONSTITUTION. In public law. The organic and fundamental law of a nation or state, which may be written or unwritten, establishing the character and conception of its government, laying the basic principles to which its internal life is to be conformed, organizing the government, and regulating, distributing, and limiting the functions of its different departments, and prescribing the extent and manner of the exercise of sovereign powers.

In a more general sense, any fundamental or important law or edict; as the Novel Constitutions of Justinian; the Constitutions of Clarendon.

In American law. The written instrument agreed upon by the people of the Union or of a particular state, as the absolute rule of action and decision for all departments and officers of the government in respect to all the points covered by it, which must control until it shall be changed by the authority which established it, and in opposition to which any act or ordinance of any such department or officer is null and void. Cooley, Const. Lim. 3.

CONSTITUTIONAL. Consistent with the constitution; authorized by the constitution; not conflicting with any provision of the constitution or fundamental law of the state. Dependent upon a constitution, or secured or regulated by a constitution; as "constitutional monarchy," "constitutional rights."

CONSTITUTIONAL LAW. 1. That branch of the public law of a state which treats of the organization and frame of government, the organs and powers of sovereignty, the distribution of political and governmental authorities and functions, the fundamental principles which are to regulate the relations of government and subject, and which prescribes generally the plan and method according to which the public affairs of the state are to be administered.

2. That department of the science of law which treats of constitutions, their establish-ment, construction, and interpretation, and of the validity of legal enactments as tested by the criterion of conformity to the fundamental law.

3. A constitutional law is one which is consonant to, and agrees with, the constitution; one which is not in violation of any provision of the constitution of the particular state.

CONSTITUTIONES. Laws promulgated, *i. e.*, enacted, by the Roman Emperor. They were of various kinds, namely, the following: (1) *Edicta;* (2) *decreta;* (3) *rescripta*, called also "*epistolæ*." Sometimes they were general, and intended to form a precedent for other like cases; at other times they were special, particular, or individual, (*personales,*) and not intended to form a precedent. The emperor had this power of irresponsible enactment by virtue of a certain *lex regia*, whereby he was made the fountain of justice and of mercy. Brown.

Constitutiones tempore posteriores potiores sunt his quæ ipsas præcesserunt. Dig. 1, 4, 4. Later laws prevail over those which preceded them.

CONSTITUTIONS OF CLARENDON. See CLARENDON.

CONSTITUTOR. In the civil law. One who, by a simple agreement, becomes responsible for the payment of another's debt.

CONSTITUTUM. In the civil law. An agreement to pay a subsisting debt which exists without any stipulation, whether of the promisor or another party. It differs from a stipulation in that it must be for an existing debt. Du Cange.

Constitutum esse eam domum unicuique nostrum debere existimari, ubi quisque sedes et tabulas haberet, suarumque rerum constitutionem fecisset. It is settled that that is to be considered the home of each one of us where he may have his habitation and account-books, and where he may have made an establishment of his business. Dig. 50, 16, 203.

CONSTRAINT. This term is held to be exactly equivalent with "restraint." 2 Tenn. Ch. 427.

In Scotch law. Constraint means duress.

CONSTRUCT. To build; erect; put together; make ready for use.

Constructio legis non facit injuriam. The construction of the law (a construction made by the law) works no injury. Co. Litt. 183; Broom, Max. 603. The law will make such a construction of an instrument as not to injure a party.

CONSTRUCTION. The process, or the art, of determining the sense, real meaning, or proper explanation of obscure or ambiguous terms or provisions in a statute, written instrument, or oral agreement, or the application of such subject to the case in question, by reasoning in the light derived from extraneous connected circumstances or laws or writings bearing upon the same or a connected matter, or by seeking and applying the probable aim and purpose of the provision.

It is to be noted that this term is properly distinguished from *interpretation*, although the two are often used synonymously. In strictness, interpretation is limited to exploring the written text, while construction goes beyond and may call in the aid of extrinsic considerations, as above indicated.

CONSTRUCTION, COURT OF. A court of equity or of common law, as the case may be, is called the court of construction with regard to wills, as opposed to the court of probate, whose duty is to decide whether an instrument be a will at all. Now, the court of probate may decide that a given instrument is a will, and yet the court of construction may decide that it has no operation, by reason of perpetuities, illegality, uncertainty, etc. Wharton.

CONSTRUCTIVE. That which is established by the mind of the law in its act of *construing* facts, conduct, circumstances, or instruments; that which has not the character assigned to it in its own essential nature, but acquires such character in consequence of the way in which it is regarded by a rule or policy of law; hence, inferred, implied, made out by legal interpretation.

CONSTRUCTIVE ASSENT. An assent or consent imputed to a party from a construction or interpretation of his conduct; as distinguished from one which he actually expresses.

CONSTRUCTIVE BREAKING INTO A HOUSE. A breaking made out by construction of law. As where a burglar gains an entry into a house by threats, fraud, or conspiracy. 2 Russ. Crimes, 9, 10.

CONSTRUCTIVE FRAUD. Constructive fraud consists (1) in any breach of duty which, without an actually fraudulent intent, gains an advantage to the person in fault, or any one claiming under him, by misleading another to his prejudice, or to the prejudice of any one claiming under him; or (2) in any such act or omission as the law specially declares to be fraudulent, without respect to actual fraud. Civil Code Cal. § 1573.

By *constructive frauds* are meant such acts or contracts as, though not originating in any actual evil design or contrivance to perpetrate a positive fraud or injury upon other persons, are yet, by their tendency to deceive or mislead other persons, or to violate private or public confidence, or to impair or injure the public interests, deemed equally reprehensible with positive fraud; and therefore are prohibited by law, as within the same reason and mischief as acts and contracts done *malo animo*. 1 Story, Eq. Jur. § 258.

CONSTRUCTIVE LARCENY. One where the felonious intent to appropriate the goods to his own use, at the time of the asportation, is made out by construction from the defendant's conduct, although, originally, the taking was not apparently felonious. 2 East, P. C. 685; 1 Leach, 212.

CONSTRUCTIVE MALICE. Implied malice; malice inferred from acts; malice imputed by law; malice which is not shown by direct proof of an intention to do injury, (express malice,) but which is inferentially established by the necessarily injurious results of the acts shown to have been committed.

CONSTRUCTIVE NOTICE. Information or knowledge of a fact imputed by law to a person, (although he may not actually have it,) because he could have discovered the fact by proper diligence, and his situation was such as to cast upon him the duty of inquiring into it.

CONSTRUCTIVE TAKING. A phrase used in the law to characterize an act not amounting to an actual appropriation of chattels, but which shows an intention to convert them to his use; as if a person intrusted with the possession of goods deals with them contrary to the orders of the owner.

CONSTRUCTIVE TOTAL LOSS. In marine insurance. This occurs where the loss or injury to the vessel insured does not amount to its total disappearance or destruction, but where, although the vessel still remains, the cost of repairing or recovering it would amount to more than its value when so repaired, and consequently the insured abandons it to the underwriters. See ACTUAL TOTAL LOSS.

CONSTRUCTIVE TREASON. Treason imputed to a person by law from his conduct or course of actions, though his deeds taken severally do not amount to actual treason. This doctrine is not known in the United States.

CONSTRUCTIVE TRUST. A trust raised by construction of law, or arising by operation of law, as distinguished from an express trust.

Wherever the circumstances of a transaction are such that the person who takes the legal estate in property cannot also enjoy the beneficial interest without necessarily violating some established principle of equity, the court will immediately raise a *constructive trust*, and fasten it upon the conscience of the legal owner, so as to convert him into a trustee for the parties who in equity are entitled to the beneficial enjoyment. Hill, Trustees, 116; 1 Spence, Eq. Jur. 511.

CONSTRUE. To put together; to arrange or marshal the words of an instrument. To ascertain the meaning of language by a process of arrangement and inference.

CONSUETUDINARIUS. In ecclesiastical law. A ritual or book, containing the rites and forms of divine offices, or the customs of abbeys and monasteries.

CONSUETUDINARY LAW. Customary law. Law derived by oral tradition from a remote antiquity. Bell.

CONSUETUDINES. In old English law. Customs. Thus, *consuetudines et assisa forestæ*, the customs and assise of the forest.

CONSUETUDINES FEUDORUM. (Lat. feudal customs.) A compilation of the law of feuds or fiefs in Lombardy, made A. D. 1170.

CONSUETUDINIBUS ET SERVICIIS. In old English law. A writ of right close, which lay against a tenant who deforced his lord of the rent or service due to him. Reg. Orig. 159; Fitzh. Nat. Brev. 151.

CONSUETUDO. Lat. A custom; an established usage or practice. Co. Litt. 58. Tolls; duties; taxes. Id. 58b.

CONSUETUDO ANGLICANA. The custom of England; the ancient common law, as distinguished from *lex*, the Roman or civil law.

Consuetudo contra rationem introducta potius usurpatio quam consuetudo appellari debet. A custom introduced against reason ought rather to be called a "usurpation" than a "custom." Co. Litt. 113.

CONSUETUDO CURIÆ. The custom or practice of a court. Hardr. 141.

Consuetudo debet esse certa; nam incerta pro nullâ habetur. Dav. 33. A custom should be certain; for an uncertain custom is considered null.

Consuetudo est altera lex. Custom is another law. 4 Coke, 21.

Consuetudo est optimus interpres legum. 2 Inst. 18. Custom is the best expounder of the laws.

Consuetudo et communis assuetudo vincit legem non scriptam, si sit specialis; et interpretatur legem scriptam, si lex sit generalis. Jenk. Cent. 273. Custom and common usage overcomes the unwritten law, if it be special; and interprets the written law, if the law be general.

Consuetudo ex certa causa rationabili usitata privat communem legem. A custom, grounded on a certain and reasonable cause, supersedes the common law. Litt. § 169; Co. Litt. 113; Broom, Max. 919.

Consuetudo, licet sit magnæ auctoritatis, nunquam tamen præjudicat manifestæ veritati. A custom, though it be of great authority, should never prejudice manifest truth. 4 Coke, 18.

Consuetudo loci observanda est. Litt. § 169. The custom of a place is to be observed.

Consuetudo manerii et loci observanda est. 6 Coke, 67. A custom of a manor and place is to be observed.

CONSUETUDO MERCATORUM. Lat. The custom of merchants, the same with *lex mercatoria*.

Consuetudo neque injuriâ oriri neque tolli potest. Lofft, 340. Custom can neither arise from nor be taken away by injury.

Consuetudo non trahitur in consequentiam. 3 Keb. 499. Custom is not drawn into consequence. 4 Jur. (N. S.) Ex. 139.

Consuetudo præscripta et legitima vincit legem. A prescriptive and lawful custom overcomes the law. Co. Litt. 113; 4 Coke, 21.

Consuetudo regni Angliæ est lex Angliæ. Jenk. Cent. 119. The custom of the kingdom of England is the law of England. See 2 Bl. Comm. 422.

Consuetudo semel reprobata non potest amplius induci. A custom once disallowed cannot be again brought forward, [or relied on.] Dav. 33.

Consuetudo tollit communem legem. Co. Litt. 33b. Custom takes away the common law.

Consuetudo volentes ducit, lex nolentes trahit. Custom leads the willing, law compels [drags] the unwilling. Jenk. Cent. 274.

CONSUL. In Roman law. During the republic, the name "consul" was given to the chief executive magistrate, two of whom were chosen annually. The office was continued under the empire, but its powers and prerogatives were greatly reduced. The name is supposed to have been derived from *consulo*, to consult, because these officers consulted with the senate on administrative measures.

In old English law. An ancient title of an earl.

In international law. An officer of a commercial character, appointed by the different states to watch over the mercantile interests of the appointing state and of its subjects in foreign countries. There are usually a number of consuls in every maritime country, and they are usually subject to a chief consul, who is called a "consul general." Brown.

The word "consul" has two meanings: (1) It denotes an officer of a particular grade in the consular service; (2) it has a broader generic sense, embracing all consular officers. 15 Ct. Cl. 64.

The official designations employed throughout this title shall be deemed to have the following meanings, respectively: *First.* "Consul general," "consul," and "commercial agent" shall be deemed to denote full, principal, and permanent consular officers, as distinguished from subordinates and substitutes. *Second.* "Deputy-consul" and "consular agent" shall be deemed to denote consular officers subordinate to such principals, exercising the powers and performing the duties within the limits of their consulates or commercial agencies respectively, the former at the same ports or places and the latter at ports or places different from those at which such principals are located respectively. *Third.* "Vice-consuls" and "vice-commercial agents" shall be deemed to denote consular officers who shall be substituted, temporarily, to fill the places of consuls general, consuls, or commercial agents, when they shall be temporarily absent or relieved from duty. *Fourth.* "Consular officer" shall be deemed to include consuls general, consuls, commercial agents, deputy-consuls, vice-consuls, vice-commercial agents, and consular agents, and none others. *Fifth.* "Diplomatic officer" shall be deemed to include ambassadors, envoys extraordinary, ministers plenipotentiary, ministers resident, commissioners, chargés d'affaires, agents, and secretaries of legation, and none others. Rev. St. U. S. § 1674.

CONSULAR COURTS. Courts held by the consuls of one country, within the territory of another, under authority given by treaty, for the settlement of civil cases between citizens of the country which the consul represents. In some instances they have also a criminal jurisdiction, but in this respect are subject to review by the courts of the home government. See Rev. St. U. S. § 4083.

CONSULTA ECCLESIA. In ecclesiastical law. A church full or provided for. Cowell.

CONSULTARY RESPONSE. The opinion of a court of law on a special case.

CONSULTATION. A writ whereby a cause which has been wrongfully removed by prohibition out of an ecclesiastical court to a temporal court is returned to the ecclesiastical court. Phillim. Ecc. Law, 1439.

A conference between the counsel engaged in a case, to discuss its questions or arrange the method of conducting it.

In French law. The opinion of counsel upon a point of law submitted to them.

CONSULTO. In the civil law. Designedly; intentionally. Dig. 28, 41.

CONSUMMATE. Completed; as distinguished from *initiate*, or that which is merely begun. The husband of a woman seised of an estate of inheritance becomes, by the birth of a child, tenant by the curtesy *initiate*, and may do many acts to charge the lands, but his estate is not *consummate* till the death of the wife. 2 Bl. Comm. 126, 128; Co. Litt. 30a.

CONSUMMATION. The completion of a thing; the completion of a marriage between two affianced persons by cohabitation.

CONTAGIOUS DISORDERS. Diseases which are capable of being transmitted by mediate or immediate contact.

CONTANGO. In English law. The commission received for carrying over or putting off the time of execution of a contract to deliver stocks or pay for them at a certain time. Wharton.

CONTEK. L. Fr. A contest, dispute, disturbance, opposition. Britt. c. 42; Kelham. *Conteckours;* brawlers; disturbers of the peace. Britt. c. 29.

CONTEMNER. One who has committed contempt of court.

CONTEMPLATION. The act of the mind in considering with attention. Continued attention of the mind to a particular subject. Consideration of an act or series of acts with the intention of doing or adopting them. The consideration of an event or state of facts with the expectation that it will transpire.

CONTEMPLATION OF BANKRUPTCY. Contemplation of a *state* of bankruptcy or a known insolvency and inability to carry on business, and a stoppage of business. 5 Reporter, 295, 299.

Something more is meant by the phrase than the expectation of insolvency; it includes the making provision against the results of it. 13 How. 150; 8 Bosw. 194.

By contemplation of bankruptcy is meant a contemplation of the breaking up of one's business, or an inability to continue it. Crabbe, 529.

CONTEMPORANEA EXPOSITIO. Lat. Contemporaneous exposition, or construction; a construction drawn from the *time* when, and the circumstances under which, the subject-matter to be construed, as a statute or custom, originated.

Contemporanea expositio est optima et fortissima in lege. Contemporaneous exposition is the best and strongest in the law. 2 Inst. 11. A statute is best explained by following the construction put upon it by judges who lived at the *time* it was made, or soon after. 10 Coke, 70; Broom, Max. 682.

CONTEMPT. Contumacy; a willful disregard of the authority of a court of justice or legislative body or disobedience to its lawful orders.

Contempt of court is committed by a person who does any act in willful contravention of its authority or dignity, or tending to impede or frustrate the administration of justice, or by one who, being under the court's authority as a party to a proceeding therein, willfully disobeys its lawful orders or fails to comply with an undertaking which he has given.

The disobedience of the defendant to the decree of that court, in this instance, is palpable, willful, and utterly inexcusable; and therefore constitutes, beyond a doubt, what is termed a "contempt," which is well described by an eminent jurist as "a disobedience to the court, by acting in opposition to the authority, justice, and dignity thereof," adding that "it commonly consists in a party doing otherwise than he is enjoined to do, or not doing what he is commanded or required by the process, order, or decree of the court; in all which cases the party disobeying is liable to be attached and committed for the contempt." 21 Conn. 199.

Contempts are of two kinds,—criminal and constructive. Criminal contempts are those committed in the immediate view and presence of the court, such as insulting language or acts of violence, which interrupt the regular proceedings in courts. Constructive contempts are those which arise from matters not transpiring in court, but in reference to failures to comply with the orders and decrees issued by the court, and to be performed elsewhere. 49 Me. 392.

Or they may be divided into such as are committed in the face of the court (*in facie curiæ*) which are punishable by commitment and fine, and such as are committed out of court, which are punishable by attachment. 1 Tidd, Pr. 479, 480. 4 Bl. Comm. 285, 286; 4 Steph. Comm. 348–353.

CONTEMPT OF CONGRESS, LEGISLATURE, or PARLIAMENT. Whatever obstructs or tends to obstruct the due course of proceeding of either house, or grossly reflects on the character of a member of either house, or imputes to him what it would be a libel to impute to an ordinary person, is a contempt of the house, and thereby a breach of privilege. Sweet.

CONTEMPTIBILITER. Lat. Contemptuously.

In old English law. Contempt, contempts. Fleta, lib. 2, c. 60, § 35.

CONTENTIOUS. Contested; adversary; litigated between adverse or contending parties; a judicial proceeding not merely *ex parte* in its character, but comprising attack and defense as between opposing parties, is so called. The litigious proceedings in ecclesiastical courts are sometimes said to belong to its "contentious" jurisdiction, in contradistinction to what is called its "voluntary" jurisdiction, which is exercised in the granting of licenses, probates of wills, dispensations, faculties, etc.

CONTENTIOUS JURISDICTION. In English ecclesiastical law. That branch of the jurisdiction of the ecclesiastical courts which is exercised upon adversary or *contentious* proceedings. See CONTENTIOUS.

CONTENTMENT, CONTENEMENT. A man's countenance or credit, which he has together with, and by reason of, his freehold; or that which is necessary for the support and maintenance of men, agreeably to their several qualities or states of life. Wharton; Cowell.

CONTENTS AND NOT-CONTENTS. In parliamentary law. The "contents" are those who, in the house of lords, express assent to a bill; the "not" or "non contents" dissent. May, Parl. Law, cc. 12, 357.

"CONTENTS UNKNOWN." Words sometimes annexed to a bill of lading of goods in cases. Their meaning is that the master only means to acknowledge the shipment, in good order, of the cases, as to their external condition. 12 How. 273.

CONTERMINOUS. Adjacent; adjoining; having a common boundary; coterminous.

CONTEST. To make defense to an adverse claim in a court of law; to oppose, resist, or dispute the case made by a plaintiff.

CONTESTATIO LITIS. In Roman law. Contestation of suit; the framing an issue; joinder in issue. The formal act of both the parties with which the proceedings *in jure* were closed when they led to a judicial investigation, and by which the neighbors whom the parties brought with them were called to testify. Mackeld. Rom. Law, § 219.

In old English law. Coming to an issue; the issue so produced. Crabb, Eng. Law, 216.

Contestatio litis eget terminos contradictarios. An issue requires terms of contradiction. Jenk. Cent. 117. To constitute an issue, there must be an affirmative on one side and a negative on the other

CONTESTATION OF SUIT. In an ecclesiastical cause, that stage of the suit which is reached when the defendant has answered the libel by giving in an allegation.

CONTESTED ELECTION. This phrase has no technical or legally defined meaning. An election may be said to be contested whenever an objection is formally urged against it which, if found to be true in fact, would invalidate it. This is true both as to objections founded upon

some constitutional provision and to such as are based on statutes. 109 Ind. 116, 10 N. E. Rep. 600.

CONTEXT. The context of a particular sentence or clause in a statute, contract, will, etc., comprises those parts of the text which immediately precede and follow it. The context may sometimes be scrutinized, to aid in the interpretation of an obscure passage.

CONTIGUOUS. In close proximity; in actual close contact. 69 N. Y. 191. Touching; bounded or traversed by. The term is not synonymous with "vicinal." 32 La. Ann. 435.

CONTINENCIA. In Spanish law. Continency or unity of the proceedings in a cause. White, New Recop. b. 3, tit. 6, c. 1.

CONTINENS. In the Roman law. Continuing; holding together. Adjoining buildings were said to be *continentia*.

CONTINENTIA. In old English practice. Continuance or connection. Applied to the proceedings in a cause. Bract. fol. 362*b*.

CONTINGENCY. An event that may or may not happen, a doubtful or uncertain future event. The quality of being contingent.

A fortuitous event, which comes without design, foresight, or expectation. A contingent expense must be deemed to be an expense depending upon some future uncertain event. 39 Barb. 272.

CONTINGENCY OF A PROCESS. In Scotch law. Where two or more processes are so connected that the circumstances of the one are likely to throw light on the others, the process first enrolled is considered as the leading process, and those subsequently brought into court, if not brought in the same division, may be remitted to it, *ob contingentiam*, on account of their nearness or proximity in character to it. The effect of remitting processes in this manner is merely to bring them before the same division of the court or same lord ordinary. In other respects they remain distinct. Bell.

CONTINGENCY WITH DOUBLE ASPECT. A remainder is said to be "in a contingency with double aspect," when there is another remainder limited on the same estate, not in derogation of the first, but as a substitute for it in case it should fail. Fearne, Rem. 373.

CONTINGENT. Possible, but not assured; doubtful or uncertain; conditioned upon the occurrence of some future event which is itself uncertain or questionable.

This term, when applied to a use, remainder, devise, bequest, or other legal right or interest, implies that no present interest exists, and that whether such interest or right ever will exist depends upon a future uncertain event. 5 Barb. 692.

CONTINGENT DAMAGES. Where a demurrer has been filed to one or more counts in a declaration, and its consideration is postponed, and meanwhile other counts in the same declaration, not demurred to, are taken as issues, and tried, and damages awarded upon them, such damages are called "contingent damages."

CONTINGENT ESTATE. An estate which depends for its effect upon an event which may or may not happen; as an estate limited to a person not *in esse*, or not yet born. 2 Crabb, Real Prop. p. 4, § 946.

CONTINGENT INTEREST IN PERSONAL PROPERTY. It may be defined as a future interest not transmissible to the representatives of the party entitled thereto, in case he dies before it vests in possession. Thus, if a testator leaves the income of a fund to his wife for life, and the capital of the fund to be distributed among such of his children as shall be living at her death, the interest of each child during the widow's life-time is *contingent*, and in case of his death is not transmissible to his representatives. Mozley & Whitley.

CONTINGENT LEGACY. A legacy given to a person at a future uncertain time, that may or may not arrive; as "at his age of twenty-one," or "if" or "when he attains twenty-one." 2 Bl. Comm. 513; 2 Steph. Comm. 259.

A legacy made dependent upon some uncertain event. 1 Rop. Leg. 506.

A legacy which has not vested.

CONTINGENT REMAINDER. An estate in remainder which is limited to take effect either to a dubious and uncertain person, or upon a dubious and uncertain event, by which no present or particular interest passes to the remainder-man, so that the particular estate may chance to be determined and the remainder never take effect. 2 Bl. Comm. 169.

A remainder limited so as to depend upon an event or condition which may never happen or be performed, or which may not happen or be performed till after the determination of the preceding estate. Fearne, Rem. 3.

CONTINGENT USE. A use limited to take effect upon the happening of some future contingent event; as where lands are conveyed to the use of A. and B., after a marriage shall be had between them. 2 Bl. Comm. 334.

CONTINUAL CLAIM. In old English law. A formal claim made by a party entitled to enter upon any lands or tenements, but deterred from such entry by menaces, or bodily fear, for the purpose of preserving or keeping alive his right. It was called "continual," because it was required to be repeated once in the space of every year and day. It had to be made as near to the land as the party could approach with safety, and, when made in due form, had the same effect with, and in all respects amounted to, a legal entry. Litt. §§ 419–423; Co. Litt. 250a; 3 Bl. Comm. 175.

CONTINUANCE. The adjournment or postponement of an action pending in a court, to a subsequent day of the same or another term.

Also the entry of a continuance made upon the record of the court, for the purpose of formally evidencing the postponement, or of connecting the parts of the record so as to make one continuous whole.

CONTINUANDO. In pleading. A word which was formerly used in a special declaration of trespass when the plaintiff would recover damages for several trespasses in the same action; and, to avoid multiplicity of actions, a man might in one action of trespass recover damages for many trespasses, laying the first to be done with a *continuando* to the whole time in which the rest of the trespasses were done; which was in this form: *Continuando* (by continuing) the trespasses aforesaid, etc., from the day aforesaid, etc., until such a day, including the last trespass. Termes de la Ley.

CONTINUING CONSIDERATION. See CONSIDERATION.

CONTINUING DAMAGES. See DAMAGES.

CONTINUOUS ADVERSE USE. Is interchangeable with the term "uninterrupted adverse use." 59 Ind. 411.

CONTINUOUS EASEMENT. One the enjoyment of which is or may be continual, without the necessity of any actual interference by man, as a water-spout, or a right of light or air; as distinguished from a *discontinuous* easement, which is one the enjoyment of which can be had only by the interference of man, as a right of way, or a right to draw water. Washb. Easem. 13; Gale, Easem. 16; 21 N. Y 505; 60 Mich. 252, 27 N. W. Rep. 512. This distinction is derived from the French law. See Civil Code, art. 688.

CONTRA. Against, confronting, opposite to; on the other hand; on the contrary. The word is used in many Latin phrases, as appears by the following titles. In the books of reports, *contra*, appended to the name of a judge or counsel, indicates that he held a view of the matter in argument *contrary* to that next before advanced. Also, after citation of cases in support of a position, *contra* is often prefixed to citations of cases opposed to it.

CONTRA BONOS MORES. Against good morals. Contracts *contra bonos mores* are void.

CONTRA FORMAM COLLATIONIS. In old English law. A writ that issued where lands given in perpetual alms to lay houses of religion, or to an abbot and convent, or to the warden or master of an hospital and his convent, to find certain poor men with necessaries, and do divine service, etc., were alienated, to the disherison of the house and church. By means of this writ the donor or his heirs could recover the lands. Reg. Orig. 238; Fitzh. Nat. Brev. 210.

CONTRA FORMAM DONI. Against the form of the grant. See FORMEDON.

CONTRA FORMAM FEOFFAMENTI. In old English law. A writ that lay for the heir of a tenant, enfeoffed of certain lands or tenements, by charter of feoffment from a lord to make certain services and suits to his court, who was afterwards distrained for more services than were mentioned in the charter. Reg. Orig. 176; Old Nat. Brev. 162.

CONTRA FORMAM STATUTI. In criminal pleading. (Contrary to the form of the statute in such case made and provided.) The usual conclusion of every indictment, etc., brought for an offense created by statute.

CONTRA JUS BELLI. Lat. Against the law of war. 1 Kent, Comm. 6.

CONTRA JUS COMMUNE. Against common right or law; contrary to the rule of the common law. Bract. fol. 48b.

Contra legem facit qui id facit quod lex prohibit; in fraudem vero qui, salvis verbis legis, sententiam ejus circumvenit. He does contrary to the law who does what the law prohibits; he acts in fraud of the law who, the letter of the law being inviolate, uses the law contrary to its intention. Dig. 1, 3, 29.

CONTRA LEGEM TERRÆ. Against the law of the land.

Contra negantem principia non est disputandum. There is no disputing against one who denies first principles. Co. Litt. 343.

Contra non valentem agere nulla currit præscriptio. No prescription runs against a person unable to bring an action. Broom, Max. 903.

CONTRA OMNES GENTES. Against all people. Formal words in old covenants of warranty. Fleta, lib. 3, c. 14, § 11.

CONTRA PACEM. Lat. Against the peace. A phrase used in the Latin forms of indictments, and also of actions for trespass, to signify that the offense alleged was committed against the public peace, *i. e.*, involved a breach of the peace. The full formula was *contra pacem domini regis*, against the peace of the lord the king. In modern pleading, in this country, the phrase "against the peace of the commonwealth" or "of the people" is used.

CONTRA PROFERENTEM. Against the party who proffers or puts forward a thing.

CONTRA TABULAS. In the civil law. Against the will, (testament.) Dig. 37, 4.

CONTRA VADIUM ET PLEGIUM. In old English law. Against gage and pledge. Bract. fol. 15b.

Contra veritatem lex nunquam aliquid permittit. The law never suffers anything contrary to truth. 2 Inst. 252.

CONTRABAND. Against law or treaty; prohibited. Goods exported from or imported into a country against its laws. Brande. Articles, the importation or exportation of which is prohibited by law. P. Enc.

CONTRABAND OF WAR. Certain classes of merchandise, such as arms and ammunition, which, by the rules of international law, cannot lawfully be furnished or carried by a neutral nation to either of two belligerents; if found in transit in neutral vessels, such goods may be seized and condemned for violation of neutrality.

A recent American author on international law says that, "by the term 'contraband of war,' we now understand a class of articles of commerce which *neutrals* are prohibited from furnishing to either one of the belligerents, for the reason that, by so doing, injury is done to the other belligerent;" and he treats of the subject, chiefly, in its relation to commerce upon the high seas. (Hall, Int. Law, 570, 592.) 4 Heisk. 345.

CONTRACAUSATOR. A criminal; one prosecuted for a crime.

CONTRACT. An agreement, upon sufficient consideration, to do or not to do a particular thing. 2 Bl. Comm. 442; 2 Kent, Comm. 449.

A covenant or agreement between two or more persons, with a lawful consideration or cause. Jacob.

A deliberate engagement between competent parties, upon a legal consideration, to do, or abstain from doing, some act. Wharton.

A contract or agreement is either where a promise is made on one side and assented to on the other; or where two or more persons enter into engagement with each other by a promise on either side. 2 Steph. Comm. 54.

A contract is an agreement by which one person obligates himself to another to give, to do, or permit, or not to do, something expressed or implied by such agreement. Civil Code La. art. 1761.

A contract is an agreement to do or not to do a certain thing. Civil Code Cal. § 1549.

A contract is an agreement between two or more parties for the doing or not doing of some specified thing. Code Ga. 1882, § 2714.

A contract is an agreement between two or more persons to do or not to do a particular thing; and the *obligation* of a contract is found in the terms in which the contract is expressed, and is the duty thus assumed by the contracting parties respectively to perform the stipulations of such contract. When that duty is recognized and enforced by the municipal law, it is one of *perfect*, and when not so recognized and enforced, of *imperfect*, obligation. 31 Conn. 265.

The writing which contains the agreement of parties, with the terms and conditions, and which serves as a proof of the obligation.

Contracts may be classified on several different methods, according to the element in them which is brought into prominence. The usual classifications are as follows:

Record, specialty, simple. Contracts are divided into three classes: (1) Contracts of record, such as judgments, recognizances, and statutes staple; (2) specialties, which are under seal, such as deeds and bonds; (3) simple contracts, or contracts by parol. There is no such fourth class as contracts in writing, distinct from verbal and sealed contracts; both verbal and written contracts are included in the class of simple contracts, and the only distinction between them is in regard to the mode of proof. Wharton.

Contracts of record are not really contracts at all, but are transactions which, being entered on the records of certain courts called "courts of record," are conclusive proof of the facts thereby appearing, and could formerly be enforced by action of law as if they had been put in the shape of a contract. They consist of judgments, recognizances, etc. Sweet.

Express and implied. When the agreement of the parties is definite and formal, and is stated either verbally or in writing, the contract is *express;* but when its terms have to be gathered by inference and deduction from facts or conduct, it is *implied.*

Executed and executory. Contracts are also distinguished into executed and executory; *executed,* where nothing remains to be done by either party, and where the transaction is completed at the moment that the arrangement is made, as where an article is sold and delivered, and payment therefor is made on the spot; *executory,* where some future act is to be done, as where an agreement is made to build a house in six months, or to do an act on or before some future day, or to lend money upon a certain interest, payable at a future time. Wharton.

An executed contract is one in which all the parties thereto have performed all the obligation which they have originally assumed. An executory contract is one in which something remains to be done by one or more parties. Code Ga. 1882, § 2715.

An executed contract is one the object of which is fully performed. All others are executory. Civil Code Cal. § 1661.

Entire and severable. An *entire* contract is one the consideration of which is entire on both sides. The entire fulfillment of the promise by either is a condition precedent to the fulfillment of any part of the promise by the other. Whenever, therefore, there is a contract to pay the gross sum for a certain and definite consideration, the contract is entire. A *severable* contract is one the consideration of which is, by its terms, susceptible of apportionment on either side, so as to correspond to the unascertained consideration on the other side, as a contract to pay a person the worth of his services so long as he will do certain work; or to give a certain price for every bushel of so much corn as corresponds to a sample. Wharton.

Principal and accessory. A *principal* contract is one which stands by itself, justifies its own existence, and is not subordinate or auxiliary to any other. *Accessory* contracts are those made for assuring the performance of a prior contract, either by the same parties or by others, such as suretyship, mortgage, and pledges. Civil Code La. art. 1764.

Unilateral and bilateral. A *unilateral* contract is one in which one party makes an express engagement or undertakes a performance, without receiving in return any express engagement or promise of performance from the other. *Bilateral* (or reciprocal) contracts are those by which the parties expressly enter into mutual engagements, such as sale or hire. Civil Code La. art. 1758; Poth. Obl. 1, 1, 1, 2.

Consensual and real. *Consensual* contracts are such as are founded upon and completed by the mere agreement of the contracting parties, without any external formality or symbolic act to fix the obligation. *Real* contracts are those in which it is necessary that there should be something more than mere consent, such as a loan of money, deposit, or pledge, which, from their nature, require a delivery of the thing, (*res.*)

Certain and hazardous. *Certain* contracts are those in which the thing to be done is supposed to depend on the will of the party, or when, in the usual course of events, it must happen in the manner stipulated. *Hazardous* contracts are those in which the performance of that which is one of its objects depends on an uncertain event. Civil Code La. 1769.

Commutative and independent. *Commutative* contracts are those in which what is done, given, or promised by one party is considered as an equivalent to or in consideration of what is done, given, or promised by the other. Civil Code La. 1761. *Independent* contracts are those in which the mutual acts or promises have no relation to each other, either as equivalents or as considerations. Civil Code La. 1762.

Gratuitous and onerous. *Gratuitous* contracts are those of which the object is the benefit of the person with whom it is made, without any profit or advantage received or promised as a consideration for it. It is not, however, the less gratuitous if it proceed either from gratitude for a benefit before received or from the hope of receiving one hereafter, although such benefit be of a pecuniary nature. Civil Code La. 1766. *Onerous* contracts are those in which something is given or promised as a consideration for the engagement or gift, or some service, interest, or condition is imposed on what is given or promised, although unequal to it in value.

Mutual interest, mixed, etc. Contracts of *mutual interest* are such as are entered into for the reciprocal interest and utility of each of the parties; as sales, exchange, partnership, and the like. *Mixed* contracts are those by which one of the parties confers a benefit on the other, receiving something of inferior value in return, such as a donation subject to a charge. Contracts *of beneficence* are those by which only one of the contracting parties is benefited; as, loans, deposit, and mandate. Poth. Obl. 1, 1, 1, 2.

CONTRACT OF BENEVOLENCE. A contract made for the benefit of one of the contracting parties only, as a mandate or deposit.

CONTRACT OF RECORD. A contract of record is one which has been declared and adjudicated by a court having jurisdiction, or which is entered of record in obedience to, or in carrying out, the judgments of a court. Code Ga. 1882, § 2716.

CONTRACT OF SALE. A contract by which one of the contracting parties, called the "seller," enters into an obligation to the other to cause him to have freely, by a title of proprietor, a thing, for the price of a certain sum of money, which the other contracting party, called the "buyer," on his part obliges himself to pay. Poth. Cont.

CONTRACTION. Abbreviation; abridgment or shortening of a word by omitting a letter or letters or a syllable, with a mark over the place where the elision occurs. This was customary in records written in the ancient "court hand," and is frequently found in the books printed in black-letter.

CONTRACTOR. This term is strictly applicable to any person who enters into a contract, but is commonly reserved to desig nate one who, for a fixed price, undertakes to procure the performance of works on a large scale, or the furnishing of goods in large quantities, whether for the public or a company or individual.

The primary meaning of the word is one who contracts; one of the parties to a bargain. He who agrees to do anything for another is a contractor. 12 N. Y. 628.

CONTRACTUS. Contract; a contract; contracts.

CONTRACTUS BONÆ FIDEI. In Roman law. Contracts of good faith. Those contracts which, when brought into litigation, were not determined by the rules of the strict law alone, but allowed the judge to examine into the *bona fides* of the transaction, and to hear equitable considerations against their enforcement. In this they were opposed to contracts *stricti juris*, against which equitable defenses could not be entertained.

CONTRACTUS CIVILES. In Roman law. Civil contracts. Those contracts which were recognized as actionable by the strict civil law of Rome, or as being founded upon a particular statute, as distinguished from those which could not be enforced in the courts except by the aid of the prætor, who, through his equitable powers, gave an action upon them. The latter were called "*contractus prætorii.*"

Contractus est quasi actus contra actum. 2 Coke, 15. A contract is, as it were, act against act.

Contractus ex turpi causa, vel contra bonos mores, nullus est. A contract founded on a base consideration, or against good morals, is null. Hob. 167.

Contractus legem ex conventione accipiunt. Contracts receive legal sanction from the agreement of the parties. Dig. 16, 3, 1, 6.

CONTRADICT. In practice. To disprove. To prove a fact contrary to what has been asserted by a witness.

CONTRADICTION IN TERMS. A phrase of which the parts are expressly inconsistent, as, *e. g.*, "an innocent murder;" "a fee-simple for life."

CONTRÆSCRITURA. In Spanish law. A counter-writing; counter-letter. A document executed at the same time with an act of sale or other instrument, and operating by way of defeasance or otherwise modifying

the apparent effect and purport of the original instrument.

CONTRAFACTIO. Counterfeiting; as *contrafactio sigilli regis*, counterfeiting the king's seal. Cowell.

CONTRAINTE PAR CORPS. In French law. The civil process of arrest of the person, which is imposed upon vendors falsely representing their property to be unincumbered, or upon persons mortgaging property which they are aware does not belong to them, and in other cases of moral heinousness. Brown.

CONTRALIGATIO. In old English law. Counter-obligation. Literally, counter-binding. *Est enim obligatio quasi contraligatio.* Fleta, lib. 2, c. 56, § 1.

CONTRAMANDATIO. A countermanding. *Contramandatio placiti*, in old English law, was the respiting of a defendant, or giving him further time to answer, by countermanding the day fixed for him to plead, and appointing a new day; a sort of imparlance.

CONTRAMANDATUM. A lawful excuse, which a defendant in a suit by attorney alleges for himself to show that the plaintiff has no cause of complaint. Blount.

CONTRAPLACITUM. In old English law. A counter-plea. Townsh. Pl. 61.

CONTRAPOSITIO. In old English law. A plea or answer. Blount. A counter-position.

CONTRARIENTS. This word was used in the time of Edw. II. to signify those who were opposed to the government, but were neither rebels nor traitors. Jacob.

Contrariorum contraria est ratio. Hob. 344. The reason of contrary things is contrary.

CONTRAROTULATOR. A controller. One whose business it was to observe the money which the collectors had gathered for the use of the king or the people. Cowell.

CONTRAROTULATOR PIPÆ. An officer of the exchequer that writeth out summons twice every year, to the sheriffs, to levy the rents and debts of the pipe. Blount.

CONTRAT. In French law. Contracts are of the following varieties: (1) *Bilateral*, or *synallagmatique*, where each party is bound to the other to do what is just and proper; or (2) *unilateral*, where the one side only is bound; or (3) *commutatif*, where one does to the other something which is supposed to be an equivalent for what the other does to him; or (4) *aléatoire*, where the consideration for the act of the one is a mere chance; or (5) *contrat de bienfaisance*, where the one party procures to the other a purely gratuitous benefit; or (6) *contrat à titre onereux*, where each party is bound under some duty to the other. Brown.

CONTRATALLIA. In old English law. A counter-tally. A term used in the exchequer. Mem. in Scacc. M. 26 Edw. I.

CONTRATENERE. To hold against; to withhold. Whishaw.

CONTRAVENING EQUITY. A right or equity, in another person, which is inconsistent with and opposed to the equity sought to be enforced or recognized.

CONTRAVENTION. In French law. An act which violates the law, a treaty, or an agreement which the party has made. That infraction of the law punished by a fine which does not exceed fifteen francs and by an imprisonment not exceeding three days. Pen. Code, 1.

In Scotch law. The act of breaking through any restraint imposed by deed, by covenant, or by a court.

CONTRECTARE. Lat. In the civil law. To handle; to take hold of; to meddle with.

In old English law. To treat. *Vel male contrectet;* or shall ill treat. Fleta, lib. 1, c. 17, § 4.

CONTRECTATIO. In the civil and old English law. Touching; handling; meddling. The act of removing a thing from its place in such a manner that, if the thing be not restored, it will amount to theft.

Contrectatio rei alienæ, animo furandi, est furtum. Jenk. Cent. 132. The touching or removing of another's property, with an intention of stealing, is theft.

CONTREFACON. In French law. The offense of printing or causing to be printed a book, the copyright of which is held by another, without authority from him. Merl. Repert.

CONTRE-MAITRE. In French marine law. The chief officer of a vessel, who, in case of the sickness or absence of the master, commanded in his place. Literally, the counter-master.

CONTRIBUTE. To supply a share or proportional part of money or property towards the prosecution of a common enterprise or the discharge of a joint obligation.

CONTRIBUTION. In common law. The sharing of a loss or payment among several. The act of any one or several of a number of co-debtors, co-sureties, etc., in reimbursing one of their number who has paid the whole debt or suffered the whole liability, each to the extent of his proportionate share.

In maritime law. Where the property of one of several parties interested in a vessel and cargo has been voluntarily sacrificed for the common safety, (as by throwing goods overboard to lighten the vessel,) such loss must be made good by the contribution of the others, which is termed "general average." 3 Kent, Comm. 232–244; 1 Story, Eq. Jur. § 490.

In the civil law. A partition by which the creditors of an insolvent debtor divide among themselves the proceeds of his property proportionably to the amount of their respective credits. Code La. art. 2522, no. 10.

Contribution is the division which is made among the heirs of the succession of the debts with which the succession is charged, according to the proportion which each is bound to bear. Civil Code La. art. 1420.

CONTRIBUTIONE FACIENDA. In old English law. A writ that lay where tenants in common were bound to do some act, and one of them was put to the whole burthen, to compel the rest to make contribution. Reg. Orig. 175; Fitzh. Nat. Brev. 162.

CONTRIBUTORY. A person liable to contribute to the assets of a company which is being wound up, as being a member or (in some cases) a past member thereof. Mozley & Whitley.

CONTRIBUTORY NEGLIGENCE. Contributory negligence, when set up as a defense to an action for injuries alleged to have been caused by the defendant's negligence, means any want of ordinary care on the part of the person injured, (or on the part of another whose negligence is imputable to him,) which combined and concurred with the defendant's negligence, and contributed to the injury as a proximate cause thereof, and as an element without which the injury would not have occurred.

CONTROLLER. A comptroller, which see.

CONTROLMENT. In old English law. The controlling or checking of another officer's account; the keeping of a counter-roll.

CONTROVER. In old English law. An inventer or deviser of false news. 2 Inst. 227.

CONTROVERSY. A litigated question; adversary proceeding in a court of law; a civil action or suit, either at law or in equity.

It differs from "case," which includes all suits, criminal as well as civil; whereas "controversy" is a civil and not a criminal proceeding. 2 Dall. 419, 431, 432.

CONTROVERT. To dispute; to deny; to oppose or contest; to take issue on.

CONTUBERNIUM. In Roman law. The marriage of slaves; a permitted cohabitation.

CONTUMACE CAPIENDO. In English law. Excommunication in all cases of contempt in the spiritual courts is discontinued by 53 Geo. III. c. 127, § 2, and in lieu thereof, where a lawful citation or sentence has not been obeyed, the judge shall have power, after a certain period, to pronounce such person contumacious and in contempt, and to signify the same to the court of chancery, whereupon a writ *de contumace capiendo* shall issue from that court, which shall have the same force and effect as formerly belonged, in case of contempt, to a writ *de excommunicato capiendo*. (2 & 3 Wm. IV. c. 93; 3 & 4 Vict. c. 93.) Wharton.

CONTUMACY. The refusal or intentional omission of a person who has been duly cited before a court to appear and defend the charge laid against him, or, if he is duly before the court, to obey some lawful order or direction made in the cause. In the former case it is called "presumed" contumacy; in the latter, "actual." The term is chiefly used in ecclesiastical law. See 3 Curt. Ecc. 1.

CONTUMAX. One accused of a crime who refuses to appear and answer to the charge. An outlaw.

CONTUSION. In medical jurisprudence. A bruise; a hurt or injury to the flesh or some part of the body by the blow of a blunt instrument, or by a fall, producing no severance of tissue or apparent wound. If the skin is broken, it is called a "contused wound."

CONTUTOR. Lat. In the civil law. A co-tutor, or co-guardian. Inst. 1, 24, 1.

CONUSANCE. In English law. Cognizance or jurisdiction. Conusance of pleas. Termes de la Ley.

CONUSANCE, CLAIM OF. See COGNIZANCE.

CONUSANT. One who knows; as, if a party knowing of an agreement in which he has an interest makes no objection to it, he is said to be conusant. Co. Litt. 157.

CONUSEE. See COGNIZEE.

CONUSOR. See COGNIZOR.

CONVENABLE. In old English law. Suitable; agreeable; convenient; fitting. Litt. § 103.

CONVENE. In the civil law. To bring an action.

CONVENIENT. Proper; just; suitable.

CONVENIT. In civil and old English law. It is agreed; it was agreed.

CONVENT. The fraternity of an abbey or priory, as *societas* is the number of fellows in a college. A religious house, now regarded as a merely voluntary association, not importing civil death. 33 Law J. Ch. 308.

CONVENTICLE. A private assembly or meeting for the exercise of religion. The word was first an appellation of reproach to the religious assemblies of Wycliffe in the reigns of Edward III. and Richard II., and was afterwards applied to a meeting of dissenters from the established church. As this word in strict propriety denotes an unlawful assembly, it cannot be justly applied to the assembling of persons in places of worship licensed according to the requisitions of law. Wharton.

CONVENTIO. In canon law. The act of summoning or calling together the parties by summoning the defendant.

In the civil law. A compact, agreement, or convention. An agreement between two or more persons respecting a legal relation between them. The term is one of very wide scope, and applies to all classes of subjects in which an engagement or business relation may be founded by agreement. It is to be distinguished from the negotiations or preliminary transactions on the object of the convention and fixing its extent, which are not binding so long as the convention is not concluded. Mackeld. Rom. Law, §§ 385, 386.

In contracts. An agreement; a covenant. Cowell.

CONVENTIO IN UNUM. In the civil law. The agreement between the two parties to a contract upon the sense of the contract proposed. It is an essential part of the contract, following the pollicitation or proposal emanating from the one, and followed by the consension or agreement of the other.

Conventio privatorum non potest publico juri derogare. The agreement of private persons cannot derogate from public right, *i. e.*, cannot prevent the application of general rules of law, or render valid any contravention of law. Co. Litt. 166*a;* Wing. Max. p. 746, max. 201.

Conventio vincit legem. The express agreement of parties overcomes [prevails against] the law. Story, Ag. § 368.

CONVENTION. In Roman law. An agreement between parties; a pact. A convention was a mutual engagement between two persons, possessing all the subjective requisites of a contract, but which did not give rise to an action, nor receive the sanction of the law, as bearing an "obligation," until the objective requisite of a solemn ceremonial, (such as *stipulatio*) was supplied. In other words, convention was the informal agreement of the parties, which formed the basis of a contract, and which became a contract when the external formalities were superimposed. See Maine, Anc. Law, 313.

"The division of conventions into contracts and pacts was important in the Roman law. The former were such conventions as already, by the older civil law, founded an obligation and action; all the other conventions were termed 'pacts.' These generally did not produce an actionable obligation. Actionability was subsequently given to several pacts, whereby they received the same power and efficacy that contracts received." Mackeld. Rom. Law, § 395.

In English law. An extraordinary assembly of the houses of lords and commons, without the assent or summons of the sovereign. It can only be justified *ex necessitate rei,* as the parliament which restored Charles II., and that which disposed of the crown and kingdom to William and Mary. Wharton.

Also the name of an old writ that lay for the breach of a covenant.

In legislation. An assembly of delegates or representatives chosen by the people for special and extraordinary legislative purposes, such as the framing or revision of a state constitution. Also an assembly of delegates chosen by a political party, or by the party organization in a larger or smaller territory, to nominate candidates for an approaching election.

CONVENTIONAL. Depending on, or arising from, the mutual agreement of parties; as distinguished from *legal,* which means created by, or arising from, the act of the law.

CONVENTIONAL ESTATES. Those freeholds not of inheritance or estates for life, which are created by the express acts of the parties, in contradistinction to those which are legal and arise from the operation of law.

CONVENTIONAL MORTGAGE. The conventional mortgage is a contract by which a person binds the whole of his property, or a portion of it only, in favor of another, to secure the execution of some engagement, but without divesting himself of possession. Civil Code La. art. 3290.

CONVENTIONE. The name of a writ for the breach of any covenant in writing, whether real or personal. Reg. Orig. 115; Fitzh. Nat. Brev. 145.

CONVENTIONS. This name is sometimes given to compacts or treaties with foreign countries as to the apprehension and extradition of fugitive offenders. See EXTRADITION.

CONVENTUAL CHURCH. In ecclesiastical law. That which consists of regular clerks, professing some order or religion; or of dean and chapter; or other societies of spiritual men.

CONVENTUALS. Religious men united in a convent or religious house. Cowell.

CONVENTUS. A coming together; a convention or assembly. *Conventus magnatum vel procerum* (the assembly of chief men or peers) was one of the names of the English parliament. 1 Bl. Comm. 148.

In the civil law. The term meant a gathering together of people; a crowd assembled for any purpose; also a convention, pact, or bargain.

CONVENTUS JURIDICUS. In the Roman law. A court of sessions held in the Roman provinces, by the president of the province, assisted by a certain number of counsellors and assessors, at fixed periods, to hear and determine suits, and to provide for the civil administration of the province. Schm. Civil Law, Introd. 17.

CONVERSANT. One who is in the habit of being in a particular place is said to be conversant there. Barnes, 162. Acquainted; familiar.

CONVERSANTES. In old English law. Conversant or dwelling; commorant.

CONVERSE. The transposition of the subject and predicate in a proposition, as: "Everything is good in its place." *Converse,* "Nothing is good which is not in its place." Wharton.

CONVERSION. In equity. The transformation of one species of property into another, as money into land or land into money; or, more particularly, a fiction of law, by which equity assumes that such a transformation has taken place (contrary to the fact) when it is rendered necessary by the equities of the case,—as to carry into effect the directions of a will or settlement,—and by which the property so dealt with becomes invested with the properties and attributes of that into which it is supposed to have been converted.

At law. An unauthorized assumption and exercise of the right of ownership over goods or personal chattels belonging to another, to the alteration of their condition or the exclusion of the owner's rights. 44 Me. 197; 36 N. H. 311; 45 Wis. 262.

Conversion is defined to be an unauthorized assumption and exercise of the right of ownership over goods belonging to another to the exclusion of the owner's rights. A *constructive* conversion takes place when a person does such acts in reference to the goods of another as amount in law to appropriation of the property to himself. Every unauthorized taking of personal property, and all intermeddling with it, beyond the extent of the authority conferred, in case a limited authority has been given, with intent so to apply and dispose of it as to alter its condition or interfere with the owner's dominion, is a conversion. 68 N. Y. 524.

"Conversion" and "carrying away" are not synonymous nor convertible terms. There may be a conversion without any carrying away. 26 Ala. 101.

CONVEY. To pass or transmit the title to property from one to another; to transfer property or the title to property by deed or instrument under seal.

To convey real estate is, by an appropriate instrument, to transfer the legal title to it from the present owner to another. 29 Conn. 356.

Convey relates properly to the disposition of real property, not to personal. 21 Barb. 551, 561.

CONVEYANCE. In pleading. Introduction or inducement.

In real property law. The transfer of the title of land from one person or class of

persons to another. 21 Barb. 551; 29 Conn. 356.

An instrument in writing under seal, (anciently termed an "assurance,") by which some estate or interest in lands is transferred from one person to another; such as a deed, mortgage, etc. 2 Bl. Comm. 293, 295, 309.

Conveyance includes every instrument in writing by which any estate or interest in real estate is created, aliened, mortgaged, or assigned, or by which the title to any real estate may be affected in law or equity, except last wills and testaments, leases for a term not exceeding three years, and executory contracts for the sale or purchase of lands. 1 Rev. St. N. Y. p. 762, § 38; Gen. St. Minn. 1878, c. 40, § 26; How. St. Mich. 1882, § 5689.

The term "conveyance," as used in the California Code, embraces every instrument in writing by which any estate or interest in real property is created, aliened, mortgaged, or incumbered, or by which the title to any real property may be affected, except wills. Civil Code Cal. § 1215.

CONVEYANCE OF VESSELS. The transfer of the title to vessels.

CONVEYANCER. One whose business it is to draw deeds, bonds, mortgages, wills, writs, or other legal papers, or to examine titles to real estate. 14 St. at Large, 118.

He who draws conveyances; especially a barrister who confines himself to drawing conveyances, and other chamber practice. Mozley & Whitley.

CONVEYANCING. A term including both the science and act of transferring titles to real estate from one man to another.

Conveyancing is that part of the lawyer's business which relates to the alienation and transmission of property and other rights from one person to another, and to the framing of legal documents intended to create, define, transfer, or extinguish rights. It therefore includes the investigation of the title to land, and the preparation of agreements, wills, articles of association, private statutes operating as conveyances, and many other instruments in addition to conveyances properly so called. Sweet.

CONVEYANCING COUNSEL TO THE COURT OF CHANCERY. Certain counsel, not less than six in number, appointed by the lord chancellor, for the purpose of assisting the court of chancery, or any judge thereof, with their opinion in matters of title and conveyancing. Mozley & Whitley.

Convicia si irascaris tua divulgas; spreta exolescunt. 3 Inst. 198. If you be moved to anger by insults, you publish them; if despised, they are forgotten.

CONVICIUM. In the civil law. The name of a species of slander or injury uttered in public, and which charged some one with some act *contra bonos mores*.

CONVICT, *v.* To condemn after judidial investigation; to find a man guilty of a criminal charge. The word was formerly used also in the sense of finding against the defendant in a civil case.

CONVICT, *n.* One who has been condemned by a court. One who has been adjudged guilty of a crime or misdemeanor. Usually spoken of condemned felons or the prisoners in penitentiaries.

Formerly a man was said to be convict when he had been found guilty of treason or felony, but before judgment had been passed on him, after which he was said to be attaint, (*q. v.*) Co. Litt. 390*b*.

CONVICTED. This term has a definite signification in law, and means that a judgment of final condemnation has been pronounced against the accused. 10 Tex. App. 469.

CONVICTION. In practice. In a general sense, the result of a criminal trial which ends in a judgment or sentence that the prisoner is guilty as charged.

Finding a person guilty by verdict of a jury. 1 Bish. Crim. Law, § 223.

A record of the summary proceedings upon any penal statute before one or more justices of the peace or other persons duly authorized, in a case where the offender has been *convicted* and sentenced. Holthouse.

Summary conviction is one which takes place before an authorized magistrate without the intervention of a jury.

In ordinary phrase, the meaning of the word "conviction" is the finding by the jury of a verdict that the accused is guilty. But, in legal parlance, it often denotes the final judgment of the court. 69 N. Y. 109.

The ordinary legal meaning of "conviction," when used to designate a particular stage of a criminal prosecution triable by a jury, is the confession of the accused in open court, or the verdict returned against him by the jury, which ascertains and publishes the fact of his guilt; while "judgment" or "sentence" is the appropriate word to denote the action of the court before which the trial is had, declaring the consequences to the convict of the fact thus ascertained. A pardon granted after verdict of guilty, but before sentence, and pending a hearing upon exceptions taken by the accused during the trial, is granted after conviction, within the meaning of a constitutional restriction upon granting pardon before conviction. When, indeed, the word "conviction" is used to describe the effect of the guilt of the accused as judicially proved in one case, when pleaded or given in evidence in another, it is sometimes used in a more comprehensive sense, including the judgment of the court upon the verdict or confession of guilt; as, for instance, in speaking of the plea of *autrefois convict*, or of the effect of guilt, judicially ascertained, as a disqualification of the convict. 109 Mass. 323. See 17 Pick. 380.

CONVIVIUM. A tenure by which a tenant was bound to provide meat and drink for his lord at least once in the year. Cowell.

CONVOCATION. In ecclesiastical law. The general assembly of the clergy to consult upon ecclesiastical matters.

CONVOY. A naval force, under the command of an officer appointed by government, for the protection of merchant-ships and others, during the whole voyage, or such part of it as is known to require such protection. Marsh. Ins. b. 1, c. 9, § 5; Park, Ins. 388; Peake, Add. Cas. 143*n;* 2 H. Bl. 551.

CO-OBLIGOR. A joint obligor; one bound jointly with another or others in a bond or obligation.

COOL BLOOD. In the law of homicide. Calmness or tranquillity; the undisturbed possession of one's faculties and reason; the absence of violent passion, fury, or uncontrollable excitement.

COOLING TIME. Time for the mind to become so calm and sedate as that it is supposed to contemplate, comprehend, and coolly act with reference to the consequences likely to ensue. 10 Tex. App. 447.

CO-OPERATION. The combined action of numbers. It is of two distinct kinds: (1) Such co-operation as takes place when several persons help each other in the same employment; (2) such co-operation as takes place when several persons help each other in different employments. These may be termed "simple co-operation" and "complex co-operation." Mill, Pol. Ec. 142.

COOPERTIO. In old English law. The head or branches of a tree cut down; though *coopertio arborum* is rather the bark of timber trees felled, and the chumps and broken wood. Cowell.

COOPERTUM. In forest law. A covert; a thicket (*dumetum*) or shelter for wild beasts in a forest. Spelman.

COOPERTURA. In forest law. A thicket, or covert of wood.

COOPERTUS. Covert; covered.

CO-OPTATION. A concurring choice; the election, by the members of a close corporation, of a person to fill a vacancy.

CO-ORDINATE and SUBORDINATE are terms often applied as a test to ascertain the doubtful meaning of clauses in an act of parliament. If there be two, one of which is grammatically governed by the other, it is said to be "subordinate" to it; but, if both are equally governed by some third clause, the two are called "co-ordinate." Wharton.

COPARCENARY. A species of estate, or tenancy, which exists where lands of inheritance descend from the ancestor to two or more persons. It arises in England either by common law or particular custom. By common law, as where a person, seised in fee-simple or fee-tail, dies, and his next heirs are two or more females, his daughters, sisters, aunts, cousins, or their representatives; in this case they all inherit, and these co-heirs are then called "coparceners," or, for brevity, "parceners" only. Litt. §§ 241, 242; 2 Bl. Comm. 187. By particular custom, as where lands descend, as in gavelkind, to all the males in equal degree, as sons, brothers, uncles, etc. Litt. § 265; 1 Steph. Comm. 319.

While joint tenancies refer to persons, the idea of coparcenary refers to the estate. The title to it is always by descent. The respective shares may be unequal; as, for instance, one daughter and two granddaughters, children of a deceased daughter, may take by the same act of descent. As to strangers, the tenants' seisin is a joint one, but, as between themselves, each is seised of his or her own share, on whose death it goes to the heirs, and not by survivorship. The right of possession of coparceners is in common, and the possession of one is, in general, the possession of the others. 1 Washb. Real Prop. *414.

COPARCENERS. Persons to whom an estate of inheritance descends jointly, and by whom it is held as an entire estate. 2 Bl. Comm. 187.

COPARTICEPS. In old English law. A coparcener.

COPARTNER. One who is a partner with one or more other persons; a member of a partnership.

COPARTNERSHIP. A partnership.

COPARTNERY. In Scotch law. The contract of copartnership. A contract by which the several partners agree concerning the communication of loss or gain, arising from the subject of the contract. Bell.

COPE. A custom or tribute due to the crown or lord of the soil, out of the lead mines in Derbyshire; also a hill, or the roof and covering of a house; a church vestment.

COPEMAN, or COPESMAN. A chapman, (*q. v.*)

COPESMATE. A merchant; a partner in merchandise.

COPIA. Lat. In civil and old English law. Opportunity or means of access.

In old English law. A copy. *Copia libelli*, the copy of a libel. Reg. Orig. 58.

COPIA LIBELLI DELIBERANDA. The name of a writ that lay where a man could not get a copy of a libel at the hands of a spiritual judge, to have the same delivered to him. Reg. Orig. 51.

COPIA VERA. In Scotch practice. A true copy. Words written at the top of copies of instruments.

COPPA. In English law. A crop or cock of grass, hay, or corn, divided into titheable portions, that it may be more fairly and justly tithed.

COPPER AND SCALES. See MANCIPATIO.

COPPICE, or COPSE. A small wood, consisting of underwood, which may be cut at twelve or fifteen years' growth for fuel.

COPULA. The corporal consummation of marriage. *Copula*, (in logic,) the link between subject and predicate contained in the verb.

Copulatio verborum indicat acceptationem in eodem sensu. Coupling of words together shows that they are to be understood in the same sense. 4 Bacon's Works, p. 26; Broom, Max. 588.

COPULATIVE TERM. One which is placed between two or more others to join them together.

COPY. The transcript or double of an original writing; as the copy of a patent, charter, deed, etc.

Exemplifications are copies verified by the

great seal or by the seal of a court. 1 Gilb. Ev. 19.

Examined copies are those which have been compared with the original or with an official record thereof.

Office copies are those made by officers intrusted with the originals and authorized for that purpose.

COPYHOLD. A species of estate at will, or customary estate in England, the only visible title to which consists of the *copies* of the *court rolls*, which are made out by the steward of the manor, on a tenant's being admitted to any parcel of land, or tenement belonging to the manor. It is an estate at the *will* of the lord, yet such a will as is agreeable to the *custom* of the manor, which customs are preserved and evidenced by the *rolls* of the several courts baron, in which they are entered. 2 Bl. Comm. 95. In a larger sense, *copyhold* is said to import every *customary* tenure, (that is, every tenure pending on the particular custom of a manor,) as opposed to free socage, or *freehold*, which may now (since the abolition of knight-service) be considered as the general or common-law tenure of the country. 1 Steph. Comm. 210.

COPYHOLD COMMISSIONERS. Commissioners appointed to carry into effect various acts of parliament, having for their principal objects the compulsory commutation of manorial burdens and restrictions, (fines, heriots, rights to timber and minerals, etc.,) and the compulsory enfranchisement of copyhold lands. 1 Steph. Comm. 643; Elton, Copyh.

COPYHOLDER. A tenant by copyhold tenure, (by copy of court-roll.) 2 Bl. Comm. 95.

COPYRIGHT. The right of literary property as recognized and sanctioned by positive law. A right granted by statute to the author or originator of certain literary or artistic productions, whereby he is invested, for a limited period, with the sole and exclusive privilege of multiplying copies of the same and publishing and selling them.

An incorporeal right, being the exclusive privilege of printing, reprinting, selling, and publishing his own original work, which the law allows an author. Wharton.

Copyright is the exclusive right of the owner of an intellectual production to multiply and dispose of copies; the sole right to the copy, or to copy it. The word is used indifferently to signify the statutory and the common-law right; or one right is sometimes called "copyright" after publication, or statutory copyright; the other copyright before

publication, or common-law copyright. The word is also used synonymously with "literary property;" thus, the exclusive right of the owner publicly to read or exhibit a work is often called "copyright." This is not strictly correct. Drone, Copyr. 100.

International copyright is the right of a subject of one country to protection against the republication in another country of a work which he originally published in his own country. Sweet.

CORAAGIUM, or CORAAGE. Measures of corn. An unusual and extraordinary tribute, arising only on special occasions. They are thus distinguished from services. Mentioned in connection with *hidage* and *carvage.* Cowell.

CORAM. Lat. Before; in presence of. Applied to persons only. Townsh. Pl. 22.

CORAM DOMINO REGE. Before our lord the king. *Coram domino rege ubicumque tunc fuerit Angliæ,* before our lord the king wherever he shall then be in England.

CORAM IPSO REGE. Before the king himself. The old name of the court of king's bench, which was originally held before the king in person. 3 Bl. Comm. 41.

CORAM NOBIS. Before us ourselves, (the king, *i. e.,* in the king's or queen's bench.) Applied to writs of error directed to another branch of the same court, *e. g.,* from the full bench to the court at *nisi prius.* 1 Archb. Pr. K. B. 234.

CORAM NON JUDICE. In presence of a person not a judge. When a suit is brought and determined in a court which has no jurisdiction in the matter, then it is said to be *coram non judice,* and the judgment is void.

CORAM PARIBUS. Before the peers or freeholders. The attestation of deeds, like all other solemn transactions, was originally done only *coram paribus.* 2 Bl. Comm. 307. *Coram paribus de vicineto,* before the peers or freeholders of the neighborhood. Id. 315.

CORAM SECTATORIBUS. Before the suitors. Cro. Jac. 582.

CORAM VOBIS. Before you. A writ of error directed by a court of review to the court which tried the cause, to correct an error in fact. 3 Md. 325; 3 Steph. Comm. 642.

CORD. A measure of wood, containing 128 cubic feet.

CO-RESPONDENT. A person summoned to answer a bill, petition, or libel, together with another respondent. Now chiefly used to designate the person charged with adultery with the respondent in a suit for divorce for that cause, and joined as a defendant with such party.

CORIUM FORISFACERE. To forfeit one's skin, applied to a person condemned to be whipped; anciently the punishment of a servant. *Corium perdere*, the same. *Corium redimere*, to compound for a whipping. Wharton.

CORN. In English law, a general term for any sort of grain; but in America it is properly applied only to maize. In the memorandum clause in policies of insurance it includes pease and beans, but not rice. Park, Ins. 112.

CORN LAWS. A species of protective tariff formerly in existence in England, imposing import-duties on various kinds of grain. The corn laws were abolished in 1846.

CORN RENT. A rent in wheat or malt paid on college leases by direction of St. 18 Eliz. c. 6. 2 Bl. Comm. 609.

CORNAGE. A species of tenure in England, by which the tenant was bound to blow a horn for the sake of alarming the country on the approach of an enemy. It was a species of grand serjeanty. Bac. Abr. "Tenure," N.

CORNER. A combination among the dealers in a specific commodity, or outside capitalists, for the purpose of buying up the greater portion of that commodity which is upon the market or may be brought to market, and holding the same back from sale, until the demand shall so far outrun the limited supply as to advance the price abnormally. 72 Pa. St. 158; 101 Mass. 145.

In surveying. An angle made by two boundary lines; the common end of two boundary lines, which run at an angle with each other.

CORNET. A commissioned officer of cavalry, abolished in England in 1871, and not existing in the United States army.

CORODIO HABENDO. The name of a writ to exact a corody of an abbey or religious house.

CORODIUM. In old English law. A corody.

CORODY. In old English law. A sum of money or allowance of meat, drink, and clothing due to the crown from the abbey or other religious house, whereof it was founder, towards the sustentation of such one of its servants as is thought fit to receive it. It differs from a pension, in that it was allowed towards the maintenance of any of the king's servants in an abbey; a pension being given to one of the king's chaplains, for his better maintenance, till he may be provided with a benefice. Fitzh. Nat. Brev. 250. See 1 Bl. Comm. 283.

COROLLARY. In logic. A collateral or secondary consequence, deduction, or inference.

CORONA. The crown. *Placita coronæ;* pleas of the crown; criminal actions or proceedings, in which the crown was the prosecutor.

CORONA MALA. In old English law. The clergy who abuse their character were so called. Blount.

CORONARE. In old records. To give the tonsure, which was done on the crown, or in the form of a crown; to make a man a priest. Cowell.

CORONARE FILIUM. To make one's son a priest. *Homo coronatus* was one who had received the first tonsure, as preparatory to superior orders, and the tonsure was in form of a corona, or crown of thorns. Cowell.

CORONATION OATH. The oath administered to a sovereign at the ceremony of crowning or investing him with the insignia of royalty, in acknowledgment of his right to govern the kingdom, in which he swears to observe the laws, customs, and privileges of the kingdom, and to act and do all things conformably thereto. Wharton.

CORONATOR. A coroner, (*q. v.*) Spelman.

CORONATORE ELIGENDO. The name of a writ issued to the sheriff, commanding him to proceed to the election of a coroner.

CORONATORE EXONERANDO. In English law. The name of a writ for the removal of a coroner, for a cause which is to be therein assigned, as that he is engaged in other business, or incapacitated by years or sickness, or has not a sufficient estate in the county, or lives in an inconvenient part of it.

D

E

F

G

H

I

J

K

L

M

CORONER. The name of an ancient officer of the common law, whose office and functions are continued in modern English and American administration. The coroner is an officer belonging to each county, and is charged with duties both judicial and ministerial, but chiefly the former. It is his special province and duty to make inquiry into the causes and circumstances of any death happening within his territory which occurs through violence or suddenly and with marks of suspicion. This examination (called the "coroner's inquest") is held with a jury of proper persons upon view of the dead body. See Bract. fol. 121; 1 Bl. Comm. 346–348; 3 Steph. Comm. 33. In England, another branch of his judicial office is to inquire concerning shipwrecks, and certify whether wreck or not, and who is in possession of the goods; and also to inquire concerning treasure trove, who were the finders, and where it is, and whether any one be suspected of having found and concealed a treasure. 1 Bl. Comm. 349. It belongs to the ministerial office of the coroner to serve writs and other process, and generally to discharge the duties of the sheriff, in case of the incapacity of that officer or a vacancy in his office.

CORONER'S COURT. In England. A tribunal of record, where a coroner holds his inquiries.

CORPORAL. Relating to the body; bodily. Should be distinguished from corporeal, (*q. v.*)

A non-commissioned officer of the lowest grade in a company of soldiers in the army.

CORPORAL OATH. An oath, the external solemnity of which consists in laying one's hand upon the Gospels while the oath is administered to him. More generally, a solemn oath.

The terms "corporal oath" and "solemn oath" are, in Indiana, at least, used synonymously; and an oath taken with the uplifted hand may be properly described by either term. 1 Ind. 184.

CORPORAL TOUCH. Bodily touch; actual physical contact; manual apprehension.

CORPORALE SACRAMENTUM. In old English law. A corporal oath.

Corporalis injuria non recipit æstimationem de futuro. A personal injury does not receive satisfaction from a future course of proceeding, [is not left for its satisfaction to a future course of proceeding.] Bac. Max. reg. 6; Broom, Max. 278.

CORPORATE. Belonging to a corporation; as a corporate name. Incorporated; as a corporate body.

CORPORATE NAME. When a corporation is erected, a name is always given to it, or, supposing none to be actually given, will attach to it by implication, and by that name alone it must sue and be sued, and do all legal acts, though a very minute variation therein is not material, and the name is capable of being changed (by competent authority) without affecting the identity or capacity of the corporation. Wharton.

CORPORATION. A franchise possessed by one or more individuals, who subsist as a body politic, under a special denomination, and are vested by the policy of the law with the capacity of perpetual succession, and of acting in several respects, however numerous the association may be, as a single individual. 2 Kent, Comm. 267.

An artificial person or being, endowed by law with the capacity of perpetual succession; consisting either of a single individual, (termed a "corporation sole,") or of a collection of several individuals, (which is termed a "corporation aggregate.") 3 Steph. Comm. 166; 1 Bl. Comm. 467, 469.

A corporation is an intellectual body, created by law, composed of individuals united under a common name, the members of which succeed each other, so that the body continues always the same, notwithstanding the change of the individuals who compose it, and which, for certain purposes, is considered a natural person. Civil Code La. art. 427.

A corporation is an artificial person created by law for specific purposes, the limit of whose existence, powers, and liabilities is fixed by the act of incorporation, usually called its "charter." Code Ga. 1882, § 1670.

Classification. According to the accepted classification of corporations, they are first divided into public and private.

A *public* corporation is one having for its object the administration of a portion of the powers of government delegated to it for that purpose; such are municipal corporations. All others are private. Code Ga. 1882, § 1672.

Corporations are either public or private. Public corporations are formed or organized for the government of a portion of the state; all other corporations are private. Civil Code Cal. § 284.

Public corporations are generally esteemed such as exist for political purposes only, such as towns, cities, parishes, and counties; and in many respects they are so, although they involve some private interest; but, strictly speaking, public corporations are such only as are founded by the government for public purposes, where the whole interests belong also to the government. If, therefore, the foundation be private, though under the charter of the government, the corporation is private, however extensive the uses may be to which it is devoted, either by the bounty of the founder or the nature and objects of the institution. The uses may, in a certain sense, be called "public," but the corporations are private, as much so, indeed, as if the franchises were vested in a single person. 4 Wheat. 518, 562; 1 Wall. Jr. 275.

All *private* corporations are divided into *ecclesiastical* and *lay;* the former are such as are composed of religious persons organized for spiritual purposes, or for administering property held for religious uses; the latter are such as exist for secular or business purposes.

Lay corporations are classified as *eleemosynary* or *civil;* the former are such as are created for the distribution of charities or for purposes falling under the head of "charitable" in its widest sense, *e. g.*, hospitals, asylums, colleges; the latter are organized for the facilitating of business transactions and the profit of the members.

Corporations are also classed as *aggregate* or *sole;* as to this division, see CORPORATION AGGREGATE; CORPORATION SOLE.

CORPORATION ACT. In English law. The statute 13 Car. II. St. 2, c. 1; by which it was provided that no person should thereafter be elected to office in any corporate town that should not, within one year previously, have taken the sacrament of the Lord's Supper, according to the rites of the Church of England; and every person so elected was also required to take the oaths of allegiance and supremacy. 3 Steph. Comm. 103, 104; 4 Bl. Comm. 58. This statute is now repealed. 4 Steph. Comm. 511.

CORPORATION AGGREGATE. A collection of several individuals united into one body, under a special denomination, and having perpetual succession under an artificial form, and vested by the policy of the law with the capacity of acting in several respects as an individual. Shelf. Mortm. 22; 1 Kyd, Corp. 13; 2 Kent, Comm. 267.

An aggregate corporation, at common law, is a collection of individuals, united into one collective body, under a special name, and possessing certain immunities, privileges, and capacities, in its collective character, which do not belong to the natural persons composing it. It is an artificial person, existing in contemplation of law, and endowed with certain powers and franchises, which, though they must be exercised through the medium of its natural members, are yet considered as subsisting in the corporation itself, as distinctly as if it were a real personage. 4 Wheat. 518, 561.

CORPORATION COURTS. Certain courts in Virginia described as follows: "For each city of the state, there shall be a court called a 'corporation court,' to be held by a judge, with like qualifications and elected in the same manner as judges of the county court." Code Va. 1887, § 3050.

CORPORATION SOLE. A corporation consisting of one person only, and his successors in some particular station, who are incorporated by law in order to give them some legal capacities and advantages, particularly that of perpetuity, which in their natural persons they could not have had. In this sense, the sovereign in England is a sole corporation, so is a bishop, so are some deans distinct from their several chapters, and so is every parson and vicar. 3 Steph. Comm. 168, 169; 2 Kent, Comm. 273.

A corporation sole consists of a single person, who is made a body corporate and politic, in order to give him some legal capacities and advantages, and especially that of perpetuity; as a bishop, dean, etc. 7 Abb. Pr. 184; 22 Pick. 122.

CORPORATOR. A member of a corporation aggregate. Grant, Corp. 48.

CORPORE ET ANIMO. Lat. By the body and by the mind; by the physical act and by the mental intent. Dig. 41, 2, 3.

CORPOREAL. A term descriptive of such things as have an objective, material existence; perceptible by the senses of sight and touch; possessing a real body. Opposed to incorporeal and spiritual.

There is a distinction between "corporeal" and "corporal." The former term means "possessing a body," that is, tangible, physical, material; the latter means "relating to or affecting a body," that is, bodily, external. Corporeal denotes the nature or physical existence of a body; corporal denotes its exterior or the co-ordination of it with some other body. Hence we speak of "corporeal hereditaments," but of "corporal punishment," "corporal touch," "corporal oath," etc.

CORPOREAL HEREDITAMENTS. Substantial permanent objects which may be inherited. The term "land" will include all such. 2 Bl. Comm. 17.

CORPOREAL PROPERTY. Such as affects the senses, and may be seen and handled by the body, as opposed to incorporeal property, which cannot be seen or handled, and exists only in contemplation. Thus a house is corporeal, but the annual rent payable for its occupation is incorporeal. Corporeal property is, if movable, capable of manual transfer; if immovable, possession of it may be delivered up. But incorporeal property cannot be so transferred, but some other means must be adopted for its transfer, of which the most usual is an instrument in writing. Mozley & Whitley.

CORPS DIPLOMATIQUE. In international law. Ambassadors and diplomatic persons at any court or capital.

CORPSE. The dead body of a human being.

CORPUS. (Lat.) Body; the body; an aggregate or mass, (of men, laws, or articles;) physical substance, as distinguished from intellectual conception; the principal sum or capital, as distinguished from interest or income.

A substantial or positive fact, as distinguished from what is equivocal and ambiguous. The *corpus delicti* (body of an offense) is the fact of its having been actually committed. Best, Pres. 269–279.

A corporeal act of any kind, (as distinguished from *animus* or mere intention,) on the part of him who wishes to acquire a thing, whereby he obtains the physical ability to exercise his power over it whenever he pleases. The word occurs frequently in this sense in the civil law. Mackeld. Rom. Law, § 248.

CORPUS CHRISTI DAY. In English law. A feast instituted in 1264, in honor of the sacrament. 32 Hen. VIII. c. 21.

CORPUS COMITATUS. The body of a county. The whole county, as distinguished from a part of it, or any particular place in it. 5 Mason, 290.

CORPUS CORPORATUM. A corporation; a corporate body, other than municipal.

CORPUS CUM CAUSA. (The body with the cause.) An English writ which issued out of chancery, to remove both the *body* and the record, touching the *cause* of any man lying in execution upon a judgment for debt, into the king's bench, there to remain until he satisfied the judgment. Cowell; Blount.

CORPUS DELICTI. The body of a crime. The body (material substance) upon which a crime has been committed, *e. g.*, the corpse of a murdered man, the charred remains of a house burned down. In a derivative sense, the substance or foundation of a crime; the substantial fact that a crime has been committed.

Corpus humanum non recipit æstimationem. The human body does not admit of valuation. Hob. 59.

CORPUS JURIS. A body of law. A term used to signify a book comprehending several collections of law. There are two principal collections to which this name is given; the *Corpus Juris Civilis*, and the *Corpus Juris Canonici*, (*q. v.*)

CORPUS JURIS CANONICI. The body of the canon law. A compilation of the canon law, comprising the decrees and canons of the Roman Church, constituting the body of ecclesiastical law of that church.

CORPUS JURIS CIVILIS. The body of the civil law. The system of Roman jurisprudence compiled and codified under the direction of the emperor Justinian, in A. D. 528–534. This collection comprises the Institutes, Digest, (or Pandects,) Code, and Novels. The name is said to have been first applied to this collection early in the seventeenth century.

CORPUS PRO CORPORE. Lat. In old records. Body for body. A phrase expressing the liability of manucaptors. 3 How. State Tr. 110.

CORRECTION. Discipline; chastisement administered by a master or other person in authority to one who has committed an offense, for the purpose of curing his faults or bringing him into proper subjection.

CORRECTION, HOUSE OF. A prison for the reformation of petty or juvenile offenders.

CORRECTOR OF THE STAPLE. In old English law. A clerk belonging to the staple, to write and record the bargains of merchants there made.

CORREGIDOR. In Spanish law. A magistrate who took cognizance of various misdemeanors, and of civil matters. 2 White, New Recop. 53.

CORREI. Lat. In the civil law. Co-stipulators; joint stipulators.

CORREI CREDENDI. Lat. In the civil and Scotch law. Joint creditors; creditors *in solido.* Poth. Obl. pt. 2, c. 4, art. 3, § 11.

CORREI DEBENDI. Lat. In Scotch law. Two or more persons bound as principal debtors to another. Ersk. Inst. 3, 3, 74.

CORRELATIVE. Having a mutual or reciprocal relation, in such sense that the existence of one necessarily implies the existence of the other. *Father* and *son* are correlative terms. *Right* and *duty* are correlative terms.

CORRESPONDENCE. Interchange of written communications. The letters written by a person and the answers written by the one to whom they are addressed.

CORROBORATE. To strengthen; to add weight or credibility to a thing by additional and confirming facts or evidence.

The expression "corroborating circumstances" clearly does not mean facts which, independent of a confession, will warrant a conviction; for then the verdict would stand not on the confession, but upon those independent circumstances. To corroborate is to strengthen, to confirm by additional security, to add strength. The testimony of a witness is said to be corroborated when it is shown to correspond with the representation of some other witness, or to comport with some facts otherwise known or established. Corroborating circumstances, then, used in reference to a confession, are such as serve to strengthen it, to render it more probable; such, in short, as may serve to impress a jury with a belief in its truth. 10 N. J. Law, 163.

Corruptio optimi est pessima. Corruption of the best is worst.

CORRUPTION. Illegality; a vicious and fraudulent intention to evade the prohibitions of the law.

The act of an official or fiduciary person who unlawfully and wrongfully uses his station or character to procure some benefit for himself or for another person, contrary to duty and the rights of others.

CORRUPTION OF BLOOD. In English law. This was the consequence of *attainder*. It meant that the attainted person could neither inherit lands or other hereditaments from his ancestor, nor retain those he already had, nor transmit them by descent to any heir, because his blood was considered in law to be corrupted. This was abolished by St. 3 & 4 Wm. IV. c. 106, and 33 & 34 Vict. c. 23; and is unknown in America. Const. U. S. art. 3, § 3.

CORSELET. Ancient armor which covered the body.

CORSE-PRESENT. A mortuary, thus termed because, when a mortuary became due on the death of a man, the best or second-best beast was, according to custom, offered or presented to the priest, and carried with the corpse. In Wales a corse-present was due upon the death of a clergyman to the bishop of the diocese, till abolished by 12 Anne St. 2, c. 6. 2 Bl. Comm. 426.

CORSNED. In Saxon law. The morsel of execration. A species of ordeal in use among the Saxons, performed by eating a piece of bread over which the priest had pronounced a certain imprecation. If the accused ate it freely, he was pronounced innocent; but, if it stuck in his throat, it was considered as a proof of his guilt. Crabb, Eng. Law, 30; 1 Reeve, Eng. Law, 21; 4 Bl. Comm. 345.

CORTES. The name of the legislative assemblies, the parliament or congress, of Spain and Portugal.

CORTEX. The bark of a tree; the outer covering of anything.

CORTIS. A court or yard before a house. Blount.

CORTULARIUM, or CORTARIUM. In old records. A yard adjoining a country farm.

CORVEE. In French law. Gratuitous labor exacted from the villages or communities, especially for repairing roads, constructing bridges, etc.

COSA JUZGADA. In Spanish law. A cause or matter adjudged, (*res judicata*.) White, New Recop. b. 3, tit. 8, note.

COSDUNA. In feudal law. A custom or tribute.

COSEN, COZEN. In old English law. To cheat. "A cosening knave." 3 Leon. 171.

COSENAGE. In old English law. Kindred; cousinship. Also a writ that lay for the heir where the *tresail, i. e.,* the father of the *besail,* or great-grandfather, was seised of lands in fee at his death, and a stranger entered upon the land and abated. Fitzh. Nat. Brev. 221.

COSENING. In old English law. An offense, mentioned in the old books, where anything was done deceitfully, whether belonging to contracts or not, which could not be properly termed by any special name. The same as the *stellionatus* of the civil law. Cowell.

COSHERING. In old English law. A feudal prerogative or custom for lords to lie and feast themselves at their tenants' houses. Cowell.

COSMUS. Clean. Blount.

COSS. A term used by Europeans in India to denote a road-measure of about two miles, but differing in different parts. Wharton.

COST. The cost of an article purchased for exportation is the price paid, with all incidental charges paid at the place of exportation. 2 Wash. C. C. 493. Cost price is that actually paid for goods. 18 N. Y. 337.

COST-BOOK. A book in which a number of adventurers who have obtained permission to work a lode, and have agreed to share the enterprise in certain proportions, enter the agreement, and from time to time the receipts and expenditures of the mine, the names of the shareholders, their respective accounts with the mine, and transfers of shares. These associations are called "Cost-Book Mining Companies," and are governed by the general law of partnership. Lindl. Partn. *147.

CO-STIPULATOR. A joint promisor.

COSTS. A pecuniary allowance, made to the successful party, (and recoverable from the losing party,) for his expenses in prosecuting or defending a suit or a distinct proceeding within a suit.

Costs and fees were originally altogether different in their nature. The one is an allowance to a *party* for expenses incurred in prosecuting or defending a suit; the other, a compensation to an *officer* for services rendered in the progress of a cause. Therefore, while an executor or administrator was not personally liable to his adversary for costs, yet, if at his instance an officer performed services for him, he had a personal demand for his fees. 11 Serg. & R. 247. There is in our statute a manifest difference between costs and fees in another respect. Costs are an allowance to a party for the expenses incurred in prosecuting or defending a suit,—an incident to the judgment; while fees are compensation to 'public officers for services rendered individuals not in the course of litigation. 58 Ala. 579.

In England, the term is also used to designate the charges which an attorney or solicitor is entitled to make and recover from his client, as his remuneration for professional services, such as legal advice, attendances, drafting and copying documents, conducting legal proceedings, etc.

COSTS DE INCREMENTO. Increased costs, costs of increase. Costs adjudged by the court in addition to those assessed by the jury. 13 How. 372.

Those extra expenses incurred which do not appear on the face of the proceedings, such as witnesses' expenses, fees to counsel, attendances, court fees, etc. Wharton.

COSTS OF THE DAY. Costs which are incurred in preparing for the trial of a cause on a specified *day*, consisting of witnesses' fees, and other fees of attendance. Archb. N. Prac. 281.

COSTUMBRE. In Spanish law. Custom; an unwritten law established by usage, during a long space of time. Las Partidas, pt. 1, tit. 2, l. 4.

CO-SURETIES. Joint sureties; two or more sureties to the same obligation.

COTA. A cot or hut. Blount.

COTAGIUM. In old English law. A cottage.

COTARIUS. In old English law. A cottager, who held in free socage, and paid a stated fine or rent in provisions or money, with some occasional personal services.

COTERELLI. Anciently, a kind of peasantry who were outlaws; robbers. Blount.

COTERELLUS. In feudal law. A servile tenant, who held in mere villenage; his person, issue, and goods were disposable at the lord's pleasure.

COTERIE. A fashionable association, or a knot of persons forming a particular circle. The origin of the term was purely commercial, signifying an association, in which each member furnished his part, and bore his share in the profit and loss. Wharton.

COTESWOLD. In old records. A place where there is no wood.

COTLAND. In old English law. Land held by a cottager, whether in socage or villenage. Cowell.

COTSETHLA. In old English law. The little seat or mansion belonging to a small farm.

COTSETHLAND. The seat of a cottage with the land belonging to it. Spelman.

COTSETUS. A cottager or cottage-holder who held by servile tenure and was bound to do the work of the lord. Cowell.

COTTAGE. In English law. A small dwelling-house that has no land belonging to it. Shep. Touch. 94; 1 Strange, 405; 2 Ld. Raym. 1015; 15 Ad. & El. (N. S.) 244.

COTTIER TENANCY. A species of tenancy in Ireland, constituted by an agreement in writing, and subject to the following terms: That the tenement consist of a dwelling-house with not more than half an acre of land; at a rental not exceeding £5 a year; the tenancy to be for not more than a month at a time; the landlord to keep the house in good repair. Landlord and Tenant Act, Ireland, (23 & 24 Vict. c. 154, § 81.)

COTUCA. Coat armor.

COTUCHANS. A term used in Domesday for peasants, boors, husbandmen.

COUCHANT. Lying down; squatting. *Couchant and levant* (lying down and rising up) is a term applied to animals trespassing on the land of one other than their owner, for one night or longer. 3 Bl. Comm. 9.

COUCHER, or COURCHER. A factor who continues abroad for traffic, (37 Edw. III. c. 16;) also the general book wherein any corporation, etc., register their acts, (3 & 4 Edw. VI. c. 10.)

COUNCIL. An assembly of persons for the purpose of concerting measures of state or municipal policy; hence called "councillors."

In American law. The legislative body in the government of cities or boroughs. An advisory body selected to aid the executive.

COUNCIL OF CONCILIATION. By the Act 30 & 31 Vict. c. 105, power is given for the crown to grant licenses for the formation of councils of conciliation and arbitration, consisting of a certain number of masters and workmen in any trade or employment, having power to hear and determine all questions between masters and workmen which may be submitted to them by both parties, arising out of or with respect to the particular trade or manufacture, and incapable of being otherwise settled. They have power to apply to a justice to enforce the performance of their award. The members are elected by persons engaged in the trade. Davis, Bldg. Soc. 232; Sweet.

COUNCIL OF JUDGES. Under the English judicature act, 1873, § 75, an annual council of the judges of the supreme court is to be held, for the purpose of considering the operation of the new practice, offices, etc., introduced by the act, and of reporting to a secretary of state as to any alterations which they consider should be made in the law for the administration of justice. An extraordinary council may also be convened at any time by the lord chancellor. Sweet.

COUNCIL OF THE NORTH. A court instituted by Henry VIII., in 1537, to administer justice in Yorkshire and the four other northern counties. Under the presi-

dency of Stratford, the court showed great rigor, bordering, it is alleged, on harshness. It was abolished by 16 Car. I., the same act which abolished the Star Chamber. Brown.

COUNSEL. 1. In practice. An advocate, counsellor, or pleader. 3 Bl. Comm. 26; 1 Kent, Comm. 307. One who assists his client with advice, and pleads for him in open court. See COUNSELLOR.

Counsellors who are associated with those regularly retained in a cause, either for the purpose of advising as to the points of law involved, or preparing the case on its legal side, or arguing questions of law to the court, or preparing or conducting the case on its appearance before an appellate tribunal, are said to be "of counsel."

2. Knowledge. A grand jury is sworn to keep secret "the commonwealth's *counsel*, their fellows', and their own."

3. Advice given by one person to another in regard to a proposed line of conduct, claim, or contention.

COUNSEL'S SIGNATURE. This is required, in some jurisdictions, to be affixed to pleadings, as affording the court a means of judging whether they are interposed in good faith and upon legal grounds.

COUNSELLOR. An advocate or barrister. A member of the legal profession whose special function is to give counsel or advice as to the legal aspects of judicial controversies, or their preparation and management, and to appear in court for the conduct of trials, or the argument of causes, or presentation of motions, or any other legal business that takes him into the presence of the court.

In some of the states, the two words "counsellor" and "attorney" are used interchangeably to designate all lawyers. In others, the latter term alone is used, "counsellor" not being recognized as a technical name. In still others, the two are associated together as the full legal title of any person who has been admitted to practice in the courts; while in a few they denote different grades, it being prescribed that no one can become a counsellor until he has been an attorney for a specified time and has passed a second examination.

In the practice of the United States supreme court, the term denotes an officer who is employed by a party in a cause to conduct the same on its trial on his behalf. He differs from an attorney at law.

In the supreme court of the United States, the two degrees of attorney and counsel were at first kept separate, and no person was permitted to practice in both capacities, but the present practice is otherwise. Weeks, Attys. at Law, 54. It is the duty of the counsel to draft or review and correct the special pleadings, to manage the cause on trial, and, during the whole course of the suit, to apply established principles of law to the exigencies of the case. 1 Kent, Comm. 307.

COUNT, *v.* In pleading. To declare; to recite; to state a case; to narrate the facts constituting a plaintiff's cause of action. In a special sense, to set out the claim or count of the demandant in a real action.

To plead orally; to plead or argue a case in court; to recite or read in court; to recite a count in court.

COUNT, *n.* In pleading. The different parts of a declaration, each of which, if it stood alone, would constitute a ground for action, are the counts of the declaration. Used also to signify the several parts of an indictment, each charging a distinct offense.

COUNT. (Fr. *comte;* from the Latin *comes.*) An earl.

COUNT AND COUNT-OUT. These words have a technical sense in a count of the house of commons by the speaker.

COUNT-OUT. Forty members form a house of commons; and, though there be ever so many at the beginning of a debate, yet, if during the course of it the house should be deserted by the members, till reduced below the number of forty, any one member may have it adjourned upon its being counted; but a debate may be continued when only one member is left in the house, provided no one choose to move an adjournment. Wharton.

COUNTEE. In old English law. The most eminent dignity of a subject before the Conquest. He was *præfectus* or *præpositus comitatûs*, and had the charge and custody of the county; but this authority is now vested in the sheriff. 9 Coke, 46.

COUNTENANCE. In old English law. Credit; estimation. Wharton.

COUNTER. The name of two prisons formerly standing in London, but now demolished. They were the Poultry Counter and Wood Street Counter.

COUNTER-AFFIDAVIT. An affidavit made and presented in contradiction or opposition to an affidavit which is made the basis or support of a motion or application.

COUNTER-BOND. In old practice. A bond of indemnity. 2 Leon. 90.

COUNTER-CLAIM. A claim presented by a defendant in opposition to or deduction from the claim of the plaintiff. A species of set-off or recoupment introduced by the codes of civil procedure in several of the states, of a broad and liberal character.

A counter-claim must be one "existing in favor of a defendant and against a plaintiff, between whom a several judgment might be had in the action, and arising out of one of the following causes of action: (1) A cause of action arising out of the contract or transaction set forth in the complaint as the foundation of the plaintiff's claim, or connected with the subject of action; (2) in an action arising on contract, any other cause of action arising also on contract, and existing at the commencement of the action." Code Proc. N. Y. § 150.

The term "counter-claim," of itself, imports a claim opposed to, or which qualifies, or at least in some degree affects, the plaintiff's cause of action. 35 Wis. 626.

A counter-claim is an opposition claim, or demand of something due; a demand of something which of right belongs to the defendant, in opposition to the right of the plaintiff. 8 How. Pr. 122.

A counter-claim is that which might have arisen out of, or could have had some connection with, the original transaction, in view of the parties, and which, at the time the contract was made, they could have intended might, in some event, give one party a claim against the other for compliance or non-compliance with its provisions. 7 Ind. 523, 524.

COUNTER-DEED. A secret writing, either before a notary or under a private seal, which destroys, invalidates, or alters a public one.

COUNTERFEIT. In criminal law. To forge; to copy or imitate, without authority or right, and with a view to deceive or defraud, by passing the copy or thing forged for that which is original or genuine. Most commonly applied to the fraudulent and criminal imitation of money.

COUNTERFEIT COIN. Coin not genuine, but resembling or apparently intended to resemble or pass for genuine coin, including genuine coin prepared or altered so as to resemble or pass for coin of a higher denomination.

COUNTERFEITER. In criminal law. One who unlawfully makes base coin in imitation of the true metal, or forges false currency, or any instrument of writing, bearing a likeness and similitude to that which is lawful and genuine, with an intention of deceiving and imposing upon mankind. 1 Stew. (Ala.) 384.

COUNTER-FESANCE. The act of forging.

COUNTER-LETTER. A species of instrument of defeasance common in the civil law. It is executed by a party who has taken a deed of property, absolute on its face, but intended as security for a loan of money, and by it he agrees to reconvey the property on payment of a specified sum. The two instruments, taken together, constitute what is known in Louisiana as an *"antichresis,"* (*q. v.*)

COUNTERMAND. A change or revocation of orders, authority, or instructions previously issued. It may be either express or implied; the former where the order or instruction already given is explicitly annulled or recalled; the latter where the party's conduct is incompatible with the further continuance of the order or instruction, as where a new order is given inconsistent with the former order.

COUNTER-MARK. A sign put upon goods already marked; also the several marks put upon goods belonging to several persons, to show that they must not be opened, but in the presence of all the owners or their agents.

COUNTERPART. In conveyancing. The corresponding part of an instrument; a duplicate or copy. Where an instrument of conveyance, as a lease, is executed in parts, that is, by having several copies or duplicates made and interchangeably executed, that which is executed by the grantor is usually called the "original," and the rest are "counterparts;" although, where all the parties execute every part, this renders them all originals. 2 Bl. Comm. 296; Shep. Touch. 50. See DUPLICATE.

COUNTER-PLEA. In pleading. A plea to some matter incidental to the main object of the suit, and out of the direct line of pleadings.

In the more ancient system of pleading, counter-plea was applied to what was, in effect, a replication to aid prayer, (*q. v.;*) that is, where a tenant for life or other limited interest in land, having an action brought against him in respect to the title to such land, prayed in aid of the lord or reversioner for his better defense, that which the de-

mandant alleged against either request was called a "counter-plea." Cowell.

COUNTER-ROLLS. In English law. The rolls which sheriffs have with the coroners, containing particulars of their proceedings, as well of appeals as of inquests, etc. 3 Edw. I. c. 10.

COUNTER-SECURITY. A security given to one who has entered into a bond or become surety for another; a countervailing bond of indemnity.

COUNTERSIGN. The signature of a secretary or other subordinate officer to any writing signed by the principal or superior to vouch for the authenticity of it.

COUNTERVAILING EQUITY. A contrary and balancing equity; an equity or right opposed to that which is sought to be enforced or recognized, and which ought not to be sacrificed or subordinated to the latter, because it is of equal strength and justice, and equally deserving of consideration.

COUNTEZ. L. Fr. Count, or reckon. In old practice. A direction formerly given by the clerk of a court to the crier, after a jury was sworn, to *number* them; and which Blackstone says was given in his time, in good English, "count these." 4 Bl. Comm. 340, note (*u.*)

COUNTORS. Advocates, or serjeants at law, whom a man retains to defend his cause and speak for him in court, for their fees. 1 Inst. 17.

COUNTRY. The portion of the earth's surface occupied by an independent nation or people; or the inhabitants of such territory.

In its primary meaning "country" signifies "place;" and, in a larger sense, the territory or dominions occupied by a community; or even waste and unpeopled sections or regions of the earth. But its metaphorical meaning is no less definite and well understood; and in common parlance, in historical and geographical writings, in diplomacy, legislation, treaties, and international codes, the word is employed to denote the population, the nation, the state, or the government, having possession and dominion over a territory. 1 Blatchf. 218, 225; 5 N. Y. Leg. Obs. 286.

In pleading and practice. The inhabitants of a district from which a jury is to be summoned; pais; a jury. 3 Bl. Comm. 349; Steph. Pl. 73, 78, 230.

COUNTY. The name given to the principal subdivisions of the kingdom of England and of most of the states of the American Union, denoting a distinct portion of territory organized by itself for political and judicial purposes. The etymology of the word shows it to have been the district anciently governed by a *count* or earl. In modern use, the word may denote either the territory marked off to form a county, or the citizens resident within such territory, taken collectively and considered as invested with political rights, or the county regarded as a municipal corporation possessing subordinate governmental powers, or an organized jural society invested with specific rights and duties.

COUNTY BRIDGE. A bridge of the larger class, erected by the county, and which the county is liable to keep in repair. 40 Iowa, 295.

COUNTY COMMISSIONERS. Officers of a county charged with a variety of administrative and executive duties, but principally with the management of the financial affairs of the county, its police regulations, and its corporate business. Sometimes the local laws give them limited judicial powers. In some states they are called "supervisors."

COUNTY CORPORATE. A city or town, with more or less territory annexed, having the privilege to be a county of itself, and not to be comprised in any other county; such as London, York, Bristol, Norwich, and other cities in England. 1 Bl. Comm. 120.

COUNTY COURT. A court of high antiquity in England, incident to the jurisdiction of the sheriff. It is not a court of record, but may hold pleas of debt or damages, under the value of forty shillings. The freeholders of the county (anciently termed the "suitors" of the court) are the real judges in this court, and the sheriff is the ministerial officer. See 3 Bl. Comm. 35, 36; 3 Steph. Comm. 395.

But in modern English law the name is appropriated to a system of tribunals established by the statute 9 & 10 Vict. c. 95, having a limited jurisdiction, principally for the recovery of small debts.

It is also the name of certain tribunals of limited jurisdiction in the county of Middlesex, established under the statute 22 Geo. II. c. 33.

In American law. The name is used in many of the states to designate the ordinary courts of record having jurisdiction for trials at *nisi prius*. Their powers generally comprise ordinary civil jurisdiction, also

the charge and care of persons and estates coming within legal guardianship, a limited criminal jurisdiction, appellate jurisdiction over justices of the peace, etc.

COUNTY PALATINE. A term bestowed upon certain counties in England, the lords of which in former times enjoyed especial privileges. They might pardon treasons, murders, and felonies. All writs and indictments ran in their names, as in other counties in the king's; and all offenses were said to be done against their peace, and not, as in other places, *contra pacem domini regis.* But these privileges have in modern times nearly disappeared.

COUNTY RATE. In English law. An imposition levied on the occupiers of lands, and applied to many miscellaneous purposes, among which the most important are those of defraying the expenses connected with prisons, reimbursing to private parties the costs they have incurred in prosecuting public offenders, and defraying the expenses of the county police. See 15 & 16 Vict. c. 81.

COUNTY-SEAT. A county-seat or county-town is the chief town of a county, where the county buildings and courts are located and the county business transacted.

COUNTY SESSIONS. In England, the court of general quarter sessions of the peace held in every county once in every quarter of a year. Mozley & Whitley.

COUPONS. Interest and dividend certificates; also those parts of a commercial instrument which are to be *cut*, and which are evidence of something connected with the contract mentioned in the instrument. They are generally attached to certificates of loan, where the interest is payable at particular periods, and, when the interest is paid, they are cut off and delivered to the payer. Wharton.

COUR DE CASSATION. The supreme judicial tribunal of France, having appellate jurisdiction only. For an account of its composition and powers, see Jones, French Bar, 22; Guyot, Repert. Univ.

COURIER. An express messenger of haste.

COURSE. A term used in surveying, meaning the direction of a line with reference to a meridian.

COURSE OF THE VOYAGE. By this term is understood the regular and customary track, if such there be, which a ship takes in going from one port to another, and the shortest way. Marsh. Ins. 185.

COURSE OF TRADE. What is customarily or ordinarily done in the management of trade or business.

COURT. In legislation. A legislative assembly. Parliament is called in the old books a court of the king, nobility, and commons assembled. Finch, Law, b. 4, c. 1, p. 233; Fleta, lib. 2, c. 2.

This meaning of the word has been retained in the titles of some deliberative bodies, such as the general court of Massachusetts, (the legislature.)

In international law. The person and suite of the sovereign; the place where the sovereign sojourns with his regal retinue, wherever that may be. The English government is spoken of in diplomacy as the court of St. James, because the palace of St. James is the official palace.

In practice. An organ of the government, belonging to the judicial department, whose function is the application of the laws to controversies brought before it and the public administration of justice.

The presence of a sufficient number of the members of such a body regularly convened in an authorized place at an appointed time, engaged in the full and regular performance of its functions. 20 Ala. 446; 20 Ark. 77.

A court may be more particularly described as an organized body with defined powers, meeting at certain times and places for the hearing and decision of causes and other matters brought before it, and aided in this, its proper business, by its proper officers, viz., attorneys and counsel to present and manage the business, clerks to record and attest its acts and decisions, and ministerial officers to execute its commands, and secure due order in its proceedings. Burrill.

The place where justice is judicially administered. Co. Litt. 58a; 3 Bl. Comm. 23.

The judge, or the body of judges, presiding over a court.

The words "court" and "judge," or "judges," are frequently used in our statutes as synonymous. When used with reference to orders made by the court or judges, they are to be so understood. 3 Ind. 239.

The term "court" may be construed to mean the judges of the court, or to include the judges and jury, according to the connection and the object of its use. 19 Vt. 478.

Classification. Courts may be classified and divided according to several methods, the following being the more usual:

Courts of record and *courts not of record;* the former being those whose acts and ju-

dicial proceedings are enrolled, or recorded, for a perpetual memory and testimony, and which have power to fine or imprison for contempt. Error lies to their judgments, and they generally possess a seal. Courts not of record are those of inferior dignity, which have no power to fine or imprison, and in which the proceedings are not enrolled or recorded.

Superior and *inferior* courts; the former being courts of general original jurisdiction in the first instance, and which exercise a control or supervision over a system of lower courts, either by appeal, error, or *certiorari;* the latter being courts of small or restricted jurisdiction, and subject to the review or correction of higher courts. Sometimes the former term is used to denote a particular group or system of courts of high powers, and all others are called "inferior courts."

To constitute a court a superior court as to any class of actions, within the common-law meaning of that term, its jurisdiction of such actions must be unconditional, so that the only thing requisite to enable the court to take cognizance of them is the acquisition of jurisdiction of the persons of the parties. 4 Bosw. 547.

An inferior court is a court whose judgments or decrees can be reviewed, on appeal or writ of error, by a higher tribunal, whether that tribunal be the circuit or supreme court. 18 Ala. 521.

Civil and *criminal* courts; the former being such as are established for the adjudication of controversies between subject and subject, or the ascertainment, enforcement, and redress of private rights; the latter, such as are charged with the administration of the criminal laws, and the punishment of wrongs to the public.

Equity courts and *law* courts; the former being such as possess the jurisdiction of a chancellor, apply the rules and principles of chancery law, and follow the procedure in equity; the latter, such as have no equitable powers, but administer justice according to the rules and practice of the common law.

As to the division of courts according to their *jurisdiction*, see JURISDICTION.

COURT-BARON. In English law. A court which, although not one of record, is incident to every manor, and cannot be severed therefrom. It was ordained for the maintenance of the services and duties stipulated for by lords of manors, and for the purpose of determining actions of a personal nature, where the debt or damage was under forty shillings. Wharton.

Customary court-baron is one appertaining entirely to copyholders.

Freeholders' court-baron is one held before the freeholders who owe suit and service to the manor. It is the court-baron proper.

COURT CHRISTIAN. The ecclesiastical courts in England are often so called, as distinguished from the civil courts. 1 Bl. Comm. 83; 3 Bl. Comm. 64; 3 Steph. Comm. 430.

COURT, CONSISTORY. See CONSISTORY COURT.

COURT FOR CONSIDERATION OF CROWN CASES RESERVED. A court established by St. 11 & 12 Vict. c. 78, composed of such of the judges of the superior courts of Westminster as were able to attend, for the consideration of questions of law reserved by any judge in a court of oyer and terminer, gaol delivery, or quarter sessions, before which a prisoner had been found guilty by verdict. Such question is stated in the form of a special case. Mozley & Whiteley; 4 Steph. Comm. 442.

COURT FOR DIVORCE AND MATRIMONIAL CAUSES. This court was established by St. 20 & 21 Vict. c. 85, which transferred to it all jurisdiction then exercisable by any ecclesiastical court in England, in matters matrimonial, and also gave it new powers. The court consisted of the lord chancellor, the three chiefs, and three senior puisne judges of the common-law courts, and the judge ordinary, who together constituted, and still constitute, the "full court." The judge ordinary heard almost all matters in the first instance. By the judicature act, 1873, § 3, the jurisdiction of the court was transferred to the supreme court of judicature. Sweet.

COURT FOR THE CORRECTION OF ERRORS. The style of a court having jurisdiction for review, by appeal or writ of error. The name was formerly used in New York and South Carolina.

COURT FOR THE RELIEF OF INSOLVENT DEBTORS. In English law. A local court which has its sittings in London only, which receives the petitions of insolvent debtors, and decides upon the question of granting a discharge.

COURT FOR THE TRIAL OF IMPEACHMENTS. A tribunal empowered to try any officer of government or other person brought to its bar by the process of impeachment. In England, the house of lords constitutes such a court; in the United States,

the senate; and in the several states, usually, the upper house of the legislative assembly.

COURT-HAND. In old English practice. The peculiar hand in which the records of courts were written from the earliest period down to the reign of George II. Its characteristics were great strength, compactness, and undeviating uniformity; and its use undoubtedly gave to the ancient record its acknowledged superiority over the modern, in the important quality of durability.

The writing of this hand, with its peculiar abbreviations and contractions, constituted, while it was in use, an art of no little importance, being an indispensable part of the profession of "clerkship," as it was called. Two sizes of it were employed, a large and a small hand; the former, called "great court-hand," being used for initial words or clauses, the *placita* of records, etc. Burrill.

COURT-HOUSE. The building occupied for the public sessions of a court, with its various offices. The term may be used of a place temporarily occupied for the sessions of a court, though not the regular court-house. 55 Mo. 181; 71 Ill. 350.

COURT-LANDS. Domains or lands kept in the lord's hands to serve his family.

COURT-LEET. The name of an English court of record held once in the year, and not oftener, within a particular hundred, lordship, or manor, before the steward of the leet; being the king's court granted by charter to the lords of those hundreds or manors. Its office was to view the frankpledges,—that is, the freemen within the liberty; to present by jury crimes happening within the jurisdiction; and to punish trivial misdemeanors. It has now, however, for the most part, fallen into total desuetude; though in some manors a court-leet is still periodically held for the transaction of the administrative business of the manor. Mozley & Whitley.

COURT-MARTIAL. A military court, convened under authority of government and the articles of war, for trying and punishing military offenses committed by soldiers or sailors in the army or navy.

COURT OF ADMIRALTY. A court having jurisdiction of causes arising under the rules of admiralty law. See ADMIRALTY.

COURT OF ANCIENT DEMESNE. In English law. A court of peculiar constitution, held by a bailiff appointed by the king, in which alone the tenants of the king's demesne could be impleaded. 2 Burrows, 1046; 1 Spence. Eq. Jur. 100; 2 Bl. Comm. 99; 1 Steph. Comm. 224.

COURT OF APPEAL, HER MAJESTY'S. The chief appellate tribunal of England. It was established by the judicature acts of 1873 and 1875, and is invested with the jurisdiction formerly exercised by the court of appeal in chancery, the exchequer chamber, the judicial committee of the privy council in admiralty and lunacy appeals, and with general appellate jurisdiction from the high court of justice.

COURT OF APPEALS. In American law. An appellate tribunal which, in Kentucky, Maryland, and New York, is the court of last resort. In Delaware and New Jersey, it is known as the "court of errors and appeals;" in Virginia and West Virginia, the "supreme court of appeals." In Texas the court of appeals is inferior to the supreme court.

COURT OF APPEALS IN CASES OF CAPTURE. A court erected by act of congress under the articles of confederation which preceded the adoption of the constitution. It had appellate jurisdiction in prize causes.

COURT OF ARBITRATION OF THE CHAMBER OF COMMERCE. A court of arbitrators, created for the convenience of merchants in the city of New York, by act of the legislature of New York. It decides disputes between members of the chamber of commerce, and between members and outside merchants who voluntarily submit themselves to the jurisdiction of the court.

COURT OF ARCHDEACON. The most inferior of the English ecclesiastical courts, from which an appeal generally lies to that of the bishop. 3 Bl. Comm. 64.

COURT OF ARCHES. See ARCHES COURT.

COURTS OF ASSIZE AND NISI PRIUS. Courts in England composed of two or more commissioners, called "judges of assize," (or of "assize and *nisi prius*,") who are twice in every year sent by the queen's special commission, on circuits all round the kingdom, to try, by a jury of the respective counties, the truth of such matters of fact as are there under dispute in the courts of Westminster Hall. 3 Steph. Comm. 421, 422; 3 Bl. Comm. 57.

AM. DICT. LAW—19

COURT OF ATTACHMENTS. The lowest of the three courts held in the forests. It has fallen into total disuse.

COURT OF AUDIENCE. Ecclesiastical courts, in which the primates once exercised in person a considerable part of their jurisdiction. They seem to be now obsolete, or at least to be only used on the rare occurrence of the trial of a bishop. Phillim. Ecc. Law, 1201, 1204.

COURT OF AUGMENTATION. An English court created in the time of Henry VIII., with jurisdiction over the property and revenue of certain religious foundations, which had been made over to the king by act of parliament, and over suits relating to the same.

COURT OF BANKRUPTCY. An English court of record, having original and appellate jurisdiction in matters of bankruptcy, and invested with both legal and equitable powers for that purpose.

COURT OF CHANCERY. A court having the jurisdiction of a chancellor; a court administering equity and proceeding according to the forms and principles of equity. In England, prior to the judicature acts, the style of the court possessing the largest equitable powers and jurisdiction was the "high court of chancery." In some of the United States, the title "court of chancery" is applied to a court possessing general equity powers, distinct from the courts of common law.

The terms "equity" and "chancery," "court of equity" and "court of chancery," are constantly used as synonymous in the United States. It is presumed that this custom arises from the circumstance that the equity jurisdiction which is exercised by the courts of the various states is assimilated to that possessed by the English courts of chancery. Indeed, in some of the states it is made identical therewith by statute, so far as conformable to our institutions. Bouvier.

COURT OF CHIVALRY, or COURT MILITARY, was a court not of record, held before the lord high constable and earl marshal of England. It had jurisdiction, both civil and criminal, in deeds of arms and war, armorial bearings, questions of precedence, etc., and as a court of honor. It has long been disused. 3 Bl. Comm. 103; 3 Steph. Comm. 335, note *l*.

COURTS OF CINQUE PORTS. In English law. Courts of limited local jurisdiction formerly held before the mayor and jurats (aldermen) of the Cinque Ports.

D

E

F

G

H

I

J

K

L

M

COURT OF CLAIMS. One of the courts of the United States, erected by act of congress. It consists of a chief justice and four associates, and holds one annual session. It is located at Washington. Its jurisdiction extends to all claims against the United States arising out of any contract with the government or based on an act of congress or regulation of the executive, and all claims referred to it by either house of congress, as well as to claims for exoneration by a disbursing officer. Its judgments are, in certain cases, reviewable by the United States supreme court. It has no equity powers. Its decisions are reported and published.

COURT OF THE CLERK OF THE MARKET. An English court of inferior jurisdiction held in every fair or market for the punishment of misdemeanors committed therein, and the recognizance of weights and measures.

COURT OF COMMISSIONERS OF SEWERS. The name of certain English courts created by commission under the great seal pursuant to the statute of sewers, (23 Hen. VIII. c. 5.)

COURT OF COMMON PLEAS. The English court of common pleas was one of the four superior courts at Westminster, and existed up to the passing of the judicature acts. It was also styled the "Common Bench." It was one of the courts derived from the breaking up of the *aula regis*, and had exclusive jurisdiction of all real actions and of *communia placita*, or common pleas, *i. e.*, between subject and subject. It was presided over by a chief justice with four puisne judges. Appeals lay anciently to the king's bench, but afterwards to the exchequer chamber. See 3 Bl. Comm. 37, et seq.

In American law. The name sometimes given to a court of original and general jurisdiction for the trial of issues of fact and law according to the principles of the common law.

COURT OF COMMON PLEAS FOR THE CITY AND COUNTY OF NEW YORK. The oldest court in the state of New York. Its jurisdiction is unlimited as respects amount, but restricted to the city and county of New York as respects locality. It has also appellate jurisdiction of cases tried in the marine court and district courts of New York city. Rap. & L.

COURTS OF CONSCIENCE. These were the same as courts of request, (*q. v.*)

COURT OF CONVOCATION. In English ecclesiastical law. A court, or assembly, comprising all the high officials of each province and representatives of the minor clergy. It is in the nature of an ecclesiastical parliament; and, so far as its judicial functions extend, it has jurisdiction of cases of heresy, schism, and other purely ecclesiastical matters. An appeal lies to the queen in council.

COURT OF THE CORONER. In English law. A court of record, to inquire, when any one dies in prison, or comes to a violent or sudden death, by what manner he came to his end. 4 Steph. Comm. 323; 4 Bl. Comm. 274. See CORONER.

COURTS OF THE COUNTIES PALATINE. In English law. A species of private court which formerly appertained to the counties palatine of Lancaster and Durham.

COURT OF COUNTY COMMISSIONERS. There is in each county of Alabama a court of record, styled the "court of county commissioners," composed of the judge of probate, as principal judge, and four commissioners, who are elected at the times prescribed by law, and hold office for four years. Code Ala. 1886, § 819.

COURT OF DELEGATES. A tribunal composed of delegates appointed by royal commission, and formerly the great court of appeal in all ecclesiastical causes. The powers of the court were, by 2 & 3 Wm. IV. c. 92, transferred to the privy council. A commission of review was formerly granted, in extraordinary cases, to revise a sentence of the court of delegates, when that court had apparently been led into material error. Brown.

COURT OF THE DUCHY OF LANCASTER. A court of special jurisdiction, held before the chancellor of the duchy or his deputy, concerning all matters of equity relating to lands holden of the king in right of the duchy of Lancaster. 3 Bl. Comm. 78.

COURT OF EQUITY. A court which has jurisdiction in equity, which administers justice and decides controversies in accordance with the rules, principles, and precedents of equity, and which follows the forms and procedure of chancery; as distinguished from a court having the jurisdiction, rules, principles, and practice of the common law.

COURT OF ERROR. An expression applied especially to the court of exchequer chamber and the house of lords, as taking cognizance of *error* brought. Mozley & Whitley. It is applied in some of the United States to the court of last resort in the state; and in its most general sense denotes any court having power to review the decisions of lower courts on appeal, error, *certiorari,* or other process.

COURT OF ERRORS AND APPEALS. The court of last resort in the state of New Jersey is so named. Formerly, the same title was given to the highest court of appeal in New York.

COURT OF EXCHEQUER. In English law. A very ancient court of record, set up by William the Conqueror as a part of the *aula regis,* and afterwards one of the four superior courts at Westminster. It was, however, inferior in rank to both the king's bench and the common pleas. It was presided over by a chief baron and four puisne barons. It was originally the king's treasury, and was charged with keeping the king's accounts and collecting the royal revenues. But pleas between subject and subject were anciently heard there, until this was forbidden by the *Articula super Chartas,* (1290,) after which its jurisdiction as a court only extended to revenue cases arising out of the non-payment or withholding of debts to the crown. But the privilege of suing and being sued in this court was extended to the king's accountants, and later, by the use of a convenient fiction to the effect that the plaintiff was the king's debtor or accountant, the court was thrown open to all suitors in personal actions. The exchequer had formerly both an equity side and a common-law side, but its equity jurisdiction was taken away by the statute 5 Vict. c. 5, (1842,) and transferred to the court of chancery. The judicature act (1873) transferred the business and jurisdiction of this court to the "Exchequer Division" of the "High Court of Justice."

In Scotch law. A court which formerly had jurisdiction of matters of revenue, and a limited jurisdiction over cases between the crown and its vassals where no questions of title were involved.

COURT OF EXCHEQUER CHAMBER. The name of a former English court of appeal, intermediate between the superior courts of common law and the house of lords. When sitting as a court of appeal from any one of the three superior courts of common law, it was composed of judges of the other two courts. 3 Bl. Comm. 56, 57;

3 Steph. Comm. 333, 356. By the judicature act (1873) the jurisdiction of this court is transferred to the court of appeal.

COURT OF GENERAL QUARTER SESSIONS OF THE PEACE. In American law. A court of criminal jurisdiction in New Jersey.

In English law. A court of criminal jurisdiction, in England, held in each county once in every quarter of a year, but in the county of Middlesex twice a month. 4 Steph. Comm. 317–320.

COURT OF GENERAL SESSIONS. The name given in some of the states (as New York) to a court of general original jurisdiction in criminal cases.

COURT OF GREAT SESSIONS IN WALES. A court formerly held in Wales; abolished by 11 Geo. IV. and 1 Wm. IV. c. 70, and the Welsh judicature incorporated with that of England. 3 Steph. Comm. 317, note.

COURT OF HUSTINGS. In English law. The county court of London, held before the mayor, recorder, and sheriff, but of which the recorder is, in effect, the sole judge. No actions can be brought in this court that are merely personal. 3 Steph. Comm. 449, note *l.*

In American law. A local court in some parts of the state of Virginia. 6 Grat. 696.

COURT OF INQUIRY. In English law. A court sometimes appointed by the crown to ascertain whether it be proper to resort to extreme measures against a person charged before a court-martial.

In American law. A court constituted by authority of the articles of war, invested with the power to examine into the nature of any transaction, accusation, or imputation against any officer or soldier. The said court shall consist of one or more officers, not exceeding three, and a judge advocate, or other suitable person, as a recorder, to reduce the proceedings and evidence to writing; all of whom shall be sworn to the performance of their duty. Rev. St. § 1342, arts. 115, 116.

COURT OF JUSTICE SEAT. In English law. The principal of the forest courts.

COURT OF JUSTICIARY. A Scotch court of general criminal jurisdiction of all offenses committed in any part of Scotland,

D

E

F

G

H

I

J

K

L

M

both to try causes and to review decisions of inferior criminal courts. It is composed of five lords of session with the lord president or justice-clerk as president. It also has appellate jurisdiction in civil causes involving small amounts. An appeal lies to the house of lords.

COURT OF KING'S BENCH. In English law. The supreme court of common law in the kingdom, now merged in the high court of justice under the judicature act of 1873, § 16.

COURT OF THE LORD HIGH STEWARD. In English law. A court instituted for the trial, during the recess of parliament, of peers indicted for treason or felony, or for misprision of either. This court is not a permanent body, but is created in modern times, when occasion requires, and for the time being, only; and the lord high steward, so constituted, with such of the temporal lords as may take the proper oath, and act, constitute the court.

COURT OF THE LORD HIGH STEWARD OF THE UNIVERSITIES. In English law. A court constituted for the trial of scholars or privileged persons connected with the university at Oxford or Cambridge who are indicted for treason, felony, or mayhem.

COURT OF MAGISTRATES AND FREEHOLDERS. In American law. The name of a court formerly established in South Carolina for the trial of slaves and free persons of color for criminal offenses.

COURT OF MARSHALSEA. A court which had jurisdiction of all trespasses committed within the verge of the king's court, where one of the parties was of the royal household; and of all debts and contracts, when both parties were of that establishment. It was abolished by 12 & 13 Vict. c. 101, § 13. Mozley & Whitley.

COURT OF NISI PRIUS. In American law. Though this term is frequently used as a general designation of any court exercising general, original jurisdiction in civil cases, (being used interchangeably with "trial-court,") it belonged as a legal title only to a court which formerly existed in the city and county of Philadelphia, and which was presided over by one of the judges of the supreme court of Pennsylvania. This court was abolished by the constitution of 1874. See COURTS OF ASSIZE AND NISI PRIUS.

COURT OF ORDINARY. In some of the United States (e. g., Georgia) this name is given to the probate or surrogate's court, or the court having the usual jurisdiction in respect to the proving of wills and the administration of decedents' estates.

COURT OF ORPHANS. In English law. The court of the lord mayor and aldermen of London, which has the care of those orphans whose parent died in London and was free of the city.

In Pennsylvania (and perhaps some other states) the name "orphans' court" is applied to that species of tribunal which is elsewhere known as the "probate court" or "surrogate's court."

COURT OF OYER AND TERMINER. In English law. A court for the trial of cases of treason and felony. The commissioners of assise and *nisi prius* are judges selected by the queen and appointed and authorized under the great seal, including usually two of the judges at Westminster, and sent out twice a year into most of the counties of England, for the trial (with a jury of the county) of causes then depending at Westminster, both civil and criminal. They sit by virtue of several commissions, each of which, in reality, constitutes them a separate and distinct court. The commission of *oyer and terminer* gives them authority for the trial of treasons and felonies; that of *general gaol delivery* empowers them to try every prisoner then in gaol for whatever offense; so that, altogether, they possess full criminal jurisdiction.

In American law. This name is generally used (sometimes, with additions) as the title, or part of the title, of a state court of criminal jurisdiction, or of the criminal branch of a court of general jurisdiction, being commonly applied to such courts as may try *felonies*, or the higher grades of crime.

COURT OF OYER AND TERMINER AND GENERAL JAIL DELIVERY. In American law. A court of criminal jurisdiction in the state of Pennsylvania.

It is held at the same time with the court of quarter sessions, as a general rule, and by the same judges. See Brightly's Purd. Dig. Pa. pp. 26, 382, 1201.

COURT OF OYER AND TERMINER, GENERAL JAIL DELIVERY, AND COURT OF QUARTER SESSIONS OF THE PEACE, IN AND FOR THE CITY AND COUNTY OF PHILA-

DELPHIA. In American law. A court of record of general criminal jurisdiction in and for the city and county of Philadelphia, in the state of Pennsylvania.

COURT OF PALACE AT WEST-MINSTER. This court had jurisdiction of personal actions arising within twelve miles of the palace at Whitehall. Abolished by 12 & 13 Vict. c. 101, 3 Steph. Comm. 317, note.

COURT OF PASSAGE. An inferior court, possessing a very ancient jurisdiction over causes of action arising within the borough of Liverpool. It appears to have been also called the "Borough Court of Liverpool." It has the same jurisdiction in admiralty matters as the Lancashire county court. Rosc. Adm. 75.

COURT OF PECULIARS. A spiritual court in England, being a branch of, and annexed to, the Court of Arches. It has a jurisdiction over all those parishes dispersed through the province of Canterbury, in the midst of other dioceses, which are exempt from the ordinary's jurisdiction, and subject to the metropolitan only. All ecclesiastical causes arising within these *peculiar* or exempt jurisdictions are originally cognizable by this court, from which an appeal lies to the Court of Arches. 3 Steph. Comm. 431; 4 Reeve, Eng. Law, 104.

COURT OF PIEPOUDRE. The lowest (and most expeditious) of the courts of justice known to the older law of England. It is supposed to have been so called from the dusty feet of the suitors. It was a court of record incident to every fair and market, was held by the steward, and had jurisdiction to administer justice for all commercial injuries and minor offenses done in that same fair or market, (not a preceding one.) An appeal lay to the courts at Westminster. This court long ago fell into disuse. 3 Bl. Comm. 32.

COURT OF PLEAS. A court of the county palatine of Durham, having a local common-law jurisdiction. It was abolished by the judicature act, which transferred its jurisdiction to the high court. Jud. Act 1873, § 16; 3 Bl. Comm. 79.

COURT OF POLICIES OF ASSURANCE. A court established by statute 43 Eliz. c. 12, to determine in a summary way all causes between merchants, concerning policies of insurance. Crabb, Eng. Law, 503.

COURTS OF PRINCIPALITY OF WALES. A species of private courts of a limited though extensive jurisdiction, which, upon the thorough reduction of that principality and the settling of its polity in the reign of Henry VIII., were erected all over the country. These courts, however, have been abolished by 1 Wm. IV. c. 70; the principality being now divided into two circuits, which the judges visit in the same manner as they do the circuits in England, for the purpose of disposing of those causes which are ready for trial. Brown.

COURT OF PROBATE. In English law. The name of a court established in 1857, under the probate act of that year, (20 & 21 Vict. c. 77,) to be held in London, to which court was transferred the testamentary jurisdiction of the ecclesiastical courts. 2 Steph. Comm. 192. By the judicature acts, this court is merged in the high court of justice.

In American law. A court having jurisdiction over the probate of wills, the grant of administration, and the supervision of the management and settlement of the estates of decedents, including the collection of assets, the allowance of claims, and the distribution of the estate. In some states the probate courts also have jurisdiction of the estates of minors, including the appointment of guardians and the settlement of their accounts, and of the estates of lunatics, habitual drunkards, and spendthrifts. And in some states these courts possess a limited jurisdiction in civil and criminal cases. They are also called "orphans' courts" and "surrogate's courts."

COURT OF QUARTER SESSIONS OF THE PEACE. In American law. A court of criminal jurisdiction in the state of Pennsylvania, having power to try misdemeanors, and exercising certain functions of an administrative nature. There is one such court in each county of the state. Its sessions are, in general, held at the same time and by the same judges as the *court of oyer and terminer and general jail delivery.* See Brightly's Purd. Dig. pp. 26, 383, § 35, p. 1198, § 1.

COURT OF QUEEN'S BENCH. See KING'S BENCH.

COURT OF RECORD. A court where the acts and judicial proceedings are enrolled on parchment or paper for a perpetual memorial and testimony; and which has power to fine and imprison for contempt of its authority. 3 Steph. Comm. 383; 3 Bl. Comm. 24.

> A court which has jurisdiction to fine and imprison, or one having jurisdiction of civil causes above forty shillings, and proceeding according to the course of the common law. 37 Me. 29.
>
> A judicial organized tribunal having attributes and exercising functions independently of the person of the magistrate designated generally to hold it, and proceeding according to the course of the common law. Bouvier.

Courts *not of record* are those of inferior dignity, which have no power to fine or imprison, and in which the proceedings are not enrolled or recorded. 3 Steph. Comm. 384.

COURT OF REGARD. In English law. One of the forest courts, in England, held every third year, for the lawing or expedition of dogs, to prevent them from running after deer. It is now obsolete. 3 Steph. Comm. 440; 3 Bl. Comm. 71, 72.

COURTS OF REQUEST. Inferior courts, in England, having local jurisdiction in claims for small debts, established in various parts of the kingdom by special acts of parliament. They were abolished in 1846, and the modern county courts (*q. v.*) took their place. 3 Steph. Comm. 283.

COURT OF SESSION. The name of the highest court of civil jurisdiction in Scotland.

It was composed of fifteen judges, now of thirteen. It sits in two divisions. The lord president and three ordinary lords form the first division; the lord justice clerk and three other ordinary lords form the second division. There are five permanent lords ordinary attached equally to both divisions; the last appointed of whom officiates on the bills, *i. e.*, petitions preferred to the court during the session, and performs the other duties of junior lord ordinary. The chambers of the parliament house in which the first and second divisions hold their sittings are called the "inner house;" those in which the lords ordinary sit as single judges to hear motions and causes are collectively called the "outer house." The nomination and appointment of the judges is in the crown. Wharton.

COURT OF SESSIONS. Courts of criminal jurisdiction existing in California, New York, and one or two other of the United States.

COURT OF STANNARIES. In English law. A court established in Devonshire and Cornwall, for the administration of justice among the miners and tinners, and that they may not be drawn away from their business to attend suits in distant courts. The stannary court is a court of record, with a special jurisdiction. 3 Bl. Comm. 79.

COURT OF STAR CHAMBER. This was an English court of very ancient origin, but new-modeled by St. 3 Hen. VII. c. 1, and 21 Hen. VIII. c. 20, consisting of divers lords, spiritual and temporal, being privy councillors, together with two judges of the courts of common law, without the intervention of any jury. The jurisdiction extended legally over riots, perjury, misbehavior of sheriffs, and other misdemeanors contrary to the laws of the land; yet it was afterwards stretched to the asserting of all proclamations and orders of state, to the vindicating of illegal commissions and grants of monopolies; holding for honorable that which it pleased, and for just that which it profited, and becoming both a court of law to determine civil rights and a court of revenue to enrich the treasury. It was finally abolished by St. 16 Car. I. c. 10, to the general satisfaction of the whole nation. Brown.

COURT OF THE STEWARD AND MARSHAL. A high court, formerly held in England by the steward and marshal of the king's household, having jurisdiction of all actions against the king's peace within the bounds of the household for twelve miles, which circuit was called the "verge." Crabb, Eng. Law, 185. It had also jurisdiction of actions of debt and covenant, where both the parties were of the household. 2 Reeve, Eng. Law, 235, 247.

COURT OF THE STEWARD OF THE KING'S HOUSEHOLD. In English law. A court which had jurisdiction of all cases of treason, misprision of treason, murder, manslaughter, bloodshed, and other malicious strikings whereby blood is shed, occurring in or within the limits of any of the palaces or houses of the king, or any other house where the royal person is abiding.

It was created by statute 33 Hen. VIII. c. 12, but long since fell into disuse. 4 Bl. Comm. 276, 277, and notes.

COURT OF SURVEY. A court for the hearing of appeals by owners or masters of ships, from orders for the detention of unsafe ships, made by the English board of trade, under the merchant shipping act, 1876, § 6.

COURT OF SWEINMOTE. In old English law. One of the forest courts, having a somewhat similar jurisdiction to that of the court of attachments, (q. v.)

COURTS OF THE UNITED STATES comprise the following: The senate of the United States, sitting as a court of impeachment; the supreme court; the circuit courts; the circuit courts of appeals; the district courts; the supreme court of the District of Columbia; the territorial courts; and the court of claims. See the several titles.

COURTS OF THE UNIVERSITIES of Oxford and Cambridge have jurisdiction in all personal actions to which any member or servant of the respective university is a party, provided that the cause of action arose within the liberties of the university, and that the member or servant was resident in the university when it arose, and when the action was brought. 3 Steph. Comm. 299; St. 25 & 26 Vict. c. 26, § 12; St. 19 & 20 Vict. c. 17 Each university court also has a criminal jurisdiction in all offenses committed by its members. 4 Steph. Comm. 325.

COURT OF WARDS AND LIVERIES. A court of record, established in England in the reign of Henry VIII. For the survey and management of the valuable fruits of tenure, a court of record was created by St. 32 Hen. VIII. c. 46, called the "Court of the King's Wards." To this was annexed, by St. 33 Hen. VIII. c. 22, the "Court of Liveries;" so that it then became the "Court of Wards and Liveries." 4 Reeve, Eng. Law, 258. This court was not only for the management of "wards," properly so called, but also of idiots and natural fools in the king's custody, and for licenses to be granted to the king's widows to marry, and fines to be made for marrying without his license. Id. 259. It was abolished by statute 12 Car. II. c. 24. Crabb, Eng. Law, 468.

COURTS OF WESTMINSTER HALL. The superior courts, both of law and equity, were for centuries fixed at Westminster, an ancient palace of the monarchs of England. Formerly, all the superior courts were held before the king's capital justiciary of England, in the *aula regis*, or such of his palaces wherein his royal person resided, and removed with his household from one end of the kingdom to another. This was found to occasion great inconvenience to the suitors, to remedy which it was made an article of the great charter of liberties, both of King John and King Henry III., that "common pleas should no longer follow the king's court, but be held in some certain place," in consequence of which they have ever since been held (a few necessary removals in times of the plague excepted) in the palace of Westminster only. The courts of equity also sit at Westminster, nominally, during term-time, although, actually, only during the first day of term, for they generally sit in courts provided for the purpose in, or in the neighborhood of, Lincoln's Inn. Brown.

COURT PREROGATIVE. See PREROGATIVE COURT.

COURT ROLLS. The rolls of a manor, containing all acts relating thereto. While belonging to the lord of the manor, they are not in the nature of public books for the benefit of the tenant.

COURTESY. See CURTESY.

COUSIN. Kindred in the fourth degree, being the issue (male or female) of the brother or sister of one's father or mother.

Those who descend from the brother or sister of the father of the person spoken of are called "paternal cousins;" "maternal cousins" are those who are descended from the brothers or sisters of the mother.

In English writs, commissions, and other formal instruments issued by the crown, the word signifies any peer of the degree of an earl. The appellation is as ancient as the reign of Henry IV., who, being related or allied to every earl then in the kingdom, acknowledged that connection in all his letters and public acts; from which the use has descended to his successors, though the reason has long ago failed. Mozley & Whitley.

COUSINAGE. See COSINAGE.

COUSTOM. Custom; duty; toll; tribute. 1 Bl. Comm. 314.

COUSTOUMIER. (Otherwise spelled "*Coustumier*" or "*Coutumier*.") In old French law. A collection of customs, unwritten laws, and forms of procedure. Two such volumes are of especial importance in juridical history, viz., the *Grand Coustumier de Normandie*, and the *Coutumier de France* or *Grand Coutumier*.

COUTHUTLAUGH. A person who willingly and knowingly received an outlaw, and cherished or concealed him; for which offense he underwent the same punishment as the outlaw himself. Bract. 128b; Spelman.

COUVERTURE, in French law, is the deposit ("margin") made by the client in the hands of the broker, either of a sum of money or of securities, in order to guaranty the broker for the payment of the securities which he purchases for the client. Arg. Fr. Merc. Law, 555.

COVENABLE. A French word signifying convenient or suitable; as covenably endowed. It is anciently written "convenable." Termes de la Ley.

COVENANT. In practice. The name of a common-law form of action *ex contractu*, which lies for the recovery of damages for breach of a covenant, or contract under seal.

In the law of contracts. An agreement, convention, or promise of two or more parties, *by deed* in writing, signed, sealed, and delivered, by which either of the parties pledges himself to the other that something is either done or shall be done, or stipulates for the truth of certain facts.

An agreement between two or more parties, reduced to writing and executed by a sealing and delivery thereof, whereby some of the parties named therein engage, or one of them engages, with the other, or others, or some of them, therein also named, that some act hath or hath not already been done, or for the performance or non-performance of some specified duty. 4 Whart. 71.

A promise by deed. 2 Steph. Comm. 108. A species of express contract, contained in a deed, to do a direct act, or to omit one. 3 Bl. Comm. 155.

Covenant is a contract, and is a writing obligatory, or parol promise, according as it is sealed or not. 8 Ala. 320.

Covenants may be classified according to several distinct principles of division. According as one or other of these is adopted, they are:

Express or implied; the former being those which are created by the express words of the parties to the deed declaratory of their intention, (Platt, Cov. 25;) while implied covenants are those which are inferred by the law from certain words in a deed which imply (though they do not express) them. Express covenants are also called covenants "in deed," as distinguished from covenants "in law."

Dependent, concurrent, and independent.

Covenants are either dependent, concurrent, or mutual and independent. The first depends on the prior performance of some act or condition, and, until the condition is performed, the other party is not liable to an action on his covenant. In the second, mutual acts are to be performed at the same time; and if one party is ready, and offers to perform his part, and the other neglects or refuses to perform his, he who is ready and offers has fulfilled his engagement, and may maintain an action for the default of the other, though it is not certain that either is obliged to do the first act. The third sort is where either party may recover damages from the other for the injuries he may have received by a breach of the covenants in his favor; and it is no excuse for the defendant to allege a breach of the covenants on the part of the plaintiff. 3 Ala. 330.

Principal and auxiliary; the former being those which relate directly to the principal matter of the contract entered into between the parties; while auxiliary covenants are those which do not relate directly to the principal matter of contract between the parties, but to something connected with it.

Inherent or collateral; the former being such as affect the particular property immediately, while the latter affect some property collateral thereto.

Joint or several. The former bind both or all the covenantors together; the latter bind each of them separately. A covenant may be both joint and several at the same time, as regards the covenantors; but, as regards the covenantees, they cannot be joint and several for one and the same cause, (5 Coke, 19*a*,) but must be either joint or several only. Covenants are usually joint or several according as the interests of the covenantees are such; but the words of the covenant, where they are unambiguous, will decide, although, where they are ambiguous, the nature of the interests as being joint or several is left to decide. Brown.

General or specific. The former relate to land generally and place the covenantee in the position of a specialty creditor only; the latter relate to particular lands and give the covenantee a lien thereon. Brown.

Executed or executory; the former being such as relate to an act already performed; while the latter are those whose performance is to be future. Shep. Touch. 161.

Affirmative or negative; the former being those in which the party binds himself to the existence of a present state of facts as represented or to the future performance of some act; while the latter are those in which the covenantor obliges himself *not* to do or perform some act.

Declaratory or obligatory; the former being those which serve to limit or direct uses; while the latter are those which are binding on the party himself. 1 Sid. 27; 1 Keb. 337.

Real or personal; the former being such as bind the heirs of the covenantor, and passing to assignees, or to the purchaser; while a personal covenant affects only the covenantor and the assets in the hands of his representatives after his death. 4 Kent, Comm. 470, 471.

Transitive or intransitive; the former being those personal covenants the duty of performing which passes over to the representatives of the covenantor; while the latter are those the duty of performing which is limited to the covenantee himself, and does not pass over to his representative. Bac. Abr. Cov.

Disjunctive covenants. Those which are for the performance of one or more of several things at the election of the covenantor or covenantee, as the case may be. Platt, Cov. 21.

COVENANT AGAINST INCUMBRANCES. A covenant that there are no incumbrances upon the land conveyed.

COVENANT COLLATERAL. A covenant which is conversant about some collateral thing that doth nothing at all, or not so immediately concern the thing granted; as to pay a sum of money in gross, etc. Shep. Touch. 161.

COVENANT FOR FURTHER ASSURANCE. An undertaking, in the form of a covenant, on the part of the vendor of real estate to do such further acts for the purpose of perfecting the purchaser's title as the latter may reasonably require. This covenant is deemed of great importance, since it relates both to the title of the vendor and to the instrument of conveyance to the vendee, and operates as well to secure the performance of all acts necessary for supplying any defect in the former as to remove all objections to the sufficiency and security of the latter. Platt, Cov.; Rawle, Cov. §§ 98, 99.

COVENANT FOR QUIET ENJOYMENT. An assurance against the consequences of a defective title, and of any disturbances thereupon. Platt, Cov. 312; Rawle, Cov. 125.

COVENANT IN DEED. A covenant expressed in words, or inserted in a deed in specific terms.

COVENANT IN LAW. A covenant implied by law from certain words in a deed which do not express it. 1 Archb. N. P. 250.

COVENANT INHERENT. A covenant which is conversant about the land, and knit to the estate in the land; as that the thing demised shall be quietly enjoyed, shall be kept in reparation, shall not be aliened, etc. Shep. Touch. 161.

COVENANT NOT TO SUE. A covenant by one who had a right of action at the time of making it against another person, by which he agrees not to sue to enforce such right of action.

COVENANT OF NON-CLAIM. A covenant sometimes employed, particularly in the New England states, and in deeds of extinguishment of ground rents in Pennsylvania, that neither the vendor, nor his heirs, nor any other person, etc., shall claim any title in the premises conveyed. Rawle, Cov. § 22.

COVENANT OF RIGHT TO CONVEY. An assurance by the covenantor that the grantor has sufficient capacity and title to convey the estate which he by his deed undertakes to convey.

COVENANT OF SEISIN. An assurance to the purchaser that the grantor has the very estate in quantity and quality which he purports to convey. 11 East, 641; Rawle, Cov. § 58. It is said that the covenant of seisin is not now in use in England, being embraced in that of a right to convey; but it is used in several of the United States. 2 Washb. Real Prop. *648.

COVENANT OF WARRANTY. An assurance by the grantor of an estate that the grantee shall enjoy the same without interruption by virtue of paramount title.

COVENANT REAL. A covenant in a deed binding the heirs of the covenantor, and passing to assignees, or to the purchaser.

It is thus distinguished from a *personal* covenant, which affects only the covenantor, and the assets in the hands of his representatives after his death. 4 Kent, Comm. 470.

A covenant real has for its object something annexed to, or inherent in, or connected with, land or other real property, and runs with the land, so that the grantee of the land is invested with it, and may sue upon it for any breach happening in his time. 6 Conn. 249.

In the old books, a covenant real is also defined to be a covenant by which a man binds himself to pass a thing real, as lands or tenements. Termes de la Ley; 3 Bl. Comm. 156.

COVENANT RUNNING WITH LAND. A covenant which goes with the

D

E

F

G

H

I

J

K

L

M

land, as being annexed to the estate, and which cannot be separated from the land, and transferred without it. 4 Kent, Comm. 472, note. A covenant is said to run with the land, when not only the original parties or their representatives, but each successive owner of the land, will be entitled to its benefit, or be liable (as the case may be) to its obligation. 1 Steph. Comm. 455. Or, in other words, it is so called when either the liability to perform it or the right to take advantage of it passes to the assignee of the land.

COVENANT TO CONVEY. A covenant by which the covenantor agrees to convey to the covenantee a certain estate, under certain circumstances.

COVENANT TO STAND SEISED. A conveyance adapted to the case where a person seised of land in possession, reversion, or vested remainder, proposes to convey it to his wife, child, or kinsman. In its terms it consists of a covenant by him, in consideration of his natural love and affection, to stand seised of the land to the use of the intended transferee. Before the statute of uses this would merely have raised a use in favor of the covenantee; but by that act this use is converted into the legal estate, and the covenant therefore operates as a conveyance of the land to the covenantee. It is now almost obsolete. 1 Steph. Comm. 532; Williams, Seis. 145.

COVENANTEE. The party to whom a covenant is made. Shep. Touch. 160.

COVENANTOR. The party who makes a covenant. Shep. Touch. 160.

COVENANTS FOR TITLE. Covenants usually inserted in a conveyance of land, on the part of the grantor, and binding him for the completeness, security, and continuance of the title transferred to the grantee. They comprise "covenants for seisin, for right to convey, against incumbrances, for quiet enjoyment, sometimes for further assurance, and almost always of warranty." Rawle, Cov. § 21.

COVENANTS IN GROSS. Such as do not run with the land.

COVENANTS PERFORMED. In Pennsylvania practice. This is the name of a plea to the action of covenant whereby the defendant, upon informal notice to the plaintiff, may give anything in evidence which he might have pleaded. 4 Dall. 439.

COVENT. A contraction, in the old books, of the word "convent."

COVENTRY ACT. The name given to the statute 22 & 23 Car. II. c. 1, which provided for the punishment of assaults with intent to maim or disfigure a person. It was so named from its being occasioned by an assault on Sir John Coventry in the street. 4 Bl. Comm. 207.

COVERT. Covered, protected, sheltered. A *pound covert* is one that is close or covered over, as distinguished from *pound overt*, which is open overhead. Co. Litt. 47b; 3 Bl. Comm. 12. A *feme covert* is so called, as being under the wing, protection, or *cover* of her husband. 1 Bl. Comm. 442.

COVERT BARON, or COVERT DE BARON. Under the protection of a husband; married. 1 Bl. Comm. 442. *La feme que est covert de baron*, the woman which is covert of a husband. Litt. § 670.

COVERTURE. The condition or state of a married woman. Sometimes used elliptically to describe the legal disability arising from a state of coverture.

COVIN. A secret conspiracy or agreement between two or more persons to injure or defraud another.

COVINOUS. Deceitful, fraudulent.

COWARDICE. Pusillanimity; fear; misbehavior through fear in relation to some duty to be performed before an enemy. O'Brien, Ct. M. 142.

CRAFT. A general term, now commonly applied to all kinds of sailing vessels, though formerly restricted to the smaller vessels. Worcester; 21 Grat. 693.

A guild.

CRANAGE. A liberty to use a crane for drawing up goods and wares of burden from ships and vessels, at any creek of the sea, or wharf, unto the land, and to make a profit of doing so. It also signifies the money paid and taken for the service. Tomlins.

CRASSA NEGLIGENTIA. Gross neglect; absence of ordinary care and diligence. 82 N. Y. 72.

CRASSUS. Large; gross; excessive; extreme. *Crassa ignorantia*, gross ignorance. Fleta, lib. 5, c. 22, § 18.

CRASTINO. The morrow, the day after. The return-day of writs; because the first day of the term was always some saint's day, and writs were returnable on the day after. 2 Reeve, Eng. Law, 56.

CRATES. An iron gate before a prison. 1 Vent. 304.

CRAVE. To ask or demand; as to crave oyer. See OYER.

CRAVEN. In old English law. A word of disgrace and obloquy, pronounced on either champion, in the ancient trial by battle, proving recreant, *i. e.*, yielding. Glanville calls it "*infestum et inverecundum verbum.*" His condemnation was *amittere liberam legem*, *i. e.*, to become infamous, and not to be accounted *liber et legalis homo*, being supposed by the event to have been proved forsworn, and not fit to be put upon a jury or admitted as a witness. Wharton.

CREAMER. A foreign merchant, but generally taken for one who has a stall in a fair or market. Blount.

CREAMUS. We create. One of the words by which a corporation in England was formerly created by the king. 1 Bl. Comm. 473.

CREANCE. In French law. A claim; a debt; also belief, credit, faith.

CREANCER. One who trusts or gives credit; a creditor. Britt. cc. 28, 78.

CREANSOR. A creditor. Cowell.

CREATE. To *create* a charter or a corporation is to make one which never existed before, while to *renew* one is to give vitality to one which has been forfeited or has expired; and to *extend* one is to give an existing charter more time than originally limited. 21 Pa. St. 188.

CREDENTIALS. In international law. The instruments which authorize and establish a public minister in his character with the state or prince to whom they are addressed. If the state or prince receive the minister, he can be received only in the quality attributed to him in his credentials. They are, as it were, his letter of attorney, his mandate patent, *mandatum manifestum.* Vattel, liv. 4, c. 6, § 76.

CREDIBILITY. Worthiness of belief; that quality in a witness which renders his evidence worthy of belief. After the competence of a witness is allowed, the consideration of his *credibility* arises, and not before. 1 Burrows, 414, 417; 3 Bl. Comm. 369.

As to the distinction between *competency* and *credibility*, see COMPETENCY.

CREDIBLE. Worthy of belief; entitled to credit. See COMPETENCY.

CREDIBLE WITNESS. One who, being competent to give evidence, is worthy of belief. 5 Mass. 229; 17 Pick. 154; 2 Curt. Ecc. 336.

CREDIT. 1. The ability of a business man to borrow money, or obtain goods on time, in consequence of the favorable opinion held by the community, or by the particular lender, as to his solvency and reliability.

2. Time allowed to the buyer of goods by the seller, in which to make payment for them.

3. The correlative of a *debt;* that is, a debt considered from the creditor's stand-point, or that which is incoming or due *to* one.

4. That which is due to a merchant, as distinguished from debit, that which is due by him.

5. That influence connected with certain social positions. 20 Toullier, n. 19.

The credit of an individual is the trust reposed in him by those who deal with him that he is of ability to meet his engagements; and he is trusted because through the tribunals of the country he may be made to pay. The credit of a government is founded on a belief of its ability to comply with its engagements, and a confidence in its honor, that it will do that voluntarily which it cannot be compelled to do. 3 Ala. 258.

Credit is the capacity of being trusted. 3 N. Y. 344, 356.

CREDIT, BILLS OF. See BILLS OF CREDIT.

CRÉDIT FONCIER. Fr. A company or corporation formed for the purpose of carrying out improvements, by means of loans and advances on real estate security.

CRÉDIT MOBILIER. Fr. A company or association formed for carrying on a banking business, or for the construction of public works, building of railroads, operation of mines, or other such enterprises, by means of loans or advances on the security of personal property.

CREDITOR. A person to whom a debt is owing by another person, called the "debtor." The creditor is called a "simple contract creditor," a "specialty creditor," a "bond creditor," or a "judgment creditor," according to the nature of the obligation giving rise to the debt; and, if he has issued execution to enforce a judgment, he is called an "execution creditor." He may also be a sole or a joint creditor. Sweet.

CREDITOR, JUDGMENT. One who has obtained a judgment against his debtor, under which he can enforce execution.

CREDITORS' BILL. In English practice. A bill in equity, filed by one or more creditors, for an account of the assets of a decedent, and a legal settlement and distribution of his estate among themselves and such other creditors as may come in under the decree.

In American practice. A proceeding to enforce the security of a judgment creditor against the property or interests of his debtor. This action proceeds upon the theory that the judgment is in the nature of a lien, such as may be enforced in equity.

A creditors' bill, strictly, is a bill by which a creditor seeks to satisfy his debt out of some equitable estate of the defendant, which is not liable to levy and sale under an execution at law. But there is another sort of a creditors' bill, very nearly allied to the former, by means of which a party seeks to remove a fraudulent conveyance out of the way of his execution. But a naked bill to set aside a fraudulent deed, which seeks no discovery of any property, chose in action, or other thing alleged to belong to the defendant, and which ought to be subjected to the payment of the judgment, is not a creditors' bill. 52 Ill. 98.

Creditorum appellatione non hi tantum accipiuntur qui pecuniam crediderunt, sed omnes quibus ex qualibet causa debetur. Under the head of "creditors" are included, not alone those who have lent money, but all to whom from any cause a debt is owing. Dig. 50, 16, 11.

CREDITRIX. A female creditor.

CREEK. In maritime law. Such little inlets of the sea, whether within the precinct or extent of a port or without, as are narrow passages, and have shore on either side of them. Call. Sew. 56.

A small stream less than a river. 12 Pick. 184.

The term imports a recess, cove, bay, or inlet in the shore of a river, and not a separate or independent stream; though it is sometimes used in the latter meaning. 38 N. Y. 103.

CREMENTUM COMITATÛS. The increase of a county. The sheriffs of counties anciently answered in their accounts for the improvement of the king's rents, above the *viscontiel* rents, under this title.

CREPARE OCULUM. In Saxon law. To put out an eye; which had a pecuniary punishment of fifty shillings annexed to it.

CREPUSCULUM. Twilight. In the law of burglary, this term means the presence of sufficient light to discern the face of a man; such light as exists immediately before the rising of the sun or directly after its setting.

Crescente malitiâ crescere debet et pœna. 2 Inst. 479. Vice increasing, punishment ought also to increase.

CREST. A term used in heraldry; it signifies the devices set over a coat of arms.

CRETINUS. In old records. A sudden stream or torrent; a rising or inundation.

CRETIO. Lat. In the civil law. A certain number of days allowed an heir to deliberate whether he would take the inheritance or not. Calvin.

CREW. The aggregate of seamen who man a ship or vessel, including the master and officers; or it may mean the ship's company, exclusive of the master, or exclusive of the master and all other officers. See 3 Sum. 209, et seq.

CREW LIST. In maritime law. A list of the crew of a vessel; one of a ship's papers. This instrument is required by act of congress, and sometimes by treaties. Rev. St. U. S. §§ 4374, 4375. It is necessary for the protection of the crews of every vessel, in the course of the voyage, during a war abroad. Jac. Sea Laws, 66, 69, note.

CRIER. An officer of a court, who makes proclamations. His principal duties are to announce the opening of the court and its adjournment and the fact that certain special matters are about to be transacted, to announce the admission of persons to the bar, to call the names of jurors, witnesses, and parties, to announce that a witness has been sworn, to proclaim silence when so directed, and generally to make such proclamations of a public nature as the judges order.

CRIEZ LA PEEZ. Rehearse the concord, or peace. A phrase used in the ancient proceedings for levying fines. It was the form of words by which the justice before whom the parties appeared directed the serjeant or countor in attendance to recite or *read aloud* the *concord* or agreement between the parties, as to the lands intended to be conveyed. 2 Reeve, Eng. Law, 224, 225.

CRIM. CON. An abbreviation for "criminal conversation," of very frequent use, denoting adultery.

CRIME. A crime is an act committed or omitted, in violation of a public law, either forbidding or commanding it; a breach or violation of some public right or duty due to a whole community, considered as a community in its social aggregate capacity, as distinguished from a civil injury. "Crime" and "misdemeanor," properly speaking, are synonymous terms; though in common usage "crime" is made to denote such offenses as are of a deeper and more atrocious dye. 4 Bl. Comm. 5.

Crimes are those wrongs which the government notices as injurious to the public, and punishes in what is called a "criminal proceeding," in its own name. 1 Bish. Crim. Law, § 43.

A crime may be defined to be any act done in violation of those duties which an individual owes to the community, and for the breach of which the law has provided that the offender shall make satisfaction to the public. Bell.

A crime or public offense is an act committed or omitted in violation of a law forbidding or commanding it, and to which is annexed, upon conviction, either of the following punishments: (1) Death; (2) imprisonment; (3) fine; (4) removal from office; or (5) disqualification to hold and enjoy any office of honor, trust, or profit in this state. Pen. Code Cal. § 15.

A crime or misdemeanor shall consist in a violation of a public law, in the commission of which there shall be a union or joint operation of act and intention, or criminal negligence. Code Ga. 1882, § 4292.

According to Blackstone, the word "crime" denotes such offenses as are of a deeper and more atrocious dye, while smaller faults and omissions of less consequence are called "misdemeanors." But the better use appears to be to make *crime* a term of broad and general import, including both felonies and misdemeanors, and hence covering all infractions of the criminal law. In this sense it is not a technical phrase, strictly speaking, (as "felony" and "misdemeanor" are,) but a convenient general term. In this sense, also, "offense" or "public offense" should be used as synonymous with it.

The distinction between a *crime* and a *tort* or civil injury is that the former is a breach and violation of the public right and of duties due to the whole community considered as such, and in its social and aggregate capacity; whereas the latter is an infringement or privation of the civil rights of individuals merely. Brown.

A crime, as opposed to a civil injury, is the violation of a right, considered in reference to the evil tendency of such violation, as regards the community at large. 4 Steph. Comm. 4.

CRIME AGAINST NATURE. The offense of buggery or sodomy.

CRIMEN. Lat. Crime. Also an accusation or charge of crime.

CRIMEN FALSI. In the civil law. The crime of falsifying; which might be committed either by writing, as by the forgery of a will or other instrument; by words, as by bearing false witness, or perjury; and by acts, as by counterfeiting or adulterating the public money, dealing with false weights and measures, counterfeiting seals, and other fraudulent and deceitful practices. Dig. 48, 10; Hallifax, Civil Law, b. 3, c. 12, nn. 56–59.

In Scotch law. It has been defined: "A fraudulent imitation or suppression of truth, to the prejudice of another." Ersk. Inst. 4, 4, 66.

At common law. Any crime which may injuriously affect the administration of justice, by the introduction of falsehood and fraud. 1 Greenl. Ev. § 373.

In modern law. This phrase is not used as a designation of any specific crime, but as a general designation of a class of offenses, including all such as involve deceit or falsification; *e. g.*, forgery, counterfeiting, using false weights or measures, perjury, etc.

Includes forgery, perjury, subornation of perjury, and offenses affecting the public administration of justice. 29 Ohio St. 358.

Crimen falsi dicitur, cum quis illicitus, cui non fuerit ad hæc data auctoritas, de sigillo regis, rapto vel invento, brevia, cartasve consignaverit. Fleta, lib. 1, c. 23. The crime of forgery is when any one illicitly, to whom power has not been given for such purposes, has signed writs or charters with the king's seal, either stolen or found.

CRIMEN FURTI. The offense of theft.

CRIMEN INCENDII. In old criminal law. The crime of burning, which included not only the modern crime of arson, (or burning of a house,) but also the burning of a man, beast, or other chattel. Britt. c. 9; Crabb, Eng. Law, 308.

CRIMEN INNOMINATUM. The nameless crime. A term for buggery or sodomy.

CRIMEN LÆSÆ MAJESTATIS. In criminal law. The crime of *lese-majesty*, or injuring majesty or royalty; high treason. The term was used by the older English law-writers to denote any crime affecting the king's person or dignity.

It is borrowed from the civil law, in which it signified the undertaking of any enterprise against the emperor or the republic. Inst. 4, 18, 3.

Crimen læsæ majestatis omnia alia crimina excedit quoad pœnam. 3 Inst. 210. The crime of treason exceeds all other crimes in its punishment.

Crimen omnia ex se nata vitiat. Crime vitiates everything which springs from it. 5 Hill, 523, 531.

CRIMEN RAPTUS. The offense of rape.

CRIMEN ROBERIÆ. The offense of robbery.

Crimen trahit personam. The crime carries the person, (*i. e.*, the commission of a crime gives the courts of the place where it is committed jurisdiction over the person of the offender.) 3 Denio, 190, 210.

Crimina morte extinguuntur. Crimes are extinguished by death.

CRIMINAL. That which pertains to or is connected with the law of crimes, or the administration of penal justice, or which relates to or has the character of crime. Also a person who has committed a crime; one who is guilty of a felony or misdemeanor.

CRIMINAL ACT. A term which is equivalent to crime; or is sometimes used with a slight softening or glossing of the meaning, or as importing a possible question of the legal guilt of the deed.

CRIMINAL ACTION. The proceeding by which a party charged with a public offense is accused and brought to trial and punishment is known as a "criminal action." Pen. Code Cal. § 683.

A criminal action is (1) an action prosecuted by the state as a party, against a person charged with a public offense, for the punishment thereof; (2) an action prosecuted by the state, at the instance of an individual, to prevent an apprehended crime, against his person or property. Code N. C. 1883, § 129.

CRIMINAL CASE. An action, suit, or cause instituted to punish an infraction of the criminal laws.

CRIMINAL CONTEMPT. A contempt of court which consists in openly insulting or resisting the powers of the court, or the persons of the judges who preside there. Otherwise called "direct" contempt. 4 Bl. Comm. 283.

CRIMINAL CONVERSATION. Adultery, considered in its aspect of a civil injury to the husband entitling him to damages; the tort of debauching or seducing of a wife. Often abbreviated to *crim. con.*

CRIMINAL INFORMATION. A criminal suit brought, without interposition of a grand jury, by the proper officer of the king or state. Cole, Crim. Inf.; 4 Bl. Comm. 398.

CRIMINAL INTENT. The intent to commit a crime; malice, as evidenced by a criminal act.

CRIMINAL LAW. That branch or division of law which treats of crimes and their punishments.

In the plural—"criminal laws"—the term may denote the laws which define and prohibit the various species of crimes and establish their punishments.

CRIMINAL LAW AMENDMENT ACT. This act was passed in 1871, (34 & 35 Vict. c. 32,) to prevent and punish any violence, threats, or molestation, on the part either of master or workmen, in the various relations arising between them. 4 Steph. Comm. 241.

CRIMINAL LAW CONSOLIDATION ACTS. The statutes 24 & 25 Vict. cc. 94–100, passed in 1861, for the consolidation of the criminal law of England and Ireland. 4 Steph. Comm. 297. These important statutes amount to a codification of the modern criminal law of England.

CRIMINAL LETTERS. In Scotch law. A process used as the commencement of a criminal proceeding, in the nature of a summons issued by the lord advocate or his deputy. It resembles a criminal information at common law.

CRIMINAL LIBEL. A libel which is punishable criminally; one which tends to excite a breach of the peace.

CRIMINAL PROCEDURE. The method pointed out by law for the apprehension, trial, or prosecution, and fixing the punishment, of those persons who have broken or violated, or are supposed to have broken or violated, the laws prescribed for the regulation of the conduct of the people of the community, and who have thereby laid themselves liable to fine or imprisonment or other punishment. 4 Amer. & Eng. Enc. Law, 730.

CRIMINAL PROCESS. Process which issues to compel a person to answer for a crime or misdemeanor. 1 Stew. (Ala.) 27.

CRIMINAL PROSECUTION. An action or proceeding instituted in a proper court on behalf of the public, for the purpose of securing the conviction and punishment of one accused of crime.

CRIMINALITER. Criminally. This term is used, in distinction or opposition to the word "*civiliter*," civilly, to distinguish a criminal liability or prosecution from a civil one.

CRIMINATE. To charge one with crime; to furnish ground for a criminal prosecution; to expose a person to a criminal charge. A witness cannot be compelled to answer any question which has a tendency to *criminate* him.

CRIMP. One who decoys and plunders sailors under cover of harboring them. Wharton.

CRO, CROO. In old Scotch law. A weregild. A composition, satisfaction, or assythment for the slaughter of a man.

CROCIA. The *crosier*, or pastoral staff.

CROCIARIUS. A cross-bearer, who went before the prelate. Wharton.

CROCKARDS, CROCARDS. A foreign coin of base metal, prohibited by statute 27 Edw. I. St. 3, from being brought into the realm. 4 Bl. Comm. 98; Crabb, Eng. Law, 176.

CROFT. A little close adjoining a dwelling house, and inclosed for pasture and tillage or any particular use. Jacob. A small place fenced off in which to keep farm-cattle. Spelman. The word is now entirely obsolete.

CROISES. Pilgrims; so called as wearing the sign of the *cross* on their upper garments. Britt. c. 122. The knights of the order of St. John of Jerusalem, created for the defense of the pilgrims. Cowell; Blount.

CROITEIR. A crofter; one holding a croft.

CROP. The products of the harvest in corn or grain. Emblements.

CROPPER. One who, having no interest in the land, works it in consideration of receiving a portion of the crop for his labor. 2 Rawle, 11.

The difference between a tenant and a cropper is: A tenant has an estate in the land for the term, and, consequently, he has a right of property in the crops. Until division, the right of property and of possession in the whole is the tenant's. A cropper has no estate in the land; and, although he has in some sense the possession of the crop, it is the possession of a servant only, and is, in law, that of the landlord, who must divide off to the cropper his share. 71 N. C. 7.

CROSS. A mark made by persons who are unable to write, to stand instead of a signature; usually made in the form of a Maltese cross.

As an adjective, the word is applied to various demands and proceedings which are connected in subject-matter, but opposite or contradictory in purpose or object.

CROSS-ACTION. An action brought by one who is defendant in a suit against the party who is plaintiff in such suit, upon a cause of action growing out of the same transaction which is there in controversy, whether it be a contract or tort.

CROSS-APPEAL. Where both parties to a judgment appeal therefrom, the appeal of each is called a "cross-appeal" as regards that of the other. 3 Steph. Comm. 581.

CROSS-BILL. In equity practice. One which is brought by a defendant in a suit against a plaintiff in or against other defendants in the same suit, or against both, touching the matters in question in the original bill. Story, Eq. Pl. § 389; Mitf. Eq. Pl. 80.

A cross-bill is a bill brought by a defendant against a plaintiff, or other parties in a former bill depending, touching the matter in question in that bill. It is usually brought either to obtain a necessary discovery of facts in aid of the defense to the original bill, or to obtain full relief to all parties in reference to the matters of the original bill. It is to be treated as a mere auxiliary suit. 17 How. 591; 35 N. H. 235.

A cross-bill is a species of pleading, used for the purpose of obtaining a discovery necessary to the defense, or to obtain some relief founded on the collateral claims of the party defendant to the original suit. 14 Ga. 167.

Also, if a bill of exchange or promissory note be given in consideration of another bill or note, it is called a "cross" or "counter" bill or note.

CROSS-COMPLAINT. In code practice. Whenever the defendant seeks affirmative relief against any party, relating to or depending upon the contract or transaction upon which the action is brought, or affecting the property to which the action relates, he may, in addition to his answer, file at the same time, or by permission of the court subsequently, a cross-complaint. The cross-complaint must be served upon the parties affected thereby, and such parties may demur or answer thereto as to the original complaint. Code Civil Proc. Cal. § 442.

CROSS-DEMAND. Where a person against whom a demand is made by another, in his turn makes a demand against that other, these mutual demands are called "cross-demands." A *set-off* is a familiar example.

CROSS-ERRORS. Errors being assigned by the respondent in a writ of error, the errors assigned on both sides are called "cross-errors."

CROSS-EXAMINATION. In practice. The examination of a witness upon a trial or hearing, or upon taking a deposition, by the party opposed to the one who produced him, upon his evidence given in chief, to test its truth, to further develop it, or for other purposes.

CROSS-REMAINDER. Where land is devised or conveyed to two or more persons as tenants in common, or where different parts of the same land are given to such persons in severalty, with such limitations that, upon the determination of the particular estate of either, his share is to pass to the other, to the entire exclusion of the ultimate remainder-man or reversioner until all the particular estates shall be exhausted, the remainders so limited are called "cross-remainders." In wills, such remainders may arise by implication; but, in deeds, only by express limitation. See 2 Bl. Comm. 381; 2 Washb. Real Prop. 233; 1 Prest. Est. 94.

CROSS-RULES. These were rules where each of the opposite litigants obtained a rule *nisi*, as the plaintiff to increase the damages, and the defendant to enter a nonsuit. Wharton.

CROSSED CHECK. A check crossed with two lines, between which are either the name of a bank or the words "and company," in full or abbreviated. In the former case, the banker on whom it is drawn must not pay the money for the check to any other than the banker named; in the latter case, he must not pay it to any other than a banker. 2 Steph. Comm. 118, note c.

CROWN. The sovereign power in a monarchy, especially in relation to the punishment of crimes. "Felony is an offense of the crown." Finch, Law, b. 1, c. 16.

An ornamental badge of regal power worn on the head by sovereign princes. The word is frequently used when speaking of the sovereign herself, or the rights, duties, and prerogatives belonging to her. Also a silver coin of the value of five shillings. Wharton.

CROWN CASES. In English law. Criminal prosecutions on behalf of the crown, as representing the public; causes in the criminal courts.

CROWN CASES RESERVED. In English law. Questions of law arising in criminal trials at the assizes, (otherwise than by way of demurrer,) and not decided there, but reserved for the consideration of the court of criminal appeal.

CROWN COURT. In English law. The court in which the crown cases, or criminal business, of the assizes is transacted.

CROWN DEBTS. In English law. Debts due to the crown, which are put, by various statutes, upon a different footing from those due to a subject.

CROWN LANDS. The demesne lands of the crown.

CROWN LAW. Criminal law in England is sometimes so termed, the crown being always the prosecutor in criminal proceedings. 4 Bl. Comm. 2.

CROWN OFFICE. The criminal side of the court of king's bench. The king's attorney in this court is called "master of the crown office." 4 Bl. Comm. 308.

CROWN OFFICE IN CHANCERY. One of the offices of the English high court of chancery, now transferred to the high court of justice. The principal official, the clerk of the crown, is an officer of parliament, and of the lord chancellor, in his non-judicial capacity, rather than an officer of the courts of law.

CROWN PAPER. A paper containing the list of criminal cases which await the hearing or decision of the court, and particularly of the court of queen's bench; and it then includes all cases arising from informations *quo warranto*, criminal informations, criminal cases brought up from inferior courts by writ of *certiorari*, and cases from the sessions. Brown.

CROWN SIDE. The criminal department of the court of queen's bench; the civil department or branch being called the "plea side." 4 Bl. Comm. 265.

CROWN SOLICITOR. In England, the solicitor to the treasury acts, in state prosecutions, as solicitor for the crown in preparing the prosecution. In Ireland there are officers called "crown solicitors" attached to each circuit, whose duty it is to get up every case for the crown in criminal prosecutions. They are paid by salaries. There is no such system in England, where prosecutions are conducted by solicitors appointed by the parish, or other persons bound over to prosecute by the magistrates on each committal; but in Scotland the still better plan exists of a crown prosecutor (called the "procurator-fiscal," and being a subordinate of the lord-advocate) in every county, who prepares every criminal prosecution. Wharton.

CROWNER. In old Scotch law. Coroner; a coroner.

CROY. In old English law. Marsh land. Blount.

CRUCE SIGNATI. In old English law. Signed or marked with a cross. Pilgrims to the holy land, or crusaders; so called because they wore the sign of the cross upon their garments. Spelman.

CRUELTY. The intentional and malicious infliction of physical suffering upon living creatures, particularly human beings; or, as applied to the latter, the wanton, malicious, and unnecessary infliction of pain upon the body, or the feelings and emotions; abusive treatment; inhumanity; outrage.

Extreme cruelty is the infliction of grievous bodily injury or grievous mental suffering upon the other by one party to the marriage. Civil Code Cal. § 94.

As between husband and wife. Those acts which affect the life, the health, or even the comfort, of the party aggrieved, and give a reasonable apprehension of bodily hurt, are called "cruelty." What merely wounds the feelings is seldom admitted to be cruelty, unless the act be accompanied with bodily injury, either actual or menaced. Mere austerity of temper, petulance of manners, rudeness of language, a want of civil attention and accommodation, even occasional sallies of passion, will not amount to legal cruelty; a fortiori, the denial of little indulgences and particular accommodations, which the delicacy of the world is apt to number among its necessaries, is not cruelty. The negative descriptions of cruelty are perhaps the best, under the infinite variety of cases that may occur, by showing what is not cruelty. 1 Hagg. Const. 35; 4 Eng. Ecc. 238, 311, 312.

AM. DICT. LAW—20

Cruelty includes both willfulness and malicious temper of mind with which an act is done, as well as a high degree of pain inflicted. Acts merely accidental, though they inflict great pain, are not "cruel," in the sense of the word as used in statutes against cruelty. 101 Mass. 34.

CRUISE. A voyage undertaken for a given purpose; a voyage for the purpose of making captures *jure belli.* 2 Gall. 538.

A voyage or expedition in quest of vessels or fleets of the enemy which may be expected to sail in any particular track at a certain season of the year. The region in which these cruises are performed is usually termed the "rendezvous," or "cruising latitude." Bouvier.

Imports a definite place, as well as time of commencement and termination, unless such construction is repelled by the context. When not otherwise specially agreed, a cruise begins and ends in the country to which a ship belongs, and from which she derives her commission. 2 Gall. 526.

CRY. To call out aloud; to proclaim; to publish; to sell at auction. "To cry a tract of land." 1 Wash. (Va.) 335, (260.)

CRY DE PAIS, or CRI DE PAIS. The hue and cry raised by the people in ancient times, where a felony had been committed and the constable was absent.

CRYER. An auctioneer. 1 Wash. (Va.) 337, (262.) One who calls out aloud; one who publishes or proclaims. See CRIER.

CRYPTA. A chapel or oratory underground, or under a church or cathedral. Du Cange.

CUCKING-STOOL. An engine of correction for common scolds, which in the Saxon language is said to signify the scolding-stool, though now it is frequently corrupted into *ducking-stool*, because the judgment was that, when the woman was placed therein, she should be plunged in the water for her punishment. It was also variously called a "trebucket," "tumbrel," or "castigatory." 3 Inst. 219; 4 Bl. Comm. 169; Brown.

CUEILLETTE. A term of French maritime law. See A CUEILLETTE.

CUI ANTE DIVORTIUM. (To whom before divorce.) A writ for a woman divorced from her husband to recover her lands and tenements which she had in fee-simple or in tail, or for life, from him to whom her husband alienated them during the marriage, when she could not gainsay it. Reg. Orig. 233.

CUI BONO. For whose good; for whose use or benefit. "*Cui bono* is ever of great weight in all agreements." Parker, C. J.,

10 Mod. 135. Sometimes translated, for what good, for what useful purpose.

Cuicunque aliquis quid concedit concedere videtur et id, sine quo res ipsa esse non potuit. 11 Coke, 52. Whoever grants anything to another is supposed to grant that also without which the thing itself would be of no effect.

CUI IN VITA. (To whom in life.) A writ of entry for a widow against him to whom her husband aliened her lands or tenements in his life-time; which must contain in it that during his life she could not withstand it. Reg. Orig. 232; Fitzh. Nat. Brev. 193.

Cui jurisdictio data est, ea quoque concessa esse videntur, sine quibus jurisdictio explicari non potest. To whomsoever a jurisdiction is given, those things also are supposed to be granted, without which the jurisdiction cannot be exercised. Dig. 2, 1, 2. The grant of jurisdiction implies the grant of all powers necessary to its exercise. 1 Kent, Comm. 339.

Cui jus est donandi, eidem et vendendi et concedendi jus est. He who has the right of giving has also the right of selling and granting. Dig. 50, 17, 163.

Cuilibet in arte sua perito est credendum. Any person skilled in his peculiar art or profession is to be believed, [i. e., when he speaks of matters connected with such art.] Co. Litt. 125a; Shelf. Mar. & Div. 206. Credence should be given to one skilled in his peculiar profession. Broom, Max. 932.

Cuilibet licet juri pro se introducto renunciare. Any one may waive or renounce the benefit of a principle or rule of law that exists only for his protection.

Cui licet quod majus, non debet quod minus est non licere. He who is allowed to do the greater ought not to be prohibited from doing the less. He who has authority to do the more important act ought not to be debarred from doing what is of less importance. 4 Coke, 23.

Cui pater est populus non habet ille patrem. He to whom the people is father has not a father. Co. Litt. 123.

Cuique in sua arte credendum est. Every one is to be believed in his own art. 9 Mass. 227.

Cujus est commodum ejus debet esse incommodum. Whose is the advantage, his also should be the disadvantage.

Cujus est dare, ejus est disponere. Wing. Max. 53. Whose it is to give, his it is to dispose; or, as Broom says, "the bestower of a gift has a right to regulate its disposal." Broom, Max. 459, 461, 463, 464.

Cujus est divisio, alterius est electio. Whichever [of two parties] has the division, [of an estate,] the choice [of the shares] is the other's. Co. Litt. 166b. In partition between coparceners, where the division is made by the eldest, the rule in English law is that she shall choose her share last. Id.; 2 Bl. Comm. 189; 1 Steph. Comm. 323.

Cujus est dominium ejus est periculum. The risk lies upon the owner of the subject. Tray. Lat. Max. 114.

Cujus est instituere, ejus est abrogare. Whose right it is to institute, his right it is to abrogate. Broom, Max. 878, note.

Cujus est solum ejus est usque ad coelum. Whose is the soil, his it is up to the sky. Co. Litt. 4a. He who owns the soil, or surface of the ground, owns, or has an exclusive right to, everything which is upon or above it to an indefinite height. 9 Coke, 54; Shep. Touch. 90; 2 Bl. Comm. 18; 3 Bl. Comm. 217; Broom, Max. 395.

Cujus est solum, ejus est usque ad coelum et ad inferos. To whomsoever the soil belongs, he owns also to the sky and to the depths. The owner of a piece of land owns everything above and below it to an indefinite extent. Co. Litt. 4.

Cujus juris (i. e., jurisdictionis) est principale, ejusdem juris erit accessorium. 2 Inst. 493. An accessory matter is subject to the same jurisdiction as its principal.

Cujus per errorem dati repetitio est, ejus consulto dati donatio est. He who gives a thing by mistake has a right to recover it back; but, if he gives designedly, it is a gift. Dig. 50, 17, 53.

Cujusque rei potissima pars est principium. The chiefest part of everything is the beginning. Dig. 1, 2, 1; 10 Coke, 49a.

CUL DE SAC. (Fr. the bottom of a sack.) A blind alley; a street which is open at one end only.

CULAGIUM. In old records. The laying up a ship in a dock, in order to be repaired. Cowell; Blount.

CULPA. A term of the civil law, meaning fault, neglect, or negligence. There are three degrees of *culpa*,—*lata culpa*, gross fault or neglect; *levis culpa*, ordinary fault or neglect; *levissima culpa*, slight fault or neglect,—and the definitions of these degrees are precisely the same as those in our law. Story, Bailm. § 18. This term is to be distinguished from *dolus*, which means fraud, guile, or deceit.

Culpa caret qui scit sed prohibere non potest. He is clear of blame who knows, but cannot prevent. Dig. 50, 17, 50.

Culpa est immiscere se rei ad se non pertinenti. 2 Inst. 208. It is a fault for any one to meddle in a matter not pertaining to him.

Culpa lata dolo æquiparatur. Gross negligence is held equivalent to intentional wrong.

Culpa tenet [teneat] suos auctores. Misconduct binds [should bind] its own authors. It is a never-failing axiom that every one is accountable only for his own delicts. Ersk. Inst. 4, 1, 14.

CULPABILIS. Lat. In old English law. Guilty. *Culpabilis de intrusione,*—guilty of intrusion. Fleta, lib. 4, c. 30, § 11.

CULPABLE. Means not only criminal, but censurable; and, when the term is applied to the omission by a person to preserve the means of enforcing his own rights, censurable is more nearly an equivalent. As he has merely lost a right of action which he might voluntarily relinquish, and has wronged nobody but himself, culpable neglect conveys the idea of neglect which exists where the loss can fairly be ascribed to the party's own carelessness, improvidence, or folly. 8 Allen, 121.

CULPABLE HOMICIDE. Described as a crime varying from the very lowest culpability, up to the very verge of murder. Lord Moncrieff, Arkley, 72.

Culpæ pœna par esto. Pœna ad mensuram delicti statuenda est. Let the punishment be proportioned to the crime. Punishment is to be measured by the extent of the offense.

CULPRIT. A person who is indicted for a criminal offense, but not yet convicted. It is not, however, a techical term of the law; and in its vernacular usage it seems to imply only a light degree of censure or moral reprobation.

Blackstone believes it an abbreviation of the old forms of arraignment, whereby, on the prisoner's pleading not guilty, the clerk would respond, "*culpabilis, prit,*" *i. e.,* he is guilty and the crown is ready. It was (he says) the *viva voce* replication, by the clerk, on behalf of the crown, to the prisoner's plea of *non culpabilis; prit* being a technical word, anciently in use in the formula of joining issue. 4 Bl. Comm. 339.

But a more plausible explanation is that given by Donaldson, (cited Whart. Lex.,) as follows: The clerk asks the prisoner, "Are you guilty, or not guilty?" Prisoner, "Not guilty." Clerk, "*Qu'il paroit,* [may it prove so.] How will you be tried?" Prisoner, "By God and my country." These words being hurried over, came to sound, "Culprit, how will you be tried?" The ordinary derivation is from *culpa.*

CULRACH. In old Scotch law. A species of pledge or cautioner, (Scotticé, *back borgh,*) used in cases of the replevin of persons from one man's court to another's. Skene.

CULTIVATED. A field on which a crop of wheat is growing is a cultivated field, although not a stroke of labor may have been done in it since the seed was put in the ground, and it is a cultivated field after the crop is removed. It is, strictly, a cultivated piece of ground. 13 Ired. 36.

CULTURA. A parcel of arable land. Blount.

CULVERTAGE. In old English law. A base kind of slavery. The confiscation or forfeiture which takes place when a lord seizes his tenant's estate. Blount; Du Cange.

Cum actio fuerit mere criminalis, institui poterit ab initio criminaliter vel civiliter. When an action is merely criminal, it can be instituted from the beginning either criminally or civilly. Bract. 102.

Cum adsunt testimonia rerum, quid opus est verbis? When the proofs of facts are present, what need is there of words? 2 Bulst. 53.

Cum aliquis renunciaverit societati, solvitur societas. When any partner renounces the partnership, the partnership is dissolved. Tray. Lat. Max. 118.

Cum confitente sponte mitius est agendum. 4 Inst. 66. One confessing willingly should be dealt with more leniently.

Cum de lucro duorum quæritur, melior est causa possidentis. When the question is as to the gain of two persons, the cause of him who is in possession is the better. Dig. 50, 17, 126.

Cum duo inter se pugnantia reperiuntur in testamento, ultimum ratum est. Where two things repugnant to each other are found in a will, the last shall stand. Co. Litt. 112b; Shep. Touch. 451; Broom, Max. 583.

Cum duo jura concurrunt in una persona æquum est ac si essent in duobus. When two rights meet in one person, it is the same as if they were in two persons.

CUM GRANO SALIS. (With a grain of salt.) With allowance for exaggeration.

Cum in corpore dissentitur, apparet nullam esse acceptionem. When there is a disagreement in the substance, it appears that there is no acceptance. 12 Allen, 44.

Cum in testamento ambigue aut etiam perperam scriptum est benigne interpretari et secundum id quod credibile est cogitatum credendum est. Dig. 34, 5, 24. Where an ambiguous, or even an erroneous, expression occurs in a will, it should be construed liberally, and in accordance with the testator's probable meaning. Broom, Max. 568.

Cum legitimæ nuptiæ factæ sunt, patrem liberi sequuntur. Children born under a legitimate marriage follow the condition of the father.

CUM ONERE. With the burden; subject to an incumbrance or charge. What is taken cum onere is taken subject to an existing burden or charge.

Cum par delictum est duorum, semper oneratur petitor et melior habetur possessoris causa. Dig. 50, 17, 154. When both parties are in fault the plaintiff must always fail, and the cause of the person in possession be preferred.

CUM PERA ET LOCULO. With satchel and purse. A phrase in old Scotch law.

CUM PERTINENTIIS. With the appurtenances. Bract. fol. 73b.

CUM PRIVILEGIO. The expression of the monopoly of Oxford, Cambridge, and the royal printers to publish the Bible.

Cum quod ago non valet ut ago, valeat quantum valere potest. 4 Kent, Comm. 493. When that which I do is of no

effect as I do it, it shall have as much effect as it can; i. e., in some other way.

CUM TESTAMENTO ANNEXO. L. Lat. With the will annexed. A term applied to administration granted where a testator makes an incomplete will, without naming any executors, or where he names incapable persons, or where the executors named refuse to act. 2 Bl. Comm. 503, 504.

CUMULATIVE. Additional; heaping up; increasing; forming an aggregate. The word signifies that two things are to be added together, instead of one being a repetition or in substitution of the other.

CUMULATIVE EVIDENCE. Additional or corroborative evidence to the same point. That which goes to prove what has already been established by other evidence. 20 Conn. 305; 28 Me. 376; 24 Pick. 246.

All evidence material to the issue, after any such evidence has been given, is in a certain sense cumulative; that is, is added to what has been given before. It tends to sustain the issue. But cumulative evidence, in legal phrase, means evidence from the same or a new witness, simply repeating, in substance and effect, or adding to, what has been before testified to. 43 Barb. 212.

Evidence is not cumulative merely because it tends to establish the same ultimate or *principally controverted* fact. Cumulative evidence is additional evidence of the same kind to the same point. 43 Iowa, 177.

CUMULATIVE LEGACIES. These are legacies so called to distinguish them from legacies which are merely *repeated*. In the construction of testamentary instruments, the question often arises whether, where a testator has twice bequeathed a legacy to the same person, the legatee is entitled to both, or only to one of them; in other words, whether the second legacy must be considered as a mere repetition of the first, or as cumulative, i. e., additional. In determining this question, the intention of the testator, if it appears on the face of the instrument, prevails. Wharton.

CUMULATIVE REMEDY. A remedy created by statute in addition to one which still remains in force.

CUMULATIVE SENTENCES. Separate sentences (each additional to the others) imposed upon a defendant who has been convicted upon an indictment containing several counts, each of such counts charging a distinct offense.

CUMULATIVE VOTING. A system of voting, by which the elector, having a number of votes equal to the number of officers to be chosen, is allowed to concentrate the whole number of his votes upon one person, or to distribute them as he may see fit. For example, if ten directors of a corporation are to be elected, then, under this system, the voter may cast ten votes for one person, or five votes for each of two persons, etc. It is intended to secure representation of a minority.

CUNADES. In Spanish law. Affinity; alliance; relation by marriage. Las Partidas, pt. 4, tit. 6, l. 5.

CUNEATOR. A coiner. Du Cange. *Cuneare*, to coin. *Cuneus*, the die with which to coin. *Cuneata*, coined. Du Cange; Spelman.

CUNTEY-CUNTEY. In old English law. A kind of trial, as appears from Bract. lib. 4, tract 3, ca. 18, and tract 4, ca. 2, where it seems to mean, one by the ordinary jury.

CUR. A common abbreviation of *curia*.

CURA. Lat. Care; charge; oversight; guardianship.

In the civil law. A species of guardianship which commenced at the age of puberty, (when the guardianship called "*tutela*" expired,) and continued to the completion of the twenty-fifth year. Inst. 1, 23, pr.; Id. 1, 25, pr.; Hallifax, Civil Law, b. 1, c. 9.

CURAGULOS. One who takes care of a thing.

CURATE. In ecclesiastical law. Properly, an incumbent who has the *cure* of souls, but now generally restricted to signify the spiritual assistant of a rector or vicar in his *cure*. An officiating temporary minister in the English church, who represents the proper incumbent; being regularly employed either to serve in his absence or as his assistant, as the case may be. 1 Bl. Comm. 393; 3 Steph. Comm. 88; Brande.

CURATEUR. In French law. A person charged with supervising the administration of the affairs of an emancipated minor, of giving him advice, and assisting him in the important acts of such administration. Duverger.

CURATIO. In the civil law. The power or duty of managing the property of him who, either on account of infancy or some defect of mind or body, cannot manage his own affairs. The duty of a curator or guardian. Calvin.

CURATOR. In the civil law. A person who is appointed to take care of anything for another. A guardian. One appointed to take care of the estate of a minor above a certain age, a lunatic, a spendthrift, or other person not regarded by the law as competent to administer it for himself. The title was also applied to a variety of public officers in Roman administrative law.

In Scotch law. The term means a guardian.

In Louisiana. A person appointed to take care of the estate of an absentee. Civil Code La. art. 50.

In Missouri. The term "curator" has been adopted from the civil law, and it is applied to the guardian of the estate of the ward as distinguished from the guardian of his person. 49 Mo. 117.

CURATOR AD HOC. In the civil law. A guardian for this purpose; a special guardian.

CURATOR AD LITEM. Guardian for the suit. In English law, the corresponding phrase is "guardian *ad litem.*"

CURATOR BONIS. In the civil law. A guardian or trustee appointed to take care of *property* in certain cases; as for the benefit of creditors. Dig. 42, 7.

In Scotch law. The term is applied to guardians for minors, lunatics, etc.

CURATORES VIARUM. Surveyors of the highways.

CURATORSHIP. The office of a curator. Curatorship differs from tutorship, (*q. v.,*) in this; that the latter is instituted for the protection of property in the first place, and, secondly, of the person; while the former is intended to protect, first, the person, and secondly, the property. 1 Lec. El. Dr. Civ. Rom. 241.

CURATRIX. A woman who has been appointed to the office of curator; a female guardian. 4 Grat. 227.

Curatus non habet titulum. A curate has no title, [to tithes.] 3 Bulst. 310.

CURE BY VERDICT. See AIDER BY VERDICT.

CURE OF SOULS. In ecclesiastical law. The ecclesiastical or spiritual charge of a parish, including the usual and regular duties of a minister in charge.

CURFEW. An institution supposed to have been introduced into England by order of William the Conqueror, which consisted in the ringing of a bell or bells at eight o'clock at night, at which signal the people were required to extinguish all lights in their dwellings, and to put out or rake up their fires, and retire to rest, and all companies to disperse. The word is probably derived from the French *couvre feu*, to cover the fire.

CURIA. In old European law. A court. The palace, household, or retinue of a sovereign. A judicial tribunal or court held in the sovereign's palace. A court of justice. The civil power, as distinguished from the ecclesiastical. A manor; a nobleman's house; the hall of a manor. A piece of ground attached to a house; a yard or court-yard. Spelman. A lord's court held in his manor. The tenants who did suit and service at the lord's court. A manse. Cowell.

In Roman law. A division of the Roman people, said to have been made by Romulus. They were divided into three tribes, and each tribe into ten *curiæ*, making thirty *curiæ* in all. Spelman.

The place or building in which each *curia* assembled to offer sacred rites.

The place of meeting of the Roman senate; the senate house.

The senate house of a province; the place where the *decuriones* assembled. Cod. 10, 31, 2. See DECURIO.

CURIA ADMIRALITATIS. The court of admiralty.

CURIA ADVISARI VULT. L. Lat. The court will advise; the court will consider. A phrase frequently found in the reports, signifying the resolution of the court to suspend judgment in a cause, after the argument, until they have deliberated upon the question, as where there is a new or difficult point involved. It is commonly abbreviated to *cur. adv. vult*, or *c. a. v.*

CURIA BARONIS, or BARONUM. In old English law. A court-baron. Fleta, lib. 2, c. 53.

Curia cancellariæ officina justitiæ. 2 Inst. 552. The court of chancery is the workshop of justice.

CURIA CHRISTIANITATIS. The ecclesiastical court.

CURIA CLAUDENDA. The name of a writ to compel another to make a fence or wall, which he was bound to make, between his land and the plaintiff's. Reg. Orig. 155. Now obsolete.

CURIA COMITATUS. The county court, (*q. v.*)

CURIA CURSUS AQUÆ. A court held by the lord of the manor of Gravesend for the better management of barges and boats plying on the river Thames between Gravesend and Windsor, and also at Gravesend bridge, etc. 2 Geo. II. c. 26.

CURIA DOMINI. In old English law. The lord's court, house, or hall, where all the tenants met at the time of keeping court. Cowell.

CURIA LEGITIME AFFIRMATA. A phrase used in old Scotch records to show that the court was opened in due and lawful manner.

CURIA MAGNA. In old English law. The great court; one of the ancient names of parliament.

CURIA MAJORIS. In old English law. The mayor's court. Calth. 144.

CURIA MILITUM. A court so called, anciently held at Carisbrook Castle, in the Isle of Wight. Cowell.

CURIA PALATII. The palace court. It was abolished by 12 & 13 Vict. c. 101.

Curia parliamenti suis propriis legibus subsistit. 4 Inst. 50. The court of parliament is governed by its own laws.

CURIA PEDIS PULVERIZATI. In old English law. The court of *piedpoudre* or *piepouders*, (*q. v.*) 3 Bl. Comm. 32.

CURIA PENTICIARUM. A court held by the sheriff of Chester, in a place there called the "*Pendice*" or "*Pentice;*" probably it was so called from being originally held under a pent-house, or open shed covered with boards. Blount.

CURIA PERSONÆ. In old records. A parsonage-house, or manse. Cowell.

CURIA REGIS. The king's court. A term applied to the *aula regis*, the *bancus*, or *communis bancus*, and the *iter* or *eyre*, as being courts of the king, but especially to the *aula regis*, (which title see.)

CURIÆ CHRISTIANITATIS. Courts of Christianity; ecclesiastical courts.

CURIALITY. In Scotch law. Curtesy. Also the privileges, prerogatives, or, perhaps, retinue, of a court.

Curiosa et captiosa interpretatio in lege reprobatur. A curious [overnice or subtle] and captious interpretation is reprobated in law. 1 Bulst. 6.

CURNOCK. In old English law. A measure containing four bushels or half a quarter of corn. Cowell; Blount.

CURRENCY. Coined money and such bank-notes or other paper money as are authorized by law and do in fact circulate from hand to hand as the medium of exchange.

CURRENT. Running; now in transit; whatever is at present in course of passage; as "the current month." When applied to money, it means "lawful;" current money is equivalent to lawful money. 1 Dall. 124.

CURRENT FUNDS. This phrase means gold or silver, or something equivalent thereto, and convertible at pleasure into coined money. 4 Ala. 90.

CURRENT MONEY. The currency of the country; whatever is intended to and does actually circulate as currency; every species of coin or currency. 5 Lea, 96. In this phrase the adjective "current" is not synonymous with "convertible." It is employed to describe money which passes from hand to hand, from person to person, and circulates through the community, and is generally received. Money is current which is received as money in the common business transactions, and is the common medium in barter and trade. 41 Ala. 321.

CURRICULUM. The year; of the course of a year; the set of studies for a particular period, appointed by a university.

CURRIT QUATUOR PEDIBUS. L. Lat. It runs upon four feet; or, as sometimes expressed, it runs upon all fours. A phrase used in arguments to signify the entire and exact application of a case quoted. "It does not follow that they run *quatuor pedibus.*" 1 W. Bl. 145.

Currit tempus contra desides et sui juris contemptores. Time runs against the slothful and those who neglect their rights. Bract. fols. 100*b*, 101.

CURSITOR BARON. An officer of the court of exchequer, who is appointed by patent under the great seal to be one of the barons of the exchequer. The office was abolished by St. 19 & 20 Vict. c. 86.

CURSITORS. Clerks in the chancery office, whose duties consisted in drawing up those writs which were of course, *de cursu,* whence their name. They were abolished by

St. 5 & 6 Wm. IV. c. 82. Spence, Eq. Jur. 238; 4 Inst. 82.

CURSO. In old records. A ridge. *Cursones terræ,* ridges of land. Cowell.

CURSOR. An inferior officer of the papal court.

Cursus curiæ est lex curiæ. 3 Bulst. 53. The practice of the court is the law of the court.

CURTESY. The estate to which by common law a man is entitled, on the death of his wife, in the lands or tenements of which she was seised in possession in fee-simple or in tail during their coverture, provided they have had lawful issue born alive which might have been capable of inheriting the estate. It is a freehold estate for the term of his natural life. 1 Washb. Real Prop. 127; 2 Bl. Comm. 126; Co. Litt. 30*a*.

CURTEYN. The name of King Edward the Confessor's sword. It is said that the point of it was broken, as an emblem of mercy. (Mat. Par. in Hen. III.) Wharton.

CURTILAGE. The inclosed space of ground and buildings immediately surrounding a dwelling-house.

In its most comprehensive and proper legal signification, it includes all that space of ground and buildings thereon which is usually inclosed within the *general fence* immediately surrounding a principal messuage and outbuildings, and yard closely adjoining to a dwelling-house, but it may be large enough for cattle to be levant and couchant therein. 1 Chit. Gen. Pr. 175.

The curtilage of a dwelling-house is a space, necessary and convenient and habitually used for the family purposes, and the carrying on of domestic employments. It includes the garden, if there be one, and it need not be separated from other lands by fence. 31 Me. 522; 10 Cush. 480; 29 N. J. Law, 474.

The curtilage is the court-yard in the front or rear of a house, or at its side, or any piece of ground lying near, inclosed and used with, the house, and necessary for the convenient occupation of the house. 10 Hun, 154.

In Michigan the meaning of curtilage has been extended to include more than an inclosure near the house. 2 Mich. 250.

CURTILES TERRÆ. In old English law. Court lands. Cowell. See COURT LANDS.

CURTILLIUM. A curtilage; the area or space within the inclosure of a dwelling-house. Spelman.

CURTIS. A garden; a space about a house; a house, or manor; a court, or palace; a court of justice; a nobleman's residence. Spelman.

CUSSORE. A term used in Hindostan for the discount or allowance made in the exchange of rupees, in contradistinction to *batta*, which is the sum deducted. Enc. Lond.

CUSTA, CUSTAGIUM, CUSTANTIA. Costs.

CUSTODE ADMITTENDO, CUSTODE AMOVENDO. Writs for the admitting and removing of guardians.

CUSTODES. In Roman law. Guardians; observers; inspectors. Persons who acted as inspectors of elections, and who counted the votes given. Tayl. Civil Law, 193.

In old English law. Keepers; guardians; conservators.

Custodes pacis, guardians of the peace. 1 Bl. Comm. 349.

CUSTODES LIBERTATIS ANGLIÆ AUCTORITATE PARLIAMENTI. The style in which writs and all judicial processes were made out during the great revolution, from the execution of King Charles I. till Oliver Cromwell was declared protector.

CUSTODIA LEGIS. In the custody of the law.

CUSTODIAM LEASE. In English law. A grant from the crown under the exchequer seal, by which the custody of lands, etc., seised in the king's hands, is demised or committed to some person as custodee or lessee thereof. Wharton.

CUSTODY. The care and keeping of anything; as when an article is said to be "in the custody of the court." Also the detainer of a man's person by virtue of lawful process or authority; actual imprisonment. 59 Pa. St. 320.

In a sentence that the defendant "be in custody until," etc., this term imports actual imprisonment. The duty of the sheriff under such a sentence is not performed by allowing the defendant to go at large under his general watch and control, but so doing renders him liable for an escape. 59 Pa. St. 320.

CUSTOM. A usage or practice of the people, which, by common adoption and acquiescence, and by long and unvarying habit, has become compulsory, and has acquired the force of a law with respect to the place or subject-matter to which it relates.

A law not written, established by long usage, and the consent of our ancestors. Termes de la Ley; Cowell; Bract. fol. 2. If it be universal, it is common law; if particular to this or that place, it is then properly *custom.* 3 Salk. 112.

Customs result from a long series of actions constantly repeated, which have, by such repetition, and by uninterrupted acquiescence, acquired the force of a tacit and common consent. Civil Code La. art. 3.

It differs from prescription, which is personal and is annexed to the person of the owner of a particular estate; while the other is local, and relates to a particular district. An instance of the latter occurs where the question is upon the manner of conducting a particular branch of trade at a certain place; of the former, where a certain person and his ancestors, or those whose estates he has, have been entitled to a certain advantage or privilege, as to have common of pasture in a certain close, or the like. The distinction has been thus expressed: "While prescription is the making of a right, custom is the making of a law." Lawson, Usages & Cust. 15, note 2.

Customs are either *general* or *particular.* General customs are such as prevail throughout a country and become the law of the country; and their existence is to be determined by the court. Particular customs are such as prevail in some county, city, town, parish, or place. 23 Me. 90.

CUSTOM-HOUSE. In administrative law. The house or office where commodities are entered for importation or exportation; where the duties, bounties, or drawbacks payable or receivable upon such importation or exportation are paid or received; and where ships are cleared out, etc.

CUSTOM-HOUSE BROKER. One whose occupation it is, as the agent of others, to arrange entries and other custom-house papers, or transact business, at any port of entry, relating to the importation or exportation of goods, wares, or merchandise. 14 St. at Large, 117.

A person authorized by the commissioners of customs to act for parties, at their option, in the entry or clearance of ships and the transaction of general business. Wharton.

Custom is the best interpreter of the law. 4 Inst. 75; 2 Eden, 74; 5 Cranch, 32; 1 Serg. & R. 106.

CUSTOM OF MERCHANTS. A system of customs or rules relative to bills of exchange, partnership, and other mercantile matters, and which, under the name of the "*lex mercatoria,*" or "law-merchant," has been ingrafted into, and made a part of, the common law. 1 Bl. Comm. 75; 1 Steph. Comm. 54; 2 Burrows, 1226, 1228.

CUSTOM OF YORK. A custom of intestacy in the province of York similar to that of London. Abolished by 19 & 20 Vict. c. 94.

CUSTOMARY COURT-BARON. A court-baron at which copyholders might transfer their estates, and where other matters relating to their tenures were transacted. 3 Bl. Comm. 33.

CUSTOMARY ESTATES. Estates which owe their origin and existence to the custom of the manor in which they are held. 2 Bl. Comm. 149.

CUSTOMARY FREEHOLD. In English law. A variety of copyhold estate, the evidences of the title to which are to be found upon the court rolls; the entries declaring the holding to be according to the custom of the manor, but it is not said to be at the will of the lord. The incidents are similar to those of common or pure copyhold. 1 Steph. Comm. 212, 213, and note.

CUSTOMARY SERVICES. Such as are due by ancient custom or prescription only.

CUSTOMARY TENANTS. Tenants holding by custom of the manor.

Custome serra prise stricte. Custom shall be taken [is to be construed] strictly. Jenk. Cent. 83.

CUSTOMS. This term is usually applied to those taxes which are payable upon goods and merchandise imported or exported. Story, Const. § 949; Bac. Abr. "Smuggling."

The duties, toll, tribute, or tariff payable upon merchandise exported or imported. These are called "customs" from having been paid from time immemorial. Expressed in law Latin by *custuma*, as distinguished from *consuetudines*, which are usages merely. 1 Bl. Comm. 314.

CUSTOMS AND SERVICES annexed to the tenure of lands are those which the tenants thereof owe unto their lords, and which, if withheld, the lord might anciently have resorted to "a writ of customs and services" to compel them. Cowell. But at the present day he would merely proceed to eject the tenant as upon a forfeiture, or claim damages for the subtraction. Brown.

CUSTOMS CONSOLIDATION ACT. The statute 16 & 17 Vict. c. 107, which has been frequently amended. See 2 Steph. Comm. 563.

CUSTOMS OF LONDON. Particular customs within the city of London, with regard to trade, apprentices, widows, orphans, and a variety of other matters. 1 Bl. Comm. 75; 1 Steph. Comm. 54, 55.

CUSTOS. A custodian, guard, keeper, or warden; a magistrate.

CUSTOS BREVIUM. The keeper of the writs. A principal clerk belonging to the courts of queen's bench and common pleas, whose office it was to keep the writs returnable into those courts. The office was abolished by 1 Wm. IV. c. 5.

CUSTOS FERARUM. A gamekeeper. Townsh. Pl. 265.

CUSTOS HORREI REGII. Protector of the royal granary. 2 Bl. Comm. 394.

CUSTOS MARIS. In old English law. Warden of the sea. The title of a high naval officer among the Saxons and after the Conquest, corresponding with *admiral*.

CUSTOS MORUM. The guardian of morals. The court of queen's bench has been so styled. 4 Steph. Comm. 377.

CUSTOS PLACITORUM CORONÆ. In old English law. Keeper of the pleas of the crown. Bract. fol. 14b. Cowell supposes this office to have been the same with the *custos rotulorum*. But it seems rather to have been another name for "coroner." Crabb, Eng. Law, 150; Bract. fol. 136b.

CUSTOS ROTULORUM. Keeper of the rolls. An officer in England who has the custody of the rolls or records of the sessions of the peace, and also of the commission of the peace itself. He is always a justice of the quorum in the county where appointed and is the principal civil officer in the county. 1 Bl. Comm. 349; 4 Bl. Comm. 272.

CUSTOS SPIRITUALIUM. In English ecclesiastical law. Keeper of the spiritualities. He who exercises the spiritual jurisdiction of a diocese during the vacancy of the see. Cowell.

Custos statum hæredis in custodia existentis meliorem, non deteriorem, facere potest. 7 Coke, 7. A guardian can make the estate of an existing heir under his guardianship better, not worse.

CUSTOS TEMPORALIUM. In English ecclesiastical law. The person to whom a vacant see or abbey was given by the king, as supreme lord. His office was, as steward of the goods and profits, to give an account to the escheator, who did the like to the exchequer.

CUSTOS TERRÆ. In old English law. Guardian, warden, or keeper of the land.

CUSTUMA ANTIQUA SIVE MAGNA. (Lat. Ancient or great duties.) The duties on wool, sheep-skin, or wool-pelts and leather exported were so called, and were payable by every merchant, stranger as well as native, with the exception that merchant strangers paid one-half as much again as natives. 1 Bl. Comm. 314.

CUSTUMA PARVA ET NOVA. (Small and new customs.) Imposts of 3d. in the pound, due formerly in England from merchant strangers only, for all commodities, as well imported as exported. This was usually called the "aliens duty," and was first granted in 31 Edw. I. 1 Bl. Comm. 314; 4 Inst. 29.

CUT. A wound made with a sharp instrument.

CUTCHERRY. In Hindu law. Corrupted from *Kachari.* A court; a hall; an office; the place where any public business is transacted.

CUTH, COUTH. Sax. Known, knowing. *Uncuth,* unknown. See COUTHUTLAUGH, UNCUTH.

CUTHRED. A knowing or skillful counsellor.

CUTPURSE. One who steals by the method of cutting purses; a common practice when men wore their purses at their girdles, as was once the custom. Wharton.

CUTTER OF THE TALLIES. In old English law. An officer in the exchequer, to whom it belonged to provide wood for the tallies, and to cut the sum paid upon them, etc.

CUTWAL, KATWAL. The chief officer of police or superintendent of markets in a large town or city in India.

CWT. A hundred-weight; one hundred and twelve pounds. 11 B. Mon. 64.

CY. In law French. Here. (*Cy-apres,* hereafter; *cy-devant,* heretofore.) Also as, so.

CYCLE. A measure of time; a space in which the same revolutions begin again; a periodical space of time. Enc. Lond.

CYNE-BOT, or CYNE-GILD. The portion belonging to the nation of the mulct for slaying the king, the other portion or *were* being due to his family. Blount.

CYNEBOTE. A mulct anciently paid by one who killed another, to the kindred of the deceased. Spelman.

CYPHONISM. That kind of punishment used by the ancients, and still used by the Chinese, called by Staunton the "wooden collar," by which the neck of the malefactor is bent or weighed down. Enc. Lond.

CY-PRES. As near as [possible.] The rule of *cy-pres* is a rule for the construction of instruments in equity, by which the intention of the party is carried out *as near as may be,* when it would be impossible or illegal to give it literal effect. Thus, where a testator attempts to create a perpetuity, the court will endeavor, instead of making the devise entirely void, to explain the will in such a way as to carry out the testator's general intention as far as the rule against perpetuities will allow. So in the case of bequests to charitable uses; and particularly where the language used is so vague or uncertain that the testator's design must be sought by construction. See 6 Cruise, Dig. 165; 1 Spence, Eq. Jur. 532; 3 Hare, 12.

CYRCE. In Saxon law. A church.

CYRICBRYCE. In Saxon law. A breaking into a church. Blount.

CYRICSCEAT. (From *cyric,* church, and *sceat,* a tribute.) In Saxon law. A tribute or payment due to the church. Cowell.

CYROGRAPHARIUS. In old English law. A cyrographer; an officer of the *bancus,* or court of common bench. Fleta, lib. 2, c. 36.

CYROGRAPHUM. A chirograph, (which see.)

CZAR. The title of the emperor of Russia, first assumed by Basil, the son of Basilides, under whom the Russian power began to appear, about 1740.

CZARINA. The title of the empress of Russia.

CZAROWITZ. The title of the eldest son of the czar and czarina.

D.

D. The fourth letter of the English alphabet. It is used as an abbreviation for a number of words, the more important and usual of which are as follows:

1. *Digestum,* or *Digesta,* that is, the Digest or Pandects in the Justinian collections of the civil law. Citations to this work are sometimes indicated by this abbreviation, but more commonly by "Dig."

2. *Dictum.* A remark or observation, as in the phrase "*obiter dictum,*" (*q. v.*)

3. *Demissione.* "On the demise." An action of ejectment is entitled "Doe *d.* Stiles v. Roe;" that is, "Doe, on the demise of Stiles, against Roe."

4. "*Doctor.*" As in the abbreviated forms of certain academical degrees. "M. D.," "doctor of medicine;" "LL.D.," "doctor of laws;" "D. C. L.," "doctor of civil law."

5. "*District.*" Thus, "U. S. Cir. Ct. W. *D.* Pa." stands for "United States Circuit Court for the Western *District* of Pennsylvania."

6. "*Dialogue.*" Used only in citations to the work called "Doctor and Student."

D. In the Roman system of notation, this letter stands for five hundred; and, when a horizontal dash or stroke is placed above it, it denotes five thousand.

D. B. E. An abbreviation for *de bene esse,* (*q. v.*)

D. B. N. An abbreviation for *de bonis non;* descriptive of a species of administration.

D. C. An abbreviation standing either for "District Court" or "District of Columbia."

D. E. R. I. C. An abbreviation used for *De ea re ita censuere,* (concerning that matter have so decreed,) in recording the decrees of the Roman senate. Tayl. Civil Law, 564, 566.

D. J. An abbreviation for "District Judge."

D. P. An abbreviation for *Domus Procerum,* the house of lords.

D. S. An abbreviation for "Deputy Sheriff."

D. S. B. An abbreviation for *debitum sine brevi,* or *debit sans breve.*

Da tua dum tua sunt, post mortem tunc tua non sunt. 3 Bulst. 18. Give the things which are yours whilst they are yours; after death they are not yours.

DABIS? DABO. Lat. (Will you give? I will give.) In the Roman law. One of the forms of making a verbal stipulation. Inst. 3, 15, 1; Bract. fol. 15*b.*

DACION. In Spanish law. The real and effective delivery of an object in the execution of a contract.

DAGGE. A kind of gun. 1 How. State Tr. 1124, 1125.

DAGUS, or DAIS. The raised floor at the upper end of a hall.

DAILY. Every day; every day in the week; every day in the week except one. A newspaper which is published six days in each week is a "daily" newspaper. 45 Cal. 30.

DAKER, or DIKER. Ten hides. Blount.

DALE and SALE. Fictitious names of places, used in the English books, as examples. "The manor of *Dale* and the manor of *Sale,* lying both in Vale."

DALUS, DAILUS, DAILIA. A certain measure of land; such narrow slips of pasture as are left between the plowed furrows in arable land. Cowell.

DAM. A construction of wood, stone, or other materials, made across a stream for the purpose of penning back the waters.

This word is used in two different senses. It properly means the work or structure, raised to obstruct the flow of the water in a river; but, by a well-settled usage, it is often applied to designate the pond of water created by this obstruction. 19 N. J. Eq. 248. See, also, 44 N. H. 78.

DAMAGE. Loss, injury, or deterioration, caused by the negligence, design, or accident of one person to another, in respect of the latter's person or property. The word is to be distinguished from its plural,—"damages,"—which means a compensation in money for a loss or damage.

An injury produces a right in them who have suffered any damage by it to demand reparation of such damage from the authors of the injury. By damage, we understand every loss or diminution of what is a man's own, occasioned by the fault of another. 1 Ruth. Inst. 399.

DAMAGE-CLEER. A fee assessed of the tenth part in the common pleas, and the twentieth part in the queen's bench and exchequer, out of all damages exceeding five marks recovered in those courts, in actions upon the case, covenant, trespass, etc., wherein the damages were uncertain; which the plaintiff was obliged to pay to the prothonotary or the officer of the court wherein he recovered, before he could have execution for the damages. This was originally a gratuity given to the prothonotaries and their clerks for drawing special writs and pleadings; but it was taken away by statute, since which, if any officer in these courts took any money in the name of damage-cleer, or anything in lieu thereof, he forfeited treble the value. Wharton.

DAMAGE FEASANT or FAISANT. Doing damage. A term applied to a person's cattle or beasts found upon another's land, doing damage by treading down the grass, grain, etc. 3 Bl. Comm. 7, 211; Tomlins. This phrase seems to have been introduced in the reign of Edward III., in place of the older expression *"en son damage,"* (*in damno suo.*) Crabb, Eng. Law, 292.

DAMAGED GOODS. Goods, subject to duties, which have received some injury either in the voyage home or while bonded in warehouse.

DAMAGES. A pecuniary compensation or indemnity, which may be recovered in the courts by any person who has suffered loss, detriment, or injury, whether to his person, property, or rights, through the unlawful act or omission or negligence of another.

A sum of money assessed by a jury, on finding for the plaintiff or successful party in an action, as a compensation for the injury done him by the opposite party. 2 Bl. Comm. 438; Co. Litt. 257a; 2 Tidd, Pr. 869, 870.

Every person who suffers detriment from the unlawful act or omission of another may recover from the person in fault a compensation therefor in money, which is called "damages." Civil Code Cal. § 3281; Civil Code Dak. § 1940.

In the ancient usage, the word "damages" was employed in two significations. According to Coke, its proper and general sense included the costs of suit, while its strict or relative sense was exclusive of costs. 10 Coke, 116, 117; Co. Litt. 257a; 9 East, 299. The latter meaning has alone survived.

Damages are either *general* or *special.* Damages for losses which necessarily result from the wrong sued for are called "general" damages, and may be shown under the *ad damnum*, or general allegation of damage; for the defendant does not need notice of such consequences to enable him to make his defense; he knows that they must exist, and will be in evidence. But if certain losses do not necessarily result from defendant's wrongful act, but, in fact, follow it as a natural and proximate consequence in the particular case, they are called "special," and must be specially alleged, that the defendant may have notice and be prepared to go into the inquiry. 28 Conn. 201, 212.

"General" damages are such as the law presumes to flow from any tortious act, and may be recovered without proof of any amount. "Special" damages are such as actually flowed from the act, and must be proved in order to be recovered. Code Ga. 1882, § 3070.

Damages may also be classed as *direct* and *consequential.* "Direct" damages are such as follow immediately upon the act done. "Consequential" damages are such as are the necessary and connected effect of the tortious act, though to some extent depending upon other circumstances. Code Ga. 1882, § 3071.

Another division of damages is into *liquidated* and *unliquidated;* the former term being applicable when the amount thereof has been ascertained by the judgment in the action or by the specific agreement of the parties; while the latter denotes such damages as are not yet reduced to a certainty in respect of amount, nothing more being established than the plaintiff's right to recover.

Damages are also either *nominal* or *substantial;* the former being trifling in amount, and not awarded as compensation for any injury, but merely in recognition of plaintiff's right and its technical infraction by defendant; while the latter are considerable in amount, and intended as real compensation for a real injury

Damages are either *compensatory* or *vindictive;* the former when nothing more is allowed than a just and exact equivalent for plaintiff's loss or injury; the latter when a greater sum is given than amounts to mere compensation, in order to punish the defendant for violence, outrage, or other circumstances of aggravation attending the transaction. Vindictive damages are also called "exemplary" or "punitive."

DAMAGES ULTRA. Additional damages claimed by a plaintiff not satisfied with those paid into court by the defendant.

DAMAIOUSE. In old English law. Causing damage or loss, as distinguished from *torcenouse*, wrongful. Britt. c. 61.

DAME. In English law. The legal designation of the wife of a knight or baronet.

DAMNA. Damages, both inclusive and exclusive of costs.

DAMNATUS. In old English law. Condemned; prohibited by law; unlawful. *Damnatus coitus*, an unlawful connection.

DAMNI INJURIÆ ACTIO. An action given by the civil law for the damage done by one who intentionally injured the slave or beast of another. Calvin.

DAMNIFICATION. That which causes damage or loss.

DAMNIFY. To cause damage or injurious loss to a person.

DAMNOSA HÆREDITAS. In the civil law. A losing inheritance; an inheritance that was a charge, instead of a benefit. Dig. 50, 16, 119.

The term has also been applied to that species of property of a bankrupt which, so far from being valuable, would be a charge to the creditors; for example, a term of years where the rent would exceed the revenue. 7 East, 342; 3 Camp. 340; 1 Esp. N. P. 234.

DAMNUM. Lat. In the civil law. Damage; the loss or diminution of what is a man's own, either by fraud, carelessness, or accident.

In pleading and old English law. Damage; loss.

DAMNUM ABSQUE INJURIA. A loss which does not give rise to an action of damages against the person causing it; as where a person blocks up the windows of a new house overlooking his land, or injures a person's trade by setting up an establishment of the same kind in the neighborhood. Broom, Com. Law, 75.

DAMNUM FATALE. In the civil law. Fatal damage; damage from fate; loss happening from a cause beyond human control, (*quod ex fato contingit*,) or an act of God, and for which bailees are not liable; such as shipwreck, lightning, and the like. Dig. 4, 9, 3, 1; Story, Bailm. § 465.

The civilians included in the phrase "*damnum fatale*" all those accidents which are summed up in the common-law expression, "Act of God or public enemies;" though, perhaps, it embraced some which would not now be admitted as occurring from an irresistible force. 8 Blackf. 535.

DAMNUM INFECTUM. In Roman law. Damage not yet committed, but threatened or impending. A preventive interdict might be obtained to prevent such damage from happening; and it was treated as a *quasi-delict*, because of the imminence of the danger.

DAMNUM REI AMISSÆ. In the civil law. A loss arising from a payment made by a party in consequence of an error of law. Mackeld. Rom. Law, § 178.

Damnum sine injuriâ esse potest. Lofft, 112. There may be damage or injury inflicted without any act of injustice.

DAN. Anciently the better sort of men in England had this title; so the Spanish *Don*. The old term of honor for men, as we now say Master or Mister. Wharton.

DANEGELT, DANEGELD. A tribute of 1s. and afterwards of 2s. upon every hide of land through the realm, levied by the Anglo-Saxons, for maintaining such a number of forces as were thought sufficient to clear the British seas of Danish pirates, who greatly annoyed their coasts. It continued a tax until the time of Stephen, and was one of the rights of the crown. Wharton.

DANELAGE. A system of laws introduced by the Danes on their invasion and conquest of England, and which was principally maintained in some of the midland counties, and also on the eastern coast. 1 Bl. Comm. 65; 4 Bl. Comm. 411; 1 Steph. Comm. 42.

DANGERIA. In old English law. A money payment made by forest-tenants, that they might have liberty to plow and sow in time of pannage, or mast feeding.

DANGEROUS WEAPON. One dangerous to life; one by the use of which a fatal wound may probably or possibly be given. As the manner of use enters into the consideration as well as other circumstances, the question is for the jury.

DANGERS OF THE RIVER. This phrase, as used in bills of lading, means only the natural accidents incident to river navigation, and does not embrace such as may be avoided by the exercise of that skill, judgment, or foresight which are demanded from persons in a particular occupation. 35 Mo. 213. It includes dangers arising from unknown reefs which have suddenly formed in the channel, and are not discoverable by care and skill. 17 Fed. Rep. 478.

E

F

G

H

I

J

K

L

M

DANGERS OF THE ROAD. This phrase, in a bill of lading, when it refers to inland transportation, means such dangers as are immediately caused by roads, as the overturning of carriages in rough and precipitous places. 7 Exch. 743.

DANGERS OF THE SEA. The expression "dangers of the sea" means those accidents peculiar to navigation that are of an extraordinary nature, or arise from irresistible force or overwhelming power, which cannot be guarded against by the ordinary exertions of human skill and prudence. 32 J. Law, 320.

The expression is equivocal. It is capable of being interpreted to mean all dangers that arise upon the seas; or may be restricted to perils which arise directly and exclusively from the sea, or of which it is the efficient cause. In insurance policies, it may have the wider meaning; but in charter-parties, an exception, introduced to limit the obligation of the charterer to return the vessel, of dangers of the seas, should be construed, since the charterer has possession, against him, and confined to the limited sense. Thus construed, it does not include destruction of the vessel by fire. 3 Ware, 215, 2 Curt. 8.

DANISM. The act of lending money on usury.

DANO. In Spanish law. Damage; the deterioration, injury, or destruction which a man suffers with respect to his person or his property by the fault (*culpa*) of another. White, New Recop. b. 2, tit. 19, c. 3, § 1.

Dans et retinens, nihil dat. One who gives and yet retains does not give effectually. Tray. Lat. Max. 129. Or, one who gives, yet retains, [possession,] gives nothing.

DAPIFER. A steward either of a king or lord. Spelman.

DARE. In the civil law. To transfer property. When this transfer is made in order to discharge a debt, it is *datio solvendi animo;* when in order to receive an equivalent, to create an obligation, it is *datio contrahendi animo;* lastly, when made *donandi animo,* from mere liberality, it is a gift, *dono datio.*

DARE AD REMANENTIAM. To give away in fee, or forever.

DARRAIGN. To clear a legal account; to answer an accusation; to settle a controversy.

DARREIN. L. Fr. Last.

DARREIN CONTINUANCE. L. Fr. In practice. The last continuance.

DARREIN PRESENTMENT. L. Fr. In old English law. The last presentment. See ASSISE OF DARREIN PRESENTMENT.

DARREIN SEISIN. (L. Fr. Last seisin.) A plea which lay in some cases for the tenant in a writ of right. See 1 Rosc. Real Act. 206.

DATA. In old practice and conveyancing. The date of a deed; the time when it was *given;* that is, executed.

Grounds whereon to proceed; facts from which to draw a conclusion.

DATE. The specification or mention, in a written instrument, of the time (day and year) when it was made. Also the time so specified.

That part of a deed or writing which expresses the day of the month and year in which it was made or *given.* 2 Bl. Comm. 304; Tomlins.

The primary signification of *date* is not time in the abstract, nor time taken absolutely, but time given or specified; time in some way ascertained and fixed. When we speak of the date of a deed, we do not mean the time when it was actually executed, but the time of its execution, as given or stated in the deed itself. The date of an item, or of a charge in a book-account, is not necessarily the time when the article charged was, in fact, furnished, but rather the time given or set down in the account, in connection with such charge. And so the expression "the date of the last work done, or materials furnished," in a mechanic's lien law, may be taken, in the absence of anything in the act indicating a different intention, to mean the time when such work was done or materials furnished, as specified in the plaintiff's written claim. 32 N. J. Law, 513.

DATE CERTAINE. In French law. A deed is said to have a *date certaine* (fixed date) when it has been subjected to the formality of registration; after this formality has been complied with, the parties to the deed cannot by mutual consent change the date thereof. Arg. Fr. Merc. Law, 555.

DATIO. In the civil law. A giving, or act of giving. *Datio in solutum;* a giving in payment; a species of accord and satisfaction. Called, in modern law, "dation."

DATION. In the civil law. A gift; a giving of something. It is not exactly synonymous with "donation," for the latter implies generosity or liberality in making a gift, while dation may mean the giving of something to which the recipient is already entitled.

DATION EN PAIEMENT. In French law. A giving by the debtor and receipt by the creditor of something in payment of a debt, instead of a sum of money.

It is somewhat like the accord and satisfaction of the common law. 16 Toullier, no. 45; Poth. Vente, no. 601.

DATIVE. A word derived from the Roman law, signifying "appointed by public authority." Thus, in Scotland, an executor-dative is an executor appointed by a court of justice, corresponding to an English *administrator*. Mozley & Whitley.

In old English law. In one's gift; that may be given and disposed of at will and pleasure.

DATUM. A first principle; a thing given; a date.

DATUR DIGNIORI. It is given to the more worthy. 2 Vent. 268.

DAUGHTER. An immediate female descendant.

DAUGHTER-IN-LAW. The wife of one's son.

DAUPHIN. In French law. The title of the eldest sons of the kings of France. Disused since 1830.

DAY. A period of time consisting of twenty-four hours, and including the solar day and the night. Co. Litt. 135a; Bract. fol. 264.

The space of time which elapses between two successive midnights. 2 Bl. Comm. 141.

That portion of time during which the sun is above the horizon, (called, sometimes, a "solar" day,) and, in addition, that part of the morning or evening during which sufficient of his light is above for the features of a man to be reasonably discerned. 3 Inst. 63; 9 Mass. 154.

The term may also denote an artificial period of time, computed from one fixed point to another twenty-four hours later, without any reference to the prevalence of light or darkness.

The word is sometimes used, in jurisprudence, in its astronomical sense of the space of time in which the earth makes one revolution upon its axis; or of the time between one midnight and the next; sometimes, in the popular sense, of the time between sunrise and sunset; and sometimes, in a conventional sense, of those hours or that recurring time which is by usage or law allotted to and deemed sufficient for the discharge of some duty or performance of some business; as where one speaks of a day's work, the whole of a business day, etc. Abbott.

In practice and pleading. A particular time assigned or given for the appearance of parties in court, the return of writs, etc. See DAYS IN BANK.

The whole of a term of court is considered as one day; and, by a legal fiction, the time between the submission and decision of a cause is also considered as but one day; so that, although a party to an action may die between the time of the decision in the cause by the supreme court of a state and the filing of the mandate of the supreme court of the United States reversing that decision, no change of parties in the state court is necessary before carrying the mandate into effect. 18 Ark. 653.

DAY-BOOK. A tradesman's account book; a book in which all the occurrences of the day are set down. It is usually a book of original entries.

DAYERIA. A dairy. Cowell.

DAYLIGHT. That portion of time before sunrise, and after sunset, which is accounted part of the day, (as distinguished from *night*,) in defining the offense of burglary. 4 Bl. Comm. 224; Cro. Jac. 106.

DAY-RULE, or DAY-WRIT. In English law. A permission granted to a prisoner to go out of prison, for the purpose of transacting his business, as to hear a case in which he is concerned at the assizes, etc. Abolished by 5 & 6 Vict. c. 22, § 12.

DAYS IN BANK. (L. Lat. *dies in banco*.) In practice. Certain stated days in term appointed for the appearance of parties, the return of process, etc., originally peculiar to the court of common bench, or bench, (bank,) as it was anciently called. 3 Bl. Comm. 277.

DAYS OF GRACE. A number of days allowed, as a matter of favor or *grace*, to a person who has to perform some act, or make some payment, after the time originally limited for the purpose has elapsed.

In old practice. Three days allowed to persons summoned in the English courts, beyond the day named in the writ, to make their appearance; the last day being called the "*quarto die post.*" 3 Bl. Comm. 278.

In mercantile law. A certain number of days (generally three) allowed to the maker or acceptor of a bill, draft, or note, in which to make payment, after the expiration of the time expressed in the paper itself. Originally these days were granted only as a matter of *grace* or favor, but the allowance of them became an established custom of merchants, and was sanctioned by the courts, (and in some cases prescribed by statute,) so that they are now demandable as of right.

DAYSMAN. An arbitrator, umpire, or elected judge. Cowell.

DAY-TIME. The time during which there is the light of day, as distinguished from night or night-time. That portion of the twenty-four hours during which a man's person and countenance are distinguishable. 9 Mass. 154; 1 Car. & P. 297.

In law, this term is chiefly used in the definition of certain crimes, as to which it is material whether the act was committed by day or by night.

DAYWERE. In old English law. A term applied to land, and signifying as much arable ground as could be plowed up in one day's work. Cowell.

DE. A Latin preposition, signifying of; by; from; out of; affecting; concerning; respecting.

DE ACQUIRENDO RERUM DOMINIO. Of (about) acquiring the ownership of things. Dig. 41, 1; Bract. lib. 2, fol. 8b.

DE ADMENSURATIONE. Of admeasurement. Thus, *de admensuratione dotis* was a writ for the admeasurement of dower, and *de admensuratione pasturæ* was a writ for the admeasurement of pasture.

DE ADVISAMENTO CONSILII NOSTRI. L. Lat. With or by the advice of our council. A phrase used in the old writs of summons to parliament. Crabb, Eng. Law, 240.

DE ÆQUITATE. In equity. *De jure stricto, nihil possum vendicare, de æquitate tamen, nullo modo hoc obtinet;* in strict law, I can claim nothing, but in equity this by no means obtains. Fleta, lib. 3, c. 2, § 10.

DE ÆSTIMATO. In Roman law. One of the innominate contracts, and, in effect, a sale of land or goods at a price fixed, (*æstimato,*) and guarantied by some third party, who undertook to find a purchaser.

DE ÆTATE PROBANDA. For proving age. A writ which formerly lay to summon a jury in order to determine the age of the heir of a tenant *in capite* who claimed his estate as being of full age. Fitzh. Nat. Brev. 257; Reg. Orig. 294.

DE ALEATORIBUS. About gamesters. The name of a title in the Pandects. Dig. 11, 5.

DE ALLOCATIONE FACIENDA, *Breve.* Writ for making an allowance. An old writ directed to the lord treasurer and barons of the exchequer, for allowing certain officers (as collectors of customs) in their accounts certain payments made by them. Reg. Orig. 192.

DE ALTO ET BASSO. Of high and low. A phrase anciently used to denote the absolute submission of all differences to arbitration. Cowell.

DE AMBITU. Lat. Concerning bribery. A phrase descriptive of the subject-matter of several of the Roman laws; as the *Lex Aufidia,* the *Lex Pompeia,* the *Lex Tullia,* and others. See AMBITUS.

DE AMPLIORI GRATIA. Of more abundant or especial grace. Townsh. Pl. 18.

DE ANNO BISSEXTILI. Of the bissextile or leap year. The title of a statute passed in the twenty-first year of Henry III., which in fact, however, is nothing more than a sort of writ or direction to the justices of the bench, instructing them how the extraordinary day in the leap year was to be reckoned in cases where persons had a day to appear at the distance of a year, as on the essoin *de malo lecti,* and the like. It was thereby directed that the additional day should, together with that which went before, be reckoned only as one, and so, of course, within the preceding year. 1 Reeve, Eng. Law, 266.

DE ANNUA PENSIONE, *Breve.* Writ of annual pension. An ancient writ by which the king, having a yearly pension due him out of an abbey or priory for any of his chaplains, demanded the same of the abbot or prior, for the person named in the writ. Reg. Orig. 265b, 307; Fitzh. Nat. Brev. 231 G.

DE ANNUO REDITU. For a yearly rent. A writ to recover an annuity, no matter how payable, in goods or money. 2 Reeve, Eng. Law, 258.

DE APOSTATA CAPIENDO, *Breve.* Writ for taking an apostate. A writ which anciently lay against one who, having entered and professed some order of religion, left it and wandered up and down the country, contrary to the rules of his order, commanding the sheriff to apprehend him and deliver him again to his abbot or prior. Reg. Orig. 71b, 267; Fitzh. Nat. Brev. 233, 234.

DE ARBITRATIONE FACTA. (Lat. Of arbitration had.) A writ formerly used when an action was brought for a cause which had been settled by arbitration. Wats. Arb. 256.

DE ARRESTANDIS BONIS NE DISSIPENTUR. An old writ which lay to seize goods in the hands of a party during the pendency of a suit, to prevent their being made away with. Reg. Orig. 126*b*.

DE ARRESTANDO IPSUM QUI PECUNIAM RECEPIT. A writ which lay for the arrest of one who had taken the king's money to serve in the war, and hid himself to escape going. Reg. Orig. 24*b*.

DE ARTE ET PARTE. Of art and part. A phrase in old Scotch law.

DE ASPORTATIS RELIGIOSORUM. Concerning the property of religious persons carried away. The title of the statute 35 Edward I. passed to check the abuses of clerical possessions, one of which was the waste they suffered by being drained into foreign countries. 2 Reeve, Eng. Law, 157; 2 Inst. 580.

DE ASSISA PROROGANDA. (Lat. For proroguing assise.) A writ to put off an assise, issuing to the justices, where one of the parties is engaged in the service of the king.

DE ATTORNATO RECIPIENDO. A writ which lay to the judges of a court, requiring them to receive and admit an attorney for a party. Reg. Orig. 172; Fitzh. Nat. Brev. 156.

DE AUDIENDO ET TERMINANDO. For hearing and determining; to hear and determine. The name of a writ, or rather commission granted to certain justices to hear and determine cases of heinous misdemeanor, trespass, riotous breach of the peace, etc. Reg. Orig. 123, et seq.; Fitzh. Nat. Brev. 110 B. See OYER AND TERMINER.

DE AVERIIS CAPTIS IN WITHERNAMIUM. Writ for taking cattle in withernam. A writ which lay where the sheriff returned to a *pluries* writ of replevin that the cattle or goods, etc., were eloined, etc.; by which he was commanded to take the cattle of the defendant in withernam, (or reprisal,) and detain them until he could replevy the other cattle. Reg. Orig. 82; Fitzh. Nat. Brev. 73, E. F. See WITHERNAM.

DE AVERIIS REPLEGIANDIS. A writ to replevy beasts. 3 Bl. Comm. 149.

AM. DICT. LAW—21

DE AVERIIS RETORNANDIS. For returning the cattle. A term applied to pledges given in the old action of replevin. 2 Reeve, Eng. Law, 177.

DE BANCO. Of the bench. A term formerly applied in England to the justices of the court of common pleas, or "bench," as it was originally styled.

DE BENE ESSE. Conditionally; provisionally; in anticipation of future need. A phrase applied to proceedings which are taken *ex parte* or provisionally, and are allowed to stand as *well done* for the present, but which may be subject to future exception or challenge, and must then stand or fall according to their intrinsic merit and regularity.

Thus, "in certain cases, the courts will allow evidence to be taken out of the regular course, in order to prevent the evidence being lost by the death or the absence of the witness. This is called 'taking evidence *de bene esse*,' and is looked upon as a temporary and conditional examination, to be used only in case the witness cannot afterwards be examined in the suit in the regular way." Hunt, Eq. 75; Haynes, Eq. 183; Mitf. Eq. Pl. 52, 149.

DE BIEN ET DE MAL. L. Fr. For good and evil. A phrase by which a party accused of a crime anciently put himself upon a jury, indicating his entire submission to their verdict.

DE BIENS LE MORT. L. Fr. Of the goods of the deceased. Dyer, 32.

DE BIGAMIS. Concerning men twice married. The title of the statute 4 Edw. I. St. 3; so called from the initial words of the fifth chapter. 2 Inst. 272; 2 Reeve, Eng. Law, 142.

DE BONE MEMORIE. L. Fr. Of good memory; of sound mind. 2 Inst. 510.

DE BONIS ASPORTATIS. For goods taken away; for taking away goods. The action of trespass for taking personal property is technically called "trespass *de bonis asportatis*." 1 Tidd, Pr. 5.

DE BONIS NON. An abbreviation of *De bonis non administratis,* (*q. v.*) 1 Strange, 34.

DE BONIS NON ADMINISTRATIS. Of the goods not administered. When an administrator is appointed to succeed another, who has left the estate partially unsettled, he is said to be granted "administration *de bonis non;*" that is, of the goods not already administered.

DE BONIS NON AMOVENDIS. Writ for not removing goods. A writ anciently directed to the sheriffs of London, commanding them, in cases where a writ of error was brought by a defendant against whom a judgment was recovered, to see that his *goods* and chattels were safely kept *without being removed*, while the error remained undetermined, so that execution might be had of them, etc. Reg. Orig. 131*b;* Termes de la Ley.

DE BONIS PROPRIIS. Of his own goods. The technical name of a judgment against an administrator or executor to be satisfied from his own property, and not from the estate of the deceased, as in cases where he has been guilty of a *devastavit* or of a false plea of *plene administravit.*

DE BONIS TESTATORIS, or IN-TESTATI. Of the goods of the testator, or intestate. A term applied to a judgment awarding execution against the property of a testator or intestate, as distinguished from the individual property of his executor or administrator. 2 Archb. Pr. K. B. 148, 149.

DE BONIS TESTATORIS AC SI. (Lat. From the goods of the testator, *if he has any,* and, if *not, from those of the executor.*) A judgment rendered where an executor falsely pleads any matter as a release, or, generally, in any case where he is to be charged in case his testator's estate is insufficient. 1 Williams' Saund. 336*b;* Bac. Abr. "Executor," B, 3; 2 Archb. Pr. K. B. 148.

DE BONO ET MALO. "For good and ill." The Latin form of the law French phrase "*De bien et de mal.*" In ancient criminal pleading, this was the expression with which the prisoner put himself upon a jury, indicating his absolute submission to their verdict.

This was also the name of the special writ of jail delivery formerly in use in England, which issued for each particular prisoner, of course. It was superseded by the general commission of jail delivery.

DE BONO GESTU. For good behavior; for good abearance.

DE CÆTERO. Henceforth.

DE CALCETO REPARANDO. Writ for repairing a causeway. An old writ by which the sheriff was commanded to distrain the inhabitants of a place to repair and maintain a causeway, etc. Reg. Orig. 154.

DE CAPITALIBUS DOMINIS FEO-DI. Of the chief lords of the fee.

DE CAPITE MINUTIS. Of those who have lost their *status,* or civil condition. Dig. 4, 5. The name of a title in the Pandects. See CAPITIS DEMINUTIO.

DE CARTIS REDDENDIS. (For restoring charters.) A writ to secure the delivery of charters or deeds; a writ of detinue. Reg. Orig. 159*b.*

DE CATALLIS REDDENDIS. (For restoring chattels.) A writ to secure the return specifically of chattels detained from the owner. Cowell.

DE CAUTIONE ADMITTENDA. Writ to take caution or security. A writ which anciently lay against a bishop who held an excommunicated person in prison for his contempt, notwithstanding he had offered sufficient security (*idoneam cautionem*) to obey the commands of the church; commanding him to take such security and release the prisoner. Reg. Orig. 66; Fitzh. Nat. Brev. 63, C.

DE CERTIFICANDO. A writ requiring a thing to be certified. A kind of *certiorari.* Reg. Orig. 151, 152.

DE CERTIORANDO. A writ for certifying. A writ directed to the sheriff, requiring him to certify to a particular fact. Reg. Orig. 24.

DE CHAMPERTIA. Writ of champerty. A writ directed to the justices of the bench, commanding the enforcement of the statute of *champertors.* Reg. Orig. 183; Fitzh. Nat. Brev. 172.

DE CHAR ET DE SANK. L. Fr. Of flesh and blood. *Affaire rechat de char et de sank.* Words used in claiming a person to be a villein, in the time of Edward II. Y. B. P. 1 Edw. II. p. 4.

DE CHIMINO. A writ for the enforcement of a right of way. Reg. Orig. 155.

DE CIBARIIS UTENDIS. Of victuals to be used. The title of a sumptuary statute passed 10 Edw. III. St. 3, to restrain the expense of entertainments. Barring. Ob. St. 240.

DE CLAMIA ADMITTENDA IN ITINERE PER ATTORNATUM. See CLAMIA ADMITTENDA, etc.

DE CLARO DIE. By daylight. Fleta, lib. 2, c. 76, § 8.

DE CLAUSO FRACTO. Of close broken; of breach of close. See CLAUSUM FREGIT.

DE CLERICO ADMITTENDO. See ADMITTENDO CLERICO.

DE CLERICO CAPTO PER STATUTUM MERCATORIUM DELIBERANDO. Writ for delivering a clerk arrested on a statute merchant. A writ for the delivery of a clerk out of prison, who had been taken and imprisoned upon the breach of a statute merchant. Reg. Orig. 147b.

DE CLERICO CONVICTO DELIBERANDO. See CLERICO CONVICTO, etc.

DE CLERICO INFRA SACROS ORDINES CONSTITUTO NON ELIGENDO IN OFFICIUM. See CLERICO INFRA SACROS, etc.

DE CLERO. Concerning the clergy. The title of the statute 25 Edw. III. St. 3; containing a variety of provisions on the subject of presentations, indictments of spiritual persons, and the like. 2 Reeve, Eng. Law, 378.

DE COMBUSTIONE DOMORUM. Of house burning. One of the kinds of appeal formerly in use in England. Bract. fol. 146b; 2 Reeve, Eng. Law, 38.

DE COMMUNI DIVIDUNDO. For dividing a thing held in common. The name of an action given by the civil law. Mackeld. Rom. Law, § 499.

DE COMON DROIT. L. Fr. Of common right; that is, by the common law. Co. Litt. 142a.

DE COMPUTO. Writ of account. A writ commanding a defendant to render a reasonable account to the plaintiff, or show cause to the contrary. Reg. Orig. 135–138; Fitzh. Nat. Brev. 117, E. The foundation of the modern action of account.

DE CONCILIO CURIÆ. By the advice (or direction) of the court.

DE CONFLICTU LEGUM. Concerning the conflict of laws. The title of several works written on that subject. 2 Kent, Comm. 455.

DE CONJUNCTIM FEOFFATIS. Concerning persons jointly enfeoffed, or seised. The title of the statute 34 Edw. I., which was passed to prevent the delay occasioned by tenants in novel disseisin, and other writs, pleading that some one else was seised jointly with them. 2 Reeve, Eng. Law, 243.

DE CONSANGUINEO, and DE CONSANGUINITATE. Writs of cosinage, (q. v.)

DE CONSILIO. In old criminal law. Of counsel; concerning counsel or advice to commit a crime. Fleta, lib. 1, c. 31, § 8.

DE CONSILIO CURIÆ. By the advice or direction of the court. Bract. fol. 345b.

DE CONTINUANDO ASSISAM. Writ to continue an assise. Reg. Orig. 217b.

DE CONTUMACE CAPIENDO. Writ for taking a contumacious person. A writ which issues out of the English court of chancery, in cases where a person has been pronounced by an ecclesiastical court to be contumacious, and in contempt. Shelf. Mar. & Div. 494–496, and notes. It is a commitment for contempt. Id.

DE COPIA LIBELLI DELIBERANDA. Writ for delivering the copy of a libel. An ancient writ directed to the judge of a spiritual court, commanding him to *deliver* to a defendant a *copy* of the libel filed against him in such court. Reg. Orig. 58. The writ in the register is directed to the Dean of the Arches, and his commissary. Id.

DE CORONATORE ELIGENDO. Writ for electing a coroner. A writ issued to the sheriff in England, commanding him to proceed to the election of a coroner, which is done in full county court, the freeholders being the electors. Sewell, Sheriffs, 372.

DE CORONATORE EXONERANDO. Writ for discharging or removing a coroner. A writ by which a coroner in England may be removed from office for some cause therein assigned. Fitzh. Nat. Brev. 163, 164; 1 Bl. Comm. 348.

DE CORPORE COMITATUS. From the body of the county at large, as distinguished from a particular neighborhood, (*de vicineto*.) 3 Bl. Comm. 360.

DE CORRODIO HABENDO. Writ for having a corody. A writ to exact a corody from a religious house. Reg. Orig. 264; Fitzh. Nat. Brev. 230. See CORODY.

DE CURIA CLAUDENDA. An obsolete writ, to require a defendant to fence in his court or land about his house, where it was left open to the injury of his neighbor's freehold. 1 Crabb, Real Prop. 314; 6 Mass. 90.

DE CURSU. Of course. The usual, necessary, and formal proceedings in an action are said to be *de cursu;* as distinguished from *summary* proceedings, or such as are incidental and may be taken on summons or motion. Writ *de cursu* are such as are issued of course, as distinguished from prerogative writs.

DE CUSTODE ADMITTENDO. Writ for admitting a guardian. Reg. Orig. 93*b*, 198.

DE CUSTODE AMOVENDO. Writ for removing a guardian. Reg. Orig. 198.

DE CUSTODIA TERRÆ ET HÆRE-DIS, *Breve.* L. Lat. Writ of ward, or writ of right of ward. A writ which lay for a guardian in knight's service or in socage, to recover the possession and custody of the infant, or the *wardship of the land and heir.* Reg. Orig. 161*b;* Fitzh. Nat. Brev. 139, B; 3 Bl. Comm. 141.

DE DEBITO. A writ of debt. Reg. Orig. 139.

DE DEBITORE IN PARTES SE-CANDO. In Roman law. "Of cutting a debtor in pieces." This was the name of a law contained in the Twelve Tables, the meaning of which has occasioned much controversy. Some commentators have concluded that it was literally the privilege of the creditors of an insolvent debtor (all other means failing) to cut his body into pieces and distribute it among them. Others contend that the language of this law must be taken figuratively, denoting a cutting up and apportionment of the debtor's *estate.*

The latter view has been adopted by Montesquieu, Bynkershoek, Heineccius, and Taylor. (Esprit des Lois, liv. 29, c. 2; Bynk. Obs. Jur. Rom. l. 1, c. 1; Heinecc. Ant. Rom. lib. 3, tit. 30, § 4; Tayl. Comm. in Leg. Decemv.) The literal meaning, on the other hand, is advocated by Aulus Gellius and other writers of antiquity, and receives support from an expression (*semoto omni cruciatu*) in the Roman code itself. (Aul. Gel. Noctes Atticæ, lib. 20, c. 1; Code, 7, 7, 8.) This is also the opinion of Gibbon, Gravina, Pothier, Hugo, and Niebuhr. (3 Gib. Rom. Emp., Am. Ed., p. 183; Grav. de Jur. Nat. Gent. et XII. Tab. § 72; Poth. Introd. Pand.; Hugo, Hist. du Droit Rom. tom. i., p. 233, § 149; 2 Niebh. Hist. Rom. p. 597; 1 Kent, Comm. 523, note.) Burrill.

DE DECEPTIONE. A writ of deceit which lay against one who acted in the name of another whereby the latter was damnified and deceived. Reg. Orig. 112.

DE DEONERANDA PRO RATA PORTIONIS. A writ that lay where one was distrained for rent that ought to be paid by others proportionably with him. Fitzh. Nat. Brev. 234; Termes de la Ley.

DE DIE IN DIEM. From day to day. Bract. fol. 205*b*.

DE DIVERSIS REGULIS JURIS ANTIQUI. Of divers rules of the ancient law. A celebrated title of the Digests, and the last in that collection. It consists of two hundred and eleven rules or maxims. Dig. 50, 17.

DE DOLO MALO. Of or founded upon fraud. Dig. 4, 3. See ACTIO DE DOLO MALO.

DE DOMO REPARANDA. A writ which lay for one tenant in common to compel his co-tenant to contribute towards the repair of the common property.

DE DONIS. Concerning gifts, (or more fully, *de donis conditionalibus,* concerning conditional gifts.) The name of a celebrated English statute, passed in the thirteenth year of Edw. I., and constituting the first chapter of the statute of Westm. 2, by virtue of which estates in fee-simple conditional (formerly known as "*dona conditionalia*") were converted into estates in fee-tail, and which, by rendering such estates inalienable, introduced perpetuities, and so strengthened the power of the nobles. See 2 Bl. Comm. 112.

DE DOTE ASSIGNANDA. Writ for assigning dower. A writ which lay for the widow of a tenant *in capite,* commanding the king's escheator to cause her dower to be assigned to her. Reg. Orig. 297; Fitzh. Nat. Brev. 263, C.

DE DOTE UNDE NIHIL HABET. A writ of dower which lay for a widow where no part of her dower had been assigned to her. It is now much disused; but a form closely resembling it is still sometimes used in the United States. 4 Kent, Comm. 63; Stearns, Real Act. 302; 1 Washb. Real Prop. 230.

DE EJECTIONE CUSTODIÆ. A writ which lay for a guardian who had been forcibly ejected from his wardship. Reg. Orig. 162.

DE EJECTIONE FIRMÆ. A writ which lay at the suit of the tenant for years against the lessor, reversioner, remainderman, or stranger who had himself deprived the tenant of the occupation of the land during his term. 3 Bl. Comm. 199.

By a gradual extension of the scope of this form of action its object was made to include not only damages for the unlawful detainer, but also the possession for the remainder of the term, and eventually the possession of land generally. And, as it turned on the right of possession, this involved a determination of the right of property, or the title, and thus arose the modern action of ejectment.

DE ESCÆTA. Writ of escheat. A writ which a lord had, where his tenant died without heir, to recover the land. Reg. Orig. 164b; Fitzh. Nat. Brev. 143, 144, E.

DE ESCAMBIO MONETÆ. A writ of exchange of money. An ancient writ to authorize a merchant to make a bill of exchange, (*literas cambitorias facere.*) Reg. Orig. 194.

DE ESSE IN PEREGRINATIONE. Of being on a journey. A species of essoin. 1 Reeve, Eng. Law, 119.

DE ESSENDO QUIETUM DE TOLONIO. A writ which lay for those who were by privilege free from the payment of toll, on their being molested therein. Fitzh. Nat. Brev. 226; Reg. Orig. 258b.

DE ESSONIO DE MALO LECTI. A writ which issued upon an essoin of *malum lecti* being cast, to examine whether the party was in fact sick or not. Reg. Orig. 8b.

DE ESTOVERIIS HABENDIS. Writ for having estovers. A writ which lay for a wife divorced *a mensa et thoro*, to recover her alimony or estovers. 1 Bl. Comm. 441; 1 Lev. 6.

DE ESTREPAMENTO. A writ which lay to prevent or stay waste by a tenant, during the pendency of a suit against him to recover the lands. Reg. Orig. 76b · Fitzh. Nat. Brev. 60.

DE EU ET TRENE. L. Fr. Of water and whip of three cords. A term applied to a neife, that is, a bond woman or female villein, as employed in servile work, and subject to corporal punishment. Co. Litt. 25b.

DE EVE ET DE TREVE. A law French phrase, equivalent to the Latin *de avo et de tritavo*, descriptive of the ancestral rights of lords in their villeins. Literally, "from grandfather and from great-grandfather's great-grandfather." It occurs in the Year Books.

DE EXCOMMUNICATO CAPIENDO. A writ commanding the sheriff to arrest one who was excommunicated, and imprison him till he should become reconciled to the church. 3 Bl. Comm. 102.

DE EXCOMMUNICATO DELIBERANDO. A writ to deliver an excommunicated person, who has made satisfaction to the church, from prison. 3 Bl. Comm. 102.

DE EXCOMMUNICATO RECAPIENDO. Writ for retaking an excommunicated person, where he had been liberated from prison without making satisfaction to the church, or giving security for that purpose. Reg. Orig. 67.

DE EXCUSATIONIBUS. "Concerning excuses." This is the title of book 27 of the Pandects, (in the *Corpus Juris Civilis.*) It treats of the circumstances which excuse one from filling the office of tutor or curator. The bulk of the extracts are from Modestinus.

DE EXECUTIONE FACIENDA IN WITHERNAMIUM. Writ for making execution in withernam. Reg. Orig. 82b. A species of *capias in withernam.*

DE EXECUTIONE JUDICII. A writ directed to a sheriff or bailiff, commanding him to do execution upon a judgment. Reg. Orig. 18; Fitzh. Nat. Brev. 20.

DE EXEMPLIFICATIONE. Writ of exemplification. A writ granted for the exemplification of an original. Reg. Orig. 290b.

DE EXONERATIONE SECTÆ. Writ for exoneration of suit. A writ that lay for the king's ward to be discharged of all suit to the county court, hundred, leet, or court-baron, during the time of his wardship. Fitzh. Nat. Brev. 158; New Nat. Brev. 352.

DE EXPENSIS CIVIUM ET BURGENSIUM. An obsolete writ addressed to the sheriff to levy the expenses of every citizen and burgess of parliament. 4 Inst. 46.

DE EXPENSIS MILITUM LEVANDIS. Writ for levying the expenses of knights. A writ directed to the sheriff for levying the allowance for knights of the shire in parliament. Reg. Orig. 191b, 192.

DE FACTO. In fact, in deed, actually. This phrase is used to characterize an officer, a government, a past action, or a state of affairs which exists actually and must be accepted for all practical purposes, but which is illegal or illegitimate. In this sense it is the contrary of *de jure,* which means rightful, legitimate, just, or constitutional. Thus, an officer, king, or government *de facto* is one who is in actual possession of the office or supreme power, but by usurpation, or without respect to lawful title; while an officer, king, or governor *de jure* is one who has just claim and rightful title to the office or power, but who has never had plenary possession of the same, or is not now in actual possession. (4 Bl. Comm. 77, 78.) So a wife *de facto* is one whose marriage is voidable by decree, as distinguished from a wife *de jure,* or lawful wife. (4 Kent, Comm. 36.) (As to the distinction between governments *de facto* and *de jure,* see GOVERNMENT. As to officers *de facto,* see that title.)

But the term is also frequently used independently of any distinction from *de jure;* thus a blockade *de facto* is a blockade which is actually maintained, as distinguished from a mere paper blockade.

In old English law. *De facto* means respecting or concerning the principal act of a murder, which was technically denominated *factum.* See Fleta, lib. 1, c. 27, § 18.

DE FACTO CONTRACT. One which has purported to pass the property from the owner to another. 74 N. Y. 575; L. R. 3 App. Cas. 459.

DE FAIRE ECHELLE. In French law. A clause commonly inserted in policies of marine insurance, equivalent to a license to touch and trade at intermediate ports. 14 Wend. 491.

DE FALSO JUDICIO. Writ of false judgment. Reg. Orig. 15; Fitzh. Nat Brev. 18. See FALSE JUDGMENT.

DE FALSO MONETA. Of false money. The title of the statute 27 Edw. I. ordaining that persons importing certain coins, called "pollards," and "crokards," should forfeit their lives and goods, and everything they could forfeit. 2 Reeve, Eng. Law, 228, 229.

De fide et officio judicis non recipitur quæstio, sed de scientia, sive sit error juris, sive facti. Concerning the fidelity and official conduct of a judge, no question is [will be] entertained; but [only] concerning his knowledge, whether the error [committed] be of law or of fact. Bac. Max. 68, reg. 17. The *bona fides* and honesty of purpose of a judge cannot be questioned, but his decision may be impugned for error either of

law or fact. Broom, Max. 85. The law doth so much respect the certainty of judgments, and the credit and authority of judges, that it will not permit any error to be assigned which impeacheth them in their *trust* and *office,* and in willful abuse of the same; but only in ignorance and mistaking either of the law, or of the case and matter of fact. Bac. Max. ubi supra. Thus, it cannot be assigned for error that a judge did that which he ought not to do; as that he entered a verdict for the plaintiff, where the jury gave it for the defendant. Fitzh. Nat. Brev. 20, 21; Bac. Max. ubi supra; Hardr. 127, arg.

DE FIDEI LÆSIONE. Of breach of faith or fidelity. 4 Reeve, Eng. Law, 99.

DE FINE FORCE. L. Fr. Of necessity; of pure necessity. See FINE FORCE.

DE FINE NON CAPIENDO PRO PULCHRE PLACITANDO. A writ prohibiting the taking of fines for beau pleader. Reg. Orig. 179.

DE FINE PRO REDISSEISINA CAPIENDO. A writ which lay for the release of one imprisoned for a re-disseisin, on payment of a reasonable fine. Reg. Orig. 222b.

DE FINIBUS LEVATIS. Concerning fines levied. The title of the statute 27 Edw. I., requiring fines thereafter to be levied, to be read openly and solemnly in court. 2 Inst. 521.

DE FORISFACTURA MARITAGII. Writ of forfeiture of marriage. Reg. Orig. 163, 164.

DE FRANGENTIBUS PRISONAM. Concerning those that break prison. The title of the statute 1 Edw. II., ordaining that none from thenceforth who broke prison should have judgment of life or limb for breaking prison only, unless the cause for which he was taken and imprisoned required such a judgment if he was lawfully convicted thereof. 2 Reeve, Eng. Law, 290; 2 Inst. 589.

DE FURTO. Of theft. One of the kinds of criminal appeal formerly in use in England. 2 Reeve, Eng. Law, 40.

DE GESTU ET FAMA. Of behavior and reputation. An old writ which lay in cases where a person's conduct and reputation were impeached.

DE GRATIA. Of grace or favor, by favor. *De speciali gratia,* of special grace or favor.

De gratia speciali certa scientia et mero motu, talis clausula non valet in his in quibus præsumitur principem esse ignorantem. 1 Coke, 53. The clause "of our special grace, certain knowledge, and mere motion," is of no avail in those things in which it is presumed that the prince was ignorant.

De grossis arboribus decimæ non dabuntur sed de sylvia cædua decimæ dabuntur. 2 Rolle, 123. Of whole trees, tithes are not given; but of wood cut to be used, tithes are given.

DE HÆREDE DELIBERANDO ILLI QUI HAPET CUSTODIAM TERRÆ. Writ for delivering an heir to him who has wardship of the land. A writ directed to the sheriff, to require one that had the body of him that was ward to another to deliver him to the person whose ward he was by reason of his land. Reg. Orig. 161.

DE HÆREDE RAPTO ET ABDUCTO. Writ concerning an heir ravished and carried away. A writ which anciently lay for a lord who, having by right the wardship of his tenant under age, could not obtain his body, the same being carried away by another person. Reg. Orig. 163; Old Nat. Brev. 93.

DE HÆRETICO COMBURENDO. (Lat. For burning a heretic.) A writ which lay where a heretic had been convicted of heresy, had abjured, and had relapsed into heresy. It is said to be very ancient. Fitzh. Nat. Brev. 269; 4 Bl. Comm. 46.

DE HOMAGIO RESPECTUANDO. A writ for respiting or postponing homage. Fitzh. Nat. Brev. 269, A.

DE HOMINE CAPTO IN WITHERNAM. (Lat. For taking a man in withernam.) A writ to take a man who had carried away a bondman or bondwoman into another country beyond the reach of a writ of replevin.

DE HOMINE REPLEGIANDO. (Lat. For replevying a man.) A writ which lies to replevy a man out of prison, or out of the custody of a private person, upon giving security to the sheriff that the man shall be forthcoming to answer any charge against him. Fitzh. Nat. Brev. 66; 3 Bl. Comm. 129.

This writ has been superseded almost wholly, in modern practice, by that of *habeas corpus;* but it is still used, in some of the states, in an amended and altered form. See 1 Kent, Comm. 404n; 34 Me. 136.

DE IDENTITATE NOMINIS. A writ which lay for one arrested in a personal action and committed to prison under a mistake as to his identity, the proper defendant bearing the same name. Reg. Orig. 194.

DE IDIOTA INQUIRENDO. An old common-law writ, long obsolete, to inquire whether a man be an idiot or not. 2 Steph. Comm. 509.

DE IIS QUI PONENDI SUNT IN ASSISIS. Of those who are to be put on assises. The title of a statute passed 21 Edw. I., defining the qualifications of jurors. Crabb, Eng. Law, 167, 189; 2 Reeve, Eng. Law, 184.

DE INCREMENTO. Of increase; in addition. Costs *de incremento*, or costs of increase, are the costs adjudged by the court in civil actions, *in addition* to the damages and nominal costs found by the jury. Gilb. Com. Pl. 260.

DE INFIRMITATE. Of infirmity. The principal essoin in the time of Glanville; afterwards called "*de malo.*" 1 Reeve, Eng. Law, 115. See DE MALO; ESSOIN.

DE INGRESSU. A writ of entry. Reg. Orig. 227b, et seq.

DE INJURIA. Of [his own] wrong. In the technical language of pleading, a replication *de injuria* is one that may be made in an action of tort where the defendant has admitted the acts complained of, but alleges, in his plea, certain new matter by way of justification or excuse; by this replication the plaintiff avers that the defendant committed the grievances in question "of his own wrong, and without any such cause," or motive or excuse, as that alleged in the plea, (*de injuria sua propria absque tali causa;*) or, admitting part of the matter pleaded, "without the rest of the cause" alleged, (*absque residuo causæ.*)

In form it is a species of traverse, and it is frequently used when the pleading of the defendant, in answer to which it is directed, consists merely of matter of excuse of the alleged trespass, grievance, breach of contract, or other cause of action. Its comprehensive character in putting in issue all the material facts of the defendant's plea has also obtained for it the title of the general replication. Holthouse.

DE INOFFICIOSO TESTAMENTO.
Concerning an inofficious or undutiful will.
A title of the civil law.   Inst. 2, 18.

DE INTEGRO.   Anew; a second time.
As it was before.

DE INTRUSIONE.   A writ of intrusion; where a stranger entered after the death
of the tenant, to the injury of the reversioner.
Reg. Orig. 233b.

DE JACTURA EVITANDA.   For
avoiding a loss.   A phrase applied to a defendant, as *de lucro captando* is to a plaintiff.
1 Litt. (Ky.) 51.

DE JUDAISMO, STATUTUM.   The
name of a statute passed in the reign of Edward I., which enacted severe and arbitrary
penalties against the Jews.

DE JUDICATO SOLVENDO.   For
payment of the amount adjudged.   A term
applied in the Scotch law to bail to the action, or special bail.

DE JUDICIIS.   Of judicial proceedings.
The title of the second part of the Digests or
Pandects, including the fifth, sixth, seventh,
eighth, ninth, tenth, and eleventh books.
See Dig. proœm. § 3.

DE JUDICIO SISTI.   For appearing
in court.   A term applied in the Scotch and
admiralty law, to bail for a defendant's appearance.

DE JURE.   Of right; legitimate; lawful;
by right and just title.   In this sense it is
the contrary of *de facto*, (which see.)   It may
also be contrasted with *de gratia*, in which
case it means "as a matter of right," as *de
gratia* means "by grace or favor."   Again
it may be contrasted with *de æquitate;* here
meaning "by law," as the latter means "by
equity."   See GOVERNMENT.

De jure decimarum, originem ducens
de jure patronatus, tunc cognitio spectat at legem civilem, i. e., communem.
Godb. 63.   With regard to the right of tithes,
deducing its origin from the right of the patron, then the cognizance of them belongs to
the civil law; that is, the common law.

DE LA PLUIS BEALE, or BELLE.
L. Fr.   Of the most fair.   A term applied to
a species of dower, which was assigned out of
the fairest of the husband's tenements.   Litt.
§ 48.   This was abolished with the military
tenures.   2 Bl. Comm. 132; 1 Steph. Comm.
252.

DE LATERE.   From the side; on the
side; collaterally; of collaterals.   Cod. 5, 5, 6.

**DE LEGATIS ET FIDEI COMMIS-
SIS.**   Of legacies and trusts.   The name of
a title of the Pandects.   Dig. 30.

DE LEPROSO AMOVENDO.   Writ
for removing a leper.   A writ to remove a
leper who thrust himself into the company
of his neighbors in any parish, in public or
private places, to their annoyance.   Reg.
Orig. 267; Fitzh. Nat. Brev. 234, E; New
Nat. Brev. 521.

DE LIBERA FALDA.   Writ of free
fold.   A species of *quod permittat*.   Reg.
Orig. 155.

DE LIBERA PISCARIA.   Writ of free
fishery.   A species of *quod permittat*.   Reg.
Orig. 155.

DE LIBERO PASSAGIO.   Writ of free
passage.   A species of *quod permittat*.   Reg.
Orig. 155.

DE LIBERTATE PROBANDA.   Writ
for proving liberty.   A writ which lay for
such as, being demanded for villeins or niefs,
offered to prove themselves free.   Reg. Orig.
87b; Fitzh. Nat. Brev. 77, F.

DE LIBERTATIBUS ALLOCANDIS.
A writ of various forms, to enable a citizen
to recover the liberties to which he was entitled.   Fitzh. Nat. Brev. 229; Reg. Orig.
262.

DE LICENTIA TRANSFRETANDI.
Writ of permission to cross the sea.   An old
writ directed to the wardens of the port of
Dover, or other seaport in England, commanding them to permit the persons named
in the writ to cross the sea from such port,
on certain conditions.   Reg. Orig. 193b.

DE LUNATICO INQUIRENDO.
The name of a writ directed to the sheriff,
directing him to inquire by good and lawful
men whether the party charged is a lunatic
or not.

DE MAGNA ASSISA ELIGENDA.
A writ by which the grand assise was chosen
and summoned.   Reg. Orig. 8; Fitzh. Nat.
Brev. 4.

De majori et minori non variant jura.
Concerning greater and less laws do not vary.
2 Vern. 552.

DE MALO.   Of illness.   This phrase
was frequently used to designate several species of essoin, (*q. v.*,) such as *de malo lecti,*

of illness in bed; *de malo veniendi*, of illness (or misfortune) in coming to the place where the court sat; *de malo villæ*, of illness in the town where the court sat.

DE MANUCAPTIONE. Writ of manucaption, or mainprise. A writ which lay for one who, being taken and imprisoned on a charge of felony, had offered bail, which had been refused; requiring the sheriff to discharge him on his finding sufficient mainpernors or bail. Reg. Orig. 268*b;* Fitzh. Nat. Brev. 249, G.

DE MANUTENENDO. Writ of maintenance. A writ which lay against a person for the offense of maintenance. Reg. Orig. 189, 182*b*.

DE MEDIETATE LINGUÆ. Of the half tongue; half of one tongue and half of another. This phrase describes that species of jury which, at common law, was allowed in both civil and criminal cases where one of the parties was an alien, not speaking or understanding English. It was composed of six English denizens or natives and six of the alien's own countrymen.

DE MEDIO. A writ in the nature of a writ of right, which lay where upon a subinfeudation the *mesne* (or middle) lord suffered his under-tenant or tenant *paravail* to be distrained upon by the lord paramount for the rent due him from the *mesne* lord. Booth, Real Act. 136.

DE MELIORIBUS DAMNIS. Of or for the better damages. A term used in practice to denote the election by a plaintiff against which of several defendants (where the damages have been assessed separately) he will take judgment. 1 Arch. Pr. K. B. 219; 8 Cow. 111.

DE MERCATORIBUS. "Concerning merchants." The name of a statute passed in the eleventh year of Edw. I., (1233,) more commonly called the "Statute of Acton Burnel," authorizing the recognizance by statute merchant. See 2 Reeve, Eng. Law, 160–162; 2 Bl. Comm. 161.

De minimis non curat lex. The law does not care for, or take notice of, very small or trifling matters. The law does not concern itself about trifles. Cro. Eliz. 353. Thus, error in calculation of a fractional part of a penny will not be regarded. Hob. 88. So, the law will not, in general, notice the fraction of a day. Broom, Max. 142.

DE MINIS. Writ of threats. A writ which lay where a person was threatened with personal violence, or the destruction of his property, to compel the offender to keep the peace. Reg. Orig. 88*b*, 89; Fitzh. Nat. Brev. 79, G, 80.

DE MITTENDO TENOREM RECORDI. A writ to send the tenor of a record, or to exemplify it under the great seal. Reg. Orig. 220*b*.

DE MODERATA MISERICORDIA CAPIENDA. Writ for taking a moderate amercement. A writ, founded on *Magna Charta*, (c. 14,) which lay for one who was excessively amerced in a court not of record, directed to the lord of the court, or his bailiff, commanding him *to take a moderate amercement* of the party. Reg. Orig. 86*b;* Fitzh. Nat. Brev. 75, 76.

DE MODO DECIMANDI. Of a *modus* of tithing. A term applied in English ecclesiastical law to a prescription to have a special manner of tithing. 2 Bl. Comm. 29; 3 Steph. Comm. 130.

De molendino de novo erecto non jacet prohibitio. Cro. Jac. 429. A prohibition lies not against a newly-erected mill.

De morte hominis nulla est cunctatio longa. Where the death of a human being is concerned, [in a matter of life and death,] no delay is [considered] long. Co. Litt. 134.

DE NATIVO HABENDO. A writ which lay for a lord directed to the sheriff, commanding him to apprehend a fugitive villein, and restore him, with all his chattels, to the lord. Reg. Orig. 87; Fitzh. Nat. Brev. 77.

De nomine proprio non est curandum cum in substantia non erretur; quia nomina mutabilia sunt, res autem immobiles. 6 Coke, 66. As to the proper name, it is not to be regarded where it errs not in substance, because names are changeable, but things immutable.

De non apparentibus, et non existentibus, eadem est ratio. 5 Coke, 6. As to things not apparent, and those not existing, the rule is the same.

DE NON DECIMANDO. Of not paying tithes. A term applied in English ecclesiastical law to a prescription or claim to be entirely discharged of tithes, and to pay no compensation in lieu of them. 2 Bl. Comm. 31.

E

F

G

H

I

J

K

L

M

DE NON PROCEDENDO AD AS-SISAM. A writ forbidding the justices from holding an assise in a particular case. Reg. Orig. 221.

DE NON RESIDENTIA CLERICI REGIS. An ancient writ where a parson was employed in the royal service, etc., to excuse and discharge him of non-residence. 2 Inst. 264.

DE NON SANE MEMORIE. L. Fr. Of unsound memory or mind; a phrase synonymous with *non compos mentis.*

DE NOVI OPERIS NUNCIATIONE. In the civil law. A form of interdict or injunction which lies in some cases where the defendant is about to erect a "new work" (*q. v.*) in derogation or injury of the plaintiff's rights.

DE NOVO. Anew; afresh; a second time. A *venire de novo* is a writ for summoning a jury for the second trial of a case which has been sent back from above for a new trial.

De nullo, quod est sua natura indivisibile, et divisionem non patitur, nullam partem habebit vidua, sed satisfaciat ei ad valentiam. Co. Litt. 32. A widow shall have no part of that which in its own nature is indivisible, and is not susceptible of division, but let the heir satisfy her with an equivalent.

De nullo tenemento, quod tenetur ad terminum, fit homagii, fit tamen inde fidelitatis sacramentum. In no tenement which is held for a term of years is there an avail of homage; but there is the oath of fealty. Co. Litt. 67b.

DE ODIO ET ATIA. A writ directed to the sheriff, commanding him to inquire whether a prisoner charged with murder was committed upon just cause of suspicion, or merely *propter odium et atiam,* (through hatred and ill will;) and if, upon the inquisition, due cause of suspicion did not appear, then there issued another writ for the sheriff to admit him to bail. 3 Bl. Comm. 128.

DE OFFICE. L. Fr. Of office; in virtue of office; officially; in the discharge of ordinary duty.

DE ONERANDO PRO RATA PORTIONE. Writ for charging according to a rateable proportion. A writ which lay for a joint tenant, or tenant in common, who was distrained for more rent than his proportion

of the land came to. Reg. Orig. 182; Fitzh. Nat. Brev. 234, H.

DE PACE ET LEGALITATE TENENDA. For keeping the peace, and for good behavior.

DE PACE ET PLAGIS. Of peace, (breach of peace,) and wounds. One of the kinds of criminal appeal formerly in use in England, and which lay in cases of assault, wounding, and breach of the peace. Bract. fol. 144; 2 Reeve, Eng. Law, 33.

DE PACE ET ROBERIA. Of peace [breach of peace] and robbery. One of the kinds of criminal appeal formerly in use in England, and which lay in cases of robbery and breach of the peace. Bract. fol. 146; 2 Reeve, Eng. Law, 37.

DE PALABRA. Span. By word; by parol. White, New Recop. b. 2, tit. 19, c. 3, § 2.

DE PARCO FRACTO. A writ or action for damages caused by a pound-breach, (*q. v.*) It has long been obsolete. Co. Litt. 47b; 3 Bl. Comm. 146.

DE PARTITIONE FACIENDA. A writ which lay to make partition of lands or tenements held by several as coparceners, tenants in common, etc. Reg. Orig. 76; Fitzh. Nat. Brev. 61, R; Old Nat. Brev. 142.

DE PERAMBULATIONE FACIENDA. A writ which lay where there was a dispute as to the boundaries of two adjacent lordships or towns, directed to the sheriff, commanding him to take with him twelve discreet and lawful knights of his county and make the perambulation and set the bounds and limits in certainty. Fitzh. Nat. Brev. 309, D.

DE PIGNORE SURREPTO FURTI, ACTIO. In the civil law. An action to recover a pledge stolen. Inst. 4, 1, 14.

DE PIPA VINI CARIANDA. A writ of trespass for carrying a pipe of wine so carelessly that it was stove, and the contents lost. Reg. Orig. 110. Alluded to by Sir William Jones in his remarks on the case of Coggs v. Barnard. Jones, Bailm. 59.

DE PLACITO. Of a plea; of or in an action. Formal words used in declarations and other proceedings, as descriptive of the particular action brought.

DE PLAGIS ET MAHEMIO. Of wounds and mayhem. The name of a criminal appeal formerly in use in England, in cases of wounding and maiming. Bract. fol. 144b; 2 Reeve, Eng. Law, 34. See Appeal.

DE PLANO. Lat. On the ground; on a level. A term of the Roman law descriptive of the method of hearing causes, when the prætor stood on the ground with the suitors, instead of the more formal method when he occupied a bench or tribunal; hence informal, or summary.

DE PLEGIIS ACQUIETANDIS. Writ for acquitting or releasing pledges. A writ that lay for a surety, against him for whom he had become surety for the payment of a certain sum of money at a certain day, where the latter had not paid the money at the appointed day, and the surety was compelled to pay it. Reg. Orig. 158; Fitzh. Nat. Brev. 137, C; 3 Reeve, Eng. Law, 65.

DE PONENDO SIGILLUM AD EXCEPTIONEM. Writ for putting a seal to an exception. A writ by which justices were formerly commanded to put their seals to exceptions taken by a party in a suit. Reg. Orig. 182.

DE POST DISSEISINA. Writ of post disseisin. A writ which lay for him who, having recovered lands or tenements by *præcipe quod reddat*, on default, or reddition, was again disseised by the former disseisor. Reg. Orig. 208; Fitzh. Nat. Brev. 190.

DE PRÆROGATIVA REGIS. The statute 17 Edw. I. St. 1, c. 9, defining the prerogatives of the crown on certain subjects, but especially directing that the king shall have ward of the lands of idiots, taking the profits without waste, and finding them necessaries. 2 Steph. Comm. 529.

DE PRÆSENTI. Of the present; in the present tense. See Per Verba de Præsenti.

DE PROPRIETATE PROBANDA. Writ for proving property. A writ directed to the sheriff, to inquire of the property or goods distrained, where the defendant in an action of replevin claims the property. 3 Bl. Comm. 148; Reg. Orig. 85b.

DE QUIBUS SUR DISSEISIN. An ancient writ of entry.

DE QUO, and DE QUIBUS. Of which. Formal words in the simple writ of entry, from which it was called a writ of entry "in the quo," or "in the quibus." 3 Reeve, Eng. Law, 33.

DE QUOTA LITIS. In the civil law. A contract by which one who has a claim difficult to recover agrees with another to give a part, for the purpose of obtaining his services to recover the rest. 1 Duval, no. 201.

DE RAPTU VIRGINUM. Of the ravishment of maids. The name of an appeal formerly in use in England in cases of rape. Bract. fol. 147; 2 Reeve, Eng. Law, 38.

DE RATIONABILI PARTE BONORUM. A writ which lay for the wife and children of a deceased person against his executors, to recover their reasonable part or share of his goods. 2 Bl. Comm. 492; Fitzh. Nat. Brev. 122, L.

DE RATIONABILIBUS DIVISIS. Writ for fixing reasonable boundaries. A writ which lay to settle the boundaries between the lands of persons in different towns, where one complained of encroachment. Reg. Orig. 157b; Fitzh. Nat. Brev. 128, M; Rosc. Real Act. 31; 3 Reeve, Eng. Law, 48.

DE REBUS. Of things. The title of the third part of the Digests or Pandects, comprising books 12–19, inclusive.

DE REBUS DUBIIS. Of doubtful things or matters. Dig. 34, 5.

DE RECORDO ET PROCESSU MITTENDIS. Writ to send the record and process of a cause to a superior court; a species of writ of error. Reg. Orig. 209.

DE RECTO. Writ of right. Reg. Orig. 1, 2; Bract. fol. 327b. See Writ of Right.

DE RECTO DE ADVOCATIONE. Writ of right of advowson. Reg. Orig. 29b. A writ which lay for one who had an estate in an advowson and his heirs in fee-simple, if he were disturbed to present. Fitzh. Nat. Brev. 30, B. Abolished by St. 3 & 4 Wm. IV. c. 27.

DE RECTO DE RATIONABILI PARTE. Writ of right, of reasonable part. A writ which lay between privies in blood, as between brothers in gavelkind, or between sisters or other coparceners for lands in fee-simple, where one was deprived of his or her share by another. Reg. Orig. 3b; Fitzh. Nat. Brev. 9, B. Abolished by St. 3 & 4 Wm. IV. c. 27.

DE RECTO PATENS. Writ of right patent. Reg. Orig. 1.

DE REDISSEISINA. Writ of redisseisin. A writ which lay where a man recovered by assise of novel disseisin land, rent, or common, and the like, and was put in possession thereof by verdict, and afterwards was disseised of the same land, rent, or common, by him by whom he was disseised before. Reg. Orig. 206b, Fitzh. Nat. Brev. 188, B.

DE REPARATIONE FACIENDA. A writ by which one tenant in common seeks to compel another to aid in repairing the property held in common. 8 Barn. & C. 269.

DE RESCUSSU. Writ of rescue or rescous. A writ which lay where cattle distrained, or persons arrested, were rescued from those taking them. Reg. Orig. 117, 118; Fitzh. Nat. Brev. 101, C, G.

DE RETORNO HABENDO. For having a return; to have a return. A term applied to the judgment for the defendant in an action of replevin, awarding him a return of the goods replevied; and to the writ or execution issued thereon. 2 Tidd, Pr. 993, 1038; 3 Bl. Comm. 149. Applied also to the sureties given by the plaintiff on commencing the action. Id. 147.

DE RIEN CULPABLE. L. Fr. Guilty of nothing; not guilty.

DE SA VIE. L. Fr. Of his or her life; of his own life; as distinguished from *pur autre vie*, for another's life. Litt. §§ 35, 36.

DE SALVA GARDIA. A writ of safeguard allowed to strangers seeking their rights in English courts, and apprehending violence or injury to their persons or property Reg. Orig. 26.

DE SALVO CONDUCTU. A writ of safe conduct. Reg. Orig. 25b, 26.

DE SCACCARIO. Of or concerning the exchequer. The title of a statute passed in the fifty-first year of Henry III. 2 Reeve, Eng. Law, 61.

DE SCUTAGIO HABENDO. Writ for having (or to have) escuage or scutage. A writ which anciently lay against tenants by knight-service, to compel them to serve in the king's wars or send substitutes, or to pay escuage; that is, a sum of money. Fitzh. Nat. Brev. 83, C. The same writ lay for one who had already served in the king's army, or paid a fine instead, against those who held of him by knight-service, to recov-

er his escuage or scutage. Reg. Orig. 88; Fitzh. Nat. Brev. 83, D, F.

DE SE BENE GERENDO. For behaving himself well; for his good behavior. Yelv. 90, 154.

DE SECTA AD MOLENDINUM. Of suit to a mill. A writ which lay to compel one to continue his custom (of grinding) at a mill. 3 Bl. Comm. 235; Fitzh. Nat. Brev. 122, M.

De similibus ad similia eadem ratione procedendum est. From like things to like things we are to proceed by the same rule or reason, [*i. e.*, we are allowed to argue from the analogy of cases.] Branch, Princ.

De similibus idem est judicandum. Of [respecting] like things, [in like cases,] the judgment is to be the same. 7 Coke, 18.

DE SON TORT. L. Fr. Of his own wrong. A stranger who takes upon him to act as an executor without any just authority is called an "executor of his own wrong," (*de son tort.*) 2 Bl. Comm. 507; 2 Steph. Comm. 244.

DE SON TORT DEMESNE. Of his own wrong. The law French equivalent of the Latin phrase *de injuria*, (*q. v.*)

DE STATUTO MERCATORIO. The writ of statute merchant. Reg. Orig. 146b.

DE STATUTO STAPULÆ. The writ of statute staple. Reg. Orig. 151.

DE SUPERONERATIONE PASTURÆ. Writ of surcharge of pasture. A judicial writ which lay for him who was impleaded in the county court, for surcharging a common with his cattle, in a case where he was formerly impleaded for it in the same court, and the cause was removed into one of the courts at Westminster. Reg. Jud. 36b.

DE TABULIS EXHIBENDIS. Of showing the tablets of a will. Dig. 43, 5.

DE TALLAGIO NON CONCEDENDO. Of not allowing talliage. The name given to the statutes 25 and 34 Edw. I., restricting the power of the king to grant talliage. 2 Inst. 532; 2 Reeve, Eng. Law, 104.

DE TEMPORE CUJUS CONTRARIUM MEMORIA HOMINUM NON EXISTIT. From time whereof the memory of man does not exist to the contrary. Litt. § 170.

DE TEMPORE IN TEMPUS ET AD OMNIA TEMPORA. From time to time, and at all times. Townsh. Pl. 17

DE TEMPS DONT MEMORIE NE COURT. L. Fr. From time whereof memory runneth not; time out of memory of man. Litt. §§ 143, 145, 170.

DE TESTAMENTIS. Of testaments. The title of the fifth part of the Digests or Pandects; comprising the twenty-eighth to the thirty-sixth books, both inclusive.

DE THEOLONIO. A writ which lay for a person who was prevented from taking toll. Reg. Orig. 103.

DE TRANSGRESSIONE. A writ of trespass. Reg. Orig. 92.

DE TRANSGRESSIONE, AD AUDIENDUM ET TERMINANDUM. A writ or commission for the hearing and determining any outrage or misdemeanor.

DE UNA PARTE. A deed *de una parte* is one where only one party grants, gives, or binds himself to do a thing to another. It differs from a deed *inter partes*, (*q. v.*) 2 Bouv. Inst. no. 2001.

DE UXORE RAPTA ET ABDUCTA. A writ which lay where a man's wife had been ravished and carried away. A species of writ of trespass. Reg. Orig. 97; Fitzh. Nat. Brev. 89, O; 3 Bl. Comm. 139.

DE VASTO. Writ of waste. A writ which might be brought by him who had the immediate estate of inheritance in reversion or remainder, against the tenant for life, in dower, by curtesy, or for years, where the latter had committed *waste* in lands; calling upon the tenant to appear and show cause why he committed waste and destruction in the place named, to the disinherison (*ad exharedationem*) of the plaintiff. Fitzh. Nat. Brev. 55, C; 3 Bl. Comm. 227, 228. Abolished by St. 3 & 4 Wm. IV. c. 27. 3 Steph. Comm. 506.

DE VENTRE INSPICIENDO. A writ to inspect the body, where a woman feigns to be pregnant, to see whether she is with child. It lies for the heir presumptive to examine a widow suspected to be feigning pregnancy in order to enable a supposititious heir to obtain the estate. 1 Bl. Comm. 456; 2 Steph. Comm. 287.

It lay also where a woman sentenced to death pleaded pregnancy. 4 Bl. Comm. 495.

This writ has been recognized in America. 2 Chand. Crim. Tr. 381.

DE VERBO IN VERBUM. Word for word. Bract. fol. 138*b*. Literally, from word to word.

DE VERBORUM SIGNIFICATIONE. Of the signification of words. An important title of the Digests or Pandects, (Dig. 50, 16,) consisting entirely of definitions of words and phrases used in the Roman law.

DE VI LAICA AMOVENDA. Writ of (or for) removing lay force. A writ which lay where two parsons contended for a church, and one of them entered into it with a great number of *laymen*, and held out the other *vi et armis;* then he that was holden out had this writ directed to the sheriff, that he remove the force. Reg. Orig. 59; Fitzh. Nat. Brev. 54, D.

DE VICINETO. From the neighborhood, or vicinage. 3 Bl. Comm. 360. A term applied to a jury.

DE WARRANTIA CHARTÆ. Writ of warranty of charter. A writ which lay for him who was enfeoffed, with clause of warranty, [in the charter of feoffment,] and was afterwards impleaded in an assise or other action, in which he could not *vouch* or call to warranty; in which case he might have this writ against the feoffor, or his heir, to compel him to warrant the land unto him. Reg. Orig. 157*b;* Fitzh. Nat. Brev. 134, D. Abolished by St. 3 & 4 Wm. IV. c. 27.

DE WARRANTIA DIEI. A writ that lay where a man had a day in any action to appear in proper person, and the king at that day, or before, employed him in some service, so that he could not appear at the day in court. It was directed to the justices, that they should not record him to be in default for his not appearing. Fitzh. Nat. Brev. 17, A; Termes de la Ley.

DEACON. In ecclesiastical law. A minister or servant in the church, whose office is to assist the priest in divine service and the distribution of the sacrament. It is the lowest order in the Church of England.

DEAD BODY. A corpse.

DEAD FREIGHT. When a merchant who has chartered a vessel puts on board a part only of the intended cargo, but yet, having chartered the whole vessel, is bound to pay freight for the unoccupied capacity, the freight thus due is called "dead freight." L. R. 6 Q. B. 528; 15 East, 547.

DEAD LETTERS. Letters which the postal department has not been able to deliver to the persons for whom they were intended. They are sent to the "dead-letter office," where they are opened, and returned to the writer if his address can be ascertained.

DEAD MAN'S PART. In English law. That portion of the effects of a deceased person which, by the custom of London and York, is allowed to the administrator; being, where the deceased leaves a widow and children, one-third; where he leaves only a widow or only children, one-half; and, where he leaves neither, the whole. This portion the administrator was wont to apply to his own use, till the statute 1 Jac. II. c. 17, declared that the same should be subject to the statute of distributions. 2 Bl. Comm. 518; 2 Steph. Comm. 254; 4 Reeve, Eng. Law, 83. A similar portion in Scotch law is called "dead's part," (*q. v.*)

DEAD-PLEDGE. A mortgage; *mortuum vadium.*

DEAD RENT. In English law. A rent payable on a mining lease in addition to a royalty, so called because it is payable although the mine may not be worked.

DEAD USE. A future use.

DEADHEAD. This term is applied to persons other than the officers, agents, or employes of a railroad company who are permitted by the company to travel on the road without paying any fare therefor. Phillips, 21.

DEADLY FEUD. In old European law. A profession of irreconcilable hatred till a person is revenged even by the death of his enemy.

DEADLY WEAPON. Such weapons or instruments as are made and designed for offensive or defensive purposes, or for the destruction of life or the infliction of injury. 8 Bush, 387.

A deadly weapon is one likely to produce death or great bodily harm. 58 Cal. 245.

A deadly weapon is one which in the manner used is capable of producing death, or of inflicting great bodily injury, or seriously wounding. 4 Tex. App. 327.

DEAD'S PART. In Scotch law. The part remaining over beyond the shares secured to the widow and children by law. Of this the testator had the unqualified disposal. Bell.

DEAF AND DUMB. A man that is born deaf, dumb, and blind is looked upon by the law as in the same state with an idiot, he being supposed incapable of any understanding. 1 Bl. Comm. 304. Nevertheless, a deaf and dumb person may be tried for felony if the prisoner can be made to understand by means of signs. 1 Leach, C. L. 102.

DEAFFOREST. In old English law. To discharge from being forest. To free from forest laws.

DEAFFORESTED. Discharged from being a forest, or freed and exempted from the forest laws.

DEAL. To traffic; to transact business; to trade. Makers of an accommodation note are deemed dealers with whoever discounts it. 17 Wend. 524.

DEALER. A dealer, in the popular, and therefore in the statutory, sense of the word, is not one who buys to keep, or makes to sell, but one who buys to sell again. 27 Pa. St. 494; 33 Pa. St. 380.

DEALINGS. Transactions in the course of trade or business. Held to include payments to a bankrupt. Moody & M. 137; 3 Car. & P. 85.

DEAN. In English ecclesiastical law. An ecclesiastical dignitary who presides over the chapter of a cathedral, and is next in rank to the bishop. So called from having been originally appointed to superintend *ten* canons or prebendaries. 1 Bl. Comm. 382; Co. Litt. 95; Spelman.

There are several kinds of deans, namely: Deans of chapters; deans of peculiars; rural deans; deans in the colleges; honorary deans; deans of provinces.

DEAN AND CHAPTER. In ecclesiastical law. The council of a bishop, to assist him with their advice in the religious and also in the temporal affairs of the see. 3 Coke, 75; 1 Bl. Comm. 382; Co. Litt. 103, 300.

DEAN OF THE ARCHES. The presiding judge of the Court of Arches. He is also an assistant judge in the court of admiralty. 1 Kent, Comm. 371; 3 Steph. Comm. 727.

DEATH. The extinction of life; the departure of the soul from the body; defined by physicians as a total stoppage of the circulation of the blood, and a cessation of the animal and vital functions consequent thereon, such as respiration, pulsation, etc.

In legal contemplation, it is of two kinds: (1) *Natural, i. e.*, the extinction of life; (2) *civil*, where a person is not actually dead, but is adjudged so by the law, as when a person is banished or abjures the realm, or enters into a monastery. Civil death also occurs where a man, by act of parliament or judgment of law, is attainted of treason or felony; for immediately upon such attainder he loses (subject, indeed, to some exceptions) his civil rights and capacities, and becomes, as it were, *civiliter mortuus.* But now, by the 33 & 34 Vict. c. 23, forfeiture for treason or felony has been abolished, but the person convicted is disqualified for offices, etc. Wharton.

Natural death is also used to denote a death which occurs by the unassisted operation of natural causes, as distinguished from a *violent* death, or one caused or accelerated by the interference of human agency.

DEATH-BED. In Scotch law. A state of sickness which ends in death. Ersk. Inst. 3, 8, 95.

DEATH-BED DEED. In Scotch law. A deed made by a person while laboring under a distemper of which he afterwards died. Ersk. Inst. 3, 8, 96. A deed is understood to be in death-bed, if, before signing and delivery thereof, the grantor was sick, and never convalesced thereafter. 1 Forbes, Inst. pt. 3, b. 2, c. 4, tit. 1, § 1. But it is not necessary that he should be actually confined to his bed at the time of making the deed. Bell.

DEATH'S PART. See DEAD'S PART; DEAD MAN'S PART.

DEATHSMAN. The executioner; hangman; he that executes the extreme penalty of the law

DEBAUCH. To entice, to corrupt, and, when used of a woman, to seduce. Originally, the term had a limited signification, meaning to entice or draw one away from his work, employment, or duty; and from this sense its application has enlarged to include the corruption of manners and violation of the person. In its modern legal sense, the word carries with it the idea of "carnal knowledge," aggravated by assault, violent seduction, ravishment. 2 Hilt. 323.

DEBENTURE. A certificate given by the collector of a port, under the United States customs laws, to the effect that an importer of merchandise therein named is enti

tled to a drawback, (*q. v.,*) specifying the amount and time when payable. See Act Cong. March 2, 1799, § 80.

In English law. A security for a loan of money issued by a public company, usually creating a charge on the whole or a part of the company's stock and property, though not necessarily in the form of a mortgage. They are subject to certain regulations as to the mode of transfer, and ordinarily have coupons attached to facilitate the payment of interest. They are generally issued in a series, with provision that they shall rank *pari passu* in proportion to their amounts.

An instrument in use in some government departments, by which government is charged to pay to a creditor or his assigns the sum found due on auditing his accounts. Brande; Blount.

DEBENTURE STOCK. A stock or fund representing money borrowed by a company or public body, in England, and charged on the whole or part of its property.

Debet esse finis litium. There ought to be an end of suits; there should be some period put to litigation. Jenk. Cent. 61.

DEBET ET DETINET. He owes and detains. Words anciently used in the original writ, (and now, in English, in the plaintiff's declaration,) in an action of debt, where it was brought by one of the original contracting parties who personally gave the credit, against the other who personally incurred the debt, or against his heirs, if they were bound to the payment; as by the obligee against the obligor, by the landlord against the tenant, etc. The declaration, in such cases, states that the defendant "*owes* to," as well as "*detains* from," the plaintiff the debt or thing in question; and hence the action is said to be "in the *debet et detinet.*" Where the declaration merely states that the defendant *detains* the debt, (as in actions by and against an executor for a debt due to or from the testator,) the action is said to be "in the *detinet*" alone. Fitzh. Nat. Brev. 119, G.; 3 Bl. Comm. 155.

DEBET ET SOLET. (Lat. He owes and is used to.) Where a man sues in a writ of right or to recover any right of which he is for the first time disseised, as of a suit at a mill or in case of a writ of *quod permittat,* he brings his writ in the *debet et solet.* Reg. Orig. 144*a;* Fitzh. Nat. Brev. 122, M.

Debet quis juri subjacere ubi delinquit. One [every one] ought to be subject to the law [of the place] where he offends. 3 Inst. 34. This maxim is taken from Bracton. Bract. fol. 154*b*.

Debet sua cuique domus esse perfugium tutissimum. Every man's house should be a perfectly safe refuge. 12 Johns. 31, 54.

Debile fundamentum fallit opus. A weak foundation frustrates [or renders vain] the work [built upon it.] Shep. Touch. 60; Noy, Max. 5, max. 12; Finch, Law, b. 1, ch. 3. When the foundation fails, all goes to the ground; as, where the cause of action fails, the action itself must of necessity fail. Wing, Max., 113, 114, max. 40; Broom, Max. 180.

DEBIT. A sum charged as due or owing. The term is used in book-keeping to denote the charging of a person or an account with all that is supplied to or paid out for him or for the subject of the account.

DEBITA FUNDI. L. Lat. In Scotch law. Debts secured upon land. Ersk. Inst. 4, 1, 11.

DEBITA LAICORUM. L. Lat. In old English law. Debts of the laity, or of lay persons. Debts recoverable in the civil courts were anciently so called. Crabb, Eng. Law, 107.

Debita sequuntur personam debitoris. Debts follow the person of the debtor; that is, they have no locality, and may be collected wherever the debtor can be found. 2 Kent, Comm. 429; Story, Confl. Laws, § 362.

DEBITOR. In the civil and old English law. A debtor.

Debitor non præsumitur donare. A debtor is not presumed to make a gift. Whatever disposition he makes of his property is supposed to be in satisfaction of his debts. 1 Kames, Eq. 212. Where a debtor gives money or goods, or grants land to his creditor, the natural presumption is that he means to get free from his obligation, and not to make a present, unless donation be expressed. Ersk. Inst. 3, 3, 93.

Debitorum pactionibus creditorum petitio nec tolli nec minui potest. 1 Poth. Obl. 108; Broom, Max. 697. The rights of creditors can neither be taken away nor diminished by agreements among the debtors.

DEBITRIX. A female debtor.

DEBITUM. Something due, or owing; a debt.

Debitum et contractus sunt nullius loci. Debt and contract are of [belong to] no place; have no particular locality. The obligation in these cases is purely personal, and actions to enforce it may be brought anywhere. 2 Inst. 231; Story, Confl. Laws, § 362; 1 Smith, Lead. Cas. 340, 363.

DEBITUM IN PRÆSENTI SOLVENDUM IN FUTURO. A debt or obligation complete when contracted, but of which the performance cannot be required till some future period.

DEBITUM SINE BREVI. L. Lat. Debt without writ; debt without a declaration. In old practice, this term denoted an action begun by original bill, instead of by writ. In modern usage, it is sometimes applied to a debt evidenced by confession of judgment without suit. The equivalent Norman-French phrase was "*debit sans breve.*" Both are abbreviated to *d. s. b.*

DEBT. A sum of money due by certain and express agreement; as by bond for a determinate sum, a bill or note, a special bargain, or a rent reserved on a lease, where the amount is fixed and specific, and does not depend upon any subsequent valuation to settle it. 3 Bl. Comm. 154.

A debt is a sum of money due by contract. It is most frequently due by a certain and express agreement, which fixes the amount, independent of extrinsic circumstances. But it is not essential that the contract should be express, or that it should fix the precise amount to be paid. 1 Pet. 145.

Standing alone, the word "debt" is as applicable to a sum of money which has been promised at a future day, as to a sum of money now due and payable. To distinguish between the two, it may be said of the former that it is a debt owing, and of the latter that it is a debt due. Whether a claim or demand is a debt or not is in no respect determined by a reference to the time of payment. A sum of money which is certainly and in all events payable is a debt, without regard to the fact whether it be payable now or at a future time. A sum payable upon a contingency, however, is not a debt, or does not become a debt until the contingency has happened. 37 Cal. 524.

The word "debt" is of large import, including not only debts of record, or judgments, and debts by specialty, but also obligations arising under simple contract, to a very wide extent; and in its popular sense includes all that is due to a man under any form of obligation or promise. 3 Metc. (Mass.) 522, 526.

"Debt" has been differently defined, owing to the different subject-matter of the statutes in which it has been used. Ordinarily, it imports a sum of money arising upon a contract, express or implied. In its more general sense, it is defined to be that which is due from one person to another, whether money, goods, or services; that which one person is bound to pay or perform to another. Under the legal-tender statutes, it seems to import any obligation by contract, express or implied, which may be discharged by money through the voluntary action of the party bound. Wherever be may be at liberty to perform his obligation by the payment of a specific sum of money, the party owing the obligation is subject to what, in these statutes, is termed "debt." 45 Barb. 613.

The word is sometimes used to denote an aggregate of separate debts, or the total sum of the existing claims against a person or company. Thus we speak of the "national debt," the "bonded debt" of a corporation, etc.

Synonyms. The term "demand" is of much broader import than "debt," and embraces rights of action belonging to the debtor beyond those which could appropriately be called "debts." In this respect the term "demand" is one of very extensive import. 2 Hill, 223.

The words "debt" and "liability" are not synonymous. As applied to the pecuniary relations of parties, liability is a term of broader significance than debt. The legal acceptation of debt is a sum of money due by certain and express agreement. Liability is responsibility; the state of one who is bound in law and justice to do something which may be enforced by action. This liability may arise from contracts either express or implied, or in consequence of torts committed. 36 Iowa, 226.

"Debt" is not exactly synonymous with "duty." A debt is a legal liability to pay a specific sum of money; a duty is a legal obligation to perform some act. 1 Minor, 120.

In practice. The name of a common-law action, which lies to recover a certain specific sum of money, or a sum that can readily be reduced to a certainty. 3 Bl. Comm. 154; 3 Steph. Comm. 461; 1 Tidd. Pr. 3.

It is said to lie in the *debet* and *detinet*, (when it is stated that the defendant owes and detains,) or in the *detinet*, (when it is stated merely that he detains.) Debt in the *detinet* for goods differs from detinue, because it is not essential in this action, as in detinue, that the specific property in the goods should have been vested in the plaintiff at the time the action is brought. Dyer, 24b.

DEBT BY SIMPLE CONTRACT. A debt or demand founded upon a verbal or implied contract, or upon any written agreement that is not under seal.

DEBT BY SPECIALTY. A debt due, or acknowledged to be due, by some deed or instrument under seal; as a deed of covenant or sale, a lease reserving rent, or a bond or obligation. 2 Bl. Comm. 465. See SPECIALTY.

DEBT EX MUTUO. A species of debt or obligation mentioned by Glanville and Bracton, and which arose *ex mutuo*, out of a certain kind of loan. Glan. lib. 10, c. 3; Bract. fol. 99. See MUTUUM; EX MUTUO.

DEBT OF RECORD. A debt which appears to be due by the evidence of a court of record, as by a judgment or recognizance. 2 Bl. Comm. 465.

DEBTEE. A person to whom a debt is due; a creditor. 3 Bl. Comm. 18; Plowd. 543. Not used.

DEBTOR. One who owes a debt; he who may be compelled to pay a claim or demand.

DEBTOR'S ACT 1869. The statute 32 & 33 Vict. c. 62, abolishing imprisonment for debt in England, and for the punishment of fraudulent debtors. 2 Steph. Comm. 159–164. Not to be confounded with the Bankruptcy Act of 1869. Mozley & Whitley.

DEBTOR'S SUMMONS. In English law. A summons issuing from a court having jurisdiction in bankruptcy, upon the creditor proving a liquidated debt of not less than £50, which he has failed to collect after reasonable effort, stating that if the debtor fail, within one week if a trader, and within three weeks if a non-trader, to pay or compound for the sum specified, a petition may be presented against him praying that he may be adjudged a bankrupt. Bankruptcy Act 1869, § 7; Robs. Bankr.; Mozley & Whitley.

DECALOGUE. The ten commandments given by God to Moses. The Jews called them the "Ten Words," hence the name.

DECANATUS. A deanery. Spelman. A company of ten persons. Calvin.

DECANIA. The office, jurisdiction, territory, or command of a *decanus*, or dean. Spelman.

DECANUS. In ecclesiastical and old European law. An officer having supervision over *ten*; a dean. A term applied not only to ecclesiastical, but to civil and military, officers. *Decanus monasticus;* a monastic dean, or dean of a monastery; an officer over ten monks. *Decanus in majori ecclesiæ;* dean of a cathedral church, presiding over ten prebendaries. *Decanus episcopi;* a bishop's or rural dean, presiding over ten clerks or parishes. *Decanus friborgi;* dean of a friborg. An officer among the Saxons who presided over a friborg, tithing, decennary, or association of ten inhabitants; otherwise called a "tithing man," or "borsholder." *Decanus militaris;* a military officer, having command of ten soldiers. Spelman.

In **Roman law.** An officer having the command of a company or "mess" of ten soldiers. Also an officer at Constantinople having charge of the burial of the dead.

DECAPITATION. The act of beheading. A mode of capital punishment by cutting off the head.

DECEASE, *n.* Death; departure from life.

DECEASE, *v.* To die; to depart life, or from life. This has always been a common term in Scotch law. "Gif ane man *deceasis.*" Skene.

DECEDENT. A deceased person; one who has lately died. Etymologically the word denotes a person who is *dying,* but it has come to be used in law as signifying any defunct person, (testate or intestate,) but always with reference to the settlement of his estate or the execution of his will.

DECEIT. A fraudulent and cheating misrepresentation, artifice, or device, used by one or more persons to deceive and trick another, who is ignorant of the true facts, to the prejudice and damage of the party imposed upon.

A subtle trick or device, whereunto may be referred all manner of craft and collusion used to deceive and defraud another by any means whatsoever, which hath no other or more proper name than *deceit* to distinguish the offense. [West Symb. § 68;] Jacob.

The word "deceit," as well as "fraud," excludes the idea of mistake, and imports knowledge that the artifice or device used to deceive or defraud is untrue. 61 Ill. 373.

In **old English law.** The name of an original writ, and the action founded on it, which lay to recover damages for any injury committed *deceitfully,* either in the name of another, (as by bringing an action in another's name, and then suffering a nonsuit, whereby the plaintiff became liable to costs,) or by a fraudulent warranty of goods, or other personal injury committed contrary to good faith and honesty. Reg. Orig. 112–116; Fitzh. Nat. Brev. 95, E, 98.

Also the name of a judicial writ which formerly lay to recover lands which had been lost by default by the tenant in a real action, in consequence of his not having been summoned by the sheriff, or by the collusion of his attorney. Rosc. Real Act. 136; 3 Bl. Comm. 166.

DECEM TALES. (Ten such; or ten tales, jurors.) In practice. The name of a writ which issues in England, where, on a trial at bar, *ten* jurors are necessary to make up a full panel, commanding the sheriff to summon the requisite number. 3 Bl. Comm. 364; Reg. Jud. 30*b*; 3 Steph. Comm. 602.

DECEMVIRI LITIBUS JUDICAN-DIS. Lat. In the Roman law. Ten persons (five senators and five *equites*) who acted as the council or assistants of the praetor, when he decided on matters of law. Hallifax, Civil Law, b. 3, c. 8. According to others, they were themselves judges. Calvin.

DECENNA. In old English law. A tithing or decennary; the precinct of a frankpledge; consisting of ten freeholders with their families. Spelman.

DECENNARIUS. Lat. One who held one-half a virgate of land. Du Cange. One of the ten freeholders in a *decennary.* Id.; Calvin. *Decennier.* One of the *decennarii,* or ten freeholders making up a tithing. Spelman.

DECENNARY. A tithing, composed of ten neighboring families. 1 Reeve, Eng. Law, 13; 1 Bl. Comm. 114.

Deceptis non decipientibus, jura subveniunt. The laws help persons who are deceived, not those deceiving. Tray. Lat. Max. 149.

DECERN. In Scotch law. To decree. "Decernit and ordainit." 1 How. State Tr. 927. "Decerns." Shaw, 16.

DECESSUS. In the civil and old English law. Death; departure.

Decet tamen principem servare leges, quibus ipse servatus est. It behoves, indeed, the prince to keep the laws by which he himself is preserved.

DECIDE. To decide includes the power and right to deliberate, to weigh the reasons for and against, to see which preponderate, and to be governed by that preponderance. 5 Gray, 253.

DECIES TANTUM. (Ten times as much.) The name of an ancient writ that was used against a juror who had taken a bribe in money for his verdict. The injured party could thus recover ten times the amount of the bribe.

DECIMÆ. In ecclesiastical law. Tenths, or tithes. The tenth part of the annual profit of each living, payable formerly to the pope. There were several valuations made of these livings at different times. The *decimæ* (tenths) were appropriated to the crown, and a new valuation established, by 26 Hen. VIII. c. 3. 1 Bl. Comm. 284. See TITHES.

Decimæ debentur parocho. Tithes are due to the parish priest.

Decimæ de decimatis solvi non debent. Tithes are not to be paid from that which is given for tithes.

Decimæ de jure divino et canonica institutione pertinent ad personam. Dal. 50. Tithes belong to the parson by divine right and canonical institution.

Decimæ non debent solvi, ubi non est annua renovatio; et ex annuatis renovantibus simul semel. Cro. Jac. 42. Tithes ought not to be paid where there is not an annual renovation, and from annual renovations once only.

DECIMATION. The punishing every tenth soldier by lot, for mutiny or other failure of duty, was termed "*decimatio legionis*" by the Romans. Sometimes only the twentieth man was punished, (*vicesimatio,*) or the hundredth, (*centesimatio.*)

DECIME. A French coin of the value of the tenth part of a franc, or nearly two cents.

Decipi quam fallere est tutius. It is safer to be deceived than to deceive. Lofft, 396.

DECISION. In practice. A judgment or decree pronounced by a court in settlement of a controversy submitted to it and by way of authoritative answer to the questions raised before it.
"Decision" is not synonymous with "opinion." A decision of the court is its judgment; the opinion is the reasons given for that judgment. 13 Cal. 27.

DECISIVE OATH. In the civil law. Where one of the parties to a suit, not being able to prove his charge, offered to refer the decision of the cause to the oath of his adversary, which the adversary was bound to ac-

cept, or tender the same proposal back again, otherwise the whole was taken as confessed by him. Cod. 4, 1, 12.

DECLARANT. A person who makes a declaration.

DECLARATION. In pleading. The first of the pleadings on the part of the plaintiff in an action at law, being a formal and methodical specification of the facts and circumstances constituting his cause of action. It commonly comprises several sections or divisions, called "counts," and its formal parts follow each other in this order: Title, venue, commencement, cause of action, counts, conclusion. The declaration, at common law, answers to the "libel" in ecclesiastical and admiralty law, the "bill" in equity, the "petition" in civil law, the "complaint" in code pleading, and the "count" in real actions.

In evidence. An unsworn statement or narration of facts made by a party to the transaction, or by one who has an interest in the existence of the facts recounted. Or a similar statement made by a person since deceased, which is admissible in evidence in some cases, contrary to the general rule, e. g., a "dying declaration."

In practice. The declaration or declaratory part of a judgment, decree, or order is that part which gives the decision or opinion of the court on the question of law in the case. Thus, in an action raising a question as to the construction of a will, the judgment or order declares that, according to the true construction of the will, the plaintiff has become entitled to the residue of the testator's estate, or the like. Sweet.

In Scotch practice. The statement of a criminal or prisoner, taken before a magistrate. 2 Alis. Crim. Pr. 555.

DECLARATION OF INDEPENDENCE. A formal declaration or announcement, promulgated July 4, 1776, by the congress of the United States of America, in the name and behalf of the people of the colonies, asserting and proclaiming their independence of the British crown, vindicating their pretensions to political autonomy, and announcing themselves to the world as a free and independent nation.

DECLARATION OF INTENTION. A declaration made by an alien, as a preliminary to naturalization, before a court of record, to the effect that it is *bona fide* his intention to become a citizen of the United

States, and to renounce forever all allegiance and fidelity to any foreign prince, potentate, state, or sovereignty whereof at the time he may be a citizen or subject.   Rev. St. § 2165.

DECLARATION OF PARIS. The name given to an agreement announcing four important rules of international law effected between the principal European powers at the Congress of Paris in 1856. These rules are: (1) Privateering is and remains abolished; (2) the neutral flag covers enemy's goods, except contraband of war; (3) neutral goods, except contraband of war, are not liable to confiscation under a hostile flag; (4) blockades, to be binding, must be effective.

DECLARATION OF RIGHT. See BILL OF RIGHTS.

DECLARATION OF TRUST. The act by which the person who holds the legal title to property or an estate acknowledges and declares that he holds the same in trust to the use of another person or for certain specified purposes. The name is also used to designate the deed or other writing embodying such a declaration.

DECLARATION OF WAR. A public and formal proclamation by a nation, through its executive or legislative department, that a state of war exists between itself and another nation, and forbidding all persons to aid or assist the enemy.

DECLARATOR. In Scotch law. An action whereby it is sought to have some right of property, or of *status*, or other right judicially ascertained and declared. Bell.

DECLARATOR OF TRUST. In Scotch law. An action resorted to against a trustee who holds property upon titles *ex facie* for his own benefit. Bell.

DECLARATORY. Explanatory; designed to fix or elucidate what before was uncertain or doubtful; as a declaratory statute, which is one passed to put an end to a doubt as to what the law is, and which declares what it is and what it has been. 1 Bl. Comm. 86.

DECLARATORY ACTION. In Scotch law. An action in which the right of the pursuer (or plaintiff) is craved to be *declared*, but nothing claimed to be done by the defender, (defendant.) Ersk. Inst. 5, 1, 46. Otherwise called an "action of declarator."

DECLARATORY DECREE. In practice. A binding declaration of right in equity without consequential relief.

DECLARATORY JUDGMENT. A declaratory judgment is one which simply declares the rights of the parties, or expresses the opinion of the court on a question of law, without ordering anything to be done.

DECLARATORY PART OF A LAW. That which clearly defines rights to be observed and wrongs to be eschewed.

DECLARE. To solemnly assert a fact before witnesses, *e. g.*, where a testator *declares* a paper signed by him to be his last will and testament.

This also is one of the words customarily used in the promise given by a person who is *affirmed* as a witness,—"sincerely and truly declare and affirm." Hence, to make a positive and solemn asseveration.

With reference to pleadings, it means to draw up, serve, and file a declaration; *e. g.*, a "rule to declare." Also to allege in a declaration as a ground or cause of action; as "he declares upon a promissory note."

DECLINATION. In Scotch law. A plea to the jurisdiction, on the ground that the judge is interested in the suit.

DÉCLINATOIRES. In French law. Pleas to the jurisdiction of the court; also of *lis pendens*, and of *connexité*, (*q. v.*)

DECLINATORY PLEA. In English practice. The plea of sanctuary, or of benefit of clergy, before trial or conviction. 2 Hale, P. C. 236; 4 Bl. Comm. 333. Now abolished. 4 Steph. Comm. 400, note; Id. 436, note.

DECLINATURE. In Scotch practice. An objection to the jurisdiction of a judge. Bell.

DECOCTION. The act of boiling a substance in water, for extracting its virtues. Also the liquor in which a substance has been boiled; water impregnated with the principles of any animal or vegetable substance boiled in it. Webster.

In an indictment "decoction" and "infusion" are *ejusdem generis;* and if one is alleged to have been administered, instead of the other, the variance is immaterial. 3 Camp. 74.

DECOCTOR. In the Roman law. A bankrupt; a spendthrift; a squanderer of public funds. Calvin.

DECOLLATIO. In old English and Scotch law. Decollation; the punishment of beheading. Fleta, lib. 1, c. 21, § 6.

DECONFES. In French law. A name formerly given to those persons who died without confession, whether they refused to confess or whether they were criminals to whom the sacrament was refused.

DECOY. A pond used for the breeding and maintenance of water-fowl. 11 Mod. 74, 130; 3 Salk. 9.

DECOY LETTER. A letter prepared and mailed for the purpose of detecting a criminal, particularly one who is perpetrating frauds upon the postal or revenue laws. 5 Dill. 39.

DECREE. In practice. The judgment of a court of equity or admiralty, answering to the judgment of a court of common law. A decree in equity is a sentence or order of the court, pronounced on hearing and understanding all the points in issue, and determining the right of all the parties to the suit, according to equity and good conscience. 2 Daniell, Ch. Pr. 986.

Decree is the judgment of a court of equity, and is, to most intents and purposes, the same as a judgment of a court of common law. A decree, as distinguished from an order, is final, and is made at the hearing of the cause, whereas an order is interlocutory, and is made on motion or petition. Wherever an order may, in a certain event resulting from the direction contained in the order, lead to the termination of the suit in like manner as a decree made at the hearing, it is called a "decretal order." Brown.

It is either interlocutory or final; the former where it passes upon some plea or issue arising in the cause, but not involving a definitive adjudication of the main question; the latter where it finally determines the whole matter in dispute.

In French law. Certain acts of the legislature or of the sovereign which have the force of law are called "*decrees;*" as the Berlin and Milan decrees.

In Scotch law. A final judgment or sentence of court by which the question at issue between the parties is decided.

DECREE DATIVE. In Scotch law. An order of a probate court appointing an administrator.

DECREE NISI. A provisional decree, which will be made absolute on motion unless cause be shown against it. In English practice, it is the order made by the court for divorce, on satisfactory proof being given in support of a petition for dissolution of marriage; it remains imperfect for at least six months, (which period may be shortened by the court down to three,) and then, unless sufficient cause be shown, it is made absolute on motion, and the dissolution takes effect, subject to appeal. Wharton.

DECREE OF CONSTITUTION. In Scotch practice. A decree by which a debt is ascertained. Bell.

In technical language, a decree which is requisite to found a title in the person of the creditor, whether that necessity arises from the death of the debtor or of the creditor. Id.

DECREE OF FORTHCOMING. In Scotch law. A decree made after an arrestment (q. v.) ordering the debt to be paid or the effects of the debtor to be delivered to the arresting creditor. Bell.

DECREE OF LOCALITY. In Scotch law. The decree of a teind court allocating stipend upon different heritors. It is equivalent to the apportionment of a tithe rent-charge.

DECREE OF MODIFICATION. In Scotch law. A decree of the teind court modifying or fixing a stipend.

DECREE OF REGISTRATION. In Scotch law. A proceeding giving immediate execution to the creditor; similar to a warrant of attorney to confess judgment.

DECREET. In Scotch law. The final judgment or sentence of a court.

DECREET ABSOLVITOR. In Scotch law. A decree dismissing a claim, or acquitting a defendant. 2 Kames, Eq. 367.

DECREET ARBITRAL. In Scotch law. An award of arbitrators. 1 Kames, Eq. 312, 313; 2 Kames, Eq. 367.

DECREET COGNITIONIS CAUSÂ. In Scotch law. When a creditor brings his action against the heir of his debtor in order to constitute the debt against him and attach the lands, and the heir appears and renounces the succession, the court then pronounces a decree *cognitionis causâ.* Bell.

DECREET CONDEMNATOR. In Scotch law. One where the decision is in favor of the plaintiff. Ersk. Inst. 4, 3, 5.

DECREET OF VALUATION OF TEINDS. In Scotch law. A sentence of the court of sessions, (who are now in the place of the commissioners for the valuation of teinds,) determining the extent and value of teinds. Bell.

DECREMENTUM MARIS. Lat. In old English law. Decrease of the sea; the receding of the sea from the land. Callis, Sewers, (53,) 65. See RELICTION.

DECREPIT. This term designates a person who is disabled, incapable, or incompetent, either from physical or mental weakness or defects, whether produced by age or other causes, to such an extent as to render the individual comparatively helpless in a personal conflict with one possessed of ordinary health and strength. 16 Tex. App. 11.

DECRETA. In the Roman law. Judicial sentences given by the emperor as supreme judge.

Decreta conciliorum non ligant reges nostros. Moore, 906. The decrees of councils bind not our kings.

DECRETAL ORDER. In chancery practice. An order made by the court of chancery, in the nature of a decree, upon a motion or petition.

An order in a chancery suit made on motion or otherwise not at the regular hearing of a cause, and yet not of an interlocutory nature, but finally disposing of the cause, so far as a decree could then have disposed of it. Mozley & Whitley.

DECRETALES BONIFACII OCTA-VI. A supplemental collection of the canon law, published by Boniface VIII. in 1298, called, also, *"Liber Sextus Decretalium,"* (Sixth Book of the Decretals.)

DECRETALES GREGORII NONI. The decretals of Gregory the Ninth. A collection of the laws of the church, published by order of Gregory IX. in 1227. It is composed of five books, subdivided into titles, and each title is divided into chapters. They are cited by using an X, (or *extra;*) thus *"Cap. 8 X de Regulis Juris,"* etc.

DECRETALS. In ecclesiastical law. Letters of the pope, written at the suit or instance of one or more persons, determining some point or question in ecclesiastical law, and possessing the force of law. The decretals form the second part of the body of canon law.

This is also the title of the second of the two great divisions of the canon law, the first being called the *"Decree,"* (*decretum.*)

DECRETO. In Spanish colonial law. An order emanating from some superior tribunal, promulgated in the name and by the authority of the sovereign, in relation to ecclesiastical matters. Schm. Civil Law, 93, note.

DECRETUM. In the civil law. A species of imperial constitution, being a judgment or sentence given by the emperor upon hearing of a cause, (*quod imperator cognoscens decrevit.*) Inst. 1, 2, 6.

In canon law. An ecclesiastical law, in contradistinction to a secular law, (*lex.*) 1 Mackeld. Civil Law, p. 81, § 93, (Kaufmann's note.)

DECRETUM GRATIANI. Gratian's decree, or *decretum.* A collection of ecclesiastical law in three books or parts, made in the year 1151, by Gratian, a Benedictine monk of Bologna, being the oldest as well as the first in order of the collections which together form the body of the Roman canon law. 1 Bl. Comm. 82; 1 Reeve, Eng. Law, 67.

DECROWNING. The act of depriving of a crown.

DECRY. To cry down; to deprive of credit. "The king may at any time *decry* or cry down any coin of the kingdom, and make it no longer current." 1 Bl. Comm. 278.

DECURIO. In the provincial administration of the Roman empire, the decurions were the chief men or official personages of the large towns. Taken as a body, the decurions of a city were charged with the entire control and administration of its internal affairs; having powers both magisterial and legislative. See 1 Spence, Eq. Jur. 54.

DEDBANA. In Saxon law. An actual homicide or manslaughter.

DEDI. (Lat. I have given.) A word used in deeds and other instruments of conveyance when such instruments were made in Latin, and anciently held to imply a warranty of title.

DEDI ET CONCESSI. I have given and granted. The operative words of conveyance in ancient charters of feoffment, and deeds of gift and grant; the English *"given and granted"* being still the most proper, though not the essential, words by which such conveyances are made. 2 Bl. Comm. 53, 316, 317; 1 Steph. Comm. 164, 177, 473, 474.

DEDICATE. To appropriate and set apart one's private property to some public use; as to make a private way public by acts evincing an intention to do so.

DEDICATION.

DEDICATION. In real property law. An appropriation of land to some public use, made by the owner, and accepted for such use by or on behalf of the public. 23 Wis. 416; 33 N. J. Law, 13.

A deliberate appropriation of land by its owner for any general and public uses, reserving to himself no other rights than such as are perfectly compatible with the full exercise and enjoyment of the public uses to which he has devoted his property. 22 Wend. 472.

In copyright law. The first publication of a work, without having secured a copyright, is a dedication of it to the public; that having been done, any one may republish it. 5 McLean, 32; 7 West. Law J. 49; 5 McLean, 328.

DEDICATION-DAY. The feast of dedication of churches, or rather the feast day of the saint and patron of a church, which was celebrated not only by the inhabitants of the place, but by those of all the neighboring villages, who usually came thither; and such assemblies were allowed as lawful. It was usual for the people to feast and to drink on those days. Cowell.

DEDIMUS ET CONCESSIMUS. (Lat. We have given and granted.) Words used by the king, or where there were more grantors than one, instead of *dedi et concessi*.

DEDIMUS POTESTATEM. (We have given power.) In English practice. A writ or commission issuing out of chancery, empowering the persons named therein to perform certain acts, as to administer oaths to defendants in chancery and take their answers, to administer oaths of office to justices of the peace, etc. 3 Bl. Comm. 447. It was anciently allowed for many purposes not now in use, as to make an attorney, to take the acknowledgment of a fine, etc.

In the United States, a commission to take testimony is sometimes termed a "*dedimus potestatem*." 3 Cranch, 293; 4 Wheat. 508.

DEDIMUS POTESTATEM DE ATTORNO FACIENDO. In old English practice. A writ, issued by royal authority, empowering an attorney to appear for a defendant. Prior to the statute of Westminster 2, a party could not appear in court by attorney without this writ.

DEDITION. The act of yielding up anything; surrender.

DEDITITII. In Roman law. Criminals who had been marked in the face or on the body with fire or an iron, so that the mark could not be erased, and subsequently manumitted. Calvin.

DEDUCTION. By "deduction" is understood a portion or thing which an heir has a right to take from the mass of the succession before any partition takes place. Civil Code La. art. 1358.

DEDUCTION FOR NEW. In marine insurance. An allowance or drawback credited to the insurers on the cost of repairing a vessel for damage arising from the perils of the sea insured against. This allowance is usually one-third, and is made on the theory that the parts restored with new materials are better, in that proportion, than they were before the damage.

DEED. A sealed instrument, containing a contract or covenant, delivered by the party to be bound thereby, and accepted by the party to whom the contract or covenant runs.

A writing containing a contract sealed and delivered to the party thereto. 3 Washb. Real Prop. 239.

In its legal sense, a "deed" is an instrument in writing, upon paper or parchment, between parties able to contract, subscribed, sealed, and delivered. 60 Ind. 572; 4 Kent, Comm. 452.

In a more restricted sense, a written agreement, signed, sealed, and delivered, by which one person conveys land, tenements, or hereditaments to another. This is its ordinary modern meaning.

The term is also used as synonymous with "fact," "actuality," or "act of parties." Thus a thing "in deed" is one that has been really or expressly done; as opposed to "in law," which means that it is merely implied or presumed to have been done.

DEED INDENTED, or INDENTURE. In conveyancing. A deed executed or purporting to be executed in parts, between two or more parties, and distinguished by having the edge of the paper or parchment on which it is written indented or cut at the top in a particular manner. This was formerly done at the top or side, in a line resembling the teeth of a saw; a formality derived from the ancient practice of dividing chirographs; but the cutting is now made either in a waving line, or more commonly by notching or nicking the paper at the edge. 2 Bl. Comm. 295, 296; Litt. § 370; Smith, Cont. 12.

DEED OF COVENANT. Covenants are sometimes entered into by a separate deed, for title, or for the indemnity of a purchaser or mortgagee, or for the production of title-deeds. A covenant with a penalty is sometimes taken for the payment of a debt, instead of a bond with a condition, but the legal remedy is the same in either case.

DEED POLL. In conveyancing. A deed of one part or made by one party only; and originally so called because the edge of the paper or parchment was *polled* or cut in a straight line, wherein it was distinguished from a deed indented or indenture.

DEED TO DECLARE USES. A deed made after a fine or common recovery, to show the object thereof.

DEED TO LEAD USES. A deed made before a fine or common recovery, to show the object thereof.

DEEM. To hold; consider; adjudge; condemn. When, by statute, certain acts are "deemed" to be a crime of a particular nature, they are such crime, and not a semblance of it, nor a mere fanciful approximation to or designation of the offense. 132 Mass. 247.

DEEMSTERS. Judges in the Isle of Man, who decide all controversies without process, writings, or any charges. These judges are chosen by the people, and are said by Spelman to be two in number. Spelman.

DEER-FALD. A park or fold for deer.

DEER-HAYES. Engines or great nets made of cord to catch deer. 19 Hen. VIII. c. 11.

DEFALCATION. The act of a defaulter; misappropriation of trust funds or money held in any fiduciary capacity; failure to properly account for such funds. Usually spoken of officers of corporations or public officials.

Also set-off. The diminution of a debt or claim by deducting from it a smaller claim held by the debtor or payor.

DEFAMATION. The taking from one's reputation. The offense of injuring a person's character, fame, or reputation by false and malicious statements. The term seems to be comprehensive of both libel and slander.

DEFAMES. L. Fr. Infamous. Britt. c. 15.

DEFAULT. The omission or failure to fulfill a duty, observe a promise, discharge an obligation, or perform an agreement.

In practice. Omission; neglect or failure. When a defendant in an action at law omits to plead within the time allowed him for that purpose, or fails to appear on the trial, he is said to *make default*, and the judgment entered in the former case is technically called a "judgment by default." 3 Bl. Comm. 396; 1 Tidd, Pr. 562.

DEFAULTER. One who makes default. One who misappropriates money held by him in an official or fiduciary character, or fails to account for such money.

DEFEASANCE. An instrument which defeats the force or operation of some other deed or estate. That which is in the same deed is called a "condition;" and that which is in another deed is a "defeasance." Com. Dig. "Defeasance."

In conveyancing. A collateral deed made at the same time with a feoffment or other conveyance, containing certain conditions, upon the performance of which the estate then created may be *defeated* or totally undone. 2 Bl. Comm. 327; Co. Litt. 236, 237.

An instrument accompanying a bond, recognizance, or judgment, containing a condition which, when performed, *defeats* or undoes it. 2 Bl. Comm. 342; Co. Litt. 236, 237.

DEFEASIBLE. Subject to be defeated, annulled, revoked, or undone upon the happening of a future event or the performance of a condition subsequent, or by a conditional limitation. Usually spoken of estates and interests in land. For instance, a mortgagee's estate is defeasible (liable to be defeated) by the mortgagor's equity of redemption.

DEFEAT. See DEFEASANCE.

DEFECT. The want or absence of some legal requisite; deficiency; imperfection; insufficiency.

DEFECTUM. Challenge *propter*. See CHALLENGE.

DEFECTUS SANGUINIS. Lat. Failure of issue.

DEFEND. To prohibit or forbid. To deny. To contest and endeavor to defeat a claim or demand made against one in a court of justice. To oppose, repel, or resist.

In covenants of warranty in deeds, it means to protect, to maintain or keep secure, to guaranty, to agree to indemnify.

DEFENDANT. The person defending or denying; the party against whom relief or recovery is sought in an action or suit.

In common usage, this term is applied to the party put upon his defense, or summoned to answer a charge or complaint, in any species of action, civil or criminal, at law or in equity. Strictly, however, it does not apply to the person against whom a real action is brought, for in that proceeding the technical usage is to call the parties respectively the "demandant" and the "tenant."

DEFENDANT IN ERROR. The distinctive term appropriate to the party against whom a writ of error is sued out.

DEFENDEMUS. Lat. A word used in grants and donations, which binds the donor and his heirs to defend the donee, if any one go about to lay any incumbrance on the thing given other than what is contained in the deed of donation. Bract. l. 2, c. 16.

DEFENDER. (Fr.) To deny; to defend; to conduct a suit for a defendant; to forbid; to prevent; to protect.

DEFENDER. In Scotch and canon law. A defendant.

DEFENDER OF THE FAITH. A peculiar title belonging to the sovereign of England, as that of "Catholic" to the king of Spain, and that of "Most Christian" to the king of France. These titles were originally given by the popes of Rome; and that of *Defensor Fidei* was first conferred by Pope Leo X. on King Henry VIII., as a reward for writing against Martin Luther; and the bull for it bears date *quinto Idus Octob.*, 1521. Enc. Lond.

DEFENDERE SE PER CORPUS SUUM. To offer duel or combat as a legal trial and appeal. Abolished by 59 Geo. III. § 46. See BATTEL.

DEFENDERE UNICÂ MANU. To wage law; a denial of an accusation upon oath. See WAGER OF LAW.

DEFENDIT VIM ET INJURIAM. He defends the force and injury. Fleta, lib. 5, c. 39, § 1.

DEFENDOUR. L. Fr. A defender or defendant; the party accused in an appeal. Britt. c. 22.

DEFENERATION. The act of lending money on usury.

DEFENSA. In old English law. A park or place fenced in for deer, and defended as a property and peculiar for that use and service. Cowell.

DEFENSE. That which is offered and alleged by the party proceeded against in an action or suit, as a reason in law or fact why the plaintiff should not recover or establish what he seeks; what is put forward to defeat an action. More properly what is *sufficient* when offered for this purpose. In either of these senses it may be either a denial, justification, or confession and avoidance of the facts averred as a ground of action, or an exception to their sufficiency in point of law.

In a stricter sense, defense is used to denote the answer made by the defendant to the plaintiff's action, by demurrer or plea at law or answer in equity. This is the meaning of the term in Scotch law. Ersk. Inst. 4, 1, 66.

Half defense was that which was made by the form "defends the force and injury, and says," (*defendit vim et injuriam, et dicit.*)

Full defense was that which was made by the form "defends the force and injury when and where it shall behoove him, and the damages, and whatever else he ought to defend," (*defendit vim et injuriam quando et ubi curia consideravit, et damna et quicquid quod ipse defendere debet, et dicit,*) commonly shortened into "defends the force and injury when," etc. Gilb. Com. Pl. 188; 8 Term. 632; 3 Bos. & P. 9, note; Co. Litt. 127b.

In matrimonial suits, in England, defenses are divided into *absolute*, i. e., such as, being established to the satisfaction of the court, are a complete answer to the petition, so that the court can exercise no discretion, but is bound to dismiss the petition; and *discretionary*, or such as, being established, leave to the court a discretion whether it will pronounce a decree or dismiss the petition. Thus, in a suit for dissolution, condonation is an absolute, adultery by the petitioner a discretionary, defense. Browne, Div. 30.

Defense also means the forcible repelling of an attack made unlawfully with force and violence.

In old statutes and records, the term means prohibition; denial or refusal. *Encounter le defense et le commandement de roy;* against the prohibition and commandment of the king. St. Westm. 1, c. 1. Also a state of severalty, or of several or exclusive occupancy; a state of inclosure.

DEFENSE AU FOND EN DROIT. In French and Canadian law. A demurrer.

DEFENSE AU FOND EN FAIT. In French and Canadian law. The general issue. 3 Low. Can. 421.

DEFENSIVA. In old English law. A lord or earl of the marches, who was the warden and defender of his country. Cowell.

DEFENSIVE ALLEGATION. In English ecclesiastical law. A species of pleading, where the defendant, instead of denying the plaintiff's charge upon oath, has any circumstances to offer in his defense. This entitles him, in his turn, to the plaintiff's answer upon oath, upon which he may proceed to proofs as well as his antagonist. 3 Bl. Comm. 100; 3 Steph. Comm. 720.

DEFENSIVE WAR. A war in defense of, or for the protection of, national rights. It may be *defensive* in its principles, though *offensive* in its operations. 1 Kent, Comm. 50, note.

DEFENSO. That part of any open field or place that was allotted for corn or hay, and upon which there was no common or feeding, was anciently said to be *in defenso;* so of any meadow ground that was laid in for hay only. The same term was applied to a wood where part was inclosed or fenced, to secure the growth of the underwood from the injury of cattle. Cowell.

DEFENSOR. In the civil law. A defender; one who assumed the defense of another's case in court. Also an advocate. A tutor or curator.

In canon law. The advocate or patron of a church. An officer who had charge of the temporalities of the church.

In old English law. A guardian, defender, or protector. The defendant in an action. A person vouched in to warranty.

DEFENSOR CIVITATIS. Lat. Defender or protector of a city or municipality. An officer under the Roman empire, whose duty it was to protect the people against the injustice of the magistrates, the insolence of the subaltern officers, and the rapacity of the money-lenders. Schm. Civil Law, Introd. 16; Cod. 1, 55, 4. He had the powers of a judge, with jurisdiction of pecuniary causes to a limited amount, and the lighter species of offenses. Cod. 1, 55, 1; Nov. 15, c. 3, § 2; Id. c. 6, § 1. He had also the care of the public records, and powers similar to those of a notary in regard to the execution of wills and conveyances.

DEFENSUM. An inclosure of land; any fenced ground. See DEFENSO.

DEFERRED LIFE ANNUITIES. In English law. Annuities for the life of the purchaser, but not commencing until a date subsequent to the date of buying them, so that, if the purchaser die before that date, the purchase money is lost. Granted by the commissioners for reduction of the national debt. See 16 & 17 Vict. c. 45. § 2. Wharton.

DEFERRED STOCK. Stock in a corporation is sometimes divided into "preferred," the holders of which are entitled to a fixed dividend payable out of the net earnings of the whole stock, and "deferred," the holders of which are entitled to all the residue of the net earnings after such fixed dividend has been paid to the holders of preferred stock. Wharton.

Deficiente uno sanguine non potest esse hæres. 3 Coke, 41. One blood being wanting, he cannot be heir. But see 3 & 4 Wm. IV. c. 106, § 9, and 33 & 34 Vict. c. 23, § 1.

DEFICIT. Someting wanting, generally in the accounts of one intrusted with money, or in the money received by him.

DEFINE. To explain or state the exact meaning of words and phrases; to settle, make clear, establish boundaries.

"An examination of our Session Laws will show that acts have frequently been passed, the constitutionality of which has never been questioned, where the powers and duties conferred could not be considered as merely explaining or making more clear those previously conferred or attempted to be, although the word 'define' was used in the title. In legislation it is frequently used in the creation, enlarging, and extending the powers and duties of boards and officers, in defining certain offenses and providing punishment for the same, and thus enlarging and extending the scope of the criminal law. And it is properly used in the title where the object of the act is to determine or fix boundaries, more especially where a dispute has arisen concerning them. It is used between different governments, as to define the extent of a kingdom or country." 36 Mich. 452.

DEFINITION. A description of a thing by its properties; an explanation of the meaning of a word or term. Webster. The process of stating the exact meaning of a word by means of other words. Worcester.

DEFINITIVE. That which finally and completely ends and settles a controversy. A definitive sentence or judgment is put in opposition to an interlocutory judgment.

A distinction may be taken between a *final* and a *definitive* judgment. The former term is applicable when the judgment exhausts the powers of the particular court in which it is rendered; while the latter word designates a judgment that is above any review or contingency of reversal. 1 Cranch 103.

DEFINITIVE SENTENCE. The final judgment, decree, or sentence of an ecclesiastical court. 3 Bl. Comm. 101.

DEFLORATION. Seduction or debauching. The act by which a woman is deprived of her virginity.

DEFORCE. In English law. To withhold wrongfully; to withhold the possession of lands from one who is lawfully entitled to them. 3 Bl. Comm. 172.

In Scotch law. To resist the execution of the law; to oppose by force a public officer in the execution of his duty. Bell.

DEFORCEMENT. Deforcement is where a man wrongfully holds lands to which another person is entitled. It therefore includes disseisin, abatement, discontinuance, and intrusion. Co. Litt. 277b, 331b. But it is applied especially to cases, not falling under those heads, where the person entitled to the freehold has never had possession; thus, where a lord has a seignory, and lands escheat to him *propter defectum sanguinis*, but the seisin is withheld from him, this is a deforcement, and the person who withholds the seisin is called a "deforceor." 3 Bl. Comm. 172.

In Scotch law. The opposition or resistance made to messengers or other public officers while they are actually engaged in the exercise of their offices. Ersk. Inst. 4, 4, 32.

DEFORCIANT. One who wrongfully keeps the owner of lands and tenements out of the possession of them. 2 Bl. Comm. 350.

DEFORCIARE. To withhold lands or tenements from the rightful owner. This is a word of art which cannot be supplied by any other word. Co. Litt. 331b.

DEFORCIATIO. In old English law. A distress, distraint, or seizure of goods for satisfaction of a lawful debt. Cowell.

DEFOSSION. The punishment of being buried alive.

DEFRAUD. To practice fraud; to cheat or trick; to deprive a person of property or any interest, estate, or right by fraud, deceit, or artifice.

DEFRAUDACION. In Spanish law. The crime committed by a person who fraudulently avoids the payment of some public tax.

DEFRAUDATION. Privation by fraud.

DEFUNCT. Deceased; a deceased person. A common term in Scotch law.

DEGASTER. L. Fr. To waste.

DEGRADATION. A deprivation of dignity; dismission from office. An ecclesiastical censure, whereby a clergyman is divested of his holy orders. There are two sorts by the canon law,—one *summary*, by word only; the other *solemn*, by stripping the party degraded of those ornaments and rights which are the ensigns of his degree. Degradation is otherwise called "deposition," but the canonists have distinguished between these two terms, deeming the former as the greater punishment of the two. There is likewise a degradation of a lord or knight at common law, and also by act of parliament. Wharton.

DEGRADATIONS. A term for waste in the French law.

DEGRADING. Reviling; holding one up to public obloquy; lowering a person in the estimation of the public.

DEGREE. In the law of descent and family relations. A step or grade, *i. e.*, the distance, or number of removes, which separates two persons who are related by consanguinity. Thus we speak of cousins in the "second degree."

In criminal law. The term "degree" denotes a division or classification of one specific crime into several grades or *stadia* of guilt, according to the circumstances attending its commission. Thus, in some states, there may be "murder in the second degree."

DEHORS. L. Fr. Out of; without; beyond; foreign to; unconnected with. *Dehors* the record; foreign to the record. 3 Bl. Comm. 387.

DEI GRATIA. Lat. By the grace of God. A phrase used in the formal title of a king or queen, importing a claim of sovereignty by the favor or commission of God. In ancient times it was incorporated in the titles of inferior officers, (especially ecclesiastical,) but in later use was reserved as an assertion of "the divine right of kings."

DEI JUDICIUM. The judgment of God. The old Saxon trial by ordeal, so called because it was thought to be an appeal to God for the justice of a cause, and it was believed that the decision was according to the will and pleasure of Divine Providence. Wharton.

DEJACION. In Spanish law. Surrender; release; abandonment; *e. g.*, the act of an insolvent in surrendering his property for the benefit of his creditors, of an heir in renouncing the succession, the abandonment of insured property to the underwriters.

DEJERATION. A taking of a solemn oath.

DEL BIEN ESTRE. L. Fr. In old English practice. Of well being; of form. The same as *de bene esse.* Britt. c. 39.

DEL CREDERE. In mercantile law. A phrase borrowed from the Italians, equivalent to our word "guaranty" or "warranty," or the Scotch term "warrandice;" an agreement by which a factor, when he sells goods on credit, for an additional commission, (called a *"del credere* commission,") guaranties the solvency of the purchaser and his performance of the contract. Such a factor is called a *"del credere* agent." He is a mere surety, liable only to his principal in case the purchaser makes default. Story, Ag. 28.

DELAISSEMENT. In French marine law. Abandonment. Emerig. Tr. des Ass. ch. 17.

DELATE. In Scotch law. To accuse. Delated, accused. *Delatit off arte and parte,* accused of being accessary to. 3 How. St. Tr. 425, 440.

DELATIO. In the civil law. An accusation or information.

DELATOR. An accuser; an informer; a sycophant.

DELATURA. In old English law. The reward of an informer. Whishaw.

DELECTUS PERSONÆ. Lat. Choice of the person. By this term is understood the right of a partner to exercise his choice and preference as to the admission of any new members to the firm, and as to the persons to be so admitted, if any.

In Scotch law. The personal preference which is supposed to have been exercised by a landlord in selecting his tenant, by the members of a firm in making choice of partners, in the appointment of persons to office, and other cases. Nearly equivalent to personal trust, as a doctrine in law. Bell.

Delegata potestas non potest delegari. 2 Inst. 597. A delegated power cannot be delegated.

DELEGATE. A person who is delegated or commissioned to act in the stead of another; a person to whom affairs are committed by another; an attorney.

A person elected or appointed to be a member of a representative assembly. Usually spoken of one sent to a special or occasional assembly or convention.

The representative in congress of one of the organized territories of the United States.

DELEGATES, THE HIGH COURT OF. In English law. Formerly the court of appeal from the ecclesiastical and admiralty courts. Abolished, upon the judicial committee of the privy council being constituted the court of appeal in such cases.

DELEGATION. A sending away; a putting into commission; the assignment of a debt to another; the intrusting another with a general power to act for the good of those who depute him.

At common law. The transfer of authority by one person to another; the act of making or commissioning a delegate.

The whole body of delegates or representatives sent to a convention or assembly from one district, place, or political unit are collectively spoken of as a "delegation."

In the civil law. A species of novation which consists in the change of one debtor for another, when he who is indebted substitutes a third person who obligates himself in his stead to the creditor, so that the first debtor is acquitted and his obligation extinguished, and the creditor contents himself with the obligation of the second debtor. Delegation is essentially distinguished from any other species of novation, in this: that the former demands the consent of all three parties, but the latter that only of the two parties to the new debt. 1 Domat, § 2318; 48 Miss. 454.

Delegation is novation effected by the intervention of another person whom the debtor, in order to be liberated from his creditor, gives to such creditor, or to him whom the creditor appoints; and such person so given becomes obliged to the creditor in the place of the original debtor. Burge, Sur. 173.

Delegatus non potest delegare. A delegate cannot delegate; an agent cannot delegate his functions to a subagent without the knowledge or consent of the principal; the person to whom an office or duty is delegated cannot lawfully devolve the duty on another, unless he be expressly authorized so to do. 9 Coke, 77; Broom, Max. 840; 2 Kent, Comm. 633; 2 Steph. Comm. 119.

DELESTAGE. In French marine law. A discharging of ballast (*lest*) from a vessel.

DELETE. In Scotch law. To erase; to strike out.

DELF. A quarry or mine. 31 Eliz. c. 7.

Deliberandum est diu quod statuendum est semel. 12 Coke, 74. That which is to be resolved once for all should be long deliberated upon.

DELIBERATE, *v.* To weigh, ponder, discuss. To examine, to consult, in order to form an opinion.

DELIBERATE, *adj.* By the use of this word, in describing a crime, the idea is conveyed that the perpetrator weighs the motives for the act and its consequences, the nature of the crime, or other things connected with his intentions, with a view to a decision thereon; that he carefully considers all these; and that the act is not suddenly committed. It implies that the perpetrator must be capable of the exercise of such mental powers as are called into use by deliberation and the consideration and weighing of motives and consequences. 28 Iowa, 524.

"Deliberation" and "premeditation" are of the same character of mental operations, differing only in degree. Deliberation is but prolonged premeditation. In other words, in law, deliberation is premeditation in a cool state of the blood, or, where there has been heat of passion, it is premeditation continued beyond the period within which there has been time for the blood to cool, in the given case. Deliberation is not only to think of beforehand, which may be but for an instant, but the inclination to do the act is considered, weighed, pondered upon, for such a length of time after a provocation is given as the jury may find was sufficient for the blood to cool. One in a heat of passion may premeditate without deliberating. Deliberation is only exercised in a cool state of the blood, while premeditation may be either in that state of the blood or in the heat of passion. 74 Mo. 249. See, also, 20 Tex. 522; 15 Nev. 178; 5 Mo. 364; 66 Mo. 13.

DELIBERATION. The act or process of deliberating. The act of weighing and examining the reasons for and against a contemplated act or course of conduct, or a choice of acts or means. See DELIBERATE.

Delicatus debitor est odiosus in lege. A luxurious debtor is odious in law. 2 Bulst. 148. Imprisonment for debt has now, however, been generally abolished.

DELICT. In the civil law. A wrong or injury; an offense; a violation of public or private duty. It will be observed that this word, taken in its most general sense, is wider in both directions than our English term "tort." On the one hand, it includes those wrongful acts which, while directly affecting some individual or his property, yet extend in their injurious consequences to the peace or security of the community at large, and hence rise to the grade of crimes or misdemeanors. These acts were termed in the Roman law "public delicts;" while those for which the only penalty exacted was compensation to the person primarily injured were denominated "private delicts." On the other hand, the term appears to have included injurious actions which transpired without any malicious intention on the part of the doer. Thus Pothier gives the name "*quasi* delicts" to the acts of a person who, without malignity, but by an inexcusable imprudence, causes an injury to another. Poth. Obl. 116. But the term is used in modern jurisprudence as a convenient synonym of "tort;" that is, a wrongful and injurious violation of a *jus in rem* or right available against all the world. This appears in the two contrasted phrases, "actions *ex contractu*" and "actions *ex delicto.*"

DELICTUM. Lat. A delict, tort, wrong, injury, or offense. Actions *ex delicto* are such as are founded on a tort, as distinguished from actions on contract.

Culpability, blameworthiness, or legal delinquency. The word occurs in this sense in the maxim, "*In pari delicto melior est conditio defendentis,*" (which see.)

A challenge of a juror *propter delictum* is for some crime or misdemeanor that affects his credit and renders him infamous. 3 Bl. Comm. 363; 2 Kent, Comm. 241.

DELIMIT. To mark or lay out the limits or boundary line of a territory or country.

DELIMITATION. The act of fixing, marking off, or describing the limits or boundary line of a territory or country.

Dilinquens per iram provocatus puniri debet mitius. 3 Inst. 55. A delinquent provoked by anger ought to be punished more mildly.

DELINQUENT. In the civil law. He who has been guilty of some crime, offense, or failure of duty.

DELIRIUM. In medical jurisprudence. Delirium is that state of the mind in which it acts without being directed **by the power** of volition, which is wholly **or partially suspended.** This happens most perfectly in dreams. But what is commonly called "delirium" is always preceded or attended by a feverish and highly diseased state of the body. The patient in delirium is wholly unconscious of surrounding objects, or conceives them to be different from what they really are. His thoughts seem to drift about, wildering and tossing amidst distracted dreams. And his observations, when he makes any, as often happens, are wild and incoherent; or, from excess of pain, he sinks into a low muttering, or silent and death-like stupor. Rush, Mind, 9, 298.

The law contemplates this species of mental derangement as an intellectual eclipse; as a darkness occasioned by a cloud of disease passing over the mind; and which must soon terminate in health or in death. 1 Bland. 386.

DELIRIUM FEBRILE. In medical jurisprudence. A form of mental aberration incident to fevers, and sometimes to the last stages of chronic diseases.

DELIRIUM TREMENS. A species of mental aberration or temporary insanity which is induced by the excessive and protracted use of intoxicating liquors.

DELITO. In Spanish law. Crime; a crime, offense, or delict. White, New Recop. b. 2, tit. 19, c. 1, § 4.

DELIVERANCE. In practice. The verdict rendered by a jury.

DELIVERY. In conveyancing. The final and absolute transfer of a deed, properly executed, to the grantee, or to some person for his use, in such manner that it cannot be recalled by the grantor. 13 N. J. Eq. 455; 1 Dev. Eq. 14.

In the law of sales. The tradition or transfer of the possession of personal property from one person to another.

Delivery is either actual or constructive. Thus, if goods cannot conveniently be actually handed from one person to another, as if they are in a warehouse or a ship, the delivery of the key of the warehouse, a delivery order, bill of lading, etc., is a constructive or symbolical delivery of the goods themselves. Williams, Pers. Prop. 87; Benj. Sales, 573.

In medical jurisprudence. The act of a woman giving birth to her offspring.

DELIVERY BOND. A bond given upon the seizure of goods (as under the revenue laws) conditioned for their restoration to the defendant, or the payment of their value, if so adjudged.

DELIVERY ORDER. An order addressed, in England, by the owner of goods to a person holding them on his behalf, requesting him to deliver them to a person named in the order. Delivery orders are chiefly used in the case of goods held by dock companies, wharfingers, etc.

DELUSION. In medical jurisprudence. An insane delusion is an unreasoning and incorrigible belief in the existence of facts which are either impossible absolutely, or, at least, impossible under the circumstances of the individual. It is never the result of reasoning and reflection; it is not generated by them, and it cannot be dispelled by them; and hence it is not to be confounded with an *opinion*, however fantastic the latter may be. 10 Fed. Rep. 170.

DEM. An abbreviation for "demise;" *e. g.*, *Doe dem. Smith*, Doe, on the demise of Smith.

DEMAIN. See DEMESNE.

DEMAND, *v.* In practice. To claim as one's due; to require; to ask relief. To summon; to call in court. "Although solemnly *demanded*, comes not, but makes default."

DEMAND, *n.* A claim: the assertion of a legal right; a legal obligation asserted in the courts. "Demand" is a word of art of an extent greater in its signification than any other word except "claim." Co. Litt. 291; 2 Hill, 220.

Demand embraces all sorts of actions, rights, and titles, conditions before or after breach, executions, appeals, rents of all kinds, covenants, annuities, contracts, recognizances, statutes, commons, etc. A release of all demands to date bars an action for damages accruing after the date from a nuisance previously erected. 1 Denio, 257.

Demand is more comprehensive in import than "debt" or "duty." 4 Johns. 536; 2 Hill, 220.

Demand, or claim, is properly used in reference to a cause of action. 32 How. Pr. 280.

An imperative request preferred by one person to another, under a claim of right, requiring the latter to do or yield something or to abstain from some act.

DEMAND IN RECONVENTION. A demand which the defendant institutes in consequence of that which the plaintiff has brought against him. Used in Louisiana.

DEMANDA. In Spanish law. The petition of a plaintiff, setting forth his demand. Las Partidas, pt. 3, tit. 10, l. 3.

DEMANDANT. The plaintiff or party suing in a real action. Co. Litt. 127.

DEMANDRESS. A female demandant.

DEMEASE. In old English law. Death.

DEMEMBRATION. In Scotch law. Maliciously cutting off or otherwise separating one limb from another. 1 Hume, 323; Bell.

DEMENS. One whose mental faculties are enfeebled; one who has lost his mind; distinguishable from *amens*, one totally insane. 4 Coke, 128.

DEMENTED. Of unsound mind.

DEMENTENANT EN AVANT. L. Fr. From this time forward. Kelham.

DEMENTIA. In medical jurisprudence. That form of insanity where the mental derangement is accompanied with a general derangement of the faculties. It is characterized by forgetfulness, inability to follow any train of thought, and indifference to passing events. 4 Sawy. 677, per Field, J.

Senile dementia is that peculiar decay of the mental faculties which occurs in extreme old age, and in many cases much earlier, whereby the person is reduced to second childhood, and becomes sometimes wholly incompetent to enter into any binding contract, or even to execute a will. It is the recurrence of second childhood by mere decay. 1 Redf. Wills, 63.

Dementia denotes an impaired state of the mental powers, a feebleness of mind caused by disease, and not accompanied by delusion or uncontrollable impulse, without defining the degree of incapacity. *Dementia* may exist without complete prostration of the mental powers. 44 N. H. 531.

DEMESNE. Domain; dominical; held in one's own right, and not of a superior; not allotted to tenants. See DEMESNE LANDS.

In the language of pleading, own; proper; original. Thus, *son assault demesne*, his own assault, his assault originally or in the first place.

DEMESNE AS OF FEE. A man is said to be seised *in his demesne as of fee* of a corporeal inheritance, because he has a property, *dominicum* or *demesne*, in the *thing* itself. But when he has no dominion in the thing itself, as in the case of an incorporeal hereditament, he is said to be *seised* as of fee, and not in his *demesne* as of fee. 2 Bl. Comm. 106; Littleton, § 10; 17 Serg. & R. 196.

DEMESNE LANDS. In English law. Those lands of a manor not granted out in tenancy, but reserved by the lord for his own use and occupation. Lands set apart and appropriated by the lord for his own private use, as for the supply of his table, and the maintenance of his family; the opposite of *tenemental* lands. Tenancy and demesne, however, were not in every sense the opposites of each other; lands held for years or at will being included among demesne lands, as well as those in the lord's actual possession. Spelman; 2 Bl. Comm. 90.

DEMESNE LANDS OF THE CROWN. That share of lands reserved to the crown at the original distribution of landed property, or which came to it afterwards by forfeiture or otherwise. 1 Bl. Comm. 286; 2 Steph. Comm. 550.

DEMESNIAL. Pertaining to a *demesne*.

DEMI. French. Half; the half. Used chiefly in composition.

DEMI-MARK. Half a mark; a sum of money which was anciently required to be tendered in a writ of right, the effect of such tender being to put the demandant, in the first instance, upon proof of the seisin as stated in his count; that is, to prove that the seisin was in the king's reign there stated. Rosc. Real Act. 216.

DEMI-OFFICIAL. Partly official or authorized. Having color of official right.

DEMI-SANGUE, or DEMY-SANGUE. Half-blood.

DEMI-VILL. A town consisting of five freemen, or frank-pledges. Spelman.

DEMIDIETAS. In old records. A half or moiety.

DEMIES. In some universities and colleges this term is synonymous with "scholars."

DEMINUTIO. In the civil law. A taking away; loss or deprivation. See CAPITIS DEMINUTIO.

DEMISE, *v.* In conveyancing. To convey or create an estate for years or life; to lease. The usual and operative word in leases: "Have granted, *demised*, and to farm let, and by these presents do grant, *demise*, and to farm let." 2 Bl. Comm. 317; 1 Steph. Comm. 476; Co. Litt. 45*a*.

DEMISE, *n.* In conveyancing. A conveyance of an estate to another for life, for years, or at will; most commonly for years; a lease. 1 Steph. Comm. 475.

Originally a posthumous grant; commonly a lease or conveyance for a term of years; sometimes applied to any conveyance, in fee, for life, or for years. Pub. St. Mass. 1882, p. 1289.

"Demise" is synonymous with "lease" or "let," except that demise *ex vi termini* implies a covenant for title, and also a covenant for quiet enjoyment, whereas lease or let implies neither of these covenants. Brown.

The word is also used as a synonym for "decease" or "death." It England it is especially employed to denote the death of the sovereign.

DEMISE AND REDEMISE. In conveyancing. Mutual leases made from one party to another on each side, of the same land, or something out of it; as when A. grants a lease to B. at a nominal rent, (as of a pepper corn,) and B. redemises the same property to A. for a shorter time at a real, substantial rent. Jacob; Whishaw.

DEMISE OF THE CROWN. The natural dissolution of the king is generally so called; an expression which signifies merely a transfer of property. By demise of the crown we mean only that, in consequence of the disunion of the king's natural body from his body politic, the kingdom is transferred or demised to his successor, and so the royal dignity remains perpetual. 1 Bl. Comm. 249; Plowd. 234.

DEMISI. I have demised or leased. *Demisi, concessi, et ad firmam tradidi;* have demised, granted, and to farm let. The usual operative words in ancient leases, as the corresponding English words are in the modern forms. 2 Bl. Comm. 317, 318.

DEMOBILIZATION. In military law. The dismissal of an army or body of troops from active service.

DEMOCRACY. That form of government in which the sovereign power resides in and is exercised by the whole body of free citizens; as distinguished from a monarchy, aristocracy, or oligarchy. According to the theory of a pure democracy, every citizen should participate directly in the business of governing, and the legislative assembly should comprise the whole people. But the ultimate lodgment of the sovereignty being the distinguishing feature, the introduction of the representative system does not remove a government from this type. However, a government of the latter kind is sometimes

specifically described as a "representative democracy."

DEMOCRATIC. Of or pertaining to democracy, or to the party of the democrats.

DEMONETIZATION. The disuse of a particular metal for purposes of coinage. The withdrawal of the value of a metal as money.

DEMONSTRATIO. Description; addition; denomination. Occurring often in the phrase, *"Falsa demonstratio non nocet,"* (a false description does not harm.)

DEMONSTRATION. Description; pointing out. That which is said or written to designate a thing or person.

In evidence. Absolutely convincing proof. That proof which excludes all possibility of error.

DEMONSTRATIVE LEGACY. A bequest of a certain sum of money, with a direction that it shall be paid out of a particular fund. It differs from a specific legacy in this respect: that, if the fund out of which it is payable fails for any cause, it is nevertheless entitled to come on the estate as a general legacy. And it differs from a general legacy in this: that it does not abate in that class, but in the class of specific legacies. 63 Pa. St. 316. See, also, 17 Ohio St. 413; 42 Ala. 9.

A legacy of quantity is ordinarily a general legacy; but there are legacies of quantity in the nature of specific legacies, as of so much money, with reference to a particular fund for payment. This kind of legacy is called by the civilians a "demonstrative legacy," and it is so far general and differs so much in effect from one properly specific that, if the fund be called in or fail, the legatee will not be deprived of his legacy, but be permitted to receive it out of the general assets; yet the legacy is so far specific that it will not be liable to abate with general legacies upon a deficiency of assets. 2 Williams, Ex'rs, 1078.

DEMPSTER. In Scotch law. A doomsman. One who pronounced the sentence of court. 1 How. State Tr. 937.

DEMUR. To present a demurrer; to take an exception to the sufficiency in point of law of a pleading or state of facts alleged.

DEMURRABLE. A pleading, petition, or the like, is said to be demurrable when it does not state such facts as support the claim, prayer, or defense put forward. 5 Ch. Div. 979.

DEMURRAGE. In maritime law. The sum which is fixed by the contract of carriage, or which is allowed, as remuneration to the owner of a ship for the detention of his vessel beyond the number of days allowed by the charter-party for loading and unloading or for sailing. Also the detention of the vessel by the freighter beyond such time. See 3 Kent, Comm. 203; 2 Steph. Comm. 185.

Demurrage is only an extended freight or reward to the vessel, in compensation for the earnings she is improperly caused to lose. Every improper detention of a vessel may be considered a demurrage, and compensation under that name be obtained for it.. 1 Holmes, 290.

Demurrage is the allowance or compensation due to the master or owners of a ship, by the freighter, for the time the vessel may have been detained beyond the time specified or implied in the contract of affreightment or the charter-party. Bell.

DEMURRANT. One who demurs; the party who, in pleading, interposes a demurrer.

DEMURRER. In pleading. The formal mode of disputing the sufficiency in law of the pleading of the other side. In effect it is an allegation that, even if the facts as stated in the pleading to which objection is taken be true, yet their legal consequences are not such as to put the demurring party to the necessity of answering them or proceeding further with the cause.

An objection made by one party to his opponent's pleading, alleging that he ought not to answer it, for some defect in law in the pleading. It admits the facts, and refers the law arising thereon to the court. 7 How. 581.

It imports that the objecting party will not proceed, but will wait the judgment of the court whether he is bound so to do. Co. Litt. 71*b;* Steph. Pl. 61.

A *general* demurrer is one which excepts to the sufficiency of a previous pleading in general terms, without showing specifically the nature of the objection; and such demurrer is sufficient when the objection is on matter of substance.

A *special* demurrer is one which excepts to the sufficiency of the pleadings of the other party, and shows specifically the nature of the objection and the particular ground of exception. Steph. Pl. 158.

In equity. An allegation of a defendant, which, admitting the matters of fact alleged by the bill to be true, shows that as they are therein set forth they are insufficient for the plaintiff to proceed upon or to oblige the defendant to answer; or that, for some reason apparent on the face of the bill, or on account of the omission of some matter which ought to be contained therein, or for want of some

circumstances which ought to be attendant thereon, the defendant ought not to be compelled to answer to the whole bill, or to some certain part thereof. Mitf. Eq. Pl. 107.

Demurrer to interrogatories is the reason which a witness tenders for not answering a particular question in interrogatories. 2 Swanst. 194. It is not, strictly speaking, a demurrer, except in the popular sense of the word. Gres. Eq. Ev. 61.

DEMURRER BOOK. In practice. A record of the issue on a demurrer at law, containing a transcript of the pleadings, with proper entries; and intended for the use of the court and counsel on the argument. 3 Bl. Comm. 317; 3 Steph. Comm. 581.

DEMURRER TO EVIDENCE. This proceeding (now practically obsolete) was analogous to a demurrer to a pleading. It was an objection or exception by one of the parties in an action at law, to the effect that the evidence which his adversary had produced was insufficient in point of law (whether true or not) to make out his case or sustain the issue. Upon joinder in demurrer, the jury was discharged, and the case was argued to the court *in banc*, who gave judgment upon the facts as shown in evidence. See 3 Bl. Comm. 372.

DEMY SANKE, DEMY SANGUE. Half-blood. A corruption of *demi-sang*.

DEN. A valley. Blount. A hollow place among woods. Cowell.

DEN AND STROND. In old English law. Liberty for ships or vessels to run aground, or come ashore. Cowell.

DENARIATE. In old English law. As much land as is worth one penny *per annum*.

DENARII. An ancient general term for any sort of *pecunia numerata*, or ready money. The French use the word *"denier"* in the same sense,—*payer de ses propres deniers*.

DENARII DE CARITATE. In English law. Customary oblations made to a cathedral church at Pentecost.

DENARII S. PETRI. (Commonly called "Peter's Pence.") An annual payment on St. Peter's feast of a penny from every family to the pope, during the time that the Roman Catholic religion was established in England.

DENARIUS. The chief silver coin among the Romans, worth 8d.; it was the seventh part of a Roman ounce. Also an English penny. The denarius was first coined five years before the first Punic war, B. C. 269. In later times a copper coin was called "*denarius.*" Smith, Dict. Antiq.

DENARIUS DEI. (Lat. "God's penny.") Earnest money; money given as a token of the completion of a bargain. It differs from *arrhæ*, in this: that *arrhæ* is a part of the consideration, while the *denarius Dei* is no part of it. The latter was given away in charity; whence the name.

DENARIUS TERTIUS COMITATÛS. In old English law. A third part or penny of the county paid to its earl, the other two parts being reserved to the crown.

DENIAL. A traverse in the pleading of one party of an allegation of fact set up by the other; a defense.

DENIER. L. Fr. In old English law. Denial; refusal. *Denier* is when the rent (being demanded upon the land) is not paid. Finch, Law, b. 3, c. 5.

DENIER A DIEU In French law. Earnest money; a sum of money given in token of the completion of a bargain. The phrase is a translation of the Latin *Denarius Dei*, (*q. v.*)

DENIZATION. The act of making one a denizen; the conferring of the privileges of citizenship upon an alien born. Cro. Jac. 540. See DENIZEN.

DENIZE. To make a man a denizen or citizen.

DENIZEN. In English law. A person who, being an alien born, has obtained, *ex donatione regis*, letters patent to make him an English subject,—a high and incommunicable branch of the royal prerogative. A denizen is in a kind of middle state between an alien and a natural-born subject, and partakes of the *status* of both of these. 1 Bl. Comm. 374; 7 Coke, 6.

The term is used to signify a person who, being an alien by birth, has obtained letters patent making him an English subject. The king may denize, but not naturalize, a man; the latter requiring the consent of parliament, as under the naturalization act, 1870, (33 & 34 Vict. c. 14.) A denizen holds a position midway between an alien and a natural-born or naturalized subject, being able to take lands by purchase or devise, (which an alien could not until 1870 do,) but not able to take lands by descent, (which a natural-born or naturalized subject may do.) Brown

The word is also used in this sense in South Carolina. See 1 McCord, Eq. 352.

A denizen, in the primary, but obsolete, sense of the word, is a natural-born subject of a country. Co. Litt. 129*a*.

DENMAN'S (LORD) ACT. An English statute, for the amendment of the law of evidence, (6 & 7 Vict. c. 85,) which provides that no person offered as a witness shall thereafter be excluded by reason of incapacity, from crime or interest, from giving evidence.

DENMAN'S (MR.) ACT. An English statute, for the amendment of procedure in criminal trials, (28 & 29 Vict. c. 18,) allowing counsel to sum up the evidence in criminal as in civil trials, provided the prisoner be defended by counsel.

DENOMBREMENT. In French feudal law. A minute or act drawn up, on the creation of a fief, containing a description of the fief, and all the rights and incidents belonging to it. Guyot, Inst. Feud. c. 3.

Denominatio fieri debet a dignioribus. Denomination should be made from the more worthy.

DENOUNCEMENT. In Mexican law. A denouncement was a judicial proceeding, and, though real property might be acquired by an alien in fraud of the law,—that is, without observing its requirements,—he nevertheless retained his right and title to it, but was liable to be deprived of it by the proper proceeding of denouncement, which in its substantive characteristics was equivalent to the inquest of office found, at common law. 26 Cal. 477.

DENSHIRING OF LAND. (Otherwise called "burn-beating.") A method of improving land by casting parings of earth, turf, and stubble into heaps, which when dried are burned into ashes for a compost. Cowell.

DENUMERATION. The act of present payment.

DENUNCIA DE OBRA NUEVA. In Spanish law. The denouncement of a new work; being a proceeding to restrain the erection of some new work, as, for instance, a building which may, if completed, injuriously affect the property of the complainant; it is of a character similar to the interdicts of possession. Escriche; 1 Cal. 63.

DENUNCIATION. In the civil law. The act by which an individual informs a public officer, whose duty it is to prosecute offenders, that a crime has been committed.

In Scotch practice. The act by which a person is declared to be a rebel, who has disobeyed the charge given on letters of horning. Bell.

DENUNTIATIO. In old English law. A public notice or summons. Bract. 202b.

DEODAND. (L. Lat. *Deo dandum*, a thing to be given to God.) In English law. Any personal chattel which was the immediate occasion of the death of any reasonable creature, and which was forfeited to the crown to be applied to *pious* uses, and distributed in alms by the high almoner. 1 Hale, P. C. 419; Fleta. lib. 1, c. 25; 1 Bl. Comm. 300; 2 Steph. Comm. 365.

DEOR HEDGE. In old English law. The hedge inclosing a deer park.

DEPART. In pleading. To forsake or abandon the ground assumed in a former pleading, and assume a new one. See DE-PARTURE.

In maritime law. To leave a port; to be out of a port. To *depart* imports more than to *sail*, or set sail. A warranty in a policy that a vessel shall *depart* on or before a particular day is a warranty not only that she shall sail, but that she shall be *out of the port* on or before that day. 3 Maule & S. 461; 3 Kent, Comm. 307, note. "To depart" does not mean merely to break ground, but fairly to set forward upon the voyage. 6 Taunt. 241.

DEPARTMENT. 1. One of the territorial divisions of a country. The term is chiefly used in this sense in France, where the division of the country into departments is somewhat analogous, both territorially and for governmental purposes. to the division of an American state into counties.

2. One of the divisions of the executive branch of government. Used in this sense in the United States, where each department is charged with a specific class of duties, and comprises an organized staff of officials; *e. g.*, the department of state, department of war, etc.

DEPARTURE. In maritime law. A deviation from the course prescribed in the policy of insurance.

In pleading. The statement of matter in a replication, rejoinder, or subsequent pleading, as a cause of action or defense, which is not pursuant to the previous pleading of the same party, and which does not support and fortify it. 2 Williams, Saund. 84a, note 1; 2 Wils. 98; Co. Litt. 304a.

A departure, in pleading, is when a party quits or departs from the case or defense which he has first made, and has recourse to another. 49 Ind. 111; 16 Johns. 205; 13 N. Y. 88, 89.

A departure takes place when, in any pleading, the party deserts the ground that he took in his last antecedent pleading, and resorts to another. Steph. Pl. 410. Or, in other words, when the second pleading contains matter not pursuant to the former, and which does not support and fortify it. Co. Litt. 304a. Hence a departure obviously can never take place till the replication. Steph. Pl. 410. Each subsequent pleading must pursue or support the former one; *i. e.*, the replication must support the declaration, and the rejoinder the plea, without departing out of it. 3 Bl. Comm. 310.

DEPARTURE IN DESPITE OF COURT. In old English practice. The tenant in a real action, having once appeared, was considered as constructively present in court until again called upon. Hence if, upon being demanded, he failed to appear, he was said to have "departed in despite [*i. e.*, contempt] of the court."

DEPASTURE. In old English law. To pasture. "If a man *depastures* unprofitable cattle in his ground." Bunb. 1, case 1.

DEPECULATION. A robbing of the prince or commonwealth; an embezzling of the public treasure.

DEPENDENCY. A territory distinct from the country in which the supreme sovereign power resides, but belonging rightfully to it, and subject to the laws and regulations which the sovereign may think proper to prescribe. 3 Wash. C. C. 286.

It differs from a *colony*, because it is not settled by the citizens of the sovereign or mother state; and from *possession*, because it is held by other title than that of mere conquest.

DEPENDENT CONTRACT. One which depends or is conditioned upon another. One which it is not the duty of the contractor to perform until some obligation contained in the same agreement has been performed by the other party. Ham. Parties, 17, 29, 30, 109.

DEPENDENT COVENANTS are those in which the performance of one depends on the performance of the other.

DEPENDING. In practice. Pending or undetermined; in progress. See 5 Coke, 47.

DEPESAS. In Spanish-American law. Spaces of ground in towns reserved for commons or public pasturage. 12 Pet. 443, note.

DEPONE. In Scotch practice. To depose; to make oath in writing.

DEPONENT. In practice. One who *deposes* (that is, testifies or makes oath in *writing*) to the truth of certain facts; one who gives under oath testimony which is reduced to writing; one who makes oath to a written statement. The party making an affidavit is generally so called.

The word "depone," from which is derived "deponent," has relation to the mode in which the oath is administered, (by the witness placing his hand upon the book of the holy evangelists,) and not as to whether the testimony is delivered orally or reduced to writing. "Deponent" is included in the term "witness," but "witness" is more general. 47 Me. 248.

DEPONER. In old Scotch practice. A deponent. 3 How. State Tr. 695.

DEPOPULATIO AGRORUM. In old English law. The crime of destroying, ravaging, or laying waste a country. 2 Hale, P. C. 333; 4 Bl. Comm. 373.

DEPOPULATION. In old English law. A species of waste by which the population of the kingdom was diminished. Depopulation of houses was a public offense. 12 Coke, 30, 31.

DEPORTATIO. Lat. In the civil law. A kind of banishment, where a condemned person was sent or carried away to some foreign country, usually to an island, (*in insulam deportatur,*) and thus taken out of the number of Roman citizens.

DEPORTATION. Banishment to a foreign country, attended with confiscation of property and deprivation of civil rights. A punishment derived from the *deportatio* (*q. v.*) of the Roman law, and still in use in France.

In Roman law. A perpetual banishment, depriving the banished of his rights as a citizen; it differed from relegation (*q. v.*) and exile, (*q. v.*) 1 Brown, Civil & Adm. Law, 125, note; Inst. 1, 12, 1, and 2; Dig. 48, 22, 14, 1.

DEPOSE. In practice. In ancient usage, to testify as a witness; to give evidence under oath.

In modern usage. To make a deposition; to give evidence in the shape of a deposition; to make statements which are written down and sworn to; to give testimony which is reduced to writing by a duly-qualified officer and sworn to by the deponent.

To deprive an individual of a public employment or office against his will. Wolffius, Inst. § 1068. The term is usually applied to the deprivation of all authority of a sovereign.

DEPOSIT. A naked bailment of goods to be kept for the depositor without reward, and to be returned when he shall require it. Jones, Bailm. 36, 117; 9 Mass. 470.

A bailment of goods to be kept by the bailee without reward, and delivered according to the object or purpose of the original trust. Story, Bailm. § 41.

A *deposit*, in general, is an act by which a person receives the property of another, binding himself to preserve it and return it in kind. Civil Code La. art. 2926.

When chattels are delivered by one person to another to keep for the use of the bailor, it is called a "deposit." The depositary may undertake to keep it without reward, or gratuitously; it is then a naked deposit. If he receives or expects a reward or hire, he is then a depositary for hire. Very variant consequences follow the differences in the contract. Code Ga. 1882, § 2103.

According to the classification of the civil law, deposits are of the following several sorts: (1) *Necessary,* made upon some sudden emergency, and from some pressing necessity; as, for instance, in case of a fire, a shipwreck, or other overwhelming calamity, when property is confided to any person whom the depositor may meet without proper opportunity for reflection or choice, and thence it is called "*miserabile depositum.*" (2) *Voluntary,* which arises from the mere consent and agreement of the parties. The common law has made no such division. There is another class of deposits called "involuntary," which may be without the assent or even knowledge of the depositor; as lumber, etc., left upon another's land by the subsidence of a flood.

The civilians again divide deposits into "simple deposits," made by one or more persons having a common interest, and "sequestrations," made by one or more persons, each of whom has a different and adverse interest in controversy touching it; and these last are of two sorts,—"conventional," or such as are made by the mere agreement of the parties without any judicial act; and "judicial," or such as are made by order of a court in the course of some proceeding.

There is another class of deposits called "irregular," as when a person, having a sum of money which he does not think safe in his own hands, confides it to another, who is to return to him, not the same money, but a like sum when he shall demand it. There is also a "*quasi* deposit," as where a person comes lawfully to the possession of another person's property by finding it; and a "special deposit" of money or bills in a bank, where the specific money, the very silver or gold, coin or bills, deposited, are to be restored, and not an equivalent. Story, Bailm. § 44, et seq.

The difference between a deposit and a mandate is that while the object of a deposit is that the thing bailed be kept, simply, the object of a mandate is that the thing may be transported from point to point, or that something be done about it. 8 Ga. 178.

Deposits made with bankers may be divided into two classes,—those in which the bank becomes bailee of the depositor, the title to the thing deposited remaining with the latter; and that kind peculiar to banking business, in which the depositor, for his own convenience, parts with the title to his money, and loans it to the banker, and the latter, in consideration of the loan of the money, and the right to use it for his own profit, agrees to refund the same amount, or any part thereof, on demand. Money collected by one bank for another, placed by the collecting bank with the bulk of its ordinary banking funds, and credited to the transmitting bank in account, becomes the money of the former. It is a deposit of the latter class. 2 Wall. 252.

Deposit, in respect to dealings of banks, includes not only a bailment of money to be returned in the same identical specie, but also all that class of contracts where money is placed in the hands of bankers to be returned, in other money, on call. 15 N. Y. 9, 166, 168.

The word is also sometimes used to designate money lodged with a person as an earnest or security for the performance of some contract, to be forfeited if the depositor fails in his undertaking.

DEPOSIT ACCOUNT. An account of sums lodged with a bank not to be drawn upon by checks, and usually not to be withdrawn except after a fixed notice.

DEPOSIT COMPANY. A company whose business is the safe-keeping of securities or other valuables deposited in boxes or safes in its building which are leased to the depositors.

DEPOSIT, GRATUITOUS. Gratuitous deposit is a deposit for which the depositary receives no consideration beyond the mere possession of the thing deposited. Civil Code Cal. § 1844.

DEPOSIT OF TITLE-DEEDS. A method of pledging real property as security for a loan, by placing the title-deeds of the land in the keeping of the lender as pledgee.

DEPOSITARY. The party receiving a deposit; one with whom anything is lodged in trust, as "depository" is the place where it is put. The obligation on the part of the depositary is that he keep the thing with reasonable care, and, upon request, restore it to the depositor, or otherwise deliver it, according to the original trust.

DEPOSITATION. In Scotch law. Deposit or *depositum*, the species of bailment so called. Bell.

DEPOSITION. The testimony of a witness taken upon interrogatories, not in open court, but in pursuance of a commission to take testimony issued by a court, or under a general law on the subject, and reduced to writing and duly authenticated, and intended to be used upon the trial of an action in court.

A deposition is a written declaration under oath, made upon notice to the adverse party for the purpose of enabling him to attend and cross-examine; or upon written interrogatories. Code Civil Proc. Cal. § 2004; Code Civil Proc. Dak. § 465.

A deposition is evidence given by a witness under interrogatories, oral or written, and usually written down by an official person. In its generic sense, it embraces all written evidence verified by oath, and includes affidavits; but, in legal language, a distinction is maintained between depositions and affidavits. 3 Blatchf. 456.

The term sometimes is used in a special sense to denote a statement made orally by a person on oath before an examiner, commissioner, or officer of the court, (but not in open court,) and taken down in writing by the examiner or under his direction. Sweet.

In ecclesiastical law. The act of depriving a clergyman, by a competent tribunal, of his clerical orders, to punish him for some offense and to prevent his acting in future in his clerical character. Ayl. Par. 206.

DEPOSITO. In Spanish law Deposit; the species of bailment so called. Schm. Civil Law, 193.

DEPOSITOR. One who makes a deposit.

DEPOSITORY. The place where a deposit (*q. v.*) is placed and kept.

DEPOSITUM. One of the four real contracts specified by Justinian, and having the following characteristics: (1) The depositary or depositee is not liable for negligence, however extreme, but only for fraud, *dolus;* (2) the property remains in the depositor, the depositary having only the possession.

Precarium and *sequestre* were two varieties of the *depositum*.

DÉPÔT. In the French law, is the *depositum* of the Roman and the deposit of the English law. It is of two kinds, being either (1) *dépôt* simply so called, and which may be either voluntary or necessary, and (2) *séquestre*, which is a deposit made either under an agreement of the parties, and to abide the event of pending litigation regarding it, or by virtue of the direction of the court or a judge, pending litigation regarding it. Brown; Civil Code La. 2897.

DEPRAVE. To defame; vilify; exhibit contempt for. In England it is a criminal offense to "deprave" the Lord's supper or the Book of Common Prayer. Steph. Crim. Dig. 99.

DEPREDATION. In French law. The pillage which is made of the goods of a decedent.

DEPRIVATION. In English ecclesiastical law. The taking away from a clergyman his benefice or other spiritual promotion or dignity, either by sentence declaratory in the proper court for fit and sufficient causes or in pursuance of divers penal statutes which declare the benefice void for some non-feasance or neglect, or some malfeasance or crime. 3 Steph. Comm. 87, 88; Burn, Ecc. Law, tit. "Deprivation."

DEPRIVE. In a constitutional provision that no person shall be *"deprived* of his property" without due process of law, this word is equivalent to the term "take," and denotes a taking altogether, a seizure, a direct appropriation, dispossession of the owner. 21 Pa. St. 147.

DEPUTIZE. To appoint a deputy; to appoint or commission one to act as deputy to an officer. In a general sense, the term is descriptive of empowering one person to act for another in any capacity or relation, but in law it is almost always restricted to the substitution of a person appointed to act for an officer of the law.

DEPUTY. A substitute; a person duly authorized by an officer to exercise some or all of the functions pertaining to the office, in the place and stead of the latter.

A deputy differs from an assignee, in that an assignee has an interest in the office itself, and does all things in his own name, for whom his grantor shall not answer, except in special cases; but a deputy has not any interest in the office, and is only the shadow of the officer in whose name he acts. And there is a distinction in doing an act

by an agent and by a deputy. An agent can only bind his principal when he does the act in the name of the principal. But a deputy may do the act and sign his own name, and it binds his principal; for a deputy has, in law, the whole power of his principal. Wharton.

DEPUTY LIEUTENANT. The deputy of a lord lieutenant of a county in England.

DEPUTY STEWARD. A steward of a manor may depute or authorize another to hold a court; and the acts done in a court so holden will be as legal as if the court had been holden by the chief steward in person. So an under steward or deputy may authorize another as subdeputy, *pro hac vice*, to hold a court for him; such limited authority not being inconsistent with the rule *delegatus non potest delegare*. Wharton.

DERAIGN. Seems to mean, literally, to confound and disorder, or to turn out of course, or displace; as deraignment or departure out of religion, in St. 31 Hen. VIII. c. 6. In the common law, the word is used generally in the sense of to prove; viz., to deraign a right, deraign the warranty, etc. Glanv. lib. 2, c. 6; Fitzh. Nat. Brev. 146. Perhaps this word "deraign," and the word "deraignment," derived from it, may be used in the sense of to prove and a proving, by disproving of what is asserted in opposition to truth and fact. Jacob.

DERECHO. In Spanish law. Law or right. *Derecho comun*, common law. The civil law is so called. A right. *Derechos*, rights.

DERELICT. Forsaken; abandoned; deserted; cast away.

Personal property abandoned or thrown away by the owner in such manner as to indicate that he intends to make no further claim thereto. 2 Bl. Comm. 9; 2 Reeve, Eng. Law, 9.

Land left uncovered by the receding of water from its former bed. 2 Rolle, Abr. 170; 2 Bl. Comm. 262; 1 Crabb, Real Prop. 109.

DERELICTION. The gaining of land from the water, in consequence of the sea shrinking back below the usual water mark; the opposite of *alluvion*, (*q. v.*) Dyer, 326b; 2 Bl. Comm. 262; 1 Steph. Comm. 419.

In the civil law. The voluntary abandonment of goods by the owner, without the hope or the purpose of returning to the possession. 12 Ga. 473; 2 Bl. Comm. 9.

Derivativa potestas non potest esse major primitiva. Noy, Max.; Wing. Max. 66. The derivative power cannot be greater than the primitive.

DERIVATIVE. Coming from another; taken from something preceding; secondary; that which has not its origin in itself, but owes its existence to something foregoing.

DERIVATIVE CONVEYANCES. Conveyances which presuppose some other conveyance precedent, and only serve to enlarge, confirm, alter, restrain, restore, or transfer the interest granted by such original conveyance. They are releases, confirmations, surrenders, assignments, and defeasances. 2 Bl. Comm. 324.

DEROGATION. The partial repeal or abolishing of a law, as by a subsequent act which limits its scope or impairs its utility and force. Distinguished from *abrogation,* which means the entire repeal and annulment of a law. Dig. 50, 17, 102.

DEROGATORY CLAUSE. In a will, this is a sentence or secret character inserted by the testator, of which he reserves the knowledge to himself, with a condition that no will he may make thereafter should be valid, unless this clause be inserted word for word. This is done as a precaution to guard against later wills being extorted by violence, or otherwise improperly obtained. By the law of England such a clause would be void, as tending to make the will irrevocable. Wharton.

Derogatur legi, cum pars detrahitur; abrogatur legi, cum prorsus tollitur. To derogate from a law is to take away part of it; to abrogate a law is to abolish it entirely. Dig. 50, 17, 102.

DESAFUERO. In Spanish law. An irregular action committed with violence against law, custom, or reason.

DESAMORTIZACION. In Mexican law. The *desamortizacion* of property is to take it out of mortmain, (dead hands;) that is, to unloose it from the grasp, as it were, of ecclesiastical or civil corporations. The term has no equivalent in English. Hall, Mex. Law. § 749.

DESCENDANT. One who is descended from another; a person who proceeds from the body of another, such as a child, grandchild, etc., to the remotest degree. The term is the opposite of "ascendant," (*q. v.*)

Descendants is a good term of description in a will, and includes all who proceed from the body of the person named; as grandchildren and great-grandchildren. Amb. 397; 2 Hil. Real. Prop. 242.

DESCENDER. Descent; in the descent. See FORMEDON.

DESCENT. Hereditary succession. Succession to the ownership of an estate by inheritance, or by any act of law, as distinguished from "purchase." Title by descent is the title by which one person, upon the death of another, acquires the real estate of the latter as his heir at law. 2 Bl. Comm. 201; Com. Dig. "Descent," A.

Descents are of two sorts,—lineal, as from father or grandfather to son or grandson; or collateral, as from brother to brother, or cousin to cousin. They are also distinguished into mediate and immediate descents. But these terms are used in different senses. A descent may be said to be a mediate or immediate descent of the estate or right; or it may be said to be mediate or immediate, in regard to the mediateness or immediateness of the pedigree or consanguinity. Thus, a descent from the grandfather, who dies in possession, to the grandchild, the father being then dead, or from the uncle to the nephew, the brother being dead, is, in the former sense, in law, immediate descent, although the one is collateral and the other lineal; for the heir is in the *per,* and not in the *per* and *cui.* On the other hand, with reference to the line of pedigree or consanguinity, a descent is often said to be immediate, when the ancestor from whom the party derives his blood is immediate, and without any intervening link or degrees; and mediate, when the kindred is derived from him *mediante altero,* another ancestor intervening between them. Thus a descent in lineals from father to son is in this sense immediate; but a descent from grandfather to grandson, the father being dead, or from uncle to nephew, the brother being dead, is deemed mediate; the father and the brother being, in these latter cases, the *medium deferens,* as it is called, of the descent or consanguinity. 6 Pet. 102.

Descent was denoted, in the Roman law, by the term "*successio,*" which is also used by Bracton, and from which has been derived the *succession* of the Scotch and French jurisprudence.

DESCENT CAST. The devolving of realty upon the heir on the death of his ancestor intestate.

DESCRIPTIO PERSONÆ. Lat. Description of the person. By this is meant a word or phrase used merely for the purpose of identifying or pointing out the person intended, and not as an intimation that the language in connection with which it occurs is to apply to him only in the official or technical character which might appear to be indicated by the word.

DESCRIPTION. **1.** A delineation or account of a particular subject by the recital of its characteristic accidents and qualities.

2. A written enumeration of items composing an estate, or of its condition, or of titles or documents; like an inventory, but with more particularity, and without involving the idea of an appraisement.

3. An exact written account of an article, mechanical device, or process which is the subject of an application for a patent.

4. A method of pointing out a particular person by referring to his relationship to some other person or his character as an officer, trustee, executor, etc.

5. That part of a conveyance, advertisement of sale, etc., which identifies the land intended to be affected.

DESERT. To leave or quit with an intention to cause a permanent separation; to forsake utterly; to abandon.

DESERTION. The act by which a person abandons and forsakes, without justification, or unauthorized, a station or condition of public or social life, renouncing its responsibilities and evading its duties.

The act of forsaking, deserting, or abandoning a *person* with whom one is legally bound to live, or for whom one is legally bound to provide, as a wife or husband.

The act by which a man quits the society of his wife and children, or either of them, and renounces his duties towards them.

"For the purposes of this case it is sufficient to say that the offense of desertion consists in the cessation of cohabitation, coupled with a determination in the mind of the offending person not to renew it." 43 Conn. 318.

An offense which consists in the abandonment of his duties by a person employed in the public service, in the army or navy, without leave, and with the intention not to return.

In respect to the military service, there is a distinction between desertion and simple absence without leave. In order to constitute desertion, there must be both an absence and an intention not to return to the service. 115 Mass. 336.

DESERTION OF A SEAMAN. The act by which a seaman deserts and abandons a ship or vessel, in which he had engaged to perform a voyage, before the expiration of his time, and without leave.

By desertion, in the maritime law, is meant, not a mere unauthorized absence from the ship without leave, but an unauthorized absence from the ship, with an intention not to return to her service, or, as it is often expressed, *animo non reverten li;* that is, with an intention to desert. 3 Story, 108.

DESHONORA. In Spanish law. Dishonor; injury; slander. Las Partidas, pt. 7, tit. 9, l. 1, 6.

DESIGN. In the law of evidence. Purpose or intention, combined with plan, or implying a plan in the mind. Burrill, Circ. Ev. 331.

As a term of art, the giving of a visible form to the conceptions of the mind, or invention. 4 Wash. C. C. 48.

Designatio justiciariorum est a rege; jurisdictio vero ordinaria a lege. 4 Inst. 74. The appointment of justices is by the king, but their ordinary jurisdiction by the law.

DESIGNATIO PERSONÆ. The description of a person or a party to a deed or contract.

Designatio unius est exclusio alterius, et expressum facit cessare tacitum. Co. Litt. 210. The specifying of one is the exclusion of another, and that which is expressed makes that which is understood to cease.

DESIGNATION. A description or descriptive expression by which a person or thing is denoted in a will without using the name.

DESIRE. This term, used in a will in relation to the management and distribution of property, is sufficient to create a trust, although it is precatory rather than imperative. 78 Ky. 123.

DESLINDE. A term used in the Spanish law, denoting the act by which the boundaries of an estate or portion of a country are determined.

DESMEMORIADOS. In Spanish law. Persons deprived of memory. White, New Recop. b. 1, tit. 2, c. 1, § 4.

DESPACHEURS. In maritime law. Persons appointed to settle cases of average.

DESPATCHES. Official communications of official persons on the affairs of government.

DESPERATE. Hopeless; worthless. This term is used in inventories and schedules of assets, particularly by executors, etc., to describe debts or claims which are considered impossible or hopeless of collection. See 11 Wend. 365.

DESPERATE DEBT. A hopeless debt; an irrecoverable obligation.

DESPITE. Contempt. *Despitz*, contempts. Kelham.

DESPITUS. Contempt. See DESPITE. A contemptible person. Fleta, lib. 4, c. 5.

DESPOJAR. A possessory action of the Mexican law. It is brought to recover possession of immovable property, of which one has been despoiled (*despojado*) by another. The word "despoil" (*despojar*) involves, in its signification, violence or clandestine means by which one is deprived of that which he possesses. 1 Cal. 268.

DESPOIL. This word involves, in its signification, violence or clandestine means by which one is deprived of that which he possesses. Its Spanish equivalent, *despojar*, is a term used in Mexican law. 1 Cal. 268.

DESPONSATION. The act of betrothing persons to each other.

DESPOSORIO. In Spanish law. Espousals; mutual promises of future marriage. White, New Recop. b. 1, tit. 6, c. 1, § 1.

DESPOT. This word, in its original and most simple acceptation, signifies *master and supreme lord;* it is synonymous with monarch; but taken in bad part, as it is usually employed, it signifies a tyrant. In some states, despot is the title given to the sovereign, as king is given in others. Enc. Lond.

DESPOTISM. That abuse of government where the sovereign power is not divided, but united in the hands of a single man, whatever may be his official title. It is not, properly, a form of government. Toullier, Dr. Civ. Fr. tit. prél. n. 32.

"Despotism" is not exactly synonymous with "autocracy," for the former involves the idea of tyranny or abuse of power, which is not necessarily implied by the latter. Every despotism is autocratic; but an autocracy is not necessarily despotic.

DESPOTIZE. To act as a despot. Webster.

DESRENABLE. L. Fr. Unreasonable. Britt. c. 121.

DESSAISISSEMENT. In French law. When a person is declared bankrupt, he is immediately deprived of the enjoyment and administration of all his property; this deprivation, which extends to all his rights, is called "*dessaisissement.*" Arg. Fr. Merc. Law, 556.

DESTINATION. The purpose to which it is intended an article or a fund shall be applied. A testator gives a destination to a legacy when he prescribes the specific use to which it shall be put.

The port at which a ship is to end her voyage is called her "port of destination." Pardessus, no. 600.

DESTRUCTION. A term used in old English law, generally in connection with *waste*, and having, according to some, the same meaning. 1 Reeve, Eng. Law, 385; 3 Bl. Comm. 223. Britton, however, makes a distinction between waste of woods and destruction of houses. Britt. c. 66.

DESUBITO. To weary a person with continual barkings, and then to bite; spoken of dogs. Leg Alured. 26, cited in Cunningham's Dict.

DESUETUDE. Disuse; cessation or discontinuance of use. Applied to obsolete statutes.

DETACHIARE. To seize or take into custody another's goods or person.

DETAINER. The act (or the juridical fact) of withholding from a person lawfully entitled the possession of land or goods; or the restraint of a man's personal liberty against his will.

The wrongful keeping of a person's goods is called an "unlawful detainer" although the original taking may have been lawful. As, if one distrains another's cattle, *damage feasant*, and before they are impounded the owner tenders sufficient amends; now, though the original taking was lawful, the subsequent detention of them after tender of amends is not lawful, and the owner has an action of replevin to recover them, in which he will recover damages for the *detention*, and not for the *caption*, because the original taking was lawful. 3 Steph. Comm. 548.

In practice. A writ or instrument, issued or made by a competent officer, authorizing the keeper of a prison to keep in his custody a person therein named. A detainer may be lodged against one within the walls of a prison, on what account soever he is there. Com. Dig. "Process," E, (3 B.) This writ was superseded by 1 & 2 Vict. c. 110, §§ 1, 2.

DETAINMENT. This term is used in policies of marine insurance, in the clause relating to "arrests, restraints, and detainments." The last two words are construed as equivalents, each meaning the effect of superior force operating directly on the vessel. 6 Mass. 109.

DETENTIO. In the civil law. That condition of fact under which one can exercise his power over a corporeal thing at his pleasure, to the exclusion of all others. It forms the substance of possession in all its varieties. Mackeld. Rom. Law, § 238.

DETENTION. The act of keeping back or withholding, either accidentally or by design, a person or thing. See DETAINER.

DETENTION IN A REFORMATORY, as a punishment or measure of prevention, is where a juvenile offender is sentenced to be sent to a reformatory school, to be there detained for a certain period of time. 1 Russ. Crimes, 82.

DETERMINABLE. That which may cease or determine upon the happening of a certain contingency. 2 Bl. Comm. 121.

DETERMINABLE FEE. (Also called a "qualified" or "base" fee.) One which has a qualification subjoined to it, and which must be determined whenever the qualification annexed to it is at an end. 2 Bl. Comm. 109.

An estate in fee which is liable to be determined by some act or event expressed on its limitation to circumscribe its continuance, or inferred by law as bounding its extent. 1 Washb. Real Prop. 62; 35 Wis. 36.

DETERMINABLE FREEHOLDS. Estates for life, which may determine upon future contingencies before the life for which they are created expires. As if an estate be granted to a woman during her widowhood, or to a man until he be promoted to a benefice; in these and similar cases, whenever the contingency happens,—when the widow marries, or when the grantee obtains the benefice,—the respective estates are absolutely determined and gone. Yet, while they subsist, they are reckoned estates for life; because they may by possibility last for life; if the contingencies upon which they are to determine do not sooner happen. 2 Bl. Comm. 121.

DETERMINATE. That which is ascertained; what is particularly designated.

DETERMINATION. The decision of a court of justice. The ending or expiration of an estate or interest in property, or of a right, power, or authority.

DETERMINE. To come to an end. To bring to an end. 2 Bl. Comm. 121; 1 Washb. Real Prop. 380.

DETESTATIO. Lat. In the civil law. A summoning made, or notice given, in the presence of witnesses, (*denuntiatio facta cum testatione.*) Dig. 50, 16, 40.

DETINET. Lat. He detains. In old English law. A species of action of debt, which lay for the specific recovery of goods, under a contract to deliver them. 1 Reeves, Eng. Law, 159.

In pleading. An action of *debt* is said to be in the *detinet* when it is alleged merely that the defendant withholds or unjustly detains from the plaintiff the thing or amount demanded.

An action of *replevin* is said to be in the *detinet* when the defendant retains possession of the property until after judgment in the action. Bull. N. P. 52; Chit. Pl. 145.

DETINUE. In practice. A form of action which lies for the recovery, *in specie,* of personal chattels from one who acquired possession of them lawfully, but retains it without right, together with damages for the detention. 3 Bl. Comm. 152.

The action of *detinue* is defined in the old books as a remedy founded upon the delivery of goods by the owner to another to keep, who afterwards refuses to redeliver them to the bailor; and it is said that, to authorize the maintenance of the action, it is necessary that the defendant should have come lawfully into the possession of the chattel, either by delivery to him or by finding it. In fact, it was once understood to be the law that *detinue* does not lie where the property had been tortiously taken. But it is, upon principle, very unimportant in what manner the defendant's possession commenced, since the gist of the action is the wrongful detainer, and not the original taking. It is only incumbent upon the plaintiff to prove property in himself, and possession in the defendant. At present, the action of *detinue* is proper in every case where the owner prefers recovering the specific property to damages for its conversion, and no regard is had to the manner in which the defendant acquired the possession. 9 Port. (Ala.) 151.

DETINUE OF GOODS IN FRANK MARRIAGE. A writ formerly available to a wife after a divorce, for the recovery of the goods given with her in marriage. Mozley & Whitley.

DETINUIT. In pleading. An action of replevin is said to be in the *detinuit* when the plaintiff acquires possession of the property claimed by means of the writ. The right to retain is, of course, subject in such case to the judgment of the court upon his title to the property claimed. Bull. N. P. 521.

DETRACTARI. To be torn in pieces by horses. Fleta, l. 1, c. 37.

DETUNICARI. To discover or lay open to the world. Matt. Westm. 1240.

DEUNX, pl. **DEUNCES.** Lat. In the Roman law. A division of the *as,* containing eleven *unciæ* or duodecimal parts; the proportion of eleven-twelfths. 2 Bl. Comm. 462, note. See As.

Deus solus hæredem facere potest, non homo. God alone, and not man, can make an heir. Co. Litt. 7*b;* Broom. Max. 516.

DEUTEROGAMY. The act, or condition, of one who marries a wife after the death of a former wife.

DEVADIATUS, or **DIVADIATUS.** An offender without sureties or pledges. Cowell.

DEVASTATION. Wasteful use of the property of a deceased person, as for extravagant funeral or other unnecessary expenses. 2 Bl. Comm. 508.

DEVASTAVERUNT. They have wasted. A term applied in old English law to waste by executors and administrators, and to the process issued against them therefor. Cowell. See DEVASTAVIT.

DEVASTAVIT. Lat. He has wasted. The act of an executor or administrator in wasting the goods of the deceased; mismanagement of the estate by which a loss occurs; a breach of trust or misappropriation of assets held in a fiduciary character; any violation or neglect of duty by an executor or administrator, involving loss to the decedent's estate, which makes him personally responsible to heirs, creditors, or legatees.

Also, if plaintiff, in an action against an executor or administrator, has obtained judgment, the usual execution runs *de bonis testatoris;* but, if the sheriff returns to such a writ *nulla bona testatoris nec propria,* the plaintiff may, forthwith, upon this return, sue out an execution against the property or person of the executor or administrator, in as full a manner as in an action against him, sued in his own right. Such a return is called a "*devastavit.*" Brown.

DEVENERUNT. A writ, now obsolete, directed to the king's escheators when any of the king's tenants *in capite* dies, and when his son and heir dies within age and in the king's custody, commanding the escheat, or that by the oaths of twelve good and lawful men they shall inquire what lands or tenements by the death of the tenant have come to the king. Dyer, 360; Termes de la Ley.

DEVEST. To deprive; to take away; to withdraw. Usually spoken of an authority, power, property, or title; as the estate is devested.

Devest is opposite to invest. As to invest signifies to deliver the possession of anything to another, so to devest signifies to take it away. Jacob.

It is sometimes written "*divest*" but "*devest*" has the support of the best authority. Burrill.

DEVIATION. In insurance. Varying from the risks insured against, as described in the policy, without necessity or just cause, after the risk has begun. 1 Phil. Ins. § 977, et seq.; 1 Arn. Ins. 415, et seq.

Any unnecessary or unexcused departure from the usual or general mode of carrying on the voyage insured. 15 Amer. Law Rev. 108.

Deviation is a departure from the course of the voyage insured, or an unreasonable delay in pursuing the voyage, or the commencement of an entirely different voyage. Civil Code Cal. § 2694.

A deviation is a voluntary departure from or delay in the usual and regular course of a voyage insured, without necessity or reasonable cause. This discharges the insurer, from the time of the deviation. 9 Mass. 436.

In contracts. A change made in the progress of a work from the original terms or design or method agreed upon.

DEVICE. In a statute against gaming devices, this term is to be understood as meaning something formed by design, a contrivance, an invention. It is to be distinguished from "substitute," which means something put in the place of another thing, or used instead of something else. 59 Ala. 91.

DEVIL ON THE NECK. An instrument of torture, formerly used to extort confessions, etc. It was made of several irons, which were fastened to the neck and legs, and wrenched together so as to break the back. Cowell.

DEVISABLE. Capable of being devised. 1 Pow. Dev. 165; 2 Bl. Comm. 373.

DEVISAVIT VEL NON. In practice. The name of an issue sent out of a court of chancery, or one which exercises chancery jurisdiction, to a court of law, to try the validity of a paper asserted and denied to be a will, to ascertain whether or not the testator did devise, or whether or not that paper was his will. **7** Brown, Parl. Cas. 437; **2** Atk. 424; **5** Pa. St. 21.

DEVISE. A gift of real property by will.

Devise properly relates to the disposal of real property, not of personal. 21 Barb. 551, 561.

Devise is properly applied to gifts of real property by will, but may be extended to embrace personal property, to execute the intention of the testator. 6 Ired. Eq. 173.

The words "devise," "legacy," and "bequest" may be applied indifferently to real or personal property, if such appears by the context of a will to have been the testator's intention. 21 N. H. 514.

Devises are *contingent* or *vested;* that is, after the death of the testator. Contingent, when the vesting of any estate in the devisee is made to depend upon some future event, in which case, if the event never occur, or until it does occur, no estate vests under the devise. But, when the future event is referred to merely to determine the time at which the devisee shall come into the use of the estate, this does not hinder the vesting of the estate at the death of the testator. **1** Jarm. Wills, c. 26.

An *executory* devise of lands is such a disposition of them by will that thereby no estate vests at the death of the devisor, but only on some future contingency. It differs from a remainder in three very material points: (1) That it needs not any particular estate to support it; (2) that by it a fee-simple or other less estate may be limited after a fee-simple; (3) that by this means a remainder may be limited of a chattel interest, after a particular estate for life created in the same. 2 Bl. Comm. 172.

DEVISEE. The person to whom lands or other real property are devised or given by will. 1 Pow. Dev. c. 7.

DEVISOR. A giver of lands or real estate by will; the maker of a will of lands; a testator.

DEVOIR. Fr. Duty. It is used in the statute of 2 Rich. II. c. 3, in the sense of duties or customs.

DEVOLUTION. In ecclesiastical law. The forfeiture of a right or power (as the right of presentation to a living) in consequence of its non-user by the person holding it, or of some other act or omission on his part, and its resulting transfer to the person next entitled.

DEVOLVE. "To devolve means to pass from a person dying to a person living; the etymology of the word shows its meaning." 1 Mylne & K. 648.

DEVY. L. Fr. Dies; deceases. Bendloe, 5.

DEXTANS. Lat. In Roman law. A division of the *as,* consisting of ten *unciæ;* ten-twelfths, or five-sixths. 2 Bl. Comm. 462, note *m.*

DEXTRARIUS. One at the right hand of another.

DEXTRAS DARE. To shake hands in token of friendship; or to give up oneself to the power of another person.

DI COLONNA. In maritime law. The contract which takes place between the owner of a ship, the captain, and the mariners, who agree that the voyage shall be for the benefit of all. The term is used in the Italian law. Emerig. Mar. Loans, § 5.

DI. ET FI. L. Lat. In old writs. An abbreviation of *dilecto et fideli,* (to his beloved and faithful.)

DIACONATE. The office of a deacon.

DIACONUS. A deacon.

DIAGNOSIS. A medical term, meaning the discovery of the source of a patient's illness.

DIALECTICS. That branch of logic which teaches the rules and modes of reasoning.

DIALLAGE. A rhetorical figure in which arguments are placed in various points of view, and then turned to one point. Enc. Lond.

DIALOGUS DE SCACCARIO. Dialogue of or about the exchequer. An ancient treatise on the court of exchequer, attributed by some to Gervase of Tilbury, by others to Richard Fitz Nigel, bishop of London in the reign of Richard I. It is quoted by Lord Coke under the name of Ockham. Crabb, Eng. Law, 71.

DIANATIC. A logical reasoning in a progressive manner, proceeding from one subject to another. Enc. Lond.

DIARIUM. Daily food, or as much as will suffice for the day. Du Cange.

DIATIM. In old records. Daily; every day; from day to day. Spelman.

DICA. In old English law. A tally for accounts, by number of cuts, (*taillees,*) marks, or notches. Cowell. See TALLIA, TALLY.

DICAST. An officer in ancient Greece answering in some respects to our juryman, but combining, on trials had before them, the functions of both judge and jury. The dicasts sat together in numbers varying, according to the importance of the case, from one to five hundred.

DICE. Small cubes of bone or ivory, marked with figures or devices on their several sides, used in playing certain games of chance. See 55 Ala. 198.

DICTATE. To order or instruct what is to be said or written. To pronounce, word by word, what is meant to be written by another. 6 Mart. (N. S.) 143.

DICTATION. In Louisiana, this term is used in a technical sense, and means to pronounce orally what is destined to be written at the same time by another. It is used in reference to nuncupative wills. 16 La. Ann. 220.

DICTATOR. A magistrate invested with unlimited power, and created in times of national distress and peril. Among the Romans, he continued in office for six months only, and had unlimited power and authority over both the property and lives of the citizens.

DICTORES. Arbitrators.

DICTUM. In general. A statement, remark, or observation. *Gratis dictum;* a gratuitous or voluntary representation; one which a party is not bound to make. 2 Kent, Comm. 486. *Simplex dictum;* a mere assertion; an assertion without proof. Bract. fol. 320.

The word is generally used as an abbreviated form of *obiter dictum,* "a remark by the way;" that is, an observation or remark made by a judge in pronouncing an opinion upon a cause, concerning some rule, principle, or application of law, or the solution of a question suggested by the case at bar, but not necessarily involved in the case or essential to its determination; any statement of the law enunciated by the court merely by way of illustration, argument, analogy, or suggestion.

Dicta are opinions of a judge which do not embody the resolution or determination of the court, and made without argument, or full consideration of the point, are not the professed deliberate determinations of the judge himself. *Obiter dicta* are such opinions uttered by the way, not upon the point or question pending, as if turning aside for the time from the main topic of the case to collateral subjects. 62 N. Y. 47, 58.

In old English law. *Dictum* meant an arbitrament, or the award of arbitrators.

In French law. The report of a judgment made by one of the judges who has given it. Poth. Proc. Civil, pt. 1, c. 5, art. 2.

DICTUM DE KENILWORTH. The edict or declaration of Kenilworth. An edict or award between King Henry III. and all the barons and others who had been in arms against him; and so called because it was made at Kenilworth Castle, in Warwickshire, in the fifty-first year of his reign, containing a composition of five years' rent for the lands and estates of those who had forfeited them in that rebellion. Blount; 2 Reeve, Eng. Law, 62.

DIE WITHOUT ISSUE. See DYING WITHOUT ISSUE.

DIEI DICTIO. Lat. In Roman law. This name was given to a notice promulgated by a magistrate of his intention to present an impeachment against a citizen before the people, specifying the day appointed, the name of the accused, and the crime charged.

DIEM CLAUSIT EXTREMUM. (Lat. He has closed his last day,—died.) A writ which formerly lay on the death of a tenant *in capite,* to ascertain the lands of which he died seised, and reclaim them into the king's hands. It was directed to the king's escheators. Fitzh. Nat. Brev. 251, K; 2 Reeve, Eng. Law, 327.

A writ awarded out of the exchequer after the death of a crown debtor, the sheriff being commanded by it to inquire by a jury when and where the crown debtor died, and what chattels, debts, and lands he had at the time of his decease, and to take and seize them into the crown's hands. 4 Steph. Comm. 47, 48.

DIES. Lat. A day; days. Days for appearance in court. Provisions or maintenance for a day. The king's rents were anciently reserved by so many days' provisions. Spelman; Cowell; Blount.

DIES A QUO. (The day from which.) In the civil law. The day from which a transaction begins; the commencement of it; the conclusion being the *dies ad quem.* Mackeld. Rom. Law, § 185.

DIES AMORIS. A day of favor. The name given to the appearance day of the term on the fourth day, or *quarto die post.* It was the day given by the favor and indulgence of the court to the defendant for his appearance, when all parties appeared in court, and had their appearance recorded by the proper officer. Wharton.

DIES CEDIT. The day begins; *dies venit*, the day has come. Two expressions in Roman law which signify the vesting or fixing of an interest, and the interest becoming a present one. Sandars' Just. Inst. (5th Ed.) 225, 232.

DIES COMMUNES IN BANCO. Regular days for appearance in court; called, also, "common return-days." 2 Reeve, Eng. Law, 57.

DIES DATUS. A day given or allowed, (to a defendant in an action;) amounting to a continuance. But the name was appropriate only to a continuance before a declaration filed; if afterwards allowed, it was called an "imparlance."

DIES DATUS IN BANCO. A day given in the *bench*, (or court of common pleas.) Bract. fols. 257b, 361. A day given in bank, as distinguished from a day at *nisi prius*. Co. Litt. 135.

DIES DATUS PARTIBUS. A day given to the parties to an action; an adjournment or continuance. Crabb, Eng. Law, 217.

DIES DATUS PRECE PARTIUM. A day given on the prayer of the parties. Bract. fol. 358; Gilb. Comm. Pl. 41; 2 Reeve, Eng. Law, 60.

DIES DOMINICUS. The Lord's day; Sunday.

Dies dominicus non est juridicus. Sunday is not a court day, or day for judicial proceedings, or legal purposes. Co. Litt. 135a; Noy, Max. 2; Wing. Max. 7, max. 5; Broom, Max. 21.

DIES EXCRESCENS. In old English law. The added or increasing day in leap year. Bract. fols. 359, 359b.

DIES FASTI. In Roman law. Days on which the courts were open, and justice could be legally administered; days on which it was lawful for the prætor to pronounce (*fari*) the *three* words, "*do*," "*dico*," "*addico*." Mackeld. Rom. Law, § 39, and note; 3 Bl. Comm. 424, note; Calvin. Hence called "*triverbial* days," answering to the *dies juridici* of the English law.

DIES FERIATI. Lat. In the civil law. Holidays. Dig. 2, 12, 2, 9.

DIES GRATIÆ. In old English practice. A day of grace, courtesy, or favor.

Co. Litt. 134b. The *quarto die post* was sometimes so called. Id. 135a.

Dies inceptus pro completo habetur. A day begun is held as complete.

Dies incertus pro conditione habetur. An uncertain day is held as a condition.

DIES INTERCISI. In Roman law. Divided days; days on which the courts were open for a part of the day. Calvin.

DIES LEGITIMUS. In the civil and old English law. A lawful or law day; a term day; a day of appearance.

DIES MARCHIÆ. In old English law. The day of meeting of English and Scotch, which was annually held on the marches or borders to adjust their differences and preserve peace.

DIES NEFASTI. In Roman law. Days on which the courts were closed, and it was unlawful to administer justice; answering to the *dies non juridici* of the English law. Mackeld. Rom. Law, § 39, note.

DIES NON. An abbreviation of *Dies non juridicus*, (*q. v.*)

DIES NON JURIDICUS. In practice. A day not juridical; not a court day. A day on which courts are not open for business, such as Sundays and some holidays.

DIES PACIS. (Lat. Day of peace.) The year was formerly divided into the days of the peace of the church and the days of the peace of the king, including in the two divisions all the days of the year. Crabb, Eng. Law, 35.

DIES SOLARIS. In old English law. A solar day, as distinguished from what was called "*dies lunaris*," (a lunar day;) both composing an artificial day. Bract. fol. 264. See DAY.

DIES SOLIS. In the civil and old English law. Sunday, (literally, the day of the sun.) See Cod. 3, 12, 7.

DIES UTILES. Juridical days; useful or available days. A term of the Roman law, used to designate those especial days occurring within the limits of a prescribed period of time upon which it was lawful, or possible, to do a specific act.

DIET. A general legislative assembly is sometimes so called on the continent of Europe.

In Scotch practice. The sitting of a court. An appearance day. A day fixed for the trial of a criminal cause. A criminal cause as prepared for trial.

DIETA. A day's journey; a day's work; a day's expenses.

DIETS OF COMPEARANCE. In Scotch law. The days within which parties in civil and criminal prosecutions are cited to appear. Bell.

DIEU ET MON DROIT. Fr. God and my right. The motto of the royal arms of England, first assumed by Richard I.

DIEU SON ACTE. L. Fr. In old law. God his act; God's act. An event beyond human foresight or control. Termes de la Ley.

DIFFACERE. To destroy; to disfigure or deface.

Difficile est ut unus homo vicem duorum sustineat. 4 Coke, 118. It is difficult that one man should sustain the place of two.

DIFFORCIARE. In old English law. To deny, or keep from one. *Difforciare rectum*, to deny justice to any one, after having been required to do it.

DIGAMA, or DIGAMY. Second marriage; marriage to a second wife after the death of the first, as "bigamy," in law, is having two wives at once. Originally, a man who married a widow, or married again after the death of his wife, was said to be guilty of bigamy. Co. Litt. 40b, note.

DIGEST. A collection or compilation, embodying the chief matter of numerous books in one, disposed under proper heads or titles, and usually by an alphabetical arrangement, for facility in reference.

As a legal term, "digest" is to be distinguished from "abridgment." The latter is a summary or epitome of the contents of a single work, in which, as a rule, the original order or sequence of parts is preserved, and in which the principal labor of the compiler is in the matter of consolidation. A digest is wider in its scope; is made up of quotations or paraphrased passages; and has its own system of classification and arrangement. An "index" merely points out the places where particular matters may be found, without purporting to give such matters *in extenso*. A "treatise" or "commentary" is not a compilation, but an original composition, though it may include quotations and excerpts.

A reference to the "Digest," or "Dig.," is always understood to designate the Digest (or Pandects) of the Justinian collection; that being the digest *par eminence*, and the authoritative compilation of the Roman law.

DIGESTA. Digests. One of the titles of the Pandects of Justinan. Inst. *proœm*, § 4. Bracton uses the singular, "*Digestum.*" Bract. fol. 19.

DIGESTS. The ordinary name of the Pandects of Justinian, which are now usually cited by the abbreviation "Dig." instead of "Ff.," as formerly. Sometimes called "Digest," in the singular.

DIGGING. Has been held as synonymous with "excavating," and not confined to the removal of earth. 1 N. Y. 316.

DIGNITARY. In canon law. A person holding an ecclesiastical benefice or dignity, which gave him some pre-eminence above mere priests and canons. To this class exclusively belonged all bishops, deans, archdeacons, etc.; but it now includes all the prebendaries and canons of the church. Brande.

DIGNITY. In English law. An honor; a title, station, or distinction of honor. Dignities are a species of incorporeal hereditaments, in which a person may have a property or estate. 2 Bl. Comm. 37; 1 Bl. Comm. 396; 1 Crabb, Real Prop. 468, et seq.

DIJUDICATION. Judicial decision or determination.

DILACION. In Spanish law. A space of time granted to a party to a suit in which to answer a demand or produce evidence of a disputed fact.

DILAPIDATION. A species of ecclesiastical waste which occurs whenever the incumbent suffers any edifices of his ecclesiastical living to go to ruin or decay. It is either voluntary, by pulling down, or permissive, by suffering the church, parsonage-houses, and other buildings thereunto belonging, to decay. And the remedy for either lies either in the spiritual court, where the canon law prevails, or in the courts of common law. It is also held to be good cause of deprivation if the bishop, parson, or other ecclesiastical person dilapidates buildings or cuts down timber growing on the patrimony of the church, unless for necessary repairs; and that a writ of prohibition will also lie against him in the common-law courts. 3 Bl. Comm. 91.

The term is also used, in the law of landlord and tenant, to signify the neglect of necessary repairs to a building, or suffering it to fall into a state of decay, or the pulling down of the building or any part of it.

Dilationes in lege sunt odiosæ. Delays in law are odious. Branch, Princ.

DILATORY DEFENSE. In chancery practice. One the object of which is to dismiss, suspend, or obstruct the suit, without touching the merits, until the impediment or obstacle insisted on shall be removed. 3 Bl. Comm. 301, 302.

DILATORY PLEAS. A class of defenses at common law, founded on some matter of fact not connected with the merits of the case, but such as might exist without impeaching the right of action itself. They were either pleas to the *jurisdiction*, showing that, by reason of some matter therein stated, the case was not within the jurisdiction of the court; or pleas in *suspension*, showing some matter of temporary incapacity to proceed with the suit; or pleas in *abatement*, showing some matter for abatement or quashing the declaration. 3 Steph. Comm. 576.

DILIGENCE. Prudence; vigilant activity; attentiveness; or care, of which there are infinite shades, from the slightest momentary thought to the most vigilant anxiety; but the law recognizes only three degrees of diligence: (1) Common or ordinary, which men, in general, exert in respect of their own concerns; the standard is necessarily variable with respect to the facts, although it may be uniform with respect to the principle. (2) High or great, which is extraordinary diligence, or that which very prudent persons take of their own concerns. (3) Low or slight, which is that which persons of less than common prudence, or indeed of no prudence at all, take of their own concerns.

The civil law is in perfect conformity with the common law. It lays down three degrees of diligence,—ordinary, (*diligentia;*) extraordinary, (*exactissima diligentia;*) slight, (*levissima diligentia.*) Story, Bailm. 19.

There may be a high degree of diligence, a common degree of diligence, and a slight degree of diligence, with their corresponding degrees of negligence, and these can be clearly enough defined for all practical purposes, and, with a view to the business of life, seem to be all that are really necessary. Common or ordinary diligence is that degree of diligence which men in general exercise in respect to their own concerns; high or great diligence is of course extraordinary diligence, or that which very prudent persons take of their own concerns; and low or slight diligence is that which persons of less than common prudence, or indeed of any prudence at all, take of their own concerns. Ordinary negligence is the want of ordinary diligence; slight, or less than ordinary,

negligence is the want of great diligence; and gross or more than ordinary negligence is the want of slight diligence. 5 Kan. 180.

In Scotch law and practice. Process of law, by which persons, lands, or effects are seized in execution or in security for debt. Ersk. Inst. 2, 11, 1. Brande. Process for enforcing the attendance of witnesses, or the production of writings. Ersk. Inst. 4, 1, 71.

DILIGIATUS. (Fr. *De lege ejectus*, Lat.) Outlawed.

DILLIGROUT. In old English law. Pottage formerly made for the king's table on the coronation day. There was a tenure in serjeantry, by which lands were held of the king by the service of finding this pottage at that solemnity.

DIME. A silver coin of the United States, of the value of ten cents, or one-tenth of the dollar.

DIMIDIA, DIMIDIUM, DIMIDIUS. Half; a half; the half.

DIMIDIETAS. The moiety or half of a thing.

DIMINUTIO. In the civil law. Diminution; a taking away; loss or deprivation. *Diminutio capitis*, loss of *status* or condition. See CAPITIS DIMINUTIO.

DIMINUTION. Incompleteness. A word signifying that the record sent up from an inferior to a superior court for review is incomplete, or not fully certified. In such case the party may suggest a "diminution of the record," which may be rectified by a *certiorari*. 2 Tidd, Pr. 1109.

DIMISI. In old conveyancing. I have demised. *Dimisi, concessi, et ad firmam tradidi*, have demised, granted, and to farm let. The usual words of operation in a lease. 2 Bl. Comm. 317, 318.

DIMISIT. In old conveyancing. [He] has demised. See DIMISI.

DIMISSORIÆ LITTERÆ. In the civil law. Letters dimissory or dismissory, commonly called "apostles," (*quæ vulgo apostoli dicuntur.*) Dig. 50, 16, 106. See APOSTOLI, APOSTLES.

DIMISSORY LETTERS. Where a candidate for holy orders has a title of ordination in one diocese in England, and is to be ordained in another, the bishop of the former diocese gives letters dimissory to the bishop of the latter to enable him to ordain the candidate. Holthouse.

DINARCHY. A government of two persons.

DINERO. In Spanish law. Money. *Dinero contado*, money counted. White, New Recop. b. 2, tit. 13, c. 1, § 1.

In Roman law. A civil division of the Roman empire, embracing several provinces. Calvin.

DIOCESAN. Belonging to a diocese; a bishop, as he stands related to his own clergy or flock.

DIOCESAN COURTS. In English law. The consistorial courts of each diocese, exercising general jurisdiction of all matters arising locally within their respective limits, with the exception of places subject to *peculiar* jurisdiction; deciding all matters of spiritual discipline,—suspending or depriving clergymen,—and administering the other branches of the ecclesiastical law. 2 Steph. Comm. 672.

DIOCESE. The territorial extent of a bishop's jurisdiction. The circuit of every bishop's jurisdiction. Co. Litt. 94; 1 Bl. Comm. 111.

DIOICHIA. The district over which a bishop exercised his spiritual functions.

DIPLOMA. In the civil law. A royal charter; letters patent granted by a prince or sovereign. Calvin.

An instrument given by colleges and societies on the conferring of any degrees.

A license granted to a physician, etc., to practice his art or profession. See 25 Wend. 469.

DIPLOMACY. The science which treats of the relations and interests of nations with nations.

Negotiation or intercourse between nations through their representatives. The rules, customs, and privileges of representatives at foreign courts.

DIPLOMATIC AGENT. In international law. A general name for all classes of persons charged with the negotiation, transaction, or superintendence of the diplomatic business of one nation at the court of another. See Rev. St. U. S. § 1674.

DIPLOMATICS. The science of diplomas, or of ancient writings and documents; the art of judging of ancient charters, public documents, diplomas, etc., and discriminating the true from the false. Webster.

DIPSOMANIA. In medical jurisprudence. An irresistible impulse to indulge in intoxication, either by the use of alcohol or of drugs such as opium. This mania or disease is classed as one of the minor forms of insanity. 19 Neb. 614, 28 N. W. Rep. 273; 1 Bish. Crim. Law, § 304.

DIPSOMANIAC. A person subject to dipsomania. One who has an irresistible desire for alcoholic liquors.

DIPTYCHA. Diptychs; tablets of wood, metal, or other substance, used among the Romans for the purpose of writing, and folded like a book of two leaves. The diptychs of antiquity were especially employed for public registers. They were used in the Greek, and afterwards in the Roman, church, as registers of the names of those for whom supplication was to be made, and are ranked among the earliest monastic records. Burrill.

DIRECT. Immediate; by the shortest course; without circuity; operating by an immediate connection or relation, instead of operating through a medium; the opposite of *indirect*.

In the usual or natural course or line; immediately upwards or downwards; as distinguished from that which is out of the line, or on the side of it; the opposite of *collateral*.

In the usual or regular course or order, as distinguished from that which diverts, interrupts, or opposes; the opposite of *cross* or contrary.

DIRECT EVIDENCE. Evidence directly proving any matter, as opposed to circumstantial evidence, which is often called "indirect." It is usually conclusive, but, like other evidence, it is fallible, and that on various accounts. It is not to be confounded with primary evidence, as opposed to secondary, although in point of fact it usually is primary. Brown.

DIRECT EXAMINATION. In practice. The first interrogation or examination of a witness, on the merits, by the party on whose behalf he is called. This is to be distinguished from an examination *in pais*, or on the *voir dire*, which is merely preliminary, and is had when the competency of the witness is challenged; from the cross-examination, which is conducted by the adverse party; and from the redirect examination, which follows the cross-examination, and is had by the party who first examined the witness.

DIRECT INTEREST. A direct interest, such as would render the interested party incompetent to testify in regard to the matter, is an interest which is certain, and not contingent or doubtful. A matter which is dependent alone on the successful prosecution of an execution cannot be considered as uncertain, or otherwise than direct, in this sense. 1 Ala. 65.

DIRECT INTERROGATORIES. On the taking of a deposition, where written interrogatories are framed, those put by the party calling the witness are named "direct interrogatories," (corresponding to the questions asked on a direct examination,) while those put by the adverse party are called "cross-interrogatories."

DIRECT LINE. Property is said to descend or be inherited in the direct line when it passes in lineal succession; from ancestor to son, grandson, great-grandson, and so on.

DIRECT TAX. A direct tax is one which is demanded from the very persons who, it is intended or desired, should pay it. Indirect taxes are those which are demanded from one person, in the expectation and intention that he shall indemnify himself at the expense of another. Mill, Pol. Econ.

Taxes are divided into "direct," under which designation would be included those which are assessed upon the property, person, business, income, etc., of those who are to pay them, and "indirect," or those which are levied on commodities before they reach the consumer, and are paid by those upon whom they ultimately fall, not as taxes, but as part of the market price of the commodity. Cooley, Tax'n, 6.

Historical evidence shows that personal property, contracts, occupations, and the like, have never been regarded as the subjects of direct tax. The phrase is understood to be limited to taxes on land and its appurtenances, and on polls. 8 Wall. 533.

DIRECTION. 1. The act of governing; management; superintendence. Also the body of persons (called "directors") who are charged with the management and administration of a corporation or institution.

2. The charge or instruction given by the court to a jury upon a point of law arising or involved in the case, to be by them applied to the facts in evidence.

3. The clause of a bill in equity containing the address of the bill to the court.

DIRECTOR OF THE MINT. An officer having the control, management, and superintendence of the United States mint and its branches. He is appointed by the president, by and with the advice and consent of the senate.

DIRECTORS. Persons appointed or elected according to law, authorized to manage and direct the affairs of a corporation or company. The whole of the directors collectively form the board of directors. Wharton.

DIRECTORY. A provision in a statute, rule of procedure, or the like, is said to be directory when it is to be considered as a mere direction or instruction of no obligatory force, and involving no invalidating consequence for its disregard, as opposed to an imperative or mandatory provision, which must be followed. The general rule is that the prescriptions of a statute relating to the performance of a public duty are so far directory that, though neglect of them may be punishable, yet it does not affect the validity of the acts done under them, as in the case of a statute requiring an officer to prepare and deliver a document to another officer on or before a certain day. Maxw. Interp. St. 330, et seq.

DIRECTORY TRUST. Where, by the terms of a trust, the fund is directed to be vested in a particular manner till the period arrives at which it is to be appropriated, this is called a "directory trust." It is distinguished from a discretionary trust, in which the trustee has a discretion as to the management of the fund. 10 Yerg. 272.

DIRIBITORES. In Roman law. Officers who distributed ballots to the people, to be used in voting. Tayl. Civil Law, 192.

DIRIMENT IMPEDIMENTS. In canon law. Absolute bars to marriage, which would make it null *ab initio*.

DISABILITY. The want of legal ability or capacity to exercise legal rights, either special or ordinary, or to do certain acts with proper legal effect, or to enjoy certain privileges or powers of free action.

At the present day, disability is generally used to indicate an incapacity for the full enjoyment of ordinary legal rights; thus married women, persons under age, insane persons, and felons convict are said to be under disability. Sometimes the term is used in a more limited sense, as when it signifies an impediment to marriage, or the restraints placed upon clergymen by reason of their spiritual avocations. Mozley & Whitley.

Disability is either *general* or *special;* the former when it incapacitates the person for the performance of all legal acts of a general class, or giving to them their ordinary legal effect; the latter when it debars him from one specific act.

Disability is also either *personal* or *absolute;* the former where it attaches to the particular person, and arises out of his *status,* his previous act, or his natural or juridical incapacity; the latter where it originates with a particular person, but extends also to his descendants or successors.

Considered with special reference to the capacity to contract a marriage, disability is either *canonical* or *civil;* a disability of the former class makes the marriage voidable only, while the latter, in general, avoids it entirely.

DISABLE. In its ordinary sense, to disable is to cause a disability, (*q. v.*)

In the old language of pleading, to disable is to take advantage of one's own or another's disability. Thus, it is "an express maxim of the common law that the party shall not disable himself;" but "this disability to disable himself * * * is personal." 4 Coke, 123*b.*

DISABLING STATUTES. These are acts of parliament, restraining and regulating the exercise of a right or the power of alienation; the term is specially applied to 1 Eliz. c. 19, and similar acts restraining the power of ecclesiastical corporations to make leases.

DISADVOCARE. To deny a thing.

DISAFFIRM. To repudiate; to revoke a consent once given; to recall an affirmance. To refuse one's subsequent sanction to a former act; to disclaim the intention of being bound by an antecedent transaction.

DISAFFIRMANCE. The repudiation of a former transaction. The refusal by one who has the right to refuse, (as in the case of a voidable contract,) to abide by his former acts, or accept the legal consequences of the same. It may either be "express" (in words) or "implied" from acts expressing the intention of the party to disregard the obligations of the contract.

DISAFFOREST. To restore to their former condition lands which have been turned into forests. To remove from the operation of the forest laws. 2 Bl. Comm. 416.

DISAGREEMENT. The refusal by a grantee, lessee, etc., to accept an estate, lease, etc., made to him; the annulling of a thing that had essence before. No estate can be vested in a person against his will. Consequently no one can become a grantee, etc., without his *agreement.* The law implies

such an agreement until the contrary is shown, but his disagreement renders the grant, etc., inoperative. Wharton.

DISALT. To disable a person.

DISAPPROPRIATION. This is where the appropriation of a benefice is severed, either by the patron presenting a clerk or by the corporation which has the appropriation being dissolved. 1 Bl. Comm. 385.

DISAVOW. To repudiate the unauthorized acts of an agent; to deny the authority by which he assumed to act.

DISBAR. In England, to deprive a barrister permanently of the privileges of his position; it is analogous to striking an attorney off the rolls. In America, the word describes the act of a court in withdrawing from an attorney the right to practise at its bar.

DISBOCATIO. In old English law. A conversion of wood grounds into arable or pasture; an assarting. Cowell. See ASSART.

DISBURSEMENTS. Money expended by an executor, guardian, trustee, etc., for the benefit of the estate in his hands, or in connection with its administration.

The term is also used under the codes of civil procedure, to designate the expenditures necessarily made by a party in the progress of an action, aside from the fees of officers and court costs, which are allowed, *eo nomine,* together with costs.

DISCARCARE. In old English law. To discharge, to unload; as a vessel. *Carcare et discarcare;* to charge and discharge; to load and unload. Cowell.

DISCARGARE. In old European law. To discharge or unload, as a wagon. Spelman.

DISCEPTIO CAUSÆ. In Roman law. The argument of a cause by the counsel on both sides. Calvin.

DISCHARGE. The opposite of *charge;* hence to release; liberate; annul; unburden; disincumber.

In the law of contracts. To cancel or unloose the obligation of a contract; to make an agreement or contract null and inoperative. As a noun, the word means the act or instrument by which the binding force of a contract is terminated, irrespective of whether the contract is carried out to the full extent contemplated (in which case the discharge is the result of *performance*) or is broken off before complete execution.

Discharge is a generic term; its principal species are rescission, release, accord and satisfaction, performance, judgment, composition, bankruptcy, merger, (*q. v.*) Leake, Cont. 413.

As applied to demands, claims, rights of action, incumbrances, etc., to discharge the debt or claim is to extinguish it, to annul its obligatory force, to satisfy it. And here also the term is generic; thus a debt, a mortgage, a legacy, may be discharged by payment or performance, or by any act short of that, lawful in itself, which the creditor accepts as sufficient. To discharge a person is to liberate him from the binding force of an obligation, debt, or claim.

Discharge by operation of law is where the discharge takes place, whether it was intended by the parties or not; thus, if a creditor appoints his debtor his executor, the debt is discharged by operation of law, because the executor cannot have an action against himself. Co. Litt. 264b, note 1; Williams, Ex'rs, 1216; Chit. Cont. 714.

In civil practice. To discharge a rule, an order, an injunction, a certificate, process of execution, or in general any proceeding in a court, is to cancel or annul it, or to revoke it, or to refuse to confirm its original provisional force.

To discharge a jury is to relieve them from any further consideration of a cause. This is done when the continuance of the trial is, by any cause, rendered impossible; also when the jury, after deliberation, cannot agree on a verdict.

In equity practice. In the process of accounting before a master in chancery, the *discharge* is a statement of expenses and counter-claims brought in and filed, by way of set-off, by the accounting defendant; which follows the *charge* in order.

In criminal practice. The act by which a person in confinement, held on an accusation of some crime or misdemeanor, is set at liberty. The writing containing the order for his being so set at liberty is also called a "discharge."

In bankruptcy practice. The discharge of the bankrupt is the step which regularly follows the adjudication of bankruptcy and the administration of his estate. By it he is released from the obligation of all his debts which were or might be proved in the proceedings, so that they are no longer a charge upon him, and so that he may thereafter engage in business and acquire property without its being liable for the satisfaction of such former debts.

In maritime law. The unlading or unlivery of a cargo from a vessel. Story, J., 2 Sum. 589, 600.

DISCLAIMER. The repudiation or renunciation of a right or claim vested in a person or which he had formerly alleged to be his. The refusal, waiver, or denial of an estate or right offered to a person. The disavowal, denial, or renunciation of an interest, right, or property imputed to a person or alleged to be his. Also the declaration, or the instrument, by which such disclaimer is published.

Of estates. The act by which a party refuses to accept an estate which has been conveyed to him. Thus, a trustee is said to disclaim who releases to his fellow-trustees his estate, and relieves himself of the trust. 1 Hil. Real Prop. 354; 13 Conn. 83.

A renunciation or a denial by a tenant of his landlord's title, either by refusing to pay rent, denying any obligation to pay, or by setting up a title in himself or a third person, and this is a distinct ground of forfeiture of the lease or other tenancy, whether of land or tithe. See 16 Ch. Div. 730.

In pleading. A renunciation by the defendant of all claim to the subject of the demand made by the plaintiff's bill. Coop. Eq. Pl. 309; Mitf. Eq. Pl. 318.

In patent law. When the title and specifications of a patent do not agree, or when part of that which it covers is not strictly patentable, because neither new nor useful, the patentee is empowered, with leave of the court, to enter a disclaimer of any part of either the title or the specification, and the disclaimer is then deemed to be part of the letters patent or specification, so as to render them valid for the future. Johns. Pat. 151.

DISCLAMATION. In Scotch law. Disavowal of tenure; denial that one holds lands of another. Bell.

DISCOMMON. To deprive commonable lands of their commonable quality, by inclosing and appropriating or improving them.

DISCONTINUANCE. In practice. The termination of an action, in consequence of the plaintiff's omitting to continue the process or proceedings by proper entries on the record. 3 Bl. Comm. 296; 1 Tidd, Pr. 678; 2 Arch. Pr. K. B. 233.

In practice, a discontinuance is a chasm or gap left by neglecting to enter a continuance. By our practice, a neglect to enter a continuance, even in a defaulted action, by no means puts an end to it;

and such actions may always be brought forward. 56 N. H. 416.

The cessation of the proceedings in an action where the plaintiff voluntarily puts an end to it, either by giving notice in writing to the defendant before any step has been taken in the action subsequent to the answer, or at any other time by order of the court or a judge.

In practice, discontinuance and dismissal import the same thing, viz., that the cause is sent out of court. 48 Mo. 235.

In pleading. That technical interruption of the proceedings in an action which follows where a defendant does not answer the whole of the plaintiff's declaration, and the plaintiff omits to take judgment for the part unanswered. Steph. Pl. 216, 217.

DISCONTINUANCE OF AN ESTATE. The termination or suspension of an estate-tail, in consequence of the act of the tenant in tail, in conveying a larger estate in the land than he was by law entitled to do. 2 Bl. Comm. 275; 3 Bl. Comm. 171. An alienation made or suffered by tenant in tail, or by any that is seised in *auter droit*, whereby the issue in tail, or the heir or successor, or those in reversion or remainder, are driven to their action, and cannot enter. Co. Litt. 325*a*. The cesser of a seisin under an estate, and the acquisition of a seisin under a new and necessarily a wrongful title. Prest. Merg. c. ii.

Discontinuare nihil aliud significat quam intermittere, desuescere, interrumpere. Co. Litt. 325. To discontinue signifies nothing else than to intermit, to disuse, to interrupt.

DISCONTINUOUS EASEMENT. One the enjoyment of which can be had only by the interference of man, as rights of way, or a right to draw water; as distinguished from a *continuous* easement, which is one the enjoyment of which is or may be continual, without the necessity of any actual interference by man, as a water-spout, or a right of light or air. Washb. Easem. 13; Gale. Easem. 16; 21 N. Y. 505; 60 Mich. 252, 27 N. W. Rep. 509. This distinction is derived from the French law. See Code Civil, art. 688.

DISCONTINUOUS SERVITUDE. See DISCONTINUOUS EASEMENT.

DISCONVENABLE. L. Fr. Improper; unfit. Kelham.

DISCOUNT. In a general sense. An allowance or deduction made from a gross sum on any account whatever. In a more limited and technical sense. The taking of interest in advance.

By the language of the commercial world and the settled practice of banks, a discount by a bank means a drawback or deduction made upon its advances or loans of money, upon negotiable paper or other evidences of debt payable at a future day, which are transferred to the bank. 8 Wheat. 338; 15 Ohio St. 87.

Although the discounting of notes or bills, in its most comprehensive sense, may mean lending money and taking notes in payment, yet, in its more ordinary sense, the discounting of notes or bills means advancing a consideration for a bill or note, deducting or discounting the interest which will accrue for the time the note has to run. 13 Conn. 248.

Discounting by a bank means lending money upon a note, and deducting the interest or premium in advance. 17 N. Y. 507, 515; 48 Mo. 189.

The ordinary meaning of the term "to discount" is to take interest in advance, and in banking is a mode of loaning money. It is the advance of money not due till some future period, less the interest which would be due thereon when payable. 42 Md. 592.

Discount, as we have seen, is the difference between the price and the amount of the debt, the evidence of which is transferred. That difference represents interest charged, being at the same rate, according to which the price paid, if invested until the maturity of the debt, will just produce its amount. 104 U. S. 276.

Discounting a note and buying it are not identical in meaning, the latter expression being used to denote the transaction when the seller does not indorse the note, and is not accountable for it. 23 Minn. 206.

In practice. A set-off or defalcation in an action. Vin. Abr. "Discount." But see 1 Metc. (Ky.) 597.

DISCOUNT BROKER. A bill broker; one who discounts bills of exchange and promissory notes, and advances money on securities.

DISCOVERT. Not married; not subject to the disabilities of coverture. It applies equally to a maid and a widow.

DISCOVERY. Invention; finding out. The finding of an island or country not previously known to geographers.

In patent law. The finding out some substance, mechanical device, improvement, or application, not previously known.

Discovery, as used in the patent laws, depends upon invention. Every invention may, in a certain sense, embrace more or less of discovery, for it must always include something that is new; but it by no means follows that every discovery is an invention. 5 Blatchf. 121.

Also used of the disclosure by a bankrupt of his property for the benefit of creditors.

In practice. The disclosure by the defendant of facts, titles, documents, or other things which are in his exclusive knowledge or possession, and which are necessary to the party seeking the discovery as a part of a cause or action pending or to be brought in another court, or as evidence of his rights or title in such proceeding.

DISCOVERY, BILL OF. In equity pleading. A bill for the discovery of facts resting in the knowledge of the defendant, or of deeds or writings, or other things in his custody or power; but seeking no relief in consequence of the discovery, though it may pray for a stay of proceedings at law till the discovery is made. Story, Eq. Pl. §§ 311, 312, and notes; Mitf. Eq. Pl. 53.

DISCREDIT. To destroy or impair the credibility of a person; to impeach; to lessen the degree of credit to be accorded to a witness or document, as by impugning the veracity of the one or the genuineness of the other; to disparage or weaken the reliance upon the testimony of a witness, or upon documentary evidence, by any means whatever.

DISCREPANCY. A difference between two things which ought to be identical, as between one writing and another; a variance, (*q. v.*)

Discretio est discernere per legem quid sit justum. 10 Coke, 140. Discretion is to know through law what is just.

DISCRETION. A liberty or privilege allowed to a judge, within the confines of right and justice, but independent of narrow and unbending rules of positive law, to decide and act in accordance with what is fair, equitable, and wholesome, as determined upon the peculiar circumstances of the case, and as discerned by his personal wisdom and experience, guided by the spirit, principles, and analogies of the law.

When applied to public functionaries, discretion means a power or right conferred upon them by law of acting officially in certain circumstances, according to the dictates of their own judgment and conscience, uncontrolled by the judgment or conscience of others. This discretion undoubtedly is to some extent regulated by usage, or, if the term is preferred, by fixed principles. But by this is to be understood nothing more than that the same court cannot, consistently with its own dignity, and with its character and duty of administering

impartial justice, decide in different ways two cases in every respect exactly alike. The question of fact whether the two cases are alike in every color, circumstance, and feature is of necessity to be submitted to the judgment of some tribunal. 18 Wend. 79, 99.

Lord Coke defines judicial discretion to be "*discernere per legem quid sit justum,*" to see what would be just according to the laws in the premises. It does not mean a wild self-willfulness, which may prompt to any and every act; but this judicial discretion is guided by the law, (see what the law declares upon a certain statement of facts, and then decide in accordance with the law,) so as to do substantial equity and justice. 13 Mo. 543.

True, it is a matter of discretion; but then the discretion is not willful or arbitrary, but legal. And, although its exercise be not purely a matter of law, yet it "*involves* a matter of law or legal inference," in the language of the Code, and an appeal will lie. 70 N. C. 171.

In criminal law and the law of torts, it means the capacity to distinguish between what is right and wrong, lawful or unlawful, wise or foolish, sufficiently to render one amenable and responsible for his acts.

DISCRETIONARY TRUSTS. Such as are not marked out on fixed lines, but allow a certain amount of discretion in their exercise. Those which cannot be duly administered without the application of a certain degree of prudence and judgment.

DISCUSSION. In the civil law A proceeding, at the instance of a surety, by which the creditor is obliged to exhaust the property of the principal debtor, towards the satisfaction of the debt, before having recourse to the surety; and this right of the surety is termed the "benefit of discussion." Civil Code La. art. 3045, et seq.

In Scotch law. The ranking of the proper order in which heirs are liable to satisfy the debts of the deceased. Bell.

DISEASE. In construing a policy of life insurance, it is generally true that, before any temporary ailment can be called a "disease," it must be such as to indicate a vice in the constitution, or be so serious as to have some bearing upon general health and the continuance of life, or such as, according to common understanding, would be called a "disease." 70 N. Y. 77.

DISENTAILING DEED. In English law. An enrolled assurance barring an entail, pursuant to 3 & 4 Wm. IV. c. 74.

DISFRANCHISE. To deprive of the rights and privileges of a free citizen; to deprive of chartered rights and immunities; to deprive of any franchise, as of the right of voting in elections, etc. Webster.

DISFRANCHISEMENT. The act of disfranchising. The act of depriving a member of a corporation of his right as such, by expulsion. 1 Bouv. Inst. no. 192.

It differs from amotion, (*q. v.*) which is applicable to the removal of an officer from office, leaving him his rights as a member. Willcock, Mun. Corp. no. 708; Ang. & A. Corp. 237.

DISGAVEL. In English law. To deprive lands of that principal quality of gavelkind tenure by which they descend equally among all the sons of the tenant. 2 Wood. Lect. 76; 2 Bl. Comm. 85.

DISGRACE. Ignominy; shame; dishonor. No witness is required to disgrace himself. 13 How. State Tr. 17, 334.

DISGRADING. In old English law. The depriving of an order or dignity.

DISGUISE. A counterfeit habit; a dress intended to conceal the person who wears it. Webster.

Anything worn upon the person with the intention of so altering the wearer's appearance that he shall not be recognized by those familiar with him, or that he shall be taken for another person.

A person lying in ambush, or concealed behind bushes, is not in "disguise," within the meaning of a statute declaring the county liable in damages to the next of kin of any one murdered by persons in disguise. 46 Ala. 118, 142.

DISHERISON. Disinheritance; depriving one of an inheritance. Obsolete.

DISHONOR. In mercantile law and usage. To refuse or decline to accept a bill of exchange, or to refuse or neglect to pay a bill or note at maturity.

A negotiable instrument is dishonored when it is either not paid or not accepted, according to its tenor, on presentment for that purpose, or without presentment, where that is excused. Civil Code Cal. § 3141.

DISINCARCERATE. To set at liberty, to free from prison.

DISINHERISON. In the civil law. The act of depriving a forced heir of the inheritance which the law gives him.

DISINHERITANCE. The act by which the owner of an estate deprives a person of the right to inherit the same, who would otherwise be his heir.

DISINTERESTED. Not concerned, in respect to possible gain or loss, in the result of the pending proceeding.

DISINTERESTED WITNESS. One who has no interest in the cause or matter in issue, and who is lawfully competent to testify.

DISJUNCTIM. Lat. In the civil law. Separately; severally. The opposite of *conjunctim*, (*q. v.*) Inst. 2, 20, 8.

DISJUNCTIVE ALLEGATION. A statement in a pleading or indictment which expresses or charges a thing alternatively, with the conjunction "or;" for instance, an averment that defendant "murdered, or caused to be murdered," etc., would be of this character.

DISJUNCTIVE TERM. One which is placed between two contraries, by the affirming of one of which the other is taken away; it is usually expressed by the word "or."

DISMES. Tenths; tithes, (*q. v.*) The original form of "dime," the name of the American coin.

DISMISS. To send away; to discharge; to cause to be removed. To dismiss an action or suit is to send it out of court without any further consideration or hearing.

DISMORTGAGE. To redeem from mortgage.

DISORDER. Turbulent or riotous behavior; immoral or indecent conduct. The breach of the public decorum and morality.

DISORDERLY HOUSE. In criminal law. A house the inmates of which behave so badly as to become a nuisance to the neighborhood. It has a wide meaning, and includes bawdy houses, common gaming houses, and places of a like character. 1 Bish. Crim. Law, § 1106; 2 Cranch, C. C. 675.

DISORDERLY PERSONS. Such as are dangerous or hurtful to the public peace and welfare by reason of their misconduct or vicious habits, and are therefore amenable to police regulation. The phrase is chiefly used in statutes, and the scope of the term depends on local regulations. See 4 Bl. Comm. 169.

DISPARAGARE. In old English law. To bring together those that are unequal, (*dispares conferre;*) to connect in an indecorous and unworthy manner; to connect in marriage those that are unequal in blood and parentage.

DISPARAGATIO. In old English law. Disparagement. *Hæredes maritentur absque* *disparagatione*, heirs shall be married without disparagement. *Magna Charta*, (9 Hen. III.) c. 6.

DISPARAGATION. L. Fr. Disparagement; the matching an heir, etc., in marriage, under his or her degree or condition, or against the rules of decency. Kelham.

DISPARAGE. To connect unequally; to match unsuitably.

DISPARAGEMENT. In old English law. An injury by union or comparison with some person or thing of inferior rank or excellence.

Marriage without *disparagement* was marriage to one of suitable rank and character. 2 Bl. Comm. 70; Co. Litt. 82b.

DISPARAGIUM. In old Scotch law. Inequality in blood, honor, dignity, or otherwise. Skene de Verb. Sign.

Disparata non debent jungi. Things unlike ought not to be joined. Jenk. Cent. 24, marg.

DISPARK. To dissolve a park. Cro. Car. 59. To convert it into ordinary ground.

DISPATCH or DESPATCH. A message, letter, or order sent with speed on affairs of state; a telegraphic message.

DISPAUPER. When a person, by reason of his poverty, is admitted to sue *in formâ pauperis*, and afterwards, before the suit be ended, acquires any lands, or personal estate, or is guilty of anything whereby he is liable to have this privilege taken from him, then he loses the right to sue *in formâ pauperis*, and is said to be dispaupered. Wharton.

Dispensatio est mali prohibiti provida relaxatio, utilitate seu necessitate pensata; et est de jure domino regi concessa, propter impossibilitatem prævidendi de omnibus particularibus. A dispensation is the provident relaxation of a *malum prohibitum* weighed from utility or necessity; and it is conceded by law to the king on account of the impossibility of foreknowledge concerning all particulars. 10 Coke, 88.

Dispensatio est vulnus, quod vulnerat jus commune. A dispensation is a wound, which wounds common law. Dav. Ir. K. B. 69.

DISPENSATION. An exemption from some laws; a permission to do something forbidden; an allowance to omit something commanded; the canonistic name for a license. Wharton.

A relaxation of law for the benefit or advantage of an individual. In the United States, no power exists, except in the legislature, to dispense with law; and then it is not so much a dispensation as a change of the law. Bouvier.

DISPERSONARE. To scandalize or disparage. Blount.

DISPLACE. This term, as used in shipping articles, means "disrate," and does not import authority of the master to discharge a second mate, notwithstanding a usage in the whaling trade never to disrate an officer to a seaman. 103 Mass. 68.

DISPONE. In Scotch law. To grant or convey. A technical word essential to the conveyance of heritable property, and for which no equivalent is accepted, however clear may be the meaning of the party. Paters. Comp.

DISPOSE. To alienate or direct the ownership of property, as disposition by will. 42 N. Y. 79. Used also of the determination of suits. 13 Wall. 664. Called a word of large extent. Freem. 177.

DISPOSING CAPACITY OR MIND. These are alternative or synonymous phrases in the law of wills for "sound mind," and "testamentary capacity," (*q. v.*)

DISPOSITION. In Scotch law. A deed of alienation by which a right to property is conveyed. Bell.

DISPOSITIVE FACTS. Such as produce or bring about the origination, transfer, or extinction of rights. They are either *investitive*, those by means of which a right comes into existence, *divestitive*, those through which it terminates, or *translative*, those through which it passes from one person to another.

DISPOSSESSION. Ouster; a wrong that carries with it the amotion of possession. An act whereby the wrong-doer gets the actual occupation of the land or hereditament. It includes abatement, intrusion, disseisin, discontinuance, deforcement. 3 Bl. Comm. 167.

DISPUNISHABLE. In old English law. Not answerable. Co. Litt. 27b. 53. 1 Steph. Comm. 245. Not punishable. "This murder is dispunishable." 1 Leon. 270.

DISPUTABLE PRESUMPTION. A presumption of law, which may be rebutted or disproved. Best, Pres. § 25.

DISPUTATIO FORI. In the civil law. Discussion or argument before a court. Mackeld. Rom. Law, § 38; Dig. 1, 2, 2, 5.

DISRATIONARE, or DIRATIONARE. To justify; to clear one's self of a fault; to traverse an indictment; to disprove. Enc. Lond.

DISSASINA. In old Scotch law. Disseisin; dispossession. Skene.

DISSECTION. The anatomical examination of a dead body.

DISSEISE. To dispossess; to deprive.

DISSEISEE. One who is wrongfully put out of possession of his lands; one who is disseised.

DISSEISIN. Dispossession; a deprivation of possession; a privation of seisin; a usurpation of the right of seisin and possession, and an exercise of such powers and privileges of ownership as to keep out or displace him to whom these rightfully belong. 3 Washb. Real Prop. 125.

It is a wrongful putting out of him that is seised of the freehold, not, as in *abatement* or *intrusion*, a wrongful entry, where the possession was vacant, but an attack upon him who is in actual possession, and turning him out. It is an ouster from a freehold in deed, as abatement and intrusion are ousters in law. 3 Steph. Comm. 386.

When one man invades the possession of another, and by force or surprise turns him out of the occupation of his lands, this is termed a "disseisin," being a deprivation of that actual seisin or corporal possession of the freehold which the tenant before enjoyed. In other words, a disseisin is said to be when one enters intending to usurp the possession, and to oust another from the freehold. To constitute an entry a disseisin, there must be an ouster of the freehold, either by taking the profits or by claiming the inheritance. Brown.

According to the modern authorities, there seems to be no legal difference between the words "seisin" and "possession," although there is a difference between the words "disseisin" and "dispossession;" the former meaning an estate gained by wrong and injury, whereas the latter may be by right or by wrong; the former denoting an ouster of the disseisee, or some act equivalent to it, whereas by the latter no such act is implied. 6 Metc. (Mass.) 439.

Equitable disseisin is where a person is wrongfully deprived of the equitable seisin of land, *e. g.*, of the rents and profits. 2 Meriv. 171; 2 Jac. & W. 166.

Disseisin by election is where a person alleges or admits himself to be disseised when he has not really been so.

Disseisinam satis facit, qui uti non permittit possessorem, vel minus commode, licet omnino non expellat. Co. Litt. 331. He makes disseisin enough who does not permit the possessor to enjoy, or makes his enjoyment less beneficial, although he does not expel him altogether.

DISSEISITRIX. A female disseisor; a disseisoress. Fleta, lib. 4, c. 12, § 4.

DISSEISOR. One who puts another out of the possession of his lands wrongfully.

DISSEISORESS. A woman who unlawfully puts another out of his land.

DISSENT. Contrariety of opinion; refusal to agree with something already stated or adjudged or to an act previously performed.

The term is most commonly used in American law to denote the explicit disagreement of one or more judges of a court with the decision passed by the majority upon a case before them. In such event, the non-concurring judge is reported as "dissenting," and sometimes files a "dissenting opinion."

DISSENTERS. Protestant seceders from the established church of England. They are of many denominations, principally Presbyterians, Independents, Methodists, and Baptists; but, as to church government, the Baptists are Independents.

DISSENTING OPINION. The opinion in which a judge announces his dissent from the conclusions held by the majority of the court, and expounds his own views.

DISSIGNARE. In old law. To break open a seal. Whishaw.

Dissimilium dissimilis est ratio. Co. Litt. 191. Of dissimilars the rule is dissimilar.

Dissimulatione tollitur injuria. An injury is extinguished by the forgiveness or reconcilement of the party injured. Ersk. Inst. 4, 4, 108.

DISSOLUTION. In contracts. The dissolution of a contract is the cancellation or abrogation of it by the parties themselves, with the effect of annulling the binding force of the agreement, and restoring each party to his original rights. In this sense it is frequently used in the phrase "dissolution of a partnership."

Of corporations. The dissolution of a corporation is the termination of its existence as a body politic. This may take place in several ways; as by act of the legislature, where that is constitutional; by surrender or forfeiture of its charter; by expiration of its charter by lapse of time; by proceedings for winding it up under the law; by loss of all its members or their reduction below the statutory limit.

In practice. The act of rendering a legal proceeding null, abrogating or revoking it; unloosing its constraining force; as when an injunction is dissolved by the court.

DISSOLUTION OF PARLIAMENT. The crown may dissolve parliament either in person or by proclamation; the dissolution is usually by proclamation, after a prorogation. No parliament may last for a longer period than seven years. Septennial Act, 1 Geo. I. c. 38. Under 6 Anne, c. 37, upon a demise of the crown, parliament became *ipso facto* dissolved six months afterwards, but under the Reform Act, 1867, its continuance is now nowise affected by such demise. May, Parl. Pr. (6th Ed.) 48. Brown.

DISSOLVE. To terminate; abrogate; cancel; annul; disintegrate. To release or unloose the binding force of anything. As to "dissolve a corporation," to "dissolve an injunction."

The phrase "dissolving a corporation" is sometimes used as synonymous with annulling the charter or terminating the existence of the corporation, and sometimes as meaning merely a judicial act which alienates the property and suspends the business of the corporation, without terminating its existence. A corporation may, for certain purposes, be considered as dissolved so far as to be incapable of doing injury to the public, while it yet retains vitality so far as essential for the protection of the rights of others. 1 Holmes, 104.

DISSUADE. In criminal law. To advise and procure a person not to do an act.

To dissuade a witness from giving evidence against a person indicted is an indictable offense at common law. Hawk. P. C. b. 1, c. 21, § 15.

DISTILLER. Every person who produces distilled spirits, or who brews or makes mash, wort, or wash, fit for distillation or for the production of spirits, or who, by any process of evaporization, separates alcoholic spirit from any fermented substance, or who, making or keeping mash, wort, or wash, has also in his possession or use a still, shall be regarded as a distiller. Rev. St. U. S. § 3247. See 16 Blatchf. 547; 2 Ben. 438.

DISTILLERY. The strict meaning of "distillery" is a place or building where alcoholic liquors are distilled or manufact-

ured; not every building where the process of distillation is used. 45 N. Y. 499.

DISTINCTE ET APERTE. In old English practice. Distinctly and openly. Formal words in writs of error, referring to the return required to be made to them. Reg. Orig. 17.

Distinguenda sunt tempora. The time is to be considered. 1 Coke, 16a; 2 Pick. 327; 14 N. Y. 380, 393.

Distinguenda sunt tempora; aliud est facere, aliud perficere. Times must be distinguished; it is one thing to do, another to perfect. 3 Leon. 243; Branch, Princ.

Distinguenda sunt tempora; distingue tempora et concordabis leges. Times are to be distinguished; distinguish times, and you will harmonize laws. 1 Coke, 24. A maxim applied to the construction of statutes.

DISTINGUISH. To point out an essential difference; to prove a case cited as applicable, inapplicable.

DISTRACTED PERSON. A term used in the statutes of Illinois (Rev. Laws Ill. 1833, p. 332) and New Hampshire (Dig. N. H. Laws, 1830, p. 339) to express a state of insanity.

DISTRACTIO. In the civil law. The sale of a pledge by a debtor. The appropriation of the property of a ward by a guardian. Calvin.

DISTRAHERE. To sell; to draw apart; to dissolve a contract; to divorce. Calvin.

DISTRAIN. To take as a pledge property of another, and keep the same until he performs his obligation or until the property is replevied by the sheriff. It was used to secure an appearance in court, payment of rent, performance of services, etc. 3 Bl. Comm. 231; Fitzh. Nat. Brev. 32, B, C, 223.

Distress is now generally resorted to for the purpose of enforcing the payment of rent, taxes, or other duties.

DISTRAINER, or DISTRAINOR. He who seizes a distress.

DISTRAINT. Seizure.

DISTRESS. The taking a personal chattel out of the possession of a wrong-doer into the custody of the party injured, to procure a satisfaction for a wrong committed; as for non-payment of rent, or injury done by cattle. 3 Bl. Comm. 6, 7; Co. Litt. 47. The taking of beasts or other personal property by way of pledge, to enforce the performance of something due from the party distrained upon. 3 Bl. Comm. 231. The taking of a defendant's goods, in order to compel an appearance in court. Id. 280; 3 Steph. Comm. 361, 363.

DISTRESS INFINITE. One that has no bounds with regard to its quantity, and may be repeated from time to time, until the stubbornness of the party is conquered. Such are distresses for fealty or suit of court, and for compelling jurors to attend. 3 Bl. Comm. 231.

DISTRIBUTEE. Distributee is admissible to denote one of the persons who are entitled, under the statute of distributions, to the personal estate of one who is dead intestate. 9 Ired. 278.

DISTRIBUTION. In practice. The apportionment and division, under authority of a court, of the remainder of the estate of an intestate, after payment of the debts and charges, among those who are legally entitled to share in the same.

DISTRIBUTIVE FINDING OF THE ISSUE. The jury are bound to give their verdict for that party who, upon the evidence, appears to them to have succeeded in establishing his side of the issue. But there are cases in which an issue may be found distributively, i. e., in part for plaintiff, and in part for defendant. Thus, in an action for goods sold and work done, if the defendant pleaded that he never was indebted, on which issue was joined, a verdict might be found for the plaintiff as to the goods, and for the defendant as to the work. Steph. Pl. (7th Ed.) 77d.

DISTRIBUTIVE JUSTICE. See JUSTICE.

DISTRICT. One of the portions into which an entire state or country may be divided, for judicial, political, or administrative purposes.

The United States are divided into judicial districts, in each of which is established a district court. They are also divided into election districts, collection districts, etc.

The circuit or territory within which a person may be compelled to appear. Cowell. Circuit of authority; province. Enc. Lond.

DISTRICT ATTORNEY. The prosecuting officer of the United States government in each of the federal judicial districts.

Also, under the state governments, the prosecuting officer who represents the state in each of its judicial districts. In some states, where the territory is divided, for judicial purposes, into sections called by some other name than "districts," the same officer is denominated "county attorney" or "state's attorney."

DISTRICT CLERK. The clerk of a district court of either a state or the United States.

DISTRICT COURTS. Courts of the United States, each having territorial jurisdiction over a *district*, which may include a whole state or only part of it. Each of these courts is presided over by one judge, who must reside within the district. These courts have original jurisdiction over all admiralty and maritime causes and all proceedings in bankruptcy, and over all penal and criminal matters cognizable under the laws of the United States, exclusive jurisdiction over which is not vested either in the supreme or circuit courts.

Inferior courts of record in California, Connecticut, Iowa, Kansas, Louisiana, Minnesota, Nebraska, Nevada, Ohio, and Texas are also called "district courts." Their jurisdiction is for the most part similar to that of county courts, (q. v.)

DISTRICT JUDGE. The judge of a United States district court; also, in some states, the judge of a district court of the state.

DISTRICT OF COLUMBIA. A territory situated on the Potomac river, and being the seat of government of the United States. It was originally ten miles square, and was composed of portions of Maryland and Virginia ceded by those states to the United States; but in 1846 the tract coming from Virginia was retroceded. Legally it is neither a state nor a territory, but is made subject, by the constitution, to the exclusive jurisdiction of congress.

DISTRICT PARISHES. Ecclesiastical divisions of parishes in England, for all purposes of worship, and for the celebration of marriages, christenings, churchings, and burials, formed at the instance of the queen's commissioners for building new churches. See 3 Steph. Comm. 744.

DISTRICT REGISTRY. By the English judicature act, 1873, § 60, it is provided that to facilitate proceedings in country districts the crown may, from time to time, by order in council, create district registries, and appoint district registrars for the purpose of issuing writs of summons, and for other purposes. Documents sealed in any such district registry shall be received in evidence without further proof, (section 61;) and the district registrars may administer oaths or do other things as provided by rules or a special order of the court, (section 62.) Power, however, is given to a judge to remove proceedings from a district registry to the office of the high court. Section 65. By order in council of 12th of August, 1875, a number of district registries have been established in the places mentioned in that order; and the prothonotaries in Liverpool, Manchester, and Preston, the district registrar of the court of admiralty at Liverpool, and the county court registrars in the other places named, have been appointed district registrars. Wharton.

DISTRICTIO. A distress; a distraint. Cowell.

DISTRINGAS. In English practice. A writ directed to the sheriff of the county in which a defendant resides, or has any goods or chattels, commanding him to *distrain* upon the goods and chattels of the defendant for forty shillings, in order to compel his appearance. 3 Steph. Comm. 567. This writ issues in cases where it is found impracticable to get at the defendant personally, so as to serve a summons upon him. Id.

A *distringas* is also used in equity, as the first process to compel the appearance of a corporation aggregate. St. 11 Geo. IV. and 1 Wm. IV. c. 36.

A form of execution in the actions of detinue and assise of nuisance. Brooke, Abr. pl. 26; 1 Rawle, 44.

DISTRINGAS JURATORES. A writ commanding the sheriff to have the bodies of the jurors, or to *distrain* them by their lands and goods, that they may appear upon the day appointed. 3 Bl. Comm. 354. It issues at the same time with the *venire*, though in theory afterwards, founded on the supposed neglect of the juror to attend. 3 Steph. Comm. 590.

DISTRINGAS NUPER VICE COMITEM. A writ to distrain the goods of one who lately filled the office of sheriff, to compel him to do some act which he ought to have done before leaving the office; as to bring in the body of a defendant, or to sell goods attached under a *fi. fa.*

DISTRINGAS VICECOMITEM. A writ of *distringas*, directed to the coroner, may be issued against a sheriff if he neglects to execute a writ of *venditioni exponas.* Arch. Pr. 584.

DISTRINGERE. In feudal and old English law. To distrain; to coerce or compel. Spelman; Calvin.

DISTURBANCE. A wrong done to an incorporeal hereditament by hindering or disquieting the owner in the enjoyment of it. Finch, 187; 3 Bl. Comm. 235.

DISTURBANCE OF COMMON. The doing any act by which the right of another to his common is incommoded or diminished; as where one who has no right of common puts his cattle into the land, or where one who has a right of common puts in cattle which are not commonable, or surcharges the common; or where the owner of the land, or other person, incloses or otherwise obstructs it. 3 Bl. Comm. 237-241; 3 Steph. Comm. 511, 512.

DISTURBANCE OF FRANCHISE. The disturbing or incommoding a man in the lawful exercise of his franchise, whereby the profits arising from it are diminished. 3 Bl. Comm. 236; 3 Steph. Comm. 510; 2 Crabb, Real Prop. p. 1074, § 2472a.

DISTURBANCE OF PATRONAGE. The hindrance or obstruction of a patron from presenting his clerk to a benefice. 3 Bl. Comm. 242; 3 Steph. Comm. 514.

DISTURBANCE OF PUBLIC WORSHIP. Any acts or conduct which interfere with the peace and good order of an assembly of persons lawfully met together for religious exercises.

DISTURBANCE OF TENURE. In the law of tenure, disturbance is where a stranger, by menaces, force, persuasion, or otherwise, causes a tenant to leave his tenancy; this disturbance of tenure is an injury to the lord for which an action will lie. 3 Steph. Comm. 414.

DISTURBANCE OF WAYS. This happens where a person who has a right of way over another's ground by grant or prescription is obstructed by inclosures or other obstacles, or by plowing across it, by which means he cannot enjoy his right of way, or at least in so commodious a manner as he might have done. 3 Bl. Comm. 241.

DISTURBER. If a bishop refuse or neglect to examine or admit a patron's clerk, without reason assigned or notice given, he is styled a "disturber" by the law, and shall not have any title to present by lapse; for no man shall take advantage of his own wrong. 2 Bl. Comm. 278.

DITCH. The words "ditch" and "drain" have no technical or exact meaning. They both may mean a hollow space in the ground, natural or artificial, where water is collected or passes off. 5 Gray, 64.

DITES OUSTER. L. Fr. Say over. The form of awarding a *respondeas ouster*, in the Year Books. M. 6 Edw. III. 49.

DITTAY. In Scotch law. A technical term in civil law, signifying the matter of charge or ground of indictment against a person accused of crime. *Taking up dittay* is obtaining informations and presentments of crime in order to trial. Skene, de Verb. Sign.; Bell.

DIVERSION. A turning aside or altering the natural course of a thing. The term is chiefly applied to the unauthorized changing the course of a water-course to the prejudice of a lower proprietor.

DIVERSITE DES COURTS. A treatise on courts and their jurisdiction, written in French in the reign of Edward III. as is supposed, and by some attributed to Fitzherbert. It was first printed in 1525, and again in 1534. Crabb, Eng. Law, 330, 483.

DIVERSITY. In criminal pleading. A plea by the prisoner in bar of execution, alleging that he is not the same who was attainted, upon which a jury is immediately impaneled to try the collateral issue thus raised, viz., the identity of the person, and not whether he is guilty or innocent, for that has been already decided. 4 Bl. Comm. 396.

DIVERSO INTUITU. Lat. With a different view, purpose, or design; in a different view or point of view; by a different course or process. 1 W. Bl. 89; 4 Kent, Comm. 211, note.

DIVERSORIUM. In old English law. A lodging or inn. Townsh. Pl. 38.

DIVERT. To turn aside; to turn out of the way; to alter the course of things. Usually applied to water-courses. Ang. Water-Courses, § 97, et seq. Sometimes to roads. 8 East, 394.

DIVES. In the practice of the English chancery division, "dives costs" are costs on the ordinary scale, as opposed to the costs formerly allowed to a successful pauper suing or defending *in formâ pauperis*, and which consisted only of his costs out of pocket. Daniell, Ch. Pr.-43.

DIVEST. Equivalent to devest, (*q. v.*)

DIVESTITIVE FACT. A fact by means of which a right is divested, terminated, or extinguished; as the right of a tenant terminates with the expiration of his lease, and the right of a creditor is at an end when his debt has been paid. Holl. Jur. 132.

Divide et impera, cum radix et vertex imperii in obedientium consensu rata sunt. 4 Inst. 35. Divide and govern, since the foundation and crown of empire are established in the consent of the obedient.

DIVIDEND. A fund to be divided. The share allotted to each of several persons entitled to share in a division of profits or property. Thus, dividend may denote a fund set apart by a corporation out of its profits, to be apportioned among the shareholders, or the proportional amount falling to each. In bankruptcy or insolvency practice, a dividend is a proportional payment to the creditors out of the insolvent estate.

In old English law. The term denotes one part of an indenture, (*q. v.*)

DIVIDENDA. In old records. An indenture; one counterpart of an indenture.

DIVINARE. Lat. To divine; to conjecture or guess; to foretell. *Divinatio*, a conjecturing or guessing.

Divinatio, non interpretatio est, quæ omnino recedit a litera. That is guessing, not interpretation, which altogether departs from the letter. Bac. Max. 18, (in reg. 3,) citing Yearb. 3 Hen. VI. 20.

DIVINE SERVICE. Divine service was the name of a feudal tenure, by which the tenants were obliged to do some special divine services in certain; as to sing so many masses, to distribute such a sum in alms, and the like. (2 Bl. Comm. 102; 1 Steph. Comm. 227.) It differed from tenure in *frankalmoign*, in this: that, in case of the tenure by divine service, the lord of whom the lands were holden might distrain for its non-performance, whereas, in case of *frankalmoign*, the lord has no remedy by distraint for neglect of the service, but merely a right of complaint to the visitor to correct it. Mozley & Whitley.

DIVISA. In old English law. A device, award, or decree; also a devise; also bounds or limits of division of a parish or farm, etc. Cowell. Also a court held on the boundary, in order to settle disputes of the tenants.

Divisibilis est semper divisibilis. A thing divisible may be forever divided.

DIVISIBLE. That which is susceptible of being divided.

A contract cannot, in general, be divided in such a manner that an action may be brought, or a right accrue, on a part of it. 2 Pa. St. 454.

DIVISIM. In old English law. Severally; separately. Bract. fol. 47.

DIVISION. In English law. One of the smaller subdivisions of a county. Used in Lincolnshire as synonymous with "riding" in Yorkshire.

DIVISION OF OPINION. In the practice of appellate courts, this term denotes such a disagreement among the judges that there is not a majority in favor of any one view, and hence no decision can be rendered on the case. But it sometimes also denotes a division into two classes, one of which may comprise a majority of the judges; as when we speak of a decision having proceeded from a "divided court."

DIVISIONAL COURTS. Courts in England, consisting of two or (in special cases) more judges of the high court of justice, sitting to transact certain kinds of business which cannot be disposed of by one judge.

DIVISUM IMPERIUM. Lat. A divided jurisdiction. Applied, e. g., to the jurisdiction of courts of common law and equity over the same subject. 1 Kent, Comm. 366; 4 Steph. Comm. 9.

DIVORCE. The legal separation of man and wife, effected, for cause, by the judgment of a court, and either totally dissolving the marriage relation, or suspending its effects so far as concerns the cohabitation of the parties.

The dissolution is termed "divorce from the bond of matrimony," or, in the Latin form of the expression, "a vinculo matrimonii;" the suspension, "divorce from bed and board," ""a mensa et thoro." The former divorce puts an end to the marriage; the latter leaves it in full force. 2 Bish. Mar. & Div. § 225.

The term "divorce" is now applied, in England,

both to decrees of nullity and decrees of dissolution of marriage, while in America it is used only in cases of divorce a mensa or a vinculo, a decree of nullity of marriage being granted for the causes for which a divorce a vinculo was formerly obtainable in England.

DIVORCE A MENSA ET THORO. A divorce from table and bed, or from bed and board. A partial or qualified divorce, by which the parties are separated and forbidden to live or cohabit together, without affecting the marriage itself. 1 Bl. Comm. 440; 3 Bl. Comm. 94; 2 Steph. Comm. 311; 2 Bish. Mar. & Div. § 225.

DIVORCE A VINCULO MATRIMONII. A divorce from the bond of marriage. A total divorce of husband and wife, dissolving the marriage tie, and releasing the parties wholly from their matrimonial obligations. 1 Bl. Comm. 440; 2 Steph. Comm. 310, 311; 2 Bish. Mar. & Div. § 225.

Divortium dicitur a divertendo, quia vir divertitur ab uxore. Co. Litt. 235. Divorce is called from divertendo, because a man is diverted from his wife.

DIXIEME. Fr. Tenth; the tenth part. Ord. Mar. liv. 1, tit. 1, art. 9.

In old French law. An income tax payable to the crown. Steph. Lect. 359.

DO. Lat. I give. The ancient and aptest word of feoffment and of gift. 2 Bl. Comm. 310, 316; Co. Litt. 9.

DO, DICO, ADDICO. Lat. I give, I say, I adjudge. Three words used in the Roman law, to express the extent of the civil jurisdiction of the prætor. Do denoted that he gave or granted actions, exceptions, and judices; dico, that he pronounced judgment; addico, that he adjudged the controverted property, or the goods of the debtor, etc., to the plaintiff. Mackeld. Rom. Law, § 39.

DO, LEGO. Lat. I give, I bequeath; or I give and bequeath. The formal words of making a bequest or legacy, in the Roman law. Titio et Seio hominem Stichum do, lego, I give and bequeath to Titius and Seius my man Stichus. Inst. 2, 20, 8, 30, 31. The expression is literally retained in modern wills.

DO UT DES. Lat. I give that you may give; I give [you] that you may give [me.] A formula in the civil law, constituting a general division under which those contracts (termed "innominate") were classed in which something was given by one party as a consideration for something *given* by the other. Dig. 19, 4; Id. 19, 5, 5; 2 Bl. Comm. 444.

DO UT FACIAS. Lat. I give that you may do; I give [you] that you may do or make [for me.] A formula in the civil law, under which those contracts were classed in which one party *gave* or agreed to give money, in consideration the other party *did* or performed certain work. Dig. 19, 5, 5; 2 Bl. Comm. 444.

In this and the foregoing phrase, the conjunction "*ut*" is not to be taken as the technical means of expressing a consideration. In the Roman usage, this word imported a *modus*, that is, a qualification; while a consideration (*causa*) was more aptly expressed by the word "*quia.*"

DOCK, *v.* To curtail or diminish, as to dock an entail.

DOCK, *n.* The cage or inclosed space in a criminal court where prisoners stand when brought in for trial.

The space, in a river or harbor, inclosed between two wharves. 17 How. 434.

DOCK-MASTER. An officer invested with powers within the docks, and a certain distance therefrom, to direct the mooring and removing of ships, so as to prevent obstruction to the dock entrances. Mozley & Whitley.

DOCK WARRANT. In English law. A warrant given by dock-owners to the owner of merchandise imported and warehoused on the dock, upon the faith of the bills of lading, as a recognition of his title to the goods. It is a negotiable instrument. Pull. Port of London, p. 375.

DOCKAGE. The sum charged for the use of a dock. In the case of a dry-dock, it has been held in the nature of rent. 1 Newb. Adm. 69.

DOCKET, *v.* To abstract and enter in a book. 3 Bl. Comm. 397, 398. To make a brief entry of any proceeding in a court of justice in the docket.

DOCKET, *n.* A minute, abstract, or brief entry; or the book containing such entries. A small piece of paper or parchment having the effect of a larger. Blount.

In practice. A formal record, entered in brief, of the proceedings in a court of justice.

A book containing an entry in brief of all the important acts done in court in the conduct of each case, from its inception to its conclusion. Pub. St. Mass. 1882, p. 1290.

The docket of judgments is a brief writing or statement of a judgment made from the record or roll, generally kept in books, alphabetically arranged, by the clerk of the court or county clerk. 1 Bradf. Sur. 343.

The name of "docket" or "trial docket" is sometimes given to the list or calendar of causes set to be tried at a specified term, prepared by the clerks for the use of the court and bar.

In the practice of some of the states there are several species of dockets, such as the "appearance docket," "judgment docket," "execution docket," etc., each containing a brief record of the class of proceedings indicated by its name.

DOCKET, STRIKING A. A phrase formerly used in English bankruptcy practice. It referred to the entry of certain papers at the bankruptcy office, preliminary to the prosecution of the fiat against a trader who had become bankrupt. These papers consisted of the affidavit, the bond, and the petition of the creditor, and their object was to obtain from the lord chancellor his fiat, authorizing the petitioner to prosecute his complaint against the bankrupt in the bankruptcy courts. Brown.

DOCTOR. This term means, simply, practitioner of physic, without respect to system pursued. A certificate of a homœopathic physician is a "doctor's certificate." 4 E. D. Smith, 1.

DOCTOR AND STUDENT. The title of a work written by St. Germain in the reign of Henry VIII. in which many principles of the common law are discussed in a popular manner. It is in the form of a dialogue between a doctor of divinity and a student in law, and has always been considered a book of merit and authority. 1 Kent, Comm. 504; Crabb, Eng. Law, 482.

DOCTORS' COMMONS. An institution near St. Paul's Churchyard, in London, where, for a long time previous to 1857, the ecclesiastical and admiralty courts used to be held.

DOCTRINE. A rule, principle, theory, or tenet of the law; as, the doctrine of merger, the doctrine of relation, etc.

DOCUMENT. An instrument on which is recorded, by means of letters, figures, or marks, matter which may be evidentially used. In this sense the term "document" applies to writings; to words printed, lithographed, or photographed; to seals, plates, or

E

F

G

H

I

J

K

L

M

stones on which inscriptions are cut or engraved; to photographs and pictures; to maps and plans. The inscription may be on stone or gems, or on wood, as well as on paper or parchment. 1 Whart. Ev. § 614.

DOCUMENTS. The deeds, agreements, title-papers, letters, receipts, and other written instruments used to prove a fact.

In the civil law. Evidence delivered in the forms established by law, of whatever nature such evidence may be. The term is, however, applied principally to the testimony of witnesses. Sav. Dr. Rom. § 165.

DODRANS. Lat. In Roman law. A subdivision of the *as*, containing nine *unciæ;* the proportion of nine-twelfths, or three-fourths. 2 Bl. Comm. 462, note.

DOE, JOHN. The name of the fictitious plaintiff in the action of ejectment. 3 Steph. Comm. 618.

DŒD-BANA. In Saxon law. The actual perpetrator of a homicide.

DOER. In Scotch law. An agent or attorney. 1 Kames, Eq. 325.

DOG-DRAW. In old forest law. The manifest deprehension of an offender against venison in a forest, when he was found drawing after a deer by the scent of a hound led in his hand; or where a person had wounded a deer or wild beast, by shooting at him, or otherwise, and was caught with a dog drawing after him to receive the same. Manwood, Forest Law, 2, c. 8.

DOG-LATIN. The Latin of illiterate persons; Latin words put together on the English grammatical system.

DOGGER. In maritime law. A light ship or vessel; *dogger-fish,* fish brought in ships. Cowell.

DOGGER-MEN. Fishermen that belong to dogger-ships.

DOGMA. In the civil law. A word occasionally used as descriptive of an ordinance of the senate. See Nov. 2, 1, 1; Dig. 27, 1, 6.

DOING. The formal word by which *services* were reserved and expressed in old conveyances; as "rendering" (*reddendo*) was expressive of *rent.* Perk. c. 10, §§ 625, 635, 638.

DOITKIN, or DOIT. A base coin of small value, prohibited by St. 3 Hen. V. c. 1. We still retain the phrase, in the common saying, when we would undervalue a man, that he is not worth a doit. Jacob.

DOLE. A part or portion of a meadow is so called; and the word has the general signification of share, portion, or the like; as "to dole out" anything among so many poor persons, meaning to deal or distribute in portions to them. Holthouse.

In Scotch law. Criminal intent; evil design. Bell, Dict. voc. "Crime."

DOLES, or DOOLS. Slips of pasture left between the furrows of plowed land.

DOLG. Sax. A wound. Spelman.

DOLG-BOTE. A recompense for a scar or wound. Cowell.

DOLI CAPAX. Lat. Capable of malice or criminal intention; having sufficient discretion and intelligence to distinguish between right and wrong, and so to become amenable to the criminal laws.

DOLI INCAPAX. Incapable of criminal intention or malice; not of the age of discretion; not possessed of sufficient discretion and intelligence to distinguish between right and wrong to the extent of being criminally responsible for his actions.

DOLLAR. The unit employed in the United States in calculating money values. It is coined both in gold and silver, and is of the value of one hundred cents.

DOLO. In Spanish law. Bad or mischievous design. White, New Recop. b. 1, tit. 1, c. 1, § 3.

Dolo facit qui petit quod redditurus est. He acts with guile who demands that which he will have to return. Broom, Max. 346.

Dolo malo pactum se non servaturum. Dig. 2, 14, 7, § 9. An agreement induced by fraud cannot stand.

Dolosus versatur in generalibus. A person intending to deceive deals in general terms. Wing. Max. 636; 2 Coke, 34a; 6 Clark & F. 699; Broom. Max. 289.

Dolum ex indiciis perspicuis probari convenit. Fraud should be proved by clear tokens. Code, 2, 21, 6; 1 Story, Cont. § 625.

DOLUS. In the civil law. Guile; deceitfulness; malicious fraud. A fraudulent address or trick used to deceive some one; a fraud. Dig. 4, 3, 1. Any subtle contrivance by words or acts with a design to circumvent. 2 Kent, Comm. 560; Code, 2, 21.

Such acts or omissions as operate as a deception upon the other party, or violate the just confidence reposed by him, whether there be a deceitful intent (*malus animus*) or not. Poth. Traité de Dépôt, nn. 23, 27; Story, Bailm. § 20*a;* 2 Kent, Comm. 506, note.

Fraud, willfulness, or intentionality. In that use it is opposed to *culpa*, which is negligence merely, in greater or less degree. The policy of the law may sometimes treat extreme *culpa* as if it were *dolus;* upon the maxim *culpa dolo comparatur.* A person is always liable for *dolus* producing damage, but not always for *culpa* producing damage, even though extreme, *e. g.*, a depositary is only liable for *dolus*, and not for negligence. Brown.

Dolus auctoris non nocet successori. The fraud of a predecessor prejudices not his successor.

Dolus circuitu non purgatur. Fraud is not purged by circuity. Bac. Max. 4; Broom, Max. 228.

DOLUS DANS LOCUM CONTRACTUI. Fraud (or deceit) giving rise to the contract; that is, a fraudulent misrepresentation made by one of the parties to the contract, and relied upon by the other, and which was actually instrumental in inducing the latter to enter into the contract.

Dolus est machinatio, cum aliud dissimulat aliud agit. Lane, 47. Deceit is an artifice, since it pretends one thing and does another.

Dolus et fraus nemini patrocinentur, (patrocinari debent.) Deceit and fraud shall excuse or benefit no man. Yearb. 14 Hen. VIII. 8; Best, Ev. p. 469, § 428; 1 Story, Eq. Jur. § 395.

Dolus latet in generalibus. Fraud lurks in generalities. Tray. Lat. Max. 162.

DOLUS MALUS. Fraud; deceit with an evil intention. Distinguished from *dolus bonus*, justifiable or allowable deceit. Calvin.; Broom, Max. 349; Mackeld. Rom. Law, § 179. Misconduct. *Magna negligentia culpa est; magna culpa dolus est*, (great negligence is a fault; a great fault is fraud.) 2 Kent, Comm. 560, note.

Dolus versatur in generalibus. Fraud deals in generalities. 2 Coke, 34*a;* 3 Coke, 81*a.*

DOM. PROC. An abbreviation of *Domus Procerum* or *Domo Procerum;* the

AM. DICT. LAW—25

house of lords in England. Sometimes expressed by the letters D. P.

DOMAIN. The complete and absolute ownership of land; a paramount and individual right of property in land. Also the real estate so owned. The inherent sovereign power claimed by the legislature of a state, of controlling private property for public uses, is termed the "right of eminent domain." 2 Kent, Comm. 339.

The public lands of a state are frequently termed the "public domain," or "domain of the state." 1 Kent, Comm. 166, 259; 2 Kent, Comm. 339, note.

A distinction has been made between "property" and "domain." The former is said to be that quality which is conceived to be in the thing itself, considered as belonging to such or such person, exclusively of all others. By the latter is understood that right which the owner has of disposing of the thing. Hence "domain" and "property" are said to be correlative terms. The one is the active right to dispose of; the other a passive quality which follows the thing and places it at the disposition of the owner. 3 Toullier, no. 83.

DOMBEC, DOMBOC. (Sax. From *dom*, judgment, and *bec, boc*, a book.) Domebook or doom-book. A name given among the Saxons to a code of laws. Several of the Saxon kings published *dombocs*, but the most important one was that attributed to Alfred. Crabb, Com. Law, 7. This is sometimes confounded with the celebrated *Domesday-Book.* See DOME-BOOK, DOMESDAY.

DOME. (Sax.) Doom; sentence; judgment. An oath. The homager's oath in the black book of Hereford. Blount.

DOME-BOOK. A book or code said to have been compiled under the direction of Alfred, for the general use of the whole kingdom of England; containing, as is supposed, the principal maxims of the common law, the penalties for misdemeanors, and the forms of judicial proceedings. It is said to have been extant so late as the reign of Edward IV., but is now lost. 1 Bl. Comm. 64, 65.

DOMESDAY, DOMESDAY - BOOK. (Sax.) An ancient record made in the time of William the Conqueror, and now remaining in the English exchequer, consisting of two volumes of unequal size, containing minute and accurate surveys of the lands in England. 2 Bl. Comm. 49, 50. The work was begun by five justices in each county in 1081, and finished in 1086.

DOMESMEN. (Sax.) An inferior kind of judges. Men appointed to doom (judge) in matters in controversy. Cowell. Suitors in a court of a manor in ancient demesne, who are judges there. Blount; Whishaw; Termes de la Ley.

DOMESTIC, *n.* Domestics, or, in full, domestic servants, are servants who reside in the same house with the master they serve. The term does not extend to workmen or laborers employed out of doors. 5 Bin. 167.

The Louisiana Civil Code enumerates as domestics those who receive wages and stay in the house of the person paying and employing them, for his own service or that of his family; such as valets, footmen, cooks, butlers, and others who reside in the house. Persons employed in public houses are not included. 6 La. Ann. 276.

DOMESTIC, *adj.* Pertaining, belonging, or relating to a home, a domicile, or to the place of birth, origin, creation, or transaction. See the following titles.

DOMESTIC ADMINISTRATOR. One appointed at the place of the domicile of the decedent; distinguished from a foreign or an ancillary administrator.

DOMESTIC ANIMALS. Horses are embraced within this description. 2 Allen, 209. But dogs are not. 75 Me. 562.

DOMESTIC ATTACHMENT. A species of attachment against resident debtors who absent or conceal themselves, as foreign attachment (*q. v.*) is against non-residents. 20 Pa. St. 144.

DOMESTIC BILL OF EXCHANGE. A bill of exchange drawn on a person residing in the same state with the drawer; or dated at a place in the state, and drawn on a person living within the state. It is the residence of the drawer and drawee which must determine whether a bill is domestic or foreign. 25 Miss. 143.

DOMESTIC COMMERCE. Commerce carried on wholly within the limits of the United States, as distinguished from foreign commerce. Also, commerce carried on within the limits of a single state, as distinguished from interstate commerce.

DOMESTIC CORPORATIONS. Such as were created by the laws of the same state wherein they transact business.

DOMESTIC COURTS. Those existing and having jurisdiction at the place of the party's residence or domicile.

DOMESTIC FACTOR. One who resides and does business in the same state or country with his principal.

DOMESTIC JUDGMENT. A judgment or decree is *domestic* in the courts of the same state or country where it was originally rendered; in other states or countries it is called *foreign.*

DOMESTIC MANUFACTURES. This term in a state statute is used, generally, of manufactures within its jurisdiction. 64 Pa. St. 100.

DOMESTICUS. In old European law. A *seneschal*, steward, or *major domo;* a judge's assistant; an assessor, (*q. v.*) Spelman.

DOMICELLA. In old English law. A damsel. Fleta, lib. 1, c. 20, § 80.

DOMICELLUS. In old English law. A better sort of servant in monasteries; also an appellation of a king's bastard.

DOMICILE. That place in which a man has voluntarily fixed the habitation of himself and family, not for a mere special or temporary purpose, but with the present intention of making a permanent home, until some unexpected event shall occur to induce him to adopt some other permanent home.

In its ordinary acceptation, a person's domicile is the place where he lives or has his home. In a strict and legal sense, that is properly the domicile of a person where he has his true, fixed, permanent home and principal establishment, and to which, whenever he is absent, he has the intention of returning. 42 Vt. 350; 9 Ired. 99.

Domicile is but the established, fixed, permanent, or ordinary dwelling-place or place of residence of a person, as distinguished from his temporary and transient, though actual, place of residence. It is his legal residence, as distinguished from his temporary place of abode; or his home, as distinguished from a place to which business or pleasure may temporarily call him. 29 Conn. 74.

Domicile is the place where a person has fixed his habitation and has a permanent residence, without any present intention of removing therefrom. 4 Barb. 504, 520.

One's domicile is the place where one's family permanently resides. 46 Ga. 277.

In international law, "domicile" means a residence at a particular place, accompanied with positive or presumptive proof of intending to continue there for an unlimited time. 32 N. J. Law, 192.

"Domicile" and "residence" are not synonymous. The domicile is the home, the fixed place of habitation; while residence is a transient place of dwelling. 5 Sandf. 44.

The domicile is the habitation fixed in any place with an intention of always staying there, while simple residence is much more temporary in its character. 4 Hun, 489.

Domicile is of three sorts,—domicile by birth, domicile by choice, and domicile by operation of law. The first is the common case of the place of birth, *domicilium originis;* the second is that which is voluntarily acquired by a party, *proprio motu;* the last is consequential, as that of the wife arising from marriage. Story, Confl. Laws, § 46.

The term "domicile of succession," as contradistinguished from a commercial, a political, or a forensic domicile, may be defined to be the actual residence of a man within some particular jurisdiction, of such character as shall, in accordance with certain well-established principles of the public law, give direction to the succession of his personal estate. 7 Fla. 81.

DOMICILE OF ORIGIN. The home of the parents. Phillim. Dom. 25, 101. That which arises from a man's birth and connections. 5 Ves. 750. The domicile of the parents at the time of birth, or what is termed the "domicile of origin," constitutes the domicile of an infant, and continues until abandoned, or until the acquisition of a new domicile in a different place. 1 Brock. 389, 393.

DOMICILED. Established in a given domicile; belonging to a given state or jurisdiction by right of domicile.

DOMICILIARY. Pertaining to domicile; relating to one's domicile. Existing or created at, or connected with, the domicile of a suitor or of a decedent.

DOMICILIATE. To establish one's domicile; to take up one's fixed residence in a given place. To establish the domicile of another person whose legal residence follows one's own.

DOMICILIUM. Domicile, (*q. v.*)

DOMIGERIUM. In old English law. Power over another; also danger. Bract. l. 4, t. 1, c. 10.

DOMINA, (DAME.) A title given to honorable women, who anciently, in their own right of inheritance, held a barony. Cowell.

DOMINANT. The tenement whose owner, as such, enjoys an easement over an adjoining tenement is called the "dominant tenement;" while that which is subject to the easement is called the "servient" one.

DOMINANT TENEMENT. A term used in the civil and Scotch law, and thence in ours, relating to servitudes, meaning the tenement or subject in favor of which the service is constituted; as the tenement over which the servitude extends is called the "servient tenement." Wharton.

DOMINATIO. In old English law. Lordship.

DOMINICA PALMARUM. (*Dominica in ramis palmarum.*) L. Lat. Palm Sunday. Townsh. Pl. 131; Cowell; Blount.

DOMINICAL. That which denotes the Lord's day, or Sunday.

DOMINICIDE. The act of killing one's lord or master.

DOMINICUM. Lat. Domain; demain; demesne. A lordship. That of which one has the lordship or ownership. That which remains under the lord's immediate charge and control. Spelman.

Property; domain; anything pertaining to a lord. Cowell.

In ecclesiastical law. A church, or any other building consecrated to God. Du Cange.

DOMINICUM ANTIQUUM. In old English law. Ancient demesne. Bract. fol. 369*b*.

DOMINION. Ownership, or right to property. 2 Bl. Comm. 1. "The holder has the dominion of the bill." 8 East, 579.

Sovereignty or lordship; as the dominion of the seas. Moll. de Jure Mar. 91, 92.

DOMINIUM. In the civil and old English law. Ownership; property in the largest sense, including both the right of property and the right of possession or use.

The mere right of property, as distinguished from the possession or usufruct. Dig. 41, 2, 17, 1; Calvin. The right which a lord had in the fee of his tenant. In this sense the word is very clearly distinguished by Bracton from *dominicum.*

The estate of a feoffee to uses. "The feoffees to use shall have the *dominium,* and the *cestui que use* the disposition." Latch, 137.

Sovereignty or dominion. *Dominium maris,* the sovereignty of the sea.

DOMINIUM DIRECTUM. In the civil law. Strict ownership; that which was founded on strict law, as distinguished from equity.

In later law. Property without use; the right of a landlord. Tayl. Civil Law, 478.

In feudal law. Right or proper ownership; the right of a superior or lord, as distinguished from that of his vassal or tenant.

The title or property which the sovereign in England is considered as possessing in all the lands of the kingdom, they being holden either immediately or mediately of him as lord paramount.

DOMINIUM DIRECTUM ET UTILE. The complete and absolute dominion in property; the union of the title and the exclusive use. 7 Cranch, 603.

DOMINIUM EMINENS. Eminent domain.

Dominium non potest esse in pendenti. Lordship cannot be in suspense, *i. e.*, property cannot remain in abeyance. Halk. Law Max. 39.

DOMINIUM PLENUM. Full ownership; the union of the *dominium directum* with the *dominium utile*. Tayl. Civil Law, 478.

DOMINIUM UTILE. In the civil law. Equitable or prætorian ownership; that which was founded on equity. Mackeld. Rom. Law, § 327, note.

In later law. Use without property; the right of a tenant. Tayl. Civil Law, 478.

In feudal law. Useful or beneficial ownership; the usufruct, or right to the use and profits of the soil, as distinguished from the *dominium directum*, (*q. v.*,) or ownership of the soil itself; the right of a vassal or tenant. 2 Bl. Comm. 105.

DOMINO VOLENTE. Lat. The owner being willing; with the consent of the owner.

DOMINUS. In feudal and ecclesiastical law. A lord, or feudal superior. *Dominus rex*, the lord the king; the king's title as lord paramount. 1 Bl. Comm. 367. *Dominus capitalis*, a chief lord. *Dominus medius*, a mesne or intermediate lord. *Dominus ligius*, liege lord or sovereign. Id.

Lord or sir; a title of distinction. It usually denoted a knight or clergyman; and, according to Cowell, was sometimes given to a gentleman of quality, though not a knight, especially if he were lord of a manor.

The owner or proprietor of a thing, as distinguished from him who uses it merely. Calvin. A master or principal, as distinguished from an agent or attorney. Story, Ag. § 3.

In the civil law. A husband. A family. Vicat.

Dominus capitalis loco hæredis habetur, quoties per defectum vel delictum

extinguitur sanguis sui tenentis. Co. Litt. 18. The supreme lord takes the place of the heir, as often as the blood of the tenant is extinct through deficiency or crime.

DOMINUS LITIS. Lat. The master of the suit; *i. e.*, the person who was really and directly interested in the suit as a party, as distinguished from his attorney or advocate. But the term is also applied to one who, though not originally a party, has made himself such, by intervention or otherwise, and has assumed entire control and responsibility for one side, and is treated by the court as liable for costs. See 1 Curt. 201.

DOMINUS NAVIS. In the civil law. The owner of a vessel. Dig. 39, 4, 11, 2.

Dominus non maritabit pupillum nisi semel. Co. Litt. 9. A lord cannot give a ward in marriage but once.

Dominus rex nullum habere potest parem, multo minus superiorem. The king cannot have an equal, much less a superior. 1 Reeves, Eng. Law, 115.

DOMITÆ. Lat. Tame; domesticated; not wild. Applied to domestic animals, in which a man may have an absolute property. 2 Bl. Comm. 391.

DOMMAGES INTERETS. In French law. Damages.

DOMO REPARANDÂ. A writ that lay for one against his neighbor, by the anticipated fall of whose house he feared a damage and injury to his own. Reg. Orig. 153.

DOMUS. Lat. In the civil and old English law. A house or dwelling; a habitation. Inst. 4, 4, 8; Townsh. Pl. 183–185.

DOMUS CAPITULARIS. In old records. A chapter-house; the chapter-house. Dyer, 26b.

DOMUS CONVERSORUM. An ancient house built or appointed by King Henry III. for such Jews as were converted to the Christian faith; but King Edward III., who expelled the Jews from the kingdom, deputed the place for the custody of the rolls and records of the chancery. Jacob.

DOMUS DEI. The house of God; a name applied to many hospitals and religious houses.

DOMUS PROCERUM. The house of lords, abbreviated into *Dom. Proc.*, or *D. P.*

Domus sua cuique est tutissimum refugium. To every man his own house is his safest refuge. 5 Coke, 91b; 11 Coke, 82; 3 Inst. 162. The house of every one is to him as his castle and fortress, as well for his defense against injury and violence as for his repose. 5 Coke, 91b; Say. 227; Broom, Max. 432. A man's dwelling-house is his castle, not for his own personal protection merely, but also for the protection of his family and his property therein. 4 Hill, 437.

Domus tutissimum cuique refugium atque receptaculum sit. A man's house should be his safest refuge and shelter. A maxim of the Roman law. Dig. 2, 4, 18.

Dona clandestina sunt semper suspiciosa. 3 Coke, 81. Clandestine gifts are always suspicious.

Donari videtur, quod nullo jure cogente conceditur. Dig. 50, 17, 82. A thing is said to be given when it is yielded otherwise than by virtue of right.

DONATARIUS. A donee; one to whom something is given.

DONATIO. Lat. A gift. A transfer of the title to property to one who receives it without paying for it. Vicat. The act by which the owner of a thing voluntarily transfers the title and possession of the same from himself to another person, without any consideration.

Its literal translation, "gift," has acquired in real law a more limited meaning, being applied to the conveyance of estates tail. 2 Bl. Comm. 316; Littleton, § 59; West. Symb. § 254; 4 Cruise, Dig. 51. There are several kinds of *donatio*, as: *Donatio simplex et pura*, (simple and pure gift without compulsion or consideration;) *donatio absoluta et larga*, (an absolute gift;) *donatio conditionalis*, (a conditional gift;) *donatio stricta et coarctura*, (a restricted gift, as an estate tail.)

DONATIO INTER VIVOS. A gift between the living. The ordinary kind of gift by one person to another. 2 Kent, Comm. 438; 2 Steph. Comm. 102. A term derived from the civil law. Inst. 2, 7, 2.

A donation *inter vivos* (between living persons) is an act by which the donee divests himself at present and irrevocably of the thing given in favor of the donee who accepts it. Civil Code La. art. 1468.

DONATIO MORTIS CAUSA. (Lat. A gift in prospect of death.) A gift made by a person in sickness, who, apprehending his dissolution near, delivers, or causes to be delivered, to another the possession of any personal goods, to keep as his own in case of the donor's decease. 2 Bl. Comm. 514.

The civil law defines it to be a gift under apprehension of death; as when anything is given upon condition that, if the donor dies, the donee shall possess it absolutely, or return it if the donor should survive or should repent of having made the gift, or if the donee should die before the donor. 1 Miles, 109–117.

A gift in view of death is one which is made in contemplation, fear, or peril of death, and with intent that it shall take effect only in case of the death of the giver. Civil Code Cal. § 1149.

A donation *mortis causa* (in prospect of death) is an act to take effect when the donor shall no longer exist, by which he disposes of the whole or a part of his property, and which is irrevocable. Civil Code La. art. 1469.

Donatio non præsumitur. A gift is not presumed. Jenk. Cent. 109.

Donatio perficitur possessione accipientis. A gift is perfected [made complete] by the possession of the receiver. Jenk. Cent. 109, case 9. A gift is incomplete until possession is delivered. 2 Kent, Comm. 438.

Donatio principis intelligitur sine præjudicio tertii. Dav. Ir. K. B. 75. A gift of the prince is understood without prejudice to a third party.

DONATIO PROPTER NUPTIAS. A gift on account of marriage. In Roman law, the bridegroom's gift to the bride in anticipation of marriage and to secure her *dos* was called "*donatio ante nuptias;*" but by an ordinance of Justinian such gift might be made after as well as before marriage, and in that case it was called "*donatio propter nuptias.*" Mackeld. Rom. Law, § 572.

DONATION. In ecclesiastical law. A mode of acquiring a benefice by deed of gift alone, without presentation, institution, or induction. 3 Steph. Comm. 81.

In general. A gift. See DONATIO.

DONATIVE ADVOWSON. In ecclesiastical law. A species of advowson, where the benefice is conferred on the clerk by the patron's deed of donation, without presentation, institution, or induction. 2 Bl. Comm. 23; Termes de la Ley.

DONATOR. A donor; one who makes a gift, (*donatio.*)

Donator nunquam desinit possidere, antequam donatorius incipiat possidere. The donor never ceases to possess, until the donee begins to possess. Bract. fol. 41b.

DONATORIUS. A donee; a person to whom a gift is made; a purchaser. Bract. fol. 13, et seq.

DONATORY. The person on whom the king bestows his right to any forfeiture that has fallen to the crown.

DONE. Distinguished from "made." "A 'deed made' may no doubt mean an 'instrument made;' but a 'deed done' is not an 'instrument done,'—it is an 'act done;' and therefore these words, 'made and done,' apply to acts, as well as deeds." Lord Brougham, 4 Bell, App. Cas. 38.

DONEE. In old English law. He to whom lands were given; the party to whom a *donatio* was made.

In later law. He to whom lands or tenements are given in tail. Litt. § 57.

In modern and American law. The party executing a power; otherwise called the "appointer." 4 Kent, Comm. 316.

DONIS, STATUTE DE. See DE DONIS, THE STATUTE.

DONNEUR D'AVAL. In French law. Guarantor of negotiable paper other than by indorsement.

DONOR. In old English law. He by whom lands were given to another; the party making a *donatio*.

In later law. He who gives lands or tenements to another in tail. Litt. § 57; Termes de la Ley.

In modern and American law. The party conferring a power. 4 Kent, Comm. 316.

DONUM. Lat. In the civil law. A gift; a free gift. Calvin. Distinguished from *munus*. Dig. 50, 16, 194.

DOOM. In Scotch law. Judicial sentence, or judgment. The decision or sentence of a court orally pronounced by an officer called a "dempster" or "deemster." In modern usage, criminal sentences still end with the words "which is pronounced for doom."

DOOMSDAY-BOOK. See DOMESDAY-BOOK.

DOOR. The place of usual entrance in a house, or into a room in the house.

DORMANT. Literally, sleeping; hence inactive; in abeyance; unknown; concealed.

DORMANT CLAIM. One which is in abeyance.

DORMANT EXECUTION. One which a creditor delivers to the sheriff with directions to levy only, and not to sell, until further orders, or until a junior execution is received.

DORMANT JUDGMENT. One which has not been satisfied, nor extinguished by lapse of time, but which has remained so long unexecuted that execution cannot now be issued upon it without first reviving the judgment.

DORMANT PARTNERS. Those whose names are not known or do not appear as partners, but who nevertheless are silent partners, and partake of the profits, and thereby become partners, either absolutely to all intents and purposes, or at all events in respect to third parties. Dormant partners, in strictness of language, mean those who are merely passive in the firm, whether known or unknown, in contradistinction to those who are active and conduct the business of the firm, as principals. See Story, Partn. § 80.

A dormant partner is one who takes no part in the business, and whose connection with the business is unknown. Both secrecy and inactivity are implied by the word. 47 N. Y. 15.

Dormiunt aliquando leges, nunquam moriuntur. 2 Inst. 161. The laws sometimes sleep, never die.

DORSUM. Lat. The back. *In dorso recordi*, on the back of the record. 5 Coke, 44b.

DORTURE. (Contracted from *dormiture*.) A dormitory of a convent; a place to sleep in.

DOS. In Roman law. Dowry; a wife's marriage portion; all that property which on marriage is transferred by the wife herself or by another to the husband with a view of diminishing the burden which the marriage will entail upon him. It is of three kinds. *Profectitia dos* is that which is derived from the property of the wife's father or paternal grandfather. That *dos* is termed *adventitia* which is not *profectitia* in respect to its source, whether it is given by the wife from her own estate or by the wife's mother or a third person. It is termed *receptitia dos* when accompanied by a stipulation for its reclamation by the constitutor on the termination of the marriage. See Mackeld. Rom. Law, §§ 561, 563.

In old English law. The portion given to the wife by the husband at the church door, in consideration of the marriage; dower; the wife's portion out of her deceased husband's estate in case he had not endowed her.

Dos de dote peti non debet. Dower ought not to be demanded of dower. Co. Litt. 31; 4 Coke, 122*b*. A widow is not dowable of lands assigned to another woman in dower. 1 Hil. Real Prop. 135.

DOS RATIONABILIS. A reasonable marriage portion. A reasonable part of her husband's estate, to which every widow is entitled, of lands of which her husband may have endowed her on the day of marriage. Co. Litt. 336. Dower, at common law. 2 Bl. Comm. 134.

Dos rationabilis vel legitima est cujuslibet mulieris de quocunque tenemento tertia pars omnium terrarum et tenementorum, quæ vir suus tenuit in dominio suo ut de feodo, etc. Co. Litt. 336. Reasonable or legitimate dower belongs to every woman of a third part of all the lands and tenements of which her husband was seised in his demesne, as of fee, etc.

DOT. (A French word, adopted in Louisiana.) The fortune, portion, or dowry which a woman brings to her husband by the marriage. 6 Mart. (N. S.) 460.

DOTAGE. Dotage is that feebleness of the mental faculties which proceeds from old age. It is a diminution or decay of that intellectual power which was once possessed. It is the slow approach of death; of that irrevocable cessation, without hurt or disease, of all the functions which once belonged to the living animal. The external functions gradually cease; the senses waste away by degrees; and the mind is imperceptibly visited by decay. 1 Bland, 389.

DOTAL. Relating to the *dos* or portion of a woman; constituting her portion; comprised in her portion.

DOTAL PROPERTY. In the civil law in Louisiana, by this term is understood that property which the wife brings to the husband to assist him in bearing the expenses of the marriage establishment. Extradotal property, otherwise called "paraphernal property," is that which forms no part of the dowry. Civil Code La. art. 2335.

DOTALITIUM. In canon and feudal law. Dower. Spelman, voc. "Doarium;" Calvin. 2 Bl. Comm. 129. Used as early as A. D. 841.

DOTATION. The act of giving a dowry or portion; endowment in general, including the endowment of a hospital or other charitable institution.

DOTE, *n.* In Spanish law. The marriage portion of a wife. White, New Recop. b. 1, tit. 6, c. 1. The property which the wife gives to the husband on account of marriage, or for the purpose of supporting the matrimonial expenses. Id. b. 1, tit. 7, c. 1, § 1; Schm. Civil Law, 75.

DOTE, *v.* "To besot" is to stupefy, to make dull or senseless, to make to dote; and "to dote" is to be delirious, silly, or insane. These are some of the meanings. 7 Ind. 441.

DOTE ASSIGNANDA. A writ which lay for a widow, when it was judicially ascertained that a tenant to the king was seised of tenements in fee or fee-tail at the day of his death, and that he held of the king in chief. In such case the widow might come into chancery, and then make oath that she would not marry without the king's leave, and then she might have this writ. These widows were called the "king's widows." Jacob; Holthouse.

DOTE UNDE NIHIL HABET. A writ which lies for a widow to whom no dower has been assigned. 3 Bl. Comm. 182. By 23 & 24 Vict. c. 126, an ordinary action commenced by writ of summons has taken its place; but it remains in force in the United States. Dower *unde nihil habet* (which title see.)

Doti lex favet; præmium pudoris est; ideo parcatur. Co. Litt. 31. The law favors dower; it is the reward of chastity; therefore let it be preserved.

DOTIS ADMINISTRATIO. Admeasurement of dower, where the widow holds more than her share, etc.

DOTISSA. A dowager.

DOUBLE AVAIL OF MARRIAGE. In Scotch law. Double the ordinary or single value of a marriage. Bell. See DUPLEX VALOR MARITAGII.

DOUBLE BOND. In Scotch law. A bond with a penalty, as distinguished from a single bond. 2 Kames, Eq. 359.

DOUBLE COMPLAINT, or DOUBLE QUARREL. A grievance made known by a clerk or other person, to the archbishop of the province, against the ordinary, for delaying or refusing to do justice in some cause ecclesiastical, as to give sentence, institute a clerk, etc. It is termed a "double complaint," because it is most commonly made against both the judge and him at whose suit justice is denied or delayed; the effect whereof is that the archbishop, taking notice of the delay, directs his letters, under his authentical seal, to all clerks of his province, commanding them to admonish the ordinary, within a certain number of days, to do the justice required, or otherwise to appear before him or his official, and there allege the cause of his delay; and to signify to the ordinary that if he neither perform the thing enjoined, nor appear nor show cause against it, he himself, in his court of audience, will forthwith proceed to do the justice that is due. Cowell.

DOUBLE COSTS. In practice. The ordinary single costs of suit, and one-half of that amount in addition. 2 Tidd, Pr. 987. "Double" is not used here in its ordinary sense of "twice" the amount. These costs are now abolished in England by St. 5 & 6 Vict. c. 97. Wharton.

DOUBLE DAMAGES. Twice the amount of actual damages as found by the verdict of a jury.

DOUBLE EAGLE. A gold coin of the United States of the value of twenty dollars.

DOUBLE ENTRY. A system of mercantile book-keeping, in which the entries in the day-book, etc., are posted *twice* into the ledger. *First*, to a *personal* account, that is, to the account of the *person* with whom the dealing to which any given entry refers has taken place; *secondly*, to an impersonal account, as "goods." Mozley & Whitley.

DOUBLE FINE. In old English law. A fine *sur done grant et render* was called a "double fine," because it comprehended the fine *sur cognizance de droit come ceo*, etc., and the fine *sur concessit.* 2 Bl. Comm. 353.

DOUBLE INSURANCE is where divers insurances are made upon the same interest in the same subject against the same risks in favor of the same assured, in proportions exceeding the value. 1 Phill. Ins. §§ 359, 366.

A double insurance exists where the same person is insured by several insurers separately in respect to the same subject and interest. Civil Code Cal. § 2641.

DOUBLE PLEADING. This is not allowed either in the declaration or subsequent pleadings. Its meaning with respect to the former is that the declaration must not, in support of a single demand, allege several distinct matters, by any one of which that demand is sufficiently supported. With respect to the subsequent pleadings, the meaning is that none of them is to contain several distinct answers to that which preceded it; and the reason of the rule in each case is that such pleading tends to several issues in respect of a single claim. Wharton.

DOUBLE POSSIBILITY. A possibility upon a possibility. 2 Bl. Comm. 170.

DOUBLE RENT. In English law. Rent payable by a tenant who continues in possession after the time for which he has given notice to quit, until the time of his quitting possession. St. 11 Geo. II. c. 19.

DOUBLE VALUE. This is a penalty on a tenant holding over after his landlord's notice to quit. By 4 Geo. II. c. 28, § 1, it is enacted that if any tenant for life or years hold over any lands, etc., after the determination of his estate, after demand made, and notice in writing given, for delivering the possession thereof, by the landlord, or the person having the reversion or remainder therein, or his agent thereunto lawfully authorized, such tenant so holding over shall pay to the person so kept out of possession at the rate of *double* the yearly value of the lands, etc., so detained, for so long a time as the same are detained. See Woodf. Landl. & Ten. (12th Ed.) 717, et seq.

DOUBLE VOUCHER. This was when a common recovery was had, and an estate of freehold was first conveyed to any indifferent person against whom the *præcipe* was brought, and then he vouched the tenant in tail, who vouched over the common vouchee. For, if a recovery were had immediately against a tenant in tail, it barred only the estate in the premises of which he was then actually seised, whereas, if the recovery were had against another person, and the tenant in tail were vouchee, it barred every latent right and interest which he might have in the lands recovered. 2 Bl. Comm. 359.

DOUBLE WASTE. When a tenant bound to repair suffers a house to be wasted, and then unlawfully fells timber to repair it, he is said to commit double waste. Co. Litt. 53.

DOUBLES. Letters-patent. Cowell.

DOUBT. The uncertainty which exists in relation to a fact, a proposition, or other thing; an equipoise of the mind arising from an equality of contrary reasons. Ayl. Pand. 121.

The term "reasonable doubt" is often used, but not easily defined. It is not mere possible doubt; because everything relating to human affairs and depending on moral evidence is open to some possible or imaginary doubt. It is that state of the case which, after the entire comparison and consideration of all the evidence, leaves the minds of jurors in such a condition that they cannot say they feel an abiding conviction, to a moral certainty, of the truth of the charge. The burden of proof is upon the prosecutor. All the presumptions of law independent of evidence are in favor of innocence; and every person is presumed to be innocent until he is proved guilty. If upon such proof there is reasonable doubt remaining, the accused is entitled to the benefit of it by an acquittal; for it is not sufficient to establish a probability, though a strong one, arising from the doctrine of chances, that the fact charged is more likely to be true than the contrary, but the evidence must establish the truth of the fact to a reasonable and moral certainty,—a certainty that convinces and directs the understanding and satisfies the reason and judgment of those who are bound to act conscientiously upon it. This is proof beyond reasonable doubt; because if the law, which mostly depends upon considerations of a moral nature, should go further than this, and require absolute certainty, it would exclude circumstantial evidence altogether. Per Shaw, C. J., in 5 Cush. 320.

DOUN. L. Fr. A gift. Otherwise written "*don*" and "*done*." The thirty-fourth chapter of Britton is entitled "*De Douns.*"

DOVE. Doves are animals *feræ naturæ*, and not the subject of larceny unless they are in the owner's custody; as, for example, in a dove-house, or when in the nest before they can fly. 9 Pick. 15.

DOWABLE. Subject to be charged with dower; as dowable lands.

Entitled or entitling to dower. Thus, a dowable interest in lands is such as entitles the owner to have such lands charged with dower.

DOWAGER. A widow who is endowed, or who has a jointure in lieu of dower. In England, this is a title or addition given to the widows of princes, dukes, earls, and other noblemen, to distinguish them from the wives of the heirs, who have right to bear the title. 1 Bl. Comm. 224.

DOWAGER-QUEEN. The widow of the king. As such she enjoys most of the privileges belonging to her as queen consort. It is not treason to conspire her death or violate her chastity, because the succession to the crown is not thereby endangered. No man, however, can marry her without a special license from the sovereign, on pain of forfeiting his lands or goods. 1 Bl. Comm. 233.

DOWER. The provision which the law makes for a widow out of the lands or tenements of her husband, for her support and the nurture of her children. Co. Litt. 30a; 2 Bl. Comm. 130; 4 Kent, Comm. 35; 1 Washb. Real Prop. 146.

Dower is an estate for the life of the widow in a certain portion of the following real estate of her husband, to which she has not relinquished her right during the marriage: (1) Of all lands of which the husband was seised in fee during the marriage; (2) of all lands to which another was seised in fee to his use; (3) of all lands to which, at the time of his death, he had a perfect equity, having paid all the purchase money therefor. Code Ala. 1886, § 1892.

The term, both technically and in popular acceptation, has reference to real estate exclusively.

"Dower," in modern use, is and should be distinguished from "dowry." The former is a provision for a widow on her husband's death; the latter is a bride's portion on her marriage.

DOWER AD OSTIUM ECCLESIÆ. Dower at the church door or porch. An ancient kind of dower in England, where a man, (being tenant in fee-simple, of full age,) openly *at the church door*, where all marriages were formerly celebrated, after affiance made and troth plighted between them, *endowed* his wife with the whole of his lands, or such quantity as he pleased, at the same time specifying and ascertaining the same. Litt. § 39; 2 Bl. Comm. 133.

DOWER BY THE COMMON LAW. The ordinary kind of dower in English and American law, consisting of one-third of the lands of which the husband was seised in fee at any time during the coverture. Litt. § 36; 2 Bl. Comm. 132; 2 Steph. Comm. 302; 4 Kent, Comm. 35.

DOWER BY CUSTOM. A kind of dower in England, regulated by custom, where the quantity allowed the wife differed from the proportion of the common law; as that the wife should have half the husband's lands; or, in some places, the whole; and, in some, only a quarter. 2 Bl. Comm. 132; Litt. § 37.

DOWER DE LA PLUIS BELLE. L. Fr. Dower of the fairest [part.] A species of ancient English dower, incident to the old tenures, where there was a guardian in chivalry, and the wife occupied lands of the heir as guardian in socage. If the wife brought a writ of dower against such guardian in chivalry, he might show this matter, and pray that the wife might be endowed *de la pluis belle* of the tenement in socage. Litt. § 48. This kind of dower was abolished with the military tenures. 2 Bl. Comm. 132.

DOWER EX ASSENSU PATRIS. Dower by the father's assent. A species of dower *ad ostium ecclesiæ*, made when the husband's father was alive, and the son, by his consent expressly given, endowed his wife with parcel of his father's lands. Litt. § 40; 2 Bl. Comm. 133.

DOWER UNDE NIHIL HABET. A writ of right which lay for a widow to whom no dower had been assigned.

DOWLE STONES. Stones dividing lands, etc. Cowell.

DOWMENT. In old English law. Endowment; dower.

DOWRESS. A woman entitled to dower; a tenant in dower. 2 P. Wms. 707.

DOWRY. The property which a woman brings to her husband in marriage; now more commonly called a "portion."

By dowry is meant the effects which the wife brings to the husband to support the expenses of marriage. Civil Code La. art. 2337.

This word expresses the proper meaning of the "*dos*" of the Roman, the "*dot*" of the French, and the "*dote*" of the Spanish, law, but is a very different thing from "dower," with which it has sometimes been confounded.

By dowry, in the Louisiana Civil Code, is meant the effects which the wife brings to the husband to support the expenses of marriage. It is given to the husband, to be enjoyed by him so long as the marriage shall last, and the income of it belongs to him. He alone has the administration of it during marriage, and his wife cannot deprive him of it. The real estate settled as dowry is inalienable during marriage, unless the marriage contract contains a stipulation to the contrary. 6 La. Ann. 786.

DOZEIN. L. Fr. Twelve; a person twelve years of age. St. 18 Edw. II.; Barring. Ob. St. 208.

DOZEN PEERS. Twelve peers assembled at the instance of the barons, in the reign of Henry III., to be privy counselors, or rather conservators of the kingdom.

DRACHMA. A term employed in old pleadings and records, to denote a groat. Townsh. Pl. 180.

An Athenian silver coin, of the value of about $7\frac{3}{4}$d. sterling.

DRACO REGIS. The standard, ensign, or military colors borne in war by the ancient kings of England, having the figure of a dragon painted thereon.

DRACONIAN LAWS. A code of laws prepared by Draco, the celebrated lawgiver of Athens. These laws were exceedingly severe, and the term is now sometimes applied to any laws of unusual harshness.

DRAFT. The common term for a bill of exchange; as being *drawn* by one person on another. 2 Bl. Comm. 467.

An order for the payment of money drawn by one person on another. It is said to be a *nomen generalissimum*, and to include all such orders. 1 Story, 30.

Draft also signifies a tentative, provisional, or preparatory writing out of any document (as a will, contract, lease, etc.) for purposes of discussion and correction, and which is afterwards to be copied out in its final shape.

DRAFTSMAN. Any one who draws or frames a legal document, *e. g.*, a will, conveyance, pleading, etc.

DRAGOMAN. An interpreter employed in the east, and particularly at the Turkish court.

DRAIN, v. To make dry; to draw off water; to rid land of its superfluous moisture by adapting or improving natural watercourses and supplementing them, when necessary, by artificial ditches. 58 Cal. 639.

DRAIN, n. A trench or ditch to convey water from wet land; a channel through which water may flow off.

The word has no technical legal meaning. Any hollow space in the ground, natural or artificial, where water is collected and passes off, is a ditch or drain. 5 Gray, 61.

The word "drain" also sometimes denotes the easement or servitude (acquired by grant or prescription) which consists in the right to drain water through another's land. See 3 Kent, Comm. 436.

DRAM. In common parlance, this term means a drink of some substance containing alcohol, something which can produce intoxication. 32 Tex. 228.

DRAM-SHOP. A drinking saloon, where liquors are sold to be drunk on the premises.

DRAMATIC COMPOSITION. A mere exhibition, spectacle, or scene is not a "dramatic composition," within the meaning of the copyright laws. 1 Abb. (U. S.) 356.

DRAW. In old criminal practice. To drag (on a hurdle) to the place of execution. Anciently no hurdle was allowed, but the criminal was actually dragged along the road to the place of execution. A part of the ancient punishment of traitors was the being thus drawn. 4 Bl. Comm. 92, 377.

In mercantile law. To draw a bill of exchange is to write (or cause it to be written) and sign it.

DRAWBACK. In the customs laws, this term denotes an allowance made by the government upon the duties due on imported merchandise when the importer, instead of selling it here, re-exports it; or the refunding of such duties if already paid. This allowance amounts, in some cases, to the whole of the original duties; in others, to a part only.

A drawback is a device resorted to for enabling a commodity affected by taxes to be exported and sold in the foreign market on the same terms as if it had not been taxed at all. It differs in this from a bounty, that the latter enables a commodity to be sold for *less* than its natural cost, whereas a drawback enables it to be sold exactly at its natural cost.

DRAWEE. A person to whom a bill of exchange is addressed, and who is requested to pay the amount of money therein mentioned.

DRAWER. The person making a bill of exchange and addressing it to the drawee.

DRAWING. In patent law. A representation of the appearance of material objects by means of lines and marks upon paper, card-board, or other substance.

DRAWING TO EXECUTION. In English criminal law. The act of drawing a condemned criminal on a hurdle from the place of prison to the place of execution. 4 Bl. Comm. 377. Where a man was hanged on an appeal of death, the wife of the person killed and all his kindred drew the felon to execution.

DRAWLATCHES. Thieves; robbers. Cowell.

DREIT-DREIT. Droit-droit. Double right. A union of the right of possession and the right of property. 2 Bl. Comm. 199.

DRENCHES, or DRENGES. In Saxon law. Tenants *in capite.* They are said to be such as, at the coming of William the Conqueror, being put out of their estates, were afterwards restored to them, on their making it appear that they were the true owners thereof, and neither *in auxilio* or *consilio* against him. Spelman.

DRENGAGE. The tenure by which the drenches, or drenges, held their lands.

DRIFT. In old English law. A driving, especially of cattle.

DRIFT-STUFF. This term signifies, not goods which are the subject of salvage, but matters floating at random, without any known or discoverable ownership, which, if cast ashore, will probably never be reclaimed, but will, as a matter of course, accrue to the riparian proprietor. 13 R. I. 641.

DRIFTLAND, DROFLAND, or DRYFLAND. A Saxon word, signifying a tribute or yearly payment made by some tenants to the king, or their landlords, for driving their cattle through a manor to fairs or markets. Cowell.

DRIFTS OF THE FOREST. A view or examination of what cattle are in a forest, chase, etc., that it may be known whether it be surcharged or not; and whose the beasts are, and whether they are commonable. These drifts are made at certain times in the year by the officers of the forest, when all cattle are driven into some pound or place inclosed, for the before-mentioned purposes, and also to discover whether any cattle of strangers be there, which ought not to common. Manwood, p. 2, c. 15.

DRIFTWAY. A road or way over which cattle are driven. 1 Taunt. 279.

DRINCLEAN. Sax. A contribution of tenants, in the time of the Saxons, towards a potation, or ale, provided to entertain the lord, or his steward. Cowell. See CERVISARII.

DRIP. A species of easement or servitude obligating one man to permit the water falling from another man's house to fall upon his own land. 3 Kent, Comm. 436.

DRIVER. One employed in conducting a coach, carriage, wagon, or other vehicle, with horses, mules, or other animals.

DROFDEN, or DROFDENNE. A grove or woody place where cattle are kept. Jacob.

DROFLAND. Sax. A quit rent, or yearly payment, formerly made by some tenants to the king, or their landlords, for *driving* their cattle through a manor to fairs or markets. Cowell; Blount.

DROIT. In French law. Right, justice, equity, law, the whole body of law; also a right.

This term exhibits the same ambiguity which is discoverable in the German equivalent, "*recht*" and the English word "*right*." On the one hand, these terms answer to the Roman "*jus*," and thus indicate law in the abstract, considered as the foundation of all rights, or the complex of underlying moral principles which impart the character of justice to all positive law, or give it an ethical content. Taken in this abstract sense, the terms may be adjectives, in which case they are equivalent to "just," or nouns, in which case they may be paraphrased by the expressions "justice," "morality," or "equity." On the other hand, they serve to point out *a* right; that is, a power, privilege, faculty, or demand, inherent in one person, and incident upon another. In the latter signification, *droit* (or *recht* or *right*) is the correlative of "duty" or "obligation." In the former sense, it may be considered as opposed to wrong, injustice, or the absence of law. *Droit* has the further ambiguity that it is sometimes used to denote the existing body of law considered as one whole, or the sum total of a number of individual laws taken together. See Jus; Recht; Right.

In old English law. A writ of right, so called in the old books. Co. Litt. 158b.

Law. The common law is sometimes termed "*common droit*." Litt. § 213; Co. Litt. 142a.

DROIT-CLOSE. An ancient writ, directed to the lord of ancient demesne on behalf of those of his tenants who held their lands and tenements by charter in fee-simple, in fee-tail, for life, or in dower. Fitzh. Nat. Brev. 23.

DROIT D'ACCESSION. In French law. That property which is acquired by making a new species out of the material of another. It is equivalent to the Roman "*specificatio.*"

DROIT D'AUBAINE. In French law. A rule by which all the property of a deceased foreigner, whether movable or immovable, was confiscated to the use of the state, to the exclusion of his heirs, whether claiming *ab intestato* or under a will of the deceased. Finally abolished in 1819.

DROIT D'EXECUTION. In French law. The right of a stockbroker to sell the securities bought by him for account of a client, if the latter does not accept delivery thereof. The same expression is also applied to the sale by a stockbroker of securities deposited with him by his client, in order to guaranty the payment of operations for which the latter has given instructions. Arg. Fr. Merc. Law, 557.

DROIT DE BRIS. A right formerly claimed by the lords of the coasts of certain parts of France, to shipwrecks, by which not only the property, but the persons of those who were cast away, were confiscated for the prince who was lord of the coast. Otherwise called "*droit de bris sur le naufrage.*" This right prevailed chiefly in Bretagne, and was solemnly abrogated by Henry III., as duke of Normandy, Aquitaine, and Guienne, in a charter granted A. D. 1226, preserved among the rolls at Bordeaux.

DROIT DE GARDE. In French feudal law. Right of ward. The guardianship of the estate and person of a noble vassal, to which the king, during his minority, was entitled. Steph. Lect. 250.

DROIT DE GITE. In French feudal law. The duty incumbent on a *roturier*, holding lands within the royal domain, of supplying board and lodging to the king and to his suite while on a royal progress. Steph. Lect. 351.

DROIT DE GREFFE. In old French law. The right of selling various offices connected with the custody of judicial records or notarial acts. Steph. Lect. 354. A privilege of the French kings.

DROIT DE MAITRISE. In old French law. A charge payable to the crown by any one who, after having served his apprenticeship in any commercial guild or brotherhood, sought to become a master workman in it on his own account. Steph. Lect. 354.

DROIT DE PRISE. In French feudal law. The duty (incumbent on a *roturier*) of supplying to the king on credit, during a certain period, such articles of domestic consumption as might be required for the royal household. Steph. Lect. 351.

DROIT DE QUINT. In French feudal law. A relief payable by a noble vassal to the king as his *seigneur*, on every change in the ownership of his fief. Steph. Lect. 350.

DROIT DE SUITE. In French law. The right of a creditor to pursue the debtor's property into the hands of third persons for the enforcement of his claim.

DROIT-DROIT. A double right; that is, the right of possession and the right of property. These two rights were, by the theory of our ancient law, distinct; and the above phrase was used to indicate the concurrence of both in one person, which concurrence was necessary to constitute a complete title to land. Mozley & Whitley.

DROIT ÉCRIT. In French law. (The written law.) The Roman civil law, or *Corpus Juris Civilis.* Steph. Lect. 130.

Droit ne done pluis que soit demaunde. The law gives not more than is demanded. 2 Inst. 286.

Droit ne poet pas morier. Right cannot die. Jenk. Cent. 100, case 95.

D R O I T S   C I V I L S. This phrase in French law denotes private rights, the exercise of which is independent of the *status* (*qualité*) of citizen. Foreigners enjoy them; and the extent of that enjoyment is determined by the principle of reciprocity. Conversely, foreigners may be sued on contracts made by them in France. Brown.

DROITS OF ADMIRALTY. Rights or perquisites of the admiralty. A term applied to goods found derelict at sea. Applied also to property captured in time of war by non-commissioned vessels of a belligerent nation. 1 Kent, Comm. 96.

DROITURAL. What belongs of right; relating to right; as real actions are either droitural or possessory,—*droitural* when the plaintiff seeks to recover the property. Finch, Law, 257.

D R O M O N E S , DROMOS, DRO-MUNDA. These were at first high ships of great burden, but afterwards those which we now call "men-of-war." Jacob.

DROP. In English practice. When the members of a court are equally divided on the argument showing cause against a rule *nisi*, no order is made, *i. e.*, the rule is neither discharged nor made absolute, and the rule is said to *drop*. In practice, there being a right to appeal, it has been usual to make an order in one way, the junior judge withdrawing his judgment. Wharton.

DROP-LETTER. A letter addressed for delivery in the same city or district in which it is posted.

DROVE-ROAD. In Scotch law. A road for driving cattle. 7 Bell, App. Cas. 43, 53, 57. A drift-road. Lord Brougham, Id.

DROVE-STANCE. In Scotch law. A place adjoining a drove-road, for resting and refreshing sheep and cattle on their journey. 7 Bell, App. Cas. 53, 57.

DROWN. To merge or sink. "In some cases a right of freehold shall *drown* in a chattel." Co. Litt. 266a, 321a.

DRU. A thicket of wood in a valley. Domesday.

DRUG. The general name of substances used in medicine; any substance, vegetable, animal, or mineral, used in the composition or preparation of medicines. The term is also applied to materials used in dyeing and in chemistry. See 79 N. C. 281; 53 Vt. 426.

DRUGGIST. A dealer in drugs; one whose business is to sell drugs and medicines. In strict usage, this term is to be distinguished from "apothecary." A druggist deals in the uncompounded medicinal substances; the business of an apothecary is to mix and compound them. But in America the two words are used interchangeably, as the same persons usually discharge both functions.

DRUMMER. A term applied to commercial agents who travel for wholesale merchants and supply the retail trade with goods, or take orders for goods to be shipped to the retail dealer. 4 Lea, 96; 34 Ark. 557.

DRUNGARIUS. In old European law. The commander of a *drungus*, or band of soldiers. Applied also to a naval commander. Spelman.

DRUNGUS. In old European law. A band of soldiers, (*globus militum.*) Spelman.

DRUNKARD. He is a drunkard whose habit it is to get drunk; whose ebriety has become habitual. The terms "drunkard" and "habitual drunkard" mean the same thing. 5 Gray, 85.

DRUNKENNESS. In medical jurisprudence. The condition of a man whose mind is affected by the immediate use of intoxicating drinks.

DRY-CRÆFT. Witchcraft; magic. Anc. Inst. Eng.

DRY EXCHANGE. In English law. A term formerly in use, said to have been invented for the purpose of disguising and covering usury; something being pretended to pass on both sides, whereas, in truth, nothing passed but on one side, in which respect it was called "dry." Cowell; Blount.

DRY-MULTURES. In Scotch law. Corn paid to the owner of a mill, whether the payers grind or not.

DRY RENT. Rent-seck; a rent reserved without a clause of distress.

DRY TRUST. A passive trust; one which requires no action on the part of the trustee beyond turning over money or property to the *cestui que trust.*

DUARCHY. A form of government where two reign jointly.

Duas uxores eodem tempore habere non licet. It is not lawful to have two wives at the same time. Inst. 1, 10, 6; 1 Bl. Comm. 436.

DUBITANS. Doubting. Dobbin, J., *dubitans.* 1 Show. 364.

DUBITANTE. Doubting. Is affixed to the name of a judge, in the reports, to signify that he doubted the decision rendered.

DUBITATUR. It is doubted. A word frequently used in the reports to indicate that a point is considered doubtful.

DUBITAVIT. Doubted. Vaughan, C. J., *dubitavit.* Freem. 150.

DUCAT. A foreign coin, varying in value in different countries, but usually worth about $2.26 of our money.

DUCATUS. In feudal and old English law. A duchy, the dignity or territory of a duke.

DUCES TECUM. (Lat. Bring with you.) The name of certain species of writs, of which the *subpœna duces tecum* is the most usual, requiring a party who is summoned to appear in court to bring with him some document, piece of evidence, or other thing to be used or inspected by the court.

DUCES TECUM LICET LANGUI-DUS. (Bring with you, although sick.) In practice. An ancient writ, now obsolete, directed to the sheriff, upon a return that he could not bring his prisoner without danger of death, he being *adeo languidus,* (so sick;) whereupon the court granted a *habeas corpus* in the nature of a *duces tecum licet languidus.* Cowell; Blount.

DUCHY COURT OF LANCASTER. A tribunal of special jurisdiction, held before the chancellor of the duchy, or his deputy, concerning all matters of equity relating to lands holden of the crown in right of the duchy of Lancaster; which is a thing very distinct from the county palatine, (which has also its separate chancery, for sealing of writs, and the like,) and comprises much territory which lies at a vast distance from it; as particularly a very large district surrounded by the city of Westminster. The proceedings in this court are the same as were those on the equity side of the court of chancery, so that it seems not to be a court of record; and, indeed, it has been holden that the court of chancery has a concurrent jurisdiction with the duchy court, and may take cognizance of the same causes. The appeal from this court lies to the court of appeal. Jud. Act 1873, § 18; 3 Bl. Comm. 78.

DUCHY OF LANCASTER. Those lands which formerly belonged to the dukes of Lancaster, and now belong to the crown in right of the duchy. The duchy is distinct from the county palatine of Lancaster, and includes not only the county, but also much territory at a distance from it, especially the Savoy in London and some land near Westminster. 3 Bl. Comm. 78.

DUCKING-STOOL. See CASTIGATORY.

DUCROIRE. In French law. Guaranty; equivalent to *del credere,* (which see.)

DUE. 1. Just; proper; regular; lawful; sufficient; as in the phrases "due care," "due process of law," "due notice."

2. Owing; payable; justly owed. That which one contracts to pay or perform to another; that which law or justice requires to be paid or done.

3. Owed, or owing, as distinguished from payable. A debt is often said to be *due* from a person where he is the party owing it, or primarily bound to pay, whether the time for payment has or has not arrived.

4. Payable. A bill or note is commonly said to be *due* when the time for payment of it has arrived. 6 Pet. 29, 36.

DUE-BILL. A brief written acknowledgment of a debt. It is not made payable to order, like a promissory note. See I. O. U.

DUE CARE. Just, proper, and sufficient care, so far as the circumstances demand it; the absence of negligence.

This term, as usually understood in cases where the gist of the action is the defendant's negligence, implies not only that a party has not been negligent or careless, but that he has been guilty of no violation of law in relation to the subject-matter or transaction which constitutes the cause of action. Evidence that a party is guilty of a violation of law supports the issue of a want of proper care; nor can it be doubted that in these and similar actions the averment in the declaration of the use of due care, and the denial of it in the answer, properly and distinctly put in issue the legality of the conduct of the party as contributing to the accident or injury which forms the groundwork of the action. No specific averment of the particular unlawful act which caused or contributed to produce the result complained of should, in such cases, be deemed necessary. 10 Allen, 18. See, also, Id. 532.

DUE COURSE OF LAW. This phrase is synonymous with "due process of law," or "the law of the land," and the general definition thereof is "law in its regular course of administration through courts of justice;" and, while not always necessarily confined to judicial proceedings, yet these words have such a signification, when used to designate the kind of an eviction, or ouster, from real estate by which a party is dispossessed, as to preclude thereunder proof of a constructive eviction resulting from the purchase of a paramount title when hostilely asserted by the party holding it. 19 Kan. 542. See, also, 34 Ala. 236; 11 Wend. 635; 63 Ala. 436; 38 Miss. 424; 3 Stew. 108; 4 Dill. 266.

DUE NOTICE. No fixed rule can be established as to what shall constitute "due notice." "Due" is a relative term, and must be applied to each case in the exercise of the discretion of the court in view of the particular circumstances. 1 McAll. 420.

DUE PROCESS OF LAW. Law in its regular course of administration through courts of justice. 3 Story, Const. 264, 661.

"Due process of law in each particular case means such an exercise of the powers of the government as the settled maxims of law permit and sanction, and under such safeguards for the protection of individual rights as those maxims prescribe for the class of cases to which the one in question belongs." Cooley, Const. Lim. 441. See, also, 12 N. Y. 209; 5 Mich. 251; 6 Cold. 233; 49 Cal. 403.

Whatever difficulty may be experienced in giving to those terms a definition which will embrace every permissible exertion of power affecting private rights, and exclude such as is forbidden, there can be no doubt of their meaning when applied to judicial proceedings. They then mean a course of legal proceedings according to those rules and principles which have been established in our systems of jurisprudence for the enforcement and protection of private rights. To give such proceedings any validity, there must be a tribunal competent by its constitution—that is, by the law of its creation—to pass upon the subject-matter of the suit; and, if that involves merely a determination of the personal liability of the defendant, he must be brought within its jurisdiction by service of process within the state, or his voluntary appearance. 95 U. S. 733.

Due process of law implies the right of the person affected thereby to be present before the tribunal which pronounces judgment upon the question of life, liberty, or property, in its most comprehensive sense; to be heard, by testimony or otherwise, and to have the right of controverting, by proof, every material fact which bears on the question of right in the matter involved. If any question of fact or liability be conclusively presumed against him, this is not due process of law. 58 Ala. 599.

These phrases in the constitution do not mean the general body of the law, common and statute, as it was at the time the constitution took effect; for that would seem to deny the right of the legislature to amend or repeal the law. They refer to certain fundamental rights, which that system of jurisprudence, of which ours is a derivative, has always recognized. 50 Miss. 468.

"Due process of law," as used in the constitution, cannot mean less than a prosecution or suit instituted and conducted according to the prescribed forms and solemnities for ascertaining guilt, or determining the title to property. 3 N. Y. 511, 517; 4 Hill, 140; 10 N. Y. 374, 397.

DUEL. A duel is any combat with deadly weapons, fought between two or more persons, by previous agreement or upon a previous quarrel. Pen. Code Cal. § 225.

DUELLUM. The trial by battel or judicial combat. See BATTEL.

DUES. Certain payments; rates or taxes.

DUKE, in English law, is a title of nobility, ranking immediately next to the Prince of Wales. It is only a title of dignity. Conferring it does not give any domain, territory, or jurisdiction over the place whence the title is taken. *Duchess*, the consort of a duke. Wharton.

DUKE OF EXETER'S DAUGHTER. The name of a rack in the Tower, so called after a minister of Henry VI., who sought to introduce it into England.

DULOCRACY. A government where servants and slaves have so much license and privilege that they domineer. Wharton.

DULY. In due or proper form or manner.

Regularly; upon a proper foundation, as distinguished from mere form.

DUM. Lat. While; as long as; until; upon condition that; provided that.

DUM BENE SE GESSERIT. While he shall conduct himself well; during good behavior. Expressive of a tenure of office not dependent upon the pleasure of the appointing power, nor for a limited period, but terminable only upon the death or misconduct of the incumbent.

DUM FERVET OPUS. While the work glows; in the heat of action. 1 Kent, Comm. 120.

DUM FUIT IN PRISONA. In English law. A writ which lay for a man who had aliened lands under duress by imprisonment, to restore to him his proper estates. 2 Inst. 482. Abolished by St. 3 & 4 Wm. IV. c. 27.

DUM FUIT INFRA ÆTATEM. (While he was within age.) In old English practice. A writ of entry which formerly lay for an infant after he had attained his full age, to recover lands which he had aliened in fee, in tail, or for life, during his infancy; and, after his death, his heir had the same remedy. Reg. Orig. 228*b;* Fitzh. Nat. Brev. 192, G; Litt. § 406; Co. Litt. 247*b.*

DUM NON FUIT COMPOS MENTIS. The name of a writ which the heirs of a person who was *non compos mentis,* and who aliened his lands, might have sued out to restore him to his rights. Abolished by 3 & 4 Wm. IV. c. 27.

DUM RECENS FUIT MALEFICIUM. While the offense was fresh. A term employed in the old law of appeal of rape. Bract. fol. 147.

DUM SOLA. While sole, or single. *Dum sola fuerit,* while she shall remain sole. *Dum sola et casta vixerit,* while she lives single and chaste. Words of limitation in old conveyances. Co. Litt. 235*a.* Also applied generally to an unmarried woman in connection with something that was or might be done during that condition.

DUMB. One who cannot speak; a person who is mute.

DUMB-BIDDING. In sales at auction, when the minimum amount which the owner will take for the article is written on a piece of paper, and placed by the owner under a candlestick, or other thing, and it is agreed that no bidding shall avail unless equal to that, this is called "dumb-bidding." Bab. Auct. 44.

DUMMODO. Provided; provided that. A word of limitation in the Latin forms of conveyances, of frequent use in introducing a reservation; as in reserving a rent.

DUN. A mountain or high open place. The names of places ending in *dun* or *don* were either built on hills or near them in open places.

DUNA. In old records. A bank of earth cast up; the side of a ditch. Cowell.

DUNGEON. Such an under-ground prison or cell as was formerly placed in the strongest part of a fortress; a dark or subterraneous prison.

DUNIO. A double; a kind of base coin less than a farthing.

DUNNAGE. Pieces of wood placed against the sides and bottom of the hold of a vessel, to preserve the cargo from the effect of leakage, according to its nature and quality. Abb. Shipp. 227.

There is considerable resemblance between dunnage and ballast. The latter is used for trimming the ship, and bringing it down to a draft of water proper and safe for sailing. Dunnage is placed under the cargo to keep it from being wetted by water getting into the hold, or between the different parcels to keep them from bruising and injuring each other. 13 Wall. 674.

DUNSETS. People that dwell on hilly places or mountains. Jacob.

Duo non possunt in solido unam rem possidere. Two cannot possess one thing in entirety. Co. Litt. 368.

Duo sunt instrumenta ad omnes res aut confirmandas aut impugnandas, ratio et authoritas. There are two instruments for confirming or impugning all things,—reason and authority. 8 Coke, 16.

DUODECEMVIRALE JUDICIUM. The trial by twelve men, or by jury. Applied to juries *de medietate linguæ.* Mol. de Jure Mar. 448.

DUODECIMA MANUS. Twelve hands. The oaths of twelve men, including himself, by whom the defendant was allowed to make his law. 3 Bl. Comm. 343.

DUODENA. In old records. A jury of twelve men. Cowell.

DUODENA MANU. A dozen hands, *i. e.,* twelve witnesses to purge a criminal of an offense.

Duorum in solidum dominium vel possessio esse non potest. Ownership or possession in entirety cannot be in two persons of the same thing. Dig. 13, 6, 5, 15; Mackeld. Rom. Law, § 245. Bract. fol. 28b.

DUPLA. In the civil law. Double the price of a thing. Dig. 21, 2, 2.

DUPLEX QUERELA. Double complaint. An ecclesiastical proceeding, which is in the nature of an appeal from an ordinary's refusal to institute, to his next immediate superior; as from a bishop to the archbishop. If the superior adjudges the cause of refusal to be insufficient, he will grant institution to the appellant. Phillim. Ecc. Law, 440.

DUPLEX VALOR MARITAGII. In old English law. Double the value of the marriage. While an infant was in ward, the guardian had the power of tendering him or her a suitable match, without disparagement, which if the infants refused, they forfeited the value of the marriage to their guardian, that is, so much as a jury would assess or any one would give to the guardian for such an alliance; and, if the infants married themselves without the guardian's consent, they forfeited double the value of the marriage. 2 Bl. Comm. 70; Litt. § 110; Co. Litt. 82b.

DUPLICATE. When two written documents are substantially alike, so that each might be a copy or transcript from the other, while both stand on the same footing as original instruments, they are called "duplicates." Agreements, deeds, and other documents are frequently executed in duplicate, in order that each party may have an original in his possession.

A duplicate is sometimes defined to be the "copy" of a thing; but, though generally a copy, a duplicate differs from a mere copy, in having all the validity of an original. Nor, it seems, need it be an exact copy. Defined also to be the "counterpart" of an instrument; but in indentures there is a distinction between *counterparts* executed by the several parties respectively, each party affixing his or her seal to only one counterpart, and *duplicate originals,* each executed by all the parties. 7 Man. & G. 91, note. The old indentures, charters, or chirographs seem to have had the character of duplicates. Burrill.

AM.DICT.LAW—26

In English law. The certificate of discharge given to an insolvent debtor who takes the benefit of the act for the relief of insolvent debtors.

The ticket given by a pawnbroker to the pawner of a chattel.

DUPLICATE WILL. A term used in England, where a testator executes two copies of his will, one to keep himself, and the other to be deposited with another person. Upon application for probate of a duplicate will, both copies must be deposited in the registry of the court of probate.

DUPLICATIO. In the civil law. The defendant's answer to the plaintiff's replication; corresponding to the rejoinder of the common law.

Duplicationem possibilitatis lex non patitur. The law does not allow the doubling of a possibility. 1 Rolle, 321.

DUPLICATUM JUS. Double right. Bract. fol. 283b. See DROIT-DROIT.

DUPLICITY. The technical fault, in pleading, of uniting two or more causes of action in one count in a writ, or two or more grounds of defense in one plea, or two or more breaches in a replication.

DUPLY, *n.* (From Lat. *duplicatio, q. v.*) In Scotch pleading. The defendant's answer to the plaintiff's replication.

DUPLY, *v.* In Scotch pleading. To rejoin. "It is *duplyed* by the panel." 3 State Trials, 471.

DURANTE. Lat. During. A word of limitation in old conveyances. Co. Litt. 234b. *Durante riduitate,* during widowhood. *Durante virginitate,* during virginity. *Durante vita,* during life.

DURANTE ABSENTIA. During absence. In some jurisdictions, administration of a decedent's estate is said to be granted *durante absentia* in cases where the absence of the proper proponents of the will, or of an executor, delays or imperils the settlement of the estate.

DURANTE BENE PLACITO. During good pleasure. The ancient tenure of English judges was *durante bene placito.* 1 Bl. Comm. 267, 342.

DURANTE MINORE ÆTATE. During minority. 2 Bl. Comm. 503; 5 Coke, 29, 30. Words taken from the old form of letters of administration. 5 Coke, ubi supra.

DURANTE VIDUITATE. During widowhood. 2 Bl. Comm. 124. *Durante casta viduitate*, during chaste widowhood. 10 East, 520.

DURBAR. In India. A court, audience, or levee. Mozley & Whitley.

DURESS, *v.* To subject to duress. A word used by Lord Bacon. "If the party *duressed* do make any motion," etc. Bac. Max. 89, reg. 22.

DURESS, *n.* Unlawful constraint exercised upon a man whereby he is forced to do some act against his will. It may be either "duress of imprisonment," where the person is deprived of his liberty in order to force him to compliance, or by violence, beating, or other actual injury, or duress *per minas*, consisting in threats of imprisonment or great physical injury or death. Duress may also include the same injuries, threats, or restraint exercised upon the man's wife, child, or parent.

Duress consists in any illegal imprisonment, or legal imprisonment used for an illegal purpose, or threats of bodily or other harm, or other means amounting to or tending to coerce the will of another, and actually inducing him to do an act contrary to his free will. Code Ga. 1882, § 2637.

By duress, in its more extended sense, is meant that degree of severity, either threatened or impending or actually inflicted, which is sufficient to overcome the mind and will of a person of ordinary firmness. Duress *per minas* is restricted to fear of loss of life, or of mayhem, or loss of limb, or other remediless harm to the person. 39 Me. 559.

DURESS OF IMPRISONMENT. The wrongful imprisonment of a person, or the illegal restraint of his liberty, in order to compel him to do some act. 1 Bl. Comm. 130, 131, 136, 137; 1 Steph. Comm. 137; 2 Kent, Comm. 453.

DURESS PER MINAS. Duress by threats. The use of threats and menaces to compel a person, by the fear of death, or grievous bodily harm, as mayhem or loss of limb, to do some lawful act, or to commit a misdemeanor. 1 Bl. Comm. 130; 4 Bl. Comm. 30; 4 Steph. Comm. 83. See METUS.

DURESSOR. One who subjects another to duress; one who compels another to do a thing, as by menace. Bac. Max. 90, reg. 22.

DURHAM. A county palatine in England, the jurisdiction of which was vested in the Bishop of Durham until the statute 6 & 7 Wm. IV. c. 19, vested it as a separate franchise and royalty in the crown. The jurisdiction of the Durham court of pleas was transferred to the supreme court of judicature by the judicature act of 1873.

DURSLEY. In old English law. Blows without wounding or bloodshed; dry blows. Blount.

DUSTUCK. A term used in Hindostan for a passport, permit, or order from the English East Indian Company. It generally meant a permit under their seal, exempting goods from the payment of duties. Enc. Lond.

DUTCH AUCTION. A method of sale by auction which consists in the public offer of the property at a price beyond its value, and then gradually lowering the price until some one becomes the purchaser. 28 Ohio St. 482.

DUTIES. In its most usual signification this word is the synonym of imposts or customs; but it is sometimes used in a broader sense, as including all manner of taxes, charges, or governmental impositions.

DUTY. In its use in jurisprudence, this word is the correlative of *right*. Thus, wherever there exists a right in any person, there also rests a corresponding duty upon some other person or upon all persons generally. But it is also used, in a wider sense, to designate that class of moral obligations which lie outside the jural sphere; such, namely, as rest upon an imperative ethical basis, but have not been recognized by the law as within its proper province for purposes of enforcement or redress. Thus, gratitude towards a benefactor is a *duty*, but its refusal will not ground an action. In this meaning "duty" is the equivalent of "moral obligation," as distinguished from a "legal obligation."

As a technical term of the law, "duty" signifies a thing due; that which is due from a person; that which a person owes to another. An obligation to do a thing. A word of more extensive signification than "debt," although both are expressed by the same Latin word "*debitum*." 26 Vt. 725, 733.

But in practice it is commonly reserved as the designation of those obligations of performance, care, or observance which rest upon a person in an official or fiduciary capacity; as the *duty* of an executor, trustee, manager, etc.

It also denotes a tax or impost due to the

government upon the importation or exportation of goods.

DUUMVIRI. (From *duo*, two, and *viri*, men.) A general appellation among the ancient Romans, given to any magistrates elected in pairs to fill any office, or perform any function. Brande.

Duumviri municipales were two annual magistrates in the towns and colonies, having judicial powers. Calvin.

Duumviri navales were officers appointed to man, equip, and refit the navy. Id.

DUX. In Roman law. A leader or military commander. The commander of an army. Dig. 3, 2, 2, pr.

In **feudal** and **old European law.** Duke; a title of honor, or order of nobility. 1 Bl. Comm. 397; Crabb, Eng. Law, 236.

In **later law.** A military governor of a province. See Cod. 1, 27, 2. A military officer having charge of the borders or frontiers of the empire, called "*dux limitis*." Cod. 1, 49, 1, pr. At this period, the word began to be used as a title of honor or dignity.

DWELL. To have an abode; to inhabit; to live in a place.

DWELLING-HOUSE. The house in which a man lives with his family; a residence; the apartment or building, or group of buildings, occupied by a family as a place of residence.

In **conveyancing.** Includes all buildings attached to or connected with the house. 2 Hil. Real Prop. 338, and note.

In **the law of burglary.** A house in which the occupier and his family usually reside, or, in other words, dwell and lie in. Whart. Crim. Law, 357.

DWELLING-PLACE. This term is not synonymous with a "place of pauper settlement." 49 N. H. 553.

Dwelling-place, or home, means some permanent abode or residence, with intention to remain; and is not synonymous with "domicile," as used in international law, but has a more limited and restricted meaning. 19 Me. 293.

DYING DECLARATIONS. Statements made by a person who is lying at the point of death, and is conscious of his approaching dissolution, in reference to the manner in which he received the injuries of which he is dying, or other immediate cause of his death, and in reference to the person who inflicted such injuries or the connection with such injuries of a person who is charged or suspected of having committed them; which statements are admissible in evidence in a trial for homicide where the killing of the declarant is the crime charged to the defendant.

DYING WITHOUT ISSUE. At common law this phrase imports an indefinite failure of issue, and not a dying without issue surviving at the time of the death of the first taker. But this rule has been changed in some of the states, by statute or decisions, and in England by St. 7 Wm. IV., and 1 Vict. c. 26, § 29.

The words "die without issue," and "die without leaving issue," in a devise of real estate, import an indefinite failure of issue, and not the failure of issue at the death of the first taker. And no distinction is to be made between the words "without issue" and "without leaving issue." 32 Barb. 328; 20 How. Pr 41; 3 Port. 69; 6 Port. 319.

In Connecticut, it has been repeatedly held that the expression "dying without issue," and like expressions, have reference to the time of the death of the party, and not to an indefinite failure of issue. 34 Me. 176.

Dying without children imports not a failure of issue at any indefinite future period, but a leaving no children at the death of the legatee. 18 N. J. Eq. 105.

DYKE-REED, or DYKE-REEVE. An officer who has the care and oversight of the *dykes* and *drains* in fenny counties.

DYSNOMY. Bad legislation; the enactment of bad laws.

DYSPEPSIA. A state of the stomach in which its functions are disturbed, without the presence of other diseases, or when, if other diseases are present, they are of minor importance. Dungl. Med. Dict.

DYVOUR. In Scotch law. A bankrupt.

DYVOUR'S HABIT. In Scotch law. A habit which debtors who are set free on a *cessio bonorum* are obliged to wear, unless in the summons and process of *cessio* it be libeled, sustained, and proved that the bankruptcy proceeds from misfortune. And bankrupts are condemned to submit to the habit, even where no suspicion of fraud lies against them, if they have been dealers in an illicit trade. Ersk. Prin. 4, 8, 18.

E.

E. As an abbreviation, this letter may stand for "Exchequer," "English," "Edward," "Equity," "East," "Eastern," "Easter," or "Ecclesiastical."

E. A Latin preposition, meaning from, out of, after, or according. It occurs in many Latin phrases; but (in this form) only before a consonant. When the initial of the following word is a vowel, *ex* is used.

E CONTRA. From the opposite; on the contrary.

E CONVERSO. Conversely. On the other hand; on the contrary. Equivalent to *e contra*.

E. G. An abbreviation of *exempli gratia*. For the sake of an example.

E MERA GRATIA. Out of mere grace or favor.

E PLURIBUS UNUM. One out of many. The motto of the United States of America.

EA. Sax. The water or river; also the mouth of a river on the shore between high and low water-mark.

Ea est accipienda interpretatio, quæ vitio caret. That interpretation is to be received [or adopted] which is free from fault [or wrong.] The law will not intend a wrong. Bac. Max. 17, (in reg. 3.)

EA INTENTIONE. With that intent. Held not to make a condition, but a confidence and trust. Dyer, 138b.

Ea quæ, commendandi causa, in venditionibus dicuntur, si palam appareant, venditorem non obligant. Those things which are said on sales, in the way of commendation, if [the qualities of the thing sold] appear openly, do not bind the seller. Dig. 18, 1, 43, pr.

Ea quæ dari impossibilia sunt, vel quæ in rerum natura non sunt, pro non adjectis habentur. Those things which are impossible to be given, or which are not in the nature of things, are regarded as not added, [as no part of an agreement.] Dig. 50, 17, 135.

Ea quæ in curia nostra rite acta sunt debitæ executioni demandari debent. Co. Litt. 289. Those things which are properly transacted in our court ought to be committed to a due execution.

Ea quæ raro accidunt non temere in agendis negotiis computantur. Those things which rarely happen are not to be taken into account in the transaction of business, without sufficient reason. Dig. 50, 17, 64.

EACH. The effect of this word, used in the covenants of a bond, is to create a several obligation. 3 Dowl. & R. 112; 5 Term 522; 2 Day, 442; 104 Mass. 217.

Eadem causa diversis rationibus coram judicibus ecclesiasticis et secularibus ventilatur. 2 Inst. 622. The same cause is argued upon different principles before ecclesiastical and secular judges.

Eadem est ratio, eadem est lex. The same reason, the same law. 7 Pick. 493.

Eadem mens præsumitur regis quæ est juris et quæ esse debet, præsertim in dubiis. Hob. 154. The mind of the sovereign is presumed to be coincident with that of the law, and with that which it ought to be, especially in ambiguous matters.

EAGLE. A gold coin of the United States of the value of ten dollars.

EALDER, or EALDING. In old Saxon law. An elder or chief.

EALDERMAN, or EALDORMAN. The name of a Saxon magistrate; alderman; analogous to *earl* among the Danes, and *senator* among the Romans. See ALDERMAN.

EALDOR-BISCOP. An archbishop.

EALDORBURG. Sax. The metropolis; the chief city. Obsolete.

EALEHUS. (Fr. *eale*, Sax., ale, and *hus*, house.) An ale-house.

EALHORDA. Sax. The privilege of assising and selling beer. Obsolete.

EAR GRASS. In English law. Such grass which is upon the land after the mowing, until the feast of the Annunciation after. 3 Leon. 213.

EAR-MARK. A mark put upon a thing to distinguish it from another. Originally and literally, a mark upon the ear; a mode of marking sheep and other animals.

Property is said to be *ear-marked* when it can be identified or distinguished from other property of the same nature.

Money has no ear-mark, but it is an ordinary term for a privy mark made by any one on a coin.

EAR-WITNESS. In the law of evidence. One who attests or can attest anything as heard by himself.

EARL. A title of nobility, formerly the highest in England, now the third, ranking between a marquis and a viscount, and corresponding with the French "*comte*" and the German "*graf.*" The title originated with the Saxons, and is the most ancient of the English peerage. William the Conqueror first made this title hereditary, giving it in fee to his nobles; and allotting them for the support of their state the third penny out of the sheriff's court, issuing out of all pleas of the shire, whence they had their ancient title "shiremen." At present the title is accompanied by no territory, private or judicial rights, but merely confers nobility and an hereditary seat in the house of lords. Wharton.

EARL MARSHAL OF ENGLAND. A great officer of state who had anciently several courts under his jurisdiction, as the court of chivalry and the court of honor. Under him is the herald's office, or college of arms. He was also a judge of the Marshalsea court, now abolished. This office is of great antiquity, and has been for several ages hereditary in the family of the Howards. 3 Bl. Comm. 68, 103; 3 Steph. Comm. 335, note.

EARLDOM. The dignity or jurisdiction of an earl. The dignity only remains now, as the jurisdiction has been given over to the sheriff. 1 Bl. Comm. 339.

EARLES-PENNY. Money given in part payment. See EARNEST.

EARNEST. The payment of a part of the price of goods sold, or the delivery of part of such goods, for the purpose of binding the contract. 108 Mass. 54.

A token or pledge passing between the parties, by way of evidence, or ratification of the sale. 2 Kent, Comm. 495, note.

EARNINGS. This term is used to denote a larger class of credits than would be included in the term "wages." 102 Mass. 235; 115 Mass. 165.

The gains of the person derived from his services or labor without the aid of capital. 20 Wis. 330. See, also, 46 N. H. 48.

"Gross" earnings are the total receipts before deducting expenditures. "As a general proposition, net earnings are the excess of the gross earnings over the expenditures defrayed in producing them, aside from, and exclusive of, the expenditure of capital laid out in constructing and equipping the works themselves." 99 U. S. 420. See, also, 44 Ohio St. 315, 7 N. E. Rep. 139; 54 Conn. 168, 5 Atl. Rep. 851.

"Surplus" earnings of a company or corporation means the amount owned by the company over and above its capital and actual liabilities. 76 N. Y. 74.

EARTH. Soil of all kinds, including gravel, clay, loam, and the like, in distinction from the firm rock. 75 N. Y. 76.

EASEMENT. A right in the owner of one parcel of land, by reason of such ownership, to use the land of another for a special purpose not inconsistent with a general property in the owner. 2 Washb. Real Prop. 25.

A privilege which the owner of one adjacent tenement hath of another, existing in respect of their several tenements, by which that owner against whose tenement the privilege exists is obliged to suffer or not to do something on or in regard to his own land for the advantage of him in whose land the privilege exists. Termes de la Ley.

A private easement is a privilege, service, or convenience which one neighbor has of another, by prescription, grant, or necessary implication, and without profit; as a way over his land, a gate-way, water-course, and the like. Kitch. 105; 3 Cruise, Dig. 484.

The land against which the easement or privilege exists is called the "servient" tenement, and the estate to which it is annexed the "dominant" tenement; and their owners are called respectively the "servient" and "dominant" owner. These terms are taken from the civil law.

At the present day, the distinction between an "easement" and a "license" is well settled and fully recognized, although it becomes difficult in some of the cases to discover a substantial difference between them. An easement, it has appeared, is a liberty, privilege, or advantage in land, without profit, and existing distinct from the ownership of the soil; and it has appeared, also, that a claim for an easement must be founded upon a deed or writing, or upon prescription, which supposes one. It is a permanent interest in another's land, with a right to enjoy it fully and without obstruction. A license, on the other hand, is a bare authority to do a certain act or series of acts upon another's land, without possessing any estate therein; and, it being founded in personal confidence, it is not assignable, and it is gone if the owner of the land who gives the license transfers his title to another, or if either party die. 3 Pin. 415.

Classification. Easements are classified as *affirmative* or *negative;* the former being those where the servient estate must permit something to be done thereon, (as to pass over it, or to discharge water upon it;) the latter being those where the owner of the servient estate is prohibited from doing something otherwise lawful upon his estate, because it will affect the dominant estate, (as interrupting the light and air from the latter by building on the former.) 2 Washb. Real Prop. 301.

They are also either *continuous* or *discontinuous;* the former depending on some natural conformation of the servient tenement, or artificial structure upon it, which constitutes the easement or the means of enjoying it; the latter being such as have no means specially constructed or appropriated for their enjoyment, and are enjoyed at intervals, leaving in the mean time no visible signs of their existence. 18 N. J. Eq. 262.

Easements are also classified as *private* or *public,* according as their enjoyment belongs to an individual or to the community.

They may also be either *of necessity* or *of convenience.* The former is the case where the easement is indispensable to the enjoyment of the dominant estate; the latter, where the easement increases the facility, comfort, or convenience of the enjoyment of the dominant estate, or of some right connected with it.

An *appurtenant* (or appendant) easement is one which is attached to and passes with the dominant tenement as an appurtenance thereof.

EAST. In the customs laws of the United States, the term "countries *east* of the Cape of Good Hope" means countries with which, formerly, the United States ordinarily carried on commercial intercourse by passing around that cape. 101 U. S. 790.

EAST GREENWICH. The name of a royal manor in the county of Kent, England; mentioned in royal grants or patents, as descriptive of the tenure of free socage.

EAST INDIA COMPANY. The East India Company was originally established for prosecuting the trade between England and India, which they acquired a right to carry on exclusively. Since the middle of the last century, however, the company's political affairs had become of more importance than their commerce. In 1858, by 21 & 22 Vict. c. 106, the government of the territories of the company was transferred to the crown. Wharton.

EASTER. A feast of the Christian church held in memory of our Saviour's resurrection. The Greeks and Latins call it "*pascha,*" (passover,) to which Jewish feast our Easter answers. This feast has been annually celebrated since the time of the apostles, and is one of the most important festivals in the Christian calendar, being that which regulates and determines the times of all the other movable feasts. Enc. Lond.

EASTER-OFFERINGS, or EASTER-DUES. In English law. Small sums of money paid to the parochial clergy by the parishioners at Easter as a compensation for personal tithes, or the tithe for personal labor; recoverable under 7 & 8 Wm. III. c. 6, before justices of the peace.

EASTER TERM. In English law. One of the four terms of the courts. It is now a fixed term, beginning on the 15th of April and ending on the 8th of May in every year, though sometimes prolonged so late as the 13th of May, under St. 11 Geo. IV. and 1 Wm. IV. c. 70. From November 2, 1875, the division of the legal year into terms is abolished so far as concerns the administration of justice. 3 Steph. Comm. 482–486; Mozley & Whitley.

EASTERLING. A coin struck by Richard II., which is supposed to have given rise to the name of "sterling," as applied to English money.

EASTERLY. This word, when used alone, will be construed to mean "due east." But that is a rule of necessity growing out of the indefiniteness of the term, and has no application where other words are used for the purpose of qualifying its meaning. Where such is the case, instead of meaning "due east," it means precisely what the qualifying word makes it mean. 32 Cal. 227.

EASTINUS. An easterly coast or country.

EAT INDE SINE DIE. In criminal practice. Words used on the acquittal of a defendant, *that he may go thence without a day, i. e.*, be dismissed without any further continuance or adjournment.

EATING-HOUSE. Any place where food or refreshments of any kind, not including spirits, wines, ale, beer, or other malt liquors, are provided for casual visitors, and sold for consumption therein. Act Cong. July 13, 1866, § 9, (14 St. at Large, 118.)

EAVES. The edge of a roof, built so as to project over the walls of a house, in order that the rain may drop therefrom to the ground instead of running down the wall.

EAVESDROPPING. In English criminal law. The offense of listening under walls or windows, or the *eaves* of a house, to hearken after discourse, and thereupon to frame slanderous and mischievous tales. 4 Bl. Comm. 168. It is a misdemeanor at common law, indictable at sessions, and punishable by fine and finding sureties for good behavior. Id.; Steph. Crim. Law, 109. See 3 Head, 300.

EBB AND FLOW. An expression used formerly in this country to denote the limits of admiralty jurisdiction. See 3 Mason, 127; 2 Story, 176; 2 Gall. 398; 4 Wall. 562; 8 Wall. 15.

EBBA. In old English law. Ebb. *Ebba et fluctus;* ebb and flow of tide; ebb and flood. Bract. fols. 255, 338. The time occupied by one ebb and flood was anciently granted to persons essoined as being beyond sea, in addition to the period of forty days. See Fleta, lib. 6, c. 8, § 2.

EBDOMADARIUS. In ecclesiastical law. An officer in cathedral churches who supervised the regular performance of divine service, and prescribed the particular duties of each person in the choir.

EBEREMORTH, EBEREMORS, EBERE-MURDER. See ABEREMURDER.

Ecce modo mirum, quod fœmina fert breve regis, non nominando virum, conjunctum robore legis. Co. Litt. 132*b*. Behold, indeed, a wonder! that a woman has the king's writ without naming her husband, who by law is united to her.

ECCHYMOSIS. In medical jurisprudence. Blackness. It is an extravasation of blood by rupture of capillary vessels, and hence it follows contusion; but it may exist, as in cases of scurvy and other morbid conditions, without the latter. Ry. Med. Jur. 172.

ECCLESIA. Lat. An assembly. A Christian assembly; a church. A place of religious worship. Spelman.

Ecclesia ecclesiæ decimas solvere non debet. Cro. Eliz. 479. A church ought not to pay tithes to a church.

Ecclesia est domus mansionalis Omnipotentis Dei. 2 Inst. 164. The church is the mansion-house of the Omnipotent God.

Ecclesia est infra ætatem et in custodia domini regis, qui tenetur jura et hæreditates ejusdem manu tenere et defendere. 11 Coke, 49. The church is under age, and in the custody of the king, who is bound to uphold and defend its rights and inheritances.

Ecclesia fungitur vice minoris; meliorem conditionem suam facere potest, deteriorem nequaquam. Co. Litt. 341. The church enjoys the privilege of a minor; it can make its own condition better, but not worse.

Ecclesia non moritur. 2 Inst. 3. The church does not die.

Ecclesiæ magis favendum est quam personæ. Godol. Ecc. Law, 172. The church is to be more favored than the parson.

ECCLESIÆ SCULPTURA. The image or sculpture of a church in ancient times was often cut out or cast in plate or other metal, and preserved as a religious treasure or relic, and to perpetuate the memory of some famous churches. Jacob.

ECCLESIARCH. The ruler of a church.

ECCLESIASTIC, *n.* A clergyman; a priest; a man consecrated to the service of the church.

ECCESIASTICAL. Something belonging to or set apart for the church, as distinguished from "civil" or "secular," with regard to the world. Wharton.

ECCLESIASTICAL AUTHORITIES. In England, the clergy, under the sovereign, as temporal head of the church, set apart from the rest of the people or laity, in order to superintend the public worship of God and the other ceremonies of religion, and to administer spiritual counsel and instruction. The several orders of the clergy are: (1) Archbishops and bishops; (2) deans and chapters; (3) archdeacons; (4) rural deans; (5) parsons (under whom are included appropriators) and vicars; (6) curates. Churchwardens or sidesmen, and parish clerks and sextons, inasmuch as their duties are connected with the church, may be considered to be a species of ecclesiastical authorities. Wharton.

ECCLESIASTICAL COMMISSIONERS. In English law. A body corporate, erected by St. 6 & 7 Wm. IV. c. 77, empowered to suggest measures conducive to the efficiency of the established church, to be ratified by orders in council. Wharton. See 3 Steph. Comm. 156, 157.

ECCLESIASTICAL CORPORATIONS. Such corporations as are composed of persons who take a lively interest in the advancement of religion, and who are associated and incorporated for that purpose. Ang. & A. Corp. § 36.

Corporations whose members are spiritual persons are distinguished from *lay* corporations. 1 Bl. Comm. 470.

ECCLESIASTICAL COURTS. A system of courts in England, held by authority of the sovereign, and having jurisdiction over matters pertaining to the religion and ritual of the established church, and the rights, duties, and discipline of ecclesiastical persons as such. They are as follows: The archdeacon's court, consistory court, court of arches, court of peculiars, prerogative court, court of delegates, court of convocation, court of audience, court of faculties, and court of commissioners of review. See those several titles; and see 3 Bl. Comm. 64–68.

ECCLESIASTICAL DIVISION OF ENGLAND. This is a division into provinces, dioceses, archdeaconries, rural deaneries, and parishes.

ECCLESIASTICAL LAW. The body of jurisprudence administered by the ecclesiastical courts of England; derived, in large measure, from the canon and civil law. As now restricted, it applies mainly to the affairs, and the doctrine, discipline, and worship, of the established church.

ECDICUS. The attorney, proctor, or advocate of a corporation. *Episcoporum ecdici;* bishops' proctors; church lawyers. 1 Reeve, Eng. Law, 65.

ECHANTILLON. In French law. One of the two parts or pieces of a wooden tally. That in possession of the debtor is properly called the "tally," the other *"echantillon."* Poth. Obl. pt. 4, c. 1, art. 2, § 8.

ECHEVIN. In French law. A municipal officer corresponding with alderman or burgess, and having in some instances a civil jurisdiction in certain causes of trifling importance.

ECHOUEMENT. In French marine law. Stranding. Emerig. Tr. des Ass. c. 12, s. 13, no. 1.

ECLAMPSIA PARTURIENTIUM. In medical jurisprudence. The name of a disease accompanied by apoplectic convulsions, and which produces aberration of mind at childbirth.

ECLECTIC PRACTICE. In medicine. That system followed by physicians who select their modes of practice and medicines from various schools. Webster.

"Without professing to understand much of medical phraseology, we suppose that the terms 'allopathic practice' and 'legitimate business' mean the ordinary method commonly adopted by the great body of learned and eminent physicians, which is taught in their institutions, established by their highest authorities, and accepted by the larger and more respectable portion of the community. By 'eclectic practice,' without imputing to it, as the counsel for the plaintiff seem inclined to, an odor of illegality, we presume is intended another and different system, unusual and eccentric, not countenanced by the classes before referred to, but characterized by them as spurious and denounced as dangerous. It is sufficient to say that the two modes of treating human maladies are essentially distinct, and based upon different views of the nature and causes of diseases, their appropriate remedies, and the modes of applying them." 34 Conn. 453.

ECRIVAIN. In French marine law. The clerk of a ship. Emerig. Tr. des Ass. c. 11, s. 3, no. 2.

ECUMENICAL. General; universal; as an ecumenical council.

EDDERBRECHE. In Saxon law. The offense of hedge-breaking. Obsolete.

EDESTIA. In old records. Buildings.

EDICT. A positive law promulgated by the sovereign of a country, and having reference either to the whole land or some of its divisions, but usually relating to affairs of state. It differs from a "public proclamation," in that it enacts a new statute, and carries with it the authority of law.

EDICTAL CITATION. In Scotch law. A citation published at the market-cross of Edinburgh, and pier and shore of Leith. Used against foreigners not within the kingdom, but having a landed estate there, and against natives out of the kingdom. Bell.

EDICTS OF JUSTINIAN. Thirteen constitutions or laws of this prince, found in most editions of the *Corpus Juris Civilis*, after the Novels. Being confined to matters of police in the provinces of the empire, they are of little use.

EDICTUM. In the Roman law. An edict; a mandate, or ordinance. An ordinance, or law, enacted by the emperor without the senate; belonging to the class of *constitutiones principis.* Inst. 1, 2, 6. An edict was a mere voluntary constitution of the emperor; differing from a rescript, in not being returned in the way of answer; and from a decree, in not being given in judgment; and from both, in not being founded upon solicitation. Tayl. Civil Law, 233.

A general order published by the prætor, on entering upon his office, containing the system of rules by which he would administer justice during the year of his office. Dig. 1, 2, 2, 10; Mackeld. Rom. Law, § 35. Tayl. Civil Law, 214. See Calvin.

EDICTUM PERPETUUM. In Roman law. The perpetual edict. A compilation or system of law in fifty books, digested by Julian, a lawyer of great eminence under the reign of Adrian, from the Prætor's edicts and other parts of the *Jus Honorarium.* All the remains of it which have come down to us are the extracts of it in the Digests. Butl. Hor. Jur. 52.

EDICTUM THEODORICI. This is the first collection of law that was made after the downfall of the Roman power in Italy. It was promulgated by Theodoric, king of the Ostrogoths, at Rome in A. D. 500. It consists of 154 chapters, in which we recognize parts taken from the Code and Novellæ of Theodosius, from the Codices Gregorianus and Hermogenianus, and the Sententiæ of Paulus. The edict was doubtless drawn up by Roman writers, but the original sources are more disfigured and altered than in any other compilation. This collection of law was intended to apply both to the Goths and the Romans, so far as its provisions went; but, when it made no alteration in the Gothic law, that law was still to be in force. Savigny, Geschichte des R. R.

EDITUS. In old English law. Put forth or promulgated, when speaking of the passage of a statute; and brought forth, or born, when speaking of the birth of a child.

EDUCATE. Includes proper moral, as well as intellectual and physical, instruction. Code Tenn. § 2521; 6 Heisk. 395.

EDUCATION. Within the meaning of a statute relative to the powers and duties of guardians, this term comprehends not merely the instruction received at school or college, but the whole course of training, moral, intellectual, and physical. 6 Heisk. 400.

Education may be particularly directed to either the mental, moral, or physical powers and faculties, but in its broadest and best sense it relates to them all. 145 Mass. 146, 13 N. E. Rep. 354.

EFFECT. The result which an instrument between parties will produce in their relative rights, or which a statute will produce upon the existing law, as discovered from the language used, the forms employed, or other materials for construing it.

The phrases "take effect," "be in force," "go into operation," etc., have been used interchangeably ever since the organization of the state. 4 Ind. 342.

EFFECTS. Personal estate or property. This word has been held to be more comprehensive than the word "goods," as including fixtures, which "goods" will not include. 7 Taunt. 188; 4 J. B. Moore, 73; 4 Barn. & A. 206.

In wills. The word "effects" is equivalent to "property," or "worldly substance," and, if used *simpliciter*, as in a gift of "all my effects," will carry the whole personal estate. Ves. Jr. 507; Ward, Leg. 209. The addition of the words "real and personal" will extend it so as to embrace the whole of the testator's real and personal estate. Cowp. 299; 3 Brown, Parl. Cas. 388.

This is a word often found in wills, and, being equivalent to "property," or "worldly substance," its force depends greatly upon the association of the adjectives "real" and "personal." "Real and personal effects" would embrace the whole estate; but the word "effects" alone must be confined to personal estate simply, unless an intention appears to the contrary. Schouler, Wills, § 509. See 1 Cowp. 304.

Effectus sequitur causam. Wing. 226. The effect follows the cause.

EFFENDI. In Turkish language. Master; a title of respect.

EFFIGY. The corporeal representation of a person.

To make the effigy of a person with an intent to make him the object of ridicule is a libel. 2 Chit. Crim. Law, 866.

EFFLUX. The running of a prescribed period of time to its end; expiration by lapse of time. Particularly applied to the termination of a lease by the expiration of the term for which it was made.

EFFLUXION OF TIME. When this phrase is used in leases, conveyances, and other like deeds, or in agreements expressed in simple writing, it indicates the conclusion or expiration of an agreed term of years specified in the deed or writing, such conclusion or expiration arising in the natural course of events, in contradistinction to the determination of the term by the acts of the parties or by some unexpected or unusual incident or other sudden event. Brown.

EFFORCIALITER. Forcibly; applied to military force.

EFFRACTION. A breach made by the use of force.

EFFRACTOR. One who breaks through; one who commits a burglary.

EFFUSIO SANGUINIS. In old English law. The shedding of blood; the mulct, fine, *wite*, or penalty imposed for the shedding of blood, which the king granted to many lords of manors. Cowell; Tomlins. See BLOODWIT.

EFTERS. In Saxon law. Ways, walks, or hedges. Blount.

EGALITY. Owelty, (*q. v.*) Co. Litt. 169a.

EGO. I; myself. This term is used in forming genealogical tables, to represent the person who is the object of inquiry.

EGO, TALIS. I, such a one. Words used in describing the forms of old deeds. Fleta, lib. 3, c. 14, § 5.

EGREDIENS ET EXEUNS. In old pleading. Going forth and issuing out of (land.) Townsh. Pl. 17.

EGYPTIANS, commonly called "Gypsies," are counterfeit rogues, Welsh or English, that disguise themselves in speech and apparel, and wander up and down the country, pretending to have skill in telling fortunes, and to deceive the common people, but live chiefly by filching and stealing, and, therefore, the statutes of 1 & 2 Mar. c. 4, and 5 Eliz. c. 20, were made to punish such as felons if they departed not the realm or continued to a month. Termes de la Ley.

Ei incumbit probatio, qui dicit, non qui negat; cum per rerum naturam factum negantis probatio nulla sit. The proof lies upon him who affirms, not upon him who denies; since, by the nature of things, he who denies a fact cannot produce any proof.

Ei nihil turpe, cui nihil satis. To him to whom nothing is enough, nothing is base. 4 Inst. 53.

EIA, or EY. An island. Cowell.

EIGNE. L. Fr. Eldest; eldest-born. The term is of common occurrence in the old books. Thus, *bastard eigne* means an illegitimate son whose parents afterwards marry and have a second son for lawful issue, the latter being called *mulier puisne*, (after-born.) *Eigne* is probably a corrupt form of the French *"ainé."* 2 Bl. Comm. 248; Litt. § 399.

EIK. In Scotch law. An addition; as, *eik* to a reversion, *eik* to a confirmation. Bell.

EINECIA. Eldership. See ESNECY.

EINETIUS. In English law. The oldest; the first-born. Spelman.

EIRE, or EYRE. In old English law. A journey, route, or circuit. Justices *in eire* were judges who were sent by commission, every seven years, into various counties to hold the assizes and hear pleas of the crown. 3 Bl. Comm. 58.

EIRENARCHA. A name formerly given to a justice of the peace. In the Digests, the word is written *"irenarcha."*

Eisdem modis dissolvitur obligatio quæ nascitur ex contractu, vel quasi, quibus contrahitur. An obligation which arises from contract, or *quasi* contract, is dissolved in the same ways in which it is contracted. Fleta, lib. 2, c. 60, § 19.

EISNE. The senior; the oldest son. Spelled, also, *"eigne," "einsne," "aisne," "eign."* Termes de la Ley; Kelham.

EISNETIA, EINETIA. The share of the oldest son. The portion acquired by primogeniture. Termes de la Ley; Co. Litt. 166b; Cowell.

EITHER. May be used in the sense of "each." 59 Ill. 87.

This word does not mean "all;" but does mean one or the other of two or more specified things. (Tex.) 4 S. W. Rep. 538.

EJECT. To cast, or throw out; to oust, or dispossess; to put or turn out of possession. 3 Bl. Comm. 198, 199, 200.

EJECTA. In old English law. A woman ravished or deflowered, or cast forth from the virtuous. Blount.

EJECTION. A turning out of possession. 3 Bl. Comm. 199.

EJECTIONE CUSTODIÆ. In old English law. Ejectment of ward. This phrase, which is the Latin equivalent for the French "*ejectment de garde*," was the title of a writ which lay for a guardian when turned out of any land of his ward during the minority of the latter. Brown.

EJECTIONE FIRMÆ. Ejection, or ejectment of farm. The name of a writ or action of trespass, which lay at common law where lands or tenements were let for a term of years, and afterwards the lessor, reversioner, remainder-man, or any stranger *ejected* or ousted the lessee of his term, *ferme*, or *farm*, (*ipsum a firma ejecit*.) In this case the latter might have his writ of *ejection*, by which he recovered at first *damages* for the trespass only, but it was afterwards made a remedy to recover back the *term* itself, or the remainder of it, with damages. Reg. Orig. 227*b*; Fitzh. Nat. Brev. 220, F, G; 3 Bl. Comm. 199; Litt. § 322; Crabb, Eng. Law, 290, 448. It is the foundation of the modern action of ejectment.

EJECTMENT. At common law, this was the name of a mixed action (springing from the earlier personal action of *ejectione firmæ*) which lay for the recovery of the possession of land, and for damages for the unlawful detention of its possession. The action was highly fictitious, being in theory only for the recovery of a term for years, and brought by a purely fictitious person, as lessee in a supposed lease from the real party in interest. The latter's title, however, must be established in order to warrant a recovery, and the establishment of such title, though nominally a mere incident, is in reality the object of the action. Hence this convenient form of suit came to be adopted as the usual method of trying titles to land. See 3 Bl. Comm. 199.

It was the only mixed action at common law, the whole method of proceeding in which was anomalous, and depended on fictions invented and upheld by the court for the convenience of justice, in order to escape from the inconveniences which were found to attend the ancient forms of real and mixed actions.

It is also a form of action by which possessory titles to corporeal hereditaments may be tried and possession obtained.

EJECTUM. That which is thrown up by the sea. Also jetsam, wreck, etc.

EJECTUS. In old English law. A whoremonger. Blount.

EJERCITORIA. In Spanish law. The name of an action lying against a ship's owner, upon the contracts or obligations made by the master for repairs or supplies. It corresponds to the *actio exercitoria* of the Roman law. Mackeld. Rom. Law, § 512.

EJIDOS. In Spanish law. Commons; lands used in common by the inhabitants of a city, pueblo, or town, for pasture, wood, threshing-ground, etc. 15 Cal. 554.

EJURATION. Renouncing or resigning one's place.

Ejus est interpretari cujus est condere. It is his to interpret whose it is to enact. Tayl. Civil Law, 96.

Ejus est nolle, qui potest velle. He who can will, [exercise volition,] has a right to refuse to will, [to withhold consent.] Dig. 50, 7, 3.

Ejus est periculum cujus est dominium aut commodum. He who has the dominion or advantage has the risk.

Ejus nulla culpa est, cui parere necesse sit. No guilt attaches to him who is compelled to obey. Dig. 50, 17, 169, pr. Obedience to existing laws is a sufficient extenuation of guilt before a civil tribunal. Broom, Max. 12, note.

EJUSDEM GENERIS. Of the same kind, class, or nature.

ELABORARE. In old European law. To gain, acquire, or purchase, as by labor and industry.

ELABORATUS. Property which is the acquisition of labor. Spelman.

ELDER BRETHREN. A distinguished body of men, elected as masters of Trinity House, an institution incorporated in the reign of Henry VIII., charged with numerous important duties relating to the marine, such as the superintendence of light-houses. Mozley & Whitley; 2 Steph. Comm. 502.

ELDER TITLE. A title of earlier date, but coming simultaneously into operation with a title of younger origin, is called the "elder title," and prevails.

ELDEST. He or she who has the greatest age.

The "eldest son" is the first-born son. If there is only one son, he may still be described as the "eldest." L. R. 7 H. L. 644.

Electa una via, non datur recursus ad alteram. He who has chosen one way cannot have recourse to another. 10 Toull. no. 170.

ELECTED. The word "elected," in its ordinary signification, carries with it the idea of a vote, generally popular, sometimes more restricted, and cannot be held the synonym of any other mode of filling a position. 5 Nev. 121.

Electio est interna libera et spontanea separatio unius rei ab alia, sine compulsione, consistens in animo et voluntate. Dyer, 281. Election is an internal, free, and spontaneous separation of one thing from another, without compulsion, consisting in intention and will.

Electio semel facta, et placitum testatum non patitur regressum. Co. Litt. 146. Election once made, and plea witnessed, suffers not a recall.

ELECTION. The act of choosing or selecting one or more from a greater number of persons, things, courses, or rights. The choice of an alternative.

The internal, free, and spontaneous separation of one thing from another, without compulsion, consisting in intention and will. Dyer, 281.

The selection of one man from among several candidates to discharge certain duties in a state, corporation, or society.

The choice which is open to a debtor who is bound in an alternative obligation to select either one of the alternatives.

In equity. The obligation imposed upon a party to choose between two inconsistent or alternative rights or claims, in cases where there is clear intention of the person from whom he derives one that he should not enjoy both. 2 Story, Eq. Jur. § 1075.

The doctrine of election presupposes a plurality of gifts or rights, with an intention, express or implied, of the party who has a right to control one or both, that one should be a substitute for the other. 1 Swanst. 394, note b; 3 Wood. Lect. 491; 2 Rop. Leg. 480–578.

In practice. The liberty of choosing (or the act of choosing) one out of several means

afforded by law for the redress of an injury, or one out of several available forms of action.

In criminal law. The choice, by the prosecution, upon which of several counts in an indictment (charging distinct offenses of the same degree, but not parts of a continuous series of acts) it will proceed.

ELECTION AUDITORS. In English law. Officers annually appointed, to whom was committed the duty of taking and publishing the account of all expenses incurred at parliamentary elections. See 17 & 18 Vict. c. 102, §§ 18, 26–28. But these sections have been repealed by the 26 Vict. c. 29, which throws the duty of preparing the accounts on the declared agent of the candidate, and the duty of publishing an abstract of it on the returning officer. Wharton.

ELECTION DISTRICT. A subdivision of territory, whether of state, county, or city, the boundaries of which are fixed by law, for convenience in local or general elections. 41 Pa. St. 403.

ELECTION JUDGES. In English law. Judges of the high court selected in pursuance of the 31 & 32 Vict. c. 125, § 11, and Jud. Act 1873, § 38, for the trial of election petitions.

ELECTION PETITIONS. Petitions for inquiry into the validity of elections of members of parliament, when it is alleged that the return of a member is invalid for bribery or any other reason. These petitions are heard by a judge of one of the common-law divisions of the high court.

Electiones fiant rite et libere sine interruptione aliqua. Elections should be made in due form, and freely, without any interruption. 2 Inst. 169.

ELECTIVE. Dependent upon choice; bestowed or passing by election. Also pertaining or relating to elections; conferring the right or power to vote at elections.

ELECTOR. He that has a vote in the choice of any officer; a constituent; also the title of certain German princes who formerly had a voice in the election of the German emperors.

ELECTORAL. Pertaining to electors or elections; composed or consisting of electors.

ELECTORAL COLLEGE. The body of princes formerly entitled to elect the emperor of Germany. Also a name sometimes given, in the United States, to the body of electors chosen by the people to elect the president and vice-president. Webster.

ELECTORS OF PRESIDENT. Persons chosen by the people at a so-called "presidential election," to elect a president and vice-president of the United States.

ELEEMOSYNA REGIS, and ELEEMOSYNA ARATRI, or CARUCARUM. A penny which King Ethelred ordered to be paid for every plow in England towards the support of the poor. Leg. Ethel. c. 1.

ELEEMOSYNÆ. Possessions belonging to the church. Blount.

ELEEMOSYNARIA. The place in a religious house where the common alms were deposited, and thence by the almoner distributed to the poor.

In old English law. The *aumerie, aumbry*, or *ambry;* words still used in common speech in the north of England, to denote a pantry or cupboard. Cowell.

The office of almoner. Cowell.

ELEEMOSYNARIUS. In old English law. An almoner, or chief officer, who received the eleemosynary rents and gifts, and in due method distributed them to pious and charitable uses. Cowell; Wharton.

The name of an officer (lord almoner) of the English kings, in former times, who distributed the royal alms or bounty. Fleta, lib. 2, c. 23.

ELEEMOSYNARY. Relating to the distribution of alms, bounty, or charity; charitable.

ELEEMOSYNARY CORPORATIONS. Such as are constituted for the perpetual distribution of the free alms and bounty of the founder, in such manner as he has directed; and in this class are ranked hospitals for the relief of poor and impotent persons, and colleges for the promotion of learning and piety, and the support of persons engaged in literary pursuits. These corporations are lay, and not ecclesiastical, even though composed of ecclesiastical persons, and although they in some things partake of the nature, privileges, and restrictions of ecclesiastical bodies. 1 Bl. Comm. 471.

Eleemosynary corporations are for the management of private property according to the will of the donors. They are private lay corporations, such as colleges, hospitals, etc. They differ from civil corporations in that the former are the mere creatures of public institution, created exclusively for the public advantage, and subject to governmental control and visitation; whereas a private corporation, especially one organized for charitable purposes, is the creature of private benefaction, endowed and founded by private individuals, and subject to their control, laws, and visitation, and not to those of the government. 4 Wheat. 518, 660.

ELEGANTER. In the civil law. Accurately; with discrimination. 3 Story, 611, 636.

ELEGIT. (Lat. He has chosen.) This is the name, in English practice, of a writ of execution first given by the statute of Westm. 2 (13 Edw. I. c. 18) either upon a judgment for a debt or damages or upon the forfeiture of a recognizance taken in the king's court. It is so called because it is in the choice or election of the plaintiff whether he will sue out this writ or a *fi. fa.* By it the defendant's goods and chattels are appraised, and all of them (except oxen and beasts of the plow) are delivered to the plaintiff, at such reasonable appraisement and price, in part satisfaction of his debt. If the goods are not sufficient, then the moiety of his freehold lands, which he had at the time of the judgment given, are also to be delivered to the plaintiff, to hold till out of the rents and profits thereof the debt be levied, or till the defendant's interest be expired. During this period the plaintiff is called "tenant by *elegit*," and his estate, an "estate by *elegit*." This writ, or its analogue, is in use in some of the United States, as Virginia and Kentucky. See 3 Bl. Comm. 418; 4 Kent, Comm. 431, 436, and notes; 10 Grat. 580.

ELEMENTS. The forces of nature. The elements are the means through which God acts, and "damages by the elements" means the same thing as "damages by the act of God." 35 Cal. 416.

ELIGIBLE. As applied to a candidate for an elective office, this term means capable of being chosen; the subject of selection or choice; and also implies competency to hold the office if chosen. 15 Ind. 331; 15 Cal. 121; 14 Wis. 497.

ELIMINATION. In old English law. The act of banishing or turning out of doors; rejection.

ELINGUATION. The punishment of cutting out the tongue.

ELISORS. In practice. Electors or choosers. Persons appointed by the court to execute writs of *venire*, in cases where both the sheriff and coroner are disqualified from acting, and whose duty is to *choose*—that is, name and return—the jury. 3 Bl. Comm. 355; Co Litt. 158; 3 Steph. Comm. 597, note.

Persons appointed to execute *any* writ, in default of the sheriff and coroner, are also called "elisors."

ELL. A measure of length, answering to the modern yard. 1 Bl. Comm. 275.

ELOGIUM. In the civil law. A will or testament.

ELOIGNE. In practice. (Fr. *éloigner*, to remove to a distance; to remove afar off.) A return to a writ of replevin, when the chattels have been removed out of the way of the sheriff.

ELOIGNMENT. The getting a thing or person out of the way; or removing it to a distance, so as to be out of reach.

ELONGATA. In practice. Eloigned; carried away to a distance. The old form of the return made by a sheriff to a writ of replevin, stating that the goods or beasts had been *eloigned*; that is, carried to a distance, to places to him unknown. 3 Bl. Comm. 148; 3 Steph. Comm. 522; Fitzh. Nat. Brev. 73, 74; Archb. N. Pract. 552.

ELONGATUS. Eloigned. A return made by a sheriff to a writ *de homine replegiando*, stating that the party to be replevied has been eloigned, or conveyed out of his jurisdiction. 3 Bl. Comm. 129.

ELONGAVIT. In England, where in a proceeding by foreign attachment the plaintiff has obtained judgment of appraisement, but by reason of some act of the garnishee the goods cannot be appraised, (as where he has removed them from the city, or has sold them, etc.,) the serjeant-at-mace returns that the garnishee has eloigned them, *i. e.*, removed them out of the jurisdiction, and on this return (called an "elongavit") judgment is given for the plaintiff that an inquiry be made of the goods eloigned. This inquiry is set down for trial, and the assessment is made by a jury after the manner of ordinary issues. Sweet.

ELOPEMENT. The act of a wife who voluntarily deserts her husband to cohabit with another man. 2 Bl. Comm. 130. To constitute an elopement, the wife must not only leave the husband, but go beyond his actual control; for if she abandons the husband, and goes and lives in adultery in a

house belonging to him, it is said not to be an elopement. 3 N. H. 42.

"ELSEWHERE." In another place; in any other place. See 1 Vern. 4, and note.

In shipping articles, this term, following the designation of the port of destination, must be construed either as void for uncertainty or as subordinate to the principal voyage stated in the preceding words. 2 Gall. 477.

ELUVIONES. In old pleading. Spring tides. Townsh. Pl. 197.

EMANCIPATION. The act by which one who was unfree, or under the power and control of another, is set at liberty and made his own master.

In Roman law. The enfranchisement of a son by his father, which was anciently done by the formality of an imaginary *sale*. This was abolished by Justinian, who substituted the simpler proceeding of a manumission before a magistrate. Inst. 1, 12, 6.

In Louisiana. The emancipation of minors is especially recognized and regulated by law.

In England. The term "emancipation" has been borrowed from the Roman law, and is constantly used in the law of parochial settlements. 7 Adol. & E. (N. S.) 574, note.

EMANCIPATION PROCLAMATION. An executive proclamation, declaring that all persons held in slavery in certain designated states and districts were and should remain free. It was issued January 1, 1863, by Abraham Lincoln, as president of the United States and commander in chief.

EMBARGO. A proclamation or order of state, usually issued in time of war or threatened hostilities, prohibiting the departure of ships or goods from some or all the ports of such state until further order. 2 Wheat. 148.

Embargo is the hindering or detention by any government of ships of commerce in its ports. If the embargo is laid upon ships belonging to citizens of the state imposing it, it is called a "civil embargo;" if, as more commonly happens, it is laid upon ships belonging to the enemy, it is called a "hostile embargo." The effect of this latter embargo is that the vessels detained are restored to the rightful owners if no war follows, but are forfeited to the embargoing government if war does follow, the declaration of war being held to relate back to the original seizure and detention. Brown.

The temporary or permanent sequestration of the property of individuals for the purposes of a government, *e. g.*, to obtain vessels for the transport of troops, the owners being reimbursed for this forced service.   Man. Int. Law, 143.

EMBASSADOR.   See AMBASSADOR.

EMBASSAGE, or EMBASSY.   The message or commission given by a sovereign or state to a minister, called an "ambassador," empowered to treat or communicate with another sovereign or state; also the establishment of an ambassador.

EMBER DAYS.   In ecclesiastical law. Those days which the ancient fathers called "*quatuor tempora jejunii*" are of great antiquity in the church.   They are observed on Wednesday, Friday, and Saturday next after Quadragesima Sunday, or the first Sunday in Lent, after Whitsuntide, Holyrood Day, in September, and St. Lucy's Day, about the middle of December.   Brit. c. 53.   Our almanacs call the weeks in which they fall the "Ember Weeks," and they are now chiefly noticed on account of the ordination of priests and deacons; because the canon appoints the Sundays next after the Ember weeks for the solemn times of ordination, though the bishops, if they please, may ordain on any Sunday or holiday.   Enc. Lond.

EMBEZZLEMENT.   The fraudulent appropriation to his own use or benefit of property or money intrusted to him by another, by a clerk, agent, trustee, public officer, or other person acting in a fiduciary character. See 4 Bl. Comm. 230, 231; 3 Kent, Comm. 194; 4 Steph. Comm. 168, 169, 219; 40 N. Y. Super. Ct. 41.

Embezzlement is the fraudulent appropriation of property by a person to whom it has been intrusted.   Pen. Code Cal. § 503; Pen. Code Dak. § 596.

Embezzlement is a species of larceny, and the term is applicable to cases of furtive and fraudulent appropriation by clerks, servants, or carriers of property coming into their possession by virtue of their employment.   It is distinguished from "larceny," properly so called, as being committed in respect of property which is not at the time in the actual or legal possession of the owner. 41 How. Pr. 294; 4 Steph. Comm. 168.

Embezzlement is not an offense at common law, but was created by statute.   "Embezzle" includes in its meaning appropriation to one's own use, and therefore the use of the single word "embezzle," in the indictment or information, contains within itself the charge that the defendant appropriated the money or property to his own use.   34 La. Ann. 1153.

EMBLEMENTS.   The vegetable chattels called "emblements" are the corn and other growth of the earth which are produced annually, not spontaneously, but by labor and industry, and thence are called "*fructus industriales.*"   64 Pa. St. 137.

The growing crops of those vegetable productions of the soil which are annually produced by the labor of the cultivator.   They are deemed personal property, and pass as such to the executor or administrator of the occupier, whether he were the owner in fee, or for life, or for years, if he die before he has actually cut, reaped, or gathered the same; and this, although, being affixed to the soil, they might for some purposes be considered, while growing, as part of the realty.   Wharton.

The term also denotes the right of a tenant to take and carry away, after his tenancy has ended, such annual products of the land as have resulted from his own care and labor.

Emblements are the away-going crop; in other words, the crop which is upon the ground and unreaped when the tenant goes away, his lease having determined; and the right to emblements is the right in the tenant to take away the away-going crop, and for that purpose to come upon the land, and do all other necessary things thereon. Brown.

EMBLERS DE GENTZ.   L. Fr.   A stealing from the people.   The phrase occurs in the old rolls of parliament: "Whereas divers murders, *emblers de gentz*, and robberies are committed," etc.

EMBRACEOR.   A person guilty of the offense of embracery, (*q. v.*)   See Co. Litt. 369.

EMBRACERY.   In criminal law.   This offense consists in the attempt to influence a jury corruptly to one side or the other, by promises, persuasions, entreaties, entertainments, *douceurs*, and the like.   The person guilty of it is called an "embraceor."   Brown.

EMENDA.   Amends; something given in reparation for a trespass; or, in old Saxon times, in compensation for an injury or crime. Spelman.

EMENDALS.   An old word still made use of in the accounts of the society of the Inner Temple, where so much in *emendals* at the foot of an account on the balance thereof signifies so much money in the bank or stock of the houses, for reparation of losses, or other emergent occasions.   Spelman.

EMENDARE.   In Saxon law.   To make amends or satisfaction for any crime or trespass committed; to pay a fine; to be fined. Spelman.   *Emendare se,* to redeem, or ransom one's life, by payment of a weregild.

EMENDATIO.   In old English law. Amendment, or correction.   The power of amending and correcting abuses, according to certain rules and measures. Cowell.

In Saxon law. A pecuniary satisfaction for an injury; the same as *emenda*, (*q. v.*) Spelman.

EMENDATIO PANIS ET CEREVISIÆ. In old English law. The power of supervising and correcting the weights and measures of bread and ale, (assising bread and beer.) Cowell.

EMERGE. To arise; to come to light. "Unless a matter happen to *emerge* after issue joined." Hale, Anal. § 1.

EMERGENT YEAR. The epoch or date whence any people begin to compute their time.

EMIGRANT. One who quits his country for any lawful reason, with a design to settle elsewhere, and who takes his family and property, if he has any, with him. Vattel, b. 1, c. 19, § 224.

EMIGRATION. The act of changing one's domicile from one country or state to another.

It is to be distinguished from "expatriation." The latter means the abandonment of one's country and renunciation of one's citizenship in it, while emigration denotes merely the removal of person and property to a foreign state. The former is usually the consequence of the latter. Emigration is also used of the removal from one section to another of the same country.

EMINENCE. An honorary title given to cardinals. They were called "*illustrissimi*" and "*reverendissimi*" until the pontificate of Urban VIII.

EMINENT DOMAIN. Eminent domain is the right of the people or government to take private property for public use. Code Civil Proc. Cal. § 1237.

The right of eminent domain is the right of the state, through its regular organization, to reassert, either temporarily or permanently, its dominion over any portion of the soil of the state on account of public exigency and for the public good. Thus, in time of war or insurrection, the proper authorities may possess and hold any part of the territory of the state for the common safety; and in time of peace the legislature may authorize the appropriation of the same to public purposes, such as the opening of roads, construction of defenses, or providing channels for trade or travel. Code Ga. 1882, § 2222.

Eminent domain is the right which a government retains over the estates of individuals to resume them for public use. Wharton.

The right of society, or of the sovereign, to dispose, in case of necessity, and for the public safety, of all the wealth contained in the state, is called "eminent domain." 2 Paine, 688.

Eminent domain is the highest and most exact idea of property remaining in the government, or in the aggregate body of the people in their sovereign capacity. It gives a right to resume the possession of the property in the manner directed by the constitution and the laws of the state, whenever the public interest requires it. 3 Paige, 45, 73.

"The exaction of money from individuals under the right of taxation, and the appropriation of private property for public use by virtue of the power of eminent domain, must not be confused. In paying taxes the citizen contributes his just and ascertained share to the expenses of the government under which he lives. But when his property is taken under the power of eminent domain, he is compelled to surrender to the public something above and beyond his due proportion for the public benefit. The matter is special. It is in the nature of a compulsory sale to the state." Black, Tax-Titles, § 3.

The term "eminent domain" is sometimes (but inaccurately) applied to the land, buildings, etc., owned directly by the government, and which have not yet passed into any private ownership. This species of property is much better designated as the "public domain," or "national domain."

EMISSARY. A person sent upon a mission as the agent of another; also a secret agent sent to ascertain the sentiments and designs of others, and to propagate opinions favorable to his employer.

EMISSION. In medical jurisprudence. The ejection or throwing out of any secretion or other matter from the body; the expulsion of urine, semen, etc.

EMIT. In American law. To put forth or send out; to issue. "No state shall *emit* bills of credit." Const. U. S. art. 1, § 10.

To issue; to give forth with authority; to put into circulation. See BILL OF CREDIT.

The word "emit" is never employed in describing those contracts by which a state binds itself to pay money at a future day for services actually received, or for money borrowed for present use. Nor are instruments executed for such purposes, in common language, denominated "bills of credit." "To emit bills of credit" conveys to the mind the idea of issuing paper intended to circulate through the community, for its ordinary purposes, as money, which paper is redeemable at a future day. 4 Pet. 410; 11 Pet. 257; 28 Ark. 369; 1 Scam. 87.

In Scotch practice. To speak out; to state in words. A prisoner is said to *emit* a declaration. 2 Alis. Crim. Pr. 560.

EMMENAGOGUES. In medical jurisprudence. The name of a class of medicines supposed to have the property of promoting the menstrual discharge, and sometimes used for the purpose of procuring abortion.

EMOLUMENT. The profit arising from office or employment; that which is received as a compensation for services, or which is annexed to the possession of office as salary, fees, and perquisites; advantage; gain, public or private. Webster. Any perquisite, advantage, profit, or gain arising from the possession of an office. 105 Pa. St. 303.

EMOTIONAL INSANITY. The species of mental aberration produced by a violent excitement of the emotions or passions, though the reasoning faculties may remain unimpaired.

EMPALEMENT. In ancient law. A mode of inflicting punishment, by thrusting a sharp pole up the fundament. Enc. Lond.

EMPANNEL. The writing or entering by the sheriff, on a parchment schedule or roll of paper, the names of a jury summoned by him. Cowell.

EMPARLANCE. See IMPARLANCE.

EMPARNOURS. L. Fr. Undertakers of suits. Kelham.

EMPEROR. The title of the sovereign ruler of an empire. This designation was adopted by the rulers of the Roman world after the decay of the republic, and was assumed by those who claimed to be their successors in the "Holy Roman Empire," as also by Napoleon. It is now used as the title of the monarch of some single countries, as lately in Brazil, and some composite states, as Germany and Austria-Hungary, and by the queen of England as "Empress of India."

The title "emperor" seems to denote a power and dignity superior to that of a "king." It appears to be the appropriate style of the executive head of a federal government, constructed on the monarchical principle, and comprising in its organization several distinct kingdoms or other *quasi* sovereign states; as is the case with the German empire at the present day.

EMPHYTEUSIS. In the Roman and civil law. A contract by which a landed estate was leased to a tenant, either in perpe-

AM. DICT. LAW—27

tuity or for a long term of years, upon the reservation of an annual rent or *canon*, and upon the condition that the lessee should improve the property, by building, cultivating, or otherwise, and with a right in the lessee to alien the estate at pleasure or pass it to his heirs by descent, and free from any revocation, re-entry, or claim of forfeiture on the part of the grantor, except for non-payment of the rent. Inst. 3, 25, 3; 3 Bl. Comm. 232; Maine, Anc. Law, 289.

The right granted by such a contract, (*jus emphyteuticum,* or *emphyteuticarium.*) The real right by which a person is entitled to enjoy another's estate as if it were his own, and to dispose of its substance, as far as can be done without deteriorating it. Mackeld. Rom. Law, § 326.

EMPHYTEUTA. In the civil law. The person to whom an *emphyteusis* is granted; the lessee or tenant under a contract of *emphyteusis.*

EMPHYTEUTICUS. In the civil law Founded on, growing out of, or having the character of, an *emphyteusis;* held under an *emphyteusis.* 3 Bl. Comm. 232.

EMPIRE. The dominion or jurisdiction of an emperor; the region over which the dominion of an emperor extends; imperial power; supreme dominion; sovereign command.

EMPIRIC. A practitioner in medicine or surgery, who proceeds on *experience only,* without science or legal qualification; a quack.

EMPLAZAMIENTO. In Spanish law. A summons or citation, issued by authority of a judge, requiring the person to whom it is addressed to appear before the tribunal at a designated day and hour.

EMPLEAD. To indict; to prefer a charge against; to accuse.

EMPLOI. In French law. Equitable conversion. When property covered by the *régime dotal* is sold, the proceeds of the sale must be reinvested for the benefit of the wife. It is the duty of the purchaser to see that the price is so reinvested. Arg. Fr. Merc. Law. 557.

EMPLOY. To engage in one's service; to use as an agent or substitute in transacting business; to commission and intrust with the management of one's affairs; and, when used in respect to a servant or hired laborer, the term is equivalent to hiring, which implies a request and a contract for a compensation, and has but this one meaning when used in the ordinary affairs and business of life. 11 N. Y. 599; 58 N. Y. 371.

EMPLOYED. This signifies both the act of doing a thing and the being under contract or orders to do it. 14 Pet. 464, 475; 2 Paine, 721, 745.

EMPLOYEE. This word "is from the French, but has become somewhat naturalized in our language. Strictly and etymologically, it means 'a person employed,' but, in practice in the French language, it ordinarily is used to signify a person in some official employment, and as generally used with us, though perhaps not confined to any official employment, it is understood to mean some permanent employment or position." 2 Lans. 453. See, also, 75 N. Y. 41; 111 Ind. 324, 12 N. E. Rep. 501.

The word is more extensive than "clerk" or "officer." It signifies any one in place, or having charge or using a function, as well as one in office. 3 Ct. Cl. 260.

EMPLOYMENT. This word does not necessarily import an engagement or rendering services for another. A person may as well be "employed" about his own business as in the transaction of the same for a principal. 43 Mo. 51; 56 Law J. Q. B. Div. 251.

EMPORIUM. A place for wholesale trade in commodities carried by sea. The name is sometimes applied to a seaport town, but it properly signifies only a particular place in such a town. Smith, Dict. Antiq.

EMPRESTITO. In Spanish law. A loan. Something lent to the borrower at his request. Las Partidas, pt. 3, tit. 18, 1. 70.

EMPTIO, EMPTION. The act of buying; a purchase.

EMPTIO BONORUM. Lat. In Roman law. A species of forced assignment for the benefit of creditors; being a public sale of an insolvent debtor's estate, whereby the purchaser succeeded to all his property, rights, and claims, and became responsible for his debts and liabilities to the extent of a quota fixed before the transfer. See Mackeld. Rom. Law, § 521.

EMPTIO ET VENDITIO. Lat. Purchase and sale; sometimes translated "emption and vendition." The name of the contract of sale in the Roman law. Inst. 3, 23; Bract. fol. 61b. Sometimes made a compound word,—*emptio-venditio.*

A consensual contract to deliver a thing for a certain price.

An agreement for the seller to part with a thing for money given to him by the buyer. 3 Salk. 61.

EMPTOR. A buyer or purchaser.

Emptor emit quam minimo potest, venditor vendit quam maximo potest. The buyer purchases for the lowest price he can; the seller sells for the highest price he can. 2 Kent, Comm. 486.

EMTIO. In the civil law. Purchase. This form of the word is used in the Digests and Code. Dig. 18, 1; Cod. 4, 49.

EMTOR. In the civil law. A buyer or purchaser; the buyer. Dig. 18, 1; Cod. 4, 49.

EMTRIX. In the civil law. A female purchaser; the purchaser. Cod. 4, 54, 1.

EN ARERE. L. Fr. In time past. 2 Inst. 506.

EN AUTRE DROIT. In the right of another. See AUTER DROIT.

EN BANKE. L. Fr. In the bench. 1 Anders. 51.

EN BREVET. In French law. An *acte* is said to be *en brevet* when a copy of it has not been recorded by the notary who drew it.

EN DECLARATION DE SIMULATION. A form of action used in Louisiana. Its object is to have a contract declared judicially a simulation and a nullity, to remove a cloud from the title, and to bring back, for any legal purpose, the thing sold to the estate of the true owner. 20 La. Ann. 169.

EN DEMEURE. In default. Used in Louisiana of a debtor who fails to pay on demand according to the terms of his obligation. See 3 Mart. (N. S.) 574.

En eschange il covient que les estates soient egales. Co. Litt. 50. In an exchange it is desirable that the estates be equal.

EN FAIT. Fr. In fact; in deed; actually.

EN GROS. Fr. In gross. Total; by wholesale.

EN JUICIO. Span. Judicially; in a court of law; in a suit at law. White, New Recop. b. 2, tit. 8, c. 1.

EN MASSE. Fr. In a mass; in a lump; at wholesale.

EN MORT MEYNE. L. Fr. In a dead hand; in mortmain. Britt. c. 43.

EN OWEL MAIN. L. Fr. In equal hand. The word "*owel*" occurs also in the phrase "*owelty* of partition."

EN RECOUVREMENT. Fr. In French law. An expression employed to denote that an indorsement made in favor of a person does not transfer to him the property in the bill of exchange, but merely constitutes an authority to such person to recover the amount of the bill. Arg. Fr. Merc. Law, 558.

EN ROUTE. Fr. On the way; in the course of a voyage or journey; in course of transportation.

EN VENTRE SA MERE. L. Fr. In its mother's womb. A term descriptive of an unborn child. For some purposes the law regards an infant *en ventre* as in being. It may take a legacy; have a guardian; an estate may be limited to its use, etc. 1 Bl. Comm. 130.

EN VIE. L. Fr. In life; alive. Britt. c. 50.

ENABLING POWER. When the donor of a power, who is the owner of the estate, confers upon persons not seised of the fee the right of creating interests to take effect out of it, which could not be done by the donee of the power unless by such authority, this is called an "enabling power." 2 Bouv. Inst. no. 1928.

ENABLING STATUTE. The act of 32 Henry VIII. c. 28, by which tenants in tail, husbands seised in right of their wives, and others, were empowered to make leases for their lives or for twenty-one years, which they could not do before. 2 Bl. Comm. 319; Co. Litt. 44*a*. The phrase is also applied to any statute enabling persons or corporations to do what before they could not.

ENACH. In Saxon law. The satisfaction for a crime; the recompense for a fault. Skene.

ENACT. To establish by law; to perform or effect; to decree. The usual introductory formula in making laws is, "*Be it enacted.*"

ENAJENACION. In Spanish and Mexican law. Alienation; transfer of property. The act by which the property in a thing, by lucrative title, is transferred, as a donation; or by onerous title, as by sale or barter. In a more extended sense, the term comprises also the contracts of emphyteusis, pledge, and mortgage, and even the creation of a servitude upon an estate. Escriche; 26 Cal. 88.

ENBREVER. L. Fr. To write down in short; to abbreviate, or, in old language, *imbreviate;* to put into a schedule. Britt. c. 1.

ENCAUSTUM. In the civil law. A kind of ink or writing fluid appropriate to the use of the emperor. Cod. 1, 23, 6.

ENCEINTE. Pregnant. See PREGNANCY.

ENCHESON. The occasion, cause, or reason for which anything is done. Termes de la Ley.

ENCLOSE. In the Scotch law. To shut up a jury after the case has been submitted to them. 2 Alis. Crim. Pr. 634. See INCLOSE.

ENCLOSURE. See INCLOSURE.

ENCOMIENDA. In Spanish law. A grant from the crown to a private person of a certain portion of territory in the Spanish colonies, together with the concession of a certain number of the native inhabitants, on the feudal principle of commendation. 2 Wools. Pol. Science, 161, 162. Also a royal grant of privileges to the military orders of Spain.

ENCOURAGE. In criminal law. To instigate; to incite to action; to give courage to; to inspirit; to embolden; to raise confidence; to make confident. 7 Q. B. Div. 258; 4 Burr. 2073. See AID.

ENCROACH. To gain unlawfully upon the lands, property, or authority of another; as if one man presses upon the grounds of another too far, or if a tenant owe two shillings rent-service, and the lord exact three. So, too, the Spencers were said to encroach the king's authority. Blount; Plowd. 94*a*.

In the law of easements. Where the owner of an easement alters the dominant tenement, so as to impose an additional restriction or burden on the servient tenement, he is said to commit an encroachment. Sweet.

ENCUMBER. See INCUMBER.

ENCUMBRANCE. See INCUMBRANCE.

END. Object; intent. Things are construed according to the end. Finch, Law, b. 1, c. 3, no. 10.

ENDENZIE, or ENDENIZEN. To make free; to enfranchise.

ENDORSE. See INDORSE.

ENDOWED SCHOOLS. In England, certain schools having endowments are distinctively known as "endowed schools;" and a series of acts of parliament regulating them are known as the "endowed schools acts." Mozley & Whitley.

ENDOWMENT. 1. The assignment of dower; the setting off a woman's dower. 2 Bl. Comm. 135.

2. In appropriations of churches, (in English law,) the setting off a sufficient maintenance for the vicar in perpetuity. 1 Bl. Comm. 387.

3. The act of settling a fund, or permanent pecuniary provision, for the maintenance of a public institution, charity, college, etc.

4. A fund settled upon a public institution, etc., for its maintenance or use.

The words "endowment" and "fund," in a statute exempting from taxation the real estate, the furniture and personal property, and the "endowment or fund" of religious and educational corporations, are *ejusdem generis*, and intended to comprehend a class of property different from the other two, not real estate or chattels. The difference between the words is that "fund" is a general term, including the endowment, while "endowment" means that particular fund, or part of the fund, of the institution, bestowed for its more permanent uses, and usually kept sacred for the purposes intended. The word "endowment" does not, in such an enactment, include real estate. 32 N. J. Law, 360.

ENDOWMENT POLICY In life insurance. A policy which is payable when the insured reaches a given age, or upon his decease, if that occurs earlier.

ENEMY, in public law, signifies either the nation which is at war with another, or a citizen or subject of such nation.

ENFEOFF. To invest with an estate by feoffment. To make a gift of any corporeal hereditaments to another. See FEOFFMENT.

ENFEOFFMENT. The act of investing with any dignity or possession; also the instrument or deed by which a person is invested with possessions.

ENFRANCHISE. To make free; to incorporate a man in a society or body politic.

ENFRANCHISEMENT. The act of making free; giving a franchise or freedom to; investiture with privileges or capacities of freedom, or municipal or political liberty. Admission to the freedom of a city; admission to political rights, and particularly the right of suffrage. Anciently, the acquisition of freedom by a villein from his lord.

The word is now used principally either of the manumission of slaves, (*q. v.,*) of giving to a borough or other constituency a right to return a member or members to parliament, or of the conversion of copyhold into freehold. Mozley & Whitley.

ENFRANCHISEMENT OF COPYHOLDS. In English law. The conversion of copyhold into freehold tenure, by a conveyance of the fee-simple of the property from the lord of the manor to the copyholder, or by a release from the lord of all seigniorial rights, etc., which destroys the customary descent, and also all rights and privileges annexed to the copyholder's estate. 1 Watk. Copyh. 362; 2 Steph. Comm. 51.

ENGAGEMENT. In French law. A contract. The obligation arising from a *quasi* contract.

The terms "obligation" and "engagement" are said to be synonymous, (17 Toullier, no. 1;) but the Code seems specially to apply the term "engagement" to those obligations which the law imposes on a man without the intervention of any contract, either on the part of the obligor or the obligee, (article 1370.) An engagement to do or omit to do something amounts to a promise. 21 N. J. Law, 369.

In English Practice. The term has been appropriated to denote a contract entered into by a married woman with the intention of binding or charging her separate estate, or, with stricter accuracy, a promise which in the case of a person *sui juris* would be a contract, but in the case of a married woman is not a contract, because she cannot bind herself personally, even in equity. Her engagements, therefore, merely operate as dispositions or appointments *pro tanto* of her separate estate. Sweet.

"ENGINE." This is said to be a word of very general signification; and, when used in an act, its meaning must be sought out from the act itself, and the language which surrounds it, and also from other acts *in pari materia*, in which it occurs. Abbott, J., 6 Maule & S. 192. In a large sense, it applies to all utensils and tools which afford the means of carrying on a trade. But in a more limited sense it means a thing of considerable dimensions, of a fixed or permanent nature, analogous to an erection or building. Id. 182.

ENGLESHIRE. A law was made by Canute, for the preservation of his Danes, that, when a man was killed, the hundred or town should be liable to be amerced, unless it could be proved that the person killed was an Englishman. This proof was called "*Engleshire.*" 1 Hale, P. C. 447; 4 Bl. Comm. 195; Spelman.

ENGLETERRE. England.

ENGLISH INFORMATION. In English law. A proceeding in the court of exchequer in matters of revenue.

"ENGLISH MARRIAGE." This phrase may refer to the place where the marriage is solemnized, or it may refer to the nationality and domicile of the parties between whom it is solemnized, the place where the union so created is to be enjoyed. 6 Prob. Div. 51.

ENGRAVE does not include the process of reproducing pictures by means of photography. 5 Blatchf. 325.

ENGROSS. To copy the rude draft of an instrument in a fair, large hand. To write out, in a large, fair hand, on parchment.

In old criminal law. To buy up so much of a commodity on the market as to obtain a monopoly and sell again at a forced price.

ENGROSSER. One who engrosses or writes on parchment in a large, fair hand.

One who purchases large quantities of any commodity in order to acquire a monopoly, and to sell them again at high prices.

ENGROSSING. In English law. The getting into one's possession, or buying up, large quantities of corn, or other dead victuals, with intent to sell them again. The total engrossing of any other commodity, with intent to sell it at an unreasonable price. 4 Bl. Comm. 158, 159. This was a misdemeanor, punishable by fine and imprisonment. Steph. Crim. Law, 95. Now repealed by 7 & 8 Vict. c. 24. 4 Steph. Comm. 291, note.

ENHANCED. This word, taken in an unqualified sense, is synonymous with "increased," and comprehends any increase of value, however caused or arising. 32 Fed. Rep. 812.

ENITIA PARS. The share of the eldest. A term of the English law descriptive of the lot or share chosen by the eldest of coparceners when they make a voluntary partition. The first choice (*primer election*) belongs to the eldest. Co. Litt. 166.

Enitia pars semper præferenda est propter privilegium ætatis. Co. Litt. 166. The part of the elder sister is always to be preferred on account of the privilege of age.

ENJOIN. To require; command; positively direct. To require a person, by writ of injunction from a court of equity, to perform, or to abstain or desist from, some act.

ENJOYMENT. The exercise of a right; the possession and fruition of a right, privilege, or incorporeal hereditament.

ENLARGE. To make larger; to increase; to extend a time limit; to grant further time. Also to set at liberty one who has been imprisoned or in custody.

ENLARGER L'ESTATE. A species of release which inures by way of enlarging an estate, and consists of a conveyance of the ulterior interest to the particular tenant; as if there be tenant for life or years, remainder to another in fee, and he in remainder releases all his right to the particular tenant and his heirs, this gives him the estate in fee. 1 Steph. Comm. 518.

ENLARGING. Extending, or making more comprehensive; as an enlarging statute, which is one extending the common law.

ENLARGING STATUTE. A remedial statute which enlarges or extends the common law. 1 Bl. Comm. 86, 87.

ENLISTMENT. The act of one who voluntarily enters the military or naval service of the government, contracting to serve in a subordinate capacity.

The words "enlist" and "enlistment," in law, as in common usage, may signify either the complete fact of entering into the military service, or the first step taken by the recruit towards that end. When used in the former sense, as in statutes conferring a right to compel the military service of enlisted men, the enlistment is not deemed completed until the man has been mustered into the service. 8 Allen, 480.

Enlistment does not include the entry of a person into the military service under a commission as an officer. 48 N. H. 280.

Enlisted applies to a drafted man as well as a volunteer, whose name is duly entered on the military rolls. 107 Mass. 282.

ENORMIA. In old practice and pleading. Unlawful or wrongful acts; wrongs. *Et alia enormia,* and other wrongs. This phrase constantly occurs in the old writs and declarations of trespass.

ENORMOUS. Aggravated. "So enormous a trespass." Vaughan, 115. Written "enormious," in some of the old books. *Enormious* is where a thing is made without a rule or against law. Brownl. pt. 2, p. 19.

ENPLEET. Anciently used for implead. Cowell.

ENQUÊTE, or ENQUEST. In canon law. An examination of witnesses, taken down in writing, by or before an authorized judge, for the purpose of gathering testimony to be used on a trial.

ENRÉGISTREMENT. In French law. Registration. A formality which consists in inscribing on a register, specially kept for the purpose by the government, a summary analysis of certain deeds and documents. At the same time that such analysis is inscribed upon the register, the clerk places upon the deed a memorandum indicating the date upon which it was registered, and at the side of such memorandum an impression is made with a stamp. Arg. Fr. Merc. Law, 558.

ENROLL. To register; to make a record; to enter on the rolls of a court; to transcribe.

ENROLLMENT. In English law. The registering or entering on the rolls of chancery, king's bench, common pleas, or exchequer, or by the clerk of the peace in the records of the quarter sessions, of any lawful act; as a recognizance, a deed of bargain and sale, and the like. Jacob.

ENROLLMENT OF VESSELS. In the laws of the United States on the subject of merchant shipping, the recording and certification of vessels employed in coastwise or inland navigation; as distinguished from the "registration" of vessels employed in foreign commerce. 3 Wall. 566.

ENS LEGIS. L. Lat. A creature of the law; an artificial being, as contrasted with a natural person. Applied to corporations, considered as deriving their existence entirely from the law.

ENSCHEDULE. To insert in a list, account, or writing.

ENSEAL. To seal. *Ensealing* is still used as a formal word in conveyancing.

ENSERVER. L. Fr. To make subject to a service or servitude. Britt. c. 54.

ENTAIL, *v.* To settle or limit the succession to real property; to create an estate tail.

ENTAIL, *n.* A fee abridged or limited to the issue, or certain classes of issue, instead of descending to all the heirs. 1 Washb. Real Prop. 66; Cowell; 2 Bl. Comm. 112, note.

Entail, in legal treatises, is used to signify an estate tail, especially with reference to the restraint which such an estate imposes upon its owner, or, in other words, the points wherein such an estate differs from an estate in fee-simple. And this is often its popular sense; but sometimes it is, in popular language, used differently, so as to signify a succession of life-estates, as when it is said that "an entail ends with A.," meaning that A. is the first person who is entitled to bar or cut off the entail, being in law the first tenant in tail. Mozley & Whitley.

ENTAILED. Settled or limited to specified heirs, or in tail.

ENTAILED MONEY. Money directed to be invested in realty to be entailed. 3 & 4 Wm. IV. c. 74, §§ 70, 71, 72.

ENTENCION. In old English law. The plaintiff's count or declaration.

ENTENDMENT. The old form of *intendment,* (*q. v.,*) derived directly from the French, and used to denote the true meaning or signification of a word or sentence; that is, the understanding or construction of law. Cowell.

ENTER. In the law of real property. To go upon land for the purpose of taking possession of it. In strict usage, the entering is preliminary to the taking possession, but in common parlance the entry is now merged in the taking possession.

In practice. To place anything before a court, or upon or among the records, in a formal and regular manner, and usually in writing; as to "enter an appearance," to "enter a judgment." In this sense the word is nearly equivalent to setting down formally in writing, in either a full or abridged form.

ENTERCEUR. L. Fr. A party challenging (claiming) goods; he who has placed them in the hands of a third person. Kelham.

ENTERING JUDGMENTS. The formal entry of the judgment on the rolls of the court, which is necessary before bringing an appeal or an action on the judgment.

ENTERING SHORT. When bills not due are paid into a bank by a customer, it is the custom of some bankers not to carry the amount of the bills directly to his credit, but to "enter them short," as it is called, *i. e.,* to note down the receipt of the bills, their amounts, and the times when they become due in a previous column of the page, and the amounts when received are carried forward into the usual cash column. Sometimes, instead of entering such bills short, bankers credit the customer directly with the amount of the bills as cash, charging interest on any advances they may make on their account, and allow him at once to draw upon them to that amount. If the banker becomes bankrupt, the property in bills entered short does not pass to his assignees, but the customer is entitled to them if they remain in his hands, or to their proceeds, if received, subject to any lien the banker may have upon them. Wharton.

ENTERTAINMENT. This word is synonymous with "board," and includes the ordinary necessaries of life. 2 Miles, 323.

ENTICE. To solicit, persuade, or procure. 12 Abb. Pr. (N. S.) 187.

ENTIRE. Whole; without division, separation, or diminution.

ENTIRE CONTRACT. Where a contract consists of many parts, which may be considered as parts of one whole, the contract is entire. When the parts may be considered as so many distinct contracts, entered into at one time, and expressed in the same instrument, but not thereby made one contract, the contract is a separable contract. But, if the consideration of the contract is single and entire, the contract must be held to be entire, although the subject of the contract may consist of several distinct and wholly independent items. 2 Pars. Cont. 517.

ENTIRE DAY. This phrase signifies an undivided day, not parts of two days. An entire day must have a legal, fixed, precise time to begin, and a fixed, precise time to end. A day, in contemplation of law, comprises all the twenty-four hours, beginning and ending at twelve o'clock at night. 43 Ala. 325.

In a statute requiring the closing of all liquor saloons during "the entire day of any election," etc., this phrase means the natural day of twenty-four hours, commencing and terminating at midnight. 7 Tex. App. 30; Id. 192.

ENTIRE INTEREST. The whole interest or right, without diminution. Where a person in selling his tract of land sells also his entire interest in all improvements upon public land adjacent thereto, this vests in the purchaser only a quitclaim of his interest in the improvements. 13 La. Ann. 410.

ENTIRE TENANCY. A sole possession by one person, called "severalty," which is contrary to several tenancy, where a joint or common possession is in one or more.

ENTIRE USE, BENEFIT, ETC. These words in the *habendum* of a trust-deed for the benefit of a married woman are equivalent to the words "sole use," or "sole and separate use," and consequently her husband takes nothing under such deed. 3 Ired. Eq. 414.

ENTIRETY. The whole, in contradistinction to a moiety or part only. When land is conveyed to husband and wife, they do not take by moieties, but both are seised of the *entirety*. 2 Kent, Comm. 132; 4 Kent, Comm. 362. Parceners, on the other hand, have not an *entirety* of interest, but each is properly entitled to the whole of a distinct moiety. 2 Bl. Comm. 188.

The word is also used to designate that which the law considers as one whole, and not capable of being divided into parts. Thus, a judgment, it is held, is an *entirety*, and, if void as to one of the two defendants, cannot be valid as to the other. So, if a contract is an *entirety*, no part of the consideration is due until the whole has been performed.

ENTITLE. In its usual sense, to entitle is to give a right or title. Therefore a person is said to be entitled to property when he has a right to it.

In ecclesiastical law. To entitle is to give a title or ordination as a minister.

ENTREBAT. L. Fr. An intruder or interloper. Britt. c. 114.

ENTREGA. Span. Delivery. Las Partidas, pt. 6, tit. 14, l. 1.

ENTREPOT. A warehouse or magazine for the deposit of goods. In France, a building or place where goods from abroad may be deposited, and from whence they may be withdrawn for exportation to another country, without paying a duty. Brande; Webster.

ENTRY. 1. In real property law. Entry is the act of going peaceably upon a piece of land which is claimed as one's own, but which is held by another person, with the intention and for the purpose of taking possession of the same.

Entry is a remedy which the law affords to an injured party ousted of his lands by another person who has taken possession thereof without right. This remedy (which must in all cases be pursued peaceably) takes place in three only out of the five species of ouster, viz., abatement, intrusion, and disseisin; for, as in these three cases the original entry of the wrong-doer is unlawful, so the wrong may be remedied by the mere entry of the former possessor. But it is otherwise upon a discontinuance or deforcement, for in these latter two cases the former possessor cannot remedy the wrong by entry, but must do so by action, inasmuch as the original entry being in these cases lawful, and therefore conferring an apparent right of possession, the law will not suffer such apparent right to be overthrown by the mere act or entry of the claimant. Brown.

An entry at common law is nothing more than an assertion of title by going on the land; or, if that was hazardous, by making continual claim. Anciently, an actual entry was required to be made and a lease executed on the land to sustain the action of ejectment; but now nothing of that kind is necessary. The entry and the lease, as well as the ouster, are fictions, and nothing is required but that the lessor should have the right to enter. A proceeding precisely analogous obtained in the civil law. 1 Ala. 660.

2. **In criminal law.** Entry is the unlawful making one's way into a dwelling or other house, for the purpose of committing a crime therein.

In cases of burglary, the least entry with the whole or any part of the body, hand, or foot, or with any instrument or weapon, introduced for the purpose of committing a felony, is sufficient to complete the offense. 3 Inst. 64.

Without reference to burglary, a breaking into a house or going upon lands with violence and circumstances of aggression is termed "forcible entry," and was a breach of the peace at common law. "Forcible entry and detainer" is made an offense by statute in many of the states.

3. **In practice.** Entry denotes the formal inscription upon the rolls or records of a court of a note or minute of any of the proceedings in an action; and it is frequently applied to the filing of a proceeding in writing, such as a notice of appearance by a defendant, and, very generally, to the filing of the judgment roll as a record in the office of the court.

4. **In commercial law.** Entry denotes the act of a merchant, trader, or other business man in recording in his account-books the facts and circumstances of a sale, loan, or other transaction. Also the note or record so made. The books in which such memoranda are first (or originally) inscribed are called "books of original entry," and are *prima facie* evidence for certain purposes.

5. **In revenue law.** The entry of imported goods at the custom house consists in submitting them to the inspection of the revenue officers, together with a statement or description of such goods, and the original

invoices of the same, for the purpose of estimating the duties to be paid thereon.

6. Under the provisions of the land laws of the United States, the term "entry" denotes the filing at the land-office, or inscription upon its records, of the documents required to found a claim for a homestead or pre-emption right, and as preliminary to the issuing of a patent for the land.

7. **In Scotch law.** The term refers to the acknowledgment of the title of the heir, etc., to be admitted by the superior.

ENTRY AD COMMUNEM LEGEM. Entry at common law. The name of a writ of entry which lay for a reversioner after the alienation and death of the particular tenant for life, against him who was in possession of the land. Brown.

ENTRY AD TERMINUM QUI PRÆTERIIT. The writ of entry *ad terminum qui præteriit* lies where a man leases land to another for a term of years, and the tenant holds over his term. And if lands be leased to a man for the term of another's life, and he for whose life the lands are leased dies, and the lessee holds over, then the lessor shall have this writ. Termes de la Ley.

ENTRY FOR MARRIAGE IN SPEECH. A writ of entry *causa matrimonii præloquuti* lies where lands or tenements are given to a man upon condition that he shall take the donor to be his wife within a certain time, and he does not espouse her within the said term, or espouses another woman, or makes himself priest. Termes de la Ley.

ENTRY IN CASU CONSIMILI. A writ of entry *in casu consimili* lies where a tenant for life or by the curtesy aliens in fee. Termes de la Ley.

ENTRY IN THE CASE PROVIDED. A writ of entry *in casu proviso* lies if a tenant in dower alien in fee, or for life, or for another's life, living the tenant in dower. Termes de la Ley.

ENTRY OF CAUSE FOR TRIAL. In English practice. The proceeding by a plaintiff in an action who had given notice of trial, depositing with the proper officer of the court the *nisi prius* record, with the panel of jurors annexed, and thus bringing the issue before the court for trial.

ENTRY ON THE ROLL. In former times, the parties to an action, personally or by their counsel, used to appear in open court and make their mutual statements *vivâ voce*, instead of as at the present day delivering their mutual pleadings, until they arrived at the issue or precise point in dispute between them. During the progress of this oral statement, a minute of the various proceedings was made on parchment by an officer of the court appointed for that purpose. The parchment then became the record; in other words, the official history of the suit. Long after the practice of oral pleading had fallen into disuse, it continued necessary to enter the proceedings in like manner upon the parchment roll, and this was called "entry on the roll," or making up the "issue roll." But by a rule of H. T. 4 Wm. IV., the practice of making up the issue roll was abolished; and it was only necessary to make up the issue in the form prescribed for the purpose by a rule of H. T. 1853, and to deliver the same to the court and to the opposite party. The issue which was delivered to the court was called the "*nisi prius record;*" and that was regarded as the official history of the suit, in like manner as the issue roll formerly was. Under the present practice, the issue roll or *nisi prius record* consists of the papers delivered to the court, to facilitate the trial of the action, these papers consisting of the pleadings simply, with the notice of trial. Brown.

ENTRY WITHOUT ASSENT OF THE CHAPTER. A writ of entry *sine assensu capituli* lies where an abbot, prior, or such as hath covent or common seal, aliens lands or tenements of the right of his church, without the assent of the covent or chapter, and dies. Termes de la Ley.

ENTRY, WRIT OF. In old English practice. This was a writ made use of in a form of real action brought to recover the possession of lands from one who wrongfully withheld the same from the demandant.

Its object was to regain the *possession* of lands of which the demandant, or his ancestors, had been unjustly deprived by the tenant of the freehold, or those under whom he claimed, and hence it belonged to the *possessory* division of real actions. It decided nothing with respect to the *right of property*, but only restored the demandant to that situation in which he was (or by law ought to have been) before the dispossession committed. 3 Bl. Comm. 180.

It was usual to specify in such writs the degree or degrees within which the writ was brought, and it was said to be "in the *per*" or "in the *per and cui*," according as there had been one or two descents or alienations from the original wrongdoer. If more than two such transfers had intervened, the writ was said to be "in the *post*." See 3 Bl. Comm. 181.

Enumeratio infirmat regulam in casibus non enumeratis. Enumeration disaffirms the rule in cases not enumerated. Bac. Aph. 17.

Enumeratio unius est exclusio alterius. The specification of one thing is the exclusion of a different thing. A maxim more generally expressed in the form "*expressio unius est exclusio alterius,*" (*q. v.*)

ENUMERATORS. Persons appointed to collect census papers or schedules. 33 & 34 Vict. c. 108, § 4.

ENURE. To operate or take effect. To serve to the use, benefit, or advantage of a person. A release to the tenant for life *enures* to him in reversion; that is, it has the same effect for him as for the tenant for life. Often written "inure."

ENVOY. In international law. A public minister of the second class, ranking next after an ambassador.

Envoys are either ordinary or extraordinary; by custom the latter is held in greater consideration.

EO INSTANTE. At that instant; at the very or same instant; immediately. 1 Bl. Comm. 196, 249; 2 Bl. Comm. 168; Co. Litt. 298*a;* 1 Coke, 138.

EO INTUITU. With or in that view; with that intent or object. Hale, Anal. § 2.

EO LOCI. In the civil law. In that state or condition; in that place, (*eo loco*.) Calvin.

EO NOMINE. Under that name; by that appellation. *Perinde ac si eo nomine tibi tradita fuisset,* just as if it had been delivered to you by that name. Inst. 2, 1, 43. A common phrase in the books.

Eodem ligamine quo ligatum est dissolvitur. A bond is released by the same formalities with which it is contracted. Co. Litt. 212*b;* Broom, Max. 891.

Eodem modo quo quid constituitur, dissolvitur. In the manner in which [by the same means by which] a thing is constituted, is it dissolved. 6 Coke, 53*b.*

EORLE. In Saxon law. An earl.

EOTH. In Saxon law. An oath.

EPIDEMIC. This term, in its ordinary and popular meaning, applies to *any* disease which is widely spread or generally prevailing at a given place and time. 36 N. Y. Super. Ct. 234.

EPILEPSY. In medical jurisprudence. A disease of the brain, which occurs in paroxysms with uncertain intervals between them.

EPIMENIA. Expenses or gifts. Blount.

EPIPHANY. A Christian festival, otherwise called the "Manifestation of Christ to the Gentiles," observed on the 6th of January, in honor of the appearance of the star to the three *magi*, or wise men, who came to adore the Messiah, and bring him presents. It is commonly called "Twelfth Day." Enc. Lond.

EPIQUEYA. In Spanish law. A term synonymous with "equity" in one of its senses, and defined as "the benignant and prudent interpretation of the law according to the circumstances of the time, place, and person."

EPISCOPACY. The office of overlooking or overseeing; the office of a bishop, who is to overlook and oversee the concerns of the church. A form of church government by diocesan bishops.

EPISCOPALIA. In ecclesiastical law. Synodals, pentecostals, and other customary payments from the clergy to their diocesan bishop, formerly collected by the rural deans. Cowell.

EPISCOPALIAN. Of or pertaining to episcopacy, or to the Episcopal Church.

EPISCOPATE. A bishopric. The dignity or office of a bishop.

EPISCOPUS. In the civil law. An overseer; an inspector. A municipal officer who had the charge and oversight of the bread and other provisions which served the citizens for their daily food. Vicat.

In medieval history. A bishop; a bishop of the Christian church.

Episcopus alterius mandato quam regis non tenetur obtemperare. Co. Litt. 134. A bishop needs not obey any mandate save the king's.

EPISCOPUS PUERORUM. It was an old custom that upon certain feasts some lay person should plait his hair, and put on the garments of a bishop, and in them pretend to exercise episcopal jurisdiction, and do several ludicrous actions, for which reason he was called "bishop of the boys;" and this custom obtained in England long after several constitutions were made to abolish it. Blount.

Episcopus teneat placitum, in curia christianitatis, de iis quæ mere sunt spiritualia. 12 Coke, 44. A bishop may hold plea in a Court Christian of things merely spiritual.

EPISTOLA. A letter; a charter; an instrument in writing for conveyance of lands or assurance of contracts. Calvin; Spelman.

EPISTOLÆ. In the civil law. Rescripts; opinions given by the emperors in cases submitted to them for decision.

Answers of the emperors to petitions.

The answers of counsellors, (*juris-consulti*,) as Ulpian and others, to questions of law proposed to them, were also called "*epistolæ*."

Opinions written out. The term originally signified the same as *literæ*. Vicat.

EPOCH. The time at which a new computation is begun; the time whence dates are numbered. Enc. Lond.

EQUALITY. The condition of possessing the same rights, privileges, and immunities, and being liable to the same duties.

Equality is equity. Fran. Max. 9, max. 3. Thus, where an heir buys in an incumbrance for less than is due upon it, (except it be to protect an incumbrance to which he himself is entitled,) he shall be allowed no more than what he really paid for it, as against other incumbrancers upon the estate. 2 Vent. 353; 1 Vern. 49; 1 Salk. 155.

EQUERRY. An officer of state under the master of the horse.

EQUES. Lat. In Roman and old English law. A knight.

EQUILOCUS. An equal. It is mentioned in Simeon Dunelm, A. D. 882. Jacob.

EQUINOXES. The two periods of the year (vernal equinox about March 21st, and autumnal equinox about September 22d) when the time from the rising of the sun to its setting is equal to the time from its setting to its rising. See Dig. 43, 13, 1, 8.

EQUITABLE. Just; conformable to the principles of natural justice and right.

Just, fair, and right, in consideration of the facts and circumstances of the individual case.

Existing in equity; available or sustainable only in equity, or only upon the rules and principles of equity.

EQUITABLE ASSETS. Equitable assets are all assets which are chargeable with the payment of debts or legacies in equity, and which do not fall under the description of legal assets. 1 Story, Eq. Jur. § 552.

Those portions of the property which by the ordinary rules of law are exempt from debts, but which the testator has voluntarily charged as assets, or which, being non-existent at law, have been created in equity. Adams, Eq. 254, et seq.

They are so called because they can be reached only by the aid and instrumentality of a court of equity, and because their distribution is governed by a different rule from that which governs the distribution of legal assets. 2 Fonbl. Eq. b. 4, pt. 2, c. 2, § 1, and notes; Story, Eq. Jur. § 552.

EQUITABLE ASSIGNMENT. An assignment which, though invalid at law, will be recognized and enforced in equity; e. g., an assignment of a chose in action, or of future acquisitions of the assignor.

EQUITABLE CONSTRUCTION. A construction of a law, rule, or remedy which has regard more to the equities of the particular transaction or state of affairs involved than to the strict application of the rule or remedy; that is, a liberal and extensive construction, as opposed to a literal and restrictive.

EQUITABLE CONVERSION. The transformation, by a doctrine of equity, of personalty into realty, in respect to its qualities and disposition, and of real estate into personalty. By this doctrine, money which, by will or agreement, is to be invested in land, is considered and treated as realty, and land which is to be turned into money is considered and treated as money. 8 Wall. 214; 45 Pa. St. 87; 61 Wis. 477, 21 N. W. Rep. 615.

EQUITABLE DEFENSE. In English practice. A defense to an action on grounds which, prior to the passing of the common-law procedure act, (17 & 18 Vict. c. 125,) would have been cognizable only in a court of equity. Mozley & Whitley.

In American practice. A defense which is available only in equity, except under the reformed codes of practice, where it may be interposed in a legal action.

EQUITABLE ESTATE. An equitable estate is an estate an interest in which can only be enforced in a court of chancery. 9 Ohio, 145.

That is properly an equitable estate or interest for which a court of equity affords the only remedy; and of this nature, especially, is the benefit of every trust, express or implied, which is not converted into a legal estate by the statute of uses. The rest are equities of redemption, constructive trusts, and all equitable charges. Burt. Comp. c. 8.

EQUITABLE MORTGAGE. A mortgage arising in equity, out of the transactions of the parties, without any deed or express contract for that special purpose. 4 Kent, Comm. 150.

A lien upon realty, which is of such a character that a court of equity will recognize it as a security for the payment of money loaned or due. 2 Story, Eq. Jur. § 1018.

A mortgage upon a purely equitable estate or interest.

In English law. The following mortgages are equitable: (1) Where the subject of a mortgage is trust property, which security is effected either by a formal deed or a written memorandum, notice being given to the trustees in order to preserve the priority. (2) Where it is an equity of redemption, which is merely a right to bring an action in the chancery division to redeem the estate. (3) Where there is a written agreement only to make a mortgage, which creates an equitable lien on the land. (4) Where a debtor deposits the title-deeds of his estate with his creditor or some person on his behalf, without even a verbal communication. The deposit itself is deemed evidence of an executed agreement or contract for a mortgage for such estate. Wharton.

EQUITABLE WASTE. Injury to a reversion or remainder in real estate, which is not recognized by the courts of law as waste, but which equity will interpose to prevent or remedy.

EQUITATURA. In old English law. Traveling furniture, or riding equipments, including horses, horse harness, etc. Reg. Orig. 100b; St. Westm. 2, c. 39.

EQUITY. 1. In its broadest and most general signification, this term denotes the spirit and the habit of fairness, justness, and right dealing which should regulate the intercourse of men with men,—the rule of doing to all others as we desire them to do to us; or, as it is expressed by Justinian, "to live honestly, to harm nobody, to render to every man his due." Inst. 1, 1, 3. It is therefore the synonym of natural right or justice. But in this sense its obligation is ethical rather than jural, and its discussion belongs to the sphere of morals. It is grounded in the precepts of the conscience, not in any sanction of positive law.

2. In a more restricted sense, the word denotes equal and impartial justice as between two persons whose rights or claims are in conflict; justice, that is, as ascertained by natural reason or ethical insight, but independent of the formulated body of law. This is not a technical meaning of the term, except in so far as courts which administer equity seek to discover it by the agencies above mentioned, or apply it beyond the strict lines of positive law.

3. In one of its technical meanings, equity is a body of jurisprudence, or field of jurisdiction, differing in its origin, theory, and methods from the common law.

It is a body of rules existing by the side of the original civil law, founded on distinct principles, and claiming incidentally to supersede the civil law in virtue of a superior sanctity inherent in those principles. Maine, Anc. Law, 27.

"As old rules become too narrow, or are felt to be out of harmony with advancing civilization, a machinery is needed for their gradual enlargement and adaptation to new views of society. One mode of accomplishing this object on a large scale, without appearing to disregard existing law, is the introduction, by the prerogative of some high functionary, of a more perfect body of rules, discoverable in his judicial conscience, which is to stand side by side with the law of the land, overriding it in case of conflict, as on some title of inherent superiority, but not purporting to repeal it. Such a body of rules has been called 'Equity.'" Holl. Jur. 59.

"Equity," in its technical sense, contradistinguished from natural and universal equity or justice, may well be described as a "portion of justice" or natural equity, not embodied in legislative enactments, or in the rules of common law, yet modified by a due regard thereto and to the complex relations and conveniences of an artificial state of society, and administered in regard to cases where the particular rights, in respect of which relief is sought, come within some general class of rights enforced at law, or may be enforced without detriment or inconvenience to the community; but where, as to such particular rights, the ordinary courts of law cannot, or originally did not, clearly afford relief. Rob. Eq.

4. In a still more restricted sense, it is a system of jurisprudence, or branch of remedial justice, administered by certain tribunals, distinct from the common-law courts, and empowered to decree "equity" in the sense last above given. Here it becomes a complex of well-settled and well-understood rules, principles, and precedents.

"The meaning of the word 'equity,' as used in its technical sense in English jurisprudence, comes back to this: that it is simply a term descriptive of a certain field of jurisdiction exercised, in the English system, by certain courts, and of which the extent and boundaries are not marked by lines founded upon principle so much as by the features of the original constitution of the English scheme of remedial law, and the accidents of its development." Bisp. Eq. § 11.

A system of jurisprudence collateral to, and in some respects independent of, "law," properly so called; the object of which is to render the administration of justice more complete, by affording relief where the courts of law are incompetent to give it, or to give it with effect, or by exercising certain branches of jurisdiction independently of them. This is equity in its proper modern sense; an elaborate system of rules and process, administered in many cases by distinct tribunals, (termed "courts of chancery,") and with exclusive jurisdiction over certain subjects. It is "still distinguished by its original and animating principle that no right should be without an adequate remedy," and its doctrines are founded upon the same basis of natural justice; but its action has become systematized, deprived of any loose and arbitrary character which might once have belonged to it, and as carefully regulated by fixed rules and precedents as the law itself. Burrill.

Equity, in its technical and scientific legal use, means neither natural justice nor even all that portion of natural justice which is susceptible of being judicially enforced. It has a precise, limited, and definite signification, and is used to denote a system of justice which was administered in a particular court,—the English high court of chancery, —which system can only be understood and explained by studying the history of that court, and how it came to exercise what is known as its extraordinary jurisdiction. Bisp. Eq. § 1.

That part of the law which, having power to enforce discovery, (1) administers trusts, mortgages, and other fiduciary obligations; (2) administers and adjusts common-law rights where the courts of common law have no machinery; (3) supplies a specific and preventive remedy for common-law wrongs where courts of common law only give subsequent damages. Chute, Eq. 4.

Equity is not the chancellor's sense of moral right, or his sense of what is equal and just, but is a complex system of established law; and an equitable maxim—as equality is equity—can only be applied according to established rules. 23 Me. 360.

5. Equity also signifies an equitable right, i. e., a right enforceable in a court of equity; hence, a bill of complaint which did not show that the plaintiff had a right entitling him to relief was said to be demurrable for want of equity; and certain rights now recognized in all the courts are still known as "equities," from having been originally recognized only in the court of chancery. Sweet.

EQUITY, COURTS OF. Courts which administer justice according to the system of equity, and according to a peculiar course of procedure or practice. See EQUITY. Frequently termed "courts of chancery." See 1 Bl. Comm. 92.

Equity delights to do justice, and that not by halves. 5 Barb. 277, 280; Story, Eq. Pl. § 72.

Equity follows the law. Talb. 52. Equity adopts and follows the rules of law in all cases to which those rules may, in terms, be applicable. Equity, in dealing with cases of an equitable nature, adopts and follows the analogies furnished by the rules of law. A leading maxim of equity jurisprudence, which, however, is not of universal application, but liable to many exceptions. Story, Eq. Jur. § 64.

Equity looks upon that as done which ought to have been done. 1 Story, Eq. Jur. § 64g. Equity will treat the subject-matter, as to collateral consequences and incidents, in the same manner as if the final acts contemplated by the parties had been executed exactly as they ought to have been; not as the parties might have executed them. Id.

EQUITY OF A STATUTE. By this phrase is intended the rule of statutory construction which admits within the operation of a statute a class of cases which are neither expressly named nor excluded, but which, from their analogy to the cases that are named, are clearly and justly within the spirit and general meaning of the law; such cases are said to be "within the equity of the statute."

EQUITY OF REDEMPTION. The right of the mortgagor of an estate to redeem the same after it has been forfeited, at law, by a breach of the condition of the mortgage, upon paying the amount of debt, interest, and costs.

Equity suffers not a right without a remedy. 4 Bouv. Inst. no. 3726.

EQUITY TO A SETTLEMENT. The equitable right of a wife, when her husband sues in equity for the reduction of her equitable estate to his own possession, to have the whole or a portion of such estate settled upon herself and her children. Also a similar right now recognized by the equity courts as directly to be asserted against the husband. Also called the "wife's equity."

EQUIVALENT. In patent law. The term "equivalent," when used of machines, has a certain definite meaning; but, when used with regard to the chemical actions of such fluids as can be discovered only by experiment, it means equally good. 7 Wall. 327.

EQUIVOCAL. Having a double or several meanings or senses. See AMBIGUITY.

EQUULEUS. A kind of rack for extorting confessions.

EQUUS COOPERTUS. A horse equipped with saddle and furniture.

ERABILIS. A maple tree. Not to be confounded with *arabilis*, (arable land.)

ERASTIANS. The followers of Erastus. The sect obtained much influence in England, particularly among common lawyers in the time of Selden. They held that offenses against religion and morality should be punished by the civil power, and not by the censures of the church or by excommunication. Wharton.

ERASURE. The obliteration of words or marks from a written instrument by rubbing, scraping, or scratching them out. Also the place in a document where a word or words have been so removed. The term is sometimes used for the removal of parts of a writing by any means whatever, as by cancellation; but this is not an accurate use.

ERCISCUNDUS. In the civil law. To be divided. *Judicium familiæ erciscundæ,* a suit for the partition of an inheritance. Inst. 4, 17, 4. An ancient phrase derived from the Twelve Tables. Calvin.

"ERECT." One of the formal words of incorporation in royal charters. "We do, incorporate, *erect*, ordain, name, constitute, and establish."

ERECTION. Raising up; building; a completed building. In a statute on the "erection" of wooden buildings, this term does not include repairing, alteration, enlarging, or removal. See 45 N. Y. 153; 27 Conn. 332; 2 Rawle, 262; 119 Mass. 254; 51 Ill. 422.

ERGO. Lat. Therefore; hence; because.

ERGOLABI. In the civil law. Undertakers of work; contractors. Cod. 4, 59.

ERIACH. A term of the Irish Brehon law, denoting a pecuniary mulct or recompense which a murderer was judicially condemned to pay to the family or relatives of his victim. It corresponded to the Saxon "weregild." See 4 Bl. Comm. 313.

F

G

H

I

J

K

L

M

ERIGIMUS. We erect. One of the words by which a corporation may be created in England by the king's charter. 1 Bl. Comm. 473.

ERMINE. By metonymy, this term is used to describe the office or functions of a judge, whose state robe, lined with ermine, is emblematical of purity and honor without stain. Webster.

ERNES. In old English law. The loose scattered ears of corn that are left on the ground after the binding.

EROSION. The gradual eating away of the soil by the operation of currents or tides. Distinguished from *submergence*, which is the disappearance of the soil under the water and the formation of a navigable body over it. 100 N. Y. 433, 3 N. E. Rep. 584.

EROTOMANIA. Sometimes also called "*Erotico-Mania*," a disease of the brain on sexual subjects. The distinction between it and *nymphomania* is that in the latter, although the condition of mind is similar, the disease is caused by a local disorder of the sexual organs reacting on the brain. Wharton.

ERRANT. Wandering; itinerant; applied to justices on circuit, and bailiffs at large, etc.

ERRATICUM. In old law. A waif or stray; a wandering beast. Cowell.

ERRONEOUS. Involving error; deviating from the law. This term is never used by courts or law-writers as designating a corrupt or evil act. 72 Ind. 338.

ERRONICE. Lat. Erroneously; through error or mistake.

ERROR. A mistaken judgment or incorrect belief as to the existence or effect of matters of fact, or a false or mistaken conception or application of the law.

Such a mistaken or false conception or application of the law to the facts of a cause as will furnish ground for a review of the proceedings upon a writ of error; a mistake of law, or false or irregular application of it, such as vitiates the proceedings and warrants the reversal of the judgment.

Error is also used as an elliptical expression for "writ of error;" as in saying that *error* lies; that a judgment may be reversed *on error*.

ERROR, WRIT OF. See WRIT OF ERROR.

Error fucatus nuda veritate in multis est probabilior; et sæpenumero rationibus vincit veritatem error. Error artfully disguised [or colored] is, in many instances, more probable than naked truth; and frequently error overwhelms truth by [its show of] reasons. 2 Coke, 73.

Error juris nocet. Error of law injures. A mistake of the law has an injurious effect; that is, the party committing it must suffer the consequences. Mackeld. Rom. Law, § 178; 1 Story, Eq. Jur. § 139, note.

ERROR NOMINIS. Error of name. A mistake of detail in the name of a person; used in contradistinction to error *de personâ*, a mistake as to identity.

Error nominis nunquam nocet, si de identitate rei constat. A mistake in the name of a thing is never prejudicial, if it be clear as to the identity of the thing itself, [where the thing intended is certainly known.] 1 Duer, Ins. 171. This maxim is applicable only where the means of correcting the mistake are apparent on the face of the instrument to be construed. Id.

ERROR OF FACT. That is called "error of fact" which proceeds either from ignorance of that which really exists or from a mistaken belief in the existence of that which has none. Civil Code La. art. 1821.

ERROR OF LAW. He is under an error of law who is truly informed of the existence of facts, but who draws from them erroneous conclusions of law. Civil Code La. art. 1822.

Error qui non resistitur approbatur. An error which is not resisted or opposed is approved. Doct. & Stud. c. 40.

Errores ad sua principia referre, est refellere. To refer errors to their sources is to refute them. 3 Inst. 15. To bring errors to their beginning is to see their last.

Errores scribentis nocere non debent. The mistakes of the writer ought not to harm. Jenk. Cent. 324.

ERRORS EXCEPTED. A phrase appended to an account stated, in order to excuse slight mistakes or oversights.

ERTHMIOTUM. In old English law. A meeting of the neighborhood to compromise differences among themselves; a court held on the boundary of two lands.

Erubescit lex filios castigare parentes. 8 Coke, 116. The law blushes when children correct their parents.

ESBRANCATURA. In old law. A cutting off the branches or boughs of trees. Cowell; Spelman.

ESCALDARE. To scald. It is said that to *scald hogs* was one of the ancient tenures in serjeanty. Wharton.

ESCAMBIO. In old English law. A writ of exchange. A license in the shape of a writ, formerly granted to an English merchant to draw a bill of exchange on another in foreign parts. Reg. Orig. 194.

ESCAMBIUM. An old English law term, signifying exchange.

ESCAPE. The departure or deliverance out of custody of a person who was lawfully imprisoned, before he is entitled to his liberty by the process of law.

The voluntarily or negligently allowing any person lawfully in confinement to leave the place. 2 Bish. Crim. Law, § 917.

Escapes are either *voluntary* or *negligent.* The former is the case when the keeper voluntarily concedes to the prisoner any liberty not authorized by law. The latter is the case when the prisoner contrives to leave his prison by forcing his way out, or any other means, without the knowledge or against the will of the keeper, but through the latter's carelessness or the insecurity of the building.

ESCAPE WARRANT. In English practice. This was a warrant granted to retake a prisoner committed to the custody of the queen's prison who had escaped therefrom. It was obtained on affidavit from the judge of the court in which the action had been brought, and was directed to all the sheriffs throughout England, commanding them to retake the prisoner and commit him to gaol when and where taken, there to remain until the debt was satisfied. Jacob; Brown.

ESCAPIO QUIETUS. In old English law. Delivered from that punishment which by the laws of the forest lay upon those whose beasts were found upon forbidden land. Jacob.

ESCAPIUM. That which comes by chance or accident. Cowell.

ESCEPPA. A measure of corn. Cowell.

Eschæta derivatur a verbo Gallico eschoir, quod est accidere, quia accidit domino ex eventu et ex insperato. Co. Litt. 93. Escheat is derived from the French word *"eschoir,"* which signifies to happen, because it falls to the lord from an event and from an unforeseen circumstance.

Eschætæ vulgo dicuntur quæ decidentibus iis quæ de rege tenent, cum non existit ratione sanguinis hæres, ad fiscum relabuntur. Co. Litt. 13. Those things are commonly called "escheats" which revert to the exchequer from a failure of issue in those who hold of the king, when there does not exist any heir by consanguinity.

ESCHEAT. In feudal law. Escheat is an obstruction of the course of descent, and consequent determination of the tenure, by some unforeseen contingency, in which case the land naturally results back, by a kind of reversion, to the original grantor, or lord of the fee. 2 Bl. Comm. 15.

It is the casual descent, in the nature of forfeiture, of lands and tenements within his manor, to a lord, either on failure of issue of the tenant dying seised or on account of the felony of such tenant. Jacob.

Also the land or fee itself, which thus fell back to the lord. Such lands were called *"excadentiæ,"* or *"terræ excadentiales."* Fleta, lib. 6, c. 1; Co. Litt. 13a.

In American law. Escheat signifies a reversion of property to the state in consequence of a want of any individual competent to inherit. The state is deemed to occupy the place and hold the rights of the feudal lord. See 4 Kent, Comm. 423, 424.

"Escheat at feudal law was the right of the lord of a fee to re-enter upon the same when it became vacant by the extinction of the blood of the tenant. This extinction might either be *per defectum sanguinis* or else *per delictum tenentis*, where the course of descent was broken by the corruption of the blood of the tenant. As a fee might be holden either of the crown or from some inferior lord, the escheat was not always to the crown. The word 'escheat,' in this country, at the present time, merely indicates the preferable right of the state to an estate left vacant, and without there being any one in existence able to make claim thereto." 29 Amer. Dec. 232, note.

ESCHEAT, WRIT OF. A writ which anciently lay for a lord, to recover possession of lands that had escheated to him. Reg. Orig. 164b; Fitzh. Nat. Brev. 143.

ESCHEATOR. In English law. The name of an officer who was appointed in every county to look after the escheats which fell due to the king in that particular county, and to certify the same into the exchequer. An escheator could continue in office for one year only, and was not re-eligible until three years. There does not appear to exist any such officer at the present day. Brown. See 10 Vin. Abr. 158; Co. Litt. 13b.

ESCHECCUM. In old English law. A jury or inquisition.

ESCHIPARE. To build or equip. Du Cange.

ESCOT. A tax formerly paid in boroughs and corporations towards the support of the community, which is called "scot and lot."

ESCRIBANO. In Spanish law. An officer, resembling a notary in French law, who has authority to set down in writing, and verify by his attestation, transactions and contracts between private persons, and also judicial acts and proceedings.

ESCRITURA. In Spanish law. A written instrument. Every deed that is made by the hand of a public *escribano,* or notary of a corporation or council (*concejo,*) or sealed with the seal of the king or other authorized persons. White, New Recop. b. 3, tit. 7, c. 5.

ESCROQUERIE. Fr. Fraud, swindling, cheating.

ESCROW. A scroll; a writing; a deed. Particularly a deed delivered by the grantor into the hands of a third person, to be held by the latter until the happening of a contingency or performance of a condition, and then by him delivered to the grantee.

A grant may be deposited by the grantor with a third person, to be delivered on the performance of a condition, and on delivery by the depositary it will take effect. While in the possession of the third person, and subject to condition, it is called an "escrow." Civil Code Cal. § 1057; Civil Code Dak. § 609.

The state or condition of a deed which is conditionally held by a third person, or the possession and retention of a deed by a third person pending a condition; as when an instrument is said to be delivered "in escrow." This use of the term, however, is a perversion of its meaning.

ESCROWL. In old English law. An escrow; a scroll. "And deliver the deed to a stranger, as an escrowl." Perk. c. 1, § 9; Id. c. 2, §§ 137, 138.

ESCUAGE. Service of the shield. One of the varieties of tenure in knight's service,

the duty imposed being that of accompanying the king to the wars for forty days, at the tenant's own charge, or sending a substitute. In later times, this service was commuted for a certain payment in money, which was then called "escuage certain." See 2 Bl. Comm. 74, 75.

ESCURARE. To scour or cleanse. Cowell.

ESGLISE, or EGLISE. A church. Jacob.

ESKETORES. Robbers, or destroyers of other men's lands and fortunes. Cowell.

ESKIPPAMENTUM. Tackle or furniture; outfit. Certain towns in England were bound to furnish certain ships at their own expense and with double *skippage* or tackle. Cowell.

ESKIPPER, ESKIPPARE. To ship.

ESKIPPESON. Shippage, or passage by sea. Spelled, also, "*skippeson.*" Cowell.

ESLISORS. See ELISORS.

ESNE. In old law. A hireling of servile condition.

ESNECY. Seniority; the condition or right of the eldest; the privilege of the eldestborn. Particularly used of the privilege of the eldest among coparceners to make a first choice of purparts upon a voluntary partition.

ESPERA. A period of time fixed by law or by a court within which certain acts are to be performed, *e. g.,* the production of papers, payment of debts, etc.

ESPERONS. L. Fr. Spurs.

ESPLEES. An old term for the products which the ground or land yields; as the hay of the meadows, the herbage of the pasture, corn of arable fields, rent and services, etc. The word has been anciently applied to the land itself. Jacob.

ESPOUSALS. A mutual promise between a man and a woman to marry each other at some other time. It differs from a marriage, because then the contract is completed. Wood, Inst. 57.

ESPURIO. Span. In Spanish law. A spurious child; one begotten on a woman who has promiscuous intercourse with many men. White, New Recop. b. 1, tit. 5, c. 2, § 1.

ESQUIRE. In English law. A title of dignity next above gentleman, and below knight. Also a title of office given to sheriffs, serjeants, and barristers at law, justices of the peace, and others. 1 Bl. Comm. 406; 3 Steph. Comm. 15, note; Tomlins.

ESSARTER. L. Fr. To cut down woods, to clear land of trees and underwood; properly to thin woods, by cutting trees, etc., at intervals. Spelman.

ESSARTUM. Woodlands turned into tillage by uprooting the trees and removing the underwood.

ESSENCE. That which is indispensable to that of which it is the essence.

ESSENCE OF THE CONTRACT. Any condition or stipulation in a contract which is mutually understood and agreed by the parties to be of such vital importance that a sufficient performance of the contract cannot be had without exact compliance with it is said to be "of the essence of the contract."

ESSENDI QUIETUM DE TOLONIO. A writ to be quit of toll; it lies for citizens and burgesses of any city or town who, by charter or prescription, ought to be exempted from toll, where the same is exacted of them. Reg. Orig. 258.

ESSOIN, *v.* In old English practice. To present or offer an excuse for not appearing in court on an appointed day in obedience to a summons; to cast an essoin. Spelman. This was anciently done by a person whom the party sent for that purpose, called an "essoiner."

ESSOIN, *n.* In old English law. An excuse for not appearing in court at the return of the process. Presentation of such excuse. Spelman; 1 Sel. Pr. 4; Com. Dig. "Exoine," B 1. Essoin is not now allowed at all in personal actions. 2 Term 16; 16 East, 7*a;* 3 Bl. Comm. 278, note.

ESSOIN DAY. Formerly the first general return-day of the term, on which the courts sat to receive essoins, *i. e.*, excuses for parties who did not appear in court, according to the summons of writs. 3 Bl. Comm. 278; Boote, Suit at Law, 130; Gilb. Com. Pl. 13; 1 Tidd, Pr. 107. But, by St. 11 Geo. IV. and 1 Wm. IV. c. 70, § 6, these days were done away with, as a part of the term.

ESSOIN DE MALO VILLÆ is when the defendant is in court the first day; but gone without pleading, and being afterwards surprised by sickness, etc., cannot attend, but sends two essoiners, who openly protest in court that he is detained by sickness in such a village, that he cannot come *pro lucrari* and *pro perdere;* and this will be admitted, for it lieth on the plaintiff to prove whether the essoin is true or not. Jacob.

ESSOIN ROLL. A roll upon which essoins were formerly entered, together with the day to which they were adjourned. Boote, Suit at Law, 130; Rosc. Real Act. 162, 163; Gilb. Com. Pl. 13.

ESSOINIATOR. A person who made an essoin.

Est aliquid quod non oportet etiam si licet; quicquid vero non licet certe non oportet. Hob. 159. There is that which is not proper, even though permitted; but whatever is not permitted is certainly not proper.

EST ASCAVOIR. It is to be understood or known; "it is to-wit." Litt. §§ 9, 45, 46, 57, 59. A very common expression in Littleton, especially at the commencement of a section; and, according to Lord Coke, "it ever teacheth us some rule of law, or general or sure leading point." Co. Litt. 16.

Est autem jus publicum et privatum, quod ex naturalibus præceptis aut gentium, aut civilibus est collectum; et quod in jure scripto jus appellatur, id in lege Angliæ rectum esse dicitur. Public and private law is that which is collected from natural precepts, on the one hand of nations, on the other of citizens; and that which in the civil law is called *"jus,"* that, in the law of England, is said to be right. Co. Litt. 558.

Est autem vis legem simulans. Violence may also put on the mask of law.

Est ipsorum legislatorum tanquam viva vox. The voice of the legislators themselves is like the living voice; that is, the language of a statute is to be understood and interpreted like ordinary spoken language. 10 Coke, 101*b*.

Est quiddam perfectius in rebus licitis. Hob. 159. There is something more perfect in things allowed.

ESTABLISH. This word occurs frequently in the constitution of the United

States, and it is there used in different meanings: (1) To settle firmly, to fix unalterably; as to establish justice, which is the avowed object of the constitution. (2) To make or form; as to establish a uniform rule of naturalization, and uniform laws on the subject of bankruptcies, which evidently does not mean that these laws shall be unalterably established as justice. (3) To found, to create, to regulate; as: "Congress shall have power to establish post-roads and post-offices." (4) To found, recognize, confirm, or admit; as: "Congress shall make no law respecting an establishment of religion." (5) To create, to ratify, or confirm; as: "We, the people," etc., "do ordain and establish this constitution." 1 Story, Const. § 454.

Establish ordinarily means to settle certainly, or fix permanently, what was before uncertain, doubtful, or disputed. 49 N. H. 230.

ESTABLISHMENT. An ordinance or statute. Especially used of those ordinances or statutes passed in the reign of Edw. I. 2 Inst. 156; Britt. c. 21.

ESTABLISHMENT OF DOWER. The assurance of dower made by the husband, or his friends, before or at the time of the marriage. Britt. cc. 102, 103.

ESTACHE. A bridge or stank of stone or timber. Cowell.

ESTADAL. In Spanish law. In Spanish America this was a measure of land of sixteen square varas, or yards. 2 White, Recop. 139.

ESTADIA. In Spanish law. Delay in a voyage, or in the delivery of cargo, caused by the charterer or consignee, for which demurrage is payable.

ESTANDARD. L. Fr. A standard, (of weights and measures.) So called because it stands constant and immovable, and hath all other measures coming towards it for their conformity. Termes de la Ley.

ESTANQUES. Wears or kiddles in rivers.

ESTATE. 1. The interest which any one has in lands, or in any other subject of property. 1 Prest. Est. 20. An estate in lands, tenements, and hereditaments signifies such interest as the tenant has therein. 2 Bl. Comm. 103. The condition or circumstance in which the owner *stands* with regard to his property. 2 Crabb, Real Prop. p. 2, § 942. In this sense, "estate" is constantly used in conveyances in connection with the words

"right," "title," and "interest," and is, in a great degree, synonymous with all of them. See Co. Litt. 345.

"Estate in land" means the kind and quantum of one's interest therein. The term is susceptible of every possible variation in which man can be related to the soil. 2 Mass. 284.

"Estate" is a very comprehensive word, and signifies the quantity of interest which a person has, from absolute ownership down to naked possession; and the quantity of interest is determined by the duration and extent of the right of possession. 9 Cow. 78, 81.

2. In another sense, the term denotes the property (real or personal) in which one has a right or interest; the subject-matter of ownership; the *corpus* of property. Thus, we speak of a "valuable estate," "all my estate," "separate estate," "trust estate," etc. This, also, is its meaning in the classification of property into "real estate" and "personal estate."

The word "estate" is a word of the greatest extension, and comprehends every species of property, real and personal. It describes both the *corpus* and the extent of interest. 55 Me. 284.

"Estate" comprehends everything a man owns, real and personal, and ought not to be limited in its construction, unless connected with some other word which must necessarily have that effect. Cam. & N. 202.

It means, ordinarily, the whole of the property owned by any one, the realty as well as the personalty. Busb. Eq. 141.

3. In a wider sense, the term "estate" denotes a man's whole financial *status* or condition,—the aggregate of his interests and concerns, so far as regards his situation with reference to wealth or its objects, including debts and obligations, as well as possessions and rights.

Here not only property, but indebtedness, is part of the idea. The estate does not consist of the assets only. If it did, such expressions as "insolvent estate" would be misnomers. Debts and assets, taken together, constitute the estate. It is only by regarding the demands against the original proprietor as constituting, together with his resources available to defray them, one entirety, that the phraseology of the law governing what is called "settlement of estates" can be justified. Abbott.

4. The word is also used to denote the aggregate of a man's financial concerns (as above) *personified.* Thus, we speak of "debts due the estate," or say that "A.'s estate is a stockholder in the bank." In this sense it is a fictitious or juridical person, the idea being that a man's business *status* continues his existence, for its special purposes, until its final settlement and dissolution.

5. In its broadest sense, "estate" signifies the social, civic, or political condition or standing of a person; or a class of persons

considered as grouped for social, civic, or political purposes; as in the phrases, "the third estate," "the estates of the realm." See 1 Bl. Comm. 153.

"Estate" and "degree," when used in the sense of an individual's personal *status*, are synonymous, and indicate the individual's rank in life. 15 Me. 122.

ESTATE AD REMANENTIAM. An estate in fee-simple. Glan. l. 7, c. 1.

ESTATE AT SUFFERANCE. The interest of a tenant who has come rightfully into possession of lands by permission of the owner, and continues to occupy the same after the period for which he is entitled to hold by such permission. 1 Washb. Real Prop. 392; 2 Bl. Comm. 150; Co. Litt. 57*b*.

ESTATE AT WILL. A species of estate less than freehold, where lands and tenements are let by one man to another, to have and to hold at the will of the lessor; and the tenant by force of this lease obtains possession. 2 Bl. Comm. 145; 4 Kent, Comm. 110; Litt. § 68. Or it is where lands are let without limiting any certain and determinate estate. 2 Crabb, Real Prop. p. 403, § 1543.

ESTATE BY ELEGIT. See ELEGIT.

ESTATE BY STATUTE MERCHANT. An estate whereby the creditor, under the custom of London, retained the possession of all his debtor's lands until his debts were paid. 1 Greenl. Cruise, Dig. 515. See STATUTE MERCHANT.

ESTATE BY THE CURTESY. Tenant by the curtesy of England is where a man survives a wife who was seised in fee-simple or fee-tail of lands or tenements, and has had issue male or female by her born alive and capable of inheriting the wife's estate as heir to her; in which case he will, on the decease of his wife, hold the estate during his life as tenant by the curtesy of England. 2 Crabb, Real Prop. § 1074.

ESTATE FOR LIFE. A freehold estate, not of inheritance, but which is held by the tenant for his own life or the life or lives of one or more other persons, or for an indefinite period, which may endure for the life or lives of persons in being, and not beyond the period of a life. 1 Washb. Real Prop. 88.

ESTATE FOR YEARS. A species of estate less than freehold, where a man has an interest in lands and tenements, and a possession thereof, by virtue of such interest, for some fixed and determinate period of time; as in the case where lands are let for the term of a certain number of years, agreed upon between the lessor and the lessee, and the lessee enters thereon. 1 Steph. Comm. 263, 264. Blackstone calls this estate a "contract" for the possession of lands or tenements for some determinate period. 2 Bl. Comm. 140.

ESTATE IN COMMON. An estate in lands held by two or more persons, with interests accruing under different titles; or accruing under the same title, but at different periods; or conferred by words of limitation importing that the grantees are to take in distinct shares. 1 Steph. Comm. 323. See TENANCY IN COMMON.

ESTATE IN COPARCENARY. An estate which several persons hold as one heir, whether male or female. This estate has the three unities of time, title, and possession; but the interests of the coparceners may be unequal. 1 Washb. Real Prop. 414; 2 Bl. Comm. 188. See COPARCENARY.

ESTATE IN DOWER. A species of life-estate which a woman is, by law, entitled to claim on the death of her husband, in the lands and tenements of which he was seised in fee during the marriage, and which her issue, if any, might by possibility have inherited. 1 Steph. Comm. 249; 2 Bl. Comm. 129; Cruise, Dig. tit. 6; 2 Crabb, Real Prop. p. 124, § 1117; 4 Kent, Comm. 35. See DOWER.

ESTATE IN EXPECTANCY. One which is not yet in possession, but the enjoyment of which is to begin at a future time; a present or vested contingent right of future enjoyment. These are remainders and reversions.

ESTATE IN FEE-SIMPLE. The estate which a man has where lands are given to him and to his heirs absolutely without any end or limit put to his estate. 2 Bl. Comm. 106; Plowd. 557; 1 Prest. Est. 425; Litt. § 1.

The word "fee," used alone, is a sufficient designation of this species of estate, and hence "simple" is not a necessary part of the title, but it is added as a means of clearly distinguishing this estate from a fee-tail or from any variety of conditional estates.

ESTATE IN FEE-TAIL, generally termed an "estate tail." An estate of inheritance which a man has, to hold to him and the heirs of his body, or to him and particular heirs of his body. 1 Steph. Comm. 228. An estate of inheritance by force of the statute *De Donis,* limited and restrained to some particular heirs of the donee, in exclusion of others. 2 Crabb, Real Prop. pp. 22, 23, § 971; Cruise, Dig. tit. 2, c. 1, § 12. See TAIL; FEE-TAIL.

ESTATE IN JOINT TENANCY. An estate in lands or tenements granted to two or more persons, to hold in fee-simple, fee-tail, for life, for years, or at will. 2 Bl. Comm. 180; 2 Crabb, Real Prop. 937. An estate acquired by two or more persons in the same land, by the same title, (not being a title by descent,) and at the same period; and without any limitation by words importing that they are to take in distinct shares. 1 Steph. Comm. 312. The most remarkable incident or consequence of this kind of estate is that it is subject to survivorship.

ESTATE IN POSSESSION. An estate whereby a present interest passes to and resides in the tenant, not depending on any subsequent circumstance or contingency. 2 Bl. Comm. 163. An estate where the tenant is in actual pernancy, or receipt of the rents and other advantages arising therefrom. 2 Crabb, Real Prop. p. 958, § 2322.

ESTATE IN REMAINDER. An estate limited to take effect in possession, or in enjoyment, or in both, subject only to any term of years or contingent interest that may intervene, immediately after the regular expiration of a particular estate of freehold previously created together with it, by the same instrument, out of the same subject of property. 2 Fearne, Rem. § 159; 2 Bl. Comm. 163; 1 Greenl. Cruise, Dig. 701.

ESTATE IN REVERSION. A species of estate in expectancy, created by operation of law, being the residue of an estate left in the grantor, to commence in possession after the determination of some particular estate granted out by him. 2 Bl. Comm. 175; 2 Crabb, Real Prop. p. 978, § 2345. The residue of an estate left in the grantor or his heirs, or in the heirs of a testator, commencing in possession on the determination of a particular estate granted or devised. 1 Rev. St. N. Y. p. 718, (723,) § 12. An estate in reversion is where any estate is derived, by grant or otherwise, out of a larger one, leaving in the original owner an ulterior estate immediately expectant on that which is so derived; the latter interest being called the "particular estate," (as being only a small

part or *particula* of the original one,) and the ulterior interest, the "reversion." 1 Steph. Comm. 290. See REVERSION.

ESTATE IN SEVERALTY. An estate held by a person in his own right only, without any other person being joined or connected with him in point of interest, during his estate. This is the most common and usual way of holding an estate. 2 Bl. Comm. 179; Cruise, Dig. tit. 18, c. 1, § 1.

ESTATE IN VADIO. An estate in gage or pledge. 2 Bl. Comm. 157; 1 Steph. Comm. 282.

ESTATE OF FREEHOLD. An estate in land or other real property, of uncertain duration; that is, either of inheritance or which may possibly last for the life of the tenant at the least, (as distinguished from a leasehold;) and held by a free tenure, (as distinguished from copyhold or villeinage.)

ESTATE OF INHERITANCE. A species of freehold estate in lands, otherwise called a "fee," where the tenant is not only entitled to enjoy the land for his own life, but where, after his death, it is cast by the law upon the persons who successively represent him *in perpetuum,* in right of blood, according to a certain established order of descent. 1 Steph. Comm. 218; Litt. § 1; 1 Rev. St. N. Y. p. 717, (722,) § 2.

ESTATE PUR AUTRE VIE. Estate for another's life. An estate in lands which a man holds for the life of another person. 2 Bl. Comm. 120; Litt. § 56.

ESTATE TAIL. See ESTATE IN FEE-TAIL.

ESTATE TAIL, QUASI. When a tenant for life grants his estate to a man and his heirs, as these words, though apt and proper to create an estate tail, cannot do so, because the grantor, being only tenant for life, cannot grant *in perpetuum,* therefore they are said to create an estate tail *quasi,* or improper. Brown.

ESTATE UPON CONDITION. An estate in lands, the existence of which depends upon the happening or not happening of some uncertain event, whereby the estate may be either originally created, or enlarged, or finally defeated. 2 Bl. Comm. 151; 1 Steph. Comm. 276; Co. Litt. 201a.

An estate having a qualification annexed to it, by which it may, upon the happening of a particular event, be created, or enlarged, or destroyed. 4 Kent, Comm. 121.

ESTATE UPON CONDITION EX-PRESSED. An estate granted, either in fee-simple or otherwise, with an express qualification annexed, whereby the estate granted shall either commence, be enlarged, or be defeated upon performance or breach of such qualification or condition. 2 Bl. Comm. 154.

An estate which is so expressly defined and limited by the words of its creation that it cannot endure for any longer time than till the contingency happens upon which the estate is to fail. 1 Steph. Comm. 278.

ESTATE UPON CONDITION IM-PLIED. An estate having a condition annexed to it inseparably from its essence and constitution, although no condition be expressed in words. 2 Bl. Comm. 152; 4 Kent, Comm. 121.

ESTATES OF THE REALM. The lords spiritual, the lords temporal, and the commons of Great Britain. 1 Bl. Comm. 153. Sometimes called the "three estates."

ESTENDARD, ESTENDART, or STANDARD. An ensign for horsemen in war.

ESTER IN JUDGMENT. To appear before a tribunal either as plaintiff or defendant. Kelham.

ESTIMATE. This word is used to express the mind or judgment of the speaker or writer on the particular subject under consideration. It implies a calculation or computation, as to *estimate* the gain or loss of an enterprise. 37 Hun, 203.

ESTOP. To stop, bar, or impede; to prevent; to preclude. Co. Litt. 352a. See Estoppel.

ESTOPPEL. A bar or impediment raised by the law, which precludes a man from alleging or from denying a certain fact or state of facts, in consequence of his previous allegation or denial or conduct or admission, or in consequence of a final adjudication of the matter in a court of law.

A preclusion, in law, which prevents a man from alleging or denying a fact, in consequence of his own previous act, allegation, or denial of a contrary tenor. Steph. Pl. 239.

An admission of so conclusive a nature that the party whom it affects is not permitted to aver against it or offer evidence to controvert it. 2 Smith, Lead. Cas. 778.

Estoppel is that which concludes and "shuts a man's mouth from speaking the truth." When a fact has been agreed on, or decided in a court of record, neither of the parties shall be allowed to call it in question, and have it tried over again at any time thereafter, so long as the judgment or decree stands unreversed; and when parties, by deed or solemn act *in pais*, agree on a state of facts, and act on it, neither shall ever afterwards be allowed to gainsay a fact so agreed on, or be heard to dispute it; in other words, his mouth is shut, and he shall not say that is not true which he had before in a solemn manner asserted to be true. Busb. 157.

Equitable estoppel (or estoppel by conduct, or *in pais*) is the species of estoppel which equity puts upon a person who has made a false representation or a concealment of material facts, with knowledge of the facts, to a party ignorant of the truth of the matter, with the intention that the other party should act upon it, and with the result that such party is actually induced to act upon it, to his damage. Bigelow, Estop. 484.

In pleading. A plea, replication, or other pleading, which, without confessing or denying the matter of fact adversely alleged, relies merely on some matter of estoppel as a ground for excluding the opposite party from the allegation of the fact. Steph. Pl. 219; 3 Bl. Comm. 308.

A plea which neither admits nor denies the facts alleged by the plaintiff, but denies his right to allege them. Gould, Pl. c. 2, § 39.

A special plea in bar, which happens where a man has done some act or executed some deed which precludes him from averring anything to the contrary. 3 Bl. Comm. 308.

ESTOPPEL BY DEED is where a party has executed a deed, that is, a writing under seal (as a bond) reciting a certain fact, and is thereby precluded from afterwards denying, in any action brought upon that instrument, the fact so recited. Steph. Pl. 197. A man shall always be *estopped* by his own deed, or not permitted to aver or prove anything in contradiction to what he has once so solemnly and deliberately avowed. 2 Bl. Comm. 295; Plowd. 434.

ESTOPPEL BY MATTER IN PAIS. An estoppel by the conduct or admissions of the party; an estoppel not arising from deed or matter of record. Thus, where one man has accepted rent of another, he will be estopped from afterwards denying, in any action with that person, that he was, at the time of such acceptance, his tenant. Steph. Pl. 197.

The doctrine of *estoppels in pais* is one which, so far at least as that term is concerned, has grown up chiefly within the last few years. But it is, and always was, a familiar principle in the law of contracts. It lies at the foundation of morals, and is a cardinal point in the exposition of promises, that one shall be bound by the state of facts which he has induced another to act upon. Redfield, C. J., 26 Vt. 366, 373.

ESTOPPEL BY MATTER OF RECORD. An estoppel founded upon matter of record; as a confession or admission made in pleading in a court of record, which precludes the party from afterwards contesting the same fact in the same suit. Steph. Pl. 197.

ESTOPPEL, COLLATERAL. The collateral determination of a question by a court having general jurisdiction of the subject.

Estoveria sunt ardendi, arandi, construendi et claudendi. 13 Coke, 68. Estovers are of fire-bote, plow-bote, house-bote, and hedge-bote.

ESTOVERIIS HABENDIS. A writ for a wife judicially separated to recover her alimony or estovers. Obsolete.

ESTOVERS. An allowance made to a person out of an estate or other thing for his or her support, as for food and raiment.

An allowance (more commonly called "alimony") granted to a woman divorced *a mensa et thoro*, for her support out of her husband's estate. 1 Bl. Comm. 441.

The right or privilege which a tenant has to furnish himself with so much wood from the demised premises as may be sufficient or necessary for his fuel, fences, and other agricultural operations. 2 Bl. Comm. 35; Woodf. Landl. & Ten. 232; 10 Wend. 639.

ESTRAY. Cattle whose owner is unknown. 2 Kent, Comm. 359; Spelman; 29 Iowa, 437. Any beast, not wild, found within any lordship, and not owned by any man. Cowell; 1 Bl. Comm. 297.

Estray must be understood as denoting a wandering beast whose owner is unknown to the person who takes it up. 27 Wis. 422; 29 Iowa, 437.

An estray is an animal that has escaped from its owner, and wanders or strays about; usually defined, at common law, as a wandering animal whose owner is unknown. An animal cannot be an estray when on the range where it was raised, and permitted by its owner to run, and especially when the owner is known to the party who takes it up. The fact of its being breachy or vicious does not make it an estray. 4 Or. 206.

ESTREAT, *v.* To take out a forfeited recognizance from the records of a court, and return it to the court of exchequer, to be prosecuted. See ESTREAT, *n.*

ESTREAT, *n.* (From Lat. *extractum.*) In English law. A copy or extract from the book of estreats, that is, the rolls of any court, in which the amercements or fines, recognizances, etc., imposed or taken by that court upon or from the accused, are set down, and which are to be levied by the bailiff or other officer of the court. Cowell; Brown.

A forfeited recognizance taken out from among the other records for the purpose of being sent up to the exchequer, that the parties might be sued thereon, was said to be estreated. 4 Bl. Comm. 253.

ESTRECIATUS. Straightened, as applied to roads. Cowell.

ESTREPE. To strip; to despoil; to lay waste; to commit waste upon an estate, as by cutting down trees, removing buildings, etc. To injure the value of a reversionary interest by stripping or spoiling the estate.

ESTREPEMENT. A species of aggravated waste, by stripping or devastating the land, to the injury of the reversioner, and especially pending a suit for possession.

ESTREPEMENT, WRIT OF. This was a common-law writ of waste, which lay in particular for the reversioner against the tenant for life, in respect of damage or injury to the land committed by the latter. As it was only auxiliary to a real action for recovery of the land, and as equity afforded the same relief by injunction, the writ fell into disuse.

ET. And. The introductory word of several Latin and law French phrases formerly in common use.

ET ADJOURNATUR. And it is adjourned. A phrase used in the old reports, where the argument of a cause was adjourned to another day, or where a second argument was had. 1 Keb. 692, 754, 773.

ET AL. An abbreviation for *et alii,* "and others."

ET ALII È CONTRA. And others on the other side. A phrase constantly used in the Year Books, in describing a joinder in issue. P. 1 Edw. II. *Prist; et alii è contra, et sic ad patriam:* ready; and others, *è contra,* and so to the country. T. 3 Edw. III. 4.

ET ALIUS. And another. The abbreviation *et al.* (sometimes in the plural written *et als.*) is affixed to the name of the person first mentioned, where there are several plaintiffs, grantors, persons addressed, etc.

ET ALLOCATUR. And it is allowed.

ET CÆTERA. And others; and other things; and so on. In its abbreviated form (*etc.*) this phrase is frequently affixed to one of a series of articles or names to show that others are intended to follow or understood to be included. So, after reciting the initiatory words of a set formula, or a clause already given in full, *etc.* is added, as an abbreviation, for the sake of convenience.

ET DE CEO SE METTENT EN LE PAYS. L. Fr. And of this they put themselves upon the country.

ET DE HOC PONIT SE SUPER PATRIAM. And of this he puts himself upon the country. The formal conclusion of a common-law plea in bar by way of traverse. The literal translation is retained in the modern form.

ET EI LEGITUR IN HÆC VERBA. L. Lat. And it is read to him in these words. Words formerly used in entering the prayer of oyer on record.

ET HABEAS IBI TUNC HOC BREVE. And have you then there this writ. The formal words directing the return of a writ. The literal translation is retained in the modern form of a considerable number of writs.

ET HABUIT. And he had it. A common phrase in the Year Books, expressive of the allowance of an application or demand by a party. Parn. *demanda la view. Et habuit,* etc. M. 6 Edw. III. 49.

ET HOC PARATUS EST VERIFICARE. And this he is prepared to verify. The Latin form of concluding a plea in confession and avoidance.

These words were used, when the pleadings were in Latin, at the conclusion of any pleading which contained new affirmative matter. They expressed the willingness or readiness of the party so pleading to establish by proof the matter alleged in his pleading. A pleading which concluded in that manner was technically said to "conclude with a verification," in contradistinction to a pleading which simply denied matter alleged by the opposite party, and which for that reason was said to "conclude to the country," because the party merely put himself upon the country, or left the matter to the jury. Brown.

ET HOC PETIT QUOD INQUIRATUR PER PATRIAM. And this he prays may be inquired of by the country. The conclusion of a plaintiff's pleading, tendering an issue to the country. 1 Salk. 6. Literally translated in the modern forms.

ET INDE PETIT JUDICIUM. And thereupon [or thereof] he prays judgment. A clause at the end of pleadings, praying the judgment of the court in favor of the party pleading. It occurs as early as the time of Bracton, and is literally translated in the modern forms. Bract. fol. 57*b;* Crabb, Eng. Law, 217.

ET INDE PRODUCIT SECTAM. And thereupon he brings suit. The Latin conclusion of a declaration, except against attorneys and other officers of the court. 3 Bl. Comm. 295.

ET MODO AD HUNC DIEM. Lat. And now at this day. This phrase was the formal beginning of an entry of appearance or of a continuance. The equivalent English words are still used in this connection.

ET NON. Lat. And not. A technical phrase in pleading, which introduces the negative averments of a special traverse. It has the same force and effect as the words *"absque hoc,"* and is occasionally used instead of the latter.

ET SEQ. An abbreviation for *et sequentia,* "and the following." Thus a reference to "p. 1, et seq." means "page first and the following pages."

ET SIC. And so. In the Latin forms of pleading these were the introductory words of a special conclusion to a plea in bar, the object being to render it positive and not argumentative; as *et sic nil debet.*

ET SIC AD JUDICIUM. And so to judgment. Yearb. T. 1 Edw. II. 10.

ET SIC AD PATRIAM. And so to the country. A phrase used in the Year Books, to record an issue to the country.

ET SIC FECIT. And he did so. Yearb. P. 9 Hen. VI. 17.

ET SIC PENDET. And so it hangs. A term used in the old reports to signify that a point was left undetermined. T. Raym. 168.

ET SIC ULTERIUS. And so on; and so further; and so forth. Fleta, lib. 2, c. 50, § 27.

ET UX. An abbreviation for *et uxor,*— "and wife." Where a grantor's wife joins him in the conveyance, it is sometimes expressed (in abstracts, etc.) to be by "A. B. *et ux."*

ETIQUETTE OF THE PROFESSION. The code of honor agreed on by mutual understanding and tacitly accepted by members of the legal profession, especially by the bar. Wharton.

Eum qui nocentem infamat, non est æquum et bonum ob eam rem condemnari; delicta enim nocentium nota esse oportet et expedit. It is not just and proper that he who speaks ill of a bad man should be condemned on that account; for it is fitting and expedient that the crimes of bad men should be known. Dig. 47, 10, 17; 1 Bl. Comm. 125.

EUNDO ET REDEUNDO. Lat. In going and returning. Applied to vessels. 3 C. Rob. Adm. 141.

EUNDO, MORANDO, ET REDEUNDO. Lat. Going, remaining, and returning. A person who is privileged from arrest (as a witness, legislator, etc.) is generally so privileged *eundo, morando, et redeundo;* that is, on his way to the place where his duties are to be performed, while he remains there, and on his return journey.

EUNOMY. Equal laws and a well-adjusted constitution of government.

EUNUCH. A male of the human species who has been castrated. See Domat, liv. prél. tit. 2, § 1, n. 10.

EVASIO. Lat. In old practice. An escape from prison or custody. Reg. Orig. 312.

EVASION. A subtle endeavoring to set aside truth or to escape the punishment of the law. This will not be allowed. If one person says to another that he will not strike him, but will give him a pot of ale to strike first, and, accordingly, the latter strikes, the returning the blow is punishable; and, if the person first striking is killed, it is murder, for no man shall evade the justice of the law by such a pretense. 1 Hawk. P. C. 81. So no one may plead ignorance of the law to evade it. Jacob.

EVASIVE. Tending or seeking to evade; elusive; shifting; as an *evasive* argument or plea.

EVENINGS. In old English law. The delivery at even or night of a certain portion of grass, or corn, etc., to a customary tenant, who performs the service of cutting, mowing, or reaping for his lord, given him as a gratuity or encouragement. Kennett, Gloss.

Eventus est qui ex causâ sequitur; et dicitur eventus quia ex causis evenit. 9 Coke, 81. An event is that which follows from the cause, and is called an "event" because it eventuates from causes.

Eventus varios res nova semper habet. Co. Litt. 379. A new matter always produces various events.

Every man must be taken to contemplate the probable consequences of the act he does. Lord Ellenborough, 9 East, 277. A fundamental maxim in the law of evidence. Best, Pres. § 16; 1 Phil. Ev. 444.

EVES-DROPPERS. See EAVES-DROPPERS.

EVICT. In the civil law. To recover anything from a person by virtue of the judgment of a court or judicial sentence.

At common law. To dispossess, or turn out of the possession of lands by process of law. Also to recover land by judgment at law. "If the land is *evicted*, no rent shall be paid." 10 Coke, 128a.

EVICTION. Dispossession by process of law; the act of depriving a person of the possession of lands which he has held, in pursuance of the judgment of a court.

Technically, the dispossession must be by judgment of law; if otherwise, it is an *ouster*.

Eviction implies an entry under paramount title, so as to interfere with the rights of the grantee. The object of the party making the entry is immaterial, whether it be to take all or a part of the land itself or merely an incorporeal right. Phrases equivalent in meaning are "ouster by paramount title," "entry and disturbance," "possession under an elder title," and the like. 5 Conn. 497.

Eviction is an actual expulsion of the lessee out of all or some part of the demised premises. 4 Cow. 581, 585.

In a more popular sense, the term denotes turning a tenant of land out of possession, either by re-entry or by legal proceedings, such as an action of ejectment. Sweet.

By a loose extension, the term is sometimes applied to the ousting of a person from the possession of chattels; but, properly, it applies only to realty.

In the civil law. The abandonment which one is obliged to make of a thing, in pursuance of a sentence by which he is condemned to do so. Poth. Contr. Sale, pt. 2, c. 1, § 2, art. 1, no. 83. The abandonment which a buyer is compelled to make of a thing purchased, in pursuance of a judicial sentence.

Eviction is the loss suffered by the buyer of the totality of the thing sold, or of a part thereof, occasioned by the right or claims of a third person. Civil Code La. art. 2500.

EVIDENCE. Any species of proof, or probative matter, legally presented at the trial of an issue, by the act of the parties and through the medium of witnesses, records, documents, concrete objects, etc., for the purpose of inducing belief in the minds of the court or jury as to their contention.

The word "evidence," in legal acceptation, includes all the means by which any alleged matter of fact, the truth of which is submitted to investigation, is established or disproved. 1 Greenl. Ev. c. 1, § 1.

That which is legally submitted to a jury, to enable them to decide upon the questions in dispute or issue, as pointed out by the pleadings, and distinguished from all comment and argument, is termed "evidence." 1 Starkie, Ev. pt. 1, § 3.

Synonyms distinguished. The term "evidence" is to be carefully distinguished from its synonyms "proof" and "testimony." "Proof" is the logically sufficient reason for assenting to the truth of a proposition advanced. In its juridical sense it is a term of wide import, and comprehends everything that may be adduced at a trial, within the legal rules, for the purpose of producing conviction in the mind of judge or jury, aside from mere argument; that is, everything that has a probative force intrinsically, and not merely as a deduction from, or combination of, original probative facts. But "evidence" is a narrower term, and includes only such kinds of proof as may be legally presented at a trial, by the act of the parties, and through the aid of such concrete facts as witnesses, records, or other documents. Thus, to urge a presumption of law in support of one's case is adducing proof, but it is not offering evidence. "Testimony," again, is a still more restricted term. It properly means only such evidence as is delivered by a witness on the trial of a cause, either orally or in the form of affidavits or depositions. Thus, an ancient deed, when offered under proper circumstances, is evidence, but it could not strictly be called "testimony." "Belief" is a subjective condition resulting from proof. It is a conviction of the truth of a proposition, existing in the mind, and induced by persuasion, proof, or argument addressed to the judgment.

The bill of exceptions states that all the "testimony" is in the record; but this is not equivalent to a statement that all the "evidence" is in the record. Testimony is one species of evidence. But the word "evidence" is a generic term which includes every species of it. And, in a bill of exceptions, the general term covering all species should be used in the statement as to its embracing the evidence, not the term "testimony," which is satisfied if the bill only contains all of that species of evidence. The statement that all the testimony is in the record may, with reference to judicial records, properly be termed an "affirmative pregnant." 60 Ind. 157.

The word "proof" seems properly to mean anything which serves, either immediately or mediately, to convince the mind of the truth or falsehood of a fact or proposition. It is also applied to the conviction generated in the mind by proof properly so called. The word "evidence" signifies, in its original sense, the state of being evident, i. e., plain, apparent, or notorious. But by an almost peculiar inflection of our language, it is applied to that which tends to render evident or to generate proof. Best, Ev. §§ 10, 11.

Classification. There are many species of evidence, and it is susceptible of being classified on several different principles. The more usual divisions are here subjoined.

Evidence is either *judicial* or *extrajudicial*. Judicial evidence is the means, sanctioned by law, of ascertaining in a judicial proceeding the truth respecting a question of fact, (Code Civil Proc. Cal. § 1823;) while extrajudicial evidence is that which is used to satisfy private persons as to facts requiring proof.

Evidence is either *primary* or *secondary*. Primary evidence is that kind of evidence which, under every possible circumstance, affords the greatest certainty of the fact in question. Thus, a written instrument is itself the best possible evidence of its existence and contents. Secondary evidence is that which is inferior to primary. Thus, a copy of an instrument, or oral evidence of its contents, is secondary evidence of the instrument and contents. Code Civil Proc. Cal. §§ 1829, 1830.

Primary evidence is such as in itself does not indicate the existence of other and better proof. *Secondary* evidence is such as from necessity in some cases is substituted for stronger and better proof. Code Ga. 1882, § 3761.

Primary evidence is that particular means of proof which is indicated by the nature of the fact under investigation, as the most natural and satisfactory; the best evidence the nature of the case admits; such evidence as may be called for in the first instance, upon the principle that its non-production gives rise to a reasonable suspicion that if produced it would tend against the fact alleged. Abbott.

Evidence is either *direct* or *indirect*. Direct evidence is that which proves the fact in dispute directly, without an inference or presumption, and which in itself, if true, conclusively establishes that fact; for example, if the fact in dispute be an agreement, the evidence of a witness who was present and witnessed the making of it is direct. Indirect evidence is that which tends to establish the fact in dispute by proving another, and which, though true, does not of itself conclusively establish that fact, but which affords an inference or presumption of its existence; for example, a witness proves an admission of the party to the fact in dispute. This proves a fact, from which the fact in dispute is inferred. Code Civil Proc. Cal. §§ 1831, 1832.

Evidence is either *intrinsic* or *extrinsic*. Intrinsic evidence is that which is derived from a document without anything to explain it. Extrinsic evidence is external evidence, or that which is not contained in the body of an agreement, contract, and the like.

In respect to its *nature*, evidence is also of the following several kinds:

Circumstantial evidence. This is proof of various facts or circumstances which usually attend the main fact in dispute, and therefore tend to prove its existence, or to sustain, by their consistency, the hypothesis claimed.

Circumstantial evidence consists in reasoning from facts which are known or proved, to establish such as are conjectured to exist. 32 N. Y. 141.

Presumptive evidence. This consists of inferences drawn by human experience from the connection of cause and effect, and observations of human conduct. Code Ga. 1882, § 3748.

Prima facie evidence. It is that which suffices for the proof of a particular fact, until contradicted and overcome by other evidence; for example, the certificate of a recording officer is *prima facie* evidence of a record, but it may afterwards be rejected upon proof that there is no such record. Code Civil Proc. Cal. § 1833.

Prima facie evidence is evidence which, standing alone and unexplained, would maintain the proposition and warrant the conclusion to support which it is introduced. 97 Mass. 230.

Partial evidence, is that which goes to establish a detached fact, in a series tending to the fact in dispute. It may be received, subject to be rejected as incompetent, unless connected with the fact in dispute by proof of other facts; for example, on an issue of title to real property, evidence of the continued possession of a remote occupant is partial, for it is of a detached fact, which may or may not be afterwards connected with the fact in dispute. Code Civil Proc. Cal. § 1834.

Satisfactory evidence. That evidence is deemed satisfactory which ordinarily produces moral certainty or conviction in an unprejudiced mind. Such evidence alone will justify a verdict. Evidence less than this is denominated "slight evidence." Code Civil Proc. Cal. § 1835.

Conclusive evidence. Conclusive or unanswerable evidence is that which the law does not permit to be contradicted; for example, the record of a court of competent jurisdiction cannot be contradicted by the parties to it. Code Civil Proc. Cal. § 1837.

Indispensable evidence is that without which a particular fact cannot be proved. Code Civil Proc. Cal. § 1836.

Documentary evidence is that derived from conventional symbols (such as letters) by which ideas are represented on material substances.

Hearsay evidence is the evidence, not of what the witness knows himself, but of what he has heard from others.

In respect to its *object*, evidence is of the following several kinds:

Substantive evidence is that adduced for the purpose of proving a fact in issue, as opposed to evidence given for the purpose of discrediting a witness, (*i. e.*, showing that he is unworthy of belief,) or of corroborating his testimony. Best, Ev. 246, 773, 803.

Corroborative evidence is additional evidence of a different character to the same point. Code Civil Proc. Cal. § 1839.

Cumulative evidence is additional evidence of the same character to the same point. Civil Code Proc. Cal. § 1838.

EVIDENCE OF DEBT. A term applied to written instruments or securities for the payment of money, importing on their face the existence of a debt. 1 Rev. St. N. Y. p. 599, § 55.

EVIDENCE OF TITLE. A deed or other document establishing the title to property, especially real estate.

EVIDENTIARY. Having the quality of evidence; constituting evidence; evidencing. A term introduced by Bentham, and, from its convenience, adopted by other writers.

EVOCATION. In French law. The withdrawal of a cause from the cognizance of an inferior court, and bringing it before another court or judge. In some respects this process resembles the proceedings upon *certiorari*.

EWAGE. (L. Fr. *Ewe*, water.) In old English law. Toll paid for water passage. The same as *aquage*. Tomlins.

EWBRICE. Adultery; spouse breach; marriage breach. Cowell; Tomlins.

EWRY. An office in the royal household where the table linen, etc., is taken care of. Wharton.

EX. 1. A Latin preposition meaning from, out of, by, on, on account of, or according to.

2. A prefix, denoting removal or cessation. Prefixed to the name of an office, relation, *status*, etc., it denotes that the person spoken of once occupied that office or relation, but does so no longer, or that he is now *out* of it. Thus, *ex*-mayor, *ex*-partner, *ex*-judge.

3. A prefix which is equivalent to "without," "reserving," or "excepting." In this use, probably an abbreviation of "except." Thus, *ex*-interest, *ex*-coupons.

"A sale of bonds 'ex. July coupons' means a sale reserving the coupons; that is, a sale in which the seller receives, in addition to the purchase price, the benefit of the coupons, which benefit he may realize either by detaching them or receiving from the buyer an equivalent consideration." 94 N. Y. 445.

EX ABUNDANTI. Out of abundance; abundantly; superfluously; more than sufficient. Calvin.

EX ABUNDANTI CAUTELA. Lat. Out of abundant caution. "The practice has arisen *abundanti cautela*." 8 East, 326; Lord Ellenborough, 4 Maule & S. 544.

EX ADVERSO. On the other side. 2 Show. 461. Applied to counsel.

EX ÆQUITATE. According to equity; in equity. Fleta, lib. 3, c. 10, § 3.

EX ÆQUO ET BONO. A phrase derived from the civil law, meaning, in justice and fairness; according to what is just and good; according to equity and conscience. 3 Bl. Comm. 163.

EX ALTERA PARTE. Of the other part.

Ex antecedentibus et consequentibus fit optima interpretatio. The best interpretation [of a part of an instrument] is made from the antecedents and the consequents, [from the preceding and following parts.] 2 Inst. 317. The law will judge of a deed or other instrument, consisting of divers parts or clauses, by looking at the whole; and will give to each part its proper office, so as to ascertain and carry out the intention of the parties. Broom, Max. *577. The whole instrument is to be viewed and compared in all its parts, so that every part of it may be made consistent and effectual. 2 Kent, Comm. 555.

EX ARBITRIO JUDICIS. At, in, or upon the discretion of the judge. 4 Bl. Comm. 394. A term of the civil law. Inst. 4, 6, 31.

EX ASSENSU CURIÆ. By or with the consent of the court.

EX ASSENSU PATRIS. By or with the consent of the father. A species of dower *ad ostium ecclesiæ*, during the life of the father of the husband; the son, by the father's consent expressly given, endowing his wife with parcel of his father's lands. Abolished by 3 & 4 Wm. IV. c. 105, § 13.

EX ASSENSU SUO. With his assent. Formal words in judgments for damages by default. Comb. 220.

EX BONIS. Of the goods or property. A term of the civil law; distinguished from *in bonis*, as being descriptive of or applicable to property not in actual possession. Calvin.

EX CATHEDRA. From the chair. Originally applied to the decisions of the popes from their *cathedra*, or chair. Hence, authoritative; having the weight of authority.

EX CAUSA. L. Lat. By title.

EX CERTA SCIENTIA. Of certain or sure knowledge. These words were anciently used in patents, and imported full knowledge of the subject-matter on the part of the king. See 1 Coke, 40*b*.

EX COLORE. By color; under color of; under pretense, show, or protection of. Thus, *ex colore officii*, under color of office.

EX COMITATE. Out of comity or courtesy.

EX COMMODATO. From or out of loan. A term applied in the old law of England to a right of action arising out of a loan, (*commodatum*.) Glanv. lib. 10, c. 13; 1 Reeve, Eng. Law, 166.

EX COMPARATIONE SCRIPTORUM. By a comparison of writings or handwritings. A term in the law of evidence. Best, Pres. 218.

EX CONCESSIS. From the premises granted. According to what has been already allowed.

EX CONSULTO. With consultation or deliberation.

EX CONTINENTI. Immediately; without any interval or delay: incontinently. A term of the civil law. Calvin.

EX CONTRACTU. From or out of a contract. In both the civil and the common law, rights and causes of action are divided into two classes,—those arising *ex contractu*, (from a contract,) and those arising *ex delicto*, (from a delict or tort.) See 3 Bl. Comm. 117; Mackeld. Rom. Law, § 384.

EX CURIA. Out of court; away from the court.

EX DEBITO JUSTITIÆ. From or as a debt of justice; in accordance with the requirement of justice; of right; as a matter of right. The opposite of *ex gratia*, (*q. v.*) 3 Bl. Comm. 48, 67.

EX DEFECTU SANGUINIS. From failure of blood; for want of issue.

EX DELICTO. From a delict, tort, fault, crime, or malfeasance. In both the civil and the common law, obligations and causes of action are divided into two great classes,—those arising *ex contractu*, (out of a contract,) and those *ex delicto*. The latter are such as grow out of or are founded upon a wrong or tort, *e. g.*, trespass, trover, replevin. These terms were known in English law at a very early period. See Inst. 4, 1, pr.; Mackeld. Rom. Law, § 384; 3 Bl. Comm. 117; Bract. fol. 101b.

Ex delicto non ex supplicio emergit infamia. Infamy arises from the crime, not from the punishment.

EX DEMISSIONE, (commonly abbreviated *ex dem.*) Upon the demise. A phrase forming part of the title of the old action of ejectment.

EX DIRECTO. Directly; immediately. Story, Bills, § 199.

Ex diuturnitate temporis, omnia præsumuntur solemniter esse acta. From length of time [after lapse of time] all things are presumed to have been done in due form. Co. Litt. 6b; Best, Ev. Introd. § 43; 1 Greenl. Ev. § 20.

EX DOLO MALO. Out of fraud; out of deceitful or tortious conduct. A phrase applied to obligations and causes of action vitiated by fraud or deceit.

Ex dolo malo non oritur actio. Out of fraud no action arises; fraud never gives a right of action. No court will lend its aid to a man who founds his cause of action upon an immoral or illegal act. Cowp. 343; Broom, Max. 729.

Ex donationibus autem feoda militaria vel magnum serjeantium non continentibus oritur nobis quoddam nomen generale, quod est socagium. Co. Litt. 86. From grants not containing military fees or grand serjeanty, a kind of general name is used by us, which is "socage."

EX EMPTO. Out of purchase; founded on purchase. A term of the civil law, adopted by Bracton. Inst. 4, 6, 28; Bract. fol. 102. See ACTIO EX EMPTO.

EX FACIE. From the face; apparently; evidently. A term applied to what appears on the face of a writing.

EX FACTO. From or in consequence of a fact or action; actually. Usually applied to an unlawful or tortious act as the foundation of a title, etc. Sometimes used as equivalent to "*de facto.*" Bract. fol. 172.

Ex facto jus oritur. The law arises out of the fact. Broom, Max. 102. A rule of law continues in abstraction and theory, until an act is done on which it can attach and assume as it were a body and shape. Best, Ev. Introd. § 1.

EX FICTIONE JURIS. By a fiction of law.

Ex frequenti delicto augetur pœna. 2 Inst. 479. Punishment increases with increasing crime.

EX GRATIA. Out of grace; as a matter of grace, favor, or indulgence; gratuitous. A term applied to anything accorded as a favor; as distinguished from that which may be demanded *ex debito*, as a matter of right.

EX GRAVI QUERELA. (From or on the grievous complaint.) In old English practice. The name of a writ (so called from its initial words) which lay for a person to whom any lands or tenements in fee were devised by will, (within any city, town, or borough wherein lands were devisable by custom,) and the heir of the devisor entered and detained them from him. Fitzh. Nat. Brev. 198, L, et seq.; 3 Reeve, Eng. Law, 49. Abolished by St. 3 & 4 Wm. IV. c. 27, § 36.

EX HYPOTHESI. By the hypothesis; upon the supposition; upon the theory or facts assumed.

EX INDUSTRIA. With contrivance or deliberation; designedly; on purpose. See 1 Kent, Comm. 818; 1 Wheat. 304.

EX INTEGRO. Anew; afresh.

EX JUSTA CAUSA. From a just or lawful cause; by a just or legal title.

EX LEGE. By the law; by force of law; as a matter of law.

EX LEGIBUS. According to the laws. A phrase of the civil law, which means according to the intent or spirit of the law, as well as according to the words or letter. Dig. 50, 16, 6. See Calvin.

EX LICENTIA REGIS. By the king's license. 1 Bl. Comm. 168, note.

EX LOCATO. From or out of lease or letting. A term of the civil law, applied to actions or rights of action arising out of the contract of *locatum*, (*q. v.*) Inst. 4, 6, 28. Adopted at an early period in the law of England. Bract. fol. 102; 1 Reeve, Eng. Law, 168.

EX MALEFICIO. Growing out of, or founded upon, misdoing or tort. This term is frequently used in the civil law as the synonym of "*ex delicto*," (*q. v.*,) and is thus contrasted with "*ex contractu.*" In this sense it is of more rare occurrence in the common law, though found in Bracton, (fols. 99, 101, 102.)

Ex maleficio non oritur contractus. A contract cannot arise out of an act radically vicious and illegal. 1 Term 734; 3 Term 422; Broom, Max. 734.

Ex malis moribus bonæ leges natæ sunt. 2 Inst. 161. Good laws arise from evil morals, *i. e.*, are necessitated by the evil behavior of men.

EX MERO MOTU. Of his own mere motion; of his own accord; voluntarily and without prompting or request. Royal letters patent which are granted at the crown's own instance, and without request made, are said to be granted *ex mero motu.* When a court interferes, of its own motion, to object to an irregularity, or to do something which the parties are not strictly entitled to, but which will prevent injustice, it is said to act *ex mero motu*, or *ex proprio motu*, or *sua sponte*, all these terms being here equivalent.

EX MORA. From or in consequence of delay. Interest is allowed *ex mora;* that is, where there has been delay in returning a sum borrowed. A term of the civil law. Story, Bailm. § 84.

EX MORE. According to custom. Calvin.

Ex multitudine signorum, colligitur identitas vera. From a great number of signs or marks, true identity is gathered or made up. Bac. Max. 103, in regula 25. A thing described by a great number of marks is easily identified, though, as to some, the description may not be strictly correct. Id.

EX MUTUO. From or out of loan. In the old law of England, a debt was said to arise *ex mutuo* when one lent another anything which consisted in number, weight, or measure. 1 Reeve, Eng. Law, 159; Bract. fol. 99.

EX NECESSITATE. Of necessity. 3 Rep. Ch. 123.

EX NECESSITATE LEGIS. From or by necessity of law. 4 Bl. Comm. 394.

EX NECESSITATE REI. From the necessity or urgency of the thing or case. 2 Pow. Dev. (by Jarman,) 308.

Ex nihilo nihil fit. From nothing nothing comes. 13 Wend. 178, 221; 18 Wend. 257, 301.

Ex nudo pacto non oritur [nascitur] actio. Out of a nude or naked pact [that is, a bare parol agreement without consideration] no action arises. Bract. fol. 99; Fleta, lib. 2, c. 56, § 3; Plowd. 305. Out of a promise neither attended with particular solemnity (such as belongs to a specialty) nor with any consideration no legal liability can arise. 2 Steph. Comm. 113. A parol agreement, without a valid consideration, cannot be made the foundation of an action. A leading maxim both of the civil and common law. Cod. 2, 3, 10; Id. 5, 14, 1; 2 Bl. Comm. 445; Smith, Cont. 85, 86.

EX OFFICIO. From office; by virtue of the office; without any other warrant or appointment than that resulting from the holding of a particular office. Powers may be exercised by an officer which are not specifically conferred upon him, but are necessarily implied in his office; these are *ex officio.* Thus, a judge has *ex officio* the powers of a conservator of the peace. Courts are bound to notice public statutes judicially and *ex officio.*

EX OFFICIO INFORMATION. In English law. A criminal information filed by the attorney general *ex officio* on behalf of the crown, in the court of queen's bench, for offenses more immediately affecting the government, and to be distinguished from informations in which the crown is the nominal prosecutor. Mozley & Whitley; **4 Steph.** Comm. 372-378.

EX OFFICIO OATH. An oath taken by offending priests; abolished by 13 Car. II. St. 1, c. 12.

Ex pacto illicito non oritur actio. From an illegal contract an action does not arise. Broom, Max. 742. See 7 Clark & F. 729.

EX PARTE. On one side only; by or for one party; done for, in behalf of, or on the application of, one party only. A judicial proceeding, order, injunction, etc., is said to be *ex parte* when it is taken or granted at the instance and for the benefit of one party only, and without notice to, or contestation by, any person adversely interested.

"*Ex parte*," in the heading of a reported case, signifies that the name following is that of the party upon whose application the case is heard.

In its primary sense, *ex parte*, as applied to an application in a judicial proceeding, means that it is made by a person who is not a party to the proceeding, but who has an interest in the matter which entitles him to make the application. Thus, in a bankruptcy proceeding or an administration action, an application by A. B., a creditor, or the like, would be described as made "*ex parte* A. B.," *i. e.*, on the part of A. B.

In its more usual sense, *ex parte* means that an application is made by one party to a proceeding in the absence of the other. Thus, an *ex parte* injunction is one granted without the opposite party having had notice of the application. It would not be called "*ex parte*" if he had proper notice of it, and chose not to appear to oppose it. Sweet.

EX PARTE MATERNA. On the mother's side; of the maternal line.

EX PARTE PATERNA. On the father's side; of the paternal line.

The phrases "*ex parte materna*" and "*ex parte paterna*" denote the line or blood of the mother or father, and have no such restricted or limited sense as from the mother or father exclusively. 24 N. J. Law, 481.

EX PARTE TALIS. A writ that lay for a bailiff or receiver, who, having auditors appointed to take his accounts, cannot obtain of them reasonable allowance, but is cast into prison. Fitzh. Nat. Brev. 129.

Ex paucis dictis intendere plurima possis. Litt. § 384. You can imply many things from few expressions.

Ex paucis plurima concipit ingenium. Litt. § 550. From a few words or hints the understanding conceives many things.

EX POST FACTO. After the fact; by an act or fact occurring after some previous act or fact, and relating thereto; by subsequent matter; the opposite of *ab initio*. Thus, a deed may be good *ab initio*, or, if invalid at its inception, may be confirmed by matter *ex post facto*.

EX POST FACTO LAW. A law passed after the occurrence of a fact or commission of an act, which retrospectively changes the legal consequences or relations of such fact or deed. By Const. U. S. art. 1, § 10, the states are forbidden to pass "any *ex post facto* law." In this connection the phrase has a much narrower meaning than its literal translation would justify, as will appear from the extracts given below.

The phrase "*ex post facto*," in the constitution, extends to criminal and not to civil cases. And under this head is included: (1) Every law that makes an action, done before the passing of the law, and which was innocent when done, criminal, and punishes such action. (2) Every law that aggravates a crime, or makes it greater than it was when committed. (3) Every law that changes the punishment, and inflicts a greater punishment than the law annexed to the crime when committed. (4) Every law that alters the legal rules of evidence, and receives less or different testimony than the law required at the time of the commission of the offense, in order to convict the offender. All these, and similar laws, are prohibited by the constitution. But a law may be *ex post facto*, and still not amenable to this constitutional inhibition; that is, provided it mollifies, instead of aggravating, the rigor of the criminal law. 16 Ga. 102; 4 Wall. 277; 2 Wash. C. C. 366; 3 N. H. 473; 3 Dall. 390; 3 Story, Const. 212.

An *ex post facto* law is one which renders an act punishable, in a manner in which it was not punishable when committed. Such a law may inflict penalties on the person, or pecuniary penalties which swell the public treasury. The legislature is therefore prohibited from passing a law by which a man's estate, or any part of it, shall be seized for a crime, which was not declared, by some previous law, to render him liable to such punishment. 6 Cranch, 87, 138.

The plain and obvious meaning of this prohibition is that the legislature shall not pass any law, after a fact done by any citizen, which shall have relation to that fact, so as to punish that which was innocent when done; or to add to the punishment of that which was criminal; or to increase the malignity of a crime; or to retrench the rules of evidence, so as to make conviction more easy. This definition of an *ex post facto* law is sanctioned by long usage. 1 Blackf. 196.

The term "*ex post facto* law," in the United States constitution, cannot be construed to include and to prohibit the enacting any law after a fact, nor even to prohibit the depriving a citizen of a vested right to property. 3 Dall. 386.

"*Ex post facto*" and "retrospective" are not convertible terms. The latter is a term of wider signification than the former and includes it. All *ex post facto* laws are necessarily retrospective, but not *e converso*. A curative or confirmatory statute is retrospective, but not *ex post facto*. Constitutions of nearly all the states contain prohibitions against *ex post facto* laws, but only a few forbid retrospective legislation in specific terms. Black, Const. Prohib. §§ 170, 172, 222.

Retrospective laws divesting vested rights are impolitic and unjust; but they are not "*ex post facto* laws," within the meaning of the constitution of the United States, nor repugnant to any other of its provisions; and, if not repugnant to the state constitution, a court cannot pronounce them to be void, merely because in their judgment they are contrary to the principles of natural justice. 2 Paine, 74.

Every retrospective act is not necessarily an *ex post facto* law. That phrase embraces only such laws as impose or affect penalties or forfeitures. 4 Wall. 172.

Retrospective laws which do not impair the obligation of contracts, or affect vested rights, or partake of the character of *ex post facto* laws, are not prohibited by the constitution. 36 Barb. 447.

Ex præcedentibus et consequentibus optima fit interpretatio. 1 Roll. 374. The best interpretation is made from the context.

EX PRÆCOGITATA MALICIA. Of malice aforethought. Reg. Orig. 102.

EX PROPRIO MOTU. Of his own accord.

EX PROPRIO VIGORE. By their or its own force. 2 Kent, Comm. 457.

EX PROVISIONE HOMINIS. By the provision of man. By the limitation of the party, as distinguished from the disposition of the law. 11 Coke, 80*b*.

EX PROVISIONE MARITI. From the provision of the husband.

EX QUASI CONTRACTU. From *quasi* contract. Fleta, lib. 2, c. 60.

EX RELATIONE. Upon relation or information. Legal proceedings which are instituted by the attorney general (or other proper person) in the name and behalf of the state, but on the information and at the instigation of an individual who has a private interest in the matter, are said to be taken "on the relation" (*ex relatione*) of such person, who is called the "relator." Such a cause is usually entitled thus: "State *ex rel.* Doe v. Roe."

In the books of reports, when a case is said to be reported *ex relatione*, it is meant that the reporter derives his account of it, not from personal knowledge, but from the relation or narrative of some person who was present at the argument.

EX RIGORE JURIS. According to the rigor or strictness of law; in strictness of law. Fleta, lib 3. c. 10, § 2.

EX SCRIPTIS OLIM VISIS. From writings formerly seen. A term used as descriptive of that kind of proof of handwriting where the knowledge has been acquired by the witness having seen letters or other documents professing to be the handwriting of the party, and having afterwards communicated personally with the party upon the contents of those letters or documents, or having otherwise acted upon them by written answers, producing further correspondence or acquiescence by the party in some matter to which they relate, or by the witness transacting with the party some business to which they relate, or by any other mode of communication between the party and the witness which, in the ordinary course of the transactions of life, induces a reasonable presumption that the letters or documents were the handwriting of the party. 5 Adol. & E. 730.

EX STATUTO. According to the statute. Fleta, lib. 5, c. 11, § 1.

EX STIPULATU ACTIO. In the civil law. An action of stipulation. An action given to recover marriage portions. Inst. 4, 6, 29.

EX TEMPORE. From or in consequence of time; by lapse of time. Bract. fols. 51, 52. *Ex diuturno tempore*, from length of time. Id. fol. 51*b*.

Without preparation or premeditation.

EX TESTAMENTO. From, by, or under a will. The opposite of *ab intestato*, (*q. v.*)

Ex tota materia emergat resolutio. The explanation should arise out of the whole subject-matter; the exposition of a statute should be made from all its parts together. Wing. Max. 238.

Ex turpi causa non oritur actio. Out of a base [illegal, or immoral] consideration, an action does [can] not arise. 1 Selw. N. P. 63; Broom, Max. 730, 732; Story, Ag. § 195.

Ex turpi contractu actio non oritur. From an immoral or iniquitous contract an action does not arise. A contract founded upon an illegal or immoral consideration cannot be enforced by action. 2 Kent, Comm. 466; Dig. 2, 14, 27, 4.

EX UNA PARTE. Of one part or side; on one side.

Ex uno disces omnes. From one thing you can discern all.

EX UTRAQUE PARTE. On both sides. Dyer, 126b.

EX UTRISQUE PARENTIBUS CONJUNCTI. Related on the side of both parents; of the whole blood. Hale, Com. Law, c. 11.

EX VI TERMINI. From or by the force of the term. From the very meaning of the expression used. 2 Bl. Comm. 109, 115.

EX VISCERIBUS. From the bowels. From the vital part, the very essence of the thing. 10 Coke, 24b; 2 Metc. (Mass.) 213. *Ex visceribus verborum*, from the mere words and nothing else. 10 Johns. 494; 1 Story, Eq. Jur. § 980.

EX VISITATIONE DEI. By the dispensation of God; by reason of physical incapacity. Anciently, when a prisoner, being arraigned, stood silent instead of pleading, a jury was impaneled to inquire whether he obstinately stood mute or was dumb *ex visitatione Dei*. 4 Steph. Comm. 394.

Also by natural, as distinguished from violent, causes. When a coroner's inquest finds that the death was due to disease or other natural cause, it is frequently phrased "*ex visitatione Dei*."

EX VISU SCRIPTIONIS. From sight of the writing; from having seen a person write. A term employed to describe one of the modes of proof of handwriting. Best, Pres. 218.

EX VOLUNTATE. Voluntarily; from free-will or choice.

EXACTION. The wrongful act of an officer or other person in compelling payment of a fee or reward for his services, under color of his official authority, where no payment is due.

Between "extortion" and "exaction" there is this difference: that in the former case the officer extorts more than his due, when something is due to him; in the latter, he exacts what is not his due, when there is nothing due to him. Co. Litt. 368.

EXACTOR. In the civil law. A gatherer or receiver of money; a collector of taxes. Cod. 10, 19.

In old English law. A collector of the public moneys; a tax gatherer. Thus, *exactor regis* was the name of the king's tax collector, who took up the taxes and other debts due the treasury.

EXACTOR REGIS. The king's collector of taxes; also a sheriff.

EXALTARE. In old English law. To raise; to elevate. Frequently spoken of water, *i. e.*, to raise the surface of a pond or pool.

EXAMEN. L. Lat. A trial. *Examen computi*, the balance of an account. Townsh. Pl. 223.

EXAMINATION. An investigation; search; interrogating.

In trial practice. The examination of a witness consists of the series of questions put to him by a party to the action, or his counsel, for the purpose of bringing before the court and jury in legal form the knowledge which the witness has of the facts and matters in dispute, or of probing and sifting his evidence previously given.

The examination of a witness by the party producing him is denominated the "direct examination;" the examination of the same witness, upon the same matter, by the adverse party, the "cross-examination." The direct examination must be completed before the cross-examination begins, unless the court otherwise direct. Code Civil Proc. Cal. § 2045.

In criminal practice. An investigation by a magistrate of a person who has been charged with crime and arrested, or of the facts and circumstances which are alleged to have attended the crime and to fasten suspicion upon the party so charged, in order to ascertain whether there is sufficient ground to hold him to bail for his trial by the proper court.

EXAMINATION DE BENE ESSE. A provisional examination of a witness; an examination of a witness whose testimony is important and might otherwise be lost, held out of court and before the trial, with the proviso that the deposition so taken may be used on the trial in case the witness is unable to attend in person at that time or cannot be produced.

EXAMINATION OF A LONG ACCOUNT. This phrase does not mean the examination of the account to ascertain the result or effect of it, but the proof by testimony of the correctness of the items composing it. 5 Daly, 63.

EXAMINATION OF BANKRUPT. This is the interrogation of a bankrupt, in the course of proceedings in bankruptcy, touching the state of his property. This is authorized in the United States by Rev. St.

§ 5086; and § 5087 authorizes the examination of a bankrupt's wife.

EXAMINATION OF INVENTION. An inquiry made at the patent-office, upon application for a patent, into the novelty and utility of the alleged invention, and as to its interfering with any other patented invention. Rev. St. U. S. § 4893.

EXAMINATION OF TITLE. An investigation made by or for a person who intends to purchase real estate, in the offices where the public records are kept, to ascertain the history and present condition of the title to such land, and its *status* with reference to liens, incumbrances, clouds, etc.

EXAMINED COPY. A copy of a record, public book, or register, and which has been compared with the original. 1 Campb. 469.

EXAMINER. In English law. A person appointed by a court to take the examination of witnesses in an action, *i. e.,* to take down the result of their interrogation by the parties or their counsel, either by written interrogatories or *viva voce.* An examiner is generally appointed where a witness is in a foreign country, or is too ill or infirm to attend before the court, and is either an officer of the court, or a person specially appointed for the purpose. Sweet.

In New Jersey. An examiner is an officer appointed by the court of chancery to take testimony in causes depending in that court. His powers are similar to those of the English examiner in chancery.

In the patent-office. An officer in the patent-office charged with the duty of examining the patentability of inventions for which patents are asked.

EXAMINER IN CHANCERY. An officer of the court of chancery, before whom witnesses are examined, and their testimony reduced to writing, for the purpose of being read on the hearing of the cause. Cowell.

EXAMINERS. Persons appointed to question students of law in order to ascertain their qualifications before they are admitted to practice.

EXANNUAL ROLL. In old English practice. A roll into which (in the old way of exhibiting sheriffs' accounts) the illeviable fines and desperate debts were transcribed, and which was *annually* read to the sheriff upon his accounting, to see what might be gotten. Cowell.

AM. DICT. LAW—29

EXCAMB. In Scotch law. To exchange. 6 Bell, App. Cas. 19, 22.

EXCAMBIATOR. An exchanger of lands; a broker. Obsolete.

EXCAMBION. In Scotch law. Exchange. 1 Forb. Inst. pt. 2, p. 173.

EXCAMBIUM. An exchange; a place where merchants meet to transact their business; also an equivalent in recompense; a recompense in lieu of dower *ad ostium ecclesiæ.*

EXCELLENCY. In English law. The title of a viceroy, governor general, ambassador, or commander in chief.

In America. The title is sometimes given to the chief executive of a state or of the nation.

EXCEPTANT. One who excepts; one who makes or files exceptions; one who objects to a ruling, instruction, or anything proposed or ordered.

EXCEPTIO. In Roman law. An exception. In a general sense, a judicial allegation opposed by a defendant to the plaintiff's action. Calvin.

A stop or stay to an action opposed by the defendant. Cowell.

Answering to the "defense" or "plea" of the common law. An allegation and defense of a defendant by which the plaintiff's claim or complaint is defeated, either according to strict law or upon grounds of equity.

In a stricter sense, the exclusion of an action that lay in strict law, on grounds of equity, (*actionis jure stricto competentis ob æquitatem exclusio.*) Heinecc. A kind of limitation of an action, by which it was shown that the action, though otherwise just, did not lie in the particular case. Calvin. A species of defense allowed in cases where, though the action as brought by the plaintiff was in itself just, yet it was unjust as against the particular party sued. Inst. 4, 13, pr.

In modern civil law. A plea by which the defendant admits the cause of action, but alleges new facts which, provided they be true, totally or partially answer the allegations put forward on the other side; thus distinguished from a mere traverse of the plaintiff's averments. Tomkins & J. Mod. Rom. Law, 90. In this use, the term corresponds to the common-law plea in confession and avoidance.

EXCEPTIO DILATORIA. In the civil law. A dilatory exception; called also "*tem-*

poralis," (temporary;) one which defeated the action for a time, (*quæ ad tempus nocet,*) and created delay, (*et temporis dilationem tribuit;*) such as an agreement not to sue within a certain time, as five years. Inst. 4, 13, 10. See Dig. 44, 1, 3.

EXCEPTIO DOLI MALI. In the civil law. An exception or plea of fraud. Inst. 4, 13, 1, 9; Bract. fol. 100*b.*

Exceptio ejus rei cujus petitur dissolutio nulla est. A plea of that matter the dissolution of which is sought [by the action] is null, [or of no effect.] Jenk. Cent. 37, case 71.

Exceptio falsi omnium ultima. A plea denying a fact is the last of all.

EXCEPTIO IN FACTUM. In the civil law. An exception on the fact. An exception or plea founded on the peculiar circumstances of the case. Inst. 4, 13, 1.

EXCEPTIO JURISJURANDI. In the civil law. An exception of oath; an exception or plea that the matter had been sworn to. Inst. 4, 13, 4. This kind of exception was allowed where a debtor, at the instance of his creditor, (*creditore deferente,*) had sworn that nothing was due the latter, and had notwithstanding been sued by him. Id.

EXCEPTIO METUS. In the civil law. An exception or plea of fear or compulsion. Inst. 4, 13, 1, 9; Bract. fol. 100*b.* Answering to the modern plea of duress.

Exceptio nulla est versus actionem quæ exceptionem perimit. There is [can be] no plea against an action which destroys [the matter of] the plea. Jenk. Cent. 106, case 2.

EXCEPTIO PACTI CONVENTI. In the civil law. An exception of compact; an exception or plea that the plaintiff had agreed not to sue. Inst. 4, 13, 3.

EXCEPTIO PECUNIÆ NON NUMERATÆ. An exception or plea of money not paid; a defense which might be set up by a party who was sued on a promise to repay money which he had never received. Inst. 4, 13, 2.

EXCEPTIO PEREMPTORIA. In the civil law. A peremptory exception; called also "*perpetua,*" (perpetual;) one which forever destroyed the subject-matter or ground of the action, (*quæ semper rem de qua agitur perimit;*) such as the *exceptio doli mali,* the

exceptio metus, etc. Inst. 4, 13, 9. See Dig. 44, 1, 3.

In common law. A peremptory plea; a plea in bar. Bract. fols. 240, 399*b.*

Exceptio probat regulam. The exception proves the rule. 11 Coke, 41; 3 Term, 722. Sometimes quoted with the addition "*de rebus non exceptis,*" ("so far as concerns the matters not excepted.")

Exceptio quæ firmat legem, exponit legem. An exception which confirms the law explains the law. 2 Bulst. 189.

EXCEPTIO REI JUDICATÆ. In the civil law. An exception or plea of matter adjudged; a plea that the subject-matter of the action had been determined in a previous action. Inst. 4, 13, 5.

This term is adopted by Bracton, and is constantly used in modern law to denote a defense founded upon a previous adjudication of the same matter. Bract. fols. 100*b,* 177; 2 Kent, Comm. 120. A plea of a former recovery or judgment.

EXCEPTIO REI VENDITÆ ET TRADITÆ. In the civil law. An exception or plea of the sale and delivery of the thing. This exception presumes that there was a valid sale and a proper tradition; but though, in consequence of the rule that no one can transfer to another a greater right than he himself has, no property was transferred, yet because of some particular circumstance the real owner is estopped from contesting it. Mackeld. Rom. Law, § 299.

Exceptio semper ultimo ponenda est. An exception should always be put last. 9 Coke, 53.

EXCEPTIO TEMPORIS. In the civil law. An exception or plea analogous to that of the statute of limitations in our law; viz., that the time prescribed by law for bringing such actions has expired. Mackeld. Rom. Law, § 213.

EXCEPTION. In practice. A formal objection to the action of the court, during the trial of a cause, in refusing a request or overruling an objection; implying that the party excepting does not acquiesce in the decision of the court, but will seek to procure its reversal, and that he means to save the benefit of his request or objection in some future proceeding.

It is also somewhat used to signify other objections in the course of a suit; for example, exception to bail is a formal objection that special bail offered by defendant are insufficient. 1 Tidd, Pr. 255.

An exception is an objection upon a matter of law to a decision made, either before or after judgment, by a court, tribunal, judge, or other judicial officer, in an action or proceeding. The exception must be taken at the time the decision is made. Code Civil Proc. Cal. § 646; 32 Cal. 307.

In admiralty and equity practice. An exception is a formal allegation tendered by a party that some previous pleading or proceeding taken by the adverse party is insufficient.

In statutory law. An exception in a statute is a clause designed to reserve or exempt some individuals from the general class of persons or things to which the language of the act in general attaches.

An exception differs from an explanation, which, by the use of a *videlicet, proviso,* etc., is allowed only to explain doubtful clauses precedent, or to separate and distribute generals into particulars. 3 Pick. 272.

In contracts. A clause in a deed or other conveyance by which the grantor excepts something out of that which he granted before by the deed.

The distinction between an exception and a reservation is that an *exception* is always of part of the thing granted, and of a thing *in esse*; a *reservation* is always of a thing not *in esse*, but newly created or reserved out of the land or tenement demised. Co. Litt. 47a; 4 Kent, Comm. 468. It has been also said that there is a diversity between an exception and a saving, for an exception exempts clearly, but a saving goes to the matters touched, and does not exempt. Plowd. 361.

In the civil law. An *exceptio* or plea. Used in this sense in Louisiana.

Declinatory exceptions are such dilatory exceptions as merely decline the jurisdiction of the judge before whom the action is brought. Code Proc. La. 334.

Dilatory exceptions are such as do not tend to defeat the action, but only to retard its progress.

Peremptory exceptions are those which tend to the dismissal of the action.

EXCEPTION TO BAIL. An objection to the special bail put in by the defendant to an action at law made by the plaintiff on grounds of the insufficiency of the bail. 1 Tidd, Pr. 255.

EXCEPTIS EXCIPIENDIS. With all necessary exceptions.

EXCEPTOR. In old English law. A party who entered an exception or plea.

EXCERPTA, or EXCERPTS. Extracts.

EXCESS. When a defendant pleaded to an action of assault that the plaintiff trespassed on his land, and he would not depart when ordered, whereupon he, *molliter manus imposuit,* gently laid hands on him, the replication of *excess* was to the effect that the defendant used more force than necessary. Wharton.

EXCESSIVE. In order that bail required (or punishment inflicted) should be described as "excessive," it must be, *per se,* unreasonably great and clearly disproportionate to the offense involved, or the peculiar circumstances appearing must show it to be so in the particular case. 44 Cal. 558; 53 Cal. 410; 39 Conn. 484.

EXCESSIVE DAMAGES. Damages awarded by a jury which are grossly in excess of the amount warranted by law on the facts and circumstances of the case; unreasonable or outrageous damages. A verdict giving excessive damages is ground for a new trial.

Excessivum in jure reprobatur. Excessus in re qualibet jure reprobatur communi. Co. Litt. 44. Excess in law is reprehended. Excess in anything is reprehended at common law.

EXCHANGE. In conveyancing. A mutual grant of equal interests, (in lands or tenements,) the one in consideration of the other. 2 Bl. Comm. 323. In the United States, it appears, exchange does not differ from bargain and sale. See 2 Bouv. Inst. 2055.

In commercial law. A negotiation by which one person transfers to another funds which he has in a certain place, either at a price agreed upon or which is fixed by commercial usage.

The profit which arises from a maritime loan, when such profit is a percentage on the money lent, considering it in the light of money lent in one place to be returned in another, with a difference in amount in the sum borrowed and that paid, arising from the difference of time and place. The term is commonly used in this sense by French writers. Hall, Emerig. Mar. Loans, 56n.

A public place where merchants, brokers, factors, etc., meet to transact their business.

EXCHANGE, BILL OF. See BILL OF EXCHANGE.

EXCHANGE OF GOODS. A commutation, transmutation, or transfer of goods for other goods, as distinguished from *sale*, which is a transfer of goods for money. 2 Bl. Comm. 446; 2 Steph. Comm. 120.

Exchange is a contract by which the parties mutually give, or agree to give, one thing for another, neither thing, or both things, being money only. Civil Code Cal. § 1804; Civil Code Dak. § 1029; Civil Code La. art. 2660.

The distinction between a sale and exchange of property is rather one of shadow than of substance. In both cases the title to property is absolutely transferred; and the same rules of law are applicable to the transaction, whether the consideration of the contract is money or by way of barter. It can make no essential difference in the rights and obligations of parties that goods and merchandise are transferred and paid for by other goods and merchandise instead of by money, which is but the representative of value or property. 14 Gray, 367.

EXCHANGE OF LIVINGS. In ecclesiastical law. This is effected by resigning them into the bishop's hands, and each party being inducted into the other's benefice. If either die before both are inducted, the exchange is void.

EXCHEQUER. That department of the English government which has charge of the collection of the national revenue; the treasury department.

It is said to have been so named from the chequered cloth, resembling a chess-board, which anciently covered the table there, and on which, when certain of the king's accounts were made up, the sums were marked and scored with counters. 3 Bl. Comm. 44.

EXCHEQUER BILLS. Bills of credit issued in England by authority of parliament. Brande. Instruments issued at the exchequer, under the authority, for the most part, of acts of parliament passed for the purpose, and containing an engagement on the part of the government for repayment of the principal sums advanced with interest. 2 Steph. Comm. 586.

EXCHEQUER CHAMBER, COURT OF. In English law. A tribunal of error and appeal.

First, it existed in former times as a court of mere debate, such causes from the other courts being sometimes adjourned into it as the judges, upon argument, found to be of great weight and difficulty, before any judgment was given upon them in the court below. It then consisted of all the judges of the three superior courts of common law, and at times the lord chancellor also.

Second, it existed as a court of error, where the judgments of each of the superior courts of common law, in all actions whatever, were subject to revision by the judges of the other two sitting collectively. The composition of this court consequently admitted of three different combinations, consisting of any two of the courts below which were not parties to the judgment appealed against. There was no given number required to constitute the exchequer chamber, but the court never consisted of less than five. One counsel only was heard on each side. Error lay from this court to the house of lords. The court is abolished, and its jurisdiction in appeals (proceedings in error in civil cases and bills of exceptions being abolished) is transferred to the court of appeal. Jud. Act 1875, § 18. Wharton.

EXCHEQUER, COURT OF. See COURT OF EXCHEQUER.

EXCHEQUER DIVISION. A division of the English high court of justice, to which the special business of the court of exchequer was specially assigned by section 34 of the judicature act of 1873. Merged in the queen's bench division from and after 1881, by order in council under section 31 of that act. Wharton.

EXCISE. An inland imposition, paid sometimes upon the consumption of the commodity, and frequently upon the retail sale. 1 Bl. Comm. 318; Story, Const. § 950.

The words "tax" and "excise," although often used as synonymous, are to be considered as having entirely distinct and separate significations, under Const. Mass. c. 1, § 1, art. 4. The former is a charge apportioned either among the whole people of the state or those residing within certain districts, municipalities, or sections. It is required to be imposed, so that, if levied for the public charges of government, it shall be shared according to the estate, real and personal, which each person may possess; or, if raised to defray the cost of some local improvement of a public nature, it shall be borne by those who will receive some special and peculiar benefit or advantage which an expenditure of money for a public object may cause to those on whom the tax is assessed. An excise, on the other hand, is of a different character. It is based on no rule of apportionment or equality whatever. It is a fixed, absolute, and direct charge laid on merchandise, products, or commodities, without any regard to the amount of property belonging to those on whom it may fall, or to any supposed relation between money expended for a public object and a special benefit occasioned to those by whom the charge is to be paid. 11 Allen, 268.

In English law. The name given to the duties or taxes laid on certain articles produced and consumed at home, among which spirits have always been the most important; but, exclusive of these, the duties on the licenses of auctioneers, brewers, etc., and on the licenses to keep dogs, kill game, etc., are included in the excise duties. Wharton.

EXCISE LAW. A law imposing excise duties on specified commodities, and providing for the collection of revenue therefrom.

In a more restricted and more popular sense, a law regulating, restricting, or taxing the manufacture or sale of intoxicating liquors.

EXCLUSA. In old English law. A sluice to carry off water; the payment to the lord for the benefit of such a sluice. Cowell.

EXCLUSIVE. Shutting out; debarring from interference or participation; vested in one person alone. An exclusive right is one which only the grantee thereof can exercise, and from which all others are prohibited or shut out.

A statute does not grant an "exclusive" privilege or franchise, unless it shuts out or excludes others from enjoying a similar privilege or franchise. 98 N. Y. 151.

EXCOMMENGEMENT. Excommunication, (*q. v.*) Co. Litt. 134*a*.

EXCOMMUNICATION. A sentence of censure pronounced by one of the spiritual courts for offenses falling under ecclesiastical cognizance. It is described in the books as twofold: (1) The *lesser* excommunication, which is an ecclesiastical censure, excluding the party from the sacraments; (2) the *greater*, which excludes him from the company of all Christians. Formerly, too, an excommunicated man was under various civil disabilities. He could not serve upon juries, or be a witness in any court; neither could he bring an action to recover lands or money due to him. These penalties are abolished by St. 53 Geo. III. c. 127. 3 Steph. Comm. 721.

EXCOMMUNICATO CAPIENDO. In ecclesiastical law. A writ issuing out of chancery, founded on a bishop's certificate that the defendant had been excommunicated, and requiring the sheriff to arrest and imprison him, returnable to the king's bench. 4 Bl. Comm. 415; Bac. Abr. "Excommunication," E.

EXCOMMUNICATO DELIBERANDO. A writ to the sheriff for delivery of an excommunicated person out of prison, upon certificate from the ordinary of his conform-

ity to the ecclesiastical jurisdiction. Fitzh. Nat. Brev. 63.

Excommunicato interdicitur omnis actus legitimus, ita quod agere non potest, nec aliquem convenire, licet ipse ab aliis possit conveniri. Co. Litt. 133. Every legal act is forbidden an excommunicated person, so that he cannot act, nor sue any person, but he may be sued by others.

EXCOMMUNICATO RECAPIENDO. A writ commanding that persons excommunicated, who for their obstinacy had been committed to prison, but were unlawfully set free before they had given caution to obey the authority of the church, should be sought after, retaken, and imprisoned again. Reg. Orig. 67.

EXCULPATION, LETTERS OF. In Scotch law. A warrant granted at the suit of a prisoner for citing witnesses in his own defense.

EXCUSABLE HOMICIDE. In criminal law. The killing of a human being, either by misadventure or in self-defense. The name itself imports some fault, error, or omission, so trivial, however, that the law excuses it from the guilt of felony, though in strictness it judges it deserving of some little degree of punishment. 4 Bl. Comm. 182.

It is of two sorts,—either *per infortunium*, by misadventure, or *se defendendo*, upon a sudden affray. Homicide *per infortunium* is where a man, doing a lawful act, without any intention of hurt, unfortunately kills another; but, if death ensue from any unlawful act, the offense is manslaughter, and not misadventure. Homicide *se defendendo* is where a man kills another upon a sudden affray, merely in his own defense, or in defense of his wife, child, parent, or servant, and not from any vindictive feeling. 4 Bl. Comm. 182.

Excusat aut extenuat delictum in capitalibus quod non operatur idem in civilibus. Bac. Max. r. 15. That may excuse or palliate a wrongful act in capital cases which would not have the same effect in civil injuries. See Broom, Max. 324.

EXCUSATIO. In the civil law. An excuse or reason which exempts from some duty or obligation.

EXCUSATOR. In English law. An excuser.

In old German law. A defendant; he who utterly denies the plaintiff's claim. Du Cange.

Excusatur quis quod clameum non opposuerit, ut si toto tempore litigii fuit ultra mare quacunque occasione. Co. Litt. 260. He is excused who does not bring his claim, if, during the whole period in which it ought to have been brought, he has been beyond sea for any reason.

EXCUSE. A reason alleged for doing or not doing a thing. Worcester.

A matter alleged as a reason for relief or exemption from some duty or obligation.

EXCUSS. To seize and detain by law.

EXCUSSIO. In the civil law. A diligent prosecution of a remedy against a debtor; the exhausting of a remedy against a principal debtor, before resorting to his sureties. Translated "discussion," (*q. v.*)

In old English law. Rescue or rescous. Spelman.

EXEAT. A permission which a bishop grants to a priest to go out of his diocese; also leave to go out generally.

EXECUTE. To finish, accomplish, make complete, fulfill. To perform; obey the injunctions of.

To make; as to execute a deed, which includes signing, sealing, and delivery.

To perform; carry out according to its terms; as to execute a contract.

To fulfill the purpose of; to obey; to perform the commands of; as to execute a writ.

To fulfill the sentence of the law upon a person judicially condemned to suffer death.

A statute is said to *execute* a use where it transmutes the equitable interest of the *cestui que use* into a legal estate of the same nature, and makes him tenant of the land accordingly, in lieu of the feoffee to uses or trustee, whose estate, on the other hand, is at the same moment annihilated. 1 Steph. Comm. 339.

EXECUTED. Completed; carried into full effect; already done or performed; taking effect immediately; now in existence or in possession; conveying an immediate right or possession. The opposite of *executory*.

EXECUTED CONSIDERATION. A consideration which is wholly past. 1 Pars. Cont. 391. An act done or value given before the making of the agreement.

EXECUTED CONTRACT. One where nothing remains to be done by either party, and where the transaction is completed at the moment that the agreement is made, as where an article is sold and delivered, and payment therefor is made on the spot. A contract is said to be *executory* where some future act is to be done, as where an agreement is made to build a house in six months, or to do an act on or before some future day, or to lend money upon a certain interest, payable at a future time. Story, Cont. 8.

EXECUTED ESTATE. An estate whereby a present interest passes to and resides in the tenant, not dependent upon any subsequent circumstance or contingency. They are more commonly called "estates in possession." 2 Bl. Comm. 162.

An estate where there is vested in the grantee a present and immediate right of present or future enjoyment.

EXECUTED FINE. The fine *sur cognizance de droit, come ceo que il ad de son done;* or a fine upon acknowledgment of the right of the cognizee, as that which he has of the gift of the cognizor. Abolished by 3 & 4 Wm. IV. c. 74.

EXECUTED REMAINDER. A remainder which vests a present interest in the tenant, though the enjoyment is postponed to the future. 2 Bl. Comm. 168; Fearne, Rem. 31.

EXECUTED TRUST. A trust of which the scheme has in the outset been completely declared. Adams, Eq. 151. A trust in which the estates and interest in the subject-matter of the trust are completely limited and defined by the instrument creating the trust, and require no further instruments to complete them. Bisp. Eq. 20.

As all trusts are executory in this sense, that the trustee is bound to dispose of the estate according to the tenure of his trust, whether active or passive, it would be more accurate and precise to substitute the terms, "perfect" and "imperfect" for "executed" and "executory" trusts. 1 Hayes, Conv. 85.

EXECUTED USE. The first use in a conveyance upon which the statute of uses operates by bringing the possession to it, the combination of which, *i. e.*, the use and the possession, form the legal estate, and thus the statute is said to execute the use. Wharton.

EXECUTED WRIT. In practice. A writ carried into effect by the officer to whom it is directed. The term "executed," applied to a writ, has been held to mean "used." Amb. 61.

EXECUTIO. Lat. The doing or following up of a thing; the doing a thing completely or thoroughly; management or administration.

In old practice. Execution; the final process in an action.

EXECUTIO BONORUM. In old English law. Management or administration of goods. *Ad ecclesiam et ad amicos pertinebit executio bonorum*, the execution of the goods shall belong to the church and to the friends of the deceased. Bract. fol. 60*b*.

Executio est executio juris secundum judicium. 3 Inst. 212. Execution is the execution of the law according to the judgment.

Executio est finis et fructus legis. Co. Litt. 289. Execution is the end and fruit of the law.

Executio juris non habet injuriam. 2 Roll. 301. The execution of law does no injury.

EXECUTION. The completion, fulfillment, or perfecting of anything, or carrying it into operation and effect. The signing, sealing, and delivery of a deed. The signing and publication of a will. The performance of a contract according to its terms.

In practice. The last stage of a suit, whereby possession is obtained of anything recovered. It is styled "final process," and consists in putting the sentence of the law in force. 3 Bl. Comm. 412. The carrying into effect of the sentence or judgment of a court.

Also the name of a writ issued to a sheriff, constable, or marshal, authorizing and requiring him to execute the judgment of the court.

At common law, executions are said to be either *final* or *quousque;* the former, where complete satisfaction of the debt is intended to be procured by this process; the latter, where the execution is only a means to an end, as where the defendant is arrested on *ca. sa.*

In criminal law. The carrying into effect the sentence of the law by the infliction of capital punishment. 4 Bl. Comm. 403; 4 Steph. Comm. 470.

EXECUTION OF DECREE. Sometimes from the neglect of parties, or some other cause, it became impossible to carry a decree into execution without the further decree of the court upon a bill filed for that purpose. This happened generally in cases where, parties having neglected to proceed upon the decree, their rights under it became so embarrassed by a variety of subsequent events that it was necessary to have the decree of the court to settle and ascertain them. Such a bill might also be brought to carry into execution the judgment of an inferior court of equity, if the jurisdiction of that court was not equal to the purpose; as in the case of a decree in Wales, which the defendant avoided by fleeing into England.

This species of bill was generally partly an original bill, and partly a bill in the nature of an original bill, though not strictly original. Story, Eq. Pl. 342; Daniell, Ch. Pr. 1429.

EXECUTION OF DEEDS. The signing, sealing, and delivery of them by the parties, as their own acts and deeds, in the presence of witnesses.

EXECUTION PAREE. In French law. A right founded on an act passed before a notary, by which the creditor may immediately, without citation or summons, seize and cause to be sold the property of his debtor, out of the proceeds of which to receive his payment. It imports a confession of judgment, and is not unlike a warrant of attorney. Code Proc. La. art. 732; 6 Toullier, no. 208; 7 Toullier, no. 99. ·

EXECUTIONE FACIENDÂ. A writ commanding execution of a judgment. Obsolete. Cowell.

EXECUTIONE FACIENDÂ IN WITHERNAMIUM. A writ that lay for taking cattle of one who has conveyed the cattle of another out of the county, so that the sheriff cannot replevy them. Reg. Orig. 82.

EXECUTIONE JUDICII. A writ directed to the judge of an inferior court to do execution upon a judgment therein, or to return some reasonable cause wherefore he delays the execution. Fitzh. Nat. Brev. 20.

EXECUTIONER. The name given to him who puts criminals to death, according to their sentence; a hangman.

EXECUTIVE. As distinguished from the legislative and judicial departments of government, the executive department is that which is charged with the detail of carrying the laws into effect and securing their due observance. The word "executive" is also used as an impersonal designation of the chief executive officer of a state or nation.

Executive officer means an officer in whom resides the power to execute the laws. 4 Cal. 127, 146.

EXECUTIVE ADMINISTRATION, or MINISTRY. A political term in England, applicable to the higher and responsible class of public officials by whom the chief departments of the government of the kingdom are administered. The number of these amounts to fifty or sixty persons. Their tenure of office depends on the confidence of a majority of the house of commons, and they are supposed to be agreed on all matters of general policy except such as are specifically left open questions. Cab. Lawy.

EXECUTOR. A person appointed by a testator to carry out the directions and requests in his will, and to dispose of the property according to his testamentary provisions after his decease.

One to whom another man commits by his last will the execution of that will and testament. 2 Bl. Comm. 503.

A person to whom a testator by his will commits the *execution*, or putting in force, of that instrument and its codicils. Fonbl. 307.

Executors are classified according to the following several methods:

They are either *general* or *special*. The former term denotes an executor who is to have charge of the whole estate, wherever found, and administer it to a final settlement; while a special executor is only empowered by the will to take charge of a limited portion of the estate, or such part as may lie in one place, or to carry on the administration only to a prescribed point.

They are either *instituted* or *substituted*. An instituted executor is one who is appointed by the testator without any condition; while a substituted executor is one named to fill the office in case the person first nominated should refuse to act.

In the phraseology of ecclesiastical law, they are of the following kinds:

Executor à lege constitutus, an executor appointed by law; the ordinary of the diocese.

Executor ab episcopo constitutus, or *executor dativus*, an executor appointed by the bishop; an administrator to an intestate.

Executor à testatore constitutus, an executor appointed by a testator. Otherwise termed "*executor testamentarius;*" a testamentary executor.

An *executor to the tenor* is one who, though not directly constituted executor by the will,

is therein charged with duties in relation to the estate which can only be performed by the executor.

In the civil law. A ministerial officer who executed or carried into effect the judgment or sentence in a cause. Calvin.

EXECUTOR DE SON TORT. Executor of his own wrong. A person who assumes to act as executor of an estate without any lawful warrant or authority, but who, by his intermeddling, makes himself liable as an executor to a certain extent.

If a stranger takes upon him to act as executor without any just authority, (as by intermeddling with the goods of the deceased, and many other transactions,) he is called in law an "executor of his own wrong," *de son tort.* 2 Bl. Comm. 507.

EXECUTOR LUCRATUS. An executor who has assets of his testator who in his life-time made himself liable by a wrongful interference with the property of another. 6 Jur. (N. S.) 543.

EXECUTORY. That which is yet to be executed or performed; that which remains to be carried into operation or effect; incomplete; depending upon a future performance or event. The opposite of *executed*.

EXECUTORY BEQUEST. See BEQUEST.

EXECUTORY CONSIDERATION. A consideration which is to be performed after the contract for which it is a consideration is made.

EXECUTORY CONTRACT. A contract which is to be executed at some future time, and which conveys only a *chose in action.* 2 Bl. Comm. 443; 2 Kent, Comm. 511, 512, note. See EXECUTED CONTRACT.

EXECUTORY DEVISE. In a general sense, a devise of a future interest in lands, not to take effect at the testator's death, but limited to arise and vest upon some future contingency. 1 Fearne, Rem. 382. A disposition of lands by will, by which no estate vests at the death of the devisor, but only on some future contingency. 2 Bl. Comm. 172.

In a stricter sense, a limitation by will of a future contingent interest in lands, contrary to the rules of the common law. 4 Kent, Comm. 263; 1 Steph. Comm. 564. A limitation by will of a future estate or interest in land, which cannot, consistently with the rules of law, take effect as a remainder. 2 Pow. Dev. (by Jarman,) 237.

By the executory devise no estate vests at the death of the devisor or testator, but only on the future contingency. It is only an indulgence to the last will and testament which is supposed to be made by one *inops consilii.* When the limitation by devise is such that the future interest falls within the rules of contingent remainders, it is a contingent remainder, and not an executory devise. 2 Bl. Comm. 173; 4 Kent, 257; 3 Term, 763.

EXECUTORY ESTATE. An estate or interest in lands, the vesting or enjoyment of which depends upon some future contingency. Such estate may be an *executory devise,* or an *executory remainder,* which is the same as a contingent remainder, because no present interest passes.

EXECUTORY FINES. These are the fines *sur cognizance de droit tantum; sur concessit;* and *sur done, grant et render.* Abolished by 3 & 4 Wm. IV. c. 74.

EXECUTORY INTERESTS. A general term, comprising all future estates and interests in land or personalty, other than reversions and remainders.

EXECUTORY LIMITATION. A limitation of a future interest by deed or will; if by will, it is also called an "executory devise."

EXECUTORY PROCESS. A process which can be resorted to in the following cases, namely: (1) When the right of the creditor arises from an act importing confession of judgment, and which contains a privilege or mortgage in his favor; (2) when the creditor demands the execution of a judgment which has been rendered by a tribunal different from that within whose jurisdiction the execution is sought. Code Prac. La. art. 732.

EXECUTORY TRUST. One which requires the execution of some further instrument, or the doing of some further act, on the part of the creator of the trust or of the trustee, towards its complete creation or full effect. An *executed* trust is one fully created and of immediate effect. These terms do not relate to the execution of the trust as regards the beneficiary.

EXECUTORY USES. These are springing uses, which confer a legal title answering to an executory devise; as when a limitation to the use of A. in fee is defeasible by a limitation to the use of B., to arise at a future period, or on a given event.

EXECUTRESS. A female executor. Hardr. 165, 473. See EXECUTRIX.

EXECUTRIX. A woman who has been appointed by will to execute such will or testament.

EXECUTRY. In Scotch law. The movable estate of a person dying, which goes to his nearest of kin. So called as falling under the distribution of an executor. Bell.

Exempla illustrant non restringunt legem. Co. Litt. 240. Examples illustrate, but do not restrain, the law.

EXEMPLARY DAMAGES. Damages on a punitive scale, given in respect of tortious acts, committed through malice or other circumstances of aggravation; damages designed not only as a compensation to the injured party, but also as a punishment to the wrong-doer for his violence, oppression, malice, or fraud.

EXEMPLI GRATIÂ. For the purpose of example, or for instance. Often abbreviated "*ex. gr.*" or "*e. g.*"

EXEMPLIFICATION. An official transcript of a document from public records, made in form to be used as evidence, and authenticated as a true copy.

EXEMPLIFICATIONE. A writ granted for the exemplification or transcript of an original record. Reg. Orig. 290.

EXEMPLUM. In the civil law. Copy; a written authorized copy. This word is also used in the modern sense of "example,"—*ad exemplum constituti singulares non trahi,* exceptional things must not be taken for examples. Calvin.

EXEMPT, *v.* To relieve, excuse, or set free from a duty or service imposed upon the general class to which the individual exempted belongs; as to exempt from militia service. See 1 St. at Large, 272.

To relieve certain classes of property from liability to sale on execution.

EXEMPT, *n.* One who is free from liability to military service; as distinguished from a *detail,* who is one belonging to the army, but detached or set apart for the time to some particular duty or service, and liable, at any time, to be recalled to his place in the ranks. 39 Ala. 379.

EXEMPTION. Freedom from a general duty or service; immunity from a general burden, tax, or charge.

A privilege allowed by law to a judgment

debtor, by which he may hold property to a certain amount, or certain classes of property, free from all liability to levy and sale on execution or attachment.

EXEMPTION LAWS. Laws which provide that a certain amount or proportion of a debtor's property shall be exempt from execution.

EXEMPTION, WORDS OF. It is a maxim of law that words of exemption are not to be construed to import any liability; the maxim *expressio unius exclusio alterius*, or its converse, *exclusio unius inclusio alterius*, not applying to such a case. For example, an exemption of the crown from the bankruptcy act 1869, in one specified particular, would not inferentially subject the crown to that act in any other particular. Brown.

EXEMPTS. Persons who are not bound by law, but excused from the performance of duties imposed upon others.

EXENNIUM. In old English law. A gift; a new year's gift. Cowell.

EXEQUATUR. Lat. Let it be executed. In French practice, this term is subscribed by judicial authority upon a transcript of a judgment from a foreign country, or from another part of France, and authorizes the execution of the judgment within the jurisdiction where it is so indorsed.

In international law. A certificate issued by the foreign department of a state to a consul or commercial agent of another state, recognizing his official character, and authorizing him to fulfill his duties.

EXERCISE. To make use of. Thus, to exercise a right or power is to do something which it enables the holder to do.

EXERCITALIS. A soldier; vassal. Spelman.

EXERCITOR NAVIS. The temporary owner or charterer of a ship.

EXERCITORIA ACTIO. In the civil law. An action which lay against the employer of a vessel (*exercitor navis*) for the contracts made by the master. Inst. 4, 7, 2; 3 Kent, Comm. 161.

EXERCITORIAL POWER. The trust given to a ship-master.

EXERCITUAL. In old English law. A heriot paid only in arms, horses, or military accouterments.

EXERCITUS. In old European law. An army; an armed force. A collection of thirty-five men and upwards.

A gathering of forty-two armed men.

A meeting of four men. Spelman.

EXETER DOMESDAY. The name given to a record preserved among the muniments and charters belonging to the dean and chapter of Exeter Cathedral, which contains a description of the western parts of the kingdom, comprising the counties of Wilts, Dorset, Somerset, Devon, and Cornwall. The Exeter Domesday was published with several other surveys nearly contemporary, by order of the commissioners of the public records, under the direction of Sir Henry Ellis, in a volume supplementary to the Great Domesday, folio, London, 1816. Wharton.

EXFESTUCARE. To abdicate or resign; to resign or surrender an estate, office, or dignity, by the symbolical delivery of a staff or rod to the alienee.

EXFREDIARE. To break the peace; to commit open violence. Jacob.

EXHÆREDATIO. In the civil law. Disinheriting; disherison. The formal method of excluding an indefeasible (or forced) heir from the entire inheritance, by the testator's express declaration in the will that such person shall be *exhæres*. Mackeld. Rom. Law, § 711.

EXHÆRES. In the civil law. One disinherited. Vicat; Du Cange.

EXHEREDATE. In Scotch law. To disinherit; to exclude from an inheritance.

EXHIBERE. To present a thing corporeally, so that it may be handled. Vicat. To appear personally to conduct the defense of an action at law.

EXHIBIT, *v.* To show or display; to offer or present for inspection. To produce anything in public, so that it may be taken into possession. Dig. 10, 4, 2.

To present; to offer publicly or officially; to file of record. Thus we speak of *exhibiting* a charge of treason, *exhibiting* a bill against an officer of the king's bench by way of proceeding against him in that court.

To administer; to cause to be taken; as medicines.

EXHIBIT, *n.* A paper or document produced and exhibited to a court during a trial or hearing, or to a commissioner taking depositions, or to auditors, arbitrators, etc.,

EXHIBIT   459   EXLEGARE

as a voucher, or in proof of facts, or as otherwise connected with the subject-matter, and which, on being accepted, is marked for identification and annexed to the deposition, report, or other principal document, or filed of record, or otherwise made a part of the case.

A paper referred to in and filed with the bill, answer, or petition in a suit in equity, or with a deposition. 16 Ga. 68.

EXHIBITANT. A complainant in articles of the peace. 12 Adol. & E. 599.

EXHIBITIO BILLÆ. Lat. Exhibition of a bill. In old English practice, actions were instituted by presenting or exhibiting a bill to the court, in cases where the proceedings were by bill; hence this phrase is equivalent to "commencement of the suit."

EXHIBITION. In Scotch law. An action for compelling the production of writings.

In ecclesiastical law. An allowance for meat and drink, usually made by religious appropriators of churches to the vicar. Also the benefaction settled for the maintaining of scholars in the universities, not depending on the foundation. Paroch. Antiq. 304.

EXIGENCE. Demand, want, need, imperativeness.

EXIGENCY OF A BOND. That which the bond demands or exacts, i. e., the act, performance, or event upon which it is conditioned.

EXIGENCY OF A WRIT. The command or imperativeness of a writ; the directing part of a writ; the act or performance which it commands.

EXIGENDARY. In English law. An officer who makes out exigents.

EXIGENT, or EXIGI FACIAS. L. Lat. In English practice. A judicial writ made use of in the process of outlawry, commanding the sheriff to *demand* the defendant, (or *cause him to be demanded, exigi faciat,*) from county court to county court, until he be outlawed; or, if he appear, then to take and have him before the court on a day certain in term, to answer to the plaintiff's action. 1 Tidd, Pr. 132; 3 Bl. Comm. 283, 284; Archb. N. Pr. 485. Now regulated by St. 2 Wm. IV. c. 39.

EXIGENTER. An officer of the English court of common pleas, whose duty it was to make out the *exigents* and proclamations in the process of outlawry. Cowell.

Abolished by St. 7 Wm. IV. and 1 Vict. c. 30. Holthouse.

EXIGI FACIAS. That you cause to be demanded. The emphatic words of the Latin form of the writ of *exigent.* They are sometimes used as the name of that writ.

EXIGIBLE. Demandable; requirable.

EXILE. Banishment; the person banished.

EXILIUM. Lat. In old English law. 1. Exile; banishment from one's country.

2. Driving away; despoiling. The name of a species of waste, which consisted in driving away tenants or vassals from the estate; as by demolishing buildings, and so compelling the tenants to leave, or by enfranchising the bond-servants, and unlawfully turning them out of their tenements. Fleta, l. 1, c. 9.

Exilium est patriæ privatio, natalis soli mutatio, legum nativarum amissio. 7 Coke, 20. Exile is a privation of country, a change of natal soil, a loss of native laws.

EXISTIMATIO. In the civil law. The civil reputation which belonged to the Roman citizen, as such. Mackeld. Rom. Law, § 135. Called a state or condition of unimpeached dignity or character, (*dignitatis inlæsæ status;*) the highest standing of a Roman citizen. Dig. 50, 13, 5, 1.

Also the decision or award of an arbiter.

EXIT. Lat. It goes forth. This word is used in docket entries as a brief mention of the issue of process. Thus, "*exit fi. fa.*" denotes that a writ of *fieri facias* has been issued in the particular case. The "*exit* of a writ" is the fact of its issuance.

EXIT WOUND. A term used in medical jurisprudence to denote the wound made by a weapon on the side where it *emerges,* after it has passed completely through the body, or through any part of it.

EXITUS. Children; offspring. The rents, issues, and profits of lands and tenements. An export duty. The conclusion of the pleadings.

EXLEGALITAS. In old English law. Outlawry. Spelman.

EXLEGALITUS. He who is prosecuted as an outlaw. Jacob.

EXLEGARE. In old English law. To outlaw; to deprive one of the benefit and protection of the law, (*exuere aliquem benefi-cio legis*.) Spelman.

EXLEX. In old English law. An out-law; *qui est extra legem*, one who is *out of* the *law's* protection. Bract. fol. 125. *Qui beneficio legis pricatur*. Spelman.

EXOINE. In French law. An act or instrument in writing which contains the reasons why a party in a civil suit, or a person accused, who has been summoned, agreeably to the requisitions of a decree, does not appear. Poth. Proc. Crim. § 3, art. 3. The same as "Essoin," (*q. v.*)

EXONERATION. The removal of a burden, charge, or duty. Particularly, the act of relieving a person or estate from a charge or liability by casting the same upon another person or estate.

A right or equity which exists between those who are successively liable for the same debt. "A surety who discharges an obligation is entitled to look to the principal for reimbursement, and to invoke the aid of a court of equity for this purpose, and a subsequent surety who, by the terms of the contract, is responsible only in case of the default of the principal and a prior surety, may claim *exoneration* at the hands of either." Bisp. Eq. § 331.

In Scotch law. A discharge; or the act of being legally disburdened of, or liberated from, the performance of a duty or obligation. Bell.

EXONERATIONE SECTÆ. A writ that lay for the crown's ward, to be free from all suit to the county court, hundred court, leet, etc., during wardship. Fitzh. Nat. Brev. 158.

EXONERATIONE SECTÆ AD CU-RIAM BARON. A writ of the same nature as that last above described, issued by the guardian of the crown's ward, and addressed to the sheriffs or stewards of the court, forbidding them to distrain him, etc., for not doing suit of court, etc. New Nat. Brev. 352.

EXONERETUR. Lat. Let him be relieved or discharged. An entry made on a bail-piece, whereby the surety is relieved or discharged from further obligation, when the condition is fulfilled by the surrender of the principal or otherwise.

EXORDIUM. The beginning or introductory part of a speech.

EXPATRIATION. The voluntary act of abandoning one's country, and becoming the citizen or subject of another. See EM-IGRATION.

EXPECT. To await; to look forward to something intended, promised, or likely to happen.

EXPECTANCY. The condition of being deferred to a future time, or of dependence upon an expected event; contingency as to possession or enjoyment.

With respect to the time of their enjoyment, estates may either be in possession or in expectancy; and of expectancies there are two sorts,—one created by the act of the parties, called a "remainder;" the other by act of law, called a "reversion." 2 Bl. Comm. 163.

EXPECTANT. Having relation to, or dependent upon, a contingency.

EXPECTANT ESTATES. Interests to come into possession and be enjoyed *in futuro*. They are of two sorts at common law,— reversions and remainders. 2 Bl. Comm. 163.

EXPECTANT HEIR. A person who has the expectation of inheriting property or an estate, but small present means. The term is chiefly used in equity, where relief is afforded to such persons against the enforcement of "catching bargains," (*q. v.*)

EXPECTATION OF LIFE, in the doctrine of life annuities, is the share or number of years of life which a person of a given age may, upon an equality of chance, expect to enjoy. Wharton.

EXPEDIMENT. The whole of a person's goods and chattels, bag and baggage. Wharton.

Expedit reipublicæ ne sua re quis male utatur. It is for the interest of the state that a man should not enjoy his own property improperly, (to the injury of others.) Inst. 1, 8, 2.

Expedit reipublicæ ut sit finis litium. It is for the advantage of the state that there be an end of suits; it is for the public good that actions be brought to a close. Co. Litt. 303*b*.

EXPEDITATÆ ARBORES. Trees rooted up or cut down to the roots. Fleta, l. 2, c. 41.

EXPEDITATE. In forest law. To cut out the ball of a dog's forefeet, for the preservation of the royal game.

EXPEDITATION. A cutting off the claws or ball of the forefeet of mastiffs, to prevent their running after deer. Spelman; Cowell.

EXPEDITIO. An expedition; an irregular kind of army. Spelman.

EXPEDITIO BREVIS. In old practice. The service of a writ. Townsh. Pl. 43.

EXPENDITORS. Paymasters. Those who expend or disburse certain taxes. Especially the sworn officer who supervised the repairs of the banks of the canals in Romney Marsh. Cowell.

EXPENSÆ LITIS. Costs or expenses of the suit, which are generally allowed to the successful party.

EXPENSIS MILITUM NON LEVANDIS. An ancient writ to prohibit the sheriff from levying any allowance for knights of the shire upon those who held lands in ancient demesne. Reg. Orig. 261.

Experientia per varios actus legem facit. Magistra rerum experientia. Co. Litt. 60. Experience by various acts makes law. Experience is the mistress of things.

EXPERTS. Persons examined as witnesses in a cause, who testify in regard to some professional or technical matter arising in the case, and who are permitted to give their opinions as to such matter on account of their special training, skill, or familiarity with it.

Persons selected by the court or parties in a cause, on account of their knowledge or skill, to examine, estimate, and ascertain things and make a report of their opinions. Merl. Repert.

Persons professionally acquainted with the science or practice in question. Strick. Ev. 408. Persons conversant with the subject-matter on questions of science, skill, trade, and others of like kind. Best, Ev. § 346.

An expert is a person who possesses peculiar skill and knowledge upon the subject-matter that he is required to give an opinion upon. 48 Vt. 366.

An expert is a skillful or experienced person; a person having skill or experience, or peculiar knowledge on certain subjects, or in certain professions; a scientific witness. 45 Me. 392; 52 Me. 68.

EXPILARE. In the civil law. To spoil; to rob or plunder. Applied to inheritances. Dig. 47, 19; Cod. 9, 32.

EXPILATIO. In the civil law. The offense of unlawfully appropriating goods belonging to a succession. It is not technically theft (*furtum*) because such property no longer belongs to the decedent, nor to the heir, since the latter has not yet taken possession.

EXPILATOR. In the civil law. A robber; a spoiler or plunderer. *Expilatores sunt atrociores fures.* Dig. 47, 18, 1, 1.

EXPIRATION. Cessation; termination from mere lapse of time; as the expiration of a lease, or statute, and the like.

EXPIRY OF THE LEGAL. In Scotch law and practice. Expiration of the period within which an adjudication may be redeemed, by paying the debt in the decree of adjudication. Bell.

EXPLEES. See ESPLEES.

EXPLETA, EXPLETIA, or EXPLECIA. In old records. The rents and profits of an estate.

EXPLICATIO. In the civil law. The fourth pleading; equivalent to the surrejoinder of the common law. Calvin.

EXPLORATOR. A scout, huntsman, or chaser.

EXPLOSION. A sudden and rapid combustion, causing violent expansion of the air, and accompanied by a report.

The word "explosion" is variously used in ordinary speech, and is not one that admits of exact definition. Every combustion of an explosive substance, whereby other property is ignited and consumed, would not be an "explosion," within the ordinary meaning of the term. It is not used as a synonym of "combustion." An explosion may be described generally as a sudden and rapid combustion, causing violent expansion of the air, and accompanied by a report. But the rapidity of the combustion, the violence of the expansion, and the vehemence of the report vary in intensity as often as the occurrences multiply. Hence an explosion is an idea of degrees; and the true meaning of the word, in each particular case, must be settled, not by any fixed standard or accurate measurement, but by the common experience and notions of men in matters of that sort. 22 Ohio St. 340.

EXPORT, *v.* To send, take, or carry an article of trade or commerce out of the country. To transport merchandise from one country to another in the course of trade. To carry out or convey goods by sea. Vaughn, 171, 172; 5 Harr. 501.

EXPORT, *n.* A thing or commodity exported. More commonly used in the plural.

F

G

H

I

J

K

L

M

EXPORTATION. The act of sending or carrying goods and merchandise from one country to another.

EXPOSE, v. To show publicly; to exhibit.

EXPOSÉ, n. Fr. A statement; account; recital; explanation. The term is used in diplomatic language as descriptive of a written explanation of the reasons for a certain act or course of conduct.

EXPOSITIO. Explanation; exposition; interpretation.

Expositio quæ ex visceribus causæ nascitur, est aptissima et fortissima in lege. That kind of interpretation which is born [or drawn] from the bowels of a cause is the aptest and most forcible in the law. 10 Coke, 24b.

EXPOSITION. Explanation; interpretation.

EXPOSITION DE PART. In French law. The abandonment of a child, unable to take care of itself, either in a public or private place.

EXPOSURE OF PERSON. In criminal law. Such an intentional exposure, in a public place, of the naked body or the private parts as is calculated to shock the feelings of chastity or to corrupt the morals of the community.

EXPRESS. Made known distinctly and explicitly, and not left to inference or implication. Declared in terms; set forth in words. Manifested by direct and appropriate language, as distinguished from that which is inferred from conduct. The word is usually contrasted with "implied."

EXPRESS ABROGATION. Abrogation by express provision or enactment; the repeal of a law or provision by a subsequent one, referring directly to it.

EXPRESS ASSUMPSIT. An undertaking to do some act, or to pay a sum of money to another, manifested by express terms.

EXPRESS COLOR. An evasive form of special pleading in a case where the defendant ought to plead the general issue. Abolished by the common-law procedure act, 1852, (15 & 16 Vict. c. 76, § 64.)

EXPRESS COMPANY. A firm or corporation engaged in the business of transporting parcels or other movable property, in the capacity of common carriers.

EXPRESS CONSIDERATION. A consideration which is distinctly and specifically named in the written contract or in the oral agreement of the parties.

EXPRESS CONTRACT. A contract the terms of which are openly uttered or declared at the time of making it. 2 Bl. Comm. 443; 2 Steph. Comm. 110. A contract made in distinct and explicit language, or by writing; as distinguished from an implied contract. 2 Kent, Comm. 450.

EXPRESS MALICE. Actual malice; malice in fact; a deliberate intention to commit an injury, evidenced by external circumstances.

EXPRESS TRUST. A trust created or declared in express terms, and usually in writing, as distinguished from one inferred by the law from the conduct or dealings of the parties.

Express trusts are those which are created in express terms in the deed, writing, or will, while implied trusts are those which, without being expressed, are deducible from the nature of the transaction, as matters of intent, or which are superinduced upon the transactions by operation of law, as matters of equity, independently of the particular intention of the parties. 56 Barb. 635.

EXPRESS WARRANTY. One expressed by particular words. 2 Bl. Comm. 300.

In the law of insurance. An agreement expressed in a policy, whereby the assured stipulates that certain facts relating to the risk are or shall be true, or certain acts relating to the same subject have been or shall be done. 1 Phil. Ins. (4th Ed.) p. 425.

Expressa nocent, non expressa non nocent. Things expressed are [may be] prejudicial; things not expressed are not. Express words are sometimes prejudicial, which, if omitted, had done no harm. Dig. 35, 1, 52; Id. 50, 17, 195. See Calvin.

Expressa non prosunt quæ non expressa proderunt. 4 Coke, 73. The expression of things of which, if unexpressed, one would have the benefit, is useless.

Expressio eorum quæ tacite insunt nihil operatur. The expression or express mention of those things which are tacitly implied avails nothing. 2 Inst. 365. A man's own words are void, when the law speaketh as much. Finch, Law, b. 1, c. 3, no. 26. Words used to express what the law will imply without them are mere words of abundance. 5 Coke, 11.

Expressio unius est exclusio alterius. The expression of one thing is the exclusion of another. Co. Litt. 210a. The express mention of one thing [person or place] implies the exclusion of another.

Expressio unius personæ est exclusio alterius. Co. Litt. 210. The mention of one person is the exclusion of another. See Broom, Max. 651.

Expressum facit cessare tacitum. That which is expressed makes that which is implied to cease, [that is, supersedes it, or controls its effect.] Thus, an implied covenant in a deed is in all cases controlled by an express covenant. 4 Coke, 80; Broom, Max. 651.

Expressum servitium regat vel declaret tacitum. Let service expressed rule or declare what is silent.

EXPROMISSIO. In the civil law. The species of novation by which a creditor accepts a new debtor, who becomes bound instead of the old, the latter being released. 1 Bouv. Inst. no. 802.

EXPROMISSOR. In the civil law. A person who assumes the debt of another, and becomes solely liable for it, by a stipulation with the creditor. He differs from a surety, inasmuch as this contract is one of novation, while a surety is jointly liable with his principal. Mackeld. Rom. Law, § 538.

EXPROMITTERE. In the civil law. To undertake for another, with the view of becoming liable in his place. Calvin.

EXPROPRIATION. This word properly denotes a voluntary surrender of rights or claims; the act of divesting oneself of that which was previously claimed as one's own, or renouncing it. In this sense it is the opposite of "appropriation." But a meaning has been attached to the term, imported from its use in foreign jurisprudence, which makes it synonymous with the exercise of the power of eminent domain, i. e., the compulsory taking from a person, on compensation made, of his private property for the use of a railroad, canal, or other public work.

In French law. Expropriation is the compulsory realization of a debt by the creditor out of the lands of his debtor, or the usufruct thereof. When the debtor is co-tenant with others, it is necessary that a partition should first be made. It is confined, in the

first place, to the lands (if any) that are in *hypothèque*, but afterwards extends to the lands not in *hypothèque*. Moreover, the debt must be of a liquidated amount. Brown.

EXPULSION. A putting or driving out. The act of depriving a member of a corporation, legislative body, assembly, society, commercial organization, etc., of his membership in the same, by a legal vote of the body itself, for breach of duty, improper conduct, or other sufficient cause.

EXPUNGE. To blot out; to efface designedly; to obliterate; to strike out wholly. Webster.

EXPURGATION. The act of purging or cleansing, as where a book is published without its obscene passages.

EXPURGATOR. One who corrects by expurging.

EXQUÆSTOR. In Roman law. One who had filled the office of *quæstor*. A title given to Tribonian. Inst. procem. § 3. Used only in the ablative case, (*exquæstore.*)

EXROGARE. (From *ex*, from, and *rogare*, to pass a law.) In Roman law. To take something from an old law by a new law. Tayl. Civil Law, 155.

EXTEND. In English practice. To value the lands or tenements of a person bound by a statute or recognizance which has become forfeited, to their full *extended* value. 3 Bl. Comm. 420; Fitzh. Nat. Brev. 131. To execute the writ of *extent* or *extendi facias,* (*q. v.*) 2 Tidd, Pr. 1043, 1044.

In taxation. Extending a tax consists in adding to the assessment roll the precise amount due from each person whose name appears thereon. "The subjects for taxation having been properly listed, and a basis for apportionment established, nothing will remain to fix a definite liability but to *extend* upon the list or roll the several proportionate amounts, as a charge against the several taxables." Cooley, Tax'n, (2d Ed.) 423.

EXTENDI FACIAS. Lat. You cause to be extended. In English practice. The name of a writ of execution, (derived from its two emphatic words;) more commonly called an "extent." 2 Tidd, Pr. 1043; 4 Steph. Comm. 43.

EXTENSION. In mercantile law. An allowance of additional time for the payment of debts. An agreement between a debtor and his creditors, by which they allow him

F

G

H

I

J

K

L

M

further time for the payment of his liabilities.

EXTENSION OF PATENT. An extension of the life of a patent for an additional period of seven years, formerly allowed by law in the United States. upon proof being made that the inventor had not succeeded in obtaining a reasonable remuneration from his patent-right. This is no longer allowed, except as to designs. See Rev. St. U. S. § 4924.

EXTENSORES. In old English law. Extenders or appraisers. The name of certain officers appointed to appraise and divide or apportion lands. It was their duty to make a survey, schedule, or inventory of the lands, to lay them out under certain heads, and then to ascertain the value of each, as preparatory to the division or partition. Bract. fols. 72b, 75; Britt. c. 71.

EXTENT. In English practice. A writ of execution issuing from the exchequer upon a debt due the crown, or upon a debt due a private person, if upon recognizance or statute merchant or staple, by which the sheriff is directed to appraise the debtor's lands, and, instead of selling them, to set them off to the creditor for a term during which the rental will satisfy the judgment.

In Scotch practice. The value or valuation of lands. Bell.

The rents, profits, and issues of lands. Skene.

EXTENT IN AID. In English practice. That kind of extent which issues at the instance and for the benefit of a debtor to the crown, for the recovery of a debt due to himself. 2 Tidd, Pr. 1045; 4 Steph. Comm. 47.

EXTENT IN CHIEF. In English practice. The principal kind of extent, issuing at the suit of the crown, for the recovery of the crown's debt. 4 Steph. Comm. 47. An adverse proceeding by the king, for the recovery of his own debt. 2 Tidd, Pr. 1045.

EXTENTA MANERII. (The extent or survey of a manor.) The title of a statute passed 4 Edw. I. St. 1; being a sort of direction for making a *survey* or terrier of a *manor*, and all its appendages. 2 Reeve, Eng. Law, 140.

EXTENUATE. To lessen; to palliate; to mitigate.

EXTENUATING CIRCUMSTANCES. Such as render a delict or crime less aggravated, heinous, or reprehensible than it would

otherwise be, or tend to palliate or lessen its guilt. Such circumstances may ordinarily be shown in order to reduce the punishment or damages.

EXTERRITORIALITY. The privilege of those persons (such as foreign ministers) who, though temporarily resident within a state, are not subject to the operation of its laws.

EXTERUS. Lat. A foreigner or alien; one born abroad. The opposite of *civis*.

Exterus non habet terras. An alien holds no lands. Tray. Lat. Max. 203.

EXTINCT. Extinguished. A rent is said to be extinguished when it is destroyed and put out. Co. Litt. 147b. See EXTINGUISHMENT.

Extincto subjecto, tollitur adjunctum. When the subject is extinguished, the incident ceases. Thus, when the business for which a partnership has been formed is completed, or brought to an end, the partnership itself ceases. Inst. 3, 26, 6; 3 Kent, Comm. 52, note.

EXTINGUISHMENT. The destruction or cancellation of a right, power, contract, or estate. The annihilation of a collateral thing or subject in the subject itself out of which it is derived. Prest. Merg. 9. For the distinction between an extinguishment and passing a right, see 2 Shars. Bl. Comm. 325, note.

"Extinguishment" is sometimes confounded with "merger," though there is a clear distinction between them. "Merger" is only a mode of extinguishment, and applies to estates only under particular circumstances; but "extinguishment" is a term of general application to rights, as well as estates. 2 Crabb, Real Prop. p. 867, § 1487.

EXTINGUISHMENT OF COMMON. Loss of the right to have common. This may happen from various causes.

EXTINGUISHMENT OF COPYHOLD. In English law. A copyhold is said to be *extinguished* when the freehold and copyhold interests unite in the same person and in the same right, which may be either by the copyhold interest coming to the freehold or by the freehold interest coming to the copyhold. 1 Crabb, Real Prop. p. 670, § 864.

EXTINGUISHMENT OF DEBTS. This takes place by payment; by accord and satisfaction; by novation, or the substitution of a new debtor; by merger, when the creditor recovers a judgment or accepts a security of a higher nature than the original obligation; by a release; by the marriage of a *feme sole* creditor with the debtor, or of an obligee with one of two joint obligors; and where one of the parties, debtor or creditor, makes the other his executor.

EXTINGUISHMENT OF RENT. If a person have a yearly rent of lands, and afterwards purchase those lands, so that he has as good an estate in the land as in the rent, the rent is *extinguished*. Termes de la Ley; Cowell; Co. Litt. 147. Rent may also be extinguished by conjunction of estates, by confirmation, by grant, by release, and by surrender. 1 Crabb, Real Prop. pp. 210–213, § 209.

EXTINGUISHMENT OF WAYS. This is usually effected by unity of possession. As if a man have a way over the close of another, and he purchase that close, the way is *extinguished*. 1 Crabb, Real Prop. p. 341, § 384.

EXTIRPATION. In English law. A species of destruction or waste, analogous to estrepement. See ESTREPEMENT.

EXTIRPATIONE. A judicial writ, either before or after judgment, that lay against a person who, when a verdict was found against him for land, etc., maliciously overthrew any house or extirpated any trees upon it. Reg. Jud. 13, 56.

EXTOCARE. In old records. To grub woodland, and reduce it to arable or meadow; "to stock up." Cowell.

EXTORSIVELY. A technical word used in indictments for extortion.

It is a sufficient averment of a corrupt intent, in an indictment for extortion, to allege that the defendant "extorsively" took the unlawful fee. 35 Ark. 438.

EXTORT. The natural meaning of the word "extort" is to obtain money or other valuable thing either by compulsion, by actual force, or by the force of motives applied to the will, and often more overpowering and irresistible than physical force. 12 Cush. 90.

Extortio est crimen quando quis colore officii extorquet quod non est debitum, vel supra debitum, vel ante tempus quod est debitum. 10 Coke, 102. Extortion is a crime when, by color of office, any person extorts that which is not due, or more than is due, or before the time when it is due.

EXTORTION. Any oppression by color or pretense of right, and particularly the exaction by an officer of money, by color of his office, either when none at all is due, or not so much is due, or when it is not yet due. 4 Conn. 480.

Extortion consists in any public officer unlawfully taking, by color of his office, from any person any money or thing of value that is not due to him, or more than his due. Code Ga. 1882, § 4507.

Extortion is the obtaining of property from another, with his consent, induced by wrongful use of force or fear, or under color of official right. Pen. Code Cal. § 518; Pen. Code Dak. § 608.

Extortion is an abuse of public justice, which consists in any officer unlawfully taking, by color of his office, from any man any money or thing of value that is not due to him, or before it is due. 4 Bl. Comm. 141.

Extortion is any oppression under color of right. In a stricter sense, the taking of money by any officer, by color of his office, when none, or not so much, is due, or it is not yet due. 1 Hawk. P. C. (Curw. Ed.) 418.

It is the corrupt demanding or receiving by a person in office of a fee for services which should be performed gratuitously; or, where compensation is permissible, of a larger fee than the law justifies, or a fee not due. 2 Bish. Crim. Law, § 390.

The distinction between "bribery" and "extortion" seems to be this: the former offense consists in the offering a present, or receiving one, if offered; the latter, in demanding a fee or present, by color of office. Jacob.

For the distinction between "extortion" and "exaction," see EXACTION.

EXTRA. A Latin preposition, occurring in many legal phrases; it means beyond, except, without, out of, outside.

EXTRA COSTS. In English practice. Those charges which do not appear upon the face of the proceedings, such as witnesses' expenses, fees to counsel, attendances, court fees, etc., an affidavit of which must be made, to warrant the master in allowing them upon taxation of costs. Wharton.

EXTRA-DOTAL PROPERTY. In Louisiana this term is used to designate that property which forms no part of the dowry of a woman, and which is also called "paraphernal property." Civil Code La. art. 2315.

EXTRA FEODUM. Out of his fee; out of the seigniory, or not holden of him that claims it. Co. Litt. 1b; Reg. Orig. 97b.

EXTRA-JUDICIUM. Extrajudicial; out of the proper cause; out of court; beyond the jurisdiction. See EXTRAJUDICIAL.

EXTRA JUS. Beyond the law; more than the law requires. *In jure, vel extra jus.* Bract. fol. 169b.

EXTRA LEGEM. Out of the law; out of the protection of the law.

Extra legem positus est civiliter mortuus. Co. Litt. 130. He who is placed out of the law is civilly dead.

EXTRA PRÆSENTIAM MARITI. Out of her husband's presence.

EXTRA QUATUOR MARIA. Beyond the four seas; out of the kingdom of England. 1 Bl. Comm. 457.

EXTRA REGNUM. Out of the realm. 7 Coke, 16a; 2 Kent, Comm. 42, note.

EXTRA SERVICES, when used with reference to officers, means services incident to the office in question, but for which compensation has not been provided by law. 21 Ind. 32.

EXTRA-TERRITORIALITY. The extra-territorial operation of laws; that is, their operation upon persons, rights, or jural relations, existing beyond the limits of the enacting state, but still amenable to its laws.

EXTRA TERRITORIUM. Beyond or without the territory. 6 Bin. 353; 2 Kent, Comm. 407.

Extra territorium jus dicenti impune non paretur. One who exercises jurisdiction out of his territory is not obeyed with impunity. Dig. 2, 1, 20; Branch, Princ.; 10 Coke, 77. He who exercises judicial authority beyond his proper limits cannot be obeyed with safety.

EXTRA VIAM. Outside the way. Where the defendant in trespass pleaded a right of way in justification, and the replication alleged that the trespass was committed outside the limits of the way claimed, these were the technical words to be used.

EXTRA VIRES. Beyond powers. See ULTRA VIRES.

EXTRACT. A portion or fragment of a writing. In Scotch law, the certified copy, by a clerk of a court, of the proceedings in an action carried on before the court, and of the judgment pronounced; containing also an order for execution or proceedings thereupon. Jacob; Whishaw.

EXTRACTA CURIÆ. In old English law. The issues or profits of holding a court, arising from the customary fees, etc.

EXTRADITION. The surrender of a criminal by a foreign state to which he has fled for refuge from prosecution to the state within whose jurisdiction the crime was committed, upon the demand of the latter state, in order that he may be dealt with according to its laws. Extradition may be accorded as a mere matter of comity, or may take place under treaty stipulations between the two nations. It also obtains as between the different states of the American Union.

Extradition between the states must be considered and defined to be a political duty of imperfect obligation, founded upon compact, and requiring each state to surrender one who, having violated the criminal laws of another state, has fled from its justice, and is found in the state from which he is demanded, on demand of the executive authority of the state from which he fled. Abbott.

EXTRAHURA. In old English law. An animal wandering or straying about, without an owner; an estray. Spelman.

EXTRAJUDICIAL. That which is done, given, or effected outside the course of regular judicial proceedings; not founded upon, or unconnected with, the action of a court of law; as extrajudicial evidence, an extrajudicial oath.

That which, though done in the course of regular judicial proceedings, is unnecessary to such proceedings, or interpolated, or beyond their scope; as an extrajudicial opinion, (*dictum.*)

That which does not belong to the judge or his jurisdiction, notwithstanding which he takes cognizance of it.

EXTRANEUS. In old English law. One foreign born; a foreigner. 7 Coke, 16.

In Roman law. An heir not born in the family of the testator. Those of a foreign state. The same as *alienus.* Vicat; Du Cange.

Extraneus est subditus qui extra terram, i. e., potestatem regis natus est. 7 Coke, 16. A foreigner is a subject who is born out of the territory, *i. e.,* government of the king.

EXTRAORDINARY. The writs of *mandamus, quo warranto, habeas corpus,* and some others are sometimes called "extraordinary remedies," in contradistinction to the ordinary remedy by action.

EXTRAORDINARY CARE is synonymous with greatest care, utmost care, highest degree of care. 54 Ill. 19. See CARE, DILIGENCE; NEGLIGENCE.

EXTRAPAROCHIAL. Out of a parish; not within the bounds or limits of any parish. 1 Bl. Comm. 113, 284.

EXTRAVAGANTES. In canon law. Those decretal epistles which were published after the Clementines. They were so called because at first they were not digested or arranged with the other papal constitutions, but seemed to be, as it were, detached from the canon law. They continued to be called by the same name when they were afterwards inserted in the body of the canon law. The first extravagantes are those of Pope John XXII., successor of Clement V. The last collection was brought down to the year 1483, and was called the "Common Extravagantes," notwithstanding that they were likewise incorporated with the rest of the canon law. Enc. Lond.

EXTREME HAZARD. To constitute extreme hazard, the situation of a vessel must be such that there is imminent danger of her being lost, notwithstanding all the means that can be applied to get her off. 1 Conn. 421.

EXTREMIS. When a person is sick beyond the hope of recovery, and near death, he is said to be *in extremis.*

Extremis probatis, præsumuntur media. Extremes being proved, intermediate things are presumed. Tray. Lat. Max. 207.

EXTRINSIC. Foreign; from outside sources; *dehors.*

EXTUMÆ. In old records. Relics. Cowell.

EXUERE PATRIAM. To throw off or renounce one's country or native allegiance; to *expatriate* one's self. Phillim. Dom. 18.

EXULARE. In old English law. To exile or banish. *Nullus liber homo, exuletur, nisi,* etc., no freeman shall be exiled, unless, etc. Magna Charta, c. 29; 2 Inst. 47.

EXUPERARE. To overcome; to apprehend or take. Leg. Edm. c. 2.

EY. A watery place; water. Co. Litt. 6.

EYDE. Aid; assistance; relief. A subsidy.

EYE-WITNESS. One who saw the act, fact, or transaction to which he testifies. Distinguished from an ear-witness, (*auritus.*)

EYOTT. A small island arising in a river. Fleta, l. 3, c. 2, § b; Bract. l. 2, c. 2.

EYRE. Justices in eyre were judges commissioned in Anglo-Norman times in England to travel systematically through the kingdom, once in seven years, holding courts in specified places for the trial of certain descriptions of causes.

EYRER. L. Fr. To travel or journey; to go about or itinerate. Britt. c. 2.

EZARDAR. In Hindu law. A farmer or renter of land in the districts of Hindoostan.

F

G

H

I

J

K

L

M

F.

F. In old English criminal law, this letter was branded upon felons upon their being admitted to clergy; as also upon those convicted of fights or frays, or of falsity. Jacob; Cowell; 2 Reeve, Eng. Law, 392; 4 Reeve, Eng. Law, 485.

F. O. B. Free on board. A term frequently inserted, in England, in contracts for the sale of goods to be conveyed by ship, meaning that the cost of shipping will be paid by the buyer. When goods are so sold in London the buyer is considered as the shipper, and the goods when shipped are at his risk. Wharton.

FABRIC LANDS. In English law. Lands given towards the maintenance, rebuilding, or repairing of cathedral and other churches. Cowell; Blount.

FABRICA. In old English law. The making or coining of money.

FABRICARE. Lat. To make. Used in old English law of a lawful coining, and also of an unlawful making or counterfeiting of coin. See 1 Salk. 342.

FABRICATE. To fabricate evidence is to arrange or manufacture circumstances or *indicia*, after the fact committed, with the purpose of using them as evidence, and of deceitfully making them appear as if accidental or undesigned; to devise falsely or contrive by artifice with the intention to deceive. Such evidence may be wholly forged and artificial, or it may consist in so warping and distorting real facts as to create an erroneous impression in the minds of those who observe them and then presenting such impression as true and genuine.

FABRICATED EVIDENCE. Evidence manufactured or arranged after the fact, and either wholly false or else warped and discolored by artifice and contrivance with a deceitful intent. See FABRICATE.

FABRICATED FACT. In the law of evidence. A fact existing only in statement, without any foundation in truth. An actual or genuine fact to which a false appearance has been designedly given; a physical object placed in a false connection with another, or with a person on whom it is designed to cast suspicion. See FABRICATE.

FABULA. In old European law. A contract or formal agreement; but particularly used in the Lombardic and Visigothic laws to denote a marriage contract or a will.

FAC SIMILE. An exact copy, preserving all the marks of the original.

FAC SIMILE PROBATE. In England, where the construction of a will may be affected by the appearance of the original paper, the court will order the probate to pass in *fac simile*, as it may possibly help to show the meaning of the testator. 1 Williams, Ex'rs, (7th Ed.) 331, 386, 566.

FACE. The face of an instrument is that which is shown by the mere language employed, without any explanation, modification, or addition from extrinsic facts or evidence. Thus, if the express terms of the paper disclose a fatal legal defect, it is said to be "void on its face."

Regarded as an evidence of debt, the face of an instrument is the principal sum which it expresses to be due or payable, without any additions in the way of interest or costs. Thus, the expression "the face of a judgment" means the sum for which the judgment was rendered, excluding the interest accrued thereon. 32 Iowa, 265.

FACERE. Lat. To do; to make. Thus, *facere defaltam*, to make default; *facere duellum*, to make the duel, or make or do battle; *facere finem*, to make or pay a fine; *facere legem*, to make one's law; *facere sacramentum*, to make oath.

FACIAS. That you cause. Occurring in the phrases "*scire facias*," (that you cause to know,) "*fieri facias*," (that you cause to be made,) etc.

FACIENDO. In doing or paying; in some activity.

FACIES. Lat. The face or countenance; the exterior appearance or view; hence, contemplation or study of a thing on its external or apparent side. Thus, *prima facie* means at the first inspection, on a preliminary or exterior scrutiny. When we speak of a "*prima facie* case," we mean one which, on its own showing, on a first examination, or without investigating any alleged defenses, is apparently good and maintainable.

FACILE. In Scotch law. Easily persuaded; easily imposed upon. Bell.

FACILITIES. This name was formerly given to certain notes of some of the banks in the state of Connecticut, which were made payable in two years after the close of the war of 1812. 14 Mass. 322.

FACILITY. In Scotch law. Pliancy of disposition. Bell.

Facinus quos inquinat æquat. Guilt makes equal those whom it stains.

FACIO UT DES. (Lat. I do that you may give.) A species of contract in the civil law (being one of the *innominate* contracts) which occurs when a man agrees to perform anything for a price either specifically mentioned or left to the determination of the law to set a value on it; as when a servant hires himself to his master for certain wages or an agreed sum of money. 2 Bl. Comm. 445.

FACIO UT FACIAS. (Lat. I do that you may do.) A species of contract in the civil law (being one of the *innominate* contracts) which occurs when I agree with a man to do his work for him if he will do mine for me; or if two persons agree to marry together, or to do any other positive acts on both sides; or it may be to forbear on one side in consideration of something done on the other. 2 Bl. Comm. 444.

FACT. A thing done; an action performed or an incident transpiring; an event or circumstance; an actual occurrence.

In the earlier days of the law "fact" was used almost exclusively in the sense of "action" or "deed;" but, although this usage survives, in some such phrases as "accessary before the fact," it has now acquired the broader meaning given above.

A fact is either a state of things, that is, an existence, or a motion, that is, an event. 1 Benth. Jud. Ev. 48.

In the law of evidence. A circumstance, event, or occurrence as it actually takes or took place; a physical object or appearance, as it actually exists or existed. An actual and absolute reality, as distinguished from mere supposition or opinion; a truth, as distinguished from fiction or error. Burrill, Circ. Ev. 218.

"Fact" is very frequently used in opposition or contrast to "law." Thus, questions of *fact* are for the jury; questions of *law* for the court. So an attorney *at law* is an officer of the courts of justice; an attorney *in fact* is appointed by the written authorization of a principal to manage business affairs usually not professional. Fraud *in fact* consists in an actual intention to defraud, carried into effect; while fraud imputed by *law* arises from the man's conduct in its necessary relations and consequences.

The word is much used in phrases which contrast it with law. Law is a principle; fact is an event. Law is conceived; fact is actual. Law is a rule of duty; fact is that which has been according to or in contravention of the rule. The distinction is well illustrated in the rule that the existence of foreign laws is matter of fact. Within the territory of its jurisdiction, law operates as an obligatory rule which judges must recognize and enforce; but, in a tribunal outside that jurisdiction, it loses its obligatory force and its claim to judicial notice. The fact that it exists, if important to the rights of parties, must be alleged and proved the same as the actual existence of any other institution. Abbott.

The terms "fact" and "truth" are often used in common parlance as synonymous, but, as employed in reference to pleading, they are widely different. A fact in pleading is a circumstance, act, event, or incident; a truth is the legal principle which declares or governs the facts and their operative effect. Admitting the facts stated in a complaint, the truth may be that the plaintiff is not entitled, upon the face of his complaint, to what he claims. The mode in which a defendant sets up that truth for his protection is a demurrer. 4 E. D. Smith, 37.

As to the classification of facts, see DISPOSITIVE FACTS.

FACTA. In old English law. Deeds. *Facta armorum*, deeds or feats of arms; that is, jousts or tournaments. Cowell.

Facts. *Facta et casus*, facts and cases. Bract. fol. 1b.

Facta sunt potentiora verbis. Deeds are more powerful than words.

Facta tenent multa quæ fieri prohibentur. 12 Coke, 124. Deeds contain many things which are prohibited to be done.

FACTIO TESTAMENTI. In the civil law. The right, power, or capacity of making a will; called "*factio activa.*" Inst. 2, 10, 6.

The right or capacity of taking by will; called "*factio passiva.*" Inst. 2, 10, 6.

FACTO. In fact; by an act; by the act or fact. *Ipso facto*, by the act itself; by the mere effect of a fact, without anything superadded, or any proceeding upon it to give it effect. 3 Kent, Comm. 55, 58.

FACTOR. A commercial agent, employed by a principal to sell merchandise consigned to him for that purpose, for and in behalf of the principal, but usually in his own name, being intrusted with the possession and control of the goods, and being remunerated by a commission, commonly called "factorage."

A factor is an agent who, in the pursuit of an independent calling, is employed by another to sell property for him, and is vested by the latter with the possession or control of the property, or authorized to receive payment therefor from the purchaser. Civil Code Cal. § 2026; Civil Code Dak. § 1168.

When the agent accompanies the ship, taking a cargo aboard, and it is consigned to him for sale, and he is to purchase a return cargo out of the proceeds, such agent is properly called a "factor." He is, however, usually known by the name of a "supercargo." Beaw. Lex. Merc. 44, 47; Liverm. Ag. 69, 70; 1 Domat, b. 1, t. 16, § 3, art. 2.

Factors are called "domestic" or "foreign," according as they reside in the same country with the principal or in a different country.

A "factor" is distinguished from a "broker" by being intrusted with the possession, management, and control of the goods, and by being authorized to buy and sell in his own name, as well as in that of his principal. Russ. Fact. 4; Story, Ag. § 33; 2 Steph. Comm. 127; 2 Barn. & Ald. 137, 143; 2 Kent, Comm. 622, note.

The term is used in some of the states to denote the person who is elsewhere called "garnishee" or "trustee." See FACTORIZING PROCESS.

FACTORAGE. The allowance or commission paid to a factor by his principal. Russ. Fact. 1; Tomlins.

FACTORIZING PROCESS. In American law. A process by which the effects of a debtor are attached in the hands of a third person. A term peculiar to the practice in Vermont and Connecticut. Otherwise termed "trustee process" and "garnishment." Drake, Attachm. § 451.

FACTORS' ACTS. The name given to several English statutes (6 Geo. IV. c. 94; 5 & 6 Vict. c. 39; 40 & 41 Vict. c. 39) by which a factor is enabled to make a valid pledge of the goods, or of any part thereof, to one who believes him to be the *bona fide* owner of the goods.

FACTORY. In English law. The term includes all buildings and premises wherein, or within the close or curtilage of which, steam, water, or any mechanical power is used to move or work any machinery employed in preparing, manufacturing, or finishing cotton, wool, hair, silk, flax, hemp, jute, or tow. So defined by the statute 7 Vict. c. 15, § 73. By later acts this definition has been extended to various other manufacturing places. Mozley & Whitley.

Also a place where a considerable number of factors reside, in order to negotiate for their masters or employers. Enc. Brit.

In American law. The word "factory" does not necessarily mean a single building or edifice, but may apply to several, where they are used in connection with each other, for a common purpose, and stand together in the same inclosure. 45 Ill. 303.

In Scotch law. This name is given to a species of contract or employment which falls under the general designation of "agency," but which partakes both of the nature of a mandate and of a bailment of the kind called *"locatio ad operandum."* 1 Bell, Comm. 259.

"FACTORY PRICES." The prices at which goods may be bought at the factories, as distinguished from the prices of goods bought in the market after they have passed into the hands of third persons or shop-keepers. 2 Mason, 90.

Facts cannot lie. 18 How. State Tr. 1187; 17 How. State Tr. 1430.

FACTUM. Lat. In old English law. A deed; a person's act and deed; anything stated or made certain; a sealed instrument; a deed of conveyance.

A fact; a circumstance; particularly a fact in evidence. Bract. fol. 1*b*.

In testamentary law. The execution or due execution of a will. The *factum* of an instrument means not barely the signing of it, and the formal publication or delivery, but proof that the party well knew and understood the contents thereof, and did give, will, dispose, and do, in all things, as in the said will is contained. 11 How. 354.

In the civil law. Fact; a fact; a matter of fact, as distinguished from a matter of law. Dig. 41, 2, 1, 3.

In French law. A memoir which contains concisely set down the fact on which a contest has happened, the means on which a party founds his pretensions, with the refutation of the means of the adverse party. Vicat.

In old European law. A portion or allotment of land. Spelman.

Factum a judice quod ad ejus officium non spectat non ratum est. An action of a judge which relates not to his office is of no force. Dig. 50, 17, 170; 10 Coke, 76.

Factum cuique suum non adversario, nocere debet. Dig. 50, 17, 155. A party's own act should prejudice himself, not his adversary.

Factum infectum fieri nequit. A thing done cannot be undone. 1 Kames, Eq. 96, 259.

FACTUM JURIDICUM. A juridical fact. Denotes one of the factors or elements constituting an obligation.

Factum negantis nulla probatio sit. Cod. 4, 19, 23. There is no proof incumbent upon him who denies a fact.

" Factum " non dicitur quod non perseverat. 5 Coke, 96. That is not called a "deed" which does not continue operative.

FACTUM PROBANDUM. Lat. In the law of evidence. The fact to be proved; a fact which is in issue, and to which evidence is to be directed. 1 Greenl. Ev. § 13.

FACTUM PROBANS. A probative or evidentiary fact; a subsidiary or connected fact tending to prove the principal fact in issue; a piece of circumstantial evidence.

Factum unius alteri noceri non debet. Co. Litt. 152. The deed of one should not hurt another.

Facultas probationum non est angustanda. The power of proofs [right of offering or giving testimony] is not to be narrowed. 4 Inst. 279.

FACULTIES, COURT OF. In English ecclesiastical law. A jurisdiction or tribunal belonging to the archbishop. It does not hold pleas in any suits, but creates rights to pews, monuments, and particular places, and modes of burial. It has also various powers under 25 Hen. VIII. c. 21, in granting licenses of different descriptions, as a license to marry, a faculty to erect an organ in a parish church, to level a church-yard, to remove bodies previously buried. 4 Inst. 337.

FACULTY. In ecclesiastical law. A license or authority; a privilege granted by the ordinary to a man by favor and indulgence to do that which by law he may not do; e. g., to marry without banns, to erect a monument in a church, etc. Termes de la Ley.

In Scotch law. A power founded on consent, as distinguished from a power founded on property. 2 Kames, Eq. 265.

FACULTY OF A COLLEGE. The corps of professors, instructors, tutors, and lecturers. To be distinguished from the board of trustees, who constitute the corporation.

FACULTY OF ADVOCATES. The college or society of advocates in Scotland.

FADERFIUM. In old English law. A marriage gift coming from the father or brother of the bride.

FÆDER-FEOH. In old English law. The portion brought by a wife to her husband, and which reverted to a widow, in case the heir of her deceased husband refused his consent to her second marriage; i. e., it reverted to her family in case she returned to them. Wharton.

FÆSTING-MEN. Approved men who were strong-armed; *habentes homines* or rich men, men of substance; pledges or bondsmen, who, by Saxon custom, were bound to answer for each other's good behavior. Cowell; Du Cange.

FAGGOT. A badge worn in popish times by persons who had recanted and abjured what was then adjudged to be heresy, as an emblem of what they had merited. Cowell.

FAGGOT VOTES. A faggot vote is where a man is formally possessed of a right to vote for members of parliament, without possessing the substance which the vote should represent; as if he is enabled to buy a property, and at the same moment mortgage it to its full value for the mere sake of the vote. Such a vote is called a "faggot vote." See 7 & 8 Wm. III. c. 25, § 7. Wharton.

FAIDA. In Saxon law. Malice; open and deadly hostility; deadly feud. The word designated the enmity between the family of a murdered man and that of his murderer, which was recognized, among the Teutonic peoples, as justification for vengeance taken by any one of the former upon any one of the latter.

FAIL. The difference between "fail" and "refuse" is that the latter involves an act of the will, while the former may be an act of inevitable necessity. 9 Wheat. 344.

FAILING OF RECORD. When an action is brought against a person who alleges in his plea matter of record in bar of the action, and avers to prove it by the record, but the plaintiff saith *nul tiel record*, viz., denies there is any such record, upon which the defendant has a day given him by the court to bring it in, if he fail to do it, then he is said to fail of his record, and the plaintiff is entitled to sign judgment. Termes de la Ley.

FAILLITE. In French law. Bankruptcy; failure; the situation of a debtor who finds himself unable to fulfill his engagements. Code de Com. arts. 442, 580; Civil Code La. art. 3522.

FAILURE. In legal parlance, the neglect of any duty may be described as a "failure." But in the language of the business world this term, applied to a merchant or mercantile concern, means an inability to pay his or their debts, from insolvency, and the word must be regarded as synonymous with "insolvency." 1 Rice, 140.

According to other authorities, "failure," in this sense, means a failure to meet current obligations at maturity. Insolvency looks to the ability to pay; failure to the fact of payment. Failure is the outward act which stands for evidence of insolvency. 13 S. C. 226. See, also, 10 Blatchf. 256; 24 Conn. 310.

FAILURE OF CONSIDERATION. The want or failure of a consideration sufficient to support a note, contract, or conveyance. It may be either partial or entire.

FAILURE OF EVIDENCE. Judicially speaking, a total "failure of evidence" means not only the utter absence of all evidence, but it also means a failure to offer proof, either positive or inferential, to establish one or more of the many facts, the establishment of *all* of which is indispensable to the finding of the issue for the plaintiff. 7 Gill & J. 28.

FAILURE OF ISSUE. The failure at a fixed time. or the total extinction, of issue to take an estate limited over by an executory devise.

A definite failure of issue is when a precise time is fixed by the will for the failure of issue, as in the case where there is a devise to one, but if he dies without issue or lawful issue living at the time of his death, etc. An indefinite failure of issue is the period when the issue or descendants of the first taker shall become extinct, and when there is no longer any issue of the issue of the grantee, without reference to any particular time or any particular event. 50 Ind. 546.

An executory devise to take effect on an indefinite failure of issue is void for remoteness. and hence courts are astute to devise some construction which shall restrain the failure of issue to the term of limitation allowed. 40 Pa. St. 18; 2 Redf. Wills, 276, note.

FAILURE OF JUSTICE. The defeat of a particular right, or the failure of reparation for a particular wrong, from the lack of a legal remedy for the enforcement of the one or the redress of the other.

FAILURE OF RECORD. Failure of the defendant to produce a record which he has alleged and relied on in his plea.

FAILURE OF TITLE. The inability or failure of a vendor to make good title to the whole or a part of the property which he has contracted to sell.

FAILURE OF TRUST. The lapsing or non-efficiency of a proposed trust, by reason of the defect or insufficiency of the deed or instrument creating it, or on account of illegality, indefiniteness, or other legal impediment.

FAINT (or FEIGNED) ACTION. In old English practice. An action was so called where the party bringing it had no title to recover, although the words of the writ were true; a *false* action was properly where the words of the writ were false. Litt. § 689; Co. Litt. 361.

FAINT PLEADER. A fraudulent, false, or collusive manner of pleading to the deception of a third person.

FAIR, *n.* In English law. A greater species of market; a privileged market. It is an incorporeal hereditament, granted by royal patent, or established by prescription presupposing a grant from the crown.

In the earlier English law, the franchise to hold a fair conferred certain important privileges; and fairs, as legally recognized institutions, possessed distinctive legal characteristics. Most of these privileges and characteristics, however, are now obsolete. In America, fairs, in the ancient technical sense, are unknown, and, in the modern and popular sense, they are entirely voluntary and non-legal, and transactions arising in or in connection with them are subject to the ordinary rules governing sales, etc.

FAIR, *adj.* Just; equitable; even-handed; equal, as between conflicting interests.

FAIR-PLAY MEN. A local irregular tribunal which existed in Pennsylvania about the year 1769, as to which see Serg. Land Laws Pa. 77; 2 Smith, Laws Pa. 195.

FAIR PLEADER. See BEAUPLEADER.

FAIRLY. Justly; rightly; equitably. With substantial correctness.

"Fairly" is not synonymous with "truly," and "truly" should not be substituted for it in a commissioner's oath to take testimony fairly. Language may be truly, yet unfairly, reported; that is, an answer may be truly written down, yet in a manner conveying a different meaning from that intended and conveyed. And language may be fairly reported, yet not in accordance with strict truth. 17 N. J. Eq. 234.

FAIT. L. Fr. Anything done. A deed; act; fact.

A deed lawfully executed. Com. Dig.

Feme de fait. A wife *de facto.*

FAIT ENROLLE. A deed enrolled, as a bargain and sale of freeholds. 1 Keb. 568.

FAIT JURIDIQUE. In French law. A juridical fact. One of the factors or elements constitutive of an obligation.

FAITH. 1. Confidence; credit; reliance. Thus, an act may be said to be done "on the faith" of certain representations.

2. Belief; credence; trust. Thus, the constitution provides that "full faith and credit" shall be given to the judgments of each state in the courts of the others.

3. Purpose; intent; sincerity; state of knowledge or design. This is the meaning of the word in the phrases "good faith" and "bad faith."

In Scotch law. A solemn pledge; an oath. "To make faith" is to swear, with the right hand uplifted, that one will declare the truth. 1 Forb. Inst. pt. 4, p. 235.

FAITOURS. Idle persons; idle livers; vagabonds. Cowell; Blount.

FALANG. In old English law. A jacket or close coat. Blount.

FALCARE. In old English law. To mow. *Falcare prata,* to mow or cut grass in meadows laid in for hay. A customary service to the lord by his inferior tenants. *Jus falcandi,* the right of cutting wood. Bract. fol. 231.

Falcata, grass fresh mown, and laid in swaths.

Falcatio, a mowing. Bract. fols. 35b, 230.

Falcator, a mower; a servile tenant who performed the labor of mowing.

Falcatura, a day's mowing.

FALCIDIA. In Spanish law. The Falcidian portion; the portion of an inheritance which could not be legally bequeathed away from the heir, viz., one-fourth.

FALCIDIAN LAW. In Roman law. A law on the subject of testamentary disposition, enacted by the people in the year of Rome 714, on the proposition of the tribune Falcidius. By this law, the testator's right to burden his estate with legacies was subjected to an important restriction. It prescribed that no one could bequeath more than three-fourths of his property in legacies, and that the heir should have at least one-fourth of the estate, and that, should the testator violate this prescript, the heir may have the right to make a proportional deduction from each legatee, so far as necessary. Mackeld. Rom. Law, § 771; Inst. 2, 22.

FALCIDIAN PORTION. That portion of a testator's estate which, by the Falcidian law, was required to be left to the heir, amounting to at least one-fourth.

FALD, or FALDA. A sheep-fold. Cowell.

FALDA. Span. In Spanish law. The slope or skirt of a hill. 2 Wall. 673.

FALDÆ CURSUS. In old English law. A fold-course; the course (going or taking about) of a fold. Spelman.

A sheep walk, or feed for sheep. 2 Vent. 139.

FALDAGE. The privilege which anciently several lords reserved to themselves of setting up folds for sheep in any fields within their manors, the better to manure them, and this not only with their own but their tenants' sheep. Called, variously, "*secta faldare,*" "fold-course," "free-fold," "*faldagii.*" Cowell; Spelman.

FALDATA. In old English law. A flock or fold of sheep. Cowell.

FALDFEY. Sax. A fee or rent paid by a tenant to his lord for leave to fold his sheep on his own ground. Blount.

FALDISDORY. In ecclesiastical law. The bishop's seat or throne within the chancel.

FALDSOCA. Sax. The liberty or privilege of foldage.

FALDSTOOL. A place at the south side of the altar at which the sovereign kneels at his coronation. Wharton.

FALDWORTH. In Saxon law. A person of age that he may be reckoned of some decennary. Du Fresne.

G

H

I

J

K

L

M

FALERÆ. In old English law. The tackle and furniture of a cart or wain. Blount.

FALESIA. In old English law. A hill or down by the sea-side. Co. Litt. 5b; Domesday.

FALK-LAND. See FOLC-LAND.

FALL. In Scotch law. To lose. To fall from a right is to lose or forfeit it. 1 Kames, Eq. 228.

FALL OF LAND. In English law. A quantity of land six ells square superficial measure.

FALLO. In Spanish law. The final decree or judgment given in a controversy at law.

FALLOW-LAND. Land plowed, but not sown, and left uncultivated for a time after successive crops.

FALLUM. In old English law. An unexplained term for some particular kind of land. Cowell.

FALSA DEMONSTRATIO. In the civil law. False designation; erroneous description of a person or thing in a written instrument. Inst. 2, 20, 30.

Falsa demonstratio non nocet, cum de corpore (persona) constat. False description does not injure or vitiate, provided the thing or person intended has once been sufficiently described. Mere false description does not make an instrument inoperative. Broom, Max. 629; 6 Term, 676; 11 Mees. & W. 189; 2 Story, 291.

Falsa demonstratione legatum non perimi. A bequest is not rendered void by an erroneous description. Inst. 2, 20, 30; Broom, Max. 645.

Falsa grammatica non vitiat concessionem. False or bad grammar does not vitiate a grant. Shep. Touch. 55; 9 Coke, 48a. Neither false Latin nor false English will make a deed void when the intent of the parties doth plainly appear. Shep. Touch. 87.

FALSA MONETA. In the civil law. False or counterfeit money. Cod. 9, 24.

Falsa orthographia non vitiat chartam, [concessionem.] False spelling does not vitiate a deed. Shep. Touch. 55, 87; 9 Coke, 48a; Wing. Max. 19.

FALSARE. In old English law. To counterfeit. *Quia falsavit sigillum*, because he counterfeited the seal. Bract. fol. 276b.

FALSARIUS. A counterfeiter. Townsh. Pl. 260.

FALSE. Untrue; erroneous; deceitful; contrived or calculated to deceive and injure. Unlawful.

In law, this word means something more than untrue; it means something designedly untrue and deceitful, and implies an intention to perpetrate some treachery or fraud. 18 U. C. C. P. 19; 7 Amer. & Eng. Enc. Law, 661.

FALSE ACTION. See FEIGNED ACTION.

FALSE CHARACTER. Personating the master or mistress of a servant, or any representative of such master or mistress, and giving a false character to the servant, is an offense punishable in England with a fine of £20. St. 32 Geo. III. c. 56.

FALSE CLAIM, in the forest law, was where a man claimed more than his due, and was amerced and punished for the same. Manw. c. 25; Tomlins.

FALSE FACT. In the law of evidence. A feigned, simulated, or fabricated fact; a fact not founded in truth, but existing only in assertion; the deceitful semblance of a fact.

FALSE IMPRISONMENT. The unlawful arrest or detention of a person without warrant, or by an illegal warrant, or a warrant illegally executed, and either in a prison or a place used temporarily for that purpose, or by force and constraint without confinement.

False imprisonment consists in the unlawful detention of the person of another, for any length of time, whereby he is deprived of his personal liberty. Code Ga. 1882, § 2990; Pen. Code Cal. § 236.

The term is also used as the name of the action which lies for this species of injury. 3 Bl. Comm. 138.

FALSE JUDGMENT. In old English law. A writ which lay when a false judgment had been pronounced in a court not of record, as a county court, court baron, etc. Fitzh. Nat. Brev. 17, 18.

In old French law. The defeated party in a suit had the privilege of accusing the judges of pronouncing a false or corrupt judgment, whereupon the issue was determined by his challenging them to the combat or *duellum*. This was called the "appeal of false judgment." Montesq. Esprit des Lois, liv. 28, c. 27.

FALSE LATIN. When law proceedings were written in Latin, if a word were significant though not good Latin, yet an indictment, declaration, or fine should not be made void by it; but if the word were not Latin, nor allowed by the law, and it were in a material point, it made the whole vicious. (5 Coke, 121; 2 Nels. 830.) Wharton.

FALSE LIGHTS AND SIGNALS. Lights and signals falsely and maliciously displayed for the purpose of bringing a vessel into danger.

FALSE NEWS. Spreading false news, whereby discord may grow between the queen of England and her people, or the great men of the realm, or which may produce other mischiefs, still seems to be a misdemeanor, under St. 3 Edw. I. c. 34. Steph. Cr. Dig. § 95.

FALSE OATH. See PERJURY.

FALSE PERSONATION. The criminal offense of falsely representing some other person and acting in the character thus unlawfully assumed, in order to deceive others, and thereby gain some profit or advantage, or enjoy some right or privilege belonging to the one so personated, or subject him to some expense, charge, or liability. See 4 Steph. Comm. 181, 290.

FALSE PLEA. See SHAM PLEA.

FALSE PRETENSES. In criminal law. False representations and statements, made with a fraudulent design to obtain money, goods, wares, or merchandise, with intent to cheat. 2 Bouv. Inst. no. 2308.

A representation of some fact or circumstance, calculated to mislead, which is not true. 19 Pick. 184.

False statements or representations made with intent to defraud, for the purpose of obtaining money or property.

A pretense is the holding out or offering to others something false and feigned. This may be done either by words or actions, which amount to false representations. In fact, false representations are inseparable from the idea of a pretense. Without a representation which is false there can be no pretense. 43 Iowa, 132.

FALSE REPRESENTATION. See FRAUD; DECEIT.

FALSE RETURN. A return to a writ, in which the officer charged with it falsely reports that he served it, when he did not, or

makes some other false or incorrect statement, whereby injury results to a person interested.

FALSE SWEARING. The misdemeanor committed in English law by a person who swears falsely before any person authorized to administer an oath upon a matter of public concern, under such circumstances that the false swearing would have amounted to perjury if committed in a judicial proceeding; as where a person makes a false affidavit under the bills of sale acts. Steph. Cr. Dig. p. 84.

FALSE TOKEN. In criminal law. A false document or sign of the existence of a fact, used with intent to defraud, for the purpose of obtaining money or property.

FALSE VERDICT. An untrue verdict. Formerly, if a jury gave a false verdict, the party injured by it might sue out and prosecute a writ of attaint against them, either at common law or on the statute 11 Hen. VII. c. 24, at his election, for the purpose of reversing the judgment and punishing the jury for their verdict; but not where the jury erred merely in point of law, if they found according to the judge's direction. The practice of setting aside verdicts and granting new trials, however, so superseded the use of attaints that there is no instance of one to be found in the books of reports later than in the time of Elizabeth, and it was altogether abolished by 6 Geo. IV. c. 50, § 60. Wharton.

FALSE WEIGHTS. False weights and measures are such as do not comply with the standard prescribed by the state or government, or with the custom prevailing in the place and business in which they are used. 7 Amer. & Eng. Enc. Law, 796.

FALSEDAD. In Spanish law. Falsity; an alteration of the truth. Las Partidas, pt. 3, tit. 26, 1. 1.

Deception; fraud. Id. pt. 3, tit. 32, 1. 21.

FALSEHOOD. A statement or assertion known to be untrue, and intended to deceive. A willful act or declaration contrary to the truth. 51 N. H. 207.

In Scotch law. A fraudulent imitation or suppression of truth, to the prejudice of another. Bell. "Something used and published falsely." An old Scottish *nomen juris*. "Falsehood is undoubtedly a nominate crime, so much so that Sir George Mackenzie and our older lawyers used no other term for the falsification of writs, and the name 'forgery' has been of modern introduction." "If there is any distinction to be made between 'forgery' and 'falsehood,' I would consider the latter to be more comprehensive than the former." 2 Broun, 77, 78.

FALSI CRIMEN. Fraudulent subornation or concealment, with design to darken or hide the truth, and make things appear otherwise than they are. It is committed (1) by words, as when a witness swears falsely; (2) by writing, as when a person antedates a contract; (3) by deed, as selling by false weights and measures. Wharton. See CRIMEN FALSI.

FALSIFICATION. In equity practice. The showing an item in the debit of an account to be either wholly false or in some part erroneous. 1 Story, Eq. Jur. § 525.

FALSIFY. To disprove; to prove to be false or erroneous; to avoid or defeat; spoken of verdicts, appeals, etc.

To counterfeit or forge; to make something false; to give a false appearance to anything.

In equity practice. To show, in accounting before a master in chancery, that a charge has been inserted which is wrong; that is, either wholly false or in some part erroneous. Pull. Accts. 162; 1 Story, Eq. Jur. § 525.

FALSIFYING A RECORD. A high offense against public justice, punishable in England by 24 & 25 Vict. c. 98, §§ 27, 28, and in the United States, generally, by statute.

FALSING. In Scotch law. False making; forgery. "Falsing of *evidentis*." 1 Pitc. Crim. Tr. pt. 1, p. 85.

Making or proving false.

FALSING OF DOOMS. In Scotch law. The proving the injustice, *falsity*, or error of the *doom* or sentence of a court. Tomlins; Jacob. The reversal of a sentence or judgment. Skene. An appeal. Bell.

FALSO RETORNO BREVIUM. A writ which formerly lay against the sheriff who had execution of process for false returning of writs. Reg. Jud. 43*b*.

FALSONARIUS. A forger; a counterfeiter. Hov. 424.

FALSUM. Lat. In the civil law. A false or forged thing; a fraudulent simulation; a fraudulent counterfeit or imitation, such as a forged signature or instrument. Also falsification, which may be either by

falsehood, concealment of the truth, or fraudulent alteration, as by cutting out or erasing part of a writing.

FALSUS. False; fraudulent; erroneous. Deceitful; mistaken.

Falsus in uno, falsus in omnibus. False in one thing, false in everything. Where a party is clearly shown to have embezzled one article of property, it is a ground of presumption that he may have embezzled others also. 1 Sumn. 329, 356; 7 Wheat. 338.

FAMA. Fame; character; reputation; report of common opinion.

Fama, fides et oculus non patiuntur ludum. 3 Bulst. 226. Fame, faith, and eyesight do not suffer a cheat.

Fama, quæ suspicionem inducit, oriri debet apud bonos et graves, non quidem malevolos et maledicos, sed providas et fide dignas personas, non semel sed sæpius, quia clamor minuit et defamatio manifestat. 2 Inst. 52. Report, which induces suspicion, ought to arise from good and grave men; not, indeed, from malevolent and malicious men, but from cautious and credible persons; not only once, but frequently; for clamor diminishes, and defamation manifests.

FAMACIDE. A killer of reputation; a slanderer.

FAMILIA. In Roman law. A household; a family. On the composition of the Roman family, see AGNATI; COGNATI; and see Mackeld. Rom. Law, § 144.

Family right; the right or *status* of being the head of a family, or of exercising the *patria potestas* over others. This could belong only to a Roman citizen who was a "man in his own right," (*homo sui juris*.) Mackeld. Rom. Law, §§ 133, 144.

In old English law. A household; the body of household servants; a quantity of land, otherwise called "*mansa*," sufficient to maintain one family.

In Spanish law. A family, which might consist of domestics or servants. It seems that a single person owning negroes was the "head of a family," within the meaning of the colonization laws of Coahuila and Texas. 9 Tex. 156.

FAMILIÆ EMPTOR. In Roman law. An intermediate person who purchased the aggregate inheritance when sold *per æs et* *libram,* in the process of making a will under the Twelve Tables. This purchaser was merely a man of straw, transmitting the inheritance to the *hæres* proper. Brown.

FAMILIÆ ERCISCUNDÆ. In Roman law. An action for the partition of the aggregate succession of a *familia,* where that devolved upon *co-hæredes.* It was also applicable to enforce a contribution towards the necessary expenses incurred on the *familia.* See Mackeld. Rom. Law, § 499.

FAMILIARES REGIS. Persons of the king's household. The ancient title of the "six clerks" of chancery in England. Crabb, Com. Law, 184; 2 Reeve, Eng. Law, 249, 251.

FAMILY. A family comprises a father, mother, and children. In a wider sense, it may include domestic servants; all who live in one house under one head. In a still broader sense, a group of blood-relatives; all the relations who descend from a common ancestor, or who spring from a common root. See Civil Code La. art. 3522, no. 16; 9 Ves. 323.

A husband and wife living together may constitute a "family," within the meaning of that word as used in a homestead law. (Fla.) 7 South. Rep. 140.

"Family," in its origin, meant "servants;" but, in its more modern and comprehensive meaning, it signifies a collective body of persons living together in one house, or within the curtilage, in legal phrase. 31 Tex. 677.

"Family" may mean children, wife and children, blood-relatives, or the members of the domestic circle, according to the connection in which the word is used. 11 Paige, 159.

"Family," in popular acceptation, includes parents, children, and servants,—all whose domicile or home is ordinarily in the same house and under the same management and head. In a statute providing that to gain a settlement in a town one must have "supported himself and his family therein" for six years, it includes the individuals whom it was the right of the head to control, and his duty to support. The wife is a member of the family, within such an enactment. 31 Conn. 326.

FAMILY ARRANGEMENT. A term denoting an agreement between a father and his children, or between the heirs of a deceased father, to dispose of property, or to partition it in a different manner than that which would result if the law alone directed it, or to divide up property without administration.

In these cases, frequently, the mere relation of the parties will give effect to bargains otherwise without adequate consideration. 1 Chit. Pr. 67; 1 Turn. & R. 13

FAMILY BIBLE. A Bible containing a record of the births, marriages, and deaths of the members of a family.

FAMILY MEETING. An institution of the laws of Louisiana, being a council of the relatives (or, if there are no relatives, of the friends) of a minor, for the purpose of advising as to his affairs and the administration of his property. The family meeting is called by order of a judge, and presided over by a justice or notary, and must consist of at least five persons, who are put under oath.

FAMOSUS. In the civil and old English law. Relating to or affecting character or reputation; defamatory; slanderous.

FAMOSUS LIBELLUS. A libelous writing. A term of the civil law denoting that species of *injuria* which corresponds nearly to libel or slander.

FANAL. Fr. In French marine law. A large lantern, fixed upon the highest part of a vessel's stern.

FANATICS. Persons pretending to be inspired, and being a general name for Quakers, Anabaptists, and all other sectaries, and factious dissenters from the Church of England. (St. 13 Car. II. c. 6.) Jacob.

FANEGA. In Spanish law. A measure of land varying in different provinces, but in the Spanish settlements in America consisting of 6,400 square varas or yards.

FAQUEER, or FAKIR. A Hindu term for a poor man, mendicant; a religious beggar.

FARANDMAN. In Scotch law. A traveler or merchant stranger. Skene.

FARDEL OF LAND. In old English law. The fourth part of a yard-land. Noy says an eighth only, because, according to him, two fardels make a nook, and four nooks a yard-land. Wharton.

FARDELLA. In old English law. A bundle or pack; a fardel. Fleta, lib. 1, c. 22, § 10.

FARDING-DEAL. The fourth part of an acre of land. Spelman.

FARE. A voyage or passage by water; also the money paid for a passage either by land or by water. Cowell.

The price of passage, or the sum paid or to be paid for carrying a passenger. 26 N. Y. 526.

G

H

I

J

K

L

M

FARINAGIUM. A mill; a toll of meal or flour. Jacob; Spelman.

FARLEU. Money paid by tenants in lieu of a heriot. It was often applied to the best chattel, as distinguished from *heriot*, the best beast. Cowell.

FARLINGARII. Whoremongers and adulterers.

FARM. A certain amount of provision reserved as the rent of a messuage. Spelman.

Rent generally which is reserved on a lease; when it was to be paid in money, it was called "*blanche firme.*" Spelman; 2 Bl. Comm. 42.

A term, a lease of lands; a leasehold interest. 2 Bl. Comm. 17; 1 Reeve, Eng. Law, 301, note. The land itself, let to farm or rent. 2 Bl. Comm. 368.

A portion of land used for agricultural purposes, either wholly or in part. 18 Pick. 553; 2 Bin. 238.

The original meaning of the word was "rent," and by a natural transition it came to mean the land out of which the rent issued.

In old English law. A lease of other things than land, as of imposts. There were several of these, such as "the sugar farm," "the silk farm," and farms of wines and currants, called "petty farms." See 2 How. State Tr. 1197–1206.

In American law. "Farm" denotes a tract of land devoted in part, at least, to cultivation, for agricultural purposes, without reference to its extent, or to the tenure by which it is held. 2 Bin. 238.

FARM LET. Operative words in a lease, which strictly mean to let upon payment of a certain rent in farm; *i. e.*, in agricultural produce.

FARM OUT. To let for a term at a stated rental. Among the Romans the collection of revenue was farmed out, and in England taxes and tolls sometimes are.

FARMER. 1. The lessee of a farm. It is said that every lessee for life or years, although it be but of a small house and land, is called "farmer." This word implies no mystery, except it be that of husbandman. Cunningham; Cowell.

2. A husbandman or agriculturist; one who cultivates a farm, whether the land be his own or another's.

3. One who assumes the collection of the public revenues, taxes, excise, etc., for a certain commission or percentage; as a *farmer* of the revenues.

FARO. An unlawful game of cards, in which all the other players play against the banker or dealer, staking their money upon the order in which the cards will lie and be dealt from the pack. Webster.

FARRAGO LIBELLI. Lat. An ill-composed book containing a collection of miscellaneous subjects not properly associated nor scientifically arranged. Wharton.

FARRIER. One whose business is to shoe horses for all such as apply to him.

FARTHING. The fourth part of an English penny.

FARTHING OF GOLD. An ancient English coin, containing in value the fourth part of a noble.

FARYNDON INN. The ancient appellation of Serjeants' Inn, Chancery lane.

FAS. Lat. Right; justice; the divine law. 3 Bl. Comm. 2; Calvin.

FASIUS. A faggot of wood.

FAST. In Georgia, a "fast" bill of exceptions is one which may be taken in injunction suits and similar cases, at such time and in such manner as to bring the case up for review with great expedition. It must be certified within twenty days from the rendering of the decision. 66 Ga. 353.

FAST-DAY. A day of fasting and penitence, or of mortification by religious abstinence. See 1 Chit. Archb. Pr. (12th Ed.) 160, et seq.

FAST ESTATE. Real property. A term sometimes used in wills. 6 Johns. 185; 9 N. Y. 502.

FASTERMANS, or FASTING-MEN. Men in repute and substance; pledges, sureties, or bondsmen, who, according to the Saxon polity, were *fast* bound to answer for each other's peaceable behavior. Enc. Lond.

FASTI. In Roman law. Lawful. *Dies fasti*, lawful days; days on which justice could lawfully be administered by the prætor. See DIES FASTI.

Fatetur facinus qui judicium fugit. 3 Inst. 14. He who flees judgment confesses his guilt.

FATHER. The male parent. He by whom a child is begotten.

FATHER-IN-LAW. The father of one's wife or husband.

FATHOM. A nautical measure of six feet in length.

FATUA MULIER. A whore. Du Fresne.

FATUITAS. In old English law. Fatuity; idiocy. Reg. Orig. 266.

FATUITY. Mental weakness; foolishness; imbecility; idiocy.

FATUM. Lat. Fate; a superhuman power; an event or cause of loss, beyond human foresight or means of prevention.

FATUOUS PERSON. One entirely destitute of reason; *is qui omnino desipit.* Ersk. Inst. 1, 7, 48.

FATUUS. An idiot or fool. Bract. fol. 420*b.*

Foolish; absurd; indiscreet; or ill considered. *Fatuum judicium,* a foolish judgment or verdict. Applied to the verdict of a jury which, though false, was not criminally so, or did not amount to perjury. Bract. fol. 289.

Fatuus, apud jurisconsultos nostros, accipitur pro non compos mentis; et fatuus dicitur, qui omnino desipit. 4 Coke, 128. Fatuous, among our jurisconsults, is understood for a man not of right mind; and he is called "*fatuus*" who is altogether foolish.

Fatuus præsumitur qui in proprio nomine errat. A man is presumed to be simple who makes a mistake in his own name. Code, 6, 24, 14; 5 Johns. Ch. 148, 161.

FAUBOURG. In French law, and in Louisiana. A district or part of a town adjoining the principal city; a suburb. See 18 La. 286.

FAUCES TERRÆ. (Jaws of the land.) Narrow headlands and promontories, inclosing a portion or arm of the sea within them. 1 Kent, Comm. 367, and note; Hale, De Jure Mar. 10; 1 Story, 251, 259.

FAULT. In the civil law. Negligence; want of care. An improper act or omission, injurious to another, and transpiring through negligence, rashness, or ignorance.

There are in law three degrees of faults,— the gross, the slight, and the very slight fault. The *gross* fault is that which proceeds from inexcusable negligence or ignorance; it is considered as nearly equal to fraud. The *slight* fault is that want of care which a prudent man usually takes of his business. The *very slight* fault is that which is excusable, and for which no responsibility is incurred. Civil Code La. art. 3556, par. 13.

FAUTOR. In old English law. A favorer or supporter of others; an abettor. Cowell; Jacob. A partisan. One who encouraged resistance to the execution of process.

In Spanish law. Accomplice; the person who aids or assists another in the commission of a crime.

FAUX. In old English law. False; counterfeit. *Faux action,* a false action. Litt. § 688. *Faux money,* counterfeit money. St. Westm. 1, c. 15. *Faux peys,* false weights. Britt. c. 20. *Faux serement,* a false oath. St. Westm. 1, c. 38.

In French law. A falsification or fraudulent alteration or suppression of a thing by words, by writings, or by acts without either. Biret.

"*Faux* may be understood in three ways. In its most extended sense it is the alteration of truth, with or without intention; it is nearly synonymous with 'lying.' In a less extended sense, it is the alteration of truth, accompanied with fraud, *mutatio veritatis cum dolo facta.* And lastly, in a narrow, or rather the legal, sense of the word, when it is a question to know if the *faux* be a crime, it is the fraudulent alteration of the truth in those cases ascertained and punished by the law." Toullier, t. 9, n. 188.

In the civil law. The fraudulent alteration of the truth. The same with the Latin *falsum* or *crimen falsi.*

FAVOR. Bias; partiality; lenity; prejudice. See CHALLENGE.

Favorabilia in lege sunt fiscus, dos, vita, libertas. Jenk. Cent. 94. Things favorably considered in law are the treasury, dower, life, liberty.

Favorabiliores rei, potius quam actores, habentur. The condition of the defendant must be favored, rather than that of the plaintiff. In other words, *melior est conditio defendentis.* Dig. 50, 17, 125; Broom, Max. 715.

Favorabiliores sunt executiones aliis processibus quibuscunque. Co. Litt. 289. Executions are preferred to all other processes whatever.

Favores ampliandi sunt; odia restringenda. Jenk. Cent. 186. Favors are to be enlarged; things hateful restrained.

FEAL. Faithful. Tenants by knight service swore to their lords to be *feal* and *leal; i. e.*, faithful and loyal.

FEAL AND DIVOT. A right in Scotland, similar to the right of turbary in England, for fuel, etc.

FEALTY. In feudal law. Fidelity; allegiance to the feudal lord of the manor; the feudal obligation resting upon the tenant or vassal by which he was bound to be faithful and true to his lord, and render him obedience and service.

Fealty signifies fidelity, the phrase "feal and leal" meaning simply "faithful and loyal." Tenants by knights' service and also tenants in socage were required to take an oath of fealty to the king or others, their immediate lords; and fealty was one of the conditions of their tenure, the breach of which operated a forfeiture of their estates. Brown.

Although foreign jurists consider fealty and homage as convertible terms, because in some continental countries they are blended so as to form one engagement, yet they are not to be confounded in our country, for they do not imply the same thing, *homage* being the acknowledgment of tenure, and *fealty*, the vassal oath of fidelity, being the essential feudal bond, and the animating principle of a feud, without which it could not subsist. Wharton.

FEAR. Apprehension of harm.

Apprehension of harm or punishment, as exhibited by outward and visible marks of emotion. An evidence of guilt in certain cases. See Burrill, Circ. Ev. 476.

FEASANCE. A doing; the doing of an act.

A making; the making of an indenture, release, or obligation. Litt. § 371; Dyer, (Fr. Ed.) 56b. The making of a statute. Keilw. 1b.

FEASANT. Doing, or making.

FEASOR. Doer; maker. *Feasors del estatute*, makers of the statute. Dyer, 3b.

FEASTS. Certain established festivals or holidays in the ecclesiastical calendar. These days were anciently used as the dates of legal instruments, and in England the quarter-days, for paying rent, are four feast-days. The terms of the courts, in England, before 1875, were fixed to begin on certain days determined with reference to the occurrence of four of the chief feasts.

FECIAL LAW. The nearest approach to a system of international law known to the ancient world. It was a branch of Roman jurisprudence, concerned with embassies, declarations of war, and treaties of peace. It received this name from the *feciales*, (*q. v.*,) who were charged with its administration.

FECIALES. Among the ancient Romans, that order of priests who discharged the duties of ambassadors. Subsequently their duties appear to have related more particularly to the declaring war and peace. Calvin.; 1 Kent, Comm. 6.

FEDERAL. In constitutional law. A term commonly used to express a league or compact between two or more states.

In American law. Belonging to the general government or union of the states. Founded on or organized under the constitution or laws of the United States.

The United States has been generally styled, in American political and judicial writings, a "federal government." The term has not been imposed by any specific constitutional authority, but only expresses the general sense and opinion upon the nature of the form of government. In recent years, there is observable a disposition to employ the term "national" in speaking of the government of the Union. Neither word settles anything as to the nature or powers of the government. "Federal" is somewhat more appropriate if the government is considered a union of the states; "national" is preferable if the view is adopted that the state governments and the Union are two distinct systems, each established by the people directly, one for local and the other for national purposes. See 92 U. S. 542; Abbott.

FEDERAL GOVERNMENT. The system of government administered in a state formed by the union or confederation of several independent or *quasi* independent states; also the composite state so formed.

In strict usage, there is a distinction between a *confederation* and a *federal government.* The former term denotes a league or permanent alliance between several states, each of which is fully sovereign and independent, and each of which retains its full dignity, organization, and sovereignty, though yielding to the central authority a controlling power for a few limited purposes, such as external and diplomatic relations. In this case, the component states are the units, with respect to the confederation, and the central government acts upon them, not upon the individual citizens. In a *federal government*, on the other hand, the allied states form a union,—not, indeed, to such an extent as to destroy their separate organization or deprive them of *quasi* sovereignty with respect to the administration of their purely local concerns, but so that the central power is erected into a true state or nation, possessing sovereignty both external and internal,—while the administration of national affairs is directed, and its effects felt, not by the separate states deliberating as units, but by the people of all, in their collective capacity, as citizens of the nation. The distinction is expressed, by the German writers, by the use of the two words "*Staatenbund*" and "*Bundesstaat;*" the former denoting a league or confederation of states, and the latter a federal government, or state formed by means of a league or confederation.

FEE. 1. A freehold estate in lands, held of a superior lord, as a reward for services, and on condition of rendering some service in return for it. The true meaning of the word "fee" is the same as that of "feud" or "fief," and in its original sense it is taken in contradistinction to "allodium," which latter is defined as a man's own land, which he possesses merely in his own right, without owing any rent or service to any superior. 2 Bl. Comm. 105. See 1 N. Y. 491.

In modern English tenures, "fee" signifies an estate of inheritance, being the highest and most extensive interest which a man can have in a feud; and when the term is used simply, without any adjunct, or in the form "fee-simple," it imports an absolute inheritance clear of any condition, limitation, or restriction to particular heirs, but descendible to the heirs general, male or female, lineal or collateral. 2 Bl. Comm. 106.

In modern English tenures, a fee signifies an estate of inheritance, and a fee-simple imports an absolute inheritance, clear of any condition or limitation whatever, and, when not disposed of by will, descends to the heirs generally. There are also limited fees: (1) Qualified or base fees; and (2) fees conditional at the common law. A base fee was confined to a person as tenant of a particular place. A conditional fee was restrained to particular heirs, as to the heirs of a man's body. 11 Wend. 259, 277.

A *determinable* fee is one which may possibly continue indefinitely, but which is liable to be determined. Plowd. 557.

A *qualified* (or base) fee is one which has a qualification subjoined thereto, and which must be determined whenever the qualification annexed to it is at an end. 2 Bl. Comm. 109.

A *conditional* fee, at the common law, was a fee restrained to some particular heirs exclusive of others. These afterwards became estates tail. 2 Bl. Comm. 110.

2. The word "fee" is also frequently used to denote the land which is held in fee.

3. The compass or circuit of a manor or lordship. Cowell.

4. **In American law.** A fee is an estate of inheritance without condition, belonging to the owner, and alienable by him, or transmissible to his heirs absolutely and simply. It is an absolute estate in perpetuity, and the largest possible estate a man can have, being, in fact, allodial in its nature.

5. A reward or wages given to one for the execution of his office, or for professional services, as those of a counsellor or physician. Cowell.

FEE-BILL. A schedule of the fees to be charged by clerks of courts, sheriffs, or other officers, for each particular service in the line of their duties.

FEE EXPECTANT. An estate where lands are given to a man and his wife, and the heirs of their bodies.

FEE-FARM. This is a species of tenure, where land is held of another in perpetuity at a yearly rent, without fealty, homage, or other services than such as are specially comprised in the feoffment. It corresponds very nearly to the "*emphyteusis*" of the Roman law.

Fee-farm is where an estate in fee is granted subject to a rent in fee of at least one-fourth of the value of the lands at the time of its reservation. Such rent appears to be called "fee-farm" because a grant of lands reserving so considerable a rent is indeed only letting lands to farm in fee-simple, instead of the usual method of life or years. 2 Bl. Comm. 43; 1 Steph. Comm. 676.

Fee-farms are lands held in fee to render for them annually the true value, or more or less; so called because a farm rent is reserved upon a grant in fee. Such estates are estates of inheritance. They are classed among estates in fee-simple. No reversionary interest remains in the lessor, and they are therefore subject to the operation of the legal principles which forbid restraints upon alienation in all cases where no feudal relation exists between grantor and grantee. 6 N. Y. 467, 497.

FEE-FARM RENT. The rent reserved on granting a fee-farm. It might be one-fourth the value of the land, according to Cowell; one-third, according to other authors. Spelman; Termes de la Ley; 2 Bl. Comm. 43.

Fee-farm rent is a rent-charge issuing out of an estate in fee; a perpetual rent reserved on a conveyance in fee-simple. 6 N. Y. 467, 495.

FEE-SIMPLE. In English law. A freehold estate of inheritance, absolute and unqualified. It stands at the head of estates as the highest in dignity and the most ample in extent; since every other kind of estate is derivable thereout, and mergeable therein, for *omne majus continet in se minus.* It may be enjoyed not only in land, but also in advowsons, commons, estovers, and other hereditaments, as well as in personalty, as an annuity or dignity, and also in an upper chamber, though the lower buildings and soil belong to another. Wharton.

In American law. An absolute or fee-simple estate is one in which the owner is entitled to the entire property, with unconditional power of disposition during his life, and descending to his heirs and legal representatives upon his death intestate. Code Ga. 1882, § 2246.

Fee-simple signifies a pure fee; an absolute estate of inheritance; that which a person holds inheritable to him and his heirs general forever. It is called "fee-simple," that is, "pure," because clear of any condition or restriction to particular heirs, being descendible to the heirs general, whether male or female, lineal or collateral. It is the largest estate and most extensive interest that can be enjoyed in land, being the entire property therein, and it confers an unlimited power of alienation. 42 Vt. 686.

A fee-simple is the largest estate known to the law, and, where no words of qualification or limitation are added, it means an estate in possession, and owned in severalty. It is undoubtedly true that a person may own a remainder or reversion in fee. But such an estate is not a fee-simple; it is a fee qualified or limited. So, when a person owns in common with another, he does not own the entire fee,—a fee-simple; it is a fee divided or shared with another. 54 Me. 426.

FEE-SIMPLE CONDITIONAL. This estate, at the common law, was a fee restrained to some particular heirs, exclusive of others. But the statute *De Donis* converted all such into estates tail. 2 Bl. Comm. 110.

FEE-TAIL. An estate tail; an estate of inheritance given to a man and the heirs of his body, or limited to certain classes of particular heirs. It corresponds to the *feudum talliatum* of the feudal law, and the idea is believed to have been borrowed from the Roman law, where, by way of *fidei commissa,* lands might be entailed upon children and freedmen and their descendants, with restrictions as to alienation. 1 Washb. Real Prop. *66.

FEED. To lend additional support; to strengthen *ex post facto.* "The interest when it accrues *feeds* the estoppel." 5 Mood. & R. 202.

FEGANGI. In old English law. A thief caught while escaping with the stolen goods in his possession. Spelman.

FEHMGERICHTE. The name given to certain secret tribunals which flourished in Germany from the end of the twelfth century to the middle of the sixteenth, usurping many of the functions of the governments which were too weak to maintain law and order, and inspiring dread in all who came within their jurisdiction. Enc. Brit. Such a court existed in Westphalia (though with greatly diminished powers) until finally suppressed in 1811.

FEIGNED ACTION. In practice. An action brought on a pretended right, when the plaintiff has no true cause of action, for some illegal purpose. In a feigned action the words of the writ are true. It differs from *false action,* in which case the words of the writ are false. Co. Litt. 361.

FEIGNED DISEASES. Simulated maladies. Diseases are generally feigned from one of three causes,—fear, shame, or the hope of gain.

FEIGNED ISSUE. An issue made up by the direction of a court of equity, (or by consent of parties,) and sent to a common-law court, for the purpose of obtaining the verdict of a jury on some disputed matter of fact which the court has not jurisdiction, or is unwilling, to decide. It rests upon a suppositious wager between the parties. See 3 Bl. Comm. 452.

FELAGUS. In Saxon law. One bound for another by oath; a sworn brother. A friend bound in the decennary for the good behavior of another. One who took the place of the deceased. Thus, if a person was murdered, the recompense due from the murderer went to the *felagus* of the slain, in default of parents or lord. Cunningham.

FELD. A field; in composition, wild. Blount.

FELE, FEAL. L. Fr. Faithful. See FEAL.

FELLOW. A companion; one with whom we consort; one joined with another in some legal *status* or relation; a member of a college or corporate body.

FELLOW-HEIR. A co-heir; partner of the same inheritance.

FELLOW-SERVANTS. "The decided weight of authority is to the effect that all who serve the same master, work under the same control, derive authority and compensation from the same common source, and are engaged in the same general business, though it may be in different grades or departments of it, are fellow-servants, who take the risk of each other's negligence." 2 Thomp. Neg. p. 1026, § 31.

Persons who are employed under the same master, derive authority and compensation from the same common source, and are engaged in the same general business, although one is a foreman of the work and the other a common laborer, are fellow-servants. 76 Me. 143.

Where two servants are employed by the same master, labor under the same control, derive their authority and receive their compensation from a common source, and are engaged in the same business, though in different departments of the common service, they are fellow-servants. 62 Tex. 597.

FELO DE SE. A felon of himself; a suicide or murderer of himself. One who deliberately and intentionally puts an end to his own life, or who commits some unlawful or malicious act which results in his own death.

FELON. One who has committed felony; one convicted of felony.

FELONIA. Felony. The act or offense by which a vassal forfeited his fee. Spelman; Calvin. *Per feloniam*, with a criminal intention. Co. Litt. 391.

Felonia, ex vi termini significat quodlibet capitale crimen felleo animo perpetratum. Co. Litt. 391. Felony, by force of the term, signifies any capital crime perpetrated with a malignant mind.

Felonia implicatur in qualibet proditione. 3 Inst. 15. Felony is implied in every treason.

FELONICE. Feloniously. Anciently an indispensable word in indictments for felony, and classed by Lord Coke among those *voces artis* (words of art) which cannot be expressed by any periphrasis or circumlocution. 4 Coke, 39; Co. Litt. 391a; 4 Bl. Comm. 307.

FELONIOUS HOMICIDE. In criminal law. The offense of killing a human creature, of any age or sex, without justification or excuse. There are two degrees of this offense, manslaughter and murder. 4 Bl. Comm. 188, 190; 4 Steph. Comm. 108, 111.

FELONIOUSLY. An indispensable word in modern indictments for felony, as *felonice* was in the Latin forms. 4 Bl. Comm. 307.

FELONY. In English law. This term meant originally the state of having forfeited lands and goods to the crown upon conviction for certain offenses, and then, by transition, any offense upon conviction for which such forfeiture followed, in addition to any other punishment prescribed by law; as distinguished from a "misdemeanor," upon conviction for which no forfeiture followed. All indictable offenses are either felonies or misdemeanors, but a material part of the distinction is taken away by St. 33 & 34 Vict. c. 23, which abolishes forfeiture for felony. Wharton.

In American law. The term has no very definite or precise meaning, except in some cases where it is defined by statute. For the most part, the state laws, in describing any particular offense, declare whether or not it shall be considered a felony. Apart from this, the word seems merely to imply a crime of a graver or more atrocious nature than those designated as "misdemeanors."

The statutes or codes of several of the states define felony as any public offense on conviction of which the offender is liable to be sentenced to death or to imprisonment in a penitentiary or state prison. Pub. St. Mass. 1882, p. 1290; Code Ala. 1886, § 3701; Code Ga. 1882, § 3404; 34 Ohio St. 301; 1 Wis. 188; 2 Rev. St. N. Y. p. 587, § 30; 1 Park. Crim. R. 39.

In feudal law. An act or offense on the part of the vassal, which cost him his fee, or in consequence of which his fee fell into the hands of his lord; that is, became forfeited. (See FELONIA.) Perfidy, ingratitude, or disloyalty to a lord.

FELONY ACT. The statute 33 & 34 Vict. c. 23, abolishing forfeitures for felony, and sanctioning the appointment of *interim curators* and *administrators* of the property of felons. Mozley & Whitley; 4 Steph. Comm. 10, 459.

FELONY, COMPOUNDING OF. See COMPOUNDING FELONY.

FEMALE. The sex which conceives and gives birth to young. Also a member of such sex.

FEME. L. Fr. A woman. In the phrase "*baron et feme*" (*q. v.*) the word has the sense of "wife."

FEME COVERT. A married woman. Generally used in reference to the legal disabilities of a married woman, as compared with the condition of a *feme sole*.

FEME SOLE. A single woman, including those who have been married, but whose marriage has been dissolved by death or divorce, and, for most purposes, those women who are judicially separated from their husbands. Mozley & Whitley; 2 Steph. Comm. 250.

FEME SOLE TRADER. In English law. A married woman, who, by the custom of London, trades on her own account, independently of her husband; so called because, with respect to her trading, she is the same as a *feme sole.* Jacob; Cro. Car. 68.

The term is applied also to women deserted by their husbands, who do business as *femes sole.* 1 Pet. 105.

FEMICIDE. The killing of a woman. Wharton.

FEMININE. Of or pertaining to females, or the female sex.

FENATIO. In forest law. The fawning of deer; the fawning season. Spelman.

FENCE, v. In old Scotch law. To defend or protect by formalities. To "fence a court" was to open it in due form, and interdict all manner of persons from disturbing their proceedings. This was called "fencing," *q. d.*, defending or protecting the court.

FENCE, n. A hedge, structure, or partition, erected for the purpose of inclosing a piece of land, or to divide a piece of land into distinct portions, or to separate two contiguous estates. See 63 Me. 308; 77 Ill. 169.

FENCE-MONTH, or DEFENSE-MONTH. In old English law. A period of time, occurring in the middle of summer, during which it was unlawful to hunt deer in the forest, that being their fawning season. Probably so called because the deer were then *defended* from pursuit or hunting. Manwood; Cowell.

FENERATION. Usury; the gain of interest; the practice of increasing money by lending.

FENGELD. In Saxon law. A tax or imposition, exacted for the repelling of enemies.

FENIAN. A champion, hero, giant. This word, in the plural, is generally used to signify invaders or foreign spoilers. The modern meaning of "fenian" is a member of an organization of persons of Irish birth, resident in the United States, Canada, and elsewhere, having for its aim the overthrow of English rule in Ireland. Webster, (Supp.)

FEOD. The same as *feud* or *fief*, being the right which the vassal had in land, or

some immovable property of his lord, to use the same and take the profits thereof, rendering unto the lord such duties and services as belonged to the particular tenure; the actual property in the soil always remaining in the lord. Spel. Feuds & Tenures.

FEODAL. Belonging to a fee or feud; feudal. More commonly used by the old writers than *feudal.*

FEODAL ACTIONS. Real actions; so called in the old books, as originally relating to *feoda*, fees, or estates in land. Mirr. c. 2, § 6; 3 Bl. Comm. 117.

FEODAL SYSTEM. See FEUDAL SYSTEM.

FEODALITY. Fidelity or fealty. Cowell. See FEALTY.

FEODARUM CONSUETUDINES. The customs of feuds. The name of a compilation of feudal laws and customs made at Milan in the twelfth century. It is the most ancient work on the subject, and was always regarded, on the continent of Europe, as possessing the highest authority.

FEODARY. An officer of the court of wards, appointed by the master of that court, under 32 Hen. VIII. c. 26, whose business it was to be present with the escheator in every county at the finding of offices of lands, and to give evidence for the king, as well concerning the value as the tenure; and his office was also to survey the land of the ward, after the office found, and to rate it. He also assigned the king's widows their dower; and received all the rents, etc. Abolished by 12 Car. II. c. 24. Wharton.

FEODATORY. In feudal law. The grantee of a *feod, feud,* or fee; the vassal or tenant who held his estate by feudal service. Termes de la Ley. Blackstone uses *"feudatory."* 2 Bl. Comm. 46.

FEODI FIRMA. In old English law. Fee-farm, (*q. v.*)

FEODI FIRMARIUS. The lessee of a fee-farm.

FEODUM. This word (meaning a feud or fee) is the one most commonly used by the older English law-writers, though its equivalent, *"feudum,"* is used generally by the more modern writers and by the *feudal* law-writers. Litt. § 1; Spelman. There were various classes of *feoda*, among which may be enumerated the following: *Feodum laicum*, a lay fee. *Feodum militare*, a knight's fee. *Feodum improprium,* an improper or derivative fee. *Feodum proprium,* a proper and original fee, regulated by the strict rules of feudal succession and tenure. *Feodum simplex,* a simple or pure fee; fee-simple. *Feodum talliatum,* a fee-tail. See 2 Bl. Comm. 58, 62; Litt. §§ 1, 13; Bract. fol. 175; Glan. 13, 23.

In old English law. A seigniory or jurisdiction. Fleta, lib. 2, c. 63, § 4.

A fee; a perquisite or compensation for a service. Fleta, lib. 2, c. 7.

FEODUM ANTIQUUM. A feud which devolved upon a vassal from his intestate ancestor.

Feodum est quod quis tenet ex quacunque causa sive sit tenementum sive reditus. Co. Litt. 1. A fee is that which any one holds from whatever cause, whether tenement or rent.

FEODUM NOBILE. A fief for which the tenant did guard and owed homage. Spelman.

FEODUM NOVUM. A feud acquired by a vassal himself.

Feodum simplex quia feodum idem est quod hæreditas, et simplex idem est quod legitimum vel purum; et sic feodum simplex idem est quod hæreditas legitima vel hæreditas pura. Litt. § 1. A fee-simple, so called because fee is the same as inheritance, and simple is the same as lawful or pure; and thus fee-simple is the same as a lawful inheritance, or pure inheritance.

Feodum talliatum, i. e., hæreditas in quandam certitudinem limitata. Litt. § 13. Fee-tail, *i. e.,* an inheritance limited in a definite descent.

FEOFFAMENTUM. A feoffment. 2 Bl. Comm. 310.

FEOFFARE. To enfeoff; to bestow a fee. The bestower was called "*feoffator,*" and the grantee or feoffee, "*feoffatus.*"

FEOFFATOR. In old English law. A feoffor; one who gives or bestows a fee; one who makes a feoffment. Bract. fols. 12*b,* 81.

FEOFFATUS. In old English law. A feoffee; one to whom a fee is given, or a feoffment made. Bract. fols. 17*b,* 44*b.*

FEOFFEE. He to whom a fee is conveyed. Litt. § 1; 2 Bl. Comm. 20.

FEOFFEE TO USES. A person to whom land was conveyed for the use of a third party. The latter was called "*cestui que use.*"

FEOFFMENT. The gift of any corporeal hereditament to another, (2 Bl. Comm. 310,) operating by transmutation of possession, and requiring, as essential to its completion, that the seisin be passed, (Watk. Conv. 183,) which might be accomplished either by investiture or by livery of seisin. 1 Washb. Real Prop. 33.

Also the deed or conveyance by which such corporeal hereditament is passed.

A feoffment originally meant the grant of a *feud* or *fee;* that is, a barony or knight's fee, for which certain services were due from the feoffee to the feoffor. This was the proper sense of the word; but by custom it came afterwards to signify also a grant (with livery of seisin) of a free inheritance to a man and his heirs, referring rather to the perpetuity of the estate than to the feudal tenure. 1 Reeve, Eng. Law, 90, 91. It was for ages the only method (in ordinary use) for conveying the freehold of land in possession, but has now fallen in great measure into disuse, even in England, having been almost entirely supplanted by some of that class of conveyances founded on the statute law of the realm. 1 Steph. Comm. 467, 468.

FEOFFMENT TO USES. A feoffment of lands to one person to the use of another.

FEOFFOR. The person making a feoffment, or enfeoffing another in fee. 2 Bl. Comm. 310; Litt. §§ 1, 57.

FEOH. This Saxon word meant originally cattle, and thence property or money, and, by a second transition, wages, reward, or fee. It was probably the original form from which the words "feod," "feudum," "fief," "feu," and "fee" (all meaning a feudal grant of land) have been derived.

FEONATIO. In forest law. The fawning season of deer.

FEORME. A certain portion of the produce of the land due by the grantee to the lord according to the terms of the charter. Spel. Feuds, c. 7.

FERÆ BESTIÆ. Wild beasts.

FERÆ NATURÆ. Lat. Of a wild nature or disposition. Animals which are by nature wild are so designated, by way of distinction from such as are naturally tame, the latter being called "*domitæ naturæ.*"

FERCOSTA. Ital. A kind of small vessel or boat. Mentioned in old Scotch law, and called "*fercost.*" Skene.

FERDELLA TERRÆ. A fardel-land; ten acres; or perhaps a yard-land. Cowell.

FERDFARE. Sax. A summons to serve in the army. An acquittance from going into the army. Fleta, lib. 1, c. 47, § 23.

FERDINGUS. A term denoting, apparently, a freeman of the lowest class, being named after the *cotseti.*

FERDWITE. In Saxon law. An acquittance of manslaughter committed in the army; also a fine imposed on persons for not going forth on a military expedition. Cowell.

FERIA. In old English law. A week-day; a holiday; a day on which process could not be served; a fair; a ferry. Cowell; Du Cange; Spelman.

FERIÆ. In Roman law. Holidays; generally speaking, days or seasons during which free-born Romans suspended their political transactions and their lawsuits, and during which slaves enjoyed a cessation from labor. All *feriæ* were thus *dies nefasti.* All *feriæ* were divided into two classes,—"*feriæ publicæ*" and "*feriæ privatæ.*" The latter were only observed by single families or individuals, in commemoration of some particular event which had been of importance to them or their ancestors. Smith, Dict. Antiq.

FERIAL DAYS. Holidays; also weekdays, as distinguished from Sunday. Cowell.

FERITA. In old European law. A wound; a stroke. Spelman.

FERLING. In old records. The fourth part of a penny; also the quarter of a ward in a borough.

FERLINGATA. A fourth part of a yard-land.

FERLINGUS. A furlong. Co. Litt. 5b.

FERM, or **FEARM.** A house or land, or both, let by lease. Cowell.

FERME. A farm; a rent; a lease; a house or land, or both, taken by indenture or lease. Plowd. 195; Vicat. See FARM.

FERMER, FERMOR. A lessee; a farmer. One who holds a term, whether of lands or an incorporeal right, such as customs or revenue.

FERMIER. In French law. One who farms any public revenue.

FERMISONA. In old English law. The winter season for killing deer.

FERMORY. In old records. A place in monasteries, where they received the poor, (*hospicio excipiebant,*) and gave them provisions, (*ferm. firma.*) Spelman. Hence the modern *infirmary,* used in the sense of a hospital.

FERNIGO. In old English law. A waste ground, or place where fern grows. Cowell.

FERRATOR. A farrier, (*q. v.*)

FERRI. In the civil law. To be borne; that is on or about the person. This was distinguished from *portari,* (to be carried,) which signified to be carried on an animal. Dig. 50, 16, 235.

FERRIAGE. The toll or fare paid for the transportation of persons and property across a ferry.

Literally speaking, it is the price or fare fixed by law for the transportation of the traveling public, with such goods and chattels as they may have with them, across a river, bay, or lake. 35 Cal. 606.

FERRIFODINA. In old pleading. An iron mine. Townsh. Pl. 273.

FERRUM. Iron. In old English law. A horse-shoe. *Ferrura,* shoeing of horses.

FERRY. A liberty to have a boat upon a river for the transportation of men, horses, and carriages with their contents, for a reasonable toll. The term is also used to designate the place where such liberty is exercised. See 42 Me. 9; 4 Mart. (N. S.) 426.

"Ferry" properly means a place of transit across a river or arm of the sea; but in law it is treated as a franchise, and defined as the exclusive right to carry passengers across a river, or arm of the sea, from one vill to another, or to connect a continuous line of road leading from one township or vill to another. It is not a servitude or easement. It is wholly unconnected with the ownership or occupation of land, so much so that the owner of the ferry need not have any property in the soil adjacent on either side. (12 C. B., N. S., 32.) Brown.

FERRYMAN. One employed in taking persons across a river or other stream, in boats or other contrivances, at a ferry. 3 Ala. 160; 8 Dana, 158.

FESTA IN CAPPIS. In old English law. Grand holidays, on which choirs wore caps. Jacob.

Festinatio justitiæ est noverca infortunii. Hob. 97. Hasty justice is the stepmother of misfortune.

FESTING-MAN. In old English law. A frank-pledge, or one who was surety for the good behavior of another. Monasteries enjoyed the privilege of being "free from festing-men," which means that they were "not bound for any man's forthcoming who should transgress the law." Cowell. See FRANK-PLEDGE.

FESTING-PENNY. Earnest given to servants when hired or retained. The same as *aries-penny.* Cowell.

FESTINUM REMEDIUM. Lat. A speedy remedy. The writ of assise was thus characterized (in comparison with the less expeditious remedies previously available) by the statute of Westminster 2, (13 Edw. I. c. 24.)

FESTUM. A feast or festival. *Festum stultorum,* the feast of fools.

FETTERS. Chains or shackles for the feet; irons used to secure the legs of convicts, unruly prisoners, etc. Similar chains securing the wrists are called "handcuffs."

FEU. In Scotch law. A holding or tenure where the vassal, in place of military service, makes his return in grain or money. Distinguished from "wardholding," which is the military tenure of the country. Bell.

FEU ANNUALS. In Scotch law. The *reddendo,* or annual return from the vassal to a superior in a feu holding.

FEU ET LIEU. Fr. In old French and Canadian law. Hearth and home. A term importing actual settlement upon land by a tenant.

FEU HOLDING. In Scotch law. A holding by tenure of rendering grain or money in place of military service. Bell.

FEUAR. In Scotch law. The tenant of a feu; a feu-vassal. Bell.

FEUD. In feudal law. An estate in land held of a superior on condition of rendering him services. 2 Bl. Comm. 105.

An inheritable right to the use and occupation of lands, held on condition of rendering services to the lord or proprietor, who himself retains the property in the lands. See Spel. Feuds, c. 1.

In this sense the word is the same as "feod," "feodum," "feudum," "fief," or "fee."

In Saxon and old German law. An enmity, or species of private war, existing between the family of a murdered man and the family of his slayer; a combination of the former to take vengeance upon the latter. See DEADLY FEUD; FAIDA.

FEUDA. Feuds or fees.

FEUDAL. Pertaining to feuds or fees; relating to or growing out of the feudal system or feudal law; having the quality of a feud, as distinguished from "allodial."

FEUDAL ACTIONS. An ancient name for *real* actions, or such as concern real property only. 3 Bl. Comm. 117.

FEUDAL LAW. The body of jurisprudence relating to feuds; the real-property law of the feudal system; the law anciently regulating the property relations of lord and vassal, and the creation, incidents, and transmission of feudal estates.

The body of laws and usages constituting the "feudal law" was originally customary and unwritten, but a compilation was made in the twelfth century, called "Feodarum Consuetudines," which has formed the basis of later digests. The feudal law prevailed over Europe from the twelfth to the fourteenth century, and was introduced into England at the Norman Conquest, where it formed the entire basis of the law of real property until comparatively modern times. Survivals of the feudal law, to the present day, so affect and color that branch of jurisprudence as to require a certain knowledge of the feudal law in order to the perfect comprehension of modern tenures and rules of real-property law.

FEUDAL POSSESSION. The equivalent of "seisin" under the feudal system.

FEUDAL SYSTEM. The system of feuds. A political and social system which prevailed throughout Europe during the eleventh, twelfth, and thirteenth centuries, and is supposed to have grown out of the peculiar usages and policy of the Teutonic nations who overran the continent after the fall of the Western Roman Empire, as developed by the exigencies of their military domination, and possibly furthered by notions taken from the Roman jurisprudence. It was introduced into England, in its completeness, by William I., A. D. 1085, though it may have existed in a rudimentary form among the Saxons before the Conquest. It formed the entire basis of the real-property law of England in medieval times; and survivals of the system, in modern days, so modify and color that branch of jurisprudence, both in England and America, that many of its principles require for their complete understanding a knowledge of the feudal system. The feudal system originated in the relations of a military chieftain and his followers, or king and nobles, or lord and vassals, and especially their relations as determined by the bond established by a grant of *land* from the former to the latter. From this it grew into a complete and intricate complex of rules for the tenure and transmission of real estate, and of correlated duties and services; while, by tying men to the land and to those holding above and below them, it created a close-knit hierarchy of persons, and developed an aggregate of social and political institutions.

For an account of the feudal system in its juristic relations, see 2 Bl. Comm. 44; 1 Steph. Comm. 160; 3 Kent, Comm. 487; Spel. Feuds; Litt. Ten.; Sull. Lect.; Spence, Eq. Jur.; 1 Washb. Real Prop. 15; Dalr. Feu. Prop. For its political and social relations, see Hall. Middle Ages; Maine, Anc. Law; Rob. Car. V.; Montesq. Esprit des Lois, bk. 30; Guizot, Hist. Civilization.

FEUDAL TENURES. The tenures of real estate under the feudal system, such as knight-service, socage, villenage, etc.

FEUDALISM. The feudal system; the aggregate of feudal principles and usages.

FEUDALIZE. To reduce to a feudal tenure; to conform to feudalism. Webster.

FEUDARY. A tenant who holds by feudal tenure. Held by feudal service. Relating to feuds or feudal tenures.

FEUDATORY. See FEODATORY.

FEUDBOTE. A recompense for engaging in a feud, and the damages consequent, it having been the custom in ancient times for all the kindred to engage in their kinsman's quarrel. Jacob.

FEUDE, or DEADLY FEUDE. A German word, signifying implacable hatred, not to be satisfied but with the death of the enemy. Such was that among the people in Scotland and in the northern parts of England, which was a combination of all the kindred to revenge the death of any of the blood upon the slayer and all his race. Termes de la Ley.

FEUDIST. A writer on feuds, as Cujacius, Spelman, etc.

FEUDO. In Spanish law. Feud or fee. White, New Recop. b. 2, tit. 2, c. 2.

FEUDUM. A feud, fief, or fee. A right of using and enjoying forever the lands of another, which the lord grants on condition that the tenant shall render fealty, military duty, and other services. Spelman. See FEODUM; FEUD.

FEUDUM ANTIQUUM. An ancient feud or fief; a fief descended to the vassal from his ancestors. 2 Bl. Comm. 212, 221. A fief which ancestors had possessed for more than four generations. Spelman.

FEUDUM APERTUM. An open feud or fief; a fief resulting back to the lord, where the blood of the person last seised was utterly extinct and gone. 2 Bl. Comm. 245.

FEUDUM FRANCUM. A free feud. One which was noble and free from talliage and other subsidies to which the *plebeia feuda* (vulgar feuds) were subject. Spelman.

FEUDUM HAUBERTICUM. A fee held on the military service of appearing fully armed at the *ban* and *arriere ban*. Spelman.

FEUDUM IMPROPRIUM. An improper or derivative feud or fief. 2 Bl. Comm. 58.

FEUDUM INDIVIDUUM. An indivisible or impartible feud or fief; descendible to the eldest son alone. 2 Bl. Comm. 215.

FEUDUM LIGIUM. A liege feud or fief; a fief held immediately of the sovereign; one for which the vassal owed fealty to his lord against all persons. 1 Bl. Comm. 367; Spelman.

FEUDUM MATERNUM. A maternal fief; a fief descended to the feudatory from his mother. 2 Bl. Comm. 212.

FEUDUM NOBILE. A fee for which the tenant did guard and owed fealty and homage. Spelman.

FEUDUM NOVUM. A new feud or fief; a fief which began in the person of the feudatory, and did not come to him by succession. Spelman; 2 Bl. Comm. 212.

FEUDUM NOVUM UT ANTIQUUM. A new fee held with the qualities and incidents of an ancient one. 2 Bl. Comm. 212.

FEUDUM PATERNUM. A fee which the paternal ancestors had held for four generations. Calvin. One descendible to heirs on the paternal side only. 2 Bl. Comm. 223. One which might be held by males only. Du Cange.

FEUDUM PROPRIUM. A proper, genuine, and original feud or fief; being of a purely military character, and held by military service. 2 Bl. Comm. 57, 58.

FEUDUM TALLIATUM. A restricted fee. One limited to descend to certain classes of heirs. 2 Bl. Comm. 112, note; 1 Washb. Real Prop. 66.

FEW. An indefinite expression for a small or limited number. In cases where exact description is required, the use of this word will not answer. 53 Vt. 600; 2 Car. & P. 300.

FI. FA An abbreviation for *fieri facias*, (which see.)

FIANCER. L. Fr. To pledge one's faith. Kelham.

FIANZA. In Spanish law. A surety or guarantor; the contract or engagement of a surety.

FIAR. In Scotch law. He that has the fee or *feu*. The proprietor is termed "fiar," in contradistinction to the life-renter. 1 Kames, Eq. Pref. One whose property is charged with a life-rent.

FIARS PRICES. The value of grain in the different counties of Scotland, fixed yearly by the respective sheriffs, in the month of February, with the assistance of juries. These regulate the prices of grain stipulated to be sold at the fiar prices, or when no price has been stipulated. Ersk. 1, 4, 6.

FIAT. In English practice. A short order or warrant of a judge or magistrate directing some act to be done; an authority issuing from some competent source for the doing of some legal act.

One of the proceedings in the English bankrupt practice, being a power, signed by the lord chancellor, addressed to the court of bankruptcy, authorizing the petitioning creditor to prosecute his complaint before it. 2 Steph. Comm. 199. By the statute 12 & 13 Vict. c. 116, fiats were abolished.

Fiat jus, ruat justitia. Let law prevail, though justice fail.

FIAT JUSTITIA. Let justice be done. On a petition to the king for his warrant to bring a writ of error in parliament, he writes on the top of the petition, "*Fiat justitia*," and then the writ of error is made out, etc. Jacob.

Fiat justitia, ruat cœlum. Let right be done, though the heavens should fall.

Fiat prout fieri consuevit, (nil temere novandum.) Let it be done as it hath used to be done, (nothing must be rashly innovated.) Jenk. Cent. 116, case 39; Branch, Princ.

FIAT UT PETITUR. Let it be done as it is asked. A form of granting a petition.

FICTIO. In Roman law. A fiction; an assumption or supposition of the law.

"*Fictio*" in the old Roman law was properly a term of pleading, and signified a false averment on the part of the plaintiff which the defendant was not allowed to traverse; as that the plaintiff was a Roman citizen, when in truth he was a foreigner. The object of the fiction was to give the court jurisdiction. Maine, Anc. Law, 25.

Fictio cedit veritati. Fictio juris non est ubi veritas. Fiction yields to truth. Where there is truth, fiction of law exists not.

Fictio est contra veritatem, sed pro veritate habetur. Fiction is against the truth, but it is to be esteemed truth.

Fictio juris non est ubi veritas. Where truth is, fiction of law does not exist.

Fictio legis inique operatur alicui damnum vel injuriam. A legal fiction does not properly work loss or injury. 3 Coke, 36; Broom, Max. 129.

Fictio legis neminem lædit. A fiction of law injures no one. 2 Rolle, 502; 3 Bl. Comm. 43; 17 Johns. 348.

FICTION. An assumption or supposition of law that something which is or may be false is true, or that a state of facts exists which has never really taken place.

A fiction is a rule of law which assumes as true, and will not allow to be disproved, something which is false, but not impossible. Best, Ev. 419.

These assumptions are of an innocent or even beneficial character, and are made for the advancement of the ends of justice. They secure this end chiefly by the extension of procedure from cases to which it is applicable to other cases to which it is not strictly applicable, the ground of inapplicability being some difference of an immaterial character. Brown.

Fictions are to be distinguished from presumptions of law. By the former, something known to be false or unreal is assumed as true; by the latter, an inference is set up, which may be and probably is true, but which, at any rate, the law will not permit to be controverted.

Mr. Best distinguishes legal fictions from presumptions *juris et de jure*, and divides them into three kinds,—affirmative or positive fictions, negative fictions, and fictions by relation. Best, Pres. p. 27, § 24.

FICTITIOUS ACTION. An action brought for the sole purpose of obtaining the opinion of the court on a point of law, not for the settlement of any actual controversy between the parties.

Courts of justice were constituted for the purpose of deciding really existing questions of right between parties; and they are not bound to answer impertinent questions which persons think proper to ask them in the form of an action on a wager. 12 East, 248.

FICTITIOUS PLAINTIFF. A person appearing in the writ or record as the plaintiff in a suit, but who in reality does not exist, or who is ignorant of the suit and of the use of his name in it. It is a contempt of court to sue in the name of a fictitious party. See 4 Bl. Comm. 134.

FIDEI-COMMISSARIUS. In the civil law this term corresponds nearly to our "*cestui que trust.*" It designates a person who has the real or beneficial interest in an estate or fund, the title or administration of which is temporarily confided to another. See Story, Eq. Jur. § 966.

FIDEI - COMMISSUM. In the civil law. A species of trust; being a gift of property (usually by will) to a person, accompanied by a request or direction of the donor that the recipient will transfer the property to another, the latter being a person not capable of taking directly under the will or gift.

FIDE-JUBERE. In the civil law. To order a thing upon one's faith; to pledge one's self; to become surety for another. *Fide-jubes? Fide-jubeo:* Do you pledge yourself? I do pledge myself. Inst. 3, 16, 1. One of the forms of stipulation.

FIDE-JUSSOR. In Roman law. A guarantor; one who becomes responsible for the payment of another's debt, by a stipulation which binds him to discharge it if the principal debtor fails to do so. Mackeld. Rom. Law, § 452; 3 Bl. Comm. 108.

The sureties taken on the arrest of a defendant, in the court of admiralty, were formerly denominated "fide-jussors." 3 Bl. Comm. 108.

FIDELIS. Faithful; trustworthy.

FIDELITAS. Fealty; fidelity.

Fidelitas. De nullo tenemento, quod tenetur ad terminum, fit homagii: fit tamen inde fidelitatis sacramentum. Co. Litt. 676. Fealty. For no tenement which is held for a term is there the oath of homage, but there is the oath of fealty.

FIDEM MENTIRI. When a tenant does not keep that fealty which he has sworn to the lord. Leg. Hen. I. c. 53.

FIDE-PROMISSOR. See FIDE-JUSSOR.

FIDES. Faith; honesty; confidence; trust; veracity; honor. Occurring in the phrase "*bona fides;*" so, also, "*mala fides.*"

Fides est obligatio conscientiæ alicujus ad intentionem alterius. Bacon. A trust is an obligation of conscience of one to the will of another.

Fides servanda est. Faith must be observed. An agent must not violate the confidence reposed in him. Story, Ag. § 192.

Fides servanda est; simplicitas juris gentium prævaleat. Faith must be kept; the simplicity of the law of nations must prevail. A rule applied to bills of exchange as a sort of sacred instruments. 3 Burrows, 1672; Story, Bills, § 15.

FIDUCIA. In the civil law. A contract by which we sell a thing to some one—that is, transmit to him the property of the thing, with the solemn forms of emancipation—on condition that he will sell it back to us. This species of contract took place in the emancipation of children, in testaments, and in pledges. Poth. Pand. h. t.

FIDUCIARIUS TUTOR. In Roman law. The elder brother of an emancipated *pupillus*, whose father had died leaving him still under fourteen years of age.

FIDUCIARY. The term is derived from the Roman law, and means (as a noun) a person holding the character of a trustee, or a character analogous to that of a trustee, in respect to the trust and confidence involved in it and the scrupulous good faith and candor which it requires. Thus, a person is a fiduciary who is invested with rights and powers to be exercised for the benefit of another person.

As an adjective it means of the nature of a trust; having the characteristics of a trust; analogous to a trust; relating to or founded upon a trust or confidence.

FIDUCIARY CONTRACT. An agreement by which a person delivers a thing to another on the condition that he will restore it to him.

FIEF. A fee, feod, or feud.

FIEF D'HAUBERT. Fr. In Norman feudal law. A fief or fee held by the tenure of knight-service; **a** knight's fee. 2 Bl. Comm. 62.

FIEF-TENANT. In old English law. The holder of **a** fief or fee; **a** feeholder or freeholder.

FIEL. In Spanish law. A sequestrator; **a** person in whose hands a thing in dispute is judicially deposited; a receiver. Las Partidas, pt. 3, tit. 9, l. 1.

FIELD. This term might well be considered as definite and certain a description as "close," and might be used in law; but it is not a usual description in legal proceedings. 1 Chit. Gen. Pr. 160.

FIELD-ALE. An ancient custom in England, by which officers of the forest and bailiffs of hundreds had the right to compel the hundred to furnish them with ale. Tomlins.

FIELD REEVE. An officer elected, in England, by the owners of a regulated pasture to keep in order the fences, ditches, etc., on the land, to regulate the times during which animals are to be admitted to the pasture, and generally to maintain and manage the pasture subject to the instructions of the owners. (General Inclosure Act, 1845, § 118.) Sweet.

FIELDAD. In Spanish law. Sequestration. This is allowed in six cases by the Spanish law where the title to property is in dispute. Las Partidas, pt. 3, tit. 3, l. 1.

FIERDING COURTS. Ancient Gothic courts of an inferior jurisdiction, so called because *four* were instituted within every inferior district or hundred. 3 Bl. Comm. 34.

FIERI. Lat. To be made; to be done. See IN FIERI.

FIERI FACIAS. (That you cause to be made.) In practice. A writ of execution commanding the sheriff to levy and make the amount of a judgment from the goods and chattels of the judgment debtor.

FIERI FACIAS DE BONIS ECCLESIASTICIS. When a sheriff to a common *fi. fa.* returns *nulla bona*, and that the defendant is a beneficed clerk, not having any lay fee, a plaintiff may issue a *fi. fa. de bonis ecclesiasticis*, addressed to the bishop of the diocese or to the archbishop, (during the vacancy of the bishop's see,) commanding him to make of the ecclesiastical goods and chattels belonging to the defendant within his diocese the sum therein mentioned. 2 Chit. Archb. Pr. (12th Ed.) 1062.

FIERI FACIAS DE BONIS TESTATORIS. The writ issued on an ordinary judgment against an executor when sued for a debt due by his testator. If the sheriff returns to this writ *nulla bona*, and a *devastavit*, (*q. v.*,) the plaintiff may sue out a *fieri facias de bonis propriis*, under which the goods of the executor himself are seized. Sweet.

FIERI FECI. (I have caused to be made.) In practice. The name given to the return made by a sheriff or other officer to a writ of *fieri facias*, where he has collected the whole, or a part, of the sum directed to be levied. 2 Tidd, Pr. 1018. The return, as actually made, is expressed by the word "Satisfied" indorsed on the writ.

Fieri non debet, (debuit,) sed factum valet. It ought not to be done, but [if] done, it is valid. Shep. Touch, 6; 5 Coke, 39; T. Raym. 58; 1 Strange, 526. A maxim frequently applied in practice. 19 Johns. 84, 92.

FIFTEENTHS. In English law. This was originally a tax or tribute, levied at intervals by act of parliament, consisting of one-fifteenth of all the movable property of the subject or personalty in every city, township, and borough. Under Edward III., the taxable property was assessed, and the value of its fifteenth part (then about £29,000) was recorded in the exchequer, whence the tax, levied on that valuation, continued to be called a "fifteenth," although, as the wealth of the kingdom increased, the name ceased to be an accurate designation of the proportion of the tax to the value taxed. See 1 Bl. Comm. 309.

FIGHT. An encounter, with blows or other personal violence, between two persons. See 73 N. C. 155.

FIGHTWITE. Sax. A mulct or fine for making a quarrel to the disturbance of the peace. Called also by Cowell "*forisfactura pugnæ*." The amount was one hundred and twenty shillings. Cowell.

FIGURES. The numerical characters by which numbers are expressed or written.

FILACER. An officer of the superior courts at Westminster, whose duty it was to file the writs on which he made process. There were fourteen filacers, and it was their duty to make out all original process.

Cowell; Blount. The office was abolished in 1837.

FILARE. In old English practice. To file. Townsh. Pl. 67.

FILE, *v.* In practice. To put upon the *files*, or deposit in the custody or among the records of a court.

"Filing a bill" in equity is an equivalent expression to "commencing a suit."

"To file" a paper, on the part of a party, is to place it in the official custody of the clerk. "To file," on the part of the clerk, is to indorse upon the paper the date of its reception, and retain it in his office, subject to inspection by whomsoever it may concern. 14 Tex. 339.

The expressions "filing" and "entering of record" are not synonymous. They are nowhere so used, but always convey distinct ideas. "Filing" originally signified placing papers in order on a thread or wire for safe-keeping. In this country and at this day it means, agreeably to our practice, depositing them in due order in the proper office. Entering of record uniformly implies writing. 2 Blackf. 247.

FILE, *n.* A thread, string, or wire upon which writs and other exhibits in courts and offices are fastened or filed for the more safe-keeping and ready turning to the same. Spelman; Cowell; Tomlins. Papers put together and tied in bundles. A paper is said also to be filed when it is delivered to the proper officer, and by him received to be kept on file. 13 Vin. Abr. 211; 1 Litt. 113; 1 Hawk. P. C. 7, 207. But, in general, "file," or "the files," is used loosely to denote the official custody of the court or the place in the offices of a court where the records and papers are kept.

FILEINJAID. Brit. A name given to villeins in the laws of Hoel Dda. Barring. Obs. St. 302.

FILIATE. To fix a bastard child on some one, as its father. To declare whose child it is. 2 W Bl. 1017.

Filiatio non potest probari. Co. Litt. 126. Filiation cannot be proved.

FILIATION. The relation of a child to its parent; correlative to "paternity."

The judicial assignment of an illegitimate child to a designated man as its father.

In the civil law. The descent of son or daughter, with regard to his or her father, mother, and their ancestors.

FILICETUM. In old English law. A ferny or bracky ground; a place where fern grows. Co. Litt. 4*b;* Shep. Touch. 95.

FILIOLUS. In old records. **A godson;** Spelman.

FILIUS. Lat. A son; a child.

A distinction was sometimes made, in the civil law, between "*filii*" and "*liberi;*" the latter word including grandchildren, (*nepotes,*) the former not. Inst. 1, 14, 5. But, according to Paulus and Julianus, they were of equally extensive import. Dig. 50, 16, 84; Id. 50, 16, 201.

Filius est nomen naturæ, sed hæres nomen juris. 1 Sid. 193. Son is a name of nature, but heir is a name of law.

FILIUS FAMILIAS. In the civil law. The son of a family; an unemancipated son. Inst. 2, 12, pr.; Id. 4, 5, 2; Story, Confl. Laws, § 61.

Filius in utero matris est pars viscerum matris. 7 Coke, 8. A son in the mother's womb is part of the mother's vitals.

FILIUS MULIERATUS. In old English law. The eldest legitimate son of a woman, who previously had an illegitimate son by his father. Glanv. lib. 7, c. 1. Otherwise called "*mulier.*" 2 Bl. Comm. 248.

FILIUS NULLIUS. The son of nobody; *i. e.,* a bastard.

FILIUS POPULI. A son of the people; a natural child.

FILL. To make full; to complete; to satisfy or fulfill; to possess and perform the duties of.

The election of a person to an office constitutes the essence of his appointment; but the office cannot be considered as actually *filled* until his acceptance, either express or implied. 2 N. H. 202.

Where one subscribes for shares in a corporation, agreeing to "take and *fill*" a certain number of shares, *assumpsit* will lie against him to recover an assessment on his shares; the word "fill," in this connection, amounting to a promise to pay assessments. 10 Me. 478.

To *fill* a prescription is to furnish, prepare, and combine the requisite materials in due proportion as prescribed. 61 Ga. 505.

FILLY. A young mare; a female colt. An indictment charging the theft of a "filly" is not sustained by proof of the larceny of a "mare." 1 Tex. App. 448.

FILUM. In old practice. A file; *i. e.,* a thread or wire on which papers were strung, that being the ancient method of filing.

An imaginary thread or line passing through the middle of a stream or road, as in the phrases "*filum aquæ,*" "*filum viæ;*" or along the edge or border, as in "*filum forestæ.*"

FILUM AQUÆ. A thread of water; a line of water; the middle line of a stream of water, supposed to divide it into two equal parts, and constituting in many cases the boundary between the riparian proprietors on each side.

FILUM FORESTÆ. Lat. The border of the forest. 2 Bl. Comm. 419; 4 Inst. 303.

FILUM VIÆ. The thread or middle line of a road. An imaginary line drawn through the middle of a road, and constituting the boundary between the owners of the land on each side. 2 Smith, Lead. Cas. (Am. Ed.) 98, note.

FIN. An end, or limit; a limitation, or period of limitation.

FIN DE NON RECEVOIR. In French law. An exception or plea founded on law, which, without entering into the merits of the action, shows that the plaintiff has no right to bring it, either because the time during which it ought to have been brought has elapsed, which is called "prescription," or that there has been a compromise, accord and satisfaction, or any other cause which has destroyed the right of action which once subsisted. Poth. Proc. Civile, pt. 1, c. 2, § 2, art. 2.

FINAL. Definitive; terminating; completed; last. In its use in jurisprudence, this word is generally contrasted with "interlocutory."

FINAL COSTS. Such costs as are to be paid at the end of the suit; costs, the liability for which depends upon the final result of the litigation.

FINAL DECISION. One from which no appeal or writ of error can be taken. 47 Ill. 167; 6 El. & Bl. 408.

FINAL DECREE. A decree in equity which fully and finally disposes of the whole litigation, determining all questions raised by the case, and leaving nothing that requires further judicial action.

FINAL DISPOSITION. When it is said to be essential to the validity of an award that it should make a "final disposition" of the matters embraced in the submission, this term means such a disposition that nothing further remains to fix the rights and obligations of the parties, and no further controversy or litigation is required or can arise on the matter. It is such an award that the party against whom it is made can perform or pay it without any further ascertainment of rights or duties. 50 Me. 401.

FINAL HEARING. This term designates the trial of an equity case upon the merits, as distinguished from the hearing of any preliminary questions arising in the cause, which are termed "interlocutory." 24 Wis. 165.

FINAL JUDGMENT. In practice. A judgment which puts an *end* to an action at law by declaring that the plaintiff either has or has not entitled himself to recover the remedy he sues for. 3 Bl. Comm. 398. So distinguished from *interlocutory* judgments, which merely establish the right of the plaintiff to recover, in general terms. Id. 397. A judgment which determines a particular cause.

A judgment which cannot be appealed from, which is perfectly conclusive upon the matter adjudicated. 24 Pick. 300. A judgment which terminates all litigation on the same right. The term "final judgment," in the judiciary act of 1789, § 25, includes both species of judgments as just defined. 2 Pet. 494; 1 Kent, Comm. 316; 6 How. 201, 209.

A judgment is final and conclusive between the parties, when rendered on a verdict on the merits, not only as to the facts actually litigated and decided, but also as to all facts necessarily involved in the issue. 26 Ala. 504.

FINAL PASSAGE. In parliamentary law. The final passage of a bill is the vote on its passage in either house of the legislature, after it has received the prescribed number of readings on as many different days in that house. 54 Ala. 613.

FINAL PROCESS. The last process in a suit; that is, writs of execution. Thus distinguished from *mesne* process, which includes all writs issued during the progress of a cause and before final judgment.

FINAL RECOVERY. The final judgment in an action. Also the final verdict in an action, as distinguished from the judgment entered upon it. 6 Allen, 243.

FINAL SENTENCE. One which puts an end to a case. Distinguished from interlocutory.

FINAL SETTLEMENT. This term, as applied to the administration of an estate, is usually understood to have reference to the order of court approving the account which closes the business of the estate, and which finally discharges the executor or administrator from the duties of his trust. 13 N. E. Rep. 131. See, also, 65 Ala. 442.

FINALIS CONCORDIA. A final or conclusive agreement. In the process of "levying a fine," this was a final agreement entered by the litigating parties upon the record, by permission of court, settling the title to the land, and which was binding upon them like any judgment of the court. 1 Washb. Real Prop. *70.

FINANCES. The public wealth of a state or government, considered either statically (as the property or money which a state now owns) or dynamically, (as its income, revenue, or public resources.) Also the revenue or wealth of an individual.

FINANCIER. A person employed in the economical management and application of public money; one skilled in the management of financial affairs.

FIND. To discover; to determine; to ascertain and declare. To announce a conclusion, as the result of judicial investigation, upon a disputed fact or state of facts; as a jury are said to "find a will." To determine a controversy in favor of one of the parties; as a jury "find for the plaintiff."

FINDER. One who discovers and takes possession of another's personal property, which was then lost.

A searcher employed to discover goods imported or exported without paying custom. Jacob.

FINDING. A decision upon a question of fact reached as the result of a judicial examination or investigation by a court, jury, referee, coroner, etc.

FINE, v. To impose a pecuniary punishment or mulct. To sentence a person convicted of an offense to pay a penalty in money.

FINE, n. In conveyancing. An amicable composition or agreement of a suit, either actual or fictitious, by leave of the court, by which the lands in question become, or are acknowledged to be, the right of one of the parties. 2 Bl. Comm. 349. Fines were abolished in England by St. 3 & 4 Wm. IV. c. 74, substituting a disentailing deed, (*q. v.*)

The party who parted with the land, by acknowledging the right of the other, was said to *levy* the fine, and was called the "cognizor" or "conusor," while the party who recovered or received the estate was termed the "cognizee" or "conusee," and the fine was said to be levied to him.

In the law of tenure. A fine is a money payment made by a feudal tenant to his lord. The most usual fine is that payable on the admittance of a new tenant, but there are also due in some manors fines upon alienation, on a license to demise the lands, or on the death of the lord, or other events. Elton, Copyh. 159.

In criminal law. Pecuniary punishment imposed by a lawful tribunal upon a person convicted of crime or misdemeanor.

It means, among other things, "a sum of money paid at the *end*, to make an *end* of a transaction, suit, or prosecution; mulct; penalty." In ordinary legal language, however, it means a sum of money imposed by a court according to law, as a punishment for the breach of some penal statute. 22 Kan. 15.

It is not confined to a pecuniary punishment of an offense, inflicted by a court in the exercise of criminal jurisdiction. It has other meanings, and may include a forfeiture, or a penalty recoverable by civil action. 11 Gray, 373.

FINE AND RECOVERY ACT. The English statutes 3 & 4 Wm. IV. c. 74, for abolishing fines and recoveries. 1 Steph. Comm. 514, et seq.

FINE ANULLANDO LEVATO DE TENEMENTO QUOD FUIT DE ANTIQUO DOMINICO. An abolished writ for disannulling a fine levied of lands in ancient demesne to the prejudice of the lord. Reg. Orig. 15.

FINE CAPIENDO PRO TERRIS. An obsolete writ which lay for a person who, upon conviction by jury, had his lands and goods taken, and his body imprisoned, to be remitted his imprisonment, and have his lands and goods redelivered to him, on obtaining favor of a sum of money, etc. Reg. Orig. 142.

FINE FOR ALIENATION. A fine anciently payable upon the alienation of a feudal estate and substitution of a new tenant. It was payable to the lord by all tenants holding by knight's service or tenants *in capite* by socage tenure. Abolished by 12 Car. II. c. 24. See 2 Bl. Comm. 71, 89.

FINE FOR ENDOWMENT. A fine anciently payable to the lord by the widow of a tenant, without which she could not be endowed of her husband's lands. Abolished under Henry I., and by *Magna Charta*. 2 Bl. Comm. 135; Mozley & Whitley.

FINE NON CAPIENDO PRO PULCHRE PLACITANDO. An obsolete writ to inhibit officers of courts to take fines for fair pleading.

FINE PRO REDISSEISINÂ CAPIENDO. An old writ that lay for the release of one imprisoned for a redisseisin, on payment of a reasonable fine. Reg. Orig. 222.

FINE SUR COGNIZANCE DE DROIT COME CEO QUE IL AD DE SON DONE. A fine upon acknowledgment of the right of the cognizee as that which he hath of the gift of the cognizor. By this the deforciant acknowledged in court a former foeffment or gift in possession to have been made by him to the plaintiff. 2 Bl. Comm. 352.

FINE SUR COGNIZANCE DE DROIT TANTUM. A fine upon acknowledgment of the right merely, and not with the circumstance of a *preceding gift* from the cognizor. This was commonly used to pass a *reversionary* interest which was in the cognizor, of which there could be no foeffment supposed. 2 Bl. Comm. 353; 1 Steph. Comm. 519.

FINE SUR CONCESSIT. A fine upon *concessit*, (he hath granted.) A species of fine, where the cognizor, in order to make an end of disputes, though he acknowledged no precedent right, yet *granted* to the cognizee an estate *de novo*, usually for life or years, by way of supposed composition. 2 Bl. Comm. 353; 1 Steph. Comm. 519.

FINE SUR DONE GRANT ET RENDER. A double fine, comprehending the fine *sur cognizance de droit come ceo* and the fine *sur concessit*. It might be used to convey particular limitations of estates, whereas the fine *sur cognizance de droit come ceo*, etc., conveyed nothing but an absolute estate, either of inheritance, or at least freehold. In this last species of fines, the cognizee, after the right was acknowledged to be in him, granted back again or rendered to the cognizor, or perhaps to a stranger, some other estate in the premises. 2 Bl. Comm. 353.

FINE-FORCE. An absolute necessity or inevitable constraint. Plowd. 94; 6 Coke, 11; Cowell.

FINEM FACERE. To make or pay a fine. Bract. 106.

FINES LE ROY. In old English law. The king's fines. Fines formerly payable to the king for any contempt or offense, as where one committed any trespass, or false-ly denied his own deed, or did anything in contempt of law. Termes de la Ley.

FINIRE. In old English law. To fine, or pay a fine. Cowell. To end or finish a matter.

FINIS. An end; a fine; a boundary or terminus; a limit.

Finis est amicabilis compositio et finalis concordia ex consensu et concordia domini regis vel justiciarum. Glan. lib. 8, c. 1. A fine is an amicable settlement and decisive agreement by consent and agreement of our lord, the king, or his justices.

Finis finem litibus imponit. A fine puts an end to litigation. 3 Inst. 78.

Finis rei attendendus est. 3 Inst. 51. The end of a thing is to be attended to.

Finis unius diei est principium alterius. 2 Bulst. 305. The end of one day is the beginning of another.

FINITIO. An ending; death, as the end of life. Blount; Cowell.

FINIUM REGUNDORUM ACTIO. In the civil law. Action for regulating boundaries. The name of an action which lay between those who had lands bordering on each other, to settle disputed boundaries. Mackeld. Rom. Law, § 499.

FINORS. Those that purify gold and silver, and part them by fire and water from coarser metals; and therefore, in the statute of 4 Hen. VII. c. 2, they are also called "parters." Termes de la Ley.

FIRDFARE. Sax. In old English law. A summoning forth to a military expedition, (*indictio ad profectionem militarem*.) Spelman.

FIRDIRINGA. Sax. A preparation to go into the army. Leg. Hen. I.

FIRDSOCNE. Sax. In old English law. Exemption from military service. Spelman.

FIRDWITE. In old English law. A fine for refusing military service, (*mulcta detrectantis militiam*.) Spelman. A fine imposed for murder committed in the army; an acquittance of such fine. Fleta, lib. 1, c. 47.

FIRE. The effect of combustion. The juridical meaning of the word does not differ from the vernacular. 1 Pars. Mar. Law, 231, et seq.

FIRE AND SWORD, LETTERS OF. In old Scotch law. Letters issued from the privy council in Scotland, addressed to the sheriff of the county, authorizing him to call for the assistance of the county to dispossess a tenant retaining possession, contrary to the order of a judge or the sentence of a court. Wharton.

FIRE-ARMS. This word comprises all sorts of guns, fowling-pieces, blunderbusses, pistols, etc.

FIREBARE. A beacon or high tower by the seaside, wherein are continual lights, either to direct sailors in the night, or to give warning of the approach of an enemy. Cowell.

FIRE-BOTE. An allowance of wood or *estovers* to maintain competent firing for the tenant. A sufficient allowance of wood to burn in a house. 1 Washb. Real Prop. 99.

FIRE INSURANCE. A contract of insurance by which the underwriter, in consideration of the premium, undertakes to indemnify the insured against all losses in his houses, buildings, furniture, ships in port, or merchandise, by means of accidental fire happening within a prescribed period. 3 Kent, Comm. 370.

FIRE ORDEAL. In Saxon and old English law. The ordeal by fire or red-hot iron, which was performed either by taking up in the hand a piece of red-hot iron, of one, two, or three pounds weight, or by walking barefoot and blindfolded over nine red-hot plowshares, laid lengthwise at unequal distances. 4 Bl. Comm. 343; Cowell.

FIRE POLICY. A contract of insurance, by which, in consideration of a single or periodical payment of premium, (as the case may be,) the company engages to pay to the assured such loss as may occur by fire to his property therein described, within the period or periods therein specified, to an amount not exceeding a particular sum fixed for that purpose by the policy. 2 Steph. Comm. 180.

FIRE-PROOF. To say of any article that it is "fire-proof" conveys no other idea than that the material out of which it is formed is incombustible. To say of a building that it is fire-proof excludes the idea that it is of wood, and necessarily implies that it is of some substance fitted for the erection of fire-proof buildings. To say of a certain portion of a building that it is fire-proof suggests a comparison between that portion and

other parts of the building not so characterized, and warrants the conclusion that it is of a different material. 102 N. Y. 459, 7 N. E. Rep. 321.

FIRKIN. A measure containing nine gallons; also a weight of fifty-six pounds avoirdupois, used in weighing butter and cheese.

FIRLOT. A Scotch measure of capacity, containing two gallons and a pint. Spelman.

FIRM. A partnership; the group of persons constituting a partnership.

The name or title under which the members of a partnership transact business.

FIRMA. In old English law. The contract of lease or letting; also the rent (or farm) reserved upon a lease of lands, which was frequently payable in provisions, but sometimes in money, in which latter case it was called "*alba firma*," white rent. A messuage, with the house and garden belonging thereto. Also provision for the table: a banquet; a tribute towards the entertainment of the king for one night.

FIRMA FEODI. In old English law. A farm or lease of a fee; a fee-farm.

FIRMAN. An Asiatic word denoting a decree or grant of privileges, or passport to a traveler.

FIRMARATIO. The right of a tenant to his lands and tenements. Cowell.

FIRMARIUM. In old records. A place in monasteries, and elsewhere, where the poor were received and supplied with food. Spelman. Hence the word "infirmary."

FIRMARIUS. L. Lat. A fermor. A lessee of a term. *Firmarii* comprehend all such as hold by lease for life or lives or for year, by deed or without deed. 2 Inst. 144, 145; 1 Washb. Real Prop. 107.

FIRMATIO. The doe season. Also a supplying with food. Cowell.

FIRME. In old records. A farm.

Firmior et potentior est operatio legis quam dispositio hominis. The operation of the law is firmer and more powerful [or efficacious] than the disposition of man. Co. Litt. 102a.

FIRMITAS. In old English law. An assurance of some privilege, by deed or charter.

FIRMURA. In old English law. Liberty to scour and repair a mill-dam, and carry away the soil, etc. Blount.

FIRST - CLASS MISDEMEANANT. In English law. Under the prisons act (28 & 29 Vict. c. 126, § 67) prisoners in the county, city, and borough prisons convicted of misdemeanor, and not sentenced to hard labor, are divided into two classes, one of which is called the "first division;" and it is in the discretion of the court to order that such a prisoner be treated as a *misdemeanant of the first division*, usually called "first-class misdemeanant," and as such not to be deemed a criminal prisoner, *i. e.*, a prisoner convicted of a crime. Bouvier.

FIRST FRUITS. In English ecclesiastical law. The first year's whole profits of every benefice or spiritual living, anciently paid by the incumbent to the pope, but afterwards transferred to the fund called "Queen Anne's Bounty," for increasing the revenue from poor livings.

In feudal law. One year's profits of land which belonged to the king on the death of a tenant *in capite;* otherwise called "*primer seisin.*" One of the incidents to the old feudal tenures. 2 Bl. Comm. 66, 67.

FIRST IMPRESSION. A case is said to be "of the first impression" when it presents an entirely novel question of law for the decision of the court, and cannot be governed by any existing precedent.

FIRST PURCHASER. In the law of descent, this term signifies the ancestor who first acquired (in any other manner than by inheritance) the estate which still remains in his family or descendants.

FISC. An Anglicized form of the Latin "*fiscus,*" (which see.)

FISCAL. Belonging to the fisc, or public treasury. Relating to accounts or the management of revenue.

FISCAL AGENT. This term does not necessarily mean depositary of the public funds, so as, by the simple use of it in a statute, without any directions in this respect, to make it the duty of the state treasurer to deposit with him any moneys in the treasury. 27 La. Ann. 29.

FISCAL JUDGE. A public officer named in the laws of the Ripuarians' and some other Germanic peoples, apparently the same as the "*Graf,*" "*reeve,*" "*comes,*" or "*count,*" and so called because charged with the collection of public revenues, either directly or by the imposition of fines. See Spelman, voc. "Grafio."

FISCUS. In Roman law. The treasury of the prince or emperor, as distinguished from "*ærarium,*" which was the treasury of the state. Spelman.

The treasury or property of the state, as distinguished from the private property of the sovereign.

In English law. The king's treasury, as the repository of forfeited property.

The treasury of a noble, or of any private person. Spelman.

FISH. An animal which inhabits the water, breathes by means of gills, swims by the aid of fins, and is oviparous.

FISH COMMISSIONER. A public officer of the United States, created by act of congress of February 9, 1871, whose duties principally concern the preservation and increase throughout the country of fish suitable for food. Rev. St. § 4395.

FISH ROYAL. These were the whale and the sturgeon, which, when thrown ashore or caught near the coast of England, became the property of the king by virtue of his prerogative and in recompense for his protecting the shore from pirates and robbers. Brown; 1 Bl. Comm. 290.

FISHERY. A place prepared for catching fish with nets or hooks. This is commonly applied to the place of drawing a seine or net. 1 Whart. 131, 132.

A right or liberty of taking fish; a species of incorporeal hereditament, anciently termed "piscary," of which there are several kinds. 2 Bl. Comm. 34, 39; 3 Kent, Comm. 409–418.

A free fishery is said to be a franchise in the hands of a subject, existing by grant or prescription, distinct from an ownership in the soil. It is an exclusive right, and applies to a public navigable river, without any right in the soil. 3 Kent, Comm. 329.

A common of fishery is not an exclusive right, but one enjoyed in common with certain other persons. 3 Kent, Comm. 329.

A several fishery is one by which the party claiming it has the right of fishing, independently of all others, so that no person can have a co-extensive right with him in the object claimed; but a partial and independent right in another, or a limited liberty, does not derogate from the right of the owner. 5 Burrows, 2814.

FISHERY LAWS. A series of statutes passed in England for the regulation of fishing, especially to prevent the destruction of fish during the breeding season, and of small fish, spawn, etc., and the employment of improper modes of taking fish. 3 Steph. Comm. 165.

FISHGARTH. A dam or wear in a river for taking fish. Cowell.

FISHING BILL. A term descriptive of a bill in equity which seeks a discovery upon general, loose, and vague allegations. Story, Eq. Pl. § 325; 32 Fed. Rep. 263.

FISK. In Scotch law. The *fiscus* or fisc. The revenue of the crown. Generally used of the personal estate of a rebel which has been forfeited to the crown. Bell.

FISTUCA, or FESTUCA. In old English law. The rod or wand, by the delivery of which the property in land was formerly transferred in making a feoffment. Called, also, "*baculum,*" "*virga,*" and "*fustis.*" Spelman.

FISTULA. In the civil law. A pipe for conveying water. Dig. 8, 2, 18.

FITZ. A Norman word, meaning "son." It is used in law and genealogy; as *Fitzherbert*, the son of Herbert; *Fitzjames*, the son of James; *Fitzroy*, the son of the king. It was originally applied to illegitimate children.

FIVE-MILE ACT. An act of parliament, passed in 1665, against non-conformists, whereby ministers of that body were prohibited from coming within five miles of any corporate town, or place where they had preached or lectured. Brown.

FIX. To liquidate or render certain. To fasten a liability upon one. To transform a possible or contingent liability into a present and definite liability.

FIXING BAIL. In practice. Rendering absolute the liability of special bail.

FIXTURE. A fixture is a personal chattel substantially affixed to the land, but which may afterwards be lawfully removed therefrom by the party affixing it, or his representative, without the consent of the owner of the freehold. 3 Nev. 82; 18 Ind. 231; 8 Iowa, 544.

Personal chattels which have been annexed to land, and which may be afterwards severed and removed by the party who has annexed them, or his personal representative, against the will of the owner of the freehold. Ferard, Fixt. 2; Bouvier.

The word "fixtures" has acquired the peculiar meaning of chattels which have been annexed to the freehold, but which are removable at the will of the person who annexed them. 1 Cromp., M. & R. 266.

"Fixtures" does not necessarily import things affixed to the freehold. The word is a modern one, and is generally understood to comprehend any article which a tenant has the power to remove. 5 Mees. & W. 174; 30 Pa. St. 185, 189.

Chattels which, by being physically annexed or affixed to real estate, become a part of and accessory to the freehold, and the property of the owner of the land. Hill.

Things fixed or affixed to other things. The rule of law regarding them is that which is expressed in the maxim, "*accessio cedit principali,*" "the accessory goes with, and as part of, the principal subject-matter." Brown.

A thing is deemed to be affixed to land when it is attached to it by roots, as in the case of trees, vines, or shrubs; or imbedded in it, as in the case of walls; or permanently resting upon it, as in the case of buildings; or permanently attached to what is thus permanent, as by means of cement, plaster, nails, bolts, or screws. Civil Code Cal. § 660.

That which is fixed or attached to something permanently as an appendage, and not removable. Webster.

That which is fixed; a piece of furniture fixed to a house, as distinguished from movable; something fixed or immovable. Worcester.

The general result seems to be that three views have been taken. One is that "fixture" means something which has been affixed to the realty, so as to become a part of it; it is fixed, irremovable. An opposite view is that "fixture" means something which appears to be a part of the realty, but is not fully so; it is only a chattel fixed to it, but removable. An intermediate view is that "fixture" means a chattel annexed, affixed, to the realty, but imports nothing as to whether it is removable; that is to be determined by considering its circumstances and the relation of the parties. Abbott.

FLACO. A place covered with standing water.

FLAG. A national standard on which are certain emblems; an ensign; a banner. It is carried by soldiers, ships, etc., and commonly displayed at forts and many other suitable places.

FLAG, DUTY OF THE. This was an ancient ceremony in acknowledgment of British sovereignty over the British seas, by which a foreign vessel struck her flag and lowered her top-sail on meeting the British flag.

FLAG OF THE UNITED STATES. By the act entitled "An act to establish the flag of the United States," (Rev. St. §§ 1791, 1792,) it is provided "that, from and after the fourth day of July next, the flag of the United States be thirteen horizontal stripes, alternate red and white; that the union be twenty stars, white in a blue field; that, on the admission of every new state into the Union, one star be added to the union of the flag; and that such addition shall take effect on the fourth day of July then next succeeding such admission."

FLAGELLAT. Whipped; scourged. An entry on old Scotch records. 1 Pitc. Crim. Tr. pt. 1, p. 7.

FLAGRANS. Burning; raging; in actual perpetration. *Flagrans bellum*, a war actually going on.

FLAGRANS CRIMEN. In Roman law. A fresh or recent crime. This term designated a crime in the very act of its commission, or while it was of recent occurrence.

FLAGRANT DÉLIT. In French law. A crime which is in actual process of perpetration or which has just been committed. Code d'Instr. Crim. art. 41.

FLAGRANT NECESSITY. A case of urgency rendering lawful an otherwise illegal act, as an assault to remove a man from impending danger.

FLAGRANTE BELLO. During an actual state of war.

FLAGRANTE DELICTO. In the very act of committing the crime. 4 Bl. Comm. 307.

FLASH CHECK. A check drawn upon a banker by a person who has no funds at the banker's, and knows that such is the case.

FLAT. A place covered with water too shallow for navigation with vessels ordinarily used for commercial purposes. 34 Conn. 370; 7 Cush. 195.

FLAVIANUM JUS. In Roman law. The title of a book containing the forms of actions, published by Cneius Flavius, A. U. C. 449. Mackeld. Rom. Law, § 39. Calvin.

FLECTA. A feathered or fleet arrow. Cowell.

FLEDWITE. A discharge or freedom from amercements where one, having been an outlawed fugitive, cometh to the place of our lord of his own accord. Termes de la Ley.

The liberty to hold court and take up the amercements for beating and striking. Cowell.

The fine set on a fugitive as the price of obtaining the king's freedom. Spelman.

FLEE FROM JUSTICE. To leave one's home, residence, or known place of abode, or to conceal one's self therein, with intent, in either case, to avoid detection or punishment for some public offense. 3 Dill. 381; 48 Mo. 240.

"FLEE TO THE WALL." A metaphorical expression, used in connection with homicide done in self-defense, signifying the exhaustion of every possible means of escape, or of averting the assault, before killing the assailant.

FLEET. A place where the tide flows; a creek, or inlet of water; a company of ships or navy; a prison in London, (so called from a river or ditch formerly in its vicinity,) now abolished by 5 & 6 Vict. c. 22.

FLEM. In Saxon and old English law. A fugitive bondman or villein. Spelman.

The privilege of having the goods and fines of fugitives.

FLEMENE FRIT, FLEMENES FRINTHE—FLYMENA FRYNTHE. The reception or relief of a fugitive or outlaw. Jacob.

FLEMESWITE. The possession of the goods of fugitives. Fleta, lib. 1, c. 147.

FLET. In Saxon law. Land; a house; home.

FLETA. The name given to an ancient treatise on the laws of England, founded mainly upon the writings of Bracton and Glanville, and supposed to have been written in the time of Edw. I. The author is unknown, but it is surmised that he was a judge or learned lawyer who was at that time confined in the Fleet prison, whence the name of the book.

FLICHWITE. In Saxon law. A fine on account of brawls and quarrels. Spelman.

FLIGHT. In criminal law. The act of one under accusation, who evades the law by voluntarily withdrawing himself. It is presumptive evidence of guilt.

FLOAT. In American land law, especially in the western states. A certificate authorizing the entry, by the holder, of a certain quantity of land. 20 How. 501, 504.

FLOATABLE. Used for floating. A floatable stream is a stream used for floating logs, rafts, etc. 2 Mich. 519.

FLOATING CAPITAL, (or circulating capital.) The capital which is consumed at each operation of production and reappears transformed into new products. At each sale of these products the capital is represented in cash, and it is from its transformations that profit is derived. Floating capital includes raw materials destined for fabrication, such as wool and flax, products in the warehouses of manufacturers or merchants, such as cloth and linen, and money for wages, and stores. De Laveleye, Pol. Ec.

Capital retained for the purpose of meeting current expenditure.

FLOATING DEBT. By this term is meant that mass of lawful and valid claims against the corporation for the payment of which there is no money in the corporate treasury specifically designed, nor any taxation nor other means of providing money to pay particularly provided. 71 N. Y. 374.

Debt not in the form of bonds or stocks bearing regular interest. Pub. St. Mass. 1882, p. 1290.

FLODE-MARK. Flood-mark, high-water mark. The mark which the sea, at flowing water and highest tide, makes on the shore. Blount.

FLOOR. A section of a building between horizontal planes. 145 Mass. 1, 12 N. E. Rep. 401.

A term used metaphorically, in parliamentary practice, to denote the exclusive right to address the body in session. A member who has been recognized by the chairman, and who is in order, is said to "have the floor," until his remarks are concluded. Similarly, the "floor of the house" means the main part of the hall where the members sit, as distinguished from the galleries, or from the corridors or lobbies.

In England, the floor of a court is that part between the judge's bench and the front row of counsel. Litigants appearing in person, in the high court or court of appeal, are supposed to address the court from the floor.

FLORENTINE PANDECTS. A copy of the Pandects discovered accidentally about the year 1137, at Amalphi, a town in Italy, near Salerno. From Amalphi, the copy found its way to Pisa, and, Pisa having submitted to the Florentines in 1406, the copy was removed in great triumph to Florence. By direction of the magistrates of the town, it was immediately bound in a superb manner, and deposited in a costly chest. Formerly, these Pandects were shown only by torch-light, in the presence of two magistrates, and two Cistercian monks, with their heads uncovered. They have been successively collated by Politian, Bolognini, and Antonius Augustinus. An exact copy of them was published in 1553 by Franciscus Taurellus. For its accuracy and beauty, this edition ranks high among the ornaments of the press. Brenchman, who collated the manuscript about 1710, refers it to the sixth century. Butl. Hor. Jur. 90, 91.

FLORIN. A coin originally made at Florence, now of the value of about two English shillings.

FLOTAGES. 1. Such things as by accident swim on the top of great rivers or the sea. Cowell.

2. A commission paid to water bailiffs. Cun. Dict.

FLOTSAM, FLOTSAN. A name for the goods which float upon the sea when cast overboard for the safety of the ship, or when a ship is sunk. Distinguished from "jetsam" and "ligan." Bract. lib. 2, c. 5; 5 Coke, 106; 1 Bl. Comm. 292.

FLOUD-MARKE. In old English law. High-water mark; flood-mark. 1 And. 88, 89.

FLOWING LANDS. This term has acquired a definite and specific meaning in law. It commonly imports raising and setting back water on another's land, by a dam placed across a stream or water-course which is the natural drain and outlet for surplus water on such land. 2 Gray, 235.

FLUCTUS. Flood; flood-tide. Bract. fol. 255.

FLUMEN. In Roman law. A servitude which consists in the right to conduct the rain-water, collected from the roof and carried off by the gutters, onto the house or ground of one's neighbor. Mackeld. Rom. Law, § 317; Ersk. Inst. 2, 9, 9. Also a river or stream.

In old English law. Flood; flood-tide.

Flumina et portus publica sunt, ideoque jus piscandi omnibus commune est. Rivers and ports are public. Therefore the right of fishing there is common to all. Day. Ir. K. B. 55; Branch, Princ.

FLUMINÆ VOLUCRES. Wild fowl; water-fowl. 11 East, 571, note.

FLUVIUS. A river; a public river; flood; flood-tide.

FLUXUS. In old English law. Flow. *Per fluxum et refluxum maris,* by the flow and reflow of the sea. Dal. pl. 10.

FLY FOR IT. On a criminal trial in former times, it was usual after a verdict of not guilty to inquire also, "Did he fly for it?" This practice was abolished by the 7 & 8 Geo. IV. c. 28, § 5. Wharton.

FLYING SWITCH. In railroading, a flying switch is made by uncoupling the cars from the engine while in motion, and throwing the cars onto the side track, by turning the switch, after the engine has passed it upon the main track. 29 Iowa, 39. See, also, 32 N. Y. 597, note.

FLYMA. In old English law. A runaway; fugitive; one escaped from justice, or who has no "hlaford."

FLYMAN-FRYMTH. In old English law. The offense of harboring a fugitive, the penalty attached to which was one of the rights of the crown.

FOCAGE. House-bote; fire-bote. Cowell.

FOCALE. In old English law. Firewood. The right of taking wood for the fire. Fire-bote. Cunningham.

FODDER. Food for horses or cattle. In feudal law, the term also denoted a prerogative of the prince to be provided with corn, etc., for his horses by his subjects in his wars.

FODERTORIUM. Provisions to be paid by custom to the royal purveyors. Cowell.

FODERUM. See FODDER.

FODINA. A mine. Co. Litt. 6*a.*

FŒDUS. In international law. A treaty; a league; a compact.

FŒMINA VIRO CO-OPERTA. A married woman; a *feme covert.*

Fœminæ ab omnibus officiis civilibus vel publicis remotæ sunt. Women are excluded from all civil and public charges or offices. Dig. 50, 17, 2; 1 Exch. 645; 6 Mees. & W. 216.

Fœminæ non sunt capaces de publicis officiis. Jenk. Cent. 237. Women are not admissible to public offices.

FŒNERATION. Lending money at interest; the act of putting out money to usury.

FŒNUS NAUTICUM. In the civil law. Nautical or maritime interest. An extraordinary rate of interest agreed to be paid for the loan of money on the hazard of a voyage; sometimes called "*usura maritima.*" Dig. 22, 2; Code, 4, 33; 2 Bl. Comm. 458.

The extraordinary rate of interest, proportioned to the risk, demanded by a person lending money on a ship, or on "bottomry," as it is termed. The agreement for such a rate of interest is also called "*fœnus nauticum.*" (2 Bl. Comm. 458; 2 Steph. Comm. 93.) Mozley & Whitley.

FŒSA. In old records. Grass; herbage. 2 Mon. Angl. 906*b;* Cowell.

FŒTICIDE. In medical jurisprudence. Destruction of the *fœtus;* the act by which criminal abortion is produced. 1 Beck, Med. Jur. 288; Guy, Med. Jur. 133.

FŒTURA. In the civil law. The produce of animals, and the fruit of other property, which are acquired to the owner of such animals and property by virtue of his right. Bowyer, Mod. Civil Law, c. 14, p. 81.

FŒTUS. In medical jurisprudence. An unborn child. An infant *in ventre sa mère.*

FOGAGIUM. In old English law. Fogage or fog; a kind of rank grass of late growth, and not eaten in summer. Spelman; Cowell.

FOI. In French feudal law. Faith; fealty. Guyot, Inst. Feod. c. 2.

FOINESUN. In old English law. The fawning of deer. Spelman.

FOIRFAULT. In old Scotch law. To forfeit. 1 How. State Tr. 927.

FOIRTHOCHT. In old Scotch law. Forethought; premeditated. 1 Pitc. Crim. Tr. pt. 1, p. 90.

FOITERERS. Vagabonds. Blount.

FOLC-GEMOTE. In Saxon law. A general assembly of the people in a town or shire. It appears to have had judicial functions of a limited nature, and also to have discharged political offices, such as deliberating upon the affairs of the commonwealth or complaining of misgovernment, and probably possessed considerable powers of local self-government. The name was also given to any sort of a popular assembly. See Spelman; Manwood; Cunningham.

FOLC-LAND. In Saxon law. Land of the folk or people. Land belonging to the people or the public.

Folc-land was the property of the community. It might be occupied in common, or possessed in severalty; and, in the latter case, it was probably parceled out to individuals in the folc-gemote or court of the district, and the grant sanctioned by the freemen who were there present. But, while it continued to be folc-land, it could not be alienated in perpetuity; and therefore, on the expiration of the term for which it had been granted, it reverted to the community, and was again distributed by the same authority. It was subject to many burdens and exactions from which boc-land was exempt. Wharton.

FOLC-MOTE. A general assembly of the people, under the Saxons. See FOLC-GEMOTE.

FOLC-RIGHT. The common right of all the people. 1 Bl. Comm. 65, 67.

The *jus commune*, or common law, mentioned in the laws of King Edward the Elder, declaring the same equal right, law, or justice to be due to persons of all degrees. Wharton.

FOLD-COURSE. In English law. Land to which the sole right of folding the cattle of others is appurtenant. Sometimes it means merely such right of folding. The right of folding on another's land, which is called "common foldage." Co. Litt. 6a, note 1.

FOLDAGE. A privilege possessed in some places by the lord of a manor, which consists in the right of having his tenant's sheep to feed on his fields, so as to manure the land. The name of foldage is also given in parts of Norfolk to the customary fee paid to the lord for exemption at certain times from this duty. Elton, Com. 45, 46.

FOLGARII. Menial servants; followers. Bract.

FOLGERE. In old English law. A freeman, who has no house or dwelling of his own, but is the follower or retainer of another, (*heorthfœst*,) for whom he performs certain predial services.

FOLGOTH. Official dignity.

FOLIO. 1. A leaf. In the ancient law-books it was the custom to number the leaves, instead of the pages; hence a folio would include both sides of the leaf, or two pages. The references to these books are made by the number of the folio, the letters "*a*" and "*b*" being added to show which of the two pages is intended; thus "Bracton, fol. 100*a*."

2. A large size of book, the page being obtained by folding the sheet of paper once only in the binding. Many of the ancient law-books are folios.

3. In computing the length of written legal documents, the term "folio" denotes a certain number of words, fixed by statute in some states at one hundred.

The term "folio," when used as a measure for computing fees or compensation, or in any legal

proceedings, means one hundred words, counting every figure necessarily used as a word; and any portion of a folio, when in the whole draft or figure there is not a complete folio, and when there is any excess over the last folio, shall be computed as a folio. Gen. St. Minn. 1878, c. 4, § 1, par. 4.

FOLK-LAND; FOLK-MOTE. See FOLC-LAND; FOLC-GEMOTE.

FONDS PERDUS. In French law. A capital is said to be invested *à fonds perdus* when it is stipulated that in consideration of the payment of an amount as interest, higher than the normal rate, the lender shall be repaid his capital in this manner. The borrower, after having paid the interest during the period determined, is free as regards the capital itself. Arg. Fr. Merc. Law, 560.

FONSADERA. In Spanish law. Any tribute or loan granted to the king for the purpose of enabling him to defray the expenses of a war.

FONTANA. A fountain or spring. Bract. fol. 233.

FOOT. 1. A measure of length containing twelve inches or one-third of a yard.

2. The base, bottom, or foundation of anything; and, by metonomy, the end or termination; as the foot of a fine.

FOOT OF THE FINE. The fifth part of the conclusion of a fine. It includes the whole matter, reciting the names of the parties, day, year, and place, and before whom it was acknowledged or levied. 2 Bl. Comm. 351.

FOOTGELD. In the forest law. An amercement for not cutting out the ball or cutting off the claws of a dog's feet, (expediting him.) To be quit of *footgeld* is to have the privilege of keeping dogs in the forest *unlawed* without punishment or control. Manwood.

FOOT-PRINTS. In the law of evidence. Impressions made upon earth, snow, or other surface by the feet of persons, or by the shoes, boots, or other covering of the feet. Burrill, Circ. Ev. 264.

FOR. In French law. A tribunal. *Le for intérieur*, the interior forum; the tribunal of conscience. Poth. Obl. pt. 1, c. 1, § 1, art. 3, § 4.

FOR THAT. In pleading. Words used to introduce the allegations of a declaration. "For that" is a positive allegation; "For that whereas" is a recital. Ham. N. P. 9.

FOR THAT WHEREAS. In pleading. Formal words introducing the statement of the plaintiff's case, by way of recital, in his declaration, in all actions except trespass. 1 Instr. Cler. 170; 1 Burrill, Pr. 127. In trespass, where there was no recital, the expression used was, "For that." Id.; 1 Instr. Cler. 202.

FOR USE. 1. For the benefit or advantage of another. Thus, where an assignee is obliged to sue in the name of his assignor, the suit is entitled "A. *for use* of B. v. C."

2. For enjoyment or employment without destruction. A loan "for use" is one in which the bailee has the right to use and enjoy the article, but without consuming or destroying it, in which respect it differs from a loan "for consumption."

"FOR WHOM IT MAY CONCERN." In a policy of marine or fire insurance, this phrase indicates that the insurance is taken for the benefit of all persons (besides those named) who may have an insurable interest in the subject.

FORAGE. Hay and straw for horses, particularly in the army. Jacob.

FORAGIUM. Straw when the corn is threshed out. Cowell.

FORANEUS. One from without; a foreigner; a stranger. Calvin.

FORATHE. In forest law. One who could make oath, *i. e.*, bear witness for another. Cowell; Spelman.

FORBALCA. In old records. A forebalk; a balk (that is, an unplowed piece of land) lying forward or next the highway. Cowell.

FORBANNITUS. A pirate; an outlaw; one banished.

FORBARRER. L. Fr. To bar out; to preclude; hence, to estop.

FORBATUDUS. In old English law. The aggressor slain in combat. Jacob.

FORBEARANCE. The act of abstaining from proceeding against a delinquent debtor; delay in exacting the enforcement of a right; indulgence granted to a debtor.

Refraining from action. The term is used in this sense, in general jurisprudence, in contradistinction to "act."

FORCE. Power dynamically considered, that is, in motion or in action; constraining power; compulsion; strength directed to an end. Usually the word occurs in such connections as to show that unlawful or wrongful action is meant.

Unlawful violence. It is either *simple*, as entering upon another's possession, without doing any other unlawful act; *compound*, when some other violence is committed, which of itself alone is criminal; or *implied*, as in every trespass, rescous, or disseisin.

Power statically considered; that is, at rest, or latent, but capable of being called into activity upon occasion for its exercise. Efficacy; legal validity. This is the meaning when we say that a statute or a contract is "in force."

In old English law. A technical term applied to a species of accessary before the fact.

In Scotch law. Coercion; duress. Bell.

FORCE AND ARMS. A phrase used in declarations of trespass and in indictments, but now unnecessary in declarations, to denote that the act complained of was done with violence. 2 Chit. Pl. 846, 850.

FORCE AND FEAR, called also "*vi metuque*," means that any contract or act extorted under the pressure of force (*vis*) or under the influence of fear (*metus*) is voidable on that ground, provided, of course, that the force or the fear was such as influenced the party. Brown.

FORCE MAJEURE. Fr. In the law of insurance. Superior or irresistible force. Emerig. Tr. des Ass. c. 12.

FORCED HEIRS. In Louisiana. Those persons whom the testator or donor cannot deprive of the portion of his estate reserved for them by law, except in cases where he has a just cause to disinherit them. Civil Code La. art. 1495.

FORCED SALE. In practice. A sale made at the time and in the manner prescribed by law, in virtue of execution issued on a judgment already rendered by a court of competent jurisdiction; a sale made under the process of the court, and in the mode prescribed by law. 6 Tex. 110.

A forced sale is a sale against the consent of the owner. The term should not be deemed to embrace a sale under a power in a mortgage. 15 Fla. 336.

FORCES. The military and naval power of the country.

FORCHEAPUM. Pre-emption; forestalling the market. Jacob.

FORCIBLE DETAINER. The offense of violently keeping possession of lands and tenements, with menaces, force, and arms, and without the authority of law. 4 Bl. Comm. 148; 4 Steph. Comm. 280.

Forcible detainer may ensue upon a peaceable entry, as well as upon a forcible entry; but it is most commonly spoken of in the phrase "forcible entry and detainer."

FORCIBLE ENTRY. An offense against the public peace, or private wrong, committed by violently taking possession of lands and tenements with menaces, force, and arms, against the will of those entitled to the possession, and without the authority of law. 4 Bl. Comm. 148; 4 Steph. Comm. 280; Code Ga. 1882, § 4524.

Every person is guilty of forcible entry who either (1) by breaking open doors, windows, or other parts of a house, or by any kind of violence or circumstance of terror, enters upon or into any real property; or (2) who, after entering peaceably upon real property, turns out by force, threats, or menacing conduct the party in possession. Code Civil Proc. Cal. § 1159.

FORDA. In old records. A ford or shallow, made by damming or penning up the water. Cowell.

FORDAL. A butt or headland, jutting out upon other land. Cowell.

FORDANNO. In old European law. He who first assaulted another. Spelman.

FORDIKA. In old records. Grass or herbage growing on the edge or bank of dykes or ditches. Cowell.

FORE. Sax. Before. Fr. Out. Kelham.

FORECLOSE. To shut out; to bar. Used of the process of destroying an equity of redemption existing in a mortgagor.

FORECLOSURE. A process in chancery by which all further right existing in a mortgagor to redeem the estate is defeated and lost to him, and the estate becomes the absolute property of the mortgagee; being applicable when the mortgagor has forfeited his estate by non-payment of the money due on the mortgage at the time appointed, but still retains the equity of redemption. 2 Washb. Real Prop. 237.

The term is also loosely applied to any of the various methods, statutory or otherwise, known in different jurisdictions, of enforcing payment of the debt secured by a mortgage, by taking and selling the mortgaged estate.

Foreclosure is also applied to proceedings founded upon some other liens; thus there are proceedings to foreclose a mechanic's lien.

FOREFAULT. In Scotch law. To forfeit; to lose.

FOREGIFT. A premium for a lease.

FOREGOERS. Royal purveyors. 26 Edw. III. c. 5.

FOREHAND RENT. In English law. Rent payable in advance; or, more properly, a species of premium or bonus paid by the tenant on the making of the lease, and particularly on the renewal of leases by ecclesiastical corporations.

FOREIGN. Belonging to another nation or country; belonging or attached to another jurisdiction; made, done, or rendered in another state or jurisdiction; subject to another jurisdiction; operating or solvable in another territory; extrinsic; outside; extraordinary.

FOREIGN ADMINISTRATOR. One appointed or qualified under the laws of a foreign state or country, where the decedent was domiciled.

FOREIGN ANSWER. In old English practice. An answer which was not triable in the county where it was made. (St. 15 Hen. VI. c. 5.) Blount.

FOREIGN APPOSER. An officer in the exchequer who examines the sheriff's *estreats*, comparing them with the records, and apposeth (interrogates) the sheriff what he says to each particular sum therein. 4 Inst. 107; Blount; Cowell.

FOREIGN ASSIGNMENT. An assignment made in a foreign country, or in another state. 2 Kent, Comm. 405, et seq.

FOREIGN ATTACHMENT. In American law. A process by which the property (lying within the jurisdiction of the court) of an absent or non-resident debtor is seized, in order to compel his appearance, or to satisfy the judgment that may be rendered, so far as the property goes.

In English law. A custom which prevails in the city of London, whereby a debt owing to a defendant sued in the court of the mayor or sheriff may be attached in the hands of the debtor.

FOREIGN BILL OF EXCHANGE.
A bill of exchange drawn in one state or country, upon a foreign state or country.

A bill of exchange drawn in one country upon another country not governed by the same homogeneous laws, or not governed throughout by the same municipal laws.

A bill of exchange drawn in one of the United States upon a person residing in another state is a foreign bill. See Story, Bills, § 22; 2 Pet. 586; 3 Kent, Comm. 94, note.

FOREIGN BOUGHT AND SOLD.
A custom in London which, being found prejudicial to sellers of cattle in Smithfield, was abolished. Wharton.

FOREIGN CHARITY. One created or endowed in a state or country foreign to that of the domicile of the benefactor. 34 N. J. Eq. 101.

FOREIGN COINS. Coins issued as money under the authority of a foreign government. As to their valuation in the United States, see Rev. St. U. S. §§ 3564, 3565.

FOREIGN COMMERCE. Commerce or trade between the United States and foreign countries. The term is sometimes applied to commerce between ports of two sister states not lying on the same coast, *e. g.*, New York and San Francisco.

FOREIGN CORPORATION. A corporation created by or under the laws of another state, government, or country.

FOREIGN COUNTY. Any county having a judicial and municipal organization separate from that of the county where matters arising in the former county are called in question, though both may lie within the same state or country.

FOREIGN COURTS. The courts of a foreign state or nation. In the United States, this term is frequently applied to the courts of one of the states when their judgments or records are introduced in the courts of another.

FOREIGN CREDITOR. One who resides in a state or country foreign to that where the debtor has his domicile or his property.

FOREIGN DIVORCE. A divorce obtained out of the state or country where the marriage was solemnized. 2 Kent, Comm. 106, et seq.

FOREIGN DOCUMENT. One which was prepared or executed in, or which comes from, a foreign state or country.

FOREIGN DOMICILE. A domicile established by a citizen or subject of one sovereignty within the territory of another.

FOREIGN DOMINION. In English law this means a country which at one time formed part of the dominions of a foreign state or potentate, but which by conquest or cession has become a part of the dominions of the British crown. 5 Best & S. 290.

FOREIGN ENLISTMENT ACT. The statute 59 Geo. III. c. 69, prohibiting the enlistment, as a soldier or sailor, in any foreign service. 4 Steph. Comm. 226. A later and more stringent act is that of 33 & 34 Vict. c. 90.

FOREIGN EXCHANGE. Drafts drawn on a foreign state or country.

FOREIGN FACTOR. A factor who resides in a country foreign to that where his principal resides.

FOREIGN-GOING SHIP. By the English merchant shipping act, 1854, (17 & 18 Vict. c. 104,) § 2, any ship employed in trading, going between some place or places in the United Kingdom and some place or places situate beyond the following limits, that is to say: The coasts of the United Kingdom, the islands of Guernsey, Jersey, Sark, Alderney, and Man, and the continent of Europe, between the river Elbe and Brest, inclusive. Home-trade ship includes every ship employed in trading and going between places within the last-mentioned limits.

FOREIGN JUDGMENT OR DECREE. A judgment rendered by the courts of a state or country politically and judicially distinct from that where the judgment or its effect is brought in question. One pronounced by a tribunal of a foreign country, or of a sister state.

FOREIGN JURISDICTION. Any jurisdiction foreign to that of the forum. Also the exercise by a state or nation of jurisdiction beyond its own territory, the right being acquired by treaty or otherwise.

FOREIGN JURY. A jury obtained from a county other than that in which issue was joined.

FOREIGN LAWS. The laws of a foreign country, or of a sister state. Foreign laws are often the suggesting occasions of changes in, or additions to, our own laws, and in that respect are called *"jus receptum."* Brown.

FOREIGN MATTER. In old practice. Matter triable or done in another county. Cowell.

FOREIGN MINISTER. An ambassador, minister, or envoy from a foreign government.

FOREIGN OFFICE. The department of state through which the English sovereign communicates with foreign powers. A secretary of state is at its head. Till the middle of the last century, the functions of a secretary of state as to foreign and home questions were not disunited.

FOREIGN PLEA. A plea objecting to the jurisdiction of a judge, on the ground that he had not cognizance of the subject-matter of the suit. Cowell.

FOREIGN PORT. A port exclusively within the sovereignty of a foreign nation. A foreign port or place is a port or place without the United States. 19 Johns. 375.

FOREIGN SERVICE, in feudal law, was that whereby a mesne lord held of another, without the compass of his own fee, or that which the tenant performed either to his own lord or to the lord paramount out of the fee. (Kitch. 299.) Foreign service seems also to be used for knight's service, or escuage uncertain. (Perk. 650.) Jacob.

FOREIGN STATE. A foreign country or nation. The several United States are considered "foreign" to each other except as regards their relations as common members of the Union.

FOREIGN VESSEL. A vessel owned by residents in, or sailing under the flag of, a foreign nation.

"Foreign vessel," under the embargo act of January, 1808, means a vessel under the flag of a foreign power, and not a vessel in which foreigners domiciled in the United States have an interest. 1 Gall. 58.

FOREIGN VOYAGE. A voyage to some port or place within the territory of a foreign nation. The *terminus* of a voyage determines its character. If it be within the limits of a foreign jurisdiction, it is a foreign voyage, and not otherwise. 1 Story, 1. See 3 Kent, Comm. 177, note; 1 Gall. 55.

FOREIGNER. In old English law, this term, when used with reference to a particular city, designated any person who was not an inhabitant of that city. According to later usage, it denotes a person who is not a citizen or subject of the state or country of which mention is made, or any one owing allegiance to a foreign state or sovereign.

FOREIN. An old form of *foreign,* (*q. v.*) Blount.

FOREJUDGE. In old English law and practice. To expel from court for some offense or misconduct. When an officer or attorney of a court was expelled for any offense, or for not appearing to an action by bill filed against him, he was said to be *forejudged the court.* Cowell.

To deprive or put out of a thing by the judgment of a court. To condemn to lose a thing.

To expel or banish.

FOREJUDGER. In English practice. A judgment by which a man is deprived or *put out* of a thing; a judgment of expulsion or banishment. See FOREJUDGE.

FOREMAN. The presiding member of a grand or petit jury, who speaks or answers for the jury.

FORENSIC. Belonging to courts of justice.

FORENSIC MEDICINE, or medical jurisprudence, as it is also called, is "that science which teaches the application of every branch of medical knowledge to the purposes of the law; hence its limits are, on the one hand, the requirements of the law, and, on the other, the whole range of medicine. Anatomy, physiology, medicine, surgery, chemistry, physics, and botany lend their aid as necessity arises; and in some cases all these branches of science are required to enable a court of law to arrive at a proper conclusion on a contested question affecting life or property." Tayl. Med. Jur. 1.

FORENSIS. In the civil law. Belonging to or connected with a court; forensic. *Forensis homo,* an advocate; a pleader of causes; one who practices in court. Calvin.

In old Scotch law. A strange man or stranger; an out-dwelling man; an "unfreeman," who dwells not within burgh.

FORESAID is used in Scotch law as *aforesaid* is in English, and sometimes, in a plural form, *foresaids.* 2 How. State Tr. 715. *Forsaidis* occurs in old Scotch records. "The Loirdis assesouris forsaidis." 1 Pitc. Crim. Tr. pt. 1, p. 107.

FORESCHOKE. Forsaken; disavowed. 10 Edw. II. c. 1.

FORESHORE. That part of the land adjacent to the sea which is alternately covered and left dry by the ordinary flow of the tides; *i. e.*, by the medium line between the greatest and least range of tide, (spring tides and neap tides.) Sweet.

FOREST. In old English law. A certain territory of wooded ground and fruitful pastures, privileged for wild beasts and fowls of forest, chase, and warren, to rest and abide in the safe protection of the prince for his princely delight and pleasure, having a peculiar court and officers. Manw. For. Laws, c. 1, no. 1; Termes de la Ley; 1 Bl. Comm. 289.

A royal hunting-ground which lost its peculiar character with the extinction of its courts, or when the franchise passed into the hands of a subject. Spelman; Cowell.

The word is also used to signify a franchise or right, being the right of keeping, for the purpose of hunting, the wild beasts and fowls of forest, chase, park, and warren, in a territory or precinct of woody ground or pasture set apart for the purpose. 1 Steph. Comm. 665.

FOREST COURTS. In English law. Courts instituted for the government of the king's forest in different parts of the kingdom, and for the punishment of all injuries done to the king's deer or *venison*, to the *vert* or greensward, and to the *covert* in which such deer were lodged. They consisted of the courts of attachments, of regard, of sweinmote, and of justice-seat; but in later times these courts are no longer held. 3 Bl. Comm. 71.

FOREST LAW. The system or body of old law relating to the royal forests.

FORESTAGE. A duty or tribute payable to the king's foresters. Cowell.

FORESTAGIUM. A duty or tribute payable to the king's foresters. Cowell.

FORESTALL. To intercept or obstruct a passenger on the king's highway. Cowell. To beset the way of a tenant so as to prevent his coming on the premises. 3 Bl. Comm. 170. To intercept a deer on his way to the forest before he can regain it. Cowell.

FORESTALLER. In old English law. Obstruction; hindrance; the offense of stopping the highway; the hindering a tenant from coming to his land; intercepting a deer before it can regain the forest. Also one who forestalls; one who commits the offense of forestalling. 3 Bl. Comm. 170; Cowell.

FORESTALLING. Obstructing the highway. Intercepting a person on the highway.

FORESTALLING THE MARKET. The act of the buying or contracting for any merchandise or provision on its way to the market, with the intention of selling it again at a higher price; or the dissuading persons from bringing their goods or provisions there; or persuading them to enhance the price when there. 4 Bl. Comm. 158. This was formerly an indictable offense in England, but is now abolished by St. 7 & 8 Vict. c. 24. 4 Steph. Comm. 291, note.

FORESTARIUS. In English law. A forester. An officer who takes care of the woods and forests. *De forestario apponendo,* a writ which lay to appoint a forester to prevent further commission of waste when a tenant in dower had committed waste. Bract. 316; Du Cange.

In Scotch law. A forester or keeper of woods, to whom, by reason of his office, pertains the bark and the hewn branches. And, when he rides through the forest, he may take a tree as high as his own head. Skene de Verb. Sign.

FORESTER. A sworn officer of the *forest*, appointed by the king's letters patent to walk the forest, watching both the vert and the venison, attaching and presenting all trespassers against them within their own bailiwick or walk. These letters patent were generally granted during good behavior; but sometimes they held the office in fee. Blount.

FORETHOUGHT FELONY. In Scotch law. Murder committed in consequence of a previous design. Ersk. Inst. 4, 4, 50; Bell.

FORFANG. In old English law. The taking of provisions from any person in fairs or markets before the royal purveyors were served with necessaries for the sovereign. Cowell. Also the seizing and rescuing of stolen or strayed cattle from the hands of a thief, or of those having illegal possession of them; also the reward fixed for such rescue.

FORFEIT. To lose an estate, a franchise, or other property belonging to one, by the act of the law, and as a consequence of some misfeasance, negligence, or omission. The further ideas connoted by this term are that it is a deprivation, (that is, against the will of the losing party,) and that the property is either transferred to another or resumed by the original grantor.

To incur a penalty; to become liable to the payment of a sum of money, as the consequence of a certain act.

FORFEITABLE. Liable to be forfeited; subject to forfeiture for non-user, neglect, crime, etc.

FORFEITURE. 1. A punishment annexed by law to some illegal act or negligence in the owner of lands, tenements, or hereditaments, whereby he loses all his interest therein, and they go to the party injured as a recompense for the wrong which he alone, or the public together with himself, hath sustained. 2 Bl. Comm. 267.

2. The loss of land by a tenant to his lord, as the consequence of some breach of fidelity. 1 Steph. Comm. 166.

3. The loss of lands and goods to the state, as the consequence of crime. 4 Bl. Comm. 381, 387; 4 Steph. Comm. 447, 452; 2 Kent, Comm. 385; 4 Kent, Comm. 426.

4. The loss of goods or chattels, as a punishment for some crime or misdemeanor in the party forfeiting, and as a compensation for the offense and injury committed against him to whom they are forfeited. 2 Bl. Comm. 420.

It should be noted that "forfeiture" is not an identical or convertible term with "confiscation." The latter is the consequence of the former. Forfeiture is the result which the law attaches as an immediate and necessary consequence of the illegal acts of the individual; but confiscation implies the action of the state; and property, although it may be forfeited, cannot be said to be confiscated until the government has formally claimed or taken possession of it.

5. The loss of office by abuser, non-user, or refusal to exercise it.

6. The loss of a corporate franchise or charter in consequence of some illegal act, or of malfeasance or non-feasance.

7. The loss of the right to life, as the consequence of the commission of some crime to which the law has affixed a capital penalty.

8. The incurring a liability to pay a definite sum of money as the consequence of violating the provisions of some statute, or refusal to comply with some requirement of law.

9. A thing or sum of money forfeited. Something imposed as a punishment for an offense or delinquency. The word in this sense is frequently associated with the word "penalty."

FORFEITURE OF A BOND. A failure to perform the condition on which the obligor was to be excused from the penalty in the bond.

FORFEITURE OF MARRIAGE. A penalty incurred by a ward in chivalry who married without the consent or against the will of the guardian. See DUPLEX VALOR MARITAGII.

FORFEITURE OF SILK, supposed to lie in the docks, used, in times when its importation was prohibited, to be proclaimed each term in the exchequer.

FORFEITURES ABOLITION ACT. Another name for the felony act of 1870, abolishing forfeitures for felony in England.

FORGABULUM, or FORGAVEL. A quit-rent; a small reserved rent in money. Jacob.

FORGE. To fabricate, construct, or prepare one thing in imitation of another thing, with the intention of substituting the false for the genuine, or otherwise deceiving and defrauding by the use of the spurious article. To counterfeit or make falsely. Especially, to make a spurious written instrument with the intention of fraudulently substituting it for another, or of passing it off as genuine; or to fraudulently alter a genuine instrument to another's prejudice; or to sign another person's name to a document, with a deceitful and fraudulent intent.

To forge (a metaphorical expression, borrowed from the occupation of the smith) means, properly speaking, no more than to make or form, but in our law it is always taken in an evil sense. 2 East, P. C. p. 852, c. 19, § 1.

To forge is to make in the likeness of something else; to counterfeit is to make in imitation of something else, with a view to defraud by passing the false copy for genuine or original. Both words, "forged" and "counterfeited," convey the idea of similitude. 42 Me. 392.

In common usage, however, *forgery* is almost always predicated of some private instrument or writing, as a deed, note, will, or a signature; and *counterfeiting* denotes the fraudulent imitation of coined or paper money or some substitute therefor.

FORGERY. In criminal law. The falsely making or materially altering, with intent to defraud, any writing which, if genuine, might apparently be of legal efficacy or the foundation of a legal liability. 2 Bish. Crim. Law, § 523.

The fraudulent making and alteration of a writing to the prejudice of another man's right. 4 Bl. Comm. 247. See FORGE.

Forgery, at common law, denotes a false making, (which includes every alteration or addition to a true instrument;) a making, *malo animo*, of any written instrument for the purpose of fraud and deceit. 2 East, P. C. 852.

The false making an instrument which purports on its face to be good and valid for the purposes for which it was created, with a design to defraud any person or persons. 1 Leach, 366.

The thing itself, so falsely made, imitated, or forged; especially a forged writing. A forged signature is frequently said to be "a *forgery.*"

In the law of evidence. The fabrication or counterfeiting of evidence. The artful and fraudulent manipulation of physical objects, or the deceitful arrangement of genuine facts or things, in such a manner as to create an erroneous impression or a false inference in the minds of those who may observe them. See Burrill, Circ. Ev. 131, 420.

FORGERY ACT, 1870. The statute 33 & 34 Vict. c. 58, was passed for the punishment of forgers of stock certificates, and for extending to Scotland certain provisions of the forgery act of 1861. Mozley & Whitley.

FORHERDA. In old records. A herdland, headland, or foreland. Cowell.

FORI DISPUTATIONES. In the civil law. Discussions or arguments before a court. 1 Kent, Comm. 530.

FORINSECUM MANERIUM. That part of a manor which lies without the town, and is not included within the liberties of it. Paroch. Antiq. 351.

FORINSECUM SERVITIUM. The payment of extraordinary aid. Kennett, Gloss.

FORINSECUS. Lat. Foreign; exterior; outside; extraordinary. *Servitium forinsecum,* the payment of aid, scutage, and other extraordinary military services. *Forinsecum manerium,* the manor, or that part of it which lies outside the bars or town, and is not included within the liberties of it. Cowell; Blount; Jacob; 1 Reeve, Eng. Law, 273.

FORINSIC. In old English law. Exterior; foreign; extraordinary In feudal law, the term "forinsic services" comprehended the payment of extraordinary aids or the rendition of extraordinary military services, and in this sense was opposed to "intrinsic services." 1 Reeve, Eng. Law, 273.

FORIS. Abroad; out of doors; on the outside of a place; without; extrinsic.

FORISBANITUS. In old English law. Banished.

FORISFACERE. Lat. To forfeit; to lose an estate or other property on account of some criminal or illegal act. To confiscate.

To act beyond the law, *i. e.,* to transgress or infringe the law; to commit an offense or wrong; to do any act against or beyond the law. See Co. Litt. 59a; Du Cange; Spelman.

Forisfacere, i. e., **extra legem seu consuetudinem facere.** Co. Litt. 59. *Forisfacere, i. e.,* to do something beyond law or custom.

FORISFACTUM. Forfeited. *Bona forisfacta,* forfeited goods. 1 Bl. Comm. 299. A crime. Du Cange; Spelman.

FORISFACTURA. A crime or offense through which property is forfeited.

A fine or punishment in money.

Forfeiture. The loss of property or life in consequence of crime.

Forisfactura plena. A forfeiture of all a man's property. Things which were forfeited. Du Cange; Spelman.

FORISFACTUS. A criminal. One who has forfeited his life by commission of a capital offense. Spelman.

Forisfactus servus. A slave who has been a free man, but has forfeited his freedom by crime. Du Cange.

FORISFAMILIARE. In old English and Scotch law. Literally, to put out of a family, (*foris familiam ponere.*) To portion off a son, so that he could have no further claim upon his father. Glanv. lib. 7, c. 3.

To emancipate, or free from paternal authority.

FORISFAMILIATED. In old English law. Portioned off. A son was said to be forisfamiliated (*forisfamiliari*) if his father assigned him part of his land, and gave him seisin thereof, and did this at the request or with the free consent of the son himself, who expressed himself satisfied with such portion. 1 Reeve, Eng. Law, 42, 110.

FORISFAMILIATUS. In old English law. Put out of a family; portioned off; emancipated; forisfamiliated. Bract. fol. 64.

FORISJUDICATIO. In old English law. Forejudger. A forejudgment. A judgment of court whereby a man is put out of possession of a thing. Co. Litt. 100b.

FORISJUDICATUS. Forejudged; sent from court; banished. Deprived of a thing by judgment of court. Bract. fol. 250*b;* Co. Litt. 100*b;* Du Cange.

FORISJURARE. To forswear; to abjure; to abandon. *Forisjurare parentilam.* To remove oneself from parental authority. The person who did this lost his rights as heir. Du Cange.

Provinciam forisjurare. To forswear the country. Spelman.

FORJUDGE. See FOREJUDGE.

FORJURER. L. Fr. In old English law. To forswear; to abjure. *Forjurer royalme,* to abjure the realm. Britt. cc. 1, 16.

FORLER-LAND. Land in the diocese of Hereford, which had a peculiar custom attached to it, but which has been long since disused, although the name is retained. But. Surv. 56.

FORM. 1. A model or skeleton of an instrument to be used in a judicial proceeding, containing the principal necessary matters, the proper technical terms or phrases, and whatever else is necessary to make it formally correct, arranged in proper and methodical order, and capable of being adapted to the circumstances of the specific case.

2. As distinguished from "substance," "form" means the legal or technical manner or order to be observed in legal instruments or juridical proceedings, or in the construction of legal documents or processes.

The distinction between "form" and "substance" is often important in reference to the validity or amendment of pleadings. If the matter of the plea is bad or insufficient, irrespective of the manner of setting it forth, the defect is one of substance. If the matter of the plea is good and sufficient, but is inartificially or defectively pleaded, the defect is one of form.

FORMA. Form; the prescribed form of judicial proceedings. *Forma et figura judicii,* the form and shape of judgment or judicial action. 3 Bl. Comm. 271.

Forma dat esse. Form gives being. Called "the old physical maxim." Lord Henley, Ch., 2 Eden, 99.

Forma legalis forma essentialis. Legal form is essential form. 10 Coke, 100.

Forma non observata, infertur adnullatio actus. Where form is not observed, a nullity of the act is inferred. 12 Coke, 7. Where the law prescribes a form, the non-observance of it is fatal to the proceeding, and the whole becomes a nullity. Best, Ev. Introd. § 59.

FORMA PAUPERIS. See IN FORMA PAUPERIS.

FORMALITIES. In England, robes worn by the magistrates of a city or corporation, etc., on solemn occasions. Enc. Lond.

FORMALITY. The conditions, in regard to method, order, arrangement, use of technical expressions, performance of specific acts, etc., which are required by the law in the making of contracts or conveyances, or in the taking of legal proceedings, to insure their validity and regularity.

FORMATA. In canon law. Canonical letters. Spelman.

FORMATA BREVIA. Formed writs; writs of form. See BREVIA FORMATA.

FORMED ACTION. An action for which a set form of words is prescribed, which must be strictly adhered to. 10 Mod. 140, 141.

FORMEDON. An ancient writ in English law which was available for one who had a right to lands or tenements by virtue of a gift in tail. It was in the nature of a writ of right, and was the highest action that a tenant in tail could have; for he could not have an absolute writ of right, that being confined to such as claimed in fee-simple, and for that reason this writ of formedon was granted to him by the statute *de donis,* Westm. 2, (13 Edw. I. c. 1,) and was emphatically called "his" writ of right. The writ was distinguished into three species, viz.: Formedon in the descender, in the remainder, and in the reverter. It was abolished in England by St. 3 & 4 Wm. IV. c. 27. See 3 Bl. Comm. 191; Co. Litt. 316; Fitzh. Nat. Brev. 255.

FORMEDON IN THE DESCENDER. A writ of formedon which lay where a gift was made in tail, and the tenant in tail aliened the lands or was disseised of them and died, for the heir in tail to recover them, against the actual tenant of the freehold. 3 Bl. Comm. 192.

FORMEDON IN THE REMAINDER. A writ of formedon which lay where a man gave lands to another for life or in tail, with remainder to a third person in tail or in fee, and he who had the particular estate died without issue inheritable, and a stranger intruded upon him in remainder, and kept him out of possession. In this case he in *remainder,* or his heir, was entitled to this writ. 3 Bl. Comm. 192.

FORMEDON IN THE REVERTER.
A writ of formedon which lay where there was a gift in tail, and afterwards, by the death of the donee or his heirs without issue of his body, the reversion fell in upon the donor, his heirs or assigns. In such case, the *reversioner* had this writ to recover the lands. 3 Bl. Comm. 192.

FORMELLA. A certain weight of above 70 lbs., mentioned in 51 Hen. III. Cowell.

FORMER ADJUDICATION, or FORMER RECOVERY. An adjudication or recovery in a former action. See RES JUDICATA.

FORMIDO PERICULI. Lat. Fear of danger. 1 Kent, Comm. 23.

FORMS OF ACTION. The general designation of the various species or kinds of personal actions known to the common law, such as trover, trespass, debt, *assumpsit*, etc. These differ in their pleadings and evidence, as well as in the circumstances to which they are respectively applicable.

FORMULA. In common-law practice, a set form of words used in judicial proceedings. In the civil law, an action. Calvin.

FORMULÆ. In Roman law. When the *legis actiones* were proved to be inconvenient, a mode of procedure called *"per formulas,"* (*i. e.*, by means of *formulæ*,) was gradually introduced, and eventually the *legis actiones* were abolished by the *Lex Æbutia*, B. C. 164, excepting in a very few exceptional matters. The *formulæ* were four in number, namely: (1) The *Demonstratio*, wherein the plaintiff stated, *i. e.*, showed, the facts out of which his claim arose; (2) the *Intentio*, where he made his claim against the defendant; (3) the *Adjudicatio*, wherein the judex was directed to assign or adjudicate the property or any portion or portions thereof according to the rights of the parties; and (4) the *Condemnatio*, in which the judex was authorized and directed to condemn or to acquit according as the facts were or were not proved. These *formulæ* were obtained from the magistrate, (*in jure*,) and were thereafter proceeded with before the judex, (*in judicio*.) Brown. See Mackeld. Rom. Law, § 204.

FORMULARIES. Collections of *formulæ*, or forms of forensic proceedings and instruments used among the Franks, and other early continental nations of Europe. Among these the formulary of Marculphus may be mentioned as of considerable interest. Butl. Co. Litt. note 77, lib. 3.

FORNAGIUM. The fee taken by a lord of his tenant, who was bound to bake in the lord's common oven, (*in furno domini*,) or for a commission to use his own.

FORNICATION. Unlawful sexual intercourse between two unmarried persons. Further, if one of the persons be married and the other not, it is fornication on the part of the latter, though adultery for the former. In some jurisdictions, however, by statute, it is adultery on the part of both persons if the woman is married, whether the man is married or not.

FORNIX. Lat. A brothel; fornication.

FORNO. In Spanish law. An oven. Las Partidas, pt. 3, tit. 32, l. 18.

FORO. In Spanish law. The place where tribunals hear and determine causes,—*exercendarum litium locus.*

FOROS In Spanish law. Emphyteutic rents. Schm. Civil Law, 309.

FORPRISE. An exception; reservation; excepted; reserved. Anciently, a term of frequent use in leases and conveyances. Cowell; Blount.
In another sense, the word is taken for any exaction.

FORSCHEL. A strip of land lying next to the highway.

FORSES. Waterfalls. Camden, Brit.

FORSPEAKER. An attorney or advocate in a cause. Blount; Whishaw.

FORSPECA. In old English law. Prolocutor; paranymphus.

FORSTAL. See FORESTALL.

Forstellarius est pauperum depressor et totius communitatis et patriæ publicus inimicus. 3 Inst. 196. A forestaller is an oppressor of the poor, and a public enemy of the whole community and country.

FORSWEAR. In criminal law. To make oath to that which the deponent knows to be untrue. This term is wider in its scope than "perjury," for the latter, as a technical term, includes the idea of the oath being taken before a competent court or officer, and relating to a material issue, which is not implied by the word "forswear."

G

H

I

J

K

L

M

FORT. This term means "something more than a mere military camp, post, or station. The term implies a fortification, or a place protected from attack by some such means as a moat, wall, or parapet." 12 Fed. Rep. 424.

FORTALICE. A fortress or place of strength, which anciently did not pass without a special grant. 11 Hen. VII. c. 18.

FORTALITIUM. In old Scotch law. A fortalice; a castle. Properly a house or tower which has a battlement or a ditch or moat about it.

FORTHCOMING. In Scotch law. The action by which an arrestment (garnishment) is made effectual. It is a decree or process by which the creditor is given the right to demand that the sum arrested be applied for payment of his claim. 2 Kames, Eq. 288, 289; Bell.

FORTHCOMING BOND. A bond given to a sheriff who has levied on property, conditioned that the property shall be forthcoming, i. e., produced, when required. On the giving of such bond, the goods are allowed to remain in the possession of the debtor. 2 Wash. (Va.) 189; 11 Grat. 522; 61 Ga. 520.

The sheriff or other officer levying a writ of *fieri facias*, or distress warrant, may take from the debtor a bond, with sufficient surety, payable to the creditor, reciting the service of such writ or warrant, and the amount due thereon, (including his fee for taking the bond, commissions, and other lawful charges, if any,) with condition that the property shall be forthcoming at the day and place of sale; whereupon such property may be permitted to remain in the possession and at the risk of the debtor. Code Va. 1887, § 3617.

FORTHWITH. As soon as, by reasonable exertion, confined to the object, a thing may be done. Thus, when a defendant is ordered to plead forthwith, he must plead within twenty-four hours. When a statute enacts that an act is to be done "forthwith," it means that the act is to be done within a reasonable time. 1 Chit. Archb. Pr. (12th Ed.) 164.

FORTIA. Force. In old English law. Force used by an accessary, to enable the principal to commit a crime, as by binding or holding a person while another killed him, or by aiding or counseling in any way, or commanding the act to be done. Bract. fols. 138, 138b. According to Lord Coke, *fortia* was a word of art, and properly signified the furnishing of a weapon of force to do the fact, and by force whereof the fact was committed, and he that furnished it was not present when the fact was done. 2 Inst. 182.

FORTIA FRISCA. Fresh force, (*q. v.*)

FORTILITY. In old English law. A fortified place; a castle; a bulwark. Cowell; 11 Hen. VII. c. 18.

FORTIOR. Lat. Stronger. A term applied, in the law of evidence, to that species of presumption, arising from facts shown in evidence, which is strong enough to shift the burden of proof to the opposite party. Burrill, Circ. Ev. 64, 66.

Fortior est custodia legis quam hominis. 2 Rolle, 325. The custody of the law is stronger than that of man.

Fortior et potentior est dispositio legis quam hominis. The disposition of the law is of greater force and effect than that of man. Co. Litt. 234a; Shep. Touch. 302; 15 East, 178. The law in some cases overrides the will of the individual, and renders ineffective or futile his expressed intention or contract. Broom, Max. 697.

FORTIORI. See A FORTIORI.

FORTIS. Strong. *Fortis et sana*, strong and sound; staunch and strong; as a vessel. Townsh. Pl. 227.

FORTLETT. A place or port of some strength; a little fort. Old Nat. Brev. 45.

FORTUIT. In French law. Accidental; fortuitous. *Cas fortuit*, a fortuitous event. *Fortuitment*, accidentally; by chance.

FORTUITOUS. Accidental; undesigned; adventitious. Resulting from unavoidable physical causes.

FORTUITOUS COLLISION. In maritime law. The accidental running foul of vessels. 14 Pet. 112.

FORTUITOUS EVENT. In the civil law. That which happens by a cause which cannot be resisted. An unforseen occurrence, not caused by either of the parties, nor such as they could prevent. In French it is called "*cas fortuit.*" Civil Code La. art. 3556, no. 15.

There is a difference between a fortuitous event, or inevitable accident, and irresistible force. By the former, commonly called the "act of God," is meant any accident produced by physical causes which are irresistible; such as a loss by lightning or storms, by the perils of the seas, by inundations and earthquakes, or by sudden death or illness. By the latter is meant such an interposition of human agency as is, from its nature and power, absolutely uncontrollable. Of this nature are losses occasioned by the inroads of a hostile army, or by public enemies. Story, Bailm. § 25.

FORTUNA. Lat. Fortune; also treasure-trove. Jacob.

Fortunam faciunt judicem. They make fortune the judge. Co. Litt. 167. Spoken of the process of making partition among coparceners by drawing lots for the several purparts.

FORTUNE-TELLERS. Persons pretending or professing to tell fortunes, and punishable as rogues and vagabonds or disorderly persons.

FORTUNIUM. In old English law. A tournament or fighting with spears, and an appeal to fortune therein.

FORTY-DAYS COURT. The court of attachment in forests, or wood-mote court.

FORUM. Lat. A court of justice, or judicial tribunal; a place of jurisdiction; a place where a remedy is sought; a place of litigation. 3 Story, 347.

In Roman law. The market place, or public paved court, in the city of Rome, where such public business was transacted as the assemblies of the people and the judicial trial of causes, and where also elections, markets, and the public exchange were held.

FORUM ACTUS. The forum of the act. The forum of the place where the act was done which is now called in question.

FORUM CONSCIENTIÆ. The forum or tribunal of conscience.

FORUM CONTENTIOSUM. A contentious forum or court; a place of litigation; the ordinary court of justice, as distinguished from the tribunal of conscience. 3 Bl. Comm. 211.

FORUM CONTRACTUS. The forum of the contract; the court of the place where a contract is made; the place where a contract is made, considered as a place of jurisdiction. 2 Kent, Comm. 463.

FORUM DOMESTICUM. A domestic forum or tribunal. The visitatorial power is called a "*forum domesticum*," calculated to determine, *sine strepitu*, all disputes that arise within themselves. 1 W. Bl. 82.

FORUM DOMICILII. The forum or court of the domicile; the domicile of a defendant, considered as a place of jurisdiction. 2 Kent, Comm. 463.

AM.DICT.LAW—33

FORUM ECCLESIASTICUM. An ecclesiastical court. The spiritual jurisdiction, as distinguished from the secular.

FORUM LIGEANTIÆ REI. The forum of defendant's allegiance. The court or jurisdiction of the country to which he owes allegiance.

FORUM ORIGINIS. The court of one's nativity. The place of a person's birth, considered as a place of jurisdiction.

FORUM REGIUM. The king's court. St. Westm. 2, c. 43.

FORUM REI. This term may mean either (1) the forum of the defendant, that is, of his residence or domicile; or (2) the forum of the *res* or thing in controversy, that is, of the place where the property is situated. The ambiguity springs from the fact that *rei* may be the genitive of either *reus* or *res*.

FORUM REI GESTÆ. The forum or court of a *res gesta*, (thing done;) the place where an act is done, considered as a place of jurisdiction and remedy. 2 Kent, Comm. 463.

FORUM REI SITÆ. The court where the thing in controversy is situated. The place where the subject-matter in controversy is situated, considered as a place of jurisdiction. 2 Kent, Comm. 463.

FORUM SECULARE. A secular, as distinguished from an ecclesiastical or spiritual, court.

FORURTH. In old records. A long slip of ground. Cowell.

FORWARDING MERCHANT, or **FORWARDER.** One who receives and forwards goods, taking upon himself the expenses of transportation, for which he receives a compensation from the owners, having no concern in the vessels or wagons by which they are transported, and no interest in the freight, and not being deemed a common carrier, but a mere warehouseman and agent. Story, Bailm. §§ 502, 509.

FOSSA. In the civil law. A ditch; a receptacle of water, made by hand. Dig. 43, 14, 1, 5.

In old English law. A ditch. A pit full of water, in which women committing felony were drowned. A grave or sepulcher. Spelman.

FOSSAGIUM. In old English law. The duty levied on the inhabitants for re pairing the moat or ditch round a fortified town.

FOSSATORUM OPERATIO. In old English law. Fosse-work; or the service of laboring, done by inhabitants and adjoining tenants, for the repair and maintenance of the *ditches* round a city or town, for which some paid a contribution, called *"fossagium."* Cowell.

FOSSATUM. A dyke, ditch, or trench; a place inclosed by a ditch; a moat; a canal.

FOSSE-WAY, or FOSSE. One of the four ancient Roman ways through England. Spelman.

FOSSELLUM. A small ditch. Cowell.

FOSTERING. An ancient custom in Ireland, in which persons put away their children to fosterers. Fostering was held to be a stronger alliance than blood, and the foster children participated in the fortunes of their foster fathers. Mozley & Whitley.

FOSTERLAND. Land given, assigned, or allotted to the finding of food or victuals for any person or persons; as in monasteries for the monks, etc. Cowell; Blount.

FOSTERLEAN. The remuneration fixed for the rearing of a foster child; also the jointure of a wife. Jacob.

FOUJDAR. In Hindu law. Under the Mogul government a magistrate of the police over a large district, who took cognizance of all criminal matters within his jurisdiction, and sometimes was employed as receiver general of the revenues. Wharton.

FOUJDARRY COURT. In Hindu law. A tribunal for administering criminal law.

FOUNDATION. The founding or building of a college or hospital. The incorporation or endowment of a college or hospital is the foundation; and he who endows it with land or other property is the founder.

FOUNDER. The person who endows an eleemosynary corporation or institution, or supplies the funds for its establishment.

FOUNDEROSA. Founderous; out of repair, as a road. Cro. Car. 366.

FOUNDLING. A deserted or exposed infant; a child found without a parent or guardian, its relatives being unknown. It has a settlement in the district where found.

FOUNDLING HOSPITALS. Charitable institutions which exist in most countries for taking care of infants forsaken by their parents, such being generally the offspring of illegal connections. The foundling hospital act in England is the 13 Geo. II. c. 29.

FOUR. In old French law. An oven or bake-house. *Four banal,* an oven, owned by the seignior of the estate, to which the tenants were obliged to bring their bread for baking. Also the proprietary right to maintain such an oven.

FOUR CORNERS. The face of a written instrument. That which is contained on the face of a deed (without any aid from the knowledge of the circumstances under which it is made) is said to be within its four corners, because every deed is still supposed to be written on one entire skin, and so to have but four corners.

To look at the *four corners* of an instrument is to examine the whole of it, so as to construe it as a whole, without reference to any one part more than another. 2 Smith, Lead. Cas. 295.

FOUR SEAS. The seas surrounding England. These were divided into the Western, including the Scotch and Irish; the Northern, or North sea; the Eastern, being the German ocean; the Southern, being the British channel.

FOURCHER. Fr. To fork. This was a method of delaying an action anciently resorted to by defendants when two of them were joined in the suit. Instead of appearing together, each would appear in turn and cast an essoin for the other, thus postponing the trial.

FOURCHING. The act of delaying legal proceedings. Termes de la Ley.

FOURIERISM. A form of socialism. See 1 Mill, Pol. Ec. 260.

FOWLS OF WARREN. Such fowls as are preserved under the game laws in warrens. According to Manwood, these are partridges and pheasants. According to Coke, they are partridges, rails, quails, woodcocks, pheasants, mallards, and herons. Co. Litt. 233.

FOX'S LIBEL ACT. In English law. This was the statute 52 Geo. III. c. 60, which secured to juries, upon the trial of indictments for libel, the right of pronouncing a general verdict of guilty or not guilty upon the whole matter in issue, and no longer bound them to find a verdict of guilty on proof of the publication of the paper charged to be a libel, and of the sense ascribed to it in the indictment. Wharton.

FOY. L. Fr. Faith; allegiance; fidelity.

FRACTIO. A breaking; division; fraction; a portion of a thing less than the whole.

FRACTION. A breaking, or breaking up; a fragment or broken part; a portion of a thing, less than the whole.

FRACTION OF A DAY. A portion of a day. The dividing a day. Generally, the law does not allow the fraction of a day. 2 Bl. Comm. 141.

Fractionem diei non recipit lex. Lofft, 572. The law does not take notice of a portion of a day.

FRACTITIUM. Arable land. Mon. Angl.

FRACTURA NAVIUM. The breaking or wreck of ships; the same as *naufragium*, (*q. v.*)

FRAIS. Fr. Expense; charges; costs. *Frais d'un procès*, costs of a suit.

FRAIS DE JUSTICE. In French and Canadian law. Costs incurred incidentally to the action.

FRAIS JUSQU'A BORD. Fr. In French commercial law. Expenses to the board; expenses incurred on a shipment of goods, in packing, cartage, commissions, etc., up to the point where they are actually put on board the vessel. 16 Fed. Rep. 336.

FRANC. A French coin of the value of a little over eighteen cents.

FRANC ALEU. In French feudal law. An allod; a free inheritance; or an estate held free of any services except such as were due to the sovereign.

FRANCHILANUS. A freeman. Chart. Hen. IV. A free tenant. Spelman.

FRANCHISE. A special privilege conferred by government upon an individual, and which does not belong to the citizens of the country generally, of common right. It is essential to the character of a franchise that it should be a grant from the sovereign authority, and in this country no franchise can be held which is not derived from a law of the state. See Ang. & A. Corp. § 104; 3 Kent, Comm. 458; 2 Bl. Comm. 37.

In England, a franchise is defined to be a royal privilege in the hands of a subject. In this country, it is a privilege of a public nature, which cannot be exercised without a legislative grant. 45 Mo. 17.

A franchise is a privilege or immunity of a public nature, which cannot be legally exercised without legislative grant. To be a corporation is a franchise. The various powers conferred on corporations are franchises. The execution of a policy of insurance by an insurance company, and the issuing a bank-note by an incorporated bank, are franchises. 15 Johns. 387.

The word "franchise" has various significations, both in a legal and popular sense. A corporation is itself a franchise belonging to the members of the corporation, and the corporation, itself a franchise, may hold other franchises. So, also, the different powers of a corporation, such as the right to hold and dispose of property, are its franchises. In a popular sense, the political rights of subjects and citizens are franchises, such as the right of suffrage, etc. 32 N. H. 484.

The term "franchise" has several significations, and there is some confusion in its use. When used with reference to corporations, the better opinion, deduced from the authorities, seems to be that it consists of the entire privileges embraced in and constituting the grant. It does not embrace the property acquired by the exercise of the franchise. 36 Conn. 255.

The term is also used, in a popular sense, to denote a political right or privilege belonging to a free citizen; as the "elective franchise."

FRANCIA. France. Bract. fol. 427*b*.

FRANCIGENA. A man born in France. A designation formerly given to aliens in England.

FRANCUS. Free; a freeman; a Frank. Spelman.

FRANCUS BANCUS. Free bench, (*q. v.*)

FRANCUS HOMO. In old European law. A free man. Domesday.

FRANCUS PLEGIUS. In old English law. A frank pledge, or free pledge. See FRANK-PLEDGE.

FRANCUS TENENS. A freeholder. See FRANK-TENEMENT.

FRANK, *v.* To send matter through the public mails free of postage, by a personal or official privilege.

FRANK, *adj.* In old English law. Free. Occurring in several compounds.

FRANK-ALMOIGNE. In English law. Free alms. A spiritual tenure whereby religious corporations, aggregate or sole, held lands of the donor to them and their successors forever. They were discharged of all other except religious services, and the *trinoda necessitas*. It differs from tenure by divine service, in that the latter required the performance of certain divine services, whereas the former, as its name imports, is free. This tenure is expressly excepted in the 12 Car. II. c. 24, § 7, and therefore still subsists in some few instances. 2 Broom & H. Comm. 203.

FRANK BANK. In old English law. Free bench. Litt. § 166; Co. Litt. 110*b*. See FREE-BENCH.

FRANK-CHASE. A liberty of free chase enjoyed by any one, whereby all other persons having ground within that compass are forbidden to cut down wood, etc., even in their own demesnes, to the prejudice of the owner of the liberty. Cowell. See CHASE.

FRANK-FEE. Freehold lands exempted from all services, but not from homage; lands held otherwise than in ancient demesne.

That which a man holds to himself and his heirs, and not by such service as is required in ancient demesne, according to the custom of the manor. Cowell.

FRANK FERM. In English law. A species of estate held in socage, said by Britton to be "lands and tenements whereof the nature of the fee is changed by feoffment out of chivalry for certain yearly services, and in respect whereof neither homage, ward, marriage, nor relief can be demanded." Britt. c. 66; 2 Bl. Comm. 80.

FRANK-FOLD. In old English law. Free-fold; a privilege for the lord to have all the sheep of his tenants and the inhabitants within his seigniory, in his fold, in his demesnes, to manure his land. Keilw. 198.

FRANK-LAW. An obsolete expression signifying the rights and privileges of a citizen, or the liberties and civic rights of a freeman.

FRANK-MARRIAGE. A species of entailed estates, in English law, now grown out of use, but still capable of subsisting. When tenements are given by one to another, together with a wife, who is a daughter or cousin of the donor, to hold in frank-marriage, the donees shall have the tenements to them and the heirs of their two bodies begotten, *i. e.*, in special tail. For the word "frank-marriage," *ex vi termini*, both creates and limits an inheritance, not only supplying words of descent, but also terms of procreation. The donees are liable to no service except fealty, and a reserved rent would be void, until the fourth degree of consanguinity be passed between the issues of the donor and donee, when they were capable by the law of the church of intermarrying. Litt. § 19; 2 Bl. Comm. 115.

FRANK-PLEDGE. In old English law. A pledge or surety for freemen; that is, the pledge, or corporate responsibility, of all the inhabitants of a tithing for the general good behavior of each free-born citizen above the age of fourteen, and for his being forthcoming to answer any infraction of the law. Termes de la Ley; Cowell.

FRANK-TENANT. A freeholder. Litt. § 91.

FRANK-TENEMENT. In English law. A free tenement, freeholding, or freehold. 2 Bl. Comm. 61, 62, 104; 1 Steph. Comm. 217; Bract. fol. 207. Used to denote both the tenure and the estate.

FRANKING PRIVILEGE. The privilege of sending certain matter through the public mails without payment of postage, in pursuance of a personal or official privilege.

FRANKLEYN, (spelled, also, "Francling" and "Franklin.") A freeman; a freeholder; a gentleman. Blount; Cowell.

FRASSETUM. In old English law. A wood or wood-ground where ash-trees grow. Co. Litt. 4*b*.

FRATER. In the civil law. A brother. *Frater consanguineus*, a brother having the same father, but born of a different mother. *Frater uterinus*, a brother born of the same mother, but by a different father. *Frater nutricius*, a bastard brother.

Frater fratri uterino non succedet in hæreditate paterna. A brother shall not succeed a uterine brother in the paternal inheritance. 2 Bl. Comm. 223; Fortes. de Laud. c. 5. A maxim of the common law of England, now superseded by the statute 3 & 4 Wm. IV. c. 106, § 9. See Broom, Max. 530.

FRATERIA. In old records. A fraternity, brotherhood, or society of religious persons, who were mutually bound to pray for the good health and life, etc., of their living brethren, and the souls of those that were dead. Cowell.

FRATERNIA. A fraternity or brotherhood.

FRATERNITY. "Some people of a place united together, in respect of a mystery and business, into a company." 1 Salk. 193.

FRATRES CONJURATI. Sworn brothers or companions for the defense of their sovereign, or for other purposes. Hoved. 445.

FRATRES PYES. In old English law. Certain friars who wore white and black garments. Walsingham, 124.

FRATRIAGE. A younger brother's inheritance.

FRATRICIDE. One who has killed a brother or sister; also the killing of a brother or sister.

FRAUD. Fraud consists of some deceitful practice or willful device, resorted to with intent to deprive another of his right, or in some manner to do him an injury. As distinguished from negligence, it is always positive, intentional. 3 Denio, 232.

Fraud, as applied to contracts, is the cause of an error bearing on a material part of the contract, created or continued by artifice, with design to obtain some unjust advantage to the one party, or to cause an inconvenience or loss to the other. Civil Code La. art. 1847.

Fraud, in the sense of a court of equity, properly includes all acts, omissions, and concealments which involve a breach of legal or equitable duty, trust, or confidence justly reposed, and are injurious to another, or by which an undue and unconscientious advantage is taken of another. 1 Story, Eq. Jur. § 187.

The unlawful appropriation of another's property, with knowledge, by design and without criminal intent. Bac. Abr.

Fraud may be *actual* or *constructive.* Actual fraud consists in any kind of artifice by which another is deceived. Constructive fraud consists in any act of omission or commission contrary to legal or equitable duty, trust, or confidence justly reposed, which is contrary to good conscience and operates to the injury of another. The former implies moral guilt; the latter may be consistent with innocence. Code Ga. 1882, § 3173. Actual fraud is otherwise called "fraud in fact." Constructive fraud is also called "fraud in law."

Actual or *positive fraud* includes cases of the intentional and successful employment of any cunning, deception, or artifice, used to circumvent, cheat, or deceive another. 1 Story, Eq. Jur. § 186.

Actual fraud or fraud in fact consists in the in-

tention to prevent creditors from recovering their just debts by an act which withdraws the property of a debtor from their reach. Fraud in law consists in acts which, though not fraudulently intended, yet, as their tendency is to defraud creditors if they vest the property of the debtor in his grantee, are void for legal fraud, and fraudulent in themselves, the policy of the law making the acts illegal. Actual fraud is always a question for the jury; legal fraud, where the facts are undisputed or are ascertained, is for the court. 64 Pa. St. 356.

The modes of fraud are infinite, and it has been said that courts of equity have never laid down what shall constitute fraud, or any general rule, beyond which they will not go, on the ground of fraud. Fraud is, however, usually divided into two large classes,—actual fraud and constructive fraud. An actual fraud may be defined to be something said, done, or omitted by a person with the design of perpetrating what he must have known to be a positive fraud. Constructive frauds are acts, statements, or omissions which operate as virtual frauds on individuals, or which, if generally permitted, would be prejudicial to the public welfare, and yet may have been unconnected with any selfish or evil design; as, for instance, bonds and agreements entered into as a reward for using influence over another, to induce him to make a will for the benefit of the obligor. For such contracts encourage a spirit of artifice and scheming, and tend to deceive and injure others. Smith, Man. Eq.

Synonyms. The term "fraud" is sometimes used as synonymous with "covin," "collusion," or "deceit." But distinctions are properly taken in the meanings of these words, for which reference may be had to the titles COVIN; COLLUSION; DECEIT.

FRAUD IN FACT. Actual, positive, intentional fraud. Fraud disclosed by matters of fact, as distinguished from constructive fraud or fraud in law.

FRAUD IN LAW. Fraud in contemplation of law; fraud implied or inferred by law; fraud made out by construction of law, as distinguished from fraud found by a jury from matter of fact; constructive fraud, (*q. v.*) See 2 Kent, Comm. 512-532.

FRAUDARE. In the civil law. To deceive, cheat, or impose upon; to defraud.

FRAUDS, STATUTE OF. This is the common designation of a very celebrated English statute, (29 Car. II. c. 3,) passed in 1677, and which has been adopted, in a more or less modified form, in nearly all of the United States. Its chief characteristic is the provision that no suit or action shall be maintained on certain classes of contracts or engagements unless there shall be a note or memorandum thereof in writing signed by the party to be charged or by his authorized agent. Its object was to close the door to the numerous frauds which were believed to be perpetrated, and the perjuries which were believed to be committed, when such obligations could be enforced upon no other evidence than the mere recollection of witnesses. It is more fully named as the "statute of frauds and perjuries."

FRAUDULENT CONVEYANCE. A conveyance or transfer of property, the object of which is to defraud a creditor, or hinder or delay him, or to put such property beyond his reach.

Every transfer of property or charge thereon made, every obligation incurred, and every judicial proceeding taken with intent to delay or defraud any creditor or other person of his demands, is void against all creditors of the debtor, and their successors in interest, and against any person upon whom the estate of the debtor devolves in trust for the benefit of others than the debtor. Civil Code Cal. § 3439.

A transfer made by a person indebted or in embarrassed circumstances, which was intended or will necessarily operate to defeat the right of his creditors to have the property applied to the payment of their demands. Abbott.

FRAUDULENT CONVEYANCES, STATUTES OF, OR AGAINST. The name given to two celebrated English statutes,—the statute 13 Eliz. c. 5, made perpetual by 29 Eliz. c. 5; and the statute 27 Eliz. c. 4, made perpetual by 29 Eliz. c. 18.

FRAUDULENT PREFERENCES. In English law. Every conveyance or transfer of property or charge thereon made, every judgment made, every obligation incurred, and every judicial proceeding taken or suffered by any person unable to pay his debts as they become due from his own moneys, in favor of any creditor, with a view of giving such creditor a preference over other creditors, shall be deemed fraudulent and void if the debtor become bankrupt within three months. 32 & 33 Vict. c. 71, § 92.

FRAUNC, FRAUNCHE, FRAUNKE. See FRANK.

FRAUNCHISE. L. Fr. A franchise.

FRAUS. Lat. Fraud. More commonly called, in the civil law, "*dolus*" and "*dolus malus*," (*q. v.*) A distinction, however, was sometimes made between "*fraus*" and "*dolus*;" the former being held to be of the most extensive import. Calvin.

FRAUS DANS LOCUM CONTRAC-TUI. Lat. A misrepresentation or conceal-ment of some fact that is material to the contract, and had the truth regarding which been known the contract would not have been made as made, is called a "fraud *dans locum contractui;*" i. e., a fraud occasioning the contract, or giving place or occasion for the contract.

Fraus est celare fraudem. It is a fraud to conceal a fraud. 1 Vern. 240; 1 Story, Eq. Jur. §§ 389, 390.

Fraus est odiosa et non præsumenda. Fraud is odious, and not to be presumed. Cro. Car. 550.

Fraus et dolus nemini patrocinari debent. Fraud and deceit should defend or excuse no man. 3 Coke, 78; Fleta, lib. 1, c. 13, § 15; Id. lib. 6, c. 6, § 5.

Fraus et jus nunquam cohabitant. Wing. 680. Fraud and justice never dwell together.

Fraus latet in generalibus. Fraud lies hid in general expressions.

FRAUS LEGIS. Lat. In the civil law. Fraud of law; fraud upon law. See IN FRAUDEM LEGIS.

Fraus meretur fraudem. Plowd. 100. Fraud merits fraud.

FRAXINETUM. In old English law. A wood of ashes; a place where ashes grow. Co. Litt. 4b; Shep. Touch. 95.

FRAY. See AFFRAY.

FRECTUM. In old English law. Freight. *Quoad frectum navium suarum,* as to the freight of his vessels. Blount.

FREDNITE. In old English law. A liberty to hold courts and take up the fines for beating and wounding. To be free from fines. Cowell.

FREDSTOLE. Sanctuaries; seats of peace.

FREDUM. A fine paid for obtaining pardon when the peace had been broken. Spelman; Blount. A sum paid the magistrate for protection against the right of revenge.

FREE. 1. Unconstrained; having power to follow the dictates of his own will. Not subject to the dominion of another. Not compelled to involuntary servitude. Used in this sense as opposed to "slave."

2. Not bound to service for a fixed term of

years; in distinction to being bound as an apprentice.

3. Enjoying full civic rights.

4. Available to all citizens alike without charge; as a free school.

5. Available for public use without charge or toll; as a free bridge.

6. Not despotic; assuring liberty; defending individual rights against encroachment by any person or class; instituted by a free people; said of governments, institutions, etc. Webster.

7. Certain, and also consistent with an honorable degree in life; as free services, in the feudal law.

8. Confined to the person possessing, instead of being shared with others; as a free fishery.

9. Not engaged in a war as belligerent or ally; neutral; as in the maxim, "Free ships make free goods."

FREE ALMS. The name of a species of tenure. See FRANK-ALMOIGNE.

FREE-BENCH. A widow's dower out of copyholds to which she is entitled by the custom of some manors. It is regarded as an excrescence growing out of the husband's interest, and is indeed a continuance of his estate. Wharton.

FREE-BORD. In old records. An allowance of land over and above a certain limit or boundary, as so much beyond or without a fence. Cowell; Blount.

The right of claiming that quantity. Termes de la Ley.

FREE BOROUGH MEN. Such great men as did not engage, like the frank-pledge men, for their decennier. Jacob.

FREE CHAPEL. In English ecclesiastical law. A place of worship, so called because not liable to the visitation of the ordinary. It is always of royal foundation, or founded at least by private persons to whom the crown has granted the privilege. 1 Burn, Ecc. Law, 298.

FREE COURSE. In admiralty law. A vessel having the wind from a favorable quarter is said to sail on a "free course."

FREE ENTRY, EGRESS, AND REGRESS. An expression used to denote that a person has the right to go on land again and again as often as may be reasonably necessary. Thus, in the case of a tenant entitled to emblements.

FREE FISHERY. A franchise in the hands of a subject, existing by grant or prescription, distinct from an ownership in the soil. It is an exclusive right, and applies to a public navigable river, without any right in the soil. 3 Kent, Comm. 410.

FREE ON BOARD. A sale of goods "free on board" imports that they are to be delivered on board the cars, vessel, etc., without expense to the buyer for packing, cartage, or other such charges.

In a contract for sale and delivery of goods "free on board" vessel, the seller is under no obligation to act until the buyer names the ship to which the delivery is to be made. 117 Pa. St. 508, 12 Atl. Rep. 32.

FREE SERVICES. In feudal and old English law. Such feudal services as were not unbecoming the character of a soldier or a freeman to perform; as to serve under his lord in the wars, to pay a sum of money, and the like. 2 Bl. Comm. 60, 61.

FREE SHIPS. In international law. Ships of a neutral nation. The phrase "free ships shall make free goods" is often inserted in treaties, meaning that goods, even though belonging to an enemy, shall not be seized or confiscated, if found in neutral ships. Wheat. Int. Law, 507, et seq.

FREE SOCAGE. In English law. A tenure of lands by certain free and honorable services, (such as fealty and rent,) and which are liquidated and reduced to a certainty. It was called "*free* socage" because the services were not only free, but honorable; whereas in *villein* socage the services, though certain, were of a baser nature. 2 Bl. Comm. 78, 79.

FREE SOCMEN. In old English law. Tenants in free socage. Glanv. lib. 3, c. 7; 2 Bl. Comm. 79.

FREE TENURE. Tenure by free services; freehold tenure.

FREE WARREN. A franchise for the preserving and custody of beasts and fowls of warren. 2 Bl. Comm. 39, 417; Co. Litt. 233. This franchise gave the grantee sole right of killing, so far as his warren extended, on condition of excluding other persons. 2 Bl. Comm. 39.

FREEDMAN. In Roman law. One who was set free from a state of bondage; an emancipated slave. The word is used in the same sense in the United States, respecting negroes who were formerly slaves.

G

H

I

J

K

L

M

FREEDOM. The state of being free; liberty; self-determination; absence of restraint; the opposite of slavery.

The power of acting, in the character of a moral personality, according to the dictates of the will, without other check, hindrance, or prohibition than such as may be imposed by just and necessary laws and the duties of social life.

The prevalence, in the government and constitution of a country, of such a system of laws and institutions as secure civil liberty to the individual citizen.

FREEHOLD. An estate in land or other real property, of uncertain duration; that is, either of inheritance or which may possibly last for the life of the tenant at the least, (as distinguished from a leasehold;) and held by a free tenure, (as distinguished from copyhold or villeinage.)

Such an interest in lands of frank-tenement as may endure not only during the owner's life, but which is cast after his death upon the persons who successively represent him, according to certain rules elsewhere explained. Such persons are called "heirs," and he whom they thus represent, the "ancestor." When the interest extends beyond the ancestor's life, it is called a "freehold of inheritance," and, when it only endures for the ancestor's life, it is a freehold not of inheritance.

An estate to be a freehold must possess these two qualities: (1) Immobility, that is, the property must be either land or some interest issuing out of or annexed to land; and (2) indeterminate duration, for, if the utmost period of time to which an estate can endure be fixed and determined, it cannot be a freehold. Wharton.

FREEHOLD IN LAW. A freehold which has descended to a man, upon which he may enter at pleasure, but which he has not entered on. Termes de la Ley.

FREEHOLD LAND SOCIETIES. Societies in England designed for the purpose of enabling mechanics, artisans, and other working-men to purchase at the least possible price a piece of freehold land of a sufficient yearly value to entitle the owner to the elective franchise for the county in which the land is situated. Wharton.

FREEHOLDER. A person who possesses a freehold estate.

FREEMAN. This word has had various meanings at different stages of history. In the Roman law, it denoted one who was either born free or emancipated, and was the opposite of "slave." In feudal law, it designated an allodial proprietor, as distinguished from a vassal or feudal tenant. In old English law, the word described a freeholder or tenant by free services; one who was not a villein. In modern legal phraseology, it is the appellation of a member of a city or borough having the right of suffrage, or a member of any municipal corporation invested with full civic rights.

A person in the possession and enjoyment of all the civil and political rights accorded to the people under a free government.

FREEMAN'S ROLL. A list of persons admitted as burgesses or freemen for the purposes of the rights reserved by the municipal corporation act, (5 & 6 Wm. IV. c. 76.) Distinguished from the Burgess Roll. 3 Steph. Comm. 197. The term was used, in early colonial history, in some of the American colonies.

FREIGHT. Freight is properly the price or compensation paid for the transportation of goods by a carrier, at sea, from port to port. But the term is also used to denote the hire paid for the carriage of goods on land from place to place, (usually by a railroad company, not an express company,) or on inland streams or lakes. The name is also applied to the goods or merchandise transported by any of the above means.

Property carried is called "freight;" the reward, if any, to be paid for its carriage is called "freightage;" the person who delivers the freight to the carrier is called the "consignor;" and the person to whom it is to be delivered is called the "consignee." Civil Code Cal. § 2110; Civil Code Dak. § 1220.

The term "freight" has several different meanings, as the price to be paid for the carriage of goods, or for the hire of a vessel under a charter-party or otherwise; and sometimes it designates goods carried, as "a freight of lime," or the like. But, as a subject of insurance, it is used in one of the two former senses. 10 Gray, 109.

The sum agreed on for the hire of a ship, entirely or in part, for the carriage of goods from one port to another. 13 East, 300. All rewards or compensation paid for the use of ships. 1 Pet. Adm. 206.

Freight is a compensation received for the transportation of goods and merchandise from port to port; and is never claimable by the owner of the vessel until the voyage has been performed and terminated. 7 Gill & J. 300.

"Dead freight" is money payable by a person who has chartered a ship and only partly loaded her, in respect of the loss of freight caused to the ship-owner by the deficiency of cargo. L. R. 2 H. L. Sc. 128.

Freight is the mother of wages. 2 Show. 283; 3 Kent, Comm. 196. Where a voyage is broken up by *vis major*, and no freight earned, no wages, *eo nomine*, are due.

FREIGHTER. In maritime law. The party by whom a vessel is engaged or chartered; otherwise called the "charterer." 2 Steph. Comm. 148. In French law, the owner of a vessel is called the "freighter," (*freteur;*) the merchant who hires it is called the "affreighter," (*affreteur.*) Emerig. Tr. des Ass. ch. 11, § 3.

FRENCHMAN. In early times, in English law, this term was applied to every stranger or "outlandish" man. Bract. lib. 3, tr. 2, c. 15.

FRENDLESMAN. Sax. An outlaw. So called because on his outlawry he was denied all help of friends after certain days. Cowell; Blount.

FRENDWITE. In old English law. A mulct or fine exacted from him who harbored an outlawed friend. Cowell; Tomlins.

FRENETICUS. In old English law. A madman, or person in a frenzy. Fleta, lib. 1, c. 36.

FREOBORGH. A free-surety, or free-pledge. Spelman. See FRANK-PLEDGE.

FREQUENT, *v.* To visit often; to resort to often or habitually. 109 Ind. 176, 9 N. E. Rep. 781.

Frequentia actus multum operatur. The frequency of an act effects much. 4 Coke, 78; Wing. Max. p. 719, max. 192. A continual usage is of great effect to establish a right.

FRERE. A brother. *Frere eyne,* elder brother. *Frere puisne,* younger brother. Britt. c. 75.

FRESCA. In old records. Fresh water, or rain and land flood.

FRESH DISSEISIN. By the ancient common law, where a man had been disseised, he was allowed to right himself by force, by ejecting the disseisor from the premises, without resort to law, provided this was done forthwith, while the disseisin was *fresh,* (*flagrante disseisina.*) Bract. fol. 162b. No particular time was limited for doing this, but Bracton suggested it should be fifteen days. Id. fol. 163. See Britt. cc. 32, 43, 44, 65.

FRESH FINE. In old English law. A fine that had been levied within a year past. St. Westm. 2, c. 45; Cowell.

FRESH FORCE. Force done within forty days. Fitzh. Nat. Brev. 7; Old Nat. Brev. 4. The heir or reversioner in a case of disseisin by *fresh force* was allowed a remedy in chancery by bill before the mayor. Cowell.

FRESH PURSUIT. A pursuit instituted immediately, and with intent to reclaim or recapture, after an animal escaped, a thief flying with stolen goods, etc.

FRESH SUIT. In old English law. Immediate and unremitting pursuit of an escaping thief. "Such a present and earnest following of a robber as never ceases from the time of the robbery until apprehension. The party pursuing then had back again his goods, which otherwise were forfeited to the crown." Staundef. P. C. lib. 3, cc. 10, 12; 1 Bl. Comm. 297.

FRESHET. A flood, or overflowing of a river, by means of rains or melted snow; an inundation. 3 Phila. 42.

FRET. Fr. In French marine law. Freight. Ord. Mar. liv. 3, tit. 3.

FRETER. Fr. In French marine law. To freight a ship; to let it. Emerig. Tr. des Ass. c. 11, § 3.

FRETEUR. Fr. In French marine law. Freighter. The owner of a ship, who lets it to the merchant. Emerig. Tr. des Ass. c. 11, § 3.

FRETTUM, FRECTUM. In old English law. The freight of a ship; freight money. Cowell.

FRETUM. A strait.

FRETUM BRITANNICUM. The strait between Dover and Calais.

FRIARS. An order of religious persons, of whom there were four principal branches, viz.: (1) Minors, Grey Friars, or Franciscans; (2) Augustines; (3) Dominicans, or Black Friars; (4) White Friars, or Carmelites, from whom the rest descend. Wharton.

FRIBUSCULUM. In the civil law. A temporary separation between husband and wife, caused by a quarrel or estrangement, but not amounting to a divorce, because not accompanied with an intention to dissolve the marriage.

FRIDBORG, FRITHBORG. Frank-pledge. Cowell. Security for the peace. Spelman.

FRIDHBURGUS. In old English law. A kind of frank-pledge, by which the lords or principal men were made responsible for their dependents or servants. Bract. fol. 124*b*.

FRIEND OF THE COURT. See AMICUS CURIÆ.

FRIENDLESS MAN. In old English law. An outlaw; so called because he was denied all help of friends. Bract. lib. 3, tr. 2, c. 12.

FRIENDLY SOCIETIES. In English law. Associations supported by subscription, for the relief and maintenance of the members, or their wives, children, relatives, and nominees, in sickness, infancy, advanced age, widowhood, etc. The statutes regulating these societies were consolidated and amended by St. 38 & 39 Vict. c. 60. Wharton.

FRIENDLY SUIT. A suit brought by a creditor in chancery against an executor or administrator, being really a suit by the executor or administrator, in the name of a creditor, against himself, in order to compel the creditors to take an equal distribution of the assets. 2 Williams, Ex'rs, 1915.

Also any suit instituted by agreement between the parties to obtain the opinion of the court upon some doubtful question in which they are interested.

FRIGIDITY. Impotence. Johnson.

FRILINGI. Persons of free descent, or freemen born; the middle class of persons among the Saxons. Spelman.

FRISCUS. Fresh uncultivated ground. Mon. Angl. t. 2, p. 56. Fresh; not salt. Reg. Orig. 97. Recent or new. See FRESH, and subsequent titles.

FRITHBORG. Frank-pledge. Cowell.

FRITHBOTE. A satisfaction or fine for a breach of the peace.

FRITHBREACH. The breaking of the peace. Cowell.

FRITHGAR. The year of jubilee, or of meeting for peace and friendship. Jacob.

FRITHGILDA. Guildhall; a company or fraternity for the maintenance of peace and security; also a fine for breach of the peace. Jacob.

FRITHMAN. A member of a company or fraternity. Blount.

FRITHSOCNE. Surety of defense. Jurisdiction of the peace. The franchise of preserving the peace. Cowell; Spelman.

FRITHSPLOT. A spot or plot of land, encircling some stone, tree, or well, considered sacred, and therefore affording sanctuary to criminals.

FRIVOLOUS. An answer or plea is called "frivolous" when it is clearly insufficient on its face, and does not controvert the material points of the opposite pleading, and is presumably interposed for mere purposes of delay or to embarrass the plaintiff.

A frivolous demurrer has been defined to be one which is so clearly untenable, or its insufficiency so manifest upon a bare inspection of the pleadings, that its character may be determined without argument or research. 40 Wis. 558.

FRODMORTEL, or FREOMORTEL. An immunity for committing manslaughter. Mon. Angl. t. 1, p. 173.

FRONTAGE—FRONTAGER. In English law a frontager is a person owning or occupying land which abuts on a highway, river, sea-shore, or the like. The term is generally used with reference to the liability of frontagers on streets to contribute towards the expense of paving, draining, or other works on the highway carried out by a local authority, in proportion to the frontage of their respective tenements. Sweet.

FRUCTUARIUS. Lat. In the civil law. One who had the usufruct of a thing; *i. e.*, the use of the fruits, profits, or increase, as of land or animals. Inst. 2, 1, 36, 38. Bracton applies it to a lessee, fermor, or farmer of land, or one who held lands *ad firmam*, for a farm or term. Bract. fol. 261.

FRUCTUS. Lat. In the civil law. Fruit, fruits; produce; profit or increase; the organic productions of a thing. *Fructus fundi*, the fruits of land. *Fructus pecudum*, the produce of flocks.

The right to the fruits of a thing belonging to another.

The compensation which a man receives from another for the use or enjoyment of a thing, such as interest or rent. See Mackeld. Rom. Law, § 167; Inst. 2, 1, 35, 37; Dig. 7, 1, 33; Id. 5, 3, 29; Id. 22, 1, 34.

Fructus augent hæreditatem. The yearly increase goes to enhance the inheritance. Dig. 5, 3, 20, 3.

FRUCTUS CIVILES. (Lat. Civil fruits.) All revenues and recompenses which, though not *fruits*, properly speaking, are recognized as such by the law.

FRUCTUS INDUSTRIALES. Industrial fruits, or fruits of industry. Those fruits of a thing, as of land, which are produced by the labor and industry of the occupant, as crops of grain; as distinguished from such as are produced solely by the powers of nature. Emblements are so called in the common law. 2 Steph. Comm. 258; 1 Chit. Gen. Pr. 92.

FRUCTUS NATURALES. Those products which are produced by the powers of nature alone; as wool, metals, milk, the young of animals.

FRUCTUS PENDENTES. Hanging fruits; those not severed. The fruits united with the thing which produces them. These form a part of the principal thing.

Fructus pendentes pars fundi videntur. Hanging fruits make part of the land. Dig. 6, 1, 44; 2 Bouv. Inst. no. 1578.

Fructus perceptos villæ non esse constat. Gathered fruits do not make a part of the farm. Dig. 19, 1, 17, 1; 2 Bouv. Inst. no. 1578.

FRUCTUS REI ALIENÆ. The fruits of another's property; fruits taken from another's estate.

FRUCTUS SEPARATI. In the civil law. Separate fruits; the fruits of a thing when they are separated from it. Dig. 7, 4, 13.

FRUGES. In the civil law. Anything produced from vines, underwood, chalk-pits, stone-quarries. Dig. 50, 16, 77.
Grains and leguminous vegetables. In a more restricted sense, any esculent growing in pods. Vicat, Voc. Jur.; Calvin.

FRUIT. The produce of a tree or plant which contains the seed or is used for food.
This term, in legal acceptation, is not confined to the produce of those trees which in popular language are called "fruit trees," but applies also to the produce of oak, elm, and walnut trees. 5 Barn. & C. 847.

FRUIT FALLEN. The produce of any possession detached therefrom, and capable of being enjoyed by itself. Thus, a next presentation, when a vacancy has occurred, is a fruit fallen from the advowson. Wharton.

FRUITS OF CRIME. In the law of evidence. Material objects acquired by means and in consequence of the commission of crime, and sometimes constituting the subject-matter of the crime. Burrill, Circ. Ev. 445; 3 Benth. Jud. Ev. 31.

Frumenta quæ sata sunt solo cedere intelliguntur. Grain which is sown is understood to form a part of the soil. Inst. 2, 1, 32.

FRUMENTUM. In the civil law. Grain. That which grows in an ear. Dig. 50, 16, 77.

FRUMGYLD. Sax. The first payment made to the kindred of a slain person in recompense for his murder. Blount.

FRUMSTOLL. Sax. In Saxon law. A chief seat, or mansion house. Cowell.

FRUSCA TERRA. In old records. Uncultivated and desert ground. 2 Mon. Angl. 327; Cowell.

FRUSSURA. A breaking; plowing. Cowell.

Frustra agit qui judicium prosequi nequit cum effectu. He sues to no purpose who cannot prosecute his judgment with effect, [who cannot have the fruits of his judgment.] Fleta, lib. 6, c. 37, § 9.

Frustra [vana] est potentia quæ nunquam venit in actum. That power is to no purpose which never comes into act, or which is never exercised. 2 Coke, 51.

Frustra expectatur eventus cujus effectus nullus sequitur. An event is vainly expected from which no effect follows.

Frustra feruntur leges nisi subditis et obedientibus. Laws are made to no purpose, except for those that are subject and obedient. Branch, Princ.

Frustra fit per plura, quod fieri potest per pauciora. That is done to no purpose by many things which can be done by fewer. Jenk. Cent. p. 68, case 28. The employment of more means or instruments for effecting a thing than are necessary is to no purpose.

Frustra legis auxilium invocat [quærit] qui in legem committit. He vainly invokes the aid of the law who transgresses the law. Fleta, lib. 4, c. 2, § 3; 2 Hale, P. C. 386; Broom, Max. 279, 297.

Frustra petis quod mox es restiturus. In vain you ask that which you will have immediately to restore. 2 Kames, Eq. 104; 5 Man. & G. 757.

Frustra petis quod statim alteri reddere cogeris. Jenk. Cent. 256. You ask

G

H

I

J

K

L

M

in vain that which you might immediately be compelled to restore to another.

Frustra probatur, quod probatum non relevat. That is proved to no purpose which, when proved, does not help. Halk. Lat. Max. 50.

FRUSTRUM TERRÆ. A piece or parcel of land lying by itself. Co. Litt. 5b.

FRUTECTUM. In old records. A place overgrown with shrubs and bushes. Spelman; Blount.

FRUTOS. In Spanish law. Fruits; products; produce; grains; profits. White, New Recop. b. 1, tit. 7, c. 5, § 2

FRYMITH. In old English law. The affording harbor and entertainment to any one.

FRYTHE. Sax. In old English law. A plain between woods. Co. Litt. 5b.
An arm of the sea, or a strait between two lands. Cowell.

FUAGE, FOCAGE. Hearth money. A tax laid upon each fire-place or hearth. An imposition of a shilling for every hearth, levied by Edward III. in the dukedom of Aquitaine. Spelman; 1 Bl. Comm. 324.

FUER. In old English law. Flight. It is of two kinds: (1) *Fuer in fait*, or *in facto*, where a person does apparently and corporally flee; (2) *fuer in ley*, or *in lege*, when, being called in the county court, he does not appear, which legal interpretation makes flight. Wharton.

FUERO. In Spanish law. A law; a code.
A general usage or custom of a province, having the force of law. *Ir contra fuero*, to violate a received custom.
A grant of privileges and immunities. *Conceder fueros*, to grant exemptions.
A charter granted to a city or town. Also designated as "*cartas pueblas.*"
An act of donation made to an individual, a church, or convent, on certain conditions.
A declaration of a magistrate, in relation to taxation, fines, etc.
A charter granted by the sovereign, or those having authority from him, establishing the franchises of towns, cities, etc.
A place where justice is administered.
A peculiar *forum*, before which a party is amenable.
The jurisdiction of a tribunal, which is entitled to take cognizance of a cause; as

fuero ecclesiastico, fuero militar. See Schm. Civil Law, Introd. 64.

FUERO DE CASTILLA. In Spanish law. The body of laws and customs which formerly governed the Castilians.

FUERO DE CORREOS Y CAMINOS. In Spanish law. A special tribunal taking cognizance of all matters relating to the post-office and roads.

FUERO DE GUERRA. In Spanish law. A special tribunal taking cognizance of all matters in relation to persons serving in the army.

FUERO DE MARINA. In Spanish law. A special tribunal taking cognizance of all matters relating to the navy and to the persons employed therein.

FUERO JUZGO. Span. The *Forum Judicium;* a code of laws established in the seventh century for the Visigothic kingdom in Spain. Some of its principles and rules are found surviving in the modern jurisprudence of that country. Schm. Civil Law, Introd. 28.

FUERO MUNICIPAL. In Spanish law. The body of laws granted to a city or town for its government and the administration of justice.

FUERO REAL. The title of a code of Spanish law promulgated by Alphonso the Learned, (*el Sabio*,) A. D. 1255. It was the precursor of the Partidas. Schm. Civil Law, Introd. 67.

FUERO VIEJO. The title of a compilation of Spanish law, published about A. D. 992. Schm. Civil Law, Introd. 65.

FUGA CATALLORUM. In old English law. A drove of cattle. Blount.

FUGACIA. A chase. Blount.

FUGAM FECIT. Lat. He has made flight; he fled. A clause inserted in an inquisition, in old English law, meaning that a person indicted for treason or felony had fled. The effect of this is to make the party forfeit his goods absolutely, and the profits of his lands until he has been pardoned or acquitted.

FUGATOR. In old English law. A privilege to hunt. Blount.
A driver. *Fugatores carrucarum,* drivers of wagons. Fleta, lib. 2, c. 78.

FUGITATE. In Scotch practice. To outlaw, by the sentence of a court; to outlaw for non-appearance in a criminal case. 2 Alis. Crim. Pr. 350.

FUGITATION. In Scotch law. When a criminal does not obey the citation to answer, the court pronounces sentence of fugitation against him, which induces a forfeiture of goods and chattels to the crown.

FUGITIVE FROM JUSTICE. A person who, having committed a crime, flies from the state or country where it transpired, in order to evade arrest and escape justice.

FUGITIVE OFFENDERS. In English law. Where a person accused of any offense punishable by imprisonment, with hard labor for twelve months or more, has left that part of her majesty's dominions where the offense is alleged to have been committed, he is liable, if found in any other part of her majesty's dominions, to be apprehended and returned in manner provided by the fugitive offenders' act, 1881, to the part from which he is a fugitive. Wharton.

FUGITIVE SLAVE. One who, held in bondage, flees from his master's power.

FUGITIVUS. In the civil law. A fugitive; a runaway slave. Dig. 11, 4; Cod. 6, 1. See the various definitions of this word in Dig. 21, 1, 17.

FULL. Complete; exhaustive; detailed. A "full" answer is as extensive a term, in describing one which is ample and sufficient, as though the term "complete" had been superadded. 22 Ala. 817

FULL AGE. In common law. The age of twenty-one years, in males and females. Litt. § 259; 1 Bl. Comm. 463.

In the civil law. The age of twenty-five years, in males and females. Inst. 1, 23, pr.

FULL BLOOD. A term of relation, denoting descent from the same couple. Brothers and sisters of *full blood* are those who are born of the same father and mother, or, as Justinian calls them, "*ex utroque parente conjuncti.*" Nov. 118, cc. 2, 3; Mackeld. Rom. Law, § 145. The more usual term in modern law is "whole blood," (*q. v.*)

FULL COURT. In practice. A court *in banc.* A court duly organized with all the judges present.

FULL DEFENSE. In pleading. The formula of defense in a plea, stated at length and without abbreviation, thus: "And the said C. D., by E. F., his attorney, comes and defends the force (or wrong) and injury when and where it shall behoove him, and the damages, and whatsoever else he ought to defend, and says," etc. Steph. Pl. p. 481.

FULL LIFE. Life in fact and in law. See IN FULL LIFE.

FULL PROOF. In the civil law. Proof by two witnesses, or a public instrument. Hallifax, Civil Law, b. 3, c. 9, nn. 25, 30; 3 Bl. Comm. 370.

Evidence which satisfies the minds of the jury of the truth of the fact in dispute, to the entire exclusion of every reasonable doubt. 38 N. J. Law, 450.

FULL RIGHT. The union of a good title with actual possession.

FULLUM AQUÆ. A fleam, or stream of water. Blount.

FUMAGE. In old English law. The same as *fuage*, or smoke farthings. 1 Bl. Comm. 324. See FUAGE.

FUNCTION. Office; duty; fulfillment of a definite end or set of ends by the correct adjustment of means. The occupation of an office. By the performance of its duties, the officer is said to fill his function. Dig. 32, 65, 1.

FUNCTIONARY. A public officer or employe. An officer of a private corporation is also sometimes so called.

FUNCTUS OFFICIO. Lat. Having fulfilled the function, discharged the office, or accomplished the purpose, and therefore of no further force or authority. Applied to an officer whose term has expired, and who has consequently no further official authority; and also to an instrument, power, agency, etc., which has fulfilled the purpose of its creation, and is therefore of no further virtue or effect.

FUND, *v.* To capitalize, with a view to the production of interest. 24 N. J. Eq. 376.

To fund a debt is to pledge a specific fund to keep down interest and reduce the principal. When extinguishment of the debt is the object prominently contemplated, the provision is called a "sinking fund." The term "fund" was originally applied to a portion of the national revenue set apart or pledged to the payment of a particular debt. Hence a funded debt was a debt for the payment of the principal or interest of which some fund was appropriated. 14 N. Y. 356, 367, 377; 21 Barb. 294.

FUND, *n.* A sum of money set apart for a specific purpose, or available for the payment of debts or claims.

In its narrower and more usual sense, "fund" signifies "capital," as opposed to "interest" or "income;" as where we speak of a corporation funding the arrears of interest due on its bonds, or the like, meaning that the interest is capitalized and made to bear interest in its turn until it is repaid. Sweet.

FUNDAMENTAL LAW. The law which determines the constitution of government in a state, and prescribes and regulates the manner of its exercise; the organic law of a state; the constitution.

FUNDAMUS. We found. One of the words by which a corporation may be created in England. 1 Bl. Comm. 473; 3 Steph. Comm. 173.

FUNDATIO. A founding or foundation.

FUNDATOR. A founder, (*q. v.*)

FUNDI PATRIMONIALES. Lands of inheritance.

FUNDING SYSTEM. The practice of borrowing money to defray the expenses of government, and creating a "sinking fund," designed to keep down interest, and to effect the gradual reduction of the principal debt.

FUNDITORES. Pioneers. Jacob.

FUNDS. 1. Money in hand; cash; money available for the payment of a debt, legacy, etc.
2. The proceeds of sales of real and personal estate, or the proceeds of any other assets converted into money. 43 N. J. Eq. 533.
3. Corporate stocks or government securities; in this sense usually spoken of as the "funds."
4. Assets, securities, bonds, or revenue of a state or government appropriated for the discharge of its debts.

FUNDUS. In the civil and old English law. Land; land or ground generally; land, without considering its specific use; land, including buildings generally; a farm.

FUNERAL EXPENSES. Money expended in procuring the interment of a corpse.

FUNGIBILES RES. Lat. A term applied in the civil law to things of such a nature as that they could be replaced by equal quantities and qualities, because, *mutua vice funguntur,* they replace and represent each other; thus, a bushel of wheat. A particular horse would not be *fungibilis res.* Sandars, Just. Inst. (5th Ed.) 322.

FUNGIBLE THINGS. Movable goods which may be estimated and replaced according to weight, measure, and number. Things belonging to a class, which do not have to be dealt with *in specie.*

Those things one specimen of which is as good as another, as is the case with half-crowns, or pounds of rice of the same quality. Horses, slaves, and so forth, are non-fungible things, because they differ individually in value, and cannot be exchanged indifferently one for another. Holl. Jur. 88.

Where a thing which is the subject of an obligation (which one man is bound to deliver to another) must be delivered *in specie,* the thing is not fungible; that very individual thing, and not another thing of the same or another class, in lieu of it, must be delivered. Where the subject of the obligation is a thing of a given class, the thing is said to be fungible; *i. e.,* the delivery of any object which answers to the generic description will satisfy the terms of the obligation. Aust. Jur. 483, 484.

FUR. Lat. A thief. One who stole secretly or without force or weapons, as opposed to robber.

FUR MANIFESTUS. Lat. In the civil law. A manifest thief. A thief who is taken in the very act of stealing.

FURANDI ANIMUS. An intention of stealing.

FURCA. A fork. A gallows or gibbet. Bract. fol. 56.

FURCA ET FLAGELLUM. In old English law. Gallows and whip. *Tenure ad furcam et flagellum,* tenure by gallows and whip. The meanest of servile tenures, where the bondman was at the disposal of his lord for life and limb. Cowell.

FURCA ET FOSSA. In old English law. Gallows and pit, or pit and gallows. A term used in ancient charters to signify a jurisdiction of punishing thieves, viz., men by hanging, women by drowning. Spelman; Cowell.

FURIGELDUM. A fine or mulct paid for theft.

Furiosi nulla voluntas est. A madman has no will. Dig. 50, 17, 40; Broom, Max. 314.

FURIOSITY. In Scotch law. Madness, as distinguished from fatuity or idiocy.

FURIOSUS. An insane man; a madman; a lunatic.

Furiosus absentis loco est. A madman is the same with an absent person, [that is, his presence is of no effect.] Dig. 50, 17, 24, 1.

Furiosus nullum negotium contrahere potest. A madman can contract nothing, [can make no contract.] Dig. 50, 17, 5.

Furiosus solo furore punitur. A madman is punished by his madness alone; that is, he is not answerable or punishable for his actions. Co. Litt. 247b; 4 Bl. Comm. 24, 396; Broom, Max. 15.

Furiosus stipulare non potest nec aliquid negotium agere, qui non intelligit quid agit. 4 Coke, 126. A madman who knows not what he does cannot make a bargain, nor transact any business.

FURLINGUS. A furlong, or a furrow one-eighth part of a mile long. Co. Litt. 5b.

FURLONG. A measure of length, being forty poles, or one-eighth of a mile.

FURLOUGH. Leave of absence; especially, leave given to a military or naval officer, or soldier or seaman, to be absent from service for a certain time. Also the document granting leave of absence.

FURNAGE. See FORNAGIUM; FOUR.

FURNITURE. This term includes that which furnishes, or with which anything is furnished or supplied; whatever must be supplied to a house, a room, or the like, to make it habitable, convenient, or agreeable; goods, vessels, utensils, and other appendages necessary or convenient for housekeeping; whatever is added to the interior of a house or apartment, for use or convenience. 27 Ind. 173.

The term "furniture" embraces everything about the house that has been usually enjoyed therewith, including plate, linen, china, and pictures. 41 N. J. Eq. 96.

The word "furniture" made use of in the disposition of the law, or in the conventions or acts of persons, comprehends only such furniture as is intended for use and ornament of apartments, but not libraries which happen to be there, nor plate. Civil Code La. art. 477.

FURNITURE OF A SHIP. This term includes everything with which a ship requires to be furnished or equipped to make her seaworthy; it comprehends all articles furnished by ship-chandlers, which are almost innumerable. 1 Wall. Jr. 369.

FURNIVAL'S INN. Formerly an inn of chancery. See INNS OF CHANCERY.

Furor contrahi matrimonium non sinit, quia consensu opus est. Insanity prevents marriage from being contracted, because consent is needed. Dig. 23, 2, 16, 2;

1 Ves. & B. 140; 1 Bl. Comm. 439; 4 Johns. Ch. 343, 345.

FURST AND FONDUNG. In old English law. Time to advise or take counsel. Jacob.

FURTHER ADVANCE. A second or subsequent loan of money to a mortgagor by a mortgagee, either upon the same security as the original loan was advanced upon, or an additional security. Equity considers the arrears of interest on a mortgage security converted into principal, by agreement between the parties, as a further advance. Wharton.

FURTHER ASSURANCE, COVENANT FOR. One of the usual agreements entered into by a vendor for the protection of the vendee's interest in the subject of purchase. It seems to be confined to an agreement that the grantor will execute any further instruments of conveyance that may be lawfully required, and not to extend to further obligations to be imposed on the covenantor by way of covenant. Sugd. Vend. 500.

FURTHER CONSIDERATION. In English practice, upon a motion for judgment or application for a new trial, the court may, if it shall be of opinion that it has not sufficient materials before it to enable it to give judgment, direct the motion to stand over for *further consideration*, and direct such issues or questions to be tried or determined, and such accounts and inquiries to be taken and made, as it may think fit. Rules Sup. Ct. xl., 10.

FURTHER DIRECTIONS. When a master ordinary in chancery made a report in pursuance of a decree or decretal order, the cause was again set down before the judge who made the decree or order, to be proceeded with. Where a master made a separate report, or one not in pursuance of a decree or decretal order, a petition for consequential directions had to be presented, since the cause could not be set down for further directions under such circumstances. See 2 Daniell, Ch. Pr. (5th Ed.) 1233, note.

FURTHER HEARING. In practice. Hearing at another time.

FURTHER MAINTENANCE OF ACTION, PLEA TO. A plea grounded upon some fact or facts which have arisen since the commencement of the suit, and which the defendant puts forward for the purpose of showing that the plaintiff should not further maintain his action. Brown.

G
H
I
J
K
L
M

FURTIVE. In old English law. Stealthily; by stealth. Fleta, lib. 1, c. 38, § 3.

FURTUM. Lat. Theft. The fraudulent appropriation to one's self of the property of another, with an intention to commit theft without the consent of the owner. Fleta, l. 1, c. 36; Bract. fol. 150; 3 Inst. 107.

The thing which has been stolen. Bract. fol. 151.

FURTUM CONCEPTUM. In Roman law. The theft which was disclosed where, upon searching any one in the presence of witnesses in due form, the thing stolen was discovered in his possession.

Furtum est contrectatio rei alienæ fraudulenta, cum animo furandi, invito illo domino cujus res illa fuerat. 3 Inst. 107. Theft is the fraudulent handling of another's property, with an intention of stealing, against the will of the proprietor, whose property it was.

FURTUM GRAVE. In Scotch law. An aggravated degree of theft, anciently punished with death. It still remains an open point what amount of value raises the theft to this serious denomination. 1 Broun, 352, note. See 1 Swint. 467.

FURTUM MANIFESTUM. Open theft. Theft where a thief is caught with the property in his possession. Bract. fol. 150b.

Furtum non est ubi initium habet detentionis per dominium rei. 3 Inst. 107. There is no theft where the foundation of the detention is based upon ownership of the thing.

FURTUM OBLATUM. In the civil law. Offered theft. *Oblatum furtum dicitur cum res furtiva ab aliquo tibi oblata sit, eaque apud te concepta sit.* Theft is called "*oblatum*" when a thing stolen is offered to you by any one, and found upon you. Inst. 4, 1, 4.

FUSTIGATIO. In old English law. A beating with sticks or clubs; one of the ancient kinds of punishment of malefactors. Bract. fol. 104b, lib. 3, tr. 1, c. 6.

FUSTIS. In old English law. A staff, used in making livery of seisin. Bract. fol. 40.

A baton, club, or cudgel.

FUTURE DEBT. In Scotch law. A debt which is created, but which will not become due till a future day. 1 Bell, Comm. 315.

FUTURE ESTATE. An estate which is not now vested in the grantee, but is to commence in possession at some future time. It includes remainders, reversions, and estates limited to commence *in futuro* without a particular estate to support them, which last are not good at common law, except in the case of chattel interests. See 2 Bl. Comm. 165.

An estate limited to commence in possession at a future day, either without the intervention of a precedent estate, or on the determination by lapse of time, or otherwise, of a precedent estate created at the same time. 1 Rev. St. N. Y. (3d Ed.) § 10.

"FUTURES." This term has grown out of those purely speculative transactions, in which there is a nominal contract of sale for future delivery, but where in fact none is ever intended or executed. The nominal seller does not have or expect to have the stock or merchandise he purports to sell, nor does the nominal buyer expect to receive it or to pay the price. Instead of that, a percentage or margin is paid, which is increased or diminished as the market rates go up or down, and accounted for to the buyer. 14 R. I. 138.

FUTURI. Those who are to be. Part of the commencement of old deeds. "*Sciant præsentes et futuri, quod ego talis, dedi et concessi,*" etc., (Let all men now living and to come know that I, A. B., have, etc.) Bract. fol. 34b.

FUZ, or FUST. A Celtic word, meaning a wood or forest.

FYHTWITE. One of the fines incurred for homicide.

FYKE. A bow-net for catching fish. Pub. St. Mass. 1882, p. 1291.

FYLE. In old Scotch law. To defile; to declare foul or defiled. Hence, to find a prisoner guilty.

FYLIT. In old Scotch practice. Fyled; found guilty. See FYLE.

FYNDERINGA. Sax. An offense or trespass for which the fine or compensation was reserved to the king's pleasure. Its nature is not known.

FYRD. The military array or land force of the whole country. Contribution to the fyrd was one of the imposts forming the *trinoda necessitas.*

FYRD-WITE. The fine incurred by neglecting to join the fyrd; one of the rights of the crown.

G.

G. In the Law French orthography, this letter is often substituted for the English W, particularly as an initial. Thus, "gage" for "wage," "garranty" for "warranty," "gast" for "waste."

GABEL. An excise; a tax on movables; a rent, custom, or service. Co. Litt. 213.

GABELLA. A tax or duty on personalty. Cowell; Spelman.

GABLATORES. Persons who paid *gabel*, rent, or tribute. Domesday; Cowell.

GABLUM. A rent; a tax. Domesday; Du Cange. The gable-end of a house. Cowell.

GABULUS DENARIORUM. Rent paid in money. Seld. Tit. Hon. 321.

GAFFOLDGILD. The payment of custom or tribute. Scott.

GAFFOLDLAND. Property subject to the gaffoldgild, or liable to be taxed. Scott.

GAFOL. The same word as "gabel" or "gavel." Rent; tax; interest of money.

GAGE, *v.* In old English law. To pawn or pledge; to give as security for a payment or performance; to wage or wager.

GAGE, *n.* In old English law. A pawn or pledge; something deposited as security for the performance of some act or the payment of money, and to be forfeited on failure or non-performance. Glanv. lib. 10, c. 6; Britt. c. 27.

A mortgage is a *dead-gage* or pledge; for, whatsoever profit it yields, it redeems not itself, unless the whole amount secured is paid at the appointed time. Cowell.

In French law. The contract of pledge or pawn; also the article pawned.

GAGE, ESTATES IN. Those held *in vadio*, or pledge. They are of two kinds: (1) *Vivum vadium*, or living pledge, or vifgage; (2) *mortuum vadium*, or dead pledge, better known as "mortgage."

GAGER DE DELIVERANCE. In old English law. When he who has distrained, being sued, has not delivered the cattle distrained, then he shall not only avow the distress, but *gager deliverance*, *i. e.*, put in surety or pledge that he will deliver them. Fitzh. Nat. Brev.

AM.DICT.LAW—34

GAGER DEL LEY. Wager of law, (*q. v.*)

GAIN. Profits; winnings; increment of value.

GAINAGE. The gain or profit of tilled or planted land, raised by cultivating it; and the draught, plow, and furniture for carrying on the work of tillage by the baser kind of *sokemen* or *villeins*. Bract. 1. i. c. 9.

GAINERY. Tillage, or the profit arising from it, or from the beasts employed therein.

GAINOR. In old English law. A sokeman; one who occupied or cultivated arable land. Old Nat. Brev. fol. 12.

GAJUM. A thick wood. Spelman.

GALE. The payment of a rent, tax, duty, or annuity.

A gale is the right to open and work a mine within the Hundred of St. Briavel's, or a stone quarry within the open lands of the Forest of Dean. The right is a license or interest in the nature of real estate, conditional on the due payment of rent and observance of the obligations imposed on the galee. It follows the ordinary rules as to the devolution and conveyance of real estate. The galee pays the crown a rent known as a "galeage rent," "royalty," or some similar name, proportionate to the quantity of minerals got from the mine or quarry. Sweet.

GALEA. In old records. A piratical vessel; a galley.

GALENES. In old Scotch law. Amends or compensation for slaughter. Bell.

GALLI-HALFPENCE. A kind of coin which, with suskins and doitkins, was forbidden by St. 3 Hen. V. c. 1.

GALLIVOLATIUM. A cock-shoot, or cock-glade.

GALLON. A liquid measure, containing 231 cubic inches, or four quarts. The *imperial* gallon contains about 277, and the ale gallon 282, cubic inches.

GALLOWS. A scaffold; a beam laid over either one or two posts, from which malefactors are hanged.

GAMACTA. In old European law. A stroke or blow. Spelman.

H I J K L M

GAMALIS. A child born in lawful wedlock; also one born to betrothed but unmarried parents. Spelman.

GAMBLE. The word "gamble" is perhaps the most apt and substantial to convey the idea of unlawful play that our language affords. It is inclusive of hazarding and betting as well as playing. 2 Yerg. 474.

GAMBLER. One who follows or practices games of chance or skill, with the expectation and purpose of thereby winning money or other property. 113 Mass. 193.

GAMBLING. See GAMING.

GAMBLING DEVICE. A machine or contrivance of any kind for the playing of an unlawful game of chance or hazard.

GAMBLING POLICY. In life insurance. One issued to a person, as beneficiary, who has no pecuniary interest in the life insured. Otherwise called a "wager policy." 50 Mo. 47.

GAME. Birds and beasts of a wild nature, obtained by fowling and hunting. Bacon, Abr. See 11 Metc. (Mass.) 79. The term is said to include (in England) hares, pheasants, partridges, grouse, heath or moor game, black game, and bustards. Brown. See 1 & 2 Wm. IV. c. 32.

A sport or pastime played with cards, dice, or other contrivance. See GAMING.

GAME-KEEPER. One who has the care of keeping and preserving the game on an estate, being appointed thereto by a lord of a manor.

GAME-LAWS. Laws passed for the preservation of game. They usually forbid the killing of specified game during certain seasons or by certain described means. As to English game-laws, see 2 Steph. Comm. 82; 1 & 2 Wm. IV. c. 32.

GAMING. The act or practice of playing games for stakes or wagers; gambling; the playing at any game of hazard. An agreement between two or more persons to play together at a game of chance for a stake or wager which is to become the property of the winner, and to which all contribute.

Gaming is an agreement between two or more to risk money on a contest or chance of any kind, where one must be loser and the other gainer. 5 Sneed, 507.

In general, the words "gaming" and "gambling," in statutes, are similar in meaning, and either one comprehends the idea that, by a bet, by chance, by some exercise of skill, or by the transpiring of some event unknown until it occurs, something of value is, as the conclusion of premises agreed, to be transferred from a loser to a winner, without which latter element there is no gaming or gambling. Bish. St. Crimes, § 858.

"Gaming" implies, when used as describing a condition, an element of illegality; and, when people are said to be "gaming," this generally supposes that the "games" have been games in which money comes to the victor or his backers. When the terms "game" or "gaming" are used in statutes, it is almost always in connection with words giving them the latter sense, and in such case it is only by averring and proving the *differentia* that the prosecution can be sustained. But when "gaming" is spoken of in a statute as indictable, it is to be regarded as convertible with "gambling." 2 Whart. Crim. Law, § 1465b.

"Gaming" is properly the act or engagement of the players. If by-standers or other third persons put up a stake or wager among themselves, to go to one or the other according to the result of the game, this is more correctly termed "betting."

GAMING CONTRACTS. See WAGER.

GAMING-HOUSES. In criminal law. Houses in which gambling is carried on as the business of the occupants, and which are frequented by persons for that purpose. They are nuisances, in the eyes of the law, being detrimental to the public, as they promote cheating and other corrupt practices. 1 Russ. Crimes, 299; Rosc. Crim. Ev. 663; 3 Denio, 101.

GANANCIAL PROPERTY. In Spanish law. A species of community in property enjoyed by husband and wife, the property being divisible between them equally on a dissolution of the marriage. 1 Burge, Confl. Law, 418. See 18 Tex. 634; 22 Mo. 254.

GANANCIAS. In Spanish law. Gains or profits resulting from the employment of property held by husband and wife in common. White, New Recop. b. 1, tit. 7, c. 5.

GANG-WEEK. The time when the bounds of the parish are lustrated or gone over by the parish officers,—rogation week. Enc. Lond.

GANGIATORI. Officers in ancient times whose business it was to examine weights and measures. Skene.

GANTELOPE, (pronounced "gauntlett.") A military punishment, in which the criminal running between the ranks receives a lash from each man. Enc. Lond. This was called "running the gauntlett."

GAOL. A prison for temporary confinement; a jail; a place for the confinement of offenders against the law.

There is said to be a distinction between "gaol" and "prison;" the former being a place for temporary or provisional confinement, or for the punishment of the lighter offenses and misdemeanors, while the latter is a place for permanent or long-continued confinement, or for the punishment of graver crimes. In modern usage, this distinction is commonly taken between the words "gaol" and "penitentiary," (or state's prison,) but the name "prison" is indiscriminately applied to either.

GAOL DELIVERY. In criminal law. The delivery or clearing of a gaol of the prisoners confined therein, by trying them. A commission of general gaol delivery is one of the four commissions under which the judges in England sit at the assizes; and it empowers them to try and *deliver* every prisoner who shall be in the *gaol*, (that is, either in actual custody, or out on bail,) when the judges arrive at the circuit town. 4 Chit. Bl. 270, and notes; 4 Steph. Comm. 333; 1 Chit. Crim. Law, 145, 146.

GAOL LIBERTIES, GAOL LIMITS. A district around a gaol, defined by limits, within which prisoners are allowed to go at large on giving security to return. It is considered a part of the gaol.

GAOLER. The master or keeper of a prison; one who has the custody of a place where prisoners are confined.

GARANDIA, or GARANTIA. A warranty. Spelman.

GARANTIE. In French law. This word corresponds to warranty or covenants for title in English law. In the case of a sale this *garantie* extends to two things: (1) Peaceful possession of the thing sold; and (2) absence of undisclosed defects, (*défauts cachés.*) Brown.

GARATHINX. In old Lombardic law. A gift; a free or absolute gift; a gift of the whole of a thing. Spelman.

GARAUNTOR. L. Fr. In old English law. A warrantor of land; a vouchee; one bound by a warranty to defend the title and seisin of his alienee, or, on default thereof, and on eviction of the tenant, to give him other lands of equal value. Britt. c. 75.

GARBA. In old English law. A bundle or sheaf. *Blada in garbis*, corn or grain in sheaves. Reg. Orig. 96; Bract. fol. 209.

GARBA SAGITTARUM. A sheaf of arrows, containing twenty-four. Otherwise called "*schaffa sagittarum.*" Skene.

GARBALES DECIMÆ. In Scotch law. Tithes of corn, (grain.) Bell.

GARBLE. In English statutes. To sort or cull out the good from the bad in spices, drugs, etc. Cowell.

GARBLER OF SPICES. An ancient officer in the city of London, who might enter into any shop, warehouse, etc., to view and search drugs and spices, and garble and make clean the same, or see that it be done. Mozley & Whitley.

GARCIO STOLÆ. Groom of the stole.

GARCIONES. Servants who follow a camp. Wals. 242.

GARD, or GARDE. Wardship; care; custody; also the ward of a city.

GARDEIN. A keeper; a guardian.

GARDEN. A small piece of land, appropriated to the cultivation of herbs, fruits, flowers, or vegetables.

GARDIA. Custody; wardship.

GARDIANUS. In old English law. A guardian, defender, or protector. In feudal law, *gardio*. Spelman.
A warden. *Gardianus ecclesiæ*, a church-warden. *Gardianus quinque portuum*, warden of the Cinque Ports. Spelman.

GARDINUM. In old English law. A garden. Reg. Orig. 1*b*, 2.

GARENE. L. Fr. A warren; a privileged place for keeping animals.

GARNESTURA. In old English law. Victuals, arms, and other implements of war, necessary for the defense of a town or castle. Mat. Par. 1250.

GARNISH, *n.* In English law. Money paid by a prisoner to his fellow-prisoners on his entrance into prison.

GARNISH, *v.* To warn or summon.
To issue process of garnishment against a person.

GARNISHEE. One garnished; a person against whom process of garnishment is issued; one who has money or property in his possession belonging to a defendant, or who owes the defendant a debt, which money, property, or debt is attached in his hands, with notice to him not to deliver or pay it over until the result of the suit be ascertained.

GARNISHMENT. In the process of attachment. A warning to a person in whose hands the effects of another are attached not

H

I

J

K

L

M

to pay the money or deliver the property of the defendant in his hands to him, but to appear and answer the plaintiff's suit. Drake, Attachm. § 451.

A "garnishment," as the word is employed in this Code, is process to reach and subject money or effects of a defendant in attachment, or in a judgment or decree, or in a pending suit commenced in the ordinary form, in the possession or under the control of a third person, or debts owing such defendant, or liabilities to him on contracts for the delivery of personal property, or on contracts for the payment of money which may be discharged by the delivery of personal property, or on a contract payable in personal property; and such third person is called the "garnishee." Code Ala. 1886, § 2994.

Garnishment is a proceeding to apply the debt due by a third person to a judgment defendant, to the extinguishment of that judgment, or to appropriate effects belonging to a defendant, in the hands of a third person, to its payment. 4 Ga. 393.

Also a warning to any one for his appearance, in a cause in which he is not a party, for the information of the court and explaining a cause. Cowell.

GARNISTURA. In old English law. Garniture; whatever is necessary for the fortification of a city or camp, or for the ornament of a thing. 8 Rymer, 328; Du Cange; Cowell; Blount.

GARSUMME. In old English law. An amerciament or fine. Cowell.

GARTER. A string or ribbon by which the stocking is held upon the leg. The mark of the highest order of English knighthood, ranking next after the nobility. This military order of knighthood is said to have been first instituted by Richard I., at the siege of Acre, where he caused twenty-six knights who firmly stood by him to wear thongs of blue leather about their legs. It is also said to have been perfected by Edward III., and to have received some alterations, which were afterwards laid aside, from Edward VI. The badge of the order is the image of St. George, called the "George," and the motto is "*Honi soit qui mal y pense.*" Wharton.

GARTH. In English law. A yard; a little close or homestead in the north of England. Cowell; Blount.

A dam or wear in a river, for the catching of fish.

GARYTOUR. In old Scotch law. Warder. 1 Pitc. Crim. Tr. pt. 1, p. 8.

GASTALDUS. A temporary governor of the country. Blount. A bailiff or steward. Spelman.

GASTEL. L. Fr. Wastel; wastel bread; the finest sort of wheat bread. Britt. c. 30; Kelham.

GASTINE. L. Fr. Waste or uncultivated ground. Britt. c. 57.

GAUDIES. A term used in the English universities to denote double commons.

GAUGE. The measure of width of a railway, fixed, with some exceptions, at 4 feet 8½ inches in Great Britain and America, and 5 feet 3 inches in Ireland.

GAUGEATOR. A gauger. Lowell.

GAUGER. A surveying officer under the customs, excise, and internal revenue laws, appointed to examine all tuns, pipes, hogsheads, barrels and tierces of wine, oil, and other liquids, and to give them a mark of allowance, as containing lawful measure. There are also private gaugers in large seaport towns, who are licensed by government to perform the same duties. Rapal. & L.

GAUGETUM. A gauge or gauging; a measure of the contents of any vessel.

GAVEL. In English law. Custom; tribute; toll; yearly rent; payment of revenue; of which there were anciently several sorts; as *gavel-corn*, *gavel-malt*, *oat-gavel*, *gavel-fodder*, etc. Termes de la Ley; Cowell; Co. Litt. 142a.

GAVELBRED. In English law. Rent reserved in bread, corn, or provision; rent payable in kind. Cowell.

GAVELCESTER. A certain measure of rent-ale. Cowell.

GAVELET. An ancient and special kind of *cessavit*, used in Kent and London for the recovery of rent. Obsolete. The statute of gavelet is 10 Edw. II. 2 Reeve, Eng. Law, c. 12, p. 298.

GAVELGELD. That which yields annual profit or toll. The tribute or toll itself. Cowell; Du Cange.

GAVELHERTE. A service of plowing performed by a customary tenant. Cowell; Du Cange.

GAVELING MEN. Tenants who paid a reserved rent, besides some customary duties to be done by them. Cowell.

GAVELKIND. A species of socage tenure common in Kent, in England, where the lands descend to all the sons, or heirs of the nearest degree, together; may be disposed of by will; do not escheat for felony; may be aliened by the heir at the age of fifteen; and dower and curtesy is given of half the land. Stim. Law Gloss.

GAVELLER. An officer of the English crown having the general management of the mines, pits, and quarries in the Forest of Dean and Hundred of St. Briavel's, subject, in some respects, to the control of the commissioners of woods and forests. He grants gales to free miners in their proper order, accepts surrenders of gales, and keeps the registers required by the acts. There is a deputy-gaveller, who appears to exercise most of the gaveller's functions. Sweet.

GAVEL-MAN. In old English law. A tenant liable to the payment of gavel or tribute. Somn. Gavelkind, 23.

GAVELMED. A customary service of mowing meadow-land or cutting grass, (*consuetudo falcandi.*) Blount.

GAVELREP. In old English law. Bedreap or bidreap; the duty of reaping at the bid or command of the lord. Somn. Gavelkind, 19, 21; Cowell.

GAVELWERK. A customary service, either *manuopera*, by the person of the tenant, or *carropera*, by his carts or carriages. Blount; Somn. Gavelkind, 24; Du Cange.

GAZETTE. The official publication of the English government, also called the "London Gazette." It is evidence of acts of state, and of everything done by the queen in her political capacity. Orders of adjudication in bankruptcy are required to be published therein; and the production of a copy of the "Gazette," containing a copy of the order of adjudication, is evidence of the fact. Mozley & Whitley.

GEBOCCED. An Anglo-Saxon term, meaning "conveyed."

GEBOCIAN. In Saxon law. To convey; to transfer *boc* land, (book-land or land held by charter.) The grantor was said to *gebocian* the alienee. See 1 Reeve, Eng. Law, 10.

GEBURSCRIPT. Neighborhood or adjoining district. Cowell.

GEBURUS. In old English law. A country neighbor; an inhabitant of the same *geburscript*, or village. Cowell.

GELD. In Saxon law. Money or tribute. A mulct, compensation, value, price. *Angeld* was the single value of a thing; *twigeld*, double value, etc. So, *weregeld* was the value of a man slain; *orfgeld*, that of a beast. Brown.

GELDABILIS. In old English law. Taxable; geldable.

GELDABLE. Liable to pay geld; liable to be taxed. Kelham.

GELDING. A horse that has been castrated, and which is thus distinguished from the horse in his natural and unaltered condition. A "ridgling" (a half-castrated horse) is not a gelding, but a horse, within the denomination of animals in the statutes. 4 Tex. App. 219.

GEMMA. Lat. In the civil law. A gem; a precious stone. Gems were distinguished by their transparency; such as emeralds, chrysolites, amethysts. Dig. 34, 2, 19, 17.

GEMOT. In Saxon law. A meeting or moot; a convention; a public assemblage. These were of several sorts, such as the *witena-gemot*, or meeting of the wise men; the *folc-gemot*, or general assembly of the people; the *shire-gemot*, or county court; the *burg-gemot*, or borough court; the *hundred-gemot*, or hundred court; the *hali-gemot*, or court-baron; the *hal-mote*, a convention of citizens in their public hall; the *holy-mote*, or holy court; the *swein-gemote*, or forest court; the *ward-mote*, or ward court. Wharton; Cunningham.

GENEALOGY. An account or history of the descent of a person or family from an ancestor; enumeration of ancestors and their children in the natural order of succession, Webst.

GENEARCH. The head of a family.

GENEATH. In Saxon law. A villein, or agricultural tenant, (*villanus villicus;*) a hind or farmer, (*firmarius rusticus.*) Spelman.

GENER. Lat. In the civil law. A son-in-law; a daughter's husband. (*Filiæ vir.*) Dig. 38, 10, 4, 6.

GENERAL. Pertaining to, or designating, the *genus* or class, as distinguished from that which characterizes the *species* or individual. Universal, not particularized; as opposed to special. Principal or central; as opposed to local. Open or available to all;

as opposed to select. Obtaining commonly, or recognized universally; as opposed to particular. Universal or unbounded; as opposed to limited. Comprehending the whole, or directed to the whole; as distinguished from anything applying to or designed for a portion only.

As a noun, the word is the title of a principal officer in the army, usually one who commands a whole army, division, corps, or brigade. In the United States army, the rank of "general" is the highest possible, next to the commander in chief, and is only occasionally created. The officers next in rank are lieutenant general, major general, and brigadier general.

GENERAL AGENT. A person who is authorized by his principal to execute all deeds, sign all contracts, or purchase all goods, required in a particular trade, business, or employment. Story, Ag. § 17.

In another sense, a person who has a general authority in regard to a particular object or thing. Id. § 18.

A general agent is one appointed to act in the affairs of his principal generally; a special agent is one appointed to act concerning some particular object. 7 Ala. 800, 804.

GENERAL APPEARANCE. An unqualified or unrestricted submission to the jurisdiction of the court. See APPEARANCE.

GENERAL ASSEMBLY. A name given in some of the United States to the senate and house of representatives, which compose the legislative body.

GENERAL ASSIGNMENT. An assignment made for the benefit of *all* the assignor's creditors, instead of a few only; or one which transfers the *whole* of his estate to the assignee, instead of a part only.

GENERAL AVERAGE. In commercial law. A contribution made by the proprietors in general of a ship or cargo, towards the loss sustained by any individual of their number, whose property has been voluntarily sacrificed for the common safety; as where, in a storm, jettison is made of any goods, or sails or masts are cut away *levandæ navis causâ,* (to lighten the vessel.) 2 Steph. Comm. 179.

The term expresses that contribution to a loss or expense voluntarily incurred for the preservation of the whole, in which all who are concerned in ship, freight, and cargo are to bear an equal part, proportionable to their respective interests. And for the loss incurred by this contribution, however small in amount, the respective owners are to be indemnified by their insurers. 4 Mass. 548.

GENERAL CHALLENGE. A species of challenge for cause, being an objection to a particular juror, to the effect that the juror is disqualified from serving in any case. Pen. Code Cal. § 1071.

GENERAL CHARACTER. See CHARACTER.

GENERAL CHARGE. A charge or instruction by the court to the jury upon the case as a whole, or upon its general features or characteristics.

GENERAL COUNCIL. (1) A council consisting of members of the Roman Catholic Church from most parts of the world, but not from every part, as an ecumenical council. (2) One of the names of the English parliament.

GENERAL COVENANT. One which relates to lands generally, and places the covenantee in the position of a specialty creditor. Brown.

GENERAL CREDIT. The character of a witness as one generally worthy of credit. According to Bouvier, there is a distinction between this and "particular credit," which may be affected by proof of particular facts relating to the particular action.

GENERAL CUSTOM. General customs are such as prevail throughout a country and become the law of that country, and their existence is to be determined by the court. Particular customs are such as prevail in some county, city, town, parish, or place; their existence is to be determined by a jury upon proof. 23 Me. 95.

GENERAL DAMAGES. In pleading and practice. Such damages as necessarily result from the injury complained of, and which may be shown under the *ad damnum,* or general allegation of damages at the end of the declaration. 2 Greenl. Ev. § 254.

GENERAL DEMURRER. In pleading. A demurrer framed in general terms, without showing specifically the nature of the objection, and which is usually resorted to where the objection is to matter of substance. Steph. Pl. 140–142; 1 Chit. Pl. 663. See DEMURRER.

GENERAL DEPOSIT. A general deposit is where the money deposited is not itself to be returned, but an equivalent in money (that is, a like sum) is to be returned. It is equivalent to a loan, and the money deposited becomes the property of the depositary. 43 Ala. 138.

GENERAL ELECTION. 1. One at which the officers to be elected are such as belong to the *general* government,—that is, the general and central political organization of the whole state; as distinguished from an election of officers for a particular locality only.

2. One held for the selection of an officer after the expiration of the full term of the former officer; thus distinguished from a *special* election, which is one held to supply a vacancy in office occurring before the expiration of the full term for which the incumbent was elected. 52 Cal. 164.

GENERAL EXECUTOR. One whose power is not limited either territorially or as to the duration or subject of his trust.

GENERAL FIELD. Several distinct lots or pieces of land inclosed and fenced in as one common field. 14 Mass. 440.

GENERAL FUND. This phrase, in New York, is a collective designation of all the assets of the state which furnish the means for the support of government and for defraying the discretionary appropriations of the legislature. 27 Barb. 575, 588.

GENERAL GAOL DELIVERY. In English law. At the assizes (*q. v.*) the judges sit by virtue of five several authorities, one of which is the commission of "general gaol delivery." This empowers them to try and deliverance make of every prisoner who shall be in the gaol when the judges arrive at the circuit town, whether an indictment has been preferred at any previous assize or not. 4 Bl. Comm. 270.

GENERAL GUARDIAN. One who has the general care and control of the person and estate of his ward.

GENERAL IMPARLANCE. In pleading. One granted upon a prayer in which the defendant reserves to himself no exceptions.

GENERAL INCLOSURE ACT. The statute 41 Geo. III. c. 109, which consolidates a number of regulations as to the inclosure of common fields and waste lands.

GENERAL INTENT. An intention, purpose, or design, either without specific plan or particular object, or without reference to such plan or object.

GENERAL INTEREST. In speaking of matters of public and general interest, the terms "public" and "general" are sometimes used as synonyms. But in regard to the admissibility of hearsay evidence, a distinction has been taken between them, the term "public" being strictly applied to that which concerns every member of the state, and the term "general" being confined to a lesser, though still a considerable, portion of the community. Tayl. Ev. § 609.

GENERAL ISSUE. In pleading. A plea which traverses and denies, briefly and in general and summary terms, the whole declaration, indictment, or complaint, without tendering new or special matter. See Steph. Pl. 155. Examples of the general issue are "not guilty," "*non assumpsit*," "*nil debet*," "*non est factum.*"

GENERAL JURISDICTION. Such as extends to all controversies that may be brought before a court within the legal bounds of rights and remedies; as opposed to *special* or *limited* jurisdiction, which covers only a particular class of cases, or cases where the amount in controversy is below a prescribed sum, or which is subject to specific exceptions.

The terms "general" and "special," applied to jurisdiction, indicate the difference between a legal authority extending to the whole of a particular subject and one limited to a part; and, when applied to the terms of court, the occasion upon which these powers can be respectively exercised. 1 N. Y. 232.

GENERAL LAND-OFFICE. In the United States, one of the bureaus of the interior department, which has charge of the survey, sale, granting of patents, and other matters relating to the public lands.

GENERAL LAW. A general law, as contradistinguished from one that is special or local, is a law that embraces a class of subjects or places, and does not omit any subject or place naturally belonging to such class. 40 N. J. Law, 1.

A law, framed in general terms, restricted to no locality, and operating equally upon all of a group of objects, which, having regard to the purposes of the legislation, are distinguished by characteristics sufficiently marked and important to make them a class by themselves, is not a special or local law, but a general law. 40 N. J. Law, 123.

GENERAL LEGACY. A pecuniary legacy, payable out of the general assets of a testator. 2 Bl. Comm. 512; Ward, Leg. 1, 16.

GENERAL LIEN. A right to detain a chattel, etc., until payment be made, not only of any debt due in respect of the particular chattel, but of any balance that may be due on general account in the same line of business. A general lien, being against the ordinary rule of law, depends entirely upon contract, express or implied, from the special usage of dealing between the parties. Wharton.

GENERAL MALICE. General malice is wickedness, a disposition to do wrong, a "black and diabolical heart, regardless of social duty and fatally bent on mischief." 11 Ired. 261.

GENERAL MEETING. A meeting of all the stockholders of a corporation, all the creditors of a bankrupt, etc.

GENERAL MONITION. In civil law and admiralty practice. A monition or summons to all parties in interest to appear and show cause against the decree prayed for.

GENERAL OCCUPANT. At common law where a man was tenant *pur auter vie*, or had an estate granted to himself only (without mentioning his heirs) for the life of another man, and died without alienation during the life of *cestui que vie*, or him by whose life it was holden, he that could first enter on the land might lawfully retain the possession, so long as *cestui que vie* lived, by right of occupancy, and was hence termed a "general" or common "occupant." 1 Steph. Comm. 415.

GENERAL ORDERS. Orders or rules of court, promulgated for the guidance of practitioners and the regulation of procedure in general, or in some general branch of its jurisdiction; as opposed to a rule or an order made in an individual case; the rules of court.

GENERAL OWNER. The general owner of a thing is he who has the primary or residuary title to it; as distinguished from a *special* owner, who has a special interest in the same thing, amounting to a qualified ownership, such, for example, as a bailee's lien.

GENERAL PARTNERSHIP. A partnership in which the parties carry on all their trade and business, whatever it may be, for the joint benefit and profit of all the parties concerned, whether the capital stock be limited or not, or the contributions thereto be equal or unequal. Story, Partn. § 74.

GENERAL PROPERTY. The right and property in a thing enjoyed by the *general owner*, (*q. v.*)

GENERAL RESTRAINT OF TRADE. One which forbids the person to employ his talents, industry, or capital in any undertaking within the limits of the state or country. 9 How. Pr. 337.

GENERAL RETAINER. A general retainer of an attorney or solicitor "merely gives a right to expect professional service when requested, but none which is not requested. It binds the person retained not to take a fee from another against his retainer, but to do nothing except what he is asked to do, and for this he is to be distinctly paid." 6 R. I. 206.

GENERAL RETURN-DAY. The day for the general return of all writs of summons, subpoena, etc., running to a particular term of the court.

GENERAL RULES. General or standing orders of a court, in relation to practice, etc. See GENERAL ORDERS.

GENERAL SESSIONS. A court of record, in England, held by two or more justices of the peace, for the execution of the authority given them by the commission of the peace and certain statutes. General sessions held at certain times in the four quarters of the year pursuant to St. 2 Hen. V. are properly called "quarter sessions," (*q. v.*,) but intermediate general sessions may also be held. Sweet.

GENERAL SHIP. Where a ship is not chartered wholly to one person, but the owner offers her generally to carry the goods of all comers, or where, if chartered to one person, he offers her to several subfreighters for the conveyance of their goods, she is called a "general" ship, as opposed to a "chartered" one. Brown.

A vessel in which the master or owners engage separately with a number of persons unconnected with each other to convey their respective goods to the place of the ship's destination. 6 Cow. 173.

GENERAL SPECIAL IMPARLANCE. An imparlance (*q. v.*) granted upon a prayer in which the defendant reserves to himself "all advantages and exceptions whatsoever." 2 Chit. Pl. 408.

GENERAL STATUTE. A statute relating to the whole community, or concerning all persons generally, as distinguished from a private or special statute. 4 Coke, 75*a;* 1 Bl. Comm. 85, 86.

GENERAL TAIL. An estate tail where one parent only is specified, whence the issue must be derived, as to A. and the heirs of his body.

GENERAL TENANCY. A tenancy which is not fixed and made certain in point of duration by the agreement of the parties. 22 Ind. 122.

GENERAL TERM. A phrase used in some jurisdictions to denote the ordinary session of a court, for the trial and determination of causes, as distinguished from a *special* term, for the hearing of motions or arguments or the despatch of various kinds of formal business, or the trial of a special list or class of cases. Or it may denote a sitting of the court *in banc.*

GENERAL TRAVERSE. One preceded by a general inducement, and denying in general terms all that is last before alleged on the opposite side, instead of pursuing the words of the allegations which it denies. Gould, Pl. vii. 5.

GENERAL USAGE. One which prevails generally throughout the country, or is followed generally by a given profession or trade, and is not local in its nature or observance.

GENERAL VERDICT. A verdict whereby the jury find either for the plaintiff or for the defendant in general terms; the ordinary form of a verdict; distinguished from a *special* verdict, (*q. v.*)

GENERAL WARRANT. A process which formerly issued from the state secretary's office in England to take up (without naming any persons) the author, printer, and publisher of such obscene and seditious libels as were specified in it. It was declared illegal and void for uncertainty by a vote of the house of commons on the 22d April, 1766. Wharton.

GENERAL WARRANTY. The name of a covenant of warranty inserted in deeds, by which the grantor binds himself, his heirs, etc., to "warrant and forever defend" to the grantee, his heirs, etc., the title thereby conveyed, against the lawful claims of all persons whatsoever. Where the warranty is only against the claims of persons claiming "by, through, or under" the grantor or his heirs, it is called a "special warranty."

GENERALE. The usual commons in a religious house, distinguished from *pietantiæ,* which on extraordinary occasions were allowed beyond the commons. Cowell.

Generale dictum generaliter est interpretandum. A general expression is to be interpreted generally. 8 Coke, 116*a.*

Generale nihil certum implicat. A general expression implies nothing certain. 2 Coke, 34*b.* A general recital in a deed has not the effect of an estoppel. Best, Ev. p. 408, § 370.

Generale tantum valet in generalibus, quantum singulare in singulis. What is general is of as much force among general things as what is particular is among things particular. 11 Coke, 59*b.*

Generalia præcedunt, specialia sequuntur. Things general precede, things special follow. Reg. Brev.; Branch, Princ.

Generalia specialibus non derogant. Jenk. Cent. 120, cited L. R. 4 Exch. 226. General words do not derogate from special.

Generalia sunt præponenda singularibus. Branch, Princ. General things are to precede particular things.

Generalia verba sunt generaliter intelligenda. General words are to be understood generally, or in a general sense. 3 Inst. 76; Broom, Max. 647.

Generalibus specialia derogant. Special things take from generals. Halk. Lat. Max. 51.

Generalis clausula non porrigitur ad ea quæ antea specialiter sunt comprehensa. A general clause does not extend to those things which are previously provided for specially. 8 Coke, 154*b.* Therefore, where a deed at the first contains special words, and afterwards concludes in general words, both words, as well general as special, shall stand.

Generalis regula generaliter est intelligenda. A general rule is to be understood generally. 6 Coke, 65.

GENERALS OF ORDERS. Chiefs of the several orders of monks, friars, and other religious societies.

GENERATIO. The issue or offspring of a mother-monastery. Cowell.

H

I

J

K

L

M

GENEROSA. Gentlewoman. Cowell; 2 Inst. 668.

GENEROSI FILIUS. The son of a gentleman. Generally abbreviated "*gen. fil.*"

GENEROSUS. Gentleman; a gentleman. Spelman.

GENICULUM. A degree of consanguinity. Spelman.

GENS. In Roman law. A tribe or clan; a group of families, connected by common descent and bearing the same name, being all free-born and of free ancestors, and in possession of full civic rights.

GENTES. People. *Contra omnes gentes*, against all people. Bract. fol. 37*b*. Words used in the clause of warranty in old deeds.

GENTILES. In Roman law. The members of a *gens* or common tribe.

GENTLEMAN. In English law. A person of superior birth.

Under the denomination of "gentlemen" are comprised all above yeoman; whereby noblemen are truly called "gentlemen." Smith de Rep. Ang. lib. 1, cc. 20, 21.

A "gentleman" is defined to be one who, without any title, bears a coat of arms, or whose ancestors have been freemen; and, by the coat that a gentleman giveth, he is known to be, or not to be, descended from those of his name that lived many hundred years since. Jacob.

GENTLEMAN USHER. One who holds a post at court to usher others to the presence, etc.

GENTLEWOMAN. A woman of birth above the common, or equal to that of a gentleman; an addition of a woman's state or degree.

GENTOO LAW. See HINDU LAW.

GENUINE. This term, when used with reference to a note, imports nothing in regard to the collectibility of the note, or in regard to its legal effect or operation, other than that the note is not false, fictitious, simulated, spurious, counterfeit, or, in short, that the apparent maker did make and deliver the note offered for sale. 37 N. Y. 487.

GENUS. In the civil law. A general class or division, comprising several species. *In toto jure generi per speciem derogatur, et illud potissimum habetur quod ad speciem directum est*, throughout the law, the species takes from the genus, and that is most particularly regarded which refers to the species. Dig. 50, 17, 80.

A man's lineage, or direct descendants.

In logic, it is the first of the universal ideas, and is when the idea is so common that it extends to other ideas which are also universal; *e. g.*, incorporeal hereditament is *genus* with respect to a *rent*, which is *species*. Woolley, Introd. Log. 45; 1 Mill, Log. 133.

GEOPONICS. The science of cultivating the ground; agriculture.

GEORGE-NOBLE. A gold coin, value 6s. 8d.

GERECHTSBODE. In old New York law. A court messenger or constable. O'Callaghan, New Neth. 322.

GEREFA. In Saxon law. Greve, reve, or reeve; a ministerial officer of high antiquity in England; answering to the *grave* or *graf* (*grafio*) of the early continental nations. The term was applied to various grades of officers, from the *scyre-gerefa*, *shire-grefe*, or *shire-reve*, who had charge of the county, (and whose title and office have been perpetuated in the modern "sheriff,") down to the *tun-gerefa*, or town-reeve, and lower. Burrill.

GERENS. Bearing. *Gerens datum*, bearing date. 1 Ld. Raym. 336; Hob. 19.

GERMAN. Whole, full, or own, in respect to relationship or descent. Brothers-german, as opposed to half-brothers, are those who have both the same father and mother. Cousins-german are "first" cousins; that is, children of brothers or sisters.

GERMANUS. Descended of the same stock, or from the same couple of ancestors; of the whole or full blood. Mackeld. Rom. Law, § 145.

GERMEN TERRÆ. A sprout of the earth. A young tree, so called.

GERONTOCOMI. In the civil law. Officers appointed to manage hospitals for the aged poor.

GERONTOCOMIUM. In the civil law. An institution or hospital for taking care of the old. Cod. 1, 3, 46, 1; Calvin.

GERSUMARIUS. Finable; liable to be amerced at the discretion of the lord of a manor. Cowell.

GERSUME. In old English law. Expense; reward; compensation; wealth. It is also used for a fine or compensation for an offense. 2 Mon. Angl. 973.

GEST. In Saxon law. A guest. A name given to a stranger on the *second night* of his entertainment in another's house. *Twa-night gest.*

GESTATION, UTERO-GESTATION. In medical jurisprudence. The time during which a female, who has conceived, carries the embryo or *fœtus* in her *uterus.*

GESTIO. In the civil law. Behavior or conduct.

Management or transaction. *Negotiorum gestio,* the doing of another's business; an interference in the affairs of another in his absence, from benevolence or friendship, and without authority. Dig. 3, 5, 45; Id. 46, 3, 12, 4; 2 Kent, Comm. 616, note.

GESTIO PRO HÆREDE. Behavior as heir. This expression was used in the Roman law, and adopted in the civil law and Scotch law, to denote conduct on the part of a person appointed heir to a deceased person, or otherwise entitled to succeed as heir, which indicates an intention to enter upon the inheritance, and to hold himself out as heir to creditors of the deceased; as by receiving the rents due to the deceased, or by taking possession of his title-deeds, etc. Such acts will render the heir liable to the debts of his ancestor. Mozley & Whitley.

GESTOR. In the civil law. One who acts for another, or transacts another's business. Calvin.

GESTU ET FAMA. An ancient and obsolete writ resorted to when a person's good behavior was impeached. Lamb. Eir. l. 4, c. 14.

GESTUM. Lat. In Roman law. A deed or act; a thing done. Some writers affected to make a distinction between "*gestum*" and "*factum.*" But the best authorities pronounced this subtile and indefensible. Dig. 50, 16, 58.

GEVILLOURIS. In old Scotch law. Gaolers. 1 Pitc. Crim. Tr. pt. 2, p. 234.

GEWINEDA. In Saxon law. The ancient convention of the people to decide a cause.

GEWITNESSA. In Saxon and old English law. The giving of evidence.

GEWRITE. In Saxon law. Deeds or charters; writings. 1 Reeve, Eng. Law, 10.

GIBBET. A gallows; the post on which malefactors are hanged, or on which their bodies are exposed. It differs from a common gallows, in that it consists of one perpendicular post, from the top of which proceeds one arm, except it be a double gibbet, which is formed in the shape of the Roman capital T. Enc. Lond.

GIFT. A voluntary conveyance of land, or transfer of goods, from one person to another, made gratuitously, and not upon any consideration of blood or money. 2 Bl. Comm. 440; 2 Steph. Comm. 102; 2 Kent, Comm. 437.

A gift is a transfer of personal property, made voluntarily and without consideration. Civil Code Cal. § 1146.

In popular language, a voluntary conveyance or assignment is called a "deed of gift."

"Gift" and "advancement" are sometimes used interchangeably as expressive of the same operation. But, while an advancement is always a gift, a gift is very frequently not an advancement. 3 Brewst. 314.

In English law. A conveyance of lands in tail; a conveyance of an estate tail in which the operative words are "I give," or "I have given." 2 Bl. Comm. 316; 1 Steph. Comm. 473.

GIFT ENTERPRISE. A scheme for the division or distribution of certain articles of property, to be determined by chance, among those who have taken shares in the scheme. The phrase has attained such a notoriety as to justify a court in taking judicial notice of what is meant and understood by it. 81 Ind. 17; 106 Mass. 422.

GIFTA AQUÆ. The stream of water to a mill. Mon. Angl. tom. 3.

GIFTOMAN. In Swedish law. The right to dispose of a woman in marriage; or the person possessing such right,—her father, if living, or, if he be dead, the mother.

GILD. In Saxon law. A tax or tribute. Spelman.

A fine, mulct, or amerciament; a satisfaction or compensation for an injury.

A fraternity, society, or company of persons combined together, under certain regulations, and with the king's license, and so called because its expenses were defrayed by the *contributions* (*geld, gild*) of its members. Spelman. In other words, a corporation; called, in Latin, "*societas,*" "*collegium,*" "*fratria,*" "*fraternitas,*" "*sodalitium,*" "*adunatio;*" and, in foreign law, "*gildonia.*" Spelman. There were various kinds of these *gilds,* as merchant or commercial *gilds,* religious *gilds,* and others. 3 Turn. Anglo

H

I

J

K

L

M

Sax. 98; 3 Steph. Comm. 173, note *u.* See
GILDA MERCATORIA.

A friborg, or decennary; called, by the Saxons, "*gyldscipes,*" and its members, "*gildones*" and "*congildones.*" Spelman.

GILD-HALL. See GUILDHALL.

GILD-RENT. Certain payments to the crown from any gild or fraternity.

GILDA MERCATORIA. A gild merchant, or merchant gild; a gild, corporation, or company of merchants. 10 Coke, 30.

GILDABLE. In old English law. Taxable, tributary, or contributory; liable to pay tax or tribute. Cowell; Blount.

GILDO. In Saxon law. Members of a *gild* or decennary. Oftener spelled "*congildo.*" Du Cange; Spelman.

GILL. A liquid measure, containing one-fourth of a pint.

GILOUR. L. Fr. A cheat or deceiver. Applied in Britton to those who sold false or spurious things for good, as pewter for silver or laten for gold. Britt. c. 15.

GIRANTE. An Italian word, which signifies the drawer of a bill. It is derived from "*girare,*" to draw.

GIRTH. In Saxon and old English law. A measure of length, equal to one yard, derived from the girth or circumference of a man's body.

GIRTH AND SANCTUARY. In old Scotch law. An asylum given to murderers, where the murder was committed without any previous design, and in *chaude mella,* or heat of passion. Bell.

GISEMENT. Agistment; cattle taken in to graze at a certain price; also the money received for grazing cattle.

GISER. L. Fr. To lie. *Gist en le bouche,* it lies in the mouth. *Le action bien gist,* the action well lies. *Gisant,* lying.

GISETAKER. An agister; a person who takes cattle to graze.

GISLE. A pledge. *Fredgisle,* a pledge of peace. *Gislebert,* an illustrious pledge.

GIST. In pleading. The essential ground or object of the action in point of law, without which there would be no cause of action. Gould, Pl. c. 4, § 12; 19 Vt. 102.

The gist of an action is the cause for which an action will lie; the ground or foundation of a suit, without which it would not be maintainable; the essential ground or object of a suit, and without which there is not a cause of action. 101 Ill. 394.

GIVE. A term used in deeds of conveyance. At common law, it implied a covenant for quiet enjoyment. 2 Hil. Real Prop. 366.

In their ordinary and familiar signification, the words "sell" and "give" have not the same meaning, but are commonly used to express different modes of transferring the right to property from one person to another. "To sell" means to transfer for a valuable consideration, while "to give" signifies to transfer gratuitously, without any equivalent. 14 Md. 184.

"GIVE AND BEQUEATH." These words, in a will, import a benefit in point of right, to take effect upon the decease of the testator and proof of the will, unless it is made in terms to depend upon some contingency or condition precedent. 9 Cush. 519; 33 Conn. 297; 8 Wheat. 538.

GIVE BAIL. To furnish or put in bail or security for one's appearance.

GIVE COLOR. To admit an apparent or colorable right in the opposite party. See COLOR.

GIVER. A donor; he who makes a gift.

GIVING IN PAYMENT. In Louisiana law. A phrase (translating the Fr. "*dation en payement*") which signifies the delivery and acceptance of real or personal property in satisfaction of a debt, instead of a payment in money. See Civil Code La. art. 2655.

GIVING RINGS. A ceremony anciently performed in England by serjeants at law at the time of their appointment. The rings were inscribed with a motto, generally in Latin.

GIVING TIME. The act of a creditor in extending the time for the payment or satisfaction of a claim beyond the time stipulated in the original contract. If done without the consent of the surety, indorser, or guarantor, it discharges him.

GLADIOLUS. A little sword or dagger; a kind of sedge. Mat. Paris.

GLADIUS. Lat. A sword. An ancient emblem of defense. Hence the ancient earls or *comites* (the king's attendants, advisers, and associates in his government) were made by being girt with swords, (*gladio succincti.*)

The emblem of the executory power of the law in punishing crimes. 4 Bl. Comm. 177.

In old Latin authors, and in the Norman laws, this word was used to signify supreme jurisdiction, (*jus gladii.*)

GLAIVE. A sword, lance, or horseman's staff. One of the weapons allowed in a trial by combat.

GLANS. In the civil law. Acorns or nuts of the oak or other trees. In a larger sense, all fruits of trees.

GLASS-MEN. A term used in St. 1 Jac. I. c. 7, for wandering rogues or vagrants.

GLAVEA. A hand dart. Cowell.

GLEANING. The gathering of grain after reapers, or of grain left ungathered by reapers. Held not to be a right at common law. 1 H. Bl. 51.

GLEBA. A turf, sod, or clod of earth. The soil or ground; cultivated land in general. Church land, (*solum et dos ecclesiæ.*) Spelman. See GLEBE.

GLEBÆ ASCRIPTITII. Villein-socmen, who could not be removed from the land while they did the service due. Bract. c. 7; 1 Reeve, Eng. Law, 269.

GLEBARIÆ. Turfs dug out of the ground. Cowell.

GLEBE. In ecclesiastical law. The land possessed as part of the endowment or revenue of a church or ecclesiastical benefice.

In Roman law. A clod; turf; soil. Hence, the soil of an inheritance; an agrarian estate. *Servi addicti glebæ* were serfs attached to and passing with the estate. Cod. 11, 47, 7, 21; Nov. 54, 1.

GLISCYWA. In Saxon law. A fraternity.

GLOMERELLS. Commissioners appointed to determine differences between scholars in a school or university and the townsmen of the place. Jacob.

GLOS. Lat. In the civil law. A husband's sister. Dig. 38, 10. 4, 6.

GLOSS. An interpretation, consisting of one or more words, interlinear or marginal; an annotation, explanation, or comment on any passage in the text of a work, for purposes of elucidation or amplification. Particularly applied to the comments on the *Corpus Juris.*

GLOSSA. A gloss, explanation, or interpretation. The *glossæ* of the Roman law are brief illustrative comments or annotations on the text of Justinian's collections, made by the professors who taught or lectured on them about the twelfth century, (especially at the law school of Bologna,) and were hence called "*glossators.*" These glosses were at first inserted in the text with the words to which they referred, and were called "*glossæ interlineares;*" but afterwards they were placed in the margin, partly at the side, and partly under the text, and called "*glossæ marginales.*" A selection of them was made by Accursius, between A. D. 1220 and 1260, under the title of "*Glossa Ordinaria,*" which is of the greatest authority. Mackeld. Rom. Law, § 90.

Glossa viperina est quæ corrodit viscera textus. 11 Coke, 34. It is a poisonous gloss which corrupts the essence of the text.

GLOSSATOR. In the civil law. A commentator or annotator. A term applied to the professors and teachers of the Roman law in the twelfth century, at the head of whom was Irnerius. Mackeld. Rom. Law, § 90.

GLOUCESTER, STATUTE OF. The statute is the 6 Edw. I. c. 1, A. D. 1278. It takes its name from the place of its enactment, and was the first statute giving costs in actions.

GLOVE SILVER. Extraordinary rewards formerly given to officers of courts, etc.; money formerly given by the sheriff of a county in which no offenders are left for execution to the clerk of assize and judges' officers. Jacob.

GLOVES. It was an ancient custom on a maiden assize, when there was no offender to be tried, for the sheriff to present the judge with a pair of white gloves. It is an immemorial custom to remove the glove from the right hand on taking oath. Wharton.

GLYN. A hollow between two mountains; a valley or glen. Co. Litt. 5*b.*

GO. To be dismissed from a court. To issue from a court. "The court said a *mandamus* must *go.*" 1 W. Bl. 50. "Let a *supersedeas go.*" 5 Mod. 421. "The writ may *go.*" 18 C. B. 35.

This word, in a statutory provision that property "shall *go* to the survivor," etc., is to be construed as equivalent to *vest.*

GO BAIL. To assume the responsibility of a surety on a bail-bond.

H

I

J

K

L

M

GO TO PROTEST. Commercial paper is said to "go to protest" when it is dishonored by non-payment or non-acceptance and is handed to a notary for protest.

GO WITHOUT DAY. Words used to denote that a party is dismissed the court. He is said to go without day, because there is no day appointed for him to appear again.

GOAT, GOTE. In old English law. A contrivance or structure for draining waters out of the land into the sea. Callis describes *goats* as "usual engines erected and built with portcullises and doors of timber and stone or brick, invented first in Lower Germany." Callis, Sewers, (91,) 112, 113. Cowell defines "gote," a ditch, sewer, or gutter.

GOD AND MY COUNTRY. The answer made by a prisoner, when arraigned, in answer to the question, "How will you be tried?" In the ancient practice he had the choice (as appears by the question) whether to submit to the trial by ordeal (by God) or to be tried by a jury, (by the country;) and it is probable that the original form of the answer was, "By God *or* my country," whereby the prisoner averred his innocence by declining neither of the modes of trial.

GOD-BOTE. An ecclesiastical or church fine paid for crimes and offenses committed against God. Cowell.

GOD-GILD. That which is offered to God or his service. Jacob.

GOD'S ACRE. A churchyard.

GOD'S PENNY. In old English law. Earnest-money; money given as evidence of the completion of a bargain. This name is probably derived from the fact that such money was given to the church or distributed in alms.

GOGING-STOLE. An old form of the word "cucking-stool," (*q. v.*) Cowell.

GOING CONCERN. A firm or corporation which, though embarrassed or even insolvent, continues to transact its ordinary business. 30 Fed. Rep. 865.

GOING OFF LARGE. This is a nautical phrase, and signifies having the wind free on either tack. 1 Newb. Adm. 8, 26; 6 McLean, 152, 170.

A vessel, in nautical technicality, "is going off large" when the wind blows from some point "abaft the beam;" is going "before the wind" when the wind is "free," comes over the stern, and the yards of the ship are braced square across. 1 Newb. Adm. 115.

GOING THROUGH THE BAR. The act of the chief of an English common-law court in demanding of every member of the bar, in order of seniority, if he has anything to move. This was done at the sitting of the court each day in term, except special paper days, crown paper days in the queen's bench, and revenue paper days in the exchequer. On the last day of term this order is reversed, the first and second time round. In the exchequer the postman and tubman are first called on. Wharton.

GOING TO THE COUNTRY. When a party, under the common-law system of pleading, finished his pleading by the words "and of this he puts himself upon the country," this was called "going to the country." It was the essential termination to a pleading which took issue upon a material fact in the preceding pleading. Wharton.

GOING WITNESS. One who is about to take his departure from the jurisdiction of the court, although only into a state or country under the general sovereignty; as from one to another of the United States, or from England to Scotland.

GOLDA. A mine. Blount. A sink or passage for water. Cowell.

GOLDSMITHS' NOTES. Bankers' cash notes (*i. e.*, promissory notes given by a banker to his customers as acknowledgments of the receipt of money) were originally called in London "goldsmiths' notes," from the circumstance that all the banking business in England was originally transacted by goldsmiths. Wharton.

GOLDWIT. A mulct or fine in gold.

GOLIARDUS. L. Lat. A jester, buffoon, or juggler. Spelman, voc. "Goliardensis."

GOMASHTAH. In Hindu law. An agent; a steward; a confidential factor; a representative.

GOOD. 1. Valid; sufficient in law; effectual; unobjectionable.

2. Responsible; solvent; able to pay an amount specified.

3. Of a value corresponding with its terms; collectible. A note is said to be "good" when the payment of it at maturity may be relied on.

Writing the word "Good" across the face of a check is the customary mode in which bankers at the present day certify that the drawer has funds to meet it, and that it will be paid on presentation for that purpose.

GOOD ABEARING. See ABEARANCE.

GOOD AND LAWFUL MEN. Those who are not disqualified for service on juries by non-age, alienage, infamy, or lunacy, and who reside in the county of the venue.

GOOD AND VALID. Reliable, sufficient, and unimpeachable in law; adequate; responsible. See GOOD.

GOOD BEHAVIOR. Orderly and lawful conduct; behavior such as is proper for a peaceable and law-abiding citizen. Surety of good behavior may be exacted from any one who manifests an intention to commit crime or is otherwise reasonably suspected of a criminal design.

GOOD CONSIDERATION. As distinguished from *valuable* consideration, a consideration founded on motives of generosity, prudence, and natural duty; such as natural love and affection.

GOOD COUNTRY. In Scotch law. Good men of the country. A name given to a jury.

GOOD FAITH. Good faith consists in an honest intention to abstain from taking any unconscientious advantage of another, even through the forms or technicalities of law, together with an absence of all information or belief of facts which would render the transaction unconscientious. Civil Code Dak. § 2105; 1 Dak. 399, 46 N. W. Rep. 1132.

As to a purchaser in good faith, see BONA FIDE PURCHASER.

GOOD JURY. A jury of which the members are selected from the list of special jurors. See L. R. 5 C. P. 155.

GOOD TITLE. This means such a title as a court of chancery would adopt as a sufficient ground for compelling specific performance, and such a title as would be a good answer to an action of ejectment by any claimant. 6 Exch. 873. See, also, 23 Barb. 370.

GOOD-WILL. The custom or patronage of any established trade or business; the benefit or advantage of having established a business and secured its patronage by the public.

The advantage or benefit which is acquired by an establishment, beyond the mere value of the capital, stocks, funds, or property employed therein, in consequence of the general public patronage and encouragement which it receives from constant or habitual customers, on account of its local position, or common celebrity, or reputation for skill or affluence or punctuality, or from other accidental circumstances or necessities, or even from ancient partialities or prejudices. Story, Partn. § 99; 33 Cal. 624.

The good-will of a business is the expectation of continued public patronage, but it does not include a right to use the name of any person from whom it was acquired. Civil Code Cal. § 992; Civil Code Dak. § 577.

The term "good-will" does not mean simply the advantage of occupying particular premises which have been occupied by a manufacturer, etc. It means every advantage, every positive advantage, that has been acquired by a proprietor in carrying on his business, whether connected with the premises in which the business is conducted, or with the name under which it is managed, or with any other matter carrying with it the benefit of the business. 61 N. Y. 226.

GOODRIGHT, GOODTITLE. The fictitious plaintiff in the old action of ejectment, most frequently called "John Doe," was sometimes called "Goodright" or "Goodtitle."

GOODS. In contracts. The term "goods" is not so wide as "chattels," for it applies to inanimate objects, and does not include animals or chattels real, as a lease for years of house or land, which "chattels" does include. Co. Litt. 118; 1 Russ. 376.

In wills. In wills "goods" is *nomen generalissimum*, and, if there is nothing to limit it, will comprehend all the personal estate of the testator, as stocks, bonds, notes, money, plate, furniture, etc. 1 Atk. 180–182.

GOODS AND CHATTELS. This phrase is a general denomination of personal property, as distinguished from real property; the term "chattels" having the effect of extending its scope to any objects of that nature which would not properly be included by the term "goods" alone, *e. g.*, living animals, emblements, and fruits, and terms under leases for years. The general phrase also embraces choses in action, as well as personalty in possession.

In wills. The term "goods and chattels" will, unless restrained by the context, pass all the personal estate, including leases for years, cattle, corn, debts, and the like. Ward, Leg. 208, 211.

GOODS SOLD AND DELIVERED. A phrase frequently used in the action of *as-*

H

I

J

K

L

M

sumpsit, when the sale and delivery of goods furnish the cause.

"GOODS, WARES, AND MERCHANDISE." A general and comprehensive designation of such chattels as are ordinarily the subject of traffic and sale. The phrase is used in the statute of frauds, and is frequently found in pleadings and other instruments. As to its scope, see 20 Pick. 9; 118 Mass. 285; 2 Mason, 407; 2 Sum. 362; 4 Blatchf. 136; 20 Mich. 357; 6 Wend. 355; 40 Ind. 593; Dudley, 28; 55 Iowa, 520, 8 N. W. Rep. 334; 2 Pars. Cont. 330; Benj. Sales, 111; 2 Kent, Comm. 510, note.

GOOLE. In old English law. A breach in a bank or sea wall, or a passage worn by the flux and reflux of the sea. St. 16 & 17 Car. II. c. 11.

GORCE, or GORS. A wear, pool, or pit of water. Termes de la Ley.

GORE. A small, narrow slip of ground. Cowell.

GOSSIPRED. In canon law. Compaternity; spiritual affinity.

GOUT. In medical jurisprudence. An inflammation of the fibrous and ligamentous parts of the joints.

GOVERNMENT. 1. The regulation, restraint, supervision, or control which is exercised upon the individual members of an organized jural society by those invested with the supreme political authority, for the good and welfare of the body politic; or the *act* of exercising supreme political power or control.

2. The system of polity in a state; that form of fundamental rules and principles by which a nation or state is governed, or by which individual members of a body politic are to regulate their social actions; a constitution, either written or unwritten, by which the rights and duties of citizens and public officers are prescribed and defined, as a monarchical government, a republican government, etc. Webster.

3. An empire, kingdom, state, or independent political community; as in the phrase, "Compacts between independent governments."

4. The sovereign or supreme power in a state or nation.

5. The machinery by which the sovereign power in a state expresses its will and exercises its functions; or the framework of political institutions, departments, and offices, by means of which the executive, judicial, legislative, and administrative business of the state is carried on.

6. The whole class or body of office-holders or functionaries considered in the aggregate, upon whom devolves the executive, judicial, legislative, and administrative business of the state.

7. In a colloquial sense, the United States, or its representatives, considered as the prosecutor in a criminal action; as in the phrase, "the government objects to the witness."

We understand, in modern political science, by "state," in its widest sense, an independent society, acknowledging no superior, and by the term "government," that institution or aggregate of institutions by which that society makes and carries out those rules of action which are necessary to enable men to live in a social state, or which are imposed upon the people forming that society by those who possess the power or authority of prescribing them. "Government" is the aggregate of authorities which rule a society. By "administration," again, we understand in modern times, and especially in more or less free countries, the aggregate of those persons in whose hands the reins of government are for the time being, (the chief ministers or heads of departments.) But the terms "state," "government," and "administration" are not always used in their strictness. The government of a state being its most prominent feature, which is most readily perceived, "government" has frequently been used for "state;" and the publicists of the last century almost always used the term "government," or "form of government," when they discussed the different political societies or states. On the other hand, "government" is often used, to this day, for "administration," in the sense in which it has been explained. Bouvier.

GOVERNMENT ANNUITIES SOCIETIES. These societies are formed in England under 3 & 4 Wm. IV. c. 14, to enable the industrious classes to make provisions for themselves by purchasing, on advantageous terms, a government annuity for life or term of years. By 16 & 17 Vict. c. 45, this act, as well as 7 & 8 Vict. c. 83, amending it, were repealed, and the whole law in relation to the purchase of government annuities, through the medium of savings banks, was consolidated. And by 27 & 28 Vict. c. 43, additional facilities were afforded for the purchase of such annuities, and for assuring payments of money on death. Wharton.

GOVERNMENT DE FACTO. A government of fact. A government actually exercising power and control in the state, as opposed to the true and lawful government; a government not established according to the constitution of the state, or not lawfully entitled to recognition or supremacy, but which has nevertheless supplanted or displaced the government *de jure.*

A government deemed unlawful, or deemed wrongful or unjust, which, nevertheless, receives presently habitual obedience from the bulk of the community.   Aust. Jur. 324.

There are several degrees of what is called "*de facto* government."

Such a government, in its highest degree, assumes a character very closely resembling that of a lawful government. This is when the usurping government expels the regular authorities from their customary seats and functions, and establishes itself in their place, and so becomes the actual government of a country. The distinguishing characteristic of such a government is that adherents to it in war against the government *de jure* do not incur the penalties of treason; and, under certain limitations, obligations assumed by it in behalf of the country or otherwise will, in general, be respected by the government *de jure* when restored.

But there is another description of government, called also by publicists a "government *de facto*," but which might, perhaps, be more aptly denominated a "government of paramount force." Its distinguishing characteristics are (1) that its existence is maintained by active military power, within the territories, and against the rightful authority, of an established and lawful government; and (2) that, while it exists, it must necessarily be obeyed in civil matters by private citizens who, by acts of obedience, rendered in submission to such force, do not become responsible, as wrong-doers, for those acts, though not warranted by the laws of the rightful government. Actual governments of this sort are established over districts differing greatly in extent and conditions. They are usually administered directly by military authority, but they may be administered, also, by civil authority, supported more or less by military force. 8 Wall. 8, 9.

The term "*de facto*," as descriptive of a government, has no well-fixed and definite sense. It is, perhaps, most correctly used as signifying a government completely, though only temporarily, established in the place of the lawful or regular government, occupying its capitol, and exercising its power, and which is ultimately overthrown, and the authority of the government *de jure* reestablished. 42 Miss. 651, 703.

A government *de facto* is a government that unlawfully gets the possession and control of the rightful legal government, and maintains itself there, by force and arms, against the will of such legal government, and claims to exercise the powers thereof. 43 Ala. 204.

GOVERNMENT DE JURE. A government of right; the true and lawful government; a government established according to the constitution of the state, and lawfully entitled to recognition and supremacy and the administration of the state, but which is actually cut off from power or control.

A government deemed lawful, or deemed rightful or just, which, nevertheless, has been supplanted or displaced; that is to say, which

receives not presently (although it received formerly) habitual obedience from the bulk of the community.   Aust. Jur. 324.

GOVERNOR. The title of the chief executive in each of the states and territories of the United States; and also of the chief magistrate of some colonies, provinces, and dependencies of other nations.

GRACE. This word is commonly used in contradistinction to "right." Thus, in St. 22 Edw. III., the lord chancellor was instructed to take cognizance of matters of grace, being such subjects of equity jurisdiction as were exclusively matters of equity.   Brown.

A faculty, license, or dispensation; also general and free pardon by act of parliament. See ACT OF GRACE.

GRACE, DAYS OF. Time of indulgence granted to an acceptor or maker for the payment of his bill of exchange or note. It was originally a gratuitous favor, (hence the name,) but custom has rendered it a legal right.

GRADATIM. In old English law. By degrees or steps; step by step; from one degree to another.   Bract. fol. 64.

GRADIENT. Moving step by step; a grade; the deviation of railways from a level surface to an inclined plane.

GRADUATES. Scholars who have taken a degree in a college or university.

GRADUS. In the civil and old English law. A measure of space. A degree of relationship.

A step or degree generally; *e. g., gradus honorum,* degrees of honor. Vicat. A pulpit; a year; a generation.   Du Cange.

A port; any place where a vessel can be brought to land.   Du Cange.

GRADUS PARENTELÆ. A pedigree; a table of relationship.

GRAFFARIUS. In old English law. A graffer, notary, or scrivener. St. 5 Hen. VIII. c. 1.

GRAFFER. A notary or scrivener. See St. 5 Hen. VIII. c. 1. The word is a corruption of the French "*greffier*," (*q. v.*)

GRAFFIUM. A writing-book, register, or cartulary of deeds and evidences. Cowell.

GRAFIO. A baron, inferior to a count. A fiscal judge. An advocate. Spelman; Cowell.

GRAFT. A term used in equity to denote the confirmation, by relation back, of the right of a mortgagee in premises to which, at the making of the mortgage, the mortgagor had only an imperfect title, but to which the latter has since acquired a good title.

GRAIL. A gradual, or book containing some of the offices of the Romish Church.

A chalice; a broad dish or vessel. The holy grail was the vessel out of which our Lord was believed to have eaten at the Last Supper. Cowell.

GRAIN. In Troy weight, the twenty-fourth part of a pennyweight. Any kind of corn sown in the ground.

GRAINAGE. An ancient duty in London under which the twentieth part of salt imported by aliens was taken.

GRAMMAR SCHOOL. In England, this term designates a school in which such instruction is given as will prepare the student to enter a college or university, and in this sense the phrase was used in the Massachusetts colonial act of 1647, requiring every town containing a hundred householders to set up a "grammar school." See 103 Mass. 97. But in modern American usage the term denotes a school, intermediate between the primary school and the high school, in which English grammar and other studies of that grade are taught.

Grammatica falsa non vitiat chartam. 9 Coke, 48. False grammar does not vitiate a deed.

GRAMMATOPHYLACIUM. (Græco-Lat.) In the civil law. A place for keeping writings or records. Dig. 48, 19, 9, 6.

GRAMME. The unit of weight in the metric system. The gramme is the weight of a cubic centimeter of distilled water at the temperature of 4° C. It is equal to 15.4341 grains troy, or 5.6481 drachms avoirdupois.

GRANATARIUS. In old English law. An officer having charge of a granary. Fleta, lib. 2, c. 82, § 1; Id. c. 84.

GRAND ASSIZE. A peculiar species of trial by jury, introduced in the time of Henry II., giving the tenant or defendant in a writ of right the alternative of a trial by battel, or by his peers. Abolished by 3 & 4 Wm. IV. c. 42, § 13. See 3 Bl. Comm. 341.

GRAND BILL OF SALE. In English law. The name of an instrument used for the transfer of a ship while she is at sea. An expression which is understood to refer to the instrument whereby a ship was originally transferred from the builder to the owner, or first purchaser. 3 Kent, Comm. 133.

GRAND CAPE. In practice. A judicial writ in the old real actions, which issued for the demandant where the tenant, after being duly summoned, neglected to appear on the return of the writ, or to cast an essoin, or, in case of an essoin being cast, neglected to appear on the adjournment day of the essoin; its object being to compel an appearance. Rosc. Real Act. 165, et seq. It was called a "cape," from the word with which it commenced, and a "grand cape" (or *cape magnum*) to distinguish it from the *petit cape*, which lay after appearance.

GRAND COUTUMIER. A collection of customs, laws, and forms of procedure in use in early times in France. See Coutumier.

GRAND DAYS. In English practice. Certain days in the terms, which are solemnly kept in the inns of court and chancery, viz., Candlemas day in Hilary term, Ascension day in Easter, St. John the Baptist's day in Trinity, and All Saints in Michaelmas; which are *dies non juridici.* Termes de la Ley; Cowell; Blount. They are days set apart for peculiar festivity; the members of the respective inns being on such occasions regaled at their dinner in the hall, with more than usual sumptuousness. Holthouse.

GRAND DISTRESS, WRIT OF. A writ formerly issued in the real action of *quare impedit*, when no appearance had been entered after the attachment; it commanded the sheriff to distrain the defendant's lands and chattels in order to compel appearance. It is no longer used. 23 & 24 Vict. c. 126, § 26, having abolished the action of *quare impedit*, and substituted for it the procedure in an ordinary action. Wharton.

GRAND JURY. A jury of inquiry, consisting of from twelve to twenty-three men, who are summoned and returned by the sheriff to each session of the criminal courts, and whose duty is to receive complaints and accusations in criminal cases, hear the evidence adduced on the part of the state, and find bills of indictment in cases where they are satisfied a trial ought to be had. They are first sworn, and instructed by the court. This is called a "grand jury" because it comprises a greater number of jurors than the ordinary trial jury or "petit jury."

GRAND LARCENY. In criminal law. In England, simple larceny was originally divided into two sorts,—*grand* larceny, where the value of the goods stolen was above twelve pence, and *petit* larceny, where their value was equal to or below that sum. 4 Bl. Comm. 229. The distinction was abolished in England by St. 7 & 8 Geo. IV. c. 29, and is not generally recognized in the United States.

GRAND SERJEANTY. A species of tenure *in capite*, resembling knight-service, as the service or render was of a free and honorable nature and military in its character. But the tenant by grand serjeanty was bound, instead of attending the king generally in his wars, to do some special honorary service to the king in person, as to carry his banner or sword, or to be his butler or champion at his coronation. Litt. § 153; 2 Bl. Comm. 73; 1 Steph. Comm. 188.

GRANDCHILD. The child of one's child.

GRANDFATHER. The father of either of one's parents.

GRANDMOTHER. The mother of either of one's parents.

GRANGE. A farm furnished with barns, granaries, stables, and all conveniences for husbandry. Co. Litt. 5a.

GRANGEARIUS. A keeper of a grange or farm.

GRANGIA. A grange. Co. Litt. 5a.

GRANT. A generic term applicable to all transfers of real property. 3 Washb. Real Prop. 181, 353.

A transfer by deed of that which cannot be passed by livery. Williams, Real Prop. 147, 149.

An act evidenced by letters patent under the great seal, granting something from the king to a subject. Cruise, Dig. tit. 33, 34.

A technical term made use of in deeds of conveyance of lands to import a transfer. 3 Washb. Real Prop. 378–380.

Though the word "grant" was originally made use of, in treating of conveyances of interests in lands, to denote a transfer by deed of that which could not be passed by livery, and, of course, was applied only to incorporeal hereditaments, it has now become a gen-

eric term, applicable to the transfer of all classes of real property. 3 Washb. Real Prop. 181.

As distinguished from a mere license, a grant passes some estate or interest, corporeal or incorporeal, in the lands which it embraces; can only be made by an instrument in writing, under seal; and is irrevocable, when made, unless an express power of revocation is reserved. A license is a mere authority; passes no estate or interest whatever; may be made by parol; is revocable at will; and, when revoked, the protection which it gave ceases to exist. 3 Duer, 255, 258.

The term "grant," in Scotland, is used in reference (1) to original dispositions of land, as when a lord makes grants of land among tenants; (2) to gratuitous deeds. Paterson. In such case, the superior or donor is said to to grant the deed; an expression totally unknown in English law. Mozley & Whitley.

By the word "grant," in a treaty, is meant not only a formal grant, but any concession, warrant, order, or permission to survey, possess, or settle, whether written or parol, express, or presumed from possession. Such a grant may be made by law, as well as by a patent pursuant to a law. 12 Pet. 410. See 9 Adol. & E. 532; 5 Mass. 472; 9 Pick. 80.

"GRANT, BARGAIN, AND SELL." Operative words in conveyances of real estate.

GRANT OF PERSONAL PROPERTY. A method of transferring personal property, distinguished from a gift by being always founded on some consideration or equivalent. 2 Bl. Comm. 440, 441. Its proper legal designation is an "assignment," or "bargain and sale." 2 Steph. Comm. 102.

GRANT TO USES. The common grant with uses superadded, which has become the favorite mode of transferring realty in England. Wharton.

GRANTEE. The person to whom a grant is made.

GRANTOR. The person by whom a grant is made.

GRANTZ. In old English law. Noblemen or grandees. Jacob.

GRASS HEARTH. In old records. The grazing or turning up the earth with a plow. The name of a customary service for inferior tenants to bring their plows, and do one day's work for their lords. Cowell.

GRASS WEEK. Rogation week, so called anciently in the inns of court and chancery.

GRASS WIDOW. A slang term for a woman separated from her husband by abandonment or prolonged absence; a woman living apart from her husband. Webster.

GRASSON, or GRASSUM. A fine paid upon the transfer of a copyhold estate.

GRATIFICATION. A gratuity; a recompense or reward for services or benefits, given voluntarily, without solicitation or promise.

GRATIS. Freely; gratuitously; without reward or consideration.

GRATIS DICTUM. A voluntary assertion; a statement which a party is not legally bound to make, or in which he is not held to precise accuracy. 2 Kent, Comm. 486; 6 Metc. (Mass.) 260.

GRATUITOUS. Without valuable or legal consideration. A term applied to deeds of conveyance.

In old English law. Voluntary; without force, fear, or favor. Bract. fols. 11, 17.

GRATUITOUS CONTRACT. In the civil law. One which tends wholly to the benefit or advantage of one of the parties, without any compensation, profit, or gain moving to the other.

GRATUITOUS DEEDS. Instruments made without binding consideration.

GRAVA. In old English law. A grove; a small wood; a coppice or thicket. Co. Litt. 4b.

A thick wood of high trees. Blount.

GRAVAMEN. The burden or gist of a charge; the grievance or injury specially complained of.

In English ecclesiastical law. A grievance complained of by the clergy before the bishops in convocation.

GRAVATIO. An accusation or impeachment. Leg. Ethel. c. 19.

GRAVE. A sepulcher. A place where a dead body is interred.

GRAVIS. Grievous; great. *Ad grave damnum*, to the grievous damage. 11 Coke, 40.

GRAVIUS. A graf; a chief magistrate or officer. A term derived from the more ancient "*grafio*," and used in combination with various other words, as an official title in Germany; as *Margravius, Rheingravius, Landgravius*, etc. Spelman.

Gravius est divinam quam temporalem lædere majestatem. It is more serious to hurt divine than temporal majesty. 11 Coke, 29.

GRAY'S INN. An inn of court. See INNS OF COURT.

GREAT CATTLE. All manner of beasts except sheep and yearlings. 2 Rolle, 173.

GREAT CHARTER. *Magna Charta*, (*q. v.*)

GREAT LAW, THE, or "The Body of Laws of the Province of Pennsylvania and Territories thereunto belonging, Past at an Assembly held at Chester, *alias* Upland, the 7th day of the tenth month, called 'December,' 1682." This was the first code of laws established in Pennsylvania, and is justly celebrated for the provision in its first chapter for liberty of conscience. Bouvier.

GREAT SEAL. In English law. A seal by virtue of which a great part of the royal authority is exercised. The office of the lord chancellor, or lord keeper, is created by the delivery of the great seal into his custody. There is one great seal for all public acts of state which concern the United Kingdom. Mozley & Whitley.

GREAT TITHES. In English ecclesiastical law. Tithes of corn, pease and beans, hay and wood. 2 Chit. Bl. Comm. 24, note; 3 Steph. Comm. 127.

GREE. Satisfaction for an offense committed or injury done. Cowell.

GREEK KALENDS. A colloquial expression to signify a time indefinitely remote, there being no such division of time known to the Greeks.

GREEN CLOTH. In English law. A board or court of justice held in the counting-house of the king's (or queen's) household, and composed of the lord steward and inferior officers. It takes its name from the green cloth spread over the board at which it is held. Wharton; Cowell.

GREEN SILVER. A feudal custom in the manor of Writtel, in Essex, where every tenant whose front door opens to Greenbury shall pay a half-penny yearly to the lord, by the name of "green silver" or "rent." Cowell.

GREEN WAX. In English law. The name of the estreats in the exchequer, delivered to the sheriff under the seal of that court, which was impressed upon green wax.

GREENBACK. The popular and almost exclusive name applied to all United States treasury issues. It is not applied to any other species of paper currency; and, when employed in testimony by way of description, is as certain as the phrase "treasury notes." 23 Ind. 21.

GREENHEW. In forest law. The same as *vert,* (*q. v.*) Termes de la Ley.

GREFFIERS. In French law. Registrars, or clerks of the courts. They are officials attached to the courts to assist the judges in their duties. They keep the minutes, write out the judgments, orders, and other decisions given by the tribunals, and deliver copies thereof to applicants.

GREGORIAN CODE. The code or collection of constitutions made by the Roman jurist Gregorius. See CODEX GREGORIANUS.

GREGORIAN EPOCH. The time from which the Gregorian calendar or computation dates; *i. e.*, from the year 1582.

GREMIO. In Spanish law. A guild; an association of workmen, artificers, or merchants following the same trade or business; designed to protect and further the interests of their craft.

GREMIUM. Lat. The bosom or breast; hence, derivatively, safeguard or protection. In English law, an estate which is in abeyance is said to be *in gremio legis;* that is, in the protection or keeping of the law.

GRENVILLE ACT. The statute 10 Geo. III. c. 16, by which the jurisdiction over parliamentary election petitions was transferred from the whole house of commons to select committees. Repealed by 9 Geo. IV. c. 22, § 1.

GRESSUME. In English law. A customary fine due from a copyhold tenant on the death of the lord. 1 Strange, 654; 1 Crabb, Real Prop. p. 615, § 778. Called also "*grassum,*" and "*grossome.*"

GRETNA GREEN MARRIAGE. A marriage celebrated at Gretna, in Dumfries, (bordering on the county of Cumberland,) in Scotland. By the law of Scotland a valid marriage may be contracted by consent alone, without any other formality. When the marriage act (26 Geo. II. c. 33) rendered the publication of banns, or a license, necessary in England, it became usual for persons who

wished to marry clandestinely to go to Gretna Green, the nearest part of Scotland, and marry according to the Scotch law; so a sort of chapel was built at Gretna Green, in which the English marriage service was performed by the village blacksmith. Wharton.

GREVA. In old records. The sea shore, sand, or beach. 2 Mon. Angl. 625; Cowell.

GRIEVED. Aggrieved. 3 East, 22.

GRITH. Peace; protection. Termes de la Ley.

GRITHBRECH. Sax. Breach of the king's peace, as opposed to *frithbrech,* a breach of the nation's peace with other nations.

GRITHSTOLE. Sax. In Saxon law. A seat, chair, or place of peace; a sanctuary; a stone within a church-gate, to which an offender might flee.

GROCER. In old English law. A merchant or trader who *engrossed* all vendible merchandise; an engrosser. St. 37 Edw. III. c. 5. See ENGROSSER.

GRONNA. In old records. A deep hollow or pit; a bog or miry place. Cowell.

GROOM OF THE STOLE. In England. An officer of the royal household, who has charge of the king's wardrobe.

GROOM PORTER. Formerly an officer belonging to the royal household. Jacob.

GROSS. Great; culpable. General. Absolute or entire. A thing *in gross* exists in its own right, and not as an appendage to another thing.

GROSS ADVENTURE. In maritime law. A loan on bottomry. So named because the lender, in case of a loss, or expense incurred for the common safety, must contribute to the *gross* or general average.

GROSS AVERAGE. In maritime law. A contribution made by the owners of a ship, its cargo, and the freight, towards the loss sustained by the voluntary and necessary sacrifice of property for the common safety, in proportion to their respective interests. More commonly called "general average," (*q. v.*) See 3 Kent, Comm. 232; 2 Steph. Comm. 179.

GROSS NEGLIGENCE. In the law of bailment. The want of slight diligence. The want of that care which every man of common sense, how inattentive soever, takes of his own property. The omission of that care which even inattentive and thoughtless men never fail to take of their own property.

GROSS WEIGHT. The whole weight of goods and merchandise, including the dust and dross, and also the chest or bag, etc., upon which tare and tret are allowed.

GROSSE AVANTURE. Fr. In French marine law. The contract of bottomry. Ord. Mar. liv. 3, tit. 5.

GROSSE BOIS. Timber. Cowell.

GROSSEMENT. L. Fr. Largely, greatly. *Grossement enseint*, big with child. Plowd. 76.

GROSSOME. In old English law. A fine, or sum of money paid for a lease. Plowd. 270, 271. Supposed to be a corruption of *gersuma*, (*q. v.*) See GRESSUME.

GROUND ANNUAL. In Scotch law. An annual rent of two kinds: *First*, the feu duties payable to the lords of erection and their successors; *second*, the rents reserved for building lots in a city, where *sub-feus* are prohibited. This rent is in the nature of a perpetual annuity. Bell.; Ersk. Inst. 11, 3, 52.

GROUND LANDLORD. The grantor of an estate on which a ground-rent is reserved.

GROUND-RENT. A perpetual rent reserved to himself and his heirs, by the grantor of land in fee-simple, out of the land conveyed. It is in the nature of an emphyteutic rent. Also, in English law, rent paid on a building lease.

GROUND WRIT. By the English common-law procedure act, 1852, c. 121, "it shall not be necessary to issue any writ directed to the sheriff of the county in which the venue is laid, but writs of execution may issue at once into any county, and be directed to and executed by the sheriff of any county, whether a county palatine or not, without reference to the county in which the venue is laid, and without any suggestion of the issuing of a prior writ into such county." Before this enactment, a *ca. sa.* or *fi. fa.* could not be issued into a county different from that in which the venue in the action was laid, without first issuing a writ, called a "ground writ," into the latter county, and then another writ, which was called a "*testatum* writ," into the former. The above enactment abolished this useless process. Wharton.

GROUNDAGE. A custom or tribute paid for the standing of shipping in port. Jacob.

GROWING CROP. A crop must be considered and treated as a *growing* crop from the time the seed is deposited in the ground, as at that time the seed loses the qualities of a chattel, and becomes a part of the freehold, and passes with a sale of it. 69 Ala. 435.

Growing crops of grain, and other annual productions raised by cultivation of the earth and industry of man, are personal chattels. Growing trees, fruit, or grass, and other natural products of the earth, are parcel of the land. 1 Denio, 550.

GROWTH HALF-PENNY. A rate paid in some places for the tithe of every fat beast, ox, or other unfruitful cattle. Clayt. 92.

GRUARII. The principal officers of a forest.

GUADIA. In old European law. A pledge. Spelman; Calvin. A custom. Spelman. Spelled also "wadia."

GUARANTEE. He to whom a guaranty is made. This word is also used, as a noun, to denote the contract of guaranty or the obligation of a guarantor, and, as a verb, to denote the action of assuming the responsibilities of a guarantor. But on the general principle of legal orthography,—that the title of the person to whom the action passes over should end in "ee," as "donee," "grantee," "payee," "bailee," "drawee," etc.,—it seems better to use this word only as the correlative of "guarantor," and to spell the verb, and also the name of the contract, "guaranty."

GUARENTIGIO. In Spanish law. A written authorization to a court to enforce the performance of an agreement in the same manner as if it had been decreed upon regular legal proceedings.

GUARANTOR. He who makes a guaranty.

GUARANTY. *v.* To undertake collaterally to answer for the payment of another's debt or the performance of another's duty, liability, or obligation; to assume the responsibility of a guarantor; to warrant. See GUARANTY, *n.*

GUARANTY. *n.* A promise to answer for the payment of some debt, or the performance of some duty, in case of the failure of another person, who, in the first instance, is liable to such payment or performance. Fell, Guar. 1; 3 Kent, Comm. 121; 60 N. Y. 438; 1 Miles, 277.

A guaranty is an undertaking by one person to be answerable for the payment of some debt, or the due performance of some contract or duty, by another person, who himself remains liable to pay or perform the same. Story, Prom. Notes, § 457.

A guaranty is a promise to answer for the debt, default, or miscarriage of another person. Civil Code Cal. § 2787.

A guaranty is a contract that some particular thing shall be done exactly as it is agreed to be done, whether it is to be done by one person or another, and whether there be a prior or principal contractor or not. 27 Conn. 31.

The definition of a "guaranty," by text-writers, is an undertaking by one person that another shall perform his contract or fulfill his obligation, or that, if he does not, the guarantor will do it for him. A guarantor of a bill or note is said to be one who engages that the note shall be paid, but is not an indorser or surety. 72 Ill. 13.

The terms "guaranty" and "suretyship" are sometimes used interchangeably; but they should not be confounded. The contract of a surety corresponds with that of a guarantor in many respects; yet important differences exist. The surety is bound with his principal as an original promisor. He is a debtor from the beginning, and must see that the debt is paid, and is held ordinarily to know every default of his principal, and cannot protect himself by the mere indulgence of the creditor, nor by want of notice of the default of the principal, however such indulgence or want of notice may in fact injure him. On the other hand, the contract of a guarantor is his own separate contract. It is in the nature of a warranty by him that the thing guarantied to be done by the principal shall be done, not merely an engagement jointly with the principal to do the thing. The original contract of the principal is not his contract, and he is not bound to take notice of its non-performance. Therefore the creditor should give him notice; and it is universally held that, if the guarantor can prove that he has suffered damage by the failure to give such notice, he will be discharged to the extent of the damage thus sustained. It is not so with a surety. 32 Ind. 11; 2 N. Y. 533.

A guaranty relating to a future liability of the principal, under successive transactions, which either continue his liability, or from time to time renew it after it has been satisfied, is called a "continuing guaranty." Civil Code Cal. § 2814.

GUARANTY INSURANCE. A guaranty or insurance against loss in case a person named shall make a designated default or be guilty of specified conduct. It is usually against the misconduct or dishonesty of an employee or officer, though sometimes against the breach of a contract. 9 Amer. & Eng. Enc. Law, 65.

GUARDAGE. A state of wardship.

GUARDIAN. A guardian is a person lawfully invested with the power, and charged with the duty, of taking care of the person and managing the property and rights of another person, who, for some peculiarity of *status*, or defect of age, understanding, or self-control, is considered incapable of administering his own affairs.

A guardian is a person appointed to take care of the person or property of another. Civil Code Cal. § 236.

One who legally has the care and management of the person, or the estate, or both, of a child during its minority. Reeve, Dom. Rel. 311.

This term might be appropriately used to designate the person charged with the care and control of idiots, lunatics, habitual drunkards, spendthrifts, and the like; but such person is, under many of the statutory systems authorizing the appointment, styled "committee," and in common usage the name "guardian" is applied only to one having the care and management of a minor.

The name "curator" is given in some of the states to a person having the control of a minor's estate, without that of his person; and this is also the usage of the civil law.

A *testamentary* guardian is one appointed by the deed or last will of the child's father; while a guardian *by election* is one chosen by the infant himself, in a case where he would otherwise be without one.

GUARDIAN AD LITEM. A guardian appointed by a court of justice to prosecute or defend for an infant in any suit to which he may be a party. 2 Steph. Comm. 342. Most commonly appointed for infant *defendants;* infant plaintiffs generally suing by *next friend*. This kind of guardian has no right to interfere with the infant's person or property. 2 Steph. Comm. 343.

GUARDIAN BY APPOINTMENT OF COURT. The most important species of guardian in modern law, having custody of the infant until the attainment of full age. It has in England in a manner superseded the guardian in socage, and in the United States the guardian by nature also. The appointment is made by a court of chancery, or probate or orphans' court. 2 Steph. Comm. 341; 2 Kent, Comm. 226.

GUARDIAN BY NATURE. The father, and, on his death, the mother, of a child. 1 Bl. Comm. 461; 2 Kent, Comm. 219. This guardianship extends only to the custody of

H

I

J

K

L

M

the person of the child to the age of twenty-one years. Sometimes called "natural guardian," but this is rather a popular than a technical mode of expression. 2 Steph. Comm. 337.

GUARDIAN BY STATUTE. A guardian appointed for a child by the deed or last will of the father, and who has the custody both of his person and estate until the attainment of full age. This kind of guardianship is founded on the statute of 12 Car. II. c. 24, and has been pretty extensively adopted in this country. 1 Bl. Comm. 462; 2 Steph. Comm. 339, 340; 2 Kent, Comm. 224–226.

GUARDIAN DE L'EGLISE. A church-warden.

GUARDIAN DE L'ESTEMARY. The warden of the stannaries or mines in Cornwall, etc.

GUARDIAN FOR NURTURE. The father, or, at his decease, the mother, of a child. This kind of guardianship extends only to the person, and determines when the infant arrives at the age of fourteen. 2 Kent, Comm. 221; 1 Bl. Comm. 461; 2 Steph. Comm. 338.

GUARDIAN IN CHIVALRY. In the tenure by knight's service, in the feudal law, if the heir of the feud was under the age of twenty-one, being a male, or fourteen, being a female, the lord was entitled to the wardship (and marriage) of the heir, and was called the "guardian in chivalry." This wardship consisted in having the custody of the body and lands of such heir, without any account of the profits. 2 Bl. Comm. 67.

GUARDIAN IN SOCAGE. At the common law, this was a species of guardian who had the custody of lands coming to the infant by descent, as also of the infant's person, until the latter reached the age of fourteen Such guardian was always "the next of kin to whom the inheritance cannot possibly descend." 1 Bl. Comm. 461; 2 Steph. Comm. 338.

GUARDIAN OF THE PEACE. A warden or conservator of the peace.

GUARDIAN OF THE POOR. In English law. A person elected by the rate-payers of a parish to have the charge and management of the parish work-house or union. See 3 Steph. Comm. 203, 215.

GUARDIAN OF THE SPIRITUALITIES. The person to whom the spiritual jurisdiction of any diocese is committed during the vacancy of the see.

GUARDIAN OF THE TEMPORALITIES. The person to whose custody a vacant see or abbey was committed by the crown.

GUARDIAN, or WARDEN, OF THE CINQUE PORTS. A magistrate who has the jurisdiction of the ports or havens which are called the "Cinque Ports," (*q. v.*) This office was first created in England, in imitation of the Roman policy, to strengthen the sea-coasts against enemies, etc.

GUARDIANSHIP. The office, duty, or authority of a guardian. Also the relation subsisting between guardian and ward.

GUARDIANUS. A guardian, warden, or keeper. Spelman.

GUARNIMENTUM. In old European law. A provision of necessary things. Spelman. A furnishing or garnishment.

GUASTALD. One who had the custody of the royal mansions.

GUBERNATOR. Lat. In Roman law. The pilot or steersman of a ship.

GUERPI, GUERPY. L. Fr. Abandoned; left; deserted. Britt. c. 33.

GUERRA, GUERRE. War. Spelman.

GUERILLA PARTY. In military law. An independent body of marauders or armed men, not regularly or organically connected with the armies of either belligerent, who carry on a species of irregular war, chiefly by depredation and massacre.

GUEST. A traveler who lodges at an inn or tavern with the consent of the keeper. Bac. Abr. "Inns," C, 5; 8 Coke, 32.

A guest, as distinguished from a boarder, is bound for no stipulated time. He stops at the inn for as short or as long time as he pleases, paying, while he remains, the customary charge. 24 How. Pr. 62.

GUEST-TAKER. An agister; one who took cattle in to feed in the royal forests. Cowell.

GUET. In old French law. Watch. Ord. Mar. liv. 4, tit. 6.

GUIA. In Spanish law. A right of way for narrow carts. White, New Recop. l. 2, c. 6, § 1.

GUIDAGE. In old English law. That which was given for safe conduct through a strange territory, or another's territory. Cowell.

The office of guiding of travelers through dangerous and unknown ways. 2 Inst. 526.

GUIDE-PLATE. An iron or steel plate to be attached to a rail for the purpose of guiding to their place on the rail wheels thrown off the track. Pub. St. Mass. 1882, p. 1291.

GUIDON DE LA MER. The name of a treatise on maritime law, by an unknown author, supposed to have been written about 1671 at Rouen, and considered, in continental Europe, as a work of high authority.

GUILD. A voluntary association of persons pursuing the same trade, art, profession, or business, such as printers, goldsmiths, wool merchants, etc., united under a distinct organization of their own, analogous to that of a corporation, regulating the affairs of their trade or business by their own laws and rules, and aiming, by co-operation and organization, to protect and promote the interests of their common vocation. In medieval history these fraternities or guilds played an important part in the government of some states; as at Florence, in the thirteenth and following centuries, where they chose the council of government of the city. But with the growth of cities and the advance in the organization of municipal government, their importance and prestige has declined. The place of meeting of a guild, or association of guilds, was called the "Guildhall." The word is said to be derived from the Anglo-Saxon "*gild*" or "*geld*," a tax or tribute, because each member of the society was required to pay a tax towards its support.

GUILD RENTS. Rents payable to the crown by any guild, or such as formerly belonged to religious guilds, and came to the crown at the general dissolution of the monasteries. Tomlins.

GUILDHALL. The *hall* or place of meeting of a *guild*, or gild.

The place of meeting of a municipal corporation. 3 Steph. Comm. 173, note. The mercantile or commercial *gilds* of the Saxons are supposed to have given rise to the present municipal corporations of England, whose place of meeting is still called the "Guildhall."

GUILDHALL SITTINGS. The sittings held in the Guildhall of the city of London for city of London causes.

GUILT. In criminal law. That quality which imparts criminality to a motive or act, and renders the person amenable to punishment by the law.

That disposition to violate the law which has manifested itself by some act already done. The opposite of innocence. See Ruth. Inst. b. 1, c. 18, § 10.

GUILTY. Having committed a crime or tort; the word used by a prisoner in pleading to an indictment when he confesses the crime of which he is charged, and by the jury in convicting.

GUINEA. A coin formerly issued by the English mint, but all these coins were called in in the time of Wm. IV. The word now means only the sum of £1. 1s., in which denomination the fees of counsel are always given.

GULE OF AUGUST. The first of August, being the day of *St. Peter ad Vincula.*

GULES. The heraldic name of the color usually called "red." The word is derived from the Arabic word "*gule,*" a rose, and was probably introduced by the Crusaders. Gules is denoted in engravings by numerous perpendicular lines. Heralds who blazoned by planets and jewels called it "Mars," and "ruby." Wharton.

GURGITES. Wears. Jacob.

GUTI. Jutes; one of the three nations who migrated from Germany to Britain at an early period. According to Spelman, they established themselves chiefly in Kent and the Isle of Wight.

GUTTER. The diminutive of a sewer. Callis, Sew. (80,) 100.

GWABR MERCHED. Maid's fee. A British word signifying a customary fine payable to lords of some manors on marriage of the tenant's daughters, or otherwise on their committing incontinence. Cowell.

GWALSTOW. A place of execution. Jacob.

GWAYF. Waif, or waived; that which has been stolen and afterwards dropped in the highway for fear of a discovery. Cowell.

GYLPUT. The name of a court which was held every three weeks in the liberty or hundred of Pathbew in Warwick. Jacob.

GYLTWITE. Sax. Compensation for fraud or trespass. Cowell.

GYNARCY, or **GYNÆCOCRACY.** Government by a woman; a state in which women are legally capable of the supreme command; e. g., in Great Britain and Spain.

GYROVAGI. Wandering monks.

GYVES. Fetters or shackles for the legs.

H.

H. This letter, as an abbreviation, stands for Henry (a king of that name) in the citation of English statutes. In the Year Books, it is used as an abbreviation for Hilary term.

H. A. An abbreviation for *hoc anno*, this year, in this year.

H. B. An abbreviation for house bill, *i. e.*, a bill in the house of representatives, as distinguished from a senate bill.

H. C. An abbreviation for house of commons, or for *habeas corpus*.

H. L. An abbreviation for house of lords.

H. R. An abbreviation for house of representatives.

H. T. An abbreviation for *hoc titulo*, this title, under this title; used in references to books.

H. V. An abbreviation for *hoc verbo* or *hac voce*, this word, under this word; used in references to dictionaries and other works alphabetically arranged.

HABE, or HAVE. Lat. A form of the salutatory expression "*Ave,*" (hail,) in the titles of the constitutions of the Theodosian and Justinianean Codes. Calvin.; Spelman.

HABEAS CORPORA JURATORUM. A writ commanding the sheriff to bring up the persons of jurors, and, if need were, to distrain them of their lands and goods, in order to insure or compel their attendance in court on the day of trial of a cause. It issued from the Common Pleas, and served the same purpose as a *distringas juratores* in the King's Bench. It was abolished by the C. L. P. Act, 1852, § 104. Brown.

HABEAS CORPUS. (You have the body.) The name given to a variety of writs, (of which these were anciently the emphatic words,) having for their object to bring a party before a court or judge. In common usage, and whenever these words are used alone, they are understood to mean the *habeas corpus ad subjiciendum*, (q. v.)

HABEAS CORPUS ACT. The English statute of 31 Car. II. c. 2, is the original and prominent *habeas corpus* act. It was amended and supplemented by St. 56 Geo. III. c. 100. And similar statutes have been enacted in all the United States. This act is justly regarded as the great constitutional guaranty of personal liberty.

HABEAS CORPUS AD DELIBERANDUM ET RECIPIENDUM. A writ which is issued to remove, for trial, a person confined in one county to the county or place where the offense of which he is accused was committed. Bac. Abr. "*Habeas Corpus,*" A; 1 Chit. Crim. Law, 132. Thus, it has been granted to remove a person in custody for contempt to take his trial for perjury in another county. 1 Tyrw. 185.

HABEAS CORPUS AD FACIENDUM ET RECIPIENDUM. A writ issuing in civil cases, to remove the cause, as also the body of the defendant, from an inferior court to a superior court having jurisdiction, there to be disposed of. It is also called "*habeas corpus cum causa.*"

HABEAS CORPUS AD PROSEQUENDUM. A writ which issues when it is necessary to remove a prisoner in order to *prosecute* in the proper jurisdiction wherein the fact was committed. 3 Bl. Comm. 130.

HABEAS CORPUS AD RESPONDENUM. A writ which is usually employed in civil cases to remove a person out of the custody of one court into that of another, in order that he may be sued and answer the action in the latter. 2 Sell. Pr. 259; 2 Mod. 198; 3 Bl. Comm. 129; 1 Tidd, Pr. 300.

HABEAS CORPUS AD SATISFACIENDUM. In English practice. A writ which issues when a prisoner has had judgment against him in an action, and the plaintiff is desirous to bring him up to some superior court, to charge him with process of execution. 3 Bl. Comm. 129, 130; 3 Steph. Comm. 693; 1 Tidd, Pr. 350.

HABEAS CORPUS AD SUBJICIENDUM. In practice. A writ directed to the person detaining another, and commanding him to produce the body of the prisoner, (or person detained,) with the day and cause of his caption and detention, *ad faciendum, subjiciendum et recipiendum*, to do, submit to, and receive whatsoever the judge or court awarding the writ shall consider in that behalf. 3 Bl. Comm. 131; 3 Steph. Comm. 695. This is the well-known remedy for deliverance from illegal confinement, called by

Sir William Blackstone the most celebrated writ in the English law, and the great and efficacious writ in all manner of illegal confinement. 3 Bl. Comm. 129.

HABEAS CORPUS AD TESTIFICANDUM. In practice. A writ to bring a witness into court, when he is in custody at the time of a trial, commanding the sheriff to have his body before the court, to testify in the cause. 3 Bl. Comm. 130; 2 Tidd, Pr. 809.

HABEAS CORPUS CUM CAUSA. (You have the body, with the cause.) In practice. Another name for the writ of *habeas corpus ad faciendum et recipiendum*, (*q. v.*) 1 Tidd, Pr. 348, 349.

Habemus optimum testem, confitentem reum. 1 Phil. Ev. 397. We have the best witness, — a confessing defendant. "What is taken *pro confesso* is taken as indubitable truth. The plea of guilty by the party accused shuts out all further inquiry. *Habemus confitentem reum* is demonstration, unless indirect motives can be assigned to it." 2 Hagg. Eccl. 315.

HABENDUM. In conveyancing. The clause usually following the granting part of the premises of a deed, which defines the extent of the ownership in the thing granted to be held and enjoyed by the grantee. 3 Washb. Real Prop. 437.

HABENDUM ET TENENDUM. In old conveyancing. To have and to hold. Formal words in deeds of land from a very early period. Bract. fol. 17*b*.

HABENTES HOMINES. In old English law. Rich men; literally, having men. The same with *fæsting-men*, (*q. v.*) Cowell.

HABENTIA. Riches. Mon. Angl. t. 1, 100.

HABERE. Lat. In the civil law. To have. Sometimes distinguished from *tenere*, (to hold,) and *possidere*, (to possess;) *habere* referring to the right, *tenere* to the fact, and *possidere* to both. Calvin.

HABERE FACIAS POSSESSIONEM. That you cause to have possession. The name of the process commonly resorted to by the successful party in an action of ejectment, for the purpose of being placed by the sheriff in the actual possession of the land recovered. It is commonly termed simply "*habere facias*," or "*hab. fa.*"

HABERE FACIAS SEISINAM. That you cause to have seisin. The writ of execution in real actions, directing the sheriff to cause the demandant to have seisin of the lands recovered. It was the proper process for giving seisin of a freehold, as distinguished from a chattel interest in lands.

HABERE FACIAS VISUM. That you cause to have a view. A writ to cause the sheriff to take a view of lands or tenements.

HABERE LICERE. Lat. In Roman law. To allow [one] to have [possession.] This phrase denoted the duty of the seller of property to allow the purchaser to have the possession and enjoyment. For a breach of this duty, an *actio ex empto* might be maintained.

HABERGEON. A diminutive of hauberk, a short coat of mail without sleeves. Blount.

HABERJECTS. A cloth of a mixed color. Magna Charta, c. 26.

HABETO TIBI RES TUAS. Have or take your effects to yourself. One of the old Roman forms of divorcing a wife. Calvin.

HABILIS. Lat. Fit; suitable; active; useful, (of a servant.) Proved; authentic, (of Book of Saints.) Fixed; stable, (of authority of the king.) Du Cange.

HABIT. A disposition or condition of the body or mind acquired by custom or a usual repetition of the same act or function.

HABIT AND REPUTE. By the law of Scotland, marriage may be established by "habit and repute" where the parties cohabit and are at the same time held and reputed as man and wife. See Bell. The same rule obtains in some of the United States.

HABITABLE REPAIR. A covenant by a lessee to "put the premises into habitable repair" binds him to put them into such a state that they may be occupied, not only with safety, but with reasonable comfort, for the purposes for which they are taken. 2 Moody & R. 186.

HABITANCY. It is difficult to give an exact definition of "habitancy." In general terms, one may be designated as an "inhabitant" of that place which constitutes the principal seat of his residence, of his business, pursuits, connections, attachments, and of his political and municipal relations. The term, therefore, embraces the fact of residence at a place, together with the intent to regard it and make it a home. The act and intent must concur. 17 Pick. 231.

HABITANT. Fr. In French and Canadian law. A resident tenant; a settler; a tenant who kept hearth and home on the seigniory.

HABITATIO. In the civil law. The right of dwelling; the right of free residence in another's house. Inst. 2, 5; Dig. 7, 8.

HABITATION. In the civil law. The right of a person to live in the house of another without prejudice to the property. It differed from a usufruct, in this: that the usufructuary might apply the house to any purpose, as of a store or manufactory; whereas the party having the right of habitation could only use it for the residence of himself and family. 1 Browne, Civil Law, 184.

In estates. A dwelling-house; a homestall. 2 Bl. Comm. 4; 4 Bl. Comm. 220.

HABITUAL CRIMINALS ACT. The statute 32 & 33 Vict. c. 99. By this act power was given to apprehend on suspicion convicted persons holding license under the penal servitude acts, 1853, 1857, and 1864. The act was repealed and replaced by the prevention of crimes act, 1871, (34 & 35 Vict. c. 112.)

HABITUAL DRUNKARD. A person given to ebriety or the excessive use of intoxicating drink, who has lost the power or the will, by frequent indulgence, to control his appetite for it. 18 Pa. St. 172.

One who has the habit of indulging in intoxicating liquors so firmly fixed that he becomes intoxicated as often as the temptation is presented by his being in the vicinity where liquors are sold is an "habitual drunkard," within the meaning of the divorce law. 35 Mich. 210.

In England, it is defined by the habitual drunkards' act, 1879, (42 & 43 Vict. c. 19,) which authorizes confinement in a retreat, upon the party's own application, as "a person who, not being amenable to any jurisdiction in lunacy, is, notwithstanding, by reason of habitual intemperate drinking of intoxicating liquor, at times dangerous to himself, or herself, or others, or incapable of managing himself or herself, or his or her affairs."

HABLE. L. Fr. In old English law. A port or harbor; a station for ships. St. 27 Hen. VI. c. 3.

HACIENDA. In Spanish law. The public domain; the royal estate; the aggregate wealth of the state. The science of administering the national wealth; public economy. Also an estate or farm belonging to a private person.

HACKNEY CARRIAGES. Carriages plying for hire in the street. The driver is liable for negligently losing baggage.

HADBOTE. In Saxon law. A recompense or satisfaction for the violation of holy orders, or violence offered to persons in holy orders. Cowell; Blount.

HADD. In Hindu law. A boundary or limit. A statutory punishment defined by law, and not arbitrary. Mozley & Whitley.

HADERUNGA. Hatred; ill will; prejudice, or partiality. Spelman; Cowell.

HADGONEL. A tax or mulct. Jacob.

HÆC EST CONVENTIO. Lat. This is an agreement. Words with which agreements anciently commenced. Yearb. H. 6 Edw. II. 191.

HÆC EST FINALIS CONCORDIA. L. Lat. This is the final agreement. The words with which the foot of a fine commenced. 2 Bl. Comm. 351.

HÆREDA. In Gothic law. A tribunal answering to the English court-leet.

HÆREDE ABDUCTO. An ancient writ that lay for the lord, who, having by right the wardship of his tenant under age, could not obtain his person, the same being carried away by another person. Old Nat. Brev. 93.

HÆREDE DELIBERANDO ALTERI QUI HABET CUSTODIUM TERRÆ. An ancient writ, directed to the sheriff, to require one that had the body of an heir, being in ward, to deliver him to the person whose ward he was by reason of his land. Reg. Orig. 161.

HÆREDE RAPTO. An ancient writ that lay for the ravishment of the lord's ward. Reg. Orig. 163.

Hæredem Deus facit, non homo. God makes the heir, not man. Co. Litt. 7b.

HÆREDES. Lat. In the civil law. Heirs. The plural of *hæres*, (q. v.)

HÆREDES EXTRANEI. In the civil law. Extraneous, strange, or foreign heirs; those who were not subject to the power of the testator. Inst. 2, 19, 3.

HÆREDES NECESSARII. In Roman law. Necessary heirs; those who, being named heirs in the will, had no election whether to accept or decline the inheritance, but were compelled to take it. This was the case with a slave who was made heir. Upon the testator's death, he at once became free, but was also obliged to take the succession.

HÆREDES PROXIMI. Nearest or next heirs. The children or descendants of the deceased.

HÆREDES REMOTIORES. More remote heirs. The kinsmen other than children or descendants.

HÆREDES SUI ET NECESSARII. In Roman law. Own and necessary heirs; *i. e.,* the lineal descendants of the estate-leaver. They were called "necessary" heirs, because it was the law that made them heirs, and not the choice of either the decedent or themselves. But since this was also true of slaves (when named "heirs" in the will) the former class were designated "*sui et necessarii,*" by way of distinction, the word "*sui*" denoting that the necessity arose from their relationship to the decedent. Mackeld. Rom. Law, § 733.

HÆREDIPETA. Lat. In old English law. A seeker of an inheritance; hence, the next heir to lands.

Hæredipetæ suo propinquo vel extraneo periculoso sane custodi nullus committatur. To the next heir, whether a relation or a stranger, certainly a dangerous guardian, let no one be committed. Co. Litt. 88*b.*

HÆREDITAS. In Roman law. The *hæreditas* was a universal succession by law to any deceased person, whether such person had died testate or intestate, and whether in trust (*ex fideicommisso*) for another or not. The like succession according to Prætorian law was *bonorum possessio.* The *hæreditas* was called "*jacens,*" until the *hæres* took it up, *i. e.,* made his *aditio hæreditatis;* and such *hæres,* if a *suus hæres,* had the right to abstain, (*potestas abstinendi,*) and, if an *extraneus hæres,* had the right to consider whether he would accept or decline, (*potestas deliberandi,*) the reason for this precaution being that (prior to Justinian's enactment to the contrary) a *hæres* after his *aditio* was liable to the full extent of the debts of the deceased person, and could have no relief therefrom, except in the case of a *damnum emergens* or *damnosa hæreditas, i. e.,* an *hæreditas* which disclosed (after the *aditio*) some enormous unsuspected liability. Brown.

In old English law. An estate transmissible by descent; an inheritance. Co. Litt. 9.

Hæreditas, alia corporalis, alia incorporalis; corporalis est, quæ tangi potest et videri; incorporalis quæ tangi non potest nec videri. Co. Litt. 9. An inheritance is either corporeal or incorporeal. Corporeal is that which can be touched and seen; incorporeal, that which can neither be touched nor seen.

HÆREDITAS DAMNOSA. A burdensome inheritance. See DAMNOSA HÆREDITAS.

Hæreditas est successio in universum jus quod defunctus habuerit. Co. Litt. 237. Inheritance is the succession to every right which the deceased had.

HÆREDITAS JACENS. In the civil law. A vacant inheritance. So long as no one had acquired the inheritance, it was termed "*hæreditas jacens;*" and this, by a legal fiction, represented the person of the decedent. Mackeld. Rom. Law, § 737.

The estate of a person deceased, where the owner left no heirs or legatee to take it, called also "*caduca;*" an escheated estate. Cod. 10, 10, 1; 4 Kent, Comm. 425.

In English law. An estate in abeyance; that is, after the ancestor's death, and before assumption of heir. Co. Litt. 342*b.* An inheritance without legal owner, and therefore open to the first occupant. 2 Bl. Comm. 259.

HÆREDITAS LUCTUOSA. In the civil law. A sad or mournful inheritance or succession; as that of a parent to the estate of a child, which was regarded as disturbing the natural order of mortality, (*turbato ordine mortalitatis.*) Cod. 6, 25, 9; 4 Kent, Comm. 397.

Hæreditas nihil aliud est, quam successio in universum jus, quod defunctus habuerit. The right of inheritance is nothing else than the faculty of succeeding to all the rights of the deceased. Dig. 50, 17, 62.

Hæreditas nunquam ascendit. An inheritance never ascends. Glanv. lib. 7, c. 1; 2 Bl. Comm. 211. A maxim of feudal origin, and which invariably prevailed in the law of England down to the passage of the statute 3 & 4 Wm. IV. c. 106, § 6, by which it was abrogated. 1 Steph. Comm. 378. See Broom, Max. 527, 528.

Hæredum appellatione veniunt hæredes hæredum in infinitum. By the title of heirs, come the heirs of heirs to infinity. Co. Litt. 9.

I

J

K

L

M

HÆRES. In Roman law. The heir, or universal successor in the event of death. The heir is he who actively or passively succeeds to the entire property of the estate-leaver. He is not only the successor to the rights and claims, but also to the estate-leaver's debts, and in relation to his estate is to be regarded as the identical person of the estate-leaver, inasmuch as he represents him in all his active and passive relations to his estate. Mackeld. Rom. Law, § 651.

It should be remarked that the office, powers, and duties of the *hæres*, in Roman law, were much more closely assimilated to those of a modern *excecutor* than to those of an heir at law. Hence "heir" is not at all an accurate translation of "*hæres*," unless it be understood in a special, technical sense.

In common law. An heir; he to whom lands, tenements, or hereditaments by the act of God and right of blood do descend, of some estate of inheritance. Co. Litt. 7*b*.

HÆRES ASTRARIUS. In old English law. An heir in actual possession.

HÆRES DE FACTO. In old English law. Heir from fact; that is, from the deed or act of his ancestor, without or against right. An heir in fact, as distinguished from an heir *de jure*, or by law.

Hæres est alter ipse, et filius est pars patris. An heir is another self, and a son is part of the father. 3 Coke. 12*b*.

Hæres est aut jure proprietatis aut jure representationis. An heir is either by right of property, or right of representation. 3 Coke, 40*b*.

Hæres est eadem persona cum antecessore. An heir is the same person with his ancestor. Co. Litt. 22; Branch, Princ. See Nov. 48, c. 1, § 1.

Hæres est nomen collectivum. "Heir" is a collective name or noun. 1 Vent. 215.

Hæres est nomen juris; filius est nomen naturæ. "Heir" is a name or term of law; "son" is a name of nature. Bac. Max. 52, in reg. 11.

Hæres est pars antecessoris. An heir is a part of the ancestor. So said because the ancestor, during his life, bears in his body (in judgment of law) all his heirs.

HÆRES EX ASSE. In the civil law. An heir to the whole estate; a sole heir. Inst. 2, 23, 9.

HÆRES EXTRANEUS. In the civil law. A strange or foreign heir; one who

was not subject to the power of the testator, or person who made him heir. *Qui testatoris juri subjecti non sunt, extranei hæredes appellantur.* Inst. 2, 19, 3.

HÆRES FACTUS. In the civil law. An heir made by will; a testamentary heir; the person created universal successor by will. Story, Confl. Laws, § 507; 3 Bl. Comm. 224. Otherwise called "*hæres ex testamento,*" and "*hæres institutus.*" Inst. 2, 9, 7; Id. 2, 14.

HÆRES FIDEICOMMISSARIUS. In the civil law. The person for whose benefit an estate was given to another (termed "*hæres fiduciarius,*" (*q. v.*) by will. Inst. 2, 23, 6, 7, 9. Answering nearly to the *cestui que trust* of the English law.

HÆRES FIDUCIARIUS. A fiduciary heir, or heir in trust; a person constituted heir by will, in trust for the benefit of another, called the "*fideicommissarius.*"

Hæres hæredis mei est meus hæres. The heir of my heir is my heir.

HÆRES LEGITIMUS. A lawful heir; one pointed out as such by the marriage of his parents.

Hæres legitimus est quem nuptiæ demonstrant. He is a lawful heir whom marriage points out as such; who is born in wedlock. Co. Litt. 7*b;* Bract. fol. 88; Fleta, lib. 6, c. 1; Broom, Max. 515.

Hæres minor uno et viginti annis non respondebit, nisi in casu dotis. Moore, 348. An heir under twenty-one years of age is not answerable, except in the matter of dower.

HÆRES NATUS. In the civil law. An heir born; one born heir, as distinguished from one made heir, (*hæres factus, q. v.;*) an heir at law, or by intestacy, (*ab intestato;*) the next of kin by blood, in cases of intestacy. Story, Confl. Laws, § 507; 3 Bl. Comm. 224.

HÆRES NECESSARIUS. In the civil law. A necessary or compulsory heir. This name was given to the heir when, being a slave, he was named "heir" in the testament, because on the death of the testator, whether he would or not, he at once became free, and was compelled to assume the heirship. Inst. 2, 19, 1.

Hæres non tenetur in Anglia ad debita antecessoris reddenda, nisi per antecessorem ad hoc fuerit obligatus, præterquam debita regis tantum. Co. Litt.

386. In England, the heir is not bound to pay his ancestor's debts, unless he be bound to it by the ancestor, except debts due to the king. But now, by 3 & 4 Wm. IV. c. 104, he is liable.

HÆRES RECTUS. In old English law. A right heir. Fleta, lib. 6, c. 1, § 11.

HÆRES SUUS. In the civil law. A man's *own* heir; a decedent's proper or natural heir. This name was given to the lineal descendants of the deceased. Inst. 3, 1, 4–5.

HÆRETARE. In old English law. To give a right of inheritance, or make the donation hereditary to the grantee and his heirs. Cowell.

HÆRETICO COMBURENDO. The statute 2 Hen. IV. c. 15, *de hæretico comburendo*, was the first penal law enacted against heresy, and imposed the penalty of death by burning against all heretics who relapsed or who refused to abjure their opinions. It was repealed by the statute 29 Car. II. c. 9. Brown. This was also the name of a writ for the purpose indicated.

HAFNE. A haven or port. Cowell.

HAFNE COURTS. Haven courts; courts anciently held in certain ports in England. Spelman.

HAGA. A house in a city or borough. Scott.

HAGIA. A hedge. Mon. Angl. tom. 2, p. 273.

HAGNE. A little hand-gun. St. 33 Hen. VIII. c. 6.

HAGNEBUT. A hand-gun of a larger description than the hagne. St. 2 & 3 Edw. VI. c. 14; 4 & 5 P. & M. c. 2.

HAIA. A park inclosed. Cowell.

HAIEBOTE. In old English law. A permission or liberty to take thorns, etc., to make or repair hedges. Blount.

HAILL. In Scotch law. Whole; the whole. "All and haill" are common words in conveyances. 1 Bell, App. Cas. 499.

HAILWORKFOLK, (*i. e.*, holywork-folk.) Those who formerly held lands by the service of defending or repairing a church or monument.

HAIMHALDARE. In old Scotch law. To seek restitution of one's own goods and gear, and bring the same *home* again. Skene de Verb. Sign.

HAIMSUCKEN. In Scotch law. The crime of assaulting a person in his own house. Bell.

HAKETON. A military coat of defense.

HALF-BLOOD. A term denoting the degree of relationship which exists between those who have the same father or the same mother, but not both parents in common. See BROTHER.

HALF-BROTHER, HALF-SISTER. Persons who have the same father, but different mothers; or the same mother, but different fathers.

HALF-CENT. A copper coin of the United States, of the value of five mills, and of the weight of ninety-four grains. The coinage of these was discontinued in 1857.

HALF-DEFENSE. In common-law pleading. The technical name of the common clause at the commencement of a defendant's plea: "And the said defendant, by ———, his attorney, *comes and defends the wrong,* (or force,) *and injury, when,*" etc. Called "*half*-defense" from its abbreviated form.

HALF-DIME. A silver (now nickel) coin of the United States, of the value of five cents.

HALF-DOLLAR. A silver coin of the United States, of the value of fifty cents, or one-half the value of a dollar.

HALF-EAGLE. A gold coin of the United States, of the value of five dollars.

HALF-ENDEAL. A moiety, or half of a thing.

HALF-KINEG. In Saxon law. Half-king, (*semi-rex.*) A title given to the aldermen of all England. Crabb, Eng. Law, 28; Spelman.

HALF-MARK. A noble, or six shillings and eight pence in English money.

HALF-PROOF. In the civil law. Proof by one witness, or a private instrument. Hallifax, Civil Law, b. 3, c. 9, no. 25; 3 Bl. Comm. 370. Or *prima facie* proof, which yet was not sufficient to found a sentence or decree.

HALF-SEAL. That which was formerly used in the English chancery for sealing of commissions to delegates, upon any appeal to the court of delegates, either in ecclesiastical or marine causes.

HALF-TIMER. A child who, by the operation of the English factory and education acts, is employed for less than the full time in a factory or workshop, in order that he may attend some "recognized efficient school." See factory and workshop act, 1878, § 23; elementary education act, 1876, § 11.

HALF-TONGUE. A jury half of one *tongue* or nationality and half of another. See De Medietate Linguæ.

HALF-YEAR. In legal computation. The period of one hundred and eighty-two days; the odd hours being rejected. Co. Litt. 135*b;* Cro. Jac. 166; Yel. 100; 1 Steph. Comm. 265.

HALIGEMOT. In Saxon law. The meeting of a hall, (*conventus aulæ*,) that is, a lord's court; a court of a manor, or court-baron. Spelman. So called from the *hall*, where the tenants or freemen met, and justice was administered. Crabb, Eng. Law, 26.

HALIMAS. In English law. The feast of All Saints, on the 1st of November; one of the cross-quarters of the year, was computed from Halimas to Candlemas. Wharton.

HALL. A building or room of considerable size, used as a place for the meeting of public assemblies, conventions, courts, etc.

In English law. A name given to many manor-houses because the magistrate's court was held in the hall of his mansion; a chief mansion-house. Cowell.

HALLAGE. In old English law. A fee or toll due for goods or merchandise vended in a hall. Jacob.

A toll due to the lord of a fair or market, for such commodities as were vended in the common hall of the place. Cowell; Blount.

HALLAZCO. In Spanish law. The finding and taking possession of something which previously had no owner, and which thus becomes the property of the first occupant. Las Partidas, 3, 5, 28; 5, 48, 49; 5, 20, 50.

HALLE-GEMOTE. Hall assembly. A species of court-baron.

HALLUCINATION. In medical jurisprudence. A species of mania; the perception of objects which have no reality, or of sensations which have no corresponding ex-

ternal cause, arising from disorder of the nervous system; delusion. Webster.

HALMOTE. See Halle-Gemote.

HALYMOTE. A holy or ecclesiastical court.

A court held in London before the lord mayor and sheriffs, for regulating the bakers.

It was anciently held on Sunday next before St. Thomas' day, and therefore called the "*holymote*," or holy court. Cowell.

HALYWERCFOLK. Sax. In old English law. Tenants who held land by the service of repairing or defending a church or monument, whereby they were exempted from feudal and military services.

HAMA. In old English law. A hook; an engine with which a house on fire is pulled down. Yel. 60.

A piece of land.

HAMBLING. In forest law. The hoxing or hock-sinewing of dogs; an old mode of laming or disabling dogs. Termes de la Ley.

HAMESECKEN. In Scotch law. The violent entering into a man's house without license or against the peace, and the seeking and assaulting him there. Skene de Verb. Sign.; 2 Forb. Inst. 139.

The crime of housebreaking or burglary. 4 Bl. Comm. 223.

HAMFARE. (Sax. From *ham*, a house.) In Saxon law. An assault made in a house; a breach of the peace in a private house.

HAMLET. A small village; a part or member of a vill. It is the diminutive of "*ham*," a village. Cowell.

HAMMA. A close joining to a house; a croft; a little meadow. Cowell.

HAMMER. Metaphorically, a forced sale or sale at public auction. "To bring to the hammer," to put up for sale at auction. "Sold under the hammer," sold by an officer of the law or by an auctioneer.

HAMSOCNE. The right of security and privacy in a man's house. Du Cange. The breach of this privilege by a forcible entry of a house is breach of the peace. Du Cange.

HANAPER. A hamper or basket in which were kept the writs of the court of chancery relating to the business of a subject, and their returns. 3 Bl. Comm. 49. According to others, the fees accruing on writs, etc., were there kept. Spelman; Du Cange.

HANAPER-OFFICE. An office belonging to the common-law jurisdiction of the court of chancery, so called because all writs relating to the business of a subject, and their returns, were formerly kept in a hamper, *in hanaperio.* 5 & 6 Vict. c. 103.

HAND. A measure of length equal to four inches, used in measuring the height of horses. A person's signature.

In old English law. An oath.

HAND DOWN. An appellate court is said to "hand down" its decision in a case, when the opinion is prepared and filed for transmission to the court below.

HAND-FASTING. Betrothment.

HAND-GRITH. Peace or protection given by the king with his own hand.

HAND MONEY. Money paid in hand to bind a bargain; earnest money.

HANDBILL. A written or printed notice displayed to inform those concerned of something to be done.

HANDBOROW. In Saxon law. A hand pledge; a name given to the nine pledges in a decennary or friborg; the tenth or chief, being called "*headborow*," (*q. v.*) So called as being an inferior pledge to the chief. Spelman.

HANDHABEND. In Saxon law. One having a thing in his hand; that is, a thief found having the stolen goods in his possession. Jurisdiction to try such thief.

HANDSALE. Anciently, among all the northern nations, shaking of hands was held necessary to bind a bargain,—a custom still retained in verbal contracts. A sale thus made was called "handsale," (*venditio per mutuam manum complexionem*.) In process of time the same word was used to signify the price or earnest which was given immediately after the shaking of hands, or instead thereof. 2 Bl. Comm. 448.

HANDSEL. Handsale, or earnest money.

HANDWRITING. The chirography of a person; the cast or form of writing peculiar to a person, including the size, shape, and style of letters, tricks of penmanship, and whatever gives individuality to his writing, distinguishing it from that of other persons.

Anything written by hand; an instrument written by the hand of a person, or a specimen of his writing.

Handwriting, considered under the law of evidence, includes not only the ordinary writing of one able to write, but also writing done in a disguised hand, or in cipher, and a mark made by one able or unable to write. 9 Amer. & Eng. Enc. Law, 264.

HANG. In old practice. To remain undetermined. "It has *hung* long enough; it is time it were made an end of." Holt, C. J., 1 Show. 77.

Thus, the present participle means pending; during the pendency. "If the tenant alien, *hanging* the *præcipe*." Co. Litt. 266a.

HANGING. In criminal law. Suspension by the neck; the mode of capital punishment used in England from time immemorial, and generally adopted in the United States. 4 Bl. Comm. 403.

HANGING IN CHAINS. In atrocious cases it was at one time usual, in England, for the court to direct a murderer, after execution, to be hanged upon a gibbet in chains near the place where the murder was committed, a practice quite contrary to the Mosaic law. (Deut. xxi. 23.) Abolished by 4 & 5 Wm. IV. c. 26. Wharton.

HANGMAN. An executioner. One who executes condemned criminals by hanging.

HANGWITE. In Saxon law. A fine for illegal hanging of a thief, or for allowing him to escape. Immunity from such fine. Du Cange.

HANIG. Customary labor.

HANSE. An alliance or confederation among merchants or cities, for the good ordering and protection of the commerce of its members. An imposition upon merchandise. Du Cange.

HANSE TOWNS, LAWS OF THE. The maritime ordinances of the Hanseatic towns, first published in German at Lubeck, in 1597, and in May, 1614, revised and enlarged.

HANSE TOWNS. The collective name of certain German cities, including Lubeck, Hamburg, and Bremen, which formed an alliance for the mutual protection and furtherance of their commercial interests, in the twelfth century. The powerful confederacy thus formed was called the "Hanseatic League." The league framed and promulgated a code of maritime law, which was known as the "Laws of the Hanse Towns," or *Jus Hanseaticum Maritimum.*

HANSEATIC. Pertaining to a hanse or commercial alliance; but, generally, the union of the Hanse towns is the one referred to, as in the expression the "Hanseatic League."

HANSGRAVE. The chief of a company; the head man of a corporation.

HANTELOD. In old European law. An arrest, or attachment. Spelman.

HAP. To catch. Thus, "hap the rent," "hap the deed-poll," were formerly used.

HAPPINESS. The constitutional right of men to pursue their "happiness" means the right to pursue any lawful business or vocation, in any manner not inconsistent with the equal rights of others, which may increase their prosperity, or develop their faculties, so as to give to them their highest enjoyment. 111 U. S. 757, 4 Sup. Ct. Rep. 652; 1 Bl. Comm. 41.

HAQUE. In old statutes. A hand-gun, about three-quarters of a yard long.

HARACIUM. In old English law. A race of horses and mares kept for breed; a stud. Spelman.

HARBINGER. In England, an officer of the royal household.

HARBOR, *v.* To receive clandestinely and without lawful authority a person for the purpose of so concealing him that another having a right to the lawful custody of such person shall be deprived of the same. 5 How. 215, 227. A distinction has been taken, in some decisions, between "harbor" and "conceal." A person may be convicted of harboring a slave, although he may not have concealed her. 24 Ala. 71.

HARBOR, *n.* A haven, or a space of deep water so sheltered by the adjacent land as to afford a safe anchorage for ships.

"Port" is a word of larger import than "harbor," since it implies the presence of wharves, or at any rate the means and opportunity of receiving and discharging cargo.

HARBOR AUTHORITY. In England a harbor authority is a body of persons, corporate or unincorporate, being proprietors of, or intrusted with the duty of constructing, improving, managing, or lighting, any harbor. St. 24 & 25 Vict. c. 47.

HARD LABOR. A punishment, additional to mere imprisonment, sometimes im-posed upon convicts sentenced to a penitentiary. But the labor is not, as a rule, any harder than ordinary mechanical labor.

HARDHEIDIS. In old Scotch law. Lions; coins formerly of the value of three half-pence. 1 Pitc. Crim. Tr. pt. 1, p. 64, note.

HARDSHIP. The severity with which a proposed construction of the law would bear upon a particular case, founding, sometimes, an argument against such construction, which is otherwise termed the "argument *ab inconvenienti.*"

HARNASCA. In old European law. The defensive armor of a man; harness. Spelman.

HARNESS. All warlike instruments; also the tackle or furniture of a ship.

HARO, HARRON. Fr. In Norman and early English law. An outcry, or hue and cry after felons and malefactors. Cowell.

HARRIOTT. The old form of "heriot," (*q. v.*) Williams, Seis. 203.

HART. A stag or male deer of the forest five years old complete.

HASP AND STAPLE. In old Scotch law. The form of entering an heir in a subject situated within a royal borough. It consisted of the heir's taking hold of the hasp and staple of the door, (which was the symbol of possession,) with other formalities. Bell; Burrill.

HASPA. In old English law. The hasp of a door; by which livery of seisin might anciently be made, where there was a house on the premises.

HASTA. Lat. A spear. In the Roman law, a spear was the sign of a public sale of goods or sale by auction. Hence the phrase "*hastæ subjicere*" (to put under the spear) meant to put up at auction. Calvin.

In feudal law. A spear. The symbol used in making investiture of a fief. Feud. lib. 2, tit. 2.

HAT MONEY. In maritime law. Primage; a small duty paid to the captain and mariners of a ship.

HAUBER. O. Fr. A high lord; a great baron. Spelman.

HAUGH, or HOWGH. A green plot in a valley.

HAUL. The use of this word, instead of the statutory word "carry," in an indictment charging that the defendant "did feloniously steal, take, and *haul* away" certain personalty, will not render the indictment bad, the words being in one sense equivalent. 108 Ind. 171, 8 N. E. Rep. 911.

HAUR. In old English law. Hatred. Leg. Wm. I. c. 16; Blount.

HAUSTUS. Lat. In the civil law. A species of servitude, consisting in the right to draw water from another's well or spring, in which the *iter*, (right of way to the well or spring,) so far as it is necessary, is tacitly included. Dig. 8, 3, 1; Mackeld. Rom. Law, § 318.

HAUT CHEMIN. L. Fr. Highway. Yearb. M. 4 Hen. VI. 4.

HAUT ESTRET. L. Fr. High street; highway. Yearb. P. 11 Hen. VI. 2.

HAUTHONER. A man armed with a coat of mail. Jacob.

HAVE. Lat. A form of the salutatory expression "*Ave*," used in the titles of some of the constitutions of the Theodosian and Justinianean codes. See Cod. 7, 62, 9; Id. 9, 2, 11.

HAVE. To possess corporally. "No one, at common law, was said to *have* or to be in possession of land, unless it were conveyed to him by the livery of seisin, which gave him the corporal investiture and bodily occupation thereof." Bl. Law Tracts, 113.

HAVE AND HOLD. A common phrase in conveyancing, derived from the *habendum et tenendum* of the old common law. See HABENDUM ET TENENDUM.

HAVEN. A place of a large receipt and safe riding of ships, so situate and secured by the land circumjacent that the vessels thereby ride and anchor safely, and are protected by the adjacent land from dangerous or violent winds; as Milford Haven, Plymouth Haven, and the like. Hale de Jure Mar. par. 2, c. 2.

HAW. A small parcel of land so called in Kent; houses. Co. Litt. 5.

HAWBERK. He who held land in France, by finding a coat or shirt of mail, with which he was to be ready when called upon. Wharton.

HAWGH, HOWGH. In old English law. A valley. Co. Litt. 5*b*.

HAWKER. A trader who goes from place to place, or along the streets of a town, selling the goods which he carries with him.

It is perhaps not essential to the idea, but is generally understood from the word, that a hawker is to be one who not only carries goods for sale, but seeks for purchasers, either by outcry, which some lexicographers conceive as intimated by the derivation of the word, or by attracting notice and attention to them, as goods for sale, by an actual exhibition or exposure of them, by placards or labels, or by a conventional signal, like the sound of a horn for the sale of fish. 12 Cush. 495.

HAWKING. The business of one who sells or offers goods for sale on the streets, by outcry, or by attracting the attention of persons by exposing his goods in a public place, or by placards, labels, or signals. 107 Ind. 505, 8 N. E. Rep. 609.

HAY-BOTE. Another name for "hedge-bote," being one of the estovers allowed to a tenant for life or years, namely, material for repairing the necessary hedges or fences of his grounds. 2 Bl. Comm. 35; 1 Washb. Real Prop. 129.

HAYWARD. In old English law. An officer appointed in the lord's court to keep a common herd of cattle of a town; so called because he was to see that they did not break or injure the hedges of inclosed grounds. His duty was also to impound trespassing cattle, and to guard against pound-breaches. Kitch. 46; Cowell.

HAZARD. An unlawful game at dice, and those who play at it are called "hazardors." Jacob.

HAZARDOUS. Exposed to or involving danger; perilous; risky.

The terms "hazardous," "extra-hazardous," "specially hazardous," and "not hazardous" are well-understood technical terms in the business of insurance, having distinct and separate meanings. Although what goods are included in each designation may not be so known as to dispense with actual proof, the terms themselves are distinct and known to be so. 88 N. Y. 364; 47 N. Y. 597.

HAZARDOUS CONTRACT. A contract in which the performance of that which is one of its objects depends on an uncertain event. Civil Code La. art. 1769. See 1 J. J. Marsh. 596.

HE. The use of this pronoun in a written instrument, in referring to a person whose Christian name is designated therein by a mere initial, is not conclusive that the person referred to is a male; it may be shown by parol that the person intended is a female. 71 Cal. 38, 11 Pac. Rep. 802.

He who has committed iniquity shall not have equity. Francis, Max.

He who seeks equity must do equity. It is in pursuance of this maxim that equity enforces the right of the wife's equity to a settlement. Snell, Eq. (5th Ed.) 374.

HEAD. Chief; leading; principal; the upper part or principal source of a stream.

HEAD OF A CREEK. This term means the source of the longest branch, unless general reputation has given the appellation to another. 2 Bibb, 110.

HEAD OF A FAMILY. A term used in homestead and exemption laws to designate a person who maintains a family; a householder.

HEADBOROUGH. In Saxon law. The head or chief officer of a borough; chief of the frankpledge tithing or decennary. This office was afterwards, when the petty constableship was created, united with that office.

HEAD-COURTS. Certain tribunals in Scotland, abolished by 20 Geo. II. c. 50. Ersk. 1, 4, 5.

HEADLAND. In old English law. A narrow piece of unplowed land left at the end of a plowed field for the turning of the plow. Called, also, "butt."

HEAD-NOTE. A syllabus to a reported case; a summary of the points decided in the case, which is placed at the *head* or beginning of the report.

HEAD-PENCE. An exaction of 40d. or more, collected by the sheriff of Northumberland from the people of that county twice in every seven years, without account to the king. Abolished in 1444. Cowell.

HEAFODWEARD. In old English law. One of the services to be rendered by a thane, but in what it consisted seems uncertain.

HEALGEMOTE. In Saxon law. A court-baron; an ecclesiastical court.

HEALSFANG. In Saxon law. A sort of pillory, by which the head of the culprit was caught between two boards, as feet are caught in a pair of stocks. Cowell.

HEALTH. Freedom from sickness or suffering. The right to the enjoyment of *health* is a subdivision of the right of personal security, one of the absolute rights of persons. 1 Bl. Comm. 129, 134. As to Injuries affecting health, see 3 Bl. Comm. 122.

HEALTH LAWS. Laws prescribing sanitary measures, and designed to promote or preserve the health of the community.

HEALTH OFFICER. The officer charged with the execution and enforcement of health laws. The powers and duties of health officers are regulated by local laws.

HEALTHY. Free from disease or bodily ailment, or any state of the system peculiarly susceptible or liable to disease or bodily ailment. 13 Ired. Law, 356.

HEARING. In equity practice. The hearing of the arguments of the counsel for the parties upon the pleadings, or pleadings and proofs; corresponding to the trial of an action at law.

The word "hearing" has an established meaning as applicable to equity cases. It means the same thing in those cases that the word "trial" does in cases at law. And the words "final hearing" have long been used to designate the trial of an equity case upon the merits, as distinguished from the hearing of any preliminary questions arising in the cause, and which are termed "interlocutory." 24 Wis. 171.

In criminal law. The examination of a prisoner charged with a crime or misdemeanor, and of the witnesses for the accused.

HEARSAY. A term applied to that species of testimony given by a witness who relates, not what he knows personally, but what others have told him, or what he has heard said by others.

Hearsay evidence is that which does not derive its value solely from the credit of the witness, but rests mainly on the veracity and competency of other persons. The very nature of the evidence shows its weakness, and it is admitted only in specified cases from necessity. Code Ga. 1882, § 3770; 1 Phil. Ev. 185.

Hearsay evidence is second-hand evidence, as distinguished from original evidence; it is the repetition at second-hand of what would be original evidence if given by the person who originally made the statement.

HEARTH MONEY. A tax levied in England by St. 14 Car. II. c. 10, consisting of two shillings on every hearth or stove in the kingdom. It was extremely unpopular, and was abolished by 1 W. & M. St. 1, c. 10. This tax was otherwise called "chimney money."

HEARTH SILVER. In English law. A species of *modus* or composition for tithes. Anstr. 323, 326.

HEAT OF PASSION. In criminal law. A state of violent and uncontrollable rage engendered by a blow or certain other provocation given, which will reduce a homicide from the grade of murder to that of manslaughter. A state of mind contradistinguished from a cool state of the blood. 66 Mo. 13; 74 Mo. 250.

HEBBERMAN. An unlawful fisher in the Thames below London bridge; so called because they generally fished at *ebbing* tide or water. 4 Hen. VII. c. 15; Jacob.

HEBBERTHEF. In Saxon law. The privilege of having the goods of a thief, and the trial of him, within a certain liberty. Cowell.

HEBBING-WEARS. A device for catching fish in ebbing water. St. 23 Hen. VIII. c. 5.

HEBDOMAD. A week; a space of seven days.

HEBDOMADIUS. A week's man; the canon or prebendary in a cathedral church, who had the peculiar care of the choir and the offices of it for his own week. Cowell.

HECCAGIUM. In feudal law. Rent paid to a lord of the fee for a liberty to use the engines called "hecks."

HECK. An engine to take fish in the river Ouse. 23 Hen. VIII. c. 18.

HEDA. A small haven, wharf, or landing place.

HEDAGIUM. Toll or customary dues at the hithe or wharf, for landing goods, etc., from which exemption was granted by the crown to some particular persons and societies. Wharton.

HEDGE-BOTE. An allowance of wood for repairing hedges or fences, which a tenant or lessee has a right to take off the land let or demised to him. 2 Bl. Comm. 35.

HEDGE-PRIEST. A vagabond priest in olden time.

HEGEMONY. The leadership of one among several independent confederate states.

HEGIRA. The epoch or account of time used by the Arabians and the Turks, who begin their computation from the day that Mahomet was compelled to escape from Mecca, which happened on Friday, July 16, A. D. 622, under the reign of the Emperor Heraclius. Wharton.

HEGUMENOS. The leader of the monks in the Greek Church.

HEIFER. A young cow which has not had a calf. 2 East, P. C. 616.

HEIR. At common law. A person who succeeds, by the rules of law, to an estate in lands, tenements, or hereditaments, upon the death of his ancestor, by descent and right of relationship.

The term "heir" has a very different signification at common law from what it has in those states and countries which have adopted the civil law. In the latter, the term is indiscriminately applied to all persons who are called to the succession, whether by the act of the party or by operation of law. The person who is created universal successor by a will is called the "testamentary heir;" and the next of kin by blood is, in cases of intestacy, called the "heir at law," or "heir by intestacy." The executor of the common law in many respects corresponds to the testamentary heir of the civil law. Again, the administrator in many respects corresponds with the heir by intestacy. By the common law, executors and administrators have no right except to the personal estate of the deceased; whereas the heir by the civil law is authorized to administer both the personal and real estate. Story, Confl. Laws, §§ 507, 508.

In the civil law. A universal successor in the event of death. He who actively or passively succeeds to the entire property or estate, rights and obligations, of a decedent, and occupies his place.

The term "heir" has several significations. Sometimes it refers to one who has formally accepted a succession and taken possession thereof; sometimes to one who is called to succeed, but still retains the faculty of accepting or renouncing, and it is frequently used as applied to one who has formally renounced. 26 La. Ann. 417.

In Scotch law. The person who succeeds to the heritage or heritable rights of one deceased. 1 Forb. Inst. pt. 3, p. 75. The word has a more extended signification than in English law, comprehending not only those who succeed to lands, but successors to personal property also. Wharton.

HEIR APPARENT. An heir whose right of inheritance is indefeasible, provided he outlive the ancestor; as in England the eldest son, or his issue, who must, by the course of the common law, be heir to the father whenever he happens to die. 2 Bl. Comm. 208; 1 Steph. Comm. 358.

HEIR AT LAW. He who, after his ancestor's death intestate, has a right to inherit all lands, tenements, and hereditaments which belonged to him or of which he was seised. The same as "heir general."

HEIR BENEFICIARY. In the civil law. One who has accepted the succession under the benefit of an inventory regularly made.

Heirs are divided into two classes, according to the manner in which they accept the successions left to them, to-wit, unconditional and beneficiary heirs. Unconditional heirs are those who inherit without any reservation, or without making an inventory, whether their acceptance be express or tacit. Beneficiary heirs are those who have accepted the succession under the benefit of an inventory regularly made. Civil Code La. art. 881.

HEIR BY CUSTOM. In English law. One whose right of inheritance depends upon a particular and local custom, such as *gavelkind*, or *borough English*. Co. Litt. 140.

HEIR BY DEVISE. One to whom lands are devised by will; a devisee of lands. Answering to the *hæres factus* (*q. v.*) of the civil law.

HEIR COLLATERAL. One who is not lineally related to the decedent, but is of collateral kin; *e. g.*, his uncle, cousin, brother, nephew.

HEIR CONVENTIONAL. In the civil law. One who takes a succession by virtue of a contract or settlement entitling him thereto.

HEIR, FORCED. One who cannot be disinherited. See FORCED HEIRS.

HEIR GENERAL. An heir at law. The ordinary heir by blood, succeeding to all the lands.

HEIR INSTITUTE. In Scotch law. One to whom the right of succession is ascertained by disposition or express deed of the deceased. 1 Forb. Inst. pt. 3, p. 75.

HEIR, IRREGULAR. In Louisiana. Irregular heirs are those who are neither testamentary nor legal, and who have been established by law to take the succession. See Civil Code La. art. 874. When there are no direct or collateral relatives surviving the decedent, and the succession consequently devolves upon the surviving husband or wife, or illegitimate children, or the state, it is called an "irregular succession."

HEIR, LEGAL. In the civil law. A legal heir is one who takes the succession by relationship to the decedent and by force of law. This is different from a testamentary

or conventional heir, who takes the succession in virtue of the disposition of man. See Civil Code La. arts. 873, 875.

HEIR-LOOMS. Such goods and chattels as, contrary to the nature of chattels, shall go by special custom to the heir along with the inheritance, and not to the executor. The termination "*loom*" (Sax.) signifies a limb or member; so that an heir-loom is nothing else but a limb or member of the inheritance. They are generally such things as cannot be taken away without damaging or dismembering the freehold; such as deer in a park, doves in a cote, deeds and charters, etc. 2 Bl. Comm. 427.

HEIR MALE. In Scotch law. An heir institute, who, though not next in blood to the deceased, is his nearest male relation that can succeed to him. 1 Forb. Inst. pt. 3, p. 76.

HEIR OF CONQUEST. In Scotch law. One who succeeds to the deceased in *conquest, i. e.,* lands or other heritable rights to which the deceased neither did nor could succeed as heir to his predecessor.

HEIR OF LINE. In Scotch law. One who succeeds lineally by right of blood; one who succeeds to the deceased in his heritage; *i. e.,* lands and other heritable rights derived to him by succession as heir to his predecessor. 1 Forb. Inst. pt. 3, p. 77.

HEIR OF PROVISION. In Scotch law. One who succeeds as heir by virtue of a particular provision in a deed or instrument.

HEIR OF TAILZIE. In Scotch law. He on whom an estate is settled that would not have fallen to him by legal succession. 1 Forb. Inst. pt. 3, p. 75.

HEIR PRESUMPTIVE. The person who, if the ancestor should die immediately, would, in the present circumstances of things, be his heir, but whose right of inheritance may be defeated by the contingency of some nearer heir being born; as a brother or nephew, whose presumptive succession may be destroyed by the birth of a child. 2 Bl. Comm. 208; 1 Steph. Comm. 358.

HEIR SPECIAL. In English law. The issue in tail, who claims *per formam doni;* by the form of the gift.

HEIR SUBSTITUTE, IN A BOND. In Scotch law. He to whom a bond is payable expressly in case of the creditor's decease, or after his death. 1 Forb. Inst. pt. 3, p. 76.

HEIR TESTAMENTARY. In the civil law. One who is named and appointed heir in the testament of the decedent. This name distinguishes him from a *legal* heir, (one upon whom the law casts the succession,) and from a *conventional* heir, (one who takes it by virtue of a previous contract or settlement.)

HEIR UNCONDITIONAL. In the civil law. One who inherits without any reservation, or without making an inventory, whether his acceptance be express or tacit. Distinguished from *heir beneficiary*, (*q. v.*)

HEIRDOM. Succession by inheritance.

HEIRESS. A female heir to a person having an estate of inheritance. When there are more than one, they are called "co-heiresses," or "co-heirs."

HEIRS. A word used in deeds of conveyance, (either solely, or in connection with others,) where it is intended to pass a fee.

HEIRS OF THE BODY. An heir begotten or borne by the person referred to; a lineal descendant. The terms "natural heirs" and "heirs of the body," in a will, and by way of executory devise, are considered as of the same legal import. 19 Conn. 112.

HEIRSHIP. The quality or condition of being heir, or the relation between the heir and his ancestor.

HEIRSHIP MOVABLES. In Scotch law. The movables which go to the heir, and not to the executor, that the land may not go to the heir completely dismantled, such as the best of furniture, horses, cows, etc., but not fungibles. Bell.

HELL. The name given to a place under the exchequer chamber, where the king's debtors were confined. Rich. Dict.

HELM. Thatch or straw; a covering for the head in war; a coat of arms bearing a crest; the tiller or handle of the rudder of a ship.

HELOWE-WALL. The end-wall covering and defending the rest of the building. Paroch. Antiq. 573.

HELSING. A Saxon brass coin, of the value of a half-penny.

HEMOLDBORH, or HELMELBORCH. A title to possession. The admission of this old Norse term into the laws of the Conqueror is difficult to be accounted for; it is not found in any Anglo-Saxon law extant. Wharton.

HENCHMAN. A page; an attendant; a herald.

HENEDPENNY. A customary payment of money instead of hens at Christmas; a composition for eggs. Cowell.

HENFARE. A fine for flight on account of murder. Domesday Book.

HENGHEN. In Saxon law. A prison, a gaol, or house of correction.

HENGWYTE. Sax. In old English law. An acquittance from a fine for hanging a thief. Fleta, lib. 1, c. 47, § 17.

HENRICUS VETUS. Henry the Old, or Elder. King Henry I. is so called in ancient English chronicles and charters, to distinguish him from the subsequent kings of that name. Spelman.

HEORDFÆTE, or HUDEFÆST. In Saxon law. A master of a family, keeping house, distinguished from a lower class of freemen, viz., *folgeras*, (*folgarii*,) who had no habitations of their own, but were house-retainers of their lords.

HEORDPENNY. Peter-pence, (*q. v.*)

HEORDWERCH. In Saxon law. The service of herdsmen, done at the will of their lord.

HEPTARCHY. A government exercised by seven persons, or a nation divided into seven governments. In the year 560, seven different monarchies had been formed in England by the German tribes, namely, that of Kent by the Jutes; those of Sussex, Wessex, and Essex by the Saxons; and those of East Anglia, Bernicia, and Deira by the Angles. To these were added, about the year 586, an eighth, called the "Kingdom of Mercia," also founded by the Angles, and comprehending nearly the whole of the heart of the kingdom. These states formed what has been designated the "Anglo-Saxon Octarchy," or more commonly, though not so correctly, the "Anglo-Saxon Heptarchy," from the custom of speaking of Deira and Bernicia under the single appellation of the "Kingdom of Northumberland." Wharton.

HERALD. In ancient law, a herald was a diplomatic messenger who carried messages between kings or states, and especially proclamations of war, peace, or truce. In English law, a herald is an officer whose duty is to keep genealogical lists and tables, adjust armorial bearings, and regulate the ceremonies at royal coronations and funerals.

HERALDRY. The art, office, or science of heralds. Also an old and obsolete abuse of buying and selling precedence in the paper of causes for hearing.

HERALDS' COLLEGE. In England. An ancient royal corporation, first instituted by Richard III. in 1483. It comprises three kings of arms, six heralds, and four marshals or pursuivants of arms, together with the earl marshal and a secretary. The heralds' books, compiled when progresses were solemnly and regularly made into every part of the kingdom, to inquire into the state of families, and to register such marriages and descents as were verified to them upon oath, are allowed to be good evidence of pedigrees. The heralds' office is still allowed to make grants of arms and to permit change of names. 3 Starkie, Ev. 843; Wharton.

HERBAGE. In English law. An easement or liberty, which consists in the right to pasture cattle on another's ground.

Feed for cattle in fields and pastures. Bract. fol. 222; Co. Litt. 46; Shep. Touch. 97. A right to herbage does not include a right to cut grass, or dig potatoes, or pick apples. 4 N. H. 303.

HERBAGIUM ANTERIUS. The first crop of grass or hay, in opposition to aftermath or second cutting. Paroch. Antiq. 459.

HERBENGER, or HARBINGER. An officer in the royal house, who goes before and allots the noblemen and those of the household their lodgings; also an innkeeper.

HERBERGAGIUM. Lodgings to receive guests in the way of hospitality. Cowell.

HERBERGARE. To harbor; to entertain.

HERBERGATUS. Harbored or entertained in an inn. Cowell.

HERBERY, or HERBURY. An inn. Cowell.

HERCIA. A harrow. Fleta, lib. 2, c. 77.

HERCIARE. To harrow. 4 Inst. 270.

HERCIATURA. In old English law. Harrowing; work with a harrow. Fleta, lib. 2, c. 82, § 2.

HERCISCUNDA. In the civil law. To be divided. *Familia herciscunda*, an inheritance to be divided. *Actio familiæ herciscundæ*, an action for dividing an inheritance. *Erciscunda* is more commonly used in the civil law. Dig. 10, 2; Inst. 3, 28, 4; Id. 4, 6, 20.

HERDEWICH. A grange or place for cattle or husbandry. Mon. Angl. pt. 3.

HERDWERCH, HEORDWERCH. Herdsmen's work, or customary labor, done by shepherds and inferior tenants, at the will of the lord. Cowell.

HEREBANNUM. In old English law. A proclamation summoning the army into the field.

A mulct or fine for not joining the army when summoned. Spelman.

A tax or tribute for the support of the army. Du Cange.

HEREBOTE. The royal edict summoning the people to the field. Cowell.

HEREDAD. In Spanish law. A piece of land under cultivation; a cultivated farm; real estate.

HEREDAD YACENTE. From Lat. *"hæreditas jacens,"* (*q. v.*) In Spanish law. An inheritance not yet entered upon or appropriated. White, New Recop. b. 2, tit. 19, c. 2, § 8.

HEREDERO. In Spanish law. Heir; he who, by legal or testamentary disposition, succeeds to the property of a deceased person. *"Hæres censeatur cum defuncto una eademque persona."* Las Partidas, 7, 9, 13.

HEREDITAGIUM. In Sicilian and Neapolitan law. That which is held by hereditary right; the same with *hereditamentum* (*hereditament*) in English law. Spelman.

HEREDITAMENTS. Things capable of being inherited, be it corporeal or incorporeal, real, personal, or mixed, and including not only lands and everything thereon, but also heir-looms, and certain furniture which, by custom, may descend to the heir together with the land. Co. Litt. 5b; 2 Bl. Comm. 17.

The two kinds of hereditaments are *corporeal*, which are tangible, (in fact, they mean the same thing as land,) and *incorporeal*, which are not tangible, and are the rights and profits annexed to or issuing out of land. Wharton.

The term includes a few rights unconnected with land, but it is generally used as the widest expression for real property of all kinds, and is therefore employed in conveyances after the words "lands" and "tenements," to include everything of the nature of realty which they do not cover. Sweet.

HEREDITARY. That which is the subject of inheritance.

HEREDITARY RIGHT TO THE CROWN. The crown of England, by the positive constitution of the kingdom, has ever been descendible, and so continues, in a course peculiar to itself, yet subject to limitation by parliament; but, notwithstanding such limitation, the crown retains its descendible quality, and becomes hereditary in the prince to whom it is limited. 1 Bl. Comm. 191.

HEREFARE. Sax. A going into or with an army; a going out to war, (*profectio militaris;*) an expedition. Spelman.

HEREGEAT. A heriot, (*q. v.*)

HEREGELD. Sax. In old English law. A tribute or tax levied for the maintenance of an army. Spelman.

HEREMITORIUM. A place of retirement for hermits. Mon. Angl. tom. 3, p. 18.

HEREMONES. Followers of an army.

HERENACH. An archdeacon. Cowell.

HERES. Heir; an heir. A form of *hæres*, very common in the civil law. See HÆRES.

HERESCHIP. In old Scotch law. Theft or robbery. 1 Pitc. Crim. Tr. pt. 2, pp. 26, 89.

HERESLITA, HERESSA, HERESSIZ. A hired soldier who departs without license. 4 Inst. 128.

HERESY. In English law. An offense against religion, consisting not in a total denial of Christianity, but of some of its essential doctrines, publicly and obstinately avowed. 4 Bl. Comm. 44, 45. An opinion on divine subjects devised by human reason, openly taught, and obstinately maintained. 1 Hale, P. C. 384. This offense is now subject only to ecclesiastical correction, and is no longer punishable by the secular law. 4 Steph. Comm. 233.

HERETOCH. A general, leader, or commander; also a baron of the realm. Du Fresne.

HERETOFORE. This word simply denotes time past, in distinction from time present or time future, and has no definite and precise signification beyond this. 40 Conn. 157.

HERETUM. In old records. A court or yard for drawing up guards or military retinue. Cowell.

HEREZELD. In Scotch law. A gift or present made or left by a tenant to his lord as a token of reverence. Skene.

HERGE. In Saxon law. Offenders who joined in a body of more than thirty-five to commit depredations.

HERIGALDS. In old English law. A sort of garment. Cowell.

HERIOT. In English law. A customary tribute of goods and chattels, payable to the lord of the fee on the decease of the owner of the land.

Heriots are divided into heriot *service* and heriot *custom*. The former expression denotes such as are due upon a special reservation in a grant or lease of lands, and therefore amount to little more than a mere rent; the latter arise upon no special reservation whatever, but depend solely upon immemorial usage and custom. 2 Bl. Comm. 422.

HERISCHILD. A species of military service, or knight's fee. Cowell.

HERISCHULDA. In old Scotch law. A fine or penalty for not obeying the proclamation made for warfare. Skene.

HERISCINDIUM. A division of household goods. Blount.

HERISLIT. Laying down of arms. Blount. Desertion from the army. Spelman.

HERISTAL. The station of an army; the place where a camp is pitched. Spelman.

HERITABLE. Capable of being taken by descent. A term chiefly used in Scotch law, where it enters into several phrases.

HERITABLE BOND. In Scotch law. A bond for a sum of money to which is added, for further security of the creditor, a conveyance of land or heritage to be held by the creditor as pledge. 1 Ross, Conv. 76; 2 Ross, Conv. 324.

HERITABLE JURISDICTIONS. In Scotch law. Grants of criminal jurisdiction formerly bestowed on great families in Scotland, to facilitate the administration of justice. Whishaw. Abolished in effect by St. 20 Geo. II. c. 50. Tomlins.

I

J

K

L

M

HERITABLE OBLIGATION. In Louisiana. An obligation is heritable when the heirs and assigns of one party may enforce the performance against the heirs of the other. Civil Code La. art. 1997.

HERITABLE RIGHTS. In Scotch law. Rights of the heir; all rights to land or whatever is connected with land, as mills, fishings, tithes, etc.

HERITAGE. In the civil law. Every species of immovable which can be the subject of property; such as lands, houses, orchards, woods, marshes, ponds, etc., in whatever mode they may have been acquired, either by descent or purchase. 3 Toullier, no. 472.

In Scotch law. Land, and all property connected with land; real estate, as distinguished from movables, or personal estate. Bell.

HERITOR. In Scotch law. A proprietor of land. 1 Kames, Eq. Pref.

HERMANDAD. In Spanish law. A fraternity formed among different towns and villages to prevent the commission of crimes, and to prevent the abuses and vexations to which they were subjected by men in power. Bouvier.

HERMAPHRODITE. An animal or human being so malformed as to have the organs of generation of both sexes.

Hermaphroditus tam masculo quam fœminæ comparatur, secundum prævalentiam sexus incalescentis. An hermaphrodite is to be considered male or female according to the predominance of the exciting sex. Co. Litt. 8; Bract. fol. 5.

HERMENEUTICS. The science or art of construction and interpretation. By the phrase "legal hermeneutics" is understood the systematic body of rules which are recognized as applicable to the construction and interpretation of legal writings.

HERMER. A great lord. Jacob.

HERMOGENIAN CODE. See CODEX HERMOGENIANUS.

HERNESCUS. A heron. Cowell.

HERNESIUM, or HERNASIUM. Household goods; implements of trade or husbandry; the rigging or tackle of a ship. Cowell.

HEROUD, HERAUD. L. Fr. A herald.

HERPEX. A harrow. Spelman.

HERPICATIO. In old English law. A day's work with a harrow. Spelman.

HERRING SILVER. This was a composition in money for the custom of supplying herrings for the provision of a religious house. Wharton.

HERUS. A master. *Servus facit ut herus det,* the servant does [the work] in order that the master may give [him the wages agreed on.] *Herus dat ut servus facit,* the master gives [or agrees to give, the wages,] in consideration of, or with a view to, the servant's doing [the work.] 2 Bl. Comm. 445.

HESIA. An easement. Du Cange.

HEST CORN. In old records. Corn or grain given or devoted to religious persons or purposes. 2 Mon. Angl. 367*b;* Cowell.

HESTA, or HESTHA. A little loaf of bread.

HETÆRARCHA. The head of a religious house; the head of a college; the warden of a corporation.

HETÆRIA. In Roman law. A company, society, or college.

HEUVELBORH. Sax. In old English law. A surety, *(warrantus.)*

HEYLODE. In old records. A customary burden upon inferior tenants, for mending or repairing hays or hedges.

HEYMECTUS. A hay-net; a net for catching conies. Cowell.

HIBERNAGIUM. The season for sowing winter corn. Cowell.

HIDAGE. An extraordinary tax formerly payable to the crown for every hide of land. This taxation was levied, not in money, but provision of armor, etc. Cowell.

HIDALGO. In Spanish law. A noble; a person entitled to the rights of nobility. By *hidalgos* are understood men chosen from good situations in life, *(de buenos lugares,)* and possessed of property, *(algo.)* White, New Recop. b. 1, tit. 5, c. 1.

HIDALGUIA. In Spanish law. Nobility by descent or lineage. White, New Recop. b. 1, tit. 5, c. 3, § 4.

HIDE. In old English law. A measure of land, being as much as could be worked with one plow. It is variously estimated at from 60 to 100 acres, but was probably determined by local usage. Another meaning was as much land as would support one family or the dwellers in a mansion-house. Also a house; a dwelling-house.

HIDE AND GAIN. In English law. A term anciently applied to arable land. Co. Litt. 85*b*.

HIDE LANDS. In Saxon law. Lands belonging to a hide; that is, a house or mansion. Spelman.

HIDEL. In old English law. A place of protection; a sanctuary. St. 1 Hen. VII. cc. 5, 6; Cowell.

HIDGILD. A sum of money paid by a villein or servant to save himself from a whipping. Fleta, l. 1, c. 47, § 20.

HIERARCHY. Originally, government by a body of priests. Now, the body of officers in any church or ecclesiastical institution, considered as forming an ascending series of ranks or degrees of power and authority, with the correlative subjection, each to the one next above. Derivatively, any body of men, taken in their public capacity, and considered as forming a chain of powers, as above described.

HIGH BAILIFF. An officer attached to an English county court. His duties are to attend the court when sitting; to serve summonses; and to execute orders, warrants, writs, etc. St. 9 & 10 Vict. c. 95, § 33; Poll. C. C. Pr. 16. He also has similar duties under the bankruptcy jurisdiction of the county courts.

HIGH COMMISSION COURT. In English law. An ecclesiastical court of very formidable jurisdiction, for the vindication of the peace and dignity of the church, by reforming, ordering, and correcting the ecclesiastical state and persons, and all manner of errors, heresies, schisms, abuses, offenses, contempts, and enormities. 3 Bl. Comm. 67. It was erected by St. 1 Eliz. c. 1, and abolished by 16 Car. I. c. 11.

HIGH CONSTABLE. In English law. An officer of public justice, otherwise called "chief constable" and "constable of the hundred," whose proper duty is to keep the king's peace within the hundred, as the petty constable does within the parish or township. 3 Steph. Comm. 46, 47. See CONSTABLE.

An officer appointed in some cities with powers generally limited to matters of police.

HIGH CONSTABLE OF ENGLAND, LORD. His office has been disused (except only upon great and solemn occasions, as the coronation, or the like) since the attainder of Stafford, Duke of Buckingham, in the reign of Henry VII.

HIGH COURT OF ADMIRALTY. In English law. This was a court which exercised jurisdiction in prize cases, and had general jurisdiction in maritime causes, on the instance side. Its proceedings were usually *in rem*, and its practice and principles derived in large measure from the civil law. The judicature acts of 1873 transferred all the powers and jurisdiction of this tribunal to the probate, divorce, and admiralty division of the high court of justice.

HIGH COURT OF DELEGATES. In English law. A tribunal which formerly exercised appellate jurisdiction over cases brought from the ecclesiastical and admiralty courts. 3 Bl. Comm. 66.

It was a court of great dignity, erected by the statute 25 Hen. VII. c. 19. It was abolished, and its jurisdiction transferred to the judicial committee of the privy council.

HIGH COURT OF ERRORS AND APPEALS. The court of last resort in the state of Mississippi.

HIGH COURT OF JUSTICE. That branch of the English supreme court of judicature (*q. v.*) which exercises (1) the original jurisdiction formerly exercised by the court of chancery, the courts of queen's bench, common pleas, and exchequer, the courts of probate, divorce, and admiralty, the court of common pleas at Lancaster, the court of pleas at Durham, and the courts of the judges or commissioners of assize; and (2) the appellate jurisdiction of such of those courts as heard appeals from inferior courts. Judicature act, 1873, § 16.

HIGH COURT OF JUSTICIARY. See COURT OF JUSTICIARY.

HIGH COURT OF PARLIAMENT. In English law. The English parliament, as composed of the house of peers and house of commons; or the house of lords sitting in its judicial capacity.

HIGH CRIMES. High crimes and misdemeanors are such immoral and unlawful acts as are nearly allied and equal in guilt to felony, yet, owing to some technical circumstance, do not fall within the definition of "felony." 6 Conn. 417.

HIGH JUSTICE. In feudal law. The jurisdiction or right of trying crimes of every kind, even the highest. This was a privilege claimed and exercised by the great lords or barons of the middle ages. 1 Robertson's Car. V., appendix, note 23.

HIGH JUSTICIER. In old French and Canadian law. A feudal lord who exercised the right called "high justice." Guyot, Inst. Feod. c. 26.

HIGH MISDEMEANORS. See MISPRISION; HIGH CRIMES.

HIGH SCHOOL. A school in which higher branches of learning are taught than in the common schools. 123 Mass. 306. A school in which such instruction is given as will prepare the students to enter a college or university.

HIGH SEAS. The ocean; public waters. According to the English doctrine, the high sea begins at the distance of three miles from the coast of any country; according to the American view, at low-water mark, except in the case of small harbors and roadsteads inclosed within the *fauces terræ*.

The open ocean outside of the *fauces terræ*, as distinguished from arms of the sea; the waters of the ocean without the boundary of any county.

Any waters on the sea-coast which are without the boundaries of low-water mark.

HIGH STEWARD, COURT OF THE LORD. In English law. A tribunal instituted for the trial of peers indicted for treason or felony, or for misprision of either, but not for any other offense. The office is very ancient, and was formerly hereditary, or held for life, or *dum benè se gesserit;* but it has been for many centuries granted *pro hâc vice* only, and always to a lord of parliament. When, therefore, such an indictment is found by a grand jury of freeholders in the queen's bench, or at the assizes before a judge of *oyer and terminer*, it is removed by a writ of *certiorari* into the court of the lord high steward, which alone has power to determine it. A peer may plead a pardon before the queen's bench, in order to prevent the trouble of appointing a high steward, merely to receive the plea, but he cannot plead any other plea, because it is possible that, in consequence of such plea, judgment of death might be pronounced upon him. Wharton.

HIGH TREASON. In English law. Treason against the king or sovereign, as distinguished from petit or petty treason, which might formerly be committed against a subject. 4 Bl. Comm. 74, 75; 4 Steph. Comm. 183, 184, note.

HIGH-WATER MARK. This term is properly applicable only to tidal waters, and designates the line on the shore reached by the water at the high or flood tide. But it is sometimes also used with reference to the waters of artificial ponds or lakes, created by dams in unnavigable streams, and then denotes the highest point on the shores to which the dams can raise the water in ordinary circumstances.

HIGH WOOD. Timber.

HIGHER AND LOWER SCALE. In the practice of the English supreme court of judicature there are two scales regulating the fees of the court and the fees which solicitors are entitled to charge. The lower scale applies (unless the court otherwise orders) to the following cases: All causes and matters assigned by the judicature acts to the queen's bench, or the probate, divorce, and admiralty divisions; all actions of debt, contract, or tort; and in almost all causes and matters assigned by the acts to the chancery division in which the amount in litigation is under £1,000. The higher scale applies in all other causes and matters, and also in actions falling under one of the above classes, but in which the principal relief sought to be obtained is an injunction. Sweet.

HIGHNESS. A title of honor given to princes. The kings of England, before the time of James I., were not usually saluted with the title of "Majesty," but with that of "Highness." The children of crowned heads generally receive the style of "Highness." Wharton.

HIGHWAY. A free and public road, way, or street; one which every person has the right to use.

"In all counties of this state, public highways are roads, streets, alleys, lanes, courts, places, trails, and bridges, laid out or erected as such by the public, or, if laid out and erected by others, dedicated or abandoned to the public, or made such in actions for the partition of real property." Pol. Code Cal. § 2618.

There is a difference in the shade of meaning conveyed by two uses of the word. Sometimes it signifies right of free passage, in the abstract, not importing anything about the character or construction of the way. Thus, a river is called a "highway;" and it has been not unusual for congress, in granting a privilege of building a bridge, to declare that it shall be a public highway. Again, it has reference to some system of law authorizing the taking a strip of land, and preparing and devoting it to the use of travelers. In this use it imports a road-way upon the soil, constructed under the authority of these laws. Abbott.

HIGHWAY ACTS, or LAWS. The body or system of laws governing the laying out, repair, and use of highways.

HIGHWAY CROSSING. A place where the track of a railroad crosses the line of a highway.

HIGHWAY-RATE. In English law. A tax for the maintenance and repair of highways, chargeable upon the same property that is liable to the poor-rate.

HIGHWAY ROBBERY. In criminal law. The crime of robbery committed upon or near a public highway. In England, by St. 23 Hen. VIII. c. 1, this was made felony without benefit of clergy, while robbery committed elsewhere was less severely punished. The distinction was abolished by St. 3 & 4 W. & M. c. 9, and in this country it has never prevailed generally.

HIGHWAY TAX. A tax for and applicable to the making and repair of highways.

HIGHWAYMAN. A bandit; one who robs travelers upon the highway.

HIGLER. In English law. A hawker or peddler. A person who carries from door to door, and sells by retail, small articles of provisions, and the like.

HIGUELA. In Spanish law. A receipt given by an heir of a decedent, setting forth what property he has received from the estate.

HIKENILD STREET. One of the four great Roman roads of Britain. More commonly called "Ikenild Street."

HILARY RULES. A collection of orders and forms extensively modifying the pleading and practice in the English superior courts of common law, established in Hilary term, 1834. Stimson.

HILARY TERM. In English law. A term of court, beginning on the 11th and ending on the 31st of January in each year. Superseded (1875) by Hilary sittings, which begin January 11th, and end on the Wednesday before Easter.

HINDENI HOMINES. A society of men. The Saxons ranked men into three classes, and valued them, as to satisfaction for injuries, etc., according to their class. The highest class were valued at 1,200s., and were called "*twelf hindmen;*" the middle class at 600s., and called "*sexhindmen;*" the lowest at 200s., called "*twyhindmen.*" Their wives were termed "*hindas.*" Brompt. Leg. Alfred. c. 12.

HINDER AND DELAY. To hinder and delay is to do something which is an attempt to defraud, rather than a successful fraud; to put some obstacle in the path, or interpose some time, unjustifiably, before the creditor can realize what is owed out of his debtor's property. 42 N. Y. Super. Ct. 63.

HINDU LAW. The system of native law prevailing among the Gentoos, and administered by the government of British India.

HINE, or HIND. A husbandry servant.

HINEFARE. The loss or departure of a servant from his master. Domesday.

HIPOTECA. In Spanish law. A mortgage of real property.

HIRCISCUNDA. See HERCISCUNDA.

HIRE, *v.* To purchase the temporary use of a thing, or to stipulate for the labor or services of another. See HIRING.

To engage in service for a stipulated reward, as to hire a servant for a year, or laborers by the day or month; to engage a man to temporary service for wages. To "employ" is a word of more enlarged signification. A man hired to labor is employed, but a man may be employed in a work who is not hired. 11 N. Y. 605.

For definitions of the various species of this class of contracts, under their Latin names, see LOCATIO and following titles.

HIRE, *n.* Compensation for the use of a thing, or for labor or services.

HIREMAN. A subject. Du Cange.

HIRER. One who hires a thing, or the labor or services of another person.

HIRING. Hiring is a contract by which one person grants to another either the enjoyment of a thing or the use of the labor and industry, either of himself or his servant, during a certain time, for a stipulated compensation, or where one contracts for the labor or services of another about a thing bailed to him for a specified purpose. Code Ga. 1882, § 2085.

Hiring is a contract by which one gives to another the temporary possession and use of property, other than money, for reward, and the latter agrees to return the same to the former at a future time. Civil Code Cal. § 1925; Civil Code Dak. § 1103.

HIRST, HURST. In old English law. A wood. Co. Litt. 4b.

HIS. The use of this pronoun in a written instrument, in referring to a person whose Christian name is designated therein by a mere initial, is not conclusive that the person referred to is a male; it may be shown by parol that the person intended is a female. 71 Cal. 38, 11 Pac. Rep. 802.

HIS EXCELLENCY. In English law. The title of a viceroy, governor general, ambassador, or commander in chief.

In American law. This title is given to the governor of Massachusetts by the constitution of that state; and it is commonly given, as a title of honor and courtesy, to the governors of the other states and to the president of the United States. It is also customarily used by foreign ministers in addressing the secretary of state in written communications.

HIS HONOR. A title given by the constitution of Massachusetts to the lieutenant-governor of that commonwealth. Const. Mass. pt. 2, c. 2, § 2, art. 1.

HIS TESTIBUS. Lat. These being witnesses. The attestation clause in old deeds and charters.

HIWISC. A hide of land.

HLAF ÆTA. Sax. A servant fed at his master's cost.

HLAFORD. Sax. A lord. 1 Spence, Ch. 36.

HLAFORDSOCNA. Sax. A lord's protection. Du Cange.

HLAFORDSWICE. Sax. In Saxon law. The crime of betraying one's lord, (*proditio domini;*) treason. Crabb, Eng. Law, 59, 301.

HLASOCNA. Sax. The benefit of the law. Du Cange.

HLOTHBOTE. In Saxon law. A fine for being present at an unlawful assembly. Spelman.

HLOTHE. In Saxon law. An unlawful assembly from eight to thirty-five, inclusive. Cowell.

HOASTMEN. In English law. An ancient gild or fraternity at Newcastle-upon-Tyne, who dealt in sea coal. St. 21 Jac. I. c. 3.

HOBBLERS. In old English law. Light horsemen or bowmen; also certain tenants, bound by their tenure to maintain a little light horse for giving notice of any invasion, or such like peril, towards the seaside. Camden, Brit.

HOC. Lat. This. *Hoc intuitu,* with this expectation. *Hoc loco,* in this place. *Hoc nomine,* in this name. *Hoc titulo,* under this title. *Hoc voce,* under this word.

HOC QUIDEM PERQUAM DURUM EST, SED ITA LEX SCRIPTA EST. Lat. (This indeed is exceedingly hard, but so the law is written; such is the written or positive law.) An observation quoted by Blackstone as used by Ulpian in the civil law; and applied to cases where courts of equity have no power to abate the rigor of the law. Dig. 40, 9, 12, 1; 3 Bl. Comm. 430.

HOC PARATUS EST VERIFICARE. Lat. This he is ready to verify.

Hoc servabitur quod initio convenit. This shall be preserved which is useful in the beginning. Dig. 50, 17, 23; Bract. 73b.

HOCCUS SALTIS. A hoke, hole, or lesser pit of salt. Cowell.

HOCK - TUESDAY MONEY. This was a duty given to the landlord that his tenants and bondmen might solemnize the day on which the English conquered the Danes, being the second Tuesday after Easter week. Cowell.

HOCKETTOR, or HOCQUETEUR. A knight of the post; a decayed man; a basket carrier. Cowell.

HODGE - PODGE ACT. A name applied to a statute which comprises a medley of incongruous subjects.

HOGA. In old English law. A hill or mountain. In old English, a *how.* *Grene hoga,* Grenehow. Domesday; Spelman.

HOGASTER. In old English law. A sheep of the second year. Fleta, lib. 2, c. 79, §§ 4, 12. A young hog. Cowell.

HOGGUS, or HOGIETUS. A hog or swine. Cowell.

HOGHENHYNE. In Saxon law. A house-servant. Any stranger who lodged three nights or more at a man's house in a decennary was called *"hoghenhyne,"* and his host became responsible for his acts as for those of his servant.

HOGSHEAD. A measure of a capacity containing the fourth part of a tun, or sixty-three gallons. Cowell. A large cask, of indefinite contents, but usually containing from one hundred to one hundred and forty gallons. Webster.

HOLD, v. 1. To possess in virtue of a lawful title; as in the expression, common in grants, "to have and to hold," or in that applied to notes, "the owner and holder."

2. To be the grantee or tenant of another; to take or have an estate from another. Properly, to have an estate on condition of paying rent, or performing service.

3. To adjudge or decide, spoken of a court, particularly to declare the conclusion of law reached by the court as to the legal effect of the facts disclosed.

4. To maintain or sustain; to be under the necessity or duty of sustaining or proving; as when it is said that a party "holds the affirmative" or negative of an issue in a cause.

5. To bind or obligate; to restrain or constrain; to keep in custody or under an obligation; as in the phrases "hold to bail," "hold for court," "held and firmly bound," etc.

6. To administer; to conduct or preside at; to convoke, open, and direct the operations of; as to hold a court, hold pleas, etc.

7. To prosecute; to direct and bring about officially; to conduct according to law; as to hold an election.

8. To possess; to occupy; to be in possession and administration of; as to hold office.

HOLD, n. In old law. Tenure. A word constantly occurring in conjunction with others, as *freehold, leasehold, copyhold,* etc., but rarely met with in the separate form.

HOLD OVER. To hold possession after the expiration of a term or lease. To retain possession of property leased, after the end of the term. To continue in possession of an office, and continue to exercise its functions, after the end of the officer's lawful term.

HOLD PLEAS. To hear or try causes. 3 Bl. Comm. 35, 298.

HOLDER. The holder of a bill of exchange, promissory note, or check is the person who has legally acquired the possession of the same, from a person capable of transferring it, by indorsement or delivery, and who is entitled to receive payment of the instrument from the party or parties liable to meet it.

HOLDER IN DUE COURSE, in English law, is "a holder who has taken a bill of exchange (check or note) complete and regular on the face of it, under the following conditions, namely: (*a*) That he became the holder of it before it was overdue, and without notice that it had been previously dishonored, if such was the fact. (*b*) That he took the bill (check or note) in good faith and for value, and that at the time it was negotiated to him he had no notice of any defect in the title of the person who negotiated it." Bills of exchange act, 1882, (45 & 46 Vict. c. 61, § 29.)

HOLDES. Sax. In Saxon law. A military commander. Spelman.

HOLDING. In English law. A piece of land held under a lease or similar tenancy for agricultural, pastoral, or similar purposes.

In Scotch law. The tenure or nature of the right given by the superior to the vassal. Bell.

HOLDING OVER. A holding beyond a term; a continuing in possession after the expiration of a term. The act of keeping possession of premises leased, after the expiration of the term of the lease, without the consent of the landlord; or of an office after the expiration of the incumbent's legal term.

HOLDING UP THE HAND. In criminal practice. A formality observed in the arraignment of prisoners. Held to be not absolutely necessary. 1 W. Bl. 3, 4.

HOLIDAY. A religious festival; a day set apart for commemorating some important event in history; a day of exemption from labor. Webster. A day upon which the usual operations of business are suspended and the courts closed, and, generally, no legal process is served.

HOLM. An island in a river or the sea. Spelman.

Plain grassy ground upon water sides or in the water. Blount. Low ground intersected with streams. Spelman.

HOLOGRAFO. In Spanish law. A holograph. An instrument (particularly a will) wholly in the handwriting of the person executing it; or which, to be valid, must be so written by his own hand.

HOLOGRAPH. A will or deed written entirely by the testator or grantor with his own hand.

HOLT. Sax. In old English law. A wood or grove. Spelman; Cowell; Co. Litt. 4*b*.

HOLY ORDERS. In ecclesiastical law. The orders of bishops, (including archbishops,) priests, and deacons in the Church of England. The Roman canonists had the orders of bishop, (in which the pope and archbishops were included,) priest, deacon, subdeacon, psalmist, acolyte, exorcist, reader, ostiarius. 3 Steph. Comm. 55, and note *a*.

HOMAGE. In feudal law. A service (or the ceremony of rendering it) which a tenant was bound to perform to his lord on receiving investiture of a fee, or succeeding to it as heir, in acknowledgment of the tenure. It is described by Littleton as the most honorable service of reverence that a free tenant might do to his lord. The ceremony was as follows: The tenant, being ungirt and with bare head, knelt before the lord, the latter sitting, and held his hands extended and joined between the hands of the lord, and said: "I become your man [*homo*] from this day forward, of life and limb and earthly honor, and to you will be faithful and loyal, and bear you faith, for the tenements that I claim to hold of you, saving the faith that I owe unto our sovereign lord the king, so help me God." The tenant then received a kiss from the lord. Homage could be done only to the lord himself. Litt. § 85; Glanv. lib. 9, c. 1; Bract. fols. 77*b*, 78-80; Wharton.

"Homage" is to be distinguished from "fealty," another incident of feudalism, and which consisted in the solemn oath of fidelity made by the vassal to the lord, whereas homage was merely an acknowledgment of tenure. If the homage was intended to include fealty, it was called "liege homage;" but otherwise it was called "simple homage." Brown.

HOMAGE ANCESTRAL. In feudal law. Homage was called by this name where a man and his ancestors had immemorially held of another and his ancestors by the service of homage, which bound the lord to warrant the title, and also to hold the tenant clear of all services to superior lords. If the tenant aliened in fee, his alienee was a tenant by homage, but not by homage ancestral. Litt. § 143; 2 Bl. Comm. 300.

HOMAGE JURY. A jury in a court-baron, consisting of tenants that do homage, who are to inquire and make presentments of the death of tenants, surrenders, admittances, and the like.

HOMAGE LIEGE. That kind of homage which was due to the sovereign alone as supreme lord, and which was done without any saving or exception of the rights of other lords. Spelman.

HOMAGER. One who does or is bound to do homage. Cowell.

HOMAGIO RESPECTUANDO. A writ to the escheator commanding him to deliver seisin of lands to the heir of the king's tenant, notwithstanding his homage not done. Fitzh. Nat. Brev. 269.

HOMAGIUM. Homage, (*q. v.*)

HOMAGIUM LIGIUM. Liege homage; that kind of homage which was due to the sovereign alone as supreme lord, and which was done without any saving or exception of the rights of other lords. Spelman. So called from *ligando*, (binding,) because it could not be renounced like other kinds of homage.

Homagium, non per procuratores nec per literas fieri potuit, sed in propria persona tam domini quam tenentis capi debet et fieri. Co. Litt. 68. Homage cannot be done by proxy, nor by letters, but must be paid and received in the proper person, as well of the lord as the tenant.

HOMAGIUM PLANUM. In feudal law. Plain homage; a species of homage which bound him who did it to nothing more than fidelity, without any obligation either of military service or attendance in the courts of his superior. 1 Robertson's Car. V., Appendix, note 8.

HOMAGIUM REDDERE. To renounce homage. This was when a vassal made a solemn declaration of disowning and defying his lord; for which there was a set form and method prescribed by the feudal laws. Bract. l. 2, c. 35, § 35.

HOMAGIUM SIMPLEX. In feudal law. Simple homage; that kind of homage which was merely an acknowledgment of tenure, with a saving of the rights of other lords. Harg. Co. Litt. note 18, lib. 2.

HOMBRE BUENO. In Spanish law. The judge of a district. Also an arbitrator chosen by the parties to a suit. Also a man in good standing; one who is competent to testify in a suit.

HOME. When a person voluntarily takes up his abode in a given place, with intention to remain permanently, or for an indefinite period of time, or without any present intention to remove therefrom, such place of abode becomes his residence or *home.* 43 Me. 418. This word has not the same technical meaning as "domicile." 19 Me. 301.

HOME, or HOMME. L. Fr. Man; a man.

Home ne sera puny pur suer des briefes en court le roy, soit il a droit ou a tort. A man shall not be punished for suing out writs in the king's court, whether he be right or wrong. 2 Inst. 228.

HOME OFFICE. The department of state through which the English sovereign administers most of the internal affairs of the kingdom, especially the police, and communicates with the judicial functionaries.

HOME PORT. A port in a state in which the owner of a vessel resides.

HOMESOKEN, HOMSOKEN. See HAMESOKEN.

HOMESTALL. A mansion-house.

HOMESTEAD. The home place; the place where the home is. It is the home, the house and the adjoining land, where the head of the family dwells; the home farm. 36 N. H. 166.

The fixed residence of the head of a family, with the land and buildings surrounding the main house.

HOMESTEAD CORPORATIONS. Corporations organized for the purpose of acquiring lands in large tracts, paying off incumbrances thereon, improving and subdividing them into homestead lots or parcels, and distributing them among the shareholders, and for the accumulation of a fund for such purposes, are known as "homestead corporations," and must not have a corporate existence for a longer period than ten years. Civil Code Cal. § 557.

HOMESTEAD EXEMPTION LAWS. Laws passed in most of the states allowing a householder or head of a family to designate a house and land as his homestead, and exempting the same homestead from execution for his general debts.

HOMICIDAL. Pertaining to homicide; relating to homicide; impelling to homicide; as a homicidal mania.

HOMICIDE. The killing any human creature. 4 Bl. Comm. 177. The act of a human being in killing another human being.

"Homicide," as a term, does not import crime. It includes crimes, such, for instance, as murder and manslaughter. But a homicide may be innocent; may even be in the performance of a duty. The execution of the sentence of death upon a criminal by the officer of the law is a homicide. The term "homicide" embraces all man-killing. 1 Park. Crim. R. 182, 186.

Justifiable homicide is such as is committed intentionally, but without any evil design, and under such circumstances of necessity or duty as render the act proper, and relieve the party from any shadow of blame; as where a sheriff lawfully executes a sentence of death upon a malefactor, or where the killing takes place in the endeavor to prevent the commission of a felony which could not be otherwise avoided.

Excusable homicide is such as is committed through misadventure or accident, without any willful or malicious intention; or by necessity, in self-defense.

Felonious homicide (which may be either murder or manslaughter) is that committed without justification or excuse in law, *i. e.,* with malice and intention, and under such circumstances as to make it punishable.

HOMICIDE PER INFORTUNIUM. In criminal law. Homicide by misfortune, or accidental homicide; as where a man doing a lawful act, without any intention of hurt, unfortunately kills another; a species of excusable homicide. 4 Bl. Comm. 182; 4 Steph. Comm. 101.

HOMICIDE PER MISADVENTURE. See HOMICIDE PER INFORTUNIUM.

HOMICIDE SE DEFENDENDO. In criminal law. Homicide in self-defense; the killing of a person in self-defense upon a sudden affray, where the slayer had no other possible (or, at least, probable) means of escaping from his assailant. 4 Bl. Comm. 183–186; 4 Steph. Comm. 103–105. A species of excusable homicide. Id.; 1 Russ. Crimes, 660.

HOMICIDIUM. Lat. Homicide, (*q. v.*) *Homicidium ex justitia,* homicide in the administration of justice, or in the execution of the sentence of the law.

Homicidium ex necessitate, homicide from inevitable necessity, as for the protection of one's person or property.

Homicidium ex casu, homicide by accident.

Homicidium ex voluntate, voluntary or willful homicide. Bract. fols. 120*b*, 121.

HOMINATIO. The mustering of men; the doing of homage.

HOMINE CAPTO IN WITHERNAMIUM. A writ to take him that had taken any bond man or woman, and led him or her out of the country, so that he or she could not be replevied according to law. Reg. Orig. 79.

HOMINE ELIGENDO. In old English law. A writ directed to a corporation, requiring the members to make choice of a man to keep one part of the seal appointed for statutes merchant, when a former is dead, according to the statute of Acton Burnell. Reg. Orig. 178; Wharton.

HOMINE REPLEGIANDO. In English law. A writ which lay to replevy a man out of prison, or out of the custody of any private person, in the same manner that chattels taken in distress may be replevied. Brown.

HOMINES. Lat. In feudal law. Men; feudatory tenants who claimed a privilege of having their causes, etc., tried only in their lord's court. Paroch. Antiq. 15.

H O M I N E S L I G I I. In feudal law. Liege men; feudal tenants or vassals, especially those who held immediately of the sovereign. 1 Bl. Comm. 367.

Hominum causa jus constitutum est. Law is established for the benefit of man.

HOMIPLAGIUM. In old English law. The maiming of a man. Blount.

HOMME. Fr. Man; a man. This term is defined by the Civil Code of Louisiana to include a woman. Article 3522, nn. 1, 2.

HOMMES DE FIEF. Fr. In feudal law. Men of the fief; feudal tenants; the peers in the lords' courts. Montesq., Esprit des Lois, liv. 28, c. 27.

HOMMES FEODAUX. Fr. In feudal law. Feudal tenants; the same with *hommes de fief,* (*q. v.*) Montesq., Esprit des Lois, liv. 28, c. 36.

HOMO. Lat. A man; a human being, male or female; a vassal, or feudal tenant; a retainer, dependent, or servant.

H O M O CHARTULARIUS. A slave manumitted by charter.

HOMO COMMENDATUS. In feudal law. One who surrendered himself into the power of another for the sake of protection or support. See COMMENDATION.

HOMO ECCLESIASTICUS. A church vassal; one who was bound to serve a church, especially to do service of an agricultural character. Spelman.

HOMO EXERCITALIS. A man of the army, (*exercitus;*) a soldier.

HOMO FEODALIS. A vassal or tenant; one who held a fee, (*feodum,*) or part of a fee. Spelman.

HOMO FISCALIS, or FISCALINUS. A servant or vassal belonging to the treasury or *fiscus.*

HOMO FRANCUS. In old English law. A freeman. A Frenchman.

HOMO INGENUUS. A free man. A free and lawful man. A yeoman.

HOMO LIBER. A freeman.

HOMO LIGIUS. A liege man; a subject; a king's vassal. The vassal of a subject.

HOMO NOVUS. In feudal law. A new tenant or vassal; one who was invested with a new fee. Spelman.

HOMO PERTINENS. In feudal law. A feudal bondman or vassal; one who *belonged* to the soil, (*qui glebæ adscribitur.*)

Homo potest esse habilis et inhabilis diversis temporibus. 5 Coke, 98. A man may be capable and incapable at different times.

HOMO REGIUS. A king's vassal.

H O M O ROMANUS. A Roman. An appellation given to the old inhabitants of Gaul and other Roman provinces, and retained in the laws of the barbarous nations. Spelman.

HOMO TRIUM LITTERARUM. A man of the three letters; that is, the three letters, "f," "u," "r;" the Latin word *fur* meaning "thief."

Homo vocabulum est naturæ; persona juris civilis. Man (*homo*) is a term of nature; person (*persona*) of civil law. Calvin.

HOMOLOGACION. In Spanish law. The tacit consent and approval inferred by law from the omission of the parties, for the space of ten days, to complain of the sentences of arbitrators, appointment of syndics, or assignees of insolvents, settlements of successions, etc. Also the approval given by the judge of certain acts and agreements for the purpose of rendering them more binding and executory. *Escriche.*

HOMOLOGARE. In the civil law. To confirm or approve; to consent or assent; to confess. *Calvin.*

HOMOLOGATE. In modern civil law. To approve; to confirm; as a court *homologates* a proceeding. See HOMOLOGATION. Literally, to use the *same words* with another; to say the like. 9 Mart. (La.) 324. To assent to what another says or writes.

HOMOLOGATION. In the civil law. Approbation; confirmation by a court of justice; a judgment which orders the execution of some act. Merl. Répert. The term is also used in Louisiana.

In English law. An estoppel *in pais.* L. R. 3 App. Cas. 1026.

In Scotch law. An act by which a person approves of a deed, the effect of which is to render that deed, though in itself defective, binding upon the person by whom it is homologated. *Bell.* Confirmation of a voidable deed.

HOMONYMIÆ. A term applied in the civil law to cases where a law was repeated, or laid down in the same terms or to the same effect, more than once. Cases of iteration and repetition. 2 Kent, Comm. 489, note.

HONDHABEND. Sax. Having in hand. See HANDHABEND.

HONESTE VIVERE. Lat. To live honorably, creditably, or virtuously. One of the three general precepts to which Justinian reduced the whole doctrine of the law, (Inst. 1, 1, 3; Bract. fols. 3, 3b,) the others being *alterum non lædere,* (not to injure others,) and *suum cuique tribuere,* (to render to every man his due.)

HONESTUS. Of good character or standing. *Coram duobus vel pluribus viris legalibus et honestis,* before two or more lawful and good men. Bract. fol. 61.

HONOR, *v.* To accept a bill of exchange, or to pay a note, check, or accepted bill, at maturity and according to its tenor.

HONOR, *n.* In English law. A seigniory of several manors held under one

baron or lord paramount. Also those dignities or privileges, degrees of nobility, knighthood, and other titles, which flow from the crown as the fountain of honor. Wharton.

In American law. The customary title of courtesy given to judges of the higher courts, and occasionally to some other officers; as "his honor," "your honor."

HONOR COURTS. Tribunals held within honors or seigniories.

HONORABLE. A title of courtesy given in England to the younger children of earls, and the children of viscounts and barons; and, collectively, to the house of commons. In America, the word is used as a title of courtesy for various classes of officials, but without any clear lines of distinction.

HONORARIUM. In the civil law. An honorary or free gift; a gratuitous payment, as distinguished from hire or compensation for service; a lawyer's or counsellor's fee. Dig. 50, 13, 1, 10–12.

An *honorarium* is a voluntary donation, in consideration of services which admit of no compensation in money; in particular, to advocates at law, deemed to practice for honor or influence, and not for fees. 14 Ga. 89.

HONORARIUM JUS. In Roman law. The law of the prætors and the edicts of the ædiles.

HONORARY CANONS. Those without emolument. 3 & 4 Vict. c. 113, § 23.

HONORARY FEUDS. Titles of nobility, descendible to the eldest son, in exclusion of all the rest. 2 Bl. Comm. 56.

HONORARY SERVICES. In feudal law. Special services to be rendered to the king in person, characteristic of the tenure by grand serjeanty; such as to carry his banner, his sword, or the like, or to be his butler, champion, or other officer, at his coronation. Litt. § 153; 2 Bl. Comm. 73.

HONORARY TRUSTEES. Trustees to preserve contingent remainders, so called because they are bound, in honor only, to decide on the most proper and prudential course. Lewin, Trusts, 408.

HONORIS RESPECTUM. By reason of honor or privilege. See CHALLENGE.

HONTFONGENETHEF. In Saxon law. A thief taken with *hondhabend;* i. e., having the thing stolen in his hand. *Cowell.*

HONY. L. Fr. Shame; evil; disgrace. *Hony soit qui mal y pense*, evil be to him who evil thinks.

HOO. A hill. Co. Litt. 5b.

HOOKLAND. Land plowed and sown every year.

HOPCON. A valley. Cowell.

HOPE. In old English law. A valley. Co. Litt. 4b.

HOPPO. A Chinese term for a collector; an overseer of commerce.

HORA AURORÆ. In old English law. The morning bell, as *ignitegium* or *coverfeu* (curfew) was the evening bell.

Hora non est multum de substantia negotii, licet in appello de ea aliquando fiat mentio. The hour is not of much consequence as to the substance of business, although in appeal it is sometimes mentioned. 1 Bulst. 82.

HORÆ JURIDICÆ, or JUDICIÆ. Hours during which the judges sat in court to attend to judicial business.

HORCA. In Spanish law. A gallows; the punishment of hanging. White, New Recop. b. 2, tit. 19, c. 4, § 1.

HORDA. In old records. A cow in calf.

HORDERA. A treasurer. Du Cange.

HORDERIUM. In old English law. A hoard; a treasure, or repository. Cowell.

HORDEUM. In old records. Barley. *Hordeum palmale*, beer barley, as distinguished from common barley, which was called "*hordeum quadragesimale.*" Blount.

HORN. In old Scotch practice. A kind of trumpet used in denouncing contumacious persons rebels and outlaws, which was done with three blasts of the horn by the king's sergeant. This was called "putting to the horn;" and the party so denounced was said to be "at the horn." Bell.

HORN-BOOK. A primer; a book explaining the rudiments of any science or branch of knowledge. The phrase "horn-book law" is a colloquial designation of the rudiments or most familiar principles of law.

HORN TENURE. In old English law. Tenure by cornage; that is, by the service of winding a horn when the Scots or other enemies entered the land, in order to warn the king's subjects. This was a species of grand serjeanty. Litt. § 156; 2 Bl. Comm. 74.

HORN WITH HORN, or HORN UNDER HORN. The promiscuous feeding of bulls and cows or all horned beasts that are allowed to run together upon the same common. Spelman.

HORNGELD. Sax. In old English law. A tax within a forest, paid for horned beasts. Cowell; Blount.

HORNING. In Scotch law. "Letters of horning" is the name given to a judicial process issuing on the decree of a court, by which the debtor is summoned to perform his obligation in terms of the decree, the consequence of his failure to do so being liability to arrest and imprisonment. It was anciently the custom to proclaim a debtor who had failed to obey such process a rebel or outlaw, which was done by three blasts of the horn by the king's sergeant in a public place. This was called "putting to the horn," whence the name.

HORREUM. Lat. A place for keeping grain; a granary. A place for keeping fruits, wines, and goods generally; a store-house. Calvin.; Bract. fol. 48.

HORS. L. Fr. Out; out of; without.

HORS DE SON FEE. L. Fr. Out of his fee. In old pleading, this was the name of a plea in an action for rent or services, by which the defendant alleged that the land in question was out of the compass of the plaintiff's fee.

HORS PRIS. L. Fr. Except. Literally translated by the Scotch "out taken."

HORS WEALH. In old English law. The wealh, or Briton who had care of the king's horses.

HORS WEARD. In old English law. A service or *corvée*, consisting in watching the horses of the lord. Anc. Inst. Eng.

HORSE. Until a horse has attained the age of four years, he is called a colt. 1 Russ. & R. 416.

The word "horse" is used in a *quasi* generic sense, to include every description of the male, in contradistinction to the female or mare, whether stallion or gelding. 38 Tex. 555.

HORSE GUARDS. The directing power of the military forces of the kingdom of Great Britain. The commander in chief, or general commanding the forces, is at the head of this department. It is subordinate to the war office, but the relations between them are complicated. Wharton.

HORTUS. Lat. In the civil law. A garden. Dig. 32, 91, 5.

HOSPES. Lat. A guest. 8 Coke, 32.

HOSPES GENERALIS. A great chamberlain.

HOSPITAL. An institution for the reception and care of sick, wounded, infirm, or aged persons: generally incorporated, and then of the class of corporations called "eleemosynary" or "charitable."

HOSPITALLERS. The knights of a religious order, so called because they built a hospital at Jerusalem, wherein pilgrims were received. All their lands and goods in England were given to the sovereign by 32 Hen. VIII. c. 24.

HOSPITATOR. A host or entertainer. *Hospitator communis.* An innkeeper. 8 Coke, 32.
Hospitator magnus. The marshal of a camp.

HOSPITIA. Inns. *Hospitia communia,* common inns. Reg. Orig. 105. *Hospitia curiæ,* inns of court. *Hospitia cancellariæ,* inns of chancery. Crabb, Eng. Law, 428, 429; 4 Reeve, Eng. Law, 120.

HOSPITICIDE. One that kills his guest or host.

HOSPITIUM. An inn; a household.

HOSPODAR. A Turkish governor in Moldavia or Wallachia.

HOST. L. Fr. An army. Britt. c. 22. A military expedition; war. Kelham.

HOSTAGE. A person who is given into the possession of the enemy, in a public war, his freedom (or life) to stand as security for the performance of some contract or promise made by the belligerent power giving the hostage with the other.

HOSTELAGIUM. In old records. A right to receive lodging and entertainment, anciently reserved by lords in the houses of their tenants. Cowell.

HOSTELER. An innkeeper. Now applied, under the form "ostler," to those who look to a guest's horses. Cowell.

HOSTES. Enemies. *Hostes humani generis,* enemies of the human race; *i. e.*, pirates.

Hostes sunt qui nobis vel quibus nos bellum decernimus; cæteri proditores vel prædones sunt. 7 Coke, 24. Enemies are those with whom we declare war, or who declare it against us; all others are traitors or pirates.

HOSTIA. In old records. The host-bread, or consecrated wafer, in the eucharist. Cowell.

HOSTICIDE. One who kills an enemy.

HOSTILARIA, HOSPITALARIA. A place or room in religious houses used for the reception of guests and strangers.

HOSTILE. Having the character of an enemy; standing in the relation of an enemy. See 1 Kent, Comm. c. 4.

HOSTILE EMBARGO. One laid upon the vessels of an actual or prospective enemy.

HOSTILE WITNESS. A witness who manifests so much hostility or prejudice under examination in chief that the party who has called him, or his representative, is allowed to cross-examine him, *i. e.*, to treat him as though he had been called by the opposite party. Wharton.

HOSTILITY. In the law of nations. A state of open war. "At the breaking out of hostility." 1 Kent, Comm. 60.
An act of open war. "When *hostilities* have commenced." Id. 56.
A hostile character. "Hostility may attach only to the person." Id.

HOT-WATER ORDEAL. In old English law. This was a test, in cases of accusation, by hot water; the party accused and suspected being appointed by the judge to put his arms up to the elbows in seething hot water, which, after sundry prayers and invocations, he did, and was, by the effect which followed, judged guilty or innocent. Wharton.

HOTCHPOT. The blending and mixing property belonging to different persons, in order to divide it equally. 2 Bl. Comm. 190.

Anciently applied to the mixing and blending of lands given to one daughter in frank marriage, with those descending to her and her sisters in fee-simple, for the purpose of dividing the whole equally among them; without which the daughter who held in frank marriage could have no share in the lands in fee-simple. Litt. §§ 267, 268; Co. Litt. 177a; 2 Bl. Comm. 190.

Hotchpot, or the *putting in hotchpot,* is applied in modern law to the throwing the amount of an advancement made to a particular child, in real or personal estate, into the common stock, for the purpose of a more equal division, or of equalizing the shares of all the children. 2 Kent, Comm. 421, 422. This answers to or resembles the *collatio bonorum*, or *collation* of the civil law.

HOTEL. An inn; a public house or tavern; a house for entertaining strangers or travelers. 54 Barb. 316; 2 Daly, 15; 46 Mo. 594.

HOUR. The twenty-fourth part of a natural day; sixty minutes of time.

HOUR OF CAUSE. In Scotch practice. The hour when a court is met. 3 How. State Tr. 603.

HOUSE. 1. A dwelling; a building designed for the habitation and residence of men.

"House" means, presumptively, a dwelling-house; a building divided into floors and apartments, with four walls, a roof, and doors and chimneys; but it does not necessarily mean precisely this. 14 Mees. & W. 181; 7 Man. & G. 122.

"House" is not synonymous with "dwelling-house." While the former is used in a broader and more comprehensive sense than the latter, it has a narrower and more restricted meaning than the word "building." 46 N. H. 61.

In the devise of a house, the word "house" is synonymous with "messuage," and conveys all that comes within the curtilage. 4 Pa. St. 93.

2. A legislative assembly, or (where the bicameral system obtains) one of the two branches of the legislature; as the "house of lords," "house of representatives." Also a quorum of a legislative body. See 2 Mich. 287.

3. The name "house" is also given to some collections of men other than legislative bodies, to some public institutions, and (colloquially) to mercantile firms or joint-stock companies.

HOUSE-BOTE. A species of estovers, belonging to a tenant for life or years, consisting in the right to take from the woods of the lessor or owner such timber as may be necessary for making repairs upon the house. See Co. Litt. 41*b*.

HOUSE-BURNING. See ARSON.

HOUSE-DUTY. A tax on inhabited houses imposed by 14 & 15 Vict. c. 36, in lieu of window-duty, which was abolished.

HOUSE OF COMMONS. One of the constituent houses of the British parliament, composed of representatives of the counties, cities, and boroughs.

HOUSE OF CORRECTION. A reformatory. A place for the imprisonment of juvenile offenders, or those who have committed crimes of lesser magnitude.

HOUSE OF ILL FAME. A bawdy-house; a brothel; a dwelling allowed by its chief occupant to be used as a resort of persons desiring unlawful sexual intercourse. 33 Conn. 91.

HOUSE OF LORDS. The upper chamber of the British parliament. It comprises the archbishops and bishops, (called "Lords Spiritual,") the English peers sitting by virtue of hereditary right, sixteen Scotch peers elected to represent the Scotch peerage under the act of union, and twenty-eight Irish peers elected under similar provisions. The house of lords, as a judicial body, has ultimate appellate jurisdiction, and may sit as a court for the trial of impeachments.

HOUSE OF REFUGE. A prison for juvenile delinquents. A house of correction or reformatory.

HOUSE OF REPRESENTATIVES. The name of the body forming the more popular and numerous branch of the congress of the United States; also of the similar branch in many of the state legislatures.

HOUSEAGE. A fee paid for housing goods by a carrier, or at a wharf, etc.

HOUSEBREAKING. In criminal law. Breaking and entering a dwelling-house with intent to commit any felony therein. If done by night, it comes under the definition of "burglary."

HOUSEHOLD. A family living together. 18 Johns. 400, 402. Those who dwell under the same roof and compose a family. Webster. A man's family living together constitutes his household, though he may have gone to another state.

Belonging to the house and family; domestic. Webster.

HOUSEHOLD FURNITURE. This term, in a will, includes all personal chattels that may contribute to the use or convenience of the householder, or the ornament of the house; as plate, linen, china, both useful and ornamental, and pictures. But goods in trade, books, and wines will not pass by a bequest of household furniture. 1 Rop. Leg. 203.

HOUSEHOLD GOODS. These words, in a will, include everything of a permanent nature (*i. e.*, articles of household which are not consumed in their enjoyment) that are used in or purchased or otherwise acquired by a testator for his house. 1 Rop. Leg. 191.

HOUSEHOLD STUFF. This phrase, in a will, includes everything which may be used for the convenience of the house, as tables, chairs, bedding, and the like. But apparel, books, weapons, tools for artificers, cattle, victuals, and choses in action will not pass by those words, unless the context of the will clearly show a contrary intention. 1 Rop. Leg. 206.

HOUSEHOLDER. The occupier of a house. Brande. More correctly, one who keeps house with his family; the head or master of a family. Webster; 18 Johns. 302. One who has a household; the head of a household.

HOUSEKEEPER. One who is in actual possession of and who occupies a house, as distinguished from a "boarder," "lodger," or "guest."

HOVEL. A place used by husbandmen to set their plows, carts, and other farming utensils out of the rain and sun. A shed; a cottage; a mean house.

H O W E. In old English law. A hill. Co. Litt. 5b.

HOY. A small coasting vessel, usually sloop-rigged, used in conveying passengers and goods from place to place, or as a tender to larger vessels in port. Webster.

HOYMAN. The master or captain of a hoy.

HUCUSQUE. In old pleading. Hitherto. 2 Mod. 24.

HUDE-GELD. In old English law. An acquittance for an assault upon a trespassing servant. Supposed to be a mistake or misprint in Fleta for "hinegeld." Fleta, lib. 1, c. 47, § 20. Also the price of one's skin, or the money paid by a servant to save himself from a whipping. Du Cange.

HUE AND CRY. In old English law. A loud outcry with which felons (such as robbers, burglars, and murderers) were anciently pursued, and which all who heard it were bound to take up, and join in the pursuit, until the malefactor was taken. Bract. fols. 115b, 124; 4 Bl. Comm. 293.

A written proclamation issued on the escape of a felon from prison, requiring all officers and people to assist in retaking him. 3 How. State Tr. 386.

HUEBRAS. In Spanish law. A measure of land equal to as much as a yoke of oxen can plow in one day. 2 White, Recop. (38,) 49; 12 Pet. 443.

HUISSERIUM. A ship used to transport horses. Also termed "uffer."

HUISSIERS. In French law. Marshals; ushers; process-servers; sheriffs' officers. Ministerial officers attached to the courts, to effect legal service of process required by law in actions, to issue executions, etc., and to maintain order during the sitting of the courts.

HULKA. In old records. A hulk or small vessel. Cowell.

HULLUS. In old records. A hill. 2 Mon. Angl. 292; Cowell.

HUMAGIUM. A moist place. Mon. Angl.

HUNDRED. Under the Saxon organization of England, each county or shire comprised an indefinite number of *hundreds*, each hundred containing ten *tithings*, or groups of ten families of freeholders or frankpledges. The hundred was governed by a high constable, and had its own court; but its most remarkable feature was the corporate responsibility of the whole for the crimes or defaults of the individual members. The introduction of this plan of organization into England is commonly ascribed to Alfred, but the idea, as well of the collective liability as of the division, was probably known to the ancient German peoples, as we find the same thing established in the Frankish kingdom under Clothaire, and in Denmark. See 1 Bl. Comm. 115; 4 Bl. Comm. 411.

HUNDRED COURT. In English law. A larger court-baron, being held for all the inhabitants of a particular *hundred*, instead of a manor. The free suitors are the judges, and the steward the registrar, as in the case of a court-baron. It is not a court of record, and resembles a court-baron in all respects except that in point of territory it is of greater jurisdiction. These courts have long since fallen into desuetude. 3 Bl. Comm. 34, 35; 3 Steph. Comm. 394, 395.

HUNDRED GEMOTE. Among the Saxons, a meeting or court of the freeholders of a hundred, which assembled, originally, twelve times a year, and possessed civil and criminal jurisdiction and ecclesiastical powers. 1 Reeve, Eng. Law, 7.

HUNDRED LAGH. The law of the hundred, or hundred court; liability to attend the hundred court. Spelman.

HUNDRED PENNY. In old English law. A tax collected from the hundred, by the sheriff or lord of the hundred. Spel. voc. "*Hundredus.*"

HUNDRED SECTA. The performance of suit and service at the hundred court.

HUNDRED SETENA. In Saxon law. The dwellers or inhabitants of a hundred. Cowell; Blount. Spelman suggests the reading of *sceatena* from Sax. "*sceat,*" a tax.

HUNDRED-WEIGHT. A denomination of weight containing, according to the English system, 112 pounds; but in this country, generally, it consists of 100 pounds avoirdupois.

HUNDREDARIUS. In old English law. A hundredary or hundredor. A name given to the chief officer of a hundred, as well as to the freeholders who composed it. Spel. voc. "*Hundredus.*"

HUNDREDARY. The chief or presiding officer of a hundred.

HUNDREDES EARLDOR, or HUNDREDES MAN. The presiding officer in the hundred court. Anc. Inst. Eng.

HUNDREDORS. In English law. The inhabitants or freeholders of a hundred, anciently the suitors or judges of the hundred court. Persons impaneled or fit to be impaneled upon juries, dwelling within the hundred where the cause of action arose. Cromp. Jur. 217. It was formerly necessary to have some of these upon every panel of jurors. 3 Bl. Comm. 359, 360; 4 Steph. Comm. 370.

The term "hundredor" was also used to signify the officer who had the jurisdiction of a hundred, and held the hundred court, and sometimes the bailiff of a hundred. Termes de la Ley; Cowell.

HURDEREFERST. A domestic; one of a family.

HURDLE. In English criminal law. A kind of sledge, on which convicted felons were drawn to the place of execution.

HURST, HYRST, HERST, or HIRST. A wood or grove of trees. Co. Litt. 4*b*.

HURTARDUS, or HURTUS. A ram or wether.

HURTO. In Spanish law. Theft. White, New Recop. b. 2, tit. 20.

HUSBAND. A married man; one who has a lawful wife living. The correlative of "wife."

Etymologically, the word signified the "house bond;" the man who, according to Saxon ideas and institutions, held around him the family, for whom he was in law responsible.

HUSBAND AND WIFE. One of the great domestic relationships; being that of a man and woman lawfully joined in marriage, by which, at common law, the legal existence of a wife is incorporated with that of her husband.

HUSBAND LAND. In old Scotch law. A quantity of land containing commonly six acres. Skene.

HUSBAND OF A SHIP. See SHIP'S HUSBAND.

HUSBANDMAN. A farmer; a cultivator or tiller of the ground. The word "farmer" is colloquially used as synonymous with "husbandman," but originally meant a tenant who cultivates *leased* ground.

HUSBANDRIA. In old English law. Husbandry. Dyer, (Fr. Ed.) 35*b*.

HUSBANDRY. Agriculture; cultivation of the soil for food; farming, in the sense of operating land to raise provisions.

HUSBREC. In Saxon law. The crime of housebreaking or burglary. Crabb, Eng. Law, 59, 308.

HUSCARLE. In old English law. A house servant or domestic; a man of the household. Spelman.

A king's vassal, thane, or baron; an earl's man or vassal. A term of frequent occurrence in Domesday Book.

HUSFASTNE. He who holds house and land. Bract. l. 3, t. 2, c. 10.

HUSGABLUM. In old records. House rent; or a tax or tribute laid upon a house. Cowell; Blount.

HUSH-MONEY. A colloquial expression to designate a bribe to hinder information; pay to secure silence.

HUSTINGS. Council; court; tribunal. Apparently so called from being held within a building, at a time when other courts were held in the open air. It was a local court. The county court in the city of London bore this name. There were hustings at York,

Winchester, Lincoln, and in other places similar to the London hustings. Also the raised place from which candidates for seats in parliament address the constituency, on the occasion of their nomination. Wharton.

In Virginia, some of the local courts are called "hustings," as in the city of Richmond. 6 Grat. 696.

HUTESIUM ET CLAMOR. Hue and cry. See HUE AND CRY.

HUTILAN. Taxes. Mon. Angl. i. 586.

HWATA, HWATUNG. In old English law. Augury; divination.

HYBERNAGIUM. In old English law. The season for sowing winter grain, between Michaelmas and Christmas. The land on which such grain was sown. The grain itself; winter grain or winter corn. Cowell.

HYBRID. A mongrel; an animal formed of the union of different species, or different genera; also (metaphorically) a human being born of the union of persons of different races.

HYD. In old English law. Hide; skin. A measure of land, containing, according to some, a hundred acres, which quantity is also assigned to it in the *Dialogus de Scaccario.* It seems, however, that the hide varied in different parts of the kingdom.

HYDAGE. See HIDAGE.

HYDROMETER. An instrument for measuring the density of fluids. Being immersed in fluids, as in water, brine, beer, brandy, etc., it determines the proportion of their density, or their specific gravity, and thence their quality. See 3 Story, U. S. Laws, 1976.

HYEMS, HIEMS. Lat. In the civil law. Winter. Dig. 43, 20, 4, 34. Written, in some of the old books, "*yems.*" Fleta, lib. 2, c. 73, §§ 16, 18.

HYPOBOLUM. In the civil law. The name of the bequest or legacy given by the husband to his wife, at his death, above her dowry.

HYPOTHEC. In Scotland, the term "hypothec" is used to signify the landlord's right which, independently of any stipulation, he has over the crop and stocking of his tenant. It gives a security to the landlord over the crop of each year for the rent of that year, and over the cattle and stocking on the farm for the current year's rent, which last continues for three months after the last con-

ventional term for the payment of the rent. Bell.

HYPOTHECA. "Hypotheca" was a term of the Roman law, and denoted a pledge or mortgage. As distinguished from the term "*pignus,*" in the same law, it denoted a mortgage, whether of lands or of goods, in which the subject in pledge remained in the possession of the mortgagor or debtor; whereas in the *pignus* the mortgagee or creditor was in the possession. Such an hypotheca might be either express or implied; express, where the parties upon the occasion of a loan entered into express agreement to that effect; or implied, as, *e. g.,* in the case of the stock and utensils of a farmer, which were subject to the landlord's right as a creditor for rent; whence the Scotch law of hypothec.

The word has suggested the term "hypothecate," as used in the mercantile and maritime law of England. Thus, under the factor's act, goods are frequently said to be "hypothecated;" and a captain is said to have a right to hypothecate his vessel for necessary repairs. Brown. See Mackeld. Rom. Law, §§ 334–359.

HYPOTHECARIA ACTIO. In the civil law. An hypothecary action; an action for the enforcement of an *hypotheca,* or right of mortgage; or to obtain the surrender of the thing mortgaged. Inst. 4, 6, 7; Mackeld. Rom. Law, § 356. Adopted in the Civil Code of Louisiana, under the name of "*l'action hypothècarie,*" (translated, "action of mortgage.") Article 3361.

HYPOTHECARII CREDITORES. In the civil law. Hypothecary creditors; those who loaned money on the security of an *hypotheca,* (*q. v.*) Calvin.

HYPOTHECARY ACTION. The name of an action allowed under the civil law for the enforcement of the claims of a creditor by the contract of hypotheca.

HYPOTHECATE. To pledge a thing without delivering the possession of it to the pledgee. "The master, when abroad, and in the absence of the owner, may *hypothecate* the ship, freight, and cargo, to raise money requisite for the completion of the voyage." 3 Kent, Comm. 171.

HYPOTHECATION. A term borrowed from the civil law. In so far as it is naturalized in English and American law, it means a contract of mortgage or pledge in which the subject-matter is not delivered

I

J

K

L

M

into the possession of the pledgee or pawnee; or, conversely, a conventional right existing in one person over specific property of another, which consists in the power to cause a sale of the same, though it be not in his possession, in order that a specific claim of the creditor may be satisfied out of the proceeds.

The term is frequently used in our text-books and reports, particularly upon the law of bottomry and maritime liens; thus a vessel is said to be hypothecated for the demand of one who has advanced money for supplies.

In the common law, there are but few, if any, cases of hypothecation, in the strict sense of the civil law; that is, a pledge without possession by the pledgee. The nearest approaches, perhaps, are cases of bottomry bonds and claims of material-men, and of seamen for wages; but these are liens and privileges, rather than hypothecations. Story, Bailm. § 288.

"Hypothecation" is a term of the civil law, and is that kind of pledge in which the possession of the thing pledged remains with the debtor, (the obligation resting in mere contract without delivery;) and in this respect distinguished from "*pignus*," in which possession is delivered to the creditor or pawnee. 24 Ark. 27. See 2 Bell, Comm. 25.

HYPOTHECATION BOND. A bond given in the contract of bottomry or *respondentia*.

HYPOTHÈQUE. In French law. Hypothecation; a mortgage on real property; the right vested in a creditor by the assignment to him of real estate as security for the payment of his debt, whether or not it be accompanied by possession. See Civil Code La. art. 3360.

It corresponds to the mortgage of real property in English law, and is a real charge, following the property into whosesoever hands it comes. It may be *légale*, as in the case of the charge which the state has over the lands of its accountants, or which a married woman has over those of her husband: *judiciaire*, when it is the result of a judg-

ment of a court of justice; and *conventionelle*, when it is the result of an agreement of the parties. Brown.

HYPOTHESIS. A supposition, assumption, or theory; a theory set up by the prosecution, on a criminal trial, or by the defense, as an explanation of the facts in evidence, and a ground for inferring guilt or innocence, as the case may be, or as indicating a probable or possible motive for the crime.

HYPOTHETICAL CASE. A combination of assumed or proved facts and circumstances, stated in such form as to constitute a coherent and specific situation or state of facts, upon which the opinion of an expert is asked, by way of evidence on a trial.

HYPOTHETICAL YEARLY TENANCY. The basis, in England, of rating lands and hereditaments to the poor-rate, and to other rates and taxes that are expressed to be leviable or assessable in like manner as the poor-rate.

HYRNES. In old English law. A parish.

HYSTEROPOTMOI. Those who, having been thought dead, had, after a long absence in foreign countries, returned safely home; or those who, having been thought dead in battle, had afterwards unexpectedly escaped from their enemies and returned home. These, among the Romans, were not permitted to enter their own houses at the door, but were received at a passage opened in the roof. Enc. Lond.

HYSTEROTOMY. The Cæsarian operation.

HYTHE. In English law. A port, wharf, or small haven to embark or land merchandise at. Cowell; Blount.

I.

I. The initial letter of the word "*Instituta*," used by some civilians in citing the Institutes of Justinian. Tayl. Civil Law, 24.

I—CTUS. An abbreviation for "*jurisconsultus*," one learned in the law; a jurisconsult.

I. E. An abbreviation for "*id est*," that is; that is to say.

I O U. A memorandum of debt, consisting of these letters, ("I owe you,") a sum of money, and the debtor's signature, is termed an "I O U."

IBERNAGIUM. The season for sowing winter corn.

Ibi semper debet fieri triatio ubi juratores meliorem possunt habere notitiam. 7 Coke, 1*b*. A trial should always be had where the jurors can be the best informed.

IBIDEM. Lat. In the same place; in the same book; on the same page, etc. Abbreviated to "*ibid.*" or "*ib.*"

ICENI. The ancient name for the people of Suffolk, Norfolk, Cambridgeshire, and Huntingdonshire, in England.

ICONA. An image, figure, or representation of a thing. Du Cange.

ICTUS. In old English law. A stroke or blow from a club or stone; a bruise, contusion, or swelling produced by a blow from a club or stone, as distinguished from "*plaga*," (a wound.) Fleta, lib. 1, c. 41, § 3.

ICTUS ORBIS. In medical jurisprudence. A maim, a bruise, or swelling; any hurt without cutting the skin.
When the skin is cut, the injury is called a "wound." Bract. lib. 2, tr. 2, cc. 5, 24.

Id certum est quod certum reddi potest. That is certain which can be made certain. 2 Bl. Comm. 143; 1 Bl. Comm. 78; 4 Kent, Comm. 462; Broom, Max. 624.

Id certum est quod certum reddi potest, sed id magis certum est quod de semetipso est certum. That is certain which can be made certain, but that is more certain which is certain of itself. 9 Coke, 47*a*.

ID EST. Lat. That is. Commonly abbreviated "*i. e.*"

Id perfectum est quod ex omnibus suis partibus constat. That is perfect which consists of all its parts. 9 Coke, 9.

Id possumus quod de jure possumus. Lane, 116. We may do only that which by law we are allowed to do.

Id quod est magis remotum, non trahit ad se quod est magis junctum, sed e contrario in omni casu. That which is more remote does not draw to itself that which is nearer, but the contrary in every case. Co. Litt. 164.

Id quod nostrum est sine facto nostro ad alium transferri non potest. That which is ours cannot be transferred to another without our act. Dig. 50, 17, 11.

Id solum nostrum quod debitis deductis nostrum est. That only is ours which remains to us after deduction of debts. Tray. Lat. Max. 227.

IDEM. Lat. The same. According to Lord Coke, "*idem*" has two significations, *sc.*, *idem syllabis seu verbis*, (the same in syllables or words,) and *idem re et sensu*, (the same in substance and in sense.) 10 Coke, 124*a*.

In old practice. The said, or aforesaid; said, aforesaid. Distinguished from "*prædictus*" in old entries, though having the same general signification. Townsh. Pl. 15, 16.

Idem agens et patiens esse non potest. Jenk. Cent. 40. The same person cannot be both agent and patient; *i. e.*, the doer and person to whom the thing is done.

Idem est facere, et non prohibere cum possis; et qui non prohibit, cum prohibere possit, in culpâ est, (aut jubet.) 3 Inst. 158. To commit, and not to prohibit when in your power, is the same thing; and he who does not prohibit when he can prohibit is in fault, or does the same as ordering it to be done.

Idem est nihil dicere, et insufficienter dicere. It is the same thing to say nothing, and to say a thing insufficiently. 2 Inst. 178. To say a thing in an insufficient man-

J

K

L

M

ner is the same as not to say it at all. Applied to the plea of a prisoner. Id.

Idem est non esse, et non apparere. It is the same thing not to be as not to appear. Jenk. Cent. 207. Not to appear is the same thing as not to be. Broom, Max. 165.

Idem est non probari et non esse; non deficit jus, sed probatio. What is not proved and what does not exist are the same; it is not a defect of the law, but of proof.

Idem est scire aut scire debere aut potuisse. To be bound to know or to be able to know is the same as to know.

IDEM PER IDEM. The same for the same. An illustration of a kind that really adds no additional element to the consideration of the question.

Idem semper antecedenti proximo refertur. Co. Litt. 685. "The same" is always referred to its next antecedent.

IDEM SONANS. Sounding the same or alike; having the same sound. A term applied to names which are substantially the same, though slightly varied in the spelling, as "Lawrence" and "Lawrance," and the like. 1 Cromp. & M. 806; 3 Chit. Gen. Pr. 171.

IDENTIFICATION. Proof of identity; the proving that a person, subject, or article before the court is the very same that he or it is alleged, charged, or reputed to be; as where a witness recognizes the prisoner at the bar as the same person whom he saw committing the crime; or where handwriting, stolen goods, counterfeit coin, etc., are recognized as the same which once passed under the observation of the person identifying them.

Identitas vera colligitur ex multitudine signorum. True identity is collected from a multitude of signs. Bac. Max.

IDENTITATE NOMINIS. In English law. An ancient writ (now obsolete) which lay for one taken and arrested in any personal action, and committed to prison, by mistake for another man of the same name. Fitzh. Nat. Brev. 267.

IDENTITY. In the law of evidence. Sameness; the fact that a subject, person, or thing before a court is *the same* as it is represented, claimed, or charged to be. See Burrill, Circ. Ev. 382, 453, 631, 644.

IDEO. Lat. Therefore. Calvin.

IDEO CONSIDERATUM EST. Therefore it is considered. These were the words used at the beginning of the entry of judgment in an action, when the forms were in Latin. They are also used as a name for that portion of the record.

IDES. A division of time among the Romans. In March, May, July, and October, the Ides were on the 15th of the month; in the remaining months, on the 13th. This method of reckoning is still retained in the chancery of Rome, and in the calendar of the breviary. Wharton.

IDIOCHIRA. Græco-Lat. In the civil law. An instrument privately executed, as distinguished from such as were executed before a public officer. Cod. 8, 18, 11; Calvin.

IDIOCY. In medical jurisprudence. That condition of mind in which the reflective, and all or a part of the affective, powers are either entirely wanting, or are manifested to the slightest possible extent. Ray, Insan. § 58; Whart. & S. Med. Jur. § 222.

There is a distinction between "idiocy" and "*dementia;*" the first being due to the fact that there are original structural defects in the brain; the second resulting from the supervention of organic changes in a brain originally of normal power. Ham. Nervous System, 338.

Idiocy is that condition in which the human creature has never had, from birth, any, the least, glimmering of reason; and is utterly destitute of all those intellectual faculties by which man, in general, is so eminently and peculiarly distinguished. It is not the condition of a deranged mind, but that of a total absence of all mind. Hence this state of fatuity can rarely ever be mistaken by any, the most superficial, observer. The medical profession seem to regard it as a natural defect, not as a disease in itself, or as the result of any disorder. In law, it is also considered as a defect; and as a permanent and hopeless incapacity. 1 Bland. Ch. 386.

IDIOT. A person who has been without understanding from his nativity, and whom the law, therefore, presumes never likely to attain any. Shelf. Lun. 2. See IDIOCY.

IDIOTA. In the civil law. An unlearned, illiterate, or simple person. Calvin. A private man; one not in office.

In common law. An idiot or fool.

IDIOTA INQUIRENDO, WRIT DE. This is the name of an old writ which directs the sheriff to inquire whether a man be an idiot or not. The inquisition is to be made by a jury of twelve men. Fitzh. Nat. Brev.

232. And, if the man were found an idiot, the profits of his lands and the custody of his person might be granted by the king to any subject who had interest enough to obtain them. 1 Bl. Comm. 303.

IDONEUM SE FACERE; IDONEARE SE. To purge one's self by oath of a crime of which one is accused.

IDONEUS. Lat. In the civil and common law. Sufficient; competent; fit or proper; responsible; unimpeachable. *Idoneus homo,* a responsible or solvent person; a good and lawful man. Sufficient; adequate; satisfactory. *Idonea cautio,* sufficient security.

IDONIETAS. In old English law. Ability or fitness, (of a parson.) Artic. Cleri, c. 13.

IF. In deeds and wills, this word, as a rule, implies a condition precedent, unless it be controlled by other words. 2 Crabb, Real Prop. p. 809, § 2152; 77 N. C. 431.

IFUNGIA. The finest white bread, formerly called "cocked bread." Blount.

IGLISE. L. Fr. A church. Kelham. Another form of *"eglise."*

IGNIS JUDICIUM. The old judicial trial by fire. Blount.

IGNITEGIUM. In old English law. The curfew, or evening bell. Cowell. See CURFEW.

IGNOMINY. Public disgrace; infamy; reproach; dishonor. Ignominy is the opposite of esteem. Wolff, § 145. See 38 Iowa, 220.

IGNORAMUS. Lat. "We are ignorant;" "We ignore it." Formerly the grand jury used to write this word on bills of indictment when, after having heard the evidence, they thought the accusation against the prisoner was groundless, intimating that, though the facts might possibly be true, the truth did not appear to them; but now they usually write in English the words "Not a true bill," or "Not found," if that is their verdict; but they are still said to *ignore* the bill. Brown.

IGNORANCE. The want or absence of knowledge.

Ignorance *of law* is want of knowledge or acquaintance with the laws of the land in so far as they apply to the act, relation, duty, or matter under consideration. Ignorance *of fact* is want of knowledge of some fact or facts constituting or relating to the subject-matter in hand.

Ignorance is not a state of the mind in the sense in which sanity and insanity are. When the mind is ignorant of a fact, its condition still remains sound; the power of thinking, of judging, of willing, is just as complete before communication of the fact as after; the essence or texture, so to speak, of the mind, is not, as in the case of insanity, affected or impaired. Ignorance of a particular fact consists in this: that the mind, although sound and capable of healthy action, has never acted upon the fact in question, because the subject has never been brought to the notice of the perceptive faculties. 28 N. J. Law, 274.

"Ignorance" and "error" are not convertible terms. The former is a lack of information or absence of knowledge; the latter, a misapprehension or confusion of information, or a mistaken supposition of the possession of knowledge. Error as to a fact may imply ignorance of the truth; but ignorance does not necessarily imply error.

Essential ignorance is ignorance in relation to some essential circumstance so intimately connected with the matter in question, and which so influences the parties, that it induces them to act in the business. Poth. Vente, nn. 3, 4; 2 Kent, Comm. 367.

Non-essential or accidental ignorance is that which has not of itself any necessary connection with the business in question, and which is not the true consideration for entering into the contract.

Involuntary ignorance is that which does not proceed from choice, and which cannot be overcome by the use of any means of knowledge known to a person and within his power; as the ignorance of a law which has not yet been promulgated.

Voluntary ignorance exists when a party might, by taking reasonable pains, have acquired the necessary knowledge. For example, every man might acquire a knowledge of the laws which have been promulgated. Doct. & Stud. 1, 46; Plowd. 343.

IGNORANTIA. Ignorance; want of knowledge. Distinguished from mistake, (error,) or wrong conception. Mackeld. Rom. Law, § 178; Dig. 22, 6. Divided by Lord Coke into *ignorantia facti* (ignorance of fact) and *ignorantia juris,* (ignorance of law.) And the former, he adds, is twofold,—*lectionis et linguæ,* (ignorance of reading and ignorance of language.) 2 Coke, 3b.

Ignorantia eorum quæ quis scire tenetur non excusat. Ignorance of those things which one is bound to know excuses not. Hale, P. C. 42; Broom, Max. 267.

Ignorantia facti excusat. Ignorance of fact excuses or is a ground of relief. 2 Coke, 3b. Acts done and contracts made under mistake or ignorance of a material fact

J

K

L

M

are voidable and relievable in law and equity. 2 Kent, Comm. 491, and notes.

Ignorantia facti excusat, ignorantia juris non excusat. Ignorance of the fact excuses; ignorance of the law excuses not. Every man must be taken to be cognizant of the law; otherwise there is no saying to what extent the excuse of ignorance may not be carried. 1 Coke, 177; Broom, Max. 253.

Ignorantia juris quod quisque tenetur scire, neminem excusat. Ignorance of the [or a] law, which every one is bound to know, excuses no man. A mistake in point of law is, in criminal cases, no sort of defense. 4 Bl. Comm. 27; 4 Steph. Comm. 81; Broom, Max. 253; 7 Car. & P. 456. And, in civil cases, ignorance of the law, with a full knowledge of the facts, furnishes no ground, either in law or equity, to rescind agreements, or reclaim money paid, or set aside solemn acts of the parties. 2 Kent, Comm. 491, and note.

Ignorantia juris sui non præjudicat juri. Ignorance of one's right does not prejudice the right. Lofft, 552.

Ignorantia legis neminem excusat. Ignorance of law excuses no one. 4 Bouv. Inst. no. 3828; 1 Story, Eq. Jur. § 111; 7 Watts, 374.

IGNORATIO ELENCHI. Lat. In logic. An overlooking of the adversary's counter-position in an argument.

Ignoratis terminis artis, ignoratur et ars. Where the terms of an art are unknown, the art itself is unknown also. Co. Litt. 2a.

IGNORE. 1. To be ignorant of, or unacquainted with.
2. To disregard willfully; to refuse to recognize; to decline to take notice of.
3. To reject as groundless, false, or unsupported by evidence; as when a grand jury *ignores* a bill of indictment.

Ignoscitur ei qui sanguinem suum qualiter redemptum voluit. The law holds him excused from obligation who chose to redeem his blood (or life) upon any terms. Whatever a man may do under the fear of losing his life or limbs will not be held binding upon him in law. 1 Bl. Comm. 131.

IKENILD STREET. One of the four great Roman roads in Britain; supposed to be so called from the *Iceni.*

ILET. A little island.

ILL. In old pleading. Bad; defective in law; null; naught; the opposite of good or valid.

ILL FAME. Evil repute; notorious bad character. Houses of prostitution, gaming houses, and other such disorderly places are called "houses of ill fame," and a person who frequents them is a person of ill fame.

ILLATA ET INVECTA. Things brought into the house for use by the tenant were so called, and were liable to the *jus hypothecæ* of Roman law, just as they are to the landlord's right of distress at common law.

ILLEGAL. Not authorized by law; illicit; unlawful; contrary to law.

Sometimes this term means merely that which lacks authority of or support from law; but more frequently it imports a violation. Etymologically, the word seems to convey the negative meaning only. But in ordinary use it has a severer, stronger signification; the idea of censure or condemnation for breaking law is usually presented. But the law implied in illegal is not necessarily an express statute. Things are called "illegal" for a violation of common-law principles. And the term does not imply that the act spoken of is immoral or wicked; it implies only a breach of the law. 1 Abb. Pr. (N. S.) 432; 48 N. H. 196; Id. 211; 3 Sneed, 64.

ILLEGAL CONDITIONS. All those that are impossible, or contrary to law, immoral, or repugnant to the nature of the transaction.

ILLEGAL CONTRACT. An agreement to do any act forbidden by the law, or to omit to do any act enjoined by the law.

ILLEGAL TRADE. Such traffic or commerce as is carried on in violation of the municipal law, or contrary to the law of nations. See ILLICIT TRADE.

ILLEGITIMACY. The condition before the law, or the social *status*, of a bastard; the state or condition of one whose parents were not intermarried at the time of his birth.

ILLEGITIMATE. That which is contrary to law; it is usually applied to bastards, or children born out of lawful wedlock.

The Louisiana Code divided illegitimate children into two classes: (1) Those born from two persons who, at the moment when such children were conceived, could have lawfully intermarried; and (2) those who are born from persons to whose marriage there existed at the time some legal impediment. Both classes, however, could be acknowledged and take by devise. 12 Rob. (La.) 56.

ILLEVIABLE. Not leviable; that cannot or ought not to be levied. Cowell.

ILLICENCIATUS. In old English law. Without license. Fleta, lib. 3, c. 5, § 12.

ILLICIT. Not permitted or allowed; prohibited; unlawful; as an *illicit* trade; *illicit* intercourse.

ILLICIT TRADE. Policies of marine insurance usually contain a covenant of warranty against "illicit trade," meaning thereby trade which is forbidden, or declared unlawful, by the laws of the country where the cargo is to be delivered.

"It is not the same with 'contraband trade,' although the words are sometimes used as synonymous. Illicit or prohibited trade is one which cannot be carried on without a distinct violation of some positive law of the country where the transaction is to take place." 1 Pars. Mar. Ins. 614.

ILLICITE. Unlawfully. This word has a technical meaning, and is requisite in an indictment where the act charged is unlawful; as in the case of a riot. 2 Hawk. P. C. c. 25, § 96.

ILLICITUM COLLEGIUM. An illegal corporation.

ILLITERATE. Unlettered; ignorant; unlearned. Generally used of one who cannot read and write.

ILLOCABLE. Incapable of being placed out or hired.

ILLUD. Lat. That.

Illud, quod alias licitum non est, necessitas facit licitum; et necessitas inducit privilegium quoad jura privata. Bac. Max. That which is otherwise not permitted, necessity permits; and necessity makes a privilege as to private rights.

Illud, quod alteri unitur, extinguitur, neque amplius per se vacare licet. Godol. Ecc. Law, 169. That which is united to another is extinguished, nor can it be any more independent.

ILLUSION. In medical jurisprudence. An image or impression in the mind, excited by some external object addressing itself to the senses, but which, instead of corresponding with the reality, is perverted, distorted, or wholly mistaken.

ILLUSORY. Deceiving by false appearances; nominal, as distinguished from substantial.

ILLUSORY APPOINTMENT. Formerly the appointment of a merely nominal share of the property to one of the objects of a power, in order to escape the rule that an exclusive appointment could not be made unless it was authorized by the instrument creating the power, was considered illusory and void in equity. But this rule has been abolished in England. (1 Wm. IV. c. 46; 37 & 38 Vict. c. 37.) Sweet.

ILLUSORY APPOINTMENT ACT. The statute 1 Wm. IV. c. 46. This statute enacts that no appointment made after its passing, (July 16, 1830,) in exercise of a power to appoint property, real or personal, among several objects, shall be invalid, or impeached in equity, on the ground that an unsubstantial, illusory, or nominal share only was thereby appointed, or left unappointed, to devolve upon any one or more of the objects of such power; but that the appointment shall be valid in equity, as at law. See, too, 37 & 38 Vict. c. 37. Wharton.

ILLUSTRIOUS. The prefix to the title of a prince of the blood in England.

IMAGINE. In English law. In cases of treason the law makes it a crime to imagine the death of the king. But, in order to complete the crime, this act of the mind must be demonstrated by some overt act. The terms "imagining" and "compassing" are in this connection synonymous. 4 Bl. Comm. 78.

IMAN, IMAM, or IMAUM. A Mohammedan prince having supreme spiritual as well as temporal power; a regular priest of the mosque.

IMBARGO. An old form of "embargo," (*q. v.*) St. 18 Car. II. c. 5.

IMBASING OF MONEY. The act of mixing the species with an alloy below the standard of sterling. 1 Hale, P. C. 102.

IMBECILITY. Weakness, or feebleness of intellect, either congenital, or resulting from an obstacle to the development of the faculties, supervening in infancy. See Whart. & S. Med. Jur. §§ 229-233.

IMBEZZLE. See EMBEZZLE.

IMBLADARE. In old English law. To plant or sow grain. Bract. fol. 176b.

IMBRACERY. See EMBRACERY.

IMBROCUS. A brook, gutter, or waterpassage. Cowell.

J

K

L

M

IMMATERIAL. Not material, essential, or necessary; not important or pertinent; not decisive.

IMMATERIAL AVERMENT. An averment alleging with needless particularity or unnecessary circumstances what is material and necessary, and which might properly have been stated more generally, and without such circumstances and particulars; or, in other words, a statement of unnecessary particulars in connection with and as descriptive of what is material. Gould, Pl. c. 3, § 188; 3 Ala. 237, 245.

IMMATERIAL ISSUE. In pleading. An issue taken on an immaterial point; that is, a point not proper to decide the action. Steph. Pl. 99, 130; 2 Tidd, Pr. 921.

IMMEDIATE. 1. Present; at once; without delay; not deferred by any interval of time. In this sense, the word, without any very precise signification, denotes that action is or must be taken either instantly or without any considerable loss of time.

Immediately does not, in legal proceedings, necessarily import the exclusion of any interval of time. It is a word of no very definite signification, and is much in subjection to its grammatical connections. 31 N. J. Law, 313.

2. Not separated in respect to place; not separated by the intervention of any intermediate object, cause, relation, or right. Thus we speak of an action as prosecuted for the "immediate benefit" of A., of a devise as made to the "immediate issue" of B., etc.

IMMEDIATE DESCENT. "A descent may be said to be mediate or immediate in regard to the mediate or immediate descent of the estate or right: or it may be said to be mediate or immediate in regard to the mediateness or immediateness of the pedigree or degrees of consanguinity." Story, J., 6 Pet. 112.

IMMEDIATELY. "It is impossible to lay down any hard and fast rule as to what is the meaning of the word 'immediately' in all cases. The words 'forthwith' and 'immediately' have the same meaning. They are stronger than the expression 'within a reasonable time,' and imply prompt, vigorous action, without any delay, and whether there has been such action is a question of fact, having regard to the circumstances of the particular case." Cockburn, C. J., 4 Q. B. Div. 471.

IMMEMORIAL. Beyond human memory; time out of mind.

IMMEMORIAL POSSESSION. In Louisiana. Possession of which no man living has seen the beginning, and the existence of which he has learned from his elders. Civil Code La. art. 762; 2 Mart. (La.) 214.

IMMEMORIAL USAGE. A practice which has existed time out of mind; custom; prescription.

IMMEUBLES. These are, in French law, the immovables of English law. Things are *immeubles* from any one of three causes: (1) From their own nature, *e. g.*, lands and houses; (2) from their destination, *e. g.*, animals and instruments of agriculture when supplied by the landlord; or (3) by the object to which they are annexed, *e. g.*, easements. Brown.

IMMIGRATION. The coming into a country of foreigners for purposes of permanent residence. The correlative term "emigration" denotes the act of such persons in leaving their former country.

IMMISCERE. Lat. In the civil law. To mix or mingle with; to meddle with; to join with. Calvin.

IMMITTERE. In the civil law. To put or let into, as a beam into a wall. Calvin.; Dig. 50, 17, 242, 1.

In old English law. To put cattle on a common. Fleta, lib. 4, c. 20, § 7.

Immobilia situm sequuntur. Immovable things follow their site or position; are governed by the law of the place where they are fixed. 2 Kent, Comm. 67.

IMMOBILIS. Immovable. *Immobilia,* or *res immobiles,* immovable things, such as lands and buildings. Mackeld. Rom. Law, § 160.

IMMORAL. Contrary to good morals; inconsistent with the rules and principles of morality which regard men as living in a community, and which are necessary for the public welfare, order, and decency.

IMMORAL CONSIDERATION. One contrary to good morals, and therefore invalid. Contracts based upon an immoral consideration are generally void.

IMMORAL CONTRACTS. Contracts founded upon considerations *contra bonos mores* are void.

IMMORALITY. That which is *cont,a bonos mores.* See IMMORAL.

IMMOVABLES. In the civil law. Property which, from its nature, destination, or the object to which it is applied, cannot move itself, or be removed.

Immovable things are, in general, such as cannot either move themselves or be removed from one place to another. But this definition, strictly speaking, is applicable only to such things as are immovable by their own nature, and not to such as are so only by the disposition of the law. Civil Code La. art. 462.

IMMUNITY. An exemption from serving in an office, or performing duties which the law generally requires other citizens to perform.

IMPAIR. To weaken, diminish, or relax, or otherwise affect in an injurious manner.

"IMPAIRING THE OBLIGATION OF CONTRACTS." For the meaning of this phrase in the constitution of the United States, see 2 Story, Const. §§ 1374–1399; 1 Kent, Comm. 413–422; Pom. Const. Law; Black, Const. Prohib. pt. 1.

IMPANEL. In English practice. To impanel a jury signifies the entering by the sheriff upon a piece of parchment, termed a "panel," the names of the jurors who have been summoned to appear in court on a certain day to form a jury of the country to hear such matters as may be brought before them. Brown.

In American practice. Besides the meaning above given, "impanel" signifies the act of the clerk of the court in making up a list of the jurors who have been selected for the trial of a particular cause.

Impaneling has nothing to do with drawing, selecting, or swearing jurors, but means simply making the list of those who have been selected. 7 How. Pr. 441.

IMPARCARE. In old English law. To impound. Reg. Orig. 92b.

To shut up, or confine in prison. *Inducti sunt in carcerem et imparcati*, they were carried to prison and shut up. Bract. fol. 124.

IMPARGAMENTUM. The right of impounding cattle.

IMPARL. To have license to settle a litigation amicably; to obtain delay for adjustment.

IMPARLANCE. In early practice, imparlance meant time given to either of the parties to an action to answer the pleading of the other. It thus amounted to a continuance of the action to a further day. Literally the term signified leave given to the parties to *talk together; i. e.*, with a view to settling their differences amicably. But in modern practice it denotes a time given to the defendant to plead.

A general imparlance is the entry of a general prayer and allowance of time to plead till the next term, without reserving to the defendant the benefit of any exception; so that after such an imparlance the defendant cannot object to the jurisdiction of the court, or plead any matter in abatement. This kind of imparlance is always from one term to another.

A general special imparlance contains a saving of all exceptions whatsoever, so that the defendant after this may plead not only in abatement, but he may also plead a plea which affects the jurisdiction of the court, as privilege. He cannot, however, plead a tender, and that he was always ready to pay, because by craving time he admits that he is not ready, and so falsifies his plea.

A special imparlance reserves to the defendant all exceptions to the writ, bill, or count; and therefore after it the defendant may plead in abatement, though not to the jurisdiction of the court. 1 Tidd, Pr. 462, 463.

IMPARSONEE. L. Fr. In ecclesiastical law. One who is inducted and in possession of a benefice. Parson imparsonee, (*persona impersonata*.) Cowell; Dyer, 40.

IMPATRONIZATION. The act of putting into full possession of a benefice.

IMPEACH. To accuse; to charge a liability upon; to sue.

To proceed against a public officer for crime or misfeasance, before a proper court, by the presentation of a written accusation called "articles of impeachment."

In the law of evidence. To call in question the veracity of a witness, by means of evidence adduced for that purpose.

IMPEACHMENT. A criminal proceeding against a public officer, before a *quasi* political court, instituted by a written accusation called "articles of impeachment;" for example, a written accusation by the house of representatives of the United States to the senate of the United States against an officer.

In England, a prosecution by the house of commons before the house of lords of a commoner for treason, or other high crimes and misdemeanors, or of a peer for any crime.

In evidence. An allegation, supported by proof, that a witness who has been examined is unworthy of credit.

IMPEACHMENT OF WASTE. Liability for waste committed; or a demand or

J

K

L

M

suit for compensation for waste committed upon lands or tenements by a tenant thereof who, having only a leasehold or particular estate, had no right to commit waste. See 2 Bl. Comm. 283.

IMPEACHMENT OF WITNESS. Proof that a witness who has testified in a cause is unworthy of credit.

IMPECHIARE. To impeach, to accuse, or prosecute for felony or treason.

IMPEDIENS. In old practice. One who hinders; an impedient. The defendant or deforciant in a fine was sometimes so called. Cowell; Blount.

IMPEDIMENTO. In Spanish law. A prohibition to contract marriage, established by law between certain persons.

IMPEDIMENTS. Disabilities, or hindrances to the making of contracts, such as coverture, infancy, want of reason, etc.

In the civil law. Bars to marriage. *Absolute impediments* are those which prevent the person subject to them from marrying at all, without either the nullity of marriage or its being punishable. *Dirimant impediments* are those which render a marriage void; as where one of the contracting parties is unable to marry by reason of a prior undissolved marriage. *Prohibitive impediments* are those which do not render the marriage null, but subject the parties to a punishment. *Relative impediments* are those which regard only certain persons with respect to each other; as between two particular persons who are related within the prohibited degrees. Bowyer, Mod. Civil Law, 44, 45.

IMPEDITOR. In old English law. A disturber in the action of *quare impedit.* St. Marlb. c. 12.

IMPENSÆ. Lat. In the civil law. Expenses; outlays. Mackeld. Rom. Law, § 168; Calvin. Divided into necessary, (*necessariæ,*) useful, (*utiles,*) and tasteful or ornamental, (*voluptuariæ.*) Dig. 50, 16, 79. See Id. 25, 1.

IMPERATIVE. See DIRECTORY.

IMPERATOR. Emperor. The title of the Roman emperors, and also of the kings of England before the Norman conquest. Cod. 1, 14, 12; 1 Bl. Comm. 242. See EMPEROR.

IMPERFECT OBLIGATIONS. Moral duties, such as charity, gratitude, etc., which cannot be enforced by law.

IMPERFECT RIGHTS. See RIGHTS.

IMPERFECT TRUST. An executory trust, (which see;) and see EXECUTED TRUST.

Imperii majestas est tutelæ salus. Co. Litt. 64. The majesty of the empire is the safety of its protection.

IMPERITIA. Unskillfulness; want of skill.

Imperitia culpæ adnumeratur. Want of skill is reckoned as *culpa;* that is, as blamable conduct or neglect. Dig. 50, 17, 132.

Imperitia est maxima mechanicorum pœna. Unskillfulness is the greatest punishment of mechanics; [that is, from its effect in making them liable to those by whom they are employed.] 11 Coke, 54a. The word *"pœna"* in some translations is erroneously rendered "fault."

IMPERIUM. The right to command, which includes the right to employ the force of the state to enforce the laws. This is one of the principal attributes of the power of the executive. 1 Toullier, no. 58.

IMPERSONALITAS. Impersonality. A mode of expression where no reference is made to any person, such as the expression *"ut dicitur,"* (as is said.) Co. Litt. 352b.

Impersonalitas non concludit nec ligat. Co. Litt. 352b. Impersonality neither concludes nor binds.

IMPERTINENCE. Irrelevancy; the fault of not properly pertaining to the issue or proceeding. The introduction of any matters into a bill, answer, or other pleading or proceeding in a suit, which are not properly before the court for decision, at any particular stage of the suit. Story, Eq. Pl. § 266.

In practice. A question propounded to a witness, or evidence offered or sought to be elicited, is called "impertinent" when it has no logical bearing upon the issue, is not necessarily connected with it, or does not belong to the matter in hand. On the distinction between pertinency and relevancy, we may quote the following remark of Dr. Wharton: "*Relevancy* is that which conduces to the proof of a *pertinent* hypothesis; a pertinent hypothesis being one which, if sustained, would logically influence the issue." 1 Whart. Ev. § 20.

IMPERTINENT. In equity pleading. That which does not belong to a pleading, interrogatory, or other proceeding; out of place; superfluous; irrelevant.

At law. A term applied to matter not necessary to constitute the cause of action or ground of defense. Cowp. 683; 5 East, 275; 2 Mass. 283. It constitutes surplusage, (which see.)

IMPESCARE. In old records. To impeach or accuse. *Impescatus*, impeached. Blount.

IMPETITIO VASTI. Impeachment of waste, (*q. v.*)

IMPETRARE. In old English practice. To obtain by request, as a writ or privilege. Bract. fols. 57, 172b. This application of the word seems to be derived from the civil law. Calvin.

IMPETRATION. In old English law. The obtaining anything by petition or entreaty. Particularly, the obtaining of a benefice from Rome by solicitation, which benefice belonged to the disposal of the king or other lay patron. Webster; Cowell.

IMPIER. Umpire, (*q. v.*)

IMPIERMENT. Impairing or prejudicing. Jacob.

IMPIGNORATA. Pledged; given in pledge, (*pignori data;*) mortgaged. A term applied in Bracton to land. Bract. fol. 20.

IMPIGNORATION. The act of pawning or putting to pledge.

Impius et crudelis judicandus est qui libertati non favet. He is to be judged impious and cruel who does not favor liberty. Co. Litt. 124.

IMPLACITARE. Lat. To implead; to sue.

IMPLEAD. In practice. To sue or prosecute by due course of law. 9 Watts, 47.

IMPLEADED. Sued or prosecuted; used particularly in the titles of causes where there are several defendants; as "A. B., impleaded with C. D."

IMPLEMENTS. Such things as are used or *employed* for a trade, or furniture of a house. 11 Metc. (Mass.) 82.

Whatever may supply wants; particularly applied to tools, utensils, vessels, instruments of labor; as, the *implements* of trade or of husbandry. 23 Iowa, 359; 6 Gray, 298.

IMPLICATA. A term used in mercantile law, derived from the Italian. In order to avoid the risk of making fruitless voyages, merchants have been in the habit of receiving small adventures, on freight, at so much per cent., to which they are entitled at all events, even if the adventure be lost; and this is called "*implicata.*" Wharton.

IMPLICATION. Intendment or inference, as distinguished from the actual expression of a thing in words. In a will, an estate may pass by mere *implication*, without any express words to direct its course. 2 Bl. Comm. 381.

An inference of something not directly declared, but arising from what is admitted or expressed.

In construing a will conjecture must not be taken for implication; but necessary implication means, not natural necessity, but so strong a probability of intention that an intention contrary to that which is imputed to the testator cannot be supposed. 1 Ves. & B. 466.

"Implication" is also used in the sense of "inference;" *i. e.*, where the existence of an intention is inferred from acts not done for the sole purpose of communicating it, but for some other purpose. Sweet.

IMPLIED. This word is used in law as contrasted with "express;" *i. e.*, where the intention in regard to the subject-matter is not manifested by explicit and direct words, but is gathered by implication or necessary deduction from the circumstances, the general language, or the conduct of the parties.

IMPLIED ABROGATION. A statute is said to work an "implied abrogation" of an earlier one, when the later statute contains provisions which are inconsistent with the further continuance of the earlier law; or a statute is impliedly abrogated when the reason of it, or the object for which it was passed, no longer exists.

IMPLIED ASSUMPSIT. An undertaking or promise not formally made, but presumed or implied from the conduct of a party. See ASSUMPSIT.

IMPLIED CONDITION. See CONDITION IMPLIED.

IMPLIED CONSIDERATION. A consideration implied or presumed by law, as distinguished from an *express* consideration, (*q. v.*)

IMPLIED CONTRACT. One not created or evidenced by the explicit agreement of the parties, but inferred by the law, as a matter of reason and justice, from their acts or conduct. For example, if A. hires B. to do any business or perform any work for him, the law implies a contract or undertaking on A.'s part to pay B. as much as his labor or service deserves. 2 Bl. Comm. 443.

IMPLIED COVENANT. One which is not set forth explicitly, but is raised by implication of law from the use of certain terms ("grant," "give," "demise," etc.) in the conveyance, contract, or lease. See COVENANT.

IMPLIED MALICE. Malice inferred by legal reasoning and necessary deduction from the *res gestæ* or the conduct of the party. Malice inferred from any deliberate cruel act committed by one person against another, however sudden. Whart. Hom. 38. What is called "general malice" is often thus inferred.

IMPLIED TRUST. A trust raised or created by implication of law; a trust implied or presumed from circumstances.

IMPLIED USE. See RESULTING USE.

IMPLIED WARRANTY. A warranty raised· by the law as an inference from the acts of the parties or the circumstances of the transaction. Thus, if the seller of a chattel have possession of it and sell it as his own, and not as agent for another, and for a fair price, he is understood to *warrant the title.* 2 Kent, Comm. 478.

A warranty implied from the general tenor of an instrument, or from particular words used in it, although no express warranty is mentioned. Thus, in every policy of insurance there is an *implied* warranty that the ship is seaworthy when the policy attaches. 3 Kent, Comm. 287; 1 Phil. Ins. 308.

IMPORTATION. The act of bringing goods and merchandise into a country from a foreign country.

IMPORTS. Importations; goods or other property imported or brought into the country from a foreign country.

IMPORTUNITY. Pressing solicitation; urgent request; application for a claim or favor which is urged with troublesome frequency or pertinacity. Webster.

IMPOSITION. An impost; tax; contribution.

IMPOSSIBILITY. That which, in the constitution and course of nature or the law, no man can do or perform.

Impossibility is of the following several sorts:

An act is *physically* impossible when it is contrary to the course of nature. Such an impossibility may be either *absolute,* i. e., impossible in any case, (e. g., for A. to reach the moon,) or *relative,* (sometimes called "impossibility in fact,") i. e., arising from the circumstances of the case, (e. g., for A. to make a payment to B., he being a deceased person.) To the latter class belongs what is sometimes called "*practical* impossibility," which exists when the act *can* be done, but only at an excessive or unreasonable cost. An act is *legally* or juridically impossible when a rule of law makes it impossible to do it; e. g., for A. to make a valid will before his majority. This class of acts must not be confounded with those which are possible, although forbidden by law, as to commit a theft. An act is *logically* impossible when it is contrary to the nature of the transaction, as where A. gives property to B. expressly for his own benefit, on condition that he transfers it to C. Sweet.

Impossibilium nulla obligatio est. There is no obligation to do impossible things. Dig. 50, 17, 185; Broom, Max. 249.

IMPOSSIBLE CONTRACTS. An impossible contract is one which the law will not hold binding upon the parties, because of the natural or legal impossibility of the performance by one party of that which is the consideration for the promise of the other. 7 Wait, Act. & Def. 124.

Impossible contracts, which will be deemed void in the eye of the law, or of which the performance will be excused, are such contracts as cannot be performed, either because of the nature of the obligation undertaken, or because of some supervening event which renders the performance of the obligation either physically or legally impossible. 10 Amer. & Eng. Enc. Law, 176.

IMPOSTS. Taxes, duties, or impositions. A duty on imported goods or merchandise. Story, Const. § 949.

Impost is a tax received by the prince for such merchandises as are brought into any haven within his dominions from foreign nations. It may in some sort be distinguished from customs, because customs are rather that profit the prince maketh of wares shipped out; yet they are frequently confounded. Cowell.

IMPOTENCE. In medical jurisprudence. The incapacity for copulation or propagating the species. Properly used of the male; but it has also been used synonymously with "sterility."

Impotentia excusat legem. Co. Litt. 29. The impossibility of doing what is required by the law excuses from the perform-ance.

IMPOTENTIAM, PROPERTY PROPTER. A qualified property, which may subsist in animals *feræ naturæ* on account of their inability, as where hawks, herons, or other birds build in a person's trees, or conies, etc., make their nests or burrows in a person's land, and have young there, such person has a qualified property in them till they can fly or run away, and then such property expires. 2 Steph. Comm. (7th Ed.) 8.

IMPOUND. To shut up stray animals or distrained goods in a pound.

To take into the custody of the law or of a court. Thus, a court will sometimes *impound* a suspicious document produced at a trial.

IMPRESCRIPTIBILITY. The state or quality of being incapable of prescription; not of such a character that a right to it can be gained by prescription.

IMPRESCRIPTIBLE RIGHTS. Such rights as a person may use or not, at pleasure, since they cannot be lost to him by the claims of another founded on prescription.

IMPRESSION. A "case of the first impression" is one without a precedent; one presenting a wholly new state of facts; one involving a question never before determined.

IMPRESSMENT. A power possessed by the English crown of taking persons or property to aid in the defense of the country, with or without the consent of the persons concerned. It is usually exercised to obtain hands for the queen's ships in time of war, by taking seamen engaged in merchant vessels, (1 Bl. Comm. 420; Maud & P. Shipp. 123;) but in former times impressment of merchant ships was also practiced. The admiralty issues protections against impressment in certain cases, either under statutes passed in favor of certain callings (*e. g.*, persons employed in the Greenland fisheries) or voluntarily. Sweet.

IMPREST MONEY. Money paid on enlisting or impressing soldiers or sailors.

IMPRETIABILIS. Lat. Beyond price; invaluable.

IMPRIMATUR. Lat. Let it be printed. A license or allowance, granted by the con-stituted authorities, giving permission to print and publish a book. This allowance was formerly necessary, in England, before any book could lawfully be printed, and in some other countries is still required.

IMPRIMERE. To press upon; to impress or press; to imprint or print.

IMPRIMERY. In some of the ancient English statutes this word is used to signify a printing-office, the art of printing, a print or impression.

IMPRIMIS. Lat. In the first place; first of all.

IMPRISON. To put in a prison; to put in a place of confinement.

To confine a person, or restrain his liberty, in any way.

IMPRISONMENT. The act of putting or confining a man in prison; the restraint of a man's personal liberty; coercion exercised upon a person to prevent the free exercise of his powers of locomotion.

It is not a necessary part of the definition that the confinement should be in a place usually appropriated to that purpose; it may be in a locality used only for the specific occasion; or it may take place without the actual application of any physical agencies of restraint, (such as locks or bars,) but by verbal compulsion and the display of available force. See 9 N. H. 491.

Any forcible detention of a man's person, or control over his movements, is imprisonment. 3 Har. (Del.) 416.

IMPRISTI. Adherents; followers. Those who side with or take the part of another, either in his defense or otherwise.

IMPROBATION. In Scotch law. An action brought for the purpose of having some instrument declared false and forged. 1 Forb. Inst. pt. 4, p. 161. The verb "improve" (*q. v.*) was used in the same sense.

IMPROPER. Not suitable; unfit; not suited to the character, time, and place. 48 N. H. 199. Wrongful. 53 Law J. P. D. 65.

IMPROPER FEUDS. These were derivative feuds; as, for instance, those that were originally bartered and sold to the feudatory for a price, or were held upon base or less honorable services, or upon a rent in lieu of military service, or were themselves alienable, without mutual license, or descended indifferently to males or females. Wharton.

IMPROPER NAVIGATION. Anything improperly done with the ship or part

J

K

L

M

of the ship in the course of the voyage. L. R. 6 C. P. 563. See, also, 53 Law J. P. D. 65.

IMPROPRIATE RECTOR. In ecclesiastical law. Commonly signifies a lay rector as opposed to a spiritual rector; just as impropriate tithes are tithes in the hands of a lay owner, as opposed to appropriate tithes, which are tithes in the hands of a spiritual owner. Brown.

IMPROPRIATION. In ecclesiastical law. The annexing an ecclesiastical benefice to the use of a lay person, whether individual or corporate, in the same way as *appropriation* is the annexing of any such benefice to the proper and perpetual use of some spiritual corporation, whether sole or aggregate, to enjoy forever. Brown.

IMPROVE. In Scotch law. To disprove; to invalidate or impeach; to prove false or forged. 1 Forb. Inst. pt. 4, p. 162.

To improve a lease means to grant a lease of unusual duration to encourage a tenant, when the soil is exhausted, etc. Bell; Stair, Inst. p. 676, § 23.

IMPROVED. Improved land is such as has been reclaimed, is used for the purpose of husbandry, and is cultivated as such, whether the appropriation is for tillage, meadow, or pasture. "Improve" is synonymous with "cultivate." 4 Cow. 190.

IMPROVEMENT. A valuable addition made to property (usually real estate) or an amelioration in its condition, amounting to more than mere repairs or replacement of waste, costing labor or capital, and intended to enhance its value and utility or to adapt it for new or further purposes.

In American land law. An act by which a locator or settler expresses his intention to cultivate or clear certain land; an act expressive of the actual possession of land; as by erecting a cabin, planting a corn-field, deadening trees in a forest; or by merely marking trees, or even by piling up a brush-heap. Burrill.

An "improvement," under our land system, does not mean a general enhancement of the value of the tract from the occupant's operations. It has a more limited meaning, which has in view the population of our forests, and the increase of agricultural products. All works which are directed to the creation of homes for families, or are substantial steps towards bringing lands into cultivation, have in their results the special character of "improvements," and, under the land laws of the United States, and of the several states, are encouraged. Sometimes their minimum extent is

defined as requisite to convey rights. In other cases not. But the test which runs through all the cases is always this: Are they real, and made *bona fide*, in accordance with the policy of the law, or are they only colorable, and made for the purpose of fraud and speculation? 37 Ark. 137.

In the law of patents. An addition to, or modification of, a previous invention or discovery, intended or claimed to increase its utility or value. See 2 Kent, Comm. 366–372.

IMPROVEMENTS. A term used in leases, of doubtful meaning. It would seem to apply principally to buildings, though generally it extends to the amelioration of every description of property, whether real or personal; but, when contained in any document, its meaning is generally explained by other words. 1 Chit. Gen. Pr. 174.

IMPROVIDENCE, as used in a statute excluding one found incompetent to execute the duties of an administrator by reason of improvidence, means that want of care and foresight in the management of property which would be likely to render the estate and effects of the intestate unsafe, and liable to be lost or diminished in value, in case the administration should be committed to the improvident person. 1 Barb. Ch. 45.

IMPRUIARE. In old records. To improve land. *Imprutamentum*, the improvement so made of it. Cowell.

IMPUBES. Lat. In the civil law. A minor under the age of puberty; a male under fourteen years of age; a female under twelve. Calvin.; Mackeld. Rom. Law, § 138.

Impunitas continuum affectum tribuit delinquendi. 4 Coke, 45. Impunity confirms the disposition to commit crime.

Impunities semper ad deteriora invitat. 5 Coke, 109. Impunity always invites to greater crimes.

IMPUNITY. Exemption or protection from penalty or punishment. 36 Tex. 153.

IMPUTATIO. In the civil law. Legal liability.

IMPUTATION OF PAYMENT. In the civil law. The application of a payment made by a debtor to his creditor.

IMPUTED NEGLIGENCE. Negligence which is not directly attributable to the person himself, but which is the negligence of a person who is in privity with him, and with whose fault he is chargeable.

IN. In the law of real estate, this preposition has always been used to denote the fact of seisin, title, or possession, and apparently serves as an elliptical expression for some such phrase as "in possession," or as an abbreviation for "*in*titled" or "*in*vested with title." Thus, in the old books, a tenant is said to be "*in* by lease of his lessor." Litt. § 82.

IN ACTION. Attainable or recoverable by action; not in possession. A term applied to property of which a party has not the possession, but only a right to recover it by action. Things in action are rights of personal things, which nevertheless are not in possession. See CHOSE IN ACTION.

IN ADVERSUM. Against an adverse, unwilling, or resisting party. "A decree not by consent, but *in adversum*." 3 Story, 318.

In ædificiis lapis male positus non est removendus. 11 Coke, 69. A stone badly placed in buildings is not to be removed.

IN ÆQUA MANU. In equal hand. Fleta, lib. 3, c. 14, § 2.

IN ÆQUALI JURE. In equal right; on an equality in point of right.

In æquali jure melior est conditio possidentis. In [a case of] equal right the condition of the party in possession is the better. Plowd. 296; Broom, Max. 713.

IN ÆQUALI MANU. In equal hand; held equally or indifferently between two parties. Where an instrument was deposited by the parties to it in the hands of a third person, to keep on certain conditions, it was said to be held *in æquali manu*. Reg. Orig. 28.

IN ALIENO SOLO. In another's land. 2 Steph. Comm. 20.

IN ALIO LOCO. In another place.

In alta proditione nullus potest esse accessorius sed principalis solummodo. 3 Inst. 138. In high treason no one can be an accessary, but only principal.

In alternativis electio est debitoris. In alternatives the debtor has the election.

In ambigua voce legis ea potius accipienda est significatio quæ vitio caret, præsertim cum etiam voluntas legis ex hoc colligi possit. In an ambiguous expression of law, that signification is to be preferred which is consonant with equity, especially when the spirit of the law can be collected from that. Dig. 1, 3, 19; Broom, Max. 576.

In ambiguis casibus semper præsumitur pro rege. In doubtful cases the presumption is always in favor of the king.

In ambiguis orationibus maxime sententia spectanda est ejus qui eas protulisset. In ambiguous expressions, the intention of the person using them is chiefly to be regarded. Dig. 50, 17, 96; Broom, Max. 567.

In Anglia non est interregnum. In England there is no interregnum. Jenk. Cent. 205; Broom, Max. 50.

IN APERTA LUCE. In open daylight; in the day-time. 9 Coke, 65*b*.

IN APICIBUS JURIS. Among the subtleties or extreme doctrines of the law. 1 Kames, Eq. 190. See APEX JURIS.

IN ARBITRIUM JUDICIS. At the pleasure of the judge.

IN ARCTA ET SALVA CUSTODIA. In close and safe custody. 3 Bl. Comm. 415.

IN ARTICULO. In a moment; immediately. Cod. 1, 34, 2.

IN ARTICULO MORTIS. In the article of death; at the point of death. 1 Johns. 159.

In atrocioribus delictis punitur affectus licet non sequatur effectus. 2 Rolle R. 82. In more atrocious crimes the intent is punished, though an effect does not follow.

IN AUTRE DROIT. L. Fr. In another's right. As representing another. An executor, administrator, or trustee sues *in autre droit*.

IN BANCO. In bank; in the bench. A term applied to proceedings in the court in bank, as distinguished from proceedings at *nisi prius*. Also, in the English court of common bench.

IN BLANK. A term applied to the indorsement of a bill or note, where it consists merely of the indorser's name, without restriction to any particular indorsee. 2 Steph. Comm. 164.

IN BONIS. Among the goods or property; in actual possession. Inst. 4, 2, 2. *In bonis defuncti*, among the goods of the deceased.

J

K

L

M

IN CAMERA. In chambers; in private. A cause is said to be heard *in camera* either when the hearing is had before the judge in his private room, or when all spectators are excluded from the court-room.

IN CAPITA. To the heads; by heads or polls. Persons succeed to an inheritance *in capita* when they individually take equal shares. So challenges to individual jurors are challenges *in capita*, as distinguished from challenges to the array.

IN CAPITE. In chief. 2 Bl. Comm. 60. Tenure *in capite* was a holding directly from the king.

In casu extremæ necessitatis omnia sunt communia. Hale, P. C. 54. In cases of extreme necessity, everything is in common.

IN CASU PROVISO. In a (or the) case provided. *In tali casu editum et provisum*, in such case made and provided. Townsh. Pl. 164, 165.

IN CAUSA. In the cause, as distinguished from *in initialibus*, (*q. v.*) A term in Scotch practice. 1 Brown, Ch. 252.

IN CHIEF. Principal; primary; directly obtained. A term applied to the evidence obtained from a witness upon his examination in court by the party producing him.
Tenure in chief, or *in capite*, is a holding directly of the king or chief lord.

In civilibus ministerium excusat, in criminalibus non item. In civil matters agency (or service) excuses, but not so in criminal matters. Lofft, 228; Tray. Lat. Max. 243.

In claris non est locus conjecturis. In things obvious there is no room for conjecture.

IN COMMENDAM. In commendation; as a commended living. 1 Bl. Comm. 393. See COMMENDA.
A term applied in Louisiana to a limited partnership, answering to the French *"en commandite."* Civil Code La. art. 2810.

In commodato hæc pactio, ne dolus præstetur, rata non est. In the contract of loan, a stipulation not to be liable for fraud is not valid. Dig. 13, 7, 17, pr.

IN COMMUNI. In common. Fleta, lib. 3, c. 4, § 2.

In conjunctivis, oportet utramque partem esse veram. In conjunctives, it is necessary that each part be true. Wing. Max. 13, max. 9. In a condition consisting of divers parts in the copulative, both parts must be performed.

IN CONSIDERATIONE INDE. In consideration thereof. 3 Salk. 64, pl. 5.

IN CONSIDERATIONE LEGIS. In consideration or contemplation of law; in abeyance. Dyer, 102b.

IN CONSIDERATIONE PRÆMISSORUM. In consideration of the premises. 1 Strange, 535.

In consimili casu, consimile debet esse remedium. Hardr. 65. In similar cases the remedy should be similar.

IN CONSPECTU EJUS. In his sight or view. 12 Mod. 95.

In consuetudinibus, non diuturnitas temporis sed soliditas rationis est consideranda. In customs, not length of time, but solidity of reason, is to be considered. Co. Litt. 141a. The antiquity of a custom is to be less regarded than its reasonableness.

IN CONTINENTI. Immediately; without any interval or intermission. Calvin. Sometimes written as one word, *"incontinenti."*

In contractibus, benigna; in testamentis, benignior; in restitutionibus, benignissima interpretatio facienda est. Co. Litt. 112. In contracts, the interpretation is to be liberal; in wills, more liberal; in restitutions, most liberal.

In contractibus, rei veritas potius quam scriptura perspici debet. In contracts, the truth of the matter ought to be regarded rather than the writing. Cod. 4, 22, 1.

In contractibus, tacite insunt [veniunt] quæ sunt moris et consuetudinis. In contracts, matters of custom and usage are tacitly implied. A contract is understood to contain the customary clauses, although they are not expressed. Story, Bills, § 143; 3 Kent, Comm. 260, note; Broom, Max. 842.

In contrahenda venditione, ambiguum pactum contra venditorem interpretandum est. In the contract of sale, an ambiguous agreement is to be interpreted against the seller. Dig. 50, 17, 172. See Id. 18, 1, 21.

In conventionibus, contrahentium voluntas potius quam verba spectari placuit. In agreements, the intention of the contracting parties, rather than the words used, should be regarded. 17 Johns. 150; Broom, Max. 551.

IN CORPORE. In body or substance; in a material thing or object.

IN CRASTINO. On the morrow. *In crastino Animarum*, on the morrow of All Souls. 1 Bl. Comm. 342.

In criminalibus, probationes debent esse luce clariores. In criminal cases, the proofs ought to be clearer than light. 3 Inst. 210.

In criminalibus, sufficit generalis malitia intentionis, cum facto paris gradus. In criminal matters or cases, a general malice of intention is sufficient, [if united] with an act of equal or corresponding degree. Bac. Max. p. 65, reg. 15; Broom, Max. 323.

In criminalibus, voluntas reputabitur pro facto. In criminal acts, the will will be taken for the deed. 3 Inst. 106.

IN CUJUS REI TESTIMONIUM. In testimony whereof. The initial words of the concluding clause of ancient deeds in Latin, literally translated in the English forms.

IN CUSTODIA LEGIS. In the custody or keeping of the law. 2 Steph. Comm. 74.

IN DELICTO. In fault. See IN PARI DELICTO, etc.

IN DIEM. For a day; for the space of a day. Calvin.

In disjunctivis sufficit alteram partem esse veram. In disjunctives it is sufficient that either part be true. Where a condition is in the disjunctive, it is sufficient if either part be performed. Wing. Max. 13, max. 9; 7 East, 272; Broom, Max. 592.

IN DOMINICO. In demesne. *In dominico suo ut de feodo*, in his demesne as of fee.

IN DORSO. On the back. 2 Bl. Comm. 468; 2 Steph. Comm. 164. *In dorso recordi*, on the back of the record. 5 Coke, 45. Hence the English *indorse, indorsement*, etc.

In dubiis, benigniora præferenda sunt. In doubtful cases, the more favorable views are to be preferred; the more liberal interpretation is to be followed. Dig. 50, 17, 56; 2 Kent, Comm. 557.

In dubiis, magis dignum est accipiendum. Branch, Princ. In doubtful cases, the more worthy is to be accepted.

In dubiis, non præsumitur pro testamento. In cases of doubt, the presumption is not in favor of a will. Branch, Princ. But see Cro. Car. 51.

IN DUBIO. In doubt; in a state of uncertainty, or in a doubtful case.

In dubio, hæc legis constructio quam verba ostendunt. In a case of doubt, that is the construction of the law which the words indicate. Branch, Princ.

In dubio, pars mitior est sequenda. In doubt, the milder course is to be followed.

In dubio, sequendum quod tutius est. In doubt, the safer course is to be adopted.

IN DUPLO. In double. *Damna in duplo*, double damages. Fleta, lib. 4, c. 10, § 1.

IN EADEM CAUSA. In the same state or condition. Calvin.

IN EMULATIONEM VICINI. In envy or hatred of a neighbor. Where an act is done, or action brought, solely to hurt or distress another, it is said to be *in emulationem vicini*. 1 Kames, Eq. 56.

In eo quod plus sit, semper inest et minus. In the greater is always included the less also. Dig. 50, 17, 110.

IN EQUITY. In a court of equity, as distinguished from a court of law; in the purview, consideration, or contemplation of equity; according to the doctrines of equity.

IN ESSE. In being. Actually existing. Distinguished from *in posse*, which means "that which is not, but may be." A child before birth is *in posse;* after birth, *in esse*.

IN EVIDENCE. Included in the evidence already adduced. The "facts in evidence" are such as have already been proved in the cause.

IN EXCAMBIO. In exchange. Formal words in old deeds of exchange.

IN EXITU. In issue. *De materia in exitu*, of the matter in issue. 12 Mod. 372.

In expositione instrumentorum, mala grammatica, quod fieri potest, vitanda est. In the construction of instruments, bad grammar is to be avoided as much as possible. 6 Coke, 39; 2 Pars. Cont. 26.

IN EXTENSO. In extension; at full length; from beginning to end, leaving out nothing.

J

L

M

IN EXTREMIS. In extremity; in the last extremity; in the last illness. 20 Johns. 502; 2 Bl. Comm. 375, 500. *Agens in extremis*, being in extremity. Bract. fol. 373*b*. Declarations *in extremis*, dying declarations. 15 Johns. 286; 1 Greenl. Ev. § 156.

IN FACIE CURIÆ. In the face of the court. Dyer, 28.

IN FACIE ECCLESIÆ. In the face of the church. A term applied in the law of England to marriages, which are required to be solemnized in a parish church or public chapel, unless by dispensation or license. 1 Bl. Comm. 439; 2 Steph. Comm. 288, 289. Applied in Bracton to the old mode of conferring dower. Bract. fol. 92; 2 Bl. Comm. 133.

IN FACIENDO. In doing; in feasance; in the performance of an act. 2 Story, Eq. Jur. § 1308.

IN FACT. Actual, real; as distinguished from implied or inferred. Resulting from the acts of parties, instead of from the act or intendment of law.

IN FACTO. In fact; in deed. *In facto dicit*, in fact says. 1 Salk. 22, pl. 1.

In facto quod se habet **ad bonum et malum, magis de bono quam de malo lex intendit.** In an act or deed which admits of being considered as both good and bad, the law intends more from the good than from the bad; the law makes the more favorable construction. Co. Litt. 78*b*.

In favorabilibus magis attenditur quod prodest quam quod nocet. In things favored, what profits is more regarded than what prejudices. Bac. Max. p. 57, in reg. 12.

IN FAVOREM LIBERTATIS. In favor of liberty.

IN FAVOREM VITÆ. In favor of life.

In favorem vitæ, libertatis, et innocentiæ, omnia præsumuntur. In favor of life, liberty, and innocence, every presumption is made. Lofft. 125.

IN FEODO. In fee. Bract. fol. 207; Fleta, lib. 2, c. 64, § 15. *Seisitus in feodo*, seised in fee. Fleta, lib. 3, c. 7, § 1.

In fictione juris semper æquitas existit. In the fiction of law there is always equity; a legal fiction is always consistent with equity. 11 Coke, 51*a*; Broom, Max. 127, 130.

IN FIERI. In being made; in process of formation or development; hence, incomplete or inchoate. Legal proceedings are described as *in fieri* until judgment is entered.

IN FINE. Lat. At the end. Used, in references, to indicate that the passage cited is at the *end* of a book, chapter, section, etc.

IN FORMA PAUPERIS. In the character or manner of a pauper. Describes permission given to a poor person to sue without liability for costs.

IN FORO. In a (or the) forum, court, or tribunal.

IN FORO CONSCIENTIÆ. In the tribunal of conscience; conscientiously; considered from a moral, rather than a legal, point of view.

IN FORO CONTENTIOSO. In the forum of contention or litigation.

IN FORO ECCLESIASTICO. In an ecclesiastical forum; in the ecclesiastical court. Fleta, lib. 2, c. 57, § 13.

IN FORO SÆCULARI. In a secular forum or court. Fleta, lib. 2, c. 57, § 14; 1 Bl. Comm. 20.

IN FRAUDEM CREDITORUM. In fraud of creditors; with intent to defraud creditors. Inst. 1, 6, pr., 3.

IN FRAUDEM LEGIS. In fraud of the law. 3 Bl. Comm. 94. With the intent or view of evading the law. 1 Johns. 424, 432.

IN FULL. Relating to the whole or *full* amount; as a receipt in full. Complete; giving all details.

IN FULL LIFE. Continuing in both physical and civil existence; that is, neither actually dead nor *civiliter mortuus*.

IN FUTURO. In future; at a future time; the opposite of *in præsenti*. 2 Bl. Comm. 166, 175.

IN GENERALI PASSAGIO. In the general passage; that is, on the journey to Palestine with the general company or body of Crusaders. This term was of frequent occurrence in the old law of essoins, as a means of accounting for the absence of the party, and was distinguished from *simplex passagium*, which meant that he was performing a pilgrimage to the Holy Land alone.

In generalibus versatur error. Error dwells in general expressions. 3 Sum. 290; 1 Cush. 292.

IN GENERE. In kind; in the same *genus* or class; the same in quantity and quality, but not individually the same. In the Roman law, things which may be given or restored *in genere* are distinguished from such as must be given or restored *in specie;* that is, identically. Mackeld. Rom. Law, § 161.

IN GREMIO LEGIS. In the bosom of the law; in the protection of the law; in abeyance. 1 Coke, 131*a;* T. Raym. 319.

IN GROSS. In a large quantity or sum; without division or particulars; by wholesale.

At large; not annexed to or dependent upon another thing. Common in gross is such as is neither appendant nor appurtenant to land, but is annexed to a man's person. 2 Bl. Comm. 34.

IN HAC PARTE. In this behalf; on this side.

IN HÆC VERBA. In these words; in the same words.

In hæredes non solent transire actiones quæ pœnales ex maleficio sunt. 2 Inst. 442. Penal actions arising from anything of a criminal nature do not pass to heirs.

In his enim quæ sunt favorabilia animæ, quamvis sunt damnosa rebus, fiat aliquando extentio statuti. In things that are favorable to the spirit, though injurious to property, an extension of the statute should sometimes be made. 10 Coke, 101.

In his quæ de jure communi omnibus conceduntur, consuetudo alicujus patriæ vel loci non est allegenda. 11 Coke, 85. In those things which by common right are conceded to all, the custom of a particular district or place is not to be alleged.

IN HOC. In this; in respect to this.

IN IISDEM TERMINIS. In the same terms. 9 East, 487.

IN INDIVIDUO. In the distinct, identical, or individual form; *in specie.* Story, Bailm. § 97.

IN INFINITUM. Infinitely; indefinitely. Imports indefinite succession or continuance.

IN INITIALIBUS. In the preliminaries. A term in Scotch practice, applied to the preliminary examination of a witness as to the following points: Whether he knows the parties, or bears ill will to either of them, or has received any reward or promise of reward for what he may say, or can lose or gain by the cause, or has been told by any person what to say. If the witness answer these questions satisfactorily, he is then examined *in causa,* in the cause. Bell, Dict. "Evidence."

IN INITIO. In or at the beginning. *In initio litis,* at the beginning, or in the first stage of the suit. Bract. fol. 400.

IN INTEGRUM. To the original or former state. Calvin.

IN INVIDIAM. To excite a prejudice.

IN INVITUM. Against an unwilling party; against one not assenting. A term applied to proceedings against an adverse party, to which he does not consent.

IN IPSIS FAUCIBUS. In the very throat or entrance. *In ipsis faucibus* of a port, actually entering a port. 1 C. Rob. Adm. 233, 234.

IN ITINERE. In eyre; on a journey or circuit. In old English law, the justices *in itinere* (or in eyre) were those who made a circuit through the kingdom once in seven years for the purposes of trying causes. 3 Bl. Comm. 58.

In course of transportation; on the way; not delivered to the vendee. In this sense the phrase is equivalent to "*in transitu.*"

IN JUDGMENT. In a court of justice; in a seat of judgment. Lord Hale is called "one of the greatest and best men who ever sat in judgment." 1 East, 306.

In judiciis, minori ætati succurritur. In courts or judicial proceedings, infancy is aided or favored. Jenk. Cent. 46, case 89.

IN JUDICIO. In Roman law. In the course of an actual trial; before a judge, (*judex.*) A cause, during its preparatory stages, conducted before the prætor, was said to be *in jure;* in its second stage, after it had been sent to a *judex* for trial, it was said to be *in judicio.*

In judicio non creditur nisi juratis. Cro. Car. 64. In a trial, credence is given only to those who are sworn.

IN JURE. In law; according to law. In the Roman practice, the procedure in an action was divided into two stages. The first was said to be *in jure;* it took place before the prætor, and included the formal and introductory part and the settlement of questions of law. The second stage was committed to the *judex*, and comprised the investigation and trial of the facts; this was said to be *in judicio.*

IN JURE ALTERIUS. In another's right. Hale, Anal. § 26.

In jure, non remota causa sed proxima spectatur. Bac. Max. reg. 1. In law, the proximate, and not the remote, cause is regarded.

IN JURE PROPRIO. In one's own right. Hale, Anal. § 26.

IN JUS VOCARE. To call, cite, or summon to court. Inst. 4, 16, 3; Calvin. *In jus vocando,* summoning to court. 3 Bl. Comm. 279.

IN KIND. In the same kind, class, or genus. A loan is returned "in kind" when not the identical article, but one corresponding and equivalent to it, is given to the lender. See IN GENERE.

IN LAW. In the intendment, contemplation, or inference of the law; implied or inferred by law; existing in law or by force of law. See IN FACT.

IN LECTO MORTALI. On the deathbed. Fleta, lib. 5, c. 28, § 12.

IN LIMINE. On or at the threshold; at the very beginning; preliminarily.

IN LITEM. For a suit; to the suit. Greenl. Ev. § 348.

IN LOCO. In place; in lieu; instead; in the place or stead. Townsh. Pl. 38.

IN LOCO PARENTIS. In the place of a parent; instead of a parent; charged, factitiously, with a parent's rights, duties, and responsibilities.

In majore summa continetur minor. 5 Coke, 115. In the greater sum is contained the less.

IN MAJOREM CAUTELAM. For greater security. 1 Strange, 105, arg.

IN MALAM PARTEM. In a bad sense, so as to wear an evil appearance.

In maleficiis voluntas spectatur, non exitus. In evil deeds regard must be had to the intention, and not to the result. Dig. 48, 8, 14; Broom, Max. 324.

In maleficio, ratihabitio mandato comparatur. In a case of malfeasance, ratification is equivalent to command. Dig. 50, 17, 152, 2.

In maxima potentia minima licentia. In the greatest power there is the least freedom. Hob. 159.

IN MEDIAS RES. Into the heart of the subject, without preface or introduction.

IN MEDIO. Intermediate. A term applied, in Scotch practice, to a fund held between parties litigant.

In mercibus illicitis non sit commercium. There should be no commerce in illicit or prohibited goods. 3 Kent, Comm. 262, note.

IN MERCY. To be in mercy is to be at the discretion of the king, lord, or judge in respect to the imposition of a fine or other punishment.

IN MISERICORDIA. The entry on the record where a party was in mercy was, "*Ideo in misericordia,*" etc. Sometimes "*misericordia*" means the being quit of all amercements.

IN MITIORI SENSU. In the milder sense; in the less aggravated acceptation. In actions of slander, it was formerly the rule that, if the words alleged would admit of two constructions, they should be taken in the less injurious and defamatory sense, or *in mitiori sensu.*

IN MODUM ASSISÆ. In the manner or form of an assize. Bract. fol. 183b. *In modum juratæ,* in manner of a jury. Id. fol. 181b.

IN MORA. In default; literally, in delay. In the civil law, a borrower who omits or refuses to return the thing loaned at the proper time is said to be *in mora.* Story, Bailm. §§ 254, 259.

In Scotch law. A creditor who has begun without completing diligence necessary for attaching the property of his debtor is said to be *in mora.* Bell.

IN MORTUA MANU. Property owned by religious societies was said to be held *in mortua manu,* or in mortmain, since religious men were *civiliter mortui.* 1 Bl. Comm. 479; Tayl. Gloss.

IN NOMINE DEI, AMEN. In the name of God, Amen. A solemn introduction, anciently used in wills and many other instruments. The translation is often used in wills at the present day.

IN NOTIS. In the notes.

In novo casu, novum remedium apponendum est. 2 Inst. 3. A new remedy is to be applied to a new case.

IN NUBIBUS. In the clouds; in abeyance; in custody of law. *In nubibus, in mare, in terra, vel in custodia legis,* in the air, sea, or earth, or in the custody of the law. Tayl. Gloss. In case of abeyance, the inheritance is figuratively said to rest *in nubibus,* or *in gremio legis.*

IN NULLIUS BONIS. Among the goods or property of no person; belonging to no person, as treasure-trove and wreck were anciently considered.

IN NULLO EST ERRATUM. In nothing is there error. The name of the common plea or joinder in error, denying the existence of error in the record or proceedings; which is in the nature of a demurrer, and at once refers the matter of law arising thereon to the judgment of the court. 2 Tidd, Pr. 1173; 7 Metc. (Mass.) 285, 287.

In obscura voluntate manumittentis, favendum est libertati. Where the expression of the will of one who seeks to manumit a slave is ambiguous, liberty is to be favored. Dig. 50, 17, 179.

In obscuris, inspici solere quod verisimilius est, aut quod plerumque fieri solet. In obscure cases, we usually look at what is most probable, or what most commonly happens. Dig. 50, 17, 114.

In obscuris, quod minimum est sequimur. In obscure or doubtful cases, we follow that which is the least. Dig. 50, 17, 9; 2 Kent, Comm. 557.

IN ODIUM SPOLIATORIS. In hatred of a despoiler, robber, or wrong-doer. 1 Gall. 174; 2 Story, 99; 1 Greenl. Ev. § 348.

In odium spoliatoris omnia praesumuntur. To the prejudice (in condemnation) of a despoiler all things are presumed; every presumption is made against a wrong-doer. 1 Vern. 452.

In omni actione ubi duae concurrunt districtiones, videlicet, in rem et in personam, illa districtio tenenda est quae magis timetur et magis ligat. In every action where two distresses concur, that is, *in rem* and *in personam,* that is to be chosen which is most dreaded, and which binds most

firmly. Bract. fol. 372; Fleta, l. 6, c. **14,** § 28.

In omni re nascitur res quae ipsam rem exterminat. In everything there arises a thing which destroys the thing itself. Everything contains the element of its own destruction. 2 Inst. 15.

IN OMNIBUS. In all things; on all points. "A case parallel *in omnibus.*" 10 Mod. 104.

In omnibus contractibus, sive nominatis sive innominatis, permutatio continetur. In all contracts, whether nominate or innominate, an exchange [of value, *i. e.,* a consideration] is implied. Gravin. lib. 2, § 12; 2 Bl. Comm. 444, note.

In omnibus obligationibus in quibus dies non ponitur, praesenti die debetur. In all obligations in which a date is not put, the debt is due on the present day; the liability accrues immediately. Dig. 50, 17, 14.

In omnibus [fere] poenalibus judiciis, et aetati et imprudentiae succurritur. In nearly all penal judgments, immaturity of age and imbecility of mind are favored. Dig. 50, 17, 108; Broom, Max. 314.

In omnibus quidem, maxime tamen in jure, aequitas spectanda sit. In all things, but especially in law, equity is to be regarded. Dig. 50, 17, 90; Story, Bailm. § 257.

IN PACATO SOLO. In a country which is at peace.

IN PACE DEI ET REGIS. In the peace of God and the king. Fleta, lib. 1, c. 31, § 6. Formal words in old appeals of murder.

IN PAIS. This phrase, as applied to a legal transaction, primarily means that it has taken place without legal proceedings. Thus a widow was said to make a request *in pais* for her dower when she simply applied to the heir without issuing a writ. (Co. Litt. 32b.) So conveyances are divided into those by matter of record and those by matter *in pais.* In some cases, however, "matters *in pais*" are opposed not only to "matters of record," but also to "matters in writing," *i. e.,* deeds, as where estoppel by deed is distinguished from estoppel by matter *in pais.* (Id. 352a.) Sweet.

IN PAPER. A term formerly applied to the proceedings in a cause before the record was made up. 3 Bl. Comm. 406; 2 Bur-

J

K

L

M

rows, 1098. Probably from the circumstance of the record being always on parchment. The opposite of "on record." 1 Burrows, 322.

IN PARI CAUSA. In an equal cause. In a cause where the parties on each side have equal rights.

In pari causa possessor potior haberi debet. In an equal cause he who has the possession should be preferred. Dig. 50, 17, 128, 1.

IN PARI DELICTO. In equal fault; equally culpable or criminal; in a case of equal fault or guilt.

In pari delicto potior est conditio possidentis, [defendentis.] In a case of equal or mutual fault [between two parties] the condition of the party in possession [or defending] is the better one. 2 Burrows, 926. Where each party is equally in fault, the law favors him who is actually in possession. Broom, Max. 290, 729. Where the fault is mutual, the law will leave the case as it finds it. Story, Ag. § 195.

IN PARI MATERIA. Upon the same matter or subject. Statutes *in pari materia* are to be construed together. 7 Conn. 456.

IN PATIENDO. In suffering, permitting, or allowing.

IN PECTORE JUDICIS. In the breast of the judge. Latch, 180. A phrase applied to a judgment.

IN PEJOREM PARTEM. In the worst part; on the worst side. Latch, 159, 160.

IN PERPETUAM REI MEMORIAM. In perpetual memory of a matter; for preserving a record of a matter. Applied to depositions taken in order to preserve the testimony of the deponent.

IN PERPETUUM REI TESTIMONIUM. In perpetual testimony of a matter; for the purpose of declaring and settling a thing forever. 1 Bl. Comm. 86.

IN PERSON. A party, plaintiff or defendant, who sues out a writ or other process, or appears to conduct his case in court himself, instead of through a solicitor or counsel, is said to act and appear *in person.*

IN PERSONAM, IN REM. In the Roman law, from which they are taken, the expressions "*in rem*" and "*in personam*" were always opposed to one another, an act or proceeding *in personam* being one done or directed against or with reference to a specific person, while an act or proceeding *in rem* was one done or directed with reference to no specific person, and consequently against or with reference to all whom it might concern, or "all the world." The phrases were especially applied to actions; an *actio in personam* being the remedy where a claim against a specific person arose out of an obligation, whether *ex contractu* or *ex maleficio*, while an *actio in rem* was one brought for the assertion of a right of property, easement, *status*, etc., against one who denied or infringed it. See Inst. 4, 6, 1; Gaius, 4, 1, 1–10; 5 Sav. Syst. 13, et seq.; Dig. 2, 14, 7, 8; Id. 4, 2, 9, 1.

From this use of the terms, they have come to be applied to signify the antithesis of "available against a particular person," and "available against the world at large." Thus, *jura in personam* are rights primarily available against specific persons; *jura in rem*, rights only available against the world at large.

So a judgment or decree is said to be *in rem* when it binds third persons. Such is the sentence of a court of admiralty on a question of prize, or a decree of nullity or dissolution of marriage, or a decree of a court in a foreign country as to the *status* of a person domiciled there.

Lastly, the terms are sometimes used to signify that a judicial proceeding operates on a thing or a person. Thus, it is said of the court of chancery that it acts *in personam*, and not *in rem*, meaning that its decrees operate by compelling defendants to do what they are ordered to do, and not by producing the effect directly. Sweet.

In personam actio est, qua cum eo agimus qui obligatus est nobis ad faciendum aliquid vel dandum. The action *in personam* is that by which we sue him who is under obligation to us to do something or give something. Dig. 44, 7, 25; Bract. 101b.

IN PIOS USUS. For pious uses; for religious purposes. 2 Bl. Comm. 505.

IN PLENA VITA. In full life. Yearb. P. 18 Hen. VI. 2.

IN PLENO COMITATU. In full county court. 3 Bl. Comm. 36.

IN PLENO LUMINE. In public; in common knowledge; in the light of day.

In pœnalibus causis benignius interpretandum est. In penal causes or cases, the more favorable interpretation should be adopted. Dig. 50, 17, (197,) 155, 2; Plowd. 86*b*, 124; 2 Hale, P. C. 365.

IN POSSE. In possibility; not in actual existence. See IN ESSE.

IN POTESTATE PARENTIS. In the power of a parent. Inst. 1, 8, pr.; Id. 1, 9; 2 Bl. Comm. 498.

IN PRÆMISSORUM FIDEM. In confirmation or attestation of the premises. A notarial phrase.

In præparatoriis ad judicium favetur actori. 2 Inst. 57. In things preceding judgment the plaintiff is favored.

IN PRÆSENTI. At the present time. 2 Bl. Comm. 166. Used in opposition to *in futuro.*

In præsentia majoris potestatis, minor potestas cessat. In the presence of the superior power, the inferior power ceases. Jenk. Cent. 214, c. 53. The less authority is merged in the greater. Broom, Max. 111.

IN PRENDER. L. Fr. In taking. A term applied to such incorporeal hereditaments as a party entitled to them was to *take* for himself; such as common. 2 Steph. Comm. 23; 3 Bl. Comm. 15.

In pretio emptionis et venditionis, naturaliter licet contrahentibus se circumvenire. In the price of buying and selling, it is naturally allowed to the contracting parties to overreach each other. 1 Story, Cont. 606.

IN PRIMIS. In the first place. A phrase used in argument.

IN PRINCIPIO. At the beginning.

IN PROMPTU. In readiness; at hand.

In propria causa nemo judex. No one can be judge in his own cause. 12 Coke, 13.

IN PROPRIA PERSONA. In one's own proper person.

In quo quis delinquit, in eo de jure est puniendus. In whatever thing one offends, in that is he rightfully to be punished. Co. Litt. 233*b;* Wing. Max. 204, max. 58. The punishment shall have relation to the nature of the offense.

IN RE. In the affair; in the matter of. This is the usual method of entitling a judicial proceeding in which there are not adversary parties, but merely some *res* concerning which judicial action is to be taken, such as

a bankrupt's estate, an estate in the probate court, a proposed public highway, etc. It is also sometimes used as a designation of a proceeding where one party makes an application on his own behalf, but such proceedings are more usually entitled "*Ex parte* ———.''

In re communi neminem dominorum jure facere quicquam, invito altero, posse. One co-proprietor can exercise no authority over the common property against the will of the other. Dig. 10, 3, 28.

In re communi potior est conditio prohibentis. In a partnership the condition of one who forbids is the more favorable.

In re dubia, benigniorem interpretationem sequi, non minus justius est quam tutius. In a doubtful matter, to follow the more liberal interpretation is not less the juster than the safer course. Dig. 50, 17, 192, 1.

In re dubia, magis inficiatio quam affirmatio intelligenda. In a doubtful matter, the denial or negative is to be understood, [or regarded,] rather than the affirmative. Godb. 37.

In re lupanari, testes lupanares admittentur. In a matter concerning a brothel, prostitutes are admitted as witnesses. 6 Barb. 320, 324.

In re pari potiorem causam esse prohibentis constat. In a thing equally shared [by several] it is clear that the party refusing [to permit the use of it] has the better cause. Dig. 10, 3, 28. A maxim applied to partnerships, where one partner has a right to withhold his assent to the acts of his copartner. 3 Kent, Comm. 45.

In re propria iniquum admodum est alicui licentiam tribuere sententiæ. It is extremely unjust that any one should be judge in his own cause.

J

In rebus manifestis, errat qui authoritates legum allegat; quia perspicue vera non sunt probanda. In clear cases, he mistakes who cites legal authorities; for obvious truths are not to be proved. 5 Coke, 67*a.* Applied to cases too plain to require the support of authority; "because," says the report, "he who endeavors to prove them obscures them."

K

L

In rebus quæ sunt favorabilia animæ, quamvis sunt damnosa rebus, fiat aliquando extensio statuti. 10 Coke, 101.

M

In things that are favorable to the spirit, though injurious to things, an extension of a statute should sometimes be made.

IN REM. A technical term used to designate proceedings or actions instituted *against the thing*, in contradistinction to personal actions, which are said to be *in personam*. See IN PERSONAM.

It is true that, in a strict sense, a proceeding *in rem* is one taken directly against property, and has for its object the disposition of property, without reference to the title of individual claimants; but, in a larger and more general sense, the terms are applied to actions between parties, where the direct object is to reach and dispose of property owned by them, or of some interest therein. Such are cases commenced by attachment against the property of debtors, or instituted to partition real estate, foreclose a mortgage, or enforce a lien. So far as they affect property in this state, they are substantially proceedings *in rem* in the broader sense which we have mentioned. 95 U. S. 734.

In rem actio est per quam rem nostram quæ ab alio possidetur petimus, et semper adversus eum est qui rem possidet. The action *in rem* is that by which we seek our property which is possessed by another, and is always against him who possesses the property. Dig. 44, 7, 25; Bract. fol. 102.

IN RENDER. A thing is said to lie *in render* when it must be rendered or given by the tenant; as rent. It is said to lie *in prender* when it consists in the right in the lord or other person to *take* something.

In republica maxime conservanda sunt jura belli. In a state the laws of war are to be especially upheld. 2 Inst. 58.

IN RERUM NATURA. In the nature of things; in the realm of actuality; in existence. In a dilatory plea, an allegation that the plaintiff is not *in rerum natura* is equivalent to averring that the person named is fictitious. 3 Bl. Comm. 301. In the civil law the phrase is applied to things. Inst. 2, 20, 7.

In restitutionem, non in pœnam hæres succedit. The heir succeeds to the restitution, not to the penalty. An heir may be compelled to make restitution of a sum unlawfully appropriated by the ancestor, but is not answerable criminally, as for a penalty. 2 Inst. 198.

In restitutionibus benignissima interpretatio facienda est. Co. Litt. 112. The most benignant interpretation is to be made in restitutions.

In satisfactionibus non permittitur amplius fieri quam semel factum est. In payments, more must not be received than has been received once for all. 9 Coke, 53.

IN SCRINIO JUDICIS. In the writing-case of the judge; among the judge's papers. "That is a thing that rests *in scrinio judicis*, and does not appear in the body of the decree." Hardr. 51.

IN SEPARALI. In several; in severalty. Fleta, lib. 2, c. 54, § 20.

IN SIMILI MATERIA. Dealing with the same or a kindred subject-matter.

IN SIMPLICI PEREGRINATIONE. In simple pilgrimage. Bract. fol. 338. A phrase in the old law of essoins. See IN GENERALI PASSAGIO.

IN SOLIDO. In the civil law. For the whole; as a whole. An obligation *in solido* is one where each of the several obligors is liable for the whole; that is, it is joint and several. Possession *in solidum* is exclusive possession.

When several persons obligate themselves to the obligee by the terms "*in solido*," or use any other expressions which clearly show that they intend that each one shall be separately bound to perform the whole of the obligation, it is called an "obligation *in solido*" on the part of the obligors. Civil Code La. art. 2082.

IN SOLIDUM. For the whole. *Si plures sint fidejussores, quotquot erunt numero, singuli in solidum tenentur*, if there be several sureties, however numerous they may be, they are individually bound for the whole debt. Inst. 3, 21, 4. *In parte sive in solidum*, for a part or for the whole. Id. 4, 1, 16. See Id. 4, 6, 20; Id. 4, 7, 2.

IN SOLO. In the soil or ground. *In solo alieno*, in another's ground. *In solo proprio*, in one's own ground. 2 Steph. Comm. 20.

IN SPECIE. Specific; specifically. Thus, to decree performance *in specie* is to decree specific performance.

In kind; in the same or like form. A thing is said to exist *in specie* when it retains its existence as a distinct individual of a particular class.

IN STATU QUO. In the condition in which it was. See STATUS QUO.

In stipulationibus cum quæritur quid actum sit verba contra stipulatorem in-

terpretanda sunt. In the construction of agreements words are interpreted against the person using them. Thus, the construction of the *stipulatio* is against the stipulator, and the construction of the *promissio* against the promissor. Dig. 45, 1, 38, 18; Broom, Max. 599.

In stipulationibus, id tempus spectatur quo contrahimus. In stipulations, the time when we contract is regarded. Dig. 50, 17, 144, 1.

IN STIRPES. In the law of intestate succession. According to the roots or stocks; by representation; as distinguished from succession *per capita*. See PER STIRPES; PER CAPITA.

IN SUBSIDIUM. In aid.

In suo quisque negotio hebetior est quam in alieno. Every one is more dull in his own business than in another's.

IN TANTUM. In so much; so much; so far; so greatly. Reg. Orig. 97, 106.

IN TERMINIS TERMINANTIBUS. In terms of determination; exactly in point. 11 Coke, 40b. In express or determinate terms. 1 Leon. 93.

IN TERROREM. In terror or warning; by way of threat. Applied to legacies given upon condition that the recipient shall not dispute the validity or the dispositions of the will; such a condition being usually regarded as a mere threat.

IN TERROREM POPULI. Lat. To the terror of the people. A technical phrase necessary in indictments for riots. 4 Car. & P. 373.

In testamentis plenius testatoris intentionem scrutamur. In wills we more especially seek out the intention of the testator. 3 Bulst. 103; Broom, Max. 555.

In testamentis plenius voluntates testantium interpretantur. Dig. 50, 17, 12. In wills the intention of testators is more especially regarded. "That is to say," says Mr. Broom, (Max., 568,) "a will will receive a more liberal construction than its strict meaning, if alone considered, would permit."

In testamentis ratio tacita non debet considerari, sed verba solum spectari debent; adeo per divinationem mentis a verbis recedere durum est. In wills an unexpressed meaning ought not to be considered, but the words alone ought to be

looked to; so hard is it to recede from the words by guessing at the intention.

IN TESTIMONIUM. Lat. In witness; in evidence whereof.

IN TOTIDEM VERBIS. In so many words; in precisely the same words; word for word.

IN TOTO. In the whole; wholly; completely; as the award is void *in toto*.

In toto et pars continetur. In the whole the part also is contained. Dig. 50, 17, 113.

In traditionibus scriptorum, non quod dictum est, sed quod gestum est, inspicitur. In the delivery of writings, not what is said, but what is done, is looked to. 9 Coke, 137a.

IN TRAJECTU. In the passage over; on the voyage over. See Sir William Scott, 3 C. Rob. Adm. 141.

IN TRANSITU. In transit; on the way or passage; while passing from one person or place to another. 2 Kent, Comm. 540–552. On the voyage. 1 C. Rob. Adm. 338.

IN VACUO. Without object; without concomitants or coherence.

IN VADIO. In gage or pledge. 2 Bl. Comm. 157.

IN VENTRE SA MERE. L. Fr. In his mother's womb; spoken of an unborn child.

In veram quantitatem fidejussor teneatur, nisi pro certa quantitate accessit. Let the surety be holden for the true quantity, unless he agree for a certain quantity. 17 Mass. 597.

In verbis, non verba, sed res et ratio, quærenda est. Jenk. Cent. 132. In the construction of words, not the mere words, but the thing and the meaning, are to be inquired after.

IN VINCULIS. In chains; in actual custody. Gilb. Forum Rom. 97.

Applied also, figuratively, to the condition of a person who is compelled to submit to terms which oppression and his necessities impose on him. 1 Story, Eq. Jur. § 302.

IN VIRIDI OBSERVANTIA. Present to the minds of men, and in full force and operation.

IN WITNESS WHEREOF. The initial words of the concluding clause in deeds: "In witness whereof the said parties have hereunto set their hands," etc. A translation of the Latin phrase "*in cujus rei testimonium.*"

INADEQUATE PRICE. A term applied to indicate the want of a sufficient consideration for a thing sold, or such a price as would ordinarily be entirely incommensurate with its intrinsic value.

INADMISSIBLE. That which, under the established rules of law, cannot be admitted or received; *e. g.*, parol evidence to contradict a written contract.

INÆDIFICATIO. In the civil law. Building on another's land with one's own materials, or on one's own land with another's materials.

INALIENABLE. Not subject to alienation; the characteristic of those things which cannot be bought or sold or transferred from one person to another, such as rivers and public highways, and certain personal rights; *e. g.*, liberty.

INAUGURATION. The act of installing or inducting into office with formal ceremonies, as the coronation of a sovereign, the inauguration of a president or governor, or the consecration of a prelate.

INBLAURA. In old records. Profit or product of ground. Cowell.

INBORH. In Saxon law. A security, pledge, or *hypotheca*, consisting of the chattels of a person unable to obtain a personal "borg," or surety.

INBOUND COMMON. An uninclosed common, marked out, however, by boundaries.

INCAPACITY. Want of capacity; want of power or ability to take or dispose; want of legal ability to act.

INCASTELLARE. To make a building serve as a castle. Jacob.

INCAUSTUM, or ENCAUSTUM. Ink. Fleta, l. 2, c. 27, § 5.

Incaute factum pro non facto habetur. A thing done unwarily (or unadvisedly) will be taken as not done. Dig. 28, 4, 1.

INCENDIARY. A house-burner; one guilty of arson; one who maliciously and willfully sets another person's building on fire.

Incendium ære alieno non exuit debitorem. Cod. 4, 2, 11. A fire does not release a debtor from his debt.

INCEPTION. Commencement; opening; initiation. The beginning of the operation of a contract or will.

Incerta pro nullis habentur. Uncertain things are held for nothing. Dav. Ir. K. B. 33.

Incerta quantitas vitiat actum. 1 Rolle R. 465. An uncertain quantity vitiates the act.

INCEST. The crime of sexual intercourse or cohabitation between a man and woman who are related to each other within the degrees wherein marriage is prohibited by law.

INCESTUOUS ADULTERY. The elements of this offense are that defendant, being married to one person, has had sexual intercourse with another related to the defendant within the prohibited degrees. 11 Ga. 53.

INCESTUOUS BASTARDY. Incestuous bastards are those who are produced by the illegal connection of two persons who are relations within the degrees prohibited by law. Civil Code La. art. 183.

INCH. A measure of length, containing one-twelfth part of a foot; originally supposed equal to three barleycorns.

INCH OF CANDLE. A mode of sale at one time in use among merchants. A notice is first given upon the exchange, or other public place, as to the time of sale. The goods to be sold are divided into lots, printed papers of which, and the conditions of sale, are published. When the sale takes place, a small piece of candle, about an inch long, is kept burning, and the last bidder, when the candle goes out, is entitled to the lot or parcel for which he bids. Wharton.

INCHARTARE. To give, or grant, and assure anything by a written instrument.

INCHOATE. Imperfect; unfinished; begun, but not completed; as a contract not executed by all the parties.

INCHOATE DOWER. A wife's interest in the lands of her husband during his life, which may become a right of dower upon his death.

INCIDENT. This word, used as a noun, denotes anything which inseparably belongs to, or is connected with, or inherent in, another thing, called the "principal." In this sense a court-baron is incident to a manor. Also, less strictly, it denotes anything which is usually connected with another, or connected for some purposes, though not inseparably. Thus, the right of alienation is incident to an estate in fee-simple, though separable in equity.

INCIDERE. Lat. In the civil and old English law. To fall into. Calvin.

To fall out; to happen; to come to pass. Calvin.

To fall upon or under; to become subject or liable to. *Incidere in legem,* to incur the penalty of a law. Brissonius.

INCILE. Lat. In the civil law. A trench. A place sunk by the side of a stream, so called because it is *cut (incidatur)* into or through the stone or earth. Dig. 43, 21, 1, 5. The term seems to have included ditches (*fossæ*) and wells, (*putei.*)

INCIPITUR. Lat. It is begun; it begins. In old practice, when the pleadings in an action at law, instead of being recited at large on the issue-roll, were set out merely by their commencements, this was described as entering the *incipitur; i. e.,* the beginning.

INCISED WOUND. In medical jurisprudence. A cut or incision on a human body; a wound made by a cutting instrument, such as a razor. Burrill, Circ. Ev. 693; Whart. & S. Med. Jur. § 808.

INCIVILE. Irregular; improper; out of the due course of law.

Incivile est, nisi tota lege perspecta, una aliqua particula ejus proposita, judicare, vel respondere. It is improper, without looking at the whole of a law, to give judgment or advice, upon a view of any one clause of it. Dig. 1, 3, 24.

Incivile est, nisi tota sententia inspecta, de aliqua parte judicare. It is irregular, or legally improper, to pass an opinion upon any part of a sentence, without examining the whole. Hob. 171*a*.

INCIVISM. Unfriendliness to the state or government of which one is a citizen.

INCLAUSA. In old records. A home close or inclosure near the house. **Paroch.** Antiq. 31; Cowell.

INCLOSE. To shut up. "To inclose a jury," in Scotch practice, is to shut them up in a room by themselves. Bell.

INCLOSED LANDS. Lands which are actually inclosed and surrounded with fences. 7 Mees. & W. 441.

INCLOSURE. In English law. Inclosure is the act of freeing land from rights of common, commonable rights, and generally all rights which obstruct cultivation and the productive employment of labor on the soil.

Also, an artificial fence around one's estate. 39 Vt. 34, 326; 36 Wis. 42. See CLOSE.

Inclusio unius est exclusio alterius. The inclusion of one is the exclusion of another. The certain designation of one person is an absolute exclusion of all others. 11 Coke, 58*b.*

INCLUSIVE. Embraced; comprehended; comprehending the stated limits or extremes. Opposed to "exclusive."

INCOLA. Lat. In the civil law. An inhabitant; a dweller or resident. Properly, one who has transferred his domicile to any country.

Incolas domicilium facit. Residence creates domicile. 1 Johns. Cas. 363, 366.

INCOME. The return in money from one's business, labor, or capital invested; gains, profit, or private revenue.

"Income" means that which comes in or is received from any business or investment of capital, without reference to the outgoing expenditures; while "profits" generally means the gain which is made upon any business or investment when both receipts and payments are taken into account. "Income," when applied to the affairs of individuals, expresses the same idea that "revenue" does when applied to the affairs of a state or nation. 4 Hill, 20; 7 Hill, 504.

INCOME TAX. A tax on the yearly profits arising from property, professions, trades, and offices. 2 Steph. Comm. 573.

Incommodum non solvit argumentum. An inconvenience does not destroy an argument.

INCOMMUNICATION. In Spanish law. The condition of a prisoner who is not permitted to see or to speak with any person visiting him during his confinement. A person accused cannot be subjected to this treatment unless it be expressly ordered by the judge, for some grave offense, and it cannot be continued for a longer period than is absolutely necessary. This precaution is resorted to for the purpose of preventing the accused from knowing beforehand the testimony of the witnesses, or from attempting to corrupt them and concert such measures as will efface the traces of his guilt. As soon, therefore, as the danger of his doing so has ceased, the interdiction ceases likewise. Escriche.

INCOMPATIBLE. Two or more relations, offices, functions, or rights which cannot naturally, or may not legally, exist in or be exercised by the same person at the same time, are said to be incompatible. Thus, the relations of lessor and lessee of the same land, in one person at the same time, are incompatible. So of trustee and beneficiary of the same property.

INCOMPETENCY. Lack of ability, legal qualification, or fitness to discharge the required duty.

As applied to evidence, the word "incompetent" means not proper to be received; inadmissible, as distinguished from that which the court should admit for the consideration of the jury, though they may not find it worthy of credence.

In French law. Inability or insufficiency of a judge to try a cause brought before him, proceeding from lack of jurisdiction.

INCONCLUSIVE. That which may be disproved or rebutted; not shutting out further proof or consideration. Applied to evidence and presumptions.

INCONSULTO. In the civil law. Unadvisedly; unintentionally. Dig. 28, 4, 1.

INCONTINENCE. Want of chastity; indulgence in unlawful carnal connection.

INCOPOLITUS. A proctor or vicar.

Incorporalia bello non adquiruntur. Incorporeal things are not acquired by war. 6 Maule & S. 104.

INCORPORAMUS. We incorporate. One of the words by which a corporation may be created in England. 1 Bl. Comm. 473; 3 Steph. Comm. 173.

INCORPORATE. 1. To create a corporation; to confer a corporate franchise upon determinate persons.

2. To declare that another document shall be taken as part of the document in which the declaration is made as much as if it were set out at length therein.

INCORPORATION. 1. The act or process of forming or creating a corporation; the formation of a legal or political body, with the quality of perpetual existence and succession, unless limited by the act of incorporation.

2. The method of making one document of any kind become a part of another separate document by referring to the former in the latter, and declaring that the former shall be taken and considered as a part of the latter the same as if it were fully set out therein. This is more fully described as "incorporation by reference." If the one document is copied at length in the other, it is called "actual incorporation."

3. In the civil law. The union of one domain to another.

INCORPOREAL. Without body; not of material nature; the opposite of "corporeal," (*q. v.*)

INCORPOREAL CHATTELS. A class of incorporeal rights growing out of or incident to things *personal;* such as patent-rights and copyrights. 2 Steph. Comm. 72.

INCORPOREAL HEREDITAMENT. Anything, the subject of property, which is inheritable and not tangible or visible. 2 Woodd. Lect. 4. A right issuing out of a thing corporate (whether real or personal) or concerning or annexed to or exercisable within the same. 2 Bl. Comm. 20; 1 Washb. Real Prop. 10.

INCORPOREAL PROPERTY. In the civil law. That which consists in legal right merely. The same as choses in action at common law.

INCORRIGIBLE ROGUE. A species of rogue or offender, described in the statutes 5 Geo. IV. c. 83, and 1 & 2 Vict. c. 38. 4 Steph. Comm. 309.

INCREASE. (1) The produce of land; (2) the offspring of animals.

INCREASE, AFFIDAVIT OF. Affidavit of payment of increased costs, produced on taxation.

INCREASE, COSTS OF. In English law. It was formerly a practice with the jury to award to the successful party in an action the nominal sum of 40s. only for his costs; and the court assessed by their own officer the actual amount of the successful party's costs; and the amount so assessed, over and above the nominal sum awarded by the jury, was thence called "costs of increase." Lush, Com. Law Pr. 775. The practice has now wholly ceased. Rapal. & Law.

INCREMENTUM. Increase or improvement, opposed to *decrementum* or abatement.

INCROACHMENT. An unlawful gaining upon the right or possession of another. See ENCROACHMENT.

INCULPATE. To impute blame or guilt; to accuse; to involve in guilt or crime.

INCULPATORY. In the law of evidence. Going or tending to establish guilt; intended to establish guilt; criminative. Burrill, Circ. Ev. 251, 252.

INCUMBENT. A person who is in present possession of an office; one who is legally authorized to discharge the duties of an office. 11 Ohio, 50.

In ecclesiastical law, the term signifies a clergyman who is in possession of a benefice.

INCUMBER. To incumber land is to make it subject to a charge or liability; *e. g.*, by mortgaging it. Incumbrances include not only mortgages and other voluntary charges, but also liens, *lites pendentes*, registered judgments, and writs of execution, etc. Sweet.

INCUMBRANCE. Any right to, or interest in, land which may subsist in third persons, to the diminution of the value of the estate of the tenant, but consistently with the passing of the fee. 8 Neb. 8; 2 Greenl. Ev. § 242.

A claim, lien, or liability attached to property; as a mortgage, a registered judgment, etc.

INCUMBRANCER. The holder of an incumbrance, *e. g.*, a mortgage, on the estate of another.

INCUR. Men contract debts; they incur liabilities. In the one case, they act affirmatively; in the other, the liability is incurred or cast upon them by act or operation of law. "Incur" means something beyond contracts,—something not embraced in the word "debts." 15 How. Pr. 48; 5 Abb. Pr. 162.

INCURRAMENTUM. The liability to a fine, penalty, or amercement. Cowell.

INDE. Lat. Thence; thenceforth; thereof; thereupon; for that cause.

Inde datæ leges ne fortior omnia posset. Laws are made to prevent the stronger from having the power to do everything. Dav. Ir. K. B. 36.

INDEBITATUS. Lat. Indebted. *Nunquam indebitatus*, never indebted. The title of the plea substituted in England for *nil debet*.

INDEBITATUS ASSUMPSIT. Lat. Being indebted, he promised or undertook. This is the name of that form of the action of *assumpsit* in which the declaration alleges a debt or obligation to be due from the defendant, and then avers that, in consideration thereof, he promised to pay or discharge the same.

INDEBITI SOLUTIO. Lat. In the civil and Scotch law. A payment of what is not due. When made through ignorance or by mistake, the amount paid might be recovered back by an action termed "*condictio indebiti.*" (Dig. 12, 6.) Bell.

INDEBITUM. In the civil law. Not due or owing. (Dig. 12, 6.) Calvin.

INDEBTEDNESS. The state of being in debt, without regard to the ability or inability of the party to pay the same. See 1 Story, Eq. Jur. 343; 2 Hill, Abr. 421.

The word implies an absolute or complete liability. A contingent liability, such as that of a surety before the principal has made default, does not constitute indebtedness. On the other hand, the money need not be immediately payable. Obligations yet to become due constitute indebtedness, as well as those already due. 9 Mo. 149.

INDECENCY. An act against good behavior and a just delicacy. 2 Serg. & R. 91.

This is scarcely a technical term of the law, and is not susceptible of exact definition or description in its juridical uses. The question whether or not a given act, publication, etc., is indecent is for the court and jury in the particular case.

INDECENT EXPOSURE. Exposure to sight of the private parts of the body in a lewd or indecent manner in a public place. It is an indictable offense at common law, and by statute in many of the states.

INDECIMABLE. In old English law. That which is not titheable, or liable to pay tithe. 2 Inst. 490.

INDEFEASIBLE. That which cannot be defeated, revoked, or made void. This term is usually applied to an estate or right which cannot be defeated.

INDEFENSUS. In old English practice. Undefended; undenied by pleading.

A defendant who makes no defense or plea. Blount.

INDEFINITE FAILURE OF ISSUE. A failure of issue not merely at the death of the party whose issue are referred to, but at any subsequent period, however remote. 1 Steph. Comm. 562. A failure of issue whenever it shall happen, sooner or later, without any fixed, certain, or definite period within which it must happen. 4 Kent, Comm. 274.

INDEFINITE NUMBER. An uncertain or indeterminate number. A number which may be increased or diminished at pleasure.

INDEFINITE PAYMENT. In Scotch law. Payment without specification. Indefinite payment is where a debtor, owing several debts to one creditor, makes a payment to the creditor, without specifying to which of the debts he means the payment to be applied. See Bell.

Indefinitum æquipollet universali. The undefined is equivalent to the whole. 1 Vent. 368.

Indefinitum supplet locum universalis. The undefined or general supplies the place of the whole. Branch, Princ.

INDEMNIFICATUS. Lat. Indemnified. See INDEMNIFY.

INDEMNIFY. To save harmless; to secure against loss or damage; to give security for the reimbursement of a person in case of an anticipated loss falling upon him.

Also to make good; to compensate; to make reimbursement to one of a loss already incurred by him.

INDEMNIS. Lat. Without hurt, harm, or damage; harmless.

INDEMNITEE. The person who, in a contract of indemnity, is to be indemnified or protected by the other.

INDEMNITOR. The person who is bound, by an indemnity contract, to indemnify or protect the other.

INDEMNITY. An indemnity is a collateral contract or assurance, by which one person engages to secure another against an anticipated loss, or to prevent him from being damnified by the legal consequences of an act or forbearance on the part of one of the parties or of some third person. See Civil Code Cal. § 2772. Thus, insurance is a contract of indemnity. So an indemnifying bond is given to a sheriff who fears to proceed under an execution where the property is claimed by a stranger.

The term is also used to denote a compensation given to make the person whole from a loss already sustained; as where the government gives indemnity for private property taken by it for public use.

A legislative act, assuring a general dispensation from punishment or exemption from prosecution to persons involved in offenses, omissions of official duty, or acts in excess of authority, is called an indemnity; strictly it is an act of indemnity.

INDEMNITY CONTRACT. An agreement between two parties, whereby the one party, the indemnitor, either agrees to indemnify and save harmless the other party, the indemnitee, from loss or damage, or binds himself to do some particular act or thing, or to protect the indemnitee against liability to, or the claim of, a third party. 10 Amer. & Eng. Enc. Law, 402.

INDEMPNIS. The old form of writing indemnis. Townsh. Pl. 19. So, indempnificatus for indemnificatus.

INDENIZATION. The act of making a denizen, or of naturalizing.

INDENT, n. In American law. A certificate or indented certificate issued by the government of the United States at the close of the Revolution, for the principal or interest of the public debt. Webster.

INDENT, v. To cut in a serrated or waving line. In old conveyancing, if a deed was made by more parties than one, it was usual to make as many copies of it as there were parties, and each was cut or indented (either in acute angles, like the teeth of a saw, or in a waving line) at the top or side, to tally or correspond with the others, and the deed so made was called an "indenture." Anciently, both parts were written on the same piece of parchment, with some word or letters written between them through which the parchment was cut, but afterwards, the word or letters being omitted, indenting came into use, the idea of which was that the genuineness of each part might be proved by its fitting into the angles cut in the other. But at length even this was discontinued, and at present the term serves only to give name to the species of deed executed by two or more parties, as opposed to a deed-poll, (*q. v.*) 2 Bl. Comm. 295.

To bind by indentures; to apprentice; as to indent a young man to a shoe-maker. Webster.

INDENTURE. A deed to which two or more persons are parties, and in which these enter into reciprocal and corresponding grants or obligations towards each other: whereas a deed-poll is properly one in which only the party making it executes it, or binds himself by it as a deed, though the grantors or grantees therein may be several in number. 3 Washb. Real Prop. 311. See IN-DENT, *v.*

INDENTURE OF APPRENTICE-SHIP. A contract in two parts, by which a person, generally a minor, is bound to serve another in his trade, art, or occupation for a stated time, on condition of being instructed in the same.

INDEPENDENCE. The state or condition of being free from dependence, subjection, or control. Political independence is the attribute of a nation or state which is entirely autonomous, and not subject to the government, control, or dictation of any exterior power.

INDEPENDENT CONTRACT. One in which the mutual acts or promises have no relation to each other, either as equivalents or considerations. Civil Code La. art. 1769; 1 Bouv. Inst. no. 699.

INDEPENDENT COVENANTS. Covenants in an instrument which are independent of each other, or where the performance of one, or the right to require its performance, or to obtain damages for its nonperformance, does not depend upon the performance of the other.

Independenter se habet assecuratio a viaggio navis. The voyage insured is an independent or distinct thing from the voyage of the ship. 3 Kent, Comm. 318, note.

INDETERMINATE. That which is uncertain, or not particularly designated; as if I sell you one hundred bushels of wheat, without stating what wheat. 1 Bouv. Inst. no. 950.

INDEX. A book containing references, alphabetically arranged, to the contents of a series or collection of volumes; or an addition to a single volume or set of volumes containing such references to its contents.

Index animi sermo. Language is the exponent of the intention. The language of a statute or instrument is the best guide to the intention. Broom, Max. 622.

INDIAN COUNTRY. This term does not necessarily import territory owned and occupied by Indians, but it means all those portions of the United States designated by this name in the legislation of congress. 4 Sawy. 121.

INDIAN TRIBE. A separate and distinct community or body of the aboriginal Indian race of men found in the United States.

INDIANS. The aboriginal inhabitants of North America.

INDICARE. In the civil law. To show or discover. To fix or tell the price of a thing. Calvin. To inform against; to accuse.

INDICATIF. An abolished writ by which a prosecution was in some cases removed from a court-christian to the queen's bench. Enc. Lond.

INDICATION. In the law of evidence. A sign or token; a fact pointing to some inference or conclusion. Burrill, Circ. Ev. 251, 252, 263, 275.

INDICATIVE EVIDENCE. This is not evidence properly so called, but the mere suggestion of evidence proper, which may possibly be procured if the suggestion is followed up. Brown.

INDICAVIT. In English practice. A writ of prohibition that lies for a patron of a church, whose clerk is sued in the spiritual court by the clerk of another patron, for tithes amounting to a fourth part of the value of the living. 3 Bl. Comm. 91; 3 Steph. Comm. 711. So termed from the emphatic word of the Latin form. Reg. Orig. 35*b*, 36.

INDICIA. Signs; indications. Circumstances which point to the existence of a given fact as probable, but not certain. For example, "*indicia* of partnership" are any circumstances which would induce the belief that a given person was in reality, though not ostensibly, a member of a given firm.

INDICIUM. In the civil law. A sign or mark. A species of proof, answering very nearly to the *circumstantial evidence* of the common law. Best, Pres. p. 13, § 11, note; Wills, Circ. Ev. 34.

INDICT. See INDICTMENT.

J

K

L

M

INDICTABLE. Proper or necessary to be prosecuted by process of indictment.

INDICTED. Charged in an indictment with a criminal offense. See INDICTMENT.

INDICTEE. A person indicted.

INDICTIO. In old public law. A declaration; a proclamation. *Indictio belli*, a declaration or indiction of war. An indictment.

INDICTION, CYCLE OF. A mode of computing time by the space of fifteen years, instituted by Constantine the Great; originally the period for the payment of certain taxes. Some of the charters of King Edgar and Henry III. are dated by indictions. Wharton.

INDICTMENT. An indictment is an accusation in writing found and presented by a grand jury, legally convoked and sworn, to the court in which it is impaneled, charging that a person therein named has done some act, or been guilty of some omission, which, by law, is a public offense, punishable on indictment. Code Iowa 1880, § 4295; Pen. Code Cal. § 917; Code Ala. 1886, § 4364.

A presentment differs from an indictment in that it is an accusation made by a grand jury of their own motion, either upon their own observation and knowledge, or upon evidence before them; while an indictment is preferred at the suit of the government, and is usually framed in the first instance by the prosecuting officer of the government, and by him laid before the grand jury, to be found or ignored. An information resembles in its form and substance an indictment, but is filed at the mere discretion of the proper law officer of the government, without the intervention or approval of a grand jury. 2 Story, Const. §§ 1784, 1786.

In Scotch law. An indictment is the form of process by which a criminal is brought to trial at the instance of the lord advocate. Where a private party is a principal prosecutor, he brings his charge in what is termed the "form of criminal letters."

Indictment de felony est contra pacem domini regis, coronam et dignitatem suam, in genere et non in individuo; quia in Angliâ non est interregnum. Jenk. Cent. 205. Indictment for felony is against the peace of our lord the king, his crown and dignity in general, and not against his individual person; because in England there is no interregnum.

INDICTOR. He who causes another to be indicted. The latter is sometimes called the "indictee."

INDIFFERENT. Impartial; unbiased; disinterested.

INDIGENA. In old English law. A subject born; one born within the realm, or naturalized by act of parliament. Co. Litt. 8a. The opposite of "*alienigena*," (*q. v.*)

INDIRECT EVIDENCE. Evidence which does not tend directly to prove the controverted fact, but to establish a state of facts, or the existence of other facts, from which it will follow as a logical inference.

Inferential evidence as to the truth of a disputed fact, not by testimony of any witness to the fact, but by collateral circumstances ascertained by competent means. 1 Starkie, Ev. 15.

INDISTANTER. Forthwith; without delay.

INDITEE. L. Fr. In old English law. A person indicted. Mirr. c. 1, § 3; 9 Coke, pref.

INDIVIDUUM. Lat. In the civil law. That cannot be divided. Calvin.

INDIVISIBLE. Not susceptible of division or apportionment; inseparable; entire. Thus, a contract, covenant, consideration, etc., may be divisible or indivisible; *i. e.*, separable or entire.

INDIVISUM. That which two or more persons hold in common without partition; undivided.

INDORSAT. In old Scotch law. Indorsed. 2 Pitc. Crim. Tr. 41.

INDORSE. To write a name on the back of a paper or document. Bills of exchange and promissory notes are indorsed by a party's writing his name on the back. 7 Pick. 117.

"Indorse" is a technical term, having sufficient legal certainty without words of more particular description. 7 Vt. 351.

INDORSEE. The person to whom a bill of exchange, promissory note, bill of lading, etc., is assigned by indorsement, giving him a right to sue thereon.

INDORSEE IN DUE COURSE. An indorsee in due course is one who, in good faith, in the ordinary course of business, and for value, before its apparent maturity or presumptive dishonor, and without knowledge of its actual dishonor, acquires a negotiable instrument duly indorsed to him, or indorsed generally, or payable to the bearer. Civil Code Cal. § 3123.

INDORSEMENT. The act of a payee, drawee, accommodation indorser, or holder of a bill, note, check, or other negotiable instrument, in writing his name upon the back of the same, with or without further or qualifying words, whereby the property in the same is assigned and transferred to another.

That which is so written upon the back of a negotiable instrument.

One who writes his name upon a negotiable instrument, otherwise than as a maker or acceptor, and delivers it, with his name thereon, to another person, is called an "indorser," and his act is called "indorsement." Civil Code Cal. § 3108; Civil Code Dak. § 1836.

An indorsement in full is one in which mention is made of the name of the indorsee. Chit. Bills, 170.

A blank indorsement is one which does not mention the name of the indorsee, and consists, generally, simply of the name of the indorser written on the back of the instrument. 1 Daniel, Neg. Inst. § 693.

A conditional indorsement is one by which the indorser annexes some condition (other than the failure of prior parties to pay) to his liability. The condition may be either precedent or subsequent. 1 Daniel, Neg. Inst. § 697.

A restrictive indorsement is one which is so worded as to restrict the further negotiability of the instrument.

A qualified indorsement is one which restrains or limits or qualifies or enlarges the liability of the indorser, in any manner different from what the law generally imports as his true liability, deducible from the nature of the instrument. Chit. Bills, (8th Ed.) 261; 7 Taunt. 160.

In criminal law. An entry made upon the back of a writ or warrant.

INDORSER. He who indorses; *i. e.*, being the payee or holder, writes his name on the back of a bill of exchange, etc.

INDUCEMENT. In contracts. The benefit or advantage which the promisor is to receive from a contract is the inducement for making it.

In criminal evidence. Motive; that which leads or tempts to the commission of crime. Burrill, Circ. Ev. 283.

In pleading. That portion of a declaration or of any subsequent pleading in an action which is brought forward by way of explanatory introduction to the main allegations. Brown.

INDUCIÆ. In international law. A truce; a suspension of hostilities; an agreement during war to abstain for a time from warlike acts.

In old maritime law. A period of twenty days after the safe arrival of a vessel under bottomry, to dispose of the cargo, and raise the money to pay the creditor, with interest.

In old English practice. Delay or indulgence allowed a party to an action; further time to appear in a cause. Bract. fol. 352*b*; Fleta, lib. 4, c. 5, § 8.

In Scotch practice. Time allowed for the performance of an act. Time to appear to a citation. Time to collect evidence or prepare a defense.

INDUCIÆ LEGALES. In Scotch law. The days between the citation of the defendant and the day of appearance; the days between the test day and day of return of the writ.

INDUCTIO. In the civil law. Obliteration, by drawing the pen or *stylus* over the writing. Dig. 28, 4; Calvin.

INDUCTION. In ecclesiastical law. Induction is the ceremony by which an incumbent who has been instituted to a benefice is vested with full possession of all the profits belonging to the church, so that he becomes seised of the temporalities of the church, and is then complete incumbent. It is performed by virtue of a mandate of induction directed by the bishop to the archdeacon, who either performs it in person, or directs his precept to one or more other clergymen to do it. Phillim. Ecc. Law, 477.

INDULGENCE. In the Roman Catholic Church. A remission of the punishment due to sins, granted by the pope or church, and supposed to save the sinner from purgatory. Its abuse led to the Reformation in Germany. Wharton. Forbearance, (*q. v.*)

INDULTO. In ecclesiastical law. A dispensation granted by the pope to do or obtain something contrary to the common law.

In Spanish law. The condonation or remission of the punishment imposed on a criminal for his offense. This power is exclusively vested in the king.

INDUMENT. Endowment, (*q. v.*)

INDUSTRIAL AND PROVIDENT SOCIETIES. Societies formed in England for carrying on any labor, trade, or handicraft, whether wholesale or retail, in-

J

K

L

M

cluding the buying and selling of land and also (but subject to certain restrictions) the business of banking.

INDUSTRIAL SCHOOLS. Schools (established by voluntary contribution) in which industrial training is provided, and in which children are lodged, clothed, and fed, as well as taught.

INDUSTRIAM, PER. Lat. A qualified property in animals *feræ naturæ* may be acquired *per industriam*, i. e., by a man's reclaiming and making them tame by art, industry, and education; or by so confining them within his own immediate power that they cannot escape and use their natural liberty. 2 Steph. Comm. 5.

INEBRIATE. A person addicted to the use of intoxicating liquors; an habitual drunkard.

Any person who habitually, whether continuously or periodically, indulges in the use of intoxicating liquors to such an extent as to stupefy his mind, and to render him incompetent to transact ordinary business with safety to his estate, shall be deemed an inebriate, within the meaning of this chapter: provided, the habit of so indulging in such use shall have been at the time of inquisition of at least one year's standing. Code N. C. 1883, § 1671.

INELIGIBILITY. Disqualification or legal incapacity to be elected to an office. Thus, an alien or naturalized citizen is ineligible to be elected president of the United States.

INELIGIBLE. Disqualified to be elected to an office; also disqualified to hold an office if elected or appointed to it. 28 Wis. 99.

Inesse potest donationi, modus, conditio sive causa; ut modus est: si conditio; quia causa. In a gift there may be manner, condition, and cause; as [*ut*] introduces a manner; if, [*si*,] a condition; because, [*quia*,] a cause. Dyer, 138.

INEST DE JURE. Lat. It is implied of right; it is implied by law.

INEVITABLE. Incapable of being avoided; fortuitous; transcending the power of human care, foresight, or exertion to avoid or prevent, and therefore suspending legal relations so far as to excuse from the performance of contract obligations, or from liability for consequent loss.

INEVITABLE ACCIDENT. An inevitable accident is one produced by an irresistible physical cause; an accident which

cannot be prevented by human skill or foresight, but results from natural causes, such as lightning or storms, perils of the sea, inundations or earthquakes, or sudden death or illness. By irresistible force is meant an interposition of human agency, from its nature and power absolutely uncontrollable. 11 La. Ann. 427. As used in the civil law, this term is nearly synonymous with "fortuitous event."

Inevitable accident is where a vessel is pursuing a lawful avocation in a lawful manner, using the proper precautions against danger, and an accident occurs. The highest degree of caution that can be used is not required. It is enough that it is reasonable under the circumstances; such as is usual in similar cases, and has been found by long experience to be sufficient to answer the end in view,—the safety of life and property. 7 Wall. 196.

Inevitable accident is only when the disaster happens from natural causes, without negligence or fault on either side, and when both parties have endeavored, by every means in their power, with due care and caution, and with a proper display of nautical skill, to prevent the occurrence of the accident. 12 Ct. Cl. 491.

INEWARDUS. A guard; a watchman. Domesday.

INFALISTATUS. In old English law. Exposed upon the sands, or sea-shore. A species of punishment mentioned in Hengham. Cowell.

INFAMIA. Lat. Infamy; ignominy or disgrace.

By *infamia juris* is meant infamy established by law as the consequence of crime; *infamia facti* is where the party is supposed to be guilty of such crime, but it has not been judicially proved. 17 Mass. 515, 541.

INFAMIS. Lat. In Roman law. A person whose right of reputation was diminished (involving the loss of some of the rights of citizenship) either on account of his infamous avocation or because of conviction for crime. Mackeld. Rom. Law, § 135.

INFAMOUS CRIME. A crime which entails infamy upon one who has committed it. See INFAMY.

The term "infamous"—i. e., without fame or good report—was applied at common law to certain crimes, upon the conviction of which a person became incompetent to testify as a witness, upon the theory that a person would not commit so heinous a crime unless he was so depraved as to be unworthy of credit. These crimes are treason, felony, and the *crimen falsi*. Abbott.

A crime punishable by imprisonment in the state prison or penitentiary, with or without hard labor, is an infamous crime, within the provision of the fifth amendment of the constitution that "no person shall be held to answer for a capital or otherwise infamous crime unless on a presentment or indictment of a grand jury." 117 U. S. 348, 6 Sup. Ct. Rep. 777.

"Infamous," as used in the fifth amendment to the United States constitution, in reference to crimes, includes those only of the class called "*crimen falsi*," which both involve the charge of falsehood, and may also injuriously affect the public administration of justice by introducing falsehood and fraud. 15 N. B. R. 325.

By the Revised Statutes of New York the term "infamous crime," when used in any statute, is directed to be construed as including every offense punishable with death or by imprisonment in a state-prison, and no other. 2 Rev. St. (p. 702, § 31,) p. 587, § 32.

INFAMY. A qualification of a man's legal *status* produced by his conviction of an infamous crime and the consequent loss of honor and credit, which, at common law, rendered him incompetent as a witness, and by statute in some jurisdictions entails other disabilities.

INFANCY. Minority; the state of a person who is under the age of legal majority,—at common law, twenty-one years. According to the sense in which this term is used, it may denote the condition of the person merely with reference to his years, or the contractual disabilities which non-age entails, or his *status* with regard to other powers or relations.

INFANGENTHEF. In old English law. A privilege of lords of certain manors to judge any thief taken within their fee.

INFANS. In the civil law. A child under the age of seven years; so called "*quasi impos fandi*," (as not having the faculty of speech.) Cod. Theodos. 8, 18, 8.

Infans non multum a furioso distat. An infant does not differ much from a lunatic. Bract. l. 3, c. 2, § 8; Dig. 50, 17, 5, 40; 1 Story, Eq. Jur. §§ 223, 224, 242.

INFANT. A person within age, not of age, or not of full age; a person under the age of twenty-one years; a minor. Co. Litt. 171b; 1 Bl. Comm. 463–466; 2 Kent, Comm. 233.

INFANTIA. In the civil law. The period of infancy between birth and the age of seven years. Calvin.

INFANTICIDE. The murder or killing of an infant soon after its birth. The fact of the birth distinguishes this act from "fœticide" or "procuring abortion," which terms denote the destruction of the *fœtus* in the womb.

INFANTS' MARRIAGE ACT. The statute 18 & 19 Vict. c. 43. By virtue of this act every infant, (if a male, of twenty, or, if a female, of seventeen, years,—section 4,) upon or in contemplation of marriage, may, with the sanction of the chancery division of the high court, make a valid settlement or contract for a settlement of property. Wharton.

INFANZON. In Spanish law. A person of noble birth, who exercises within his domains and inheritance no other rights and privileges than those conceded to him. Escriche.

INFEFT. In Scotch law. To give seisin or possession of lands; to invest or enfeoff. 1 Kames, Eq. 215.

INFEFTMENT. In old Scotch law. Investiture or infeudation, including both charter and seisin. 1 Forb. Inst. pt. 2, p. 110.

In later law. *Saisine,* or the instrument of possession. Bell.

INFENSARE CURIAM. An expression applied to a court when it suggested to an advocate something which he had omitted through mistake or ignorance. Spelman.

INFEOFFMENT. The act or instrument of feoffment. In Scotland it is synonymous with "*saisine*," meaning the instrument of possession. Formerly it was synonymous with "investiture." Bell.

INFERENCE. In the law of evidence. A truth or proposition drawn from another which is supposed or admitted to be true. A process of reasoning by which a fact or proposition sought to be established is deduced as a logical consequence from other facts, or a state of facts, already proved or admitted.

An inference is a deduction which the reason of the jury makes from the facts proved, without an express direction of law to that effect. Code Civil Proc. Cal. § 1958.

INFERENTIAL. In the law of evidence. Operating in the way of inference; argumentative. Presumptive evidence is sometimes termed "inferential." 4 Pa. St. 272.

INFERIOR. One who, in relation to another, has less power and is below him; one who is bound to obey another. He who makes the law is the superior; he who is

J

K

L

M

bound to obey it, the inferior. 1 Bouv. Inst. no. 8.

INFERIOR COURT. This term may denote any court subordinate to the chief appellate tribunal in the particular judicial system; but it is commonly used as the designation of a court of special, limited, or statutory jurisdiction, whose record must show the existence and attaching of jurisdiction in any given case, in order to give presumptive validity to its judgment. See Cooley, Const. Lim. 508.

The English courts of judicature are classed generally under two heads,—the superior courts and the inferior courts; the former division comprising the courts at Westminster, the latter comprising all the other courts in general, many of which, however, are far from being of inferior importance in the common acceptation of the word. Brown.

INFEUDATION. The placing in possession of a freehold estate; also the granting of tithes to laymen.

INFICIARI. Lat. In the civil law. To deny; to deny one's liability; to refuse to pay a debt or restore a pledge; to deny the allegation of a plaintiff; to deny the charge of an accuser. Calvin.

INFICIATIO. Lat. In the civil law. Denial; the denial of a debt or liability; the denial of the claim or allegation of a party plaintiff. Calvin.

INFIDEL. One who does not believe in the existence of a God who will reward or punish in this world or that which is to come. Willes, 550. One who professes no religion that can bind his conscience to speak the truth. 1 Greenl. Ev. § 368.

INFIDELIS. In old English law. An infidel or heathen.

In feudal law. One who violated fealty.

INFIDELITAS. In feudal law. Infidelity; faithlessness to one's feudal oath. Spelman.

INFIDUCIARE. In old European law. To pledge property. Spelman.

INFIHT. Sax. An assault made on a person inhabiting the same dwelling.

Infinitum in jure reprobatur. That which is endless is reprobated in law. 12 Coke, 24. Applied to litigation.

INFIRM. Weak, feeble. The testimony of an "infirm" witness may be taken *de bene esse* in some circumstances. See 1 P. Wms. 117.

INFIRMATIVE. In the law of evidence. Having the quality of diminishing force; having a tendency to weaken or render infirm. 3 Benth. Jud. Ev. 14; Best, Pres. § 217.

INFIRMATIVE CONSIDERATION. In the law of evidence. A consideration, supposition, or hypothesis of which the criminative facts of a case admit, and which tends to weaken the inference or presumption of guilt deducible from them. Burrill, Circ. Ev. 153–155.

INFIRMATIVE FACT. In the law of evidence. A fact set up, proved, or even supposed, in opposition to the criminative facts of a case, the tendency of which is to weaken the force of the inference of guilt deducible from them. 3 Benth. Jud. Ev. 14; Best, Pres. § 217, et seq.

INFIRMATIVE HYPOTHESIS. A term sometimes used in criminal evidence to denote an hypothesis or theory of the case which assumes the defendant's innocence, and explains the criminative evidence in a manner consistent with that assumption.

INFORMAL. Deficient in legal form; inartificially drawn up.

INFORMALITY. Want of legal form.

INFORMATION. In practice. An accusation exhibited against a person for some criminal offense, without an indictment. 4 Bl. Comm. 308.

An accusation in the nature of an indictment, from which it differs only in being presented by a competent public officer on his oath of office, instead of a grand jury on their oath. 1 Bish. Crim. Proc. § 141.

The word is also frequently used in the law in its sense of communicated knowledge, and affidavits are frequently made, and pleadings and other documents verified, on "information and belief."

In French law. The act or instrument which contains the depositions of witnesses against the accused. Poth. Proc. Civil, § 2, art. 5.

INFORMATION IN THE NATURE OF A QUO WARRANTO. A proceeding against the usurper of a franchise or office. See Quo Warranto.

INFORMATION OF INTRUSION. A proceeding instituted by the state prosecuting officer against intruders upon the public domain. See Gen. St. Mass. c. 141; 3 Pick. 224; 6 Leigh, 588.

INFORMATUS NON SUM. In practice. I am not informed. A formal answer made by the defendant's attorney in court to the effect that he has not been advised of any defense to be made to the action. Thereupon judgment by default passes.

INFORMER. A person who informs or prefers an accusation against another, whom he suspects of the violation of some penal statute.

A common informer is a person who sues for a penalty which is given to any person who will sue for it, as opposed to a penalty which is only given to a person specially aggrieved by the act complained of. 3 Bl. Comm. 161.

INFORTIATUM. The name given by the glossators to the second of the three parts or volumes into which the Pandects were divided. The glossators at Bologna had at first only two parts, the first called "*Digestum Vetus*," (the Old Digest,) and the last called "*Digestum Novum*," (the New Digest.) When they afterwards received the middle or second part, they separated from the *Digestum Novum* the beginning it had then, and added it to the second part, from which *enlargement* the latter received the name "*Infortiatum*." Mackeld. Rom. Law, § 110.

INFORTUNIUM, HOMICIDE PER. Where a man doing a lawful act, without intention of hurt, unfortunately kills another.

INFRA. Lat. Below; underneath; within. This word occurring by itself in a book refers the reader to a subsequent part of the book, like "*post.*" It is the opposite of "*ante*" and "*supra*," (*q. v.*)

INFRA ÆTATEM. Under age; not of age. Applied to minors.

INFRA ANNOS NUBILES. Under marriageable years; not yet of marriageable age.

INFRA ANNUM. Under or within a year. Bract. fol. 7.

INFRA ANNUM LUCTÛS. (Within the year of mourning.) The phrase is used in reference to the marriage of a widow within a year after her husband's death, which was prohibited by the civil law.

INFRA BRACHIA. Within her arms. Used of a husband *de jure*, as well as *de facto*. 2 Inst. 317. Also *inter brachia*. Bract. fol. 148*b*. It was in this sense that a woman could only have an appeal for murder of her husband *inter brachia sua*.

INFRA CIVITATEM. Within the state. 1 Camp. 23, 24.

INFRA CORPUS COMITATUS. Within the body (territorial limits) of a county. In English law, waters which are *infra corpus comitatus* are exempt from the jurisdiction of the admiralty.

INFRA DIGNITATEM CURIÆ. Beneath the dignity of the court; unworthy of the consideration of the court. Where a bill in equity is brought upon a matter too trifling to deserve the attention of the court, it is demurrable, as being *infra dignitatem curiæ*.

INFRA FUROREM. During madness; while in a state of insanity. Bract. fol. 19*b*.

INFRA HOSPITIUM. Within the inn. When a traveler's baggage comes *infra hospitium, i. e.*, in the care and under the custody of the innkeeper, the latter's liability attaches.

INFRA JURISDICTIONEM. Within the jurisdiction. 2 Strange, 827.

INFRA LIGEANTIAM REGIS. Within the king's ligeance. Comb. 212.

INFRA METAS. Within the bounds or limits. *Infra metas forestæ*, within the bounds of the forest. Fleta, lib. 2, c. 41, § 12. *Infra metas hospitii*, within the limits of the household; within the verge. Id. lib. 2, c. 2, § 2.

INFRA PRÆSIDIA. Within the protection; within the defenses. In international law, when a prize, or other captured property, is brought into a port of the captors, or within their lines, or otherwise under their complete custody, so that the chance of rescue is lost, it is said to be *infra præsidia*.

INFRA QUATUOR MARIA. Within the four seas; within the kingdom of England; within the jurisdiction.

INFRA QUATUOR PARIETES. Within four walls. 2 Crabb, Real Prop. p. 106, § 1089.

INFRA REGNUM. Within the realm.

INFRA SEX ANNOS. Within six years.

J

K

L

M

INFRA TRIDUUM. Within three days. Formal words in old appeals. Fleta, lib. 1, c. 31, § 6; Id. c. 35, § 3.

INFRACTION. A breach, violation, or infringement; as of a law, a contract, a right or duty.

In French law, this term is used as a general designation of all punishable actions.

INFRINGEMENT. A breaking into; a trespass or encroachment upon; a violation of a law, regulation, contract, or right. Used especially of invasions of the rights secured by patents, copyrights, and trademarks.

INFUGARE. To put to flight.

INFULA. A coif, or a cassock. Jacob.

INFUSION. In medical jurisprudence. The process of steeping in liquor; an operation by which the medicinal qualities of a substance may be extracted by a liquor without boiling. Also the product of this operation. "Infusion" and "decoction," though not identical, are *ejusdem generis* in law. 3 Camp. 74. See DECOCTION.

INGE. Meadow, or pasture. Jacob.

INGENIUM. (1) Artifice, trick, fraud; (2) an engine, machine, or device. Spelman.

INGENUITAS. Liberty given to a servant by manumission.

INGENUITAS REGNI. In old English law. The freemen, yeomanry, or commonalty of the kingdom. Cowell. Applied sometimes also to the barons.

INGENUUS. In Roman law. A person who, immediately that he was born, was a free person. He was opposed to *libertinus,* or *libertus,* who, having been born a slave, was afterwards manumitted or made free. It is not the same as the English law term "*generosus,*" which denoted a person not merely free, but of good family. There were no distinctions among *ingenui;* but among *libertini* there were (prior to Justinian's abolition of the distinctions) three varieties, namely: Those of the highest rank, called "*Cives Romani;*" those of the second rank, called "*Latini Juniani;*" and those of the lowest rank, called "*Dediticii.*" Brown.

INGRATITUDE. In Roman law, ingratitude was accounted a sufficient cause for revoking a gift or recalling the liberty of a freedman. Such is also the law of France,

with respect to the first case. But the English law has left the matter entirely to the moral sense.

INGRESS, EGRESS, AND REGRESS. These words express the right of a lessee to enter, go upon, and return from the lands in question.

INGRESSU. In English law. An ancient writ of entry, by which the plaintiff or complainant sought an entry into his lands. Abolished in 1833.

INGRESSUS. In old English law. Ingress; entry. The relief paid by an heir to the lord was sometimes so called. Cowell.

INGROSSATOR. An engrosser. *Ingrossator magni rotuli,* engrosser of the great roll; afterwards called "clerk of the pipe." Spelman; Cowell.

INGROSSING. The act of making a fair and perfect copy of any document from a rough draft of it, in order that it may be executed or put to its final purpose.

INHABITANT. One who resides actually and permanently in a given place, and has his domicile there.

"The words 'inhabitant,' 'citizen,' and 'resident,' as employed in different constitutions to define the qualifications of electors, mean substantially the same thing; and one is an inhabitant, resident, or citizen at the place where he has his domicile or home." Cooley, Const. Lim. *600. But the terms "resident" and "inhabitant" have also been held not synonymous, the latter implying a more fixed and permanent abode than the former, and importing privileges and duties to which a mere resident would not be subject. 40 Ill. 197.

INHABITED HOUSE DUTY. A tax assessed in England on inhabited dwelling-houses, according to their annual value, (St. 14 & 15 Vict. c. 36; 32 & 33 Vict. c. 14, § 11,) which is payable by the occupier, the landlord being deemed the occupier where the house is let to several persons, (St. 48 Geo. III. c. 55, Schedule B.) Houses occupied solely for business purposes are exempt from duty, although a care-taker may dwell therein, and houses partially occupied for business purposes are to that extent exempt. Sweet.

INHERENT POWER. An authority possessed without its being derived from another. A right, ability, or faculty of doing a thing, without receiving that right, ability, or faculty from another.

INHERETRIX. The old term for "heiress." Co. Litt. 13a.

INHERIT. To take by inheritance; to take as heir on the death of the ancestor. "To inherit *to*" a person is a common expression in the books. 3 Coke, 41; 2 Bl. Comm. 254, 255.

INHERITABLE BLOOD. Blood which has the purity (freedom from attainder) and legitimacy necessary to give its possessor the character of a lawful heir; that which is capable of being the medium for the transmission of an inheritance.

INHERITANCE. An estate in things real, descending to the heir. 2 Bl. Comm. 201.

Such an estate in lands or tenements or other things as may be inherited by the heir. Termes de la Ley.

An estate or property which a man has by descent, as heir to another, or which he may transmit to another, as his heir. Litt. § 9.

A perpetuity in lands or tenements to a man and his heirs. Cowell; Blount.

"Inheritance" is also used in the old books where "hereditament" is now commonly employed. Thus, Coke divides inheritances into corporeal and incorporeal, into real, personal, and mixed, and into entire and several.

In the civil law. The succession of the heir to all the rights and property of the estate-leaver. It is either testamentary, where the heir is created by will, or *ab intestato*, where it arises merely by operation of law. Heinec. § 484.

INHERITANCE ACT. The English statute of 3 & 4 Wm. IV. c. 106, by which the law of inheritance or descent has been considerably modified. 1 Steph. Comm. 359, 500.

INHIBITION. In ecclesiastical law. A writ issuing from a superior ecclesiastical court, forbidding an inferior judge to proceed further in a cause pending before him. In this sense it is closely analogous to the writ of *prohibition* at common law.

Also the command of a bishop or ecclesiastical judge that a clergyman shall cease from taking any duty.

In Scotch law. A species of diligence or process by which a debtor is prohibited from contracting any debt which may become a burden on his heritable property, in competition with the creditor at whose instance the inhibition is taken out; and from granting any deed of alienation, etc., to the prejudice of the creditor. Brande.

In the civil law. A prohibition which the law makes or a judge ordains to an individual. Hallifax, Civil Law, p. 126.

INHIBITION AGAINST A WIFE. In Scotch law. A writ in the sovereign's name, passing the signet, which prohibits all and sundry from having transactions with a wife or giving her credit. Bell; Ersk. Inst. 1, 6, 26.

INHOC. In old records. A nook or corner of a common or fallow field, inclosed and cultivated. Kennett, Par. Antiq. 297, 298; Cowell.

INHONESTUS. In old English law. Unseemly; not in due order. Fleta, lib. 1, c. 31, § 8.

Iniquissima pax est anteponenda justissimo bello. The most unjust peace is to be preferred to the justest war. 18 Wend. 257, 305.

INIQUITY. In Scotch practice. A technical expression applied to the decision of an inferior judge who has decided contrary to law; he is said to have committed iniquity. Bell.

Iniquum est alios permittere, alios inhibere mercaturam. It is inequitable to permit some to trade and to prohibit others. 3 Inst. 181.

Iniquum est aliquem rei sui esse judicem. It is wrong for a man to be a judge in his own cause. Branch, Princ.; 12 Coke, 113.

Iniquum est ingenuis hominibus non esse liberam rerum suarum alienationem. It is unjust that freemen should not have the free disposal of their own property. Co. Litt. 223a; Hob. 87; 4 Kent, Comm. 131.

INITIAL. That which *begins* or stands at the *beginning*. The first letter of a man's name.

INITIALIA TESTIMONII. In Scotch law. Preliminaries of testimony. The preliminary examination of a witness, before examining him in chief, answering to the *voir dire* of the English law, though taking a somewhat wider range. Wharton.

INITIATE. Commenced; inchoate. *Curtesy initiate* is the interest which a husband has in the wife's lands after a child is born who may inherit, but before the wife dies.

J

K

L

M

INITIATIVE. In French law. The name given to the important prerogative conferred by the *charte constitutionnelle*, article 16, on the late king to propose through his ministers projects of laws. 1 Toullier, no. 39.

INJUNCTION. A prohibitive writ issued by a court of equity, at the suit of a party complainant, directed to a party defendant in the action, or to a party made a defendant for that purpose, forbidding the latter to do some act, or to permit his servants or agents to do some act, which he is threatening or attempting to commit, or restraining him in the continuance thereof, such act being unjust and inequitable, injurious to the plaintiff, and not such as can be adequately redressed by an action at law.

An injunction is a writ or order requiring a person to refrain from a particular act. It may be granted by the court in which the action is brought, or by a judge thereof, and when made by a judge it may be enforced as an order of the court. Code Civil Proc. Cal. § 525.

Mandatory injunctions command defendant to do a particular thing. *Preventive*, command him to refrain from an act.

An injunction is called "preliminary" or "provisional," or an "injunction *pendente lite*," when it is granted at the outset of a suit brought for the purpose of restraining the defendant from doing the act threatened, until the suit has been heard and the rights of the parties determined. It is called "final" or "perpetual" when granted upon a hearing and adjudication of the rights in question, and as a measure of permanent relief.

INJURIA. Injury; wrong; the privation or violation of right. 3 Bl. Comm. 2.

INJURIA ABSQUE DAMNO. Injury or wrong without damage. A wrong done, but from which no loss or damage results, and which, therefore, will not sustain an action.

Injuria fit ei cui convicium dictum est, vel de eo factum carmen famosum. An injury is done to him of whom a reproachful thing is said, or concerning whom an infamous song is made. 9 Coke, 60.

Injuria illata judici, seu locum tenenti regis, videtur ipsi regi illata maxime si fiat in exercentem officium. 3 Inst. 1. An injury offered to a judge, or person representing the king, is considered as offered to the king himself, especially if it be done in the exercise of his office.

Injuria non excusat injuriam. One wrong does not justify another. Broom, Max. 395. See 6 El. & Bl. 47.

Injuria non præsumitur. Injury is not presumed. Co. Litt. 232. Cruel, oppressive, or tortuous conduct will not be presumed. Best. Ev. p. 336, § 298.

Injuria propria non cadet in beneficium facientis. One's own wrong shall not fall to the advantage of him that does it. A man will not be allowed to derive benefit from his own wrongful act. Branch, Princ.

Injuria servi dominum pertingit. The master is liable for injury done by his servant. Lofft, 229.

INJURIOUS WORDS. In Louisiana. Slander, or libelous words. Civil Code La. art. 3501.

INJURY. Any wrong or damage done to another, either in his person, rights, reputation, or property.

In the civil law. A delict committed in contempt or outrage of any one, whereby his body, his dignity, or his reputation is maliciously injured. Voet, Com. ad Pand. 47, t. 10, no. 1.

Injustum est, nisi tota lege inspecta, de una aliqua ejus particula proposita judicare vel respondere. 8 Coke, 117b. It is unjust to decide or respond as to any particular part of a law without examining the whole of the law.

INLAGARE. In old English law. To restore to protection of law. To restore a man from the condition of outlawry. Opposed to *utlagare*. Bract. lib. 3, tr. 2, c. 14, § 1; Du Cange.

INLAGATION. Restoration to the protection of law. Restoration from a condition of outlawry.

INLAGH. A person within the law's protection; contrary to *utlagh*, an outlaw. Cowell.

INLAND. Within a country, state, or territory; within the same country.

In old English law, inland was used for the demesne (*q. v.*) of a manor; that part which lay next or most convenient for the lord's mansion-house, as within the view thereof, and which, therefore, he kept in his own hands for support of his family and for hospitality; in distinction from outland or utland, which was the portion let out to tenants. Cowell; Kennett; Spelman.

INLAND BILL OF EXCHANGE. A bill of which both the drawer and drawee reside within the same state or country. Otherwise called a "domestic bill," and distinguished from a "foreign bill."

INLAND NAVIGATION. Within the meaning of the legislation of congress upon the subject, this phrase means navigation upon the rivers of the country, but not upon the great lakes. 24 How. 1; 6 Biss. 364.

INLAND TRADE. Trade wholly carried on at home; as distinguished from commerce, (which see.)

INLANTAL, INLANTALE. Demesne or inland, opposed to *delantal*, or land tenanted. Cowell.

INLAUGHE. Sax. In old English law. Under the law, (*sub lege*,) in a frank-pledge, or decennary. Bract. fol. 125*b*.

INLAW. To place under the protection of the law. "Swearing obedience to the king in a leet, which doth *inlaw* the subject." Bacon.

INLEASED. In old English law. Entangled, or ensnared. 2 Inst. 247; Cowell; Blount.

INLIGARE. In old European law. To confederate; to join in a league, (*in ligam coire*.) Spelman.

INMATE. A person who lodges or dwells in the same house with another, occupying different rooms, but using the same door for passing in and out of the house. Webster; Jacob.

INN. An inn is a house where a traveler is furnished with everything which he has occasion for while on his way. 3 Barn. & Ald. 283. See 5 Sandf. 242; 35 Conn. 183.

Under the term "inn" the law includes all taverns, hotels, and houses of public general entertainment for guests. Code Ga. 1882, § 2114.

The words "inn," "tavern," and "hotel" are used synonymously to designate what is ordinarily and popularly known as an "inn" or "tavern," or place for the entertainment of travelers, and where all their wants can be supplied. A restaurant where meals only are furnished is not an inn or tavern. 54 Barb. 311; 1 Hilt. 193.

An inn is distinguished from a private boarding-house mainly in this: that the keeper of the latter is at liberty to choose his guests, while the innkeeper is obliged to entertain and furnish all travelers of good conduct and means of payment with what they may have occasion for, as such travelers, while on their way. 33 Cal. 557.

The distinction between a boarding-house and an inn is that in the former the guest is under an express contract for a certain time at a certain rate; in the latter the guest is entertained from day to day upon an implied contract. 2 E. D. Smith, 148.

INNAMIUM. A pledge.

INNAVIGABILITY. In insurance law. The condition of being *innavigable*, (*q. v.*) The foreign writers distinguish "innavigability" from "shipwreck." 3 Kent, Comm. 323, and note. The term is also applied to the condition of streams which are not large enough or deep enough, or are otherwise unsuited, for navigation.

INNAVIGABLE. As applied to streams, not capable of or suitable for navigation; impassable by ships or vessels.

As applied to vessels in the law of marine insurance, it means unfit for navigation; so damaged by misadventures at sea as to be no longer capable of making a voyage. See 3 Kent, Comm. 323, note.

INNER BARRISTER. A serjeant or queen's counsel, in England, who is admitted to plead within the bar.

INNER HOUSE. The name given to the chambers in which the first and second divisions of the court of session in Scotland hold their sittings. See OUTER HOUSE.

INNINGS. In old records. Lands recovered from the sea by draining and banking. Cowell.

INNKEEPER. One who keeps an *inn*, or house for the lodging and entertainment of travelers. The keeper of a common inn for the lodging and entertainment of travelers and passengers, their horses and attendants, for a reasonable compensation. Story, Bailm. § 475. One who keeps a tavern or coffee-house in which lodging is provided. 2 Steph. Comm. 133.

One who receives as guests all who choose to visit his house, without any previous agreement as to the time of their stay, or the terms. His liability as innkeeper ceases when his guest pays his bill, and leaves the house with the declared intention of not returning, notwithstanding the guest leaves his baggage behind him. 5 Sandf. 242.

INNOCENCE. The absence of guilt.
The law presumes in favor of innocence.

INNOCENT CONVEYANCES. A technical term of the English law of conveyancing, used to designate such conveyances as may be made by a leasehold tenant without working a forfeiture. These are said to be lease and re-lease, bargain and sale, and, in case of a life-tenant, a covenant to stand seised. See 1 Chit. Pr. 243.

INNOMINATE. In the civil law. Not named or classed; belonging to no specific class; ranking under a general head. A term applied to those contracts for which no certain or precise remedy was appointed, but a general action on the case only. Dig. 2, 1, 4, 7, 2; Id. 19, 4, 5.

INNOMINATE CONTRACTS, literally, are the "unclassified" contracts of Roman law. They are contracts which are neither *re, verbis, literis,* nor *consensu* simply, but some mixture of or variation upon two or more of such contracts. They are principally the contracts of *permutatio, de æstimato, precarium,* and *transactio.* Brown.

INNONIA. In old English law. A close or inclosure, (*clausum, inclausura.*) Spelman.

INNOTESCIMUS. Lat. We make known. A term formerly applied to letters patent, derived from the emphatic word at the conclusion of the Latin forms. It was a species of exemplification of charters of feoffment or other instruments not of record. 5 Coke, 54*a.*

INNOVATION. In Scotch law. The exchange of one obligation for another, so as to make the second obligation come in the place of the first, and be the only subsisting obligation against the debtor. Bell. The same with "novation," (*q. v.*)

INNOXIARE. In old English law. To purge one of a fault and make him innocent.

INNS OF CHANCERY. So called because anciently inhabited by such clerks as chiefly studied the framing of writs, which regularly belonged to the cursitors, who were officers of the court of chancery. There are nine of them,—Clement's, Clifford's, and Lyon's Inn; Furnival's, Thavies, and Symond's Inn; New Inn; and Barnard's and Staples' Inn. These were formerly preparatory colleges for students, and many entered them before they were admitted into the inns of court. They consist chiefly of solicitors, and possess corporate property, hall, chambers, etc., but perform no public functions like the inns of court. Wharton.

INNS OF COURT. These are certain private unincorporated associations, in the nature of collegiate houses, located in London, and invested with the exclusive privilege of calling men to the bar; that is, conferring the rank or degree of a barrister. They were founded probably about the beginning of the fourteenth century. The principal inns of court are the Inner Temple,

Middle Temple, Lincoln's Inn, and Gray's Inn. (The two former originally belonged to the Knights Templar; the two latter to the earls of Lincoln and Gray respectively.) These bodies now have a "common council of legal education," for giving lectures and holding examinations. The inns of chancery, distinguishable from the foregoing, but generally classed with them under the general name, are the buildings known as "Clifford's Inn," "Clement's Inn," "New Inn," "Staples' Inn," and "Barnard's Inn." They were formerly a sort of collegiate houses in which law students learned the elements of law before being admitted into the inns of court, but they have long ceased to occupy that position.

INNUENDO. This Latin word (commonly translated "meaning") was the technical beginning of that clause in a declaration or indictment for slander or libel in which the application of the language charged to the plaintiff was pointed out. Hence it gave its name to the whole clause; and this usage is still retained, although an equivalent English word is now substituted. Thus, it may be charged that the defendant said "he (*meaning* the said plaintiff) is a perjurer."

The word is also used, (though more rarely,) in other species of pleadings, to introduce an explanation of a preceding word, charge, or averment.

It is said to mean no more than the words "*id est,*" "*scilicet,*" or "meaning," or "aforesaid," as explanatory of a subject-matter sufficiently expressed before; as "such a one, *meaning* the defendant," or "such a subject, *meaning* the subject in question." Cowp. 683. It is only explanatory of some matter already expressed. It serves to point out where there is precedent matter, but never for a new charge. It may *apply* what is *already expressed,* but cannot add to or enlarge or change the sense of the previous words. 1 Chit. Pl. 422.

INOFFICIOSUM. In the civil law. Inofficious; contrary to natural duty or affection. Used of a will of a parent which disinherited a child without just cause, or that of a child which disinherited a parent, and which could be contested by *querela inofficiosi testamenti.* Dig. 2, 5, 3, 13; Paulus, lib. 4, tit. 5, § 1.

INOFFICIOUS TESTAMENT. A will not in accordance with the testator's natural affection and moral duties. Williams, Ex'rs, (7th Ed.) 38.

INOFICIOCIDAD. In Spanish law. Everything done contrary to a duty or obligation assumed, as well as in opposition to the piety and affection dictated by nature. Escriche.

INOPS CONSILII. Lat. Destitute of counsel; without legal counsel. A term applied to the acts or condition of one acting without legal advice, as a testator drafting his own will.

INORDINATUS. An intestate.

INPENY and OUTPENY. In old English law. A customary payment of a penny on entering into and going out of a tenancy, (*pro exitu de tenura, et pro ingressu.*) Spelman.

INQUEST. 1. A body of men appointed by law to inquire into certain matters. The grand jury is sometimes called the "grand inquest."

2. The judicial inquiry made by a jury summoned for the purpose is called an "inquest." The finding of such men, upon an investigation, is also called an "inquest."

3. The inquiry by a coroner, termed a "coroner's inquest," into the manner of the death of any one who has been slain, or has died suddenly or in prison.

4. This name is also given to a species of proceeding under the New York practice, allowable where the defendant in a civil action has not filed an affidavit of merits nor verified his answer. In such case the issue may be taken up, out of its regular order, on plaintiff's motion, and tried without the admission of any affirmative defense.

An inquest is a trial of an issue of fact where the plaintiff alone introduces testimony. The defendant is entitled to appear at the taking of the inquest, and to cross-examine the plaintiff's witnesses; and, if he do appear, the inquest must be taken before a jury, unless a jury be expressly waived by him. 6 How. Pr. 118.

INQUEST OF OFFICE. In English practice. An inquiry made by the king's (or queen's) officer, his sheriff, coroner, or escheator, *virtute officii*, or by writ sent to them for that purpose, or by commissioners specially appointed, concerning any matter that entitles the king to the possession of lands or tenements, goods or chattels; as to inquire whether the king's tenant for life died seised, whereby the reversion accrues to the king; whether A., who held immediately of the crown, died without heir, in which case the lands belong to the king by escheat; whether B. be attainted of treason, whereby his estate is forfeited to the crown; whether C., who has purchased land, be an alien, which is another cause of forfeiture, etc. 3 Bl. Comm. 258. These *inquests of office* were more frequent in practice during the continuance of the military tenures than at present; and were devised by law as an authentic means to give the king his right by solemn matter of record. Id. 258, 259; 4 Steph. Comm. 40, 41. Sometimes simply termed "*office*," as in the phrase "office found," (*q. v.*) See 7 Cranch, 603.

INQUILINUS. In Roman law. A tenant; one who hires and occupies another's house; but particularly, a tenant of a hired house in a city, as distinguished from *colonus*, the hirer of a house or estate in the country. Calvin.

INQUIRENDO. An authority given to some official person to institute an inquiry concerning the crown's interests.

INQUIRY. The writ of inquiry is a judicial process addressed to the sheriff of the county in which the venue is laid, stating the former proceedings in the action, and, "because it is unknown what damages the plaintiff has sustained," commanding the sheriff that, by the oath of twelve men of his county, he diligently inquire into the same, and return the inquisition into court. This writ is necessary after an interlocutory judgment, the defendant having let judgment go by default, to ascertain the *quantum* of damages. Wharton.

INQUISITIO. In old English law. An inquisition or inquest. *Inquisitio post mortem*, an inquisition after death. An inquest of office held, during the continuance of the military tenures, upon the death of every one of the king's tenants, to inquire of what lands he died seised, who was his heir, and of what age, in order to entitle the king to his marriage, wardship, relief, primer seisin, or other advantages, as the circumstances of the case might turn out. 3 Bl. Comm. 258. *Inquisitio patriæ*, the inquisition of the country; the ordinary jury, as distinguished from the grand assise. Bract. fol. 15*b*.

INQUISITION. In practice. An inquiry or inquest; particularly, an investigation of certain facts made by a sheriff, together with a jury impaneled by him for the purpose.

INQUISITOR. A designation of sheriffs, coroners *super visum corporis*, and the like,

J

K

L

M

who have power to inquire into certain matters.

INROLL. A form of "enroll," used in the old books. 3 Rep. Ch. 63, 73; 3 East, 410.

INROLLMENT. See ENROLLMENT.

INSANE. Unsound in mind; of unsound mind; deranged, disordered, or diseased in mind. Violently deranged; mad.

INSANITY. A manifestation of disease of the brain, characterized by a general or partial derangement of one or more faculties of the mind, and in which, while consciousness is not abolished, mental freedom is perverted, weakened, or destroyed. Ham. Nervous System, 332.

The prolonged departure, without any adequate cause, from the states of feeling and modes of thinking usual to the individual in health. Bouvier.

This is not, strictly speaking, a legal term, but it is commonly used to denote that state of mind which prevents a person from knowing right from wrong, and, therefore, from being responsible for acts which in a sane person would be criminal. Pope, Lun. 6, 19, 356.

By insanity is not meant a total deprivation of reason, but only an inability, from defect of perception, memory, and judgment, to do the act in question. So, by a lucid interval is not meant a perfect restoration to reason, but a restoration so far as to be able, beyond doubt, to comprehend and to do the act with such reason, memory, and judgment as to make it a legal act. 2 Del. Ch. 263.

Insanus est qui, abjecta ratione, omnia cum impetu et furore facit. He is insane who, reason being thrown away, does everything with violence and rage. 4 Coke, 128.

INSCRIBERE. Lat. In the civil law. To subscribe an accusation. To bind one's self, in case of failure to prove an accusation, to suffer the same punishment which the accused would have suffered had he been proved guilty. Calvin.

INSCRIPTIO. Lat. In the civil law. A written accusation in which the accuser undertakes to suffer the punishment appropriate to the offense charged, if the accused is able to clear himself of the accusation. Calvin.; Cod. 9, 1, 10; Id. 9, 2, 16, 17.

INSCRIPTION. In evidence. Anything written or engraved upon a metallic or other solid substance, intended for great durability; as upon a tombstone, pillar, tablet, medal, ring, etc.

INSCRIPTIONES. The name given by the old English law to any written instrument by which anything was granted. Blount.

INSENSIBLE. In pleading. Unintelligible; without sense or meaning, from the omission of material words, etc. Steph. Pl. 377.

INSETENA. In old records. An inditch; an interior ditch; one made within another, for greater security. Spelman.

INSIDIATORES VIARUM. Lat. Highwaymen; persons who lie in wait in order to commit some felony or other misdemeanor.

INSIGNIA. Ensigns or arms; distinctive marks; badges; *indicia*; characteristics.

INSILIARIUS. An evil counsellor. Cowell.

INSILIUM. Evil advice or counsel. Cowell.

INSIMUL. Lat. Together; jointly. Townsh. Pl. 44.

INSIMUL COMPUTASSENT. They accounted together. The name of the count in *assumpsit* upon an account stated; it being averred that the parties had settled their accounts together, and defendant engaged to pay plaintiff the balance.

INSIMUL TENUIT. One species of the writ of *formedon* brought against a stranger by a coparcener on the possession of the ancestor, etc. Jacob.

INSINUACION. In Spanish law. The presentation of a public document to a competent judge, in order to obtain his approbation and sanction of the same, and thereby give it judicial authenticity. Escriche.

INSINUARE. Lat. In the civil law. To put into; to deposit a writing in court, answering nearly to the modern expression "to file." *Si non mandatum actis insinuatum est*, if the power or authority be not deposited among the records of the court. Inst. 4, 11, 3.

To declare or acknowledge before a judicial officer; to give an act an official form.

INSINUATIO. Lat. In old English law. Information or suggestion. *Ex insinuatione*, on the information. Reg. Jud. 25, 50.

INSINUATION. In the civil law. The transcription of an act on the public registers, like our recording of deeds. It was not necessary in any other alienation but that appropriated to the purpose of donation. Inst. 2, 7, 2.

INSINUATION OF A WILL. In the civil law. The first production of a will, or the leaving it with the registrar, in order to its probate. Cowell; Blount.

INSOLVENCY. The condition of a person who is insolvent; inability to pay one's debts; lack of means to pay one's debts. Such a relative condition of a man's assets and liabilities that the former, if all made immediately available, would not be sufficient to discharge the latter. Or the condition of a person who is unable to pay his debts as they fall due, or in the usual course of trade and business. See 2 Kent, Comm. 389; 4 Hill, 652; 15 N. Y. 141, 200; 3 Gray, 600; 2 Bell, Comm. 162.

As to the distinction between bankruptcy and insolvency, see BANKRUPTCY.

INSOLVENCY FUND. In English law. A fund, consisting of moneys and securities, which, at the time of the passing of the bankruptcy act, 1861, stood, in the Bank of England, to the credit of the commissioners of the insolvent debtors' court, and was, by the twenty-sixth section of that act, directed to be carried by the bank to the account of the accountant in bankruptcy. Provision has now been made for its transfer to the commissioners for the reduction of the national debt. Robs. Bankr. 20, 56.

INSOLVENT. One who cannot or does not pay; one who is unable to pay his debts; one who is not solvent; one who has not means or property sufficient to pay his debts.

A debtor is "insolvent," within the meaning of the bankrupt act, when he is unable to pay his debts and meet his engagements in the ordinary course of business, as persons in trade usually do. 3 Ben. 153; Id. 520; 1 Abb. (U. S.) 440; 1 Dill. 186.

A trader is insolvent when he is not in a condition to meet his engagements or pay his debts in the usual and ordinary course of business. His solvency or insolvency does not depend upon the simple question whether his assets at the date alleged will or will not satisfy all the demands against him, due and to become due. 33 Cal. 625.

INSOLVENT LAW. A term applied to a law, usually of one of the states, regulating the settlement of insolvent estates, and according a certain measure of relief to insolvent debtors.

INSPECTATOR. A prosecutor or adversary.

INSPECTION. The examination or testing of food, fluids, or other articles made subject by law to such examination, to ascertain their fitness for use or commerce.

Also the examination by a private person of public records and documents; or of the books and papers of his opponent in an action, for the purpose of better preparing his own case for trial.

INSPECTION LAWS. Laws authorizing and directing the inspection and examination of various kinds of merchandise intended for sale, especially food, with a view to ascertaining its fitness for use, and excluding unwholesome or unmarketable goods from sale, and directing the appointment of official inspectors for that purpose. See Const. U. S. art. 1, § 10, cl. 2; Story, Const. § 1017, et seq.

INSPECTION OF DOCUMENTS. This phrase refers to the right of a party, in a civil action, to inspect and make copies of documents which are essential or material to the maintenance of his cause, and which are either in the custody of an officer of the law or in the possession of the adverse party.

INSPECTION, TRIAL BY. A mode of trial formerly in use in England, by which the judges of a court decided a point in dispute, upon the testimony of their own senses, without the intervention of a jury. This took place in cases where the fact upon which issue was taken must, from its nature, be evident to the court from ocular demonstration, or other irrefragable proof; and was adopted for the greater expedition of a cause. 3 Bl. Comm. 331.

INSPECTORS. Officers whose duty it is to examine the quality of certain articles of merchandise, food, weights and measures, etc.

INSPECTORSHIP, DEED OF. In English law. An instrument entered into between an insolvent debtor and his creditors, appointing one or more persons to inspect and oversee the winding up of such insolvent's affairs on behalf of the creditors.

INSPEXIMUS. Lat. In old English law. We have inspected. An exemplification of letters patent, so called from the emphatic word of the old forms. 5 Coke, 53b.

INSTALLATION. The ceremony of inducting or investing with any charge, office, or rank, as the placing a bishop into his see, a dean or prebendary into his stall or seat, or a knight into his order. Wharton.

INSTALLMENTS. Different portions of the same debt payable at different successive periods as agreed. Brown.

J

K

L

M

INSTANCE. In pleading and practice. Solicitation, properly of an earnest or urgent kind. An act is often said to be done at a party's "special *instance* and request."

In the civil and French law. A general term, designating all sorts of actions and judicial demands. Dig. 44, 7, 58.

In ecclesiastical law. Causes of *instance* are those proceeded in at the solicitation of some party, as opposed to causes of office, which run in the name of the judge. Hallifax, Civil Law, p. 156.

In Scotch law. That which may be insisted on at one diet or course of probation. Wharton.

INSTANCE COURT. In English law. That division or department of the court of admiralty which exercises all the ordinary admiralty jurisdiction, with the single exception of prize cases, the latter belonging to the branch called the "Prize Court."

The term is sometimes used in American law for purposes of explanation, but has no proper application to admiralty courts in the United States, where the powers of both instance and prize courts are conferred without any distinction. 3 Dall. 6; 1 Gall. 563; 3 Kent, Comm. 355, 378.

INSTANCIA. In Spanish law. The institution and prosecution of a suit from its commencement until definitive judgment. The first instance, "*primera instancia*," is the prosecution of the suit before the judge competent to take cognizance of it at its inception; the second instance, "*secunda instancia*," is the exercise of the same action before the court of appellate jurisdiction; and the third instance, "*tercera instancia*," is the prosecution of the same suit, either by an application of revision before the appellate tribunal that has already decided the cause, or before some higher tribunal, having jurisdiction of the same. Escriche.

INSTANTER. Immediately; instantly; forthwith; without delay. Trial *instanter* was had where a prisoner between attainder and execution pleaded that he was not the same who was attainted.

When a party is ordered to plead *instanter*, he must plead the same day. The term is usually understood to mean within twenty-four hours.

INSTAR. Lat. Likeness; the likeness, size, or equivalent of a thing. *Instar dentium*, like teeth. 2 Bl. Comm. 295. *Instar omnium*, equivalent or tantamount to all. Id. 146; 3 Bl. Comm. 231.

INSTAURUM. In old English deeds. A stock or store of cattle, and other things; the whole stock upon a farm, including cattle, wagons, plows, and all other implements of husbandry. 1 Mon. Angl. 548*b*; Fleta, lib. 2, c. 72, § 7. *Terra instaurata*, land ready stocked.

INSTIGATION. Incitation; urging; solicitation. The act by which one incites another to do something, as to commit some crime or to commence a suit.

INSTIRPARE. To plant or establish.

INSTITOR. Lat. In the civil law. A clerk in a store; an agent.

INSTITORIA ACTIO. Lat. In the civil law. The name of an action given to those who had contracted with an *institor* (*q. v.*) to compel the principal to performance. Inst. 4, 7, 2; Dig. 14, 3, 1; Story, Ag. § 426.

INSTITORIAL POWER. The charge given to a clerk to manage a shop or store. 1 Bell, Comm. 506, 507.

INSTITUTE, *v.* To inaugurate or commence; as to institute an action.

To nominate, constitute, or appoint; as to institute an heir by testament. Dig. 28, 5, 65.

INSTITUTE, *n.* In the civil law. A person named in the will as heir, but with a direction that he shall pass over the estate to another designated person, called the "substitute."

In Scotch law. The person to whom an estate is first given by destination or limitation; the others, or the heirs of tailzie, are called "substitutes."

INSTITUTES. A name sometimes given to text-books containing the elementary principles of jurisprudence, arranged in an orderly and systematic manner. For example, the Institutes of Justinian, of Gaius, of Lord Coke.

INSTITUTES OF GAIUS. An elementary work of the Roman jurist Gaius; important as having formed the foundation of the Institutes of Justinian, (*q. v.*) These Institutes were discovered by Niebuhr in 1816, in a *codex rescriptus* of the library of the cathedral chapter at Verona, and were first published at Berlin in 1820. Two editions have since appeared. Mackeld. Rom. Law, § 54.

INSTITUTES OF JUSTINIAN. One of the four component parts or principal divisions of the *Corpus Juris Civilis*, being an elementary treatise on the Roman law, in four books. This work was compiled from earlier sources, (resting principally on the Institutes of Gaius,) by a commission composed of Tribonian and two others, by command and under direction of the emperor Justinian, and was first published November 21, A. D. 533.

INSTITUTES OF LORD COKE. The name of four volumes by Lord Coke, published A. D. 1628. The first is an extensive comment upon a treatise on tenures, compiled by Littleton, a judge of the common pleas, *temp.* Edward IV. This comment is a rich mine of valuable common-law learning, collected and heaped together from the ancient reports and Year Books, but greatly defective in method. It is usually cited by the name of "Co. Litt.," or as "1 Inst." The second volume is a comment upon old acts of parliament, without systematic order; the third a more methodical treatise on the pleas of the crown; and the fourth an account of the several species of courts. These are cited as 2, 3, or 4 "Inst.," without any author's name. Wharton.

INSTITUTIO HÆREDIS. Lat. In Roman law. The appointment of the *hæres* in the will. It corresponds very nearly to the nomination of an executor in English law. Without such an appointment the will was void at law, but the *prætor* (*i. e.*, equity) would, under certain circumstances, carry out the intentions of the testator. Brown.

INSTITUTION. The commencement or inauguration of anything. The first establishment of a law, rule, rite, etc. Any custom, system, organization, etc., firmly established An elementary rule or principle.

In practice. The commencement of an action or prosecution; as, A. B. has instituted a suit against C. D. to recover damages for trespass.

In political law. A law, rite, or ceremony enjoined by authority as a permanent rule of conduct or of government. Webster.

A system or body of usages, laws, or regulations, of extensive and recurring operation, containing within itself an organism by which it effects its own independent action, continuance, and generally its own further development. Its object is to generate, effect, regulate, or sanction a succession of acts, transactions, or productions of a peculiar kind or class. We are likewise in the habit of calling single laws or usages "institu-

tions," if their operation is of vital importance and vast scope, and if their continuance is in a high degree independent of any interfering power. Lieb. Civil Lib. 300.

In corporation law. An organization or foundation, for the exercise of some public purpose or function; as an asylum or a university. By the term "institution" in this sense is to be understood an establishment or organization which is permanent in its nature, as distinguished from an enterprise or undertaking which is transient and temporary. 29 Ohio St. 206; 24 Ind. 391.

In ecclesiastical law. A kind of investiture of the spiritual part of the benefice, as induction is of the temporal; for by institution the care of the souls of the parish is committed to the charge of the clerk. Brown.

In the civil law. The designation by a testator of a person to be his heir.

In jurisprudence. The plural form of this word ("institutions") is sometimes used as the equivalent of "institutes," to denote an elementary text-book of the law.

INSTITUTIONES. Works containing the elements of any science; institutions or institutes. One of Justinian's principal law collections, and a similar work of the Roman jurist Gaius, are so entitled. See INSTITUTES.

INSTRUCT. To convey information as a client to an attorney, or as an attorney to a counsel; to authorize one to appear as advocate; to give a case in charge to the jury.

INSTRUCTION. In French criminal law. The first process of a criminal prosecution. It includes the examination of the accused, the preliminary interrogation of witnesses, collateral investigations, the gathering of evidence, the reduction of the whole to order, and the preparation of a document containing a detailed statement of the case, to serve as a brief for the prosecuting officers, and to furnish material for the indictment.

INSTRUCTIONS. In common law. Orders given by a principal to his agent in relation to the business of his agency.

In practice. A detailed statement of the facts and circumstances constituting a cause of action made by a client to his attorney for the purpose of enabling the latter to draw a proper declaration or procure it to be done by a pleader.

INSTRUMENT. A written document; a formal or legal document in writing, such as a contract, deed, will, bond, or lease.

J

K

L

M

In the law of evidence. Anything which may be presented as evidence to the senses of the adjudicating tribunal. The term "instruments of evidence" includes not merely documents, but witnesses and living things which may be presented for inspection. 1 Whart. Ev. § 615.

INSTRUMENT OF APPEAL. The document by which an appeal is brought in an English matrimonial cause from the president of the probate, divorce, and admiralty division to the full court. It is analogous to a petition. Browne, Div. 322.

INSTRUMENT OF EVIDENCE. Instruments of evidence are the *media* through which the evidence of facts, either disputed or required to be proved, is conveyed to the mind of a judicial tribunal; and they comprise persons, as well as writings. Best, Ev. § 123.

INSTRUMENT OF SAISINE. An instrument in Scotland by which the delivery of "saisine" (*i. e.*, seisin, or the feudal possession of land) is attested. It is subscribed by a notary, in the presence of witnesses, and is executed in pursuance of a "precept of saisine," whereby the "grantor of the deed" desires "any notary public to whom these presents may be presented" to give saisine to the intended grantee or grantees. It must be entered and recorded in the registers of saisines. Mozley & Whitley.

INSTRUMENTA. That kind of evidence which consists of writings not under seal; as court-rolls, accounts, and the like. 3 Co. Litt. 487.

INSUCKEN MULTURES. A quantity of corn paid by those who are thirled to a mill. See THIRLAGE.

INSUFFICIENCY. In equity pleading. The legal inadequacy of an answer in equity which does not fully and specifically reply to some one or more of the material allegations, charges, or interrogatories set forth in the bill.

INSULA. An island; a house not connected with other houses, but separated by a surrounding space of ground. Calvin.

INSUPER. Moreover; over and above. An old exchequer term, applied to a charge made *upon* a person in his account. Blount.

INSURABLE INTEREST. Such a real and substantial interest in specific property as will sustain a contract to indemnify the person interested against its loss. If the assured had no real interest, the contract would be a mere wager policy.

Every interest in property, or any relation thereto, or liability in respect thereof, of such a nature that a contemplated peril might directly damnify the insured, is an insurable interest. Civil Code Cal. § 2546.

INSURANCE. A contract whereby, for a stipulated consideration, one party undertakes to compensate the other for loss on a specified subject by specified perils. The party agreeing to make the compensation is usually called the "insurer" or "underwriter;" the other, the "insured" or "assured;" the agreed consideration, the "premium;" the written contract, a "policy;" the events insured against, "risks" or "perils;" and the subject, right, or interest to be protected, the "insurable interest." 1 Phil. Ins. §§ 1–5.

Insurance is a contract whereby one undertakes to indemnify another against loss, damage, or liability arising from an unknown or contingent event. Civil Code Cal. § 2527; Civil Code Dak. § 1474.

Various classes or kinds of insurance are in use. *Marine* insurance applies to vessels, cargoes, and property exposed to maritime risks. *Fire* insurance covers buildings, merchandise, and other property on land exposed to injury by fire. *Life* insurance means the engagement to pay a stipulated sum upon the death of the insured, or of a third person in whose life the insured has an interest, either whenever it occurs, or in case it occurs within a prescribed term. *Accident* and *health* insurance include insurances of persons against injury from accident, or expense and loss of time from disease. Many other forms might exist, and several others have been to a limited extent introduced in recent times; such as insurance of valuables against theft, insurance of the lives and good condition of domestic animals, insurance of valuable plate-glass windows against breakage. Abbott.

INSURANCE AGENT. An agent employed by an insurance company to solicit risks and effect insurances.

Agents of insurance companies are called "general agents" when clothed with the general oversight of the companies' business in a state or large section of country, and "local agents" when their functions are limited and confined to some particular locality.

INSURANCE BROKER. A broker through whose agency insurances are effected. 3 Kent, Comm. 260. See BROKER.

INSURANCE COMPANY. A corporation or association whose business is to make contracts of insurance. They are either mutual companies or stock companies.

INSURANCE POLICY. See POLICY.

INSURE. To engage to indemnify a person against pecuniary loss from specified perils. To act as an insurer.

INSURED. The person who obtains insurance on his property, or upon whose life an insurance is effected.

INSURER. The underwriter or insurance company with whom a contract of insurance is made.

The person who undertakes to indemnify another by a contract of insurance is called the "insurer," and the person indemnified is called the "insured." Civil Code Cal. § 2538.

INSURGENT. One who participates in an insurrection; one who opposes the execution of law by force of arms, or who rises in revolt against the constituted authorities.

A distinction is often taken between "insurgent" and "rebel," in this: that the former term is not necessarily to be taken in a bad sense, inasmuch as an insurrection, though extralegal, may be just and timely in itself; as where it is undertaken for the overthrow of tyranny or the reform of gross abuses. According to Webster, an insurrection is an incipient or early stage of a rebellion.

INSURRECTION. A rebellion, or rising of citizens or subjects in resistance to their government. See INSURGENT.

Insurrection shall consist in any combined resistance to the lawful authority of the state, with intent to the denial thereof, when the same is manifested, or intended to be manifested, by acts of violence. Code Ga. 1882, § 4315.

INTAKERS. In old English law. A kind of thieves inhabiting Redesdale, on the extreme northern border of England; so called because they *took in* or received such booties of cattle and other things as their accomplices, who were called "outparters," brought in to them from the borders of Scotland. Spelman; Cowell.

INTAKES. Temporary inclosures made by customary tenants of a manor under a special custom authorizing them to inclose part of the waste until one or more crops have been raised on it. Elton, Common, 277.

INTEGER. Whole; untouched. *Res integra* means a question which is new and undecided. 2 Kent, Comm. 177.

INTEMPERANCE. Habitual intemperance is that degree of intemperance from the use of intoxicating drinks which disqualifies the person a great portion of the time from properly attending to business, or which would reasonably inflict a course of great mental anguish upon an innocent party. Civil Code Cal. § 106.

INTEND. To design, resolve, purpose. To apply a rule of law in the nature of presumption; to discern and follow the probabilities of like cases.

INTENDANT. One who has the charge, management, or direction of some office, department, or public business.

INTENDED TO BE RECORDED. This phrase is frequently used in conveyances, when reciting some other conveyance which has not yet been recorded, but which forms a link in the chain of title. In Pennsylvania, it has been construed to be a covenant, on the part of the grantor, to procure the deed to be recorded in a reasonable time. 2 Rawle, 14.

INTENDENTE. In Spanish law. The immediate agent of the minister of finance, or the chief and principal director of the different branches of the revenue, appointed in the various departments in each of the provinces into which the Spanish monarchy is divided. Escriche.

INTENDMENT OF LAW. The true meaning, the correct understanding or intention of the law; a presumption or inference made by the courts. Co. Litt. 78.

INTENT. In criminal law and the law of evidence. Purpose; formulated design; a resolve to do or forbear a particular act; aim; determination. In its literal sense, the stretching of the mind or will towards a particular object.

"Intent" expresses mental action at its most advanced point, or as it actually accompanies an outward, corporal act which has been determined on. *Intent* shows the presence of *will* in the act which consummates a crime. It is the exercise of intelligent will, the mind being fully aware of the nature and consequences of the act which is about to be done, and with such knowledge, and with full liberty of action, willing and electing to do it. Burrill, Circ. Ev. 284, and notes.

INTENTIO. Lat. In the civil law. The formal complaint or claim of a plaintiff before the prætor.

In old English law. A count or declaration in a real action, (*narratio.*) Bract. lib. 4, tr. 2, c. 2; Fleta, lib. 4, c. 7; Du Cange.

J

K

L

M

Intentio cæca mala. A blind or obscure meaning is bad or ineffectual. 2 Bulst. 179. Said of a testator's intention.

Intentio inservire debet legibus, non leges intentioni. The intention [of a party] ought to be subservient to [or in accordance with] the laws, not the laws to the intention. Co. Litt. 314a, 314b.

Intentio mea imponit nomen operi meo. Hob. 123. My intent gives a name to my act.

INTENTION. Meaning; will; purpose; design. "The *intention* of the testator, to be collected from the whole will, is to govern, provided it be not unlawful or inconsistent with the rules of law." 4 Kent, Comm. 534.

"Intention," when used with reference to the construction of wills and other documents, means the sense and meaning of it, as gathered from the words used therein. Parol evidence is not ordinarily admissible to explain this. When used with reference to civil and criminal responsibility, a person who contemplates any result, as not unlikely to follow from a deliberate act of his own, may be said to intend that result, whether he desire it or not. Thus, if a man should, for a wager, discharge a gun among a multitude of people, and any should be killed, he would be deemed guilty of intending the death of such person; for every man is presumed to intend the natural consequence of his own actions. Intention is often confounded with motive, as when we speak of a man's "good intentions." Mozley & Whitley.

INTENTIONE. A writ that lay against him who entered into lands after the death of a tenant in dower, or for life, etc., and held out to him in reversion or remainder. Fitzh. Nat. Brev. 203.

INTER. Lat. Among; between.

INTER ALIA. Among other things. A term anciently used in pleading, especially in reciting statutes, where the whole statute was not set forth at length. *Inter alia enactatum fuit*, among other things it was enacted. See Plowd. 65.

Inter alias causas acquisitionis, magna, celebris, et famosa est causa donationis. Among other methods of acquiring property, a great, much-used, and celebrated method is that of gift. Bract. fol. 11.

INTER ALIOS. Between other persons; between those who are strangers to a matter in question.

INTER APICES JURIS. Among the subtleties of the law. See APEX JURIS.

INTER BRACHIA. Between her arms. Fleta, lib. 1, c. 35, §§ 1, 2.

INTER CÆTEROS. Among others; in a general clause; not by name, (*nominatim.*) A term applied in the civil law to clauses of disinheritance in a will. Inst. 2, 13, 1; Id. 2, 13, 3.

INTER CANEM ET LUPUM. (Lat. Between the dog and the wolf.) The twilight; because then the dog seeks his rest, and the wolf his prey. 3 Inst. 63.

INTER CONJUGES. Between husband and wife.

INTER CONJUNCTAS PERSONAS. Between conjunct persons. By the act 1621, c. 18, all conveyances or alienations between conjunct persons, unless granted for onerous causes, are declared, as in a question with creditors, to be null and of no avail. Conjunct persons are those standing in a certain degree of relationship to each other; such, for example, as brothers, sisters, sons, uncles, etc. These were formerly excluded as witnesses, on account of their relationship; but this, as a ground of exclusion, has been abolished. Tray. Lat. Max.

INTER PARTES. Between parties. Instruments in which two persons unite, each making conveyance to, or engagement with, the other, are called "papers *inter partes.*"

INTER QUATUOR PARIETES. Between four walls. Fleta, lib. 6, c. 55, § 4.

INTER REGALIA. In English law. Among the things belonging to the sovereign. Among these are rights of salmon fishing, mines of gold and silver, forests, forfeitures, casualties of superiority, etc., which are called "*regalia minora*," and may be conveyed to a subject. The *regalia majora* include the several branches of the royal prerogative, which are inseparable from the person of the sovereign. Tray. Lat. Max.

INTER RUSTICOS. Among the illiterate or unlearned.

INTER SE, INTER SESE. Among themselves. Story, Partn. § 405.

INTER VIRUM ET UXOREM. Between husband and wife.

INTER VIVOS. Between the living; from one living person to another. Where property passes by conveyance, the transaction is said to be *inter vivos*, to distinguish it from a case of succession or devise. So an ordinary gift from one person to another is called a "gift *inter vivos*," to distinguish it from a donation made in contemplation of death, (*mortis causa*.)

INTERCALARE. In the civil law. To introduce or insert among or between others: to introduce a day or month into the calendar; to intercalate. Dig. 50, 16, 98, pr.

INTERCEDERE. In the civil law. To become bound for another's debt.

INTERCHANGEABLY. By way of exchange or interchange. This term properly denotes the method of signing deeds, leases, contracts, etc., executed in duplicate, where each party signs the copy which he delivers to the other.

INTERCOMMON. To enjoy a common mutually or promiscuously with the inhabitants or tenants of a contiguous township, vill, or manor. 2 Bl. Comm. 33; 1 Crabb, Real Prop. p. 271, § 290.

INTERCOMMONING. When the commons of two adjacent manors join, and the inhabitants of both have immemorially fed their cattle promiscuously on each other's common, this is called "intercommoning." Termes de la Ley.

INTERCOMMUNING. Letters of intercommuning were letters from the Scotch privy council passing (on their act) in the king's name, charging the lieges not to reset, supply, or intercommune with the persons thereby denounced; or to furnish them with meat, drink, house, harbor, or any other thing useful or comfortable; or to have any intercourse with them whatever,—under pain of being reputed art and part in their crimes, and dealt with accordingly; and desiring all sheriffs, bailies, etc., to apprehend and commit such rebels to prison. Bell.

INTERCOURSE. Communication; literally, a *running* or passing *between* persons or places; commerce.

INTERDICT. In Roman law. A decree of the prætor by means of which, in certain cases determined by the edict, he himself directly commanded what should be done or omitted, particularly in causes involving the right of possession or a *quasi* possession. In the modern civil law, interdicts are regarded precisely the same as actions, though they give rise to a summary proceeding. Mackeld. Rom. Law, § 258.

Interdicts are either prohibitory, restorative, or exhibitory; the first being a prohibition, the second a decree for restoring possession lost by force, the third a decree for the exhibiting of accounts, etc. Heinec. § 1206.

An interdict was distinguished from an "action," (*actio*,) properly so called, by the circumstance that the prætor himself decided in the first instance, (*principaliter*,) on the application of the plaintiff, without previously appointing a *judex*, by issuing a decree commanding what should be done, or left undone. Gaius, 4, 139. It might be adopted as a remedy in various cases where a regular action could not be maintained, and hence interdicts were at one time more extensively used by the prætor than the *actiones* themselves. Afterwards, however, they fell into disuse, and in the time of Justinian were generally dispensed with. Mackeld. Rom. Law, § 258; Inst. 4, 15, 8.

In ecclesiastical law. An ecclesiastical censure, by which divine services are prohibited to be administered either to particular persons or in particular places.

In Scotch law. An order of the court of session or of an inferior court, pronounced, on cause shown, for stopping any act or proceedings complained of as illegal or wrongful. It may be resorted to as a remedy against any encroachment either on property or possession, and is a protection against any unlawful proceeding. Bell.

INTERDICTION. In French law. Every person who, on account of insanity, has become incapable of controlling his own interests, can be put under the control of a guardian, who shall administer his affairs with the same effect as he might himself. Such a person is said to be "*interdit*," and his *status* is described as "interdiction." Arg. Fr. Merc. Law, 562.

In the civil law. A judicial decree, by which a person is deprived of the *exercise* of his civil rights.

INTERDICTION OF FIRE AND WATER. Banishment by an order that no man should supply the person banished with fire or water, the two necessaries of life.

INTERDICTUM SALVIANUM. Lat. In Roman law. The Salvian interdict. A process which lay for the owner of a farm to obtain possession of the goods of his tenant who had pledged them to him for the rent of the land. Inst. 4, 15, 3.

I n t e r d u m evenit ut exceptio quæ prima facie justa videtur, tamen inique noceat. It sometimes happens that a plea which seems *prima facie* just, nevertheless is injurious and unequal. Inst. 4, 14, 1, 2.

J

K

L

M

INTERESSE. Lat. Interest. The interest of money; also an interest in lands.

INTERESSE TERMINI. An interest in a term. That species of interest or property which a lessee for years acquires in the lands demised to him, before he has actually become possessed of those lands; as distinguished from that property or interest vested in him by the demise, and also reduced into possession by an actual entry upon the lands and the assumption of ownership therein, and which is then termed an "estate for years." Brown.

INTEREST. In property. The most general term that can be employed to denote a property in lands or chattels. In its application to lands or things real, it is frequently used in connection with the terms "estate," "right," and "title," and, according to Lord Coke, it properly includes them all. Co. Litt. 345b.

More particularly it means a right to have the advantage accruing from anything; any right in the nature of property, but less than title; a partial or undivided right; a title to a share.

The terms "interest" and "title" are not synonymous. A mortgagor in possession, and a purchaser holding under a deed defectively executed, have, both of them, absolute as well as insurable interests in the property, though neither of them has the legal title. 29 Conn. 20.

In the law of evidence. "Interest," in a statute that no witness shall be excluded by interest in the event of the suit, means "concern," "advantage," "good," "share," "portion," "part," or "participation." 11 Barb. 471; 11 Metc. (Mass.) 390.

A relation to the matter in controversy, or to the issue of the suit, in the nature of a prospective gain or loss, which actually does, or presumably might, create a bias or prejudice in the mind, inclining the person to favor one side or the other.

For money. Interest is the compensation allowed by law or fixed by the parties for the use or forbearance or detention of money. Civil Code Cal. § 1915.

Legal interest is the rate of interest established by the law of the country, and which will prevail in the absence of express stipulation; *conventional* interest is a certain rate agreed upon by the parties. 2 Cal. 568.

Simple interest is that which is paid for the principal or sum lent, at a certain rate or allowance, made by law or agreement of parties. *Compound* interest is interest upon interest, where accrued interest is added to the principal sum, and the whole treated as a new principal, for the calculation of the interest for the next period.

INTEREST, MARITIME. See MARITIME INTEREST.

INTEREST OR NO INTEREST. These words, inserted in an insurance policy, mean that the question whether the insured has or has not an insurable interest in the subject-matter is waived, and the policy is to be good irrespective of such interest. The effect of such a clause is to make it a *wager* policy.

INTEREST POLICY. In insurance. One which actually, or *prima facie*, covers a substantial and insurable interest; as opposed to a *wager* policy.

Interest reipublicæ ne maleficia remaneant impunita. It concerns the state that crimes remain not unpunished. Jenk. Cent. pp. 30, 31, case 59; Wing. Max. 501.

Interest reipublicæ ne sua quis male utatur. It concerns the state that persons do not misuse their property. 6 Coke, 36a.

Interest reipublicæ quod homines conserventur. It concerns the state that [the lives of] men be preserved. 12 Coke, 62.

Interest reipublicæ res judicatas non rescindi. It concerns the state that things adjudicated be not rescinded. 2 Inst. 360. It is matter of public concern that solemn adjudications of the courts should not be disturbed. See Best, Ev. p. 41, § 44.

Interest reipublicæ suprema hominum testamenta rata haberi. It concerns the state that men's last wills be held valid, [or allowed to stand.] Co. Litt. 236b.

Interest reipublicæ ut carceres sint in tuto. It concerns the state that prisons be safe places of confinement. 2 Inst. 589.

Interest (imprimis) reipublicæ ut pax in regno conservetur, et quæcunque paci adversentur provide declinentur. It especially concerns the state that peace be preserved in the kingdom, and that whatever things are against peace be prudently avoided. 2 Inst. 158.

Interest reipublicæ ut quilibet re sua bene utatur. It is the concern of the state that every one uses his property properly.

Interest reipublicæ ut sit finis litium. It concerns the state that there be an end of lawsuits. Co. Litt. 303. It is for the general welfare that a period be put to litigation. Broom, Max. 331, 343.

INTEREST SUIT. In English law. An action in the probate branch of the high court of justice, in which the question in dispute is as to which party is entitled to a grant of letters of administration of the estate of a deceased person. Wharton.

INTEREST UPON INTEREST. Compound interest, (*q. v.*)

INTERFERENCE. In patent law, this term designates a collision between rights claimed or granted; that is, where a person claims a patent for the whole or any integral part of the ground already covered by an existing patent or by a pending application.

INTERIM. In the mean time; meanwhile. An assignee *ad interim* is one appointed between the time of bankruptcy and appointment of the regular assignee. 2 Bell, Comm. 355.

INTERIM COMMITTITUR. Lat. "In the mean time, let him be committed." An order of court (or the docket-entry noting it) by which a prisoner is committed to prison and directed to be kept there until some further action can be taken, or until the time arrives for the execution of his sentence.

INTERIM CURATOR. A person appointed by justices of the peace to take care of the property of a felon convict, until the appointment by the crown of an administrator or administrators for the same purpose. Mozley & Whitley.

INTERIM FACTOR. In Scotch law. A judicial officer elected or appointed under the bankruptcy law to take charge of and preserve the estate until a fit person shall be elected trustee. 2 Bell, Comm. 357.

INTERIM OFFICER. One appointed to fill the office during a temporary vacancy, or during an interval caused by the absence or incapacity of the regular incumbent.

INTERIM ORDER. One made in the mean time, and until something is done.

INTERIM RECEIPT. A receipt for money paid by way of premium for a contract of insurance for which application is made. If the risk is rejected, the money is refunded, less the *pro rata* premium.

INTERLAQUEARE. In old practice. To link together, or interchangeably. Writs

were called "*interlaqueata*" where several were issued against several parties residing in different counties, each party being summoned by a separate writ to warrant the tenant, together with the other warrantors. Fleta, lib. 5, c. 4, § 2.

INTERLINEATION. The act of writing between the lines of an instrument; also what is written between lines.

INTERLOCUTOR. In Scotch practice. An order or decree of court; an order made in open court. 2 Swint. 362; Arkley, 32.

INTERLOCUTOR OF RELEVANCY. In Scotch practice. A decree as to the relevancy of a libel or indictment in a criminal case. 2 Alis. Crim. Pr. 373.

INTERLOCUTORY. Provisional; temporary; not final. Something intervening between the commencement and the end of a suit which decides some point or matter, but is not a final decision of the whole controversy.

INTERLOCUTORY COSTS. In practice. Costs accruing upon proceedings in the intermediate stages of a cause, as distinguished from final costs; such as the costs of motions. 3 Chit. Gen. Pr. 597.

INTERLOCUTORY DECREE. In equity practice. A provisional or preliminary decree, which is not final and does not determine the suit, but directs some further proceedings preparatory to the final decree. A decree pronounced for the purpose of ascertaining matter of law or fact preparatory to a final decree. 1 Barb. Ch. Pr. 326, 327.

INTERLOCUTORY JUDGMENT. A judgment which is not final is called "interlocutory;" that is, an interlocutory judgment is one which determines some preliminary or subordinate point or plea, or settles some step, question, or default arising in the progress of the cause, but does not adjudicate the ultimate rights of the parties, or finally put the case out of court. Thus, a judgment or order passed upon any provisional or accessory claim or contention is, in general, merely interlocutory, although it may finally dispose of that particular matter. 1 Black, Judgm. § 21.

INTERLOCUTORY ORDER. "An order which decides not the cause, but only settles some intervening matter relating to it; as when an order is made, on a motion in chancery, for the plaintiff to have an injunction to quiet his possession till the hearing of

J

K

L

M

the cause. This or any such order, not being final, is interlocutory." Termes de la Ley.

INTERLOCUTORY SENTENCE. In the civil law. A sentence on some indirect question arising from the principal cause. Hallifax, Civil Law, b. 3, ch. 9, no. 40.

INTERLOPERS. Persons who run into business to which they have no right, or who interfere wrongfully; persons who enter a country or place to trade without license. Webster.

INTERN. To restrict or shut up a person, as a political prisoner, within a limited territory.

INTERNATIONAL LAW. The law which regulates the intercourse of nations; the law of nations. 1 Kent, Comm. 1, 4. The customary law which determines the rights and regulates the intercourse of independent states in peace and war. 1 Wildm. Int. Law, 1.

The system of rules and principles, founded on treaty, custom, precedent, and the consensus of opinion as to justice and moral obligation, which civilized nations recognize as binding upon them in their mutual dealings and relations.

Public international law is the body of rules which control the conduct of independent states in their relations with each other.

Private international law is that branch of municipal law which determines before the courts of what nation a particular action or suit should be brought, and by the law of what nation it should be determined; in other words, it regulates private rights as dependent on a diversity of municipal laws and jurisdictions applicable to the persons, facts, or things in dispute, and the subject of it is hence sometimes called the "conflict of laws." Thus, questions whether a given person owes allegiance to a particular state where he is domiciled, whether his *status*, property, rights, and duties are governed by the *lex sitûs*, the *lex loci*, the *lex fori*, or the *lex domicilii*, are questions with which private international law has to deal. Sweet.

INTERNUNCIO. A minister of a second order, charged with the affairs of the papal court in countries where that court has no nuncio.

INTERNUNCIUS. A messenger between two parties; a go-between. Applied to a broker, as the agent of both parties. 4 C. Rob. Adm. 204.

INTERPELATION. In the civil law. The act by which, in consequence of an agreement, the party bound declares that he will not be bound beyond a certain time. Wolff, Inst. Nat. § 752.

INTERPLEADER. When two or more persons claim the same thing (or fund) of a third, and he, laying no claim to it himself, is ignorant which of them has a right to it, and fears he may be prejudiced by their proceeding against him to recover it, he may file a bill in equity against them, the object of which is to make them litigate their title between themselves, instead of litigating it with him, and such a bill is called a "bill of interpleader." Brown.

By the statute 1 & 2 Wm. IV. c. 58, summary proceedings at *law* were provided for the same purpose, in actions of *assumpsit*, debt, detinue, and trover. And the same remedy is known, in one form or the other, in most or all of the United States.

Under the Pennsylvania practice, when goods levied upon by the sheriff are claimed by a third party, the sheriff takes a rule of interpleader on the parties, upon which, when made absolute, a feigned issue is framed, and the title to the goods is tested. The goods, pending the proceedings, remain in the custody of the defendant upon the execution of a forthcoming bond. Bouvier.

INTERPOLATE. To insert words in a complete document.

INTERPOLATION. The act of interpolating; the words interpolated.

INTERPRET. To construe; to seek out the meaning of language; to translate orally from one tongue to another.

Interpretare et concordare leges legibus, est optimus interpretandi modus. To interpret, and [in such a way as] to harmonize laws with laws, is the best mode of interpretation. 8 Coke, 169a.

Interpretatio chartarum benigne facienda est, ut res magis valeat quam pereat. The interpretation of deeds is to be liberal, that the thing may rather have effect than fail. Broom, Max. 543.

Interpretatio fienda est ut res magis valeat quam pereat. Jenk. Cent. 198. Such an interpretation is to be adopted that the thing may rather stand than fall.

Interpretatio talis in ambiguis semper fienda est ut evitetur inconveniens et absurdum. In cases of ambiguity, such an interpretation should always be made that what is inconvenient and absurd may be avoided. 4 Inst. 328.

INTERPRETATION. The discovery and representation of the true meaning of any signs used to convey ideas. Lieb. Herm.

"Construction" is a term of wider scope than "interpretation;" for, while the latter is concerned only with ascertaining the sense and meaning of the subject-matter, the former may also be directed to explaining the legal effects and consequences of the instrument in question. Hence interpretation precedes construction, but stops at the written text.

Close interpretation (*interpretatio restricta*) is adopted if just reasons, connected with the formation and character of the text, induce us to take the words in their narrowest meaning. This species of interpretation has generally been called "literal," but the term is inadmissible. Lieb. Herm. 54.

Extensive interpretation (*interpretatio extensiva*, called, also, "liberal interpretation") adopts a more comprehensive signification of the word. Id. 58.

Extravagant interpretation (*interpretatio excedens*) is that which substitutes a meaning evidently beyond the true one. It is therefore not genuine interpretation. Id. 59.

Free or unrestricted interpretation (*interpretatio soluta*) proceeds simply on the general principles of interpretation in good faith, not bound by any specific or superior principle. Id. 59.

Limited or restricted interpretation (*interpretatio limitata*) is when we are influenced by other principles than the strictly hermeneutic ones. Id. 60.

Predestined interpretation (*interpretatio predestinata*) takes place if the interpreter, laboring under a strong bias of mind, makes the text subservient to his preconceived views or desires. This includes artful interpretation, (*interpretatio vafer*,) by which the interpreter seeks to give a meaning to the text other than the one he knows to have been intended. Id. 60.

It is said to be either "legal," which rests on the same authority as the law itself, or "doctrinal," which rests upon its intrinsic reasonableness. Legal interpretation may be either "authentic," when it is expressly provided by the legislator, or "usual," when it is derived from unwritten practice. Doctrinal interpretation may turn on the meaning of words and sentences, when it is called "grammatical," or on the intention of the legislator, when it is described as "logical." When logical interpretation stretches the words of a statute to cover its obvious mean-

ing, it is called "extensive;" when, on the other hand, it avoids giving full meaning to the words, in order not to go beyond the intention of the legislator, it is called "restrictive." Holl. Jur. 344.

INTERPRETATION CLAUSE. A section of a statute which defines the meaning of certain words occurring frequently in the other sections.

INTERPRETER. A person sworn at a trial to interpret the evidence of a foreigner or a deaf and dumb person to the court.

INTERREGNUM. An interval between reigns. The period which elapses between the death of a sovereign and the election of another. The vacancy which occurs when there is no government.

INTERROGATOIRE. In French law. An act which contains the interrogatories made by the judge to the person accused, on the facts which are the object of the accusation, and the answers of the accused. Poth. Proc. Crim. c. 4, art. 2, § 1.

INTERROGATORIES. A set or series of written questions drawn up for the purpose of being propounded to a party in equity, a garnishee, or a witness whose testimony is taken on deposition; a series of formal written questions used in the judicial examination of a party or a witness. In taking evidence on depositions, the interrogatories are usually prepared and settled by counsel, and reduced to writing in advance of the examination.

Interrogatories are either *direct* or *cross*, the former being those which are put on behalf of the party calling a witness; the latter are those which are interposed by the adverse party.

INTERRUPTIO. Lat. Interruption. A term used both in the civil and common law of prescription. Calvin.

Interruptio multiplex non tollit præscriptionem semel obtentam. 2 Inst. 654. Frequent interruption does not take away a prescription once secured.

INTERRUPTION. The occurrence of some act or fact, during the period of prescription, which is sufficient to arrest the running of the statute of limitations. It is said to be either "natural" or "civil," the former being caused by the act of the party; the latter by the legal effect or operation of some fact or circumstance.

J

K

L

M

Interruption of the possession is where the right is not enjoyed or exercised continuously; interruption of the right is where the person having or claiming the right ceases the exercise of it in such a manner as to show that he does not claim to be entitled to exercise it.

In Scotch law. The true proprietor's claiming his right during the course of prescription. Bell.

INTERSECTION. The point of intersection of two roads is the point where their middle lines intersect. 73 Pa. St. 127.

INTERSTATE COMMERCE. Traffic, intercourse, commercial trading, or the transportation of persons or property between or among the several states of the Union, or from or between points in one state and points in another state; commerce between two states, or between places lying in different states.

INTERSTATE COMMERCE ACT. The act of congress of February 4, 1887, designed to regulate commerce between the states, and particularly the transportation of persons and property, by carriers, between interstate points, prescribing that charges for such transportation shall be reasonable and just, prohibiting unjust discrimination, rebates, draw-backs, preferences, pooling of freights, etc., requiring schedules of rates to be published, establishing a commission to carry out the measures enacted, and prescribing the powers and duties of such commission and the procedure before it.

INTERSTATE COMMERCE COMMISSION. A commission created by the interstate commerce act (q. v.) to carry out the measures therein enacted, composed of five persons, appointed by the President, empowered to inquire into the business of the carriers affected, to enforce the law, to receive, investigate, and determine complaints made to them of any violation of the act, make annual reports, hold stated sessions, etc.

INTERVENER. An intervener is a person who voluntarily interposes in an action or other proceeding with the leave of the court.

INTERVENING DAMAGES. Such damages to an appellee as result from the delay caused by the appeal. 1 Tyler, 267.

INTERVENTION. In international law. Intervention is such an interference between two or more states as may (according to the event) result in a resort to force; while mediation always is, and is intended to

be and to continue, peaceful only. Intervention between a sovereign and his own subjects is not justified by anything in international law; but a remonstrance may be addressed to the sovereign in a proper case. Brown.

In English ecclesiastical law. The proceeding of a third person, who, not being originally a party to the suit or proceeding, but claiming an interest in the subject-matter in dispute, in order the better to protect such interest, interposes his claim. 2 Chit. Pr. 492; 3 Chit. Commer. Law, 633; 2 Hagg. Const. 137; 3 Phillim. Ecc. Law, 586.

In the civil law. The act by which a third party demands to be received as a party in a suit pending between other persons.

The intervention is made either for the purpose of being joined to the plaintiff, and to claim the same thing he does, or some other thing connected with it; or to join the defendant, and with him to oppose the claim of the plaintiff, which it is his interest to defeat. Poth. Proc. Civile, pt. 1, c. 2, § 7, no. 3.

INTESTABILIS. A witness incompetent to testify. Calvin.

INTESTABLE. One who has not testamentary capacity; e. g., an infant, lunatic, or person civilly dead.

INTESTACY. The state or condition of dying without having made a valid will.

INTESTATE. Without making a will. A person is said to die intestate when he dies without making a will, or dies without leaving anything to testify what his wishes were with respect to the disposal of his property after his death. The word is also often used to signify the person himself. Thus, in speaking of the property of a person who died intestate, it is common to say "the intestate's property;" i. e., the property of the person dying in an intestate condition. Brown.

Besides the strict meaning of the word as above given, there is also a sense in which intestacy may be partial; that is, where a man leaves a will which does not dispose of his whole estate, he is said to "die intestate" as to the property so omitted.

INTESTATE SUCCESSION. A succession is called "intestate" when the deceased has left no will, or when his will has been revoked or annulled as irregular. Therefore the heirs to whom a succession has fallen by the effects of law only are called "heirs *ab intestato*." Civil Code La. art. 1096.

INTESTATO. In the civil law. Intestate; without a will. Calvin.

INTESTATUS. In the civil and old English law. An intestate; one who dies without a will. Dig. 50, 17, 7.

Intestatus decedit, qui aut omnino testamentum non fecit; aut non jure fecit; aut id quod fecerat ruptum irritumve factum est; aut nemo ex eo hæres exstitit. A person dies intestate who either has made no testament at all or has made one not legally valid; or if the testament he has made be revoked, or made useless; or if no one becomes heir under it. Inst. 3, 1, pr.

INTIMATION. In the civil law. A notification to a party that some step in a legal proceeding is asked or will be taken. Particularly, a notice given by the party taking an appeal, to the other party, that the court above will hear the appeal.

In Scotch law. A formal written notice, drawn by a notary, to be served on a party against whom a stranger has acquired a right or claim; e. g., the assignee of a debt must serve such a notice on the debtor, otherwise a payment to the original creditor will be good.

INTIMIDATION. In English law. Every person commits a misdemeanor, punishable with a fine or imprisonment, who wrongfully uses violence to or *intimidates* any other person, or his wife or children, with a view to compel him to abstain from doing, or to do, any act which he has a legal right to do, or abstain from doing. (St. 38 & 39 Vict. c. 86, § 7.) This enactment is chiefly directed against outrages by trades-unions. Sweet. There are similar statutes in many of the United States.

INTIMIDATION OF VOTERS. This, by statute in several of the states, is made a criminal offense. Under an early Pennsylvania act, it was held that, to constitute the offense of intimidation of voters, there must be a preconceived intention for the purpose of intimidating the officers or interrupting the election. 3 Yeates, 429.

INTITLE. An old form of "*entitle*." 6 Mod. 304.

INTOL AND UTTOL. In old records. Toll or custom paid for things imported and exported, or bought in and sold out. Cowell.

INTOXICATE. Generally relates to the use of strong drink. "Intoxicated," used without words of qualification, signifies a

condition produced by drinking intoxicating spirituous liquor, and is equivalent to "drunk." No additional word is needed to convey this idea. It is sometimes said that a person is intoxicated with opium, or with ether, or with laughing-gas; but this is an unusual or forced use of the word. A complaint, under a statute authorizing proceedings against persons found intoxicated, which avers that defendant was found intoxicated, is in this respect sufficient, and need not allege upon what he became so. 47 Vt. 294.

INTOXICATING LIQUORS. Those the use of which is ordinarily or commonly attended with entire or partial intoxication. 6 Park. Crim. R. 355.

The terms "intoxicating liquor" and "spirituous liquor" are not synonymous. All spirituous liquor is intoxicating, but all intoxicating liquor is not spirituous. Fermented liquor, though intoxicating, is not spirituous, because not distilled. 2 Gray, 501; 4 Gray, 18.

INTRA. Lat. In; near; within. "*Infra*" or "*inter*" has taken the place of "*intra*" in many of the more modern Latin phrases.

INTRA ANNI SPATIUM. Within the space of a year. Cod. 5, 9, 2. *Intra annale tempus.* Id. 6, 30, 19.

INTRA FIDEM. Within belief; credible. Calvin.

INTRA LUCTUS TEMPUS. Within the time of mourning. Cod. 9, 1, auth.

INTRA MŒNIA. Within the walls (of a house.) A term applied to domestic or *menial* servants. 1 Bl. Comm. 425.

INTRA PARIETES. Between walls; among friends; out of court; without litigation. Calvin.

INTRA PRÆSIDIA. Within the defenses. See INFRA PRÆSIDIA.

INTRA QUATUOR MARIA. Within the four seas. Shep. Touch. 378.

INTRA VIRES. An act to said to be *intra vires* ("within the power") of a person or corporation when it is within the scope of his or its powers or authority. It is the opposite of *ultra vires*, (q. v.)

INTRARE MARISCUM. To drain a marsh or low ground, and convert it into herbage or pasture.

INTRINSECUM SERVITIUM. Common and ordinary duties with the lord's court.

INTRINSIC VALUE. The intrinsic value of a thing is its true, inherent, and essential value, not depending upon accident, place, or person, but the same everywhere and to every one. 5 Ired. 698.

INTRODUCTION. The part of a writing which sets forth preliminary matter, or facts tending to explain the subject.

INTROMISSION. In Scotch law. The assumption of authority over another's property, either legally or illegally. The irregular intermeddling with the effects of a deceased person, which subjects the party to the whole debts of the deceased, is called *"vitious intromission."* Kames, Eq. b. 3, c. 8, § 2.

INTROMISSIONS. Dealings in stock, goods, or cash of a principal coming into the hands of his agent, to be accounted for by the agent to his principal. 29 Eng. Law & Eq. 391.

INTRONISATION. In French ecclesiastical law. Enthronement. The installation of a bishop in his episcopal see.

INTRUDER. A stranger who, on the death of the ancestor, enters on the land, unlawfully, before the heir can enter.

INTRUSION. A species of injury by ouster or amotion of possession from the freehold, being an entry of a stranger, after a particular estate of freehold is determined, before him in remainder or reversion.

The name of a writ brought by the owner of a fee-simple, etc., against an intruder. New Nat. Brev. 453. Abolished by 3 & 4 Wm. IV. c. 57.

INTUITUS. A view; regard; contemplation. *Diverso intuitu,* (q. v.,) with a different view.

INUNDATION. The overflow of waters by coming out of their bed.

INURE. To take effect; to result.

INUREMENT. Use; user; service to the use or benefit of a person. 100 U. S. 583.

Inutilis labor et sine fructu non est effectus legis. Useless and fruitless labor is not the effect of law. Co. Litt. 127b. The law forbids such recoveries whose ends are vain, chargeable, and unprofitable. Id; Wing. Max. p. 110, max. 38.

INVADIARE. To pledge or mortgage lands.

INVADIATIO. A pledge or mortgage.

INVADIATUS. One who is under pledge; one who has had sureties or pledges given for him. Spelman.

INVALID. Vain; inadequate to its purpose; not of binding force or legal efficacy; lacking in authority or obligation.

INVASION. An encroachment upon the rights of another; the incursion of an army for conquest or plunder. Webster.

INVASIONES. The inquisition of serjeanties and knights' fees. Cowell.

INVECTA ET ILLATA. Lat. In the civil law. Things carried in and brought in. Articles brought into a hired tenement by the hirer or tenant, and which became or were pledged to the lessor as security for the rent. Dig. 2, 14, 4, pr. The phrase is adopted in Scotch law. See Bell.

Inveniens libellum famosum et non corrumpens punitur. He who finds a libel and does not destroy it is punished. Moore, 813.

INVENT. To find out something new; to devise, contrive, and produce something not previously known or existing, by the exercise of independent investigation and experiment; particularly applied to machines, mechanical appliances, compositions, and patentable inventions of every sort.

INVENTIO. In the civil law. Finding; one of the modes of acquiring title to property by occupancy. Heinecc. lib. 2, tit. 1, § 350.

In old English law. A thing found; as goods, or treasure-trove. Cowell. The plural, *"inventiones,"* is also used.

INVENTION. In patent law. The act or operation of finding out something new; the process of contriving and producing something not previously known or existing, by the exercise of independent investigation and experiment. Also the article or contrivance or composition so invented.

An "invention" differs from a "discovery." The former term is properly applicable to the contrivance and production of something that did not before exist; while discovery denotes the bringing into knowledge and use of something which, although it existed, was before unknown. Thus, we speak of the "discovery" of the properties of light, electricity, etc., while the telescope and the electric motor are the results of the process of "invention."

INVENTOR. One who finds out or contrives some new thing; one who devises some new art, manufacture, mechanical appliance, or process; one who invents a patentable contrivance.

INVENTORY. A detailed list of articles of property; a list or schedule of property, containing a designation or description of each specific article; an itemized list of the various articles constituting a collection, estate, stock in trade, etc., with their estimated or actual values. In law, the term is particularly applied to such a list made by an executor, administrator, or assignee in bankruptcy.

INVENTUS. Lat. Found. *Thesaurus inventus*, treasure-trove. *Non est inventus*, [he] is not found.

INVERITARE. To make proof of a thing. Jacob.

INVEST. To loan money upon securities of a more or less permanent nature, or to place it in business ventures or real estate, or otherwise lay it out, so that it may produce a revenue or income.

To clothe one with the possession of a fief or benefice. See INVESTITURE.

INVESTITIVE FACT. The fact by means of which a right comes into existence; *e. g.*, a grant of a monopoly, the death of one's ancestor. Holl. Jur. 132.

INVESTITURE. A ceremony which accompanied the grant of lands in the feudal ages, and consisted in the open and notorious delivery of possession in the presence of the other vassals, which perpetuated among them the *æra* of their new acquisition at the time when the art of writing was very little known; and thus the evidence of the property was reposed in the memory of the neighborhood, who, in case of disputed title, were afterwards called upon to decide upon it. Brown.

In ecclesiastical law. Investiture is one of the formalities by which the election of a bishop is confirmed by the archbishop. See Phillim. Ecc. Law, 42, et seq.

INVESTMENT. Money invested.

INVIOLABILITY. The attribute of being secured against violation. The persons of ambassadors are inviolable.

INVITO. Lat. Being unwilling. Against or without the assent or consent.

Invito beneficium non datur. A benefit is not conferred on one who is unwilling to receive it; that is to say, no one can be compelled to accept a benefit. Dig. 50, 17, 69; Broom, Max. 699, note.

INVITO DEBITORE. Against the will of the debtor.

INVITO DOMINO. The owner being unwilling; against the will of the owner; without the owner's consent. In order to constitute larceny, the property must be taken *invito domino*.

INVOICE. In commercial law. An account of goods or merchandise sent by merchants to their correspondents at home or abroad, in which the marks of each package, with other particulars, are set forth. Marsh. Ins. 408; Dane, Abr. Index.

A list or account of goods or merchandise sent or shipped by a merchant to his correspondent, factor, or consignee, containing the particular marks of each description of goods, the value, charges, and other particulars. Jac. Sea Laws, 302.

A writing made on behalf of an importer, specifying the merchandise imported, and its true cost or value. And. Rev. Law, § 294.

INVOICE BOOK. A book in which invoices are copied.

INVOICE PRICE of goods means the prime cost. 7 Johns. 343.

INVOLUNTARY. An involuntary act is that which is performed with constraint (*q. v.*) or with repugnance, or without the will to do it. An action is involuntary, then, which is performed under duress. Wolff. Inst. Nat. § 5.

INVOLUNTARY MANSLAUGHTER. The unintentional killing of a person by one engaged in an unlawful, but not felonious, act. 4 Steph. Comm. 52.

IOTA. The minutest quantity possible. Iota is the smallest Greek letter. The word "jot" is derived therefrom.

Ipsæ leges cupiunt ut jure regantur. Co. Litt. 174. The laws themselves require that they should be governed by right.

IPSE. Lat. He himself; the same; the very person.

IPSE DIXIT. He himself said it; a bare assertion resting on the authority of an individual.

IPSISSIMIS VERBIS. In the identical words; opposed to "substantially." 7 How. 719; 5 Ohio St. 346.

IPSO FACTO. By the fact itself; by the mere fact. By the mere effect of an act or a fact.

J

K

L

M

In English ecclesiastical law. A censure of excommunication in the ecclesiastical court, immediately incurred for divers offenses, after lawful trial.

IPSO JURE. By the law itself; by the mere operation of law. Calvin.

Ira furor brevis est. Anger is a short insanity. 4 Wend. 336, 355.

IRA MOTUS. Moved or excited by anger or passion. A term sometimes formerly used in the plea of *son assault demesne.* 1 Tidd, Pr. 645.

IRE AD LARGUM. To go at large; to escape; to be set at liberty.

IRENARCHA. In Roman law. An officer whose duties are described in Dig. 5, 4, 18, 7. See Id. 48, 3, 6; Cod. 10, 75. Literally, a peace-officer or magistrate.

IRREGULAR. Not according to rule; improper or insufficient, by reason of departure from the prescribed course.

IRREGULAR DEPOSIT. A species of deposit which arises when a party, having a sum of money which he does not think safe in his own hands, confides it to another, (*e. g.,* a bank,) who is to return to him not the same money, but a like sum, when he shall demand it. An irregular deposit differs from a *mutuum* simply in this respect: that the latter has principally in view the benefit of the borrower, and the former the benefit of the bailor. Story, Bailm. § 84; Poth. du Depot. 82, 83.

IRREGULAR PROCESS. Sometimes the term "irregular process" has been defined to mean process absolutely void, and not merely erroneous and voidable; but usually it has been applied to all process not issued in strict conformity with the law, whether the defect appears upon the face of the process, or by reference to extrinsic facts, and whether such defects render the process absolutely void or only voidable. 2 Ind. 252.

IRREGULARITY. Violation or non-observance of established rules and practices. The want of adherence to some prescribed rule or mode of proceeding; consisting either in omitting to do something that is necessary for the due and orderly conducting of a suit, or doing it in an unseasonable time or improper manner. 1 Tidd, Pr. 512. "Irregularity" is the technical term for every defect in practical proceedings, or the mode of conducting an action or defense, as distinguishable from defects in pleadings. 3 Chit. Gen. Pr. 509.

The doing or not doing that, in the conduct of a suit at law, which, conformably with the practice of the court, ought or ought not to be done. 2 Ind. 252.

In canon law. Any impediment which prevents a man from taking holy orders.

IRRELEVANCY. The absence of the quality of relevancy in evidence or pleadings.

Irrelevancy, in an answer, consists in statements which are not material to the decision of the case; such as do not form or tender any material issue. 18 N. Y. 315, 321.

IRRELEVANT. In the law of evidence. Not relevant; not relating or applicable to the matter in issue; not supporting the issue.

IRREMOVABILITY. The *status* of a pauper in England, who cannot be legally removed from the parish or union in which he is receiving relief, notwithstanding that he has not acquired a settlement there. 3 Steph. Comm. 60.

IRREPARABLE INJURY. This phrase does not mean such an injury as is beyond the possibility of repair, or beyond possible compensation in damages, or necessarily great damage, but includes an injury, whether great or small, which ought not to be submitted to, on the one hand, or inflicted, on the other; and which, because it is so large or so small, or is of such constant and frequent occurrence, cannot receive reasonable redress in a court of law. 76 Ill. 322.

Wrongs of a repeated and continuing character, or which occasion damages that are estimated only by conjecture, and not by any accurate standard, are included. 3 Pittsb. R. 204.

IRREPLEVIABLE. That cannot be replevied or delivered on sureties. Spelled, also, "irreplevisable." Co. Litt. 145.

IRRESISTIBLE FORCE. A term applied to such an interposition of human agency as is, from its nature and power, absolutely uncontrollable; as the inroads of a hostile army. Story, Bailm. § 25.

IRREVOCABLE. Which cannot be revoked or recalled.

IRRIGATION. The operation of watering lands for agricultural purposes by artificial means.

IRRITANCY. In Scotch law. The happening of a condition or event by which a charter, contract, or other deed, to which a clause irritant is annexed, becomes void.

IRRITANT. In Scotch law. Avoiding or making void; as an irritant clause. See IRRITANCY.

IRRITANT CLAUSE. In Scotch law. A provision by which certain prohibited acts specified in a deed are, if committed, declared to be null and void. A *resolutive* clause dissolves and puts an end to the right of a proprietor on his committing the acts so declared void.

IRROGARE. In the civil law. To impose or set upon, as a fine. Calvin. To inflict, as a punishment. To make or ordain, as a law.

IRROTULATIO. An enrolling; a record.

IS QUI COGNOSCIT. Lat. The cognizor in a fine. *Is cui cognoscitur*, the cognizee.

ISH. In Scotch law. The period of the termination of a tack or lease. 1 Bligh, 522.

ISLAND. A piece of land surrounded by water.

ISSINT. A law French term, meaning "thus," "so," giving its name to part of a plea in debt.

ISSUABLE. In practice. Leading to or producing an issue; relating to an issue or issues.

ISSUABLE PLEA. A plea to the merits; a traversable plea. A plea such that the adverse party can join issue upon it and go to trial.

It is true a plea in abatement is a plea, and, if it be properly pleaded, issues may be found on it. In the ordinary meaning of the word "plea," and of the word "issuable," such pleas may be called "issuable pleas," but, when these two words are used together, "issuable plea," or "issuable defense," they have a technical meaning, to-wit, pleas to the merits. 44 Ga. 434.

ISSUABLE TERMS. In the former practice of the English courts, Hilary term and Trinity term were called "issuable terms," because the issues to be tried at the assizes were made up at those terms. 3 Bl. Comm. 353. But the distinction is superseded by the provisions of the judicature acts of 1873 and 1875.

ISSUE, *v.* To send forth; to emit; to promulgate; as, an officer *issues* orders, process *issues* from a court. To put into circulation; as, the treasury *issues* notes.

ISSUE, *n.* The act of issuing, sending forth, emitting, or promulgating; the giving a thing its first inception; as the issue of an order or a writ.

In pleading. The disputed point or question to which the parties in an action have narrowed their several allegations, and upon which they are desirous of obtaining the decision of the proper tribunal. When the plaintiff and defendant have arrived at some specific point or matter affirmed on the one side, and denied on the other, they are said to be at issue. The question so set apart is called the "issue," and is designated, according to its nature, as an "issue in fact" or an "issue in law." Brown.

Issues arise upon the pleadings, when a fact or conclusion of law is maintained by the one party and controverted by the other. They are of two kinds: (1) Of law; and (2) of fact. Code N. Y. § 243; Rev. Code Iowa 1880, § 2737; Code Civil Proc. Cal. § 588.

Issues are classified and distinguished as follows:

General and *special.* The former is raised by a plea which briefly and directly traverses the whole declaration, such as "not guilty" or "*non assumpsit.*" The latter is formed when the defendant chooses one single material point, which he traverses, and rests his whole case upon its determination.

Material and *immaterial.* They are so described according as they do or do not bring up some material point or question which, when determined by the verdict, will dispose of the whole merits of the case, and leave no uncertainty as to the judgment.

Formal and *informal.* The former species of issue is one framed in strict accordance with the technical rules of pleading. The latter arises when the material allegations of the declaration are traversed, but in an inartificial or untechnical mode.

Real or *feigned.* A real issue is one formed in a regular manner in a regular suit for the purpose of determining an actual controversy. A feigned issue is one made up by direction of the court, upon a supposed case, for the purpose of obtaining the verdict of a jury upon some question of fact collaterally involved in the cause.

Common issue is the name given to the issue raised by the plea of *non est factum* to an action for breach of covenant.

In real law. Descendants. All persons who have descended from a common ancestor.

3 Ves. 257; 17 Ves. 481; 19 Ves. 547; 1 Rop. Leg. 90.

In this sense, the word includes not only a child or children, but all other descendants in whatever degree; and it is so construed generally in deeds. But, when used in wills, it is, of course, subject to the rule of construction that the intention of the testator, as ascertained from the will, is to have effect, rather than the technical meaning of the language used by him; and hence issue may, in such a connection, be restricted to children, or to descendants living at the death of the testator, where such an intention clearly appears. Abbott.

In business law. A class or series of bonds, debentures, etc., comprising all that are emitted at one and the same time.

ISSUE IN FACT. In pleading. An issue taken upon or consisting of matter of *fact*, the fact only, and not the law being disputed, and which is to be tried by a jury. 3 Bl. Comm. 314, 315; Co. Litt. 126*a*; 3 Steph. Comm. 572. See Code Civil Proc. Cal. § 590.

ISSUE IN LAW. In pleading. An issue upon matter of law, or consisting of matter of law, being produced by a demurrer on the one side, and a joinder in demurrer on the other. 3 Bl. Comm. 314; 3 Steph. Comm. 572, 580. See Code Civil Proc. Cal. § 589.

ISSUE ROLL. In English practice. A roll upon which the issue in actions at law was formerly required to be entered, the roll being entitled of the term in which the issue was joined. 2 Tidd, Pr. 733. It was not, however, the practice to enter the issue at full length, if triable by the country, until after the trial, but only to make an *incipitur* on the roll. Id. 734.

ISSUES. In English law. The goods and profits of the lands of a defendant against whom a writ of *distringas* or *distress infinite* has been issued, taken by virtue of such writ, are called "issues." 3 Bl. Comm. 280; 1 Chit. Crim. Law, 351.

ITA EST. Lat. So it is; so it stands. In modern civil law, this phrase is a form of attestation added to exemplifications from a notary's register when the same are made by the successor in office of the notary who made the original entries.

ITA LEX SCRIPTA EST. Lat. So the law is written. Dig. 40, 9, 12. The law must be obeyed notwithstanding the apparent rigor of its application. 3 Bl. Comm. 430. We must be content with the law as it stands, without inquiring into its reasons. 1 Bl. Comm. 32.

ITA QUOD. In old practice. So that. Formal words in writs. *Ita quod habeas corpus,* so that you have the body. 2 Mod. 180.

The name of the stipulation in a submission to arbitration which begins with the words "so as [*ita quod*] the award be made of and upon the premises."

In old conveyancing. So that. An expression which, when used in a deed, formerly made an estate upon condition. Litt. § 329. Sheppard enumerates it among the three words that are most proper to make an estate conditional. Shep. Touch. 121, 122.

Ita semper fiat relatio ut valeat dispositio. 6 Coke, 76. Let the interpretation be always such that the disposition may prevail.

ITA TE DEUS ADJUVET. Lat. So help you God. The old form of administering an oath in England, generally in connection with other words, thus: *Ita te Deus adjuvet, et sacrosancta Dei Evangelia,* So help you God, and God's holy Evangelists. *Ita te Deus adjuvet et omnes sancti,* So help you God and all the saints. Willes, 338.

Ita utere tuo ut alienum non lædas. Use your own property and your own rights in such a way that you will not hurt your neighbor, or prevent him from enjoying his. Frequently written, "*Sic utere tuo,*" etc., (*q. v.*)

ITEM. Also; likewise; again. This word was formerly used to mark the beginning of a new paragraph or division after the first, whence is derived the common application of it to denote a separate or distinct particular of an account or bill.

The word is sometimes used as a verb. "The whole [costs] in this case that was thus *itemed* to counsel." Bunb. p. 164, case 233.

ITER. In the civil law. A way; a right of way belonging as a servitude to an estate in the country, (*prædium rusticum.*) The right of way was of three kinds: (1) *iter,* a right to walk, or ride on horseback, or in a litter; (2) *actus,* a right to drive a beast or vehicle; (3) *via,* a full right of way, comprising right to walk or ride, or drive beast or carriage. Heinec. § 408. Or, as some think, they were distinguished by the width of the objects which could be rightfully carried over the way; e. g., *via,* 8 feet; *actus,* 4 feet, etc. Mackeld. Rom. Law, § 290; Bract. fol. 232; 4 Bell, H. L. Sc. 390.

In old English law. A journey, especially a circuit made by a justice in eyre, or itinerant justice, to try causes according to his own mission. Du Cange; Bract. lib. 3, cc. 11, 12, 13.

In maritime law. A way or route. The route or direction of a voyage; the route or way that is taken to make the voyage assured. Distinguished from the voyage itself.

Iter est jus eundi, ambulandi hominis; non etiam jumentum agendi vel vehiculum. A way is the right of going or walking, and does not include the right of driving a beast of burden or a carriage. Co. Litt. 56*a*; Inst. 2, 3, pr.; Mackeld. Rom. Law, § 318.

ITERATIO. Repetition. In the Roman law, a bonitary owner might liberate a slave, and the quiritary owner's repetition (*iteratio*) of the process effected a complete manumission. Brown.

ITINERA. Eyres, or circuits. 1 Reeve, Eng. Law, 52.

ITINERANT. Wandering; traveling; applied to justices who make circuits.

IULE. In old English law. Christmas.

J

K

I

M

J.

J. The initial letter of the words "judge" and "justice," for which it frequently stands as an abbreviation. Thus, "J. A.," judge advocate; "J. J.," junior judge; "L. J.," law judge; "P. J.," president judge; "F. J.," first judge; "A. J.," associate judge; "C. J.," chief justice or judge; "J. P.," justice of the peace; "JJ.," judges or justices; "J. C. P.," justice of the common pleas; "J. K. B.," justice of the king's bench; "J. Q. B.," justice of the queen's bench; "J. U. B.," justice of the upper bench.

This letter is sometimes used for "I," as the initial letter of "Institutiones," in references to the Institutes of Justinian.

JAC. An abbreviation for "*Jacobus*," the Latin form of the name James; used principally in citing statutes enacted in the reigns of the English kings of that name; *e. g.*, "St. 1 Jac. II." Used also in citing the second part of Croke's reports; thus, "Cro. Jac." denotes "Croke's reports of cases in the time of James I."

JACENS. Lat. Lying in abeyance.

JACENS HÆREDITAS. An inheritance in abeyance. See HÆREDITAS JACENS.

JACET IN ORE. In old English law. It lies in the mouth. Fleta, lib. 5, c. 5, § 49.

JACK. A kind of defensive coat-armor worn by horsemen in war; not made of solid iron, but of many plates fastened together. Some tenants were bound by their tenure to find it upon invasion. Cowell.

JACOBUS. A gold coin worth 24s., so called from James I., who was king when it was struck. Enc. Lond.

JACTITATION. A false boasting; a false claim; assertions repeated to the prejudice of another's right. The species of defamation or disparagement of another's title to real estate known at common law as "slander of title" comes under the head of jactitation, and in some jurisdictions (as in Louisiana) a remedy for this injury is provided under the name of an "action of jactitation."

JACTITATION OF A RIGHT TO A CHURCH SITTING appears to be the boasting by a man that he has a right or title to a pew or sitting in a church to which he has legally no title.

JACTITATION OF MARRIAGE. In English ecclesiastical law. The boasting or giving out by a party that he or she is married to some other, whereby a common reputation of their matrimony may ensue. To defeat that result, the person may be put to a proof of the actual marriage, failing which proof, he or she is put to silence about it. 3 Bl. Comm. 93.

JACTITATION OF TITHES is the boasting by a man that he is entitled to certain tithes to which he has legally no title.

JACTIVUS. Lost by default; tossed away. Cowell.

JACTURA. In the civil law. A throwing of goods overboard in a storm; jettison. Loss from such a cause. Calvin.

JACTUS. A throwing goods overboard to lighten or save the vessel, in which case the goods so sacrificed are a proper subject for general average. Dig. 14, 2, "*de lege Rhodia de Jactu.*"

JACTUS LAPILLI. The throwing down of a stone. One of the modes, under the civil law, of interrupting prescription. Where one person was building on another's ground, and in this way acquiring a right by *usucapio*, the true owner challenged the intrusion and interrupted the prescriptive right by throwing down one of the stones of the building before witnesses called for the purpose. Tray. Lat. Max.

JAIL. A gaol; a prison; a building designated by law, or regularly used, for the confinement of persons held in lawful custody. See GAOL.

JAIL DELIVERY. See GAOL DELIVERY.

JAIL LIBERTIES. See GAOL LIBERTIES.

JAILER. A keeper or warden of a prison or jail.

JAMBEAUX. Leg-armor. Blount.

JAMMA, JUMMA. In Hindu law. Total amount; collection; assembly. The total of a territorial assignment.

JAMMABUNDY, JUMMABUNDY. In Hindu law. A written schedule of the whole of an assessment.

JAMPNUM. Furze, or grass, or ground where furze grows; as distinguished from "arable," "pasture," or the like. Co. Litt. 5a.

JAMUNLINGI, JAMUNDILINGI. Freemen who delivered themselves and property to the protection of a more powerful person, in order to avoid military service and other burdens. Spelman. Also a species of serfs among the Germans. Du Cange. The same as *commendati*.

JANITOR. In old English law. A door-keeper. Fleta, lib. 2, c. 24.

In modern law. A janitor is understood to be a person employed to take charge of rooms or buildings, to see that they are kept clean and in order, to lock and unlock them, and generally to care for them. 84 N. Y. 352.

JAQUES. In old English law. Small money.

JAVELIN-MEN. Yeomen retained by the sheriff to escort the judge of assize.

JAVELOUR. In Scotch law. Jailer or gaoler. 1 Pitc. Crim. Tr. pt. 1, p. 33.

JEDBURGH JUSTICE. Lynch law.

JEMAN. In old records. Yeoman. Cowell; Blount.

JEOFAILE. L. Fr. I have failed; I am in error. An error or oversight in pleading.

Certain statutes are called "statutes of amendments and jeofailes" because, where a pleader perceives any slip in the form of his proceedings, and acknowledges the error, (jeofaile,) he is at liberty, by those statutes, to amend it. The amendment, however, is seldom made; but the benefit is attained by the court's overlooking the exception. 3 Bl. Comm. 407; 1 Saund. p. 228, no. 1.

Jeofaile is when the parties to any suit in pleading have proceeded so far that they have joined issue which shall be tried or is tried by a jury or inquest, and this pleading or issue is so badly pleaded or joined that it will be error if they proceed. Then some of the said parties may, by their counsel, show it to the court, as well after verdict given and before judgment as before the jury is charged. And the counsel shall say: "This inquest ye ought not to take." And if it be after verdict, then he may say: "To judgment you ought not to go." And, because such niceties occasioned many delays in suits, divers statutes are made to redress them. Termes de la Ley.

JEOPARDY. Danger; hazard; peril. Jeopardy is the danger of conviction and punishment which the defendant in a crim-inal action incurs when a valid indictment has been found, and a petit jury has been impaneled and sworn to try the case and give a verdict.

JERGUER. In English law. An officer of the custom-house who oversees the waiters. Techn. Dict.

JESSE. A large brass candlestick, usually hung in the middle of a church or choir. Cowell.

JET. Fr. In French law. Jettison. Ord. Mar. liv. 3, tit. 8; Emerig. Traité des Assur. c. 12, § 40.

JETSAM. A term descriptive of goods which, by the act of the owner, have been voluntarily cast overboard from a vessel, in a storm or other emergency, to lighten the ship. 1 C. B. 113.

Jetsam is where goods are cast into the sea, and there sink and remain under water. 1 Bl. Comm. 292.

Jetsam differs from "flotsam," in this: that in the latter the goods float, while in the former they sink, and remain under water. It differs also from "ligan."

JETTISON. The act of throwing overboard from a vessel part of the cargo, in case of extreme danger, to lighten the ship. The same name is also given to the thing or things so cast out.

A carrier by water may, when in case of extreme peril it is necessary for the safety of the ship or cargo, throw overboard, or otherwise sacrifice, any or all of the cargo or appurtenances of the ship. Throwing property overboard for such purpose is called "jettison," and the loss incurred thereby is called a "general average loss." Civil Code Cal. § 2148; Civil Code Dak. § 1245.

JEUX DE BOURSE. In French law. Speculation in the public funds or in stocks; gambling speculations on the stock exchange; dealings in "options" and "futures."

JEWEL. By "jewels" are meant ornaments of the person, such as ear-rings, pearls, diamonds, etc., which are prepared to be worn. Brown, Ch. 467. See, further, 43 N. Y. 539; 36 Barb. 70; 14 Pick. 370; 33 Fed. Rep. 709.

JOB. The whole of a thing which is to be done. "To build by plot, or to work by the job, is to undertake a building for a certain stipulated price." Civil Code La. art. 2727.

JOBBER. One who buys and sells goods for others; one who buys or sells on the stock exchange; a dealer in stocks, shares, or securities.

JOCALIA. In old English law. Jewels. This term was formerly more properly applied to those ornaments which women, although married, call their own. When these *jocalia* are not suitable to her degree, they are assets for the payment of debts. 1 Rolle, Abr. 911.

JOCELET. A little manor or farm. Cowell.

JOCUS. In old English law. A game of hazard. Reg. Orig. 290.

JOCUS PARTITUS. In old English practice. A divided game, risk, or hazard. An arrangement which the parties to a suit were anciently sometimes allowed to make by mutual agreement upon a certain hazard, (*sub periculo;*) as that one should lose if the case turned out in a certain way, and, if it did not, that the other should gain, (*quod unus amittat si ita sit, et si non sit, quod alius lucretur.*) Bract. fols. 211*b*, 379*b*, 432, 434, 200*b*.

JOHN DOE. The name which was usually given to the fictitious lessee of the plaintiff in the mixed action of ejectment. He was sometimes called "Goodtitle." So the Romans had their fictitious personages in law proceedings, as *Titius, Seius.*

JOINDER. Joining or coupling together; uniting two or more constituents or elements in one; uniting with another person in some legal step or proceeding.

JOINDER IN DEMURRER. When a defendant in an action tenders an issue of law, (called a "demurrer,") the plaintiff, if he means to maintain his action, must accept it, and this acceptance of the defendant's tender, signified by the plaintiff in a set form of words, is called a "joinder in demurrer." Brown.

JOINDER IN ISSUE. In pleading. A formula by which one of the parties to a suit joins in or accepts an issue in fact tendered by the opposite party. Steph. Pl. 57, 236. More commonly termed a "*similiter.*" (*q. v.*)

JOINDER IN PLEADING. Accepting the issue, and mode of trial tendered, either by demurrer, error, or issue in fact, by the opposite party.

JOINDER OF ACTIONS. This expression signifies the uniting of two or more demands or rights of action in one action; the statement of more than one cause of action in a declaration.

JOINDER OF ERROR. In proceedings on a writ of error in criminal cases, the joinder of error is a written denial of the errors alleged in the assignment of errors. It answers to a joinder of issue in an action.

JOINDER OF OFFENSES. The uniting of several distinct charges of crime in the same indictment or prosecution.

JOINDER OF PARTIES. The uniting of two or more persons as co-plaintiffs or as co-defendants in one suit.

JOINT. United; combined; undivided; done by or against two or more unitedly; shared by or between two or more.

JOINT ACTION. An action in which there are two or more plaintiffs, or two or more defendants.

JOINT ADVENTURE. A commercial or maritime enterprise undertaken by several persons jointly. See ADVENTURE.

JOINT AND SEVERAL BOND. A bond in which the obligors bind themselves both jointly and individually to the obligee, and which may be enforced either by a joint action against all or separate actions against each.

JOINT BOND. One in which the obligors (two or more in number) bind themselves jointly, but not severally, and which must therefore be prosecuted in a joint action against all the obligors.

JOINT COMMITTEE. A joint committee of a legislative body comprising two chambers is a committee consisting of representatives of each of the two houses, meeting and acting together as one committee.

JOINT CONTRACT. One made by two or more promisors, who are jointly bound to fulfill its obligations, or made to two or more promisees, who are jointly entitled to require performance of the same.

JOINT CREDITORS. Persons jointly entitled to require satisfaction of the same debt or demand.

JOINT DEBTOR ACTS. Statutes enacted in many of the states, which provide that judgment may be given for or against one or more of several plaintiffs, and for or against one or more of several defendants, and that, "in an action against several defendants, the court may, in its discretion, render judgment against one or more of them, leaving the action to proceed against the others, whenever a several judgment is proper." The name is also given to statutes providing that where an action is instituted against two or more defendants upon an alleged joint liability, and some of them are served with process, but jurisdiction is not obtained over the others, the plaintiff may still proceed to trial against those who are before the court, and, if he recovers, may have judgment against all of the defendants whom he shows to be jointly liable. 1 Black, Judgm. §§ 208, 235.

JOINT DEBTORS. Persons united in a joint liability or indebtedness.

JOINT EXECUTORS. Co-executors; two or more who are joined in the execution of a will.

JOINT FIAT. In English law. A fiat in bankruptcy, issued against two or more trading partners.

JOINT FINE. In old English law. "If a whole vill is to be fined, a joint fine may be laid, and it will be good for the necessity of it; but, in other cases, fines for offenses are to be severally imposed on each particular offender, and not jointly upon all of them." Jacob.

JOINT HEIR. A co-heir.

JOINT INDICTMENT. When several offenders are joined in the same indictment, such an indictment is called a "joint indictment;" as when principals in the first and second degree, and accessaries before and after the fact, are all joined in the same indictment. 2 Hale, P. C. 173; Brown.

JOINT LIVES. This expression is used to designate the duration of an estate or right which is granted to two or more persons to be enjoyed so long as they both (or all) shall live. As soon as one dies, the interest determines.

JOINT-STOCK BANKS. In English law. Joint-stock companies for the purpose of banking. They are regulated, according to the date of their incorporation, by charter, or by 7 Geo. IV. c. 46; 7 & 8 Vict. cc. 32, 113; 9 & 10 Vict. c. 45, (in Scotland and Ireland;) 20 & 21 Vict. c. 49; and 27 & 28 Vict. c. 32; or by the "Joint-Stock Companies Act, 1862," (25 & 26 Vict. c. 89.) Wharton.

JOINT-STOCK COMPANY. An unincorporated association of individuals for business purposes, resembling a partnership in many respects, but possessing a common fund or capital stock, divided into shares, which are apportioned among the members according to their respective contributions, and which are assignable by the owner without the consent of the other members.

An association of a large number of persons united together for the common purpose of carrying on a trade or some useful enterprise capable of yielding profit. The common property of the members, applicable to the purposes of the company, is called its "joint stock." Wharton.

The words "joint-stock company" have never been used as descriptive of a corporation created by special act of the legislature, and authorized to issue certificates of stock to its shareholders. They describe a partnership made up of many persons acting under articles of association, for the purpose of carrying on a particular business, and having a capital stock, divided into shares transferable at the pleasure of the holder. 121 Mass. 526.

JOINT-STOCK CORPORATION. This differs from a joint-stock *company* in being regularly incorporated, instead of being a mere partnership, but resembles it in having a capital divided into shares of stock. Most business corporations (as distinguished from eleemosynary corporations) are of this character.

JOINT TENANCY. An estate in joint tenancy is an estate in fee-simple, fee-tail, for life, for years, or at will, arising by purchase or grant to two or more persons. Joint tenants have one and the same interest, accruing by one and the same conveyance, commencing at one and the same time, and held by one and the same undivided possession. The grand incident of joint tenancy is survivorship, by which the entire tenancy on the decease of any joint tenant remains to the survivors, and at length to the last survivor. Pub. St. Mass. 1882, p. 1292.

A joint interest is one owned by several persons in equal shares, by a title created by a single will or transfer, when expressly declared in the will or transfer to be a joint tenancy, or when granted or devised to executors or trustees as joint tenants. Civil Code Cal. § 683.

JOINT TENANTS. Two or more persons to whom are granted lands or tenements to hold in fee-simple, fee-tail, for life, for years, or at will. 2 Bl. Comm. 179.

Persons who own lands by a joint title created expressly by one and the same deed or will. 4 Kent, Comm. 357. Joint tenants have one and the same interest, accruing by

K

L

M

one and the same conveyance, commencing at one and the same time, and held by one and the same undivided possession. 2 Bl. Comm. 180.

JOINT TRESPASSERS. Two or more who unite in committing a trespass.

JOINT TRUSTEES. Two or more persons who are intrusted with property for the benefit of one or more others.

JOINTRESS, JOINTURESS. A woman who has an estate settled on her by her husband, to hold during her life, if she survive him. Co. Litt. 46.

JOINTURE. A freehold estate in lands or tenements secured to the wife, and to take effect on the decease of the husband, and to continue during her life at the least, unless she be herself the cause of its determination. 21 Me. 369.

A competent livelihood of freehold for the wife of lands and tenements to take effect presently in possession or profit, after the decease of the husband, for the life of the wife at least. Co. Litt. 36*b;* 2 Bl. Comm. 137.

A jointure strictly signifies a joint estate limited to both husband and wife, and such was its original form; but, in its more usual form, it is a sole estate limited to the wife only, expectant upon a life-estate in the husband. 2 Bl. Comm. 137; 1 Steph. Comm. 255.

JONCARIA, or JUNCARIA. Land where rushes grow. Co. Litt. 5*a.*

JORNALE. As much land as could be plowed in one day. Spelman.

JOUR. A French word, signifying "day." It is used in our old law-books; as "*tout jours,*" forever.

JOUR EN BANC. A day *in banc.* Distinguished from "*jour en pays,*" (a day in the country,) otherwise called "*jour en nisi prius.*"

JOUR IN COURT. In old practice. Day in court; day to appear in court; appearance day. "Every process gives the defendant a day in court." Hale, Anal. § 8.

JOURNAL. A daily book; a book in which entries are made or events recorded from day to day. In maritime law, the journal (otherwise called "log" or "log-book") is a book kept on every vessel, which contains a brief record of the events and occurrences of each day of a voyage, with the nautical observations, course of the ship, account of the weather, etc. In the system of double-entry book-keeping, the journal is an account-book into which are transcribed, daily or at other intervals, the items entered upon the day-book, for more convenient posting into the ledger. In the usage of legislative bodies, the journal is a daily record of the proceedings of either house. It is kept by the clerk, and in it are entered the appointments and actions of committees, introduction of bills, motions, votes, resolutions, etc., in the order of their occurrence.

JOURNEY. The original signification of this word was a day's travel. It is now applied to a travel by land from place to place, without restriction of time. But, when thus applied, it is employed to designate a travel which is without the ordinary habits, business, or duties of the person, to a distance from his home, and beyond the circle of his friends or acquaintances. 53 Ala. 521.

JOURNEY-HOPPERS. In English law. Regrators of yarn. 8 Hen. VI. c. 5.

JOURNEYMAN. A workman hired by the day, or other given time.

JOURNEYS ACCOUNTS. In English practice. The name of a writ (now obsolete) which might be sued out where a former writ had abated without the plaintiff's fault. The length of time allowed for taking it out depended on the length of the *journey* the party must make to reach the court; whence the name.

JUBERE. Lat. In the civil law. To order, direct, or command. Calvin. The word *jubeo,* (I order,) in a will, was called a "word of direction," as distinguished from "precatory words." Cod. 6, 43, 2.

To assure or promise.

To decree or pass a law.

JUBILACION. In Spanish law. The privilege of a public officer to be retired, on account of infirmity or disability, retaining the rank and pay of his office (or part of the same) after twenty years of public service, and on reaching the age of fifty.

JUDÆUS, JUDEUS. Lat. A Jew.

JUDAISMUS. The religion and rites of the Jews. Du Cange. A quarter set apart for residence of Jews. A usurious rate of interest. 1 Mon. Angl. 839; 2 Mon. Angl. 10, 665. *Sex marcus sterlingorum ad acquietandam terram prædictum de Judaismo, in quo fuit impignorata.* Du Cange. An income anciently accruing to the king from the Jews. Blount.

JUDEX. Lat. In Roman law. A private person appointed by the prætor, with the consent of the parties, to try and decide a cause or action commenced before him. He received from the prætor a written formula instructing him as to the legal principles according to which the action was to be judged. Calvin. Hence the proceedings before him were said to be *in judicio*, as those before the prætor were said to be *in jure*.

In later and modern civil law. A judge, in the modern sense of the term.

In old English law. A juror. A judge, in modern sense, especially—as opposed to *justiciarius, i. e.*, a common-law judge—to denote an ecclesiastical judge. Bract. fols. 401, 402.

JUDEX A QUO. In modern civil law. The judge *from* whom, as *judex ad quem* is the judge *to* whom, an appeal is made or taken. Hallifax, Civil Law, b. 3, c. 11, no. 34.

JUDEX AD QUEM. A judge to whom an appeal is taken.

Judex æquitatem semper spectare debet. A judge ought always to regard equity. Jenk. Cent. p. 45, case 85.

Judex ante oculos æquitatem semper habere debet. A judge ought always to have equity before his eyes.

Judex bonus nihil ex arbitrio suo faciat, nec proposito domesticæ voluntatis, sed juxta leges et jura pronunciet. A good judge should do nothing of his own arbitrary will, nor on the dictate of his personal inclination, but should decide according to law and justice. 7 Coke, 27a.

Judex damnatur cum nocens absolvitur. The judge is condemned when a guilty person escapes punishment.

JUDEX DATUS. In Roman law. A judge given, that is, assigned or appointed, by the prætor to try a cause.

Judex debet judicare secundum allegata et probata. The judge ought to decide according to the allegations and the proofs.

JUDEX DELEGATUS. A delegated judge; a special judge.

Judex est lex loquens. A judge is the law speaking, [the mouth of the law.] 7 Coke, 4a.

JUDEX FISCALIS. A fiscal judge; one having cognizance of matters relating to the *fiscus*, (q. v.)

Judex habere debet duos sales,—salem sapientiæ, ne sit insipidus; et salem conscientiæ, ne sit diabolus. A judge should have two salts,—the salt of wisdom, lest he be insipid; and the salt of conscience, lest he be devilish.

Judex non potest esse testis in propria causa. A judge cannot be a witness in his own cause. 4 Inst. 279.

Judex non potest injuriam sibi datam punire. A judge cannot punish a wrong done to himself. See 12 Coke, 114.

Judex non reddit plus quam quod petens ipse requirit. A judge does not give more than what the complaining party himself demands. 2 Inst. 286.

JUDEX ORDINARIUS. In the civil law. An ordinary judge; one who had the right of hearing and determining causes as a matter of his own proper jurisdiction, (*ex propria jurisdictione*,) and not by virtue of a delegated authority. Calvin.

JUDEX PEDANEUS. In Roman law. The judge who was commissioned by the prætor to hear a cause was so called, from the low seat which he anciently occupied at the foot of the prætor's tribunal.

JUDGE. A public officer, appointed to preside and to administer the law in a court of justice; the chief member of a court, and charged with the control of proceedings and the decision of questions of law or discretion. "Judge" and "justice" (q. v.) are often used in substantially the same sense.

JUDGE ADVOCATE. An officer of a court-martial, whose duty is to swear in the other members of the court, to advise the court, and to act as the public prosecutor; but he is also so far the counsel for the prisoner as to be bound to protect him from the necessity of answering criminating questions, and to object to leading questions when propounded to other witnesses.

JUDGE ADVOCATE GENERAL. The adviser of the government in reference to courts-martial and other matters of military law. In England, he is generally a member of the house of commons and of the government for the time being.

JUDGE-MADE LAW. A phrase used to indicate judicial decisions which construe away the meaning of statutes, or find meanings in them the legislature never intended. It is sometimes used as meaning, simply, the law established by judicial precedent. Cooley, Const. Lim. 70, note.

JUDGE ORDINARY. By St. 20 & 21 Vict. c. 85, § 9, the judge of the court of probate was made judge of the court for divorce and matrimonial causes created by that act, under the name of the "judge ordinary."

In Scotland, the title "judge ordinary" is applied to all those judges, whether supreme or inferior, who, by the nature of their office, have a fixed and determinate jurisdiction in all actions of the same general nature, as contradistinguished from the old Scotch privy council, or from those judges to whom some special matter is committed; such as commissioners for taking proofs, and messengers at arms. Bell.

JUDGE'S CERTIFICATE. In English practice. A certificate, signed by the judge who presided at the trial of a cause, that the party applying is entitled to costs. In some cases, this is a necessary preliminary to the taxing of costs for such party.

A statement of the opinion of the court, signed by the judges, upon a question of law submitted to them by the chancellor for their decision. See 3 Bl. Comm. 453.

JUDGE'S MINUTES, or NOTES. Memoranda usually taken by a judge, while a trial is proceeding, of the testimony of witnesses, of documents offered or admitted in evidence, of offers of evidence, and whether it has been received or rejected, and the like matters.

JUDGE'S ORDER. An order made by a judge at chambers, or out of court.

JUDGER. A Cheshire juryman. Jacob.

JUDGMENT. The official and authentic decision of a court of justice upon the respective rights and claims of the parties to an action or suit therein litigated and submitted to its determination.

The conclusion of law upon facts found, or admitted by the parties, or upon their default in the course of the suit. Tidd, Pr. 930; 32 Md. 147.

The decision or sentence of the law, given by a court of justice or other competent tribunal, as the result of proceedings instituted therein for the redress of an injury. 3 Bl. Comm. 395; 12 Minn. 437, (Gil. 326.)

A judgment is the final determination of the rights of the parties in the action. Code N. Y. § 245; Code Civil Proc. Cal. § 577; Code Civil Proc. Dak. § 228.

A judgment is the final consideration and determination of a court of competent jurisdiction upon the matter submitted to it, and it is only evidenced by a record, or that which is by law, as the files and journal entries of this state, substituted in its stead. An order for a judgment is not the judgment, nor does the entry of such order partake of the nature and qualities of a judgment record. This must clearly ascertain not only the determination of the court upon the subject submitted, but the parties in favor of and against whom it operates. 3 Mich. 88.

The term "judgment" is also used to denote the reason which the court gives for its decision; but this is more properly denominated an "opinion."

Classification. Judgments are either *in rem* or *in personam;* as to which see JUDGMENT IN REM, JUDGMENT IN PERSONAM.

Judgments are either *final* or *interlocutory.* See Code N. C. § 384.

A *final* judgment is one which puts an end to the action, or disposes of the whole case, finally and completely, by declaring either that the plaintiff is entitled to recover a specific sum or that he cannot recover, and leaving nothing to be done but the execution of the judgment.

A final judgment is one that disposes of the case, either by dismissing it before a hearing is had upon the merits, or, after the trial, by rendering judgment either in favor of the plaintiff or defendant; but no judgment or order which does not determine the rights of the parties in the cause, and preclude further inquiry as to their rights in the premises, is a final judgment. 7 Neb. 398.

An *interlocutory* judgment is one given in the progress of a cause upon some plea, proceeding, or default which is only intermediate, and does not finally determine or complete the suit. 3 Bl. Comm. 396.

A judgment may be *upon the merits,* or it may not. A judgment on the merits is one which is rendered after the substance and matter of the case have been judicially investigated, and the court has decided which party is in the right; as distinguished from a judgment which turns upon some preliminary matter or technical point, or which, in consequence of the act or default of one of the parties, is given without a contest or trial.

Of judgments rendered without a regular

trial, or without a complete trial, the several species are enumerated below. And *first:*

Judgment *by default* is a judgment obtained by one party when the other party neglects to take a certain necessary step in the action (as, to enter an appearance, or to plead) within the proper time. In Louisiana, the term "*contradictory* judgment" is used to distinguish a judgment given after the parties have been heard, either in support of their claims or in their defense, from a judgment by default. 11 La. 366.

Judgment *by confession* is where a defendant gives the plaintiff a *cognovit* or written confession of the action (or "confession of judgment," as it is frequently called) by virtue of which the plaintiff enters judgment.

Judgment *nil dicit* is a judgment rendered for the plaintiff when the defendant "says nothing;" that is, when he neglects to plead to the plaintiff's declaration within the proper time.

Judgment by *non sum informatus* is one which is rendered when, instead of entering a plea, the defendant's attorney says he is not informed of any answer to be given to the action. Steph. Pl. 130.

Judgment of *nonsuit* is of two kinds,— voluntary and involuntary. When plaintiff abandons his case, and consents that judgment go against him for costs, it is voluntary. But when he, being called, neglects to appear, or when he has given no evidence on which a jury could find a verdict, it is involuntary. Freem. Judgm. § 6.

Judgment of *retraxit.* A judgment rendered where, after appearance and before verdict, the plaintiff voluntarily goes into court and enters on the record that he "withdraws his suit." It differs from a nonsuit. In the latter case the plaintiff may sue again, upon payment of costs; but a *retraxit* is an open, voluntary renunciation of his claim in court, and by it he forever loses his action.

Judgment of *nolle prosequi.* This judgment is entered when plaintiff declares that he will not further prosecute his suit, or entry of a *stet processus,* by which plaintiff agrees that all further proceedings shall be stayed.

Judgment of *non pros. (non prosequitur)* is one given against the plaintiff for a neglect to take any of those steps which it is incumbent on him to take in due time.

Judgment of *cassetur breve* or *billa* (that the writ or bill be quashed) is a judgment rendered in favor of a party pleading in abatement to a writ or action. Steph. Pl. 130, 131.

Judgment of *nil capiat per breve* or *per billam* is a judgment in favor of the defendant upon an issue raised upon a declaration or peremptory plea.

Judgment *quod partes replacitent.* This is a judgment of repleader, and is given if an issue is formed on so immaterial a point that the court cannot know for whom to give judgment. The parties must then reconstruct their pleadings.

Judgment of *respondeat ouster* is a judgment given against the defendant, requiring him to "answer over," after he has failed to establish a dilatory plea upon which an issue in law has been raised.

Judgment *quod recuperet* is a judgment in favor of the plaintiff, (that he do recover,) rendered when he has prevailed upon an issue in fact or an issue in law other than one arising on a dilatory plea. Steph. Pl. 126.

Judgment *non obstante veredicto* is a judgment entered for the plaintiff "notwithstanding the verdict" which has been given for defendant; which may be done where, after verdict and before judgment, it appears by the record that the matters pleaded or replied to, although verified by the verdict, are insufficient to constitute a defense or bar to the action.

Special, technical names are given to the judgments rendered in certain actions. These are explained as follows:

Judgment *quod computet* is a judgment in an action of account-render that the defendant do account.

Judgment *quod partitio fiat* is the interlocutory judgment in a writ of partition, that partition be made.

Judgment *quando acciderint.* If on the plea of *plene administravit* in an action against an executor or administrator, or on the plea of *riens per descent* in an action against an heir, the plaintiff, instead of taking issue on the plea, take judgment of assets *quando acciderint,* in this case, if assets afterwards come to the hands of the executor or heir, the plaintiff must first sue out a *scire facias,* before he can have execution. If, upon this *scire facias,* assets be found for part, the plaintiff may have judgment to recover so much immediately, and the residue of the assets *in futuro.* 1 Sid. 448.

Judgment *de melioribus damnis.* Where, in an action against several persons for a joint tort, the jury by mistake sever the damages by giving heavier damages against one defendant than against the others, the plaintiff may cure the defect by taking judgment for the greater damages (*de melioribus damnis*)

L

M

against that defendant, and entering a *nolle prosequi* (*q. v.*) against the others. Sweet.

Judgment *in error* is a judgment rendered by a court of error on a record sent up from an inferior court.

JUDGMENT-BOOK. A book required to be kept by the clerk, among the records of the court, for the entry of judgments. Code N. Y. § 279.

JUDGMENT CREDITOR. One who is entitled to enforce a judgment by execution. (*q. v.*) The owner of an unsatisfied judgment.

JUDGMENT DEBTOR. A person against whom judgment has been recovered, and which remains unsatisfied.

JUDGMENT DEBTOR SUMMONS. Under the English bankruptcy act, 1861, §§ 76–85, these summonses might be issued against both traders and non-traders, and, in default of payment of, or security or agreed composition for, the debt, the debtors might be adjudicated bankrupt. This act was repealed by 32 & 33 Vict. c. 83, § 20. The 32 & 33 Vict. c. 71, however, (bankruptcy act, 1869,) provides (section 7) for the granting of a "debtor's summons," at the instance of creditors, and, in the event of failure to pay or compound, a petition for adjudication may be presented, unless in the events provided for by that section. Wharton.

JUDGMENT DEBTS. Debts, whether on simple contract or by specialty, for the recovery of which judgment has been entered up, either upon a *cognovit* or upon a warrant of attorney or as the result of a successful action. Brown.

JUDGMENT DOCKET. A list or docket of the judgments entered in a given court, methodically kept by the clerk or other proper officer, open to public inspection, and intended to afford official notice to interested parties of the existence or lien of judgments.

JUDGMENT IN PERSONAM. A judgment against a particular person, as distinguished from a judgment against a thing or a right or *status*. The former class of judgments are conclusive only upon parties and privies; the latter upon all the world. See next title.

JUDGMENT IN REM. A judgment *in rem* is an adjudication, pronounced upon the *status* of some particular subject-matter, by a tribunal having competent authority for that purpose. It differs from a judgment *in personam*, in this: that the latter judgment is in form, as well as substance, between the parties claiming the right; and that it is so *inter partes* appears by the record itself. It is binding only upon the parties appearing to be such by the record, and those claiming by them. A judgment *in rem* is founded on a proceeding instituted, not against the person, as such, but against or upon the thing or subject-matter itself, whose state or condition is to be determined. It is a proceeding to determine the state or condition of the thing itself; and the judgment is a solemn declaration upon the *status* of the thing, and it *ipso facto* renders it what it declares it to be. 2 Vt. 73.

Various definitions have been given of a judgment *in rem*, but all are criticised as either incomplete or comprehending too much. It is generally said to be a judgment declaratory of the *status* of some subject-matter, whether this be a person or a thing. Thus, the probate of a will fixes the *status* of the document as a will. The personal rights and interests which follow are mere incidental results of the *status* or character of the paper, and do not appear on the face of the judgment. So, a decree establishing or dissolving a marriage is a judgment *in rem*, because it fixes the *status* of the person. A judgment of forfeiture, by the proper tribunal, against specific articles or goods, for a violation of the revenue laws, is a judgment *in rem*. But it is objected that the customary definition does not fit such a case, because there is no fixing of the *status* of anything, the whole effect being a seizure, whatever the thing may be. In the foregoing instances, and many others, the judgment is conclusive against all the world, without reference to actual presence or participation in the proceedings. If the expression "strictly *in rem*" may be applied to any class of cases, it should be confined to such as these. "A very able writer says: 'The distinguishing characteristic of judgments *in rem* is that, wherever their obligation is recognized and enforced as against *any* person, it is equally recognized and enforced as against *all* persons.' It seems to us that the true definition of a 'judgment *in rem*' is 'an adjudication' against some person or thing. or upon the *status* of some subject-matter; which, wherever and whenever binding upon *any* person, is equally binding upon *all* persons." 10 Mo. App. 78.

JUDGMENT NISI. At common law, this was a judgment entered on the return of the *nisi prius* record, which, according to the terms of the *postea*, was to become absolute *unless* otherwise ordered by the court within the first four days of the next succeeding term.

JUDGMENT NOTE. A promissory note, embodying an authorization to any attorney, or to a designated attorney, or to the holder, or the clerk of the court, to enter an appearance for the maker and confess a judgment against him for a sum therein named, upon default of payment of the note.

JUDGMENT PAPER. In English practice. A sheet of paper containing an *incipitur* of the pleadings in an action at law, upon which final judgment is signed by the master. 2 Tidd, Pr. 930.

JUDGMENT RECORD. In English practice. A parchment roll, on which are transcribed the whole proceedings in the cause, deposited and filed of record in the treasury of the court, after signing of judgment. 3 Steph. Comm. 632. In American practice, the record is signed, filed, and docketed by the clerk.

JUDGMENT ROLL. In English practice. A roll of parchment containing the entries of the proceedings in an action at law to the entry of judgment inclusive, and which is filed in the treasury of the court. 1 Arch. Pr. K. B. 227, 228; 2 Tidd, Pr. 931. See ROLL.

Judicandum est legibus, non exemplis. Judgment is to be given according to the laws, not according to examples or precedents. 4 Coke, 33*b;* 4 Bl. Comm. 405.

JUDICARE. In the civil and old English law. To judge; to decide or determine judicially; to give judgment or sentence.

JUDICATIO. In the civil law. Judging; the pronouncing of sentence, after hearing a cause. Hallifax, Civil Law, b. 3, c. 8, no. 7.

JUDICATORES TERRARUM. Persons in the county palatine of Chester, who, on a writ of error, were to consider of the judgment given there, and reform it; otherwise they forfeited £100 to the crown by custom. Jenk. Cent. 71.

JUDICATURE. 1. The state or profession of those officers who are employed in administering justice; the judiciary.

2. A judicatory, tribunal, or court of justice.

3. Jurisdiction; the right of judicial action; the scope or extent of jurisdiction.

JUDICATURE ACTS. The statutes of 36 & 37 Vict. c. 66, and 38 & 39 Vict. c. 77, which went into force November 1, 1875, with amendments in 1877, c. 9; 1879, c. 78; and 1881, c. 68,—made most important changes in the organization of, and methods of procedure in, the superior courts of England, consolidating them to-

gether so as to constitute one supreme court of judicature, consisting of two divisions,—her majesty's high court of justice, having chiefly original jurisdiction; and her majesty's court of appeal, whose jurisdiction is chiefly appellate.

Judices non tenentur exprimere causam sententiæ suæ. Jenk. Cent. 75. Judges are not bound to explain the reason of their sentence.

JUDICES ORDINARII. In the civil law. Ordinary *judices;* the common *judices* appointed to try causes, and who, according to Blackstone, determined only questions of fact. 3 Bl. Comm. 315.

JUDICES PEDANEI. In the civil law. The ordinary *judices* appointed by the prætor to try causes.

JUDICES SELECTI. In the civil law. Select or selected *judices* or judges; those who were used in criminal causes, and between whom and modern *jurors* many points of resemblance have been noticed. 3 Bl. Comm. 366.

Judici officium suum excedenti non paretur. A judge exceeding his office is not to be obeyed. Jenk. Cent. p. 139, case 84. Said of void judgments.

Judici satis pœna est, quod Deum habet ultorem. It is punishment enough for a judge that he has God as his avenger. 1 Leon. 295.

JUDICIA. Lat. In Roman law. Judicial proceedings; trials. *Judicia publica,* criminal trials. Dig. 48, 1.

Judicia in curia regis non adnihilentur, sed stent in robore suo quousque per errorem aut attinctum adnullentur. Judgments in the king's courts are not to be annihilated, but to remain in force until annulled by error or attaint. 2 Inst. 539.

Judicia in deliberationibus crebro maturescunt, in accelerato processu nunquam. Judgments frequently become matured by deliberations, never by hurried process or precipitation. 3 Inst. 210.

Judicia posteriora sunt in lege fortiora. 8 Coke, 97. The later decisions are the stronger in law.

Judicia sunt tanquam juris dicta, et pro veritate accipiuntur. Judgments are, as it were, the sayings of the law, and are received as truth. 2 Inst. 537.

K

L

M

JUDICIAL. Belonging to the office of a judge; as *judicial* authority.

Relating to or connected with the administration of justice; as a *judicial* officer.

Having the character of judgment or formal legal procedure; as a *judicial* act.

Proceeding from a court of justice; as a *judicial* writ, a *judicial* determination.

JUDICIAL ACTION. Action of a court upon a cause, by hearing it, and determining what shall be adjudged or decreed between the parties, and with which is the right of the case. 12 Pet. 718.

JUDICIAL ACTS. Acts requiring the exercise of some judicial discretion, as distinguished from ministerial acts, which require none.

JUDICIAL ADMISSIONS. Admissions made voluntarily by a party which appear of record in the proceedings of the court.

JUDICIAL AUTHORITY. The power and authority appertaining to the office of a judge; jurisdiction; the official right to hear and determine questions in controversy.

JUDICIAL COMMITTEE OF THE PRIVY COUNCIL. In English law. A tribunal composed of members of the privy council, being judges or retired judges, which acts as the queen's adviser in matters of law referred to it, and exercises a certain appellate jurisdiction, chiefly in ecclesiastical causes, though its power in this respect was curtailed by the judicature act of 1873.

JUDICIAL CONFESSION. In the law of evidence. A confession of guilt, made by a prisoner before a magistrate, or in court, in the due course of legal proceedings. 1 Greenl. Ev. § 216.

JUDICIAL CONVENTIONS. Agreements entered into in consequence of an order of court; as, for example, entering into a bond on taking out a writ of sequestration. 6 Mart. (N. S.) 494.

JUDICIAL DECISIONS. The opinions or determinations of the judges in causes before them, particularly in appellate courts.

JUDICIAL DISCRETION. The power confided to a judge to exercise his individual discrimination and opinion in deciding certain minor or collateral matters. This power is not arbitrary, but is confined within narrow limits, within which, however, its exercise is not subject to review.

"Judicial discretion" means a discretion to be exercised in discerning the course prescribed by law. 26 Wend. 143.

JUDICIAL DOCUMENTS. Proceedings relating to litigation. They are divided into (1) judgments, decrees, and verdicts; (2) depositions, examinations, and inquisitions taken in the course of a legal process; (3) writs, warrants, pleadings, etc., which are incident to any judicial proceedings. See 1 Starkie, Ev. 252.

JUDICIAL MORTGAGE. In the law of Louisiana. The lien resulting from judgments, whether rendered on contested cases or by default, whether final or provisional, in favor of the person obtaining them. Civil Code La. art. 3321.

JUDICIAL NOTICE. The act by which a court, in conducting a trial, or framing its decision, will, of its own motion, and without the production of evidence, recognize the existence and truth of certain facts, having a bearing on the controversy at bar, and which, from their nature, are not properly the subject of testimony, or which are universally regarded as established by common notoriety, *e. g.*, the laws of the state, international law, historical events, the constitution and course of nature, main geographical features, etc.

JUDICIAL OFFICER. A person in whom is vested authority to decide causes or exercise powers appropriate to a court.

JUDICIAL POWER. The authority vested in courts and judges, as distinguished from the executive and legislative power.

JUDICIAL PROCEEDINGS. A general term for proceedings relating to, practiced in, or proceeding from, a court of justice; or the course prescribed to be taken in various cases for the determination of a controversy or for legal redress or relief.

JUDICIAL SALE. A judicial sale is one made under the process of a court having competent authority to order it, by an officer duly appointed and commissioned to sell, as distinguished from a sale by an owner in virtue of his right of property. 8 How. 495.

JUDICIAL SEPARATION. A separation of man and wife by decree of court, less complete than an absolute divorce; otherwise called a "limited divorce."

JUDICIAL STATISTICS. In English law. Statistics, published by authority, of the civil and criminal business of the United Kingdom, and matters appertaining thereto. Annual reports are published separately for England and Wales, for Ireland, and for Scotland.

JUDICIAL WRITS. In English practice. Such writs as issue under the private seal of the courts, and not under the great seal of England, and are tested or witnessed, not in the king's name, but in the name of the chief judge of the court out of which they issue. The word "judicial" is used in contradistinction to "original;" original writs being such as issue out of chancery under the great seal, and are witnessed in the king's name. See 3 Bl. Comm. 282.

JUDICIARY, *adj.* Pertaining or relating to the courts of justice, to the judicial department of government, or to the administration of justice.

JUDICIARY, *n.* That branch of government invested with the judicial power; the system of courts in a country; the body of judges; the bench.

JUDICIARY ACT. The name commonly given to the act of congress of September 24, 1789, (1 St. at Large, 73,) by which the system of federal courts was organized, and their powers and jurisdiction defined.

Judiciis posterioribus fides est adhibenda. Faith or credit is to be given to the later judgments. 13 Coke, 14.

JUDICIO SISTI. A caution, or security, given in Scotch courts for the defendant to abide judgment within the jurisdiction. Stim. Law Gloss.

Judicis est in pronuntiando sequi regulam, exceptione non probata. The judge in his decision ought to follow the rule, when the exception is not proved.

Judicis est judicare secundum allegata et probata. Dyer, 12. It is the duty of a judge to decide according to facts alleged and proved.

Judicis est jus dicere, non dare. It is the province of a judge to declare the law, not to give it. Lofft, Append. 42.

Judicis officium est opus diei in die suo perficere. It is the duty of a judge to finish the work of each day within that day. Dyer, 12.

Judicis officium est ut res, ita tempora rerum, quærere. It is the duty of a judge to inquire into the times of things, as well as into things themselves. Co. Litt. 171.

JUDICIUM. Lat. Judicial authority or jurisdiction; a court or tribunal; a judicial hearing or other proceeding; a verdict or judgment.

Judicium a non suo judice datum nullius est momenti. 10 Coke, 70. A judgment given by one who is not the proper judge is of no force.

JUDICIUM CAPITALE. In old English law. Judgment of death; capital judgment. Fleta, lib. 1, c. 39, § 2. Called, also, "*judicium vitæ amissionis*," judgment of loss of life. Id. lib. 2, c. 1, § 5.

JUDICIUM DEI. Lat. In old English and European law. The judgment of God; otherwise called "*divinum judicium*," the "divine judgment." A term particularly applied to the ordeals by fire or hot iron and water, and also to the trials by the cross, the eucharist, and the corsned, and the *duellum* or trial by battle, (*q. v.,*) it being supposed that the interposition of heaven was directly manifest, in these cases, in behalf of the innocent. Spelman; Burrill.

Judicium est quasi juris dictum. Judgment is, as it were, a declaration of law.

Judicium non debet esse illusorium; suum effectum habere debet. A judgment ought not to be illusory; it ought to have its proper effect. 2 Inst. 341.

JUDICIUM PARIUM. In old English law. Judgment of the peers; judgment of one's peers; trial by jury. Magna Charta, c. 29.

Judicium redditur in invitum. Co. Litt. 248*b*. Judgment is given against one, whether he will or not.

Judicium (semper) pro veritate accipitur. A judgment is always taken for truth, [that is, as long as it stands in force it cannot be contradicted.] 2 Inst. 380; Co. Litt. 39*a*, 168*a*.

JUG. In old English law. A watery place. Domesday; Cowell.

JUGE. In French law. A judge.

JUGE DE PAIX. In French law. An inferior judicial functionary, appointed to decide summarily controversies of minor importance, especially such as turn mainly on questions of fact. He has also the functions of a police magistrate. *Ferrière.*

JUGERUM. An acre. Co. Litt. 5*b.* As much as a yoke (*jugum*) of oxen could plow in one day.

JUGES D'INSTRUCTION. In French law. Officers subject to the *procureur impérial* or *général,* who receive in cases of criminal offenses the complaints of the parties injured, and who summon and examine witnesses upon oath, and, after communication with the *procureur impérial,* draw up the forms of accusation. They have also the right, subject to the approval of the same superior officer, to admit the accused to bail. They are appointed for three years, but are re-eligible for a further period of office. They are usually chosen from among the regular judges. *Brown.*

JUGULATOR. In old records. A cutthroat or murderer. *Cowell.*

JUGUM. In the civil law. A yoke; a measure of land; as much land as a yoke of oxen could plow in a day. Nov. 17, c. 8.

JUGUM TERRÆ. In old English law. A yoke of land; half a plow-land. Domesday; Co. Litt. 5*a;* Cowell.

JUICIO. In Spanish law. A trial or suit. White, New Recop. b. 3, tit. 4, c. 1.

JUICIO DE APEO. In Spanish law. The decree of a competent tribunal directing the determining and marking the boundaries of lands or estates.

JUICIO DE CONCURSO DE ACREEDORES. In Spanish law. The judgment granted for a debtor who has various creditors, or for such creditors, to the effect that their claims be satisfied according to their respective form and rank, when the debtor's estate is not sufficient to discharge them all in full. *Escriche.*

JUMENT. In old Scotch law. An ox used for tillage. 1 Pitc. Crim. Tr. pt. 2, p. 89.

JUMENTA. In the civil law. Beasts of burden; animals used for carrying burdens. This word did not include "oxen." Dig. 32, 65, 5.

JUMP BAIL. To abscond, withdraw, or secrete one's self, in violation of the obligation of a bail-bond. The expression is colloquial, and is applied only to the act of the principal.

JUNCARIA. In old English law. The soil where rushes grow. Co. Litt. 5*a;* Cowell.

Juncta juvant. United they aid. A portion of the maxim, "*Quæ non valeant singula juncta juvant,*" (*q. v.,*) frequently cited. 8 Man. & G. 99.

JUNGERE DUELLUM. In old English law. To join the *duellum;* to engage in the combat. Fleta, lib. 1, c. 21, § 10.

JUNIOR. Younger. This has been held to be no part of a man's name, but an addition by use, and a convenient distinction between a father and son of the same name. 10 Paige, 170; 7 Johns. 549; 2 Caines, 164.

JUNIOR BARRISTER. A barrister under the rank of queen's counsel. Also the junior of two counsel employed on the same side in a case. *Mozley & Whitley.*

JUNIOR COUNSEL. The younger of the counsel employed on the same side of a case, or the one lower in standing or rank, or who is intrusted with the less important parts of the preparation or trial of the cause.

JUNIOR CREDITOR. One whose claim or demand accrued at a date posterior to that of a claim or demand held by another creditor.

JUNIOR EXECUTION. One which was issued after the issuance of another execution, on a different judgment, against the same defendant.

JUNIOR JUDGMENT. One which was rendered or entered after the rendition or entry of another judgment, on a different claim, against the same defendant.

JUNIOR WRIT. One which is issued, or comes to the officer's hands, at a later time than a similar writ, at the suit of another party, or on a different claim, against the same defendant.

JUNIPERUS SABINA. In medical jurisprudence. This plant is commonly called "savin."

JUNK-SHOP. A shop where old cordage and ships' tackle, old iron, rags, bottles, paper, etc., are kept and sold. A place where odds and ends are purchased and sold. 12 Rich. Law, 470.

JUNTA, or JUNTO. A select council for taking cognizance of affairs of great consequence requiring secrecy; a cabal or faction. This was a popular nickname applied to the Whig ministry in England, between 1693–1696. They clung to each other for mutual protection against the attacks of the so-called "Reactionist Stuart Party."

JURA. Rights; laws. 1 Bl. Comm. 123. See Jus.

Jura ecclesiastica limitata sunt infra limites separatos. Ecclesiastical laws are limited within separate bounds. 3 Bulst. 53.

Jura eodem modo destituuntur quo constituuntur. Laws are abrogated by the same means [authority] by which they are made. Broom, Max. 878.

JURA FISCALIA. In English law. Fiscal rights; rights of the exchequer. 3 Bl. Comm. 45.

JURA IN RE. In the civil law. Rights in a thing; rights which, being separated from the *dominium*, or right of property, exist independently of it, and are enjoyed by some other person than him who has the *dominium*. Mackeld. Rom. Law, § 237.

JURA MIXTI DOMINII. In old English law. Rights of mixed dominion. The king's right or power of jurisdiction was so termed. Hale, Anal. § 6.

Jura naturæ sunt immutabilia. The laws of nature are unchangeable. Branch, Princ.

JURA PERSONARUM. Rights of persons; the rights of persons. Rights which concern and are annexed to the persons of men. 1 Bl. Comm. 122.

JURA PRÆDIORUM. In the civil law. The rights of estates. Dig. 50, 16, 86.

Jura publica anteferenda privatis. Public rights are to be preferred to private. Co. Litt. 130*a*. Applied to protections.

Jura publica ex privato [privatis] promiscue decidi non debent. Public rights ought not to be decided promiscuously with private. Co. Litt. 130*a*, 181*b*.

JURA REGALIA. In English law. Royal rights or privileges. 1 Bl. Comm. 117, 119; 3 Bl. Comm. 44.

JURA REGIA. In English law. Royal rights; the prerogatives of the crown. Crabb, Com. Law, 174.

Jura regis specialia non conceduntur per generalia verba. The special rights of the king are not granted by general words. Jenk. Cent. p. 103.

JURA RERUM. Rights of things; the rights of things; rights which a man may acquire over external objects or things unconnected with his person. 1 Bl. Comm. 122; 2 Bl. Comm. 1.

Jura sanguinis nullo jure civili dirimi possunt. The right of blood and kindred cannot be destroyed by any civil law. Dig 50, 17, 9; Bac. Max. reg. 11; Broom, Max 533; 14 Allen, 562.

JURA SUMMI IMPERII. Rights of supreme dominion; rights of sovereignty. 1 Bl. Comm. 49; 1 Kent, Comm. 211.

JURAL. 1. Pertaining to natural or positive right, or to the doctrines of rights and obligations; as "jural relations."

2. Of or pertaining to jurisprudence; juristic; juridical.

3. Recognized or sanctioned by positive law; embraced within, or covered by, the rules and enactments of positive law. Thus, the "jural sphere" is to be distinguished from the "moral sphere;" the latter denoting the whole scope or range of ethics or the science of conduct, the former embracing only such portions of the same as have been made the subject of legal sanction or recognition.

4. Founded in law; organized upon the basis of a fundamental law, and existing for the recognition and protection of rights. Thus, the term "jural society" is used as the synonym of "state" or "organized political community."

JURAMENTÆ CORPORALES. Corporal oaths, (*q. v.*)

JURAMENTUM. Lat. In the civil law. An oath.

JURAMENTUM CALUMNIÆ. In the civil and canon law. The oath of calumny. An oath imposed upon both parties to a suit, as a preliminary to its trial, to the effect that they are not influenced by malice or any sinister motives in prosecuting or defending the same, but by a belief in the justice of their cause. It was also required of the attorneys and proctors.

Juramentum est indivisibile; et non est admittendum in parte verum et in parte falsum. An oath is indivisible; it is not to be held partly true and partly false. 4 Inst. 274.

JURAMENTUM IN LITEM. In the civil law. An assessment oath; an oath taken by the plaintiff in an action, that the extent of the damages he has suffered, estimated in money, amounts to a certain sum, which oath, in certain cases, is accepted in lieu of other proof. Mackeld. Rom. Law, § 376.

JURAMENTUM JUDICIALE. In the civil law. An oath which the judge, of his own accord, defers to either of the parties.

It is of two kinds: *First*, that which the judge defers for the decision of the cause, and which is understood by the general name "*juramentum judiciale*," and is sometimes called "suppletory oath," *juramentum suppletorium; second*, that which the judge defers in order to fix and determine the amount of the condemnation which he ought to pronounce, and which is called "*juramentum in litem.*" Poth. Obl. p. 4, c. 3, § 3, art. 3.

JURAMENTUM NECESSARIUM. In Roman law. A compulsory oath. A disclosure under oath, which the prætor compelled one of the parties to a suit to make, when the other, applying for such an appeal, agreed to abide by what his adversary should swear. 1 Whart. Ev. § 458; Dig. 12, 2, 5, 2.

JURAMENTUM VOLUNTARIUM. In Roman law. A voluntary oath. A species of appeal to conscience, by which one of the parties to a suit, instead of proving his case, offered to abide by what his adversary should answer under oath. 1 Whart. Ev. § 458; Dig. 12, 2, 34, 6.

JURARE. To swear; to take an oath.

Jurare est Deum in testem vocare, et est actus divini cultus. 3 Inst. 165. To swear is to call God to witness, and is an act of religion.

JURAT. The clause written at the foot of an affidavit, stating when, where, and before whom such affidavit was sworn.

JURATA. In old English law. A jury of twelve men sworn. Especially, a jury of the common law, as distinguished from the *assisa*.

The jury clause in a *nisi prius* record, so called from the emphatic words of the old forms: "*Jurata ponitur in respectum*," the jury is put in respite. Townsh. Pl. 487.

Also a jurat, (which see.)

JURATION. The act of swearing; the administration of an oath.

Jurato creditur in judicio. He who makes oath is to be believed in judgment. 3 Inst. 79.

JURATOR. A juror; a compurgator, (q. v.)

Juratores debent esse vicini, sufficientes, et minus suspecti. Jurors ought to be neighbors, of sufficient estate, and free from suspicion. Jenk. Cent. 141.

Juratores sunt judices facti. Jenk. Cent. 61. Juries are the judges of fact.

JURATORY CAUTION. In Scotch law. A description of caution (security) sometimes offered in a suspension or advocation where the complainer is not in circumstances to offer any better. Bell.

JURATS. In English law. Officers in the nature of aldermen, sworn for the government of many corporations. The twelve assistants of the bailiff in Jersey are called "jurats."

JURE. Lat. By right; in right; by the law.

JURE BELLI. By the right or law of war. 1 Kent, Comm. 126; 1 C. Rob. Adm. 289.

JURE CIVILI. By the civil law. Inst. 1, 3, 4; 1 Bl. Comm. 423.

JURE CORONÆ. In right of the crown.

JURE DIVINO. By divine right. 1 Bl. Comm. 191.

JURE ECCLESIÆ. In right of the church. 1 Bl. Comm. 401.

JURE EMPHYTEUTICO. By the right or law of *emphyteusis*. 3 Bl. Comm. 232. See EMPHYTEUSIS.

JURE GENTIUM. By the law of nations. Inst. 1, 3, 4; 1 Bl. Comm. 423.

Jure naturæ æquum est neminem cum alterius detrimento et injuria fieri locupletiorem. By the law of nature it is not just that any one should be enriched by the detriment or injury of another. Dig. 50, 17, 206.

JURE PROPINQUITATIS. By right of propinquity or nearness. 2 Crabb, Real Prop. p. 1019, § 2398.

JURE REPRESENTATIONIS. By right of representation; in the right of another person. 2 Bl. Comm. 224, 517; 2 Crabb, Real Prop. p. 1019, § 2398.

JURE UXORIS. In right of a wife. 3 Bl. Comm. 210.

Juri non est consonum quod aliquis accessorius in curia regis convincatur antequam aliquis de facto fuerit attinctus. It is not consonant to justice that any accessary should be convicted in the king's court before any one has been attainted of the fact. 2 Inst. 183.

JURIDICAL. Relating to administration of justice, or office of a judge.

Regular; done in conformity to the laws of the country and the practice which is there observed.

JURIDICAL DAYS. Days in court on which the laws are administered.

JURIDICUS. Lat. Relating to the courts or to the administration of justice; juridical; lawful. *Dies juridicus*, a lawful day for the transaction of business in court; a day on which the courts are open.

JURIS. Lat. Of right; of law.

Juris affectus in executione consistit. The effect of the law consists in the execution. Co. Litt. 289b.

JURIS ET DE JURE. Of law and of right. A presumption *juris et de jure*, or an irrebuttable presumption, is one which the law will not suffer to be rebutted by any counter-evidence, but establishes as conclusive; while a presumption *juris tantum* is one which holds good in the absence of evidence to the contrary, but may be rebutted.

JURIS ET SEISINÆ CONJUNCTIO. The union of seisin or possession and the right of possession, forming a complete title. 2 Bl. Comm. 199, 311.

Juris ignorantia est cum jus nostrum ignoramus. It is ignorance of the law when we do not know our own rights. 9 Pick. 130.

JURIS POSITIVI. Of positive law; a regulation or requirement of positive law, as distinguished from natural or divine law. 1 Bl. Comm. 439; 2 Steph. Comm. 286.

Juris præcepta sunt hæc: Honeste vivere; alterum non lædere; suum cuique tribuere. These are the precepts of the law: To live honorably; to hurt nobody; to render to every one his due. Inst. 1, 1, 3; 1 Bl. Comm. 40.

JURIS PRIVATI. Of private right; subjects of private property. Hale, Anal. § 23.

JURIS PUBLICI. Of common right; of common or public use; such things as, at least in their own use, are common to all the king's subjects; as common highways, common bridges, common rivers, and common ports. Hale, Anal. § 23.

JURIS UTRUM. In English law. An abolished writ which lay for the parson of a church whose predecessor had alienated the lands and tenements thereof. Fitzh. Nat. Brev. 48.

JURISCONSULT. A jurist; a person skilled in the science of law, particularly of international or public law.

JURISCONSULTUS. Lat. In Roman law. An expert in juridical science; a person thoroughly versed in the laws, who was habitually resorted to, for information and advice, both by private persons as his clients, and also by the magistrates, advocates, and others employed in administering justice.

Jurisdictio est potestas de publico introducta, cum necessitate juris dicendi. Jurisdiction is a power introduced for the public good, on account of the necessity of dispensing justice. 10 Coke, 73a.

JURISDICTION. The power and authority constitutionally conferred upon (or constitutionally recognized as existing in) a court or judge to pronounce the sentence of the law, or to award the remedies provided by law, upon a state of facts, proved or admitted, referred to the tribunal for decision, and authorized by law to be the subject of investigation or action by that tribunal, and in favor of or against persons (or a *res*) who present themselves, or who are brought, before the court in some manner sanctioned by law as proper and sufficient. 1 Black, Judgm. § 215.

Jurisdiction is a power constitutionally conferred upon a judge or magistrate to take cognizance of and determine causes according to law, and to carry his sentence into execution. 6 Pet. 591; 9 Johns. 239; 2 Neb. 135.

The authority of a court as distinguished from the other departments; judicial power considered with reference to its scope and extent as respects the questions and persons subject to it; power given by law to hear and decide controversies. Abbott.

Jurisdiction is the power to hear and determine the subject-matter in controversy between parties to the suit; to adjudicate or exercise any judicial power over them. 12 Pet. 657, 717.

Jurisdiction is the power to hear and determine a cause; the authority by which judicial officers take cognizance of and decide causes. 43 Tex. 440.

JURISDICTION CLAUSE. In equity practice. That part of a bill which is in-

K

L

M

tended to give jurisdiction of the suit to the court, by a general averment that the acts complained of are contrary to equity, and tend to the injury of the complainant, and that he has no remedy, or not a complete remedy, without the assistance of a court of equity, is called the "jurisdiction clause." Mitf. Eq. Pl. 43.

JURISDICTIONAL. Pertaining or relating to jurisdiction; conferring jurisdiction; showing or disclosing jurisdiction; defining or limiting jurisdiction; essential to jurisdiction.

JURISINCEPTOR. A student of the civil law.

JURISPERITUS. Skilled or learned in the law.

JURISPRUDENCE. The philosophy of law, or the science which treats of the principles of positive law and legal relations.

"The term is wrongly applied to actual systems of law, or to current views of law, or to suggestions for its amendment, but is the name of a science. This science is a formal, or analytical, rather than a material, one. It is the science of actual or positive law. It is wrongly divided into 'general' and 'particular,' or into 'philosophical' and 'historical.' It may therefore be defined as the formal science of positive law." Holl. Jur. 12.

In the proper sense of the word, "jurisprudence" is the science of law, namely, that science which has for its function to ascertain the principles on which legal rules are based, so as not only to classify those rules in their proper order, and show the relation in which they stand to one another, but also to settle the manner in which new or doubtful cases should be brought under the appropriate rules. Jurisprudence is more a formal than a material science. It has no direct concern with questions of moral or political policy, for they fall under the province of ethics and legislation; but, when a new or doubtful case arises to which two different rules seem, when taken literally, to be equally applicable, it may be, and often is, the function of jurisprudence to consider the ultimate effect which would be produced if each rule were applied to an indefinite number of similar cases, and to choose that rule which, when so applied, will produce the greatest advantage to the community. Sweet.

JURISPRUDENTIA. In the civil and common law. Jurisprudence, or legal science.

Jurisprudentia est divinarum atque humanarum rerum notitia, justi atque injusti scientia. "Jurisprudence" is the knowledge of things divine and human, the science of what is right and what is wrong. Dig. 1, 1, 10, 2; Inst. 1, 1, 1. This definition is adopted by Bracton, word for word. Bract. fol. 3.

Jurisprudentia legis communis Angliæ est scientia socialis et copiosa. The jurisprudence of the common law of England is a science social and comprehensive. 7 Coke, 28a.

JURIST. One who is versed or skilled in law; answering to the Latin "*jurisperitus,*" (q. v.)

One who is skilled in the civil law, or law of nations. The term is now usually applied to those who have distinguished themselves by their *writings* on legal subjects.

JURISTIC. Pertaining or belonging to, or characteristic of, jurisprudence, or a jurist, or the legal profession.

JURISTIC ACT. One designed to have a legal effect, and capable thereof.

JURNEDUM. In old English law. A journey; a day's traveling. Cowell.

JURO. In Spanish law. A certain perpetual pension, granted by the king on the public revenues, and more especially on the salt-works, by favor, either in consideration of meritorious services, or in return for money loaned the government, or obtained by it through forced loans. Escriche.

JUROR. One member of a jury. Sometimes, one who takes an oath; as in the term "non-juror," a person who refuses certain oaths.

JUROR'S BOOK. A list of persons qualified to serve on juries.

JURY In practice. A certain number of men, selected according to law, and *sworn* (*jurati*) to inquire of certain matters of fact, and declare the truth upon evidence to be laid before them. This definition embraces the various subdivisions of juries; as *grand jury, petit jury, common jury, special jury, coroner's jury, sheriff's jury,* (q. v.)

A jury is a body of men temporarily selected from the citizens of a particular district, and invested with power to present or indict a person for a public offense, or to try a question of fact. Code Civil Proc. Cal. § 190.

The terms "jury" and "trial by jury," as used in the constitution, mean twelve competent men, disinterested and impartial, not of kin, nor personal dependents of either of the parties, having their homes within the jurisdictional limits of the court, drawn and selected by officers free from all bias in favor of or against either party, duly impaneled and sworn to render a true verdict according to the law and the evidence. 11 Nev. 89.

A *grand* jury is a body of men, (twelve to twenty-three in number,) returned in pursuance of law, from the citizens of a county, or city and county, before a court of competent jurisdiction, and sworn to inquire of public offenses committed or triable within the county, or city and county. Code Civil Proc. Cal. § 192.

A *trial* jury is a body of men returned from the citizens of a particular district before a court or officer of competent jurisdiction, and sworn to try and determine, by verdict, a question of fact. Code Civil Proc. Cal. § 193.

JURY-BOX. In practice. The place in court (strictly an inclosed place) where the jury sit during the trial of a cause. 1 Archb. Pr. K. B. 208; 1 Burrill, Pr. 455.

JURY COMMISSIONER. An officer charged with the duty of selecting the names to be put into the jury wheel, or of drawing the panel of jurors for a particular term of court.

JURY-LIST. A paper containing the names of jurors impaneled to try a cause, or it contains the names of all the jurors summoned to attend court.

JURY OF MATRONS. In common-law practice. A jury of twelve matrons or discreet women, impaneled upon a writ *de ventre inspiciendo*, or where a female prisoner, being under sentence of death, pleaded her pregnancy as a ground for staying execution. In the latter case, such jury inquired into the truth of the plea.

JURY PROCESS. The process by which a jury is summoned in a cause, and by which their attendance is enforced.

JURY WHEEL. A machine containing the names of persons qualified to serve as grand and petit jurors, from which, in an order determined by the hazard of its revolutions, are drawn a sufficient number of such names to make up the panels for a given term of court.

JURYMAN. A juror; one who is impaneled on a jury.

JURYWOMAN. One member of a jury of matrons, (q. v.)

JUS. Lat. In Roman law. Right; justice; law; the whole body of law; also a right. The term is used in two meanings:

1. "*Jus*" means "law," considered in the abstract; that is, as distinguished from any specific enactment, the science or department of learning, or *quasi* personified factor in human history or conduct or social development, which we call, in a general sense, "the law." Or it means the law taken as a system, an aggregate, a whole; "the sum total of a number of individual laws taken together." Or it may designate some one particular system or body of particular laws; as in the phrases "*jus civile*," "*jus gentium*," "*jus prætorium*."

2. In a second sense, "*jus*" signifies "a right;" that is, a power, privilege, faculty, or demand inherent in one person and incident upon another; or a capacity residing in one person of controlling, with the assent and assistance of the state, the actions of another. This is its meaning in the expressions "*jus in rem*," "*jus accrescendi*," "*jus possessionis*."

It is thus seen to possess the same ambiguity as the words "*droit*," "*recht*," and "*right*," (which see.)

The continental jurists seek to avoid this ambiguity in the use of the word "*jus*," by calling its former signification "objective," and the latter meaning "subjective." Thus Mackeldey (Rom. Law, § 2) says: "The laws of the first kind [compulsory or positive laws] form law [*jus*] in its objective sense, [*jus est norma agendi*, law is a rule of conduct.] The possibility resulting from law in this sense to do or require another to do is law in its subjective sense, [*jus est facultas agendi*, law is a license to act.] The voluntary action of man in conformity with the precepts of law is called 'justice,' [*justitia*.]"

Some further meanings of the word are:

An action. Bract. fol. 3. Or, rather, those proceedings in the Roman action which were conducted before the prætor.

Power or authority. *Sui juris*, in one's own power; independent. Inst. 1, 8, pr.; Bract. fol. 3. *Alieni juris*, under another's power. Inst. 1, 8, pr.

The profession (*ars*) or practice of the law. *Jus ponitur pro ipsa arte.* Bract. fol. 2b.

A court or judicial tribunal, (*locus in quo redditur jus.*) Id. fol. 3.

JUS ABUTENDI. The right to abuse. By this phrase is understood the right to do exactly as one likes with property, or having full dominion over property. 3 Toullier, no. 86.

JUS ACCRESCENDI. The right of survivorship. The right of the survivor or survivors of two or more joint tenants to the tenancy or estate, upon the death of one or more of the joint tenants.

K

L

M

Jus accrescendi inter mercatores, pro beneficio commercii, locum non habet. The right of survivorship has no place between merchants, for the benefit of commerce. Co. Litt. 182a; 2 Story, Eq. Jur. § 1207; Broom, Max. 455. There is no survivorship in cases of partnership, as there is in joint-tenancy. Story, Partn. § 90.

Jus accrescendi præfertur oneribus. The right of survivorship is preferred to incumbrances. Co. Litt. 185a. Hence no dower or curtesy can be claimed out of a joint estate. 1 Steph. Comm. 316.

Jus accrescendi præfertur ultimæ voluntati. The right of survivorship is preferred to the last will. Co. Litt. 185b. A devise of one's share of a joint estate, by will, is no severance of the jointure; for no testament takes effect till after the death of the testator, and by such death the right of the survivor (which accrued at the original creation of the estate, and has therefore a priority to the other) is already vested. 2 Bl. Comm. 186; 3 Steph. Comm. 316.

JUS AD REM. A term of the civil law, meaning "a right to a thing;" that is, a right exercisable by one person over a particular article of property in virtue of a contract or obligation incurred by another person in respect to it, and which is enforceable only against or through such other person. It is thus distinguished from *jus in re*, which is a complete and absolute dominion over a thing available against all persons.

The disposition of modern writers is to use the term "*jus ad rem*" as descriptive of a right without possession, and "*jus in re*" as descriptive of a right accompanied by possession. Or, in a somewhat wider sense, the former denotes an inchoate or incomplete right to a thing; the latter, a complete and perfect right to a thing.

In canon law. A right to a thing. An inchoate and imperfect right, such as is gained by nomination and institution; as distinguished from *jus in re*, or complete and full right, such as is acquired by corporal possession. 2 Bl. Comm. 312.

JUS ÆLIANUM. A body of laws drawn up by Sextus Ælius, and consisting of three parts, wherein were explained, respectively: (1) The laws of the Twelve Tables; (2) the interpretation of and decisions upon such laws; and (3) the forms of procedure. In date, it was subsequent to the *jus Flavianum,* (*q. v.*) Brown.

JUS ÆSNECIÆ. The right of primogeniture, (*q. v.*)

JUS ALBINATUS. The *droit d'aubaine,* (*q. v.*) See ALBINATUS JUS.

JUS ANGLORUM. The laws and customs of the West Saxons, in the time of the Heptarchy, by which the people were for a long time governed, and which were preferred before all others. Wharton.

JUS AQUÆDUCTUS. In the civil law. The name of a servitude which gives to the owner of land the right to bring down water through or from the land of another.

JUS BANCI. In old English law. The right of bench. The right or privilege of having an elevated and separate *seat of judgment*, anciently allowed only to the king's judges, who hence were said to administer *high* justice, (*summam administrant justitiam.*) Blount.

JUS BELLI. The law of war. The law of nations as applied to a state of war, defining in particular the rights and duties of the belligerent powers themselves, and of neutral nations.

The right of war; that which may be done without injustice with regard to an enemy. Gro. de Jure B. lib. 1, c. 1, § 3.

JUS BELLUM DICENDI. The right of proclaiming war.

JUS CANONICUM. The canon law.

JUS CIVILE. Civil law. The system of law peculiar to one state or people. Inst. 1, 2, 1. Particularly, in Roman law, the civil law of the Roman people, as distinguished from the *jus gentium*. The term is also applied to the body of law called, emphatically, the "civil law."

The *jus civile* and the *jus gentium* are distinguished in this way. All people ruled by statutes and customs use a law partly peculiar to themselves, partly common to all men. The law each people has settled for itself is peculiar to the state itself, and is called "*jus civile*," as being peculiar to that very state. The law, again, that natural reason has settled among all men,—the law that is guarded among all peoples quite alike,—is called the "*jus gentium*," and all nations use it as if law. The Roman people, therefore, use a law that is partly peculiar to itself, partly common to all men. Hunter, Rom. Law, 38.

But this is not the only, or even the general, use of the words. What the Roman jurists had chiefly in view, when they spoke of "*jus civile*," was not local as opposed to cosmopolitan law, but the old law of the city as contrasted with the newer law introduced by the prætor, (*jus prætorium, jus honorarium.*) Largely, no doubt, the *jus gentium* corresponds with the *jus prætorium;* but the correspondence is not perfect. Id. 89.

Jus civile est quod sibi populus constituit. The civil law is what a people establishes for itself. Inst. 1, 2, 1; 1 Johns. 424, 426.

JUS CIVITATUS. The right of citizenship; the freedom of the city of Rome. It differs from *jus quiritium*, which comprehended all the privileges of a free native of Rome. The difference is much the same as between "denization" and "naturalization" with us. Wharton.

JUS CLOACÆ. In the civil law. The right of sewerage or drainage. An easement consisting in the right of having a sewer, or of conducting surface water, through the house or over the ground of one's neighbor. Mackeld. Rom. Law, § 317.

JUS COMMUNE. In the civil law. Common right; the common and natural rule of right, as opposed to *jus singulare*, (*q. v.*) Mackeld. Rom. Law, § 196.

In English law. The common law, answering to the Saxon "*folcright.*" 1 Bl. Comm. 67.

Jus constitui oportet in his quæ ut plurimum accidunt non quæ ex inopinato. Laws ought to be made with a view to those cases which happen most frequently, and not to those which are of rare or accidental occurrence. Dig. 1, 3, 3; Broom, Max. 43.

JUS CORONÆ. In English law. The right of the crown, or to the crown; the right of succession to the throne. 1 Bl. Comm. 191; 2 Steph. Comm. 434.

JUS CUDENDÆ MONETÆ. In old English law. The right of coining money. 2 How. State Tr. 118.

JUS CURIALITATIS. In English law. The right of curtesy. Spelman.

JUS DARE. To give or to make the law; the function and prerogative of the legislative department.

JUS DELIBERANDI. In the civil law. The right of deliberating. A term granted by the proper officer at the request of him who is called to the inheritance, (the heir,) within which he has the right to investigate its condition and to consider whether he will accept or reject it. Mackeld. Rom. Law, § 742; Civil Code La. art. 1028.

Jus descendit, et non terra. A right descends, not the land. Co. Litt. 345.

JUS DEVOLUTUM. The right of the church of presenting a minister to a vacant parish, in case the patron shall neglect to exercise his right within the time limited by law.

JUS DICERE. To declare the law; to say what the law is. The province of a court or judge. 2 Eden, 29; 3 P. Wms. 485.

JUS DISPONENDI. The right of disposing. An expression used either generally to signify the right of alienation, as when we speak of depriving a married woman of the *jus disponendi* over her separate estate, or specially in the law relating to sales of goods, where it is often a question whether the vendor of goods has the intention of reserving to himself the *jus disponendi; i. e.*, of preventing the ownership from passing to the purchaser, notwithstanding that he (the vendor) has parted with the possession of the goods. Sweet.

JUS DIVIDENDI. The right of disposing of realty by will. Du Cange.

JUS DUPLICATUM. A double right; the right of possession united with the right of property; otherwise called "*droit-droit.*" 2 Bl. Comm. 199.

Jus est ars boni et æqui. Law is the science of what is good and just. Dig. 1, 1, 1, 1; Bract. fol. 2*b*.

Jus est norma recti; et quicquid est contra normam recti est injuria. Law is a rule of right; and whatever is contrary to the rule of right is an injury. 3 Bulst. 313.

Jus et fraus nunquam cohabitant. Right and fraud never dwell together. 10 Coke, 45*a*. Applied to the title of a statute. Id.; Best, Ev. p. 250, § 205.

Jus ex injuria non oritur. A right does (or can) not arise out of a wrong. 4 Bing. 639; Broom, Max. 738, note.

JUS FALCANDI. In old English law. The right of mowing or cutting. Fleta, lib. 4, c. 27, § 1.

JUS FECIALE. In Roman law. The law of arms, or of heralds. A rudimentary species of international law founded on the rites and religious ceremonies of the different peoples.

JUS FIDUCIARIUM. In the civil law. A right in trust; as distinguished from *jus legitimum*, a legal right. 2 Bl. Comm. 328.

K

L

M

JUS FLAVIANUM. In old Roman law. A body of laws drawn up by Cneius Flavius, a clerk of Appius Claudius, from the materials to which he had access. It was a popularization of the laws. Mackeld. Rom. Law, § 39.

JUS FLUMINUM. In the civil law. The right to the use of rivers. Locc. de Jure Mar. lib. 1, c. 6.

JUS FODIENDI. In the civil and old English law. A right of digging on another's land. Inst. 2, 3, 2; Bract. fol. 222.

JUS GENTIUM. The law of nations. That law which natural reason has established among all men is equally observed among all nations, and is called the "law of nations," as being the law which all nations use. Inst. 1, 2, 1; Dig. 1, 1, 9; 1 Bl. Comm. 43; 1 Kent, Comm. 7; Mackeld. Rom. Law, § 125.

Although this phrase had a meaning in the Roman law which may be rendered by our expression "law of nations," it must not be understood as equivalent to what we now call "international law," its scope being much wider. It was originally a system of law, or more properly equity, gathered by the early Roman lawyers and magistrates from the common ingredients in the customs of the old Italian tribes,—those being the nations, *gentes*, whom they had opportunities of observing, —to be used in cases where the *jus civile* did not apply; that is, in cases between foreigners or between a Roman citizen and a foreigner. The principle upon which they proceeded was that any rule of law which was common to all the nations they knew of must be intrinsically consonant to right reason, and therefore fundamentally valid and just. From this it was an easy transition to the converse principle, viz., that any rule which instinctively commended itself to their sense of justice and reason must be a part of the *jus gentium*. And so the latter term came eventually to be about synonymous with "equity," (as the Romans understood it,) or the system of prætorian law.

Modern jurists frequently employ the term "*jus gentium privatum*" to denote private international law, or that subject which is otherwise styled the "conflict of laws;" and "*jus gentium publicum*" for public international law, or the system of rules governing the intercourse of nations with each other as persons.

JUS GLADII. The right of the sword; the executory power of the law; the right, power, or prerogative of punishing for crime. 4 Bl. Comm. 177.

JUS HABENDI. The right to have a thing. The right to be put in actual possession of property. Lewin, Trusts, 585.

JUS HABENDI ET RETINENDI. A right to have and to retain the profits, tithes, and offerings, etc., of a rectory or parsonage.

JUS HÆREDITATIS. The right of inheritance.

JUS HAURIENDI. In the civil and old English law. The right of drawing water. Fleta, lib. 4, c. 27, § 1.

JUS HONORARIUM. The body of Roman law, which was made up of edicts of the supreme magistrates, particularly the prætors.

JUS IMAGINIS. In Roman law. The right to use or display pictures or statues of ancestors; somewhat analogous to the right, in English law, to bear a coat of arms.

JUS IMMUNITATIS. In the civil law. The law of immunity or exemption from the burden of public office. Dig. 50, 6.

JUS IN PERSONAM. A right against a person; a right which gives its possessor a power to oblige another person to give or procure, to do or not to do, something.

JUS IN RE. In the civil law. A right in a thing. A right existing in a person with respect to an article or subject of property, inherent in his relation to it, implying complete ownership with possession, and available against all the world. See JUS AD REM.

Jus in re inhærit ossibus usufructuarii. A right in the thing cleaves to the person of the usufructuary.

JUS IN RE PROPRIA. The right of enjoyment which is incident to full ownership or property, and is often used to denote the full ownership or property itself. It is distinguished from *jus in re alienâ*, which is a mere easement or right in or over the property of another.

JUS INCOGNITUM. An unknown law. This term is applied by the civilians to obsolete laws. Bowyer, Mod. Civil Law, 33.

JUS INDIVIDUUM. An individual or indivisible right; a right incapable of division. 36 Eng. Law & Eq. 25.

Jus jurandi forma verbis differt, re convenit; hunc enim sensum habere debet: ut Deus invocetur. Grot. de Jur. B., l. 2, c. 13, § 10. The form of taking an oath differs in language, agrees in meaning; for it ought to have this sense: that the Deity is invoked.

JUS LATII. In Roman law. The right of Latium or of the Latins. The principal privilege of the Latins seems to have been the use of their own laws, and their not being subject to the edicts of the prætor, and that they had occasional access to the freedom of Rome, and a participation in her sacred rites. Butl. Hor. Jur. 41.

JUS LATIUM. In Roman law. A rule of law applicable to magistrates in Latium. It was either *majus Latium* or *minus Latium,*—the *majus Latium* raising to the dignity of Roman citizen not only the magistrate himself, but also his wife and children; the *minus Latium* raising to that dignity only the magistrate himself. Brown.

JUS LEGITIMUM. A legal right. In the civil law. A right which was enforceable in the ordinary course of law. 2 Bl. Comm. 328.

JUS MARITI. The right of a husband; especially the right which a husband acquires to his wife's movable estate by virtue of the marriage. 1 Forb. Inst. pt. 1, p. 63.

JUS MERUM. In old English law. Mere or bare right; the mere right of property in lands, without either possession or even the right of possession. 2 Bl. Comm. 197; Bract. fol. 23.

JUS NATURÆ. The law of nature. See JUS NATURALE.

JUS NATURALE. The natural law, or law of nature; law, or legal principles, supposed to be discoverable by the light of nature or abstract reasoning, or to be taught by nature to all nations and men alike; or law supposed to govern men and peoples in a state of nature, *i. e.,* in advance of organized governments or enacted laws. This conceit originated with the philosophical jurists of Rome, and was gradually extended until the phrase came to denote a supposed basis or substratum common to all systems of positive law, and hence to be found, in greater or less purity, in the laws of all nations. And, conversely, they held that if any rule or principle of law was observed in common by all peoples with whose systems they were acquainted, it must be a part of the *jus naturale,* or derived from it. Thus the phrases "*jus naturale*" and "*jus gentium*" came to be used interchangeably.

Jus naturale est quod apud homines eandem habet potentiam. Natural right is that which has the same force among all mankind. 7 Coke, 12.

JUS NAVIGANDI. The right of navigating or navigation; the right of commerce by ships or by sea. Locc. de Jure Mar. lib. 1, c. 3.

JUS NECIS. In Roman law. The right of death, or of putting to death. A right which a father anciently had over his children.

Jus non habenti tute non paretur. One who has no right cannot be safely obeyed. Hob. 146.

Jus non patitur ut idem bis solvatur. Law does not suffer that the same thing be twice paid.

JUS NON SCRIPTUM. The unwritten law. 1 Bl. Comm. 64.

JUS PAPIRIANUM. The civil law of Papirius. The title of the earliest collection of Roman *leges curiatæ,* said to have been made in the time of Tarquin, the last of the kings, by a *pontifex maximus* of the name of Sextus or Publius Papirius. Very few fragments of this collection now remain, and the authenticity of these has been doubted. Mackeld. Rom. Law, § 21.

JUS PASCENDI. In the civil and old English law. The right of pasturing cattle. Inst. 2, 3, 2; Bract. fols. 53*b*, 222.

JUS PATRONATUS. In English ecclesiastical law. The right of patronage; the right of presenting a clerk to a benefice. Blount.

A commission from the bishop, where two presentations are offered upon the same avoidance, directed usually to his chancellor and others of competent learning, who are to summon a jury of six clergymen and six laymen to inquire into and examine who is the rightful patron. 3 Bl. Comm. 246; 3 Steph. Comm. 517.

JUS PERSONARUM. Rights of persons. Those rights which, in the civil law, belong to persons as such, or in their different characters and relations; as parents and children, masters and servants, etc.

JUS PORTUS. In maritime law. The right of port or harbor.

JUS POSSESSIONIS. The right of possession.

JUS POSTLIMINII. In the civil law. The right of postliminy; the right or claim of a person who had been restored to the possession of a thing, or to a former condition, to be considered as though he had never been deprived of it. Dig. 49, 15, 5; 3 Bl. Comm. 107, 210.

K

L

M

In international law. The right by which property taken by an enemy, and recaptured or rescued from him by the fellow-subjects or allies of the original owner, is restored to the latter upon certain terms. 1 Kent, Comm. 108.

JUS PRÆSENS. In the civil law. A present or vested right; a right already completely acquired. Mackeld. Rom. Law, § 191.

JUS PRÆTORIUM. In the civil law. The discretion of the prætor, as distinct from the *leges*, or standing laws. 3 Bl. Comm. 49. That kind of law which the prætors introduced for the purpose of aiding, supplying, or correcting the civil law for the public benefit. Dig. 1, 1, 7. Called, also, "*jus honorarium*," (*q. v.*)

JUS PRECARIUM. In the civil law. A right to a thing held for another, for which there was no remedy. 2 Bl. Comm. 328.

JUS PRESENTATIONIS. The right of presentation.

JUS PRIVATUM. The civil or municipal law of Rome.

JUS PROJICIENDI. In the civil law. The name of a servitude which consists in the right to build a projection, such as a balcony or gallery, from one's house in the open space belonging to one's neighbor, but without resting on his house. Dig. 50, 16, 242; Id. 8, 2, 2; Mackeld. Rom. Law, § 317.

JUS PROPRIETATIS. The right of property, as distinguished from the *jus possessionis*, or right of possession. Bract. fol. 3. Called by Bracton "*jus merum*," the mere right. Id.; 2 Bl. Comm. 197; 3 Bl. Comm. 19, 176.

JUS PROTEGENDI. In the civil law. The name of a servitude. It is a right by which a part of the roof or tiling of one house is made to extend over the adjoining house. Dig. 50, 16, 242, 1; Id. 8, 2, 25; Id. 8, 5, 8, 5.

Jus publicum et privatum quod ex naturalibus præceptis aut gentium aut civilibus est collectum; et quod in jure scripto jus appellatur, id in lege Angliæ rectum esse dicitur. Co. Litt. 185. Public and private law is that which is collected from natural principles, either of nations or in states; and that which in the civil law is called "*jus*," in the law of England is said to be "right."

Jus publicum privatorum pactis mutari non potest. A public law or right cannot be altered by the agreements of private persons.

JUS QUÆSITUM. A right to ask or recover; for example, in an obligation there is a binding of the obligor, and a *jus quæsitum* in the obligee. 1 Bell, Comm. 323.

JUS QUIRITIUM. The old law of Rome, that was applicable originally to patricians only, and, under the Twelve Tables, to the entire Roman people, was so called, in contradistinction to the *jus prætorium*, (*q. v.,*) or equity. Brown.

Jus quo universitates utuntur est idem quod habent privati. The law which governs corporations is the same which governs individuals. 16 Mass. 44.

JUS RECUPERANDI. The right of recovering [lands.]

JUS RELICTÆ. In Scotch law. The right of a relict; the right or claim of a relict or widow to her share of her husband's estate, particularly the movables. 2 Kames, Eq. 340; 1 Forb. Inst. pt. 1, p. 67.

JUS REPRESENTATIONIS. The right of representing or standing in the place of another, or of being represented by another.

JUS RERUM. The law of things. The law regulating the rights and powers of persons over things; how property is acquired, enjoyed, and transferred.

Jus respicit æquitatem. Law regards equity. Co. Litt. 24*b*; Broom, Max. 151.

JUS SCRIPTUM. In Roman law. Written law. Inst. 1, 2, 3. All law that was actually committed to writing, whether it had originated by enactment or by custom, in contradistinction to such parts of the law of custom as were not committed to writing. Mackeld. Rom. Law, § 126.

In English law. Written law, or statute law, otherwise called "*lex scripta*," as distinguished from the common law, "*lex non scripta*." 1 Bl. Comm. 62.

JUS SINGULARE. In the civil law. A peculiar or individual rule, differing from the *jus commune*, or common rule of right, and established for some special reason. Mackeld. Rom. Law, § 196.

JUS STAPULÆ. In old European law. The law of staple; the right of staple. A right or privilege of certain towns of stopping imported merchandise, and compelling it to be offered for sale in their own markets. Locc. de Jure Mar. lib. 1, c. 10.

JUS STRICTUM. Strict law; law interpreted without any modification, and in its utmost rigor.

Jus superveniens auctori accrescit successori. A right growing to a possessor accrues to the successor. Halk. Lat. Max. 76.

JUS TERTII. The right of a third party. A tenant, bailee, etc., who pleads that the title is in some person other than his landlord, bailor, etc., is said to set up a *jus tertii.*

Jus testamentorum pertinet ordinario. Yearb. 4 Hen. VII., 13*b*. The right of testaments belongs to the ordinary.

JUS TRIPERTITUM. In Roman law. A name applied to the Roman law of wills, in the time of Justinian, on account of its threefold derivation, viz., from the prætorian edict, from the civil law, and from the imperial constitutions. Maine, Anc. Law, 207.

Jus triplex est,—proprietatis, possessionis, et possibilitatis. Right is threefold, —of property, of possession, and of possibility.

JUS TRIUM LIBERORUM. In Roman law. A right or privilege allowed to the parent of *three* or more *children.* 2 Kent, Comm. 85; 2 Bl. Comm. 247. These privileges were an exemption from the trouble of guardianship, priority in bearing offices, and a treble proportion of corn. Adams, Rom. Ant. (Amer. Ed.) 227.

JUS UTENDI. The right to use property without destroying its substance. It is employed in contradistinction to the *jus abutendi.* 3 Toullier, no. 86.

JUS VENANDI ET PISCANDI. The right of hunting and fishing.

Jus vendit quod usus approbavit. Ellesm. Postn. 35. The law dispenses what use has approved.

JUSJURANDUM. Lat. An oath.

Jusjurandum inter alios factum nec nocere nec prodesse debet. An oath made between others ought neither to hurt nor profit. 4 Inst. 279.

JUST. Right; in accordance with law and justice.

"The words 'just' and 'justly' do not always mean 'just' and 'justly' in a moral sense, but they not unfrequently, in their connection with other words in a sentence, bear a very different signification. It is evident, however, that the word 'just' in the statute [requiring an affidavit for an attachment to state that plaintiff's claim is *just*] means 'just' in a moral sense; and from its isolation, being made a separate subdivision of the section, it is intended to mean 'morally just' in the most emphatic terms. The claim must be *morally* just, as well as *legally* just, in order to entitle a party to an attachment." 5 Kan. 300.

JUST COMPENSATION. As used in the constitutional provision that private property shall not be taken for public use without "just compensation," this phrase means a full and fair equivalent for the loss sustained by the taking for public use. It may be more or it may be less than the mere money value of the property actually taken. The exercise of the power being necessary for the public good, and all property being held subject to its exercise when and as the public good requires it, it would be unjust to the public that it should be required to pay the owner more than a fair indemnity for the loss he sustains by the appropriation of his property for the general good. On the other hand, it would be equally unjust to the owner if he should receive less than a fair indemnity for such loss. To arrive at this fair indemnity, the interests of the public and of the owner, and all the circumstances of the particular appropriation, should be taken into consideration. Lewis, Em. Dom. § 462.

JUST TITLE. By the term "just title," in cases of prescription, we do not understand that which the possessor may have derived from the true owner, for then no true prescription would be necessary, but a title which the possessor may have received from any person whom he honestly believed to be the real owner, provided the title were such as to transfer the ownership of the property. Civil Code La. art. 3484.

JUSTA. In old English law. A certain measure of liquor, being as much as was sufficient to drink at once. Mon. Angl. t. 1, c. 149.

JUSTA CAUSA. In the civil law. A just cause; a lawful ground; a legal transaction of some kind. Mackeld. Rom. Law, § 283.

K

L

M

JUSTICE, v. In old English practice. To do justice; to see justice done; to summon one to do justice.

JUSTICE, n. In jurisprudence. The constant and perpetual disposition to render every man his due. Inst. 1, 1, pr.; 2 Inst. 56. The conformity of our actions and our will to the law. Toull. Droit Civil Fr. tit. prél. no. 5.

In the most extensive sense of the word, it differs little from "virtue;" for it includes within itself the whole circle of virtues. Yet the common distinction between them is that that which, considered positively and in itself, is called "virtue," when considered relatively and with respect to others has the name of "justice." But "justice," being in itself a part of "virtue," is confined to things simply good or evil, and consists in a man's taking such a proportion of them as he ought. Bouvier.

Commutative justice is that which should govern contracts. It consists in rendering to every man the exact measure of his dues, without regard to his personal worth or merits, *i. e.,* placing all men on an equality. *Distributive* justice is that which should govern the distribution of rewards and punishments. It assigns to each the rewards which his personal merit or services deserve, or the proper punishment for his crimes. It does not consider all men as equally deserving or equally blameworthy, but discriminates between them, observing a just proportion and comparison. This distinction originated with Aristotle. (Eth. Nic. V.) See Fonbl. Eq. 3; Toull. Droit Civil Fr. tit. prél. no. 7.

In Norman French. Amenable to justice. Kelham.

In feudal law. Jurisdiction; judicial cognizance of causes or offenses.

In common law. The title given in England to the judges of the king's bench and the common pleas, and in America to the judges of the supreme court of the United States and of the appellate courts of many of the states. It is said that this word in its Latin form (*justitia*) was properly applicable only to the judges of common-law courts, while the term "*judex*" designated the judges of ecclesiastical and other courts. See Leg. Hen. I. §§ 24, 63; Co. Litt. 71b.

The same title is also applied to some of the judicial officers of the lowest rank and jurisdiction, such as police justices and justices of the peace.

JUSTICE AYRES, (or AIRES.) In Scotch law. Circuits made by the judges of the justiciary courts through the country, for the distribution of justice. Bell.

JUSTICE IN EYRE. From the old French word "*eire,*" *i. e.,* a journey. Those justices who in ancient times were sent by commission into various counties, to hear more especially such causes as were termed "pleas of the crown," were called "justices in eyre." They differed from justices in oyer and terminer, inasmuch as the latter were sent to one place, and for the purpose of trying only a limited number of special causes; whereas the justices in eyre were sent through the various counties, with a more indefinite and general commission. In some respects they resembled our present justices of assize, although their authority and manner of proceeding differed much from them. Brown.

JUSTICE OF THE PEACE. In American law. A judicial officer of inferior rank, holding a court not of record, and having (usually) civil jurisdiction of a limited nature, for the trial of minor cases, to an extent prescribed by statute, and for the conservation of the peace and the preliminary hearing of criminal complaints and the commitment of offenders.

In English law. Judges of record appointed by the crown to be justices within a certain district, (e. g., a county or borough,) for the conservation of the peace, and for the execution of divers things, comprehended within their commission and within divers statutes, committed to their charge. Stone, J. Pr. 2.

JUSTICE SEAT. In English law. The principal court of the forest, held before the chief justice in eyre, or chief itinerant judge, or his deputy; to hear and determine all trespasses within the forest, and all claims of franchises, liberties, and privileges, and all pleas and causes whatsoever therein arising. 3 Bl. Comm. 72; 4 Inst. 291; 3 Steph. Comm. 440.

JUSTICEMENTS. An old general term for all things appertaining to justice.

JUSTICER. The old form of *justice.* Blount.

JUSTICES' COURTS. Inferior tribunals, not of record, with limited jurisdiction, both civil and criminal, held by justices of the peace. There are courts so called in many of the states.

JUSTICES OF APPEAL. The title given to the ordinary judges of the English court of appeal. The first of such ordinary judges are the two former lords justices of appeal in chancery, and one other judge appointed by the crown by letters patent. **Jud. Act 1875, § 4.**

JUSTICES OF ASSIZE. These justices, or, as they are sometimes called, "justices of *nisi prius*," are judges of the superior English courts, who go on circuit into the various counties of England and Wales for the purpose of disposing of such causes as are ready for trial at the assizes. See ASSIZE.

JUSTICES OF GAOL DELIVERY. Those justices who are sent with a commission to hear and determine all causes appertaining to persons, who, for any offense, have been cast into gaol. Part of their authority was to punish those who let to mainprise those prisoners who were not bailable by law, and they seem formerly to have been sent into the country upon this exclusive occasion, but afterwards had the same authority given them as the justices of assize. Brown.

JUSTICES OF LABORERS. In old English law. Justices appointed to redress the frowardness of laboring men, who would either be idle or have unreasonable wages. Blount.

JUSTICES OF NISI PRIUS. In English law. This title is now usually coupled with that of *justices of assize;* the judges of the superior courts acting on their circuits in both these capacities. 3 Bl. Comm. 58, 59.

JUSTICES OF OYER AND TERMINER. Certain persons appointed by the king's commission, among whom were usually two judges of the courts at Westminster, and who went twice in every year to every county of the kingdom, (except London and Middlesex,) and, at what was usually called the "assizes," heard and determined all treasons, felonies, and misdemeanors. Brown.

JUSTICES OF THE BENCH. The justices of the court of common bench or common pleas.

JUSTICES OF THE FOREST. In old English law. Officers who had jurisdiction over all offenses committed within the forest against vert or venison. The court wherein these justices sat and determined such causes was called the "justice seat of the forest." They were also sometimes called the "justices in eyre of the forest." Brown.

JUSTICES OF THE HUNDRED. Hundredors; lords of the hundreds; they who had the jurisdiction of hundreds and held the hundred courts.

AM.DICT.LAW—43

JUSTICES OF THE JEWS. Justices appointed by Richard I. to carry into effect the laws and orders which he had made for regulating the money contracts of the Jews. Brown.

JUSTICES OF THE PAVILION. In old English law. Judges of a pyepowder court, of a most transcendent jurisdiction, anciently authorized by the bishop of Winchester, at a fair held on St. Giles' hills near that city. Cowell; Blount.

JUSTICES OF TRAIL-BASTON. In old English law. A kind of justices appointed by King Edward I. upon occasion of great disorders in the realm, during his absence in the Scotch and French wars. They were a kind of justices in eyre, with great powers adapted to the emergency, and which they exercised in a summary manner. Cowell; Blount.

JUSTICESHIP. Rank or office of a justice.

JUSTICIABLE. Proper to be examined in courts of justice.

JUSTICIAR. In old English law. A judge or justice. One of several persons learned in the law, who sat in the *aula regis,* and formed a kind of court of appeal in cases of difficulty.

JUSTICIARII ITINERANTES. In English law. Justices in eyre, who formerly went from county to county to administer justice. They were so called to distinguish them from justices residing at Westminister, who were called "*justicii residentes.*" Co. Litt. 293.

JUSTICIARII RESIDENTES. In English law. Justices or judges who usually resided in Westminister. They were so called to distinguish them from justices in eyre. Co. Litt. 293.

JUSTICIARY. An old name for a judge or justice. The word is formed on the analogy of the Latin "*justiciarius*" and French "*justicier.*"

K

JUSTICIARY COURT. The chief criminal court of Scotland, consisting of five lords of session, added to the justice general and justice clerk; of whom the justice general, and, in his absence, the justice clerk, is president. This court has a jurisdiction over all crimes, and over the whole of Scotland. Bell.

L

M

JUSTICIATUS. Judicature; prerogative.

JUSTICIES. In English law. A writ directed to the sheriff, empowering him, for the sake of dispatch, to try an action in his county court for a larger amount than he has the ordinary power to do. It is so called because it is a commission to the sheriff to do the party justice, the word itself meaning, "You may do justice to ———." 3 Bl. Comm. 36; 4 Inst. 266.

JUSTIFIABLE. Rightful; warranted or sanctioned by law; that which can be shown to be sustained by law; as justifiable homicide.

JUSTIFIABLE HOMICIDE. Such as is committed intentionally, but without any evil design, and under such circumstances of necessity or duty as render the act proper, and relieve the party from any shadow of blame; as where a sheriff lawfully executes a sentence of death upon a malefactor, or where the killing takes place in the endeavor to prevent the commission of a felony which could not be otherwise avoided.

JUSTIFICATION. A maintaining or showing a sufficient reason in court why the defendant did what he is called upon to answer, particularly in an action of libel. A defense of justification is a defense showing the libel to be true, or in an action of assault showing the violence to have been necessary. See Steph. Pl. 184.

In practice. The proceeding by which bail establish their ability to perform the undertaking of the bond or recognizance.

JUSTIFICATORS. A kind of compurgators, (q. v.,) or those who by oath justified the innocence or oaths of others; as in the case of wager of law.

JUSTIFYING BAIL consists in proving the sufficiency of bail or sureties in point of property, etc.

The production of bail in court, who there justify themselves against the exception of the plaintiff.

JUSTINIANIST. A civilian; one who studies the civil law.

JUSTITIA. Lat. Justice. A jurisdiction, or the office of a judge.

Justitia debet esse libera, quia nihil iniquius venali justitia; plena, quia justitia non debet claudicare; et celeris, quia dilatio est quædam negatio. Justice ought to be free, because nothing is more iniquitous than venal justice; full, because justice ought not to halt; and speedy, because delay is a kind of denial. 2 Inst. 56.

Justitia est constans et perpetua voluntas jus suum cuique tribuendi. Justice is a steady and unceasing disposition to render to every man his due. Inst. 1, 1, pr.; Dig. 1, 1, 10.

Justitia est duplex, viz., severe puniens et vere præveniens. 3 Inst. Epil. Justice is double; punishing severely, and truly preventing.

Justitia est virtus excellens et Altissimo complacens. 4 Inst. 58. Justice is excellent virtue and pleasing to the Most High.

Justitia firmatur solium. 3 Inst. 140. By justice the throne is established.

Justitia nemini neganda est. Jenk. Cent. 178. Justice is to be denied to none.

Justitia non est neganda non differenda. Jenk. Cent. 93. Justice is neither to be denied nor delayed.

Justitia non novit patrem nec matrem; solam veritatem spectat justitia. Justice knows not father nor mother; justice looks at truth alone. 1 Bulst. 199.

JUSTITIA PIEPOUDROUS. Speedy justice. Bract. 333b.

JUSTITIUM. In the civil law. A suspension or intermission of the administration of justice in courts; vacation time. Calvin.

JUSTITIUM FACERE. To hold a plea of anything.

JUSTIZA. In Spanish law. The name anciently given to a high judicial magistrate, or supreme judge, who was the ultimate interpreter of the laws, and possessed other high powers.

JUSTS, or JOUSTS. Exercises between martial men and persons of honor, with spears, on horseback; different from *tournaments*, which were military exercises between many men in troops. 24 Hen. VIII. c. 13.

Justum non est aliquem antenatum mortuum facere bastardum, qui pro tota vita sua pro legitimo habetur. It is not just to make a bastard after his death one elder born who all his life has been accounted legitimate. 8 Coke, 101.

JUXTA. Lat. Near; following; according to.

JUXTA CONVENTIONEM. According to the covenant. Fleta, lib. 4, c. 16, § 6.

JUXTA FORMAM STATUTI. According to the form of the statute.

JUXTA RATAM. At or after the rate. Dyer, 82.

JUXTA TENOREM SEQUENTEM. According to the tenor following. 2 Salk. 417. A phrase used in the old books when the very words themselves referred to were set forth. Id.; 1 Ld. Raym. 415.

JUZGADO. In Spanish law. The judiciary; the body of judges; the judges who concur in a decree.

K

L

M

Printed in Great Britain
by Amazon

44740141R00381